# THE HANDBOOK
## of
# PUBLIC AFFAIRS

# Advisory Board

# THE HANDBOOK
## of
# PUBLIC AFFAIRS

*Edited by*
PHIL HARRIS
and CRAIG S. FLEISHER

SAGE Publications
London ● Thousand Oaks ● New Delhi

First published 2005

SAGE Publications Ltd
1 Oliver's Yard
55 City Road
London EC1Y 1SP

SAGE Publications Inc
2455 Teller Road
Thousand Oaks, California 91320

SAGE Publications India Pvt Ltd
B-42, Panchsheel Enclave
Post Box 4109
New Delhi 110 017

**Library of Congress Control Number: 2004116093**
A catalogue record for this book is available from the British Library

ISBN 0 7619 4396 5

Typeset by C&M Digital (P) Ltd., Chennai, India
Printed in Great Britain by The Cromwell Press Ltd, Trowbridge, Wiltshire

To Irene, Angela, Zachary, Austin, and Kieren

Thanks for making it possible

# Contents

# List of Illustrations

# List of Tables

# List of Exhibits

# Contributors

**Geoff Allen** pioneered research and teaching in business–government relations and the political environment of business in Australia. He has taught MBA and executive programs as a full-time or part-time academic for thirty years, and is an adjunct professor at the Melbourne Business School. He has also been at the center of the business–politics relationship over a long career as a civil servant, senior political advisor, co-founder and foundation CEO of Australia's large-company business organization (Business Council of Australia), and as management consultant for business and government. He has chaired a number of major state and federal government advisory bodies and is currently chair of the Australian government's Trade Policy Advisory Council. He is director of a number of companies and is deputy chairman of the board of the Melbourne Business School. In 1988 he founded the economics and public policy consultancy the Allen Consulting Group, and in 1990 founded the Centre for Corporate Public Affairs, of which he is chairman. He is Asia-Pacific regional editor of the *Journal of Public Affairs*.

**Leighton Andrews** is a former head of Public Affairs at the BBC. He has been a consultant to many major media companies. Immediately before his election, he lectured at the School of Journalism at Cardiff University, where he is now Honorary Professor. He is also a member of the Editorial Board of the *Journal of Public Affairs*. He was elected to the National Assembly for Wales as Assembly Member for the Rhondda in 2003 and now sits on the National Assembly's Economic Development, Culture and Audit committees. He is married with two children.

**Archie B. Carroll** is Professor of Management and holder of the Robert W. Scherer Chair of Management and Corporate Public Affairs in the Terry College of Business, University of Georgia, Athens, GA. He is the senior co-author of *Business and Society: Ethics and Stakeholder Management,* sixth edition (2006), as well as ten other books and dozens of scholarly journal articles. Dr Carroll has served in many professional capacities. He has been President of the Society for Business Ethics (1998–1999), Chairman of the Social Issues in Management (SIM) division of the Academy of Management (1976–1977) and has served on the editorial review boards of the *Academy of Management Review* and the *Journal of Management.* He is on the editorial review boards of *Business Ethics Quarterly, Business and Society, Journal of Management,* and the *Journal of Public Affairs.* A multiple award-winning scholar, his research and teaching interests embrace business ethics, moral leadership, corporate social performance, corporate citizenship, non-profit management, and stakeholder theory.

**Scott A. Castleman** is General Manager of Legislative Demographic Services (LDS) based in Fairfax, VA, a position he assumed after having served as the firm's

Director of Operations. LDS was the first company to match zip codes to political jurisdictions and has, since 1982, been on the cutting edge of providing technology for tracking issues and mobilizing constituents. As Director of Operations, Scott developed much of the cutting edge web-based products LDS offers.

**Craig S. Fleisher** holds the Odette Research Chair in Business and is Professor of Management (Strategy & Entrepreneurship) at the Odette School of Business, University of Windsor, Ontario, Canada. He was previously President of the Canadian Council for Public Affairs Advancement and a board member of the Center for Public Affairs Management (Washington, DC), Public Affairs Association of Canada, and George Washington University Graduate School of Political Management. He is currently the Regional Editor for the Americas of the *Journal of Public Affairs*, Editor of the *Journal of Competitive Intelligence and Management*, a member of the Institute for Public Relations Commission on Public Relations Measurement and Evaluation, and an editorial board member of the *Asia Pacific Public Relations Journal* and *International Journal of Technology Intelligence and Planning*.

An award-winning instructor in strategy, competitive analysis, and social issues in management, he is an active speaker and advisor to senior executives in organizations around the globe. He has written several acclaimed books, including *Assessing, Managing and Maximizing Public Affairs Performance* (1997), *Public Affairs Benchmarking: A Comprehensive Guide* (1995), *Strategic and Competitive Analysis* (2003), and has also published over 150 articles and chapters. He has previously served as dean, graduate programme director, chair, and/or professor at the Universities of Calgary, New Brunswick, Wilfrid Laurier (Canada), and Sydney (Australia). His holds a PhD in Business Administration from the Katz Graduate School of Business, University of Pittsburgh.

**Edward A. Grefe** is Adjunct Professor of Issues Management and Grassroots Politics at the Graduate School of Political Management at George Washington University and President of Legislative Democratic Services (LDS) Communications Group. In 1995, the Public Affairs Council cited him as the person who "helped 'invent' grassroots public affairs." That accolade was based on his two books on grassroots advocacy as well as countless articles on how to identify and mobilize constituents. In the early 1980s, with a programmer-partner, he developed GAMBIT, the first ever relational database management program to track issues and the activities of activists on both sides of an issue.

**Jennifer J. Griffin** is Associate Professor of Strategic Management and Public Policy at the George Washington University School of Business in Washington, DC. She teaches courses in business and public policy, managing strategic issues and corporate strategy. A "Faculty of the Year" MBA teaching award winner, she was also designated a GW Institute of Public Policy Research Scholar in 2002. Her research interests are in corporate public affairs, political strategy, capacity building, and social impact management. She has published numerous management journal articles and has been an invited speaker at the Public Affairs Council, the Canadian Conference Board, and the Washington Campus, among others. Jennifer served as a Trustee of the Board for the Foundation for Public Affairs, board member of the International Association for Business and Society (IABS), Academy of Management member, past president of the GW chapter of Beta Gamma Sigma Business Honorary, and Tau Beta Pi engineering honorary member.

**Irene Harris** is Director of Academic Projects at the School of Business, University of Otago, Dunedin, New Zealand. She has responsibility for a number of projects, including academic accreditation. Her teaching and research interests include management development, management learning and government interventions in training and development. She holds a Business Studies degree, a Masters in Management Learning and a Post Graduate Diploma in Education. She is a member of the Chartered Institute of Personnel and Development.

**Phil Harris** is Chair and Professor of the Department of Marketing at the School of Business, University of Otago, Dunedin, New Zealand. Before moving to New Zealand in 2004 he had been joint founder and Director of the highly regarded Centre for Corporate and Public Affairs at Manchester Metropolitan University Business School. From 1999 to 2002 he was Chairman of the Academy of Marketing. He is a member of the Chartered Institute of Marketing Academic Senate and International Board of Trustees. In addition he is a board member of the Global Marketing Special Interest Group of the American Marketing Association and International Research Director of the European Centre for Public Affairs and a past chairman of its Research Committee. Phil is also a Fellow of the Royal Society of Arts and Manufacturers and was made a Fellow of the Institute of Public Relations in recognition of his international work in developing the public affairs discipline.

He is joint founding editor of the *Journal of Public Affairs* and a member of a number of international editorial and advisory boards. He has published over 150 articles and papers. His most recent books include *European Business and Marketing*, co-authored with Frank McDonald (Sage, 2004) and *Machiavelli, Marketing and Management* (Routledge, 2000). He was a parliamentary candidate both at the national and the European level and has been a campaign advisor in the last four UK general elections. He is one of the founders of the recently launched US-based *Journal of E-Government* and the *Journal of Political Marketing*. He is a consultant and advisor to various organizations in the corporate, government and not-for-profit sectors.

**Brian Hawkinson** serves the corporate public affairs community in two capacities: as Director of the Center for Public Affairs Management (CPAM), a unit of the Washington DC-based Public Affairs Council—the leading professional association for public affairs executives; and as Executive Director of the Foundation for Public Affairs. The CPAM is the analytical, applied research and management-consulting arm of the Council. In that regard, it advances the field of public affairs through collecting and analyzing data, assessing best practices, and providing professional assistance to member organizations in the areas of strategic planning and management, organizational structure, performance measurement and evaluation. The Foundation for Public Affairs conducts and supports research on emerging public policy issues and trends that affect the practice of public affairs. Brian holds a BBA degree in management and marketing from James Madison University and an MBA from the Pamplin College of Business at Virginia Tech.

**Pursey P.M.A.R. Heugens** (PhD, Erasmus University) is an Assistant Professor of Organization Theory at the Utrecht School of Economics (the Netherlands). His research interests include public affairs, business ethics, and organization theory. He has published some twenty-five peer-reviewed articles in journals such as *Academy of Management Review, Organization Studies*, the *Journal of Business Ethics*, the *Journal of Management Studies*, and *Strategic Organization*, and book chapters with publishers such as Oxford University Press, Sage, and Blackwell. Dr. Heugens has guest-edited special issues of the *Journal of Public Affairs*, the *Journal of Business Ethics*, and *Corporate Reputation Review*, and sits on the editorial boards of four scholarly journals.

**John M. Holcomb** is Associate Professor of Business Ethics and Legal Studies at the Daniels College of Business, University of Denver. He has over twenty-five years of teaching experience and has been a consultant for several corporations, trade associations, and think-tanks. In 1975, he organized the Foundation for Public Affairs in Washington, DC and was its first executive director. He has written extensively on corporate governance, corporate social responsibility and political strategy, campaign finance law, and social movements and political interest groups. He teaches courses on law, ethics, and public policy; on global values; and on international business law. He is a member of the Colorado Commission on Judicial Discipline and is past president of the Rocky Mountain Academy of Legal Studies in Business. He has a JD from Georgetown University Law Center and an MA in Political Science from Vanderbilt University.

**Gerry Keim** is Associate Dean (MBA) and Professor of Management, WP Carey School of Business, Arizona State University. He previously taught at the Ivey Business School, Texas A&M and the Stanford Graduate School of Business. An award-winning instructor and frequent consultant and speaker for executive audiences throughout the Americas and Europe, he is a regular visiting professor in the International Management Institute of Austria's Johannes Kepler University and core faculty member of the Washington Campus. His research, teaching and consulting centers on the interface between business and its external political, social and economic environment and developing entrepreneurial capabilities in existing business organizations. His research is published in leading journals including the *Academy of Management Journal, Academy of Management Review, Strategic Management Journal, Sloan Management Review, Journal of Management, Public Choice, Journal of Politics*, and *California Management Review*. He serves on the Board of Trustees of the Public Affairs Foundation, Washington, DC.

**Andreas Lederer** lives in Vienna, Austria, and works for Christian Scheucher Consulting Ltd as a political consultant on election campaigns and for corporations in Central and Eastern Europe. He studied political science, philosophy and marketing in Vienna, Copenhagen, London and Los Angles and holds a Masters in Political Science from the University of Vienna. He has published various articles on international political consulting and campaigning. He has also commented on political issues and elections on television.

**Niombo Lomba** works as a public affairs consultant in Berlin, Germany. She holds a Masters in Political Science from the University of Augsburg and is a former member of the national executive board of the Green Party in Germany.

**Burdett Loomis** is a professor of political science at the University of Kansas. He is currently on leave, serving as the Director of Communications for the Governor of Kansas. He has written extensively on organized interests, the Congress, public policy, and political careers, and has edited or written in more than twenty-five books, including seven editions of *Interest Group Politics* (with Allan Cigler). He served as an American Political Science Association Congressional Fellow (1975–76) and has been a guest scholar at the Brookings Institution.

**Conor McGrath** has been Lecturer in Political Lobbying and Public Affairs at the University of Ulster in Northern Ireland since 1999. He served in 2000 as the founding chairman of the Northern Ireland Government Affairs Group. In addition, he acts as Head of Education at the Public Relations Institute of Ireland. Before becoming an academic he worked for a Conservative MP in London and a Republican Congressman, as Public Affairs Director at a PR company, and as a self-employed political consultant. His research interests include the education and training of lobbyists, the fictional representation of lobbyists, international and transnational lobbying, the communication dimension of lobbying, lobbying as a form of political marketing, and the personal characteristics and professional skills of lobbyists. His book *Perspectives on Lobbying: Washington, London, Brussels*, is published in 2005.

**Lord Tom McNally** was elected the leader of the Liberal Democrats in the UK House of Lords in October 2004. He has served as Party spokesman on trade, broadcasting and home affairs. He has also been Deputy Leader in the Lords since 2001. He has served on the Select Committees on Freedom of Information and on the Public Service, as well as the Puttnam Committee on the Communications Bill. From 1969 to 1974 he was International Secretary of the Labour Party, and from 1974 to 1979 was Political Secretary to the Rt Hon. James Callaghan. From 1979 to 1983 he was MP for Stockport South. He left the Labour Party to join the SDP in 1981 and served on the Federal Executive of the Liberal Democrats from the formation of the Party in 1988 until 1998. He also served as political advisor to the Rt Hon. Paddy Ashdown, 1988–98. Out of Parliament, he was appointed a Parliamentary advisor to GEC (1983–84) and then Director General of the British Retail Consortium (1985–87). In 1987, he joined public relations firm Hill and

Knowlton as Director of Public Affairs, before moving to a similar position at Shandwick Public Relations in 1993. He subsequently became Vice-Chairman of Shandwick. In 2003, he was appointed to the new post of non-executive Vice-Chairman of Weber Shandwick following the take-over of Shandwick by American communications giant Interpublic.

**Martin Meznar** received his PhD in International Business from the University of South Carolina. He is currently an Associate Professor of Management in the School of Global Management and Leadership, Arizona State University in Phoenix. A highly regarded instructor, his teaching responsibilities are in the areas of strategic management and international business. His research interests include corporate social responsibility and public affairs management in multinational corporations. A long-contributing member of the Academy of International Business, Academy of Management, and International Association of Business & Society, his work has been published in a variety of outlets including the *Academy of Management Journal, Business & Society,* the *Journal of International Management,* and the *Journal of Public Affairs.*

**Dr Bruce I. Newman** is currently Professor of Marketing at DePaul University, founding Editor-in-Chief of the *Journal of Political Marketing*; and recently Visiting Scholar at the Institute of Government at the University of California-Berkeley and in the Department of Political Science at Stanford University. He has published nine books (including *The Marketing of the President* and *Handbook of Political Marketing*) and numerous articles on the subjects of political marketing and consumer psychology. Dr Newman lectures around the world on the topics of political and business marketing, and is represented by World Class Speakers & Entertainers (www.speak.com). In 1993, Dr Newman received the Ehrenring (Ring of Honor) from the Austrian Advertising Research Association in Vienna for his research in political marketing, and during 1995–1996 he advised the Clinton White House on communication strategy.

**William D. Oberman** is Associate Professor of Business in the John L. Grove College of Business, Shippensburg University, Pennsylvania. He received his PhD from the University of Pittsburgh's Katz Graduate School of Business and has been on the faculties at the Universities of New Mexico, Penn State, and Pittsburgh. He has published many articles on business–government relations and has continuing research interests in the areas of social networks, conceptions of corporate social responsibility and business involvement in the public policy process. He teaches MBA and undergraduate courses in business and society, business ethics, business and public policy, and strategic management. He is a long-time contributing member of the Social Issues in Management division of the Academy of Management and the International Association of Business and Society.

**Robin Pedler** is an Associate Fellow of Templeton College, Oxford University. He is also Academic Director of the European Training Institute, Brussels. He had a career in international management, becoming Director, External Relations Europe, with

Mars. In 1991 he returned to academic life. He has conducted 'EU Presidency' training with government officials in Belgium, Finland, Sweden and the UK. He has worked extensively in recently joined states. Publications include *European Union Lobbying: Changes in the Arena – 14 Case Studies* and *Shaping European Law and Policy – the role of committees and comitology in the political process.*

**Douglas G. Pinkham** is the president of the Public Affairs Council of America. Under his leadership, the Council has expanded its Internet-based services, management consulting practice and research on emerging public affairs trends. Prior to joining the Council, Mr Pinkham was vice president of communications for the American Gas Association (AGA). He is also an accredited member of the Public Relations Society of America. He serves on the boards of the Center for Ethics in Government, the Boston College Center for Corporate Citizenship, and the European Centre for Public Affairs. He is also a judge in the Points of Light Foundation's Awards of Excellence in Corporate Community Service. He has authored numerous articles for trade and professional magazines around the world and is a frequent speaker on public affairs issues, politics, communications and corporate management.

**Rinus van Schendelen** has been Professor in Political Science at Erasmus University, Rotterdam, since 1980. He has written many books and articles on lobbying and public affairs management, particularly at the EU level. His most recent books are *Machiavelli in Brussels: The Art of Lobbying the EU* (2002) and (co-editor) *The Unseen Hand: Unelected EU Legislators* (2003). He frequently trains lobby groups at the EU level.

**Christian Scheucher** holds Masters degrees from Harvard and the University of Vienna. He currently runs Christian Scheucher Consulting Ltd, a political and public affairs consulting firm working internationally for candidates and corporations. Political consulting focuses on election campaigns in Central and Eastern Europe to the Caucasian States. Corporate work on CEO-level only includes clients in health care, communications and infrastructure. He is also the European Editor for the *Journal of Public Affairs.*

**James Shaw** is Community Affairs Manager at Nexen Inc., based in Calgary, Alberta, Canada. From his early start in the petroleum industry as a surface land negotiator, Jim has tirelessly sought resolution to stakeholder issues through open dialogue, clear communication and innovative engagement initiatives. His successes in stakeholder engagement have made him a sought-after speaker on the subject, having presented in Canada, Europe and South America. Jim has studied at the University of Calgary, holds an advanced certificate in Corporate Community Involvement from Boston College and is a Canadian Registered Safety Professional.

**Patrick Shaw** was a senior research fellow at the Melbourne Business School (MBS) in the 1970s and has established successful stakeholder engagement initiatives for several major Canadian projects. He is managing director of Quorum Strategic

Inc., a management consulting and strategic communications firm (www. quorumstrategic.com). His practice includes clients in natural resource, financial services, health care and technology organizations where he helps establish communication-leveraged change, inside and outside. His work often draws upon the disciplines of stakeholder engagement, issues management, risk, and crisis communication. Pat has been an active member of the International Association of Business Communicators and has served as president of the 1,400 member Toronto chapter. He is a member of the Institute of Corporate Directors of Canada. He holds a BScAg from the University of Alberta.

**Amy Showalter** heads the Showalter Group, Inc., and is employed by leading organizations to help improve their grassroots and PAC effectiveness. Her clients include national trade associations and Fortune 500 companies including Southwest Airlines, American Heart Association, New York Life Insurance, Kraft Foods, National Federation of Independent Business, ConocoPhillips, and the Dow Chemical Company, among others. She is a faculty member of the US Chamber's Institute for Organization Management, as well as The Capitol.Net. She serves on the Board of the Washington Area State Relations Group and the Government Relations Section Council of the American Society of Association Executives. Amy is the co-founder and producer of Innovate to Motivate, the largest national conference for grassroots and PAC professionals, author of *Beyond Fundraisers and Fly-Ins—105 Ways to Keep in Touch with Your Elected Officials All Year* as well as more than 50 articles on grassroots and PAC development.

**Thomas Spencer** is Executive Director of the European Centre for Public Affairs at the SEMS School of Management, University of Surrey, Guildford and Visiting Professor of Public Affairs at Brunel University, Uxbridge. As a committed environ-mentalist he was, from 1995 to 1999, President of GLOBE International (Global Legislators Organization for a Balanced Environment) that links four hundred members of parliament worldwide. From 2002 to 2003 he was Chairman of Counterpart Europe, an NGO active in sixty countries. He was also a Commissioner of the Commission on Globalization between 2000 and 2003, and Co-Moderator of the "National Sovereignty and Universal Challenges: Choices for the World after Iraq" conference held in Brussels in June 2003.

Tom Spencer writes, lectures and broadcasts widely. He holds the Great Golden Medal for Merit of the Republic of Austria (1996) and the Forum for the Future's Green Ribbon Award (1999). He is a member of the Council of Federal Trust and a Trustee of the Friends of Europe organization.

**Clive S. Thomas** is Professor of Political Science and Chair of the Department of Social Science at the University of Alaska, Juneau. His publications include books, articles and chapters on interest groups, most recently the *Research Guide to US and International Interest Groups* (2004). He has been a volunteer lobbyist and teaches seminars on lobby organization and tactics. During 1997–1998 and spring 2000 he was a Fulbright Senior Research Scholar in Brussels, studying American interest groups operating in the European Union. He has also received Fulbright awards to the Slovak Republic and to Argentina and Peru.

**Simon Titley** studied International Relations at the University of Keele, and has been an active member of the British Liberal and Liberal Democrat parties since 1975. He began his professional career in 1979 in the national headquarters of the Liberal Party, and subsequently worked in various political and NGO campaign roles. He has been a public affairs consultant since 1993, based in both London and Brussels, specializing in designing and organizing grassroots and media campaigns. From 1998 to 1999, he was one of the organizers of the Save Duty Free Campaign, the first major application of pressure group-style campaign techniques to an EU business lobbying effort.

**Duane Windsor** is Lynette S. Autrey Professor of Management in Rice University's Jesse H. Jones Graduate School of Management, Houston, Texas. He teaches courses in leadership and business ethics in the MBA for Executives program and an MBA elective in public–nonprofit financial and strategic management. Previously he taught required MBA courses in legal and government processes and in strategy. His published work emphasizes anti-corruption efforts, corporate social responsibility, and stakeholder theory. His publications include "Public Affairs, Issues Management, and Political Strategy: Opportunities, Obstacles, and Caveats", *Journal of Public Affairs* (January 2002) and "The Development of International Business Norms", *Business Ethics Quarterly* (October 2004). He co-authored, with Lee E. Preston, *The Rules of the Game in the Global Economy: Policy Regimes for International Business* (1997, 1992). He earned his BA from Rice University (Political Science); AM and PhD from Harvard University (Political Economy and Government).

# Foreword

*Douglas G. Pinkham*

It's remarkable that a working knowledge of public affairs is not required of every business school graduate. Students learn the essentials of finance, marketing, and operations management, but many don't do more than dip a toe into the waters of politics, regulation, corporate reputation, and social responsibility.

Why? For one thing, public affairs trends and outcomes are difficult to measure and analyze. It's not easy to turn case studies about a company's business environment into flow charts and predictive models. The externalities faced by a business are numerous and oftentimes unique to that company's history, industry sector, location, and place in the market.

This is not to say that business schools ignore the subject altogether. Indeed, many offer electives on "Business and the Environment," "Social Issues in Management," and "Legal Issues in Management" or "Business Law." Some even focus directly on the role of government in society. But if a financial manager (and future CEO) goes into graduate school with the goal of studying finance, he or she can do just that—and gain only minimal exposure to the ways in which public policy and public opinion affect an organization's success.

As a result, many of the world's most influential companies are run and managed by individuals who lack an understanding of public affairs.

These are very bright people, however. When they see the collapse of the GE–Honeywell merger, antitrust suits facing Microsoft, local opposition to the opening of new Wal-Mart stores, or the global protests against McDonald's and Citibank, they know that something difficult and unpredictable is going on.

Many corporate leaders are now realizing that the externalities facing their business models are as vexing as their operational or competitive challenges. The problem is that many have not integrated public affairs considerations into their overall business strategy. That means their decisions and organization's responses may be ineffective or counterproductive.

To make matters worse, corporations are still living in the shadow of Enron, Global Crossing, WorldCom, $6,000 shower curtains, insider trading, and other corporate scandals. Unfortunately, the public's distrust of business will probably get worse before it gets better. It is interesting to note that a 2004 poll by Harris Interactive showed that 74 percent of the public believes Corporate America's reputation is either "not good" or "terrible." It should come as no surprise that even a well-meaning business leader from a reputable company may find him- or herself facing hostile consumers, investors, and employees.

At the same time, it has become apparent to even the most free-market-thinking top executive that government and its influence are here to stay. The government decides how business is conducted, who owns information, who merges or acquires another firm and who pays what taxes. The rise of globalization, concerns about homeland security, and governance rules created by the Sarbanes-Oxley Act have actually done much to expand the role of government in the United States. In state capitals, in Brussels, in Washington, DC—everywhere—there are many responsible people hard at work developing and implementing public policies.

Companies that do understand the public affairs challenges often face internal tests. The pace of business often makes it difficult to think and act in the long term—or to coordinate complex enterprises and relationships. According to research conducted by the Foundation for Public Affairs (Washington, DC), more than one-third of corporations don't highly coordinate the activities of government relations and corporate communications departments. At a minimum, this means they are leaving business opportunities on the table. But it also means that they may not be doing a good job of managing the company's risk levels in the marketplace.

In this environment, companies (as well as non-profit organizations) need to understand all aspects of public affairs strategy. *The Handbook of Public Affairs* is a comprehensive guide to best knowledge and practices in the field. It explains the relationship between public policy and business performance, public affairs tools and tactics, and effective management systems. Case studies are used to examine how public affairs and politics intersect in North America, the European Union and other regions of the world. In its final section the book ties together cutting-edge scholarly developments in the public affairs field with real-world trends in business and government.

The net effect is an authoritative source of knowledge about a vitally important management function. Everyone—from business school deans to chief executive officers to seasoned public affairs executives—can find information in *The Handbook of Public Affairs* to help them achieve their reputation and public policy-related goals.

# Foreword

*Lord Tom McNally*

If you count in my time as a student politician I have spent forty years in active politics. During that time I have worked as a party official, a civil servant, a Member of Parliament, as in-house advisor to a large manufacturing company, as director-general of a major trade association and as director of public affairs for two of the world's largest PR agencies, Hill & Knowlton and Weber Shandwick. For the last nine years I have also been a member of the House of Lords.

I give that brief outline of my career to explain why it gives me such pleasure to contribute alongside Douglas Pinkham a foreword to this *Handbook of Public Affairs*. My forty-year odyssey through public life has given me a front-row seat to watch the development of public affairs from a minor monitoring service to a full-blown profession. The bringing together in this publication of both academic and hands-on professional expertise is a welcome sign of that coming of age. Public affairs is now carried out by trained practitioners working to the highest standards of professional ethics. The service they provide is based on research, analysis, and experience. Over the last forty years public affairs has moved from being an optional extra for the PR department to being an operational necessity in the boardroom. It is as much flying blind in the modern corporate world to take decisions without public affairs advice as it would be to do so without financial or legal advice.

We live in a world of instant 24/7 communication which makes the capacity to absorb, analyze, and advise on developing events a key asset for public affairs practitioners. So too is an understanding of political decision making at local, regional, national, and international level. The power and reach of regulators and their capacity to adopt best practice from each other, the pace and direction of international trade agreements, the likely impact of new technologies, the opening up of new markets, all need a public affairs understanding and input.

So too does the work of non-governmental organizations and pressure groups. Reputation management and corporate social responsibility are all concepts relatively new to the boardroom agenda. Yet miscalculations and mistakes in these areas can have catastrophic impacts on the bottom line. Neither should we assume that this handbook will be for boardroom reading only. The NGOs and pressure groups have become increasingly sophisticated and professional in presenting their cases.

In the end this increase in professionalism on all sides is a major contribution to better governance. It was an American practitioner who said that where one lobbyist is at work the public interest may be under threat but where many are at work the public interest is enhanced. I have seen the truth of that observation from both sides of the fence. I have used my professional experience to enable a client to make the right case to the right person at the right time to make sure that a particular piece of legislation came out in a way helpful to a company. As a parliamentarian I have used the expert briefing of lobbyists to test and probe the likely effectiveness of proposed legislation.

Public Affairs today is an essential ingredient both in good corporate governance and of more effective and efficient law making. Some of the damage done to public affairs by scandals in the past were part of the growing pains of a profession which grew too fast for its own and external regulation to cope. Today, however, on both sides of the Atlantic, and more widely internationally, there are legal frameworks and professional codes of conduct which safeguard the interests of both clients and public affairs professionals.

Greater transparency, increased professionalism, and increased academic study and support all come together to underpin a profession now enjoying maturity. *The Handbook of Public Affairs* is both a testament to that maturity and an invaluable working manual for those working in or wishing to understand public affairs.

# Preface

A prudent man must always follow in the footsteps of great men and imitate those who have been outstanding. If his own prowess fails to compare with theirs, at least it has an air of greatness about it.

(Niccolo Machiavelli)

*The Handbook of Public Affairs* has been designed and planned to be a high-quality pivotal text of leading-edge articles, which will act as the core reference point for those practising in, researching, or studying public affairs in Europe, America, and Australasia. There are increasing amounts of published research in this field and it is an area of professional practice that has seen substantial growth over the past decade. Public affairs, and particularly government relations/lobbying, have evolved from a tactic adopted by organizations to amend occasional legislation to become a major international managerial strategy to achieve competitive advantage.

The rapidly increasing strategic role of public affairs has been spurred on by the trend towards deregulation, privatization, and regulation. This, together with the globalization of business operations and a surge in transnational government legislation (European Union, North American Free Trade Area, World Trade Organization) has forced organizations of all types to pay greater attention to their relationship with government—at all levels. The formal approval of acquisitions, alliances, mergers, standard setting, and takeovers is increasingly under scrutiny of government as it attempts to regulate markets and trade. The regulation of auditing and the large accountancy groups is now much on the world public affairs agenda and exercising leading corporate, political, and research minds as they attempt to produce good corporate governance.

The increasing role of government as regulator as old corporatist linkages break down under globalization is a phenomenon that public affairs practitioners and corporations have to deal with on a daily and yet strategic basis. The transfer of publicly owned businesses to the private sector such as energy, telecommunications, and water utilities has directly stimulated the increasing importance of the public affairs area.

In addition the growth of increasingly powerful and well organized pressure groups, which are capable of mobilizing strong opposition to organizations whose policies they disagree with, has further stimulated public affairs work, stakeholder programs, political campaigning, and lobbying activity. Technological advances within the media now allow events in virtually any part of the world to be screened almost instantaneously, subjecting the behaviour of organizations even in the most remote parts of the globe to worldwide media and public scrutiny. The global dialogue on trade, commerce, and investment involves business executives, government officials, and representatives of non-governmental organizations. Not surprisingly, this dialogue often includes environmental (ecological), social, sustainability, and community issues. Thus the entire business–government–society relationship is open to discussion, debate, and redefinition throughout the world.

Businesses, government agencies, and NGOs have a stake in cultivating a dialogue that is informed, fact-driven, and progressive. Population growth, the need for improved quality of life, military security, human rights, and sustainable economic and ecological practices are among the broad issues shaping the public agenda for nations across the globe. Constructive dialogue depends on accurate information, commitment to human interaction, and the willingness to think long as well as short term.

If you have any suggestions for improvements to *The Handbook of Public Affairs* please let us know, as we intend to update this cutting edge work on a regular basis.

Phil Harris and Craig S. Fleisher

# Acknowledgments

In putting together the first *Handbook of Public Affairs* there are many people we owe thanks to. It has been a long task and one which at times has seemed very daunting. "Where do you start and where do you end?" we kept on saying. The discipline is an evolving and dynamic one and we hope we have done it credit in an international context. Thanks are due to many. First our advisory board, which represents many of the leading figures in the field; Geoff Allen, Tim Clement-Jones, Mark Hatcher, Raymond Hoewing, Andrew Lock, John Mahon, Tom McNally, Danny Moss, Bruce Newman, James Post, Tom Spencer, and Teresa Yancey Crane, whose support, kindness, and singleminded support have been very important to us. There are the unsung heroes who typed and did background research for us, invariably at the last moment and at breakneck speed. These included Anna Gunnell, Victor Knip, Heather Lings, May Nhan, Maddie Maher, Jessica Smith, and the library and research staff of our respective institutions. We also would particularly like to thank the support of our respective business schools in Canada (Odette), Manchester (MMUBS), and New Zealand (Otago) without whose support and research funding we would never have been able to produce what we believe is a groundbreaking guide to effective international public affairs. Also to organizations across the world such as the Academy of Marketing Political Marketing Group, the Australian Centre for Corporate Public Affairs, Canadian Council for Public Affairs Advancement, European Centre for Public Affairs, International Association of Business and Society, International Association of Business Communicators, International Public Relations Research Symposium, Public Affairs Association of Canada, UK Centre for Corporate and Public Affairs at Manchester Metropolitan University, US Center for PA Management (Washington, DC) and the *Journal of Public Affairs* and its publishers, Henry Stewart, of London. The latter, which is becoming the leading journal in the field, helped in the development and underpinning of the work.

Most importantly we thank Sage and our superbly encouraging editor, Delia Alfonso Martinez, who encouraged and supported us at every stage of the development of the *Handbook* regardless of the time and other pressures. Finally, and perhaps most important to us, can we thank Irene Harris, Angela, Zachary, Austin, and Kieren Fleisher for their patience, support, and good humour. It was freely given and gratefully received.

Phil and Craig

# Introduction

## The Development of a Sub-discipline and Major Area of Research

*Phil Harris and Craig S. Fleisher*

One change leaves the way open for the introduction of others.

Niccolo Machiavelli, *The Prince*

*The Handbook of Public Affairs* is the first international research-focused book to capture the true depth and essence of this rapidly growing and strategically important management discipline. We hope it will act as the core reference point for those practicing in, researching or studying public affairs in Europe, North America, and the wider world. We believe it reflects the leading practice and thinking in this rapidly growing area of strategic management. All the chapters have been specially commissioned and reviewed to ensure they reflect the best of international practice in public affairs.

The book is laid out in four parts: I The Environments of Public Affairs, II Tools, Techniques and Organizing for Public Affairs, III Case Studies in Public Affairs, IV Scholarship and Theory Building in Public Affairs. Each part has a comprehensive introduction and linking section, which outlines the content of each section. To underpin the depth of the area we have deliberately extended Part III, Case Studies in Public Affairs, to enable the reader to appreciate national and international practice fully.

Public affairs strategy we see as being dominated by the need to influence policy. There are three broad historic definitions of public affairs. The first is that it is the policy formulation process of public and corporate stakeholder programmes. For instance, in the United Kingdom most broadcasting franchise holders such as Granada, Channel 4, etc., have developed regular practical programs to ensure good two-way dialog with all commercial, political, and regional interests to maintain and strengthen their position both alongside the franchise offerer (government) and the regulator. The second is that it is the corporate consideration of the impact of environmental (in its broadest sense), political, and social developments on a company and the opinion-leader contact programs which follow. For example, both in Brussels and in Whitehall it is interesting to see which takeovers and mergers are favored or frowned upon by government regulators controlled by politicians. The same can be seen in the United States, with politicians being more inclined to support one airline company than another. Planned airline mergers and the operation of through ticketing initiatives can be supported or not by politicians, and much of this support or lack of it is gained over a period of time. The final definition is more focused and has very strong North American origins. It is the totality of government affairs or relations. The latter in Europe would mean government at local, regional, national, and transnational levels, operated by elected and/or appointed officials, whilst in the United States the focus is on Washington and/or the state legislatures.

This handbook touches upon the first two definitions but for its direction focuses on the strategic use of government affairs as the core component of modern public affairs work. The reason for taking this approach is simply that it is often the most strategically important area to the company or organization and invariably reflects those issues that could be considered under the first two definitions. The reason for the hegemony of government affairs within the public affairs function is that government activity has grown dramatically in the last twenty years at all levels, a result of internationalism, deregulation, and regulation across all sectors of business. Increasingly the area of public affairs is playing a strategic role within the company or organization as it attempts to position itself in changing environments where government is responding to various environmental pressures to modify policy.

## BUSINESS ORGANIZATIONS

For companies in the private sector, the influence of government is ever present, whether in the form of tax payments to be made, technical standards to be met, or safety, health, and environmental laws that need to be complied with, and so on. The United Kingdom's membership of the European Union has meant even more additional legislation and directives coming from the Commission, Parliament and other European bodies on common issues, such as environmental legislation. It has been argued that over 70 percent of domestic legislation in this area comes from Brussels; for instance, setting standards on water quality, air pollution, and packaging standards all comes from this source. While businesses have to ensure they are always up to date on all legislation and policy decisions, they also need to identify issues which might result in legislation if they are not addressed early and well enough.

However, rather than just monitoring developments in one's immediate business environment, one needs to be proactive and take an active part in the policy formulation process, by using one's right to express one's views and concerns. Only then is one able to shape the outcome, to amend, to delay or prevent legislation altogether. Here, for example, carbon taxes coming from legislators and their respective governments can have a significant impact on the profitability and viability of chemical and oil companies. Thus a dialog about implementation, the impact of tax on countries' interests, the level of tax and giving background data on the implications of a program in this area can be vital for the strategic success and direction of the organization. For companies operating in such regulated markets as telecommunications, the media or pharmaceuticals, it is vital that they have this regular two-way dialog with government or face legislation which may be against their strategic interest.

In the case of public sector organizations, government has more direct control over the strategic direction and shape of their operation. Consequently there is a need to ensure government listens to the organization's corporate views, but it must be remembered that sometimes determined politicians do not want to hear strategic views from state organizations.

Despite the surge in privatization policies across the world over the last two decades many privatized industries and public service providers are still under indirect government control as they are frequently answerable to regulatory bodies which set and review prices and quality standards for the products and services of many of the industries. To discuss any desired or threatening change in regulation, these regulators have to be approached and are thus regularly exposed to extensive lobbying.

The importance of influencing government policy for the corporate entity is essential at a number of levels, as it frequently impacts upon the direction and strategy of the company. Examples are that government can be a source of income, as customer (defense equipment procurement is an obvious example) or finance provider by offering support in the form of grants or export credits to underpin preferred policy initiatives. In takeover, merger, and corporate cooperation activity it can have a direct impact by considering referral to the various national and international competition authorities or even the World Trade Organization. A referral or long delay at one of these bodies can cause serious damage to a company, which could be reflected in its share value, which might be part of a planned competitor's activity. Thus it is essential that ahead of any action in this area the relevant regulatory authorities are sounded out to check out their reaction to anticipated corporate action. By taking this approach one can reduce risk and increase the likelihood of being given government approval for the planned merger/cooperation activity or, alternatively, decide not to progress with what will almost certainly not be given approval. In addition one can use this area of government regulation to apply pressure to fend off unwanted takeovers.

For charities, NGOs, and pressure groups, legislation is also important, but often in a more positive way than for business organizations, since it can help to protect or support their beneficiaries. In addition, charities can make officials pay attention to small but important details, as, for example, the need to remember at the planning stage to make buildings accessible to disabled people.

The core reasons for the growth and rising importance of public affairs as a management discipline would appear to be:

1  Increased internationalization and competition in business markets increases the importance of governments creating a competitive business environment.
2  Importation and influence of a more structured corporate lobbying system from the United States whose objective is to influence legislation affecting business markets.

3   Increased corporate acquisition, merger, strategic alliance, and joint venture
    activity.
4   The growth of international and transnational government is generating sub-
    stantial legislation affecting businesses, for example on the environment. This
    has brought lobbying at an international and national level to ensure business's
    voice is heard when proposals are being formulated.

Shaping the external environment by influencing government through lobbying
activities or corporate campaigning is now typical of strategic marketing management
practice, whether it be for business, public or not-for-profit sectors. The relevance of
such activities stems, of course, from the fact that there is hardly an item of legislation
passed through the EU, UK or US legislatures which does not in some way encroach
upon business interests or impinge on organizational goals. The proposal to tax audio
tapes (Harris and Lock, 1996), for example, would have affected a variety of organizations, including educationalists and charities such as the Royal National Institute for
the Blind (RNIB), not to mention a large number of consumers of blank tapes.
Discreet organizing via a commercial lobbyist company funded as part of a coalition
of interests by the European Japanese Electronic Manufacturers Association resulted
in the proposals being substantially amended. Changing the wording of a proposal or
the insertion of a special exception in regulations can be worth millions of dollars,
euros or pounds to commercial organizations and be crucial to the survival of non-
profit organizations' activities.

The "golden rule" of lobbying is to get involved as early as possible. Also, one
should not expect to enter a consultation and be able to demand changes.
Government officials and servants need to be cultivated *before* they are needed,
which means one has to invest in building good personal relationships of trust, not
by wining and dining them but by supplying reliable and sufficient information
whenever asked and keeping them generally well informed about relevant developments and concerns. Once the need to influence policy arises, one has to have a well
prepared and strongly argued case. Length and depth of the relationships established with key figures are important but if one is asking for a favor without convincing arguments to found it on, it is difficult for the other side to see one's point.

One also has to be prepared to compromise. Even a small step into the desired
direction is often a success, compared with achieving nothing because one is not
ready to negotiate. "Cooperation, not confrontation" should always be the motto.

## TARGETING

To approach government effectively, the key people involved in the relevant decision-
making process need to be identified as clearly as possible, which requires knowledge of government structure and the relation of each element to the overall
policy-making process. Listed below is a taxonomy of situations in which government is involved, and the suggested relative importance of public affairs in influencing outcomes.

1   *Government as purchaser or allocator:*

  (a)   *Winner takes all.* In a number of situations, there is only one contract or opportunity to be bid for. Lottery franchises are a good example. Price is rarely the sole criterion. The public decision is usually very visible and lobbying is rife.

  (b)   *Large, infrequent contracts.* Defense and large public works contracts are typical of this category. Increasingly failure to obtain such contracts threatens the very existence of the company or a strategic business unit with a visible and politically delicate impact on employment.

  (c)   *Regularly supplied items.* Apart from highly specialized items, these are usually supplied through standard purchasing procedures, notably by competitive tender. These procedures leave little scope for lobbying, except in so far as it may be necessary to qualify a supplier to be included in the approved list or to pass any other pre-tender hurdles.

2   *Government as legislator and framer of regulations.* Legislation on matters such as product safety, trademarks and intellectual property, and fair trading are obvious targets for business lobbying, to ensure that legitimate interests are protected. However, it is easily forgotten that a great many matters that affect specific businesses are enacted through regulations under enabling legislation. Visible examples are vehicle Construction and Use regulations, and regulations affecting food and agriculture. Lobbying is important here to ensure that regulations are sensibly framed and represent an appropriate balance of business and other pressure group interests.

3   *Government as initiator of action.* There are a number of explicit circumstances in which the relevant secretary of state initiates action by a quango or similar body. The most familiar case is the Monopolies and Mergers Commission in the UK. In other examples, where a quango can initiate action itself, the government of the day exerts some influence in terms of matters that are taken up and is frequently the final arbiter in terms of action upon the recommendations it receives. Lobbying in terms of provision of information as well as persuasive communication plays an important role in shaping the progress of events.

4   *Government and European legislation and regulation.* With the increasing influence of US and European directives and regulations upon product markets, proper representation of manufacturers' interests has become critical in those areas which the EU and the US is seeking to regulate.

5   *Government as decision maker.* There are a range of other situations where the government has *de facto* or *de jure* powers to take decisions which affect business.

We have conducted extensive research with politicians, government officials, and public affairs professionals in America and Europe and what emerges is that organizations can be seriously disadvantaged if they are not providing information to support their long-term business positions or counter their national and international corporate competitors by providing information to relevant bodies. This may well sound very logical, but the reality is that a number of interests and companies lack the know-how or understanding of the various EU, UK or US government processes and their ability to develop policy and regulations which impact upon them and the markets in which they operate. This puts them at a serious disadvantage.

In certain markets it is more important for the corporation or organization to be involved in supplying information to the government process because of regulation or deregulation. Major business areas where lobbying is essential are pharmaceuticals, broadcasting, utilities, transport and infrastructure contracts, etc. The need to lobby and influence government policy as the world internationalizes is increasing rather than decreasing, and lobbying is becoming a highly professionalized, invariably ethical, and increasingly regulated part of business strategy. *The Handbook of Public Affairs* with its quality advice from some of the world's leading figures and researchers will allow you to understand the discipline more and practice it even better.

## REFERENCES

Harris, P., and A. Lock (1996). "Machiavellian Marketing: The Development of Corporate Lobbying in the UK," *Journal of Marketing Management* 12 (4).
Machiavelli, Niccolo (1532). *The Prince*, trans. G. Bull. London: Penguin (1961).

# PART I

# The Environments of Public Affairs

A prince also wins prestige for being a true friend or a true enemy …

Revealing himself without reservation in favor of one against another. This policy is always more advantageous than neutrality.

Niccolo Machiavelli

## THE ENVIRONMENTS OF PUBLIC AFFAIRS

This first part of *The Handbook of Public Affairs* is designed to appeal to those trying to gain an international perspective into the history of the discipline and how it is evolving. In its chapters it gives the background to the evolution of public affairs in America and Europe and how it is developing. Chapters by Pedlar and Hawkinson will particularly appeal to the practitioner, whilst statesmen and politicians will appreciate the comments of Spencer and Harris. Oberman and Holcomb's work shows the impressive evolution of the discipline, whilst Fleisher points to the way the discipline is evolving internationally. Each chapter is by a recognized expert in the field and outlines the best in modern thinking in the area. This part encompasses seven subject matter areas related to public affairs and business-government relations more generally, including:

1 History and critique of US public affairs.
2 History of public affairs in the European Union and United Kingdom.
3 Internationalization and importance of public affairs.
4 Public policy processes in North America.
5 Public policy processes in the European Union.
6 State of public affairs in the United States.
7 Public affairs practice in the United Kingdom.

In the first chapter, "The Global Development of Public Affairs," joint editor Professor Craig Fleisher of the Odette School of Business, University of Windsor, Ontario, argues that the onset of the twenty-first century arrived with a concomitant need for business organizations to effectively interact with international public policy stakeholders and issues. Crafting managerial responses to the complexity, dynamism, and uncertainty created by the global convergence and increased interdependence of financial markets, information and technology has become a common challenge to contemporary executives. Boundary-spanning activities like international public affairs and government relations (PA/GR) linking aspects of international business, corporate political activity, and strategic management serve essential managerial roles. Although it has not been the recipient of voluminous systematic thinking, the application of new ideas and perspectives related to the PA/GR function as performed in international or global contexts has emerged as a valuable topic of consideration to business practitioners and scholars.

Policy concerns related to international business are frequently high-priority public and business policy items in most nation-states. These concerns may, for example, be about trade agreements and conflicts, the flows of people, financial resources, and goods, the opening of or restrictions on markets (e.g., protectionism, standards setting, tariff/non-tariff or trade barriers, dumping, export subsidies, etc.), or rulings against market offenders (e.g., penalties or sanctions), and the like. Some of the more prominent public policy concerns facing international businesses are listed.

In Chapter 2, "Public Affairs in North America: US Origins and Development," John Holcomb of the Daniels College of Business, University of Denver, Colorado, argues that business and politics have always had an interesting and dynamic coexistence in the United States. The chapter looks at the historical development of public affairs as it has occurred in the United States up to the present day. It identifies the societal events and trends particularly in the United States throughout the twentieth century that led business to organize PA efforts.

Holcomb's work looks at those key events or trends that led to the formation and reformation of corporate and association-based PA structures, as well as institutional factors that have created forces—both accelerators and inhibitors—affecting its evolution. Particular attention is given to the development of the field itself, noting its individual champions, leading practitioners, and scholarly associations (i.e., foundations, research centers, and think tanks), educational providers, and consultancy base.

Robin Pedler of Templeton College, Oxford, one of the leading European lobbying educators and writers, in Chapter 3, "The History and Development of Public Affairs in the European Union and United Kingdom," argues that just as in the United States, business and politics have also had an interesting and dynamic coexistence in Europe and the United Kingdom.

Pedler assesses the historical development of public affairs as it has occurred in the

European Union and United Kingdom up to the present time. It identifies the societal events and trends throughout the twentieth century that led business to organize and the formation and reformation of corporate and association-based PA structures, as well as institutional factors that have created forces—both accelerators and inhibitors—affecting its evolution. Special attention is given to the development of the field in the European Union itself, noting its individual champions, leading practitioners, and scholarly associations (i.e., foundations, research centers, and think tanks), educational providers, and consultancy base.

In the fourth chapter, "The External Environment of Public Affairs in North America: Public Policy Process and Institutions," William Oberman of Shippensburg University (USA) outlines how corporate and association-based "public affairs takes place in a macro-environmental context of public policy processes and institutions ... with which its practices interact. Public policy processes and institutions include the social, political, and legal arrangements that structure interactions outside of, but also in conjunction with, agreements and exchanges made in private markets."

This chapter specifically provides the reader with a working understanding of how issues evolve through public policy processes such as law making, regulation, and legal review. It also provides descriptions of the purpose and structuring of the stakeholder-based institutions in which competing stakeholders contest issues and impact business, including the principal public entities such as the executive branch, legislatures, judiciary, and regulatory and administrative agencies as well as the non-governmental such as the media and public opinion. Last but not least, the chapter concludes by portraying the recent development of international organizations such as the World Trade Organization that are increasingly shaping North American public affairs.

In Chapter 5, "The External Environment of Public Affairs in the European Union and the United Kingdom: Public Policy Process and Institutions," that committed internationalist Tom Spencer, the chairman of the European

Centre for Public Affairs and past chairman of the European Parliament Foreign Affairs Committee, argues that:

> Philosophers tell us that it is logically impossible to "step into the same river twice." For lobbyists it is equally true that you never lobby the same European Union twice. The process of change is continuous, subtle and unrelenting. Treaties are the milestones by which the Union marks the passage of current practice into legal form. Each act of lobbying and the response to it creates new precedents and opens new possibilities. The Union is a vast dance to the music of power. Prime Ministers, parliamentarians, diplomats, consultants, civil society, and corporations constantly form new patterns and learn new steps. The speed and complexity of this continent-wide barn dance has accelerated in 2004—the Year of Change. The coincidence of the end of the quinquennial cycle of the Union with both a major enlargement and a new Constitutional Treaty has kept everyone on their toes. The study of public affairs is a valuable exercise in its own right but it can also tell us a great deal about the societies which play host to public affairs practice. This chapter seeks to shine light on the European system of public affairs by comparing it with the American model and by examining commonly expressed criticisms of both.

It has been suggested that "Public Affairs takes place in a macro-environmental context of public policy processes and institutions (a.k.a. the "non-market" environment) with which its practices interact. Public policy processes and institutions include the social, political and legal arrangements that structure interactions outside of, but also in conjunction with, agreements and exchanges made in private markets." Such a concept has its roots in the American experience and should be interpreted very differently in the European context.

In Chapter 6, "The Internal Environment of Public Affairs: Organization, Process, and Systems," Brian Hawkinson, of the US Public Affairs Council, argues that there is a term for a particular style of management—"Management by Walking Around." It refers to the art of getting out among the people engaged in the day-to-day activity of the enterprise to see what is going on, what successes are being achieved and what problems need to be dealt with. It gives managers insight into individual performance, but, more important, into broader issues and trends that affect the performance of the larger enterprise.

At the Public Affairs Council and Foundation for Public Affairs they practice a variation of that approach which he calls "Management by Asking Around," or MBAA.

> By observing and asking our member-company public affairs executives a lot of questions about their work—what they do, how they do it, what resources they devote to achieving what goals, we are able to understand how they apply the skills and resources of an integrated public affairs function to shaping public policy and public opinion in order to create market advantage for their companies. We are also able to identify and understand the issues and trends that affect the practice of corporate public affairs on a broad scale.
>
> Part of "Management by Asking Around" entails finding out not only what public affairs executives engage in but also which specific activities matter most to their success. The Public Affairs Council has been doing this "asking" partly through the regular administration of a comprehensive survey called the *State of Corporate Public Affairs*, three of which were conducted during the 1990s, in 1992, 1996 and 1999. In the most recent edition of the *State of Corporate Public Affairs Survey*, conducted by the Foundation for Public Affairs (2002a), we asked around nearly 600 of the prime US-based member organizations on this topic and got some interesting replies.

In the final chapter co-editor Phil Harris explores developments in UK public affairs and how the need to raise funding by the political parties has meant their conferences are increasingly an opportunity for the PA industry to explore policy options and meet activists, etc. United Kingdom PA management practice and its use of issues management are explored.

# 1

# The Global Development of Public Affairs

CRAIG S. FLEISHER

The onset of the twenty-first century arrived with a concomitant need for business organizations to effectively interact with international public policy stakeholders and issues. Crafting managerial responses to the complexity, dynamism, and uncertainty created by the global convergence and increased interdependence of financial markets, information, and technology has become a common challenge to contemporary executives. Boundary-spanning activities like international public affairs and government relations (PA/GR) linking aspects of international business, corporate political activity, and strategic management serve essential managerial roles. Although it has not been the recipient of voluminous systematic thinking, the application of new ideas and perspectives related to the PA/GR function as performed in international or global contexts has emerged as a valuable topic of consideration to business practitioners and scholars.

Policy concerns related to international business are frequently high-priority public and business policy items in most nation-states. These concerns may, for example, be about trade agreements and conflicts, the flows of people, financial resources, and goods, the opening of or restrictions to markets (e.g., protectionism, standards setting, tariff/non-tariff or trade barriers, dumping, export subsidies, etc.), or rulings against market offenders (e.g., penalties or sanctions), and the like. A select listing of some of the more prominent public policy concerns facing international businesses is provided in Exhibit 1.1.

---

**Exhibit 1.1 Selected International Public Policy Issues Affecting Business Interests and Organizations**

- Bribery, questionable payments to and/or corruption of government/public officials.
- Corporate social irresponsibility and unethical behaviors/practices.
- Disputes over land rights and claims.
- Environmental degradation and unsustainable practices.
- Exploiting workers (e.g., sweatshops).

- Export of outlawed products/services.
- Failure to abide by internationally accepted codes of business conduct.
- Funding of "front" or false activist groups.
- Insensitivity to local consumer and stakeholder interests and needs.
- Introduction of genetically modified food products.
- Irresponsible business practices, marketing, and sales.
- Manufacturing and trading military arms.
- Money laundering.
- Support of oppressive regimes.
- Unsafe working conditions.

Companies and industries intent on providing goods or services for the global market are nearly always impacted by the actions (or inaction) of governments and their political agents. This makes it incumbent upon businesses and business groups to interact with public policy decisions and decision-making processes, as well as public policy institutions and stakeholders in both their home (i.e., where they are headquartered) and host (i.e., where they maintain operations) countries in which they operate business activities. This PA/GR interaction commonly takes the form of environmental scanning/monitoring and intelligence development, sociopolitical and legal advising/counseling, lobbying (both formal and informal in nature), and sociopolitical communication/marketing or promotion processes.

Despite the increased need to effectively manage multinational and global issues and stakeholders and the challenges and opportunities they create for business organizations, the management and practice of PA/GR have received little scholarly attention in an international, global, cross-national, and/or comparative perspective. Very few books have been written on the topic, the results of a moderate number of research projects have been published, and only a few practitioner-focused articles have examined the topic in any appreciable depth. As a means for moving the development of an effective scholarly response forward, the author of this *Handbook of Public Affairs* chapter specifically intends to:

1　Examine the published literature on public affairs practice as it occurs around the globe.
2　Identify areas of the literature that offer promise for future study.
3　Establish avenues for conducting and improving future research.

## BACKGROUND AND DEFINITIONS

A useful question with which to begin our examination is whether the relative paucity of PA/GR scholarship could be caused by a lack of global PA practice. Are phenomena in the issue and stakeholder environment global, international, or cross-national by their natures? If the determination is made that stakeholders and/or issues do actually operate across borders, this leads to an important question. Do companies actually employ PA practices, processes or structures to address these matters on a global, as opposed to a more localized, basis?

There is often some definitional confusion when looking at the geographic nature or scope of a firm. This confusion arises because defining whether a firm is transnational, multinational, or global can depend upon what variables are being used to make the distinctions. Differences in these definitions can depend on items such as origin of ownership, headquarters location, national backgrounds of senior executives, the nature of the business strategy employed, or where the majority of customers or processes exist. As in many newer fields of business inquiry, the study of international business is beginning to arrive at agreed-upon definitions and consensual understanding of the critical terms.

Domestic companies are typically understood to conduct their operations wholly within the borders of a single nation-state. Once the company does business and horizontally operates across another border outside its host country, it internationalizes and therefore crosses the line to being an international, multinational, transnational, or global corporation. Hill (2003) defines an international business as "any firm that engages in international trade or investment." *Multinational corporations* ("MNCs" or "multinational enterprises") are conceptually different than "international corporations." Multinational corporations are now viewed to be single enterprises that operate beyond the borders of a single country and accomplish their objectives by deriving at least a moderate degree of their profits or revenues from outside their home region (Vernon and Wells, 1986).[1] "Transnational" is a term traditionally used by the United Nations to refer to MNCs, but recent usage often equates a "transnational" with a "global" enterprise as opposed to a "multinational" one (Wartick and Wood, 1998). Last but not least are attempts to describe "global" or "globalized" organizations. Sociologists such as Giddens (1999) define the term "global" more broadly than business or management scholars and see globalization as being related to worldwide interconnections at several levels that result from the elimination of communication and trade barriers and processes whereby cultural, economic, political, and social factors converge and create interdependences.

Some business experts claim that too much attention is given to "global" facets of commerce and that the word may be used in ways that are actually not accurate. For example, Rugman (2001) claims that globalization is mostly misunderstood and that one world trade zone has never actually existed in practice and that firms do not offer uniform or consistent products or services across all parts of the globe. If this view is indeed correct, then the existence of global public affairs and public policy-affective forces might also not be global in nature, given that commerce itself cannot be globally practiced. Rugman argues instead that government regulations and cultural differences divide the world into three major regional blocs of North America, the European Union and Japan, following up on arguments made previously by Ohmae (1985) of the importance of these three geographic clusters in the larger scheme of commerce. If the triad view is valid, scholars should have uncovered evidence that MNCs would have PA/GR decision makers, or at least responsibility centers, in the three triad areas. There is no empirical research of which the author is aware that has actually identified PA operations as being organized structurally or strategically along "triad" lines.

Working to some degree against these non-globalization arguments is the operation of stakeholders who simultaneously operate in multiple countries on single issues—such as the operations of Greenpeace relative to greenhouse gas issues or the operations of the World Wildlife Fund (WWF) relative to the issue of protecting wildlife within and across many national borders. Communication technology, facilitated to a heavy extent through the development of advanced telecommunications and the Internet and their subsequent use by global organizations, has created the theoretical, if not practically attained, ability for business and non-market stakeholders to operate in a global fashion. Also, a number of non-government organizations (NGOs) have certainly taken up the cause of anti-globalization and decry the activities of organizations, businesses in the form of MNCs and quasi-governmental bodies such as the International Monetary Fund (IMF) and World Trade Organization (WTO), that appear to exert much power in terms of influencing nation-state-level public policy decisions and, according to their views, negatively impact consumers, human rights, less developed countries, the natural environment, and workers.

The PA/GR activities of an international business will differ from those conducted in a purely domestic context. At the most simple level, differences arise from the fact that the cultural, economic, legal, political, and social systems in separate nation-states are different. If these distinctions and the organization's operations are important enough, it can potentially mean that the business may need to vary its PA/GR plans and activities on a country-by-country basis. International PA/GR is also more complex than purely domestic PA/GR. This arises not only from a greater number of issues and stakeholders but also from the need to coordinate and control responses across these different countries as well as between the organization's own headquarters/subsidiary units. Last but not least, governments and public policy makers frequently treat companies differently, depending on whether they call a country home or not.

Managing IPA/GR activities can be a most complex task because MNEs are not only single organizations operating in a global environment, but at the same time are also collections of interlinked subsidiaries that operate in a diversity of national environments (Drogendijk, 2004). Preston (1993) has noted that this complexity involves a series of international linkages among trade and investment relations, management links, and policy linkages. In light of this evolving context within which businesses operate, PA/GR practice and practitioners have been challenged to respond in helping organizations to positively address and engage issues and stakeholders that cross national boundaries. The next section of the chapter reviews trends impacting global PA/GR practice.

## PROMINENT TRENDS IN INTERNATIONAL PUBLIC AFFAIRS/GOVERNMENT RELATIONS

There is no shortage of books, journals, conferences, and articles describing the growing managerial challenges and opportunities created by the internationalization or globalization of business. The growth of the scholarly field of international business studies, proliferation of international business degrees, subjects and courses, as well as the emergence of scholarly associations such as the Association of International Business Studies (AIBS), attest to the recognition by business educators of the importance of the disciplinary area. Notwithstanding these impressive developments, knowledge of the effects of international business on the management of organizational, sociopolitical, non-market or PA activities remains relatively limited. I'll outline four major areas and trends that demonstrate why there is a need for businesses and management practitioners to acquire a better understanding of this important area.

## The Existence of Conflicted Attitudes Toward Government and Business

1   There exists an ever-present and long-standing tension whereby publics want their governments to do more for them, and yet these same publics often do not want their governments doing too much either. Public policy makers are constantly struggling to achieve a balance between these contrasting poles.

2   In many nation-states the institutions of business and government are trusted less to produce beneficial outcomes by various stakeholder groups than they have been in the past (Boggs, 2001). These levels of trust can significantly vary from year to year. The most recent Edelman Trust Barometer reports (available online at www.edelman.com/events/Trust/startwm.html) show how opinion leaders' trust of institutions can vary from time to time in various nations.

3   Lower voter turnouts (compared with historically high levels) in recent Canadian and American federal elections suggest that electoral outcomes are being made by increasingly lower percentages/proportions of eligible voters and, as such, the results of elections may not represent the "will of the majority" (Boggs, 2001).

4 Citizens in a number of prominent nation-states have experienced growing feelings of disempowerment. For example, in the United States there have been questions about whether their vote actually matters and whether one person can "make a difference" in political and public policy matters (Dunham *et al.*, 2004).

5 Angst exists in, for example, Australia, the Philippines, Poland, and numerous other countries over decisions about whether one's nation should be involved in regional and/or international conflicts like the ones that have been going on in Middle Eastern countries in the 1990s and twenty-first century to date. Voters attempts to resolve this angst can even sway national elections, as occurred in Spain in 2004.

## Growing Distrust of Business

1 In some countries the public perceive that some individuals or groups wield undue influence through campaign-financing activities. This has caused many challenges for PA practitioners, particularly in the United States, where such perceptions have received the greatest media coverage (Birnbaum, 2000; Lewis, 2004; Silverstein, 1998).

2 Business interests are viewed by some people as "using" government as another factor of production, supplier of inputs, or as an agent that needs to be managed in its pursuit of competitive success (Boddewyn and Brewer, 1994).

3 Corporate governance scandals and ethics failures like Enron, Arthur Andersen, WorldCom, etc., are caused by business-people who don't understand the deep connections between business, government, and society (Waddock, 2004). These highly visible scandals and failures undermine the building of public trust in business as a beneficial institution.

4 Perceived inability of the public and private sectors to work well together in many countries in meeting public demands in health care and infrastructure. Many issues, especially the type that internationally oriented PA/GR practitioners must interact with, appear as intractable as ever. Some collaborative as well as individual attempts by the private and public sector have made little progress. This can be evidenced on environmental matters (like greenhouse gases or water purity) that don't respect borders, ongoing cross-border trade conflicts, and social matters related to long-held distrust and ill will between national and/or religious groups.

5 Transparency and disclosure are now the norm. Companies that used to operate on a "need to know" basis with stakeholders now are essentially impelled by stakeholders employing information and communication technologies to operate on a "need to disclose" basis (Tapscott and Ticoll, 2003).

## Increasingly Powerful Convergence of Information, Communications, and Technology

1 Media operate in seven-second sound bites—requiring constant monitoring of news on and off the Internet as well as use of push and pull news capture methods (Holtz, 1999). News bites get transmitted around the world in a matter of minutes, 24/7. This creates an imperative for PA/GR practitioners to react more swiftly than ever to developments across the globe, as well as to implement issue management strategies and tactics on the fly (Hoewing, 2000).

2 People increasingly rely on the Internet for news and current events. This has empowered a number of newly effective activist groups as well as having re-energized what had otherwise been declining consumer, shareholder and union groups (Holtz, 1999).

3 Political processes now include Web components whether it be Web pages dedicated to groups, issues or stakeholder causes, blogs focused on sociopolitical matters of interest to business organizations, online

voting in elections, political fund raising over the Web, video spots meant for non-broadcast audiences, and the like (Hoewing, 2000; Holtz, 1999).

## Rising Tensions Experienced by People between Localization and Globalization Forces

1   The impact of the Internet on increasing the general public's awareness of issues has led businesses to rely more upon grassroots and grasstops approaches. This means that PA/GR practitioners must be able to manage issues on a global or worldwide basis while still remaining sensitive and attuned to the concerns and views of local stakeholders (Grefe, 2001).

2   There is a growing societal expectation that more *local* levels of government (state/province, cities, townships, etc.) can be trusted to meet citizens' needs. More local activism at the grassroots level can be seen in country after country, leading to a greater importance being attributed to more local levels (i.e., community, provincial/state, regional, etc.) of GR activities.

3   Activist groups have become more sophisticated at simultaneously operating both globally and locally. Many of the better organized groups have the resources and demonstrated abilities to coordinate their efforts to address key issues simultaneously in multiple nation-states and regions (Keck and Sikkink, 1998).

4   While some individuals have actively sought to take advantage of the new relationships and worlds opened up by information and communication technologies, others have steadily retreated into enclaves or self-made "cocoons," walled communities, and the relative safety of their neighborhood localities (Boggs, 2001).

Although these four areas are certainly not the only ones of interest to businesses and practitioners, they do communicate how emerging globalization can impact major institutions like business and government. Among the more prominent implications are that:

1   Businesses and executives must become more knowledgeable, skilled and capable of effectively addressing international business and public policy phenomena (Lenn, 1996).

2   PA/GR practitioners will need to develop particular "global" or "international" competencies if they are to be successful in the present and future (Fleisher, 2003).

3   Long-established organizational processes and structures may need to be modified to correspond to shifting global strategies, stakeholder actions, and issues (Johnson, 1995; Meznar, 1995).

4   Processes need to be established to allow organizations to maintain constant ($365 \times 24 \times 7$) monitoring of global developments (Hoewing, 2000). Similar enhancements need to be made by practitioners in analyzing the flow of data and information once it is gathered (Fleisher, 2002) so that timely recommendations can be made in terms of worthwhile organizational responses to important developments.

These needs are being intermittently recognized and addressed by PA/GR researchers and scholars, although their ability to offer cogent description, explanation, and prescriptions have been achieved only to varying degrees of effectiveness. International PA/GR competencies required by practitioners are elaborated later in this chapter. The following section will elaborate on the state of academic research into international and multinational PA/GR phenomena.

## BRIEF REVIEW OF THE LITERATURE ON MULTINATIONAL ENTERPRISE, INTERNATIONAL AND/OR GLOBAL PUBLIC AFFAIRS[2]

Although there is a substantial amount of academic research published on corporate

Table 1.1 *Key contributions to the scholarly literature specifically focused on international or multinational PA/GR subject matter*

| Time period | Authors |
|---|---|
| 1970s | Boddewyn and Kapoor (1972) |
| | Boddewyn (1973a) |
| | Boddewyn (1973b) |
| | Dunn, Cahill and Boddewyn (1979) |
| | International Conference on Public Affairs (1971) |
| | Kapoor and Boddewyn (1973) |
| 1980s | Blake (1981) |
| | Bergner (1982) |
| | Boddewyn (1988) |
| | Gladwin and Walter (1980) |
| | Lusterman (1985) |
| | Mahini and Wells (1986) |
| 1990s | Boddewyn and Brewer (1994) |
| | Gladwin and Kennelly (1995) |
| | Griffin and Lenn (1998) |
| | Johnson (1995) |
| | Kennelly and Gladwin (1995) |
| | Lenn et al., 1993 |
| | Lenn (1996) |
| | Lenn (1990) |
| | Meznar and Johnson (1996) |
| | Meznar (1995) |
| | Public Affairs Council (1997) |
| | Ring, Lenway and Govekar (1990) |
| 2000+ | Berg and Holtbrugge (2001) |
| | Blumentritt (2003) |
| | Fleisher (2003) |

The full publication details of the particular citations included in this table are provided in the reference section.

public affairs/government relations (for an overview, see Griffin *et al.*, 2001a, b), most of it has been generated by scholars from the United States about American phenomena. There have been a few notable scholarly attempts to illustrate and detail the *international* activities of the PA/GR function, most commonly those occurring in American MNCs. These began appearing in the business academic literature starting in the late 1960s and have occurred sporadically since that time. A summary of these efforts between 1970 and the current time can be found in Table 1.1.

As can be observed by examining Table 1.1, especially when compared against the comprehensive listings generated by Griffin *et al.*, 2001a, b), there is a relative paucity of research that has been produced on international public affairs or of public affairs/government relations

in MNCs. Additionally, the number of different scholars studying these phenomena is also limited, with only a couple of scholars, those being Boddewyn and Lenn, having published the results of three or more different studies over the thirty-plus-year period encompassed by this review. Few of these scholars, Boddewyn being the lone exception, have been active in researching and publishing PA/GR papers beyond one decade. No research centers, to the best of the author's knowledge, exist with their primary purpose being dedicated to studying international public affairs/government relations or business-government relations phenomena.

There is also a plethora of literature focusing on public affairs/government relations as specifically practiced in a variety of democratic countries, including coverage of its status in

Table 1.2  *Literature citing empirical studies of PA/GR practice in specific nation-states*

| Nation | Studies |
| --- | --- |
| Australia | Centre for Corporate Public Affairs (1996) |
| | Post and The Centre for Public Affairs (1993) |
| | Sekuless (1991, 1984) |
| Canada | Baetz (1993) |
| | Canadian Council for Public Affairs Advancement (1999, 1996) |
| | Stanbury (1993) |
| | Taylor (1991) |
| | Wright and DuVernet (1988) |
| Europe | Andersen and Eliassen (1995) |
| | Gardner (1991) |
| | Haug and Koppang (1997) |
| | Hawkins (2004) |
| | MacMillan (1991) |
| | Mazey and Richardson (1993) |
| | Naerts (1990) |
| | Newman (1990) |
| | Oomens and van den Bosch (1999) |
| | Patterson (1983) |
| | Pedler (2002) |
| | Pedler and Van Schendelen (1994) |
| | Steel (1990) |
| | Van Schendelen (2002, 1990) |
| United Kingdom | Aerts and Verhaege (2001) |
| | Johns (2002) |
| | Rogers (1986) |
| United States | Foundation for Public Affairs (2002, 1999) |
| | Post, Dickie, Murray and Mahon (1983, 1982) |
| | Public Affairs Council (1997) |

several regions or nation-states, listed in Table 1.2. In general, there is very little research published on PA/GR activities in former or present communist countries, most of Africa (outside South Africa), South and Central America, less developed countries—an exception is Akinsaya (1984)—and most of Asia (including the subcontinent). There are a few exceptions to this generalization, most of which have been produced since 2000, including:

1  How European companies influence Asian countries (Aggarwal, 2001).
2  German companies' public affairs/government relations in India (Berg and Holtbrugge, 2001).
3  Government relations in China (Kennedy, forthcoming).

It should also be noted that the public relations and communication (PR&C) literature has a higher quantity of published research than the PA/GR field on MNC and international phenomena, but little of this research is focused specifically on international GR, sociopolitical issue management, or MNC lobbying activity—the stock and parcel of PA/GR practice. Elements of the research that makes up the body of international and MNC PR&C knowledge may be amenable for applications to PA/GR scholars and should be considered for those purposes.

This is not to suggest that the basic processes underlying PA/GR activities as previously described do not occur in most nation-states. Most nation-states do host varying levels of PA/GR activity; instead, the nature of formal

PA/GR activities in these places has not been systematically studied, researched and/or published. The following section attempts to elaborate on difficulties that are encountered in the scholarly study of international PA/GR phenomena as well as, in some cases, providing suggestions for overcoming or minimizing these constraints.

## THE STATE OF CONTEMPORARY INTERNATIONAL PUBLIC AFFAIRS/GOVERNMENT RELATIONS RESEARCH

The following are a dozen prominent observations on the state of contemporary international public affairs/government relations (hereafter referred to as IPA) research. It should be recognized that this analysis is not based on a systematic literature analysis, but rather is based on the author's review of the area literature as captured in recent comprehensive bibliographic efforts (see, for example, Griffin *et al.*, 2001a, b; Getz, 2002). This task, among many that are about to be noted in the points below, are opportunities available for scholars to address.

### Key IPA Concepts Lack Definitional Consensus and Definitional Specificity

International public affairs/government relations means different things to different individuals in different industries in different countries. For example, there are multiple definitions of any of the following PA/GR-related terms: "public affairs," "international," "public policy environment" (PPE), "non-market," "corporate political activity," "sociopolitical," or "non-commercial environment." Research performed in the IPA area should always explicitly define crucial terms such as these and should, whenever possible, refer to previous scholarly use of the terms. This activity must be performed for informing research participants

as well as in the dissemination of research findings.

### Absence of Coherent Formal Theory and the Relative Absence of Working Theories

A good deal of the research in international public affairs/government relations has been either atheoretical or is subject to the frequent use of fragmented theoretical perspectives (Keim, 2002; Schuler, 2002; Windsor, 2002); consequently, the field is not able to progress to a grand or unifying model. For the field to progress forward, it is important that scholars tie their research into (1) existing organizational theoretical frameworks such as has been done in prior research efforts predominantly using resource dependence, resource-based views, exchange, agency, transaction costs; (2) existing working theories of international PA/GR phenomena; and/or (3) into previously performed grounded theory work. It is self-defeating with respect to field development for IPA researchers not to perform this task. There is still a wide variety of theoretical perspectives that remain relatively untapped in describing international PA/GR phenomena, including but not limited to: bargaining power, behavioral theory of the firm, chaos theory, cognitive theory, competitive dynamics, contingency, game theory, industrial organizational (i.e., I/O) economics, institutional theory—historical or sociological, interest group, network theory, organizational ecology, rational choice, sociological, and strategic choice. The application of multiparadigmatic approaches whereby the researcher attempts to integrate otherwise disparate theoretical approaches can be valuable in developing new insights (Lewis and Grimes, 1999).

### Excessive Reliance on Descriptive Research Designs

It is essential that international PA/GR researchers continue to strive to apply more sophisticated correlational and causal-comparative designs; consequently, this necessitates the utilization and development of relevant qualitative and/or quantitative databases. Having noted this, researchers using quantitative data in public affairs/government relations should also aim to avoid relying too heavily on univariate and bivariate (i.e., mostly *t* tests) statistical techniques. The bulk of scholarly efforts to date have been of an historical or descriptive nature, although work since the early 1990s appears to be moving in the direction of more sophisticated correlational or causal-comparative designs. The continued development of the scholarship base in public affairs/government relations continues to require movement toward greater utilization of more sophisticated methods (i.e., multivariate analytical methods versus univariate ones).

## Overabundance of Cross-sectional, Qualitative IPA Research

The bulk of the IPA research conducted to date has been static in nature; researchers have examined the phenomena of interest at a single point in time. In light of the observation that the larger contexts in which IPA phenomena are being studied (i.e., issue, organizational, nonmarket, stakeholder, etc.) are ever-dynamic and evolving, advancement in the IPA field requires researchers to employ longitudinal research designs, thus allowing analysis of response continuity and changes over time. There is a promising opportunity for researchers to perform panel, processual, or trend studies. Also, there is a strong need for historical research perspectives on many facets of IPA activity.

## Overreliance on Questionnaires and Single-type Respondents for Data Gathering

In light of the sensitive, proprietary, and competitive nature of the work within which IPA practitioners are typically engaged, it is no surprise that researchers resort to custom-developed and single-application questionnaires for gathering specific data; nevertheless,

advancement of IPA knowledge requires the use and application of other data-gathering techniques beside questionnaires. IPA practitioners have been seen to use content analysis, depth interviews, focus groups, and various field observation techniques to better understand the international PA/GR environment. Why don't academic researchers?

Not only are questionnaires heavily used in IPA research, but researchers also tend to over-rely on one particular respondent category to generate responses about IPA phenomena, that being the senior PA/GR officer. Senior PA/GR officers are generally the primary IPA study data source to the exception of line managers and senior executives who often perform significant and strategic PA/GR organizational roles. International PA/GR activities are performed frequently by the grassroots, by line managers, and by organizational spokespeople, not to mention consultants and networks of grassroots-based friends and supporters. Researchers should capture their perspectives in addition to the top PA/GR official in order to gain a deeper, richer understanding of often complex IPA phenomena.

## Absence of IPA Databases (and/or Database Sharing)

Despite the constraints described in the first sentence of the above point, it is essential that researchers share data with one another at every opportunity. This will allow the cumulative development of knowledge as well as the further refinement and testing of concepts and propositions. Also, some researchers may look to build public databases on IPA items (i.e., data on staffing, organizational structure arrangements, types of IPA interventions used, etc.). One opportunity that researchers should look to capture involves working with some of the IPA professional associations (e.g., the Center for Corporate Public Affairs, European Center for Public Affairs, Public Affairs Council) who perform regular research and have begun to develop databases among their memberships.

## Under- or Non-reporting of Validity and Reliability

Reporting on these concerns is critical in helping readers make a determination of the quality of the research. Even if it is not required for publication, researchers should keep records of these items for future reference by other interested scholars. It also helps other researchers who may utilize portions of a questionnaire, conceptual operationalizations or measures developed in the research.

## Lack of Detailed Case Study Research

Case study research designs are particularly beneficial techniques that allow the researcher to intensively investigate one or a few situations with similar characteristics to the researcher's problem situation. Although this technique would appear to hold high potential for IPA researchers, this is another area with a dearth of academic contributions. There have been a few case study descriptions published in the *Journal of Public Affairs* or communications/public relations books (e.g., Moss and DeSanto, 2002; Pedler, 2002; Pedler and Van Schendelen, 1994). These are typically not focused on questions of international PA/GR structure, process or policy development, but rather are more commonly corporate efforts to shape policy and address single issues across national boundaries.

## A Convenience Mentality for Doing Research Only in Our Backyards

The convenience mentality is also often referred to by the acronym NIMBY (i.e., Not In My Back Yard) problem or NOTE (i.e., "Not Over There Either"). It is certainly easier to deal with familiar concepts and institutions than unfamiliar ones. Meznar (2002) describes the lack of IPA perspectives as a result of "ethnocentric bias." He sees this as having occurred because the vast majority of IPA research has been conducted by North American scholars, examining North American data and subjects, and presented and published in the dominant American group's journals. Certain parts of the world have been subject to scant scholarly exploration into PA/GR phenomena. Africa, the Middle East, Eastern Europe, and Latin America, among some Asian locations as well, are geographic contexts that offer researchers a myriad of opportunity.

These limitations of the extant IPA scholarship can be partially overcome through collaborative efforts with international organizations and researchers, who can act as sounding boards and contacts for future research efforts. The recent growth of European and Asian journals and scholarly activity might bring some new methodological and theoretical perspectives to the IPA knowledge base, benefiting the field's intellectual diversity.

## Career Problems for Academics Performing IPA Research

Although it may not be politically correct to state this, few scholars have been able to build their academic careers in business or management schools based on the cumulative excellence of their contributions to the IPA field. The problems here relate to issues of budget, timing, and incentives. International PA/GR research, particularly employing some of the designs called for in previous points, can require a substantial quantity and quality of financial, human and temporal resources to produce effective research outcomes. Other problems include researchers not having enough research dollars to acquire or develop needed databases, the practical career need (i.e., tenure decisions that commonly arise within half a dozen years in an academic's career development) for producing immediate results, and current incentives for publishing easy-to-do quantitative research that demonstrates sophisticated statistical manipulation but adds little to conceptual, pragmatic, or theoretical progress in the IPA field. The number of highly reputable journals amenable to IPA research has increased in recent years, with IPA researchers occasionally publishing in outlets such as *Academy of Management Review, Academy of Management Journal, Administrative Science Quarterly, Journal of International Business Studies, Journal of Management, Organization Science,* and *Strategic Management Journal,* but it still lacks the cumulative mass or number of researchers to be a regular contributor to these most prestigious publishing outlets. The relatively recent additions of refereed academic outlets such as the *Journal of Public Affairs* (UK), *Journal of Political Marketing* (US), and *Business and Politics* (UK) and scholarly books such as this *Handbook of Public Affairs* should help generate further development of IPA scholarship.

## Scholarly Irrelevance

The problem being observed here is that IPA practitioners are often light years ahead of IPA scholars in terms of activity conceptualization. Unless researchers actively stay on top of IPA developments (including regularly interacting and networking with leading-edge professionals, organizations, and their activities), the field loses the advantage of observational experience by which to leverage a useful research program. Most IPA practitioners face major deadlines, difficult work loads, and lack the time needed to deeply reflect upon the efficacy of their past activities and actions. Although many IPA practitioners have advanced degrees, few are capable of the specialized insight and rigor that academics bring to the examination of relevant phenomena. If academics cannot offer time-challenged IPA practitioners something useful, they will see little or no reason to participate in what they will perceive as time-consuming, unproductive research projects.

## Lack of Emphasis on Certain Economic Sectors/Industries and an Almost Exclusive Focus on Large Organizations

There has also tended to be over-reliance on studying PA/GR phenomena in certain industries (e.g., steel, natural resources, heavy and light manufacturing, forest products, computers, chemicals/pharmaceuticals) with little examination of these activities in service industries (e.g., accounting, hospitality and tourism, legal services, media, and telecom). Also, large companies and organizations have been studied almost to the exclusion of small and medium-sized enterprises that also face PA/GR phenomena, if not by themselves then also through their participation in larger trade or industry associations. There is much to be gained by looking at these increasingly popular and important industries and the ways they address IPA/GR phenomena.

In summary, international perspectives are not prominent or plentiful in IPA/GR research. Researchers have a responsibility, and opportunity, to improve this state of affairs by keeping in mind some key prescriptions for doing research, and properly modifying their approach to address the complexities created by studying complex phenomena in international contexts. The next section of this chapter offers a number of ideas to help researchers keep these considerations central in their efforts.

## ADDITIONAL IDEAS FOR IMPROVING INTERNATIONAL PUBLIC AFFAIRS/GOVERNMENT RELATIONS RESEARCH

How can researchers improve their ability to achieve satisfactory outcomes when studying IPA/GR phenomena? It is important to remember, potential respondents judge research quality often as vigorously as any top journal reviewer. Poor research design can both antagonize the very people you desire to participate in your well meaning projects and produce inconclusive, invalid and/or "ungeneralizable" results which inhibit scholarly progress in our field. My caveat in this discussion will be that IPA research of the nature just described can be a waste of time and money, and is generally counterproductive.

An important prerequisite to performing research effectively is to take the appropriate amount of front-end time to clarify the design and objectives of your research initiative. Among the more prominent issues that need to be carefully considered are the aspects of the respondent's experience to be measured. International PA/GR researchers need to be careful to operationalize concepts that respondents can understand in their own terms. An example of a problem commonly encountered in IPA research is identifying which individuals actually perform IPA/GR activities. Public affairs/government relations to the Canadian professional in the telecommunications industry who is dealing with the Mexican government has a much greater public communications component than that practiced by the American telecommunications professional dealing with EU public policy makers in Brussels.

These situations create several key issues surrounding sampling and population definitions. Public affairs researchers have noticeably avoided defining these ideas in their research. For example, when you are speaking of international "public affairs" practitioners or activities, what boundaries are being established around the referenced population? For example, will the sample include those people only with PA/GR titles? Will those individuals with titles such as Corporate Affairs be sampled or not? Will it include line managers at the business unit level who perform a significant number of PA/GR activities in the course of their job responsibilities? How about the chief executive officers or managing directors who, according to some accounts, spend upwards of two-thirds of their time dealing with public policy environment stakeholders?

The answers to these questions have clear implications for both sample size and questionnaire design decisions. The key aspect the researcher must recognize is that not all IPA/GR practitioners or activities are similar, and in reality even those similarly named or similarly constructed are often significantly different. There is a strong need in this stream of research to divide and subdivide these research targets. Hence, it is crucial that researchers clearly and specifically define: (1) their concepts; (2) public affairs; (3) what is meant in the study by the concept "international"; (4) the boundaries surrounding the sampling choices.

## Sampling Considerations

Problems of sampling can weigh heavy in the minds of those contemplating IPA research projects. For example, the number of research contacts to be sought and made will be determined by a number of factors, primarily the number of potential respondents in the defined population, the degree of accuracy that is required, and, inevitably, the budget available to do the research. For every subdivision of the respondent base for which individual measurements are required, a significant sample is needed.

Respondent bases, especially in an area as heterogeneous as international public affairs/government relations, often need to be subdivided many times, thereby resulting in measurable jumps in the amount of resources required to do the research. For some researchers, the total picture of international public affairs, let alone any important subgroups within it, would not be sufficient to support research on any grand scale. A considerable degree of pragmatism needs to be adopted, and a more qualitative than quantitative stance may be appropriate to take in such circumstances. Although statistical rules cannot effectively be applied to really small samples, those of logic can, and such samples can potentially offer robust insights. Any researcher who receives responses from ten of the thirteen, for example, American PA telecommunications lobbyists operating on a specific policy issue in Brussels may not receive the statistician's blessing, but probably should feel confident enough to offer reasonable confidence in the quality of their findings based on these numbers.

The researcher's task is aided if some of the segments have been previously researched, and if the population and sampling decisions were clearly spelled out, allowing them to compare and possibly extend some previous researchers' findings. As previously described, unfortunately there has not been much accumulation of systematic scholarly research in the IPA area. The field has a plethora of one-shot case studies, interviews with executives dealing with IPA issues, business journal anecdotes or characterizations of IPA conditions and so forth, but too little systematic, scholarly research.

## Research Design Choices

Research design refers to the "master" plan for organizing the collection and analytical activities researchers perform to answer research questions. Every research design choice brings with it some inherent advantages and disadvantages that the researcher must consider. There are a variety of general research design modes researchers interested in IPA/GR phenomena may pursue, including:

1   *Historical.* This design is often accomplished through content analysis or retrospective interviewing. An obvious difficulty researchers face in doing this in an IPA context is that the phenomena often occur in undocumented or unpublished formats. Much IPA activity goes on in "back rooms," lobbies or behind the scenes and is purposefully kept out of the public's view. Few of the strategic assumptions and true values underlying policy making decisions made by corporations with respect to PA/GR issues are ever made public, even among non-executive members of the organization. Another difficulty inherent in employing historical design approaches is that the actions and speeches of individuals associated with communicating about an organization's PA/GR positions and actions may intentionally (i.e., through deception) or unintentionally belie the organization's true intentions.

2   *Descriptive.* This design often involves theory building or grounded research. Most descriptive IPA studies have been cross-sectional

(collecting data at one point in time) in nature, achieved through the use of single-shot questionnaires or case research. The use of these is problematic with respect to: (a) understanding contexts surrounding PA activity and decision making; (b) the difficulty of interpreting data; (c) the necessity to assess and discuss the tests of measure reliability within the survey instrument. International public affairs researchers need to build upon this base. They should consider ways of conducting more longitudinal research. One area that IPA researchers should aim to conduct in is designing panel studies whereby they systematically survey the same individuals on several occasions over an extended period of time. Of course, these researchers must combat the problem of experimental mortality whereby participants (if not the organization itself) drop out of scrutiny during the course of the study.

3   *Correlational.* Some researchers choose to employ correlational methods in their IPA studies. When they are done in the typical manner evidenced in the scholarship, researchers have demonstrated a high reliance on less sophisticated statistical correlative techniques such as Kendall's tau, Spearman's rho, etc. These less sophisticated techniques will likely be of lesser value in helping to describe, or explain, the more complex nature of most strategic IPA phenomena.

4   *Causal-comparative.* Very little IPA research has been done using these designs either. One reason for this is that the base created through the application of the prior three designs has not allowed an accumulation of knowledge upon which many causal-comparative studies can be fruitfully pursued. These designs also typically require researchers to employ both quantitative and qualitative data, raising the level of complexity and resources beyond the point where some researchers are comfortable.

5   *Experimental/quasi-experimental.* These approaches have been successfully used in studying economic and public policy phenomena, but precious few individuals have

considered their potential applications to IPA research questions. Some new possibilities to do this research have arisen with the relatively recent development of realistic public policy and legislative process simulations like the US National Association of Manufacturers' *Legislative Insight* package that allows the controlled manipulation of limited numbers of variables and can capture the dynamic pathing options (i.e., tactics) taken by PA/GR officers. These may prove to be uniquely attractive if researchers are fortunate enough to get agreement for officials to take the time to participate in these studies.

## Data-gathering Methods

Without getting into a philosophical debate on the advantages or disadvantages of quantitative versus qualitative approaches, the following section will review a few approaches that are particularly suitable for IPA research at this point in its theoretical development.

1  *Content analysis.* This approach involves the objective, systematic, and quantitative description of the content of documents, including print media and broadcast media coverage. Especially on the public policy side of corporate IPA/GR work, there is a plethora of documents such as congressional or administrative committee minutes, policy circulars, issue briefs, and voting records, offered both in paper and electronic formats, that offer substantive evidence of organizations' issue positioning as well as the stakeholders' positions.

2  *Depth interviews (individual focus sessions).* This data-gathering approach involves using an open-ended interview in which respondents are encouraged to discuss an IPA issue, problem, or question in his or her own terms. These are ideally driven by the respondent being interviewed. A number of the IPA researchers identified in Table 1.1 have successfully employed these methods. Although doing these interviews usually prerequires a substantial amount of ethical review as well as personal contacts and trust in identifying willing participants, they can be most valuable for the IPA researcher to get behind the veil of published and public information to understand the motives and antecedents of IPA activity and strategy.

3  *Focus groups.* Focus groups involve targeted discussions led by a moderator typically involving six to twelve individuals. They are best suited for unstructured explorations of issues in the participants' own terms and are particularly well suited for pretesting survey instruments before being used in field testing. International public affairs researchers can take advantage of this design, particularly when working collaboratively with the larger professional associations in the PA/GR field who can facilitate these kinds of sessions more conveniently than most researchers can do on their own.

4  *Field observations.* The broad category of field observations functions as a label which serves as an umbrella for several techniques, including field studies, certain types of case studies, and participant observation. It is particularly difficult to conduct these in the IPA field unless the researcher can get permission to "shadow" an official. The observer literally needs to be "in the room" when policy decisions are being considered. Also, researchers are being blitzed by millions of pieces of data, increasing the problems of subjectivity and bias. These methods provide a contextual richness to IPA phenomena unrivalled by most other observation techniques.

5  *The questionnaire.* The workhorse observation technique of IPA research, the questionnaire, is a written, structured series of questions or probes that collect information from our respondents. These can be done in self-administered, face-to-face, telephone, or mailed formats. Their use in studying IPA phenomena has been increasingly limited due to the work and time demands being faced by prospective

respondents, as well as the proliferation of organizational policies that preclude members from responding to unsolicited surveys.

## Samples of Potential Topics for Further IPA/GR Study

This section lists some examples of studies that can potentially be conducted in examining IPA phenomena. These are shared mainly for illustration purposes, but should give the prospective researcher some useful ideas that they might incorporate into their own research agendas and planning.

1   *Historical/descriptive.* The researcher might conduct longitudinal studies of an organization's IPA modifications—possibly in terms of structure, staffing, resources, plans, and actions etc.—over time (e.g., five years prior to five years hence) to deal with the emergence of new trade zones (EU, NAFTA), WTO rounds, or other similar multinational issues.

2   *Comparative.* The researcher can perform intra-industry studies of the IPA actions and strategies used by companies in different countries (e.g., how Merck deals with the European Union, Japan and South America versus how its competitor Pfizer does it). The researcher would consider what differences are there in the respective organization's IPA techniques, strategies, staffing, structure, reporting relationships, etc., and the always interesting dependent variable of which organization is more successful.

3   *Comparative.* Here the researcher would compare different IPA modes, such as looking at whether a communications-oriented, community relations-oriented, or a government relations-oriented approach is more successful in dealing with Third World countries? Another slant at this topic would be to look at a company that had tried multiple IPA approaches over time in

one or more countries to examine their relative experiences and performance.

4   *Comparative.* Here the researcher would question which industries have been/are most successful dealing with a specific country's public policy institutions and processes? For example, the researcher might want to examine the Korean computer industry versus its auto industry in gaining freer access to Japanese markets. The researcher would be challenged to describe and demonstrate the differences between the respective industries' public policy environment influence strategies. Another slant on this topic would be to have the researcher look at what companies within an industry have been most successful in influencing the outcome of a particular issue debate that cuts across multiple countries.

5   *Descriptive.* The researcher can examine the issue of how companies have sought to staff (could also look at structural questions) their IPA offices in home and host countries. They might want to describe staff backgrounds, qualifications, career paths (decision making centralization, reporting relationships, line and staff distinctions), etc. Another question the researcher might examine related to this first topic is whether IPA personnel have a significant influence on the organization's (e.g., subsidiary) performance in a particular nation-state or set of countries?

6   *Descriptive.* Here the researcher might examine a specific IPA issue, for example, environmental standard setting affecting the global chemical industry. They would compare organizations' strategies with respect to influencing the issue. Which worked successfully? Which did not?

7   *Quasi-experimental.* The researcher could design a hypothetical IPA issue. They would have IPA officers (International Public Affairs Officers, or IPAOs) of different firms respond to how they would design a strategy to handle the issue (i.e., before). They could then change a key parameter of issue (intervention/treatment)

and have IPAOs respond (after). Compare responses before and after treatment. The use of a legislative or public policy-making simulation software package would be particularly amenable to this form of research.

There are virtually no conceptual or theoretical limits to the research possibilities that might be pursued in the IPA/GR domain. Of course, there are a variety of pragmatic and practitioner issues that might limit what the researcher can imagine, but that should not stop researchers from envisioning important IPA questions to study. One of the questions that has faced researchers is to examine whether IPA practitioners need to have a unique set of competences in order to effectively practice their craft. The next section describes this challenge further.

## COMPETENCIES NEEDED FOR INTERNATIONAL AND MULTINATIONAL PUBLIC AFFAIRS

There has been a growing interest expressed by some companies in organizing for international public affairs (Lindsay, 2003). As was previously described in the opening sections of this chapter, the practice of public affairs/government relations is different outside one's home nation because, among other things, other nations have different governance systems, historical developments, public policy institutions and processes, and social structures and values. Unique political and value systems, in particular, have major implications for the management of the PA/GR process (Mack, 1997). As such, it is likely useful to develop a list of globally oriented PA/GR knowledge and competencies that all international PA/GR managers should acquire.

Although this topic is clearly ripe for several extensive research studies, my list of international PA/GR competencies would include the following (Fleisher, 2003).

## Development of Intercultural Competence

International public affairs are always intercultural public affairs. It is critical that the PA manager gains familiarity with how the practice of public affairs in different nation-states is impacted by cultural variations. These cultural variations can be reflected as differences in behaviors, concepts of time, lifestyles, patterns of decision making, perceptions, and values, among other things (Starling, 1996). To gain this familiarity, PA managers must first understand their own cultural underpinnings before they can gain a constructive understanding of other cultures (Hofstede, 1991). Comparisons between one's own culture and context and other nations' cultures and contexts help PA managers to understand often subtle differences that shape different public policy environments (Hall, 1976). Cultural variation also affects the development of the practice of international public affairs at the societal level. Similar to the reactions of individuals, nation-states often respond to public issues in culturally specific ways; therefore, societal factors are important for the PA manager to understand as well. Last but not least, it is incumbent upon the PA/GR manager to gain an understanding of the historical antecedents of other countries' cultural and social development.

## Impact of Societal Factors on Public Affairs

There are a number of societal factors that will impact almost any international PA/GR effort. Some of the more obvious ones would include:

1 *State-to-state relations.* Public policy makers and politicians attempt to influence stakeholders not only in their own nations, but often in others as well. This is particularly pertinent to a discussion of regional policy bodies and multination trade agreements.
2 *Nature of social networks.* Much public policy change comes through the influence of key individuals or groups of individuals. In some

countries, these key parties can be identified and nurtured to support organizational goals. In other nations, it may be more difficult for the corporation to have its "voice heard" over other established institutions.

3   *Level of economic development.* An underlying objective of public affairs is to influence and support the achievement of an organization's business goals. These business goals are addressed within the context of a nation-state's economy and economic fabric.

4   *Political ideologies.* Business issues are highly impacted by the practice and practitioners of politics (Wartick and Wood, 1998). The vast majority of PA/GR issues they will face will arise due to the result of political forces and decisions.

5   *Nature of social change.* Nation-states approach social change at different paces (some slow, some more rapid), using different mechanisms (ranging from formal legal systems to militaristic or anarchic means), and promulgated by different forms of activist groups.

6   *The overall business-government relationship.* Some national governments work very closely with and are heavily influenced by the business community, while in other nations the national government goes out of its way to keep business at arm's length and to maintain as much "distance" between it and business as possible.

7   *Nature and activism of organized interest groups.* In light of the information and communication technologies (ICTs) available today, it is a rare nation-state that isn't impacted by well informed and organized interest groups of all stripes pushing for changes to public policy. Many of these interest groups operate both globally and multinationally. Many groups have an anti-business ideological slant, while some are pro-development. Recognizing the "friends" from the "foes" is critical.

8   *Legal system and structure.* Many nation-states have well-developed bodies of law and structure that provide explicit detail relative to what is and isn't allowable in their

particular jurisdictions. Other nations' legal systems are not well developed and are ambiguous, leaving open to discretion the alternative actions organizations may take.

9   *Nature of the media and public communication channels.* Many countries allow free and unfettered activity by the media and journalistic establishments, while others impose tight controls and restraints upon these sectors.

10  *Nature of regulatory mechanisms.* Different nation-states can wield a vast array of broadly defined regulatory mechanisms and structures, ranging from allowing self-regulation of most business activity to strictly controlled regulatory regimes.

11  *View of the natural environment and geographic factors.* Much business activity has impacts on the physical or ecological context of a nation-state. Some nation-states are actively protective of their natural resources while others see these resources as being beneficial in their economic development.

Many of the key knowledge factors that internationally active PA/GR managers should be aware of are captured in Exhibit 1.2.

## Understanding Local Public Policy Institutions and Processes

The globally competent PA manager will understand other nations' form of government, legal systems, the structure of the state, national politics, political culture, public policy process and recent public policy developments.

## Nation-state-specific Applications of PA/GR Functions

The PA manager needs to understand how community relations, government relations, investor relations and all forms of stakeholder relations uniquely take place in relevant nation-states (Lenn, 1996). Ideally, the identification of best practices in these areas would bring even greater benefit.

---

### Exhibit 1.2 Major Factors Businesses Need to Understand About a Nation-state's Public Policy Environment

- *Administrative divisions*—formation of states/provinces, municipalities, districts, etc.
- *Branches of government/political structure*—executive (e.g., Cabinet, chief/head of state, head of government, etc.), judicial, legislative, etc.
- *Capital*—the location of the seat of government (note: there may be more than one in terms of historical, judicial, legislative, political, and/or titular locations).
- *Constitution*—including its basis, historical origin and development, and process for modification.
- *Economy and trade*—including debt, education, employment, financial institutions, GDP, imports and exports, infrastructure, major industries, rates and flows, health and welfare.
- *Elections*—suffrage, funding, timing, representation, and process.
- *Form of state*—there is a wide variety of structures by which nation-states adopt and administer public policy, among them examples are commonwealth, confederacy, democracy, federal, monarchy, parliamentary, republic, theocracies, etc.
- *Issues*—matters of political concern or controversy impacting the electorate. These often arise from unique cultural, historical, linguistic, political or sociological origins.
- *Legal system*—including its basis, historical development, jurisdiction and role in government.
- *Media*—major broadcasters and media channels, journalist, news (dailies and weeklies), periodicals, etc.
- *Participation in international organizations* (e.g., International Monetary Fund, United Nations, World Trade Organization, etc.).
- *Political parties and leaders*—ruling and opposition groups.
- *Political pressure groups and leaders*—stakeholders not standing for political election yet desiring political change.

---

### Language Skills (Corbett, 1991)

In some parts of the globe, particularly in the EU capital of Brussels, the inability to speak multiple languages puts the PA/GR manager at a large disadvantage relative to those individuals who are multilingual. Despite recent advances in translation technologies, much discussion and dialogue that underpins many public policy development processes still relies upon stakeholder conversations and dialogue, quite often infused with local nuances that only a multilingual speaker can pick up.

### Understanding of Ethics in a Global/International Context

The question "When in Rome should we do as the Romans do?" remains important to the management and practice of public affairs. In light of a number of highly visible ethical transgressions by corporations, it is clearer than ever before that PA/GR managers need to be leaders in establishing, communicating and maintaining the ethical guidelines and conscience of their corporation both at home and abroad.

## Managing International Consultants, Alliances and Issue Partners

Despite the adage "Think global and act local," there are times that every PA/GR unit requires specialist assistance that can come only from local experts, groups or associations. This will be especially true when first entering a country or with first efforts to expand the reach of the organization into a new nation-state.

There always remains the underlying question of where and how practitioners will develop the above listed competencies. In Part III, the author outlines arguments around the education of PA/GR practitioners. The answer as to where and to whom practitioners can turn is likely to be found among the for-profit and not-for-profit entities active in guiding business organizations and practitioners' national and transnational PA/GR practice. The section that follows outlines these entities and the range of activities with which they are involved.

## PROFESSIONAL ASSOCIATIONS ACTIVE IN NATION-STATE-FOCUSED AND INTERNATIONAL PUBLIC AFFAIRS/GOVERNMENT RELATIONS

Where and to whom can practitioners turn to get help in dealing with IPA/GR matters? There is undoubtedly a variety of PA/GR activities that occur both in various nation-states as well as in multinational contexts. One stream of evidence, that being the activities of professional associations the missions of which specifically focus on serving the PA/GR community, provides some support for the institutionalization of PA/GR activities in different countries. These groups usually provide products, programs, and services designed to improve practitioner's understanding of and competence in plying PA/GR. The majority of these groups were birthed since 1990, but a few have been around in one form or another much longer.

There are associations or foundations of corporate public affairs practitioners in several major (predominantly English-speaking) countries. These are listed in Table 1.3. Many of the more traditional national or transnational public relations and corporate communications professional associations (e.g., the Canadian Public Relations Society, the Confederation Européenne des Relations Publiques, the Council of PR Firms, the International Association of Political Consultants, the International Public Relations Association, the Institute for Public Relations, the International Association of Business Communicators, the Public Relations Society of America (see Dennis, 1996, etc.) will frequently have chapters, interest groups, or professional sections representing the portion of their membership groups that includes PA/GR practitioners and their interests.

Most nation-states lack the professional bodies that provide guidance for PA/GR practice, regulation and standards setting. Indeed, the author is unaware of a single group that has managed to establish publicly accepted guidelines for PA/GR practice, examination of PA/GR competency/skills or knowledge, regulate the flow of members into and out of the profession, and/or to certify the qualifications of PA/GR practitioners in their nation-state. Having said this, many GR practitioners, particularly those that have a major portion of their work responsibilities in lobbying government or governmental entities on behalf of their organization, are already required or will soon be required to register or seek licensure in order to practice their trade. The PA side of the PA/GR equation has almost universally remained outside the regulatory auspices of governmental authorities, which may be viewed either as a good (i.e., it allows the free flow of individuals and ideas into and out of the practice area) or a negative factor (e.g., sometimes the ideas or persons who are flowing into or out of the profession cause significant harm or damage to various PA/GR issue stakeholders).

Table 1.3   *Associations or foundations of corporate public affairs practitioners*

| Region | Organization |
|---|---|
| **AUSTRALIA**<br>One association primarily aims to meet the specific needs of Australian and New Zealand PA/GR practitioners | • Australian Centre for Corporate Public Affairs (ACCPA, www.accpa.com.au) headquartered in Melbourne was established in 1990 and is Australia and New Zealand's largest professional association serving PA/GR practitioners |
| **CANADA**<br>Four organizations primarily serve or have served Canadian PA/GR practitioners | • Canadian Council for Public Affairs Advancement (CCPAA, founded 1994, www.ccpaa.org)<br>• Government Relations Institute of Canada (GRIC, established 1994, www.gric-irgc.ca) |
| **EUROPE**<br>Associations that serve European PA/GR practitioners | • Public Affairs Association of Canada (PAAC, founded 1984, www.publicaffairs.ca) headquartered in Toronto<br>• Conference Board of Canada's Council of Public Affairs Executives (Ottawa, www.conferenceboard.ca) |
| **TRANSNATIONAL**<br>Two organizations aim to meet the needs of globally active PA/GR practitioners | |
| **UNITED KINGDOM**<br>Two groups provide benefits and networking opportunities for UK-based PA/GR practitioners | • European Centre for Public Affairs (ECPA, www.publicaffairs.ac) headquartered in Belgium and London (established in 1986)<br>• European Association of Political Consultants (1996, headquartered in Vienna, www.eapc.com) |
| **UNITED STATES**<br>Virtually all of these groups are headquartered in the greater Washington, DC, area and provide assistance to US-based PA/GR practitioners | • Global Public Affairs institute (GPAI, established 1988, www.gpai.org)<br>• International Association of Political Consultants (established 1969, www.iapc.org) |
| | • Association of Professional Political Consultants (APPC, established 1994—www.appc.org.uk) is headquartered in London<br>• PubAffairs (an informal but well-established networking group of PA/GR practitioners) headquartered in Westminster and the Web at www.pubaffairs.org |
| | • American Association of Political Consultants (AAPC, established 1969, www.theaapc.org)<br>• American League of Lobbyists (ALL, established in 1979, www.alldc.org)<br>• Issue Management Council in Leesburg, VA, has been around since the 1980s and can be found on the Web at www.issuemanagement.org<br>• Public Affairs Council (PAC, established 1954, www.pac.org) and its two divisions: (a) Center for Public Affairs Management (CPAM) and (b) Foundation for Public Affairs (FPA)<br>• State Government Affairs Council (SGAC) |

## Consultancies

There is a variety of consultancies who claim to provide PA/GR services on a multicountry or international basis. These would include, most prominently among a larger group, the following: Brodeur Worldwide, BSMG, Burson-Marstellar, Edelman, Fleishman-Hilliard, GCI Group/ APCO Associates, Hill and Knowlton, Manning, Selvage and Lee, Ogilvy, Porter Novelli, and Ruder Finn. Many businesses and corporate bodies rely upon outsourcing the capabilities of firms such as these to assist them in their international PA/GR challenges. This mode of

Table 1.4  *Prominent public affairs-focused periodicals*

| Media type | Nation of origin | Examples |
| --- | --- | --- |
| Academic journals | United Kingdom | *Journal of Public Affairs* |
| | | *Business and Politics* |
| Directories | Australia | |
| | United States | *Federal Lobbyists* |
| Periodicals | United Kingdom | *National Directory of Corporate Public Affairs* |
| | | *Directory of Political Lobbying* |
| | Australia | *Government Affairs Group Handbook* |
| | United States | |
| | Canada | *Corporate Public Affairs* (ACCPA) |
| | Global | *Impact* (Public Affairs Council) |
| | | *Influence: The Business of Lobbying* |
| | | *Campaigns and Elections* |
| | | *Hill Times* |
| | | *Lobby Monitor* |
| | | *PR Week* |

practice has associated benefits and drawbacks that must be taken into active consideration compared to the utilization of in-house (i.e., business or corporate) PA/GR capabilities (Post and Griffin, 1999). Businesses are also benefited by the assistance provided through international trade associations, chambers of commerce, government offices, and other groups focused on assisting organizations to navigate multinational business government relations and public policy issues.

### Publishers of IPA Subject Matter

Last but not least, the international PA/GR community is frequently served by the producers of various media that cater to their interests and needs. A number of academic journals, regularly published directories, Internet/World Wide Web sites and periodicals, also bring nation-state-specific and multinational perspectives to the practice and knowledge of public affairs/government relations. Table 1.4 summarizes a number of the more prominent IPA-related publications.

### CONCLUSION

International PA/GR should be having an important influence on the development of all forms of PA/GR practice and scholarship.

There are numerous challenges and opportunities confronting both practitioners and scholars intent on developing a greater mastery of this uniquely challenging facet of public affairs/government relations. Distinctive social, political, linguistic, historical, and cultural factors suggest that frameworks and understandings that guide practice in one part of the world may not be effective in different geographic contexts. The scholarly base of PA/GR understanding remains somewhat embryonic by nature and will need continued progress for it to be of greater utility and value to business organizations and their decision makers.

### NOTES

1 Many economists' definitions of "multinational" suggest that at least 25–30 percent of the firm's revenues or profits should come from outside of its "home region" for it to be classified as a true multinational.

2 The author is, unfortunately, restricting his observations to that of English-language published literature, fully recognizing that there are some fine pieces of literature published in other languages that are beyond the scope of this chapter's review.

### REFERENCES

Aerts, S., and S. Verhaege (2001). *Improving the Government Relations Function.* Guildford: European Centre for Public Affairs.

Aggarwal, V.K. (2001). *Winning Asia, European Style: Market and non-Market Strategies for Success.* New York: Palgrave Macmillan.

Akinsaya, A.A. (1984). *Multinationals in a Changing Environment: Business–Government Relations in the Third World.* New York: Praeger.

Andersen, S., and K. Eliassen (1995). "EU Lobbying: The New Research Agenda," *European Journal of Political Research* 27 (4): 427–441.

Baetz, M.C. (1993). *Canadian Cases in Business-Government Relations.* Toronto, ON: Nelson.

Berg, N., and D. Holtbrugge (2001). "Public Affairs Management Activities of German Multinational Corporations in India," *Journal of Business Ethics* 30 (1): 105–119.

Bergner, D.J. (1982). "The Role of Strategic Planning in International Public Affairs," *Public Relations Journal* 38: 32–39.

Birnbaum, J. (2000). *The Money Men: The Real Story of Fund Raising's Influence on Political Power in America.* New York: Random House.

Blake, D.H. (1981). "How to Get Operating Managers to Manage Public Affairs in Foreign Subsidiaries," *Columbia Journal of World Business* 16 (spring): 61–67.

Blumentritt, T.P. (2003). "Foreign Subsidiaries' Government Affairs Activities: The Influence of Management and Resources," *Business and Society* 42 (2): 202–233.

Boddewyn, J.J. (1973a). "External Affairs at Four Levels in US Multinationals," *Industrial Relations* 12 (2): 239–247.

Boddewyn, J.J. (1973b). "The External Affairs Function in American Multinational Corporations," in J. Fayerweather (ed.), *International Business-Government Affairs.* New York: Ballinger.

Boddewyn, J.J. (1988). "International Public Affairs," in I. Walter (ed.), *Handbook of International Management.* New York: Wiley.

Boddewyn, J.J., and T.L. Brewer (1994). "International Business Political Behavior: New Theoretical Directions," *Academy of Management Review* 19 (1): 119–143.

Boddewyn, J.J., and A. Kapoor (1972). "The External Relations of American Multinational Enterprises," *International Studies Quarterly* 16 (4): 433–453.

Boggs, C. (2001). *The End of Politics: Corporate Power and the Decline of the Public Sphere.* New York: Guilford Press.

Canadian Council for Public Affairs Advancement (1996). *Corporate Public Affairs Management: The 1996 Survey of Canadian Practice.* Waterloo, ON: Canadian Council for Public Affairs Advancement.

Canadian Council for Public Affairs Advancement (1999). *The 1998 State of Corporate Public Affairs Survey.* Toronto, ON: Canadian Council for Public Affairs Advancement.

Centre for Corporate Public Affairs (1996). *Report of Australia and New Zealand Corporate Public Affairs Survey.* Sydney: Centre for Corporate Public Affairs.

Corbett, W.J. (1991). "EC 92: Communicating in the New Europe," *Public Relations Quarterly* 36 (winter): 7–13.

Dennis, L.B. (1996). *Practical Public Affairs in an Era of Change: A Communications Guide for Business, Government, and College.* Lanham, MD: University Press of America.

Drogendijk, R. (2004). "The Public Affairs of Internationalization: Balancing Pressures from Multiple Environments," *Journal of Public Affairs* 4 (1): 44–55.

Dunham, R.S., L. Walczak, P. Dwyer, M. McNamee, and A. Starr (2004). "Does Your Vote Matter?" *Business Week* (3887), June 14, pp. 60–75.

Dunn, S.W., M.F. Cahill, and J.J. Boddewyn (1979). *How Fifteen Transnational Corporations Manage Public Affairs.* Chicago: Crain Books.

Fleisher, C.S. (2002). "Analysis and Analytical Tools for Managing Corporate Public Affairs," *Journal of Public Affairs* 2 (3): 167–172.

Fleisher, C.S. (2003). "The Development of Competencies in International Public Affairs," *Journal of Public Affairs* 3 (1): 76–82.

Foundation for Public Affairs (1999). *1999–2000 State of Corporate Public Affairs.* Washington, DC: Public Affairs Council.

Foundation for Public Affairs (2002). *The State of Corporate Public Affairs: Final Report.* Washington, DC: Foundation for Public Affairs.

Gardner, J. (1991). *Effective Lobbying in the EC.* Deventer: Kluwer.

Getz, K.A. (2002). "Public Affairs and Political Strategy: Theoretical Foundations," *Journal of Public Affairs* 1–2 (4–1): 305–329.

Giddens, A. (1999). *Runaway World: How Globalization is Reshaping our Lives.* London: Profile Books.

Gladwin, T.N., and J.J. Kennelly (1995). *Patterns and Trends in the Management of Global Public Affairs.* Global Public Affairs Institute Occasional Paper, New York: Global Public Affairs Institute.

Gladwin, T.N., and I. Walter (1980). "How Multinationals can Manage Social and Political Forces," *Journal of Business Strategy* 1 (1): 54–68.

Grefe, E.A. (2001). *Global Grassroots is a Reality.* Management Report Series, Washington, DC: Public Affairs Council.

Griffin, J.J., and D.J. Lenn (1998). "Corporate Public Affairs: A Cross-national Comparison," *Proceedings of the International Association for Business and Society (IABS)*. Kailua-Kona, HI, June 11–14.

Griffin, J., C.S. Fleisher, S., Brenner, and J. Boddewyn (2001a). "Corporate Public Affairs Research: A Chronological Reference list I, 1985–2000," *Journal of Public Affairs* 1 (1): 9–32.

Griffin, J., C.S. Fleisher, S. Brenner, and J. Boddewyn (2001b). "Corporate Public Affairs Research: A Chronological Reference List II, 1958–1984," *Journal of Public Affairs* 1 (2): 167–186.

Hall, E.T. (1976). *Beyond Culture*. Garden City, NY: Anchor Press.

Haug, M., and H. Koppang (1997). "Lobbying and Public Relations in a European Context," *Public Relations Review* 23 (3): 233–247.

Hawkins, A. (2004). "The State of Public Affairs," presentation given to the third annual conference of the European Centre for Public Affairs, Brussels, February.

Hill, C.W.L. (2003). *International Business: Competing in the Global Marketplace*, 4th edn. New York: McGraw-Hill Irwin.

Hoewing, L. (2000). *Using the Internet in a Corporate Public Affairs Office*. Management Report series, Washington, DC: Public Affairs Council.

Hofstede, G. (1991). *Cultures and Organizations: The Software of the Mind*. New York: McGraw-Hill.

Holtz, S. (1999). *Public Relations on the Net: Winning Strategies to Inform the Media, the Investment Community, the Government, the Public, and More!* New York: AMACOM, a division of American Management Association.

International Conference on Public Affairs (1971). *Public Affairs in the US and Europe*. New York: Conference Board.

Johns, S. (2002). *The Persuaders: When Lobbyists Matter*. Basingstoke: Palgrave Macmillan.

Johnson, J. (1995). "Public Affairs and Internationalization: How Multinational Firms Implement Strategies to Manage their Stakeholder Environment," in *International Association of Business and Society Proceedings*, Vienna.

Kapoor, A., and J.J. Boddewyn (1973). *International Business-Government Relations: US Corporate Experience in Asia and Western Europe*. New York: AMACOM.

Keck, M.E., and K. Sikkink (1998). *Activists beyond Borders: Advocacy Networks in International Politics*. Ithaca, NY: Cornell University Press.

Keim, G.D. (2002). "Managing Business Political Activities in the USA: Bridging between Theory and Practice," *Journal of Public Affairs* 1 (4): 362–375.

Kennedy, S. (2005). *The Business of Lobbying in China*. Cambridge, MA: Harvard University Press.

Kennelly, J., and T. Gladwin (1995). "Patterns and Trends in the Management of Global Public Affairs," in *International Association of Business and Society Proceedings*, Vienna.

Lenn, D.J. (1990). "Managing Government Relations: A Typology of Multinational Enterprise Strategy and Structure," in D. Wood and W. Martello (eds), *1990 IABS Annual Proceedings*. San Diego, CA: 102–113.

Lenn, J. (1996). "International Public Affairs: Managing within the Global Village," in LB. Dennis (ed.), *Practical Public Affairs in an Era of Change: A Communications Guide for Business, Government, and College*. Lanham, MD: University Press of America.

Lenn, D.J., S.N. Brenner, L. Burke, D. Dodd-McCue, C.S. Fleisher, L.J. Lad, D.R. Palmer, K.S. Rogers, S.A. Waddock, and R.E. Wokutch (1993). "Managing Corporate Public Affairs and Government Relations: US Multinational Corporations in Europe," in J.E. Post (ed.), *Research in Corporate Social Performance and Policy* XIV. Greenwich, CT: JAI Press.

Lewis, C. (2004). *The Buying of the President, 2004: Who's Really Bankrolling Bush and his Democratic Challengers—and What They Expect in Return (Buying of the President)*. Washington, DC: Center for Public Integrity.

Lewis, M.W., and A.J. Grimes (1999). "Metatriangulation: Building Theory from Multiple Paradigms," *Academy of Management Review* 24 (4): 672–690.

Lindsay, A. (2003). "Public Affairs Integrates Further into Business Strategy—and Networks Skills and Structure into Key Line Areas," *Corporate Public Affairs* (Australian Centre for Corporate Public Affairs) 13 (3–4): 1–25.

Lusterman, S. (1985). *Managing International Public Affairs*. New York: The Conference Board.

Mack, C.S. (1997). *Business, Politics, and the Practice of Government Relations*. Westport, CT: Quorum Books.

MacMillan, K. (1991). *The Management of European Public Affairs*. ECPA Occasional Series, Templeton College, Oxford: European Centre for Public Affairs.

Mahini, A., and L.T. Wells (1986). "Government Relations in the Global Firm," in M.E. Porter (ed.), *Competition in Global Industries*. Boston, MA: Harvard Business School Press.

Mazey, S., and J. Richardson (1993). *Lobbying in the EC.* Oxford: Oxford University Press.

Meznar, M. (1995). "Public Affairs Practices in Multinational Corporations: A Description and Preliminary Analysis," in *International Association of Business and Society Proceedings,* Vienna.

Meznar, M. (2002). "The Theoretical Foundations of Public Affairs and Political Strategy: Where Do We Go From Here?" *Journal of Public Affairs* 1–2 (4–1): 330–335.

Meznar, M.B., and J.H. Johnson (1996). "Multinational Operations and Stakeholder Management: Internationalization, Public Affairs Strategies, and Economic Performance," *Journal of International Management* 2 (4): 233–261.

Moss, D., and B. DeSanto (2002). *Public Relations Cases: International Perspectives.* London: Routledge.

Naets, G. (1990). "Lobbying in the European Communities: A Booming Business," *Business Journal,* 20–23. Cited in Anderson, C. (1992). *Influencing the European Community: Guidelines for a Successful Business Strategy.* London: Kogan Page, p. 344.

Newman, D. (1990). "Lobbying in the EC," *Business Journal,* 12–15. Cited in Anderson, C. (1992). *Influencing the European Community: Guidelines for a Successful Business Strategy.* London: Kogan Page, p. 344.

Ohmae, K. (1985). *Triad Power.* New York: Free Press.

Oomens, M.J.H., and F.A.J. van den Bosch (1999). "Strategic Issue Management in Major European-based Companies," *Long Range Planning* 32 (1): 49–57.

Patterson, B. (1983). "Lobbying in Europe." Public Relations Consultants' Association Guidance Paper, London: Public Relations Consultants' Association.

Pedler, R.H. (2002). *European Union Lobbying: Changes in the Arena.* Basingstoke: Palgrave Macmillan.

Pedler, R.H., and M.P.C.M. Van Schendelen (1994). *Lobbying the European Union: Companies, Trade Associations and Issue Groups.* Ipswich: Ipswich Book Co.

Post, J.E., and Centre for Public Affairs (1993). "Australian Public Affairs Practice: Results of the 1992 National Public Affairs Survey," in J.E. Post (ed.), *Research in Corporate Social Performance and Policy* XIV. Greenwich, CT: JAI Press.

Post, J.E., and J.J. Griffin (1999). *Outsourcing Public Affairs: Issues for Public Affairs Officers.* Management Report series, Washington, DC: Public Affairs Council.

Post, J.E., R.B. Dickie, E.A. Murray, Jr., and J.F. Mahon (1982). "The Public Affairs Function in American Corporations: Development and Relations with Corporate Planning," *Long Range Planning* 15 (2): 12–21.

Post, J.E., R.B. Dickie, E.A., Murray, Jr. and J.F. Mahon (1983). "Managing Public Affairs: The Public Affairs Function," *California Management Review* 26 (1): 135–50.

Preston, L.E. (1993). "Policy Regimes for International Business: Concepts and Prospects," in *Occasional Paper No. 7.* College Park, Maryland: Center for International Business Education and Research, College of Business and Management, University of Maryland.

Public Affairs Council (1997). *1996 Survey of International Public Affairs.* Washington, DC: Center for Public Affairs Management.

Ring, P.S., S.A. Lenway, and M. Govekar. (1990). "Management of the Political Imperative in International Business," *Strategic Management Journal* 11 (2): 141–151.

Rogers, W. (1986). *Government and Industry: A Business Guide to Westminster, Whitehall, and Brussels.* Brentford: Kluewer.

Rugman, A. (2001). "The Myth of Global Strategy," *International Marketing Review* 18 (6): 583–588.

Schuler, D.A. (2002). "Public Affairs, Issues Management and Political Strategy: Methodological Approaches that Count," *Journal of Public Affairs* 1–2 (4–1): 336–355.

Sekuless, P. (1984). *The Lobbyists: Using them in Canberra.* Sydney: Allen and Unwin.

Sekuless, P. (1991). *Lobbying Canberra in the Nineties: The Government Relations Game.* Sydney: Allen and Unwin.

Silverstein, K. (1998). *Washington on $10 Million a Day: How Lobbyists Plunder the Nation.* Monroe, ME: Common Courage Press.

Stanbury, W. (1993). *Business-Government Relations in Canada: Influencing Public Policy.* Scarborough, ON: Nelson.

Starling, G. (1996). *The Changing Environment of Business,* 4th edn. Cincinnati, OH: Southwestern.

Steel, R. (1990). "Getting Your Company's Views Heard in Brussels," *Journal of European Business* 2: 37–43.

Tapscott, D., and D. Ticoll (2003). *The Naked Corporation: How the Age of Transparency will Revolutionize Business.* New York: Free Press.

Taylor, D.W. (1991). *Business and Government Relations: Partners in the 1990s.* Toronto, ON: Gage.

Van Schendelen, M.P. (1990). "Business and Govern-
  ment Relations in Europe," *European Affairs* 2:
  81–82.
Van Schendelen, M.P. (2002). *Machiavelli in
  Brussels: The Art of Lobbying the EU.* Amsterdam:
  Amsterdam University Press.
Vernon, R., and L.T. Wells, Jr. (1986). *Manager in the
  International Economy,* 5th edn. Englewood
  Cliffs, NJ: Prentice Hall.
Waddock, S. (2004). "Hollow Men at the Helm,"
  *BizEd* 3 (5): 24–29.

Wartick, S., and D. Wood (1998). *International
  Business and Society.* New York: Blackwell.
Windsor, D. (2002). "Public Affairs, Issue Management
  and Political Strategy: Opportunities, Obstacles
  and Caveats," *Journal of Public Affairs* 1–2 (4–1):
  382–415.
Wright, W.J., and C. DuVernet (1988). *The Canadian
  Public Affairs Handbook.* Agincourt, ON: Carswell.

# 2

# Public Affairs in North America

## US Origins and Development

JOHN M. HOLCOMB

The period of the late 1960s through the 1970s witnessed a rise and evolution of corporate social responsibility (CSR). While the focus was narrower and the concepts and tools were more rudimentary than are found in some companies in the new century, the efforts and initiatives of that time provided a foundation for more serious endeavors in subsequent decades. In another sense, the pressures from the social movements of the 1960s and 1970s on corporations were more intense and often more aggressive than those of contemporary interest groups, and the responses by companies were often more immediate and launched with more conviction than those of today. While not as sophisticated and not as well structured as the social responsibility initiatives of the new century, the programs of the late 1960s and 1970s were often innovative and ground-breaking, given the corporate mind set of the times. They also spurred new thinking among academics and consultants, leading to criticisms and refinements of the theories and approaches underlying corporate social responsibility.

Written from the perspective of a former staff member of the Public Affairs Council (PAC), the association of corporate public affairs executives, this chapter will trace the evolution and activities of corporations during the decade of the 1970s. James Post and other scholars from Boston University, in cooperation with the Council, have studied the staffing, budget, and programming patterns of corporate public affairs departments during that era (Post *et al.*, 1982, 1983; Post and Griffin, 1997). Others have studied the patterns of public affairs staffing as well (Marcus and Irion, 1987). This chapter focuses more on the activities of the Council itself, however, as a reflection of the demands and priorities of its corporate members. Further, this chapter will compare the state of corporate social responsibility in the 1970s to that in the early stages of the new century.

Prior to the 1970s, corporate public affairs had a more traditional focus on politics and government relations, at both the federal and state levels. The very mission of the Public Affairs Council, called the Effective Citizens Organization at its founding by Richard Armstrong in 1954, was to promote the political education and involvement of executives. That mission was reflected in the board composition of the Council, as the corporate Vice-presidents of Public Affairs that steered the organization placed a heavy emphasis on government relations and lobbying in their own departmental activities. The mission was also in keeping with the quiescent period of the 1950s, prior to the social upheavals of the 1960s.

This is not to say that community and social issues were irrelevant to corporate public affairs in the 1950s and even earlier. Community relations had always been a component of public affairs, but it did not assume compelling significance until the urban riots and social upheavals of the late 1960s and early 1970s. The very term "urban affairs" connoted a more activist stance by corporations, as opposed to the earlier and more constant label "community relations." Most large corporations retained the titles Community Relations Department and Community Relations Officer but the emphasis had clearly shifted in the "urban" direction. It reflected the reality that most large corporations were headquartered in large urban centers, that social needs and social tensions surrounded those locations, and that the political priorities of that period heavily focused on urban revitalization. The term "urban affairs" was also very often a euphemism for "minority relations," as the urban problems of the era often beset minority populations most heavily, and the pressures felt by corporations to respond were often brought by civil rights groups, especially those representing the interests of African-Americans.

While one study of corporate executives during that era (Buehler and Shetty, 1974) found that CSR motivations involved enlightened self-interest and legal compliance more than "forestalling violence" (Buehler and Shetty, 1974), those statements and findings do shroud an underlying reality. The reality of the time was that the concern for and significance of urban and minority issues dramatically increased along with the riots in the cities in the late 1960s.

## CORPORATE URBAN AFFAIRS AND MINORITY RELATIONS

There are several indicators from the late 1960s through the early 1970s that demonstrate the definition of "corporate social responsibility" had an "urban affairs" emphasis. In addition to the Public Affairs Council, other leading peak associations, such as the Chamber of Commerce of the United States and the National Association of Manufacturers, also for the first time hired urban affairs staff specialists to serve member company needs during that period. Though most of the PAC board members had a keener interest in government relations, a faction of the board felt strongly that the Council should address the urban tensions and challenges of the day. Under the continuing leadership of Sam Convissor of the RCA Corporation, the Council formed an Urban Affairs Committee of the board. Also serving as members at various times were such public affairs executives as Russell Laxson of Honeywell, A. Ruric Todd of Pacific Gas & Electric Company, Martha McKay of McKay & Associates, Ted Curtis of Eastman Kodak, Susan Decker of Joseph Seagram & Sons, and Harold Sims of Johnson & Johnson. (See Appendix 2.1 for a more complete list of corporate urban affairs executives of the late 1960s and 1970s.) The Council launched an Urban Affairs function in 1968 and, indicating its evolution and broadening focus over time, renamed that function Urban Affairs and Corporate Responsibility in 1973.

The Public Affairs Council annually sponsored an "urban affairs training seminar" for staff newly hired in that area by member companies. The "minority relations" aspect of that function was partially reflected by the race of participants in those seminars, a large percentage of whom were usually African-American. The attendance at the seminars ranged from forty to eighty new corporate staff, and the training program was held annually or semiannually between 1968 and 1975. Some of the functions of the Council at the time are now fulfilled by the Boston College Center for Corporate Citizenship (earlier called the Center for Corporate Community Relations). The Public Affairs Council also initiated a monthly newsletter for its roughly 500 corporate members, called *Corporation and Community*, which reported on urban policy trends and described innovative corporate initiatives in urban affairs.

The agendas of those seminars, the information requests received by Council staff, and the topics of its newsletter articles also depict the urban and minority emphasis of social responsibility of that era. Discrimination, affirmative action, and minority enterprise were consistently important agenda items on training seminar programs. Exemplary corporate programs at the Standard Oil Company of Indiana (later to become Amoco Oil Company), Borden, and the Quaker Oats Company were often featured. Speakers at the time included Philip Drotning of Standard Oil, who had designed a model minority purchasing program; Carlton Spitzer of Borden, who was also President of the National Minority Purchasing Council; Tom Roeser of Quaker Oats, who served for a time in the Nixon administration as Director of the Office of Minority Business Enterprise in the Department of Commerce; and Elmer Young of First Pennsylvania Bank. Model corporate programs were also featured in *Corporation and Community*, as was the litigation then being directed at General Electric and AT&T, which led to the first landmark affirmative action settlements.

The Council also featured and publicized the efforts of the National Alliance of Business, an organization formed by corporate CEOs like Henry Ford to promote the hiring of the long-term unemployed after the urban riots. In a related manner, PAC also tracked the issue of discriminatory social clubs and luncheon clubs. The Council addressed litigation surrounding private clubs in its newsletter and also surveyed its member companies regarding their policies on subsidizing such clubs.

Another issue of "urban affairs" significance often discussed at Council seminars and addressed in newsletter articles was facility site location and inner-city plants. Two member companies that were leaders in those fields at the time were the Control Data Corporation, where the efforts were represented by Gary Lohn, and the Jewel Food Company, where Bob Jones was the company urban affairs representative. Control Data located some of its facilities in inner cities and on Native American reservations, and Jewel Food sustained a commitment to inner-city store locations.

One major organization and think tank at the time, the Suburban Action Institute (SAI), examined and publicized the racial impact of corporate relocation policies. Paul Davidoff, the city planning expert who founded SAI, was a frequent speaker at Council seminars. The Council staff also followed land use litigation in *Corporation and Community* and publicized the reform efforts of the Urban Land Institute, an organization of real estate developers, planners, regulators, and advisors dedicated to responsible land use planning and industry best practices. Metropolitan segregation and desegregation efforts, along with constructive roles corporations might play, were also issues of concern to several PAC member companies. The Hon. Andrew Young, a member of Congress and later Mayor of Atlanta, once spent a full day discussing those issues with a handful of select companies. Through its newsletter, PAC also followed the controversies surrounding the headquarters relocations of companies like General Electric (from New York City to Fairfield, CT) and American Airlines (from New York City to Dallas, TX) at the time.

One other "urban affairs"-related issue always addressed at training seminars, and a frequent topic of information requests, was that of community audits. George Valli of Babcock and Wilcox was an authority and frequent speaker on the subject at PAC meetings. Martha McKay, a key PAC board member and consultant, would do studies of community power structures for a member company when that firm was about to expand to a new urban location.

Related to the needs assessment issue was also the evaluation issue. The Public Affairs Council sponsored one of the earliest meetings on the corporate social audit in 1970 at the Massachusetts Institute of Technology (MIT) and brought in the leading academic experts and corporate practitioners. ABT Associates of Cambridge, MA, and Eastern Gas & Fuel Associates, led by Eli Goldston, were two of the earliest examples of corporate social audits. The Council also featured on its conferences and in its newsletter the efforts of James Hetland of First Minneapolis Bank, who annually conducted both a community profile and corporate social impact report for his company.

Another "urban affairs" issue of significance to PAC member companies was city government reform and metropolitan reorganization. The Council featured in its programs and/or its publications those organizations promoting reform and business-government partnership, such as the Hartford Process, the Philadelphia Partnership, Chicago United, and Central Atlanta Progress.

Another indicator of the "urban affairs" emphasis in the CSR lexicon of that day was the requests Council staff would receive about organizations and interest groups. The Council had files on 2,500 to 3,000 organizations in the early 1970s, and the most frequent requests were received on organizations that emphasized urban affairs or civil rights. The Council tracked the programs and activities of leading groups like the National Urban League, the NAACP, Operation PUSH, La Raza, and the League of United Latin American Citizens. Leaders of such organizations, including Rev. Jesse Jackson, then head of Operation PUSH, also spoke at Council conferences of their efforts to either pressure or help companies to more fully address urban/minority issues. Rev. Jackson later established covenants with various corporations to promote minority hiring and promotion, corporate board memberships, and business relationships. Council staff also represented its member companies on an advisory committee to the National Urban Coalition, and on another advisory council on minority affairs to the Corporation for Public Broadcasting. The Council also worked with Msgr. Geno Baroni, head of the National Center for Urban Ethnic Affairs at Catholic University, and with the American Jewish Committee to promote corporate respect for ethnic groups and religious diversity. The Public Affairs Council also worked with the community relations service at the Department of Justice to promote peaceful community conflict resolution.

The Council was also active on other issues related to the urban agenda and the impact on minorities. Corrections reform and ex-inmate hiring programs were part of PAC's focus, as it sponsored two conferences on the issue in the early 1970s and published newsletter articles, which featured the involvement of companies like Polaroid and its public affairs director, Robert Palmer. The Council also worked with the staff of Senator Charles Percy (Rep., Illinois) and with the American Bar Association to promote and publicize prison industries legislation. In a similar political vein, the Council also worked with corporate officers and representatives of various government agencies and Nixon administration staff through a periodic informal gathering called the "Madison Group," to build an agenda of progressive domestic policy initiatives.

## CORPORATIONS AND WOMEN'S RIGHTS

While the activities of PAC in the area of corporate social responsibility in the 1970s clearly had an urban and community affairs thrust, the issue of women's rights was also significant in the Council's CSR efforts. In fact, while the Council did not have a minority board member in the early 1970s, it at least had two female board members—Martha McKay of McKay & Associates and Susan Decker of Joseph Seagram & Sons. That is a paltry number compared to the much greater number of women on PAC's board in 2004, but at least it exceeded the lack of representation for racial minorities. Later in the 1970s, Harold Sims of Johnson & Johnson, former Executive Director of the National Urban League, joined the PAC board.

Through Martha McKay's leadership efforts, the Council addressed diversity issues and the promotion of women in its programs. Ms McKay was also personally involved in "glass ceiling" issues, and in helping major corporate members like AT&T address the promotion of women through the "Womanagement" program she designed for that company. She was also head of the North Carolina chapter of the National Women's Political Caucus and served as a liaison for the Council to such groups as the Southern Regional Council.

PAC addressed the women's rights agenda through other means as well. In addition to addressing affirmative action in its urban affairs training seminars, the Council featured industry day care programs in that seminar and in its newsletter coverage, presenting to its members such model corporate efforts as Control Data's Northside Child Development Center in Minneapolis. The Council also featured in *Corporation and Community* the programs and initiatives of major women's groups, such as the National Organization for Women, the National Women's Political Caucus, the National Women's Policy Center, and Women Employed.

Further, through its information clearinghouse, the Council also assisted its corporate members in locating viable female candidates for corporate board positions. It would track the current leading women board members and refer member companies to organizations like Catalyst, headed by Felice Schwartz, to identify other female candidates.

## CORPORATE PHILANTHROPY AND EMPLOYEE VOLUNTEERISM

In addition to the Council's focus on urban affairs, minority relations, and women's rights in its programming and support for corporate members during the 1970s, it also focused on the universal staple of CSR—corporate philanthropy. Strategic philanthropy and its connection to core business functions joined corporate volunteer programs as features of all urban affairs training seminars in the 1970s. The Council featured model contributions programs of various banks and of the exemplary Dayton Hudson Foundation in its training seminars, and discussed innovations in corporate philanthropy in *Corporation and Community*. Robert MacGregor, director of the Dayton Hudson Foundation and later director of Chicago United, a consortium of fifty large corporations headquartered in Chicago, spoke frequently at PAC seminars. James Johnson, later a top aide to Walter Mondale and to the 2004 presidential campaign of John Kerry, succeeded MacGregor as director of the Dayton

Hudson Foundation in the 1970s and was also a speaker at PAC urban affairs seminars.

Further, the Council also reviewed and publicized critical studies of corporate philanthropy, such as one conducted by the CORO Foundation of California, that recommended ways to make corporate giving more systematic. That study was supported by the United Bank of California and its top public affairs executive, PAC board member Lloyd Dennis. PAC also followed public policy initiatives that would affect the future of philanthropy, such as the recommendations of that time by the Filer Commission on Private Philanthropy and Public Needs. John Filer was then CEO of the Aetna Insurance Company, and Burt Knauft, Vice-president of CSR for Aetna, frequently discussed corporate philanthropy at PAC training seminars.

In the 1970s, loaned executive programs were also becoming more common as part of CSR initiatives, and PAC often featured at its conferences model programs of such companies as IBM and Xerox. IBM also used its program as a companion to its diversity initiatives by sponsoring an executive–faculty exchange program with traditionally black colleges and universities. Likewise, it targeted some of its philanthropy to serve the diversity cause, by extending aid for engineering scholarships to black institutions of higher learning. The Council also featured in its newsletter such novel programs as the loaned executive program sponsored by the Economic Development Council of New York City. Through that program, corporate executives would assist city government agencies in streamlining the transportation and court systems of New York, making each more efficient.

The Council also featured innovative corporate volunteer programs in both its seminars and in its newsletter. Such prototypes as the decentralized Community Involvement Teams organized by the Levi Strauss Company became models for corporate efforts forty years later. Bill Funk of the United Bank of Denver was also a frequent panelist who discussed corporate volunteer programs in the west.

## OTHER SOCIAL ISSUES AND CORPORATE INITIATIVES

Beyond the foregoing high-priority items in the Council's CSR programming, it also occasionally examined other social issues and their impact on corporations. Corporate drug abuse programs that emphasized education and treatment were sometimes discussed at training seminars. C. Douglas Ades of the Chemical Bank frequently discussed his bank's innovative community banking program, with decentralized branches in minority neighborhoods. The Council also addressed through its newsletter and conferences the issue of redlining by banks and insurance companies, whereby companies would deny loans and insurance policies to minority neighborhoods, literally drawing a red line of exclusion around them. PAC also addressed legislative remedies like the Community Reinvestment Act, and featured national critic and protest leader Gail Cincotta of the National Housing Information Center at some of its meetings.

The Council also examined the progress and promise of community development corporations (CDCs) in its conferences and newsletter, as well as how major companies could assist CDCs. Corporations such as the Bank of America and the Pacific Gas & Electric Company, with efforts led by Fred Martin, Fletcher Chan, and Edmund Sajor, were leaders in supporting Low-income Support Corporations in the 1970s. Experts on education reform, transportation policy, and housing policy also addressed PAC seminars, as part of the urban agenda of that era. The Council also sponsored two major conferences in the 1970s, one on quality of work life, the other on corporate governance, as its focus broadened from the urban agenda to a wider scope of emerging issues.

## THE FOUNDATION FOR PUBLIC AFFAIRS AND THE BROADER CSR AGENDA

In 1976, the Council developed its Foundation for Public Affairs as a research foundation that also focused more broadly on emerging issues and political interest groups. From its more narrow focus in the early 1970s on civil rights activism and the urban agenda, the Foundation became a major repository and resource center on social movements and political interest groups of all varieties. It pioneered a biannual analysis of 100 to 250 interest groups, known as *Public Interest Profiles*, spun off in the 1980s to Congressional Quarterly Press.

The Foundation's evolution and studies on political interest groups and broader issues of corporate responsibility paralleled the growing interest by PAC's corporate members in that expanding agenda. Two forward-looking PAC board members, who later became presidents of the Foundation, were chiefly responsible for moving the Foundation into serious research and program efforts on crucial emerging issues. Those two astute public affairs executives were Stephen K. Galpin of the General Electric Company and Francis W. Steckmest of the Shell Oil Company. Steckmest also wrote a major book on corporate performance sponsored by the Business Roundtable (Steckmest, 1982). Together, and along with the two top operating officers of the Public Affairs Council—President Richard Armstrong and Vice-president Raymond Hoewing—they really changed the direction and focus of the organization. Due to the relatively small size of the organization (it had less than twenty staff members) and its leadership's willingness to be innovative and take risks, the Council adapted to pressing issues and changing priorities more rapidly than any other comparable business association.

Under the leadership of Armstrong and Hoewing, a combination that worked together for over twenty years, the Council also adapted to other challenges facing its member companies during the decade of the 1970s. In the middle of that decade, they moved the Council's programming and the Foundation's research to focus on the evolving area of issues management. While most corporate public affairs executives in that day grew up using only the traditional tools of government relations, including lobbying connections and campaign contributions, many realized the value of issues analysis, forecasting, and management. Member companies like IBM, with a sophisticated Washington office staff that specialized and divided labor according to various issue arenas, were prototypes for other corporations to consider. The Council increasingly included issues management as an agenda item in its training seminars and sponsored special conferences on issues management as well, while the Foundation gathered organizational materials that companies could share among one another. Such experts as Graham Molitor of Public Policy Forecasting and Jan Dauman of an operation called Matrix in the United Kingdom assisted the Council in building its first issues management conferences. Eventually, these efforts led to the formation of a separate organization, the Issues Management Association, founded by PAC board member W. Howard Chase, to meet the needs of specialists in the field.

As many of the Council's corporate members fanned out throughout the globe, and multinational corporations grew in number, PAC also adapted to their concerns by sponsoring international public affairs conferences in foreign capitals like Brussels, Tokyo, and Sydney. Raymond Hoewing took the lead in developing this vital new component within the Council, discovering how companies were organizing their efforts, ascertaining member company needs, and lining up experts throughout the globe to advise and guide corporate operations. As PAC member companies faced a rising tide of state government activism in the 1970s, the Council also expanded its operations and conferences on state government relations.

Given the interest of most member companies in campaign contributions and electoral politics, the Council also gave advice and counsel to companies that wished to form political action committees. It also worked with and commissioned studies by Herbert Alexander, then head of the Citizen's Research Foundation and one of the nation's leading experts on campaign finance reform laws. It also followed with interest and featured the work of Edwin Epstein, another leading expert in the field and then head of the Business and Public Policy Department at the Haas School of Business of the University of California, Berkeley.

## MISSING CSR INGREDIENTS

While the Council, with its corporate members, emphasized and understood the urban affairs agenda of the early 1970s better than most business associations and then evolved into a broader emerging issues and corporate responsibility agenda in the late 1970s, there were understandably two missing ingredients along the way. While the Council had the expertise and the information to respond to member requests about other social movements, such as consumerism and environmentalism, it did not heavily emphasize these in its conferences. The simple reason was that more often than not those issues fell outside the purview of corporate Public Affairs Departments. During the 1970s, corporate consumer affairs departments and environmental affairs departments were also forming, and were served by new organizations such as the Society of Consumer Affairs Professionals (SOCAP).

Of course, corporate Public Affairs Departments would still deal with the political dimensions and media/PR dimensions of those issues, so the Foundation for Public Affairs became an important source of information in that respect. The vast amounts of information continually gathered and managed by the Foundation staff from the interest groups active on those issues became an extremely valuable resource for corporate members. It assisted them in their own issues management and analysis, as well as coalition-building efforts, as attested by the growing number of requests logged by the Foundation on a daily basis in the late 1970s.

## LINK TO ACADEMIC LITERATURE AND THEORIES

### Urban versus Environmental and Consumer Issues

The rise of corporate urban affairs activities and departments in the late 1960s and early 1970s did coincide with some studies of the emerging area, but they were few and far between and not commensurate with the activity then unfolding in the corporate world. The focus of most of the "Business and Society" texts at the time was on the concepts of public policy and corporate social responsibility, and on what later would become known as stakeholder concerns—most prominently urban, environmental, and consumer issues (Aram, 1986; Elkins and Callahan, 1981; Greenwood, 1977; Starling, 1988). All of those areas, along with women's rights and the corporate world, were treated in a rudimentary manner, as determined by the limited studies then being conducted.

There were a few studies that at least partially focused on corporate urban initiatives at the time, and those few were published mostly in the *Academy of Management Journal* or the *Academy of Management Review*. They found outlets mainly through proceedings. One study published in the *Academy of Management Journal* surveyed executives to determine the various motivations for corporate social action, and the correlation between motivation on the one hand and industry and firm size on the other (Buehler and Shetty, 1974). That study included the usual litany of urban, environmental, and consumer affairs in its definition of corporate social action, and included among urban affairs such corporate activities as "equal employment opportunities; training and employment of minorities and the disadvantaged; fostering economic development of urban areas including minority owned businesses; promoting physical development of housing, transportation, schools, and medical facilities; supporting the arts and cultural improvements" (Buehler and Shetty, 1974).

Among publications in proceedings, one study of social responsibility activities of small companies (Gomulka, 1975) defined such activities as "contributions to education and the arts, minority hiring and training, hard core hiring and training, civil rights, ecology, urban renewal, consumer complaints, understanding accounting statements, truth in advertising, fair and just prices, guarantees and warranties, etc." Obviously included among those activities is a fair amount of those depicted earlier as part of the traditional "urban affairs" agenda of the day. Another study of "Corporate Social Involvement at the Local Level" included among the initiatives studied donation of employee time, urban renewal, equal opportunity and training, employment of the disadvantaged, support of minority enterprise and small business, and contributions to charity and social welfare organizations (Reeder, 1978). Both of the foregoing studies were surveys of unspecified executives that yielded some descriptive data and moderately interesting correlations to company size, industry, firm history, and program structure. However, no study at the time captured the feel or essence of corporate urban initiatives, explained how they worked, or explained and evaluated their importance.

Another of the earlier studies in an *Academy Proceedings* explored the Polaroid Corporation's more muted response to the treatment of women than to more traditional minority concerns, and applied business policy and pressure-response models (Post and Mellis, 1976). Rarely would a business ethics case book contain a vignette or case on community/urban issues, such as the case "Shutdown at Eastland," on the impact of plant closings (Beauchamp and Bowie, 2003). Only one major text has consistently given serious attention to corporation and urban/community issues (Post *et al.*, 2002), with a chapter on "The Community and the Corporation" and case studies titled "Abbott Laboratories helps Habitat for Humanity" and "Walt Disney and the License to Operate." Perhaps other text authors will follow if urban issues once again become a crisis. Virtually all of the other ethics or Business and Society texts and case books over time have had chapters or sections on the environment, consumerism, and employee rights/diversity, but have ignored urban and community issues (Buchholz, 1986; Hoffman and Frederick, 1995; Donaldson *et al.*, 2001; Jennings, 2003; Sethi *et al.*, Falbe, 1997; Sturdivant and Robinson, 1981; Beauchamp, 2003).

The dearth of discussion and attention is impressive. It is ironic that the issue that drove much of the activity and growth of corporate social responsibility during the 1970s now gets scant attention in the business and society literature. Perhaps new issues and a new agenda have simply supplanted the old issues for corporations, or perhaps the Business and Society field is just focusing on new trends, at the expense of important issues in the community and urban milieu. Much to its credit, a previously mentioned organization, the Boston College Center for Corporate Citizenship, continues to sponsor conferences and studies on corporate community affairs.

There is, of course, a vast literature on philanthropy. There are also a few studies by scholars in three areas of needed research: (1) corporate community involvement in a specific urban or geographic area (Burke *et al.*, 1986; Logan, 1994); (2) the role of business in education reform (Waddock, 1994, 1995); and the important area of private-public partnerships (Committee for Economic Development, 1982; Peterson and Sundblad, 1994). The role of business consortia and community coalitions, such as the aforementioned Chicago United, the Philadelphia Partnership, and Hartford Process also deserved attention at one time through such case analyses but were largely ignored by the academic community. Donor forums exist in various cities throughout the country and also merit serious examination. There are also too few scholars in business schools throughout the country who focus much of their work on urban and regional economic development (Gittell and Thompson, 2002, 1999; Gittell and Vidal, 1998; Gittell *et al.*, 1996; Gittell, 1992), and their work deserves more attention by corporate practitioners. That work really lies at the heart of what was once the most pivotal element of the CSR agenda.

More than surveys of executive opinions and community relations priorities, grounded studies and cases (Miles, 1987) would also be more helpful to practitioners, to illuminate the impact and importance of business on urban life and the community. Studies such as Sonnenfeld (1981), that examined the public affairs efforts of the forest products industry and its interaction with stakeholders, and made useful comparisons among competitors in the industry, provide models of the type of studies that would most help companies if

translated into a focus on community relations and urban affairs. They would also provide applied and practical guidance to companies and might advance the state of the art.

## Corporate Social Responsibility

While PAC's staff and corporate members focused on the heightened importance of urban affairs, they were also cognizant of the growing focus on the broader field of corporate social responsibility (Committee for Economic Development, 1971). The Council invited such speakers from the academic world as William Frederick and S. Prakash Sethi to address its membership and explain the concepts of corporate social responsibility (CSR 1), corporate social responsiveness (CSR 2), and corporate social policy (Ackerman, 1973; Ackerman and Bauer, 1976; Carroll, 1979; Epstein, 1979; Frederick, 1978; Sethi, 1975, 1979; Wartick and Cochran, 1985) then evolving in the literature. The thinking and concepts of the day did help corporate practitioners better understand the context of their efforts. Practitioners could instinctively appreciate the importance of the concept of responsiveness (Ackerman, 1973; Carroll, 1979; Frederick, 1978) since it correlated with their function of defining corporate social activities as responses to social pressures and social activists, and as a managerial and pragmatic approach to the outside world. As urban or community affairs directors increasingly grew to serve as internal consultants to top management and corporate line officers on key social issues, and to serve as filters of social demands from outside groups, the "window in" role discussed by Wartick and Cochran (1985) resonated with them.

At the same time, some PAC members had strong reservations about the language then being used to describe the broad reality they faced. The first reservation concerned the very use of the term "social." While business might be a subset of the social system, some felt it did not have "social responsibilities" as such. "Social" connotes societal responsibilities which do not belong solely to business. Responsibility and responsiveness, yes, but not with the adjective "social" attached. The term seemed to contradict the managerial and pragmatic approach some advocated for corporations in being more "responsive."

The term "social" also seemed to carry a stigma that might serve to undermine the internal legitimacy that public affairs executives strive so diligently to attain within their corporations. When dealing with hard-headed and pragmatic managers, negotiating with them while carrying the mantle of a "social worker" may not communicate the right message when trying to gain acceptance for one's budget and programs. Trying to "save the world" is not the proper corporate mission in the eyes of most managers. Further, the term "social" may be ideologically charged, implying from "the left," which is also not the best way to gain the empathy and support of practical managers. The era of the 1970s preceded later efforts to transform the term "corporate social responsibility" into a strategic concept.

The Council's Urban Affairs Committee were fully aware of the baggage that went along with the term "social responsibility" when it discussed renaming the job and department title at the Council. Realizing that the label should be conceptually valid and clear, the corporate representatives also understood the importance of the package. The label must send the proper message to gain some internal legitimacy within their departments and corporations. Hence, the committee members opted for the term "corporate responsibility," rather than "corporate social responsibility." That decision sent two desirable messages. First, the agenda must be narrower than "all social issues" or "saving society" in order to be credible, and this new label better communicated that concern. Second, the issues on the still far-flung public affairs agenda are not merely "social," as in fluff or appendages to the corporation. They are instead central to corporate functions and survival, and the term "corporate responsibility" better communicated that message. The term "corporate social responsibility" too often communicated appendage efforts such as philanthropy, often not centrally related to the core functions of the firm.

The Council's corporate members also frequently expressed reservations with the term "proactive." Instead of reactionaries, are we now to become "proactionaries"? some would quip. Again, the concept seemed to be almost too grandiose and unrealistic to many. It might indeed overstate the possibilities of their own function within the corporation. The concept derived from the work of Carroll (1979), who discussed the continuum from reactive to defensive to accommodative to proactive. He in turn adapted the concept from the work of Ian Wilson (1975), the former top issues management director of General Electric during the era of Reginald Jones. Despite its distinguished lineage, the term rankled some. Hence, the term "interactive," brought to life by certain authors and works (Post, 1978; Sonnenfeld, 1981), and undoubtedly used in many speeches by executives, was a welcome relief and realistic alternative to some in the Council staff and membership. It more modestly communicated what is possible and what public affairs executives actually do on a daily basis. They interact with other group representatives, with community representatives, and with public officials. They don't dictate solutions but rather help formulate resolutions through a process of interaction. They bargain and compromise. They are part of the political process, perhaps both inside the organization and as liaisons with outside groups and institutions.

## Critique of Corporate Social Responsibility

In effect, the Council and its corporate membership had perhaps moved ahead of the academic discussion, to where that discussion would wind up twenty years later. The concepts of social responsibility, social responsiveness, and social policy spawned critiques in academic circles, led by Preston and Post (1975, 1981). By developing the concept of "public responsibility" as an alternative to social responsibility, they brought the field and corporate efforts to a more realistic terrain. It was also less presumptuous territory, less defined by the ethics of top management, and was also at least a partial solution to the boundary problem posed by the concept of CSR (Wartick and Cochran, 1985). Further, companies forming board-level committees to monitor and oversee their responses to external issues often used the label "public responsibility" for those committees, as revealed in a study published in the *Harvard Business Review* (Lovdal *et al.*, 1977). Major companies such as American Express and Texaco preferred that label for their board committees.

However, the term "public responsibility" may also have been the half-way point to a better solution, at least in the eyes of many. That solution was the concept of stakeholder management—conceptually clear and with language that is widely used and seen to be legitimate in the corporate world. The groundbreaking work by Freeman (1984) has also stimulated a wide range of literature that has further developed, amplified, and evaluated the concept (Clarkson, 1995; Mitchell *et al.*, 1997; Donaldson and Preston, 1995; Freeman, 1999; Harrison and Freeman, 1999; Jones, 1995). In criticizing "the inclusive and vague meaning of the word social" Clarkson (1995) gives voice to the corporate pragmatists who resist the use of the adjective "social" for any of their efforts, but who find stakeholder terminology useful and meaningful. The formulator and developer of the concept (Freeman, 1999) acknowledges its instrumental value, one reason it is so easily embraced by the corporate world.

Though Clarkson and others place government and public authorities among primary stakeholders, while placing the media and interest groups among secondary stakeholders, public affairs practitioners see all of them as vital entities to which they must relate. They might argue about which to place in the primary or secondary categories, since any external stakeholder or interest group can affect corporate survival, depending upon the situation. Stakeholder relations, however, is undeniably the central aspect of their job responsibilities. One can even find the term "stakeholder engagement" in the job title of some executives since the year 2000.

## Corporate Social Audit

The shift in focus from CSR to stakeholder management has also been accompanied by a less drastic shift from the early days of the corporate social audit. The academic literature on the social audit (Bauer and Fenn, 1972; Corson and Steiner, 1974; American Institute for Certified Public Accountants, 1977) closely tracked the period of its slow progress in the corporate world and among Council members. Despite some early believers and adopters, it was not widely accepted or utilized and still is not.

Nonetheless, the literature on corporate social performance and its evaluation has moved ahead (Abbott and Monsen, 1979; Alexander and Buchholz, 1978; Aupperle *et al.*, 1985; Coffey and Fryxell, 1991; Arlow and Gannon, 1982; Cochran and Wood, 1984; Graves and Waddock, 1994; Greening and Turban, 2000; Griffin and Mahon, 1997; Kaplan and Norton, 1992; McGuire *et al.*, 1988; Turban and Greening, 1997; Waddock and Smith, 2000; Wood, 1991). Even though corporations have been slow to recognize the importance of corporate social performance, there are at least two driving forces behind its progress. First, there has been a natural curiosity regarding the possible link between social performance and financial performance. Despite the mixed results of the studies, the hope persists that a solid case can be made for a positive financial impact and return from "better" corporate social performance. Second, the rise of social investment funds has created a need for data on corporate social performance, as well as a demonstrated link with positive financial performance. This second factor especially was only in its infancy during the earlier years of the 1970s.

## Issues Management

Just as the Council developed its Foundation research activities in 1976 and began its programs on issues management, the literature as well began to unfold. Howard Chase launched the Issues Management Association, and he followed that with publications of his own (Chase, 1977, 1984). In addition, the Conference Board published a study of its own during the same time period (Brown, 1979). Others followed with later studies in the 1980s (Kaufman et al., 1989; Lenz and Engledow, 1986; Wartick and Rude, 1986).

In the 1990s another study followed that confirmed the importance of the Council's earlier development of an emphasis on interest groups. The link between issues management and analysis of interest group activities became apparent in the work of Greening and Gray (1994). Their study analyzed the connection between external institutional pressures from the media, interest groups, and corporate crises, to the organizational capabilities of issues management. The authors examined such dependent variables as a distinct issues management function, the extent of resource commitment, the use of task forces and committees, the integration of issues management with corporate planning, and the integration of issues management with line management. The authors state their hypothesis as, "The extent to which an organization develops dimensions of issues management structures is expected to depend on three institutional factors: issue-related media exposure, interest group pressure, and the severity of the crises experienced. Generally, our argument is that the greater these institutional pressures, the more a firm will exhibit a highly developed issues management structure." The study found that, of the three factors, interest group pressures were most associated with a serious issues management program and effort.

Along with the growing field of issues management, a literature on corporate crisis management also unfolded from the 1970s onward. Even when internal corporate failures generated these disasters, they often affected a wide range of corporate stakeholders, provoked responses from political interest groups, and contained a public policy dimension (Dutton and Ottensmeyer, 1987; Heath and Nelson, 1984; Marcus and Goodman, 1991; Mitroff et al., 1987; Shrivastava, 1987; Shrivastava and Mitroff, 1987). Hence, they often involved Public Affairs Departments and executives as part of the corporate response.

## Environmental Affairs

As previously noted, the corporate public affairs professional was, in many respects, really at the fringes of the environmental agenda, dating back to the first Earth Day of 1970. Corporations later developed environmental affairs departments or components to more seriously address that agenda. Even so, environmental issues affected corporations as political, legal, and regulatory issues in the 1970s, and hence Public Affairs Departments had some responsibility over them. Community relations officers might also find local environmental issues and groups to be within their domain of concerns. Therefore, even though environmentalism was not a major part of the Public Affairs Council's agenda, it did follow the various issues and groups as part of the Foundation's research activities.

The corporate need for information and assistance exceeded the ability of business schools and the Business and Society field to supply that information and analysis. That at least was the tendency until the 1990s, when leading Business and Society scholars turned their attention in that direction, mainly through articles, texts, and case books (Buchholz, 1993; Buchholz et al., 1992; Hoffman et al., 1990; Post, 1991; Shrivastava, 1995a, b; 1996). Under the leadership of Starik and others, the Academy of Management formed its interest group, Organization and the Natural Environment (ONE) at that time, and scholars began to devote more attention to environmental sustainability as a legitimate and even mainstream concern of business management (Elkington, 1994; Gladwin, 1992; Hart, 1995, 1997). The World Business Council for Sustainable Development also formed and published major works (Ayres, 1995; Schmidheiny, 1992). JAI Press published one of its important series of research volumes on business and sustaining the natural environment in 1995 (Collins et al., 1995), and the Academy of Management devoted a special edition of its journal in 2000 (Starik and Marcus, 2000) to articles written by various ONE scholars on business and the natural environment.

However, while the environmental movement, philosophers, and political scientists had been focusing on the environmental and sustainability agenda since the 1970s, most of the citations by business scholars started only in the 1990s. In that sense, business scholars did not do very well at anticipating the direction the agenda would take and the needs of the business community. Rather, most of the research was published after some leading corporations had already seen the light and began to innovate to meet the sustainability challenge (Starik and Marcus, 2000).

## THE FUTURE FOR CORPORATE PUBLIC AFFAIRS AND ACADEMIC RESEARCH

Of all the publications mentioned in this chapter, there are three that stand out in this author's estimation as being helpful guides through the evolution of the literature related to the issues central to corporate public affairs. For a summary of the thinking and literature related to all aspects of corporate social responsibility, one should read Wartick and Cochran (1985), even if one does not believe in a paradigm of corporate social policy. For a critique of corporate social responsibility and a solid foundation for the literature on stakeholder management, Clarkson (1995) is most helpful. Finally, for a summary of the literature and a sensible empirical study of corporate issues management, Greening and Gray (1994) is most helpful.

In trying to get an idea of the roadmap for the future, this author found that the article by Waddock *et al.* (2002) provides the right guidance and connects many of the strands of recent trends that will affect corporations in the future. Through its title, "Responsibility: The New Business Imperative," it also strikes the right rhetorical chord with this author. The term "social" does not appear in that title. Given the recent wave of corporate scandals and violations, basic responsibility now seems at the core of corporate and public concerns. Also, the term "stakeholder" is widely accepted by now and almost implicit as an underlying adjective for the term "responsibility," especially since the damage done by scandals has been felt by so many stakeholders and by society and the economy at large.

Beyond its title, the content of the article and its survey of trends stimulate the following thoughts and observations about what is different in the business environment today and what challenges corporations and public affairs executives will have to meet in the future:

1 Stakeholder activism remains a constant and growing pressure for corporations. Environmental and human rights groups are more prominent than they were in the 1970s, but civil rights and community groups have by no means lost their fervor. Which sectors are more militant, more creative, more difficult, and more resourceful than others still deserves study, and the answer may often depend on the situation and the industry. The international networks of such groups may complicate life for corporations and lead to other questions, such as "Are these groups dominated by Western thinking and often just as parochial as the corporations they target?"

2 The trappings of corporate responsibility are far more evident in 2004 than they were in the 1970s. There are more corporate codes, industry codes, and training programs. In this age, there is even online training in the area of ethics and corporate responsibility. Does this mean that corporate responsibility is or will be any more "institutionalized" than it has been in the past?

3 Social performance evaluation may still have a long way to go, but it has made giant strides since the 1970s. More investment funds, non-governmental organizations (NGOs), and international organizations have established their own standards and benchmarks, not at all consistent with one another. The demands and pressures are now more precise than they were in the 1970s. What should a transnational corporation do when faced with conflicting standards?

4   There are far more data available by
    which to measure or evaluate corporate
    responsibility than there were in the 1970s.
    Consultants, international organizations,
    and NGOs are all developing metrics by
    which to evaluate corporate governance,
    environmental impact, and other aspects of
    "social" performance. Should corporations
    disclose, debate, or contest such metrics?

5   The motivations underlying corporate
    responsibility may have changed from
    the emphasis on legal compliance and
    enlightened self-interest in the 1970s to an
    emphasis on strategic thinking or even
    integrity-based management in 2004, or
    perhaps there are just more mixed motives
    and complex motives today. How does the
    more complex set of motives affect the
    development of overall corporate strategy
    on a macro basis and the training of indi-
    vidual employees on a micro basis?

6   For large corporations, the global arena is
    ever more complex than it was in the 1970s.
    The spread of the rule of law and democracy
    has made for sophisticated governments and
    complex laws in some areas of the world,
    while the threat of primitive and corrupt
    governments also remains. NGOs continue
    to proliferate on a global basis, and interna-
    tional organizations focus more on cor-
    porate responsibility issues. With the great
    variations in culture from one country and
    region to another, how is a company to prac-
    tice responsible community relations?

7   With the spread of globalization and the
    rise of codes passed by international orga-
    nizations, there has been a growing ten-
    dency for courts to rely on such codes as
    "soft law" in their decisions. As the distance
    between the "hard law" of statutes and court
    precedents and the "soft law" of codes nar-
    rows, so also does the distance between legal
    obligations and voluntary self-regulation.
    How then do corporations define the range
    of various corporate responsibilities?

8   The distinctions between internal and
    external stakeholders, or between primary
    and secondary stakeholders, seemed fairly
    clear in the 1970s. Some, such as suppliers,
    were given only passing attention, while

acknowledged to be economic or internal
stakeholders. Currently, however, the relations are more complex as NGOs press a
corporation to impose a broader range of
responsibilities on its suppliers. From the
supplier's or purchaser's viewpoint, which
stakeholders now fall into the primary or
secondary category?

## CONCLUSION

Of all the social movements and tensions of
the 1960s and early 1970s that propelled the
concept of corporate social responsibility at
the time, the urban tensions and race relations
in the country were foremost. Community
relations officers were at the forefront of dealing with such pressures and tensions, and the
field of corporate urban affairs developed in
response. Employment, purchasing, investment,
and philanthropic policies were all heavily
affected. Even international investment decisions, such as a decision whether to stay or
invest in South Africa, were dramatically
affected by the domestic politics driven by civil
rights groups in the United States. Relations
between business and government were also
affected, as companies formed private-public
partnerships to address urban issues, and
companies assisted government agencies and
influenced public policy to address such issues.
Other social movements also adopted the
successful model and tactics of the civil rights
movement to advance their own causes.

In the 1970s, more emphasis in academic
studies on the business response to urban and
community pressures might have both helped
business forge a better response and signified
the real importance of the urban agenda at the
time. The academic community and literature,
especially in business schools, instead developed a broader concern with corporate social
responsibility that only partially appreciated
the significance of the corporate urban challenges and initiatives. The concepts and language developed also posed practical problems
for corporate public affairs and community
affairs executives as they tried to create a

legitimate base to influence corporate policies and actions. The later evolution of "public responsibility," "stakeholder management," and then "corporate responsibility" has likely alleviated some of the earlier credibility problems posed by use of the term "social."

While late in responding to other stakeholder pressures as well, such as the environmental agenda, business school scholars did more immediately study and track the unfolding fields of issues management and crisis management. That is a tribute to the group of scholars at Boston University that focused on the growth of corporate public affairs and to the later group of scholars at Penn State University that focused on the development of the issues management field.

For the future, both corporations and business scholars must adapt to the growing pressures of globalization and to the growth of new standards, both legal and non-legal, by a host of countries, organizations, and NGOs. There are a great variety of global and societal pressures to be analyzed, along with new forms of corporate organization and governance. With all the work ahead, we may not be able to afford the luxury of spending any more time debating the proper terminology to be used in discussing the essence of "corporate responsibility".

## APPENDIX 2.1 LEADING CORPORATE EXECUTIVES WITH URBAN AFFAIRS RESPONSIBILITIES IN THE 1970S

| | |
|---|---|
| C. Douglas Ades | Chemical Bank |
| Fletcher Chan | Bank of America |
| Sam Convissor | RCA Corporation |
| Chuck Curry | Quaker Oats |
| Ted Curtis | Eastman Kodak |
| Jack Davies | Chase Manhattan Bank |
| Susan Decker | Joseph Seagram and Sons |
| Lloyd Dennis | United California Bank |
| Philip Drotning | Standard Oil Company of Indiana |
| William Duke | Atlantic Richfield |
| Robert Dunn | Levi Strauss |
| Myrlie Evers | Atlantic Richfield |

| | |
|---|---|
| William Ewald | IBM |
| Thomas Fassett | Xerox |
| Eileen Fox | Bankers Trust |
| William Funk | United Bank of Denver |
| Gary Garrison | Massachusetts Mutual Life Insurance Company |
| James Hetland | First Minneapolis Bank |
| Levi Jackson | Ford Motor Company |
| Robert Jones | Jewell Food |
| William Kandel | Singer Company |
| Burt Knauft | Aetna Life & Casualty |
| Russell Laxson | Honeywell |
| Ellen Lipez | Lever Brothers |
| Gary Lohn | Control Data Corporation |
| Robert MacGregor | Dayton Hudson Foundation |
| Fred Martin | Bank of America |
| Martha McKay | McKay & Associates |
| Robert Palmer | Polaroid |
| William Patrick | AT&T |
| William Perry | S.C. Johnson Company |
| Tom Roeser | Quaker Oats |
| Edmund Sajor | Pacific Gas & Electric Company |
| Harold Sims | Johnson & Johnson |
| Ronald Speed | Honeywell |
| Carlton Spitzer | Borden |
| A. Ruric Todd | Pacific Gas & Electric Company |
| George Valli | Babcock & Wilcox Company |
| Elmer Young | First Pennsylvania Bank |

## REFERENCES

Abbott, W.F., and R.J. Monsen (1979). "On the Measurement of Corporate Social Responsibility: Self-report Disclosure as Method of Measuring Social Involvement," *Academy of Management Journal* 22: 501–515.

Ackerman, R.W. (1973). "How Companies Respond to Social Demands," *Harvard Business Review* 51 (4): 88–98.

Ackerman, R.W., and R.A. Bauer (1976). *Corporate Social Responsiveness: The Modern Dilemma.* Reston, VA: Reston Publishing.

Alexander, G.J., and R.A. Buchholz (1978). "Corporate Social Responsibility and Stock

Market Performance," *Academy of Management Journal* 21 (3): 479–486.

American Institute of Certified Public Accountants (1977). *Measurement of Corporate Social Performance*. New York: American Institute of Certified Public Accountants.

Aram, J.D. (1986). *Managing Business and Public Policy: Concepts, Issues, and Cases*. White Plains, NY: Pitman.

Arlow, P., and M.J. Gannon (1982). "Social Responsiveness, Corporate Structure and Economic Performance," *Academy of Management Review* 7 (2): 235–241.

Aupperle, K.E., A.B., Carroll, and J.D. Hatfield (1985). "An Empirical Examination of the Relationship between Corporate Social Responsibility and Profitability," *Academy of Management Journal* 28: 446–463.

Ayres, R.U. (1995). *Achieving Eco-efficiency in Business. Report of the WBCSD Second Antwerp Eco-efficiency Workshop, March 1995*. Geneva: World Business Council for Sustainable Development, UN Environment Program.

Bauer, R.A., and D.H. Fenn (1972). *The Corporate Social Audit*. New York: Russell Sage Foundation.

Beauchamp, T.L. (2003). *Case Studies in Business, Society, and Ethics*. Englewood Cliffs, NJ: Prentice Hall.

Beauchamp, T.L., and N.E. Bowie (eds) (2004). *Ethical Theory and Business*. Upper Saddle River, NJ: Pearson.

Brown, J.K. (1979). *The Business of Issues: Coping with the Company's Environments*. New York: Conference Board.

Buchholz, R.A. (1986). *Business Environment and Public Policy: Implications for Management and Strategy Formulation*. Englewood Cliffs, NJ: Prentice Hall.

Buchholz, R.A. (1993). *Principles of Environmental Management: The Greening of Business*. Englewood Cliffs, NJ: Prentice Hall.

Buchholz, R., A. Marcus, and J. Post (1992). *Managing Environmental Issues: A Case Book*. Englewood Cliffs, NJ: Prentice Hall.

Buehler, V.M., and Y.K. Shetty (1974). "Motivations for Corporate Social Action," *Academy of Management Journal* 17 (4): 767–771.

Burke, L., J. Logsdon, and D. Vogel (1986). "Corporate Community Involvement in the San Francisco Bay Area," *California Management Review* 28 (3): 122–141.

Carroll, A.B. (1979). "A Three-dimensional Conceptual Model of Corporate Performance," *Academy of Management Review* 4 (4): 497–505.

Chase, H.W. (1977). "Public Issues Management: The New Science," *Public Relations Journal* 33 (5): 25–26.

Chase, H.W. (1984). *Issues Management: Origins of the Future*. Stamford, CT: Issues Action Publications.

Clarkson, M.E. (1995). "A Stakeholder Framework for Analyzing and Evaluating Corporate Social Performance," *Academy of Management Review* 20 (1): 92–117.

Cochran, P.L., and R.A. Wood (1984). "Corporate Social Responsibility and Financial Performance," *Academy of Management Journal* 27 (1): 42–56.

Coffey, B.S., and G.E. Fryxell (1991). "Institutional Ownership of Stock and Dimensions of Corporate Social Performance: An Empirical Examination," *Journal of Business Ethics* 10: 437–444.

Collins, D., M. Starik, J.E. Post, and W.C. Frederick (eds) (1995). "Research in Corporate Social Performance and Policy: Sustaining the Natural Environment: Empirical Studies on the Interface Between Nature and Organizations," *Research in Social and Corporate Performance*, Supplement 1. Greenwich, CT: JAI Press.

Committee for Economic Development (1971). *Social Responsibilities of Business Corporations*. New York: Committee for Economic Development.

Committee for Economic Development (1982). *Public-Private Partnership: An Opportunity for Urban Communities*. New York: Committee for Economic Development.

Corson, J.J., and G.A. Steiner (1974). *Measuring Business Social Performance: The Corporate Social Audit*. New York: Committee for Economic Development.

Donaldson, T., and L.E. Preston (1995). "The Stakeholder Theory of the Corporation: Concepts, Evidence, and Implications," *Academy of Management Review* 20 (1): 65–91.

Donaldson, T., P.H. Werhane, and M. Cording (eds) (2001). *Ethical Issues in Business: A Philosophical Approach*. Upper Saddle River, NJ: Pearson.

Dutton, J.E., and E. Ottensmeyer (1987). "Strategic Issues Management Systems: Forms, Functions, and Contexts," *Academy of Management Review* 12 (2): 355–365.

Elkington, J. (1994). "Towards the Sustainable Corporation," *California Management Review* 36 (2): 90–100.

Elkins, A., and D.W. Callaghan (1981). *A Managerial Odyssey: Problems in Business and its Environment*. Reading, MA: Addison Wesley.

Epstein, E.M. (1979). "Societal, Managerial, and Legal Perspectives on Corporate Social Responsibility," *Hastings Law Journal* 30 (5): 1287–1320.

Frederick, W.C. (1978). *From CSR 1 to CSR 2: The Maturing of Business and Society Thought.* Working Paper 279, Pittsburgh, PA: Graduate School of Business, University of Pittsburgh.

Freeman, R.E. (1984). *Strategic Management: A Stakeholder Approach.* Boston, MA: Pitman.

Freeman, R.E. (1999). "Response: Divergent Stakeholder Theory," *Academy of Management Review* 24 (2): 233–236.

Gittell, R.J. (1992). *Renewing Cities.* Princeton, NJ: Princeton University Press.

Gittell, R., and P. Thompson (1999). "Inner City Business Development and Entrepreneurship: New Frontiers for Policy and Research," in R.F. Ferguson and W.T. Dickens (eds), *Urban Problems and Community Development.* Washington, DC: Brookings Institution Press.

Gittell, R., and J.P. Thompson (2002). "Making Social Capital Work: Social Capital and Community Economic Development," in S. Saegert, J.P. Thompson, and M.R. Warren (eds), *Social Capital and Poor Communities.* New York: Russell Sage Foundation.

Gittell, R., and A. Vidal (1998). *Community Organizing: Building Social Capital as a Development Strategy.* Newbury Park, CA: Sage.

Gittell. R., A. Kaufman, and M. Merenda (1996). "Rationalizing State Economic Development," in U. Staber, N. Schaefeer, and B. Sharma (eds), *Business Networks: Prospects for Regional Development.* Berlin: De Gruyter.

Gladwin, T.N. (1992). *Building the Sustainable Corporation: Creating Environmental Sustainability and Competitive Advantage.* Washington, DC: National Wildlife Federation.

Gomulka, E.G. (1975). "An Analysis of Social Responsibility Activities Undertaken by Small Business Companies," *Academy of Management Proceedings* 18: 336–338.

Graves, S.B., and S.A. Waddock (1994). "Institutional Owners and Corporate Social Performance," *Academy of Management Journal* 37 (4): 1034–1046.

Greening, D.W., and B. Gray (1994). "Testing a Model of Organizational Response to Social and Political Issues," *Academy of Management Journal* 37 (3): 467–498.

Greening, D.W., and D.B. Turban (2000). "Corporate Social Performance as a Competitive Advantage in Attracting a Quality Workforce," *Business and Society* 39 (3): 254–280.

Greenwood, W.T. (1977). *Issues in Business and Society.* Boston, MA: Houghton Mifflin.

Griffin, J.J., and J.F. Mahon (1997). "The Corporate Social Performance and Corporate Financial Performance Debate: Twenty-five Years of Incomparable Research," *Business and Society* 36 (1): 5–31.

Harrison, J.S., and R.E. Freeman (1999). "Stakeholders, Social Responsibility, and Performance: Empirical Evidence and Theoretical Perspectives," *Academy of Management Journal* 42 (5): 479–487.

Hart, S.L. (1995). "A Natural Resource-based View of the Firm," *Academy of Management Review* 20 (4): 986–1014.

Hart, S.L. (1997). "Beyond Greening: Strategies for a Sustainable World," *Harvard Business Review* 75 (1): 65–76.

Heath, R.L., and R.A. Nelson (1984). *Issues Management: Corporate Public Policymaking in an Information Society.* Beverly Hills, CA: Sage.

Hoffman, W.M., and R.E. Frederick (eds) (1995). *Business Ethics: Readings and Cases in Corporate Morality.* New York: McGraw-Hill.

Hoffman, W.M., R. Frederick, and E.S. Petry (1990). *The Corporation, Ethics, and the Environment.* New York: Quorum Books.

Jennings, M.M. (ed.) (2003). *Business Ethics: Case Studies and Selected Readings.* Mason, OH: West Legal Studies.

Jones, T.M. (1995). "Instrumental Stakeholder Theory: A Synthesis of Ethics and Economics," *Academy of Management Review* 20 (2): 404–437.

Kaplan, R.S., and D.P. Norton (1992). "The Balanced Scorecard: Measures that Drive Performance," *Harvard Business Review* 70 (1): 71–79.

Kaufman, A.M., E.J. Englander, and A.A. Marcus (1989). "Structure and Implementation in Issues Management: Transaction Costs and Agency Theory," in L.E. Preston and J.E. Post (eds), *Research in Corporate Social Performance and Policy* XI. Greenwich, CT: JAI Press.

Lenz, R.T., and J.L. Engledow (1986). "Environmental Analysis Units and Strategic Decision Making: A Field Study of Selected Leading-edge Corporations," *Strategic Management Journal* 7: 69–89.

Logan, D. (1994). *Community Involvement of Foreign-owned Companies in the United States.* Research Report 1089–94, New York: Conference Board.

Lovdal, M.L., R.A. Bauer, and N.H. Treverton (1977). "Public Responsibility Committees of the Board," *Harvard Business Review* 55 (3): 40–66.

Marcus, A., and R.S. Goodman (1991). "Victims and Shareholders: The Dilemmas of Presenting Corporate Policy during a Crisis," *Academy of Management Journal* 34 (2): 281–305.

Marcus, A., and M.S. Irion (1987). "The Continued Growth of the Corporate Public Affairs Function," *Academy of Management Executive* 1 (3): 212–249.

McGuire, J.B., A. Sundgren, and T. Schneeweis (1988). "Corporate Social Responsibility and Firm Financial Performance," *Academy of Management Journal* 31 (4): 854–872.

Miles, R.H. (1987). *Managing the Corporate Social Environment: A Grounded Theory.* Englewood Cliffs, NJ: Prentice Hall.

Mitchell, R.K., B.R. Agle, and D.J. Wood (1997). "Toward a Theory of Stakeholder Identification and Salience: Defining the Principle of Who and What Really Counts," *Academy of Management Review* 22 (4): 853–886.

Mitroff, I., P. Shrivastava, and F. Udwadia (1987). "Effective Crisis Management," *Academy of Management Executive* 1 (3): 283–292.

Peterson, G., and D. Sundblad (1994). *Corporations as Partners in Strengthening Urban Communities.* Research Report 1079–94, New York: Conference Board.

Post, J.E. (1978). *Corporate Behavior and Social Change.* Reston, VA: Reston Publishing.

Post, J.E. (1991). "Management as if the Earth Mattered," *Business Horizons* 34 (4): 32–38.

Post, J.E., and J.J. Griffin (1997). *The State of Corporate Public Affairs.* Washington, DC: Foundation for Public Affairs.

Post, J.E., and M. Mellis (1976). "Corporate Responsiveness and Organizational Learning," *California Management Review* 20: 57–63.

Post, J.E., A.T. Lawrence, and J. Weber (2002). *Business and Society: Corporate Strategy, Public Policy, and Ethics.* Boston, MA: McGraw-Hill.

Post, J.E., E.A. Murray, Jr, R.B. Dickie, and J.F. Mahon (1982). "The Public Affairs Function in American Corporations: Development and Relations with Corporate Planning," *Long Range Planning* 15 (2): 12–21.

Post, J.E., E.A. Murray, Jr, R.B. Dickie, and J.F. Mahon (1983). "The Public Affairs Function," *California Management Review* 28 (1): 135–150.

Preston, L.E., and J.E. Post (1975). *Private Management and Public Policy: The Principle of Public Responsibility.* Englewood Cliffs, NJ: Prentice Hall.

Preston, L.E., and J.E. Post (1981). "Private Management and Public Policy," *California Management Review* 23 (3): 56–62.

Reeder, J. (1978). "Corporate Social Involvement at the Local Level," *Academy of Management Proceedings* 21: 256–259.

Schmidheiny, S. (1992). *Changing Course: A Global Business Perspective on Development and the Environment.* Cambridge, MA: MIT Press.

Sethi, S.P. (1975). "Dimensions of Corporate Social Responsibility," *California Management Review* 17 (3): 58–84.

Sethi, S.P. (1979). "Conceptual Framework for Environmental Analysis of Social Issues and Evaluation of Business Response Patterns," *Academy of Management Review* 4 (1): 63–74.

Sethi, S.P., P. Steidlmeier, and C.M. Falbe (eds) (1997). *Scaling the Corporate Wall: Readings in Business and Society.* Upper Saddle River, NJ: Prentice Hall.

Shrivastava, P. (1987). *Bhopal: Anatomy of a Crisis.* Cambridge, MA: Ballinger.

Shrivastava, P. (1995a). "Ecocentric Management in a Risk Society," *Academy of Management Review* 20: 118–137.

Shrivastava, P. (1995b). "The Role of Corporations in Achieving Ecological Sustainability," *Academy of Management Review* 20 (4): 936–960.

Shrivastava, P. (1996). *Greening Business: Toward Sustainable Corporations.* Cincinnati, OH: Thompson Executive Press.

Shrivastava, P., and I. Mitroff (1987). "Strategic Management of Corporate Crises," *Columbia Journal of World Business* 22 (1): 5–12.

Sonnenfeld, J.A. (1981). *Corporate Views of the Public Interest: Perceptions of the Forest Industry.* Boston, MA: Auburn.

Starik, M., and A. Marcus (2000). "Introduction to the Special Research Forum on the Management of Organizations in the Natural Environment: A Field Emerging from Multiple Paths, with Many Challenges Ahead," *Academy of Management Journal* 43 (4): 539–546.

Starling, G. (1988). *The Changing Environment of Business: A Managerial Approach.* Boston, MA: PWS-Kent.

Steckmest, F.W. (1982). *Corporate Performance: The Key to Public Trust.* New York: McGraw-Hill.

Sturdivant, F.D., and L.M. Robinson (1981). *The Corporate Social Challenge: Cases and Commentaries.* Homewood, IL: Irwin.

Turban, D.B., and D.W. Greening (1997). "Corporate Social Performance and Organizational Attractiveness to Prospective Employees," *Academy of Management Journal* 40 (3): 658–672.

Waddock, S.A. (1994). *Business and Education Reform: The Fourth Wave.* Research Report 1091–94. New York: Conference Board.

Waddock, S.A. (1995). *Not by Schools Alone: Sharing Responsibility for America's School Reform.* New York: Praeger.

Waddock, S., and N. Smith (2000). "Corporate Responsibility Audits: Doing Well by Doing Good," *Sloan Management Review* 41 (2): 75–83.

Waddock, S.A., C.B. Bodwell, and S. Graves (2002). "Responsibility: The New Business Imperative," *Academy of Management Executive* 16 (2): 132–148.

Wartick, S.L., and P.L. Cochran (1985). "The Evolution of the Corporate Social Performance Model," *Academy of Management Review* 10 (4): 758–769.

Wartick, S.L., and R. Rude (1986). "Issues Management: Corporate Fad or Corporate Function?" *California Management Review* 29 (1): 124–140.

Wilson, I. (1975). "Societal change and the planning process", presented at the AAAS Annual Meeting, New York, 31 January.

Wood, D.J. (1991). "Corporate Social Performance Revisited," *Academy of Management Review* 16 (4): 691–718.

## ACKNOWLEDGMENT

This chapter is dedicated to Raymond Hoewing and to the memory of Richard Armstrong, leaders of the Public Affairs Council. Together, they were entrepreneurs with vision who built an organization, adapted it to changing conditions, nurtured and sustained it through the years, and treated their employees with fairness and respect. They were "leaders" of their profession in the best and truest sense of that term.

# 3

# The History and Development of Public Affairs in the European Union and the United Kingdom

ROBIN PEDLER

Government relations have existed for as long as people have been trying to do business. Traditionally, however, they were part of the role of the head of the business. Influence could be pronounced and could produce serious effects. The colourful history of the eighteenth century is peppered with wars involving the Dutch, French, Spanish, and English as they sought to promote the interests of their sugar planters and spice merchants. Perhaps the most blatant of these was the War of Jenkins' Ear.

In the EU context, at the time of the establishment of the European Coal and Steel Community (ECSC) in the early 1950s, "In France, the steelmasters were used to thinking of themselves as the aristocracy of employers. Their association, under government authority, fixed supplies to firms, output quotas and deliveries to customers ... The President, Jacques Aubrun, complained that Monnet excluded the steelmasters from talks, whereas *all other governments kept industry in close touch*" (Duchêne, 1994: 221). The ECSC

began the development of the European Community/Union and served as a model for the broader communities that followed.

The historical questions therefore become: "When did the desire to influence government develop into a discrete and recognized arm of management?" "When did 'gentlemen lobbyists' become 'warriors'?"

## LOBBYING IN THE EUROPEAN UNION

### A Formal Structure to Incorporate Government Affairs?

When the European Community was established in 1958, its structure included a body called the Economic and Social Committee (ECOSOC). While not a full institution it had, and still has, a role in the development of policy. Like many of the EU institutions, it owes its origin partly to a French model—the Economic and Social Council. It is a tripartite body, with representatives appointed by member state governments from industry, trade unions and "other interests." It is a requirement of the decision-making process that the Council of Ministers may not take a decision until it has received the opinion of ECOSOC. To that extent, the founding fathers of the Community recognized the need to take account of the views of civil society. In practice, however, ECOSOC duplicated the functions of the European Parliament, and as that body gained power, so ECOSOC declined. Its influence is assessed as having been considerable until the 1970s, especially on social issues, and then to have declined steadily, to disappear in the early 1990s (although the body still exists and issues opinions).

## Individual and Commercial Lobbying

Both the leading Brussels lobbyists interviewed for this chapter[1] concur with the tradition of the high-level "gentleman lobbyist" and go on to place the birth of Public Affairs as a discrete management practice in the European Union in the late 1970s.

Up to that time, "diplomatic lobbying" at the highest levels remained the rule. There were very few lobbyists involved in the system and the word "representation" was rarely used. There was already a substantial number of business associations active and officials tended to focus any consultations that took place through them. At that time, law firms, even US law firms, were not involved in lobbying, though there were a few political consultancies, mainly British.

The event that sparked the explosion of public affairs was the first direct election to the European Parliament in 1979. Up till then, the European Parliament consisted of members delegated from national parliaments. For the next seven years, however, Parliament acted purely in an advisory role and most decisions in the Council of Ministers had to be unanimous. Nevertheless, decision making was becoming more complex, and companies increasingly felt the need of an expert local presence to "find out what's going on." So the foundation of public affairs was the need to provide information. From that developed the need to influence the process effectively.

In those early days, client companies already had lists of up to fifty issues that were being debated in the Community context and wanted to know "What's happening that affects me?" The industry associations, typically federations of national federations, though numerous, proved weak when it came to providing focused information. The first association to address this problem was CEFIC, the chemical industry association, which put through a reform in the early 1980s giving its multinational company members direct membership and a role in the decision-making process alongside the national federations.

## Agricultural Interests

The strength of the agricultural lobby in the European Union is widely recognized. It is well and critically described by Bruno Julien (1988). Their first European association, COPA, had indeed been set up before the European Community was established and played an important role in the structure and implementation of the Common Agricultural Policy (CAP). Within the agricultural community, a very powerful but separate voice is that of the sugar producers' association, CEFS. It again was established in 1953 and played its part in the design of the sugar regime, an especially restrictive part of the CAP. CEFS, though European, maintained its offices in Paris until 1988, but then moved to Brussels "because of the Single Market project" (Guéguen) (see below). From then on, the operations of CEFS provide an interesting case study in how it set about first establishing and then protecting the sugar regime.[2] They did not, unlike large and effective organizations described below, issue statements. They concentrated on systematic networking. To build and maintain their networks, they raised the level of people attending meetings for them and made sure these people were very communicative and very technical. They formed a "war machine" into which they incorporated outside experts and lawyers, as indicated.

By these means they were able to establish a "partnership" with the Directorate General of

Agriculture within the Commission. The Commission believed that the quota system on which the regime is based was "good." Its first major challenge came with the GATT Uruguay Round (1987–95). There CEFS with the Commission were able proactively to establish self-financing of sugar exports.

## Commercial Interests: the Vredeling Proposal

In December 1980, Commissioner Davignon and MEP Vredeling brought forward a measure for a Europe-wide system of compulsory information and consultation, to be achieved through works councils. This provoked shocked opposition from business, especially from US-owned firms. There was strenuous lobbying and the measure was defeated in Parliament.

## THE SINGLE EUROPEAN MARKET

Heavy lobbying over information and consultation was, however, the exception rather than the rule in the early 1980s. In 1985 the real launch was in reaction to the Delors-Cockfield proposals to create a single European market. This remains the ongoing spur of lobbying activity. From an institutional point of view, the first step in the process was provided by the Single European Act of 1986, which both created the qualified majority vote for taking decisions in the Council of Ministers and enhanced the role of the European Parliament.

"The industry of public affairs was created for the Single Market," says Stanley Crossick. He goes on to emphasize that his own first lobbying was for himself. He would say to his official contacts: "Please call me a 'lobbyist' and talk about lobbying as part of the democratic process. Strong advocacy for different players is in the interest of good government."

The development of public affairs was not confined to the representation of individual companies. The single market also engendered two interesting and powerful associations. The

first of these was the European Round Table of Industrialists. This may look like, and to some extent is, the formalization of the chairman's role in intergovernment relations, since membership is limited to the chairmen of fifty of Europe's largest companies, by personal invitation. While their presence undoubtedly gives weight to their views, it is significant that they found it necessary to come together as an association and present those views collectively to the European institutions, rather than rely on close relations with member-state governments. It should also be noted that there is an active role within the Round Table for the Public Affairs Directors of the companies represented, who, in the role of "sherpas," research and write up the reports that are the public representation of their chairmen's collective views. The European Round Table is widely credited with conceiving the idea of the single market and then driving the institutions to put it into effect.

The other association engendered by the single market project was the "American Chamber of Commerce in Belgium—EU Committee." While the chamber was a long established organization, its EU committee was a new and semi-independent body that earned itself a name for effective lobbying. To some extent, its foundation may have been provoked by the refusal of the Round Table to countenance the membership of the heads of US companies. (This restriction did not apply to the heads of non-EU European companies. The chairman of Nestlé Switzerland was a founding member, as was Per Gyllenhammer, then chairman of Volvo, twelve years before Sweden joined the European Union.)

The work of the AmCham EU Committee is very much more "classic" public affairs than is that of the Round Table. The US chairmen very rarely appear or take part. The work is done by their European Public Affairs Directors, very few of whom are American. As with the Round Table work, a great deal of their effectiveness rests on the quality of their research and writing. They have also developed a good use of the "round table" which brings together senior Commission officials and leading representatives of US firms for a public debate early in the process of developing policy. This approach was frequently used during the single market process.

## "THE BRUSSELS LANDSCAPE"— A CROWDED PICTURE

This chapter has so far focused on the development of commercial lobbying. But companies are but one of a number of interesting players seeking to influence the process. Justin Greenwood (2003) identifies and describes five different sets of players. While the first are "business interests," and he devotes twice as much space to them as to any of the others, they coexist and not infrequently clash with representatives of professions, labour, public interests, and regional interests. Each of these groups has tended to grow and gain importance as the European Union has expanded and its processes have become more complicated.

The most dramatic rise among these groups has been that of public interests, in the main represented by NGOs. Their increase in numbers and effectiveness and their increasing acceptance into the decision-making process has been driven, over twenty years, by the European Union's concern that it has a "democratic deficit" and is too far removed from its citizens and too little understood. From an historical point of view, the rise in influence may be judged by the representation in Brussels of the World Wide Fund for Nature (WWF). Tony Long set up its Brussels office on his own in the late 1980s. He still heads it, but now employs twenty five professional colleagues, including lawyers and economists. This should be contrasted with the staff employed by even large companies in their EU representations, where "[Most] corporate public affairs offices are small affairs with two or three people, with anything more than five exceptional" (Greenwood, 2003: 123).

NGOs have enhanced their influence by becoming masters at helping the European Union to set the agenda in which policy decisions are taken. This approach is clearly described by Long *et al.* (2002)

## HOW MANY LOBBYISTS CROWD THE LANDSCAPE?

In the thirty-year history of active lobbying in the European Union, there has been a rapid development in the number of lobbyists. The first attempt to gauge how many there might be was that by the Secretariat General of the European Commission. They contributed to Jacques Delors's proposal *An Open and Structured Dialogue* (1992) and estimated that there were 10,000 lobbyists active in Brussels. Separate research by the author and Justin Greenwood has suggested that there was little statistical base for this estimate, which was in fact largely based on the work of a Norwegian academic. Since there is no official register of lobbyists in Brussels (unlike Washington) their number remains a matter of speculation. Debates continue. While some argue that the 10,000 figure is too high, Guéguen for one argues that it is far too low and that the true figure is three times as high. Much lies in the definition of "lobbyist." Are the civil servants and diplomats who represent their member states in the Permanent Representations to the European Union lobbying on behalf of their governments? Many of them freely use the word. Some statistical base can be established from the *European Public Affairs Directory*, the most complete work of its kind. This sets out not only corporate lobbyists but also twelve different categories of "professional" associations and federations, many European, some international.[3] Since, however, the *Directory* does not list the full staff of each body, trying to use it as a statistical base remains an estimate.

The May 2004 enlargement of the European Union to include a further ten central and south European states will undoubtedly prove to have been an historic event. It will also influence the history of public affairs, since those countries bring with them a wide range of different cultures and political traditions.

## PUBLIC AFFAIRS IN
## THE UNITED KINGDOM

The profession's development in the United Kingdom is also a post-war phenomenon. As in Brussels, the speciality was developed by consultancies before it moved "in house." The first of these was founded by Commander Christopher Powell in the 1950s. Michael Burrell says of Powell: "[He] was a brilliant, if somewhat arrogant, man whose knowledge of how Parliament works was unrivalled" (2001: 6).

Powell remained a lonely practitioner for some years. As in Brussels, it was not until the 1970s that the practice became more widespread. Ian Greer and Charles Barker both began as lobbyists in that decade and GJW was founded in 1980. While the profession has continued, with both consultancies and in-house managers active, it has not seen the exponential expansion noted in Brussels. This may well be indirect evidence of the extent to which decisions that affect the bottom line for business have increasingly come to be taken in Brussels, so that the influence is channelled there.

Historically, public affairs in the United Kingdom will probably be remembered for major scandals over the 1990s. The first became known as "cash for questions." The central figures were the political consultant Ian Greer and the Egyptian-born entrepreneur, Mohamed Al Fayed. Ian Greer had expanded his operation by setting up a consultancy, Ian Greer Associates, in 1982. "It became an extraordinary success, with an unrivalled client list of blue-chip companies, but the seeds of its destruction were planted just three years after its foundation, when Ian Greer met the Egyptian-born owner of Harrod's, Mohamed Al Fayed" (Burrell, 2001). The story continued as Al Fayed became involved in a bitter battle with another entrepreneur, Tiny Rowland, and employed Ian Greer to organize the support he felt he needed in the House of Commons. Two Conservative members in particular were contacted and agreed to help—Neil Hamilton and Tim Smith. Hamilton in particular put down questions designed to discredit Rowland. The campaign, however, did not develop well.

In May 1987 there was a general election. Greer asked for financial support from Al Fayed and received £12,000 "which he used to support the constituency campaigns of Conservative MPs" (Burrell, 2001: 7). Margaret Thatcher won the election and the Al Fayed campaign continued. "By 1988, Fayed says, he was handing over money in cash to Hamilton (the 'cash for questions')" (Burrell, 2001: 7).

The Conservatives went on to win another election in 1992 under John Major. Neil Hamilton became a junior Minister but did not answer Al Fayed's letter of congratulation. Shortly after that the Home Office rejected Mohamed Al Fayed's application for British citizenship.

"Fayed was furious, both about what he saw as his betrayal by Neil Hamilton and by the Government's rejection of his citizenship application. He approached the editor of the *Guardian*, Peter Preston, and so triggered the *Guardian* investigation that culminated in the downfall of Tim Smith, Neil Hamilton and Ian Greer" (Burrell, 2001). Smith and Hamilton both resigned from their positions as junior Ministers and both lost their seats in the 1997 election. Ian Greer issued a writ for libel against the *Guardian* but on subsequent legal advice withdrew it. "Released from the constraints of the case, the *Guardian* published further damaging material. IGA's clients and staff deserted in droves. Just before the end of 1996 the company went into voluntary liquidation" (Burrell, 2001: 7).

There were two lasting results from the "cash for questions" scandal. The first was that in 1994 John Major set up the Nolan Committee on Standards in Public Life, which led on the establishment of the House of Commons Select Committee on Standards in Public Life. This led to a code of conduct for MPs, published in 1996 and updated in 2002.

The second consequence of "cash for questions" was that five of Greer's colleagues as political consultants, concerned by the damage that the affair had caused to their image and reputation, set up in 1994 the Association of Professional Political Consultants (APPC). A decade later the membership had increased to twenty five companies. ACCP is a self-regulatory body. Its members all sign up to a code of conduct that forbids any financial relationship with politicians. It also pursues openness by publishing a twice-yearly register of consultancy clients.

Work by the European Parliament shows that this system of self-regulation is one of the few that exists in member states of the European Union to control the activities of lobbyists (DG Research, 2003). Of the other member state parliaments, only the German Bundestag maintains an official register of organizations wishing to "express or defend their interests." The register is published annually. Denmark takes careful note of interest groups which express opinions, but does not publish a list. The other twelve member states surveyed have no official rules in their parliaments.

So the history of public affairs is brief, though it already includes its moments of crisis as well as opportunity. The practice is increasingly focused on the processes of the European Union, and this concentration is likely to continue.

## NOTES

1 Stanley Crossick, European Policy Centre, and Daniel Guéguen, CLAN Public Affairs.

2 My thanks to Daniel Guéguen in this connection.

3 The twelve categories of professional associations are:

1   European trade and professional associations
2   Interest groups
3   Chambers of Commerce
4   National Employers' Federations
5   Regions
6   Think tanks and training
7   Labour unions
8   International organizations
9   Law firms specializing in EU matters
10  Consultants specializing in EU matters: Political, Economic and Management, Public Relations
11  National Trade and Professional Organizations
12  National Associations of Chambers of Commerce.

## REFERENCES

Burrell, Michael (2001). *Lobbying and the Media: Working with Politicians and Journalists.* London: Hawksmere.

Delors, Jacques (1992). *An Open and Structured Dialogue between the Commission and Interest Groups.* SEC (92) 2272 final. Brussels: CEC.

DG Research (2003). *Lobbying in the European Union: Current Rules and Practices.* Brussels: DG Research.

Duchêne, François (1994). *Jean Monnet: The First Statesman of Interdependence.* New York: Norton.

*European Public Affairs Directory* (2004). Brussels: Landmarks.

Greenwood, Justin (2003). *Interest Group Representation in the European Union.* London: Palgrave Macmillan.

Julien, Bruno (1988). *Les Groupes de pression américains. Le lobby agro-alimentaire à l'assaut du pouvoir.* Paris.

Long, Tony, Liam Salter, and Stephen Singer (2002). "WWF: European and Global Climate Policy," in Robin Pedler (ed.), *European Union Lobbying: Changes in the Arena.* London: Palgrave Macmillan.

# 4

# The External Environment of Public Affairs in North America

## *Public Policy Process and Institutions*

WILLIAM D. OBERMAN

This chapter provides an introduction to the public policy-making environment in North America, with a focus on the institutions and processes of policy-making in the United States. The goal is to supply a practical intellectual background on the US political system, particularly for readers who are not specialists in American politics, against which the concepts and issues discussed in following chapters can be viewed. The chapter is divided into two sections. The first describes the formal institutions, procedures, and organizations associated with policy making. Governmental institutions, the procedures they follow, and the interest groups that seek to influence them are covered. The second section is organized around a typical public policy process model and uses that model to integrate important conceptualizations of the policy process and the informal structures that emerge from it, including agendas and policy subsystems.

## FORMAL INSTITUTIONS, PROCEDURES, AND ORGANIZATIONS

The United States differs from most other representative democracies in its governmental structure. The US constitution creates a system divided horizontally by federalism and vertically by a separation of powers. In contrast to the more common parliamentary systems which blend the executive and legislative functions, the functions of law making, execution, and interpretation are separated into distinct governmental branches in the United States. This creates a unique dynamic in policy making that will be apparent throughout the chapter. Even from a constitutional perspective, however, the separation is not complete, as a system of checks and balances gives each branch some control over the others. In practical policy-making terms the separation is still less complete; all three branches participate in the process, although, theoretically, it is a legislative or law-making function. This joint policy making, nevertheless, has constitutional bounds, and attempts by one branch to reach too far into the functions of another are likely to be struck down. An example is the Supreme Court decision declaring unconstitutional the "legislative veto" included in a number of 1970s statutes which gave Congress the power to void decisions made in the executive branch.

Another dimension is added to the US public policy environment by the federal system. Power and authority are constitutionally divided between the state and federal governments and public policies are formulated and implemented at both levels. An implication of this system is that one type of "interest group" trying to exert influence on national policy is made up of state and local governments. In addition to elected officials of individual states and localities, associations have formed to lobby the federal government. The National League of Cities, the National Governors' Association, and the National Association of State Budget Officers are examples of these intergovernmental lobbying groups (Nice and Fredericksen, 1995). Direct federal spending in a state or locality, federal grants, revenue sharing, and "unfunded mandates" to the states by the federal government to implement federal programs are among the areas of federal policy that impact lower levels of government.

In a later section on public policy process, we will discuss how policy advocates seek to expand or contain the "scope" of conflict on the issues in which they are involved. One component of scope in a federal system is the governmental level at which a policy issue is debated and resolved (Nice and Fredericksen, 1995). The general trend since the early days of the republic has been toward increasing nationalization. This trend has been driven by the broadening scale of problems, the recognition by state governments that some higher level of authority was required to solve collective action problems among the states themselves, and by policy advocates looking for a more sympathetic audience for their cause (for example, civil rights advocates in the early 1960s) or attempting to employ a more efficient lobbying strategy (for example, the successful movement by anti-drunk driving forces to raise the legal drinking age in the states by tying it to federal highway funding rather than lobbying state by state). However, the management of conflict scope by policy proponents can also work in the opposite direction when particular policy proposals are perceived as more likely to be received favorably at the state level (Kernell and Jacobson, 2000).

## Congress

Based on its constitutional and organizational capacity to function independent of the executive, the US Congress has been described as "far and away the most powerful" (Gilmour, 2001) of the world's national legislative bodies. The Congress consists of two Houses, the Senate and the House of Representatives. A Bill must be passed in identical form by both Houses before it can be sent to the President to sign into law. A presidential veto can be overridden on a two-thirds vote by both Houses. Two senators are elected from each state for six-year terms. House members serve two-year terms and are elected from districts based on population. House members win re-election more than 90 percent of the time, senators more than 80 percent of the time. The US electoral system limits the ability of party leaders to discipline members.

A major difference in procedure between the House and the Senate is the lack of a time limit on debate in the latter, allowing a minority group of senators or even a single senator to indefinitely delay a vote on a Bill (and the work of the whole Senate) through filibustering tactics. In the House of Representatives, the majority party-controlled Rules Committee wields "staggering" power to determine the conditions under which a Bill favorably reported from committee can be debated, amended, and voted on by the full House in order to ensure the position favored by majority party will prevail (Gilmour, 2001). While the House works according to a strict system of rules and carefully constructed majorities, passing legislation in the Senate requires consensus building and sensitivity to the demands of minorities and individual senators. Thus, in the Senate, important legislation is brought to the floor under unanimous consent agreements, rather than rules imposed by the majority party leadership.

Both houses of Congress are organized into standing committees and subcommittees responsible for specific areas of legislation and oversight. Committees and their chairs essentially control which proposed legislation will reach a vote before the full House. Committee assignments are made by the party leadership, with the interests of the individual members taken into account. Members of Congress often become experts in specialized policy areas related to their committee. Committee chairpersons are members of the majority party, normally, but not exclusively, selected on the basis of seniority. Large professional committee staffs of subject-matter experts do much of the work and contribute substantially to the development of legislation. In addition to committee and subcommittee staffs, the staffs of individual members and the institutional staff agencies of the Congress, such as the General Accounting Office and Congressional Budget Office, contribute to the capacity of the Congress to make policy independent of executive branch or interest group expertise (Anderson, 2003).

Oleszek (1978) notes four enduring features of the congressional decision-making process: decentralization, multiple decision points, the necessity for compromise, and time pressure. In order to become law, a Bill has to be negotiated through more than 100 specific steps (Oleszek, 1978). Along the way it will require several majority committee and subcommittee votes—each of which is likely to demand compromise and bargaining—and will be vulnerable at any step to derailment by opponents. This journey takes place in an environment of decentralized power, characterized by members who represent widely diverse constituencies, a system of fragmented and overlapping committee jurisdiction, and weak party discipline. The situation necessitates a "constant cycle of coalition building" and bargaining which is made possible by the non-legislative objectives of members (such as desire for re-election, committee appointments, nicer offices, etc.) and the diverse constituencies they represent (Oleszek, 1978). Meanwhile, the congressional term clock is running; all Bills must pass the House and Senate by the end of the two-year term.

A common view of members of Congress is that with the exception of a few "saints" their primary motive is re-election (Mayhew, 1974; Fiorina, 1989). The most important consideration for a legislator in deciding how to vote on the record according to this view is the maximization of approval in the home district, although when no clear constituency interest is at stake, "the congressman may take into account the general welfare of the country" (Fiorina, 1989). While there are many opportunities in the committee and subcommittee process to quietly vote, even against constituent opinion, engaging in substantive policy making can be risky and thankless in terms of re-election. Any recorded vote is going to alienate some segment of a legislator's constituency. At the same time, as one among hundreds, it is difficult for an individual legislator to take credit for popular laws. This gives Congress an incentive to shift policy making to the bureaucracy, allowing members to focus on activities that make them popular in their home districts such as pork barrel legislation and case work. Bringing home federal money for local projects may attract some criticism but is generally popular with the voters that count. Case work, which usually involves helping a constituent navigate the federal bureaucracy, creates goodwill with voters and has no down side. (The beauty for members of Congress in delegating policy making to the bureaucracy is that it not only transfers the anger of those dissatisfied with policy to the bureaucracy, but also allows the legislators to use case work to ingratiate themselves with constituents facing problems generated by the increasing bureaucracy the legislators themselves create.) This may be an unfair caricature of congressional behavior, but it nevertheless reflects the strong incentives for conflict avoidance on substantive policy matters in the Congress and the way these incentives have affected the process of policy making.

The conventional wisdom (Matthews, 1960; Bauer et al., 1963) is that lobbyists focus their activity on politicians already on their side, paying little attention to those opposed or uncommitted. More recent research (for example, Schlozman and Tierney, 1986) asserts, however, that lobbyists expend much effort on the undecided and those weakly committed for or against their position. There is even some argument and evidence that lobbyists target legislators hostile to their position and only speak to friendly ones to counter the lobbying of opposing groups (Austin-Smith and Wright, 1994).

The research on the influence of campaign contributions is equally contradictory. Some researchers claim campaign contributions have little effect on voting, some have found significant effects, and others have described mixed effects. Smith (1995) reviews a number of common explanations for the conflicting research findings. The most common is that contributions are really aimed at obtaining access, not votes. This is supported by anecdotal evidence and some quantitative research (Langbein, 1986), but little is known about the quality of that access. Another explanation is that contributions affect recorded voting only under certain conditions, such as on issues that are low-visibility, technical, or non-partisan, or when the public is indifferent or divided. A third explanation is that contributions influence activities that take place out of public view such as the drafting and introduction of legislation and amendments, and the markup process in committees and subcommittees (Conway, 1991; Sorauf, 1992).

## The Executive

The term "executive" refers not only to the President personally, but to the entire apparatus of what has come to be termed the "institution-alized presidency." This includes the Cabinet, the White House staff (numbering about 400), and the Executive Office of the President (EOP). The Office of Management and Budget (OMB) and the National Security Council (NSC) are part of the EOP. The executive influences the public policy process through the use of formal and informal powers. Formally, the President selects several thousand political appointees for the top positions in administrative agencies, issues Executive Orders to the bureaucracy, and can veto legislation passed by Congress. Informally, but most visibly, the President sets the major policy agenda. The President occupies a "bully pulpit" and popular Presidents who are effective communicators can sway the policy preferences of the public and pressure other policy makers (Page and Shapiro, 1985).

The President is expected to lead: the Congress is fragmented and parochial; the President represents the national interest. An important part of presidential leadership is setting before Congress and the nation a public policy agenda. The presidential agenda signals what the President believes are the most important issues facing the country, the most appropriate alternatives for dealing with them, and their priority (Light, 1999). The agenda is an instrument of power that sets the terms of political debate and embodies a conception of how limited governmental resources should be allocated. How successful the President is in obtaining legislative support for this agenda depends on the resources at the President's disposal. Resources are based on internal policy and policy-making expertise as well as external political capital. Light (1999) sees the process of putting the President's agenda into action taking place in the context of two often out-of-phase policy cycles: the "cycle of decreasing influence" and the "cycle of increasing effectiveness." While learning and "effectiveness" increase over time, political capital generally decreases. These two cycles create cross-pressures: move fast to improve the chance of political success versus take your time to improve the chance of creating good policy. The result, according to Light (1999), has been the development of a "No Win Presidency."

The executive influences the public policy process in many less visible ways. The President appoints the top-level leadership of administrative agencies charged with implementing policy. These political appointees presumably share the President's policy preferences, but those working for administrative branch agencies can also be fired if they waiver. (Some appointees are regulatory commissioners who have judge-like status and can be removed only for cause.) The executive also possesses administrative powers over the policy process. Since the 1940s, legislative proposals going to Congress from anywhere in the executive branch have required clearance through the OMB (and its predecessor). Since the 1980s, the OMB has reviewed proposed regulatory rules. Executive orders give an administration power to "shape the substance of individual regulations" (West and Cooper, 1985). President Reagan's Executive Order 12291 required agencies to submit a regulatory impact analysis (RIA) containing a detailed cost–benefit analysis to the OMB for any rule having an economic impact of more than $100 million. Although the RIA review was supposed to have been purely technical, there were allegations of political factors entering into the process (West and Cooper, 1985). The method was changed during the Clinton administration under Executive Order 12866, which required fewer rules to be submitted for review, but led to the approval of a much smaller proportion of them without modification. The OMB under the second Bush administration continued to operate under 12866, but began to issue "return" and "prompt" letters to agencies which seem to expand its role. Return letters reject a rule outright and specify what needs to done to win approval; prompt letters suggest areas where rule making might be beneficial (Kerwin, 2003).

## Administrative Agencies

There are four varieties of administrative agencies in the federal government of the United States: executive departments, headed by Cabinet secretaries (for example, the State Department and Commerce Department); independent regulatory commissions, headed by multimember boards (for example, the Interstate Commerce Commission and Federal Reserve Board); independent agencies (for example, the Environmental Protection Agency and Central Intelligence Agency); and government corporations (for example, the US Post Office and Federal Deposit Insurance Corporation). These agencies conduct four types of activities associated with policy making and implementation: rule making, adjudication, law enforcement, and program operations (Anderson, 2003). In rule making, agencies assume the quasi-legislative function of formulating the operational details necessary to implement laws. The rules created have the force of law. Agencies assume a quasi-judicial role through adjudication by making decisions

on when to apply or how to interpret a particular rule or law in a given case. Even seemingly routine enforcement and operations can function as modes of policy making.

Rule-making procedures are structured by the Administrative Procedure Act of 1946 (APA), which outlines formal, "on the record," and less formal, "notice and comment," procedures. Congress has the option of specifying "on the record" rule making, but has not usually done so. The commonly used form, "notice and comment" or "informal" rule making, is governed by Section 553 of the APA. Prior to the making of any rule, Section 503 requires publication of a general notice of proposed rulemaking in the *Federal Register*, including the time, place, legal authority under which the rule is proposed, and the terms or substance of the proposed rule. Interested parties must be given the opportunity to participate through the submission of written data, opinions or arguments, and possibly oral presentation. Publication of a rule is required not less than thirty days before it is to go into effect. Section 706 of the APA provides for judicial review of agency rules on substantive or procedural grounds.

The APA was a result of a New Deal era conflict between advocates of a large, active government capable of efficient policy implementation and conservative forces that sought to guard individual and property rights though common law due process requirements. Kerwin (2003) notes that although the proponents of big government won the battle in drafting the APA, "over the next several decades, they would lose the war." While "notice and comment" rule making has not generally been replaced with the "on the record" form, many forces have combined to impose a "creeping judicialization" on the process (Kerwin, 2003). Hybrid procedures are now common. The APA itself says little about the information the agency must consider in making a rule, but information requirements have been increasingly specified by policy-authorizing statutes, information statutes (such as the National Environmental Policy Act, which requires environmental impact statements when proposed rules have potentially significant impacts on the environment), and executive orders. Section 553 of the APA also does not detail participation requirements or require open hearings, but executive orders, authorizing statutes, and court decisions have moved in the direction of mandating more time for comment, the use of advisory committees, and public hearings, sometimes with provision for rebuttal or cross-examination (Kerwin, 2003). A number of more recent laws have required "on the record" procedures.

West (1984) views the creeping judicialization described above as part of an attempt by the Congress, courts, and executive branch to "structure administrative discretion" as increased policy-making authority has been delegated from Congress to administrative agencies. This attempt has been reflective of two underlying values: rationality and responsiveness. Concerns for responsiveness have expanded administration into a forum for interest representation in the policy-making and judicial review process. Rationality concerns have led to requirements for cost-benefit analyses and impact statements. Strengthened due process requirements attempt to address both values. Statutes now often mandate hearings and final rules based on "substantial evidence." Courts can overturn a rule made according to the provisions of Section 553 on substantive grounds only if it is found to represent an "arbitrary and capricious abuse of discretion." The standard of substantive evidence is much stricter, demanding that agencies pay closer attention to the arguments of interested parties and to the scientific and legal premises of any rules promulgated. This has increased the cost of rule making and the opportunities for groups to delay the process.

In addition to their quasi-legislative role as rule makers, administrative agencies assume a quasi-judicial role when they apply existing rules or laws to a particular case. In regulatory settings, if a party is charged with violating a law or rule, and no settlement can be reached, a non-jury trial will be held before an administrative law judge. The judge's decision is final, but can be appealed within the agency and then to the federal courts. Agencies sometimes choose to make policy incrementally through the development of case precedent and employ adjudication as a substitute for rule making.

The manner in which a regulatory agency enforces laws or policies can be a form of policy making in its own right. Decisions to undertake vigorous or lax enforcement of a statute, to informally decide to pursue only those who violate the law by a certain degree (for example, giving speeding tickets only to those exceeding legal speed limits by more than 10 m.p.h.), or to cease to enforce a law completely are all regularly occurring forms of *de facto* policy making.

## The Courts

Federal judges are nominated by the President and confirmed by the Senate. Once on the bench, they hold lifetime tenure. They are part of the public policy-making process in a number of ways. First, through interpreting the constitution—decisions like *Brown v. Board of Education* and *Roe v. Wade* have had tremendous consequences for public policy, both in terms of their effect on existing policy and in their shaping of debate for decades. Many lesser known decisions on cases related to school busing, employment law, due process requirements, and a host of other issues have led to commentators such as Glazer (1975) to remark that "judges decree the sea must not advance, and weary administrators—hectored by … lawyers for public advocacy centers— must go through the motions to show the courts they are trying."

Courts also affect the public policy process directly through the judicial review of legislative and administrative policy—and the prospect of that review on the formulation of policy. The Supreme Court may declare an Act of Congress unconstitutional, but a more common intervention is in the review of administrative action. Legal challenge of rules is most frequently encountered by social regulatory agencies, such as the EPA and OSHA, whose policies are made in conflictual environments and have far-reaching impacts (Kerwin, 2003). Section 706 of the APA provides that courts can (1) compel an agency action that has been unlawfully or unreasonably delayed and (2) set aside agency actions and conclusions that are arbitrary and capricious, unconstitutional, in excess of statutory authority, without observance of lawful procedure, or unsupported by substantial evidence when on-the-record rule making is required. There have been conflicting Supreme Court opinions on the extent to which judges can second-guess the detailed substance of agency rule making (Kerwin, 2003). The generally accepted standard is that courts should defer to the policy judgments of agencies when they are "reasonable" and the result of "reasoned decision-making" (Lubbers, 1998). However, this standard is sufficiently vague that it can be used to justify both interventionist and non-interventionist judicial opinions.

## Interests, Groups, and Organizations

In addition to the formal institutions of government, the other major class of participant in the public policy process is made up of the interests seeking representation and influence. How and if interests obtain representation and influence are critical questions in democratic systems. The assumptions made regarding these questions have evolved over the years and have been the subject of continuing debate.

Concern with group interests in American politics can be traced back to James Madison's analysis of factions in *The Federalist Papers* and John C. Calhoun's antebellum defense of states' rights and factional interests (Ornstein and Elder, 1978). The modern approach to political interest groups was pioneered by Bentley (1908), but his ideas were largely ignored until Truman (1951) rediscovered and expanded them. Truman's work inspired other researchers, and interest groups became a focus of political thought in the 1950s. In contrast to earlier critics of faction, group theorists of that era generally cast groups in a positive light. Interest groups were seen as emerging to express political demands and communicate those demands to decision makers. They were portrayed as facilitating consensus and assisting the mutual adjustment of interests (McKenna, 1976).

Truman believed the formation of an organized interest group begins when a group of individuals experiences some disturbance to an established pattern of behavior and its members feel they have been disadvantaged. They may believe they have claims upon another group or groups. To stabilize the disturbed relationships within the group and with members of other groups, an association is formed. The association may seek redress from the government. As modern society becomes ever more diverse and specialized, and as rapid change frustrates expectations, these types of associations will multiply. They will appear in waves as the formation of one association sparks counter-organization among rival groups. In Truman's (1951) words, "the proliferation of associations is inescapable." In this view, the problems of representation are minimized. Any group that believes itself to be disadvantaged will organize to defend its interests. Plural democracy will work smoothly as competing interests make their voices heard in the government and as "special interests" are automatically counterbalanced.

This outlook was challenged by analysts like Schattschneider (1960), who charged that there was an upper-class bias in representation that less advantaged groups could not overcome, and Bachrach and Baratz (1962), who held that much real power was derived from control of the policy agenda. Another type of challenge, and one that set the terms of debate for many years, came from an economics-oriented perspective. Olson's (1965) "logic of collective action" called into question the ability of groups to organize in the facile manner assumed by group theorists like Truman. Olson identified an inconsistency in the reasoning of the group theorists, who expected that people understood by the group theorists themselves to be primarily interested in their own welfare would voluntarily sacrifice to help their group obtain its objectives. Olson equates this thinking with the "hopelessly eccentric" belief of anarchists that, in the absence of an oppressive state, a natural human order of cooperation and mutual aid will spontaneously emerge (Olson, 1965).

The "free rider" problem is at the heart of Olson's skepticism. Members of large groups will perceive their individual contributions to group success to be small and the absence of an individual contribution unlikely to be noticed. At the same time they know that as members of the group they will share in any collective benefits the group obtains regardless of whether they contribute. The tendency for any self-interested actor in this situation will be to withhold contributions and "free-ride" on the contributions of others. Of course, this makes the organization of large-scale interest groups problematic. Groups can be presumed to organize only when it is in the interest and within the capabilities of one member to absorb the whole cost of organization. Olson terms these "privileged" groups. Groups in which no single member has an incentive to bear the entire cost of organization, but which are relatively small, making individual contributions meaningful and easily monitored, may or may not be able to organize. These are labeled "intermediate" groups. Large groups are termed "latent" and will never be able to organize in the absence of some "selective incentive" that can "stimulate a rational individual … to act in a group-oriented way" (Olson, 1965). A selective incentive can be a positive reward to contributors beyond the collective benefit sought by the group or a negative sanction on free riders.

Olson (1965) offered a "by-product" theory of political pressure groups. According to this theory, all large economic groups with lobbying organizations, such as labor unions and professional organizations, were originally formed for some purpose other than lobbying and maintain themselves through the distribution of selective incentives. Thus, lobbying is a "by-product." Industry lobbies were seen as representing privileged or, perhaps, intermediate groups. Olson (1965) believed that large, latent, "forgotten groups," such as taxpayers, consumers, and white-collar workers, were doomed to "suffer in silence."

Olson's reasoning shattered the pluralist assumption that any disadvantaged group in society would be able to organize to defend its interests and undermined all existing theories of group formation (Salisbury, 1975). It became clear that social forces alone could not generate interest group formation. What then could explain the large numbers of organized interest groups that were emerging by the late 1960s? Exchange theory (Salisbury, 1969) offers one explanation by focusing on the role of entrepreneurs. Salisbury (1969) argues that "groups must be organized by organizers investing capital." People with similar preferences, a collective interest, exist only as a potential group until an organizer, or "entrepreneur," invests in the selective benefits necessary to attract them to an organization. The benefits provided may be material, solidary (socializing, status, identification, sense of belonging), or expressive (opportunities to express values) (Clark and Wilson, 1961). There is an exchange between the entrepreneur and the members; the members get the selective benefits and the entrepreneur receives at least enough membership support to keep the benefits flowing plus a profit (material or expressive). Some of these profits may be spent in lobbying to serve the personal values of the entrepreneur and/or to meet the demands of the membership for collective benefits.

Starting with the collective action framework of Olson and incorporating a broad view of incentives similar to Salisbury's, Moe (1980) added the notion of "efficacy" to develop what he considered a more balanced perspective on group membership. Efficacy refers to an individual's subjective estimate of the costs and benefits of political success, the belief that his or her contributions can make a difference. When efficacy is low and the interest is primarily economic or material, Olson's reasoning holds. However, when people believe, perhaps irrationally, that their contributions matter, the situation changes. Also of great importance is the fact that many "purposive" incentives, derived from ideological or moral principles, are more important than material gain. Group membership in support of a deeply held principle may actually serve as a selective incentive in itself. The addition of individual perceptions and strongly held beliefs to collective action reasoning, produces a more complex, less deterministic view of group formation that no longer makes sweeping predictions about group behavior (Moe, 1980).

Neither the comfortable assurance of the group theorists in the efficiency of representation nor the bleak pessimism of Olson and others is warranted. Group interests may find representation, but the ability of leaders to influence perceptions and manipulate rewards is at least as important as disruptive social forces in stimulating the organization of this representation.

## Institutions

Traditionally, discussions of interest advocacy have revolved around interest groups, but many of the "groups" participating in the public process are not in fact groups but "institutions" (Salisbury, 1984). In other words, they are not membership-based interest groups as discussed above, but formal organizations such as corporations, local governments, and universities. Salisbury sees institutions of this sort as dominating interest representation in Washington and believes that many of the problems which critics such as Schattschneider (1960) have attributed to interest group politics actually derive from the power of institutions. Institutional actors as defined by Salisbury generally have a wider range of policy concerns than interest groups and employ multiple specialized representatives to interact with governmental officials. Their managers possess more discretionary resources and have less need to justify their actions to their members than the leaders of membership groups. Little else needs to be said in this chapter about institutional representation, as that in essence is the subject of the rest of this book.

## THE POLICY PROCESS AND INFORMAL INSTITUTIONS

The preceding section can be thought of as having provided a description of the major players in the public policy game and the rules by which they play. This section looks at the structure of the game. The discussion will be organized around a sequential model of the policy-making process. Models of this sort depict the development of a policy from the first recognition of a problem through the stages of development of a public policy to address that problem. Whether or not this linear sequencing reflects the reality of the manner in which most public policies originate, it provides a logical and frequently employed way to discuss the necessary steps in the process. We will also use it to organize of a number of important conceptualizations of various aspects of policy making.

## Process and Problems

A standard, and typical, representation of public policy making in the American political system (Anderson et al., 1978) divides the process into six stages: problem formation, policy agenda, policy formulation, policy adoption, policy implementation, and policy evaluation. A policy problem is defined by Anderson (2003) as "a condition or situation that produces needs or dissatisfaction among people and for which relief or redress by governmental action in sought." During the first stage of the process, some person or group decides that some condition, such as the downloading of music from the Internet, the rising cost of health care, or the threat of international terrorism, is a problem that government should address. The "translation" from condition to problem involves value-based judgments, comparisons to conditions elsewhere (for example, prescription drugs being cheaper in Canada), and how the condition comes to be categorized or defined (Kingdon, 1984). Often a dramatic triggering event, such as an industrial accident, natural disaster, or act of war, draws attention to a condition, turning it into a problem in the public mind.

## Agenda Access

The second stage of the public policy process involves gaining access to the policy agenda. A good definition of the policy agenda is the "list of subjects or problems to which government officials, and people outside of government closely associated with those officials, are paying serious attention to at any given time" (Kingdon, 1984). A distinction is usually made between the systemic or governmental agenda and the institutional or decision agenda (Cobb and Elder, 1972; Kingdon, 1984). Items on the systemic or governmental agenda are widely discussed as problems warranting governmental attention, but only items on the institutional or decision agenda of some governmental unit are under active decision-making consideration by policy makers. Cobb and Ross (1997) describe three paths through which problems reach the agenda: (1) the "outside initiative model," in which an individual or group outside the government seeks a governmental solution to a condition it defines as a problem—the civil rights movement would be an example; (2) the "mobilization model," in which public officials campaign for attention and support on an issue—an example would be the "war on terrorism"; and (3) the "inside access model," in which a narrow group of political insiders seeks to place an item on a decision agenda with little public attention.

The transformation of a condition from a problem perceived by some individual or group to an issue on the public policy agenda is a critical step, particularly when the initiative comes from the outside. It was recognized by Bachrach and Baratz (1962) that control of the agenda was a "second face of power" that kept many potential issues that challenged existing privilege from getting broad public attention and consideration by government policy makers. Following Schattschneider (1960), Cobb and Elder (1972) take a conflict perspective on the problem of gaining agenda access. In this view, problems are converted into issues when they involve conflict between groups over scarce resources or positions (such as power or respect). In order to get their problems on the agenda, groups who want to change the existing balance must expand the conflict to broader publics. Successful conflict expansion requires defining the issue in a manner that convinces a politically significant number of people that something must be done about a given condition and that this something should be done by a governmental unit. To broaden concern, the issue should be defined in abstract terms, drawing on "potent" political symbols. It should be made to seem highly significant, of enduring importance, not too complex, and unique. Conversely, opponents will seek to contain the issue, denying agenda status by promoting the narrowest possible definition of the issue (Cobb and Ross, 1997).

## Formulation

The policy formulation stage involves the development of proposals to deal with a problem or issue. Once an issue reaches open discussion on the systemic agenda, proposed solutions to the underlying problem may come from a variety of sources, including interest groups, members of Congress, congressional staff organizations, the administration, executive branch agencies, academics, and think tanks. The types of policy proposals that can emerge at this stage have been classified as incremental, branching, and inventive (Starling, 1979). The incremental approach to public policy, based on successive limited comparisons as opposed to comprehensive analysis, was championed by Lindblom (1959), who questioned the intellectual capacity of humans to deal with the complexity of public policy problems. The branching approach seeks solutions by analogizing from one area of public policy to another. Inventive solutions are based on creative and productive applications of existing knowledge and make a sharp break with past practice (Starling, 1979).

The question of how particular proposals emerge at a given time to be associated with specific problems was explored by Kingdon (1984). Kingdon refers to the activities at the formulation stage as the "alternative specification" process and sees it as linked to the agenda-setting process, but distinct. In Kingdon's description of policy making, inspired by the "garbage can model" of organizational decision making (Cohen et al., 1972), the government is seen as an "organized anarchy" characterized by "problematic preferences, unclear technology, and fluid participation" (Kingdon, 1984). Through this anarchy flows three largely independent process streams:

a problem recognition stream, a policy proposal stream, and a political stream. A constant flow of problems, driven by triggering events and issue activists, gain public attention. At the same time, communities of policy specialists based inside and outside of government continually generate policy proposals. Ideas confront each other and float around in a "policy primeval soup" (Kingdon, 1984). In the third stream, changes in the national mood and electoral challenges for presidential administrations and the Congress flow independent of the problem and proposal streams. Occasionally, the three separate streams come together, a "policy window" opens, and proposals can be become coupled with problems in the presence of an opportunity for political action. Of note in Kingdon's (1984) view is that policy alternatives are developed independent of the problems for which they are ultimately proposed as solutions. For example, proponents of urban mass transit first promoted it as a solution to the problem of traffic congestion, then to pollution, and then to energy shortages as each of these problems caught public attention. This challenges the linear thinking behind life cycle models of the public policy process and issue evolution (including the one used to structure this discussion).

## Adoption

In the policy adoption stage, a decision is made by a governmental authority to adopt, modify, or reject one of the proposed policy alternatives (Anderson, 2003). Many problems never reach the stage in which a proposed solution is adopted. They may have never achieved agenda status, there may have been no viable solutions proposed, or government decision makers may have rejected all proposed alternatives. As Cobb and Ross (1997) point out, "opponents need a victory at only one point in the policy process to prevail." The informal institutional structure of governmental decision making has much to do with the likelihood of any newly identified problem becoming the subject of public policy.

Public policies in the United States tend to be made within specialized subsystems. One perspective, which characterizes these venues as "iron triangles," "whirlpools" (Griffith, 1939), or "subgovernments" (Freeman, 1965), is that they are closed, stable systems which allow likeminded special interest groups, bureaucrats, and legislators to dominate the policy process to the detriment of democratic representation (Lowi, 1979; McConnell, 1966). Baumgartner and Jones (1993) refer to institutional structures of this type as "policy monopolies." To create a "monopoly on political understandings concerning the policy of interest, and an institutional arrangement that reinforces that understanding" is the wish of every policy entrepreneur (Baumgartner and Jones, 1993).

In the 1970s and 1980s an alternative picture of the institutional structure of policy making began to emerge. Heclo (1978) argued that the iron triangle view was "disastrously incomplete." Factors such as the growth in government since the 1950s, the increasing complexity of issues, and the proliferation of fluid interest groups able to mobilize for political action had strained the stability of subgovernments and transformed them into webs of influence. Heclo termed these webs "issue networks." Issue networks are characterized by fluid participation, participant motivation based more on intellectual or emotional commitment than material interest, and uncertain control. Similarly, Gais et al. (1984) found that the "autonomous and impervious iron triangles" had evolved into "conflictual, permeable, and unpredictable" systems as growing middle-class involvement in politics and developments in communication technology allowed citizen groups to mobilize and broaden political debate.

Not everyone agreed that the iron triangle was dead. For example, McCool (1989) suggested that the changes in the structure of policy making may have increased the power of subgovernments. The fragmentation in Congress and the executive branch since the 1960s, seen in the proliferation of subcommittees and new agencies, combined with the growth in the number of public interest and single interest groups, was said by McCool to actually increase the possibility of clientele relationships.

According to Berry (1989), the debate among public policy scholars was not about whether there exist only iron triangles or only issue networks, but about which view most typically describes policy making in the American government. More recent scholarship has recast the debate into dynamic terms, looking at how institutional structures are created, destroyed, and replaced. Baumgartner and Jones (1993) picture the American political system as a "mosaic of continually reshaping systems of limited participation." The focus is not on whether relatively closed systems exist, but rather on the stability of those systems.

The theory of "punctuated equilibria" proposed by Baumgartner and Jones (1993) seeks to explain the presence in the US policy system of both stability and rapid change. According to this theory, democratic political systems can never be in general equilibrium, which implies not only stability, but a movement back to the equilibrium point after a disturbance. However, there can be points of partial equilibria. These areas of partial stability are policy monopolies or subgovernments in which stability is maintained by the structure of political institutions and the shared definition of the issues dealt with by members of those institutions. This is termed "structure-induced equilibrium." The "driving force" for both stability and instability is issue definition or policy image. Changing the definition of an issue can mobilize previously apathetic citizens, destabilize an existing partial equilibria, and drive policy making for the issue to a new institutional arena or venue. This new venue will have different institutional rules favoring a different interpretation of the issue and a different set of interests. Thus, while a snapshot look at the policy-making system may reveal subsystems that have the characteristics of closed, policy monopolies, a second look a few years later may find a different landscape, with old monopolies destroyed and new ones created. In the Baumgartner and Jones (1993) model of policy making, the agenda setting and issue definition process is not just about attracting enough public attention to an issue to put it on the agenda of some governmental institution,

it is about choosing, creating, and destroying institutions. Process and institution in this model are inseparable.

## Implementation

Policy making and policy implementation are often inseparable as well. In ideal constitutional and Weberian terms, legislatures would be expected to create policy and executive branch administrative agencies to carry it out. The reality is much more complex. The term "implementation" was formally introduced into the public policy literature by Pressman and Wildavsky (1973) to refer to the "interaction between the setting of goals and the actions geared to achieve them." Interaction is the key term here, for there is no clear line of demarcation between the legislative and the implementation process. The specialized subsystems from which policies emerge, be they iron triangles or issue networks, include legislators, bureaucrats, and other interested parties. In a more formal sense, the administrative agencies delegated as the authority to implement the laws passed by the legislature are dependent on the legislature for their budgets and subject to the oversight of legislative committees. Thus, the reach of the legislative branch extends into the policy implementation stage, notwithstanding the unconstitutionality of a formal "legislative veto."

The reach of the administrative agencies extends backwards into the policy formulation and adoption stages, as well. (For the "inside access" model, the reach would extend as far as the agenda-building stage.) Many of the policy alternatives considered in the formulation stage emerge from policy specialists within administrative agencies. At the adoption stage, considerable policy-making discretion is regularly delegated to administrators. The legislative mandates given to administrative agencies by the Congress are often broad and ill defined. One set of reasons for this is resource-related. Congress has neither the time nor the technical expertise and resources of an administrative agency to craft the details of policy.

A second set of reasons is political. The political compromise and bargaining required to obtain majority approval for a piece of legislation usually make a certain amount of ambiguity necessary. The avoidance of conflict is also important. As previously noted, many charge that legislators would rather concern themselves with activities that enhance their chances for re-election than make tough policy choices that are bound to dissatisfy some portion of the electorate. Hayes (1981) proposed that in the presence of a "conflictual demand pattern" in an area of public policy, re-election-minded and conflict-avoiding legislators will delegate authority to administrators. This shifts the still unresolved conflict from the legislature to an administrative agency and insulates legislators from the ill will of either side. The bottom line is that a significant amount of policy making takes place at the agency level.

Other actors are not idle at the implementation stage either. The White House, individual members of Congress and congressional committees, courts, other agencies, interest groups, state and local governments, and the media are all constituencies forming the political environment in which agencies implement policies (Anderson, 2003). Agencies must respond to and balance pressures emanating from its various constituencies. A particularly important constituency is an agency's clientele group. The nature of the clientele-agency relationship and the environment of implementation in general are influenced to a large extent by the type of policy the agency is charged with implementing.

Lowi (1964) identified three types of domestic policies: distributive, redistributive, and regulatory. Others have modified this typology—Hayes (1981) adds self-regulation and non-decision types; Ripley and Franklin (1991) divide regulatory into competitive and protective forms—but Lowi's list remains the basis for most discussions. Distributive polices are associated with "pork barrel" politics and involve government subsidization of private activities. Regulatory policies establish behavioral rules and set conditions for activities. Redistributive policies transfer wealth or other scarce resources between groups.

Distributive policies tend to be created in response to a "consensual demand pattern" in which the groups seeking the benefits are concentrated and politically well organized, while the general public who will pay the costs is not (Wilson, 1973; Hayes, 1981). Thus, an agency implementing a distributive program operates in an atmosphere in which everyone is on the same page—all benefit from increased levels of benefits—and the potential opposition is largely unrepresented. Clientele groups are generally supportive of the agency. According to Ripley and Franklin (1991), subgovernments dominate distributive policy making; participation will be stable over time, decision making will be relatively invisible, and relationships will be cooperative, with little sense of competition for scarce resources. The only constituencies with significant influence are the agency itself, the relevant congressional subcommittee, and the subsidized group—the classic "iron triangle." (Of course, as we have been informed by Baumgartner and Jones, stability does not imply immortality.)

With little to offer in the form of benefits either to regulated industries or to public interest groups, regulatory agencies receive less clientele support than other agencies (Meier, 1987). As Anderson (2003) plainly states, "most people obviously prefer receiving benefits to being restricted or controlled." The implementation of regulatory policy is usually conflictual, with organized interests arrayed on opposing sides of regulatory issues. Closed subgovernments are not the norm. Congressional involvement often goes beyond the subcommittee level to the full committee, even to the full House or Senate (Ripley and Franklin, 1991). The White House may become involved, along with the full range of other constituencies. Any significant regulatory implementation action is likely to dissatisfy some group and invite litigation, drawing the courts into the process.

## Evaluation

Policy evaluation can be formal or informal. Anyone is free to informally evaluate the positive and negative effects of a public policy and communicate that evaluation to whoever will listen. Formal evaluation may be undertaken by various governmental entities, such as the implementing agency itself, the General Accounting Office associated with the Congress, and specialized governmental commissions. Ongoing Congressional oversight of administrative agencies and their activities can also be considered a form of policy evaluation. Much more or less formal evaluation is performed outside of the government. University-based academics, the media, research organizations, and interest groups all evaluate public policy. Just as adoption and implementation are often in a practical sense inseparable, evaluation is not usually a distinct stage in the life of public policy. Except when a specific "sunset clause" has been mandated, there is usually no point of the policy cycle at which evaluation and possible major change or termination are viewed as the natural step. Evaluations become part of the constant flow of inputs into a continually recycling system.

## CONCLUSION

The goal of this chapter was to provide a sort of condensed textbook covering major US public policy-making institutions and processes for non-specialists in American politics. As such, it is necessarily incomplete. Every perspective could not be included. Important actors in the process, such as the mass media, may have been mentioned only in passing or by implication. Emerging international arenas for policy making, such as the World Trade Organization, have not been mentioned at all. However, it is hoped that this overview will be helpful to readers in gaining a fuller appreciation of the chapters to follow.

## REFERENCES

Anderson, J.E. (2003). *Public Policymaking: An Introduction.* New York: Houghton Mifflin.

Anderson, J.E., D.W. Brady, and C. Bullock III (1978). *Public Policy and Politics in America.* Monterey, CA: Brooks Cole.

Austin-Smith, D., and J.R. Wright (1994). "Counteractive Lobbying," *American Journal of Political Science* 38 (1): 25–44.

Bachrach, P., and M. Baratz (1962). "The Two Faces of Power," *American Political Science Review* 56 (4): 947–952.

Bauer, R.A., I. de Sola Poole, and A.L. Dexter (1963). *American Business and Public Policy.* New York: Atherton.

Baumgartner, F.R., and B.D. Jones (1993). *Agendas and Instability in American Politics.* Chicago: University of Chicago Press.

Bentley, A.F. (1908). *The Process of Government.* Chicago: University of Chicago Press.

Berry, J.M. (1989). "Subgovernments, Issue Networks, and Political Conflict," in R.A. Harris and S.M. Milkis (eds), *Remaking American Politics.* Boulder, CO: Westview Press.

Clark, P.B., and J.Q. Wilson (1961). "Incentive Systems: A Theory of Organizations," *Administrative Science Quarterly* 6 (2): 129–166.

Cobb, R.W., and C.D. Elder (1972). *Participation in American Politics: The Dynamics of Agenda Building.* Baltimore, MD: Johns Hopkins University Press.

Cobb, R.W., and M.H. Ross (1997). *Cultural Strategies of Agenda Denial: Avoidance, Attack, and Redefinition.* Lawrence, KS: University of Kansas Press.

Cohen, M.D., J.G. March, and J.P. Olsen (1972). "A Garbage Can Model of Organizational Choice," *Administrative Science Quarterly* 17 (1): 1–25.

Conway, M.M. (1991). "PACs in the Political Process," in A.J. Cigler and B.A. Loomis (eds), *Interest Group Politics.* Washington, DC: Congressional Quarterly Press.

Fiorina, M.P. (1989). *Congress: Keystone of the Washington Establishment.* New Haven, CT: Yale University Press.

Freeman, J.L. (1965). *The Political Process.* New York: Random House.

Gais, T.L., M.A. Peterson, and J.L. Walker (1984). "Interest Groups, Iron Triangles, and Representative Institutions in American National Government," *British Journal of Political Science* 14 (March): 161–185.

Gilmour, J.B. (2001). "The Powell Voting Amendment Cycle: An Obituary," *Legislative Studies Quarterly* 26 (May): 249–262.

Glazer, N. (1975). "Towards an Imperial Judiciary," *Public Interest* 41 (fall): 104–123.

Griffith, E. (1939). *Impasse of Democracy.* New York: Harrison-Hilton.

Hayes, M.T. (1981). *Lobbyists and Legislators: A Theory of Political Markets.* New Brunswick, NJ: Rutgers University Press.

Heclo, H. (1978). "Issue Networks and the Executive Establishment," in A. King (ed.), *The New

*American Political System.* Washington, DC: American Enterprise Institute.

Kernell, S., and G.C. Jacobson (2000). *The Logic of American Politics.* Washington, DC: Congressional Quarterly Press.

Kerwin, C.M. (2003). *Rulemaking: How Government Agencies Write Law and Make Policy,* 3rd edn. Washington, DC: Congressional Quarterly Press.

Kingdon, J.W. (1984). *Agendas, Alternatives, and Public Policies.* Boston, MA: Little Brown.

Langbein, L.I. (1986). "Money and Access: Some Empirical Evidence," *Journal of Politics* 48 (4): 1052–1062.

Light, P.C. (1999). *The President's Agenda: Domestic Policy Choice from Kennedy to Clinton.* Baltimore, MD: Johns Hopkins University Press.

Lindblom, C.E. (1959). "The Science of 'Muddling Through'," *Public Administration Review* 19 (2): 79–88.

Lowi, T.J. (1964). "American Business, Public Policy, Case Studies, and Political Theory," *World Politics* 16 (4): 677–715.

Lowi, T.J. (1979). *The End of Liberalism: The Second Republic of the United States.* New York: Norton.

Lubbers, J.S. (1998). *A Guide to Federal Agency Rulemaking.* Chicago: American Bar Association.

Matthews, D.R. (1960). *US Senators and their Worlds.* New York: Vintage.

Mayhew, D.R. (1974). *Congress: The Electoral Connection.* New Haven, CT: Yale University Press.

McConnell, G. (1966). *Private Power and American Democracy.* New York: Knopf.

McCool, D. (1989). "Subgovernments and the Impact of Policy Fragmentation and Accommodation," *Policy Studies Review* 8 (winter): 264–287.

McKenna, G. (1976). *American Politics: Ideals and Realities.* New York: McGraw-Hill.

Meier, K.J. (1987). *Politics and the Bureaucracy: Policymaking in the Fourth Branch of Government.* Monterey, CA: Brooks Cole.

Moe, T.M. (1980). "A Calculus of Group Membership," *American Journal of Political Science* 24 (November): 593–632.

Nice, D.C., and P. Fredericksen (1995). *The Politics of Intergovernmental Relations.* Chicago: Nelson-Hall.

Oleszek, W.J. (1978). *Congressional Procedures and the Policy Process.* Washington, DC: Congressional Quarterly Press.

Olson, M. (1965). *The Logic of Collective Action: Public Goods and the Theory of Groups.* Cambridge, MA: Harvard University Press.

Ornstein, N.J., and S. Elder (1978). *Interest Groups, Lobbying, and Policymaking.* Washington, DC: Congressional Quarterly Press.

Page, B.I., and R.Y. Shapiro (1985). "Presidential Leadership through Public Opinion," in G.C. Edwards III, S.A. Shull, and N.C. Thomas (eds), *The Presidency and Public Policy Making.* Pittsburgh, PA: University of Pittsburgh Press.

Pressman, J.L., and A.B. Wildavsky (1973). *Implementation.* Berkeley, CA: University of California Press.

Ripley, R.B., and G.A. Franklin (1991). *Congress, the Bureaucracy, and Public Policy.* Pacific Grove, CA: Brooks Cole.

Salisbury, R.H. (1969). "An Exchange Theory of Interest Groups," *Midwest Journal of Political Science* 13 (1): 1–32.

Salisbury, R.H. (1975). "Interest Groups," in F.I. Greenstein and N.W. Polsby (eds), *Handbook of Political Science* IV, *Nongovernmental Politics.* Reading, MA: Addison Wesley.

Salisbury, R.H. (1984). "Interest Representation: The Dominance of Institutions," *American Political Science Review* 78 (1): 64–76.

Schattschneider, E.E. (1960). *The Semisovereign People: A Realist's Guide to Democracy in America.* New York: Holt.

Schlozman, K.L., and J.T. Tierney (1986). *Organized Interests and American Democracy.* New York: Harper & Row.

Smith, R.A. (1995). "Interest Group Influence in the US Congress," *Legislative Studies Quarterly* 20 (1): 89–139.

Sorauf, F.J. (1992). *Inside Campaign Finance: Myths and Realities.* New Haven, CT: Yale University Press.

Starling, G. (1979). *The Politics and Economics of Public Policy: An Introductory Analysis with Cases.* Homewood, IL: Dorsey Press.

Truman, D.B. (1951). *The Governmental Process.* New York: Knopf.

West, W.F. (1984). "Structuring Administrative Discretion: The Pursuit of Rationality and Responsiveness," *American Journal of Political Science* 28 (2): 340–360.

West, W.F., and J. Cooper (1985). "The Rise of Administrative Clearance," in G.C. Edwards III, S.A. Shull, and N.C. Thomas (eds), *The Presidency and Public Policy Making.* Pittsburgh, PA: University of Pittsburgh Press.

Wilson, J.Q. (1973). *Political Organizations.* New York: Basic Books.

# 5

# The External Environment of Public Affairs in the European Union and the United Kingdom

## Public Policy Process and Institutions

THOMAS SPENCER

Philosophers tell us that it is logically impossible to "step into the same river twice." For lobbyists it is equally true that you never lobby the same European Union twice. The process of change is continuous, subtle and unrelenting. Treaties are the milestones by which the Union marks the passage of current practice into legal form. Each act of lobbying and the response to it creates new precedents and opens new possibilities. The Union is a vast dance to the music of power. Prime Ministers, parliamentarians, diplomats, consultants, civil society, and corporations constantly form new patterns and learn new steps. The speed and complexity of this continent-wide barn dance accelerated in 2004—the Year of Change. The coincidence of the end of the quinquennial cycle of the Union with both a major enlargement and a new Constitutional Treaty has kept everyone on their toes. The study of public affairs is a valuable exercise in its own right but it can also tell us a great deal about the societies which play host to public affairs practice. This chapter seeks to shine a light on the European system of public affairs by comparing it with the American model and by examining commonly expressed criticisms of both.

It has been suggested that:

> Public Affairs takes place in a macro-environmental context of public policy processes and institutions (a.k.a. the "non-market" environment) with which its practices interact. Public policy processes and institutions include the social, political and legal arrangements that structure interactions outside of, but also in conjunction with, agreements and exchanges made in private markets.

Such a concept has its roots in the American experience and should be interpreted very differently in the European context.

This "non-market" environment for public affairs in the United States operates in the context of a single, albeit federal, state with an old written constitution, a galaxy of lawyers and a tradition of litigation. Of course the system can be amended and it changes naturally as society shifts and evolves. There is clearly a difference between the functioning of the American political system as taught in the 1950s as a stable model of checks and balances and the current unhappy state of a system dominated by interests. However, the evolution is of a straight-line nature and can be tracked and examined in a single political culture.

The situation in the European Union is very different. The Union is composed of different states. Each nation has developed a different approach to the role of the state, in some cases dating back more than a thousand years. Perhaps above all, each of the twenty-five states was exposed to extreme traumas in the twentieth century from fascism to communism, via occupation, civil war, and loss of empire. The European Union that emerged from the experiences of 1914–45, aptly described as Europe's Second Thirty Years War, has advanced by international treaty. The treaty process from 1949 onwards was not a straight-line advance dictated at a gathering of a few founding fathers. Rather it advanced along the lines of least resistance, sector by sector. This "journey to an unknown destination" danced to an essentially federalist vision. However, each individual step was dictated by functionalist compromise, resulting in cumulative complex treaty documents. Each successive treaty enshrined current practice and short-term aspiration. Only in the twenty first century has the Union given birth to the so-called "Constitutional Treaty" which aspires to give Europe a single, logical and transparent constitutional document.

This path towards a constitution has been influenced by public affairs at every stage in a complex series of feedback mechanisms. For example, there was much more reference to transport than to agriculture in the Treaty of Rome, of 1957, yet primary agricultural lobbies were successful in creating the huge structure of the Common Agricultural Policy, whereas transport remained of little interest in the Union until comparatively recently. The European Union as it exists in 2004 is a shifting compromise between the supranational "community method" and various forms of intergovernmentalism. In a Europe of twenty

five nations there are now twenty six forms of public affairs. It is the twenty sixth variant that is the most important to master for public affairs success. This is the practice of public affairs in the European institutions—the Council of Ministers, the European Commission, the European Parliament, the European Court and the range of agencies and institutions scattered across the European landscape in the American tradition of pork barrel.

The European Union may have something approaching a single internal market, a substantially common currency and jointly conducted negotiations on external trade, but its divisions are much more deeply rooted than the equivalent divisions apparent inside the United States. To influence this behemoth the public affairs practitioner needs a sense of history and cultural empathy, in addition to the toolkit of public affairs skills that apply in any political market. Good public affairs practice at the level of the Union requires sensitivity to national, regional, and local identities, since sensitivity to ethnic and religious factors is built into the national structure of each state in a way that is not true in the melting-pot of America. There is a much wider range of living standard between the poorest and wealthiest states of the European Union than is the case in the United States. The countries of the Union overwhelmingly use Roman law, which often sits uncomfortably with the cultural inheritance of the Anglosphere. Perhaps the sheer difference of Europe is underlined by the fact that the Union now operates with a total of twenty official languages.

The European Centre for Public Affairs owes its birth to the first great *cause célèbre* of European public affairs. In 1980 the so-called Vredeling Directive, on which the author served as European Parliamentary *rapporteur*, was an attempt to insert Dutch and German models of worker involvement into the boards of multinational companies. In the face of such provocation, many blue-chip American companies dispatched phalanxes of Washington-trained experts to Brussels. The result was a tragi-comedy. Their lack of empathy for a complex political system that they did not understand proved instantly counterproductive, but brilliantly illustrated the gulf between different political systems and traditions on either side of the Atlantic. After nearly twenty years of teaching by the European Centre for Public Affairs such mistakes are seldom made nowadays in either direction.

The European Centre for Public Affairs defines public affairs as "organised attempts to influence decision-making within a political system." The phrase is therefore used to cover a much wider range of activities than is the case in the United States. It embraces corporate communications, government affairs, regulatory affairs, media relations, aspects of public relations, and corporate social responsibility. The public affairs specialist in Europe is expected to be omnicompetent, from monitoring and research through strategy setting and coalition building up to the 10 percent of the activity that involves lobbying contact with the target decision maker or stakeholder.

If the non-market environment is so different on both sides of the Atlantic, what can we say about the practice of public affairs in each society? In a well-established state, public affairs functions discreetly and without undue public comment. It plays a role similar to the plumbing of a house. One is only aware of it when it breaks down. In recent years the public affairs plumbing of the US political system has come to be regarded as the cause of just such a stink. Fareed Zakaria devotes a chapter to this subject in his book *The Future of Freedom* (2003). Writers as diverse as Thomas Barnett (*The Pentagon's New Map*, 2004), and Timothy Garton Ash (*Free World*, 2004) all refer to the impact of new lobbying processes on the way in which American policies are shaped. Garton Ash in particular draws our attention to the way in which the commercial and political marketplace of Washington differs from that of Brussels.

As analysts jostle for attention in the crowded market for ideas, they have to shout loudly like traders on the floor of a stock exchange. Shouting loudly to clinch an intellectual "trade" requires overstatement. It means taking a grand, simplifying idea and, egged-on by your magazine editor or book publisher, pushing it further: The End Of History! The Clash Of Civilisations! Europeans Are From Venus! …

He further draws our attention to the political marketplace: "in Washington, some three to five thousand jobs in government are filled by political appointees every time a new administration comes to power." In a land rich in communication, the impact of public affairs on American opinion helps to shape the world view of the United States and thus, via the conveyor belt of globalization, has a direct impact on the rest of the world. This is especially true given the emaciated state of those few institutions of political globalization—as opposed to economic globalization—which currently function. Conversely, the widespread sense of the ill health of the American political system has also played a great part in shaping the world's view of the United States, the declining respect in which it is held, and the collapse of faith in its benevolent intentions.

In the US Congress continuous gerrymandering by both major parties, substantially aided by computers, has produced a political system with very few swing seats. The country now reflects an almost perfect division between red and blue, with the power of incumbency ever more influential. Participation levels have continued to drop. The direct power of money as expressed through Political Action Committees has continued to grow. The Democrat and Republican party structures have in essence become "Potemkin" parties, with only a passing reality during the primary season. This is not to argue that the interest groups are all-powerful in the system. The tobacco companies have certainly been forced back in recent years despite their sophisticated and well-funded public affairs efforts, and it seems likely that the food companies will face a similar road on the issue of obesity. If one were to believe American commentators' criticisms of their own political system, these trends have clearly created a permanent government by "interests" and an end to the separation of powers. These great entrenched interests make it very difficult for the American system to adapt to changes in the political environment. Defense policy was immensely slow to change after the Cold War and continued to reflect traditional assumptions about the desirability of big ticket spending, even if this produced armed forces ill equipped to deal with the asymmetrical angst of a Bin Laden. Similarly the power of certain fossil fuel companies to block both America's and the world's transition to a fossil fuel-free, climate-friendly energy policy has been on display in administrations both Democrat and Republican. There is a vigorous debate about the failings of the American political system and the dominance of money which seems to coexist quite happily with the continued functioning of the much criticized system. This is not the place to examine the details of this money culture. It is in any case a much more subtle animal than is usually admitted by Europeans. Luigi Graziano in his excellent book *Lobbying, Pluralism and Democracy* (2001) is a fine example in the tradition of de Tocquville of a European with empathy producing new insights into the way America works. If one was to pick one particularly salient cause, among a range of other issues, for the dominance of monied interests in the American political system, it would be the freedom to produce political television advertising and the exorbitant cost of doing so.

This is not to say that money plays no role in the political contests of European states, and of course there are criticisms of the way European politics is run, especially from the traditional left. There are well-documented cases of corruption at the highest level in Italy, France and—perhaps most surprisingly—Germany, in the case of Chancellor Kohl. There are sleazy transactions in Britain, slush funds in Slovakia and backhanders in Belgium. And of course it would be foolish to overlook the influence of state-owned and parastatal companies in certain European states, and the intimate relationship between politics, business, and administration in many European political cultures. One could detect some early signs of the Americanization of the European political process in the late 1990s. Silvio Berlusconi capitalized on the collapse of the Italian post-war political system and used his money and media influence to create his own party, Forza Italia, which propelled him into the Prime Minister's office in a rather un-European way. Similarly, wealthy individuals such as Sir James Goldsmith and his Referendum Party had and will continue to have a major influence on the European debate by their articulation of Euroskepticism. The UK Independence Party, with its funds drawn largely from a single euroskeptic Yorkshire businessman, used American political techniques and advice to take 15 percent of the popular vote in the European Parliament elections of 2004. However, nowhere in Europe is the political process as centered around the gathering of election funds as is the case in the United States. And at the level of the European institutions elections are still cheaper to run and less influential in outcome. Politicians take their seats in the European Parliament more on the basis of party position than on their individual ability to raise money and run. Put quite simply, elections are vastly cheaper in Europe, and politicians devote less time to gathering in cash. In consequence, European complaints about the practice of public affairs are rarely systemic. They tend to revolve around individual cases of overaggressive lobbying or improper behavior. Only on the far left is there extensive criticism of the practice of public affairs, a viewpoint perhaps best documented in *Europe, Inc.*, produced by the Corporate Europe Observatory in Amsterdam.

How will the practice of public affairs in the European Union continue to change along with its political evolution? As the European corridors of power become more crowded with new arrivals and new issues the professional public affairs community may need to review whether the current level of self-regulation is sufficient. Notwithstanding the Martin Report on corporate lobbying in the European Parliament and the stupidity of individual lobbyists in the case of chocolate eggs, there is no reason why the European Parliament and the other institutions should adopt an aggressive stance towards lobbying of all kinds. If they do so it will be because public affairs practitioners have failed to explain the validity of their craft. Much better that professional lobbyists propose any changes, rather than wait for some heavyhanded imposition in response to an as yet unknown idiocy—an idiocy perpetrated by individuals who neither understand nor respect the current delicate balance, based as it is on the interinstitutional need for elegant information flow. Journalists and public affairs practitioners are essential lubricants of the European political system. Both must be alert to the need for change in their behavior in this new Europe.

Similar changes are visible in the public affairs of the other key European institutions. Nowadays the power of the European Commission depends more than ever on the personality and credibility of its leadership. If the Commission can collectively succeed in recovering from it mid-life crisis, it may yet exercise as much influence as in its heyday. The complexity of the new system will be its ally. The fragile flower of its morale depends, however, on a shared ability to visualize what kind of institution it will be in ten years. It will remain, however, the paramount target for proactive lobbyists, who are themselves part of the Commission's decision making in the underground chambers of Commission-led comitology. It is the Council of Ministers for whom the next five years look most challenging and where creative lobbyists could fish convincingly for power and influence. Working at the level of twenty-five nations is more than a numerical adjustment for the Council. It requires new practice, much of it centered around the increased significance of the Council secretariat. New mechanisms for influencing the European debate in twenty five capitals will also need to be developed. This will be a challenge for public affairs practitioners of all kinds, whether they style themselves diplomats, civil servants or civil society activists. Despite the high profile of corporate lobbying, public affairs in the European Union is overwhelmingly a matter of both member states and third-country governments lobbying each other.

Taken together, these myriad challenges should be an invitation for Europe-based lobbyists to think of new ways of reaching their goals. Those who believe that more of the same will be sufficient in a Union of twenty-five, heading towards thirty-five, will be painfully disappointed. The merely mechanical is doomed to lose out to the innovative and the courageous. Effective public affairs, whether by diplomats, civil society, trade associations or officials, can no longer be "learned on the job." Every player in the game should now be setting themselves training and competence targets for the next five years. It is generally agreed that a Europe of fifteen member states represented the outer limit of instinct and amateurism in European public affairs. In reality nobody can now claim credibly to understand the public affairs of twenty-five nations. The day of the Renaissance public affairs prince who, armed with a decent education and three languages, could make a good fist of universal European coverage is now past. It is not just the formal structures of the Union which need to adapt to the new challenges. European public affairs is now a team effort requiring preparation and planning.

Only the congenitally foolhardy make long-term predictions about the future of public affairs. Logically, the continued evolution of a global political space to match the economic integration of existing globalization should produce a convergence of practice among the different traditions of public affairs around the world. Many of the great international public affairs practices are ultimately owned by American companies and in so far as public affairs is taught at all at universities and business schools it tends to be American models which predominate. On the other hand, it is apparent that European and American world views are on divergent trajectories. If this is the case in 2004, in what remains a predominantly Atlantic world, how much more will it be the case in 2050 in a multipolar world where the public affairs traditions of Asia are of at least equal importance?

# 6

# The Internal Environment of Public Affairs

## Organization, Process, and Systems

BRIAN HAWKINSON

There is a term for a particular style of management—"Management by Walking Around." It refers to the art of getting out among the people engaged in the day-to-day activity of the enterprise to see what is going on, what successes are being achieved, and what problems need to be dealt with. It gives managers insight into individual performance, but, more importantly, into broader issues and trends that affect the performance of the larger enterprise.

At the Public Affairs Council and Foundation for Public Affairs we practice a variation of that approach. I'll call it "Management by Asking Around" or MBAA. By observing and asking our member-company public affairs executives a lot of questions about their work—what they do, how they do it, what resources they devote to achieving what goals—we are able to understand how they apply the skills and resources of an integrated public affairs function to shaping public policy and public opinion in order to create market advantage for their companies. We are also able to identify and understand the issues and trends that affect the practice of corporate public affairs on a broad scale.

Part of "Management by Asking Around" entails finding out not only what Public Affairs executives engage in but also which specific activities matter most to their success. The Public Affairs Council has been doing this "asking" partly through the regular administration of a comprehensive organizational survey called the *State of Corporate Public Affairs*, three of which were conducted during the 1990s, in 1992, 1996 and 1999. In the most recent edition of the *State of Corporate Public Affairs Survey*, conducted by the Public Affairs Council and the Foundation for Public Affairs (2002a), we asked around nearly 600 of our primarily US-based member organizations about this topic and got some interesting replies. These are shared in the sections to follow.

## THE STATE OF CORPORATE PUBLIC AFFAIRS

The survey (Public Affairs Council and Foundation for Public Affairs, 2002a) asked

Table 6.1    *Political involvement activities of US companies* (*n* = 112)

| Activities | % of companies engaging in | Most important |
|---|---|---|
| Political action committee contributions to federal candidates | 82% | • |
| Visits to company locations by candidates/public officials | 82% | |
| Participation in coalitions | 79% | • |
| Lobbying or relationship building by CEO/senior executives | 78% | • |
| Candidate fund raisers | 67% | |
| Lobbying or relationship building by other employees (other than PA executives) | 67% | • |
| Political action committee contributions to state candidates | 65% | |
| Grassroots and/or grasstops activism | 65% | • |
| Political action committee contributions to political parties | 52% | |
| Voter registration/get-out-the-vote efforts | 52% | |
| Employee newsletter on political/legislative affairs | 51% | |
| Corporate contributions to candidates in states where permissible | 46% | |
| Corporate contributions to national political parties ("soft money" funds) | 44% | |
| Corporate contributions to state political parties where permissible | 43% | |
| Employee political involvement training | 24% | |
| Issue advocacy advertising | 23% | |
| Independent expenditures | 18% | |
| Candidate fairs/debates | 18% | |
| Express advocacy communications/endorsement of candidates | 13% | |
| Other: | | |
| Activity in trade/professional associations | 4% | |
| Lobbying or relationship building by public affairs staff | 3% | |

*Source* Public Affairs Council and Foundation for Public Affairs (2002a).

responding companies about their political activities. The full list of political involvement activities in which US companies engage is shown in Table 6.1. More than half of the companies participating in the survey engaged in at least eleven discrete political involvement activities. Among those, five were identified as the most important to achieving the public affairs function's goals:

1  Political Action Committee (PAC) contributions to federal candidates.
2  Participation in coalitions.
3  Lobbying or relationship building by the CEO and senior executives.
4  Lobbying or relationship building by employees other than public affairs executives.
5  Grassroots and/or grasstops activism.

In the discussion that follows, an exploration into the reasons why these five political involvement activities were cited as the most important yields rich insights into the practice of public affairs in the United States.

## POLITICAL ACTION COMMITTEE CONTRIBUTIONS TO FEDERAL CANDIDATES

There are two constants in all US federal elections: recurrence and money. Federal elections are held at two-year intervals for all seats in the House of Representatives and one-third of all seats in the Senate where the terms last six years. Presidential elections are held every four years. These elections are expensive to plan and conduct due in part to the size of the country, the sophistication of messages created and the mix of media used to deliver them.

Size is an issue. Elections for members of the House of Representatives are done by district (each district represents approximately

Table 6.2   *The cost of US elections, 2004*

| Federal election campaign type | Expenditures ($) |
| --- | --- |
| Presidential | 827,826,017 |
| US Senate* | 14,427,145 |
| US House of Representatives* | 1,479,894 |

* Average amount.

*Source* Center for Responsive Politics (2005).

600,000 people). Senate elections are statewide and presidential elections are nationwide. It's no surprise, then, that Senate election campaigns tend to be more expensive than House election campaigns, and that presidential election campaigns are the most expensive of all.

Table 6.2 details the total amount spent by candidates for the most recent federal elections in the United States. Expenditures for the presidential election include those made by all candidates; for Senate and House elections, the expenditures cited represent the average amount spent by contestants for an individual seat.

But there is another reason that presidential elections are so expensive, and it has to do with the electoral process itself. Unlike elections for the House and Senate, where outcomes are determined by the aggregate number of popular votes across the district or state, the outcomes of presidential elections are determined by a relatively complex structured process called the "Electoral College". In the Electoral College, each of the 50 state delegations is apportioned a number of votes equal to that state's number of federal representatives in the House of Representatives and Senate. The presidential candidate who receives the most electoral votes wins the election. That makes presidential elections actually a collection of separate, state-specific contests.

A golf analogy offers clarity in describing this electoral process. There are various ways that golf matches can be scored. The two most common are referred to as "stroke play" and "match play." Under "stroke play" rules, the player that takes the fewest total number of strokes over the course of the match is the winner. Under "match play" rules, players contest each hole separately. The player that takes the fewest number of strokes on a hole wins that hole; the player that wins the most number of holes over the course of the match is the winner of the match—irrespective of the total number of strokes taken by either contestant. The concept of "stroke play" provides an effective descriptor for US House or Senate elections, whereas the concept of "match play" effectively describes the basis by which the winners of presidential elections are determined.

Messages matter, too. Elections are about choosing between competing world views. They are contests between competing ideas about the nation's direction and priorities. In political campaigns, those competing ideas attract money necessary to deliver the messages that will compel voters to make a choice. Good ideas tend to attract more money than do bad ideas. To be more specific, bad ideas tend not to attract money in the political marketplace of campaign ideas any better than bad products attract money in the commercial marketplace.

The high costs associated with conducting election campaigns make political funding an economic reality. The Federal Election Campaign Act prohibits corporations and labor unions from using their general treasury funds to make contributions or expenditures in connection with federal elections. However, the Act does permit them to set up political committees, which may make contributions to and expenditures on behalf of federal candidates and their campaign committees. Federal election law refers to such a corporate or labor union committee as a "separate segregated fund," though it is more commonly called a "political action committee" or PAC.

Those eligible to contribute to a corporate PAC are currently defined in the Federal Election Campaign Act as "The corporation's executive and managerial personnel, the stockholders (only those with voting rights), and the

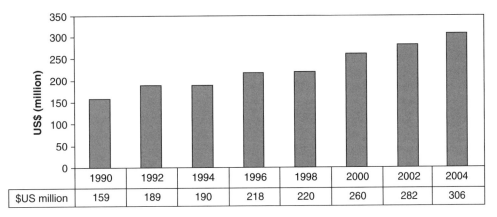

| $US million | 159 | 189 | 190 | 218 | 220 | 260 | 282 | 306 |

*(years: 1990, 1992, 1994, 1996, 1998, 2000, 2002, 2004)*

Figure 6.1   *Total federal political action committee contributions, 1990–2004.*
Source *Federal Election Commission (2004)*

families of the above two groups" (Federal Election Campaign Act, Federal Election Commission, found at www.fec.gov).

Campaign finance reform, specifically the Bipartisan Campaign Reform Act of 2002 (BCRA), created the first change in more than twenty years to the way that federal election campaigns are funded. Among those changes are:

1  The elimination of so-called "soft money", large contributions by companies, labor unions, interest groups and individuals to political parties for their use in "party building" purposes.
2  An increase in the amounts that individuals can contribute to PACs and candidates.

The result is that PACs have become more important than ever as vehicles to raise the funds necessary to finance election campaigns. Total contributions to federal PACs have increased steadily over the past ten years. In Figure 6.1 total PAC contributions (corporate, labor union and interest group) are shown for the past eight elections.

Businesses, their industry associations and pro-business group PACs have been successful in raising funds to support pro-business candidates. The business, industry association and pro-business PACs that raised the most amount of money during the 2001–02 federal election cycle are identified in Table 6.3.

Since elections are basically contests between competing world views, those organizations that have historically opposed pro-business public policy have been busy raising funds to support their preferred candidates, as well. In fact, companies, industry associations and pro-business groups have their work cut out for them when it comes to raising PAC funds. As Table 6.4 reflects, the PACs of organizations historically opposed to the interests of business have also demonstrated successful fund-raising efforts.

Candidates who receive contributions from corporate PACs tend to be selected based on intersections of business interest, rather than based on party affiliation. Table 6.5 lists the most often cited criteria driving contribution decisions.

The above discussion of the reasons for PAC contributions to federal candidates reveals the tight relationship between politics and business. Recurrence of elections, scope and size of elections, election costs, and the institutionalized opportunity to affect the turn of elections, all combine to weave the spheres of politics and business ever closer. So much so that often the boundaries between capitalism and democracy bleed into one another and become blurred at best and virtually indistinguishable at worst. Politics and business intertwine to form two of the most significant threads in the larger sociopolitical environmental tapestry that will

Table 6.3   *Top ten business, trade association, and pro-business group political action committees during the 2001–2002 federal election cycle*

| Name of PAC | Federal PAC receipts ($) |
| --- | --- |
| New Republican Majority Fund | 6,377,809 |
| National Association of Realtors | 5,193,903 |
| United Parcel Service | 4,695,501 |
| American Medical Association | 4,393,761 |
| Dealers Election Action Committee of the National Auto Dealers Association | 3,313,548 |
| Credit Union Legislative Action Council | 3,243,894 |
| Americans for a Republican Majority | 3,042,623 |
| Federal Express | 2,952,518 |
| Build PAC of the National Association of Home Builders | 2,413,492 |
| National Beer Wholesalers Association | 2,235,095 |
| Deloitte and Touche Federal | 2,142,126 |

*Source* Federal Election Commission (2004).

Table 6.4   *Top ten labor, trial lawyer, and liberal interest-group political action committees during the 2001–2002 federal election cycle*

| Name of PAC | Federal PAC receipts ($) |
| --- | --- |
| Emily's List | 16,723,791 |
| Democrat Republican Independent Voter Education (International Brotherhood of Teamsters) | 9,881,958 |
| International Brotherhood of Electrical Workers Committee on Political Education | 9,160,503 |
| United Auto Workers Voluntary Community Action Program | 9,046,130 |
| American Federation of State, County and Municipal Employees— PEOPLE Qualified | 8,881,820 |
| Service Employees International Union Political Action Committee | 8,371,266 |
| Voice of Teachers Committee on Political Education, New York State United Teachers | 7,428,246 |
| Association of Trial Lawyers of America | 7,419,866 |
| National Education Association Fund for Children and Public Education | 6,855,862 |
| American Federation of Teachers AFL-CIO Committee on Political Education | 5,997,616 |
| Communications Workers of America Political Contributions Committee | 5,705,194 |

*Source* Federal Election Commission (2004).

Table 6.5   *Political action committee contribution criteria*

| Criteria for making federal PAC contributions | % of PACs |
| --- | --- |
| Membership on key legislative committees | 95 |
| Voting record consistent with company's goals | 93 |
| Leadership position (on legislative committees or within the political party) | 89 |
| Company has a plant/operating facility in recipient's district (or state for Senate candidates) | 84 |
| Likelihood of getting elected | 62 |
| Incumbent status | 53 |
| Recommended by PAC member | 47 |
| Financial need | 45 |
| Party affiliation | 18 |
| Other | 6 |

$n = 103$.

*Source* Public Affairs Council and Foundation for Public Affairs (2003a).

Table 6.6  *Frequency of use of coalitions by US corporations*

| Use of coalitions for | n | % yes | % no |
|---|---|---|---|
| Federal government relations work | 60 | 100 | |
| State government relations work | 92 | 93 | 7 |

*Sources* Public Affairs Council and Foundation for Public Affairs (2003b, 2001).

increasingly define the business environment facing corporate public affairs practitioners in the twenty first century.

## PARTICIPATION IN COALITIONS

Coalitions have become major players in shaping public policy. By pulling together diverse but allied groups for a common purpose, coalitions can, amongst other things:

1  Provide strength in numbers.
2  Present a consistent message across a broad cross-section of interests.
3  Make a particular message more credible.
4  Save money and time by eliminating duplication of effort among coalition members.

The use of coalitions for public affairs or government relations work is nearly universal, according to research. Table 6.6 details the frequency of use of coalitions by US corporations at the federal and state levels. It is interesting to note the kinds of coalition partners that respondent companies typically work with. At the federal level, these companies predominantly partner with "Other companies in our industry" (97 percent of the group) and/or "Associations" (92 percent); more than half work with "Companies in other industries" and "Advocacy groups" (68 percent and 55 percent, respectively). Figure 6.2 reflects the increasing diversity of coalition partners with which corporations are partnering.

Figure 6.2 underscores the increasingly complex and interdependent market dynamic facing public affairs practitioners. As macro-environmental relationships intensify, due in part to globalization and to technological advancements as well, companies are finding many other cooperative and even supportive stakeholders sharing mutual agendas both upstream and downstream in their value chains. What is most interesting and worthy of further exploration is that some companies find coalition partners in the sociopolitical arena that would be their opponents in the commercial or retail marketplaces for goods and services.

## LOBBYING OR RELATIONSHIP BUILDING BY THE CHIEF EXECUTIVE OFFICER AND SENIOR EXECUTIVES

Legislators make the "rules" of the marketplace and regulators enforce these rules. Their decisions affect companies in many ways, including but not limited to:

1  Providing them the freedom to operate.
2  Affecting their operating costs.
3  Impacting their access to markets.
4  Influencing their ability to innovate.

Accordingly, it is critical in the policy development process for the people who make and enforce the rules of the marketplace to understand what outcomes their decisions will result in. The chief executive officer (CEO) is uniquely positioned to educate legislators and regulators about the company, its interests, and the effect that impending legislation or regulation may have on it. In addition, nothing sends a message that specific public policy issues are important to a company better than having the CEO commit his or her time and attention to it.

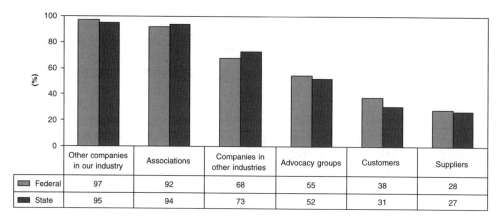

| | Other companies in our industry | Associations | Companies in other industries | Advocacy groups | Customers | Suppliers |
|---|---|---|---|---|---|---|
| Federal | 97 | 92 | 68 | 55 | 38 | 28 |
| State | 95 | 94 | 73 | 52 | 31 | 27 |

Figure 6.2    *Types of coalition partners.* Source *Public Affairs Council and Foundation for Public Affairs (2001, 2003)*

Table 6.7    *Politically engaged CEOs*

| Political involvement activities engaged in by CEO | % of companies |
|---|---|
| Written communications with legislators/regulators at the federal level | 81 |
| Actively participated in trade/business association(s) | 80 |
| Endorsed PAC | 74 |
| Direct lobbying at the federal level | 70 |
| Attended candidate fundraisers | 62 |
| Written communications with legislators/regulators at the state level | 51 |
| Direct lobbying at the state level | 44 |
| Endorsed grassroots participation | 36 |
| Endorsed get-out-the-vote activities | 32 |
| Testified before legislative/regulatory body(ies) | 25 |
| None | 2 |
| Other: | |
|    Encouraged political activities by his direct reports | 1 |
|    Met with visiting elected officials | 1 |

$n = 114$.
*Source* Public Affairs Council and Foundation for Public Affairs (2002a).

Research shows that CEOs are indeed engaged in political activity on behalf of their companies. Nearly all (98 percent) of the CEOs whose companies participated in the 2002 *State of Corporate Public Affairs Survey* (Foundations for Public Affairs, 2002) engaged in at least one political involvement activity. The three most often reported activities were: "Written communications with legislators/regulators at the federal level" (81 percent); "Active participation in trade/business association(s)" (80 percent); "Direct

lobbying at the federal level" (70 percent). Table 6.7 presents the wide range of political activities engaged in by CEOs of respondent corporations.

The active engagement of CEOs in a wide spectrum of political activities as demonstrated in Table 6.7 reflects the importance they apparently place on effectively managing the sociopolitical strategy of their respective firms and industries. By directly attending to a diverse portfolio of sociopolitical assets, these forward-looking CEOs and senior executives are acting

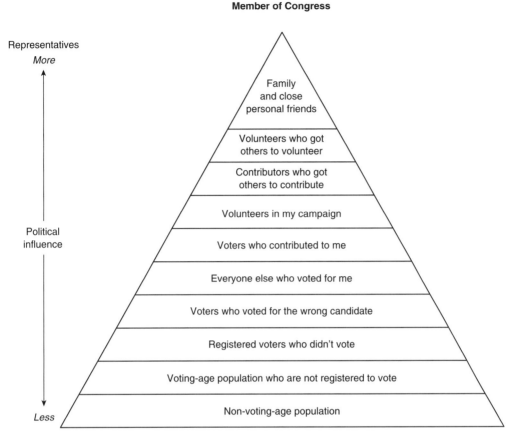

Figure 6.3    *Political influence pyramid. Average US congressional district: 600,000 people.*
*The model can apply to lawmakers at the federal, state, or local level.* Source *Michael E.*
*Dunn & Associates, Inc.* © 2004

to optimize the prospects of their respective firms in a politically charged marketplace.


## LOBBYING OR RELATIONSHIP BUILDING BY EMPLOYEES OTHER THAN PUBLIC AFFAIRS EXECUTIVES

It's not surprising that legislators receive input on public policy issues from lots of different people and groups. The challenge in shaping public policy is to find the right person to deliver the best message to the appropriate legislator at the right time. But who among

those people and groups are viewed by legislators as important messengers? Figure 6.3 details the hierarchy of people and groups who are considered influential by members of the US House of Representatives.

It makes sense that the people who can have the greatest influence on legislators' decision making are the people that they know best and trust most. Following the hierarchy detailed above, it's clear that you don't have to be a CEO or corporate lobbyist to have the legislator's attention. While you can't do much to become a legislator's family member or close friend, anyone who volunteers for or contributes to a legislator's election campaign, or votes for the

Table 6.8    *Grassroots constituents*

| Groups recruited for grassroots participation | % of companies |
|---|---|
| Employees | 90 |
| Retirees | 34 |
| Customers | 29 |
| Allied interest groups | 26 |
| Community where the firm has an economic presence | 24 |
| Suppliers | 17 |
| Shareholders | 8 |
| General public | 7 |
| Other | 5 |
|    Independent sales representatives/agents | 1 |
|    Community advisory panel | |

$n = 86$.
*Source* Foundation for Public Affairs and Foundation for Public Affairs (2002b).

Table 6.9    *Top five grassroots activities*

| Activity | % of companies |
|---|---|
| Write/e-mail a legislator | 95 |
| Call a legislator | 75 |
| Meet with a legislator | 37 |
| Write a letter to a newspaper editor | 19 |
| Attend a political rally | 4 |

$n = 81$.
*Source* Public Affairs Council and Foundation for Public Affairs (2002).

legislator *or for his or her opponent* can have their voice heard.

Employees from throughout the organization who take the time to build relationships with legislators, therefore, have the opportunity to help shape public policy decisions that affect the company and its ability to compete successfully. This discussion about the importance and place of grassroots activity is elaborated further in Chapter 24 of this *Handbook*.

## GRASSROOTS AND/OR GRASSTOPS ACTIVISM

Grassroots can be defined, for the purposes of this chapter, as organized efforts by organizations to inform, recruit and deploy political power from constituents. These constituents, who can be recurring or itinerant in their frequency of activity, can emanate from either inside or outside the organization.

Who are the "constituents" that US corporations recruit in order to deploy political power? They tend to be the people who have the largest stake in the success of the company—current employees, retirees and customers. Research as shown in Table 6.8 demonstrates that nearly all (90 percent) of companies recruit their own employees for grassroots efforts. Approximately one-third also recruit former employees in the form of retirees and even their customers (34 percent and 29 percent, respectively).

As might be expected from most motivational research, grassroots members need to have a purpose. So what, exactly, do companies ask these recruited people to do? As Table 6.9 indicates, nearly all organizations (95 percent) ask their grassroots members to write or e-mail legislators regarding specific issues or pieces of legislation. Three-quarters ask members to place a phone call to legislators for the same purpose.

Grassroots members, especially employees and customers, are busy people. Contacting legislators to discuss specific legislative initiatives or issues is time-consuming. How often can companies go to the well in asking grassroots members to act? On average, our informal discussions among our members at various meetings of grassroots organizers and managers have found that corporations ask their grassroots members to take action (in response to so-called "calls to action") four times a year.

## CONCLUSION

Looking ahead, it would appear that there are two principal forces shaping the US practice of corporate public affairs as it evolves in the mid-2000s:

1   Increased government and media scrutiny of corporate behavior.
2   Campaign finance reform.

Increased government and media scrutiny of corporate behavior—whether it relates to issues of governance, perceived excesses in compensation and benefits, insider trading, or the movement of domestic jobs overseas—makes it critical that corporations act proactively to shape public policy about the commercial marketplace and public perception about the role of corporations in society.

To be successful, the efforts of companies to shape public policy and public perception will necessarily include elements of the political involvement activities discussed in this chapter. Participation in coalitions, lobbying, and relationship building by the CEO and employees other that public affairs executives, including grassroots activism, will continue to be important.

It is also reasonable to examine how future trends could shape the relative importance of the main political activities organizations employ in public affairs efforts. For an optimal public affairs strategy, it is imperative that organizations pursue an holistic approach to corporate political action with an eye on strategically using a variety of activities, participants, stakeholders, and targets, etc. Organizations must remain ever vigilant as to the constant change that takes place in evergreen sociopolitical environments that define democracies such as the one found in the United States. Consequently, the public affairs professional both today and in the future will need to constantly monitor the firm's public affairs and sociopolitical strategy and adjust both the mixture and type of inputs to address the inherent dynamism. Those individuals and organizations able to effectively manage these adjustments in real-time stand the greater chance of having public affairs success and better enabling their organizations to achieve successful competitive product market outcomes.

## REFERENCES

Center for Responsive Politics (2005). Found March 2004 at http://www.opensecrets.org/. Washington, DC: Center for Responsive Politics.

Federal Election Commission (2004a). *Campaign Finance Reports and Data.* Washington, DC: Federal Election Commission, http://www.fec.gov/finance_reports.html.

Foundation for Public Affairs (2002). *The State of Corporate Public Affairs: Final Report.* Washington, DC: Foundation for Public Affairs.

Michael E. Dunn & Associates (undated) © *The Influence Pyramid.* Arlington, VA: Michael E. Dunn & Associates http://www.dunnassoc.com/index.html.

Public Affairs Council and Foundation for Public Affairs (2001). *State–Government Relations Benchmarking Project.* Washington, DC: Public Affairs Council.

Public Affairs Council and Foundation for Public Affairs (2002a). *State of Corporate Public Affairs Survey.* Washington, DC: Public Affairs Council.

Public Affairs Council and Foundation for Public Affairs (2002b). *Corporate, Trade, and Professional Grassroots Benchmarking Project.* Washington, DC: Public Affairs Council.

Public Affairs Council and Foundation for Public Affairs (2003a). *Corporate PAC Benchmarking Project.* Washington, DC: Public Affairs Council.

Public Affairs Council and Foundation for Public Affairs (2003b). *Corporate Government Relations Washington Office Benchmarking Project.* Washington, DC: Public Affairs Council.

# 7

# The Management of Public Affairs in the United Kingdom

PHIL HARRIS

Good lobbying is like growing asparagus, one should have started three years ago.

(Michael Shea, in Harris and Lock, 1996)

The core objective of this chapter is to assess and review the development, evolution, and increasing use of corporate political lobbying as a major strategic feature of business management practice in the United Kingdom. This chapter proposes a number of theoretical constructs for a fuller appreciation of political lobbying and public affairs work by the management discipline. This stimulated the development of a number of subsidiary and supportive objectives to underpin the inquiry and thrust of the study. This included an assessment of published definitions and terms used to describe political lobbying, political marketing, and public affairs. These were distilled from the published and current research and used to define and set the parameters of the study and subsequent theorizing. A realistic assessment of what is a very broad, somewhat disparate, and eclectic literature covering the research area has been undertaken and reflects a number of academic disciplinary positions (e.g. Pluralism, Reformed Pluralism and Neopluralism (Smith, 1993, 1995)) and traditions (e.g. journalistic inquiry, management science, marketing, political science,

public administration, public relations, etc.). This review has led to a number of issues arising for further inquiry, for instance the impact of the emergence of the regulatory state, the organization and extent of corporate lobbying by FTSE 200 companies, "not for profit" organizations and small to medium-sized enterprises (SMEs) and the effect of globalization on existing practice.

A grounded and ideographic methodology was used throughout the study based on Layders (1993) "Research Map." This adopted the approach of using context (macro social organization), setting (intermediate social organization), situated activity (social activity), and self (self-identity and individuals' social experience) as the basis for the planning and ongoing formulation of field research, which has theory generation as a primary aim. To aid the conceptualization process and theory development the research used network and interaction models associated with the work of Häkansson (1982) and the IMP group of researchers as the most fruitful for understanding this relationship-rich area. This has been augmented by the use of Strandvik and Törnroos's (1995) "Kite Model" concept to ensure the research has a clear understanding of the temporal dimensions of the area of study.

A particular gap in empirical research suggested by applying these methods was the lack of knowledge of party political conferences as a significant marketplace for business-to-business marketing and corporate political lobbying activity. A longitudinal research study covering the period 1994–2003 of these activities at party political conferences has been undertaken and its key findings have been outlined elsewhere. Core issues that emerged from this study were the role of private and "not for profit" interests in championing causes and interests at these events and the way the annual gathering is being used as a networking opportunity to communicate on and resolve complex issues between business and government.

The growth and development of corporate political lobbying (public affairs) was explored with senior managers and lobbyists during the period of research both at interview and during party political conferences. This suggested that for large organizations (particularly FTSE 200 companies, major charities, and pressure groups) an organized strategic approach to political lobbying was being adopted to gain competitive or market advantage. It found that highly qualified individuals were usually employed in this increasingly important profession in the United Kingdom who had considerable experience of the political process and understood how associated networks of power and influence worked. Personal integrity, ethics, honesty, and truth were seen by informants as essential prerequisites of individuals operating in what is usually seen as a long-term approach to business strategy and positive political policy development. Issues management techniques (Heath, 1990) were seen as important strategic tools to allow senior management to plan, prioritize, and target political lobbying. The seniority and influence of the individual lobbyist within the organization were noted as important for effective political lobbying. Advanced preparation, the supply of quality information, and access to networks of decision makers and policy advisors and administrators (particularly civil servants) were deemed essential for effective lobbying. It was broadly agreed that corporate lobbying had grown significantly over the 1990s in response to national and transnational government regulation activity, globalization, and environmental pressures. In addition it was felt that coalition building and collaboration with other interested organizations were often a way of bringing more leverage or pressure on government by a political lobbying campaign.

Interviews held with politicians and civil servants confirmed the dramatic growth in lobbying activity, much of which—for instance, non-targeted mail shots—was deemed non-effective and sometimes counterproductive. The impact a parliamentarian can have on an issue was reviewed and was found to be dependent on the advocacy and character of the individual concerned, majority of the ruling party (government) awareness and appreciation of the temporal nature of networks and the decision-making process. In addition the complex moral issues that political decision-making and advocating certain causes can make on the individual's integrity were explored. This is especially apposite given the sitting of the Committee on Standards in Public Life (especially Nolan's recommendations).

In this chapter the research findings from party conferences are evaluated with the interviews from respondents who have outlined detailed comment on the relative scale, size, and process of lobbying. These research findings in turn are assessed against the literature and methods applied throughout the study. Research interviews by participant observation of public affairs work and the continuous collection of primary and secondary source material gathered and observed throughout the period of research are used where appropriate to underpin the analysis and conceptualization process of the chapter. Research theories and relevant theoretical concepts of associated social science (Grant, 1989) and marketing theory (Häkansson, 1982) are employed in this section to assess their relevance to the phenomena being researched. The application of the trade show literature (Bonoma, 1983; Williams et al., 1993; Gopalakrishna et al., 1995) to commercial exhibitions and associated activity at political party conferences is then used to show the commonality and symmetry between marketing and political lobbying.

Additional influences on public affairs work, the legal profession, and increases in regulatory activities and the growth of politically oriented consultancies in the United Kingdom are assessed. Is this coincidental or are we seeing the importation of US-style political consultancies (Gould, 1998) that as well as managing campaigning directly exert influence on government policy development? The role of market research techniques such as the "focus group" in defining political campaigning and associated political marketing warfare priorities is widely reported (Newman, 1994; Maarek, 1995). Focus groups and opinion polling are now being widely used to discover the acceptance rate of lobbyists' propositions and government and think-tank policy options by politicians, journalists, public servants, and the public (Morris, 1999). The market testing of new strategic policy products is just another example of the direct linkage of political lobbying and relationship marketing.

Can the interface between business and politics be managed effectively for competitive advantage? The chapter proposes some ways in which some practical considerations can be used to reduce risk for the modern organization operating in environments increasingly influenced by government. In addition issues management approaches (Chase, 1984; Heath, 1997) are used in conjunction with interactionalist and network perspectives derived from the IMP group of researchers of marketing to explore and explain the modern role of public affairs work for the organization.

## TWO OF A KIND: POLITICAL LOBBYING AND THE RELATIONSHIP TO POLITICAL MARKETING IN THE UNITED KINGDOM

The term used in preference in this study is to describe the area as *political lobbying*. This emerged from the research both through participant observation and at interview with respondents and, it is argued, is a more accurate descriptor of the main activities carried out by participants and practitioners in the area of study. The somewhat prosaic and widely used term "public affairs" tends to add to the ambiguity of the area and is open to

many interpretations. This is evident in the range of job titles and departmental terms used by informants throughout the research. Interestingly public affairs was perceived as a high-status, almost generic term for the area by respondents and was also seen by a number as rather ambiguous and perhaps deliberately so.

The term "political lobbying" was generally recognized by informants as the core activity and functional title to describe the area. The use of the term "public affairs" by practitioners may be deliberate and suits individuals and organizations who seek anonymity for their activities in this area. Alternatively they may wish to avoid being pilloried by the press and/or gain the odium of politicians who frequently negatively criticize as a result of public antipathy (Greer, 1997). Lobbying is commonly perceived by the public as being a relatively devious, underhand, and low-esteem profession, whilst public affairs sounds much more personable and acceptable.

The former Conservative government Cabinet Minister the Rt Hon. Michael Portillo sums up many of these attitudes and sentiments, but also indicates the relative importance of political lobbying to government and parliamentary system: "Lobbyists are as essential to the political system, as sewers are to the modern city" (*Marketing*, February 16, 1995, p. 16). This also suggests that the activity is a communication process and that it is about the selling and communication of ideas and interests across relationships, a marketing communication process. Reflecting these arguments, views, and research, the original question inherent in the title of the thesis could be refined further: "Is political lobbying part of modern marketing?" The answer that emerges from this research is that the strategic use of lobbying by corporate and "not for profit" interests is very much a marketing-focused activity which is part of the development of relationships and in particular political marketing. Evidence that emerges from the research is as follows:

1   Informants saw political lobbying as a form of selling interests, policy alternatives, and solutions and information to a more regulatory oriented government.

2   Party conferences have increasingly emerged as a marketplace to exhibit and sell business and "not for profit" interests to political decision makers and influencers.

3   The increasing financial scale of political campaigning, which the Neill Committee report (1998a, b) indicated exceeded £50 million in the 1997 general election, has resulted in political parties having to raise substantial income above traditional sources of finance. As has been argued by Sabato (1981), O'Shaughnessy (1990) and others for the United States, but is increasingly the case for the United Kingdom, the need for campaign funds has stimulated improved access for organized interests to sell their needs and positions to government.

4   The growth in regulation by government has resulted in business and "not for profit" interests having a need to market their ideas and interests to government and politicians or lose position.

To further substantiate this case a broad definition of marketing is adopted and an *a priori* argument proposed that the marketing concept is fully applicable, regularly used, and easily transferable for use in political markets (Butler and Collins, 1995; Lock and Harris, 1996; O'Cass, 1996). In outlining the adoption of the marketing concept by political markets it is important to recognize the latter's special features and characteristics. Political markets, for instance, generally show consideration for the collective good of society rather than of just a few members (Butler and Collins, 1995; Chapman and Cowdell, 1998) and are invariably extensively regulated (Baines *et al.*, 1999). Butler and Collins (1995) have argued that these processes are interlinked, since the policy process usually commences ahead of general elections, when parties develop new ideas for party policy. This is most probably due to the fact that there is a need to retain competitive advantage in order to win election campaigns and form a government. This has caused politicians in the past to put forward policies that are popular regardless of their subsequent cost (Self, 1993).

Marketing relationships, as marketing research phenomena, are probably as old as trade relationships (Möller and Halinen-Kaila, 1998). As the research suggests lobbying and public affairs activity for strategic ends seems to fit within the broad marketing literature and particularly relationship marketing theory relating to the organization and its interaction in the wider environment. Möller and Halinen-Kaila (1998), in their review of the research roots and future directions of relationship marketing, argue that most firms (or organizations) have to master several modes of marketing. Most have to master traditional aspects of marketing management such as brand management, segmentation, and competitive positioning as well as what they call "Interorganizational/Extensive Relationship Marketing" and the "Consumer/Limited Relationship Marketing." They see relationship marketing dividing into these two main bodies of theory for scholarly inquiry, that of "Interorganizational/Extensive Relationship Marketing" and "Consumer/Limited Relationship Marketing." Research on party conferences indicates the scale and size of the multitude of relationships being established with the political parties to market and influence policy making and show substantial "Interorganizational Marketing" activity. "Extensive Relationship Marketing" was clearly seen as vital by informants and is very evident in interviews with political lobbyists, politicians, and civil servants. These relationships certainly would suggest that lobbying and public affairs work fit within the concept of Interorganizational/Extensive Relationship Marketing theory.

If we accept having previously reviewed the development of the marketing concept and researched the growth of strategic public affairs that political lobbying is an integral part of marketing and thus management then where does this phenomenon and its transaction network fit into relationship marketing theory? Do we need to refine our definitions?

To fit these developments a philosophy of marketing exchange theory that can be applied to these specialist exchanges and buyer-seller interactions in these networks is used. "Political marketing is the facilitation of exchanges between political entities and their environment and amongst those entities" (Harris and Lock, cited in Harris, 1996, p. 18.).

The definition was developed to strengthen the term "political marketing" by allowing it to take account of modern developments such as the emergence of environmental, political cause and pressure-group campaigning, political lobbying, the impact of referenda and aspects of cause and social marketing. This definition fits well the phenomena researched in this study and suggests that modern marketing theory and practice encompass much of what we regard as public affairs and especially strategic lobbying. Not just the promotional and marketing communications aspects of the area but the application of the full marketing concept to strategically shape and even develop new and old markets. This is clearly supported by the research and is very evident in the comments from lobbyists on amending governmental subvention policy on commercial television and comments on the advocacy of what constitutes chocolate. Among politicians the advocacy of more international landing slots at Manchester Airport is a good example.

## STRATEGIC POLITICAL LOBBYING AND RELATIONSHIP MARKETING THEORY

In assessing "business-to-business marketing" and lobbying activity at political party conferences, research with senior managers in public affairs, and similarly with politicians and public servants, a number of features emerge. To make sense of these a network approach based on the work of the IMP group of researchers (Häkansson, 1982) and the embeddedness concept (Anderson et al., 1994; Halinen and Törnroos, 1995) can be applied throughout to evaluate phenomena observed and to develop a realistic theoretical construct.

### The Direct Influence of Individual Parliamentarians

The research confirms the literature (Doig and Wilson, 1995) that elected representatives, particularly MPs but also peers and MEPs, have limited individual direct influence on decision and policy making by government. The late

Richard Crossman argued in his diaries (Crossman, 1975) that he saw MPs as powerless ciphers, but they do have privileged access to confidential information, to draft legislation, and to the wider decision-making process. The value of this access has grown to interest groups and lobbyists since 1979. This increasing importance was stimulated by reforming Conservative governments pushing their own legislative programme through rather than accepting what was emerging from a long deliberative Whitehall-led consultative process. The Blair government has maintained this momentum through its major policy changes such as devolution and a move towards a US model of government, with over fifty Labour political special advisors being appointed to Whitehall departments (MacAskill, 1997a). Collectively MPs can exert increased influence on the executive because of its need for their continued support and consequent votes to back its legislation programme. The power of MPs at times of small or no overall majority governments in the United Kingdom can increase dramatically because of the executive's reliance on their support. Small groups of MPs and even individual ones can exert significant influence on government. This was seen very clearly in pressure exerted by the activities of the Conservative Euroskeptic MPs on the last Tory government (Norton, 1997). Individual MPs and peers have the opportunity to influence indirectly via a network of contacts. These can include access points to decision makers, memberships, and positions of responsibility held within the party, parliamentary committees, professional affiliations, trade associations, local government, business groups, trade union linkages, and a broad range of connections with other organizations and contacts.

### The Significance of the Embeddedness Concept

The extent of this web of activity, potential access, and influence points of parliamentary representatives can be clearly seen in the Register of Members' Interests published each year (HMSO, 1997, 1996, 1995, 1994). It is detailed in biographies and pen portraits such as *Dod's Parliamentary Companion* (1993, 1998).

Elected representatives appear from the research results at their most effective when they are an active advocate and/or representative participant within a network or number of networks. The degree of embeddedness of the representative within the network (Granovetter, 1985; Grabher, 1993; Halinen and Törnroos, 1995) is important to allow individuals to champion certain causes across and within a number of networks. Sir Malcolm Thornton, then a Conservative MP, in conversation with this author, included a good example of the embeddedness concept in action and practice. His remarks also highlight well the importance of Ahrne's "centaur concept" as a useful metaphorical tool for analysis in the area:

> There are other ways of doing this and if I am not a Minister, finding some way to get into the government machinery. And as a Member of Parliament I know the way the system works and therefore I have got to use whatever tools I can find to put a case. Using lobbying techniques openly, overtly, above board, on the table—whatever expression that might be useful—that side of things too and I think that, well, Thornton would, wouldn't he, become involved in this in the first place.
>
> As a North West MP supporting Manchester Airport the case is overwhelmingly in favour of this issue of gaining access to routes. Not just because it was Singapore Airlines but because it was going to benefit Liverpool and the North West. No reason at all to do this, other than I believed in Manchester Airport and the right for it to have long-haul air routes. In my view this is one way in which a constituency member can make a difference.

Individuals who act like Ahrne's (1994) so-called organizational "centaurs" who champion or act on behalf of interests and organizations within their web of networks can clearly be very effective at exerting influence on decision making. The level of activity and number of networks which the "centaur" enters are dependent upon the amount of interaction the individual engages in. These actors can create their own networks which extend far beyond the company by which they are employed and Ahrne argues they have their family and friends, and they make personal contacts through membership of voluntary associations such as political parties, trade unions, or sports clubs. This research is used to explain industrial networks but can equally be applied to public affairs work and the actors that operate in those arenas, particularly parliamentarians, government officials, and lobbying practitioners. The able parliamentarian, official, or lobbyist can access a number of networks and individuals to influence decision or policy making (Searing, 1994). If we continue to apply interactionalist marketing theory to this phenomenon then Halinen and Törnroos (1998) would underpin the point by emphasizing that personal networks are likely to influence business exchange. This can be seen very clearly in Figure 7.1. The complexity of decision making in this figure lends itself to a network perspective.

## WEAK AND STRONG LINKAGES AND THE OPERATION OF POLITICAL LOBBYING NETWORKS

Granovetter (1973, 1974) uses the concept of weak linkages as a powerful concept in seeking to understand the dynamics in social networks. In his view the strong ties between individuals or groups, e.g. kin, friends, and close workmates, seem to stabilize relationships in social networks. Weak ties among those not in frequent contact, on the other hand, seem to stimulate change by adding new information and new dimensions to social interaction (see Granovetter, 1974; Scott, 1991). This theory of weak and strong linkages can be seen to apply equally to political interaction and lobbying effectiveness in the interviews held as part of the research. Access to and linkage with political networks are one of the reasons why there was a premium price being paid for the recruitment of former Labour Party researchers to commercial lobbying organizations prior to the election of a Labour government in 1997. Many businesses and agencies realized that having a

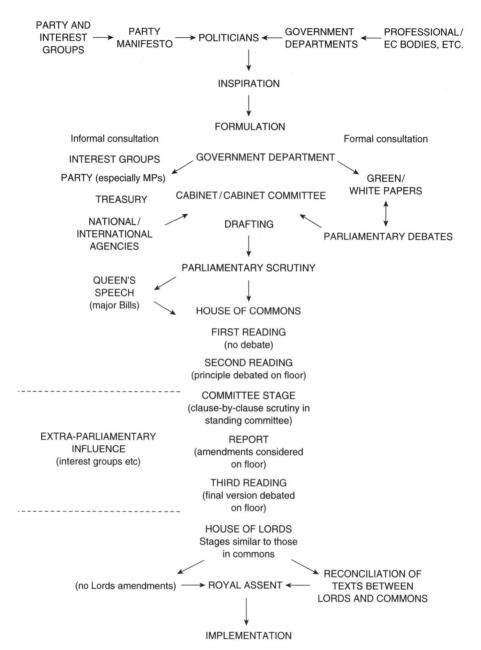

Figure 7.1    *The Principal Stages in the Legislative Process for UK Government Bills*
Source *Foreign and Commonwealth Office*

lobbyist supporting their organization with strong ties to Labour would be useful to their cause, as it would allow improved access to government. In 1996 Mike Craven, former personal assistant to John Prescott, MP, joined the lobbyists Market Access. Rex Osbourne, Labour's polling strategist, and Mike Lee, David Blunkett's former researcher, joined the strategic lobbying organization Westminster Strategy (Clarke, 1996). In-house within organizations the same process has occurred in that stronger linkages to the governing party have been developed, for instance, a utility company allegedly moved a member of staff to public affairs work from a technical management role because of the individual's strong Labour Party links (non-attributable source). Granovetter's argument of the importance of having insider status in the policy-making process is strongly supported by the research. Comments by Anthony Weale, then of ICI, show the importance of having acceptable linkages into policy and decision-making networks by legislators and public servants:

> If you reach a point where you can't cope, I can always get someone else to help.
>
> We don't use outsiders. We don't use consultants. Not at all.
>
> We always do it ourselves, on the basis that parliamentarians particularly, but civil servants as well, would find it very odd for a company like ICI to have to use outsiders to do its work for it.
>
> I mean, there are areas where consultants are very handy, but not in this function.

If we apply Granovetter's concept to parliamentarians, civil servants, and public affairs practitioners, we can see that it leads us to argue that regular and consistent contact is the key to successful influence or lobbying. Sudden irregular contact frequently sends the wrong signals and does not work, as it suggests panic (crisis) and that the participants raising the issue have not been monitoring the policy-making process effectively and could have short-term opportunist ambitions. Alternatively, one can argue that the group or people involved in the issue may not be an inclusive group within the policy-making process. For instance, they may not have access to or be part of the network which is affecting them. (See Harris and O'Shaughnessy, 1997, or Ratzan, 1998).

Ministers and members of government who are decision makers have only limited time available to be lobbied because of the protection given them by civil servants, their Ministry, the party, their own political staff and the increasing constraints on their time. Access to these decision makers is normally gained only by introduction via parliamentarians, officials,

other intermediaries, or by formal channels and routes. However, access is usually limited and the consultation process restricted unless concerted pressure is exerted on the government policy-making process. As a result the more able elected representatives apply what marketing researchers would call a "network approach" (Häkansson, 1982) to be most effective at exerting pressure on the executive. Parliamentarians and those operating within public affairs to succeed in influencing a decision will bring about a coalition of interests (Mack, 1997) and/or networks to exert pressure on the Minister or government to bring about change in a policy initiative or a review of a particular area. A good example is the case Sir Malcolm Thornton outlined at interview about exerting pressure to gain government approval for additional runway slots at Manchester Airport. A further example is the analysis of the coalition of interests and networks which were used to achieve competitive advantage by large retail marketing interests on Sunday trading, which has been well cited. The approach adopted in both instances is more a relationship marketing approach than a transactional one and clearly fits Möller and Halinen-Kaila's earlier (1998) definition of Interorganizational/Extensive Relationship Marketing.

## PICTURES AT AN EXHIBITION: PARTY CONFERENCES AS MARKETPLACES FOR POLITICAL LOBBYING

UK political party conferences are places where given the combination of exhibition area, fringe meetings, hotels and restaurants, politicians, media, and business interests regularly meet and exchange views, which have an impact on policy and decisions taken. It emerged from the research that party political conferences have become one of the key networking events of the year, with many of the senior figures who play roles in policy and government decision making being present and those trying to influence those decisions consequently attending.

There is only limited recognition of the growing role of party conferences as core contact points where strategic lobbying can be carried out. Berry (1991) has carried out some initial work, but this is limited as it is based on only one year's collection of data, is very qualitatively oriented and primarily looks at why various organizations exhibit or attend rather than the scale and types of activity. In addition at the time of Berry's research the Labour Party was still broadly averse to commercial activity at its conferences and business participation was relatively restricted. And further, the need to generate substantial income from party conferences was less of an imperative at the time of Berry's original research (1990–91). Neill (1998a) has indicated that the three main UK political parties need to regularly generate at least £60 million to fund their general election campaigns, and evidence from 2001 and probably 2005 seems to support this view. A sizable proportion of this income comes from party conferences and the author estimates that for the Labour Party up to one-third of this funding comes directly or indirectly from party conferences. Private estimates in 1998 suggested that the Labour Party allegedly generated a £2 million surplus from its 1998 Blackpool conference (non-attributable source). This level of income seems to be being maintained throughout recent years, with the largest surges of income being immediately prior and post a general election by the governing party (Labour throughout the period). The Conservatives, income from these activities has stayed static or marginally declined during this period.

## Gaining Context, Activity, Temporality and Self (CATS) at Party Conferences

The research includes ten years' attendance at all major political party conferences over the period 1994–2003 as participant observer and researcher with consequent analysis. As a result through active immersion in these conferences and associated events (fringe meetings, receptions, etc.) the researcher was able to observe not just the scale of lobbying and marketing activity but also a change of governing party (1997) and its impact and the build-up in policy development and election campaigning

(1995 and 1996). The data give a clear indication of the scale, size, and type of business-to-business marketing communication activity at party conferences.

This is the first time that lobbying and business-to-business marketing activity have been assessed and quantified over a realistic time period to form a longitudinal data set for research. In addition all conferences in 2004 were monitored to check out the assertions drawn from the data set and to maintain the database, which is being added to and maintained for further research.

## The Marketplace Provided by Party Conferences

As a result of the conferences being of a directly political nature, Ministers and government members attend their own party events as active politicians and have less constraints of access put on them by the civil service in these surroundings. In addition organized business and "not for profit" interests use the opportunity to gain discreet and relatively easy access to decision makers to informally talk through the issues that impact upon them. Interestingly the range, scale, and variety of events at party conferences produce a certain anonymity and great camouflage opportunities to facilitate private meetings and encounters between organizations, politicians, and officials. In addition regular contact is maintained with representatives of the political party and decision makers who have either access to or can influence on a local, national, or European level political decision making and government. As a result of the gathering of the politicians, media, business, public and voluntary sector interests in one place, much swapping of information and intelligence gathering is completed. For many participants at party conferences it is an opportunity to catch up with contacts, renew acquaintances, gather information, and extend their business and political networks (BBC Radio 4 *Today* programme, Thursday, October 1, 1998). As MacAskill (1998) has argued, the "conference season produces a dizzying array of options, a fringe programme to rival the

Edinburgh Festival and a host of receptions" (p. 3.); this gives some flavour and insight into the opportunities for lobbying and public affairs work. The relevant importance of the political conferences to lobbyists and public affairs practitioners is in direct correlation to the party's position in relation to government. The evidence for this can be seen in the levels of political lobbying activity seen at party conferences from 1994 to 2003.

Organized interests take a proactive role at party conferences and the exhibition stand frequently doubles as an effective operations base for lobbying and selling-type initiatives deemed as priorities by the participating organization at the conference. This reflects the published literature and marketing research on perceived practice at commercial exhibitions/trade shows (Bonoma, 1983; Black, 1989; Williams *et al.*, 1993; Kronvall and Törnroos, 1998). When the stand is used as a base for both advertising the product or service, at party conferences this is invariably a cause, policy or organizational interest. In the marketing literature the stand or event acts as a meeting place between clients and sales force to foster business and contact interactions to organize further sales activities and the coordination of staff. At party conferences these interactions take place in exhibition areas and fringe meetings between representatives of the party and members of the exhibiting organization. This was observed as a feature of the better run stands at conferences; the RSPCA even confirmed to the author that they operate a shift system to facilitate this process and have stand operations and planning events ahead of the event. The leading stands invariably have gifts, special offers, special guests, or a competition to attract delegates and attendees (for instance, a pair of first-class tickets to a distant but warm destination was the normal British Airways lure observed during the period of prime research from 1993 to 2003). The need by political parties to generate substantial income to fund campaigning and associated operations has led to a fostering and consequent growth of commercial activity at party conferences. This in turn has led to more regular liaison between senior party officials and representatives

(including Ministers), commercial exhibitors, and sponsors of fringe events and other aspects of the conference.

As part of this process of contact the Prime Minister, Tony Blair, Mrs Cherie Blair, Gordon Brown, Mo Mowlam, and various members of the Cabinet visited individually every exhibition stand during the Labour Party 1998 conference to thank them for attending and supporting the event. This activity provides excellent photo opportunities for all concerned and consequently allegedly makes the organizations' attendances financially more justifiable internally (non-attributable informant). A similar style of "thank you for your support" operation, but on a smaller scale, is carried out at the Conservative and Liberal Democrat conferences. Each political conference hosts a special reception for exhibitors and sponsors, which is attended by senior party figures where annual prizes for the best stands are normally presented. In addition sponsored party dinners at conferences to raise party funds with senior government figures in attendance have grown dramatically since Labour was elected in 1997. It was reported to the researcher that Labour's conference dinner in 1998 had 500 guests attending at £500 per head and that allegedly a well known publicly owned transport utility had booked a table for twenty people to attend. The guests of the company were made up of ten Labour Party members who included appropriate senior Ministers, MPs, senior councillors, and party figures. One Minister who was a guest at the dinner visited the stand of the organization to thank them for their hospitality and allegedly was considerably more open and amenable to the organization after the event (non-attributable source). In 2002 Labour held a major fund-raising dinner which former US President Bill Clinton attended in Blackpool; individual tickets were close to £1,000. The example shows how clearly marketing practice and in particular theory on buyer and consumer behaviour (Howard and Sheth, 1969; Baker and Parkinson, 1986; O'Shaughnessy, 1987, 1992; Foxall, 1994; Schmitz, 1995, etc.). Managing trust as part of sales management (Morgan and Hunt, 1994; Doney and Cannon, 1997; Donaldson, 1998, etc.), relationship marketing (Christopher *et al.*, 1991; Ramsey and Sohi, 1997, etc.) and interaction and particularly networking theory (Weitz, 1981; Häkansson, 1982; Turnbull and Valla, 1986; Ford, 1990; Horan *et al.*, 1998) are all aspects of this practical case of public affairs work.

## ROLE OF CIVIL SERVANTS

Civil servants operate by certain codes and procedures and are members of a complex web of officials employed by government to develop, manage, and steer executive policy. At a preliminary and/or early stage in policy or decision making cogent advice and information can be given to civil servants to influence particular decisions and policy imperatives. Ben Chapman, then a civil servant and now MP, made this point very tellingly at interview:

> It is a fact of life that, in my view at least, in policy making he who writes the first paper sets the course of the forces before you. After that you are in the business of trying to amend effectively an established position and that is more difficult. So you have to get in before the paper.

Respondents felt that the importance of influencing civil servants and their thinking was not recognized effectively in the literature on lobbying. Supplying regular and tailored sources of information and proposing potential solutions for complex areas of policy were seen as particularly effective ways of influencing government officials. It also emerged in the research that it was better to contact officials at a lower level of authority and work one's way up the system than the other way round and to start too high, where there is less room for manoeuvre which could consequently be counterproductive.

## THE GROWTH AND DEVELOPMENT OF PUBLIC AFFAIRS

Public affairs practitioners indicated that there had been a steady and consistent growth of lobbying and associated work over the 1980s and 1990s (Jordan, 1991; Nolan, 1995a, b; Harris and Lock, 1995; Moloney, 1996; Souza, 1998). The research underpins this and argues that much of the growth in public affairs has come from the impact of globalization, government deregulation (Gabriel and Lang, 1995), privatization policy, the development of transnational government (the European Union, etc.), and the increasing awareness of businesses' need to influence government policy to gain commercial advantage (Moloney, 1996). Public affairs practitioners of major companies frequently have a career profile which reflects a background in government service, politics, and/or some knowledge of the legal profession. In addition senior figures invariably have a strong background in high-level financial and general management.

The ability to connect and understand the political process will be explored more fully later in this chapter, but it is worth noting that the skill of being able to understand and link into political networks easily is a common personal background feature among senior practitioners.

### The Long Arm of the Law: The Use of a Legal Training for Political Lobbying Work

Mack (1997: 101) argues that in the United States:

> The increasing intimacy of many issues raises the question of whether a lobbyist need necessarily be an attorney, a member of a profession focused on detail. In many cases, lawyers make effective lobbyists for many of the same reasons that attorneys predominate as legislators.

However, he argues that non-legally trained individuals may be equally good provided they have these traits and access to a lawyer for detailed guidance. Interestingly there is a steady trend in the United Kingdom, where legally trained lobbyists are on the increase. A good example of this is the launch in the United Kingdom and Brussels of APCO, the US lawyer-led public affairs and strategic communications company. Evidence from the large commercial law companies is that they are considering extending their services into corporate lobbying. In addition public affairs practitioners see their role as contributing directly to the competitiveness and profitability of their company or group of organizations. There has been a steady professionalization of the public affairs role within many organizations as they have faced increasing regulation or increased corporate competition. The increase in legislation and regulation both from the UK legislature and increasingly the European Union is making it more important for the competitive organization to be proactive in terms of its public profile and public affairs work.

## Defining Public Affairs and Lobbying

To understand the role of public affairs it is essential to have knowledge of how the function operates and the prime reasons for its existence. There is a great deal of debate about the precise role but if research sees it as being about lobbying and community interests this seems to have wide-scale support both in the literature (Harris et al., 1999) and among practitioners.

The definition which is preferred in this study covering the areas explored and is robust enough to cover both in-company and consultancy activity is that by Van Schendelen (1993), who argues that lobbying can cover a multitude of practices and in particular: "The informal exchange of information with public authorities, as a minimal description on the one hand, and as trying informally to influence public authorities on the other hand" (p. 3). This allows for both informal and formal contact. In regard to commercial and political campaigning for a particular cause, issue, or coalition of interests the following definition was formulated after wide consultation with practitioners and reference to the published research in the area: "mobilizing opinion to exert pressure on public authorities or bodies for commercial gain or competitive advantage."

It is important to note that the majority of influencing and lobbying that takes place to obtain strategic gain is covert and aimed at the policy-making process and administration of government. The definition taken to describe lobbying by this study is: "The specific effort to influence public decision making either by pressing change in policy or seeking to prevent such change" (Institute of Public Relations, 1994).

Grunig and Hunt (1984), who see lobbying as being able to provide sufficient data to a legislature so that all of the facts can be known before a vote is cast, reinforce this. They see lobbying as running in a continuum from the more pure version, by arranging social opportunities to mix business with pleasure, to the downright corrupt and buying votes with money and/or favours. The increasing need for political parties in the United Kingdom to raise substantial sums to pay for modern media election campaigning is beginning to show signs of moving in this direction (Challen, 1998; Ramsey, 1998; Baines et al., 1999).

## PUBLIC AFFAIRS AND ISSUES MANAGEMENT

At interview a number of senior figures in public affairs suggested that one of the key features of the profession was good issues management. One respondent went so far as to suggest diagramatically the importance of this to his company and industry. Issues management has a number of definitions, especially at corporate level (Hainsworth and Meng, 1988), due primarily to senior management perceptions and interpretations of what issues impact upon their organization's operations. In addition the fact that the subject area is still relatively new in the United Kingdom has led to a wide diversity of constructs of definitions and a consequent number of interpretations, which has led to some ambiguity among practitioners and the literature (L'Etang, 1996).

This research takes as a starting point in the need to assess the application of issues management to public affairs Cutlipp et al.'s (1994) definition, "Issues management is the proactive process of anticipating, identifying, evaluating and responding to public policy issues that affect organizations and their publics" (p. 16).

Issues management was originally introduced and conceptualized by W. Howard Chase (1977), a public relations consultant who saw it as identifying issues, setting priorities, selecting program strategies, implementing programs of action and communication, and the evaluation of effectiveness. Chase reconceptualized this in 1984 with what he termed his Chase/Jones Issue Management Process model, which outlined five steps to manage public policy issues:

1  Issue identification.
2  Issue analysis.
3  Issue change strategy options.
4  Issue Action programming.
5  Evaluation of results.

This is more fully explored in Chapter 28.

Clearly this process has a number of striking similarities with the marketing management concept. This had been developed much earlier by Borden (1964), who in turn grounded it on the arguments of Culliton (1948) and his perception of the marketer as a mixer of ingredients. However, where issues management theory varies is that unlike the marketing concept it is not a dominant producer-oriented model (Gronroos, 1994a; Laycock, 1983) but instead it has the ability to respond to outside environmental change. It is reflective and can permeate the philosophy and awareness of many organizations, especially if they operate in regulated markets. Heath (1990) has put together a theoretical basis to underpin the theory. He argues that issues management is underpinned by much of social exchange theory, which "involves the transference of resources" (Roloff, 1981: 25):

> If relationships cost more than they are worth, they are more likely to be abandoned or reformed; if the cost is great and they cannot be terminated, sanctions and constraints are likely to be used to force change, thereby leading to new, ostensibly more favourable, cost-benefit ratios.
>
> (Heath, 1998: xiii)

He argues that because of the stress on resource management, social exchange theory brings to the fore the norms of reciprocity basic to each relationship. He moves issues management into the wider public community field by arguing that:

> Managements are well served by issues managers who know the costs that can result from strained relationships, whereby key stakeholders believe that the costs associated with the organization or industry outweigh the social and material benefits.
>
> (Heath, 1998: xiii)

The literature appears to argue that issues management's prime role is to understand policy likely to emerge from government and the public domain. Thus issues management covers a large part of public affairs work. Hainsworth and Meng (1988) have emphasized this even more strongly in suggesting:

> [it] seeks to identify potential or emerging issues (legislative, regulatory, political or social) that may impact upon the organization then mobilises and co-ordinates organizational resources to strategically influence the development of those issues.
>
> (Hainsworth and Meng, 1988: 28–9)

Thus the ultimate aim of issues management is to shape and respond to public policy for the benefit of the organization. This theory appears to fit very comfortably with the assessment of policy risk commonly utilized by practitioners. In addition in discussion with informants a number confirmed that they used these types of technique to assess the impact of a policy issue on the organization and its competitiveness. This fits comfortably within Möller and Halinen-Kaila's earlier (1998) definition of Interorganizational/Extensive Relationship Marketing.

Issues research is important in developing well understood positions and action plans by organizations on emerging public policy, whether the issues being assessed are offensive or defensive, current or emerging. Mack (1997: 27) suggests that in the United States the aim in government relations is to use issues management to understand: "What is happening and why, what the impact is internally (on the company or among the organizations' members) and also the significance externally—on friends, foes and potential allies."

This appears to equally apply in the United Kingdom, especially among organizations who take a proactive public affairs stance (confirmed by respondents). Mack suggests a checklist of questions (Exhibit 7.1), which the government relations researcher should be asking to develop sound intelligence on current issues. These can be adapted for the United Kingdom. The questions can be developed to build a basic audit for the development of effective public affairs management practice.

---

### Exhibit 7.1 Checklist for Effective Strategic Public Affairs Management

- What is the issue all about?
- What are the key Bills, directives or regulatory proposals?
- What are their provisions?
- What is their significance?
- How/will it affect us?
- Who are its governmental sponsors?
- What interest groups are backers and allies, both actual and potential?
- What part and/or level of government is stimulating this development (local, regional, national or transnational)?
- What is the underlying rationale behind the proposal and motivations of its supporters?
- What are the issues and who are the opponents, now and in the future?
- What is the relative motivation of opponents over time?
- What relevant background documents and reports are there on this issue?
- What are the prospects for the issue?
- What are the political implications of this issue?
- Is it part of some wider trend or development in policy?
- How does it fit alongside important interest groups, political leaders and candidates, parties, think tanks or European initiatives?
- What is the best estimate of time scales for this policy development: short, medium or long term?
- What is the life cycle of the issue, based upon a current assessment of risk?
- Will evidence or soundings be taken by the government or promoters of this policy?
- How can this be influenced?
- Is it possible to locate influential government officials in this policy area?
- As the policy develops over time will it be possible to move amendments or refine certain areas?
- What are the short, medium, and long-term implications for our organization?
- Costs or gains this policy option would generate for our business (internally and externally)?
- How would this affect our overall competitive position?
- Are there initiatives that could be taken either to promote or curtail action on this issue?
- Who are potential coalition partners and opponents on this issue?

*Source* Author's revised schema of questions developed from interviews with respondents and adapted from the work of Mack (1998).

## VIRTUAL REALITY: CYBERSPACE AND PUBLIC AFFAIRS

Effective issues management requires good access to a range of complex and detailed information sources to provide an understanding and appreciation of public policy development for the organization. Communication and technology advances have meant that it is now possible to search Web sites that can provide a high-quality range of information on business interests, government, and the growing plethora of "not for profit" organizations and interests. (A good example in the United Kingdom is Government on Line, www.open.gov.uk.) This makes it infinitely easier to assess the above questions and calculate the likely risk, loss, and gain, using issues management techniques. In addition there is a range of networks of individuals and groups who are capable of answering issue-related questions or can provide appropriate information that can be extremely useful in this process. These may include government officials, parliamentary staff, quangos, NGOs, trade and professional association personnel. Other options include researchers with think tanks, policy research organizations such as the Wellcome Trust (this in fact operates a scientific grant-awarding and information network via the World Wide Web on www.wellcome.ac.uk), academic institutions, journalists, and researchers in the media as useful providers of information and intelligence sources. Also staff of non-business organizations such as trade unions, environmental groups, consumer organizations, and "not for profit" organizations can be very useful suppliers of quality information for the assessment process.

In addition, background data and research on policy development as part of information technology development can be obtained increasingly on line. Sources of government information are also increasingly being put on line on the Net for a range of complex reasons, which include accessibility, accountability to the electorate, and electronic democracy programmes. This process of making easily available electronic access points to government data has also made good public affairs research easier.

## UTILIZING ISSUES MANAGEMENT TO GAIN COMPETITIVE ADVANTAGE

A number of respondents reported that they bought in privately the services of one of these organizations to keep abreast of policy developments and issues likely to affect their interests (non-attributable comment). The voting record of parliamentarians in the United Kingdom can increasingly be analysed and seen on line by those interested in lobbying. It was also confirmed to the author that voting records by issue and surveys of attendance by politicians at events were allegedly kept by one private agency as a potential service to appropriate lobbyists or causes. It is well known that the anti-abortion and Pro-life campaigns (as they have done in Eire and the United States), the RSPCA, the RSPB and many other pressure groups keep sophisticated and long-term records on parliamentarians' voting records and opinions. During elections and when policy issues affecting the pressure or interest group emerge, information on candidate or parliamentarian attitude is passed on to active campaigners to exert pressure on them. Throughout the research parliamentarians indicated that their postbags were dominated by abortion campaigning and animal rights-related letters. Respondents also outlined the scale of this process and its effectiveness when used to support campaigns against the movement of live animals, animal testing, hunting, and abortion.

Emerging issues identification is used to assess the likelihood of a particular policy being adopted. This usually includes a complex appraisal of all sources of information and trends that are emerging in society and economic life. The steady increase in environmentalism has been relatively easy to perceive over the last twenty years, but its exact individual impact on particular products and businesses has been very difficult to assess. Meng (1992) argues that there are five stages in the life cycles of issues:

1  *Potential issue.* Isolated events develop into a pattern; interest groups adopt the problem as a cause.

2   *Emerging issue.* The issue develops a broader base of supporters. It begins to generate media attention.

3   *Current issue.* The issue has become current; it is brought to the attention of legislators, politicians, and regulators.

4   *Crisis stage.* Various policy alternatives compete and one will be adopted.

5   *Dormancy.* The issue has metamorphosized into a law and is in the hands of the regulators.

By the time issues reach the fourth stage (legislative or other policy action) they are well advanced in their evolutionary cycle and are more difficult to influence. This supports the earlier argument that it is best to get in as early as possible with government to influence its direction. Issues management argues that the advanced organization will be scanning, tracking, screening, and evaluating all data and sources of information available to it, to assess the likely impact of each potential issue on the company's existing or planned lines of business, markets, products, or services. In trade associations and other membership groups the impact analysis is somewhat broader, concentrating on examining the industry's future development or current planned programs.

The next stage of the issues management process in public affairs is to disseminate the issue analysis to decision makers as part of the strategic and business planning process. Traverse-Healey (1978) suggested seven questions which should be asked of emerging issues to decide their relevant importance to the organization. The respondents in the research confirmed at interview that broadly the same criteria apply but that these can be adapted and modified as follows:

1   Will the issue/s affect the bottom line?

2   What is the probability and time scale of this issue impacting on us?

3   Can corporate action change the outcome?

4   In the light of this analysis are our present corporate policies and practices correct?

5   Do we have the resources and the will to do something on this at present?

6   What will be the cost to influence this?

7   What are the financial or policy benefits to us of doing this?

8   What can we learn from this for the benefit of our organization?

9   How can we evaluate the effectiveness of our actions?

10   What can we learn from this situation to ensure future competitiveness?

The competitive organization (whether it is "not for profit" or private) builds this issues management procedure into its planning and policy-making process. Senior management see it as a critical strategic business activity to maintain competitiveness.

CONCLUSION

The chapter argues that political lobbying is part of modern political marketing activity and fits within what has come to be called "relationship marketing". The role and relative significance of parliamentarians and civil servants within the government decision-making process has been analysed and outlined. It has been found that the individual qualities and power of networks open to parliamentarians play a significant factor in their relative effectiveness. It was generally agreed that the earlier one started planning and understanding a particular policy area the more effective lobbying would be in that domain. It also emerged from the research that it is invariably more fruitful for effectiveness to deal with the civil service at an early point rather than leaving it late and in the hands of parliamentarians when the bulk of the issue has already been decided.

The annual party conferences and exhibitions are emerging as increasing centres for business-to-business marketing and political lobbying activity. The size and scale of activity reflect the fact that political parties have to fund campaigning and this is forcing a need to generate income from private and "not for profit" sector interest. Public affairs has moved from a small-scale and relatively specialist functional area to one which has become much more strategic, planned, and thought out to give commercial and organizational advantage to modern interests. Political lobbying was seen as being essential both to maintain competitive advantage for the organization and to provide accurate and quality information to government for decision making.

## REFERENCES

Ahrne, G. (1994). *Social Organizations: Interaction Inside, Outside and Between Organizations*. London: Sage.

Anderson, J.C., H. Häkansson, and J. Johanson (1994). "Dyadic Business Relationships within a Business Network Context," *Journal of Marketing* 58: 1–15.

Andrews, L. (1996a). "The Relationship of Political Marketing to Political Lobbying: An Examination of the Devonport Campaign for the *Trident* Refitting Contract," *European Journal of Marketing* 30 (10–11): 76–99.

Andrews, L. (1996b). "New Labour, New England," in M. Perryman (ed.), *The Blair Agenda*. London: Lawrence & Wishart.

Baines, P.R., P. Harris, and B.I. Newman (1999). "New *Real Politik*: Political marketing. Campaigning and the Application of Political Marketing towards a Cross-cultural Model," in *Proceedings of the Twenty-eighth European Marketing Academy Conference*, May 12–14, Berlin: Humboldt University.

Baker, M.J., and S.T. Parkinson (1986). *Organizational Buying Behaviour: Purchasing and Marketing Management Implications*. London: Macmillan.

Berry, S.P. (1991). "The Growth and Development of the Commercial Lobbying Industry in Britain during the 1980s." Unpublished doctoral dissertation, Birkbeck College, London University.

Black, S. (1989). *Introduction to Public Relations*. London: Modino.

Bonoma, T.V. (1983). "Getting More out of Your Trade Shows," *Harvard Business Review* 61: 75–83.

Borden, N. (1964). "The Concept of the Marketing Mix," *Journal of Advertising Research*, June, pp. 2–7.

Butler, P., and N. Collins (1995). "Marketing Public Sector Services: Concepts and Characteristics. *Journal of Marketing Management* 11 (1–3): 83–96.

Challen, C. (1998). *Price of Power: The Secret Funding of the Tory Party*. London: Vision Paperbacks.

Chapman, D., and T. Cowdell (1998). *New Public Sector Marketing*. London: Pitman.

Chase, W.H. (1977). "Public Issue Management: The New Science," *Public Relations Journal* 33 (10): 25–26.

Chase, W.H. (1984). *Issue Management: Origins of the Future*. Stamford, CT: Issue Action Publications.

Christopher, M., A. Payne, and D. Ballantyne (1991). *Relationship Marketing*. Oxford: Butterworth Heinemann.

Clarke, P. (1996). "Knowledge Means Power for the Insider Lefties," *Sunday Times* (Scottish edition), August 18, p. 6.

Crossman, R. (1975). *Diaries of a Cabinet Minister* I, *Lord President of the Council and Leader of the House of Commons, 1966–1968*. London: Hamish Hamilton and Jonathan Cape.

Culliton, J.W. (1948). *The Management of Marketing Costs*. Boston, MA: Harvard University Press.

Cutlip, S.M., A.H. Center, and G.M. Broom (1994). *Effective Public Relations*, 7th edn. Upper Saddle River, NJ: Prentice Hall.

Dod (1993). *Dod's Parliamentary Companion 1993*. Hurst Green: Dod's Parliamentary Companion.

Dod (1998). *Dod's Parliamentary Companion 1998*. Hurst Green: Dod's Parliamentary Companion.

Doig, A., and J. Wilson (1995). "Untangling the Threads," F.F. Ridley and A. Doig (eds), *Sleaze: Politicians, Private Interests and Public Relations*. Oxford: Oxford University Press, pp. 14–30.

Donaldson, B. (1998). *Sales Management: Theory and Practice*. London: Macmillan.

Doney, P.M., and J.P. Cannon (1997). "An Examination of the Nature of Trust in Buyer-Seller Relationships," *Journal of Marketing* 61 (April): 35–51.

Ford, D. (ed.) (1990). *Understanding Business Markets: Interaction, Relationships, Networks*. London: Academic Press.

Foxall, G.R. (1994). "Environment-impacting Consumer Behaviour: A Framework for Social Marketing and Demarketing," in M.J. Baker (ed.), *Perspectives on Marketing Management* IV. Chichester: Wiley.

Gabriel, Y., and T. Lang (1995). *The Unmanageable Consumer*. London: Sage.

Gopalakrishna, S., J. Williams, G. Lilien, and I.K. Sequeira (1995). "Do trade shows pay off?" *Journal of Marketing* 59 (3): 75–83.

Gould, P. (1998). *The Unfinished Revolution: How the Modernizers Saved the Labour Party*. London: Little Brown.

Grabher, G. (1993). "Rediscovering the Social in the Economics of Interfirm Relations," in G. Grabner (ed.), *The Embedded Firm: On the Socioeconomics of Industrial Networks*. London: Routledge.

Granovetter, M. (1973). "The Strength of Weak Ties," *American Journal of Sociology* 78: 1360–1381.

Granovetter, M. (1974). *Getting a Job.* Cambridge, MA: Harvard University Press.

Granovetter, M. (1985). "Economic Action and Social Structure: The Problem of Embeddedness," *American Journal of Sociology* 91: 481–510.

Grant, W. (1989). *Pressure Groups, Politics and Democracy in Britain.* London: Philip Alan.

Greer, I. (1997). *One Man's Word: The Untold Story Of the Cash-for-Questions Affair.* London: Andre Deutsch.

Gronroos, C. (1994a). "From Marketing Mix to Relationship Marketing: Towards a Paradigm Shift in Marketing," *Management Decision* 32 (2): 4–20.

Gronroos, C. (1994b). "Quo Vadis, Marketing? Toward a Relationship Marketing Paradigm," *Journal of Marketing Management* 10 (5): 347–361.

Grunig, J., and T. Hunt (1984). *Managing Public Relations.* Fort Worth, TX: Harcourt Brace Jovanovich.

Hainsworth, B., and M. Meng (1988). "How Corporations Define Issue Management," *Public Relations Review* 14 (4): 18–30.

Häkansson, H. (ed.) (1982). *International Marketing and Purchasing of Industrial Goods: An Interaction Approach.* Chichester: Wiley.

Häkansson, H., and J. Johanson (1992), "A Model of Industrial Networks," in B. Axelsson and G. Easton (eds), *Industrial Networks: A New View of Reality.* London: Routledge.

Halinen, A., and J-A. Törnroos (1995). "The Meaning of Time in the Study of Buyer-Seller Relationships," in K.E. Moller and D.T. Wilson (eds), *Business Marketing: An Interaction and Network Approach.* Boston, MA: Kluwer.

Halinen, A., and J-A. Törnroos (1998). "The Role of Embeddedness in the Evolution of Business Networks," *Scandinavian Journal of Management* 14 (3): 187–205.

Harris, P., and A. Lock (1995). "Machiavellian Network Marketing: Corporate Political Lobbying and Industrial Marketing in the UK," in P. Turnbull, D. Yorke, and P. Naude (eds), *Interaction, Relationships and Networks: Proceedings of the Eleventh IMP Conference* III, September 7–9, Manchester Federal School of Business and Management.

Harris, P., and A. Lock (1996). "Machiavellian Marketing: The Development of Corporate Lobbying in the UK," *Journal of Marketing Management* 12 (4): 313–28.

Harris, P., and N. O'Shaughnessy (1997). "BSE and Marketing Communication Myopia: Daisy and the Death of the Sacred Cow," *Journal of Risk Decision and Policy* 2 (1): 29–39.

Harris, P., D. Moss, and N. Vetter (1999). "Machiavelli's Legacy to Public Affairs: A Modern Tale of Servants and Princes in UK Organizations," *Journal of Communication Management* 3 (3): 201–217.

Heath, R.L. (1990). "Corporate Issues Management: Theoretical Underpinnings and Research Foundation," *Public Relations Research Annual* 2: 29–65.

Heath, R.L. (1997). *Strategic Issues Management: Organizations and Public Policy Challenges.* Thousand Oaks, CA: Sage.

HMSO (1994). *Register of Members' Interests as at 31st January 1994,* London: HMSO.

HMSO (1995). *Register of Members' Interests as at 31st January 1995,* London: HMSO.

HMSO (1996). *Register of Members' Interests as at 31st March 1996,* London: HMSO.

HMSO (1997). *Register of Members' Interests as at 31st March 1997.* London: HMSO.

Horan, C.P., D. McLoughlin, and S. DeBurca (1998). "A Preliminary Assessment of the Impact of IMP Literature on Scholarly Research: A Citation Analysis," in *Proceedings of the Fourteenth IMP Annual Conference, Interactions, Relationships, and Networks.* September 3–5, Turku: School of Business Administration.

Howard, J.A., and J.N. Sheth (1969). *Theory of Buyer Behavior.* New York: Wiley.

Institute of Public Relations (1994). *The Registration of Political Lobbyists.* London: IPR.

Jordan, G. (ed.) (1991). *The Commercial Lobbyists.* Aberdeen: Aberdeen University Press.

Kronvall, M., and J-A. Törnroos (1998). *Understanding Event Marketing Management: A Case Study of Nokia Balalaika Show in Berlin,* Meddelandeden Working Papers, No. 372, Helsinki: Swedish School of Economics and Business Administration.

Laycock, P.J. (1983). "The Four Ps: A Production Orientated Approach to the Study and Teaching of Marketing," in M. Christopher, M.H.B. McDonald, and A. Rushton (eds), *Proceedings of the 1983 Marketing Education Group Annual Conference, Back to Basics: The Four Ps Revisited,* Cranfield Institute of Technology, July.

Layder, D. (1993). *New Strategies in Social Research.* Cambridge: Polity Press.

L'Etang, J. (1996). "Corporate Responsibility and Public Relations Ethics," in J. L'Etang and D. Layder (eds), *New Strategies in Social Research.* Cambridge: Polity Press.

Lock, A., and P. Harris (1996). "Political Marketing: Vive la Différence!" *European Journal of Marketing* 30 (10–11): 21–31.

Maarek, P.J. (1995). *Political Marketing and Communication.* London: Libbey.

MacAskill, E. (1997a). "Civil Service makes way for Blair's Elite," *Guardian*, June 3, p. 3.

MacAskill, E. (1997b). "Ministers Plan Further Measures on Eradication of Landmines," *Guardian*, October 29, p. 9.

MacAskill, E. (1998). "Do Party Conferences Matter Any More?" London: *Guardian* Media supplement, September 21, pp. 1–3.

Mack, C.S. (1997). *Business, Politics, and the Practice of Government Relations*. Westport, CT: Quorum.

Meng, M. (1992). "Early Identification Aids Issues Management," *Public Relations Journal* 47 (3): 22–24.

Möller, K., and A. Halinen-Kaila (1998). "Relationship Marketing: Its Disciplinary Roots and Future Directions," *Proceedings of the Twenty-seventh European Marketing Academy Conference (EMAC)*, Stockholm, 20th–23rd May.

Moloney, K. (1996). *Lobbyists for Hire*. Aldershot: Dartmouth.

Morgan, R.M., and S.D. Hunt (1994). "The Commitment-Trust theory of Relationship Marketing," *Journal of Marketing* 58 (July): 20–38.

Morris, D. (1999). *Behind the Oval Office: Getting Re-elected against All Odds*. Los Angeles: Renaissance Books.

Neill, Lord (1998a). *Fifth Report of the Committee on Standards in Public Life, The Funding of Political Parties in the UK* I, *Report*, CM 4057-I. London: TSO.

Neill, Lord (1998b). *Fifth Report of the Committee on Standards in Public Life, The Funding of Political Parties in the UK* II, *Evidence*, CM 4057-II. London: TSO.

Newman, B. (1994). *The Marketing of the President*. Thousand Oaks, CA: Sage.

Nolan, Lord (1995a). *First Report of the Committee on Standards in Public Life* I, *Report*, CM 2850-I. London: HMSO.

Nolan, Lord (1995b). *First Report of the Committee on Standards in Public Life* II, *Transcripts of Oral Evidence*, CM 2850-II. London: HMSO.

Norton, P. (1997). "Parliamentary Oversight," in P. Dunleavy, A. Gamble, I. Holliday, and G. Peele (eds), *Developments in British Politics*. London: Macmillan.

O'Cass, A. (1996). "Political Marketing and the Marketing Concept," *European Journal of Marketing* 30 (10–11): 62–75.

O'Shaughnessy, J. (1987). *Why People Buy*. Oxford: Oxford University Press.

O'Shaughnessy, J. (1992). *Competitive Marketing: A Strategic Approach*, 2nd edn. London: Routledge.

O'Shaughnessy, N. (1990). "High Priesthood, Low Priestcraft: The Role of Political Consultants," *European Journal of Marketing* 24 (2): 7–23.

Ramsey, R. (1998). *Prawn Cocktail Party: The Hidden Power behind New Labour*. London: Vision Paperbacks.

Ramsey, R.P., and R.S. Sohi (1997). "Listening to your Customers: The Impact of Perceived Salesperson Listening Behaviour on Relationship Outcomes," *Journal of the Academy of Marketing Science* 25 (2): 127–137.

Ratzan, S.C. (ed.) (1998). *The Mad Cow Crisis: Health and the Public Good*. London: UCL Press.

Roloff, M.E. (1981). *Interpersonal Communication: The Social Exchange Approach*. Beverly Hills, CA: Sage.

Sabato, L. (1981). *The Rise of Political Consultants*. New York: Basic Books.

Schmitz, J.M. (1995). "Understanding the Persuasion Process between Industrial Buyers and Sellers." *Industrial Marketing Management* 24 (4): 83–90.

Scott, J. (1991). *Social Network Analysis: A Handbook*. London: Sage.

Searing, D.D. (1994). *Westminster's World: Understanding Political Roles*. Cambridge, MA: Harvard University Press.

Self, P. (1993). *Government by the Market? The Politics of Public Choice*. London: Macmillan.

Smith, M.J. (1993). *Pressure Power and Policy: State Autonomy and Policy Networks in Britain and the United States*. Hemel Hempstead: Harvester Wheatsheaf.

Smith, M.J. (1995). *Pressure Groups*. Manchester: Baseline Books.

Souza, C. (1998). *So You Want to be a Lobbyist? The Inside Story of the Political Lobbying Industry*. London: Politicos.

Strandvik, T., and J-A. Törnroos (1995). "Studying Relationships in Industrial and Services Marketing." Paper presented at the Eleventh IMP Conference, Manchester Federal School of Business and Management, September 7–9.

Traverse-Healey, T. (1978). *The Rationale, Methodology and Management of Public Affairs and Public Relations and Practical Issue Management*. Oxford: Centre for Public Affairs.

Turnbull, P.W., and J.P. Valla (1986). *Strategies for International Industrial Marketing*. London: Croom Helm.

Van Schendelen, M.P.C.M. (ed.) (1993). *National, Public and Private EC Lobbying*. Aldershot: Dartmouth.

Weitz, B.A. (1981). "Effectiveness in Sales Interactions: A Contingency Framework," *Journal of Marketing* 45 (winter): 85–103.

Williams, J.D., S. Gopalakrishna, and J.M. Cox (1993). "Trade Show Guidelines for smaller Firms." *Industrial Marketing Management* 22: 265–275.

# PART II

# Tools, Techniques, and Organizing for Public Affairs

Tender your advice with modesty.

(Niccolo Machiavelli)

The field of corporate public affairs (PA) has transitioned from its origins some five decades ago to becoming a more mature field. Although public affairs has not yet achieved the status of a "professional" field (Fleisher, 1998b), the nature of the managerial activities, processes, and tools and techniques employed by PA practitioners have evolved and become more sophisticated. Contemporary PA tools and techniques reflect an improved understanding and means for addressing varied issue and stakeholder-based challenges and opportunities. This part of *The Handbook of Public Affairs* examines the range of tools and techniques employed in PA practice. It provides discussion, examples, and observations about the contexts in which they are used and their efficacy.

Chapter 8 by Amy Showalter and Craig Fleisher provides a helpful introduction to the evolution of strategies and tactics for influencing public policy making. The tools and techniques of public affairs, some of which are state-of-the-art while others are "tried and true" classics, include the range of activities, functions, practices, processes, and/or tactics designed to help an organization to achieve its non-market strategy. Many of these activities have been adopted from other fields, such as political science and political studies,

social organizing, legal affairs, and political management, and have been adapted expressly for business or corporate public affairs purposes. In some cases, the business or corporate PA applications have come to constitute leading-edge practice and are expanding the envelope beyond some of the technique's original intentions or capabilities.

The authors examine a wide range of organizational public affairs techniques such as lobbying, environmental (including issue and stakeholder) monitoring and scanning, grass roots, constituency building, electoral techniques like "Get Out The Vote" (GOTV), issue advertising, political action committees, PA and corporate social audits, judicial influence techniques such as Strategic Lawsuits Against Public Participation (SLAPPs), advisory panels and speaker's bureaus, volunteerism, sponsorships, Web activism, coalitions and alliances, and community investment, among others. The authors emphasize the necessity for PA practitioners to be aware of the various tools at their disposal and to know when, where and how they can best be utilized. One thing that should help them know these contingencies is the increasing number of meetings held by professional associations and other groups in various countries that are dedicated to discussing the contexts and nature of their use.

The second chapter in this part, by Patrick Shaw, president of the consultancy firm

Quorum Strategic, of Toronto, introduces a strategic approach to how PA practitioners can plan and manage their career paths. Shaw emphasizes the importance of how a successful PA or PR professional must think about themselves and their careers if they are to maximize the opportunities available to them in the field. Shaw notes that opportunities are expected to increase for PA practitioners in the foreseeable future, and how the roles are expected to be dispersed through existing career tracks in organizations as well as in distinct PA-related paths as well. He notes the wide range of organizational roles PA practitioners can adopt, such as change communications, executive counseling, issue analysis and management, and research and measurement, among others. Shaw offers evidence that suggests these will be increasingly utilized by senior executives in knowledge-based enterprises.

Shaw provides a number of hands-on, active-oriented exercises that the practitioner can use to help better understand the ways in which they can benefit their organizations. Included among these are suggestions for identifying capabilities, improving interview skills, and for honing one's personal marketing approach. He ends the chapter by describing the nature of compensation earned by practitioners, which is not too dissimilar from other more established managerial positions in fields like marketing and advertising, for example, and may potentially increase at a better rate in the future as organizations recognize the unique attributes that practitioners can bring to the decision-making table and/or as the field better organizes to continue professionalizing itself (see also Fleisher, 2003, 2002a, b, c, 1998b).

Craig Fleisher offers the third chapter in this part, in which he looks at the ways in which PA performance can be assessed. He notes that decision makers have long wondered how to appropriately resource the function of public affairs and have struggled with decisions about establishing proper budgets and allocating satisfactory resources to the area. Practitioners have also struggled with this, as surveys often disclose that they are unable to demonstrate their value or worth to executives in tangible ways that easily fit in with existing notions of

value creation or generation in businesses (Ferraro, 2000). The ubiquitous hope of finding the measurement Holy Grail, shooting the evaluation silver bullet, or acquiring the public affairs ROI calculation on a disk have made many practitioners feel akin to Don Quixote tilting at windmills.

Fleisher notes that there is hope on the horizon, as has been demonstrated through both research and practice. He notes that there have been several research studies that have been conducted into this area that have shed light on what works and doesn't work as well in terms of providing convincing evidence to individuals outside of the area that PA management is being conducted effectively and efficiently, if not efficaciously (Fleisher, 1998a, 1997, 1995; Grunig and Grunig, 2001; Lindenmann, 2001). Fleisher further brings into focus the key practical and scholarly challenges facing those trying to accurately assess PA performance as well as some guidance already generated for those intent on doing it better than their current practice allows. He concludes his chapter by providing guidance to managers who are focused on improving their management of the process of PA performance assessment as well as providing direction to researchers who are intent on improving their understanding of this often seemingly intractable area.

Chapter 11 by Grefe and Castleman is on one of the practices of public affairs that has likely shown the greatest development since the 1990s, that being the use and application of information and communications systems and technologies (ICSTs). The authors begin by relating a story they experienced and how the effective application of ICSTs had allowed some organizations to clearly stay ahead of the curve. Others, lacking the applications, were similarly disadvantaged in trying to influence the public policy process using the old-style tactics that failed to utilize ICSTs. The authors make a convincing case that ICSTs are not a fad and are becoming an institutionalized and accepted part of the public policy process and that the failure to recognize or employ them is similar to riding horse-drawn carriages on superhighways.

The authors proceed to identify some of the more interesting ICSTs that have been employed in business and corporate PA applications. Included among these are the use of Web monitoring for sociopolitical intelligence, grassroots databases to motivate an organization's friends and family on key issues, e-mail, cellular telecommunication, and online advocacy tools. The authors note that the future looks even more promising in terms of being able to employ ICSTs like personalized portals and instant text messaging in PA practice as practitioners, public policy officials, and PA ICST providers and specialists better understand how to work with and effectively employ developing technologies and systems in creating and forging powerful relationships that make the difference in terms of achieving positive policy outcomes. Practitioners and organizations who fail to heed the changes wrought by technology will increasingly fail to win public policy battles where their issue adversaries have learned to effectively employ these systems and technologies.

Chapter 12, on structuring the PA function, by Martin Meznar, examines the question of how public affairs is organized or structured in organizations. Because it serves the role of a boundary spanning function, Meznar insightfully notes that the ideal structure for public affairs in an organization is ofttimes dependent on the organization's larger strategy as well as the nature of the environmental context in which the organization operates. Meznar reviews a number of the key studies conducted on strategy-structure-environment configurations, particularly as it impacts the establishment of the organization's appropriate sociopolitical strategy and structure configuration.

Meznar and Nigh (1995) suggested that *bridging* (attempting to change the organization to fit the environment) and *buffering* (attempting to change the environment to fit the organization) could be considered PA strategies, although the two strategies are not necessarily exclusive and firms could practice both of them to varying degrees (Meznar and Nigh, 1993). Meznar proceeds to look at the impacts of the environment on PA strategy, and PA strategy on PA structure, as well as the

need for matching or aligning strategy, structure, and environment. Meznar ends his chapter by noting the critical implications that the complexity and turbulence caused by globalization will have on future PA structure and strategy decisions. He suggests that there is no "one right way" to structure a PA function, and that it will be wise for organizational and PA decision makers to consider the different structural configuration choices in light of evolving strategic and environmental conditions.

This section encompasses a wide range of tools and techniques that affect how public affairs is practiced in contemporary organizations. It makes a strong case that PA practice will require insightful managerial decisions and continuous learning on the part of practitioners. The challenges facing future PA practitioners will surely require a level of knowledge, skills, and abilities that will supersede that being demonstrated in today's practice. The tools and techniques employed in future PA practice may or may not be available today, and those organizations that show the innovativeness to try new tools and techniques in resolving the PA issues facing them may indeed achieve some temporary nonmarket or sociopolitical advantages. More permanent forms of advantage will be acquired by those organizations that learn to continuously stay on the leading edge of the developments in these areas and that have developed the appropriate strategies and structures for navigating their business and public policy challenges.

## REFERENCES

Ferraro, R. (2000). *Considerations for Measuring Public Affairs' Value*. Public Affairs Management Report, Washington, DC: Public Affairs Council.

Fleisher, C.S. (1995). *Public Affairs Benchmarking: A Comprehensive Guide*. Washington, DC: Public Affairs Council.

Fleisher, C.S. (1997). *Assessing, Managing, and Maximizing Public Affairs Performance*. Washington, DC: Public Affairs Council.

Fleisher, C.S. (1998a). "A Benchmarked Assessment of the Strategic Management of Corporate Communications," *Journal of Marketing Communications* 4 (3): 163–76.

Fleisher, C.S. (1998b). "Do Public Affairs Practitioners Constitute a Profession?" in *Proceedings of the Fifth Annual International Public Relations Symposium*, Bled, Slovenia.

Fleisher, C.S. (2002a). "The State of North American Higher Education in Corporate Public affairs," *Journal of Public Affairs* 2 (1): 436–40.

Fleisher, C.S. (2002b). "The Evolving Profile, Qualification and Roles of the Senior Public Affairs Officer," *Journal of Public Affairs* 2 (2): 90–4.

Fleisher, C.S. (2002c). "Analysis and Analytical Tools for Managing Corporate Public Affairs," *Journal of Public Affairs* 2 (3): 167–72.

Fleisher, C.S. (2003). "The Development of Competencies in International Public Affairs," *Journal of Public Affairs* 3 (1): 76–82.

Grunig, J., and L. Grunig (2001). *Guidelines for Formative and Evaluative Research in Public Affairs: A Report for the Department of Energy Office of Science.* College Park, MD: White Paper.

Lindenmann, W. (2001). *Public Relations Research for Planning and Evaluation.* Commission on PR Measurement and Evaluation, special report. Gainsville, FL: Institute of Public Relations.

Meznar, M., and D. Nigh (1993). "Managing Corporate Legitimacy: Public Affairs Activities, Strategies, and Effectiveness," *Business and Society* 32 (1): 30–43.

Meznar, M., and D. Nigh (1995). "Buffer or Bridge? Environmental and Organizational Determinants of Public Affairs Activities in American Firms," *Academy of Management Journal* 38 (4): 975–96.

# 8

# The Tools and Techniques of Public Affairs

AMY SHOWALTER AND CRAIG S. FLEISHER

Corporate public policy management, strategies, and tactics for influencing public policy making continuously evolve. The tools and techniques of public affairs (PA), some of which are state-of-the-art while others are "tried and true" classics, include the activities, functions, practices, processes, and/or tactics designed to achieve organizational non-market strategy. This chapter describes and discusses the practices of organizational public affairs techniques such as lobbying, environmental (including issue and stakeholder) monitoring and scanning, grassroots, constituency building, electoral techniques like "Get out the Vote" (GOTV), issue advertising, political action committees, public affairs and corporate social audits, judicial influence techniques such as Strategic Lawsuits Against Public Participation (SLAPPs), advisory panels and speaker's bureaus, voluntarism, sponsorships, Web activism, coalitions and alliances, and community investment. Among the authors' key intentions is to highlight the necessity for PA practitioners to be aware of the various tools at their disposal and to know how, when and where they can best be utilized.

## LOBBYING

What once was the exclusive domain of the professional lobbyist to influence public policy is now comprised of numerous tools and techniques, each calling for its own staff expertise. From direct lobbying to PAC contributions to "Get out the Vote" drives, organizations now enjoy a myriad of tactics to advance their cause with their stakeholders, the public, the media, and, most important, their elected representatives. The triumvirate tools of grassroots, political action committees (PACs) and lobbying still reign supreme, but there are numerous tools for the progressive public affairs professional that, adeptly engaged, can result in short- and long-term project success.

When most fledgling advocacy groups want to impact the public policy process, they think first of lobbyists, and quickly hire one. Lobbyists have enjoyed the spotlight for infinity, it seems. With the plethora of input from constituents, the media, other legislators, and legislative staff, lobbyists represent an agile, focused source of expertise on their particular industry or cause.

The term "lobbyist" evolved in the early nineteenth century. From stories of "lobby agents" in the New York State Capitol to the more commonly known story of the Willard Hotel in Washington, DC, serving as the meeting site for legislators and those seeking favors, by the mid-1800s the term had been shortened to "lobbyist" and a new profession was born.

In a strict sense, lobbyists are utilized to articulate the effects of proposed legislation on their organization to legislators, as well as to promote legislation that will grow market share, and provide compelling reasons why legislators should defeat certain proposals.

However, their role involves much more than simply sharing this information and persuading legislators. They are often called upon to coordinate meetings between elected officials and organization leaders, to research the short- and long-term impact of proposed legislation and regulations, attend legislative and regulatory hearings, work with coalitions interested in the same issues, and educate organization leaders on the impact and status of their legislative priorities.

Some politically partisan lobbyists also host fund raisers and raise money for legislators. In organizations with few resources, they also administer the organization's political action committee and grassroots programs.

Lobbyists who coalesce philosophically with certain legislators are also called upon to help draft legislation, amendments, and public policy pronouncements. The actual implementing legislation for the Contract with America was written, in part, by a group of lobbyists who financially supported the Republican Party and who agreed to support the entire Contract that came out of the process. The American Petroleum Institute helped draft legislation that would reduce liabilities from toxic wastes. Lobbyists for corporations wrote the legislation on regulatory relief that limited the ability of the bureaucracy to enforce existing environmental and worker safety rules (Greider, 1992).

Because lobbyists' effectiveness is often determined by the breadth and quality of their legislator relationships, one of the inherent challenges to the professional lobbyist is how to advance their issues—and, frankly, their career—when the electorate determines who they work with and the positions of power they occupy. Particular obstacles to lobbying success revolve around the term-limited legislator. At the most recent count, eighteen states limit the number of terms a state legislator can serve in a particular legislative chamber. It is difficult for the lobbyist to maintain relationships with an ever changing cadre of legislative committee chairpersons and legislative leaders.

## GRASSROOTS LOBBYING

Grassroots lobbying involves engaging group members and/or others with a stake in an issue to persuade lawmakers to support the group's public policy goals. Because legislators depend on voters to advance their career through re-election, constituent grassroots input is a potent tool to influence legislators to vote with their constituents.

It's no longer a matter of if, but when, an organization will mobilize its members or stakeholders to get involved in their legislative cause. In the 1980s and early 1990s grassroots lobbying was considered an advantage in the legislative influence process. Now, it's essential for accomplishing favorable legislative outcomes. The wildly successful use of grassroots lobbying in the Clinton health care reform proposals and NAFTA in 1993 and 1994 made true believers out of many who believed that grassroots activism was "nice but not necessary" for winning legislative issues.

One of the main strengths of an active grassroots organization is that it gives an elected official a compelling reason to support the organization's point of view. Legislators understand the language of constituent concern, and in some high-profile issues, understand that constituent concern translates into votes on election day.

There are several varieties of grassroots communications and organizing. There are internal programs, where an organization communicates with and mobilizes its employees and/or association members. "Third-party" grassroots communications and organizing is a term used for engaging ancillary groups that may be peripherally impacted by an issue. *Ad hoc* grassroots communications and organizing is, unfortunately, a very common grassroots tactic that is initiated when an issue critical to an organization or interest arises. *Ad hoc* grassroots is characterized by reaction and hastily prepared communications.

Because virtually every organization with a stake in the public policy process has some kind of grassroots capability, the enduring challenge and potential weakness of grassroots tools is the lack of grassroots communications authenticity. This is commonly referred to as an "astroturf" approach to grassroots involvement. The Competitive Long Distance Coalition, later named the Unity Coalition, called individuals who used certain companies' long-distance services and asked them questions about their services. The coalition then sent multiple letters on behalf of those whose answers were in agreement with the coalitions' positions. It was later revealed that many of these grassroots "advocates" did not know that information was being sent on their behalf. Legislators, rightly, are trying to ascertain the sincerity and authenticity of constituent communications. Thus, the organizations that facilitate the development of committed, sincere advocates will have an advantage in the legislative process.

Another constant challenge is the belief by many organizations that their advocacy Web site, annual legislative reception, or Action Alerts comprise a true grassroots program, thereby neglecting the necessary ingredients for a continuous, authentic grassroots presence. These events or features are certainly *ingredients* of a successful program, but as stand-alone features they do not constitute a true grassroots *program*. A program is a continuous effort not only to persuade people to become advocates for your issues, but also to educate them about the legislative process, provide access to elected representatives, create a sense of teamwork, and recognize stellar advocates.

There are numerous ingredients of a successful grassroots program. Very generally, the essential disciplines are advocate persuasion, recruitment, retention, motivation, recognition, mobilization, and target persuasion. No matter what tools are used in grassroots organizing, mastery of these disciplines will help to determine a group's grassroots success.

## ELECTORAL TECHNIQUES

The erosion of voter turnout has resulted in organizations taking responsibility for mobilizing voters sympathetic to their cause. Associations and, increasingly, corporations conduct voter registration and "Get out the Vote" (GOTV) drives to engage their supporters during the election season.

There has been a steady decline in the size and number of non-partisan voter organizations. In the mid-1960s, 2.4 of every 1,000 women over the age of twenty belonged to the League of Women Voters, compared with 0.79 in 1998 (Putnam, 2000). Virtually every membership organization has witnessed a decline in members. Thus, the electoral efforts of associations and corporations serve a necessary and vital role in mobilizing voters.

Ultimately, the goal of mobilizing organization members and employees should be not only to get them to the polls, but for them to vote for candidates who support their public policy issues. There is no body of research to prove that this goal is uniformly achieved, especially within the corporate setting.

Anecdotally, the 2000 Kentucky congressional race won by freshman Republican Ernie Fletcher versus former Republican Scotty Baesler (D) was in part attributed to a grassroots voter mobilization effort among business people. The US Chamber of Commerce expanded its voter mobilization efforts in 2000 due to the numerous competitive races with candidates who exhibited distinct philosophical views. The chamber targeted twenty-five House races and ten Senate contests. The organization mailed thousands of voter toolkits to state and local chambers as well as to businesses that wanted to participate in the effort (Malbin *et al.*, 2002).

Increasingly, organizations use these techniques to organize likeminded individuals, regardless of whether they belong to their organization. Once they have their names from their response to a grassroots call to action, they can also encourage their favorable voting behavior.

The advantages of voter mobilization are realized not only on election day. If the organization has a structure to support the newly mobilized voters, it can leverage its electoral involvement toward greater grassroots activity when critical issues come before legislators. Citizens for a Sound Economy (CSE) routinely focused their electoral techniques on television advertising. In 1996, that changed. They recognized the need to build a sustainable grassroots network, rather than to invest in campaigns without catapulting that investment into a viable grassroots community. After the 1996 election, they established state chapters throughout the country that now mobilize on issues related to taxation and free enterprise (Malbin *et al.*, 2002).

Groups that use only one technique to mobilize do not usually realize the long-term benefits of an ongoing grassroots network. With the ease of technology tools, many novices neglect the powerful yet still under-utilized electoral mobilization technique: personal voter contact. Labor unions, known for their personal approach to political organizing, have formalized this approach with real results. In the 2000 election, union members made over 8 million phone calls and sent out more than 14 million pieces of mail. David Broder remarked on this achievement in a 2000 post-election column:

> What has been a seat-of-the-pants judgment is now drawing strong support from controlled experiments conducted by political scientists. Eighty-one percent of union members who received a personal contact at work or at home supported the labor-endorsed candidates last year. The union household share of the electorate increased from 23 percent to 26 percent.

## PUBLIC POLICY ENVIRONMENTAL MONITORING, RESEARCH AND SCANNING

Many public affairs practitioners have two primary missions in life: monitor or scan the public policy environment for changes in direction and fulfill the immediate needs of superiors and internal customers when they ask for specific data on public policy actions and events. One of these activities happens day to day and is ongoing in nature while the other occurs on an as-needed basis and takes place in the form of *ad hoc* requests or stakeholder research in the form of focus groups, (stakeholder) opinion polling, or surveys.

This dichotomy characterizes the complex nature of modern public affairs (PA). On the one hand, the pace of constant change in public policy markets and within firms makes it necessary for companies to continuously leverage new knowledge they learn about issues and the environment, while they struggle to fulfill research requests coming from front-line policy makers and field personnel that need mission-critical public affairs to execute more immediate business goals. This continuum of information gathering creates a PA process that at once must capture insight as events occur and integrate this "fresh" understanding with existing repositories of public policy data that might be months or even years old. These two very different processes form the core of how organizations act on the public affairs that is made available to the firm and can be described in two discrete forms of PA work flow: Environmental Scanning/Monitoring and Research.

Since some PA units are chartered during times of strife, PA managers often begin by attacking a small number of event-driven research objectives with very short deadlines and great importance to the long-term health of the firm. Here's an example: the firm's lobbyist knows from discussion with regulatory committee members that a new foreign competitor wants to enter the domestic market with a new, unregulated technology—presenting a competitive threat to the firm's established line of business. Management will often find its strategy lacking about how to react to this new entrant and "draft" a sales manager, PA specialist, and/or legal expert to head up the research effort. Usually the project is accompanied by the absurdly vague mission of "finding out everything there is to know about ..." the research target and the technology.

The results of such a project tend to be highly speculative and are often out of date by the time the project is complete. One reason causing this is that each of the experts drafted will have a unique perspective for addressing the threat. Furthermore, the concept of reacting to competitor initiatives in the public policy and competitive marketplaces becomes troublesome in terms of strategy and planning—the goal is to anticipate. If the PA unit is lucky enough to survive this first, scattershot project, this *ad hoc* quality of initial event-driven research eventually becomes much more seamlessly integrated with the PA objectives of the organization. Once customers learn how to make requests that get results and processes are developed to manage PA activities more appropriately, the PA unit begins to learn the subtleties of its sister discipline, environmental scanning.

Environmental scanning is usually the next phase of development for the sophomore PA unit. This process involves regular, ongoing monitoring of the public policy environment, issues, and stakeholder initiatives, so as to avoid surprises. Environmental scanning also involves monitoring other central public policy issues important to the firm that might either present new opportunities or threaten the firm's position in the marketplace. This includes topics such as federal or state legislation and regulation, technological advances made outside the industry, or investments made by the various industry organizations associated with the sector.

However, environmental scanning does not necessarily turn up immediately useful nuggets for decision makers. For example, a pharmaceuticals firm might learn that its competitor has recently cited previous technologies in a patent application filed in Europe (patent applications are public documents in Europe, unlike the United States), while, at the same time, they've begun importing particular organic compounds from Brazil (available in public records as well) and have begun hiring scientists with specialties in a particular field of antibiotic drug approval. None of these pieces of information means much on its own; it is the synthesis of the various bits of information that might lead the pharmaceuticals firm to begin drawing some conclusions about where their competitor is headed—perhaps foreshadowing the introduction of a new antibiotic compound some years hence.

This is very much the nature of scanning one's environment—bringing together the parts of an equation that represent meaningful "foreknowledge" of where a competitor or stakeholders might be headed in the future, rather than where they've already been. The firm that begins to integrate the workflow processes of *ad hoc*, event-driven research with those of environmental scanning begins to realize the true power of proactive public affairs. This involves nothing less than the ability to predict the probable futures with which issues will evolve and stakeholders will behave and formulate countervailing strategies to help the organization beat them to new opportunities.

Once a company has regularized the scanning and *ad hoc* processes with internal customers, it can begin to automate collection of primary (i.e., lobbyists and executives) and secondary research sources (i.e., roll calls, congressional agendas, regulatory committee coverage, etc.) and delivery mechanisms to end users. *Ad hoc* research is rarely an automated or self-service kind of procedure. By definition, *ad hoc* research is event-driven in terms of specifically defining the objectives of the research request and communicating interim results of the research to the internal client as the project unfolds. *Ad hoc* projects benefit a great deal from being as diligent as possible with customers, even to the point of knowing "why" the research is sought after by the customer in order to add context and give clues to the analyst about the best techniques for collection. So how can *ad hoc* PA research be applied to a self-service context?

Self-service research is best applied to locating *ad hoc* public affairs that has already been conducted or by connecting the PA client with a subject-matter expert that may have either made such a request or previously conducted her own research. This way, *ad hoc* requests can be fulfilled by existing documents on the network that have already been authored or by the authors of those documents themselves. Many modern corporate information or knowledge-based systems—PC Docs/Fulcrum, Dataware, Lotus among others—help users identify subject-matter experts based upon the documents that others have authored. For example, a company seeking out an expert on "mergers and acquisitions activity in the financial services sector in Southeast Asia" might simply find the author of any number of topically similar documents and ask them the questions they seek answered. In this context, public affairs has left the PA unit altogether and gone to the periphery, usually accelerating the pace of delivery and improving its "actionability". When PA users are able to connect with one another rather than using the PA unit as a broker, organizations can begin to realize the true value of public policy environment knowledge. As they begin to materialize, these internal, de facto subject-matter experts can also become very important PA sources for the public affairs staff as well.

Environmental scanning activities are much better suited to self-service or automated methods of delivery. Because internal PA consumers are now able to search against a lexicon of similar keywords to isolate density of terms within a document or digital source, the consumer can automate the process of retrieving updates on their own. Or, the PA staff can customize a delivery profile for news items they discover during their scanning for delivery in a daily e-mail message, on a personal home page or using push technology.

One of the most exciting areas of change in the self-service and automation of public affairs comes in the form of intelligent agents. Intelligent agents search for new information on a particular range of subject matter and deliver it to users as it appears, rather than hoping the user will perform a fresh search on their own. While simple agent-like effects can be built into search engines, like adding a date field to the search engine which will run new searches, the most exciting agent technology detects changes in documents and alerts users to those changes when they appear. For example, there are many free services which will track changes to Web sites and deliver an e-mail message to users when a change of any kind is detected.

The PA research process potentially brings critical insight to business decision making. It monitors organizational stakeholders' strategic intent while interpreting important trends in the overall business and public policy environment to identify opportunities and threats. In this way, PA research can be used as a tool for managing and making sense of the vital information buried in an increasingly complex and crowded external environment.

The process will define elements of the information value chain and establish the key topical needs. Prior to delivering information to its customers, a PA unit:

1  Talks with its customers about their true information requirements.
2  Works with them to prioritize the topics according to relative value.
3  Identifies appropriate meetings to maintain presence in planning loops.
4  Communicates current issues to the field to focus collection efforts.
5  Coordinates all forms of information collection.
6  Develops techniques to monitor the topics.
7  Analyzes the results looking for patterns and nuggets of true public policy environment intelligence.
8  Creates appropriate action-oriented reports.

Public affairs focuses on creating value by targeting the needs of its customers so as to deliver customized services and products. It is critical to an organization's understanding of stakeholders' actions, issues and customers' desires. It integrates with the planning process so that there is a constant feedback and refreshment mechanism. Done well, this tool is one of the best to connect PA strategy to business strategy and for demonstrating business impact.

## POLITICAL ACTION COMMITTEES

Political action committees (PACs) constitute one of the "big three" of public affairs tools, the others being lobbying and grassroots. Political action committees represent a fund for political contributions made up of money from an organization's members and/or employees. Ostensibly, the money goes to candidates and legislators who exhibit favorable behaviors toward an organization's public policy goals. Ideally, PACs are a way for organizations to elect candidates that promote their public policy positions and agree philosophically with their legislative beliefs. Unfortunately, many organizations utilize them to obtain access to candidates and elected officials, which solidifies the public's belief that PACs are a nefarious aspect of the political system.

An effective PAC enables an organization to elect and keep candidates with similar philosophies in office. When a PAC accomplishes this goal, its lobbying and grassroots efforts are easier. Lobbying elected officials who essentially agree with your organization's goals takes less time and effort.

The most successful PACs are constantly recruiting new contributors. *Ad hoc* PAC recruitment tactics are usually exhibited by groups who do not embrace a culture of positive political participation. An *ad hoc* approach is a major shortcoming of any PAC. The very capricious nature of the recruitment process communicates to members that the PAC isn't very important. Another weakness is not in the PAC itself, but in how it's used. Again, giving PAC contributions for access attenuates its unsavory image in the eyes of contributors.

The fundamentals of PAC development and management include, in the case of corporations, securing senior management support, and in the case of associations, securing board member support of the PAC (Kennerdell, 2001). "Support" in meaning not only their contributions to the PAC, but their *active advocacy* on behalf of the PAC.

A formal recruitment plan is essential. Without it, potential PAC contributors are not aware of the PAC except when they are asked for money, and as expected, they have no impression of it at all, or a negative one by virtue of the media's coverage of PACs.

The PAC recruitment is enhanced when accompanied by a consistently executed employee or member education program. The education component can be facilitated through the grassroots program, or be independent of the grassroots, as certain information can only be provided to an organization's PAC-eligible employees. For example, a PAC can inform its members and PAC-eligible employees of the candidates endorsed by the PAC, as well as engage in express advocacy, whereby it urges PAC members to vote for certain candidates.

The effective PAC also has clear, written, and easily accessible criteria for candidate contributions. Lack of criteria adds to a negative PAC image. Written criteria also give assistance to the lobbyist who is constantly pursued by candidates and legislators seeking a PAC contribution, yet do not exhibit the voting behavior of a PAC-worthy candidate or legislator.

## JUDICIAL INFLUENCE TECHNIQUES

As evidenced by the ongoing battles over the use of tobacco products, the consumption of fast food, or the constitutionality of tort reform legislation, the courts have emerged as another tool for organizations to achieve their public affairs goals. The judicial system, while normally thought of as a last resort for resolving public policy goals, is becoming an increasingly common tactic in addressing what a legislative body either will not address, or won't address to a group's satisfaction, and most commonly, in attempting to overturn enacted legislation. As a result, judicial influence techniques have been growing exponentially.

The intentions behind involvement in judicial elections are not dissimilar to the strategies behind giving financial contributions to candidates. An interest group's mission is accomplished with more ease if individuals with similar philosophies serve in legislative office and the judiciary.

From a state perspective, judicial politics interest groups took a more active role in judicial elections in the early 1990s. This may have been due to the intense media scrutiny in Alabama's judicial politics. Alabama received media attention for the costly battles between trial lawyers and civil defense interests in Alabama Supreme Court elections. The 1994 Alabama Supreme Court elections saw an acrimonious battle between trial lawyers and business groups who backed different candidates for the available seats. The genesis of this increased engagement was a 1993 Supreme Court decision that had declared unconstitutional the package of tort reform legislation enacted by the Alabama state legislature (*Henderson X. Roe Hartsfield v. Alabama Power Company*, 627 So.2d 878, Alabama, 1993).

Ohio has also faced intense interest-group involvement in judicial races. Business groups and the trial bar regularly battle for their chosen candidates to serve on the State Supreme Court. The Ohio elections have been so high-profile that they were one of the four states chosen by the Constitution Project of Washington, DC, to conduct extensive voter education efforts on court races.

The Michigan Chamber of Commerce, the Michigan State Medical Society, and Michigan trade associations created an organization to influence Michigan judicial elections in the mid-1990s.

On a national level, the American Tort Reform Association, a national pro-business-interest group, and the Michigan group have published evaluations of the Michigan Supreme Court to determine the extent to which judges reflect pro-business values (Ankeny, 1998). Wary of aligning themselves with a potentially negative media image, many industries now pay for specific research to clarify the decisions of state Supreme Court judges and analyze them for their degree of industry support.

The continuing emphasis of state judicial elections is further demonstrated by the US Chamber of Commerce's development of the Institute for Legal Reform to support the election of pro-business judges in Alabama, Illinois, Michigan, Mississippi, and Ohio. The institute will make direct campaign contributions and pay for issue advertising.

Interest groups are also involved beyond making campaign contributions to judicial candidates. One drawback to the increased interest group activism in the courts is that the new

"judicial politics" has resulted in a perception among the public of less justice. A survey (Champagne, 2001) of public opinion on the judicial system found that 81 percent of respondents believe that "judges' decisions are influenced by political considerations." Seventy-eight percent believe that "elected judges are influenced by having to raise campaign funds." These national survey findings are supported by state surveys.

## CORPORATE OR ISSUE ADVERTISING

*Time* magazine published a special January 11, 1999, edition about the future of medicine. This particular issue contained nearly forty pages of eye-catching advertisements sponsored by Pfizer, a global pharmaceutical firm headquartered in New York. Pfizer's institutional advertising included both product-focused ads as well as a number of ad pages aimed at promoting a favorable public image of the firm. Readers learned about Pfizer's history, its concern for family and women's health, innovative research programs and its long-standing commitment to service and improving American life. On one of the issue's final pages, Pfizer shifted its focus toward editorializing against government-led reform or renewed regulation of the health care system and shared its view that the free market provided a superior health care environment. This effort by Pfizer is an example of how corporate or issue advertising can be used by an organization in support of PA objectives.

Corporate or issue advertising has as its primary objective the promotion of the corporation and its interests as a whole (Marchand, 1987, 1998). This contrasts with product/service advertisements which specifically try to sell particular commercial offerings (Margulies, 1981). While conceptually this distinction is fairly straightforward, there are cases where it is difficult to distinguish one from the other, particularly in the case of what have been termed "hybrid ads" which explicitly deal with both dimensions simultaneously (Winkleman, 1985).

It is not surprising that the resources devoted to product/service ads greatly outweigh resources devoted to corporate advertising—regarding both practice and research (Schumann *et al.*, 1991). It is well established that product/service advertising has much wider use and emphasis in current corporate practice and that corporate advertising dealing with the promotion of the corporation as a whole is ill defined, misunderstood, and confused in the minds of many business practitioners (Margulies, 1981). Nevertheless, corporate or issue ads have been identified as an important tool for improving the corporate image, particularly in the area of overcoming public distrust of business (Berry, 1984). It is also expected that, given greater pressure to be responsive to such issues as environmental responsibility, gender equality, and health and safety, corporations will increasingly turn to corporate ads to improve their images and reputations with the general public (MacKiewicz, 1993).

Several typologies exist which differentiate various types of corporate ads. Schumann *et al.* (1991) use a typology developed by Rothschild (1987), arguing that it provides a "convenient categorization" for organizing the major forms of corporate advertising. The categories used in the typology are as follows: image, financial, special opportunity message, and issue/advocacy. The most important distinction is between image and issue advertisements. However, Rothschild further differentiates image messages as those directed to the financial community and also addresses unique opportunities as separate categories. The benefits of advertising to the financial community have been debated. Some argue that the financial community is likely to be neutral, if not negative, towards resources spent on corporate ads (Garbet, 1981). Some limited studies, however, indicate at least temporary stock price and financial reputation advantages to companies using corporate ads (Berkman and Gilson, 1987; Zetti, 1983). One conceptual problem with focusing on the financial community as a target is differentiating whether the investment decision makers are personally influenced by the ads, or whether they anticipate a positive public response which would, in turn, impact the performance of the company performance.

Another typology, developed by Meadow (1981) arises from his efforts to assess the impact of corporate advertising on the political process. The ten categories Meadow uses for this are: (1) image, (2) informative, (3) public interest, (4) participation, (5) patriotic, (6) free enterprise, (7) controversy, (8) equal time, (9) advertorial, (10) recruitment. This typology offers interesting delineations of corporate advertising types with specific implications to the political and public policy developmental process; however, there is considerable overlap and confusion in defining corporate advertising with this amount of detail. For example, an ad concerning taxation of a certain industrial sector could be simultaneously included in the categories of controversy, public interest, and advertorial. Empirical research utilizing detailed categorical treatments of this nature is likely to result in only small increments of understanding as compared with using fewer and broader categories based on previous studies on this topic (Meadow, 1983).

A commonly accepted distinction within corporate advertising is between image and issue ads (Reisman, 1989). Image ads focus on trying to directly shape how the corporation is perceived and viewed in the public image. Issue advertising, on the other hand, involves the corporation communicating a position on a controversial issue. "Issue advertising" is commonly used interchangeably with the term "advocacy advertising" (Sethi, 1987).

An important distinction within both issue and image advertising is that they can either be related or unrelated to direct corporate actions. For example, related image ads emphasize good practices associated with the business activities of the company (e.g., quality, employee relations, sourcing policies), whereas, unrelated image ads focus on good deeds done by the company which go beyond regular business activities (e.g., philanthropy, cause support, corporate giving). This distinction is clearly aligned with Preston and Post's (1975) distinction of primary and secondary involvements, related ads being associated with primary involvements and unrelated ads associated with secondary (or tertiary) involvements.

An example of an unrelated image ad by a foreign-owned MNC is the series of print ads which tout Toyota's philanthropic donations to the United Negro College Fund. In contrast, a related image ad by Honda emphasizes the amount of goods they export back to Japan, with the intention of emphasizing the good they do for the US balance of payments.

Similarly, issue ads may be related to issues confronting the company (e.g., taxation, regulation, foreign competition), or they may be unrelated and thereby directed towards issues which do not directly impact the firm (e.g., patriotism, drug abuse, battered wives). Just as with the differences between product/service and corporate ads, with each distinction mentioned there may be some disagreement on the fringes requiring expert judgment in the operationalization of distinctions.

In their comprehensive summary of the research in corporate advertising, Schumann et al. (1991) summarize the theory and practice of the corporate advertising form. They note that while annual totals of corporate advertising spending have reached well over US $100 million in certain years, this is relatively small as a percentage of total advertising spending, comprising less than 1 percent of the total. An important point to remember, however, is that the bulk of corporate advertising is done in print media, which are considerably less expensive than television in terms of both production and time slots. These authors also argue that such public image mechanisms are likely to increase in the future and have been shown to function as an effective and persuasive public affairs tool.

## WEB ACTIVISM

What once was accomplished through direct mail and newsletters has been transferred to the Internet, or, in the case of a corporation, its company intranet. Web activism is fast, inexpensive, and saves time. Interest groups are using it to inform and mobilize the public, their own members, and third-party groups who have an ancillary interest in their issues.

Some have predicted that Web activism would be the great equalizer between established interest groups and those with less financial and human resources. However, a comparison of the sites of established groups and those with fewer resources demonstrates that resource-rich groups are more likely to have sites that exhibit more content, more attractive graphics, and more technical innovations. Wealthy organizations have the luxury of updating their sites daily, and are more likely to have interactive features (Davis, 1999).

There are several challenges to effective Web activism. Keeping the Web site current, and providing information that can't be readily accessed elsewhere are paramount. There must be value and exclusivity in the site's content. Password-protected access for exclusive, strategic information is necessary. Also, links should be provided not only to likeminded organizations, but to the sites of one's legislative opponents. Virtually every organization with an advocacy Web site includes links to form letters and e-mails that, by typing in one's zip code, can be automatically sent to their elected representatives.

The greatest challenge, and reward, of Web activism is to create an offline community of local advocates with broad geographic reach. This is the apex of Web activism. This most recently has been exemplified by US presidential candidate Howard Dean's online momentum in 2004. While the campaign's electronic communications and fund raising were impressive, the electronic organizing was used to create groups of local supporters who informed each other of campaign events, met to attend rallies, wrote personal letters to Dean supporters in other states, and so forth. This is perhaps the ultimate advantage of Web activism: to create a *community* of committed grassroots advocates.

Electronic mobilization via e-mail is fast and inexpensive. However, the immutable challenge in any grassroots communications medium is ever present in e-mail communications: keeping the attention of the intended audience. Great care should be taken to encourage advocates to open and read e-mail communications. The subject line must reveal why an issue is urgent, as well as why the e-mail should be opened. According to learning expert and author Abby Marks-Beale, people read 25 percent slower on the screen than traditional print. Therefore, PA professionals should be cognizant of an e-mail message's length, font size, and color, the amount of graphics that must be downloaded, and so forth. For an in-depth exploration of this topic, see Chapter 11.

## COALITIONS

Coalitions are one of the most frequently utilized tools of public affairs. The rise in coalition participation is due to the dramatic difference in the way that the Congress, state legislatures, and even local governments conduct business. It is also a product of the realization that every interest group has its own constituency that can bring pressure to bear on a legislator, therefore making it harder for them to say no to that interest group member than to another interest group that is not a member of a coalition.

Coalitions allow organizations to have a greater influence reach among their targeted legislators. In the formerly strict congressional seniority system, people could rely heavily on relationships between a committee chairperson and an industry lobbyist. Now there may be as many as five or six committees and their attendant subcommittees have jurisdiction over specific issues. This puts many interest groups in a precarious influence position when they do not have grassroots presence with those particular legislators. Thus, the coalition creates more reach and access.

A coalition is simply an alliance of organizations representing different perspectives, all with a common issue. They are formed around a common interest or problem in order to unite resources and maximize each one's influence with a particular legislative body.

The best coalitions have the involvement and commitment of all stakeholders, clear leadership, group agreement on the vision and mission for the coalition, and assessment of member needs and identification of member resources. Once these initial building blocks are established, the effective coalition creates short- and long-term objectives, develops an action plan and implements it, and evaluates the group's work and goal attainment.

Ideally, a major coalition priority is to develop an explicit policy goal around which the groups can coalesce. Often it's somewhat nebulous, such as promoting school vouchers, or preventing tax increases on a particular product, but it must be clear enough so that the organizations can identify themselves as being for or against it. One flaw of coalition development is the lack of principles guiding the coalition. For example, an organization should be able to point to guiding principles driving an issue so that they can quickly mobilize their support.

Kevin Hula's research with interest group leaders for his book *Lobbying Together* (1999) noted that many group leaders admitted that a key rationale for coalition membership is to "Show their membership that the Washington staff is busy." Hula surmises that "some group leaders view participation in a coalition as a low-cost trophy that they can deliver to their membership to demonstrate activity on issues."

Some coalitions are permanent, some are formal and enduring. Some are predictable, such as environmental groups working together on the Arctic National Wildlife Refuge Drilling Proposal; others are more intriguing, as when the Christian Coalition and the American Civil Liberties Union (ACLU) joined forces to oppose lobby reform legislation.

Many coalitions adopt names and frame their mission in terms of the public interest, but they may be led and financed by narrow interests. For example, the National Wetlands Coalition is a group of oil drillers, land developers, and major gas companies. The Consumer Federation is dominated by Sears (Hernson *et al.*, 1997). Nevertheless, many coalitions are authentic, cooperative initiatives, such as the Asbestos Alliance. The Asbestos Alliance is a non-profit organization composed of asbestos defendant companies, trade associations, insurers, and others seeking congressional legislation to solve America's asbestos litigation crisis.

## CORPORATE COMMUNITY RELATIONS, INVESTMENT AND VOLUNTARISM

What is corporate community relations (CCR) and why is it an important tool available to the PA practitioner? Two scholars who have studied the field offer the following definition in that CCR refers to the relations between an organization and the communities (local, national, and/or global) in which it resides or has an impact. They suggest that it encompasses programs which advance the mutual interests of the organization and its stakeholding communities through the provision of all kinds of financial donations and contributions, employee voluntarism, community-based programs, relationships with civic, professional, and non-profit organizations, and corporate citizenship activities (Waddock and Boyle, 1995).

Companies get involved in CCR for a large number of reasons. Among the more prominent ones are self-interest, direct and indirect benefits, reputation, and image. More specifically, they might also be done in order to:

1  Demonstrate corporate citizenship/statesmanship.
2  Improve the business environment.
3  Offer employees new benefits.
4  Generate public relations/marketing/image benefits.
5  Be altruistic.
6  Show stakeholders the nature of the commitment of senior officers or directors.
7  Respond to pressure from stakeholders.
8  Favorably influence human resources (especially those given to education).
9  Respond to mandates from various levels of government (banks and the Community Reinvestment Act).
10  Counteract negative images.

Companies carry out CCR in one of two basic ways:

1  *Community involvement programs.* This is voluntarism in the form of an organization donating the time and talent of its managers and employees. Among the more commonly used activities would be voluntary programs, literacy programs, technical assistance, organizational board memberships, disaster relief, and executive loan programs.
2  *Corporate giving/charitable contributions/philanthropy or social investing.* This involves primarily the giving of financial or product/service donations. It mainly includes giving to the third sector (non-profits), fund raising for the United Way and other collective fund raising efforts and matching gifts, or even institutional advertising aimed at benefiting community organizations.

A major facet of most CCR programs is to make social investments. These investments are made in a variety of different causes, among other things:

1  Educational institutions or causes (continues to be the primary recipient) primarily focused on math, science, engineering, and technology learning.
2  Social services, health and human services.
3  Civic/urban community affairs.
4  The arts, cultural organizations.
5  Other (patriotic activities, religious, special athletic events).

A number of prominent organizations have utilized CCR to distinguish themselves in their community environments. These companies are often recognized through benchmarking exercises as being "best practice" CCR organizations (Fleisher, 1995). Examples of these include the following:

1  Hewlett Packard, Intel, Motorola, Apple, TI: educational efforts in local communities.
2  Home Depot: assists with making available affordable housing, provides materials grants.
3  Microsoft: information technology for underserved populations, library online.
4  Proctor & Gamble: provides cash, products and land to food banks, the American Red Cross, and the United Way.

Those PA operations that will succeed using CCR in the future will have a number of distinctive characteristics, including:

1 *Strategy.* Public affairs will seek to actively connect CCR activities and operations to competitive advantage. In order to achieve this, it will need better systems for understanding the links between stakeholder and corporate competitive needs. The organizational move toward strategic contributions, strategic CCR, and strategic voluntarism will have been permanently institutionalized. This is to suggest not that some organizations will stop pursuing CCR activities just on the moral/ethical merits of good citizenship, but that the best funded and best managed programs will increasingly be in organizations which utilize a "strategic" approach because they are encouraged to be accountable for the resources spent on CCR activities. CCR activities will be increasingly viewed by senior executives and operating division managers as providing a competitive edge that results in marketplace advantages, since the traditional market-based sources of competitive advantage have been imitated faster and easier than before.

2 *Staffing.* Successful PA operations actively link CCR activities and operations to other infrastructural functions. In other words, all CCR activities may potentially have marketing, communications, public affairs, government relations, planning and human resource management implications. For this connection to occur, organizations need to continue to raise the knowledge, skills, and abilities of CCR personnel. Increasingly in the future the typical CCR professional will have either come from another of these functions (if moving internally) or will be a serious contender for key positions as they become available in these functions. There will also be greater recognition of the value of CCR activities in a number of important university programs, mostly in the larger US cities (e.g., New York, Boston, Philadelphia, and Washington, DC) which experience a unique set of community issues. This will mean that students get exposed to CCR concepts, if not direct CCR study streams, within not only management or business school programs but also programs of social work, urban planning, political science, and sociology among others.

3 *Structural changes toward virtual organizations.* In order for organizations to respond to community needs (not just the geographically neighboring community but communities from all over the globe) CCR and PA functions will need to change toward virtualized forms. Such structural efforts will allow these organizations to balance the meeting of local and global needs, both within the organization and within the community.

4 *Systems.* Successful CCR departments will increasingly use technology to support their activities, including such things as communicating with internal and external stakeholders via the Internet and intranets, using electronic means for communicating funding/grant criteria, and taking contribution requests electronically, among other things.

5 *Style and posture.* Corporate community relations activities may eventually be part of a larger function in the organization responsible for organizational relationships which combines all the traditional stakeholder-focused functions, including all communications, CCR, environmental, government relations, investor relations, media relations, and public relations. These functions could optimally fall under the aegis of a Chief Relationship Officer reporting direct to the highest level of organizational decision makers and a member of the most important executive-level committees.

6 *Shared values.* Tomorrow's effective CCR practitioners will not face the almost constant legitimacy challenges their predecessors faced. They will increasingly be viewed as a partner at the strategic decision-making table because they have general management competencies on top of their specific CCR capabilities. Business units will seek out CCR and PA professionals as a welcomed and invited partner at the strategic decision-making table.

## CONCLUSION

Public affairs practitioners and departments have a large and varied arsenal of tools available to them in order to influence the public policy environment as well as to accomplish their organizations' business objectives. Many of these tools are long-standing staples of the practitioner (e.g., lobbying, grassroots, political action committees), while others are more modern responses to the changing public policy environment (e.g., Web activism). This chapter has looked at several of these tools in order to give the reader a flavor of the variety available and the way in which they can be used. The successful PA professional and unit will be aware of the full range of tools available to them and is responsible for understanding how and when to most effectively apply them.

## REFERENCES

Ankeny, R. (1998). "Consumer groups, trial lawyers upset over evaluations", *Crain's Detroit Business* 2 November, p. 44.

Berkman, H., and C. Gilson (1987). *Advertising.* New York: Random House.

Berry, W. (1984). "Overcoming Public Distrust of Business," *Business Forum,* winter, pp. 15–19.

Broder, David (2000). "Politicos Rediscover the Direct Approach," *Chicago Tribune.*

Champagne, A. (2001). "Interest Groups in Judicial Elections," Summit on Improving Judicial Selection, *Loyola of Los Angeles Law Review* 34 (4): 1411–1427.

Davis, R. (1999). *The Web of Politics: The Internet's Impact on the American Political System.* New York: Oxford University Press.

Fleisher, C.S. (1995). *Public Affairs Benchmarking: A Comprehensive Guide.* Washington, DC: Public Affairs Council.

Garbet, T. (1981). *Corporate Advertising: The What, Why and the How.* New York: McGraw-Hill.

Greider, W. (1992). *Who will Tell the People?* New York: Simon & Schuster.

Hernson, P.S., R.G. Shaiko, and C. Wilcox (eds) (1997). *The Interest Group Connection: Electioneering, Lobbying, and Policymaking in Washington.* Chatham, NJ: Chatham House.

Hula, K. (1999). *Lobbying Together: Interest Group Coalitions in the Legislative Process.* Washington, DC: Georgetown University Press.

Kennerdell, P. (2001). *The Corporate PAC Handbook, 2001.* Washington, DC: Public Affairs Council.

MacKiewicz, A. (1993). *The Economist Intelligence Unit Guide to Building a Global Image.* New York: McGraw-Hill.

Malbin, M.J., C. Wilcox, M.J. Rozell, and R. Skinner (2002). *New Interest Group Strategy: A Preview of post-McCain-Feingold Politics.* Washington, DC: Campaign Finance Institute.

Marchand, R. (1987). "The Fitful Career of Advocacy Advertising: Political Protection, Client Cultivation, and Corporate Morale," *California Management Review* 24 (2): 128–156.

Marchand, R. (1998). *Creating the Corporate Soul: The Rise of Public Relations and Corporate Imagery in American Big Business.* Berkeley, CA: University of California Press.

Margulies, W. (1981). "A Stepsister to Consumer," *Advertising Age,* July 6.

Meadow, R.G. (1981). "The Political Dimensions of Non-product Advertising," *Journal of Communication* 31 (3): 69–82.

Meadow, R.G. (1983). "Political Advertising as Grassroots Lobbying: New Forms of Corporate Political Participation," *Social Science Journal* 20 (4): 49–63.

Preston, L., and J. Post (1975). *Private Management and Public Policy.* Englewood Cliffs, NJ: Prentice Hall.

Putnam, R. (2000). *Bowling Alone.* New York: Simon & Schuster.

Reisman, J. (1989). "Corporate Advertising," *Public Relations Journal* 45 (September): 21–26.

Rothschild, M. (1987). *Advertising.* Boston, MA: Heath.

Schumann, D.M., J.M. Hathcote, and S. West (1991). "Corporate Advertising in America: A Review of Published Studies on Use, Measurement and Effectiveness," *Journal of Advertising* 20 (3): 35–56.

Sethi, P. (1987). *Handbook of Advocacy Advertising.* Cambridge, MA: Ballinger.

Waddock, S.A., and M-E. Boyle (1995). "The Dynamics of Change in Corporate Community Relations," *California Management Review* 37 (4): 125–140.

Winkleman, M. (1985). "Corporate Advertising," *Public Relations Journal* 42 (December): 38–39.

Zetti, E. (1983). "Reading between the lines of corporate ads", *Advertising Age* 24 January, M9–M16.

# 9

# The Human Resource Dimensions of Public Affairs

*Staffing, Training, Career Paths, Competencies, and Salaries*

PATRICK SHAW

This chapter introduces a strategic approach to planning and managing your public affairs (PA) or public relations (PR) career. In it, we will review how a successful PA or PR professional must think about themselves, and about their career, in order to achieve all that they can be in their chosen field.

The US Bureau of Labor Statistics (BLS) (Franklin, 1997) reports that employment of marketing, advertising, and public relations (including, more broadly, public affairs) managers is expected to increase faster than average for all occupations through the year 2006. According to the US Bureau of Labor Statistics (2004), public relations specialists held about 158,000 jobs in 2002.

## ROLES IN PUBLIC AFFAIRS/PUBLIC RELATIONS

The increased importance of human resources (HR) for PA and PR tracks closely with the rising importance and diverse reach of the public affairs and relations functions. Public Relations is looked upon to deliver two-way communications; providing messages to external and internal audiences as well as returning gathered intelligence and a competitive perspective to management.

> Public relations, at its best, not only tells an organization's 'story' to its publics, but also helps shape the organization and the way it performs. Through research, measurement and evaluation, public relations professionals determine the concerns and expectations of the organization's publics and explain them to management. A responsible and effective public relations program is based on the understanding and support of its publics.
>
> (Public Relations Society of America, www.prsa.org/_resources/profession/careeroverview.asp?ident=profz)

The role of PA or PR professionals continues to be firmly rooted in core skills of writing excellence, general communication and relationship building, and the establishment of trust between parties.

PA or PR jobs, and whole careers, can be found in a range of areas with considerable scope in fulfilling widely described and generally accepted duties. For today's career professional seeking to maximize their contribution to the organization's mandate, it is important to seek opportunities beyond the specific assignment as your role cannot be fully captured in any single job description generally available to management. Few in the organization really comprehend the diverse and wide-reaching impact that a true PA or PR professional can have on management capabilities and the success of the franchise they represent.

PA or PR has many faces in any organization, including:

1 *Communication counsel.* Providing advice to executive or line management in terms of understanding audience or stakeholder concerns, relationship building, and communications coaching in order to achieve the desired business outcomes.

2 *Research and measurement.* Determining and assessing the attitudes, causes and behaviors of key publics in order to support allocation of resources, implement, and measure acceptance or change in behavior or attitudes.

3 *Writing.* The ability to clearly and succinctly present an organization's views or perspective in plain and understandable language is one of the core criteria for an effective public relations career. A wide range of writing and editing expertise is required as you will write for news releases, speeches, video script, Web sites, newsletters, and technical and trade materials.

4 *Media relations.* Understanding of, and relating with, the many streams of business, trade and electronic media in seeking publicity for an organization or in responding to media enquiries and issues.

5 *Marketing and special events.* Combining activities designed to create awareness, sell a product, service or idea, including advertising, the overall look and feel of collateral materials, publicity, promotion, displays, trade shows, and uniquely developed special events.

6 *Employee relations.* Informing an organization's employees or members to ensure they have the appropriate information to effectively understand and represent the organization, serving as point of access to inform management of emerging and upcoming issues.

7 *Change communications.* Working closely with executive, HR, and line management to create understanding and motivation for accepting and implementing change within an organization.

8 *Community relations.* Serving as an 'ambassador' in the community to build relationships, establish trust, understanding, and dialogue between key community members and the organization in order to maintain or enhance interactions to the benefit of an organization and the community where it operates.

9 *Government affairs.* Establishing an understanding of government programs and policies and their impact upon the organization and then working directly with legislatures and regulatory agencies to ensure fair and balanced application and outcomes. Actively involving senior management in public policy development; informing and assisting the organization in adapting to changes in public expectations.

10 *Issues and crisis management.* Identifying and addressing issues of public interest in which an organization is, or should be, concerned before they escalate to crisis proportions. Developing crisis communications plan and response preparedness.

11 *Investor and financial relations.* Building relationships with buy and sell side brokers, establishing communications and timely disclosure programs to support investor confidence and building positive relationships with institutional and retail shareholders. Managing annual meeting and annual report processes.

12 *Philanthropy and development funding.* Developing and implementing policies and procedures to contribute to socially responsible programs and causes that will reflect well upon the organization, its employees, and business purpose.

Encouraging an organization's members, employees, and other supporters to volunteer time and resources toward targeted causes.

This is a functional list of PA or PR roles. Others will evolve as new industries and technologies emerge, as well as there being hybrid roles that cut across a number of these areas. With such a range of roles, the PA or PR professional could progress systematically among them throughout her/his career. Professional development might mean moving through increasingly responsible or complex duties within any given role, or a move across the PA or PR organization to learn and apply skills for a broadly different PA or PR contribution.

## TAKING A STRATEGIC APPROACH TO UNDERSTANDING YOURSELF

It is important that practitioners start with the end in mind. At the same time a blessing and a curse, this course of advice is meant to get us thinking about more than our job interests or career goals, but particularly about our personal goals, values, and principles. These are essential considerations in preparing to step into, or up to, increasingly responsible roles in the public relations area of any organization. With an understanding of these essential truths, you will have the strength, endurance, and the insight to work through the ethical dilemmas or social and business conundrums that will seem to block your path or restrict your effectiveness.

Long before you prepare your first crisis communication or grassroots lobbying plan, you will be dealing with business and ethical issues. Especially for the PA or PR professional, crises reveal character, they don't build it! Getting your personal elements clarified arms you with the level of understanding needed to move into and along your career choice with greater confidence. The familiar maxim rings true: "To thine own self be true."

Human Resources for public affairs or public relations starts with you. Whether you are a recent college grad or a twenty-year veteran, you will benefit personally and professionally from taking time to understand about yourself. Why? Well, when you are doing work that aligns with your personal interests or integrity, you will be more productive and more effective—and a whole lot happier. The more you understand about yourself, the better you will be able to understand, relate to, and connect with others. Wherever you go, employers, coworkers, and audiences like to work with people who like doing what they do. That usually ties to knowing why you are doing what you are doing—again, from the personal and the professional perspective.

The shoemaker's children don't really need to go barefoot. It is a great disservice to the PA or PR profession that practitioners so often constrain their professional efforts to developing reputation plans for employers or clients. Get started on this as an introspective exercise first. Articulate your very own mission and vision or sense of purpose. Be clear on your values and principles. These are essential elements in any strategic communication plan and they are "must do," not simply "would be nice to do," exercises for you to be a strategic career communicator.

Do you have what it takes? There are a few quick assessment tools that can help you grasp the meaning and the significance of your personal preferences style. Your unique approach to dealing with detail, accepting ambiguity, working under pressure, or taking direction, near-term perspective or longer-horizon view, and a host of other personality traits are already developed or well along the way to being solidly embedded in your persona. Unfortunately for us, these characteristics are often easier to see in others than in our own self. Yet when we have a grasp of the vocabulary that goes to describe these traits and their relative prominence in how we respond to the world around us or implement our own plans, we can be much more effective in our own career management and workplace.

The Personal Style Indicator (PSI) is a self-administered and self-scored tool that helps you better understand your own personality style and how it 'fits' in the world around you. It can be purchased and even administered online.

Table 9.1    *Personality trait checklist*

| ✓ | Personal traits | ✓ | Personal traits | ✓ | Personal traits | ✓ | Personal traits |
|---|---|---|---|---|---|---|---|
| | Active | | Decisive | | Intuitive | | Resourceful |
| | Adaptable | | Demanding | | Inventive | | Restless |
| | Adventurous | | Dependable | | Leader | | Rigid |
| | Aggressive | | Diligent | | Loyal | | Sarcastic |
| | Alert | | Diplomatic | | Open-minded | | Self-controlled |
| | Ambitious | | Direct | | Opportunistic | | Sensible |
| | Analytical | | Dominant | | Optimistic | | Serious |
| | Appreciative | | Dynamic | | Organized | | Sincere |
| | Argumentative | | Efficient | | Outgoing | | Sound Judgment |
| | Artistic | | Empathetic | | Outspoken | | Spontaneous |
| | Assertive | | Enthusiastic | | Patient | | Stable |
| | Attentive | | Extravert | | Persevering | | Supportive |
| | Boastful | | Factual | | Pervasive | | Sympathetic |
| | Calm | | Firm | | Philosophical | | Systematic |
| | Carefree | | Flexible | | Playful | | Tactful |
| | Caring | | Frank | | Polite | | Talkative |
| | Cautious | | Fussy | | Practical | | Tenacious |
| | Confident | | Generous | | Problem solver | | Tidy |
| | Conscientious | | Humorous | | Punctual | | Tolerant |
| | Cooperative | | Idealistic | | Realistic | | Tough |
| | Creative | | Imaginative | | Relaxed | | Trusting |
| | Critical | | Independent | | Reliable | | Versatile |
| | Curious | | Introversive | | Reserved | | Visionary |

The Meyers Briggs Personality Type Indicator® (MBTI) is the granddaddy of the Carl Jung-based psychological or personality testing tools. It should be administered by a trained and qualified leader. The debrief that accompanies a properly administered MBTI-type assessment can be comprehensive and very insightful.

The MBTI also has a communications style component. This helps establish a vocabulary around communications that you, your coworkers, and internal networks will find to be empowering and time-saving as you advance your PR initiatives.

A simple and quick assessment of your personality traits can be seen from a self-selection from commonly recognized personality characteristics. In Table 9.1 place a check (✓) beside the top ten to fifteen most prominent personal traits that you think are reflected to others around you. (Ask three to five people who know you or your work habits to complete the worksheets that follow and compare their input to your self assessment—the variances will give you insights to the areas to focus on emphasizing or changing. Ask people who are peers, subordinates, and supervisors. Differences in reporting perceptions are valuable insights too.)

Especially in the PA or PR field, where you are continually attempting to influence others' perception of a service, product, change, or choice, it is important that you have a good grasp of how others view you and of how you see yourself. With this list of the leading traits you perceive yourself to possess or demonstrate, you will be able to better understand how you are viewed by others as you interact in work situations. That understanding will empower your ability to earn the trust of others and influence the actions needed to deliver the outcomes you seek to deliver.

Table 9.2  *Personal values in your work*

| ✓ | Personal values | ✓ | Personal values |
|---|---|---|---|
| | Adventure | | Innovation |
| | Affiliation | | Intellectual challenge |
| | Advancement | | Tranquility |
| | Autonomy | | Knowledge |
| | Challenging issues | | Decision making |
| | Variety | | Fulfillment |
| | Collegiality | | Power |
| | Competition | | Performance rewards |
| | Recognition | | Excitement |
| | Security | | Stability |
| | Speed | | Status |
| | Excitement | | Freedom |
| | Friendship | | Independence |
| | Influence | | Stress |
| | Integrity | | Ethics |
| | Teamwork | | Opportunity |
| | Clarity | | Wealth |
| | Promotions | | Other: |

Public affairs or public relations people often help their organizations define their mission, vision, and values. In thinking strategically about your PA or PR career you need to do likewise for yourself, focusing on the brand of *you*. In Table 9.2, the idea behind this exercise is to identify with a check (✓) the top five values from the following list that you feel are most important to you.

Understanding your personal motivations will help you define your passion for pursuing a particular stream of PA or PR or a specific workplace engagement. With a fundamental understanding of those things important to yourself, you are ready to assess the PR field for the opportunities to contribute your professional capabilities and to further develop your career.

## CAREER DEVELOPMENT

To contribute at a professional level requires a core set of skills and capabilities. To advance in the PA or PR business, either in terms of increasing responsibility or in terms of complexity of organization, it is extremely important to develop the capacity to think analytically, build a true empathy for the players in every situation, portray confidence even under pressure, and present thoughtful, practical solutions grounded in an understanding of legal and practical constraints that can lead to simple, clear, and measurable solutions. These capabilities are developed throughout a PR career as practitioners encounter opportunities to practice their trade, understand their organization's business or interest position, and establish personal and professional integrity essential to further advancement.

In their study of career development among professionals, termed *Novations* by Gene Dalton and Paul Thompson (1993) they describe two concepts that have played out in the career of PA or PR professionals in North America since the transition of the role from that of a mere editorial function to that of trusted executive counsel. The perspective of career *Novations* applies equally for PA or PR practitioners around the globe. The first is the observation that careers develop in distinct stages, each with distinct activities, skills, and relationship requirements. The second realization is that between each distinct state there is an essential renegotiation of expectations and obligations with those around them.

Dalton and Thompson describe four major stages of career growth—what they call the "apprentice," the "colleague," the "mentor," and the "director" stages. They observe that most professionals move readily from "apprentice"

to "colleague," the most common stage and generally associated with what we refer to as the "professional (or seasoned)" PA or PR practitioner. Organizations in different parts of the world use a variety of position descriptions to describe similar PA or PR jobs. For the most part, we could approximate the four stages for the PA or PR role as coordinator, manager, director, and executive or vice-president responsible for PA or PR. Exhibit 9.1 provides a descriptive schematic of these four roles.

---

### Exhibit 9.1 Characteristics of Career Stages

#### STAGE 1 COORDINATOR (APPRENTICE)

- Works under the supervision and direction of a more senior professional.
- Work/assignments are a part of a larger project or activity overseen by a senior professional.
- Generally lacks experience and status in the organization.
- Expected to willingly accept direction.
- Expected to do most of the detailed and routine work on a project.
- Exercises "directed" creativity.
- Learns to work under pressure.

#### STAGE 2 MANAGER (COLLEAGUE)

- Goes into depth on one problem area.
- Assumes responsibility for a definable portion of a project, process, or client.
- Works independently and produces significant results.
- Develops credibility and a personal reputation.
- Develops own resources to solve problems.
- Increases confidence and ability.

#### STAGE 3 DIRECTOR (MENTOR)

- Makes significant technical contributions in own area and begins working in more than one area.
- Greater breadth of technical skills and application of those skills.
- Stimulates others through ideas and information.
- Involved in developing people:

    o Acts as an idea leader for a small group.
    o Serves as a mentor to younger professionals.
    o Assumes a formal supervisory position.

- Deals with the outside to benefit others in the organization.

STAGE 4 VICE-PRESIDENT OR EXECUTIVE (DIRECTOR)

- Provides direction for the organization by:

  o "Mapping" the environment to highlight opportunities and dangers.
  o Focusing activities in areas of "distinctive competence."
  o Managing the process by which decisions are made.

- Exercises formal and informal power to:

  o Initiate action and influence decisions.
  o Obtain resources and approvals.

- Represents the organization to individuals and groups at different levels inside and outside the organization.
- Sponsors promising individuals to test and prepare them for key roles.

*Source* Dalton and Thompson (1993).

Depending upon the individual, and the size and breadth of the organization they are in, there may well be considerable overlap between stages and jobs. There is often more career opportunity in the white space of the organization chart, the undefined territory in the department, than there is within the boxes or specific role or job descriptions.

Public Affairs, Corporate Communications, Public Relations, Corporate Affairs—the function covers a variety of staff services with very similar needs and skill requirements, regardless of the name. It commands specific expertise in many areas, with some demanding specialization and focus, and yet each requires a wide perspective on the industry or issue you are engaged in. Table 9.3 provides a useful diagnostic to objectively compare a self-assessment of PA/PR skills against how a peer and a superior assess your skills.

The seasoned PR professional is first and foremost a 'counselor' whose advice and services are sought by other executives to help their organization implement change of some manner or form. Change of attitude, legislative design, consumer behavior, employee loyalty, public acceptance—everything gets captured in the change perspective.

A PA or PR career could see you working for almost any size corporation; a for-profit or not-for-profit; one listed on a major stock exchange or one privately held, maybe a family corporation; local, regional, or national government, political assistant, or civil servant. There is no single, comprehensive or interchangeable set of qualifications or experience that describes the ideal individual for a career in public affairs or public relations with such a variety of endpoints.

Most think of PR executives as highly articulate, attuned to public issues; individuals of great character and sound judgment, able to build trusting relationships with a wide range of publics. Public affairs or public relations professionals are problem solvers, strategists, creative thinkers, implementers, facilitators, organizers, writers and editors, negotiators, front-line spokespersons and, more often than not, the public face and conscience of an organization. Table 9.4 provides a list of several core organizational competencies in which PA and PR professionals must be adept.

## DEFINING THE PUBLIC AFFAIRS OR PUBLIC RELATIONS POSITION

At some point in your career you will be asked to write, or rewrite, your job description. It may be when you have been in your current role for some time already. It could be that you are just interested in having some better boundaries

Table 9.3   *Core functional public affairs/public relations competencies*

| Core functional PA/PR competency | Assessment | | | Difference and comments |
| --- | --- | --- | --- | --- |
| | Self | Peer | Superior | |
| Communications issues advice and counsel | 1 2 3 4 5 | 1 2 3 4 5 | 1 2 3 4 5 | |
| Effective writing | 1 2 3 4 5 | 1 2 3 4 5 | 1 2 3 4 5 | |
| External networking with PA/PR experts | 1 2 3 4 5 | 1 2 3 4 5 | 1 2 3 4 5 | |
| Internal networking with supporting groups | 1 2 3 4 5 | 1 2 3 4 5 | 1 2 3 4 5 | |
| Oral communications techniques | 1 2 3 4 5 | 1 2 3 4 5 | 1 2 3 4 5 | |
| Understanding our organization | 1 2 3 4 5 | 1 2 3 4 5 | 1 2 3 4 5 | |
| Communications research and evaluation | 1 2 3 4 5 | 1 2 3 4 5 | 1 2 3 4 5 | |
| Appropriate use of communications technology | 1 2 3 4 5 | 1 2 3 4 5 | 1 2 3 4 5 | |
| Media relations procedures, practices and terminology | 1 2 3 4 5 | 1 2 3 4 5 | 1 2 3 4 5 | |
| Philanthropy and contributions management | 1 2 3 4 5 | 1 2 3 4 5 | 1 2 3 4 5 | |
| Generate relevant creative ideas | 1 2 3 4 5 | 1 2 3 4 5 | 1 2 3 4 5 | |
| The in-house role of PA/PR | 1 2 3 4 5 | 1 2 3 4 5 | 1 2 3 4 5 | |
| The role of PA/PR consultants | 1 2 3 4 5 | 1 2 3 4 5 | 1 2 3 4 5 | |
| PA/PR's relationship with other marketing and planning disciplines | 1 2 3 4 5 | 1 2 3 4 5 | 1 2 3 4 5 | |
| Understand how to define measurable PA/PR objectives | 1 2 3 4 5 | 1 2 3 4 5 | 1 2 3 4 5 | |
| Understand the different PA/PR approaches and techniques appropriate for different market sectors | 1 2 3 4 5 | 1 2 3 4 5 | 1 2 3 4 5 | |
| Produce SWOT analyses, competitor analyses and market positioning data | 1 2 3 4 5 | 1 2 3 4 5 | 1 2 3 4 5 | |
| Understand research techniques and social research demographics and audience behavior/opinion | 1 2 3 4 5 | 1 2 3 4 5 | 1 2 3 4 5 | |
| Write proposals, evaluation reports, speeches and presentations | 1 2 3 4 5 | 1 2 3 4 5 | 1 2 3 4 5 | |
| Develop programs for financial analysts, financial media and shareholders | 1 2 3 4 5 | 1 2 3 4 5 | 1 2 3 4 5 | |
| The techniques used in all aspects of public relations | 1 2 3 4 5 | 1 2 3 4 5 | 1 2 3 4 5 | |
| The regulations and regulatory bodies which govern public relations and marketing activities | 1 2 3 4 5 | 1 2 3 4 5 | 1 2 3 4 5 | |
| The regulations and bodies which govern the media | 1 2 3 4 5 | 1 2 3 4 5 | 1 2 3 4 5 | |
| The basics of law as it affects PA/PR initiatives | 1 2 3 4 5 | 1 2 3 4 5 | 1 2 3 4 5 | |

around what you are expected to do. It could be that the organization is "re-engineering," "refocusing," or "resizing." With the insights gained through the exercises outlined in this chapter you will be well along the way to defining your preferred job or describing the key characteristics of the position you determine the organization needs in the pursuit of its mandate. The position analysis questionnaire in Appendix 9.1 will help guide you through a level of dispatched detail that is often difficult for PA or PR professionals to scribe in reference to their own duties. It will provide details on the size and impact of your role, enabling it to be measured in relation to other roles within the organization. The questionnaire can also be used to help you prepare a formal job description for your role.

## PREPARING FOR A CAREER IN PUBLIC AFFAIRS OR PUBLIC RELATIONS

### Academic Qualifications

A university or college degree is an essential starting point for careers in public affairs or public relations. Many stalwart PR professionals made their start with journalism, english, history, communications or commerce degrees.

Table 9.4    *Core organizational competencies*

| Core organizational competency | Self | Peer | Superior | Difference and comments |
|---|---|---|---|---|
| | | Assessment | | |
| How organizations structure themselves and operate within their industry | 1 2 3 4 5 | 1 2 3 4 5 | 1 2 3 4 5 | |
| The legal and ethical responsibilities of a member of the board of directors | 1 2 3 4 5 | 1 2 3 4 5 | 1 2 3 4 5 | |
| Prioritize work load and meeting deadlines | 1 2 3 4 5 | 1 2 3 4 5 | 1 2 3 4 5 | |
| Work as part of a team | 1 2 3 4 5 | 1 2 3 4 5 | 1 2 3 4 5 | |
| Present yourself and your ideas clearly in meetings and presentations | 1 2 3 4 5 | 1 2 3 4 5 | 1 2 3 4 5 | |
| Build good working relationships with clients, media and suppliers | 1 2 3 4 5 | 1 2 3 4 5 | 1 2 3 4 5 | |
| Organize and chair meetings | 1 2 3 4 5 | 1 2 3 4 5 | 1 2 3 4 5 | |
| Set and manage budgets | 1 2 3 4 5 | 1 2 3 4 5 | 1 2 3 4 5 | |
| Give feedback and coach individuals and/or teams | 1 2 3 4 5 | 1 2 3 4 5 | 1 2 3 4 5 | |
| Manage own learning and/or learning of others | 1 2 3 4 5 | 1 2 3 4 5 | 1 2 3 4 5 | |
| Influence and/or manage acceptance of change in the workplace | 1 2 3 4 5 | 1 2 3 4 5 | 1 2 3 4 5 | |
| Business and economic fundamentals | 1 2 3 4 5 | 1 2 3 4 5 | 1 2 3 4 5 | |
| Business practices and controls | 1 2 3 4 5 | 1 2 3 4 5 | 1 2 3 4 5 | |
| Appropriate interpersonal communications | 1 2 3 4 5 | 1 2 3 4 5 | 1 2 3 4 5 | |
| Presentations, negotiation, and interview skills | 1 2 3 4 5 | 1 2 3 4 5 | 1 2 3 4 5 | |
| Understanding and application of ethics in the business environment | 1 2 3 4 5 | 1 2 3 4 5 | 1 2 3 4 5 | |
| Managing stress and conflict resolution | 1 2 3 4 5 | 1 2 3 4 5 | 1 2 3 4 5 | |
| Valuing others and working with diversity | 1 2 3 4 5 | 1 2 3 4 5 | 1 2 3 4 5 | |
| Project management capabilities | 1 2 3 4 5 | 1 2 3 4 5 | 1 2 3 4 5 | |
| Leading teams | 1 2 3 4 5 | 1 2 3 4 5 | 1 2 3 4 5 | |
| The management of organizations, including mission, vision, and operating culture | 1 2 3 4 5 | 1 2 3 4 5 | 1 2 3 4 5 | |
| Results focus and awareness of organizational outcomes | 1 2 3 4 5 | 1 2 3 4 5 | 1 2 3 4 5 | |
| Regulations and bodies that affect the operations of the organization | 1 2 3 4 5 | 1 2 3 4 5 | 1 2 3 4 5 | |
| Confidence and management presence | 1 2 3 4 5 | 1 2 3 4 5 | 1 2 3 4 5 | |

There is a strong case to be made for economics, psychology, education and law as solid educational backgrounds in public relations. Many PA professionals start their career with degrees in business, commerce, management, political science, pre-law, public administration, or several of the more traditional arts disciplines such as psychology or sociology. The road quickly converges for those who engage with an organization that encourages continued professional education.

Professional development is readily available in most major centers through academic continuing education programs at universities or colleges and through groups like the Public Relations Society of America (PRSA), International Association of Business Communicators (IABC), Public Affairs Council (PAC), Canadian Public Relations Society (CPRS), Issue Management Association (IMA), Institute for Public Relations (IPR), the Public Relations Institute of Australia (PRIA), and many other global 'communities of practice' in public affairs or public relations.

According to a Government of Canada (2003) employment and career reference Web site, professional occupations in public relations and communications require the following education, training, and experience:

You usually need a university degree or college diploma in public relations, communications, journalism or a field related to a particular subject. To be a public relations practitioner, you may need an APR (Accredited in Public Relations) designation. With additional training and experience, you may move up the ranks to become a manager in public relations, fundraising or communications. Most recent entrants have an undergraduate university degree, and almost one in ten has a graduate degree.

While the graduate degree is increasingly attractive for employers, in the early stages of your PA or PR career the 'applied science' aspect has led many organizations to seek candidates who bring together the liberal thinking elements often associated with a university degree and the specific and tactical expertise more often associated with a college or trade school education. There are many programs now combining critical elements of each, with solid theory and liberal arts exposure of the university curriculum inextricably linked to a practical communications sequence at an affiliated college.

## Volunteering

Many secondary or high schools have instituted community service requirements in order for students to graduate. Universities are considering these contributions in their entry criteria, looking for well rounded personalities, wanting individuals who have not only achieved academic excellence but who were also involved in their communities in meaningful ways. They want people in their schools who already have a record of contributing through sports teams, church groups, multi-ethnic organizations, school or community committees, etc. The model also holds true in most cases for the PA or PR function.

When a candidate can show commitment and passion not only in the pursuit of their PA or PR career but also in their profession or the community where they live, they are differentiating themselves from hundreds of other candidates less inclined. Besides differentiation, the individual acquires a set of organizational experiences, contacts, and skills that can also be beneficial to them in future PA or PR roles.

## Finding Your PA or PR Job

No job is more demanding than the task of finding a job. As a PA or PR person, you have or will dedicate your working life to promoting the good or needs of others—your organization, special interest group, boss, whatever. Rarely do PA or PR people apply their PA or PR skills to their own career needs. But that is exactly what you must do. If it is your first job, or if you are a consultant and constantly looking for the next assignment, you need to reflect those same PA or PR skills which you bring to the table for your employer toward helping you connect with that next employment opportunity.

The core competency of research will serve you well in your job search. There are many excellent online resources, tools, and listings. The Web is an excellent source for information about your target organization too.

A common rule of thumb states that, 80 percent of the time, employers fill a position before they ever have to go to an agency or place an ad in the career sections of the newspapers. You need to network to find those soon-to-be-filled jobs. The four-stage model of the Hidden Job Opportunity shown in Figure 9.1 depicts the significance of the need to market yourself before jobs are posted.

## Networking

Networking is about maintaining, developing, and expanding relationships with people you know, or would like to know, for the purpose of exchanging mutually beneficial information. One of the most effective methods for gathering and exchanging information is through networking. If you are looking for a career in public affairs or public relations you need to get good at this. It will be your networks that help land the job, and it will certainly be your networks that enable you to successfully execute the many and diverse tasks you will face in your role. There are six key networking functions or purposes: advise, sponsor, inform, teach, nurture, and connect. At different times, each of these elements will take on a more meaningful and urgent character in your career.

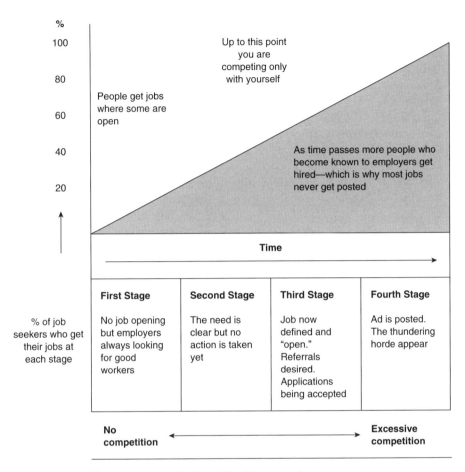

The four-stage model of the hidden job opportunity

Figure 9.1   *The hidden job market.* Source *KPMG Consulting Services*

Networking needs to be deliberate, focused, and reciprocal. It is not spontaneous, manipulative, or one-sided. Networking requires that you know what you want: you must have a clear objective, and then move ahead in a deliberate yet engaging manner. Networking is a reciprocal endeavor. People who devote their time and insight to you deserve something in return, so listen carefully in those sessions to learn what it is you can offer them. Anticipate your networking target's response, needs, distractions. Prepare and rehearse your initial call and contact script just as you would prepare for a job interview. Exhibit 9.2 provides ten useful rules of networking that will assist job seekers in exploring opportunities in the PA/PR sector.

---

### Exhibit 9.2 Ten Rules for Building and Nurturing an Effective Network

1  There are really only twenty people in the world who count. You may need to contact 2,000 to figure out who the twenty are, and then focus your efforts.
2  Keep a personal mailing list up to date. You can't start without it.

3   Practice Malthusian math—1, 2, 4, 8, 16 … Never leave a meeting/interview without two other contact names.
4   Write a thank-you note. Thank those who take the time to talk to you about your issue. Always open the door to people younger than you.
5   Keep in touch but not with junk. Send something that is of value to that person—something they wouldn't have yet seen but would appreciate.
6   Give books, not booze. If you are giving something as a gift, make it something that they will remember, appreciate, but are not likely to pick up for themselves or have access to.
7   Volunteer and work in the community. Combine your interest and skills, but don't work on speculation just with the hope of getting the job. Remember the twenty person rule.
8   Court the media. Give them what they need – information or story ideas.
9   Court the head hunters. Why rob banks? Because that's where the money is! Head hunters are job collectors. Stay in touch.
10  Host your favorite heroes. Arrange luncheons that will align you with influential speakers that you may have access to but your clients/customers don't. They will remember you for this favor! Hook on to stars in the business sense.

*Source* Ramsay (1997).

## Interviewing: Success Stories

It is widely and commonly noted that 87 percent of communication is non-verbal. So why emphasize telling a great story? The answer is that all the non-verbal excellence will go for nothing if the facts don't support the "face" you put on the situation. Certainly, applicants need to be well groomed, confident, and firm in their entrance and initial interaction. Interviewers commonly claim they can size up a candidate in the first few minutes of an interview. The stories offered by the candidate, however, need to be deliberate and on target too.

Probably the most common request in any interview is "Tell me about yourself." This is at the same time terrifying and yet a terrific opening, if you are adequately prepared. As the interviewee, you have the chance to deliver a two-minute uninterrupted pitch on your fit for the job at hand. This is the time to *focus on the three to five strengths* you want the interviewer to recall long after you leave.

Telling your success stories requires using active language to describe your capabilities and interests. Review the interests and skills

listed in Table 9.5 and add others you might come up with. Then work through the entire list; in the column in front of the skill or capability indicate a P (primary) or S (secondary) skill or strength you are strongest or most interested in. From Table 9.5 select the top five items that best describe you, your interests and capabilities. Identifying the skill areas you are most interested or capable in is but one step. Now write out specific examples of how you used that skill or developed that interest area.

Skill or interest No. 1

Example of how you used skill or interest No. 1

Skill or interest No. 2

Example of how you used sill or interest No. 2

Skill or interest No. 3

Table 9.5   *Interests and skills relevant for public affairs/public relations*

| P/S | Skill | P/S | Skill | P/S | Skill | P/S | Skill | P/S | Skill |
|-----|-------|-----|-------|-----|-------|-----|-------|-----|-------|
| | Acting | | Consulting | | Fund raising | | Modeling | | Restoring |
| | Advising | | Controlling | | Generating | | Motivating | | Revising |
| | Allocating | | Coordinating | | Guiding | | Negotiating | | Rewarding |
| | Analyzing | | Corresponding | | Imagining | | Newness | | Risk assessing |
| | Arranging | | Costing | | Improving | | Numbers | | Risk taking |
| | | | Counseling | | Innovating | | Persuading | | Scheduling |
| | Assembling | | Creating | | Inspecting | | Photographing | | Selling |
| | Assessing | | Customer care | | Interpreting | | Piloting | | Serving |
| | Auditing | | Debating | | Interviewing | | Planning | | Sketching |
| | Bargaining | | Deciding | | Inventing | | Playing | | Sorting |
| | Budgeting | | Defining | | Investigating | | Preparing | | Speaking |
| | Building | | Delegating | | Isolating | | Presenting | | Speed |
| | Buying | | Demonstrating | | Documenting | | Printing | | Supervising |
| | Calculating | | Designing | | Drafting | | Problem solving | | Talking |
| | Calling | | Directing | | Driving | | Programming | | Testing |
| | Changing | | Displaying | | | | Promoting | | Timing |
| | Challenging | | Distributing | | Leading | | Proof reading | | Training |
| | Coordinating | | Editing | | Listening | | Purchasing | | Translating |
| | Coaching | | Encouraging | | Maintaining | | Questioning | | Troubleshooting |
| | Collecting | | Estimating | | Managing | | Reading | | Tutoring |
| | Competing | | Experimenting | | Marketing | | Reconciling | | Typing |
| | Compiling | | Evaluating | | Measuring | | Recording | | Writing |
| | Composing | | Filing | | Meeting | | Recruiting | | Other |
| | Computers | | Following | | Memorizing | | Reducing | | |
| | Constructing | | Forecasting | | Mentoring | | Repairing | | |

Example of how you used skill or interest No. 3

Skill or interest No. 4

Example of how you used skill or interest No. 4

Skill or interest No. 5

Example of how you used skill or interest No. 5

Use these active interest examples to help describe past situations you have encountered that are particularly relevant to the role being considered. Identify and link appropriate strengths and skills to the job at hand. Close

your monologue with a summary comment of your current situation and interest in the contribution you would like to make to the organization. Then ask a friend to listen to your speech and give you some feedback on the top three things they take away from hearing you say it like you mean it.

## Be a STAR

In preparing your success stories, and in responding to questions in an interview, be prepared to demonstrate how your past behavior affected the results you were looking for. Interviewers observe how your past actions and achievements may predict future behavior and how that might apply to their needs. The STAR method of responding to interview questions (shown in Exhibit 9.3) is a tried and true approach for giving structure to your response, enabling you to stay on track and your interviewer to follow and focus on your skills and capabilities.

---

### Exhibit 9.3 **The STAR Interview Method**

| | |
|---|---|
| **S is for Situation** | Succinctly describe the circumstance that existed. |
| **T is for Task** | Your analysis or assessment of what needed to be done. |
| **A is for Action** | What and how you applied one of the skills you want the interviewer to be able to recall at the end of the interview. |
| **R is for Results** | The outcome or measurable achievement and how that benefited your organization. |

---

Whenever possible cite quantifiable data as part of the outcomes—you will see the interviewer make notes immediately. It is far more compelling, and simpler, to record numbers than words. When preparing for an interview, consider the exercise from the interviewer's perspective. Think about the position description: what are the defined requirements of the role? Identify the key responsibilities, qualifications and skills. Consider a position analysis: determine the skills that would be success factors for effective performance. Anticipate the questions: for each anticipated success factor anticipate at least one question the interviewer may ask. And finally, prepare answers using the STAR approach and practice rigorously beforehand. Prepare the script of your success stories, write it out, edit it, draft it like you are submitting it for publication. Then practice it out loud, until you are fluent and comfortable with the delivery of this important oral history of your business effectiveness without actually memorizing it. It is important to be enthusiastic and to deliver your story with passion, not as a recital.

## Salaries

Professional associations often conduct compensation studies. You can access these through your membership or for a one-time access fee. They are broad benchmark references only. Do not undersell yourself, but also be realistic regarding the market and capabilities you really have to contribute. It is a greater problem living up to expectations generated from an inflated

salary than it is to seek equitable compensation for exceptional work delivered and sustained over time.

According to the Public Relations Society of America (see www.prsa.org), the average entry-level salary (US$) in public relations for a person with a baccalaureate degree is approximately $18,000—$22,000. PSRA reports that an account executive of a consulting firm can earn upwards of $35,000, as will a person with a comparable responsibility in a company's PR department. A PR director for a small to medium-sized organization may earn $35,000 to $40,000, while the range for the large corporation more likely would be $40,000 to $60,000. Salaries from $75,000 to $150,000 are earned by a number of seasoned PR executives, who often carry the title of vice-president.

In Canada the popular job search Web site Monster.co.uk reported in June 2004 that a typical Public Relations Director working in Toronto earns a median base salary of $110,510. Half of the people in this job earn between $92,901 and $129,809. A typical Public Affairs or Relations Manager earns a median base salary of $74,492. Half of the people in this job earn between $65,460 and $89,155.

The Monster.co.uk site in June 2004 lists marketing and PR jobs ranging from £16,000 sterling for an entry-level marketing campaign assistant through a range of mid-career PR functions from £30,000 to £60,000. The most senior marketing manager role can reach £90,000 in salary compensation.

Salaries for PR professionals vary depending upon the industry and the location of the organization. Recently, the higher-paying jobs have been in the larger population centres and among the financial services and health care industries. Most senior positions, certainly director and above, have additional "at risk" salary components. Commonly referred to as "salary bonus" or "performance incentive," these amounts are usually tied to corporate and individual performance towards meeting predetermined goals. Bonuses can add from 25 percent to 50 percent to a person's annual salary. Hiring bonus at the senior level can be 10 percent of a base salary. Other incentives may include car allowance, a loan to purchase company stock and a wide range of other incentives. These vary significantly by industry and the size of the community where you are seeking employment.

For the senior PA or PR professional wondering how to set an appropriate consulting rate, a simple rule is to take your salary, without benefits or allowances, multiply by three (to allow for benefits, office allocations, etc.), and then divide by the number of work days in your business calendar. A person making $100,000 per year would divide 300,000 by say 1,700 hours in the work year, for an hourly rate of, say, $175. This may sound high to the individual starting out or to the corporate PA or PR person retaining counsel. This fee accounts for all those elements otherwise included though not reflected in the annual salary of a staff PA or PR person: things like pension, professional development, technology support, etc.

The financial rewards of working in public affairs or public relations are not only about salary. Having company-sponsored insurance or savings plans may be important. Ensuring flexibility in the work environment and the availability of technology that will support your effectiveness may need to be negotiated and agreed to ahead of moving into a new position. Vacation allowances, fitness or lifestyle aspects, parking, professional development fees, and travel and expense account procedures should all be fully considered and agreed to.

The PA or PR career is a very demanding profession. Timelines are rarely set by the practitioner. Crises happen. The PA or PR professional is nearly always on call, ready to step in and assist senior management on a moment's notice. The rewards can be significant if this is the right fit for your personality and passion.

## THE CAREER COACH

A coach or mentor is a partner with whom you have a trust relationship. They are someone who helps you clarify what most matters in your work and in your life. The coach helps you think through and then organize action steps that let you achieve those meaningful professional and even personal results.

Coaching is about momentum much more than about motivation. Fundamentally you, as the PA or PR professional, need to have an open mind and a strategic approach to your career for a coach to make a significant contribution to your success. A coach helps you sustain action by helping reframe problems or situations in terms of the opportunities and challenges for you to tackle and learn from. The coach helps you clarify "next steps" and then helps you strive for the needed results even when you don't much feel like it. The coach is not someone you take every little issue or problem to. They are a strategic mentor who can help you think through the difficult or complex dilemmas you may face.

## CONCLUSION

This chapter introduced a strategic approach to planning and managing a career in public affairs (PA) and/or public relations (PR). The PA/PR role is growing both in total numbers employed and in the diversity of roles for which practitioners are responsible. These developments are presenting opportunities for PA and PR professionals to make important contributions to their affiliated organizations and to society in general. In order to optimize these contributions and, indeed, to enhance self-actualization, it is imperative that PA or PR professionals exercise a high level of professionalism in their career management.

Such an approach to career management is comprised of many facets to which PA and PR professionals must explicitly attend. Aspiring PA and PR professionals must engage in 'due diligence' to determine if their personal values, skills, personality traits, and motivations mesh closely with the dynamics and requirements of the profession. In addition to stressing the importance of finding a "good fit" between personal characteristics and career requirements, this chapter has also encouraged PA/PR professionals to actively manage their career development. This means developing a practical toolkit stocked with techniques and approaches that can be useful at all stages in one's career, including: educational qualifications, volunteering, mining the hidden job market, networking, successful interviewing, salary negotiation, career coaching, and managing career development through increasing "stages" of responsibility.

With both a creative and systematic approach to career management, PA and PR professionals can expect to continue to have diverse and wide-reaching impacts on management capabilities and the success of the franchise they represent.

## APPENDIX 9.1 POSITION ANALYSIS QUESTIONNAIRE

### Guidelines for Completing the Position Analysis Questionnaire

- Complete the following questions as they relate to your role.
- Use clear and specific language rather than generalities. If a statement does not add to the reader's knowledge of your position, then leave it out, change it, or add an example.
- Use the active tense and active verbs. Do not use qualifiers (e.g., typically manage complex assignments that are very challenging).
- Do not use personal judgments. For example, do not write, "I run the HR Department"; rather, give the facts that will allow the reader to draw their own conclusions.
- Use simple and concise language supported by examples. Avoid jargon, acronyms or "buzz words."
- Text in italics is offered as examples only.

Name: _____       Date: _____

| | |
|---|---|
| Position title: | *[E.g.] Communications Coordinator* |
| Department: | *Public Affairs* |
| Reports to (name and title): | *Director, Corporate Communications* |
| Receive supervision, direction or work assignments from: | *VP Public Affairs and Government Relations, Director Corporate Communications* |

### Position purpose

Summarize (one or two sentences) the main purpose of your position (i.e. answers to "Why does the position exist?").

**Example A** (Accounts Payable Clerk). *To compile, classify, process, and maintain data and payments to accounts payable records.*

**Example B** (Project Management Trainer). *To provide project management expertise to members to ensure that projects are delivered on time, on budget, and to quality specifications.*

*[E.g.] The communications coordinator supports communications department management in the delivery of key communications programs, plans, and initiatives in alignment with the corporation's business objectives.*

## Responsibilities

* **Purpose.** To understand your position by breaking it down into its key responsibility components. Information provided should be focused on duties that support end results.

    List the most important duties of your position in order of significance. Be as brief and concise as possible. Give a general description and leave out the details. Estimate the average amount of each day you spend on these (see below). A simple trick is to copy applicable tasks from job descriptions you may find on the Internet.

* **Time estimation aid**

| | | | | | |
|---|---|---|---|---|---|
| One hour/day | 14% | One day/week | 20% | One week/month | 23% |
| One hour/week | 3% | One day/month | 4% | One week/year | 2% |
| Two hours/month | 1% | Two days/year | 1% | One month/year | 8% |

* **List what you do, how it is achieved and why**                                   **% of time**

    **Example.** *Manage the recruitment and selection process of new staff*                    %

    **How this is achieved?**   (a)   *Coordinate the recruitment and selection of senior positions and supervise the process for junior positions*
    (b)   *Assess resumés and develop shortlists of candidates to interview*
    (c)   *Conduct candidate interviews and manage the feedback process to ensure that the candidate is communicated with in a timely manner*

1.  **Specific duty description:** _____ %
    _____
    _____

    **How this is achieved:**   (a) _____
    (b) _____
    (c) _____

2.  **Specific duty description:** _____ %
    _____
    _____

    **How this is achieved:**   (a) _____
    (b) _____
    (c) _____

*Continue describing your important duties (typically less than 7 in total) in this manner until you account for 100% of your time (do not exceed 100%).*

## Qualifications

- **Purpose.** To identify the combination of education and experience required to successfully perform your position at the fully competent level.
- **State** the *minimum* amount of formal education and/or specific training normally required to satisfactorily perform the duties of your position. Indicate any special skills, licenses, technical requirements, certification, designation or degrees required:

- **State** the *minimum* amount of experience required to perform the duties of your position. Indicate if there is anything particular about that experience (e.g. supervisory, systems, etc.).

- Is any other special skill or knowledge required for your position?

## Communication and contacts

- **Purpose.** To describe the internal and external stakeholders that your position comes in contact with (e.g. other staff/departments, suppliers, the public, etc.) and to describe the active communication skills needed to perform at a fully competent level in your position.
  Describe the types of regular internal and external contacts made in the performance of your duties:

- **Position/Person contacted**          **Purpose of contact**

  *Legal services*                        *Advice on contracts*

  *Suppliers for office supplies*         *Order supplies and negotiate bulk discounts*

- **Describe** the most difficult/complex "Stakeholder Management" (internal and external) situations that you must deal with. How frequently do they occur? Give examples.

*Example A.* Must resolve situations where the client expectation of the time and project resources required to complete a project is not realistic.

*Example B.* As a communications specialist, I ensure that we are communicating to external stakeholders on a regular basis. I must work very closely with internal staff to ensure the timeliness and accuracy of all communications. Often I am competing with conflicting priorities and the time constraints of the internal staff. Clarifying the need for information early and setting and enforcing deadlines are required to ensure timely access to the information.

- Does any part of your position require negotiation or persuasive ability? Does it require the resolution of conflict and/or complaints? Give examples.

  *Example A.* Regularly negotiate with members on the project scope as it relates to the investment that the organization has made.

  *Example B.* The project that I lead requires inputs and information from other internal departments. I must persuade the department representatives to deliver the inputs, data, or feedback on time or the project timelines will slip. I have no authority over the department representatives so must continue to communicate the shared benefits of providing timely information and feedback.

## Leadership and Scope

- **Purpose.** To describe your position's requirement to direct and/or control activities or resources—such as people, projects or information—in order to produce results. Leadership may be exercised directly or indirectly.
- **List** the position titles of anyone you assign work to, direct and/or guide in their work (indicate the number of individuals; FT/PT; direct/indirect reports).

| Position | Number | Fulltime/Contract, Direct or Indirect Reports |
|---|---|---|
| | | |

- Describe the key dimensions of your job. These may include:

| Key dimension | Description |
|---|---|
| Operating budget: | |
| Investments managed: | |
| Buying volume: | |
| Key vendor/supplier relationships managed: | |
| Alliances/member relationships managed: | |

Costs controlled:

Facilities and equipment managed:

Other (Please describe):

## Problem Solving/Judgement

- **Purpose.** To describe the type and scope of problems encountered in the role and the problem solving skills and judgment that that are required to resolve these issues.
- **Describe** the most complex/difficult problems that you must solve without consulting your supervisor. What policies, procedures, and guidelines are available to you in dealing with problems and decisions? Give examples.
  *Example. I will work directly with media representatives to create opportunities for senior management to be interviewed or contribute articles.*

- **Describe** the types of problems for which you would seek supervisory help. How frequently do they occur? Give examples.
  *Example A. Need to negotiate terms and conditions with a supplier for contracts that exceed my signing authority—quarterly.*
  *Example B. Final approval of communications for external audiences—weekly.*

- **Describe** the types of errors (probable, not possible) that may occur in your work, the likely consequences (fiscal, client, operational efficiency, public relations) of those errors and what may be required to correct them. Give examples.
  *Example A. On a very complex project, where there is significant coordination across different departments, I could go over budget or not meet time deadlines.*
  *Example B. If information is released to the public which is incorrect it may cause embarrassment and loss of credibility to the organization.*

- **Describe** the job demands (e.g. deadlines, work load, tediousness of certain work, changing priorities, constant troubleshooting, and multiple reporting relationships) that occur in the performance of the tasks in your position. Give examples of the causes.

*Example.* *The deadlines in my department are always tight to begin with and often the direction will change part way through a project. This results in a lot of rework being done and a lot of late nights in order to meet the deadline.*

## Working Environment

- **Purpose.** To identify the physical and mental demands that are involved in your position that can produce physical stress and fatigue, risk of accident, ill health or discomfort.
- **List** machines, tools and equipment regularly used. Include all equipment used to perform specific position tasks such as maintenance equipment, ladders, etc.

- **Describe** the physical effort required in your position. This may involve extended standing, sitting, lifting, etc. Give examples of frequency and type of physical effort.
  *Example A.* *Repetitive physical motion for extended periods using keyboard.*
  *Example B.* *Required to sit for long periods of time.*

- **Describe** the type (local, air) and frequency of any travel required by your job.

- **Describe** the visual attention required in your position. Give examples of type, frequency and duration.
  **Example.** *Entering media data in e-mail distribution lists every day.*

# REFERENCES

Dalton, G.W., and P.H. Thompson (1993). *Novations: Strategies for Career Management.* Boston, MA: Novations Group.

Franklin, J.C. (1997). "Industry Outlook and Employment Projections to 2006," *Monthly Labor Review,* US Bureau of Labor Statistics, November. http://www.bls.gov/opub/mlr/1997/11/art4full.pdf.

Government of Canada (2003). *Professional Occupations in Public Relations and Communications (NOC 5124): Education, Training and Experience.* http://jobfutures.ca/noc/5124p2.shtml.

KPMG (1998). *Building Contacts and Networking.* Toronto, ON: KPMG Consulting Services.

Public Relations Society of America (2004). *Careers in Public Relations: An Overview.* New York: PRSA. http://www.prsa.org/_Resources/profession/career overview.asp?ident=prof2.

Ramsay, B. (1997). "Ramsay Writes," International Association of Business Communicators (IABC) Career Development Workshop, Toronto.

US Bureau of Labor Statistics (2004). "Public Relations Specialists," in *Occupational Outlook Handbook 2004–05.* http://www.bls.gov/oco/ocos086.htm.

# 10

# The Measurement and Evaluation of Public Affairs Process and Performance

CRAIG S. FLEISHER

This chapter addresses a question likely as old as commerce itself: how can decision makers be sure they are expending the appropriate amount of resources on the right kind of activities so that stakeholder value can be maximized? Intensified competitive environments and increasing stakeholder concerns have created pressure on firms to enhance spending effectiveness and efficiency wherever possible. Senior management almost always wants to see the tangible results of their investments in given activities (e.g., public affairs, hereafter abbreviated PA), and often complains about the lack of understanding of how a given activity actually contributes to the bottom line. Increasingly, numbers-driven chief executive officers (CEOs) and chief financial officers (CFOs) demand to know how efficiently their firms' PA dollars are being put to use.

Companies are increasingly concerned with ensuring that all activities are making a tangible contribution to the bottom line, especially activities such as public affairs that have a dynamic effect on the organization over time. However, public affairs does not have a body of procedures established that allows appropriate accounting of the net effect on the investments and uses of PA resources as other functions

have been accustomed to. In general, PA practice and performance have always been more of an art than a science, more qualitative than quantitative, and more conjectural than empirical. Similar to what occurs with their advertising practices and investments, many companies intrinsically know that some portion of their PA investment hits their intended targets, they just cannot confidently identify which portion hits and if they succeeded with any accuracy or consistency.

Each dollar invested in public affairs may eventually be challenged by shareholders and board-pressured executives to demonstrate bottom-line or at least top-line performance. Questions are being asked such as "Just what is PA's contribution to our profitability? Increased sales? Expense reductions?" Most PA executives have felt that they had little choice but to throw more or new resources at their problems and at least some of these investments would pay off. That kind of thinking, however, is changing. Most companies have difficulty in assessing the performance of their PA function, if they attempt to do so formally at all.

Assessing PA performance by conducting evaluation and measurement of organizational interactions among stakeholders acting within the public policy environment (PPE but also known as the "non-market" environment) is important to firms seeking to improve both their market and their non-market performance. Examples abound of firms whose performance ran foul of their PPE stakeholders' expectations. Several instances were associated with significant short- and long-term economic and/or reputation damage to the offending firms (e.g., Ford and Bridgestone Tire, Arthur Andersen, Enron, Parmalat, etc.). This nature of performance outcome is often viewed in terms of deteriorating levels of corporate social performance (CSP) (Wartick and Cochran, 1985).

Managers of corporate public affairs (CPA) units often have the most significant organizational responsibility for ensuring that their organizations maintain effective relationships with stakeholders in the PPE. Several empirical studies have been conducted examining the relationship between PA units and effective CSP (see, for example, Waddock and Graves, 1997; Roman *et al.*, 1999; Preston and O'Bannon, 1997). Each study provided a unique glimpse into selected aspects of the relationship between PA unit activities and the achievement of various levels of CSP.

Over a decade has passed since the last comprehensive study was undertaken of CPA management, measurement, and assessment processes (Fleisher, 1993a, b). That study produced a refined model that demonstrated that managerial behaviors and decisions were directly affected by PPE forces and the PA unit's influence. The result of managerial behaviors and decisions, combined with the effects made on these by the PA management subsystem, led the organization to exhibit certain PPE behaviors. Whether these behaviors are effective or not is dependent on how the organization views its PPE relationships, which is commonly reflected by the approach it takes in evaluating PA management. This chapter seeks to answer how professionals in the field of corporate public affairs are assessing their function's value or worth, and whether contemporary practices have changed or advanced since they were studied over a decade ago.

## BACKGROUND

Leaders of organizational staff groups such as finance, marketing, public affairs, or purchasing are routinely asked by senior executives responsible for their organization's budget allocations to demonstrate their function's impact on corporate performance. All functions that have a need for using corporate funds are asked to account for their utilization of scarce funds, and some functions have commonly had more success in demonstrating accountability than others. This demonstration takes on increased importance during more difficult economic cycles or periods when budget cuts, corporate downsizing, and restructuring are persistent (Fleisher and Hoewing, 1992).

The desire and need for assessing organizational performance have visibly grown since the 1990s, both within and outside of the PA field (Neely, 2002). Indeed, several research centers or foundations (e.g., the Centre for Business Performance at Cranfield School of Management in the United Kingdom, or the Foundation for Performance Measurement in the United States) and associations (e.g., the Performance Measurement Association, of which the author is a member; the British Academy of Management which has a Performance Management Special Interest Group) were established during this time period (Neely *et al.*, 1995). Several performance assessment tools, particularly the balanced scorecard, customer surveys, activity-based costing and management (ABC or ABM), benchmarking, performance dashboards, pay-for-performance, and the performance prism have reached varying levels of popularity and use (Rigby, 2003; Neely, 2002; Ittner and Larker, 1998).

Despite the increased level of interest expressed in the topic, definitions and consensus around the scope of "performance assessment" still remain elusive. Neely (1998) defines performance measurement as "the process of quantifying the efficiency and effectiveness of past actions through acquisition, collation, sorting, analysis, interpretation, and dissemination of appropriate data." Moulin (2002) defines it as "evaluating how well organizations are managed and the value they deliver for customers and other stakeholders." Definition remains so elusive that several authors have noted that "performance" is a word in which everyone places the concepts that suit them, letting the context take care of the definition (Lebas and Euske, 2002).

The concept of corporate public affairs has also tended to remain elusive to definitional agreements. The definition and scope of corporate public affairs need to be clearly understood before any attempts can be made to develop measures with which to evaluate it. In this chapter, I define corporate public affairs as *a management function that facilitates exchanges between an organization and its social and political stakeholders* (Fleisher and Blair, 1999). Corporate public affairs officers (PAOs) are actively involved with monitoring the external environment and managing issues that arise in the organization's relations with political, societal, and economic forces—and are the organization's key managers of issues and stakeholders.

Performance is not an easy subject, and there is clearly a need to study and rethink what is meant by it and how to measure it (Meyer, 2002). Performance in this chapter is broadly defined as both the comparative economic (i.e., market-based, commercial transaction exchange-based) and the non-economic (i.e., issue, non-market, public policy, stakeholder) perceptions placed upon organizations by their stakeholders. Common market measures include metrics such as return on investment (ROI), internal rate of return (IRR) market share, product/service quality, investment intensity, marketing expenditures, or economic value added (EVA), while common non-market measures would include, among other things, corporate image or reputation, community investment, corporate social performance or responsibility (CSR), and/or political influence.

This chapter addresses the concept of performance assessment in public affairs, thereby increasing the need to make distinctions between the primary underlying social science facets of the process, these being evaluation, measurement, and research (Lindenmann, 2001). Research is a basic tool for fact and opinion gathering that focuses on the entire PA process and examines the nature of transactional relationships that exist among and between institutions and their key stakeholders. For the public affairs officer, a useful definition of PA *research* is that it is a planned and systematic effort using primary and secondary sources to discover, confirm, and/or understand through an objective appraisal the facts or opinions pertaining to a specified problem, situation, or opportunity. *Evaluation* means determining the relative effectiveness, performance, or value of a PA program or strategy, ordinarily done by measuring outputs and outcomes against a predetermined set of objectives. *Measurement* is the process of assigning a specific quantitative or numerical indicator to a PA activity or process. Research underlies PA performance assessment methods or techniques and provides support and assistance to measurement and evaluation efforts.

Performance assessment is conceptually part of the ordinary work process that a public affairs officer would undertake. Together, the components form a cycle, from fact finding, research, and formulation to implementation of the PA activities and programs, commonly known as Research—Objectives—Planning—Evaluation (ROPE) in public relations (PR) circles (Hendrix, 1997). After implementation of activities or programs, the results that are obtained must be monitored, and the results become an input to the formulation process on the next cycle. Thus the PA process is supposed to be continuous, although it does not always work in practice in the neat and sequential way it is typically presented in the academic textbooks. Indeed, parts of the process are often skipped entirely, like, for example, the research or assessment portions. Sometimes there is so little time in between stages that barely any time is left to actually or properly conduct one or more of these steps. As such, many successfully or unsuccessfully realized PA plans and actions can be more accurately described as "emergent" rather than "intended."

Performance assessment is nearly always important in management, and particularly so in highly competitive, complex, global and/or dynamic environments, where PA managers are expected to have a strong grasp on dozens of issues. This is a vital part of the planning and accountability process for those public affairs officers who are in high PA-intensity industries such as pharmaceuticals, high-technology, fast-moving consumer goods, as well as resource-intense industries such as energy or forest products. Public affairs officers in organizations within these industries have a greater corresponding need to effectively assess performance than their counterparts in slower-moving, less global, less complex, and less competitive industries.

Public affairs officers, and the executives to whom they report, have frequently expressed dissatisfaction with the evaluation and measurement or performance assessment of PA activities (Ferraro, 2000; Fleisher and Mahaffy, 1997; Fleisher, 1993b). Failure to adequately measure PA performance often results in a loss of accountability for public affairs officers and their units. This inability to demonstrate valued results can also give rise to declining roles and responsibilities for public affairs within the organization, a subsequent loss of influence and/or impact, and sometimes even career (Laird, 1996). As such, it is important to identify and describe those reasons that have kept public affairs officers from experiencing satisfaction with this critical work process.

### Aims of the 1991 Study

In response to these issues and as a means for understanding what PA professionals were doing with respect to their assessments of PA performance, I led a comprehensive and extensive research study of public affairs officers in the United States during the second half of 1991. The study was designed to probe the following questions:

1  What was the role of evaluation and measurement in public affairs?
2  How were PA units being assessed?
3  Who performed PA evaluation?
4  What activities were being assessed?

5  What evaluation methods were being used?
6  What problems were being encountered in assessing public affairs?
7  How was the performance assessment activity related to other PA activities?

The study was not expressly designed to address specific steps in how evaluation was conducted or to develop methods for improving the applicability of specific performance measures. The research aimed to outline the diverse set of activities and contexts that surrounded PA performance assessment. As in most empirical studies of public affairs, there were difficulties in determining just what it was (i.e., it means different things to different people in different organizations and industries) and what constitute evaluation (Fleisher, 1993a). The survey was part of an ongoing research project into PA evaluation and measurement that also included case studies, interviews, and expert discussions (Fleisher, 1995, 1997, 1998; Fleisher and Burton, 1995, 1996). Over 1,000 US-based public affairs officers participated in the research. This was, and likely still is, viewed to be the largest number of practitioners ever to participate in an academic study of PA evaluation and measurement (E&M) practices (Griffin *et al.*, 2001a, b).

### Summary of Findings from the 1991 Study

The following were among the most important of the findings out of this previous research. In recognition that these results have been published extensively elsewhere, I have excerpted a five-point summary of the key findings below:

1  Most public affairs officers intentionally evaluated their PA units. In general, this evaluation was of an informal, qualitative nature.
2  Public affairs officer respondents generally believed that increasing emphasis should be placed on conducting more formal and rigorous evaluation of their unit's activities; however, many felt that greater

emphasis on evaluation would not add value in terms of significantly improving their unit's performance.

3 There was a significant association between the formality and analytical rigor of PA evaluation and top management's support of quality management or rigorous performance management or measurement principles. Organizations which utilized quality management techniques were more likely to pursue rigorous, analytical evaluation of public affairs.

4 Effectiveness for the majority of PA units was measured by the degree of achievement of previously established goals—using management by objectives (MBO) type approaches. Many firms actively mated goal achievement and stakeholder satisfaction measures.

5 Most firms regularly evaluated the performance of their individual PA professionals; however, few evaluated the performance of their overall PA unit or the organization's PPE performance.

A positive overall appraisal of and by public affairs officers in this survey was that public affairs had come a long way up to that point in time in terms of its accountability within organizations. This was reflected, in one proxy measure, by the increasing number and proportion of public affairs officers who frequently communicated and interacted at the uppermost decision-making levels of their firms. Respondents commented that public affairs generally was well perceived by organizational decision makers and that continuing, albeit gradual, progress was being made in addressing its impact on bottom-line concerns.

Notwithstanding the positive perceptions, most of the public affairs officers still claimed that a sizable gap existed between the current state and the intended destination. Public affairs professionals generally remained dissatisfied with their ability to conduct defensible evaluations of public affairs, quantifying its effect on the bottom line, and in designing specific standards for measurement. I concluded that further research and discussion was needed to address these concerns. That is what served as the premise of the recent set of studies where I began to revisit the status of performance assessment by PA practitioners in contemporary circumstances. I summarized my findings at the time as such (Fleisher, 1997):

> Most performance measurement systems used in public affairs departments today are ineffective in helping managers make decisions so as to simultaneously improve both departmental and organizational performance. The relative absence of effectively performing assessment systems will continue to exacerbate the difficulties that PA decision-makers face in demonstrating their organizational value and legitimacy. To the extent that these difficulties result in inadequate resource allocation to public affairs, it becomes a Catch-22 situation. The catch is that it requires resources to install and operate these systems and yet without these systems, it is difficult to make a sound case for the provision of these resources to the function!

## WHAT PUBLIC AFFAIRS OFFICERS PERCEIVE TO BE UNSATISFACTORY WITH RESPECT TO CONTEMPORARY PUBLIC AFFAIRS PERFORMANCE ASSESSMENT

I am in the process of revisiting the questions and replicating much of the process I used to study the phenomenon of PA performance assessment in the early 1990s. What I am presenting below is a preliminary summary of the findings to date. A major part of this research, a comprehensive written survey, is still yet to be disseminated and is scheduled for release in the near future.

Based on a series of focus groups held in both the United States and Canada in 2000–2004, a comprehensive review of the contemporary literature and conference proceedings, as well as utilizing the results of several proprietary benchmarking studies, I would suggest that the following major issues remain *unre*solved at this point over a decade after the first study. I have not presented them here in any particular priority order other than to note that these themes have been the ones which have been most prominent to date within the data that have been analyzed.

## Using Information Technology to Support PA Performance Assessment

Executives, who are often obsessed with quantification, have attempted any number of organizational information technology (IT) initiatives to improve their ability to assess, manage, and maximize their organizational performance (Neely, 2002). The problem with most enterprise-wide resource planning and reporting systems today is that what they offer is ordinarily data—reshuffled, recatalogued, reallocated, but rarely offering information or insight (Fleisher, 2002). They provide so much data that executives are often heard exclaiming that they are drowning in them. Among the bigger problems today is not that we are necessarily assessing the wrong things, but that we are assessing too many things and that the organization ends up falling into the all too common trap of simply trying to capture and assess too much data.

Public affairs officers consistently expressed that they have seldom been assisted by their organization's adoption and use of information technology to help them assess and/or manage their performance. Unsurprisingly, they are rarely involved in the organization's decision-making processes associated with acquiring IT assets for information management purposes. Most recently adopted performance reporting systems have provided balanced scorecard, customer, financial, or market-based information, but hardly any offer the issue or stakeholder-based performance metrics and insights that public affairs officers need to assess the full range of their performance contributions. There are some new IT solutions that ostensibly could promote the development and management of non-market measures, particularly in the areas of grassroots management, media tracking, image or reputation monitoring, but few of these have been widely adopted by organizations and most of them remain outside of the

domain of those individuals (in accounting, finance, or executive management) who are primarily responsible for performance management in most corporations. Several organizations have developed proprietary systems for automating the capture and circulation of PA performance data, but nearly all of these are embryonic in their development (Hoewing, 2000). There are several PA-dedicated IT vendors but none to my respondents' knowledge have managed to provide performance reporting modules that are integral with the organization's larger performance management systems.

## Assessing the Return on Investment of PA Activities

The basic question behind PA return on investment (ROI) calculations is whether organizations can recover investment costs in public affairs and achieve measurable benefits from the function. The equation for calculating PA return on investment is deceptively simple and is as follows: *ROI percent = [Value of benefits generated by PA–Cost of PA]/Cost of PA × 100 percent.* Despite the need for this clarity, ROI calculations in public affairs are not commonly conducted. The most common reasons given by PAO respondents for not conducting formal ROI analysis of public affairs include the following:

1 The costs of tracking and measuring the costs and benefits of public affairs may not be worth the effort, especially because public affairs is carried out both in an ongoing and episodic (i.e., project-based) manner.
2 While PA costs are known up front, both before and during PA interventions, benefits may not appear immediately and often accrue over extended time periods.
3 The benefits of PA interventions are often viewed to be "soft" or "intangible," difficult to quantify and convert accurately into dollars.
4 The benefits generated by public affairs are usually not solely due to public affairs's efforts nor can they be evenly or objectively allocated across the organization.

5 Adverse findings in an ROI calculation could be damaging to the PA function and its practitioners and result in less resources and support from top management.

Most public affairs officers recognize that return on investment isn't the panacea they seek despite the recognition that it is important to develop an ROI mindet. Other factors are also critical in business decisions, including that risks must be assessed against rewards, PA undertakings must be congruent with the organization's strategy, short-term goals need to be balanced out against long-term ones, and that scarce resources are invariably affected by internal politics. Last but not least, most public affairs officers continue to question how to develop ROI measures on non-events, whereby their actions prevented certain activities from occurring (e.g., lobbying that resulted in legislation that ostensibly prevented a competitor from entering the competitive marketplace) in the marketplace. They recognize that any good calculation of PA return on investment must account for some reasonable levels of conditional probability and risk.

### Effectively Measuring Changes in Non-Financial Capital

Much of what public affairs officers do is to regularly address (i.e., attract, build, grow, or maintain) the balance of human, relational, or structural capital accumulated within their organizations. *Human capital* is the knowledge that employees take with them when they depart from the organization. It includes employees' knowledge, skills, experience, and abilities. *Relational capital* is all those resources that are linked to an organization's external relationships and its stakeholders—the primary area of capital expected to be influenced by public affairs officers. It comprises the part of human and structural capital involved with the organization's relations with its stakeholders plus the perceptions they hold about the organization. *Structural capital* is the knowledge that stays within the organization at the end of every working day. It includes the organization's routines and procedures.

Successful public affairs officers and PA operations spend the lion's share of organizational resources allocated to them engaging in networking activities. These activities lead to relationships that are counted upon by decision makers in the organization to provide the organization with the opportunity to influence the public policy environment at some indefinite point in the future. Very few companies have done an effective job in capturing, managing, and monitoring their stocks of non-financial capital. If and when this begins to catch on, public affairs officers need to be at the forefront with those who are developing the systems and metrics by which this is to be accomplished, since they, like most of the rest of the organization's boundary-spanning agents, stand to benefit the most from the regular accounting for these items.

### Demonstrating the Value of Intangibles

Much PA work is based on improving not only the types of capital described in the point above, but also on improving relationship capital with a variety of stakeholders, enhancing goodwill, expanding the corporate reputation, or on growing the amount of brand/corporate equity that customers perceive in the organization. Accounting systems were originated a millennium ago to help people account for land, labor, and capital—the tangible items exchanged as part of commerce and commercial transactions. The last few decades have witnessed a major shift toward valuing the exchange of less tangible things like credibility, reputation, innovativeness, flexibility, knowledge, and trust (Lev, 2001). There is little doubt that the outcome of much PA work would be to address the total value of the intangibles the organization brings to the table for its proposed and desired exchanges (Ferraro, 2000). Unfortunately, there has been little progress made in determining, or in reporting, the value of intangibles that underlie an organization's thrusts into stakeholder exchanges or addressing issues in the non-marketplace.

Companies that show the greatest market value today are often those that cannot show large amounts of land, labor, and/or capital.

Successful firms like Intel, Microsoft, or Nokia are valuable more for the intangibles they bring to the marketplace, phenomena which are not adequately captured by accounting concepts such as "goodwill," which typically come into play only (and if) the organization is to be sold on the open market. These successful companies have growing experience with the budgeting and practice of intangible activities and invest heavily in them.

Managing and practicing intangible activities can lead to robust performance outcomes. The difference between the market and book values of successful intangible managing organizations can be immense, and it is not too difficult or much of a stretch to make an argument that the PA activities conducted by firms such as these have been a prominent contributor to their success and correspondingly high market values. Nevertheless, unless investors, analysts, and/or executives demand the regular assessment and communication of the performance of these intangibles, public affairs officers will continue to struggle in demonstrating the nature of their contributions.

## Institutionalizing Performance Assessment with Other Routine PA Activities

In numerous studies of public relations (see the review in Watson, 2001) as well as corporate public affairs (Ferraro, 2000; Fleisher, 1993a, 1997; Fleisher and Nickel, 1995; Fleisher and Burton, 1995), it has been demonstrated that planning, research, or evaluation tend to get short-changed for budget and time resources relative to other PA activities. Assessment, measurement, and evaluation are performed as though they are discretionary activities by the vast majority of public affairs officers—despite the fact that they also claim these activities are vital to the successful performance of their jobs.

My research, as well as that of many others (Watson, 2001), has described the common barriers that prevent these practitioners from doing the level of assessment they think is ideal. The barriers range from not knowing how to do it, lacking proficiency in the analytical tools and techniques of performance assessment

(Fleisher, 2002), not having the time or money to do it, inability to develop appropriate measures, a view of the cost/benefit of performance assessment not making it worth the resources expended, or inability to communicate the nature of PA performance to executives who don't well understand the function and its tasks in the first place (Fleisher, 1997). As such, PA performance assessment remains outside of the core activities that public affairs officers perform on a regular basis, most commonly done only when it is either demanded of them or their budget is threatened in the absence of these results.

## Balancing and Maximizing the Time Spent Doing PA Performance Assessment Activities

Most public affairs officers claim that they still do not properly manage their time allocation between research, planning, implementation, and assessment—the four major spokes in a hypothetical wheel describing their activities (Fleisher, 1997). Most still claim to spend the vast majority of their time fire-fighting or working on tactical activities, although the vast majority claim they wish they had more time available to them to perform more strategic, research, or assessment-oriented roles (Fleisher and Nickel, 1995).

This situation brings up the proverbial Catch-22 for public affairs officers. Since they do not take the time to plan and perform their assessment, they won't have the time to do it properly either. Over time, most senior executives need their public affairs officers to do more things with fewer resources. It is difficult for the public affairs officers to make the business case for more resources when they lack the time or wherewithal to develop and deliver the business case for better functional resourcing in the first place.

## Public Affairs Still Lacks Forward-Facing Performance Indicators

Measures are the language of progress. They provide a sense not only of where the organization is at relative to its current PA environment, but also where it might be headed in the future. This is one of the biggest problems in PA performance assessment, as there is a serious lack of leading—versus a plethora of lagging—measures. This situation points to the lack of formative research in particular, but it is compounded by the lack of evaluative research that many public affairs officers fail to conduct.

Variances in PA performance are important enough to be explained. For example, why did only 48 percent of the eligible work force take part in the last grassroots lobbying campaign when 74 percent had done so during the previous effort? Much more important is whether a given situation is improving and whether it would be satisfactory in a future period, which, in the previous example, it clearly was not. Truly effective performance indicators should serve as an *early warning device* regarding key PA variables, and communicate progress and potential problems both to public affairs officers and to the top management team. They should also communicate to implementers whether the PA department is headed toward accomplishing its mission, strategy, and vision or not.

### The Need to Systematically Select a Set of Synergistic Assessment Approaches to Utilize on an Ongoing Basis

Most organizations utilize an overriding assessment approach or two across their organization, whether it is benchmarking, MBO, strategic (quality award) approaches, internal market economy, profit-centered approach, client or customer-focused approach, research-based approach, critical variables (e.g., $2 \times 2$ matrices), wins/losses, reputation indices, etc. Most public affairs officers use one or two overriding performance assessment approaches, typically those in current favor within their larger organization. Unfortunately, some of these approaches, when applied to and used in public affairs, do not generate the same level of credibility or applicability that they do in the line-oriented organizational functions that they were particularly designed for.

The difficulty with this situation is that most of the approaches favored by the larger organization do not adequately account for PA performance outputs, outgrowths, or outcomes. Another frustrating facet of this situation is that many organizations jump from one performance assessment approach to another approach every few years, never actually giving any particular approach the proper amount of time needed for it to be institutionalized and to infuse itself within the fabric of the entire organization. This makes it more critical for public affairs officers to be cognizant of how to make the appropriate connection between their work and systems and the larger organization's assessment processes. Building a variety of useful performance assessment approaches into the fabric of the ongoing PA operation is usually the key to creating an effective function, but few PA teams have managed to do this successfully on a sustained basis.

### Finding an Appropriate Balance of Qualitative and Quantitative Measures

The tendency in most measurement and assessment circles in recent years has been heavily toward the quantification of everything (i.e., if you cannot measure it, you cannot manage it). The dominant view was that all dimensions of performance could be measured, which by default tended to mean that all phenomena could be placed in numerical terms. For those public affairs officers who have attempted to take up the challenge, this led to their counting most PA activities—in terms of things like the number of meetings held with key stakeholders, the number of letters sent to key public policy committee personnel, the number of issues being actively monitored, wins and losses, the number of bills being tracked, the number of persons involved in the grassroots program, etc.

Counting is not equivalent to and is only the starting point of measurement, which generally requires a baseline zero point and other points for comparison to be useful. Also, all the counts that were accumulated by public affairs officers generally only provided snapshot measures of how busy they were. Few senior decision makers would suggest a strong positive correlation between "busy-ness" and positive strategic value—indeed, too much activity on the wrong issues, too many meetings with inappropriate stakeholders, and the organization could easily perform badly in a PA context.

## Breaking Away from Historicist Models of Assessment

This is the kind of assessment that is done as it is because it always has been done that way. Public affairs practitioners relying on this inadequate approach realize that it does not improve their performance or add value to their organization. Instead, it meets the minimal standard of having a "performance-based contract" and ensuring that basic tasks are completed. The problem continually mentioned in my research is that many public affairs officers do not have examples, mentors, or benchmarks to provide them with guidelines for establishing useful performance assessment systems; hence, they revert back to the common denominator of doing it the same way that their predecessors did it, recognizing that it probably will not move the function or the organization forward the way that a useful system could.

The historicist model generally emphasizes PA *products* over *processes* and *outcomes*. As mentioned in the prior point, counting things does not provide an adequate means of assessing PA performance. Such measures ignore the real successes public affairs can achieve in terms of quality and relationships (Grunig and Grunig, 2001). Also, if public affairs officers and their organization's top management teams have expressed continuing dissatisfaction with their performance assessment, it would behoove them to try different, innovative, and potentially more useful approaches and methods. Few public affairs officers seem to know where to begin this journey.

## IMPLICATIONS FOR MANAGERS

Managers continue to have their work cut out for them in terms of demonstrating PA performance. The following items all addressing PA performance system implementation were deemed to be the most important ones raised by managers during several benchmarking efforts that sought to determine proven practices in developing, managing, and improving PA performance assessment systems.

## Be Aware of Political Ramifications

All performance assessment efforts in organizations can potentially impact the allocation of resources, recognition, and/or rewards. As such, there will be various individuals and groups that may view the assessment system as their means for achieving local goals as opposed to organizational ones. This suggests that the PA decision makers should work in conjunction with other senior executives in making sure that the assessment system used locally by public affairs as well as those used locally by others are all part and parcel of the larger organization-wide performance assessment system and that the impacts created by these assessment systems can be fairly determined and addressed by the senior executives responsible for allocating resources.

## Build Ongoing Communications

The establishment of the performance assessment system needs to be accomplished through the efforts of many individuals and groups. Stakeholders who affect and are affected by PA performance assessment systems include the managers responsible for the function, the employees responsible for delivering the objectives and outcomes sought, other groups who work with public affairs in achieving the organization's public policy goals, as well as the senior executives who must steward the organization's overall efforts. As such, all of these stakeholders need to be constantly communicated with in terms of the system process, outputs, and outcomes so that they can assist in its development and in the development of effective public policy outcomes. No stakeholder group should be surprised about what is transpiring; consequently, regular and ongoing communication can serve to avoid negative surprises and to lessen the possibility of the area being beset by adverse internal political ramifications.

## Grow the Effort from the Ground Up

One thing that managers repeatedly commented upon in looking at performance assessment processes was the need to build in the system as opposed to "bolting on" systems that were developed for other functions or for other purposes than what was required within public affairs. No manager stated that an "off the shelf" system was immediately or even easily applicable for effective performance assessment. None of the managers interviewed claimed to be aware of a software application that solved their performance assessment problems and difficulties. As such, it is critical to understand the basics of establishing performance assessment, to recognize the critical facets of the organization's current and future strategy and performance for which PA performance assessment requires accounting, and to know which features of organizational change management processes need to be considered as the system rolls out.

## Measures Need to be Chosen Wisely

Many PA managers were liable to first trying to adopt so-called "easy" assessment systems such as balanced scorecards, performance dashboards, or other simplified (e.g., $2 \times 2$) matrices that were supposed to help them manage and improve their performance. Most of the managers who attempted this were quickly disappointed with the results of their efforts and recognized that they needed to put in the amount of work and thought necessary to develop and customize measures that worked particularly for their PA efforts, their organization's strategy, and the larger public policy environment. A system that works for a competitor in the same industry likely would not work for another organization, since each organization has a unique strategy-performance configuration that needs to be accounted for in assessment system development.

## Provide Resources for Training and Support

A PA performance assessment system will impact all PA stakeholders, also including less obvious parties such as hired lobbyists, contracted communication specialists, grassroots solutions providers, as well as the more obvious employees and volunteers in the program. As such, time, funds and educational sessions need to be planned and resourced if the system will achieve the things for which it is designed. Several PA managers in the benchmarking efforts shared that they had acquired resources budgeted for the origination of the system but lacked them after the first year and were unable to sustain the emphasis that the system required in order to be effective.

## Regularly Evaluate Your Performance Assessment System

It is rare for a system to be effective and optimized from its origination. Most systems require tweaking and annual assessment to determine how they might be improved over time. If nothing else, the system needs to be able to reflect changes in structuring and strategy that ordinarily impact an organization on a regular basis. This evaluation should be conducted by someone who both uses and manages the system as well as someone who has expertise in the design and maintenance of performance assessment systems who is not directly associated with the organization's PA activities.

## Remain Patient for the Effort to Bear Fruit

Most of our respondents, who felt as though their performance assessment efforts were bearing fruit, and who had the appropriate documentation to support this view, spent from three to five years getting the effort moving before they felt as though it were institutionalized and effective. The first twelve to eighteen months were viewed to be among the most critical because that is the time frame within which the majority of these efforts are most likely going to be abandoned, if that is the eventual result. For those groups and functions that saw benefits from the systems, they needed to have multi-year planning processes supporting the use and institutionalization of their system along with the demonstrated patience of both users and consumers of the system outputs.

## IMPLICATIONS FOR SCHOLARS

As readers may surmise from the findings presented in this chapter, there is still a great deal of research that needs to be done on assessing PA performance. The subject matter domain area of assessing corporate staff performance, and the performance of PA groups more specifically, are rich with opportunities for research. Among the most critical questions that still need to be further examined, and the nature of studies that I suggest should be attempted, there are included:

1   *Exploratory studies:*

   (a)   What percentages of companies employ and have institutionalized their PA performance assessment systems?
   (b)   What do organizational decision makers (e.g., CEOs, CFOs) and resource allocation executives perceive about PA performance?
   (c)   Do senior executives need better evidence of performance than they are currently receiving?
   (d)   Are PA unit heads and/or organizational decision makers satisfied with the performance assessment attempts already tried?

2   *Descriptive studies:*

   (a)   Are there any examples of organizations that can be identified and publicized that have fully operational and consistently successful PA performance assessment systems?
   (b)   Can these so-called "best practice" systems be adapted or generalized among other PA units or groups?

3   *Longitudinal studies:*

   (a)   What are the evolutionary processes, activities, and practices that a PA operation would need to undertake in order to build a fully operational and consistently successful PA performance assessment system?
   (b)   How does the organizational context need to develop over time to support effective PA performance management?

4   *Correlative/comparative studies:*

   (a)   Are PA units that have fully operational and consistently successful PA performance assessment systems better able than their counterparts that lack them to gain better and greater access to organizational decision makers?
   (b)   Are they able to gain greater year-to-year increases in budget allocations than units that lack these systems?
   (c)   Are they able to demonstrate greater levels of PA staff productivity and/or satisfaction than units lacking these systems?
   (d)   Are companies that employ ISO (International Standards Organization), balanced scorecard, or quality performance systems more likely to institutionalize PA performance assessment systems?

5   *Causal studies:*

   (a)   Do PA performance management systems lead to better PA unit or organizational strategic/tactical performance?
   (b)   Do organizational performance management programs lead to the establishment of PA performance management programs?

6   *Conceptual/theoretical studies:*

   (a)   Can we/how can we define, identify, and operationalize PA performance?
   (b)   Can we/how can we conceptualize and operationalize PA performance management systems?
   (c)   What are the ways in which PA performance management and organizational performance management can be linked?

(d) What existing theories of organization, management, and/or strategy (e.g., resource dependence, agency, transaction costs, institutional, etc.) can be utilized to better conceptualize PA performance management?

In performing these studies, scholars will need to be careful in their consideration of certain facets of the phenomena that have been known to complicate previous studies. The most prominent of these would include the following.

## Conceptual/Definitional Issues

1 Clearly and comprehensively define terms such as "assessment," "evaluation," "measurement," "public affairs," and "value" as utilized in the research. Wherever possible, researchers should compare and contrast their definitions of these terms against the existing literature, preferably carrying forward definitions that have already become well entrenched in the scholarship and that have already benefited from the accumulated conduct of empirical studies.

2 Identify and describe assumptions underlying the broader public policy environmental context as well as the organizational context in which PA is being studied. Many earlier PA studies were performed on activities within particular industries (e.g., Baysinger *et al.*, 1987; Bhambri and Sonnenfeld, 1988; Sonnenfeld, 1982).

3 Seek to associate research questions with existing theories and conceptualizations. Researchers may want to consider utilizing relevant advances made in associated areas such as corporate political strategy, business and public policy, corporate social performance and responsibility, management accounting, performance management, and business policy scholarship.

4 Couch research findings in terms of relevant theoretical concepts. This should become increasingly easier since there is now a growing literature and scholarly base focused on assessing non-traditional forms of performance in organizations.

## Research Design Issues

1 Those researchers utilizing questionnaires or survey instruments should describe measures taken to address instrumental validity and reliability concerns. Authors should also make questionnaires available to other researchers for subsequent studies.

2 Researchers doing case studies should recommend steps that subsequent research should accomplish to further generalize findings across other samples and/or over time.

3 Scholars should seek to perform more studies of a correlational, causal-comparative, and/or experimental research nature as opposed to primarily descriptive ones. Researchers intent on conducting descriptive studies should seek means to augment the use of existing databases or create databases that will be shared with other researchers so that a cumulative body of knowledge can grow more quickly and reliably.

4 Sampling design opportunities should include studies of a wider range of industries (including service industries), activities conducted in multiple states and/or regions. Sampling should include all individuals involved in the organizational PA effort, not just public affairs officers.

5 Creative selection of research methodologies to generate better fine- and coarse-grained understandings of PA phenomena. Researchers should generally avoid the performance of large-scale surveys, with their decreasing response rates, unless they have abundant resources or are complementing these findings through triangulation methods.

## CONCLUSION

When I studied the state of performance assessment in public affairs over a decade ago, it was clear that progress had been made since previous decades, and that public affairs officers and their top management teams had come to plainly recognize the need for improvement in their performance assessment. There was a degree of optimism that the "corner would be turned" and that this dissatisfying situation would hopefully be resolved. I initiated a study of the current status of performance assessment recently to see if this optimism, expressed by public affairs officers back in the early 1990s, was warranted or not.

Unfortunately, the state of performance assessment in public affairs does not actually look all that much better than it did over a decade ago. Despite the increased emphasis on performance assessment in organizations in general, most public affairs officers continue to struggle with effectively demonstrating and communicating the value or worth of their efforts to the larger organizations. They remain optimistic, generally, but many of the same phenomena that were so evident over a decade ago remain just as evident today.

There is a clear challenge presented by these findings for students, scholars, and practitioners of public affairs. There needs to be new research, new experiments, new conceptualizations, and new ways of acting applied to this difficult area. The historicist or "old way of doing things" with respect to PA performance assessment has not, and will not, suffice. Unless there is a systematic and organized means for making progress in this area, similar to what has been done in terms of the professionalization of related fields, the situation is unlikely to reflect all that much difference a decade from now.

## REFERENCES

Baysinger, B.D., G.D. Keim and C.P. Zeithaml (1987). "Constituency Building as a Political Strategy in the Petroleum Industry," in A. Marcus, A. Kaufman and D. Beam (eds), *Business Strategy and Public Policy*. New York: Quorum.

Bhambri, A., and J. Sonnenfeld (1988). "Organization Structure and Corporate Social Performance: A Field Study in Two Contrasting Industries," *Academy of Management Journal* 31 (3): 642–662.

Ferraro, R. (2000). *Considerations for Measuring Public Affairs' Value*. Public Affairs Management Report, Washington, DC: Public Affairs Council.

Fleisher, C.S. (1993a). "Public Affairs Management Performance: An Empirical Analysis of Evaluation and Measurement," in J. Post (ed.), *Research in Corporate Social Performance and Policy* xiv. Greenwich, CT: JAI Press.

Fleisher, C.S. (1993b). "Assessing the Effectiveness of Corporate Public Affairs Efforts," in B.M. Mitnick (ed.), *Corporate Political Agency: The Construction of Competition in Public Affairs*. Newbury Park, CA: Sage.

Fleisher, C.S. (1995). *Public Affairs Benchmarking: A Comprehensive Guide*. Washington, DC: Public Affairs Council.

Fleisher, C.S. (1997). *Assessing, Managing, and Maximizing Public Affairs Performance*. Washington, DC: Public Affairs Council.

Fleisher, C.S. (1998). "A Benchmarked Assessment of the Strategic Management of Corporate Communications," *Journal of Marketing Communications* 4 (3): 163–176.

Fleisher, C.S. (2002). "Analysis and Analytical Tools for Managing Corporate Public Affairs," *Journal of Public Affairs* 2 (3): 167–172.

Fleisher, C.S., and N. Blair (1999). "Tracing the Parallel Evolution of Public Affairs and Public Relations: An Examination of Practice, Scholarship and Teaching," *Journal of Communication Management* 3 (3): 276–292.

Fleisher, C.S., and S. Burton (1995). "Taking Stock of Corporate Management Benchmarking Practices: The Next Panacea or Pandora's Box?" *Public Relations Review* 21 (1): 1–21.

Fleisher, C.S., and S. Burton (1996). "Benchmarking: Evaluating the Public Affairs Function/Operation," in L.B. Dennis (ed.), *Practical Public Affairs in an Era of Change*. New York: University Press of America.

Fleisher, C.S., and R. Hoewing (1992). "Strategically Managing Corporate Public Affairs: New Challenges and Opportunities," *Journal of Strategic Change* 1 (5): 287–296.

Fleisher, C.S., and D. Mahaffy (1997). "A Balanced Scorecard Approach to Public Relations Management Assessment," *Public Relations Review* 23 (2): 117–142.

Fleisher, C.S., and J. Nickel (1995). "Attempting TQM in Organizational Staff Areas: TQM as Managerial Innovation in Public Affairs," *Canadian Journal of Administrative Sciences* 12 (2): 116–127.

Griffin, J.J., C.S. Fleisher, S.N. Brenner, and J.J. Boddewyn (2001a). "Corporate Public Affairs Research: Chronological Reference List I, 1985–2000," *Journal of Public Affairs* 1 (1): 9–32.

Griffin, J.J., C.S. Fleisher, S.N. Brenner, and J.J. Boddewyn (2001b). "Corporate Public Affairs Research: Chronological Reference List II, 1958–1984," *Journal of Public Affairs* 1 (2): 169–186.

Grunig, J., and L. Grunig (2001). *Guidelines for Formative and Evaluative Research in Public Affairs: A Report for the Department of Energy Office of Science.* College Park, MD: White Paper.

Hendrix, J. (1997). *Public Relations Cases,* 4th edn. New York: Thompson Learning.

Hoewing, L. (2000). *Using the Internet in a Corporate Public Affairs Office.* Public Affairs Management report, Washington, DC: Public Affairs Council.

Ittner, C.D., and D.F. Larker (1998). "Innovations in Performance Measurement: Trends and Research Implications," *Journal of Management Accounting Research* 10: 205–238.

Laird, N. (1996). "Public Affairs: Profit Center?" in L. Dennis (ed.), *Practical Public Affairs in an Era of Change.* New York: University Press of America.

Lebas, M., and K. Euske (2002). "Delineation of Performance," in A. Neely (ed.), *Business Performance Measurement: Theory and Practice.* Cambridge: Cambridge University Press.

Lev, B. (2001). "Measuring the Value of Intellectual Property," *Ivey Business Journal,* March–April, pp. 16–20.

Lindenmann, W. (2001). *Public Relations Research for Planning and Evaluation,* Commission on PR Measurement and Evaluation, special report. Gainesville, FL: Institute for Public Relations.

Meyer, M. (2002). "Finding Performance: The New Discipline in Management," in A. Neely (ed.), *Business Performance Measurement: Theory and Practice.* Cambridge: Cambridge University Press.

Moulin, M. (2002). *Delivering Excellence in Health and Social Care.* Buckingham: Open University Press.

Neely, A. (1998). *Measuring Business Performance.* London: Profile Books.

Neely, A. (2002). *Business Performance Measurement: Theory and Practice.* Cambridge: Cambridge University Press.

Neely, A.D., M. Gregory, and K. Platts (1995). "Performance Measurement System Design: A Literature Review and Research Agenda," *International Journal of Operations and Production Management* 15 (4): 80–116.

Preston, L., and D. O'Bannon (1997). "The Corporate Social-Financial Performance Relationship: A Typology and Analysis," *Business and Society* 36 (4): 419–429.

Rigby, D. (2003). *Management Tools 2003.* White Paper, Boston, MA: Bain.

Roman, R., S. Hayibor, and B. Agle (1999). "The Relationship between Financial and Social Performance: Repainting a Portrait," *Business and Society* 38 (1): 109–125.

Sonnenfeld, J.A. (1982). "Structure, Culture and Performance in Public Affairs: A Study of the Forest Products Industry," in L. Preston (ed.), *Research in Corporate Social Performance and Policy* IV. Greenwich, CT: JAI Press.

Waddock, S., and S. Graves (1997). "Quality of Management and Quality of Stakeholder Relations: Are they Synonymous?" *Business and Society* 36 (3): 250–279.

Wartick, S., and P. Cochran (1985). "The Evolution of the Corporate Social Performance Model," *Academy of Management Review* 10 (4): 758–769.

Watson, T. (2001). "Integrating Planning and Evaluation: Evaluating the Public Relations Practice and Public Relations Programs," in R. Heath (ed.), *Handbook of Public Relations.* Thousand Oaks, CA: Sage.

# 11

# Information, Communications Systems, and Technology in Public Affairs

EDWARD A. GREFE AND SCOTT A. CASTLEMAN

Two events, more than a decade apart, set the stage for this chapter. The first event took place in Albany, NY, in the late 1980s; the second in the office of the senior issues manager for a multinational oil company in late 2003. Their connection is eerie.

The Albany episode brought together representatives of the Mars Candy Company and the Hershey Foods Corporation. (Among the representatives of Hershey present at the meeting in Albany was one of the authors.) Mars wanted approval to sell liquor-filled candy in the State of New York. The repeal of prohibition had kept in place legal restraints on liquor-filled products crossing state lines and the company was seeking similar approval in every state in order to sell a new line of products.

Hershey was not opposed to the sale of such candy. But, Hershey's view was that the candy should be sold in sufficiently large quantities and at a price whereby the product could be sold only as a novelty in special gift stores. Hershey hoped to avoid the possibility of an inexpensive product being displayed and sold side-by-side with their own candy, an actuality that had occurred when Mars had been successful in two states before Hershey got

organized. Among other reasons, Hershey argued, was the possible enticement of a less expensive, readily available, liquor-filled product to children, and the consequent backlash among parents against all candy companies.

The legislator chairing the meeting that day asked what Hershey wanted in terms of amendments. Three were offered. Immediately, the Mars representative replied, "I doubt that my client will agree to any of these proposed amendments." Whereupon the Hershey representative responded: "That's odd. Mars agreed to all three amendments just yesterday in Tallahassee, Florida, and in Austin, Texas."

To say that the reaction of the Mars lobbyist was one of shock would be to put it mildly. He had no knowledge of what Mars had agreed to elsewhere because the culture of that company—at least at that time—was to not share information. Hershey, by contrast, had built a nationwide computer system which allowed it to track legislative issues on a minute-by-minute basis. That enabled Hershey to mount a national strategy on any issue.

Fast forward to the second related event, nearly a decade later. The oil company executive smiled when he heard this story and then related his own version. His example reflected what we believe—and he confirmed—is going on globally today. (This second event comes from an interview conducted by one of the authors with the oil company executive.)

His story involved showing up in Bolivia to try and help the local affiliate deal with a public affairs problem that had arisen when a group of local Bolivians mounted opposition to a program the oil company was about to undertake. The local manager's reaction was familiar to those of us who worked political campaigns throughout the United States in the late 1960s and early 1970s when the political campaign consultant industry was born. At the dawn of the political consultant business, this new breed was generally met with suspicion and skepticism from the locals.

True to form, the Bolivian manager said: "What can corporate offer? This is a local matter. We do politics differently here than is done anywhere else. You could not possibly understand nor be able to help us. We can handle it ourselves." The view that "we do things differently here" mirrored precisely the reaction US political campaign consultants experienced when arriving to handle a campaign in a state in which they had not previously worked—or later, when first arriving in a foreign nation.

Realizing the Bolivian manager's sensitivity, the corporate manager from London responded: "You may be right, but as we read your report on the tactics being used we see an identical pattern to those employed in two other nations and in two US states. That suggests that those locally who are proposing this action did not on their own come up with either a strategy or an implementation plan. Our guess is that your Bolivian group has consulted with and is being coached by others. We believe the Internet is being used to communicate and link this plan globally. So it is no longer a local issue, one you can solve by yourself. Rather, it is a global issue that must be dealt with by a strategy developed at headquarters and executed locally."

As these two events reflect, today the political stage is global. And while all politics may be local—a point we shall make repeatedly—the impact of local politics in one nation is felt in local communities in other nations almost immediately.

Often the mistaken notion is that one can segregate one's issues and the strategy for dealing with them on a jurisdiction-by-jurisdiction basis. That notion is the old politics, and is no more true today within the confines of the fifty United States—as the lobbyist from Mars learned to his embarrassment and dismay—than it is within the confines of the nations throughout the world, be they 'united' or not.

Today the Internet is fueling issues and the mobilization of adherents to those issues. International grassroots groups with an agenda operate on the notion: "Act locally, but think globally." And just as many organizations were slow to recognize or to grasp the adaptation of political organizing techniques by their critics in the latter part of the twentieth century, so too many organizations today seem equally baffled on how to recognize and respond to their critics who now mount efforts in many international settings simultaneously and with great speed.

This chapter will focus on the new possibilities available to the public affairs community. We will discuss the technology that now enables organizations to monitor issue activity and mount a response. A look at the public affairs industry, today, is a look at the information-sharing realities of the Information Economy, a new generation of stakeholders, and the challenge of managing a message in this environment. We will emphasize the need to make the technology subordinate to the strategy and the message. But, we will focus on how to use the technology to achieve—if nothing else—a place at the table where decisions are made rather than be a bystander to the decision-making process while it is controlled by one's critics.

## NEW POSSIBILITIES

The focus of this chapter is information and communications systems and technologies (ICSTs) and their integration into the practice of public affairs. ICSTs have changed what is possible in terms of executing outreach tactics in both *ad hoc* campaigns as well as formal advocacy programs. This is true for associations, issue groups, and the corporation. Old tactics—including leaving decisions on how to handle issues up to local managers—no longer apply. Communication tools and information technologies have, likewise, offered new possibilities to the individual stakeholder, requiring public affairs managers to adapt to maintain control. The new possibilities created by ICSTs now enable advocacy to embrace tactics not logistically available twenty years ago and are making the entire public affairs discipline expand rapidly.

Before looking at the ICSTs themselves and where they are headed, it is interesting to look at the manner in which they are affecting the public affairs profession overall. There may be some fundamental effects that technology integration is having on the practice, discipline, and art of public affairs. Perspective, however, is important. There is a significant difference between changing a profession's core goals and purposes as opposed to changing the tools and tactics used to achieve them. Even more significant would be changes to the profession's relevance within the world—especially to its practitioners.

In this chapter's introduction, a story was told recounting two events—the candy company lobbyist discovering he was disconnected from his organization's strategy as it evolved; and the oil executive voicing the folly of coordinating advocacy tactics by assuming geopolitical vacuums exist. Universally, public affairs professionals face obstacles in managing and executing strategy. Embracing new tactics and recognizing new possibilities are a must. The lobbyist for Mars Candy was blindsided in the late 1980s by what the global oil company's senior issues manager, by 2003, inherently knew. That is that campaign tactics are by necessity executed locally, but managers must plan and coordinate campaign tactics from a vantage point where there is 360° view. Why? Information and tactics are easily packaged, rapidly distributed, and universally available through ICSTs.

Every place is connected to every other place through technology. Your opposition's message and tactics are sent to stakeholders around the globe in seconds. What takes place in one locality now echoes nationally, if not globally. More and more outreach tactics are imported from other geographic areas, where they have been tested and refined. Your advocates are seeing events that have already been scripted somewhere else.

The moral of the story is that things like ICSTs showing up can, and do, change the world. And public affairs managers must be willing to change as well. It is, therefore, not enough to simply digest the best practices of integrating ICSTs. For one, those best practices are still being written. Second, any lessons, are only temporary as the world and the industry continue to change. There cannot be, for these reasons, a magic playbook, manual, or guidebook. We are far enough down the path of integrating ICSTs to understand that, as a discipline, public affairs not only must be able to identify stakeholders, but must also identify new possibilities.

New possibilities today, as is often the case, are tomorrow's realities. This is the process of innovation and integration that recurs time and time again. Not so long ago continuously staying connected to ever shifting strategies was not viable. And neither was executing tactics locally but coordinating tactics nationally or globally. Both were emerging new possibilities in the 1980s, but are realities today.

## The Electronic Town Hall: Connecting the Governed with the Governing

At the dawn of the so-called "New Economy" of the 1990s, the "Dot-com Bubble" to some, the Internet and World Wide Web were fueling a frantic rethinking of the way all business and communications processes were structured. Beyond the massive numbers of people trying to predict the business and economic implications, there was a much smaller number of technological and political purists who had a more profound assessment of what the future held. ICSTs were, according to their measure, empowering the weak, removing corruption, and offering true democracy. True democracy, created by unrestricted access to ideas and unfiltered expression of opinions—available to both the governing and the governed—would be enabled by technology. Thinking along these lines is still occurring. Joe Trippi wrote about the effect that the Internet is having on the way political candidates in the United States win elections in the September 2004 issue of *Wired* magazine, opening his article with the following:

> The Internet has been revolutionizing business and culture for years—and that was just a side effect. What's really going on is a political phenomenon, a democratic movement that flows naturally from our civic lives and spills over into the music we hear, the clothes we buy, the causes we support.

> (2004: 97–98)

H. Ross Perot proposed, during his unsuccessful bid for President of the United States, the concept of the "electronic town hall." The electronic town hall was a place in the virtual world, the World Wide Web, where citizens could be educated and voice their opinion on a myriad of issues great and small. Perot saw ICSTs as a way to take away the distortion and influence of unions, associations, lobbyists, special interests, political parties, and any layers that separated the decision makers from the people. This separation was causing distortion and political shaping—leaving the opinions of the individual citizen unheard. Incorporating ICSTs into the infrastructure of governance would allow the unfiltered "true voices" of the people to be heard.

What has come from these ideas and predictions thanks, in part, to ICST integration? The practice of public affairs, particularly grassroots advocacy, will always be fundamentally about finding and nurturing one-to-one relationships with stakeholders. Efforts to identify the stakeholders, acquiring or capturing demographic and psychographic data about them, are more efficient using relational databases—the foundation of the ICSTs in use today. By utilizing the Internet medium, ICSTs are fundamental in mobilizing stakeholders—from one individual to millions—through applications like e-mail and text messaging. Public sites, extranets, intranets, and blogs on the World Wide Web now educate on issues and offer analysis and opinions from those who have them. The Internet is surpassing traditional mass media as the primary global source of all types of information. Effortlessly and without the need for substantial direct mail, call center, or other distribution budgets, ICSTs accomplish tasks whose costs had for a long time kept broad advocacy out of the reach of many organizations.

Grassroots tactics in particular, the activity of reaching out directly to individual stakeholders rather than smaller numbers of authority figures above them, have steadily increased as a cornerstone strategy because ICSTs make those tactics financially viable. At the fundamental level the integration of ICSTs has been significantly beneficial to the basic functions of building advocacy programs—recruiting, educating, motivating, and mobilizing. The one-to-one relationship, with human contact, remains the strongest and most enduring relationship that organizations can forge with a stakeholder. Public affairs managers, as yet, still have a place between the advocate and those in positions of authority—a space where they can practice their profession. But again, it is not a change in the goals and fundamentals of practicing public affairs that has been the catalyst for growth and new possibilities.

Bill Clinton ultimately prevailed over H. Ross Perot in the 1992 US presidential election—and electronic town halls as envisioned by Perot were essentially abandoned. A few years later the Dot-com Bubble began to burst and the New Economy began to fall. Fortunately, ICSTs survived—and the "Information Economy" has replaced the "New Economy." The Information Economy covets the value inherent in being able to capture, manage, and share information. The Information Economy, and the changes it is having on our stakeholders, are the catalyst for new possibilities and value the same "information unfiltered" principles behind the electronic town hall. The environment our industry attempts to influence and manage, therefore, is what is changing and it is this that necessitates new tactics.

In short, new possibilities are not created by virtue of ICSTs changing the public affairs discipline—but rather by ICSTs having already changed the world. The process of innovation and integration never stops. The electronic town hall did not become reality, but the possibility it was based on—advocacy that bypasses the layers of organized groups to get the stakeholder directly to the authority holder—has become a reality.

## Heterarchies: Acting Locally and Coordinating Globally

The events surrounding the initiation of military action against Iraq by the United States, following the 9/11 terrorist attacks in the United States, illustrate new possibilities that have arrived. All of us engaged in the political advocacy business are still examining and evaluating the February 15, 2002, anti-war protests that occurred in front of the United Nations and simultaneously in cities worldwide.

International political issues spurring sudden and widespread political grassroots movements are not new. Such movements, as well, have used the Internet and other ICSTs to educate, recruit, and mobilize broadly and rapidly. Maude Barlow, a seasoned international activist whose campaign against ratification of the Multilateral Agreement on Investment (MAI) in the mid-1990s, is a fitting example. The agreement was not finalized at the 1996 meeting of the World Trade Organization (WTO) in Singapore and was transferred to the Organization of Economic Cooperation and Development (OECD), known by most as the "G-8", to be discreetly negotiated. The grassroots movement is in some degree credited with preventing G-8 adoption of the agreement.

But two aspects of the Iraq anti-war protests are of particular interest. The first is the unparalleled growth rate in terms of the recruiting of the participants, considering it was not created by a seasoned international activist; and, second, the speed and synchronization with which participants were mobilized, considering there was no central coordinating entity to directly manage local execution.

The *New York Times* writer Jennifer Lee used the word "heterarchies" when describing the headless structure of these Iraq anti-war protests. "Heterarchy" is a term she borrowed from social theorists who use it to describe decentralized social networks (Lee, 2003). Lee investigated the protests and worldwide rallies because what began with a single e-mail written by a twenty-two-year-old activist by the name of Eli Pariser became, in *three months'* time, a total number of activists equal to that which took anti-Vietnam War organizers *three years* to build. Lee was intrigued by what may be the fastest-growing movement in American history.

On the same subject, another piece, written by George Parker, catalogued the chronology of events beginning with Pariser's September 12, 2001, e-mail to a group of friends asking them to contact their legislators to urge a restrained response to the previous day's terrorist attacks (Parker, 2003). Within three days of that e-mail, Pariser and a recent graduate from the University of Chicago named David Pickering, who had 1,000 names on an online petition, decided to join forces. By September 18, 2001, Pariser and Pickering had launched a Web site and over 120,000 people from 180 countries had signed their online petition. By October 9, as their campaign crested, Pariser and Pickering were able to submit to several world leaders on October 9, 2001, a petition containing over half a million online signatures requiring over 3,000 pages for a printout. The success of this campaign is credited to the power of the Internet Web sites and e-mail.

As Parker (2003) noted in his article:

> Internet democracy allows citizens to find one another directly, without phone trees or meetings of chapter organizations, and it amplifies their voices in the electronic storms or "smart mobs" (masses summoned electronically) that it seems able to generate in a few hours. With cell phones and instant messaging, the time frame of protest might soon be the nanosecond.

While Parker (2003) focused on the growth of the movement, Lee (2003) tracked how the non-centralized organization, relying on e-mails, Web sites, and text messages, was able to direct a grassroots "heterarchy" with these information and communications systems tying the group together.

Like the electronic town hall, heterarchies do away with a centralized, top-down organizing body—typical of protests and grassroots movement in the past and of virtually all corporate and trade associations' public affairs efforts—that is hierarchical in structure. Both, however, illustrate that ICST integration has enabled a new type of activism, much different than the advocacy we know from traditional public affairs campaigns or even broad protests from the Vietnam era, the Million Man March, or labor disputes. This new tactic puts out the message and nothing stands between the stakeholders and the targets, or between stakeholders and each other.

Lee (2003) cautions that before organization gurus dismiss these movements as headless and therefore unmanageable, they must realize decentralized organization does *not* mean loss of control. To reinforce her point she notes a delay that was orchestrated before the more than 2 million people in over 175 cities worldwide staged their simultaneous protest. At the last minute, some of the US-based organizers decided to wait and see what Colin Powell had to say in his presentation to the United Nations. The delay was carried off without a hitch by supplementing the updated demonstration schedule going out via alternative radio stations with e-mails, text messaging, and Web sites focused on spreading the word from one activist to the next regarding the new timetable.

It used to be true that only those organizations with substantial enough budgets could communicate with the masses, but now ICSTs have made one-to-many communication easily executable by anyone, even the individual stakeholders. Direct communication from stakeholder to stakeholder, advocate to advocate, or protestor to protestor, one-to-one, is called "P2P communication", where P2P is short for "peer to peer" (similar to B2B, short for "business to business"). ICSTs have enabled both one-to-many and P2P on a large scale, and this represents two things that are both at the heart of this new activism: (1) the underlying idea of ICSTs removing barriers between the governed and

governing, and (2) relinquishing some amount of their direct control is something the public affairs practitioner must embrace in order to continue reaching out to those stakeholders within programs that face the technical reality of the modern day by pushing global coordination of local tactics.

Whether we discuss "e-activism," "Internet democracy," or "dot-org politics", the introduction of information and communications systems technologies integrating e-mail, database, Internet, cellular, Web, and text-messaging systems is now here for public affairs practitioners to ponder and, hopefully, to master. Some have done so successfully. The underlying concept of the electronic town hall, heterarchical protests, one-to-many communication, and P2P is the most important concept for public affairs to master … the *online community*. In 2004, Howard Dean's presidential campaign and the advocacy group MoveOn.org both showed that online communities can translate into effective political influence centers. We will look at this more specifically later in this chapter.

Communicating with stakeholders, as well as the individual performing the role as advocate, is easier and more convenient than ever in history—possibly too easy. The use of ICSTs has expanded the scale of the profession and shrunken the world of the stakeholder because the governing and the governed are only a click away. For those who endeavor to inspire and communicate, ICSTs mean more can be done with less. This is efficiency and growth—more geographic reach, more volume, less time, and less money. At the most basic level the fundamental impact of ICSTs on the public affairs industry, campaign tactics, and advocacy in general is "growth." Just in terms of scale, they are all bigger. More activity is possible and more activists are available.

Growth is making public affairs a more challenging profession in three undeniable ways, the first being that business demands on public affairs managers are now to produce more with fewer resources. The world is smaller and faster and they are expected to keep up. A single e-mail and a single Web site can carry a message beyond impact levels of traditional public relations (PR) tactics such as television and print advertising. Public affairs managers are being expected to provide bigger impact and increased influence on the community and the government.

Stakeholders having technological means and access, which most do, can engage in activist activity at will, which leaves less space for the public affairs manager to coordinate them. Electronic town hall ideas that inspire realities such as heterarchically orchestrated protests are creating another, second, challenge for public affairs managers—maintaining control. Think in terms of the question "What is more problematic—an apathetic stakeholder who will not get involved or a motivated activist who does not stick to the message?"

The fact that ICSTs have made it viable for public affairs campaigns to incorporate large-scale tactics has also made it easy and convenient for the stakeholder to perform at their end. The third challenge which public affairs, the entire profession, must manage is that of what could be termed "constituent devaluation." As one might expect, this growth—in terms of scale, volume, and numbers of activist contacts, correspondence, and activities—has resulted in more political noise. Those we are trying to influence with write-your-legislator, petition drive, phone bank, direct mail, etc., tactics know this is the case. Online surveys may be given less attention since they could represent the opinions of undetermined individuals from unknown corners of the Internet, or at least could be perceived as such. Some recipients may ignore e-mails received in droves by rationalizing, that if these constituents truly cared about the issue, they would have spent more effort than the thirty seconds it takes to send an all but pre-written e-mail correspondence. The same could be thought of phone "patch through" efforts. Even online surveys and polls present public affairs managers with a double-sided problem—on the one hand, the more advocacy activity there is the more it takes to rise above the fray and create impact; on the other hand, as advocacy tactics are easier for stakeholders to get involved in, overall results may be diminished in the eyes of those they are trying to influence as being insincere or artificially inflated.

There is little doubt for those who are suspicious of ICST impact that the public affairs discipline is "crafting the message" above all else. There is also no question about the notion that the role of the public affairs practitioner includes establishing relationships and managing the communications process with those individual stakeholders. Technology has not changed that. What technology has changed, however, is the tactics available for implementation into the execution of public affairs campaigns. How these tactics alter the campaign management process itself, and how technology has accentuated engaging more individual stakeholders in advocacy programs, is more defined. One cannot truly say that "globalization" is an accurate term for public affairs programs since most organizations' issues and the relevant governing influences are most often well within geographic boundaries of some type. Execution remains true to the timeless statement by former US Congressman Tip O'Neill that "All politics is local" but the coordination of tactics is no longer necessary at the local level, as the Bush campaign of 2004 proved—with national direction of precinct and sub-precinct operations.

There remains much to be learned about what works and what does not work. Even these lessons will be temporary, as the integration of technology to assist the public affairs craft continues to evolve. Our public affairs profession, as it is today, sprang from the type of political consulting, which did not emerge in the United States until the 1960s and 1970s, that borrows lessons learned in business marketing tactics and advises matching a narrower message to targeted constituencies. The computer and information technology innovations that were the foundation for modern day ICST's were developing at nearly the same time.

The story of public affairs and ICSTs is just beginning. The profession has found paths to efficiency and growth, no doubt about it. But is bigger also translating into better? That is a matter of opinion, but this is a story with no ending. It is a story about a relatively young profession adopting and adapting recent innovations, a recurring process, and finding new possibilities as it does so.

To buttress this point, we reference Michael Cornfield's *Politics Moves Online*, in which he notes:

> A revolutionary theory of online politics projects greater popular involvement in politics out of the notion that because more people *can* see more information in time to act on it, they *will*, and their efforts will be decisive. If men (and women) were smart voters, no campaigning would be necessary. Although the Internet makes it easier for individuals to act on what they see, it does not revise what Mancur Olson postulated as the logic of collective action: "rational, self-interested individuals will not act to achieve their common or group interests" unless the number of individuals is quite small or "unless there is coercion or some other special device."
>
> The Net is, in some respects, that special service. It makes easier the work of grassroots organizers in trying to overcome the inertia attributed to the logic of collective action. In their digital-era reconsideration of Olson's theory, Arthur Lupia and Gisela Sin conclude that, "by increasing noticeability, decreasing organization costs, or increasing the range over which credible commitments are possible, evolving technologies can transform formerly unattractive partners into attractive ones." But the Net is not so special as to eliminate the need for organizers. Someone still has to come up with the revelation.
>
> (Cornfield, 2004: 21)

## ICST INTEGRATION DOES NOT CHANGE THE FUNDAMENTALS OF PUBLIC AFFAIRS

There is no question that technology and public affairs come together and that, symbiotically, they will remain linked as partners in communication far into the future. We are witnessing just now only the early stages of technology's integration into public affairs. It is important, however, to be conscious of the limits of ICST integration when setting expectations and when creating strategy.

Nearly all public affairs professionals today are aware of what communications systems and technologies are in existence and are equally aware of how these technologies provide communications conduits to stakeholders. The ability to communicate with large numbers of stakeholders quickly and at a viable cost has been commonplace for some time, as has their assistance with the staples of building advocacy programs. As a profession, seeing the growth and efficiencies ICSTs offer, the public affairs profession has been active and eager to take advantage.

We have looked at the manner that ICSTs are affecting the public affairs profession as an overall industry:

1 Bringing advocacy tactics within reach of more organizations.
2 Enabling new tactics.
3 Enhancing the convenience for stakeholders becoming activists.
4 Overall growth in the amount, and frequency, of advocacy tactic use.

From a broad perspective the increase in efficiency for the cornerstone activities of outreach programs—identifying, educating, motivating—has pushed public affairs campaigns into the Information Economy. To understand the integration of ICSTs it is necessary to also explore deeper than these macro-views, or previously articulated observations, and consider the ground level of public affairs campaigns, from the perspective of a public affairs manager. From that perspective the importance of knowing the limits of ICSTs is extremely important.

Both challenges and new possibilities for public affairs managers have, and will continue to be, presented. Growth like the public affairs industry has experienced is both hard to manage and hard to cope with for a public affairs practitioner attempting to stay in control. As such, public affairs managers are asking if bigger is translating into better.

Advocacy and grassroots programs are becoming fundamental strategies at a rapidly expanding number of organizations, even among those that have a long-standing culture that traditionally relied on only lobbying to navigate the political seas. As such, a more crowded and efficient advocacy arena has evolved enabling all combatants to do more with less. As Dennis Johnson noted in *Congress OnLine*:

> The electronic advocacy revolution has made it possible for marginally-funded organizations to spend relatively little money to reach their own members, like-minded citizens, and then to reach Members of Congress, the White House, and the agencies of the Executive Branch. A new class of activists has emerged: individuals who perhaps otherwise would not become involved, would not write to Congress and who would not take time off work to protest an issue. The online activist is asked to do something relatively simple: read the e-mail, and if you believe in what we say, click on the name of your legislator, and write an e-mail, or click onto our website, choose paragraphs and phrases that best fit your sentiments, and then send the message to Congress.
>
> (2004: 59–60)

But, the advocacy arena, more than ever, can leave scars. It is increasingly difficult to generate impact and rise above the noise of opinions, e-mails, transmissions, and Web hits. The pressure is turned up on public affairs programs, which are asked for greater results while expending fewer resources. Goals are tough and budgets are even tougher. One public affairs manager lamented to us in a meeting in Washington, DC, that the more her department accomplishes, the more it takes to win.

Most practitioners have realized, by trial and error, that even the most sophisticated technologies cannot provide "public affairs in a box"—some practitioners, unfortunately, do erroneously make this very assumption. There are numerous examples of organizations, for example, publishing Web sites and integrating online advocacy tools into those sites without regard to basic public affairs best practices for recruiting and motivating. Low participation and certainly no real results are equally common. With participation rates below any acceptable level, no overall impact on the issue is made; and generally an embarrassing waste of stakeholders' time and the organization's resources results. Outreach tactics and programs

can get a bad name at these organizations who sometimes conclude that they do not work.

John Heino, a federal affairs professional at Minnesota Power, explained the basic public affairs principle in this area as follows:

> Because people are motivated by different things, you need to build a variety of rewards and recognition opportunities into your grassroots program. Perception is critical. People have to believe that involvement actually produces results. Finally, you have to minimize barriers so busy employees don't view participation as more trouble than it's worth.
>
> (Heino, 2000)

ICSTs do, as we have discussed, minimize barriers to stakeholders, so many organizations just implement Web sites and online advocacy tools, without regard to the considerations Heino specified.

Issues can many times be underexplained on Web sites, or provide only direct links to draft legislation—without explanation, analysis, or linkage to the stakeholder. Stakeholders may not be effectively recruited, using messages and connections that directly appeal to them. Even more frequently "public affairs in a box" mentalities leave stakeholders poorly prepared, if at all, for advocacy roles because they don't train away or dispel common fears and misconceptions about the political process. Those that have participated go unthanked and those that did not participate are not asked why. Public affairs professionals should, even at the entry level, know the value of these types of activities! Yet, we see sophisticated corporations and associations integrate ICSTs while looking for public affairs guidance in their server's user manual!

A little more than half, approximately 60 percent, of qualified citizens in the United States are registered to vote. Somewhere in the region of 60–80 percent (US Census Bureau, 2002: 3–4) of those who are registered will cast a ballot in any particular election. This aspect of the American political system is often a lure for election-year outreach programs designed to weigh influence in the election and to recruit new political advocates. ICSTs are being employed extensively to do just that. Voter registration drives as part of Get-out-the-Vote (GOTV) campaigns target every attractive demographic in their relational databases. Intranets and Web pages distribute the necessary voter forms and candidate score cards—personalized according to the individual addresses—advertisements, Web sites, blast e-mails and phone banks urge filling out and submitting those forms while stressing which candidates in their districts are preferred and why. Every effort is made to make registering and learning the candidates quick, easy, and more convenient. Voter registration increases are celebrated by organizations as outreach successes.

Newly registered voters' commitment and allegiance, however, go unquestioned—and unconfirmed after the election, despite readily available voter data. The amount of activity is lauded, but often the actual results are not given equal attention. In many cases, no real relationship was made with the stakeholder that lasted past the election. The point is that the fundamental public affairs skills needed to forge relationships, and not just a mastering of the tools of the craft, are what make the public affairs profession indispensable … if bigger is to be, indeed, better. Public affairs managers, in terms of function and capability, are more important than ever.

Person-to-person communications, outside of organized online communities, intensify the challenge for public affairs managers of staying in control of the message. Few have effectively managed online community advocacy and, thus, have not harnessed the possibility. Instead, they are experiencing the challenges of being left behind, tactically. Advocates can use Web sites, message boards, chat rooms, and blogs to sidestep organized campaign programs to express opinions directly with CEOs, legislators, and each other. Heterarchical protests, as previously discussed, also demonstrate stakeholders executing tactics, without an organization providing coordinating management. After protestors' feet are on the street, real-time coordination is possible without organizational aid, through text messaging, resulting in what have been termed "smart mobs."

(Note: Aside from the lack of traditional organizing structures, or the P2P communications that enable them to succeed without structure, little focus in this chapter has been put on ICSTs and their specific utility in the logistics of large rallies and protests—such as the role of text-messaging in the 2001 protests in the Philippines ousting President Joseph Estrada, for example. The reason is that such protests and rallies are not a likely tactic of the vast majority of public affairs professionals. Instead, tactics that require as little of their stakeholders, and their own organization, as possible are—the preference that an electronic mob of correspondence over a physical mob of activists will arrive on the doorstep of decision makers. It is also uncertain how much feet-on-the-street protests will continue to be utilized now that virtual, fingers-on-the-keyboard protests are gaining in popularity.)

Using ICSTs is not a new concept for public affairs professionals. Even so, many professionals with years of experience incorporating ICSTs into campaign tactics still feel unsure about the role that technology should occupy in their organization. This is understandable. Mixed experiences from campaign to campaign show that there is no set of best practices that will ensure positive results. Why do some campaigns see positive results while others using the same technology do not? Was the technology better or flawed in some manner in each case? Is the problem outside the technology—human fallibility? The answer is, of course, is that ICSTs are going to benefit public affairs practitioners to the extent that they are put in their proper role, skillfully integrated, and masterfully operated.

While it is necessary to have a functional understanding of ICSTs, as tools of the public affairs craft, it is even more important to reserve a rightful role for them. It is a point we cannot stress enough as the single most important, overriding guiding principle: *Technology must be subservient to communications strategy and secondary to crafting of the message.* Technology, in our view, must serve the strategy and message, developed by public affairs professionals, for the benefit of their campaigns.

There are concrete limits, as of now, to what ICSTs can do in public affairs efforts—the rest relies on us humans and the relationships we make. One of the most comprehensive and available resources for help with public affairs fundamentals is published by the Public Affairs Council in Washington, DC (http://www.pac.org), in a book entitled *Winning at the Grassroots* (Heino, 2000), which includes advice and experience from prominent practitioners on many of the common activities in public affairs programs. We strongly suggest it for all practitioners. Again, the reality is that integrating ICSTs can assuredly make any public affairs program *bigger*, but public affairs fundamentals are the key to making them *better*. As P2P online communities and other tactics are approached this remains a concern.

Keeping in mind the limits of technology and the need to reserve a rightful role for ICSTs, what is out there and how is it being used? When discussing public affairs and technology, one invariably runs into many of the same gray areas we see when trying to define the public affairs discipline itself. There is general acceptance that the public affairs discipline is a profession of building and managing relationships. ICSTs are useful only within the context of supporting these efforts. In our view, the most effective way to approach the technologies is to categorize their use into two ways:

1  *Ad hoc campaigns.* ICSTs are integrated to facilitate a linear strategy that has a definite beginning and end. There is generally no tie-in with other campaigns or their ICST requirements. In this aspect the ICSTs are implemented as *tools* to do specific tasks. *Ad hoc* campaigns utilize ICSTs for their automation and efficiency benefits more than their ability to integrate and share information.
2  *Formal advocacy programs.* In a formal advocacy program there is a volunteer/opt-in membership aspect, the program itself has a distinct identity and brand, pursues long-term goals, and will be founded on a mission statement. As such, these environments integrate ICSTs as *systems* or *infrastructures* that are designed to support

public affairs life cycles through multiple years, campaigns, and tactics. A requirement is placed on the ICST configuration to be able to perform *ad hoc* campaigns, but also to support the formal program's needs as well—that of providing a 360° view of activity and results.

No matter how one may choose to categorize ICSTs, it is essential that limits on the technology be considered. While many old tactics may no longer apply, the fundamentals of our profession still do.

## AD HOC CAMPAIGN TOOLS

An *ad hoc* campaign can be thought of as a battle without the context of an overall war. Winning or losing does not affect a larger public affairs goal or campaign—*ad hoc* campaigns start when an issue arises and end when the issue is over. Most often defensive—or at least reactionary—in nature, an *ad hoc* campaign can be an effective tactic for handling crisis situations. They are not and should not be the strategy, on the other hand, of organizations that are effectively attempting to bring about long-term political change. That is not to say *ad hoc* campaigns are lesser in value, as they do reflect a willingness to reach out to stakeholders when their organization is threatened by something critical and specific. ICSTs have added tremendous value to the *ad hoc* campaign manager but have limited staying power.

Previously we pointed out that many organizations new to advocacy outreach tactics have embraced them. The integration of ICSTs as effective enablers of *ad hoc* campaign tactics represents the primary reason for this growth. Political crisis, therefore, is the most common incentive for adding grassroots advocacy and outreach tactics to existing communications efforts. Something comes up that, if not dealt with, may have disastrous consequences. An *ad hoc* campaign is initiated using ICSTs that make it viable and cost-effective. Just a few examples of situations where *ad hoc* campaigns, at least in the United States, are popular reactions: legislation, legal actions, executive appointments, public relations problems, appropriations Bills, redistricting battles, elections, etc. Once the crisis is past, everything stops and the *ad hoc* campaign is concluded.

Significant beneficiarias of *ad hoc* campaigns are single-issue advocacy groups, interests, and movements. They are focused and passionate, for one thing, and, secondly, perpetually in crisis mode. They use *ad hoc* campaigns well and the emotional connection they have with their stakeholders often translates into successful results.

While not able to sustain effective results, like formal advocacy programs, the appeal of *ad hoc* campaigns is easy to understand. For a variety of situations, specifically, they are an effective method of addressing them. They are also appealing because they are linear, easy to understand, less difficult to sell within an organization, and can be executed by a small resource base. As we look at how ICSTs are used in *ad hoc* campaigns, much of the discussion is from the perspective of activity in the United States. Executing locally—in other areas of the world—is subject to the nuances and technical development available in those areas.

For the *ad hoc* program, most often, it is a matter of quickly alerting the stakeholder about the issue, offering the necessary background information, and asking for support by performing some very specific action. This usually includes either attending a rally or a march, donating money, making contact with the legislator, or writing the local media. The initial alert to stakeholders is usually in an urgent tone and the message is of some significant result looming if stakeholders do not take action. This is fairly common among *ad hoc* campaigns. The differences, rather, from one campaign to the next, are most often in the identifying of stakeholders and the type of information shared with them to educate them on the issue. The mobilization, or "call to action," aspects have fewer variations.

Exhibit 11.1 shows the basic skeleton of a common *ad hoc* campaign and its integrated ICSTs.

---

### Exhibit 11.1 A Common *Ad Hoc* Campaign with Integrated Information and Communication Systems

LOCATE

*Stakeholder database.* No matter whether the data are purchased from the market or derived from existing membership, accounting, customer, voter, and/or employee records, the first ICST integrated is the stakeholder database. Depending on the campaign's purpose there may be a need to associate each stakeholder in the database with their respective legislative districts and the legislators that represent those districts. From this "legislative match" the ability to direct the stakeholder to specific and relevant legislators is derived, when requesting that they take action. Many stakeholders, possibly most of your stakeholders, will not know who their legislators are, or how to contact them. More sophisticated stakeholder database products have legislative matching as an inherent activity within the system.

EDUCATE

*Public Web sites.* Beyond being the environment for online advocacy tools, public Web sites are simply fundamental in all public affairs campaigns. Once built, they share information, can administer online surveys, facilitate quick polls, organize chat rooms/newsgroups, and utilize identity-enforcing graphics. They differ from extranets and intranets only in the fact that they are accessible to everyone—without any sort of permission challenge, such as a user name and password—and thus are "public." Public Web sites may ask for user names and passwords but it is only to establish the stakeholder identity within the stakeholder database and is not a function of whether they have permission to view the Web site. Far cheaper and more effective than any other method, the public Web site is the tool for sharing information about your organization and what it stands for … as well as what it is doing to achieve its goals.

## MOTIVATE

*Online advocacy tool.* The belief by a stakeholder not only that they *should* take action, but that they easily *can* take action is powerful motivation, especially if they have just learned about how an issue affects them. Online advocacy tools acquired and ultimately embedded into normal Web pages serve as the environment for stakeholders to take action by writing correspondence to legislators and media over the Internet. Legislative matching can be an integrated function of online advocacy tools, targeting outgoing correspondence based on the stakeholder address, which they enter in the process of using the online advocacy tool. The system can be linked to e-mail and fax services to allow the correspondence to be e-mailed, faxed, or simply printed by the stakeholder. The public affairs manager by providing online advocacy tools offers the stakeholder the ability to learn about the issue, find out why it is important that the stakeholder supports the organization on the issue, obtain educational materials, and take action, all at a single place on the World Wide Web. For this, the stakeholders that use the tool provide back to the public affairs manager, via server logs tracking their activity, a picture of activity levels. The primary purpose is to efficiently spell out the issue to the stakeholder, make a strong enough impact on the stakeholder that they will be motivated to take action, and then enable the stakeholder to act on that motivation.

## ACTIVATE

*Blast messaging.* The "call to action" drives the stakeholders to the Web site and its embedded tools. Either directly—through bulk mail, text messaging, blast fax/e-mail, or phone banks— or broadly; through public relations and advertising the stakeholder is driven back to an online environment that the public affairs manager controls. Many times the education aspect can begin in the initial call to action by previewing the issue and stating its importance to the stakeholder. Stakeholder databases facilitate personalization of the call to action where specific issues, Web sites, and other portions of the call to action can be tailored to fit each stakeholder.

## An *Ad Hoc* Campaign

In the wake of the infamous September 11, 2001, attack on the World Trade Center in New York, there was widespread fear and anxiety in nearby Westchester County about the security of the two nuclear power plants at the Indian Point Energy Center (IPEC) that had been recently acquired by Entergy. This concern was manipulated and fanned by traditional anti-nuclear activist groups whose goal was to force the closure of the Indian Point plants. In the midst of near panic among some citizens, the owner of IPEC—Entergy Services—faced the daunting task of mounting a grassroots community education and outreach effort virtually overnight. In response, the company used technological resources to mount a campaign that heavily relied upon the success of grassroots organizing and public advocacy efforts.

The results were impressive:

1   Nine hundred employees, employee families, and others turned out for a February 2002 rally in Poughkeepsie, complete with pro-Indian Point balloons, banners, and buttons.
2   When the Westchester County Board of Legislators held its first public hearing on a resolution to close Indian Point in March 2002, four hundred chanting, sign-waving grassroots volunteers gathered in opposition.

3  Letters-to-the-editor campaigns began in conjunction with calls to action on various legislative initiatives via e-mail, phone, and fax.
4  One employee created a listserv to help keep supporters informed about the issues surrounding Indian Point.

In addition, the company created an Internet Web site (www.safesecurevital. org) to tell its positive Indian Point story and assisted employee activists at the plants with their own informative website (www. proindianpoint.com).

The employees' *ad hoc* advocacy efforts have been remarkable. Public support for keeping Indian Point open stabilized, the US Nuclear Regulatory Commission and Federal Emergency Management Administration rejected requests to close Indian Point, the progress of anti-nuclear forces was slowed, major daily newspapers came out in support of keeping the plants open and federal and state legislation that the company regarded as an overreaction to public fears about Indian Point were defeated or softened. It was a successful *ad hoc* effort that proved the efficacy of having the right technology in place to mobilize supporters and direct their activities.

Provided that the stakeholder-to-target matching capabilities are strong enough, *ad hoc* campaigns, as outlined in the table, can be executed anywhere and coordinated either nationally or globally. The Internet connects those acting locally, the stakeholders, to the public affairs manager, providing the technology. (The Westchester effort, for example, was directed from the corporation's headquarters in New Orleans, while still empowering local people to participate in the on-the-ground decision making.) ICSTs have been able to broker a mutually agreeable deal between the public affairs manager and the potential activist. As public affairs managers provide convenience through things like online advocacy tools or online surveys, more stakeholders have agreed to become active, especially in times of crisis.

Many *ad hoc* campaigns are undertaken as a numbers game, determining success or failure

based on the amount of phone calls, letters, faxes, and e-mails they were able to generate. In a sense, therefore, ICSTs have been instrumental to public affairs managers who need to produce a "show of strength" behind their position. As we have already touched on, there can be some real concerns when integrating ICSTs in this manner. It is broadly known that organizations can be effective at generating significant levels of stakeholder activity by their calls to action. That is the concern … it can be viewed as *activity* rather than solid *support*.

E-mail activity, in particular, has issues that deserve special attention. Prior to 2003, stakeholders sending legislators a fax was estimated by most to be more effective than sending those same legislators an e-mail. Now e-mail is seen as more effective, a sign that the fax machine is losing its prominent position in the halls of government. This has further increased what can only be termed as an explosion in the number of e-mails that legislators have received since the new millennium. The growth has been so pronounced that many of the normal constituent communications handling processes no longer work. There are four things to strongly consider:

1  *Accuracy.* There is no assurance the e-mail was received, read, or appeared as you sent it. Despite the popular assumption, a sending e-mail system cannot guarantee the e-mail made it intact to its destination and, therefore, does not send a failure notification in every instance. The recipient's network, in fact, may receive the message but fail to deliver it to an e-mail inbox. The recipient's e-mail system, and not the sender's, determines what the formatting of the e-mail is. E-mail has evolved into one of the most complicated and layered applications that is broadly utilized today. There are many places for failure and some e-mails have been reported to have taken four days to be delivered.
2  *Constituent services vary.* From office to office and organization to organization there are different standards and processes for handling incoming e-mails. It may go through a process that results in a regular

letter being sent back to the stakeholder, taking several weeks. E-mails may be read at scheduled internals and not daily. Variations in how e-mails are handled are something to consider in *ad hoc* campaigns that have a tight timeline.

3  *Web forms.* Due to the increased number of e-mails being sent by activists, many organizations have stopped publishing an e-mail address and have opted for incoming messages to be sent by filling out a form on the Web. Online advocacy tools that transparently interact with Web forms, instead of allowing stakeholders to do so, may fail to properly fill out and submit the form should there be any change in the location of the form, the structure of the form, or any protective measures built into the form to prevent anything other than a human filling it out. One common example is the presence of an image of a word on the form. In order to submit the form, the word in the image must be manually entered into a particular field in the form.

4  *Spamming.* There are groups in the anti-spammer community who do not view e-mail-based calls to action in the same way as public affairs managers do. Unfortunately, if the anti-spam community (or any member of it) decides that your blast e-mail is spam, you can be given the "black hat" label. Once the black hat label is applied, your network has a decent probability of being targeted for hacker attacks, and it can take months of explaining to get the "white hat" label again. There can be organization-wide disruptions and costs if this occurs. It is critical to know and adhere to spam laws in all geographic areas if blast communication, especially e-mail, is to be used in *ad hoc* campaigns.

With the power that ICSTs give to *ad hoc* campaigns, the public affairs manager should be aware of the price for that power. Jurisdictions are passing stringent controls on the communications that are allowed. Formal advocacy programs are much more effective at steering clear of trouble in this sense, as they rely less on stakeholders that *should* be interested, but rather rely more heavily on stakeholders that have voluntarily stated that they *are* interested. This distinction also highlights the limits of ICSTs for the *ad hoc* campaign.

One organization in the metropolitan Washington DC area that represents the policy concerns of retail tobacco dealers across the United States integrated online advocacy into its existing Web site. Most of the battlegrounds for this association are at the state level, rather than the federal level, and span nearly all of the fifty states. Their strategy was to facilitate their members writing e-mails and faxes to their state's legislators that represented the districts in which they live. The association, after only one month, had a 1.5 percent participation rate among its members. This continued for a full year before they sought professional advice. The problems were glaring. They were simply presenting the Bills being proposed and where the organization stood on each one. There was no training for how to read the Bill, what to include in the correspondence, and what the impact of the proposed legislation promised to be.

Survey responses from the members illustrated that while the online advocacy tool that was integrated could have sent millions of correspondences, that is not enough. The members told the organization, once it asked them, that they were simply intimidated by the act of writing a politician and that they felt so poorly educated on the legislation that they could not engage in even a basic conversation. The integration was done poorly from the start but the reality is that participation rates are incredibly hard to sustain in *ad hoc* campaigns, if they are active for an extended amount of time. Further, it is equally difficult to have a relationship with a group of stakeholders who are asked to repeatedly participate in *ad hoc* campaigns, without any sort of "big picture" or "ultimate goal" of why they should continue to support the possibly numerous demands on their time.

It has already begun, and is expected in our view to continue, that more public affairs managers, who are realizing that their goals are more long term than their tactics, are shying away from *ad hoc* campaign tactics. Those of us in the United States have seen evidence of this even in the most traditional *ad hoc* efforts:

elections. For most of American political history, between election cycles, candidates and parties generally did not reach out to individual stakeholders. Candidate campaign committee and political party Web sites, newsletters, e-mail blasts, and extranets are open for business perpetually. The *ad hoc* campaign tactic of asking for a constituent's vote before the election has been replaced by asking for a longer-term relationship throughout the term.

## FORMAL ADVOCACY PROGRAMS

Formal advocacy programs seek a 360° view of their goals, stakeholders, and environment. The manner in which they integrate ICSTs reflects this desire. Technology is viewed less in terms of tools to perform particular functions than as integrated parts of a machine. Properly done, this type of integration can aid public affairs managers' deal with the challenges of the new activism and the new politics.

Where many *ad hoc* campaigns target volume, formal advocacy programs seek depth. Their use of technology shows this desire. Stakeholder databases are used to track much more information about individuals, and great pains are taken to keep the database records up to date. The reason for this is being able to move beyond broadcast communications, and even beyond traditional segmentation, to more meaningful and effective communications programs. Looking for more useful commonalities, on an issue-by-issue or campaign-by-campaign basis, from a larger pool of stakeholders, and then communicating with the whole by communicating with the resulting groups separately is sometimes referred to as either "narrowcasting" or "micro-targeting." ICSTs make it not only possible, but also rather easy. Benefits abound from this approach and can begin at the very inception of the formal advocacy program.

Formal advocacy programs have an identity, mission, and goals. Involvement by the stakeholder begins by joining the program as a volunteer, thus opting in, to participate. With a proper stakeholder database, in-depth information about the stakeholder can be captured during the process. It is common for surveys to be administered to get a profile of the new stakeholder, what their interests are and what they are willing to do (e.g., write legislators, speak to the media, recruit within their community, etc.). These stakeholder profiles are stored in the stakeholder database and can be searched in innumerable ways to support narrowcasting based on both geographic and psychographic matrices. Activism levels among their stakeholders—their participation—can also become a filtering data layer in narrowcasting, but this raises a common problem throughout the industry.

Traditionally, grassroots and other advocacy outreach professionals are entry to mid-level professionals, compared to the media, PR, and government relations positions often reserved for more experienced public affairs professionals. This is problematic on a technical level, as most public affairs professionals are far less adept at the fundamentals of database management and data processing. More experience, albeit not directly technical, does help tremendously, as lessons do get learned along the way about the pitfalls and traps in using, and implementing, stakeholder databases. Less experienced public affairs professionals often fail to see obstacles far enough in advance to avoid them. There is a common saying, "Garbage in: garbage out," that sums up these problems. Expecting to maintain a formal and ongoing advocacy program based on a database of stakeholder profiles that is not properly maintained and constantly updated is folly. Further, it represents a failure to adhere to a fundamental public affairs practice—continually strengthening and reinforcing the established relationships with stakeholders.

The stakeholder database should be singled out for expanded discussion. It is where 90 percent of any public affairs campaign holds value. There are numerous database platforms, from basic contact management solutions to powerful enterprise resource management (ERM) systems. The basic function of databases for public affairs efforts is to organize and manipulate information about, and for, the stakeholders. Stakeholder information remains the core of all advocacy tactics, and databases remain the foundation of nearly all public affairs technologies. More information about stakeholders is being researched and gathered than ever before, including district matching results: the legislative districts in which they live, and the contact information for legislators that represent them at the federal, state, county, and municipal levels. This translates, for the public affairs manager, a stakeholder address list into a meaningful political "footprint."

This "district matching" or "legislative matching", in the United States, is possible using a combination of census data to aid in establishing zip code-to-legislative district tables and address correction technologies to "correct" or normalize constituent addresses to determine zip+4 assignments. Almost universally, vendors provide the necessary district matching data and tools, rather than organizations developing these technologies themselves. With database technology growing more and more powerful, a wide variety of other data sources and data types is now included in communications efforts. The following are just a few of the more common examples:

1   Survey responses.
2   Polling responses.
3   Profiles: the person's educational background, hobbies, Church affiliation, community organization memberships, spouse, children, etc.
4   Legislator information: who represents the person at multiple levels of government.
5   District assignments.
6   Activist records: letters they have written, e-mails sent, phone calls made, meetings attended.
7   Donor files: contributions to candidates or to causes.
8   Voter files: whether or not a person voted; *not* for whom they voted.
9   Demographic data: concerning the area in which the person lives, to use for comparison.
10  Psychographic data: concerning the area in which the person lives, to use for comparison.
11  Financial information.
12  Employee records.
13  Opt-in e-mail lists.
14  Consumer behavior: purchases made.
15  Media market data: local print and broadcast outlets.
16  Census data.

This information can be manipulated—the popular term is "sliced and diced"—in many ways to design, plan, execute, and ultimately analyze outreach activities' effectiveness. The database is the single most necessary technology in grassroots communications. In most cases, however, stakeholders do not interact directly with the database, but their use of other technologies will fill the database up with information they provide and information gained from research about them. By filling out Web forms, taking online surveys and using online advocacy tools, for example, the stakeholders interact indirectly with the "back end" (i.e. database) of their organization's Web site.

For the public affairs manager, the public Web site represents a bit of a dilemma. On the one hand, grassroots communicators find public Web sites valuable because they allow the message to be presented within the context of the formal advocacy program's identity and brand. On the other hand, this is a far cry from the one-to-one communications that grassroots professionals desire. Nevertheless, many outreach efforts use public Web sites as the primary method to communicate with stakeholders, particularly those who are expected to be on their side of the issue.

There is limited capacity to recruit neutral stakeholders to a position by making a connection on an intellectual, community interest, or political concern level by educating these "strangers" about the issue(s) and how they are affected. The limitation of public Web sites is that sensitive and privileged information cannot be safely protected, should that be a need, without some sort of security protections that would almost always rely on a previously established relationship between the stakeholder and the organization.

In such cases, the *extranet* and *intranet* are often integrated. Anyone familiar with associations has seen the nearly obligatory "Members Only" section on their public Web sites. These sections are access-controlled. Both extranets and intranets are simply access-controlled Web sites, the only differentiator being their target audience. The intranet is meant for trusted individuals inside the organization: members, employees, staff, and consultants. Their relationship with the organization is explicit and direct. Organizational codes of conduct and other policies bind their behavior. The extranet is meant for trusted relationships outside of the organization: suppliers, partners, customers, consultants, and employee families. Anyone who has logged onto their bank for online banking services, by using their Web browser, did so through the bank's extranet. The bank's employees, by contrast, may use their Web browser to fill out their timesheet on the bank's intranet.

In all forms of Web sites—public, extranet, or intranet—a successful grassroots communications strategist understands the following limitations of the site:

1    Constituents must proactively come to view the content—that is, to see the message—whether the person be friend, foe, or uninterested stranger.
2    The message is unlikely to be tailored to their interests, and few genuine relationships are begun in this manner.
3    And no Web site substitutes for person-to-person communication.

Allowances are made by supplementing one's approach with at least the following:

1    Use of other grassroots communications tools to drive potential constituents to the Web site.
2    Use of alternative grassroots communications media—such as direct mail, phone banks, and one-on-one presentations—to add "hits" to the frequency of hearing the message being carried by the Web site.

Databases are the backbone behind persistent advocacy programs and narrowcasting. Narrowcasting is effective because it keeps communications relevant and within the boundaries of the initial connection with stakeholders, the

foundation of the relationship. Based on information stored in the stakeholder database, content and user (i.e. message and stakeholder) are aligned. The American Civil Liberties Union (ACLU) and the American Association of Retired Persons (AARP) are both examples of organizations that embrace targeting a message to a specific, narrow group of their overall membership. These are also organizations that invest in sophisticated Web sites to convey information to their members and would-be members. There are hundreds, possibly thousands, of organizations who also do this to some degree—each in a different manner.

The ACLU has members on the basis of a wide array of issues from general First Amendment rights to group-specific discrimination issues. There is no umbrella issue that binds all of its stakeholders together (except that they all have decided to participate in the ACLU). The relationship the ACLU has with its members could be called "intellectual," compared to the AARP and its members. The AARP also exerts influence on a wide variety of issues; however, the membership has an umbrella commonality—they are all senior citizens. Whether the issue is prescription drug coverage or social security reform, AARP's relationships with the members are broadly relevant and meaningful, because of this common bond they share. Less intellectual, the relationship between the AARP and its members could be described as more personal. Each organization will endeavor to acquire and maintain a different set of data on its members. Formal advocacy programs are continuous and can effectively tell much about each of its stakeholders with each communication. This is a significant benefit of formal programs over *ad hoc* campaigns. The information in the stakeholder database can be invaluable.

Nothing occurring right now in the integration of ICSTs into public affairs, in our opinion, is as significant as the proliferation of online communities. Online communities hark back to the electronic town hall—destinations in the virtual world where opinions and discussion flow free and unfiltered. They are, as well, the world of the newest journalistic and political rising star—the "blogger."

The rise in blogs is generally estimated to be around 400,000 and some attract a larger readership than newspapers in all but the largest American cities. Their impact to gather and distribute information exceeds that of network television media, such as the CBS network. The news media industry is faced with a similar effect from this phenomenon as is the public affairs industry. That effect is that the new activism we have discussed has so empowered individual stakeholders that the role of journalist is now as readily within their reach as is the role of activist.

This was illustrated when bloggers caught the use of bogus documents by CBS anchor Dan Rathers during a television news program; a *Sixty Minutes* story about President George W. Bush's service in the Air National Guard. *Washington Post* writer Howard Kurtz wrote about the story in a piece titled "After Blogs Got Hits, CBS Got a Black Eye" and explained:

> In the last two years, the blogosphere—a vast, free-floating, often quirky club open to anyone with a modem and some opinions—has been growing in influence, with some one-man operations boasting followings larger than those of small newspapers. Many sites are seething with partisan passion, often directed at the media. But they are also two-way portals for retired military officers, computer techies, former IBM Selectric salespeople and just about anyone else to challenge and fact-check media claims.
>
> (Kurtz, 2004)

As Dan Rather and CBS discovered, the new "blogger" is every bit as powerful as any anchorman or network, perhaps even more powerful.

Formal advocacy programs, being enduring in purpose, are well suited to effectively integrate Web technologies, like blogs, because they view technology not as a tool but as a component of a larger, purposeful infrastructure. Online *community* replaces the notion of online advocacy alone being all that public affairs managers need to offer their stakeholders. Instead, online advocacy is but one of many functions and activities available to stakeholders through ICSTs. The online community is a place where the stakeholder can go to be reconnected with the organization and other stakeholders.

## Online Communities

The medium where online communities exist is the World Wide Web. Web sites are universally used as a communications tool by public affairs campaigns already. Outreach efforts utilize the three basic types of Web sites: public sites, extranets, and intranets. All three types provide an online environment where online communities are constructed using various tools such as blogs, chat rooms, online advocacy tools, etc. Online community infrastructure is built when there is a blending of the public Web site, intranet, and extranet functionality, in order to cast a wider net to capture the attention and participation of stakeholders. Commonly referred to as "portals," Web sites can act as doorways to a broad swath of information and resources. Anyone looking for the definition to a technical term or label should consider using http://www.webopedia.com as a resource. The definition of "portal" at webopedia.com is as follows:

> Commonly referred to as simply a portal, a Web site or service that offers a broad array of resources and services, such as e-mail, forums, search engines, and on-line shopping malls. The first Web portals were online services, such as AOL, that provided access to the Web, but by now most of the traditional search engines have transformed themselves into Web portals to attract and keep a larger audience.
>
> (www.webopedia.com)

By incorporating many singular functions and technologies into a single place on the World Wide Web, a portal, the infrastructure for an online community, is implemented. Sustaining the online community is a matter of attracting and retaining stakeholders by embracing the fundamentals of public affairs relationship-building practices, and by extending technology tools to stakeholders to foster the new activism tactics of P2P and heterarchical behavior. Tip O'Neill's famous dictum has not been replaced, merely enhanced so that public affairs managers are now encouraged "to act locally but think and plan globally." If stakeholders cannot communicate with each other freely through your organization, where will they go to do so—and will that place be supportive of your organization's goals?

A public Web site is what most people commonly think of when they think of a Web site, and is used primarily for recruiting new stakeholders by presenting the issue(s), providing information, and facilitating the ultimate "call to action." As such, Web sites are well suited to this task. They are able to present endless content and information in a variety of formats that are graphically flexible. For formal outreach programs they also provide an environment for chat rooms, newsgroups, blogs, voter tools, and online advocacy tools, among other things.

Chat rooms, newsgroups, and blogs are also examples of P2P and heterarchical advocacy, concepts we have already looked at, where the stakeholder acts independently to communicate both laterally and with decision makers. The ability to express opinions and even carry on conversations offers the stakeholder a way to "publish" their thoughts on to the Web without significant technical infrastructure of their own. It also provides the public affairs practitioner with an environment to gather the opinions of their stakeholders, as well as others. As it is a public site, the entire world has access to the output. For those unfamiliar with chat rooms, newsgroups, and blogs, their construct and function are fairly simple.

A chat room, as the name implies, is a place on the Web where people may post statements and other people may read and respond to those statements—or chat—forming what is called a "thread" (meaning a string of related postings and responses). A thread may be thought of as analogous to the transcript of a conversation between two or more people. This is slightly different than newsgroups and bulletin board systems, where the stakeholder needs reader software to fully participate, but the principle purpose is similar—a place to exchange thoughts on topical interest areas.

Chats are organized topically into rooms containing multiple discussion threads and newsgroups into forums containing multiple discussion threads, with each room or forum dedicated to a specific topic and each thread a discussion on that topic. For example, a Web site containing chat rooms or newsgroup forums dedicated to politics may have rooms or forums such as: Conservative Politics, Liberal Politics, Election News, Federal Election Commission, and Political Gossip. Others might have rooms and forums dedicated to particular political commentators and their writings.

All of these might be moderated or unmoderated. Moderated rooms and forums have rules that must be adhered to, in order to participate. If somebody breaks the rules, their access to the system may be cut off and their postings (i.e. comments) removed. Most of the guidelines, or rules, are simply to post things in rooms related to the topic of your statement and to be sure to explain what you are talking about so that your comment does not completely rely on previous postings for context. But there are also some definite taboos. "Spamming" and "flaming" are the two most serious, in most cases. "Spamming" is a term that just means junk information or unsolicited transmission of that information. If the chat is about the next G-8 summit, spam would be posting a comment about how important stopping global pollution is to the ozone layer, or any other comment that is self-serving and unrelated to the topic being discussed. Spamming often inspires what is called "flaming." Flaming is overly harsh and poignant criticism that is directed at another participant to the point that it is beyond the topic area and is a personal attack. Both spamming and flaming are not tolerated in moderated situations, and likewise, occur regularly in unmoderated areas.

For more information about chat rooms and newsgroup forums, just type into any search engine the topic and the word "chat" and/or "newsgroup." To cover all types of topic and/or discussion Web sites you may also consider http://directory.google.com and search more broadly.

A "blog" is different from both chat rooms and newsgroup forums in that it is a one-sided expression, with no ongoing discussion inherent. In this regard a blog is similar to the writings and views expressed by an opinion editorial columnist. Each is a "one-to-many" communication process, or, in the case of the blog, a one-to-many technology. Blog is short for "Web log" and is basically a regularly updated online journal. Many political writers, pundits, and politicos have blogs to get their thoughts out to the masses. As the document authentication mistake made by CBS caught and publicized by two bloggers highlighted, so do many individuals. Any individual, in fact, can launch a blog of his or her own for under US $500.

What should be taken away from the size and influence of the blogosphere is that it is part of the new activism, in spirit and practice. As an integrated technology, blogs can, and in fact are, a part of the public affairs environment— because they are a rapidly growing part of the political mix. The individuals who participate in blogs, chat rooms, and newsgroups are likely among the ranks of any organization's stakeholders.

Participation is a good thing, no matter if it is P2P communications within your online community or writing legislators in support of your position. Public affairs managers who have trouble motivating must re-evaluate the message— not the technology that delivers it. Having a realistic idea of what an online community can do for your organization is the critical first step, assessing it as a unified infrastructure.

We have already mentioned one example of an organization with a healthy and effective formal advocacy program—the Entergy Corporation in the United States—when we discussed *ad hoc* advocacy programs. Headquartered in New Orleans, LA, it is an integrated electric and nuclear power company, whose formal grassroots program, called EnPOWER, reaches out to employees, retirees, and the community. Its stakeholders include mechanics, engineers, office professionals, low-income community members, and the communities at large for whom they provide electric power services. The long-term program was enhanced and expanded once the need for it became abundantly clear following its *ad hoc* use when the company confronted anti-nuclear activists in Westchester County, New York. Now seen as a

way to organize employees and others at all the company's locations and to encourage the involvement of their people in all the issues the company encounters, the formal structure of their program represents, we believe, a model of what corporations should be doing.

The public affairs and government affairs management illustrated progressive thinking on how to integrate old tactics and new tactics using their existing program. One of the premier cable television channels in the United States, Home Box Office (HBO), aired a documentary about the company's struggle at IPEC that had been at the core of a grassroots struggle. The documentary examined this notion and did not arrive at any conclusion other than that the reactor continues to be a concern for some, continuing however to suggest it posed a significant threat. The documentary, palpably biased, in Entergy's assessment, was deserving of some sort of response.

Entergy had several options in responding to the insinuation that its reactor posed a direct threat to the community, included protesting to HBO directly or investing in a regional mass media campaign to distribute a message that the reactor was in fact safe, secure, and vital to the energy needs of the New York area. Such traditional tactics had been shown by the program as organizing rallies supporting the reactor, directly lobbying legislators, and mobilizing stakeholders to educate members of the community and recruit their peers. Instead, EnPOWER activated its stakeholders by sending them an e-mail with the link to the bulletin board on the HBO Web site to post in the discussion threads about the documentary. EnPOWER members became e-activists, entering into the P2P conversations about the documentary. The fact that Entergy continually invests in a formal advocacy program gave it this flexibility—its stakeholders had already been organized and had received advocacy training by EnPOWER in the past on writing, speaking, and recruiting.

While this example illustrates both how a program moves from *ad hoc* to formal as well as how a well conceived formal advocacy program is an invaluable asset for organizations in dealing with the new tactics of public affairs today, the question remains: where do online communities in general serve a role? Or, do online communities serve a general role that both corporations and other types of organizations, like associations, benefit from? If so, how should an organization implement an online community?

While these ICSTs certainly have been integrated by public affairs campaigns already, there is a strong sense that the industry is still trying to understand how stakeholders relate to one technology versus another. This is an important consideration when building an online community infrastructure and making technology investment decisions. Would stakeholder participation rates increase if normal e-mail communication was supplemented by integrating chat forums or discussion boards? In turn, is it effective to have stakeholders communicating with each other in these online communities, or does that take away valuable time and energy better spent taking action on important issues and other similar external calls to action? Any stakeholder can be scared, bullied, or tricked into taking action on an issue, but only once will it likely work. Formal advocacy programs, as we have reinforced repeatedly, are ongoing and persistent. They cannot rely on this type of motivation. The fundamentals of public affairs apply, and these carry into decision-making processes regarding ICST integration.

Both the American Civil Liberties Union and the Association for the Advancement of Retired Persons utilize online communities that fit their respective organizations' goals and outreach strategies. Both have paid attention to the useful segments within their memberships. Both organizations narrowcast messages and content. And both also utilize online communities to provide a common place for their entire stakeholder base to communicate. But, as previously stated, the necessary ICSTs must have an environment in which to operate—Web sites.

The ACLU (www.aclu.org) Web site is organized into approximately twenty policy areas that help its online visitors find the information they are interested in. A small sampling of the policy areas includes: death penalty, drug policy, free speech, national security, women's

rights. The amount of policy and legislativ information and related calls to action is substantial enough that a search function is needed to narrow down, by either state of residence or general topic, what is to be presented. The ability to join the ACLU Action Network, their formale-activist program, is also provided.

The AARP (www.aarp.org) Web site, in contrast, is organized around lifestyle areas such as health and wellness, tips and travel, money and work, and learning. The AARP policy-oriented section of the Web site presents a small number of top-priority policy and legislative issues and calls to action—and membership-wide interest in all of them is assumed. You can become a member of their formal advocacy program, AARP Grassroots America, through the site.

Both organizations have e-mail updates and/or newsletters that keep their members up to date and motivated based on areas of interest. Both organizations provide online advocacy tools in their Web sites to allow members to take action on the issues presented. It is also true that both enable stakeholders to join their formal grassroots programs and provide ICSTs for that purpose—expending considerable resources to make sure information is acquired, shared, and distributed. In short, they are both doing the basic technology integration that most sophisticated Web sites serving in a public affairs role tend to do. There is little variation between organizations in these areas simply because these integrations are efficient through automation enhancements and not strategic in nature. The differences in strategy, however, from one organization to another are the driving forces in the manner in which online communities are implemented.

The online communities start to show some differences, strategically, between the organizations. The ACLU has integrated discussion board technology under the name "ACLU Forums," while the AARP calls its the "Online Community." While both the ACLU Forums and the AARP Online Community are basically the same technology to enable P2P communications, and both are moderated systems and have rules, the use of them shows contrasts between the strategic visions behind them.

The ACLU Forums are a "free-speech zone" where the rules are a list of things not to do:

1 Spamming.
2 Posting offsite links that violate policy or present technical threat.
3 Derailing the debate.
4 Posting advertisements.
5 Expecting the ACLU to take action against offensive language.
6 Soliciting of names, addresses, and phone numbers.
7 Violating ISP (Internet Service Provider) rules and policies.
8 Encrypting postings so the ACLU cannot read them.
9 Posting materials that violate copyright.
10 Using ignorance of the above policies as an excuse for violating them.

The AARP Online Community rules, by contrast, are a list of etiquette tips and protocol:

1 Understand your environment and go with the flow of the community.
2 Be clear and concise and refer back to, or even quote, the post you are responding to so that others will know what your are talking about.
3 Treat others the way you want to be treated.
4 No selling.
5 Watch what you say and do not transmit anything that is vulgar, unlawful, abusive, threatening, hateful, harassing, defamatory, obscene, or racially or ethnically objectionable.

While the environment of the ACLU Forums is positioned as an intellectually spirited free-speech zone, the AARP Online Community is managed to be a more comfortable place to seek and provide advice and information. The ACLU has approximately 400,000 members and deals with a significant number of policy issues on their behalf. The AARP has 35 million members and also deals with a significant number of policy issues on behalf of its members. Both organizations have content-rich Web sites, formal advocacy programs, extend advocacy tools and technologies to the

stakeholder, and embrace the online community notion. What is, then, the significant thing to take away from the manner in which both of these organizations has integrated ICSTs into their public affairs strategies? Both organizations have chosen formal advocacy program tactics to build a persistent and flexible enough advocacy base to address a myriad of issues. And both have established a clear identity, mission, and goals that guide their integration of technology, as it does their policy positions. Most important, however, they have seemingly realized that P2P communication is a fact of life and have adapted it for the good of the organization. By providing an online community infrastructure, ACLU and AARP have ensured that their stakeholders do not need to go somewhere else to find the information and opinions held by other stakeholders on topics and issues important to them.

It is useful to step back and assess where the ACLU and AARP both draw power from, in order to better understand why their online communities are structured as they are.

The ACLU influences policy through its ability to persuade via legal might and intellectual prowess. As such, the organization's outreach strategy is to relationships created by connecting with stakeholders on an intellectual level. It has integrated its online community in line with this strategy. The ACLU Forum is a place to find information and opinion, support and dissent, in a topical structure. The rules reinforce free speech and the organization as a protector of it. Its stakeholders want to learn and express themselves. The ACLU has provided an environment for them—which is preferable to those same stakeholders going somewhere else to do so.

The AARP, as an organization, influences policy by its sheer size and number of members—and the ability to move 35 million individuals as a unified constituent bloc. The stakeholder relationships are intimate and personal. It cements the organization-to-individual relationships by connecting to stakeholders on the issues and challenges of life they each face as senior citizens. The AARP's strategy is to unify its stakeholders to fight and celebrate together. Its online community aids this strategy.

The AARP Online Community is a place where stakeholders can find information and advice from other senior citizens. The AARP manages its online community to be courteous, positive, and protective of stakeholders—the exact image they want stakeholders to have of the organization itself.

What has been done effectively by both organizations is the taking of the fundamentals of public affairs and the applying of them to their use of technology, and then the integrating of technology in harmony with their overall strategies. Formal advocacy programs and online communities turn stakeholders into capable advocates and keep them connected with the organization.

## THE FUTURE: MANAGING STAKEHOLDER DUALITY

Looking forward and attempting to ascertain where ICSTs integration is taking the public affairs industry can be difficult for public affairs managers. And to some extent it is a daunting task. While one must always make room for the unexpected, there is much that is fairly evident after examining what is occurring now and finding the fundamental effects of ICSTs on our craft. Public affairs managers should consider that ICST integration—online communities in particular—calls for new tactics because of two fundamental realities. First of all, the world is smaller and more connected today. Planners must accommodate the global reach of information for those acting locally. And, second, the global connection is forcing stakeholders to have dual identities—the real *person* and the virtual *user*.

The new activism we have been discussing, created by ICST integration, is fundamentally changing the role of the activist by introducing the virtual identity. The new activism is about recognizing and embracing the dual existence of stakeholders in the analog world and in the virtual world. Attending rallies, writing letters, speaking in public, or telephoning decision makers is done by the real-world person but P2P communication is often done using "online

identities" or "user names" which represent a separate identity from the stakeholder in your stakeholder database. This separation is present even inside the stakeholder's psyche. People are generally less inhibited and more confident in saying things and participating while in this alternative virtual identity—a trait that is useful in an activist. The technology offers a separation, or distance, that can be comforting. Public affairs must apply the same fundamental practices to both identities that their stakeholders possess. This applies to strategy, ICST integration, and message alike.

The future of our discipline is, in part, to continue to seek the efficiencies that automation via technology offers but also to integrate ICSTs in such manner that they effectively serve in their subservient role of fostering relationships, both with the real-world individual and the virtual personas of stakeholders.

### Personalized Portals: Beyond Narrowcasting

A "broadcast" is a message from one to many. A "narrowcast" is a communication from one to some. And P2P is a direct expression that is one-to-one. P2P is specifically peer-to-peer and the public affairs manager is not a peer of the stakeholder. "Personalization" is the next step beyond narrowcasting, where the public affairs manager integrates ICSTs in such a manner that communicating one-to-one with an individual stakeholder occurs. The move from narrowcasting to personalization is perhaps the most significant shift that is being explored and tested in the industry in terms of automation. As personalization grows, the changes will be wide-sweeping and will affect the Web sites used in a public affairs role.

Public Web sites today are generally tasked with broadcasting information that is consistent from one person to the next, without change. Extranets and intranets begin to move towards narrowcasting by establishing the identity of the visitor and allowing access to only the information and tools that apply to that person. There is little true personalization in public affairs currently. Lists may be segmented for e-mail blasts, and the stakeholder's name and some other data merged into the message—but many others will have received substantially the same communication.

Portals, as we have defined, are Web sites that offer a breadth of content and resources and where personalization can be enabled. As stakeholders visit portals they will see the general broadcast information that is relevant broadly before moving deeper into the portal for Web pages specifically for them—not for a small group of people like them in some way but meant for them as specific individuals. The virtual-world persona joins the real-world person as access to the communications they have with the organization and other stakeholders are made available, access to intranet/extranet resources is given, and entry for the virtual persona into the online community is facilitated. Public affairs strategies may find that this is the only time and place where their stakeholder's real-world identities and their virtual persona coexist.

## Increased Move Toward Formal Advocacy Programs

Out of necessity, more organizations are going to have to move towards formal advocacy programs to be able to effectively influence policy. The new activism and new tactics are going to demand public affairs efforts that can both invest in the information gathering and distribution technologies used to feed an online community but also can attract and train stakeholders that are broadly flexible in utility and ability to handle many real-world and virtual-world advocacy tactics. Further, stakeholders are going to have to be more able to effectively serve the advocacy demands outside of the sanctioned activities of the advocacy program, such as debating policy on an online forum or recruiting in a chat room.

One might find this assessment to be a contradiction to previous statements that ICSTs have made it more viable to engage in outreach and grassroots tactics and it is easier to be an activist. These things are true, but "bigger is not better" is true also. The period of growth is a swing of a pendulum. Those who are more

capable at public affairs will raise the bar industry-wide and begin to cull out the weaker participants. This is a healthy cycle, and by and large the craft benefits from it.

## Beyond Grassroots: Internet Intelligence

Up to this point, we have examined public affairs technologies as they relate to communication and management tools. There is another emerging application of technology being pioneered by Convy & Associates, a leading grassroots advocacy technology provider in Washington, DC, that focuses on "Internet intelligence," which is a narrower version of Fleisher's concept of public policy competitive intelligence (Fleisher, 1999) or even larger scholarly concepts of corporate political strategy.

Convy's team has built a system that allows the user to gain insight from the Internet by "reading the Internet." Users scan interest-group sites, message boards, chat rooms, published media, and legislative activity. By searching thousands of postings each hour, they can discover what's out there that's relevant to an issue or legislative action, in real time. That information can then be interpreted and structured into a decision-making model and delivered to decision makers via e-mail, instant messaging, short messaging service, text message, etc.

'Internet intelligence' is described by company president John Convy (www.convyassociates. com) as "the evolution of grassroots, made possible by the unique nature of the Internet." In this context, grassroots is described as the 'how,' as in "We've got an issue, and this is *how* we can respond to it." Convy has broadened the process into a proactive and full-cycle intelligence gathering, issue monitoring, and grassroots engagement program. The premise is that one can now address the basic questions of "who, what, when, where, and why" there *might* be a problem, *before* they erupt, again giving more time to prepare for the 'how' of a plan for dealing with the emerging crisis. This enables the public affairs practitioner to get out in front of the issue and define, frame, and, hopefully, diffuse it.

This approach also allows a client to use Internet intelligence to advance their own agenda while protecting their position and reputation. While the Internet offers unique opportunities to advance an organization's position, there is a dark side, where online rumors and misinformation are rampant. The damage that an Internet attack can cause has been proven, and its costs can be staggering in terms of legislator mind share, shareholder equity, and reputation. It's also hard to lobby members while they are getting hammered by Internet-fueled opposition. To counteract these rumors and attacks, we believe—and the technology Convy provides supports this— that users should actively participate in the forums to make sure their positions are articulated properly.

When interviewed by us in preparation for this chapter and asked why it's important to practice Internet intelligence, Convy responded:

1   The Internet is the largest source of content in existence.
2   The Internet shapes opinions and reputations.
3   Certain opinion leaders use the Internet as their primary publishing medium.
4   Stories can appear online up to twenty four hours before the offline press.
5   Sensitive content is often leaked online.

In addition, it can be used for:

1   Early warning and emerging issue identification.
2   Real-time evaluation of potential and current threats.
3   Media and legislative monitoring and evaluation.
4   Stakeholder identification and tracking.
5   Opposition research.

## CONCLUSION

Relationships are still created by one-to-one communication and founded upon some connection to the issue(s); grassroots technologies have not changed the underlying principles by which constituents are located, educated, and

motivated. The same basic ideas for motivating people to get involved are as prevalent today as they have been for more than a century. Witness our ability to ignore an incoming call when the caller's number is not recognized, and to delete unwelcome e-mail. People still respond to people they know as opposed to strangers.

So far, cementing stakeholder relationships with a piece of technology has not been a substitute for one-on-one relationships with other humans, at least in the world of grassroots politics. There is no such thing as, in our opinion— and may never be—a grassroots-in-a-box solution to communications. Communicators still have to get out there and make the one-to-one connections. Grassroots is still intense and grassroots professionals still have a lot to do. What they should be pleased to know is that *once the relationship has been established* it is becoming easier to maintain and reinforce that relationship with modern technology, correctly applied.

If public affairs managers are going to be successful in coping with the changes in the size and scope of their industry, they must integrate ICSTs effectively. There is more activism and it is a new activism where P2P and heterarchical structures are working. It is assuredly true that efficiency and growth in advocacy outreach tactics has occurred—due to the reach and speed that databases, e-mail, Web sites and other electronic communications tools offer. The aspect of all of this that is important is that bigger is not better, necessarily. This is a question we have hedged throughout this chapter and it deserves an answer. Considering how ICSTs have been integrated to foster the new activism, they have, indeed, made advocacy and outreach tactics better. Through the hard work and initiative of both public affairs manager and stakeholder this promises to be the case for a long time.

## REFERENCES

Cornfield, M. (2004). *Politics Moves Online.* New York: Century Foundation.
Fleisher, C. (1999). "Public Policy Competitive Intelligence," *Competitive Intelligence Review* 10 (2): 23–36.

Heino, J. (2000). "Motivation: The Difference between Grassroots Activists and No-shows," in T. Kramer (ed.), *Winning at the Grassroots*. Washington, DC: Public Affairs Council.

Johnson, D.W. (2004). *Congress OnLine*. New York: Routledge.

Kurtz, H. (2004). "After Blogs Got Hits, CBS Got a Black Eye", *Washington Post*, September 20, p. 8, col. 1.

Lee, J. (2003). "How the Protestors Mobilized," *New York Times Magazine*, February 23.

Parker, G. (2003). "Smart-mobbing the War", *New York Times Magazine*, March 6, pp. 46–49.

Pottruk, D.S., and T. Pearce (2000). *Clicks and Mortar*. New York: Jossey Bass.

Trippi, J. (2004). "Power to the People," *Wired*, September 12.

US Census Bureau (2002). *United States Department of Commerce, Economics and Statistics Administration Report, Voting and Registration in the Election of November 2002*, Washington, DC: Bureau of the Census.

# 12

# The Organization and Structuring of Public Affairs

## MARTIN B. MEZNAR

The appropriate structural configuration of any organizational function depends on a variety of factors. In order to understand the organization and structuring of public affairs (PA) activities we must consider the context in which those activities are carried out. Research in organization theory has demonstrated that both internal and environmental characteristics help determine the appropriate functional structure for organizational activities. This chapter discusses the impact of the firm's general environment and the firm's PA strategy on the way the PA function is structured. Specifically, the chapter will examine how characteristics of the firm's sociopolitical environment affect a firm's PA strategy and how environment and strategy affect the firm's PA structure (as depicted in Figure 12.1).

## THE PUBLIC AFFAIRS FUNCTION

The PA function serves a boundary-spanning role in organizations. As Post et al. (1982: 12) assert: the "essential role of the public affairs unit appears to be that of a *window out* of the corporation through which management can perceive, monitor, and understand external change, and simultaneously, a *window in* through which society can influence corporate policy and practice."

The PA function manages the interface between the firm and a specific segment of the firm's external environment. Marx (1990: 9) noted that "the assessment of the company's external sociopolitical environment ... [is] primarily the responsibility of public affairs specialists." Different boundary-spanning functions concentrate on different segments of the firm's environment. Community relations and government relations are most often considered the primary responsibilities of the PA function (Post et al., 1982). Consequently, PA structure and activities are largely influenced by the socio (community)-political (government) environment in which the firm operates. The sociopolitical environment is comprised primarily of governmental and social stakeholders.

## THE IMPACT OF THE ENVIRONMENT ON PUBLIC AFFAIRS STRUCTURE

### The Environment

In its boundary-spanning capacity, the PA function must be structured in a way that reflects

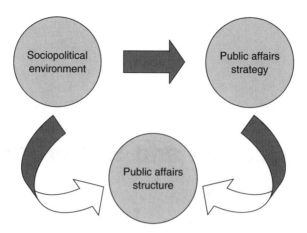

Figure 12.1    *Determinants of Public Affairs Structure*

the attributes of the external environment. A key concept in developing propositions concerning the relationship between organizational structure and environment is the notion of "requisite variety" (Ashby, 1956; Hedberg *et al.*, 1976), which contends that, in order to deal with complex situations, complex systems are required. Complicated environments will require complicated PA structures, simple environments will require simple structures. Building on this perspective, Katz and Kahn (1978) argue that sectors of the environment vary in terms of their stability/turbulence and uniformity/diversity. The two key dimensions of the sociopolitical environment which affect the structure of the PA function are the environment's level of *turbulence* and diversity (or *complexity*). Complexity deals with the number of relevant actors, relationships, and issues in the firm's sociopolitical environment, while turbulence deals with the stability of actors, relationships, and issues in the environment.

A complex environment is one in which there are many issues and many stakeholder groups involved in the discussion of the issues. Working through the issues and managing stakeholder relations is a tedious, time-consuming process requiring a significant amount of corporate resources. A turbulent environment, however, is one where change occurs frequently. It is a dynamic environment. Issues change quickly. The stakeholders the

firm deals with change often. The firm is continually faced with changing external expectations about corporate practices. The group of stakeholders the firm is dealing with today may be entirely different from the group of stakeholders a month from now. A turbulent environment typically requires quick responses and flexibility on the part of the firm.

## PA Structure

There is a considerable body of work done on the structure of the PA function—particularly in American firms (Mahon, 1982; Post *et al.*, 1983; Greening and Gray, 1994; Schuler and Rehbein, 1997; Rehbein and Schuler, 1999). These studies define structure in a variety of different ways. Rehbein and Shuler for example, define PA structure around whether or not the firm has a Washington, DC, office. Greening and Gray define PA structure as the level of formalization of PA activities. Others (e.g., Dunn *et al.*, 1979) consider the level of autonomy (decentralization) of the function as a key aspect of structure. In this chapter, "PA structure" refers to the level of formalization and decentralization of PA activities.

According to Miles (1980, 1987), when the environment in which the firm operates is stable and homogeneous, boundary spanning (PA) can be developed into a routine activity whose performers have relatively little power

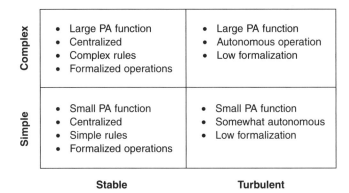

Figure 12.2   *Environment characteristics and public affairs structure.* Source *Adapted from Miles (1980)*

or influence. But when the environment is more complex and turbulent, boundary-spanning activities will tend to be more non-routine and boundary-spanning functions will tend to be more powerful within the organization. In turbulent environments the firm is more vulnerable to environmental change. In such instances, the role of PA officials is elevated from following a set of prescribed rules to creatively managing the stakeholder relations in a way that maintains the firm's legitimacy. It is in such instances that public affairs becomes most strategically important to the success of the firm. Applying Miles's (1980, 1987) reasoning to the structure of the PA function, it would be expected that in turbulent and complex environments the PA function would be large and would be given greater autonomy in decision making with fewer standard operating rules. Stable and simple environments would be associated with smaller, less autonomous PA units operating under a formal set of rules and procedures (as depicted in Figure 12.2).

If the environment is complex but stable, formal rules developed over time may be used to administer the function, and decision-making authority can remain at a central location. As the environment becomes more turbulent, however, the rapid modification of formal rules that is required tends to overburden the decision makers at the center—creating pressure for delegation of authority. Furthermore, rapidly changing contexts often require

rapid responses. Quicker responses are possible when decision-making authority is moved away from the center and toward those responsible for managing the interface with the environment.

The environment is only one of the critical determinants of organizational structure. A firm's strategy is another widely recognized factor which affects structure (Miller, 1987, 1988; Harris and Ruefli, 2000; Love *et al.*, 2002). Before proceeding with a discussion of the impact of a firm's PA strategy on its PA structure, however, it must be considered how a firm's PA strategy is affected by the sociopolitical environment within which the firm operates.

## THE IMPACT OF THE ENVIRONMENT ON PUBLIC AFFAIRS STRATEGY

### The Environment

Thompson (1967) argued that boundary-spanning units are used by organizations to reduce environmental uncertainty. In this role, the objective of the boundary-spanning unit is to *buffer* the organization's technical core from an unstable environment. Examples of *buffering* activities range from carrying high levels of inventory to deal with demand volatility without having to alter the production process (thereby protecting the "technical core"), to lobbying the government to block new laws (e.g., reductions in the emission of pollutants)

**Emphasis on bridging**

|  | Low | High |
|---|---|---|
| **Low** | **Low activity**<br><br>(low emphasis on all<br>public affairs activities) | **Buffering**<br><br>(concentrates on<br>defending technical core) |
| **High** | **Bridging**<br><br>(concentrates on<br>accomodation) | **High activity**<br><br>(high emphasis on all<br>public affairs activities) |

(Left axis label: Emphasis on bridging)

Figure 12.3   *Public affairs strategy classification.* Source *Meznar and Nigh (1993)*

which would require changes in the production process. Several researchers have noted that boundary-spanning units are not limited only to buffering activities. They also serve a *bridging* role (Thompson, 1967; Fennell and Alexander, 1987; Aldrich and Herker, 1977) wherein they promote organizational adaptation to changes in the environment. In the earlier quote (Post *et al.*, 1982), it was stated that public affairs, as a boundary-spanning function, is not just a *window out* of the organization, it is also "a *window in* through which society can influence corporate policy and practice." A firm's PA strategy is defined by the degree to which the PA function allows (or disallows) society to influence corporate activities. Addressing the same issue, Pfeffer and Salancik (1978) state that "there are two broadly defined contingent adaptive (corporate) responses—the organization can adapt and change to fit the environmental requirements (i.e., *bridge*), or the organization can attempt to alter the environment so that it fits the organization's capabilities (i.e., *buffer*)." The PA function, in its dual capacity as a *window out* and a *window in*, is instrumental in determining which adaptive response the firm will pursue.

## PA Strategies

"Strategy" can be defined as "the basic characteristics of the match an organization achieves with its environment" (Hofer and Schendel,

1978: 4). Thus, how the PA function chooses to match its activities with external demands can be considered a *public affairs strategy*. Following this line of reasoning, Meznar and Nigh (1995) suggested that *bridging* (attempting to change the organization to fit the environment) and *buffering* (attempting to change the environment to fit the organization) could be considered PA strategies. However, since buffering and bridging activities are not mutually exclusive (that is, firms can at the same time adapt their behavior and try to change their environment) Meznar and Nigh (1993) proposed the PA strategy classification shown in Figure 12.3.

This classification follows closely the research stream initiated by Carroll (1979). Carroll argued that "social responsiveness [interpreted here as PA activities] can range on a continuum from no response (do nothing) to a proactive response (do much)." Building on the work of Wilson (1975) and McAdam (1973), Carroll also highlighted four strategies which range along a social responsiveness continuum. The *do nothing* approach is called a *reaction strategy*. Next is the *defense strategy*, where a firm does only what is required. Third is the *accommodation strategy*, where the firm is open to change and is law-abiding. Finally, the *do much* approach is called by Carroll a *proaction strategy*. Though they are similar, a fundamental difference between Carroll's social responsiveness framework and Meznar and Nigh's framework (depicted in Figure 12.3) is that Meznar and Nigh classify PA activities

|  | Stable | Turbulent |
|---|---|---|
| **Complex** | **Bridging**<br><br>(accomodation) | **High activity**<br><br>(high emphasis on all<br>public affairs activities) |
| **Simple** | **Low activity**<br><br>(low emphasis on all<br>public affairs activities) | **Buffering**<br><br>(defense) |

Figure 12.4   *Environment characteristics and public affairs strategies*

along two dimensions (buffering and/or bridging) and not just one (social responsiveness). These strategies (both Carroll's and Meznar and Nigh's) have "no moral or ethical connotations but (are) concerned only with the managerial process of response" (Carroll, 1979: 502). That is, no one strategy is necessarily more moral or ethical than another. These strategies are simply alternative ways of "matching" the organization's competencies with the opportunities and threats in its sociopolitical environment.

There is a logical connection between the strategies depicted in Figure 12.3 and the environmental characteristics depicted in Figure 12.2. When the sociopolitical environment is characterized by high levels of complexity and high levels of turbulence, firms need all the weapons in their PA arsenal to cope with managing their many and rapidly changing stakeholders. In such environments firms are likely to adopt a *high activity* strategy. Conversely, in stable and simple environments the corporate PA function tends to be small, and new demands and expectations of external stakeholders are minimal. In such an environment a *low activity* strategy is common. Complex stable environments are conducive to *bridging* strategies because the actors and issues, though many, remain stable over time and compromise resolutions are possible. Firms benefit from engaging in a dialogue with stakeholders that have a long-term interest in the organization's activity and role in society. Managing *complex* environments requires a significant amount of corporate resources (a large investment in PA efforts), but these efforts are often directed at

matching corporate practice with stakeholder expectations. *Turbulent* environments are by far the most difficult to manage. In situations where environmental change is rapid and unpredictable, it becomes almost impossible for firms to effectively pursue a bridging strategy. Changing expectations may invalidate previous corporate attempts to comply with stakeholder pressure. Changing stakeholder groups make it difficult to establish long-term, mutually beneficial relationships. Such instances, as Thompson (1967) notes, may be most effectively handled by corporate efforts to insulate themselves from external pressures and concentrate on buffering to protect the technical core. The relationship between environment characteristics and PA strategies is summarized in Figure 12.4. The mapping in Figure 12.4 is not intended to be deterministic. Firms may successfully pursue a variety of PA strategies across a variety of environment types (depending in part on how the firm defines success). Firms in the same industry often pursue different PA strategies. Figure 12.4 is intended only to illustrate, in a general way, the impact that environmental characteristics may have on PA strategies.

## THE IMPACT OF PUBLIC AFFAIRS STRATEGY ON PUBLIC AFFAIRS STRUCTURE

How is it, then, that PA strategies affect PA structures? Empirical research in this area has been limited, in part by the lack of consensus about PA strategy classifications. If we follow the classification in Figure 12.3, a variety of structural implications can be drawn.

## Low Activity Strategy

Low activity strategies imply a minimal commitment of organizational resources to the PA function. This makes sense because public affairs is a less vital function in stable and simple sociopolitical environments. Firms pursuing this strategy may not even have a formal PA department. Activities associated with public affairs may be dispersed across a variety of organizational units.

For example, in industries where changes to regulatory requirements are rarely considered or where corporate activities have minimal impact on the community or other social stakeholders there is little incentive to fund a boundary-spanning unit concentrating exclusively on the social-political environment. In such circumstances, if a PA unit exists at all in the organization, its activities will be considered relatively unimportant to the firm. Activities will tend to be routinized (or formalized) and public affairs activities will tend to be centralized (autonomy is not delegated to a small, peripheral, functional area). Such a structure is consistent with the pursuit of a "low activity" strategy.

Of course, the greatest danger to firms pursuing a low activity strategy is that their simple, stable, sociopolitical environment may suddenly change and, because of their neglect in boundary spanning, the changes will arrive unforeseen and have a significant (negative) impact on corporate performance. Firms pursuing a low activity strategy are the most likely to outsource sociopolitical boundary-spanning activities.

## Buffering Strategy

Firms pursuing a buffering strategy are typically those that face a turbulent environment. The rapid change in issues and stakeholders the firm must deal with makes it difficult to pursue other PA strategies. The turbulent sociopolitical environment requires a lot of attention on the part of corporate decision makers. The firm

may perceive itself as being buffeted by an unending stream of issues and stakeholder groups. Though the firm might prefer to adapt and resolve the issues, it sees little hope of resolution due to the ever-changing nature of the environment. In such instances, the firm tends to adapt its internal activities in order to "buffer" itself from the turbulence in its environment. In the terminology of Pfeffer and Salancik (1978), instead of adapting itself to the environment, in order to survive, the firm will focus on changing the environment. Firms pursuing a buffering strategy concentrate on environment-changing activities such as advocacy advertising, lobbying, making PAC contributions (and so on) in an effort to influence the external environment to change in their favor.

Clearly, PA activities are very important to the buffering firm. The PA department is vital in maintaining the firm's legitimacy in a difficult sociopolitical milieu. Significant organizational resources are devoted to PA activities. The type of PA activities pursued changes as the issues and relevant stakeholder groups change. The PA function will tend to be large, well funded, and strategically important to the firm. Given the need for lobbying and influence (as the firm attempts to exert some control over its environment), buffering firms will often have a DC public affairs office. Public affairs officers will tend to occupy high positions within the overall corporate structure. The PA function will have more autonomy to make its own decisions. Public affairs issues will be considered in the firm's strategic planning. Buffering activities (advocacy advertising, PAC contributions, lobbying, etc.) tend to be somewhat easier to routinize than bridging activities (discussed ahead), so PA activities will usually be moderately formalized. Formalization is only moderate because the environment is turbulent and the function needs to retain an appropriate level of flexibility in order to respond quickly to changes in the environment.

## Bridging Strategy

The bridging strategy fits best with complex but stable environments (Figure 12.3). The complex environment requires that the firm commit significant resources to PA activities. Bridging firms will tend to have a formal Public Affairs Department with a large, stable staff. The bridging organization attempts to adapt and change to fit the environmental requirements (Pfeffer and Salancik, 1978). This attempt to "bridge" requires that the firm be attuned to changing external expectations in order to promote prompt organizational realignment with new external expectations. Such firms emphasize identifying and dealing with issues quickly and in a way that is responsive to stakeholder concerns. Typically they see their corporate reputation as an important asset and strive to aggressively improve and promote that reputation.

As with the buffering firm, the bridging firm's PA function is strategically important to the organization. It tends to be well funded and is the responsibility of high-level organizational officers. The stability of the environment allows the function to be more long term in its outlook. Building long-term partnerships with external stakeholders is key to the PA function's success. Where the buffering firm may hold to an "us versus them" approach to PA management, the bridging firm's approach is more oriented toward working together with external stakeholders. The PA function will have a moderate amount of autonomy to make its own decisions. Bridging activities (quick adaptation to changing external expectations, prompt regulatory compliance, building positive relationships with external stakeholder groups, etc.) are often difficult to routinize and quantify. Consequently bridging firms will give their PA function some flexibility in how it carries out its duties.

## High Activity Strategy

Firms pursuing a high activity strategy will have the largest, most active PA functions. These firms combine buffering and bridging strategies within the same department. The complex and turbulent nature of the environment requires that these firms pursue a wide range of activities (both buffering and bridging) as they seek to manage the interface between the firm and its sociopolitical environment. Such firms would be the ones with the largest amount of corporate resources committed to managing public affairs. The PA departments in "high activity" firms would be those with the most significant impact on the firm's performance and long-term legitimacy.

The gambit of PA activities pursued by such firms requires a large amount of autonomy (decentralization) for the PA function. Public affairs decision makers are highly regarded throughout the organization, wielding considerable power and influence over other functional areas within the firm. The top PA officer would likely be a member of the top management team and have significant influence in overall strategy formulation and implementation. Public affairs activities are formalized when possible, but much of the daily operations of the function would be structured in a way to promote flexibility and adaptation to the complex and turbulent environment facing the firm. The function is characterized by the ability to respond quickly and forcefully to environmental change. Aggressive and thorough environmental scanning and analysis are critical to the function's effectiveness. Competence in public affairs can be the source of a distinct competitive advantage in the industry.

## THE IMPORTANCE OF MATCHING STRUCTURE, STRATEGY, AND ENVIRONMENT

In order for a PA function to effectively carry out its responsibilities and contribute positively to the overall performance of the firm, there must be a "match" (or "fit") between the firm's PA structure, PA strategy, and sociopolitical environment. The structure of the PA function cannot be evaluated or understood in a vacuum.

For example, the firm operating in a simple, stable environment (something of a rarity today—as discussed in the next section) could be wasting organizational resources by overfunding the PA function or allowing it too much influence over the activities of other functional areas more critical to the firm. Pursuing a "high activity" strategy in a simple, stable environment is unlikely to be the source of a competitive advantage for the firm. Rather it may put the firm at a competitive disadvantage if the emphasis on public affairs detracts from appropriate attention to other more critically important (in this environment) functions.

Similarly, the firm operating in a turbulent environment that seeks exclusively to pursue a bridging (accommodative) strategy may find itself ineffective and, perhaps, doomed to fail. Bridging works best in stable environments where issues and stakeholders don't change overnight. In turbulent environments firms must be able to insulate themselves from passing fads and be able to weather social pressure on issues that would destroy the firm's technical core. If the firm devotes all its resources to learning the rules (bridging) and the rules change every month, those resources may be misspent. In such instances, the firm needs to devote resources to define the rules (buffering). A firm's PA strategy must be appropriate to the firm's environment.

The same is true for the relationship between strategy and structure. Firms pursuing a high activity strategy need to structure the PA function in a way that provides it sufficient resources, authority, and flexibility to carry out the strategy. Adopting a structure that works well with a low activity strategy (that is, a highly formalized, centralized PA structure, where PA managers have little influence on corporate strategic decisions) is likely to doom a high activity strategy to failure and have serious repercussions for the survival of the firm. The same would be true for firms that adopt a structure conducive to buffering for a strategy pursuing bridging. The key to the success of the PA function is not utilizing a particular structure. It is adopting a structure that fits the PA strategy and the external environment.

## FIT IN THE FUTURE: GLOBALIZATION AND PUBLIC AFFAIRS STRUCTURE

Globalization is characterized by the increasing interconnectedness between national economies and cultures. This interconnectedness is having a significant impact on how firms perceive their sociopolitical environment. In general, globalization tends to increase the number of relevant stakeholder groups dealing with the firm. NGOs, foreign governments, labor organizations, social and environmental activists are becoming increasingly relevant in the firm's sociopolitical environment as the firm's operations spread across an increasing number of national boundaries. There is little doubt that globalization has increased the complexity of the sociopolitical environment for firms expanding internationally.

This change in the external environment appears to be leading to significant structural changes within organizations. Public affairs departments seem to be growing larger and more complex (as the law of requisite variety would predict). Unless the pendulum swings back rapidly and we find national economies becoming more insular and independent (which seems very unlikely), the importance of the PA function in large corporations is almost certain to grow along with increasing environmental complexity.

### Complexity and Globalization

Though greater environmental complexity is currently a by-product of globalization, this may only be temporary. A number of international (or supranational) efforts exist to harmonize business practices across countries. International certification efforts (such as ISO 14000 environmental standards, for example) may eventually lead to a consistent set of stakeholder expectations across multiple countries which will make managing the job of the PA function easier. Most such efforts, however, are still several years away from being widely accepted and adopted. It appears that, at least for now, globalization and environmental complexity go hand in hand.

### Turbulence and Globalization

A well organized globalization process need not increase turbulence in a firm's sociopolitical environment. However, what we observe occurring at many international economic meetings (for example, World Trade Organization, International Monetary Fund, Organization of American States, Organization for Economic Cooperation and Development, or the World Economic Forum meetings) is anything but a well organized process. Protests, demonstrations, inflamed rhetoric, North-South confrontations, and the like have led to greater turbulence in an already very complex environment. If this trend continues, it will accelerate the importance of PA activities to corporate survival and success. Such turbulence may lead more firms to emphasize buffering activities in their PA function. We are likely to see an increase in "us versus them" attitudes between firms and sociopolitical stakeholders. The increased turbulence is likely to lead firms to engage in more buffering in order to insulate themselves from external chaos. Such developments will present great challenges for corporate PA officers. The low activity strategy is likely to be more and more inappropriate. Firms that have historically adopted a bridging (accommodative) strategy may find the implementation of such a strategy increasingly difficult. Bridging will require greater resources and effort on the part of the PA staff as the environment changes.

How will such changes affect the structure of public affairs in multinational corporations? The PA function will continue to grow in importance and size. Public affairs officials will require more autonomy and more resources to successfully carry out the task of maintaining a "fit" between the firm's sociopolitical environment and corporate practice. The tasks of the PA function will become increasingly difficult to formalize. Successful PA departments will be those with the authority and flexibility to respond quickly to changing external expectations and stakeholders.

## CONCLUSION

As with other organizational functions, there is no "one right way" to structure public affairs.

Public affairs structure is largely the result of the PA strategy adopted by the organization and the sociopolitical environment in which the firm operates. This chapter offered only a brief overview of some aspects of the relationship between environment, strategy, and PA structure.

Because the sociopolitical environment varies between industries, it is natural that we observe industry differences in PA structures. Highly regulated industries (complex but stable environments) are often characterized by firms which emphasize bridging (see Figure 12.4). These firms tend to have a large, centralized PA department, with formalized operational rules (Figure 12.2). Deregulated industries tend to be more turbulent, and we observe less centralization and formalization of the PA function.

Ultimately, the most successful PA departments are those where the PA structure is designed to correspond with the characteristics of the firm's external environment and to carry out the firm's PA strategy. A misinterpreted environment and/or a misguided PA strategy will almost certainly lead to an ineffective PA function.

## REFERENCES

Aldrich, H., and D. Herker (1977). "Boundary Spanning Roles and Organizational Structure," *Academy of Management Review* 2 (2): 217–230.

Ashby, W.R. (1956). *An Introduction to Cybernetics.* London: Chapman & Hall.

Carroll, A.B. (1979). "A Three-dimensional Conceptual Model of Corporate Social Performance," *Academy of Management Review* 4 (4): 497–505.

Dunn, S.W., M.F. Cahill, and J.J. Boddewyn (1979). *How Fifteen Transnational Corporations Manage Public Affairs.* Chicago: Crain Books.

Fennell, M., and J.A. Alexander (1987). "Organizational Boundary Spanning in Institutionalized Environments," *Academy of Management Journal* 30 (3): 456–476.

Greening, W., and B. Gray (1994). "Testing a Model of Organizational Response to Social and Political Issues," *Academy of Management Journal* 37 (3): 467–498.

Harris, I.C., and T.W. Ruefli (2000). "The Strategy/Structure Debate: An Examination of the Performance Implications," *Journal of Management Studies* 37 (4): 587–603.

Hedberg, B.L.T., P.C. Nystrom, and W.H. Starbuck (1976). "Camping on See-saws: Prescription for a Self-organizing Organization," *Administrative Science Quarterly* 21 (1): 41–65.

Hofer, C., and D. Schendel (1978). *Strategy Formulation: Analytical Concepts.* St Paul, MN: West.

Katz, D., and R. Kahn (1978). *The Social Psychology of Organization.* New York: Wiley.

Love, L., R. Priem, and G. Lumpkin (2002). "Explicitly Articulated Strategy and Firm Performance under Alternative Levels of Centralization," *Journal of Management* 28 (5): 611–627.

Mahon, J.F. (1982). "The Corporate Public Affairs Office: Structure, Behavior, and Impact." Unpublished doctoral dissertation, Boston, MA: Boston University School of Management.

Marx, T.G. (1990). "Strategic Planning for Public Affairs," *Long Range Planning* 23 (1): 9–16.

McAdam, T. (1973). "How to Put Corporate Responsibility into Practice," *Business and Society Review* 6 (summer): 8–16.

Meznar, M., and D. Nigh (1993). "Managing Corporate Legitimacy: Public Affairs Activities, Strategies, and Effectiveness," *Business and Society* 32 (1): 30–43.

Meznar, M., and D. Nigh. (1995). "Buffer or Bridge? Environmental and Organizational Determinants of Public Affairs Activities in American Firms," *Academy of Management Journal* 38 (4): 975–996.

Miles, R.H. (1980). *Macro-organizational Behavior.* Santa Monica, CA: Goodyear.

Miles, R.H. (1987). *Managing the Corporate Social Environment: A Grounded Theory.* Englewood Cliffs, NJ: Prentice Hall.

Miller, D. (1987). "Strategy Making and Structure: Analysis and Implications for Performance," *Academy of Management Journal* 30 (1): 7–32.

Miller, D. (1988). "Relating Porter's Business Strategies to Environment and Structure: Analysis and Performance Implications," *Academy of Management Journal* 31(2): 280–308.

Pfeffer, J., and J.R. Salancik (1978). *The External Control of Organizations: A Resource Dependence Perspective.* New York: Harper & Row.

Post, J.E., E.A. Murray, R.B. Dickie, and J.F. Mahon (1982). "The Public Affairs Function in American Corporations: Development and Relations with Corporate Planning," *Long Range Planning* 15 (2): 12–21.

Post, J.E., E.A. Murray, R.B. Dickie, and J.F. Mahon (1983). "Managing Public Affairs: The Public Affairs Function," *California Management Review* 26 (1): 135–150.

Rehbein, K., and D. Schuler (1999). "Testing the Firm as a Filter," *Business and Society* 38 (2): 144–166.

Schuler, D., and K. Rehbein (1997). "The Filtering Role of the Firm in Corporate Political Involvement," *Business and Society* 36 (2): 116–139.

Thompson, J.D. (1967). *Organizations in Action: Social Science Bases of Administrative Science.* New York: McGraw-Hill.

Wilson, I. (1975). "What One Company is Doing about Today's Demands on Business," in G. Steiner (ed.), *UCLA Conference on Changing Business-Society Relationships.* Los Angeles: Graduate School of Management, UCLA.

# PART III

# Case Studies in Public Affairs

Everyone sees what you appear to be: few experience what you really are.

Niccolo Machiavelli

Part III deals with that essential area of public affairs, lobbying, and includes advice and analysis from some of the leading practitioners, researchers, and writers in this discrete and immense area internationally. Lobbying has grown as a profession significantly over the 1990s from its original prime home, the United States, to embrace the European Union and increasingly the rest of the world, and this section outlines much of that development. It has been widely argued that for every dollar spent on political campaigning in the United States ten times that amount is spent on lobbying the legislature in one way or another by public bodies, corporates, or not-for-profit organizations.

There are distinct differences between US lobbying and that which is dominant in the European Union but increasingly "Brusselington" (as Brussels has been called) is the focus of European lobbying as the home of the transnational decision makers in Europe. Evidence suggests that lobbying in Europe concurs with the US experience in that it is equal to ten times campaign election expenditure and that the business in its entirety is a multibillion-euro one. It is also where much transnation lobbying is coordinated by multinational organizations wishing to influence individual state legislatures.

Lobbying outside the dominant trading blocs of North America and the European Union is very different and there is still a limited body of knowledge in this area. One good source of material is Australasia, as a bridgehead into Asia, and experiences from the Pacific are explored in this part of the book. Because of the scale of lobbying in the United States and European Union cases from these markets dominate. The issue of the fundamental synergy between political marketing, campaigning, and lobbying is fully explored. We believe this part outlines a fundamental area of public affairs which is still underresearched. We wonder why.

Chapter 13 is introduced by Rinus van Schendelen, Professor of Political Science at the Erasmus University, Rotterdam. He is a long-standing advocate of quality PA training and is a founding member of the European Centre for Public Affairs and regularly trains lobby groups throughout Europe. Among his published works is *Machiavelli in Brussels*. In this chapter Van Schendelen introduces how it is possible to influence the European Union and achieve a desired result. He identifies lobby groups such as those based in Brussels or operating from their home country as the means of doing so. The lobby groups are seen as birds and bees: smelling the scents of the flowers of "Brussels" they try to get closer in order to achieve desired legislative, financial, and/or other end results. The focus of the chapter is the questions of how these groups try to score and how they can improve their scores. The institutions are outlined and effective strategies that can be adopted using a PA management approach are discussed and highlighted, using modern case studies.

Chapter 14 is by Simon Titley, a public affairs consultant, based in London and Brussels, who specializes in designing and organizing grassroots and media campaigns. In 1998–99, he was one of the organizers of the Save Duty Free Campaign, the first major application of pressure group-style campaign techniques to an EU business lobbying effort. Chapter 14 explores the success of NGOs and pressure groups within the European Union. The chapter attempts to explain how the success of NGOs has meant a gradual shift in power within the European Union from producer interests towards consumer interests, with a consequent shift in political focus from product to the impact of production.

In Chapter 15 the political and governmental scenes are outlined by Phil and Irene Harris. The former has written extensively in the area of public affairs and political marketing and was the joint founding editor of the *Journal of Public Affairs*. Both currently reside at the University of Otago. This chapter explores UK public affairs development and the growth of UK party conferences as regular meeting places for lobbyists and policy makers. The chapter outlines the use of party conferences both as a fundraising event and market place for public affairs communication into the policy-making process. Data gathered over the period 1993–2004 is presented and reviewed on this unique phenomenon.

Chapter 16 introduces a case study of political lobbying, by Leighton Andrews, AM, the member of the Welsh Assembly for the Rhondha and former lobbyist and Public Affairs Director of the BBC. He explores the history and development of the BBC from initially government controlled state radio broadcaster through to terrestrial television supplier and into the Digital Age. The chapter looks at the organizational structure of the BBC and its varied stakeholder base, its representative structure, and the evolving needs of the environment in which it operates. The case highlights the specialist public provision needs

demanded of the corporation, such as age, disability, ethnic, gender, and geographic needs. It outlines the complex politics and pressures from commercial competitors around the BBC and explores the corporation's commercialization and evolving role as a world news purveyor. The case outlines the coalition building and PA campaign to win a 10-year extension of the charter for the BBC in 1996.

Chapter 17 is by Conor McGrath, whose research interests include the education and training of lobbyists and lobbying as a form of political marketing, and he is currently a lecturer in Political Communication and Public Affairs at the University of Ulster. He explores the development of the National Beer Wholesalers Association (NBWA) in the United States. The NBWA is one of the most powerful lobbying groups on Capitol Hill. This case study outlines how the National Beer Wholesalers Association has transformed itself into one of the most powerful groups in Washington, through the initiation and implementation of a positive, proactive, and professional government affairs strategy.

Chapter 18 is by Clive S. Thomas, Professor of Political Science and Chair, Department of Social Science University of Alaska Southeast Juneau, Alaska. He is a long-time volunteer lobbyist and teaches seminars on lobby organization and tactics. In this chapter he introduces an overview on lobbying in the United States. The chapter explores how the activities of lobbying are universal, whether it is in Washington, DC, or Lisbon. Yet what are different are the processes, the institutional structure and the political cultural values.

Chapter 19 is by Burdett Loomis, who is currently acting as the Director of Communications for the Governor of Kansas. He is also Professor and Chair of the Department of Political Science, University of Kansas. In this chapter, Loomis introduces the maturing United States lobbying industry. The chapter explores this growing industry, its structure, and the processes required to lobby successfully both domestically and internationally in the United States.

Chapter 20 is by Jim and Patrick Shaw, who are both successful in stakeholder engagement initiatives. Jim Shaw is currently the Community Affairs Manager at Nexen Inc., based in Calgary, Canada, while Patrick is the Managing Director of Quorum Strategic Inc. The chapter introduces a Canadian case study in public affairs, based on how the Canadian energy company Nexen Inc. managed stakeholder relationships associated with the drilling and the production of natural gas in one of Canada's major cities. It explores the principles and supporting strategies for effective participative community consultation.

Chapter 21 continues to explore public affairs with an examination of the evolution of public affairs in Australia. This was conducted by senior research fellow at the Melbourne Business School Geoff Allen, who has pioneered research and teaching in business-government relations and the political environment of business in Australia. He argues that the geographic distances and diversity of climate in the Australian subcontinent have led to their own dynamic politics and business systems. The political system is a parliamentary one with a federal government and associated upper and lower Houses as well as powerful state legislatures. The study explores how Australia has borrowed PA ideas and practices from the United States and United Kingdom yet the philosophical underpinnings and language of Australian business draw on both traditions, and have selected for application elements from each which suit Australian circumstances. Thus coalition building is explored and the benefits for corporate members, government, and Australian consumers are identified.

Chapter 22 continues to explore the role of public affairs, this time identifying the role of public relations in emerging markets. Andreas Lederer, Niombo Lomba, and Christian Scheucher explore the predominantly German-speaking lobbying world focusing on Berlin and Vienna. The former is the recently re-established capital of the largest state in Europe in terms of economy and population. It explores both regional interests and structures but also looks at the way lobbying and influence are emerging in this relatively newly reunified state. The issues of lobbying in Central Europe are more fully explored in a number of cases which look at the newly emerging European Union and its enlargement with associated issues of access to markets, ecological variation, and economic generation. This chapter addresses what the bases of these branches are and the role they play recognizing the potential for future developments.

Chapter 23 links the extensive political marketing literature and research to that of public affairs. Bruce Newman of De Paul University, Chicago, perhaps the leading writer in the field of political marketing, introduces the major linkages there have been in political party funding and the use of leverage to gain contracts. In the United States this is via PACs, etc., and has evolved into a major financial operation to successfully fund campaigns. Political campaigning and its literature are explored alongside the ever inflating costs of campaigning in the United States. International comparisons are made and the ethics of campaign budgets and tactics explored.

# 13

# Managing Government Relations in the European Union

RINUS VAN SCHENDELEN

## EU LOBBYING: AN OLD PRACTICE IN A NEW SYSTEM

Although the world of lobbying is only 150 years new (Milbrath, 1963), the essence of it belongs to all times and places. It refers to *the use of unorthodox means by interest groups, in order to get a desired outcome from government.* The definition deserves a short elaboration here (Van Schendelen, 2002: 40–49, 203–206). The "government" stands at least for every public official, unit, or institution entitled to make a formally binding decision. It may even be a mid-level civil servant or a committee of experts empowered to make such a decision. One can broaden it even to those not formally entitled but in practice able to bind others, such as groups at home ("internal lobby") or in society ("social lobby"). An "interest group" is a group interested in the outcome, in short a stakeholder. Private groups like companies, trade associations, and non-governmental organizations (NGOs) like citizens' groups or Amnesty have the old reputation of lobbying. But parts of government, so-called "public interest groups," have garnered the new reputation. At the level of the European Union (EU) one can find all these private groups (business and NGO) and public

ones (central and decentralized). If an interest group tries to get a desired outcome by unorthodox means, it is a lobby group. The "unorthodox means" fall outside the standard patterns of permitted or invited behavior, such as voting, taking a seat in a body or going to the Court. They are characterized by subtleties such as informal, silent, indirect, and supplying behavior and come close to classical diplomacy (De Callières, 1716). By means of well intended "wait and see" behavior they may even remain invisible. A "desired outcome" may be anything as desired by the lobby group, for example a law, subsidy, procurement, procedure, or position benefiting the group and at the very least, not the competitor. As such lobbying constitutes selfish behavior.

The concept of lobbying falls under three headings of political science. One is *influence.* Lobbying is only an effort and not sufficient for making a difference or becoming influential. Many factors may intervene between the effort and the result, such as the quality of lobbying, the competition of others, and the accessibility of the officials. Lobbying is not even necessary, as long as more orthodox means remain available and effective as well, for example a formal petition, a hearing, or the ballot box. But lobbying is frequently most helpful in increasing the chances of getting a desired outcome from government. Lobbying falls, secondly, under political *participation*. It is different from both conventional (orthodox) participation through the electoral process and protest behavior ("exit, voice, and loyalty," Hirschman, 1970). It can best be seen as a matter of "entry, support, and loyalty": one enters an interesting arena, negotiates about support, and owes loyalty to those who support. The participation is seldom a single activity, but usually an interactive process. Regarding both participation and influence the question of decisive resources remains relevant. We arrive here at the conclusion that the quality of preparatory homework is the single most decisive factor of success. Finally there is the heading of *democracy*. On this too we can come to the conclusion that a few lobby groups can endanger democracy but a thousand or more can enhance it.

Lobbying is of all times and places. One can find it in all political systems of the past, but frequently without a special name for it, as it is widely seen as the crux of politics, not needing its own name. It is about getting from a power holder a desired outcome and about achieving this by more unorthodox means, which potentially give a lead over competitors. One can find it at all places of governance, from the family, street, and work to various forms of association in the private or public domains of society. Conscious lobbying, however, is not a constant but a *variable* phenomenon. Paradoxically, it is relatively widespread in both highly and less formalized political systems. The first category tends to be rather closed to rising groups supporting new values, demands, and interests and having to find new ways and back doors to get their demands satisfied, in short to use unorthodox ways. Less formalized systems are rather open to all interest groups and set a premium on the use of unorthodox means providing the edge over others in the game of getting a desired outcome. The United States may be seen as an example of a highly formalized system, requiring smart lobbying. The European Union is a less formalized system, attracting countless initiatives of lobbying.

## THE EUROPEAN UNION AS AN IRRESISTIBLE FIELD FOR LOBBYING

In comparison to other Western political systems, the European Union is a very open one. It receives its basic formal *skeleton* (powers and institutions) from its component parts, these being the member-state governments. Almost all people working inside it are recruited from the member countries, either by election (members of the European Parliament, MEPs), selection (the members of the College of Commissioners, the Economic and Social Committee, the Committee of the Regions, and the Court), open competition (civil servants) or serving in dual roles (Council of Ministers). They transport demands and interests from their various countries, regions, sectors, and groups into the system and make this different by *flesh and blood*. In these respects the European Union, or as a metaphor "Brussels", is as open as the national systems. But two characteristics particularly make it even more open.

One is the heterogeneous *composition* of all the people inside the institutions. They hold very different values, norms, interests, loyalties, and a great deal more, related to their different backgrounds. They have to accommodate each other, but in their mutual competition they try to get support from others inside and outside. They open their windows and doors for information and support from all sorts of public and private interests groups, ranging from national Ministries to city officials and from companies to NGOs. From their side they also distribute information and support to these, thus building up a coalition in favour of their policy position. For example, the Commission frequently launches a "call for interests," by which it invites interested groups to participate in the process, and the Parliament does so by means of hearings and intergroups. By the early publication of agendas, minutes, drafts, and "what is in the pipeline" the Commission, Parliament and even the Council are much more transparent than their equivalents in most member countries.

The other special factor of openness is the *small size* of the EU engine, the Commission, which holds the "exclusive monopoly" of making proposals for legislation, having in fact veto power. It has, in all, about 11,500 civil servants for policy-related activities, plus about 8,500 people for translating, secretarial, and technical work. Its policy staff is smaller than that of many a single Ministry in one member state. On average, in each of about twenty Directorates General (DGs, mini-Ministries) fewer than 600 people are in charge of the policy process. In a policy unit inside, on average, about twenty five people run a policy domain, such as maritime safety, social security schemes, or animal nutrition. Of course, they can't do this on their own. Their solution is to insource experts from outside, representing larger interest families and brought together into an expert committee (Van Schendelen and Scully, 2003). At the moment there are estimated to be about 1,800 such committees with 80,000 experts in all, coming fifty-fifty from domestic governments (roughly two-thirds national and one-third decentralized layers) and private organizations (two-thirds profit-oriented and one-third NGO). They all help the *chef de dossier* of a policy unit to draft Green Papers (defining "the problem"), White Papers (suggesting "the solution" for the problem) and the final proposals for legislation. A small part of the proposals (15 percent, so-called "secondary legislation") has to be adopted by the Council and the Parliament, under co-decision with the legislators; the Council does so mainly through approximately 300 working groups and the Parliament using its mechanism of *rapporteurs*. The largest part (85 percent) is legislation delegated by previous secondary laws to the Commission, which mainly acts through the involvement of about 450 special committees ("comitology"). In short, all sorts of interest groups can get a semi-formal position inside the Commission. The integration of Europe largely takes place here.

Not surprisingly, many interest groups consider the European Union to be an *irresistible* playing field. It is seen as highly relevant for its "honey and money": the honey to be gained from EU legislation overruling domestic legislation and the money from subsidies and procurements. As the costs of influencing are frequently much less than the costs of passive adaptation to an outcome, the acting on the playing field is considered efficient as well. Here the interest group can also easily find allies for sharing costs and building up a coalition. Not least, "Brussels" is an open and permeable place. Nobody can stop an interest group on its way to "Brussels." Most groups travel now and then to the EU locations and act through intermediaries like European federations (EuroFeds). About 3,000 interest groups also have a permanent office in downtown Brussels, all together employing more than 10,000 people, with the following distribution: 32 percent EuroFeds, 20 percent commercial consultants, 13 percent companies, 11 percent NGOs, 10 percent national associations, 6 percent regional offices, 5 percent international organizations and 1 percent think tanks (Fallik, 2003). Besides these, there are the permanent representations (PRs) of the member-state governments and more than 150 delegations from foreign governments. The variable costs (location and facilities) of a modest office are about €100,000 a year (Greenwood, 1997: 103). In the past the Brussels office was mainly the concern of national governments (the PRs) and the companies and NGOs with a multinational position. Runners-up appear as the offices of smaller-sized NGOs, regions, associations of small-and-medium-sized enterprises (SMEs), national agencies, and foreign interest groups. Even single Ministries sometimes open their own office outside the national PR and run it as a lobby "apartment" under low profile.

## PATTERNS OF EUROPEAN UNION LOBBYING

There exists, of course, a wide *variety* of EU lobbying activities, styles, and results. Is there some pattern of behavior? Until the end of the 1980s most interest groups, except the multinationals, took the route to Brussels primarily via their domestic capital. Here they had to merge their interests and to follow so-called "national coordination." That made some sense as well: the European Union looked far away and complex and at that time most proposals by the Commission had to be adopted by the Council, acting through unanimity. The national capital could at least provide effective protection against undesired outcomes. During these decades the domestic interest groups behaved more or less "typically" nationally (Spinelli, 1966). That time is over. The Council, now largely acting under co-decision with the Parliament and voting by (qualified) majority, is no longer the national shield. Most proposals are substantially made and largely adopted under the management of the Commission. Interest groups had to find their own early ways to Brussels. *Self-reliance* has replaced national coordination. Member states have, in fact, become member countries. Only very weakly organized groups and those with interests falling under national veto power still visit the national capital as the platform for Brussels.

In consequence, something like a "national style" of lobbying has become less visible. Popular reputations such as the "loud Italians", "formalistic Germans", "tough Polish" and "sneaky French" have, in fact, become fairy tales. Also the belief that groups from a big country have the edge over those from a small one has become largely invalid, as most (around 90 percent) Commission civil servant, MEP and Council votes do not "belong" to one single country. The self-reliant behavior of interest groups produces, in consequence, more *idiosyncrasies*. For example, groups with multinational roots frequently behave differently from those without, as the former can more easily organize concerted action. Associations and governmental groups are usually sensitive to interventions from their members and publics. Some Ministries, like Industry or the Environment, tend to feel more at home in Brussels than Justice or Education. Companies in concentrated sectors (like chemicals and electronics) behave differently from those in more fragmented sectors (like construction and agriculture). Every interest group has, however, its own profile of such idiosyncrasies. In short, no general patterns of behavior based on traditional background characteristics can be found. But two new factors give rise to new patterns of EU lobbying.

One has to do with the rise of self-reliance, now causing overcrowding at the gateways to the European Union. At the receiving end the Commission civil servants, MEPs and Council officials have become reluctant to receive one interest group after another with regard to the same dossier. They require an aggregation of interests and, in fact, set the different groups to the work of integrating Europe. Its feedback effect results in more *collective action* (Greenwood, 2003). Groups with a more or less common interest establish or join a sort of EuroFed, ranging from a rather heterogeneous umbrella like UNICE (all national employers' organizations) to a more homogeneous *ad hoc* formation like the ECOBP (against biotechnology). A collective action can also crosscut domains, sectors, and regions. To give a few examples: trade unions and employers' groups together make deals for legislation under the Social Chapter, big airlines and consumer groups have constructed their EACF and authorities, companies and unions in steel producing regions have established their RETI. Many interest groups are members of a small number of collective actions. By these they lose some of their idiosyncrasies, get more common values and interests, and produce more patterned behavior. Common structures like a secretariat, board and committee stabilize the pattern.

The second main factor of more patterned behavior is, increasingly, the interest at stake. The self-interest drives the action. Of course, many groups are merely political tourists or adventurers searching for a fast piece of honey and money. Only by sheer luck do they sometimes get that. The amateur lobbyists go poorly prepared to Brussels, open doors at the wrong time and place, behave in an arrogant and demanding way, and do many more things that irritate those from whom they hope to get a desired outcome. Those who have invested in resources like a Brussels office frequently have a reputation for *professionalism*, resulting in a better balance of EU profits and losses. Their main characteristic is not their full-time job in influencing the EU process, let alone their possible commercial status, but only the more thoughtful management of their public affairs, quality not necessarily inherent in full-time or commercial people. They are pushed by the need to meet expectations at home and to account for the investments made, and they are pulled by the logic of playing on a hugely relevant, complex, and dynamic field full of competitive arenas. This is disciplining their behavior. The professional players are small in number, as the premier league is in every sport. Their composition is also variable, as a reputation can be won and lost. At one time the German company Siemens, the French Ministry of Finance, Greenpeace, the region of Lombardia and the American Chamber of Commerce may be part of it, but at another time they can be out of the arena. Interestingly, on the EU playing field the more amateur groups frequently take the professional ones as examples to follow. This cue taking makes their behavior more patterned too. For this reason we shall now elaborate the professional working methods.

## PROFESSIONAL LOBBYING

Interest groups wanting to get a desired outcome of EU decision making can, if they belong to a member country, place their hopes on institutional procedures and platforms. Groups from central government and party politics frequently do so, as they believe in their formal position as insides. But most groups do not have such a position in the College, the Parliament or the Council. Semi-institutional vehicles, like expert committees and working groups, bring them closer to the playing field. The unorthodox (non-institutional) ways and means of lobbying bring them as close as possible to those who are in charge of making the decision. Starting with the latter is usually also the *best order,* giving the best result. The lobby element of informality especially can create a relationship of trust, necessary for mutual listening and agreeing. This informal outcome can be laid down in a semi-formal text, for example a White Paper or a proposal. An interest group only wanting to block an undesired outcome (negative lobbying) and having got its viewpoint in such a text, can stop its lobby actions here, but has to remain watchful as to

whether the final text will remain in line. If it wants to push its desire (positive lobbying), however, it needs formal signatures from the Commission, Parliament and/or Council for a final result. Lobby groups want to draft the substantial text and to leave only the signatures to the authorities.

The day-to-day lobbying is full of *dilemmas* for an interest group wanting to apply unorthodox ways and means. The leading question every day is: to whom must it direct its lobby actions, where, on what particular issue, when and how? It cannot do everything at the same time and therefore has always to be selective. For example, it cannot approach at the same time both the *chef de dossier* and the head of unit, belonging to the Commission's policy unit in charge of a dossier of interest, as this might destroy at least one relationship. Neither can it remain silent and make noises on the same issue at the same time. In short, every detail of lobbying is full of dilemmas and for each there is a menu of choices. For example, if one wants to approach some Commission official more indirectly, one has the option of going through his/her staff or friends, a colleague or a superior, another unit or even a DG, a EuroFed, an *ad hoc* formation, a befriended interest group or making one U-turn out of many. Such detailed dilemmas and options exist for every question.

The *type of answer* makes a big difference between amateur and professional groups. The former just do something, at random, and are going to make unforced errors or blunders. Slightly better are the semi-professional groups and individuals, who rely on rules of thumb and hearsay wisdom, like "keep it low-key", "be early" or "be brief and clear," or who only do what officials prefer, for example "come to me" (and not to another), "give support" and "provide more information." From the professionals they can learn that there are many specific circumstances under which they can better do the opposite of what is generally recommended. These professionals have only one answer to the aforementioned leading question: "We don't know yet, as it depends on the situation." For them the situation is the combat *arena* around a dossier, which may start with a debate for a Green Paper, be formalized as a EU law, and continue under an inspection procedure. The arena is a collection of interrelated interests, in Europe always being contested and thus at issue, with interested groups (so-called "stakeholders") behind them. Time can always change the composition of an arena and bring in new (or remove old) stakeholders and interests. All these components of an arena the professionals make subject to closer scrutiny and study, before they feel sure what it is best to do. As stakeholders themselves they also have to define in advance their desired outcomes and next-best scenarios precisely.

The professional lobbyist is a rational player like Machiavelli (Harris *et al.*, 2000; Van Schendelen, 2002). Before he can solve dilemmas of behavior prudently, he has to study the dossier-related arena and to define the specific ambitions of his interest group. All together this is much more than the old-fashioned corridor lobbying and better covered by the new label of *public affairs management*, referring to the management of one's public agenda (*res publica*). In theory the professional may prefer to set out the aims first, to make the arena study subsequently, and to do what is best thereafter. But in practice most of the professional lobby groups make their conclusions regarding their ambitions, the arena, and the best actions in a more or less simultaneous way. The reason is that they may prefer to change the arena and even their own aims before the action starts, thus reversibly adapting these two variables to the best possible actions at the very minimum. Indeed, many prefer the higher chance of a satisfactory outcome by a low effort (high efficiency) rather than the small chance of a full win after strenuous lobbying. This balancing between effectiveness and efficiency is part of rationality too. The three main ingredients of professional lobbying we shall now elaborate on briefly.

## Aims

If one does not know what must be achieved, one cannot act. Setting the targets is, however, a complex and painful process. It starts with the preceding question of whether the European Union has relevant challenges in its pipeline at all. If not, one can at best remain passive. The definition of a *challenge* is always subjective, as it depends on perceptions of reality, ones own values and norms, and the differences between the two, being either positive (opportunity, dream outcome) or negative (threat, nightmare outcome). In defining their EU challenges interest groups can behave very differently from each other. In hierarchically led groups, as are common in the south of Europe, the chairman, CEO, or Minister defines these challenges by decree and leaves the solving of the threat or the seizing of the opportunity to his servants. In more horizontally run groups, to be found in the northern countries, all that is a matter of home politics or the internal arena. In professional circumstances a specialist Public Affairs (PA) unit invites rank-and-file people to say what they fear or desire from the European Union and then it tries to draft a sort of common agenda.

In most groups a long list of dreams and nightmares is the result. But at the EU level every group is too small to play more than a handful of chessboards itself. One has to be selective, by downsizing the long list to a manageable *short list*. Many variations can be found once again, from a top-down decision to a bottom-up outcome. Professional groups sift through a number of rational criteria used negatively, such as (not) damaging internal cohesion, having a poor cost-benefit ratio, solvable by a free ride, and promising a good chance. Here they fast forward to the arena study and the most prudent form of action. The differences between the long and the short list, they try to entrust to befriended stakeholders. Subsequently they translate every dossier on the short list into a number of specific *aims*, either positive or negative. Their leadership approves the short list and gives its PA unit a time-bound mandate for realizing it. Non-professional groups keep it all mixed up. They chase their long list, without clear targets, and in fact go out shopping at random, usually returning with only souvenirs. Selection, in short, is complex because it is about assessing oneself, and painful because it is mostly about giving things up.

Not least, every group has also to fulfill internal *requisites* for EU action. It must possess realistic knowledge of EU processes, back doors, and people, particularly regarding the specific arena at stake. It must have some basic resources or, if these are absent, the skills to get them, such as networks, specialist people, and a basic budget. The internal cohesion must remain sufficiently stable and supportive. Because one can't make aims interesting to other stakeholders with only a demand side ("position paper"), one has to prepare a supply side, full of items interesting to others. The group must always keep its nerves under control, even if the dream fades and the nightmare comes nearer. All this and more is strenuous. According to practitioners the "home front" usually requires 60 percent of their energy (Van Schendelen, 2002: 167). If they neglect it, they can hardly return with a serious prize, as is the fate of their amateur colleagues. Groups that score high on homogeneity and resources, for example multinationals like Shell and Greenpeace (Jordan, 1997), can more easily meet these requisites than those scoring low can. Domestic governments and associations especially often have difficulty with that. They usually have a very long list of challenges, can hardly select due to pressure from their publics, and fall short of sufficient internal cohesion, expertise and resources, the supply side, and control of their emotions.

## Study

In the plural area of Europe every interest is always contested by others and is thus at issue. An interest group never has a one-to-one relationship with the official empowered to sign a binding decision. In between there always stands many other stakeholders with very different backgrounds and interests. For example, the Postal Services Directive, adopted under co-decision in 2002, has been challenged by, among others, private post companies, state-run post organizations, US-led and European couriers, mail-order firms, consumer groups, and trade unions, all acting both individually and through their associations and domestic Ministries, coming from both inside Europe

and abroad, and all having both friends and enemies inside any of the decision-making institutions. Every interest group seriously wanting to win or at least not to lose its interest has to study the arena to which it belongs both before and repeatedly during the fight. A lobby campaign is, in this respect, no different from a military one; only the weapons and the manners have become civilized. It requires a lot of scouting and spying or, in polite terms, monitoring and going *window-out* (PARG, 1981). One has to lobby for information about the stakeholders, their own interests, the time schedules, and the possibly changing composition of the arena, because present stakeholders can leave and new ones enter, the former taking their interests along with them.

The purpose of the preparatory work is to find promising ways to realize one's reasoned ambitions by identifying friends, enemies, and their potential coalitions, as based on more or less common interests and specified for a particular moment and arena composition. The insight delivers the summary information on whether the aforementioned situation, "on which the best lobbying always depends," is mainly friendly, unfriendly, or indeterminate for oneself, as part of the arena. From here the interest group can start to go *window-in*, which means lobbying for support for its interest, by entering coalitions, negotiations, and suitable deals with others. The best practices of lobbying are dependent on the type of situation and take note of the management of stakeholders, issues, time schedule, and arena composition. For example, if the situation is substantially friendly, one should try to take a free ride, keep the issues high, speed up the process, and play dumb; if unfriendly, one should try to approach wavering stakeholders, reframe the issue at stake, delay the process, and mobilize new stakeholders, for example by indirectly causing a stir; if indeterminate, one can best wait and see for the moment, but invest more in preparatory scenarios for when the situation turns either friendly or unfriendly.

All this is difficult indeed, and requires skilled people. Collecting useful information already requires lobbying expertise. Of course, there are plenty of free sources like Web sites, but fine-tuned information usually comes from relationships and networks. Consultancy firms sell lots of information, even that regarding the internal and private affairs of groups and people. A potential gold mine is the corporate memory (including archives), but only a few professionals make use of this great source. Of course, no group can get a complete, reliable, and valid overview of any arena. Some degree of *uncertainty* always remains, thus urging continued study. Amateur groups neglect the window-out work, march unprepared into the ambush, and survive only by sheer luck. Most groups fall short of a good arena study. A frequent mistake is the overlooking of the different stakeholders or interests involved. In the postal services case, the privatized post companies of Britain and the Netherlands, after having successfully influenced the proposals of the Internal Market Directorate, introvertedly neglected the very different interests (of employment and public service) of their state-run competitors in France and Germany, and in the end got much less than they hoped for. Professional groups study the arena carefully, not only for their short list, but by a quick scan also for their long list, in order to eliminate such cases as "dead duck" and "free ride," for which it isn't rational to lobby oneself.

## Prudence

Lobbying the European Union clearly requires a lot of preparation. On this very competitive playing field, full of dilemmas, there is no serious alternative for it. Ambition and study are necessary for getting a good chance of success, but not sufficient in themselves. They give at best a reasoned direction to the choosing of the best ways and means of lobbying in a particular situation—in short, a sort of educated guess. Many factors can make the guess false, for example a poorly defined aim, an incomplete arena study, lack of information, better prepared opponents, an unforeseen event changing the arena or an unexpected reaction from an important stakeholder. For this reason *prudence* is the third main ingredient of professional EU lobbying. It implies not only continual scrutiny of the chosen aim and previous

study, but also critical concern about the potential effects of real lobbying. The formally intended effect remains, of course, to make a difference in the desired direction. But effectiveness is seldom acceptable at any price. Boomerangs and scandals especially must be avoided. A boomerang is a counterproductive effect of a previous act (or non-act) of lobbying that outweighs the costs of influencing. A scandal is (rightly or wrongly) a very negative and publicly launched assessment of ones behavior by others that impairs ones licence to operate. Such costs one can better prevent.

Before a lobby group starts its real lobbying of an arena, it can play a special game beforehand. Every arena has some structure, determined by specific procedures, positions, and people, in short "Triple P." They may be formal, as laid down in a treaty text or regulations, but also may be semi-formal, like internal rules, and even informal, by unwritten acceptance in practice. They prescribe the ways a single issue or a full dossier should be decided, which sorts of interests should be positioned in that procedure, and which people are entitled to sit in these positions. In fact, they are comparable with the pickets on a playing field. They always offer some room for interpretation, and hence for fighting or lobbying and for rearranging the goalposts. Even a small change of the goalposts can make much difference for the outcome, as the following examples demonstrate. Under effective German pressure on the Court of Justice the Commission had to revise in 2000 the legal basis of its Tobacco Ban Directive. The transfer of the portfolio on genetically modified organisms (GMOs) from the Environment Directorate to the Consumer Affairs Directorate in 2001 gave industrial and consumer groups a stronger position. And the inclusion of people from private companies on the board of the European Food Safety Authority in 2002 gave them the driving seat. A lobby group can play Triple P not only reactively, by challenging current procedures, positions and people, but also proactively, long before an issue or portfolio is rising up the official agenda. Successfully changing the goalposts helps to net the ball subsequently.

A lobby group has always, sooner or later, to solve the above-mentioned leading question "whom, where, on what, when, and how" so it can lobby today. To the amateur group this remains the first question, but to the professional one it is, after preparatory work, also the last question. By this time it may have solved most or all of the dilemmas and now shows what it is best to do and not to do, but still it has to choose its best activities from the great variety of menus or from its own kitchen. Lobbying in real life requires *fine-tuning*, as fine as possible. When a lobby group knows to whom it should address its activities, it must also define which interests should be raised when, where, and how. A good lobby is tailor-made, never ready-made. The preparatory work can yield its second pay-off here, as it informs about the interests of others, the time schedule, the networks and maybe even the idiosyncrasies of others. For example, a phone call, a lunch, and a private letter are all informal techniques, but their effects can be very different on the same person. Both a EuroFed and a scientific panel are indirect ways to submit supportive evidence, but these channels differ by quality, power, and linkage and may have different effects. A supply side must have not only elements of substantial interest, but also personal warmth and trust. Menus representing collected experiences are useful as checklists for making better choices. Prudent creativity and some good luck are indispensable for the finishing touch. Successful lobbying is like playing chess: maybe 40 percent can be learnt, 50 percent depends on professional method and the last 10 percent is an art.

In direct contrast from the popular view, successful lobbying in the European Union is not just "going around the corridors of power" but also requires a lot of professional activities: considered aims, careful study of the arena, and highly prudent behavior. The two aforementioned ingredients are a precondition for the third. The corridors can, of course, remain a tool of lobbying for information and support, but are only one of many. Successful lobbying is, in short, particularly dependent on intelligent behavior or *brains* and, again different from popular conceptions, is much less dependent on characteristics like wealth, size, or legal status. All lobbying is itself as well only

one important way to become influential, as the semi-formal layers and formal approaches remain equally optional also. Case studies at the EU level suggest that combining a mixture of ways usually gives the best results (Pedler and Van Schendelen, 1994; Wallace and Young, 1997; Claeys *et al.*, 1998; Pedler, 2002). For positive lobbying one anyhow has to get the formal signatures. Professional lobbying at the EU level is still exceptional by reason of the quantity of interest groups, but by quality it functions as a dominant example followed by the many, thus giving a pattern to their behavior at the EU level.

## FOUR DEPENDENT VARIABLES OF EU LOBBYING

EU lobbying has not only many causes as outlined before (multi-causality), but also many effects (multi-finality). Here we focus on the latter. One relevant dependent variable is the assumed effectiveness or influence. Is there evidence for it? A second potentially relevant effect regards the quality of decision making. Does lobbying contribute to better and more legitimate EU policies? A third and critically debated dependent variable is EU democracy. Do lobby groups have positive, negative, or maybe neutral effects on this? Finally we shall discuss European integration as a variable dependent on lobbying. These four possible effects are widely under discussion, but of course are chosen out of many more. Some of these are, for example, the effects of lobbying on the efficiency of EU decision making, the growth of welfare, the distribution of public goods, the europeanization of member countries, to mention only these.

### Effectiveness

The best criterion of effectiveness is the realization of a desired outcome. An excellent indicator of this is the inclusion of one's proposed line in a draft text. There are many examples of such an event, occurring for example formally through the Parliament, semi-formally in an expert committee, or informally via lobbying. But the substantial question always is whether the effect can to be contributed to the effort. Regarding social life strict causality can, by the lack of a control situation, never be fully proven and is at the best *plausible* (Hume, 1748). There is, indeed, a lot of plausible evidence. Aforementioned case studies of lobbying reveal a lot of success stories, but also disappointments and failures, for the one or other group. The same holds true for the case of lobbying via expert committees and comitology, where difference of formal powers does not correlate with influence, a paradox partially caused by the lobbying of their members (Van Schendelen, 1998). A few reputable studies among both senders (lobbyists) and receivers (officials) also ascribe influence in particular to groups lobbying by means of excellent timing, supply of information, or aggregation of broader interests (Kohler-Koch, 1998; Burson-Marsteller, 2001). Journalists and mass publics tend to ascribe influence to lobby groups as well, but their evidence is frequently only an impression or hearsay. An indirect indicator is the rise of lobbying and lobby offices. Apparently many more groups believe that their lobby efforts and investments are worthwhile.

Many interest groups also apply two next-best criteria of effectiveness. One is the strengthening of their position in an arena, the other the improvement of their organization at home. Apparently they sometimes suffer a loss on the first criterion and then have to take a next-best one. In fact, at this point they add the time perspective. Having lost a specific interest now, they may yet believe they have gained a better chance for the near future, thanks for example to the respect and trust they have earned from important stakeholders or their new support and mandate from their home organization. They have compensated for their primary loss. This also indicates that wins and losses can be very *volatile*. Only for a short time is an interest group or coalition usually a winner in a policy arena, as happened to the "Green coalition" in the late 1980s (environmental policies), exporting companies in the early 1990s (the open market), and the British government in the late 1990s (priority to

enlargement). But that glorious moment is long gone when the environment has to compete with the values of consumers and industry, the open market is confronted with proposals for the protection of "public services," and enlargement is followed by a strengthening of the institutions. There is no evidence, in short, that the distribution of wins and losses is cumulative among the lobbying interest groups.

This volatile distribution of influence can be explained theoretically. Lobbying, now seen as a process of communication between a sender and a receiver, making use of channels coming together in an arena and cautiously watched within an environment, is *full of limits*. Its main elements are constantly in a variable condition. The sender may have human and organizational shortcomings, like mythical beliefs regarding the EU playing field or lack of leadership inside the home organization. The receiver can be desperate for new information or disorganized by internal problems. The channels can have a distorting power or simply result in a dead end. The arena may be highly divided or constantly changing in composition and thus remains indeterminate. And there is usually some intervention from the environment, for example by the mass media scandalizing an event and outside groups interfering in the process. Professional lobby groups are, however, more able to cope with these limitations than amateur groups are. By their prudence they take them more into account. Thanks to their preparatory work, they can sometimes move them. They can also use the limitations to influence competitors and opponents.

## Quality of Outcomes

Do the many pressures from lobby groups result in better and more legitimate EU policy comes? The problem here is with the popular word "better". Of course, a lobby group having to give in to an opponent will probably complain that the resulting policy outcome is inferior to what it could have been without opposition. Being the sole winner always yields the best policy, according to the winner. But there is no objective criterion enabling us to conclude that the one policy value, for example a Green environment, is better or worse than another, like industrial activity or traffic mobility. The word "better" can only be translated into the ways of policy making (procedure or process), not into substantial content. Here we replace it with the *fairness* of decision making regarding the content of policy. In an extremely plural Europe, where every interest is always contested, fairness implies that all the different interest groups have a good chance to get their interest taken into account. As a consequence the EU mechanism of decision making must be open and competitive. If so, then any policy outcome represents the best possible quality, to compare with the "best possible price" on a perfectly open and competitive market. The European Union is like any market, however; not fully perfect in practice, but compared to most member countries it is very open and competitive. In the past it has had different reputations, for example that a farmers' cartel made the agricultural policies or that industrial groups more than other ones lobbied MEPs. But reputations can have their own imperfection. Agriculture has been a rather closed domain, but also a highly competitive one internally (Rieger, 2000), and industrial groups had to lobby MEPs intensely after losing at the Commission.

A good measure of fairness is the *discursiveness* of the policy debates for decision making. The concept refers to debates fully open to new evidence, argumentation, and persuasion among participants from inside and outside (Besette, 1994). The many different officials and interest groups at the EU level make the debates highly discursive. The various formal bodies and parts inside each make their own contribution of facts, arguments, and persuasion, as do the many expert committees and the thousands of lobby groups. All together they permanently influence the framing of a dossier, from Green Paper to final Act. The GMO dossier, for example, has been reframed from issues of industrial policy initially to environment policy subsequently and consumer policy now, resulting in very different outcomes. In the debates of the Parliament a very high level

of discursiveness, with variation for different dossiers, has been observed (D'Hollander, 2003). Almost every stakeholder can get its interests taken into account somehow.

The wide participation of stakeholders and the discursiveness of the debates also create an indicator of perceived fairness, namely *legitimacy*. In comparison to many a domestic government there is surprisingly little protest from interest groups at the outcome side of EU decision making, once a decision has been taken. The explanation probably lies in the degree of openness. At EU level the interest groups are openly invited to bring in their interest through experts and lobbying and to become part of the system. At the domestic level they frequently find the doors more or less closed by civil servants. To keep their ticket inside the EU system the professional lobby groups, more so than the amateur ones, are normally willing to take an eventual loss as being "all in the game and better luck next time," an attitude eased by the volatile distribution of wins and losses. Most officials and MEPs also consider lobbying as legitimate, as long as it is well prepared and attuned to their needs (Koeppl, 2001), especially those MEPs from the northern areas belonging to the largest parties, who like lobbyists for their information, aggregation of interests, and support for grassroots activities (Kohler-Koch, 1998). Journalists and mass publics are usually positive about the wide inclusion of different interests and negative if a few are neglected. They want to hear a wide-ranging debate.

## Democracy

Do lobby groups have positive, negative, or maybe neutral effects on democracy at the EU level? The difficult word here is, of course, "democracy." Every member country has its own set of notions and practices for so-called "democracy," usually contested and changing over time. All countries have together created at the EU level a *long list of notions*, each being pushed or contested by one or the other country or parts of it in the form of sectors and regions. One example is the following. For some the

Parliament is the basis of democracy, for others it is only one among many in an interest-group democracy, as is the current mixture in most countries. As to the Parliament itself, some people take as criterion its formal powers, others its representation or something else. Comparing it with the formal powers of their national parliament, some conclude there is a "democratic deficit," others a "democratic surplus." All this regards only one notion, parliamentary democracy, as it applies for only a few issues. In addition, there are different notions of democracy as pluralistic competition, transparency, elected authority, limited government, citizenship and freedoms, to mention only a very few here (Van Schendelen, 2002: 279–317). Many notions are not even readily consistent with each other and need a mixed balance. Examples are the notions of competition by either elections or interest groups, decision making either by majority or consensus, and legitimacy by either authorized officials or fairness of process.

Somewhere inside the European Union all these notions have their support groups and somehow all have already been put into practice at the EU level, now getting its own sort of democracy *sui generis*. The treaties may codify this europeanization of democracy formally, but unwritten practices and a lot of lobbying contribute to it substantially. Sometimes lobby groups try to influence it specifically, as the Vatican did for the 2003 convention, the presumed forerunner of the next treaty. But usually their impacts on EU democracy are only a side effect of their self-interested lobbying. Indeed, these impacts can be negative for example when they effectively make the system closed to new competitors, create a policy cartel with a few others, prevent accountability or limit the freedoms of citizens. Many (but never all) people will consider the resulting imperfections of openness, competition, accountability, and freedom as negative for the value of democracy. Lobby groups, however, frequently also create contrary side effects, for example by mobilizing new entrants, breaking a cartel, enhancing discursiveness, or promoting citizenship. Their self-interestedness, has, in short,

many different side effects, including highly appreciated ones (Mandeville, 1705). In addition there are the correction mechanisms belonging to the EU system itself and shown by the following examples. Civil servants, MEPs and other officials have a selfish interest in keeping the doors open, in order to collect information and support and thus to take over the driving seat. In their mutual competition lobby groups exert strong social control over each other. The smoke from lobby fights attracts mass media and new interest groups. Scandals bring the ultimate correction.

The negative side effects on democracy are frequently caused more by the interest groups that are passive, incidental, and amateur than by the active, established, and professional ones. The former leave the arenas to others, go for all or nothing, and are poorly prepared, while the latter enhance democracy by their participation, longer-term perspective, and prepared prudence. As *The Federalist* stated long ago (1788: paper 10), democracy benefits the majority as the number of active, established, and professional interest groups increases to the maximum having the highest variety. A few lobby groups may endanger democracy, but thousands of them strengthen it. The preconditions for a democratic system are thus external openness and internal competition. They are already stimulated by the correction mechanisms built into the current system. In addition, amateur groups are now following the example of the professionals, incidental groups are establishing themselves better, and formerly passive groups are becoming more active. The remainder nowadays consists of interests not yet organized as a serious interest group at the EU level, such as immigrant businessmen and retired people. Sooner or later they will be pushed or pulled on to the playing field too.

## Integration

Bringing parts together into a larger whole can be taken as the most general definition of integration. In the early 1950s six central governments in Europe concluded the Coal and Steel Treaty, the forerunner of the current EU treaties. The objective was to speed up the reconstruction of their countries devastated by war, for which raw materials such as coal and steel were then necessary, by pooling their domestic production in a larger framework. This treaty was given a common High Authority (now the Commission), an Assembly (now the Parliament) and a Court. For themselves the central governments kept the final say as the Council of Ministers. This new *transnational* framework is still the basic skeleton of the current European Union. But its "flesh and blood" have become very different since those early days. The Commission is now the main engine for the making of decisions and policies, the Parliament has become an influential body, the Court has been given expanded powers and the Council together with the Parliament is now the formal co-legislator for "only" the 15 percent of secondary laws. Their size, composition, workings, and impacts have greatly changed. From only coal and steel, most domestic policy fields now fall more or less under EU governance. Numerous semi-formal committees and working groups have been established, with people also from decentralized governments and private interest groups sitting around the table. The corridors inside the buildings and the places around are full of lobby groups. In short, integration has moved from the level of member-state governments to that of organized groups from member countries.

Willy-nilly the lobby groups contribute much to European integration. They aggregate their interests by entering a collective action. They have to, as they will scarcely be heard otherwise. They also inform both each other and officials about what they, acting close to the citizens, are doing, experiencing, fearing, and desiring. By their social control they make this information more complete and reliable. Besides, they give support to one or the other proposal, thus also binding themselves and providing more legitimacy to the outcomes. By their selfish competition they permanently search for new allies by entering new coalitions with incumbent groups and stimulating outside groups to participate as well, thus crossing and widening the arenas. Not least, they make

by-products of integration, such as mixing domestic cultures, getting a better understanding of different people, making non-political deals and engaging social networks.

The missing link in European integration can be said to be the hundreds of millions of European *citizens*. Given the problem of size (Dahl and Tufte, 1973), these millions can become more integrated only by representation and acculturation. Regarding both mechanisms lobby groups play important roles. On the EU input side they claim to be representative of a segment of European society and on the output side they have to explain to their people why an outcome is inevitably a compromise among different cultures. Professional groups usually play these roles much better than amateur ones. They know that their claim to act on behalf of others needs substance before it may become challenged and that any compromise can reasonably be justified as a clash of cultures, thus saving their own face in both situations. Amateur groups tend to be nonchalant about their legitimacy of representation and their explanation in terms of acculturation. Because amateur groups outnumber the professional ones, there is still a lot of room for improvement here also.

## REFERENCES

Besette, J. (1994). *The Mild Voice of Reason*. Chicago, IL: University of Chicago Press.

Burson-Marsteller (2001). *A Guide to Effective Lobbying of the European Parliament*. Brussels: BKSH.

Claeys, P., *et al.* (eds) (1998). *Lobbying, Pluralism and European Integration*. Brussels: EIP.

Dahl, R., and E. Tufte (1973). *Size and Democracy*. Stanford, CA: Stanford University Press.

De Callières, M. (1716). *On the Manner of Negotiating with Princes*. Washington, DC: University Press of America (1963).

D'Hollander, H. (2003). "Democratic Legitimacy in European Decision-making." Ph.D., in Dutch, Brussels: Belgian Parliament.

Fallik, A. (2003). *European Public Affairs Directory*. Brussels: Landmarks.

*Federalist Papers* (1788). London: New English Library (1961).

Greenwood, J. (1997). *Representing Interests in the European Union.* London: Macmillan.

Greenwood, J. (2003). *Interest Representation in the European Union.* London: Palgrave.

Harris, P., *et al.* (eds) (2000). *Machiavelli, Marketing and Management.* London: Routledge.

Hirschman, A. (1970). *Exit, Voice, and Loyalty.* Cambridge, MA: Harvard University Press.

Hume, D. (1748). *An Enquiry Concerning Human Understanding.* London: Cadell.

Jordan, A. (1997). *The Protest Business.* Manchester: Manchester University Press.

Koeppl, P. (2001). "The Acceptance, Relevance and Dominance of Lobbying the European Commission," *Journal of Public Affairs* 1 (1): 69–80.

Kohler-Koch, B. (1998). "Organised Interests in the European Union and the European Parliament," in P. Claeys *et al.* (eds), *Lobbying, Pluralism and European Integration.* Brussels: EIP.

Mandeville, B. (1705). *The Fable of the Bees: Private Vices, Public Benefits.* London: Garman (1934).

Milbrath, L. (1963). *The Washington Lobbyists.* Chicago: Rand MacNally.

PARG (1981). *Public Affairs Offices and their Functions.* Boston, MA: Public Affairs Research Group, Boston University.

Pedler, R. (2002). *EU Lobbying: Changes in the Arena.* Basingstoke: Palgrave.

Pedler, R., and R. van Schendelen (eds) (1994). *Lobbying the European Union.* Aldershot: Dartmouth.

Rieger, E. (2000). "The Common Agricultural Policy," in H. Wallace and W. Wallace (eds), *Policy-making in the European Union.* Oxford: Oxford University Press.

Schendelen, R. van (ed.) (1998). *EU Committees as Influential Policymakers.* Aldershot: Ashgate.

Schendelen, R. van (2002). *Machiavelli in Brussels: The Art of Lobbying the European Union.* Amsterdam: Amsterdam University Press.

Schendelen, R. van and R. Scully (eds) (2003). *The Unseen Hand: Unelected EU Legislators.* London: Frank Cass.

Spinelli, A. (1965). *The Eurocrats.* Baltimore, MD: Johns Hopkins University Press.

Wallace, H., and A. Young (eds) (1997). *Participation and Policymaking in the European Union.* Oxford: Clarendon Press.

# 14

# The Rise of the NGOs in the EU

SIMON TITLEY

Much has been written about public affairs in Europe but few will admit the obvious—that most business advocacy in the European Union is a failure. It is NGOs and pressure groups that are setting the agenda in most areas of EU business regulation. Or, to be more accurate, it is NGOs and pressure groups that are more successful at identifying and channeling popular opinion and popular demands.

This chapter attempts to explain why this is so. Principally, Western societies have undergone profound change in recent decades. NGOs tend to understand this change and know how to work with the grain, whereas business tends not to. The consequence has been a gradual shift in power within the European Union from producer interests towards consumer interests, with a consequent shift in political focus from production to the impact of production.

I conclude by suggesting some potentially profitable new areas of academic study. Scholarly work on the European Union has been a product of traditional political science, with a focus on institutional structures and procedures. I suggest that some very different academic disciplines must be brought to bear if the European Union's political process is to be truly understood.

## A EUROPEAN FABLE

Conventional accounts of industry advocacy in the European Union usually follow a narrative along the following lines.

The European widget industry discovers that the European Commission is proposing legislation that would outlaw the use of bat guano in the production of brass widgets. Immediate action is taken: the European Association of Widget Manufacturers holds a committee meeting. Three months later, one of its young policy wonks produces a position paper. Thanks to the Association's "contacts" in the EU institutions, there is a series of meetings in which the industry's leading scientific experts produce a detailed, rational, science-based case for the retention of bat guano. An amendment is secured in the European Parliament which would outlaw the use of bat guano in five years' time instead of two years as originally proposed. The widget industry hails this vote as a great victory and claims that it has shared popular concern about bat guano all along. To add weight to this account, flow charts and diagrams are produced, demonstrating the complexity of the EU institutions and the various stages that legislation must pass through. A generous helping of EU acronyms and jargon is thrown in, to show just how knowledgeable the storyteller is.

Here's my alternative story—and it doesn't sound very academic. The widget industry has been shafted. Comprehensively. By a pressure group.

No one in the widget industry saw what was coming until it was too late. The industry took ages to arrive at a common position. It failed to make a political case. It succeeded only in achieving a minor amelioration of a business-critical political decision. Fundamentally, the industry did not understand the political dynamic driving the issue and was therefore unable to respond effectively.

The story I have outlined is imaginary. But similar cases can be found in Brussels every day. Business advocacy in the EU is a failure. And it's an expensive failure. Each year, industry spends more than a billion euros on EU advocacy, and most of it is ineffective. The winners are the consumer and environmental NGOs, who have succeeded in setting the political agenda with a fraction of the resources available to industry. To understand why this has happened, we have to examine not the formal structures and procedures of the EU institutions, but the fundamental social, economic and political changes that have happened in recent decades. NGOs, by and large, understand what has changed and know how to campaign successfully. Industry, by and large, does not.

## THE BIG STORY: WHO SETS THE AGENDA?

A quick glance at the headline stories on the EurActiv.com news portal Web site provides a snapshot of the major issues being debated within the European Union. Leaving aside EU institutional issues such as enlargement or the proposed new constitution, the major issues at the time of writing include the following:

1   REACH (the proposed system for regulating chemicals).
2   Maritime pollution.
3   The working time directive.

4   Internet "spam" (junk e-mails).
5   Energy efficiency.
6   Air pollution.
7   Genetically modified organisms (GMOs).
8   Farm subsidies.

In most if not all of these cases, the pressure for reform has come from NGOs and pressure groups. These issues have arisen from genuine popular concerns, about the environment, health and safety, privacy, employee rights and Third World poverty. Generally, regulatory issues tend to be placed on the EU agenda against the wishes of business, which finds itself fighting some kind of rearguard action intended to delay or ameliorate proposed regulation.

If one still needed proof of NGO influence, the single best example would be the adoption by the European Union of the 'precautionary principle', which is having a profound effect on EU policy making and regulation. It has shifted the burden on to the proponents of a new activity to prove that it is safe, rather than placing the burden on regulators or the public to prove that it is unsafe.

## THE FUNCTION OF EU ADVOCACY

The relative failure of business is, in part, a failure of imagination. Business has tended to adopt a narrow definition of politics and consequently has a limited idea of what advocacy might achieve.

The function of EU advocacy, as in all forms of public affairs, is the management of issues by adapting to and influencing public behavior, attitudes, and policy. Traditionally, however, most business advocacy has focused more narrowly on the European Union's formal legislative process. Business interests have tended to limit themselves to lobbying the EU institutions to win favorable amendments to proposed legislation.

But there is also an important social role for advocacy. A major function of the European Union is to reconcile the need for wealth creation with social, environmental, and other ethical objectives. The Union operates on the basis of consensus (formalized through the concept of "social partners") but can achieve a consensus only if all the interested parties fully engage in the political process in the first place.

One might imagine that NGOs and pressure groups would be pleased with a situation in which they can consistently outmaneuver business interests. This is not the case. Most of the mainstream NGOs are not "anti-capitalist" or violent protesters but are political realists, attempting to negotiate some form of justice within the established political and economic system. Informal conversations with NGO and pressure group advocates indicate widespread frustration at their inability to find a partner on the business side with whom they can negotiate effectively.

The other important function of EU advocacy, so far as business is concerned, is the strategic role it plays in helping to establish and maintain corporations' brand values and popular trust. Over the past twenty or so years, business equity has shifted from tangibles (bricks and mortar, plant, and equipment) into intangibles (brand values and corporate reputation). Furthermore, we live in a world in which, of the 100 largest economies, more than half are business corporations rather than geographic sovereign states.

In this world of brand values, it is crucial for a corporation to maintain trust to stay in business. As the stock of politicians and government sinks, people perceive business, especially multinational corporations, as alternative locations of political power. Business is finding that it needs popular consent to operate. The less business is perceived to be trustworthy, the more it will face public pressure to modify its behavior.

Public affairs, then, has an important role to play in demonstrating the trustworthiness of business. How a corporation or industry sector conducts itself politically has a significant impact on popular perceptions and thus the pressure for regulation. It is this vulnerability that NGOs and pressure groups are adroit at exploiting.

It is noteworthy that, within most business corporations, the people responsible for marketing their company's products and services are acutely aware of popular perceptions and trends and how these relate to the brand, whereas their public affairs colleagues seem divorced from this intellectual process. An in-house public affairs person is more likely to have a working relationship with his company's scientists than he is with his company's brand managers.

## THE SIZE OF THE EU PUBLIC AFFAIRS AND LOBBYING INDUSTRY

Another way to judge the comparative effectiveness of business and NGOs is to look at their respective staff and budgets dedicated to EU advocacy.

How big is the EU lobbying industry overall? The simple response is that no one has a precise answer. There is no central register of lobbyists (apart from those with passes to the European Parliament) and, in any case, there are various ambiguities and disagreements over definitions.

The industry is also relatively immature, having really begun to develop only in the 1980s. It remains dominated by anglophones, having been consciously modeled on Anglo-Saxon lobbying industries in Washington, DC, and London.

What is extraordinary is the relatively large size of the EU public affairs and lobbying industry and the relatively small proportion employed on behalf of NGOs and pressure groups. Business interests employ public affairs and lobbying specialists in various ways: directly (as part of an in-house public affairs, corporate affairs, or government relations team), indirectly (employed by an EU business association) or hired via a consultancy (public affairs agencies, management consultancies, and law firms).

Most published estimates put the number of people employed in EU public affairs and lobbying somewhere between 10,000 and 15,000 but it is impossible to put a precise figure on it.

For example, most estimates would include the administrative staff of public affairs consultancies, who are not lobbyists themselves but rely on lobbying for their employment. Conversely, most estimates exclude the staff of regional government offices in Brussels or foreign diplomats accredited to the European Union, who are lobbyists for most practical purposes. And should one include the staff of think tanks, who influence EU policy but not necessarily on behalf of any interest group?

Let us assume that the true figure is between 10,000 and 15,000. To put this in context, the EU institutions employ approximately 25,000 people, 10,000 of whom are interpreters or translators. In other words, the ratio of advocates to EU *fonctionnaires* is roughly one-to-one.

The number of EU business associations is staggering. Greenwood (2002a, b) estimates that there are 950 such associations, at least 750 of which are headquartered in Brussels. Conversely, EurActiv.com lists only 250 European NGOs and think tanks combined. Probably fewer than 100 NGOs and pressure groups (or their European federations) maintain any permanent presence in Brussels, in most cases with few staff.

Despite the vague nature of these figures, two things are clear. First, that business interests, collectively, are spending a large sum of money on EU advocacy. (Based on staff numbers, and taking into account other costs, I would estimate at least €750 million and probably more than €1 billion per year.) Second, that the amount spent by business interests dwarfs that of NGOs and pressure groups.

## POLITICAL CHANGE WITHIN THE EUROPEAN UNION

Three broad political trends are changing the world of public affairs in the European Union. These trends tip the balance of power away from traditional elites, to the advantage of NGOs and pressure groups.

1   *Breaking down of national boundaries.* This is not just a function of the European Union. As the economy globalizes, so issues are less and less likely to be confined to one country. Significantly, hostile campaigns are also globalizing, through the growing capacity of pressure groups to mobilize on an international basis. The Internet is playing a significant part, by enabling consumers and pressure groups to share intelligence, mobilize, and communicate globally.

2   *A shift in the balance of power.* Four factors are taking power away from traditional elites and spreading it to a variety of stakeholders. These factors explain the apparent paradox between EU integration and devolution. The fact that the European Union is integrating does not necessarily mean that power is centralizing.

   (a)   *The Internet* is changing the way politics works. It does not necessarily increase the number of activists. What it does is to empower consumers and activists by providing easier access to intelligence, by making it easier and faster to mobilize, and by making it easier and faster to communicate. The Internet not only changes the rules but also lowers the "price of entry," so that there are more new political actors and the old elites are losing their advantages.

   (b)   There is a shift in the way policy is initiated, away from traditional policy-making elites towards *policy networks*. These include think tanks, the media, and NGOs. This means more varied sources of intelligence and pressure points, and an increasing need for large-scale coalition-building campaigns.

   (c)   Within the *EU institutions*, power is shifting from the bureaucracy to elected politicians. The policy environment is becoming less technocratic and more politicized. The European

Parliament is acquiring power at the expense of the European Commission. This means that, to be effective, one can no longer rely on elite lobbying but must also address a variety of constituency interests.

(d) Within most of the EU member states, there has been a trend of *devolving power* from national government towards regional and local government. There is a trend towards stronger local identities and a revival of local culture and language, in part as a reaction to globalization. Individual regions and large cities are growing in influence and forming cross-border alliances. This increases the need for local knowledge and local cultural understanding, with approaches tailored accordingly.

3 *Changing public attitudes.* The growth of brands means that companies are effectively demanding an emotional commitment from consumers. As national governments lose power, European consumers are increasingly demanding that companies take on social and ethical responsibilities. In response, corporate social responsibility (CSR) or "corporate citizenship" has become a first-rank concern for companies and their corporate reputations. Companies are developing new nonfinancial metrics to enable them to measure their performance against new criteria. Companies need to address stakeholder relationships with groups such as NGOs, local politicians, and local communities. A further trend is in popular attitudes to risk. The public has become obsessed with safety, and a "blame culture" is evolving, even though fears are often irrational. Political decisions are not always based on sound science. Instead, politicians and NGOs are able to use the 'precautionary principle' to justify decisions.

## SOCIAL CHANGE AS A SOURCE OF PRESSURE

Elsewhere (Titley, 2003), I have argued that the most significant change to have occurred in Western societies in the past fifty years is the transformation of the self. This change is a product of increased affluence and education. It underpins the shift in power from producer interests towards consumer interests.

As long as most Europeans were preoccupied with the daily battle for survival, the primary determinant of their political allegiances was the group (community, family, class, church) and people to a large extent subsumed their individual needs and identities within their group. With the spread of affluence and education, a profound change has taken place and, increasingly, people see their lives in terms of self-actualization. They define their own identities and their peer groups, and no longer buy their political opinions "off the shelf" from their traditional groups.

The traditional role of politicians was both to promote a sectoral/ideological interest but also to work to reconcile competing interests. As long as most people defined themselves in terms of group allegiances, politicians retained popular respect. Now that people are pursuing more individualistic and consumerist goals, and expect more immediate gratification, it is impossible for politicians to satisfy all these individualized wants simultaneously. With the disappearance of major ideological divides, politicians have been reduced to following rather than leading public opinion. They increasingly compete to agree with public opinion and have little political incentive to support any case unless it can demonstrate public support.

This social change provides the basis for the success of pressure groups. Unlike politicians, pressure groups pursue a single interest and have no competing constituency interests to reconcile. This gives pressure groups the freedom to satisfy individual emotional impulses. Crucially, pressure groups understand that the trick is to mobilize public opinion to create a compelling political case.

## DIFFERENCES BETWEEN EU AND US POLITICAL CULTURES

Most American observers of EU politics find the influence of NGOs and pressure groups (particularly consumer and environmental groups) over the EU decision-making process an extraordinary phenomenon. Loewenberg (2001) reports a cultural gulf and a consequent catalog of high-profile lobbying failures, notably the GEC-Honeywell merger proposal and Monsanto's GMO debacle.

There are seven key differences between Washington and Brussels political cultures which have often led US-owned multinational business interests to adopt inappropriate techniques and leave the field clear for their NGO opponents.

1   The European Union's political system is essentially consensual rather than adversarial. It is usually more important to reach agreement than for one side to "win." In any case, there are usually too many "sides" for any single one to emerge as the sole victor.
2   The prevailing political culture throughout the European Union is social democratic. By comparison with the United States, this means a commitment to free markets but with extensive social and labor market regulation. In general, business and especially multinational companies are perceived much less favorably by politicians than is the case in the United States.
3   Consumer and environmental lobbies are a powerful force, with mass popular support. In general, NGOs are perceived more favorably by the public than business and tend to enjoy the benefit of the doubt in any conflict.
4   EU politicians get involved in quite technical aspects of legislation that in the United States would be the preserve of regulatory agencies.
5   When lobbying in the European Union, technical knowledge and a good case are more important than "access." EU politicians and officials need access to expertise, so they want to meet the clients, not their hired lobbyists.
6   Few EU lobbyists are lawyers, and law firms are not major players in the Brussels lobbying market. Lawyers are generally confined to regulatory issues, mostly competition and antitrust.
7   In EU lobbying, "campaign contributions" are not a weapon in the lobbyist's armory. Custom and law limit the scope for corporate donations and, in any case, the campaign costs of individual politicians are very low compared with their US counterparts. Television advertising (the most expensive tactic in US elections) is not used in most European elections.

## HOW PRESSURE GROUPS SUCCEED

What is it that has equipped NGOs and pressure groups to outwit business even though they have fewer resources?

1   *Leveraging the self.* Single-issue pressure groups have succeeded primarily because they are more in tune with the new political and social climate. They have no formal responsibilities like an elected politician, are free to focus on a single issue, and thus are better able to satisfy public opinion.
2   *Making a political case.* Pressure groups understand the importance of an emotional appeal and do not rely solely on rational argument. It is normal for elected politicians to want to be re-elected. The arguments they wish to hear are those that will resonate with their electors rather than some desiccated scientific treatise. This trend is amplified by the increasing reliance of the media on the emotionally appealing "sound bite".
3   *A genuine case.* Most successful pressure groups in the European Union represent authentic and widely held concerns. Environmentalism, for example, is not a fringe concern but is now an established part of the political consensus in Europe, because large numbers of Europeans are passionate gardeners, walkers, bird watchers, or anglers who take a keen interest in the preservation of traditional landscapes and the protection of wildlife.

4  *Acting politically.* Pressure groups are not afraid to involve themselves in grassroots politics. Indeed, it is their life blood. Their strength is in local networks of committed volunteers. They do not franchise all their political action to a group of professionals in Brussels. Their ability to mobilize grassroots popular support creates a sense of momentum, a compelling narrative for media consumption, and a compelling case for elected politicians. This enables them to set the agenda rather than wait for events to happen.

5  *Agility.* Most pressure groups, surprisingly, are less democratic in a formal sense than their counterparts in the EU business associations. There are no lengthy consultation processes or consensus-building procedures. This enables them to respond quickly without having to wait for any internal processes to crank into gear.

6  *Leveraging brand vulnerability.* Leading pressure groups understand fully the importance to their corporate rivals of the brand. Through the growth in importance of the brand, business is demanding a more emotional attachment from consumers, rather than a rational assessment of the functional benefits of products. But, in its reliance on emotion, business has got more than it bargained for. It has become more vulnerable to criticism that has a popular emotional resonance. Increasingly, citizens are holding companies responsible for their actions, and pressure groups understand how to exploit the emotional side of these popular concerns. Pressure groups also benefit from a climate of opinion in Europe in which big business (particularly US-owned multinationals) is generally mistrusted.

Attacks on the brand are such a powerful weapon that some NGOs are bypassing the formal political system entirely. Why bother with an elaborate lobbying campaign, or a lengthy battle to amend laws and regulations, when you can change corporate behavior through, for example, a mass consumer boycott?

The result of these pressure group advantages is that business interests, not only individual corporations (e.g. McDonald's) but also entire industries (e.g. biotechnology), have found their corporate reputation to be at the mercy of grassroots pressure group campaigns.

## REASONS FOR FAILURE

The easiest way to explain the relative failure of business advocacy in Europe is simply to say that business either does not or cannot exploit the techniques that successful pressure groups use. Why should this be so?

1  *Failure of imagination.* Most business interests fail to take an holistic view of politics. Politics is more than laws and regulations. Political issues don't begin in political institutions, but usually start at the grassroots level with a local issue or campaign, which is amplified by the media and eventually reaches the national or even international stage. Political stakeholders with an interest in such issues are increasing in number and influence. A change in public opinion can be sufficient to impact on a company's business, without any formal policy changes necessarily taking place. Without the necessary imagination, tactics replace strategy and business lobbyists seek to minimize regulation on an *ad hoc* basis with little regard for the broader political and social context.

2  *Elitism.* A positive barrier to taking a more holistic view of politics, or engaging public opinion, is elitism. Elite lobbying is a comfortable and predictable world in which to work, and a premium is set on "contacts." Public protest is regarded as a nuisance, so it becomes hard to grasp that any policy change can spring from grassroots sentiment rather than political or bureaucratic elites.

3  *Too many "wonks".* The NGOs and pressure groups have shown that, to lobby effectively, one must campaign. They do not rely on elite lobbying as a tactic, but engage in stakeholder relations and

coalition building, grassroots and Internet campaigning, media relations, and creative use of the Internet. Unfortunately, most of the people hired by business (whether directly or indirectly through agencies) are policy wonks, with two or three university degrees and experience as a *stagiaire* (intern) in the EU institutions, but with no campaigning or media experience. To keep salary costs down, most of these wonks are also too young, lacking in experience and wisdom. Bureaucratic inertia has evolved, with wonks hiring more wonks.

4   *EU business associations are ineffective.* Most companies channel their lobbying efforts through European business associations, either directly (as a member) or at one remove (via their national association). There are logical reasons for doing so: the European Commission prefers to deal with a consensus industry view, and none but the largest corporations can afford to maintain their own in-house public affairs operation in Brussels. But business associations have increasingly suffered from paralysis. Their tortuous internal decision-making procedures make any fast response impossible. Decisions, when they are arrived at, are often a lowest common denominator point of view which has little political impact. Much of the day-to-day activity is ritualized (for example, committee meetings and position papers). The inability to reach meaningful decisions is causing many associations to splinter into smaller and more specialized associations.

## FUTURE ACADEMIC STUDY

Most academic study of EU politics has a traditional political science perspective and places too much emphasis on the political structures and formal procedures. Given the increasing tendency for issues to arise at a grassroots level, and the growing complexity of the web of policy networks, there is considerable scope for academic study into mapping the "influencers" in each EU country and thus laying the intellectual foundation for a more successful public affairs industry, especially in non-Anglo Saxon markets.

We have seen how elitist attitudes blind many senior business people to the importance of political events at a grassroots level. Here, our understanding would benefit from the attention of management psychologists or perhaps even anthropologists. We have also seen the phenomenon of the "policy wonk" and the company scientist, both committed to purely rational argument, who have difficulty with emotional concepts and wish to avoid public engagement. Are these people mildly autistic? Are such professions attractive to autistic people? Perhaps a psychologist would care to let us know.

## CONCLUSION

Throughout Western democracies, political issues are being driven increasingly by public opinion. This is a consequence of a number of political, social, and technological developments, in particular:

1   An increasing tendency for politicians to follow rather than lead public opinion.
2   A better educated, more affluent, more demanding, self-centered and fickle public, which trusts pressure groups more than business or politicians.
3   The rapid growth of the Internet, which empowers the public and NGOs, lowers the "price of entry" for political influence, deprives old elites of their advantages, and accelerates the speed at which issues develop.
4   Increased competition in the media, resulting in an emphasis on emotionally appealing "sound bites" rather than rational argument.

Politicians increasingly compete to agree with public opinion. They have little political incentive to support any case unless it can demonstrate public support. NGOs tend to understand these new rules of engagement, while business tends not to. This is why NGOs, with fewer resources than business, have enjoyed more political success.

# REFERENCES

Greenwood, J. (2002a). *Inside the EU Business Associations*. Basingstoke: Palgrave.

Greenwood, J. (ed.) (2002b). *The Effectiveness of EU Business Associations*. Basingstoke: Palgrave.

Loewenberg, S. (2001). "Lobbying, Euro-Style", *National Journal* (36).

Titley, S. (2003). "How Political and Social Change will transform the EU Public Affairs Industry", *Journal of Public Affairs* 3 (1).

# 15

# Lobbying in the United Kingdom

PHIL HARRIS AND IRENE HARRIS

Laws are like sausages. It is better not to see them being made.

(Count Otto von Bismarck)

UK political party conferences are one of the most visible areas where businesses, organizations, and political parties can be seen interacting with each other. UK party conferences as a result provide a good research laboratory in which to investigate strategic public affairs and how it functions using not only interviews and observation, but also data collection and subsequent analysis. The party conference environment acts as a communications conduit for the sharing and swapping of information as well as an opinion exchange and policy positioning forum.

Of particular relevance to public affairs is the way in which conferences act as a marketplace where politicians, organizations and interest groups can gain easy access to each other and exchange views and ideas. It is perhaps the ultimate network opportunity for those interested in government, political processes, and the formation of policy. The annual party conference is a forum where businesses, "not for profit" organizations and other organized interest groups can communicate their views to politicians and supporters and directly feed them into the party decision- and policy-making process.

## PREVIOUS RESEARCH ON BUSINESS OR LOBBYING ACTIVITIES AT POLITICAL PARTY CONFERENCES

Surprisingly there is very little published research on business or "not for profit" organizational activity and exhibitions at party conferences and even less on the effectiveness or use of lobbying at these major political events. The work which has been published is relatively recent and limited to a descriptive overview of marketing features at party conferences by Harris and Lock (1995), lobbying activities by the same authors or conferences as an avenue for interest group activity in support of the Devonport dockyard lobbying campaign in Andrews (1996). The great bulk of written material about party conferences and rallies in the United Kingdom has, not surprisingly, been written by political journalists, and has concentrated on the popular reportage of the politics. Anthony Bevins (1996) of the *Independent* provides a good example in his article "Shirt-sleeved Major Rallies the Tories to his Cause," reporting on the casual style of John Major at a Conservative Party conference rally.

In addition, the press report the occasional feature article on a topical issue. During the period of the research examples were: Andrew Adonis and Patrick Wintour of the *Observer*, on "Paddy Ashdown and his Plans" (1996); Michael Jones of the *Sunday Times* on the "Battle for the Middle Class Vote" (1994); Peter Riddell and Philip Webster of the *Times* on Norman Tebbit's advice to John Major on how to beat Labour (1996). On a day-to-day basis the journalists concentrate on output to be broadcast or printed in the short term, for instance Andrew Rawnsley of the *Guardian* "On ditching electoral liabilities" (1994); Ewen MacAskill, then of the *Scotsman,* on the conference appeal of Tony Blair (1994); and Michael White of the *Guardian* on over media-conscious politicians (1996). This output of journalistic writing inevitably focuses on political events, issues and politicians of interest to their audience and in the case of the specialist press their focused readers. In addition, there are thumbnail sketches of the conference, which often include reportage on characters and interesting moments interpreted and observed during the event. Examples of this style of journalism can be seen in Matthew Parris (1996) of the *Times* on Chancellor Kenneth Clarke's speech or Simon Hoggart (1996) of the *Guardian* on artificially stimulated applause for Cabinet Minister performances and presentations. The sketch writers have also occasionally teamed up with cartoonists to produce a book full of insights into the presentation of political personalities at party conferences. Bell and Hoggart's *Live Briefs* (1996) is a good example of this style and the former now publishes regular popular books of best cartoons from his *Guardian* work.

In addition many journalists have written well reviewed books on aspects of the Thatcher, Major, and Blair election campaigns and can provide useful sources of secondary data. These works have occasional sections on, and often specifically refer to, events at party conferences (Fairlie, 1968; Watkins, 1991), but are increasingly being dominated by the reporting of the use of conferences as presentational platforms for the marketing of leaders and their policies (Thatcher, 1983; Tyler, 1987; Pearce, 1992; Jones, 1995; Cathcart, 1997; Jones, 1997). A number of leading journalists and political commentators have been attending conferences for many years and see the

three weeks of the prime party conferences (normally from the third week in September to the second week in October) as an annual campaign. These commentators use this as an opportunity to see how the parties and their respective supporters are responding to the pressures of power or lack of it. Professor Anthony King of Essex University writes during the conference season for the *Daily Telegraph.* He commented to the author that he had been attending party conferences for more than thirty years and could remember the start of commercial activity at party conferences (Anthony King, October 9, 1996, in conversation, Conservative Party Conference). John Cole, the former chief political correspondent of the BBC, also expressed his personal view that the conference season was very tiring for journalists, who in many instances also cover the pre-party conference Trade Union Congress (TUC) and post-party season Confederation of British Industry (CBI) conferences. Cole said that he had been "doing the party conference round for over twenty years and it took its toll, physically and mentally on you" (John Cole, October 3, 1994, in conversation, Labour Party Conference). He confirmed that some journalists got bored and/or irritated if there was nothing interesting to report while they were on this campaign schedule, "therefore some of them might try and make the news or force individuals to reveal or say things they might regret." Cole also supported the view that all conferences "were becoming increasingly presentational" and "increasing amounts of corporate activity and lobbying were a trend" at party conferences, but that serious journalists would usually be interested in reporting only key political events, insights into decision making or personalities rather than public affairs work. Until the early twenty-first century public affairs activity has gone largely unreported, although it has often become one of the prime reasons for many to attend them.

Many leading commentators have substantial reflective experiences to build into any analysis of lobbying and marketing activity at party conferences. Unfortunately much of that observation and knowledge has not been recorded or is only available orally to researchers. Reportage of political conferences is increasingly focused on the presentational aspects and personalities at the event. This is facilitated by spin doctoring, and the production deadlines of the more structured media, with not only the desire to serve readers or viewers but also an element of laziness on the part of journalists (Holmes, 1997; Bourdieu, 1998). This has meant reportage of commercial activities at conferences has been seen as peripheral unless such activities add to the main story like "sleaze" as an issue in John Major's government. However, conversations with journalists and business figures do indicate that the growth of commercial activity in the party conferences area began in the United Kingdom in the 1980s, first at Conservative Party conferences and then at the new Social Democratic Party (SDP) events. This commercial activity from 1990 onwards emerged as a feature at Liberal Democrat and Labour Party conferences. Interestingly the Labour Party was slow to develop this area for a number of reasons, one of which was that various interest groups did not want to sell exhibition space to what they saw as groups opposed to their members' views or the party's policy. For example, the unions associated with the then state-owned Royal Mail in the 1990s (the Communications Union and its forerunners) did not want private competitors attending the Labour Party Conference, so they ensured that private commercial carriers such as DHL and UPS were not allowed to exhibit. In addition Rupert Murdoch's News International and its associated organizations like TNT were effectively *persona non grata* for a number of years at Labour Party conferences. This tactic of "blocking" various exhibitors clearly caused some confusion and image problems for Labour when it came to sell exhibition space. The problem has disappeared with the so-called "modernization" of the Labour Party resulting in the 1997 conference commercial exhibition area being then the largest event of this sort ever seen in the United Kingdom.

A significant source of useful information on party conference activity is politicians' biographies. There have been a large number of these

in recent years, the most well received being those by Healey (1990), Jenkins (1991), Lawson (1992), Baker (1993), Thatcher (1993) and of course Clark (1993). However, most of the material published by these authors is focused, primarily, on political events or incidents and gives little insight into commercial activities at conferences. The exceptions are one or two who do refer to sponsored receptions they attended, who they saw, and how they experienced the intensity and pressures of the conference and the headquarters hotel (Baker, 1993: 292–299). The Rt Hon. Alan Clark, MP, is perhaps the most illuminating about what Ministers get out of conferences. He wrote on Tuesday, October 4, 1983, that he had a new boyish-looking haircut that made him look younger and "am looking forward to Conference next week at Blackpool. My first as a Minister, to swagger and ponce" (1993: 44). Alan Clark's piece is typically idiosyncratic and sardonically amusing. However, most autobiographical and biographical works in this area give little insight into commercial activity or lobbying at party conferences. A number have been criticized for being poorly written, if not ghosted, and they are often egotistical, with some evidence of selective memory retention evident (Rosenbaum, 1997).

The bulk of academic research on party conferences has come from political scientists and focuses primarily on political issues, although Kelly (1989, 1994) has researched the organizational structure of Conservative Party conferences and associated policy making. Jones and Kavanagh (1998) have assiduously commented that they see the role of the conference as an annual rallying of the faithful and a public relations exercise in which the leader receives a standing ovation, "a regulation ten minutes for Margaret Thatcher in the 1980s and an impression of euphoric unity is assiduously cultivated for public consumption" (pp. 188–189). Much of this adoration of the Leader has continued throughout the 1990s and early twenty-first century as Tony Blair has dominated the political scene and been adored at his party's annual conference.

Kavanagh (1996a) has noted the continued unrepresentative nature of delegates at party conferences, which, he believes, has led increasingly to isolated political leaders misjudging public opinion.

> From being the best seaside blood sport in the early 1980s, Labour Conferences now resemble the Conservative Conference which Labour once ridiculed. The object of the gathering is less to debate policy or political strategy than to project an image of party unity and strong leadership—above all on television.
>
> (Kavanagh, 1996a: 29)

Since Labour gained its first election for government in 1997 after eighteen years in opposition, the conference has become predominantly a five-day rally for activists and a leadership policy forum.

There is little in the political science area which sheds light on commercial activities at party conferences. The bulk of secondary source material on these events focuses on political communication issues and just occasionally organizational management. Political scientists tend to concentrate and focus on political phenomena and the rituals of conferences rather than the events and features which are emerging outside the main conference hall.

However, Kline (1997) reflects on the use of the conference for political marketing and the use of seasoned communications professionals to shape the campaign into a consistent and coherent communication process. He argues that there is a long-standing flow of agency and public relations experts and gives examples of Tony Schwartz and the Saatchis' involvement. Kline argues that these professionals and personalities "transferred their experience and ideas from the promotional sector into the back rooms" of political campaigning. Kline advocates that they are a primary indication of a bridge between the previously discrete spheres of consumer and political marketing—forging a more synthetic political marketing paradigm (p. 139).

An early indication of this overlap with the advertising and communications world can be seen in Scammell (1995), who has written about the use of media management and professionalism at party conferences to market clear political messages. She reports the introduction at the 1982 Conservative conference of the head-up display unit, known as the sincerity machine, which had been pioneered by Ronald Reagan. It allows the speaker to read his/her text from unobtrusive, transparent perspex screens, creating the illusion that the orator is speaking without notes. Scammell in her book *Designer Politics* highlights the increased professionalism being applied to the projection of coherent political messages at party conferences, and argues that increasingly the marketing concept is being vigorously applied to these events and all political campaigning.

More recently, Stanyer and Scammell (1996) have carried out research on political fringe meetings at party conferences and their consequent impact on the media and policy development. Although the prime focus of the work is on the evaluation and promotion of new policy ideas and issues through the use of the fringe by the Conservative and Labour Parties, and their consequent reportage by the media, they also highlight the growth of commercial interests at party conferences. Their research assesses the number of fringe meeting events held, by subcategory, at the 1986 and 1995 conferences. What emerges from the preliminary analysis is that there has been a large-scale increase in corporate pressure-group activity and associated lobbying at party conferences, indicated by the number of fringe meetings sponsored at each event. Stanyer and Scammell (1996) compare data from 1986 and 1995 and show that there has been a 73 percent rise at Conservative Party conferences and a 75 percent increase at Labour Party conferences in fringe meeting activity over the period. They argue that 70 percent of this growth of new fringe meetings at the Labour Party Conference was organized by corporate interests, pressure groups, charities, trade unions, trade associations, the media, and research centres or think tanks. The study is driven by the need to look at how policy is being formulated, and, only as a by-product, notes the growth of corporate activity at conferences.

If we look at journalistic output in the area, writers very rarely comment on the business and organizational activities at party conferences. They may include a passing reference to some of the exhibition stands as a background pastiche to an article on the conference but there is little more depth than that. Occasionally there has been a piece on the formal lobbying of Conference in the press, and articles from the 1997 conference season included Animal Rights protests (*Times*, October 3, 1997), anti-land mine campaigning (*Guardian*, October 3, 1997), and pensioners (*Times*, October 2, 1997).

Lobbying of conferences by angry farmers (organized by the NFU) campaigning for government support for the beef industry (Conservative Party, 1996) and workers protesting at the closure of their pits (South Wales miners) or steel mill (Gartcosh) have all been observed during the ten years of research in this area.

However, the less overt activity of discreet organizational lobbying at party conferences has rarely been reported or researched. There has been one recent notable exception and that is the work carried out by the respected BBC political correspondent Michael Cockerell and his television documentary report for the BBC *A Word in the Right Ear* (1997). In it he looks at the campaign to stop Post Office privatization as a case study in political campaigning and lobbying. The campaign was discreetly managed by Lowe Bell on behalf of the Communications Workers' Union from 1994 to 1997. The documentary has a section which looks at the growth of commercial activities at party conferences and how such activities are increasingly important for the political parties as income generators and as suppliers of information to the decision- and policy-making process. Cockerell argues that the counter-Post Office privatization campaign made decisive use of the party conferences and activists to stop the then President of the Board of Trade, Michael Heseltine, MP, from privatizing Royal Mail.

Cockerell reports that the then Sir Tim Bell (now the life peer Lord Bell) took personal charge of the campaign. He was a strong supporter of Margaret Thatcher and known to dislike Michael Heseltine, who he perceived as having brought about her downfall. Neil Lawson was the campaign manager within Lowe Bell for Royal Mail. Lawson is a former

aide to a later Chancellor, Gordon Brown, MP, and has close links with the new Labour government team via HM Treasury. Lawson now runs his own public affairs company, which reflects very much the embeddedness concept in operation. Cockerell argues that there were more lobbyists at the 1996 Conservative Party Conference than delegates, which although difficult to validate, this author would deem highly probable and increasingly the norm at the prime UK governing party conference.

The annual party conferences in the United Kingdom are the largest yearly political gatherings or rallies in Europe, with over 21,000 people being reported as having attended the post-election victory Labour Party Conference in Brighton in September 1997 (*Guardian*, October 1, p. 3; *Economist*, October 4, p. 20). Much of the research published on party conferences (Minkin, 1978; Kelly, 1989, 1994; Morris, 1991; Kavanagh, 1996b; Stanyer and Scammell, 1996, etc.) and extensive press coverage concentrates on the communication of political messages to delegates and members, the media, and the electorate.

The literature and research in the area of commercial activities at party conferences as has been argued earlier is very limited. There has been no systematic attempt to observe or measure what is happening in terms of lobbying or business activity at party conferences. However, there is a distinct area of research which has emerged in recent years on the use of marketing techniques and their incorporation into the promotion of not only politicians but also policy and the effective use of the managed rally or conference for political marketing purposes. An assessment of business and organizational lobbying and associated activities at the party conferences has so far not been carried out. The following attempts to bridge that gap in knowledge.

## RESEARCH AT THE 1994–2003 CONFERENCES: CONTEXT AND SETTING

The annual party conferences originally developed as a policy-making forum and meeting place for activists, members, party interests, and politicians alike. Increasingly the role of the conference has changed. The Conservative conference has long been a platform for the presentation of party policy and politicians. It is stage-managed for maximum media impact and has very little member debate. The recent exception to this purely presentational trend is the post-election defeat debate at the party conference in Blackpool in 1997. A similar trend highlighting the lack of debate has increasingly become the norm in the Labour Party since its 1992 election defeat and is increasingly the case within the third party, the Liberal Democrats, as it gets closer to power.

## Political Rally or Annual Business Lobbying Convention?

Party conferences are formal annual events with their own set of rituals and rules, and part of that process is being seen and making contacts at key meeting points in the event, especially receptions or private parties. Such venues also provide an ideal opportunity for people to meet from the business and political world and keep up to date their network of contacts and information sources. Party conferences now see substantial attendance from key figures in industry, charities, and the public sector. At the 1996 Labour Party Conference ahead of the 1997 general election, major figures from industry were observed as part of the research and reported in many instances by the press. These included the chief executives of British Airways, BAA, the Granada Group, Sainsbury's, United Utilities, etc., Richard Branson of Virgin, Rupert Murdoch of News International and senior members of Liffe, Europe's largest futures and options exchange, who were all reported at the post-election Labour Party Conference in September 1997 (*Guardian*, September 29, p. 9). In 2002 again these organizations and senior members from Tesco's, Sainsbury's, Marks & Spencer, Granada, Diageo, and a growing host of other organizations were seen active at the conferences.

This is not surprising as party conferences are annual events that can be planned ahead in diaries and scheduled for decision makers and influencers to attend. In addition, certain points on an agenda are obvious attractors to various interest groups. For instance, the Prime Minister's and the Chancellor of the Exchequer's key speeches, as well as those of their opposite numbers in the other parties, are scheduled on days which have particular appeal to foreign dignitaries and businesses, not only because of the perceived status they receive, but also because of the insight into the workings of government and the development of policy. Such policies could impact upon their organization (see Exhibit 15.3 on page 242) and interests in attending particular policy sessions. At the 1997 post-election victory conference held by the Labour Party, the session, which included the new Prime Minister, Tony Blair's, speech, was an all-ticket event in the conference hall, with the less well connected or known watchers and apparatchiks being given access to one of three nearby overflow cinemas in a multiplex where they were able to hear and view the address. Ambassadors, senior visiting dignitaries, leading correspondents (especially those deemed influential or sympathetic to Labour), and leading business figures were given seats in the main conference hall, or in the case of Labour supporters were sold seats in return for a party donation. This has become the norm for all Labour Party Conferences and is very similar to the style of sponsorship expected at the Democrat and Republican conventions in the United States in a presidential election year.

## Research Access to Party Conferences

Research was undertaken at all the major annual UK party conferences between September 1994 and October 2003 and was supported by Granada Television. Granada's support was crucial in gaining entry to the conferences as an accredited member of the media, which allowed privileged access to the press office, political press briefings, full copies of politicians' speeches, and easy entry to receptions and fringe events. This enabled quality research to be conducted by participant observation and the collection of substantial primary and secondary data throughout the events.

A good example of the research advantages of such access can be assessed by the accuracy and quality of the data obtained. Accurate information could be gained directly from the press office; and if they could not answer queries they would find somebody who could. This level of access and detailed communication response is designed to specifically service media needs and is not available to the normal party delegate or those with observer status. (This latter category covers the majority of exhibitors, researchers and occasional attendees at party conferences.) During the research it was found through participant observation that journalists, lobbyists, and politicians gave their time more readily to accredited media representatives than to those with observer or delegate status. This was partly the result of privileged access to events or parts of the conference at which these individuals and groups congregated. Moreover the media are seen as being of particular interest to people attending the conference because of their prime communications role and consequent privileged position (Packard, 1957; McLuhan, 1964; Curran and Seaton, 1997). In addition, not being a party delegate or observer, but a *bona fide* representative of a major television group, meant that research access and information were readily made available by other members of the media, lobbyists, "not for profit" campaigners, business interests, party members, diplomats, and foreign visiting dignitaries. These people invariably liked talking or being associated with the media, consequently substantial amounts of background information and data for the research were obtained, which allowed a more rigorous conceptualization of the theoretical constructs necessary to assess lobbying and business-to-business marketing activity at party conferences.

A good example of quality access and information in the "not for profit" area is that at one point the research was able to assess rapidly how and why the "Movement of Live Animals" campaign had developed. To explore this issue,

information was obtained from the Royal Society for the Prevention of Cruelty to Animals (RSPCA) exhibition stand which was supported by a full briefing from their then chief parliamentary officer (now with British Telecom), who outlined the various stages in the campaign and made available the latest briefing paper on the subject. The research issue was further explored by visiting the Royal Society for the Protection of Birds (RSPB) stand and interviewing a director of the International Fund for Animal Welfare who was relaxing there. He gave a very full global pressure-group perspective on the topic. The research was then strengthened by interviewing an official of the National Farmers' Union (NFU) to obtain the farmers' perspective on the issue and subsequent attendance at the European Commission reception and fringe meeting. A comprehensive briefing session was attended and observed on the European perspective on the transportation of animals. Additional research was gained at fringe meetings and receptions throughout that week which covered the subject or interest area of animal welfare or campaigning. This access allowed a realistic and rounded picture of the policy issues and decision-making procedure on the transportation of animals to be obtained in a few hours from informed opinion which otherwise would have been very difficult to obtain in such depth. In addition, the people one discussed these issues with were often regarded as the leading experts in their respective fields.

Attendance at the party conferences allows complex strategic business issues to be explored, a greater depth of inquiry to be obtained and interesting issues and avenues more fully researched. An example of this was at London Weekend Television's (LWT) select lunchtime reception for senior Conservative politicians and officials at the 1995 Conservative conference in Bournemouth. An interview with a junior Minister and, separately, one of his officials about how lobbying worked in information technology industries was obtained. The interviews confirmed earlier research observations and findings. The research was further strengthened by attendance at a fringe meeting on information technology where a presentation by Ian Taylor, MP, the then Under-Secretary for Trade and Technology at the Department of Trade and Industry, was observed which confirmed that certain corporate industries (telecoms predominantly) and interests had directly influenced the development of a particular policy. These interests were represented at the back of the room, watching the Minister outline how he saw policy unfolding.

## The Increasing Scale of Party Conferences

The statistics are startling. On top of the 1,317 accredited delegates, 14,500 visitors and 2,000 journalists, party staff and police bring the total to 23,000—the largest political conference in Britain.

(Michael White, *Guardian*, September 29, 1997, p. 9)

Labour's Conference in 1997 was quite exceptional. It was packed full of political watchers and professional voyeurs and was very much the national victory celebration after the party had been out of power for eighteen years. It had a new, young leader and followed one of the largest-ever electoral landslides in UK political history. Conservative and Labour Party conferences during the period of the research had attendances in excess of 10,000 people, with those ahead of the 1997 and 2001 general elections being significantly larger than usual.

The Conservative conference held in Bournemouth in 1996 gives some interesting insights into the scale of party conferences. Conservative Central Office issued the background statistics in Exhibit 15.1 during the event. The data correlate with the information that Michael Cockerell of the BBC collected for the documentary discussed earlier.

The Liberal Democrat party conferences are scaled-down versions of the larger two parties' events but still attract interest on a wide scale. An indication of the size of Liberal Democrat conferences can be seen in Table 15.1. One can assume that with day visitors, observers, exhibitors, guests, media, etc., this is likely to rise by a factor of at least three. This would mean the total attendance at the Brighton 1997 conference would be in the order of 7,000–8,000 people (confirmed to author by Liberal Democrat Party sources) and this level of attendance was maintained to 2003.

Watchers and lobbyists are attracted by certain key informative sessions of party conferences. Conference days with special statements or presentations by Ministers on their policy portfolios, e.g. health, the environment, disability, trade and industry, science, the arts, aid, education, etc., attract the interests and lobbies associated with the respective policy area, although normally policy is well defined ahead of most speeches. However, there is a view that to be present when Ministers make public statements, and to be near them and their

---

### Exhibit 15.1 Relevant Statistics on the 1995 Conservative Party Conference

- Over 11,000 people were accredited to attend the conference.
- 2,000 press and media passes were issued.
- Nearly 300 events, meetings and receptions took place during conference week.
- Only four towns or cities are large enough to accommodate the Conservative conference—Bournemouth, Birmingham, Blackpool and Brighton.
- The CPC bookshop transports 5,500 items from London to its conference stand.
- In 1994, 16,000 guests attended eighty receptions during conference week in the Highcliff Hotel.

*Source* 113th Conservative Party Conference 1996, conference document, 66.

Table 15.1　*Attendance of representatives at Liberal Democrat conferences,*
*1992–1997*

| Year | Venue | No. |
|------|-------|-----|
| 1992 | Harrogate | 1,475 |
| 1993 | Torquay | 1,596 |
| 1994 | Brighton | 1,747 |
| 1996 | Glasgow | 1,369 |
| 1997 | Brighton | 1,753 |

*Source* "The Role and Operation of the Party Conference," background paper for consultative session tabled at 1997 Liberal Democrat conference, Brighton, p. 7.

associated advisors and government servants when statements are made, gives insight into policy thinking and future interpretation and can aid influence. (This view was confirmed at interview with business and "not for profit" lobbyist informants.) Interested organizations will invariably have a reception ahead of a particular ministerial policy address to gather support and gauge opinion among activists or sometimes afterwards as part of an ongoing commitment to reviewing issues that impact upon their organization. The research noted PowerGen, Safeways, BAA and Sallingbury Casey (a lobbyist group) in operation at the 1996 Conservative Party Conference ahead of sessions in the conference that might be of interest to them.

If the organization has an exhibition stall it may well use this as a base from which to promote the organization's views or to provide information. A good example of how this works can be seen in Exhibit 15.2. The conference fringe

can be used to host a meeting on the cause or policies you favour or support with other organizations. In addition, advertisements may be taken in the parties' publications supporting a particular view or championing a cause. In 1996 the anti-gun lobby was very active using these tactics to support initiatives, post the Dunblane school massacre, to urge the abolition of hand guns.

An overview of the shape of party conferences can be seen in Exhibit 15.3 on page 242, which outlines the 1996 Labour Party Conference agenda by policy issue and known key groups represented at the conference who had a strong interest in a particular section of the conference agenda. The exhibit highlights the potential corporate and "not for profit" groups with an interest in particular parts of the conference proceedings. It is worth noting that many of the utility companies held meetings ahead of, or after, not only the main trade and industry debate but also post the session on the environment. The utility companies

---

**Exhibit 15.2 North East of England Supermarket Case**

At the 1996 Labour Conference, research observed a public affairs manager of a large supermarket, being approached by a North East of England councillor who said that a rival supermarket had been blocked from gaining planning permission to build in their town. The council, it was argued, would prefer the public affairs manager's company to develop the site and would the retailer like to put in an application? The public affairs manager thanked the councillor and got on her mobile phone to the company's group site planning department to feed the information back. Indeed, they were very interested, and two years later the company's supermarket is on that site and trading. Public affairs work in support of retail location acquisition and planning has been one of the fastest-growing areas of the UK discipline in the last ten years.

were watching for statements on increasing competition in their sector, enhanced powers for regulators, the future extent and direction of windfall profit taxes, as well as pollution and environmental protection initiatives. One major utilities company board and selected senior managers had a private dinner at the main Blackpool conference hotel with Labour politicians and policy advisors on the evening after the environment debate. (Based on research observation and non-attributable discussion with utilities employees.)

## ASSESSING LOBBYING AND MARKETING ACTIVITY AT PARTY CONFERENCES: ISSUES AND RESULTS

In addition to interviews and secondary sources, our research deliberately concentrated on observable and measurable phenomena at the conferences to ascertain whether corporate lobbying was in evidence. This falls into three observable categorizations of data, which have, to date, not been researched before. These are the number of advertisements, fringe meetings, and exhibitions purchased or held at the conferences to promote a cause or an organization and its interests. The rest of this section focuses on these observable features of conferences.

The quantifiable data are drawn from a comprehensive review of registered interests gathered by research through attendance at the 1994–2003 conferences. The data were collated systematically over ten years' attendance at party conferences and reflect the range, scale, and intensity of lobbying and "business to business" marketing interests represented at these events. The data set outlines recorded information for the period 1994–2003; this was checked for accuracy and emerging trends and will be re-evaluated in 2004. An earlier version of this data and associated issues has been published in Harris and Lock (1995). This is the first and only systematic database of the lobbying and "business to business" activity at party conferences.

In addition, party conferences were regularly attended from 1975 to 1993 as a member of the Liberal Party, Liberal Democrat Party and of the Alliance groupage of parties, which included joint rallies and attendance at SDP events. Historical background research and phenomenological grounding in the processes to be evaluated had been obtained prior to the study through membership of the national executive and conference organizing committee of one of the political parties (Phil Harris). This provided valuable insight into the operation of modern political conferences and added to research credibility and levels of mutual understanding at these events.

To assess lobbying activity at party conferences, research data had to be gathered to quantify the scale of operations of lobbyists at conferences. For, as has been stated earlier, conferences are meeting places where politicians and business and "not for profit" groups can meet and talk. Many of these meetings are difficult to observe or quantify using traditional research methods, as the interest or organization will not want them observed or recorded. Falling into this category are private receptions, especially those not advertised. These meetings and events can be observed discreetly or by luck, perseverance, or personal invitation, but it is normally impossible to measure how many of them there are or what they are about. At one point an attempt was made to gather data by listing in note form these types of private events which are usually discreetly advertised on hotel event boards to give directions for the benefit of attendees. However, it became apparent that this would not elicit meaningful results and the conclusion was reached that to obtain a realistic sample would be practically impossible. For example, in Blackpool at conference time there would be at least eleven main conference hotels holding receptions and fringe meetings. These would have to be visited in a very short period of time four times a day (simultaneously at breakfast, lunch, early evening, and late evening times to observe fringe meetings, meals, and receptions) for the four or five days of the conference over a distance of three miles. Even with a large field research team this would have been practically impossible to achieve.

Table 15.2    *Advertisements placed in official party publications, 1994–1997*

| Party | Public | NFP | UPA | Private | Party | Total |
|---|---|---|---|---|---|---|
| | | | **1994** | | | |
| Conservative | 4 | 7 | 10 | 23 | 4 | 48 |
| Liberal Democrat | 3 | 6 | 10 | 10 | 1 | 30 |
| Labour | 7 | 7 | 12 | 24 | 2 | 52 |
| | | | **1995** | | | |
| Conservative | 4 | 8 | 13 | 21 | 9 | 55 |
| Liberal Democrat | 3 | 5 | 10 | 15 | 9 | 42 |
| Labour | 5 | 5 | 6 | 12 | 9 | 37 |
| | | | **1996** | | | |
| Conservative | 8 | 16 | 9 | 29 | 4 | 56 |
| Liberal Democrat | 7 | 13 | 11 | 10 | 7 | 48 |
| Labour | 15 | 27 | 22 | 27 | 11 | 102 |
| | | | **1997** | | | |
| Conservative | 5 | 12 | 7 | 14 | 4 | 42 |
| Liberal Democrat | 6 | 9 | 8 | 11 | 6 | 40 |
| Labour | 1 | 9 | 6 | 22 | 1 | 39 |
| **Total** | **68** | **124** | **124** | **218** | **67** | **591** |

## Advertising

Therefore the research focused on primary data collection that could be obtained legitimately and verified independently. Thus research focused on looking at the features of commercial activity at party conferences that could be measured (advertisements, exhibitions, and fringe meetings). The first of these consisted of advertisements purchased in official party publications by outside organizations.

These ranged from full or half-page color advertisements such as that placed by Sainsbury's in all party conference agenda documents in 1996 and 1997 entitled "J. Sainsbury, grocer. Part of the local community," showing a cross-section of society which included lollipop ladies (school road crossing assistants), disabled people, judges, mothers, and children, which was designed to show the community commitment and spirit of the retailer, to a small black-and-white advertisement placed for Slater Menswear of Glasgow at the 1995 Liberal Democrat conference extolling the virtue of the good prices on men's clothes which could be obtained from the store by those present at the event.

The core advertisements by category are listed in Table 15.2. The typology of organizations by interest is based upon earlier work by Presthus (1973, 1974), Schmitter and Streeck (1981), Whiteley and Winyard (1987), Jordan (1994) and that of Stanyer and Scammell (1996) previously referred to and the authors' personal categorization of the three types of advertiser, exhibitor, and fringe event sponsor. These categories are amalgamations of a disparate group of interests and, of course, some could fit into a number of sectors. For instance, private company sponsorship of a Conservative fringe meeting or the General and Municipal Boilermakers' Union (GMB) stand sponsored by Vauxhall Motors at the 1995 Labour conference, in each case the example could fit into two subcategories. To aid the clarity of the data the authors have taken the most visible sponsor, exhibitor, or advertiser and listed them as the main organization behind the particular event or feature. In the case where there is no one clear promoter of the advert, event or exhibition all organizations are listed. The five broad categorizations used to subdivide data collected at conferences are as follows:

1  *Public sector.* Government-controlled, owned, or sponsored agencies or organizations (e.g., the Arts Council, the BBC, the

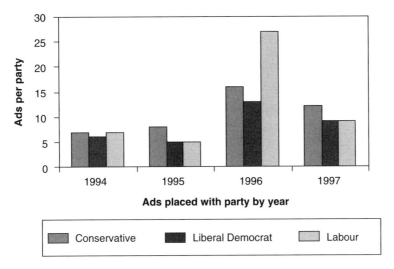

Figure 15.1    *Not-for-profit advertisements in official party conference publications,*
*1994–1997*

Campaign for Racial Equality, the Government of Gibraltar, the Post Office, etc.) and interests controlled or owned by local authorities (e.g., the Local Government Association or Bilston College).

2   *"Not for profit".* Charitable trusts, recognized pressure groups, and think tanks. For instance, Age Concern, the Child Poverty Action Group, Greenpeace, the Leonard Cheshire Foundation, the RSPB, and in the latter category Demos, the Institute for Public Policy Research (IPPR) and the Social Market Foundation (SMF).

3   *Unions and professional associations.* Traditional trade unions such as the TGWU, Unison, etc., through to professional associations and federations, for instance the British Medical Association (BMA), the Police Federation of England and Wales, and the Advertising Association.

4   *Private sector.* Public limited companies, industry groups, and associated interests. For instance, Boot's the Chemist, the Cable Television Association, Guinness, Manchester Airport and the Railfreight Group.

5   *Party-associated organizations.* Groups and organizations in this sector cover predominantly official political party organizations such as interest groups or campaigning parts of the organization. This category includes

the ALDC (Association of Liberal Democrat Councillors), the Conservative Anti-hunt Council, the Conservative Medical Society, the European Parliamentary Labour Party through to the Welsh Night (traditional entertainment organized by the Welsh Liberal Democrats).

As one would expect there is a surge of activity in purchased advertisements in election years allowing organizations to raise their awareness and issues ahead of an election. This is particularly marked in the "not for profit" sector, where advertising in Labour publications increased 450 percent from five to twenty seven over the period 1995 to 1996, which suggests that the sector was very much wanting to push forward issues and policy options into the future Labour government's agenda.

The trade unions and professional associations also increased their expenditure on advertisements at the 1996 and 2000 conferences ahead of the 1997 and 2001 general elections. As can be seen in Figure 15.1, the most dramatic rise in advertising support was by this sector at the Labour conference of 1996. This also occurred in 2000, indicating that advertisers wanted to be associated with that party and its policies particularly. The data also suggest that the parties are more focused on

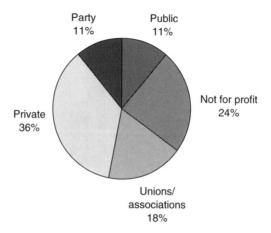

Figure 15.2    *Advertisements at party conferences, by sector, 1994–2003*

raising money from earnings from sold advertising space in the run-up to the election than they are outside the campaign period. In addition, there is a tendency by advertisers to want to be associated with the victorious party in an election, also it must be added that a significant number of advertisers in this period back the leading two parties and in some cases all three.

The research also showed clearly that the Labour Party benefited ahead of the 1997 general election in 1996 from a surge in advertisements from the private sector placed in its conference publications. There was also a small increase for the Conservatives.

All sectors show that there is a surge of interest just ahead of an election by advertisement purchases and that this tapers off once the electoral process is complete. Total advertising expenditure by category for the period of research can be seen in Figure 15.2. The private sector is the largest purchaser of advertisements at party conferences and much of this activity is focused ahead of a general election. The next largest sectors are "not for profit", trade unions, and professional associations, which are equal in size over the four-year cycle of conferences. However, when one looks in detail at Table 15.2, one can see that the latter group has been in steady decline whilst the "not for profit" group of interests has become much more evident ahead of the general election.

The results from the data gathered at party conferences on adverts are difficult to assess, because of the scale of activity and the clear influence of the general election leading to a surge of interest in 1996 and 2000. There is one dramatic feature of such interest that emerges, though, and that is that by the 1996 conference season Labour was the clear favourite of advertisers in that it had seen a 175 percent increase in sales of ads over 1995, whilst the Conservative Party had remained static and the Liberal Democrats had shown a marginal increase. This suggests that purchases of advertisements were very much wanted to gain favour with the most likely winner of the 1997 election—Labour.

## Exhibitors

Commercial exhibitions at party conferences have grown in significance as both an income generator for the political organization and as a provider of information for party activists and apparatchiks. A further indication of the size of this business activity at party conferences can be found by analysing the financial accounts and reports of the respective political organizations presented at the annual conferences. For instance, the commercial operations of the Labour Party (conference exhibition income is by far the largest component according to the author's sources) made a net contribution to party funds of £513,000 in 1996 (Labour Party, 1997: 19). In the same document it was reported that all exhibition space for the 1997 conference was sold out within three hours of going on sale. This was the largest-ever commercial exhibition held at a party conference in the United Kingdom. Such was the scrabble for exhibition space that, like oversubscribed trade shows, late applicants and bookings found themselves on poor sites tucked away in an alcove in a secondary hotel, where their ability to meet attendees and do business was limited. Labour conference exhibition space remains at a premium and is sold out normally a year ahead of the event.

Even the third major party, the Liberal Democrat Party, reported an income of £263,756 from commercial sources at its 1996 conference, which was 17 percent up on 1995 (Liberal Democrat Party, 1997: 19). At the 1997 Conservative conference (post their election defeat, demand was down) it was estimated that the party had made a surplus from this activity of £160,000 in the previous year. This suggests that organizations are much more interested in buying exhibition space the year before a general election. In recent years the Conservative Party, the former party of government, has had to hide unsold exhibition space at conferences, and this has done little to assure exhibitors.

Senior Ministers of the leading parties normally have responsibility for visiting exhibition stands during the Party Conference. In addition, exhibitions are one of the most visible signs of the promotion of a corporate or organizational interest at the party conferences. Over the ten conference seasons of the research a steady improvement in the quality, size, and professionalism of the exhibitions at the conferences was observed. This growth in overall quality paralleled similar developments in trade show activity, being seen at commercial exhibitions in Europe (Cope, 1989; Shipley et al., 1993; Dekimpe et al., 1997). Exhibition stands that attracted the most attention and interest had proactive staff, were well manned and underpinned by regular promotion ahead of and during the conference. At party

conferences national and international organizations clearly could exert the power of a brand over lesser known organizations, which concurs with the findings of the trade show research of Gopalakrishna et al. (1995).

The size of stand can vary significantly. The small party organization or charity may have one standard stall and even share it with other organizations to reduce costs, whilst Sky, British Airways or the Cable Communications Association (now not exhibiting) have had large multimedia-driven stands bolstered by a large number of staff and regular promotional events to enhance perception and knowledge among delegates.

Exhibitions are one of the most visual features of commercial lobbying and interest group behaviour at party conferences. Table 15.3 summarizes exhibitors at party conferences over the period 1994–1997. A number of key features emerge from this large sample of interests exhibiting at party conferences. First, exhibitors are conservative with a small "c" and like to attend the usual national venues, and anything outside of the three main conference sites tends not to be supported. In 1995 the Liberal Democrats followed their federalist instincts and political convictions and decided to hold their conference in Glasgow. As a result they suffered a dramatic decline in exhibitors, who were not prepared to travel to somewhere perhaps a little more interesting than the usual out-of-season conference resort. Interestingly one can see this phenomenon repeated again in 1997 when the Liberal Democrats went to Eastbourne rather than one of the "three Bs" (Bournemouth, Blackpool, or Brighton). Even though it is close to London it is perhaps perceived as being out of the way and not taken seriously by exhibitors. The post-general election situation just exacerbates this tendency for the Liberal Democrats, who lose a revenue-earning opportunity once again. The Liberal Party suffered a similar lack of support when it went to Dundee in the 1980s (non-attributable source).

Another clear feature that emerges is that over the period 1994 to 1997 there is a drift away from the Conservative Party by conference exhibitors in the run-up to the May 1997 general election and an even more marked

Table 15.3   *Exhibitors at party conferences, 1994–1997*

| Party | Public | NFP | UPA | Private | Party | Total |
|---|---|---|---|---|---|---|
| **1994** | | | | | | |
| Conservative | 17 | 23 | 8 | 44 | 8 | 100 |
| Liberal Democrat | 12 | 21 | 9 | 19 | 29 | 90 |
| Labour | 16 | 27 | 15 | 31 | 20 | 109 |
| **1995** | | | | | | |
| Conservative | 12 | 15 | 9 | 40 | 10 | 86 |
| Liberal Democrat | 4 | 15 | 5 | 16 | 29 | 69 |
| Labour | 15 | 25 | 20 | 36 | 15 | 111 |
| **1996** | | | | | | |
| Conservative | 12 | 15 | 7 | 37 | 10 | 81 |
| Liberal Democrat | 10 | 19 | 4 | 18 | 31 | 82 |
| Labour | 17 | 24 | 19 | 38 | 13 | 111 |
| **1997** | | | | | | |
| Conservative | 8 | 13 | 6 | 31 | 11 | 69 |
| Liberal Democrat | 5 | 15 | 4 | 13 | 31 | 68 |
| Labour | 12 | 40 | 15 | 47 | 13 | 127 |
| **Total** | 140 | 252 | 121 | 370 | 220 | 1,103 |

decline thereafter. The net beneficiaries are the Labour Party, where one can see a noticeable trend of growing support as private-sector exhibitors steadily increase from 1995 to 1997. This has resulted in Labour dominating the exhibition scene much like the Conservatives had done previously in 1994 and before. Conservative Party Conference exhibitors declined 30 percent over that period whilst Labour increased by 51 percent from a lower base level.

The data clearly show that levels of exhibition activity increase ahead of a general election and decline immediately after, with the exception to the case being the governing party. If data were gathered over a longer period of time it would be possible to observe whether this is equally the case for new governments, as in Labour's case post the 1997 general election. As shown in advertisements, the public sector and trade union/professional association sectors appear in relative decline.

It is also worth noting that those parties with the least financial resources have the greatest number of voluntary activist groups at party conferences and this is particularly apparent at Liberal Democrat conferences. However, it also highlights the fact that much stall space at the third party's conferences is filled by party supporters rather than interested private-sector, public-sector, unions and associations or "not for profit" organizations. Income is thus accordingly limited for the third party from this activity.

Figure 15.3 is a total picture in percentages of all exhibitors at party conferences over the period and indicates that the bulk of activity is quite clearly in the private and "not for profit" sectors. We know from earlier analysis in this chapter that the category "party organizations" is a group that can be just a reflection of the status, professionalism, and voluntarism of the party organization. This group could be a reflection of large numbers of volunteers or enthusiasts within the party who may not even pay much of a fee for their stall. In addition, we know from the previous analysis of advertisements and the data in Table 15.3 on exhibitions that the public sector and unions and professional associations are in relative decline at conferences. Consequently, what we are observing is that increasingly activity by outside groups at conferences is coming from the private sector and "not for profit" categories. All of these groups are normally at the conference to exert influence or communicate messages to government and politicians through the use of

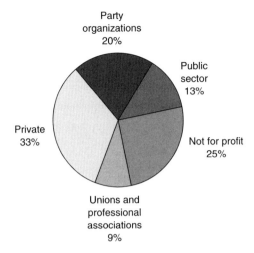

Figure 15.3    *Exhibitors at party conferences, by sector, 1994–2003*

one medium or another. There has been a steady growth in activities by not for profit organizations over the ten-year period of the study and a slow but steady decline among public-sector, unions and professional association interests. This indicates the increasing competitiveness and awareness of effective political lobbying by the private sector (normally reflective of large-scale organizations rather than small to medium-sized enterprises, SMEs) and "not for profit" organizations (which have invariably been dominated by a number of prime issues, e.g., animal welfare).

An analysis of the data underpinning Table 15.3 starkly shows the decline in attractiveness of the Conservative Party Conference against a commensurate rise in interest in Labour, reflecting the growing strength and attractiveness of Labour to the commercial and pressure group interests at conferences. It is surprising to find a steady decline in commercial/"not for profit" activity at the Liberal Democrat conferences at a time when relatively speaking they have had more influence and power than before.

A particular feature that emerges is a steady decline in public-sector interests being represented at Conservative Party conferences. At the end of the period of research these had more than halved from seventeen to eight over the period of the data collection. The Conservatives have also seen a steady decline in

"not for profit" exhibitors over the same period, from twenty three to thirteen. Another feature is the 65 percent of all union and professional association stalls at the Labour Party conferences, showing the historic link between the Labour Party and trade unions.

The number of exhibitors in total at conferences is relatively static, although there is some evidence that Labour's increased commercialization of its conference is beginning to reverse any potential decline. However, it should be noted that many of the stalls and exhibitions are becoming more sophisticated and considerably more is being spent on renting exhibition space. It is known that there is a significant cost differentiation on stands and the actual site within exhibition areas and that space is at a premium at Labour conferences (Labour Party, 1997: 19). Interestingly, the research observed less pressure on exhibition space at the defeated Conservatives' conference, and certainly this was the case at the Liberal Democrats, who have clearly a significant way to go to market these spaces, as the data indicate.

## Fringe Meetings

Fringe meetings are those meetings and events outside the main conference hall which are held at breakfast, lunchtime, and early and late evening times by parties for the benefit of giving

Table 15.4   *Fringe events at party conferences, 1994–1997*

| Party | Public | NPA | UPA | Private | Party | Total |
|---|---|---|---|---|---|---|
| | | | **1994** | | | |
| Conservative | 15 | 39 | 23 | 32 | 5 | 114 |
| Liberal Democrat | 11 | 32 | 19 | 16 | 7 | 85 |
| Labour | 15 | 33 | 26 | 22 | 16 | 112 |
| | | | **1995** | | | |
| Conservative | 6 | 32 | 17 | 21 | 50 | 126 |
| Liberal Democrat | 9 | 28 | 14 | 20 | 54 | 125 |
| Labour | 13 | 39 | 24 | 27 | 108 | 211 |
| | | | **1996** | | | |
| Conservative | 12 | 45 | 14 | 21 | 34 | 126 |
| Liberal Democrat | 12 | 36 | 18 | 20 | 48 | 134 |
| Labour | 12 | 42 | 24 | 27 | 107 | 212 |
| | | | **1997** | | | |
| Conservative | 9 | 38 | 14 | 22 | 39 | 122 |
| Liberal Democrat | 10 | 35 | 16 | 18 | 57 | 136 |
| Labour | 14 | 35 | 23 | 32 | 82 | 186 |
| **Total** | 138 | 434 | 232 | 278 | 607 | 1,689 |

a platform to organizations, interests, and speakers to discuss ideas and areas of common interest with those attending conferences. They can include alternative policy issues, be a platform for well-known politicians, or provide a forum for individuals and organizations to consider particular policy issues or concerns. Recently many of the events have become platforms for coalitions of interests to consider a particular issue, for example Europe, animal welfare, or health care. Table 15.4 outlines the number of these events by category held at the various conferences between 1994 and 1997.

This is a difficult area to assess as the Conservative fringe until recent times was very limited, but this type of event had become established by the 1994 conference and has grown remarkably since then. It should be noted that the overall figures are distorted by the large number of party organization meetings at the Labour and Liberal Democrat conferences. These meetings are invariably used as election and candidate training meetings whilst the Conservatives have tended to use private professionally run events. An interesting phenomenon which emerges is the steady increase in private-sector events and the sponsorship of fringe meetings. Labour's growth in privately sponsored fringe meetings is

in marked contrast to the Conservatives' relative decline, which parallels the findings of the previous data set cited. The "not for profit" sector, as one would expect, is the largest provider of fringe meetings and these become more pronounced just ahead of the general election, as can be seen in the figures for the 1996 conference season. The total figure for fringe meetings by sector is indicated in Figure 15.4.

The broad trends that emerge from the data for fringe meeting activity at conferences parallel that reported previously on the other observed features of party conferences (advertisements and exhibitions). That is that public-sector activity has been in steady decline at Conservative conferences and that there was a surge of interest in the Labour Party ahead of the 1997 general election, shown by the increased activity levels at the 1996 party conference and at the post-election conference in 1997. There is a significant move of private-sector-supported fringe meetings from the Conservative Party to the Labour Party over the period of research. Party member organizations representing campaigning and associated activity are much more significant at Labour and Liberal Democrat party conferences, reflecting the more voluntary nature of those parties.

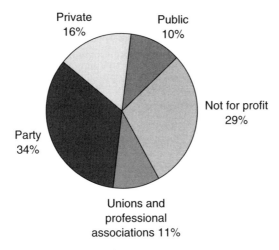

Figure 15.4    *Fringe events at party conferences, by sector, 1994–2003*

## RELATIONSHIP MARKETING AT PARTY CONFERENCES

The data gathered from the party conferences on business activities show a substantial interest in the promotion of messages, interests, policies, and themes to the political process. Research shows (see www.Phil-Harris.com) the complete range of sponsors and advertisements, fringe meetings, and exhibitions taking place at the conferences. This now shows only a limited portion of overt lobbying at party conferences and as has been argued previously much lobbying at these events is difficult to monitor, quantify, or tabulate. The three data sets featured in this work measuring data sets of advertisements, exhibitions, and fringe meetings show both the diversity and the vibrancy of selling messages by the sponsors to politicians and public decision makers.

The core features of lobbying and marketing activity are indicated in Figure 15.5, which outlines the use of the relationship marketing approach and network theory at party conferences. This outlines the key events, fora, and media that can be used to gain access to politicians and decision makers at party conferences. Clearly, a well structured marketing communication plan to use these opportunities as part of an overall strategy can be very effective. The well prepared campaign will use a combination of fringe meetings, receptions, advertisements, and an exhibition stand supported by informal briefings, lobbying and dinners to get the required message over. This is all part of a well geared public affairs or political lobbying campaign to provide information and/or exert influence on government decision making.

## CONCLUSION

The scale of business and marketing activities at party conferences grew considerably in the 1990s. Media and political attention remains focused on the activities of politicians at party conferences, but there is only limited research on the vast amount of lobbying and business marketing activity at these events. Levels of activity have been measured and observed over the period 1994–1998 and point to the increasing role of the party conference as an interface between business and politics. In fact, it emerges as an annual marketplace where political lobbying can be seen at first hand. This chapter confirms the growing level and importance of business lobbying and associated relationship marketing at party conferences.

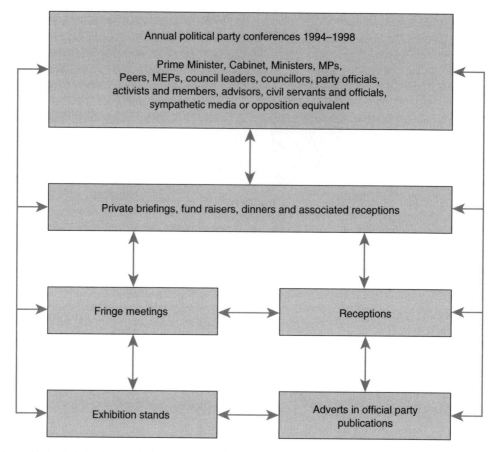

Figure 15.5   *Relationship marketing at party conferences: the new policy network*

---

**Exhibit 15.3 Policy Sessions and Interests in Attendance at the Labour Party Conference, Blackpool, September 30 to October 3, 1996**

**Monday September 30**

Official Conference opening

*Health and Community Care* (Chris Smith, MP). British Medical Association (BMA), Royal College of Nursing (RCN), Royal College of Midwives (RCM), Unison (Health Service workers' union), etc.

*Stakeholder Economy* (Gordon Brown, MP). Co-operative Wholesale Society (CWS), British Nuclear Fuels (BNFL), Sainsbury's, various utility companies, Federation of Small Businesses, Institute of Directors (IOD), Lloyd's, etc.

*Economic Policy* (Margaret Beckett, MP). Cable Television, Sky Television, Scotch Whisky Association, Sears and many others.

*Rights at Work.* Communication Workers' Union, Transport and General Workers' Union (TGWU), MSF, IOD, etc.

## Tuesday October 1

*Representation of Women.* MSF, Body Shop, Fawcett Society.

*Europe* (Robin Cook, MP). Channel Tunnel, Eurostar, British Airways, Scottish Fishermen's Association.

Speaker from European Socialist Group.

*Parliamentary report and Leader's speech.* All.

*Party business.* Very little external interest.

## Wednesday October 2

*Transport* (Andrew Smith, MP). BAA, London Rail Development, Sea Containers, Virgin, Manchester Airport, London Luton Airport, etc.

*Education* (David Blunkett, MP). ATL, National Association of Head Teachers (NAHT), National Union of Teachers (NUT), National Council for Voluntary Qualifications (NCVQ), Open University, Committee of Vice-Chancellors and Principals (CVCP).

*Housing.* Chartered Institute of Housing and National Housing Federations, National House Building Confederation, All-party Group on Homelessness and Housing.

*General election campaign.*

*Operation Victory* (John Prescott, MP).

*One Nation Society.*

Deputy Prime Minister of Italy.

*Environment* (Frank Dobson, MP). British Aggregate Construction Materials Industries; Anglia Water, Boot's, United Utilities and other utility companies.

*Food and agriculture.* NFU, Country Landowners, Compassion in World Farming.

*Fair taxes/benefits* (Harriet Harman, MP). Shelter (housing charity), Carers' Alliance, Church Action on Poverty, Child Poverty Action Group, and many more.

## Thursday October 3

*Defence* (David Clark, MP). Yeoman (Plessey/Siemens), Racal, British Aerospace, Westland, GEC.

*Leadership in the World (Third World), including the Middle East and Burma.* War on Want, Water Aid, Oxfam Sweat Shop Campaign.

*Overseas Development* (Clare Short, MP). CAFOD, etc.

*Arms trade/Human rights/Iran.* Campaign against the Arms Trade.

*Reforming Democracy.* Association of Local Government (regional government and reform), Sainsbury's, Boot's, Combined Heat and Power Association.

*Home Affairs, including abuse* (Jack Straw, MP). Law Society, Portman Group.

*Gun control.* Gun Control Network Dunblane.

*Snowdrop.* Petition, Prison Officers' Association.

*Equalities.* Commission on Racial Equality, Stonewall (homosexual rights).

*Crime.* Police Federation, Royal Automobile Club (RAC), etc.

*Local Democracy and Accountability.* Sainsbury's, Safeway, Tesco, ASDA, KPMG.

*Northern Ireland.* Various.

*Scottish Affairs.* Various.

*Welsh Affairs.* Various.

*Civil Rights.* Amnesty, Liberty, etc.

*Nigeria.* Amnesty, Body Shop, Shell.

*Animal Welfare.* Country Landowners' Association, RSPCA.

*Kashmir and Jammu.* Sikh and Khalsa Human Rights Punjab subcommittee.

### Friday 4 October

*Building a Dynamic Party.* Charter 88.

*Party campaigns.* Lobbyists and communications specialists.

*Deputy Leader finale/speech* (John Prescott, MP). Media and delegates.

## REFERENCES

Adonis, A., and Wintour, P. (1996). "Ashdown's Grand Plan," *Observer*, September 22, p. 15.

Andrews, L. (1996). "The Relationship of Political Marketing to Political Lobbying: An Examination of the Devonport Campaign for the *Trident* Refitting Contract," *European Journal of Marketing* 30 (10–11): 76–99.

Baker, K. (1993). *The Turbulent Years: My Life in Politics.* London: Faber.

Bell, S., and Hoggart, S. (1996). *Live Briefs.* London: Methuen.

Bevins, A. (1996). "Shirt-sleeved Major Rallies the Tories to his Cause," *Independent*, October 10, p. 1.

Bourdieu P. (1998). *On Television and Journalism.* London: Pluto Press.

Cathcart, B. (1997). *Were you still up for Portillo?* London: Penguin.

Clark, A. (1993). *Diaries*. London: Weidenfeld and Nicolson.

Cockerell, M. (1997). *A Word in the Right Ear*. Television documentary for BBC 2, 9.00 p.m., January 9.

Conservative Party (1996). *113th Conference Agenda*. London: Conservative and Unionist Party.

Cope, N. (1989). "Putting on a Show for the Trade," *Business*, December, pp. 119–124.

Curran, J., and J. Seaton (1997). *Power without Responsibility*, 5th edn. London: Routledge.

Dekimpe, M., P. Francois, S. Gopalakrishna, G. Lillien, and C. Van den Bulte (1997). *Generalizing about Trade Show Effectiveness: A Cross-national Comparison*. ISBM, Report 5-1997, Penn State University.

*Economist* (1997). October 4, p. 20.

Fairlie, H. (1968). *The Life of Politics*. London: Methuen.

Gopalakrishna, S., J. Williams, G. Lilien, and I.K. Sequeira (1995). "Do trade shows pay-off?" *Journal of Marketing* 59 (3): 75–83.

*Guardian* (1997). September 29, p. 9.

*Guardian* (1997). October 1, p. 3.

Harris, P., and A. Lock (1995). "Machiavellian Network Marketing: Corporate Political Lobbying and Industrial Marketing in the UK," in P. Turnbull, D. Yorke, and P. Naude (eds), *Interaction, Relationships and Networks: Proceedings of the Eleventh IMP Conference III, September 7–9*, Manchester Federal School of Business and Management.

Healey, D. (1990). *The Time of My Life*. London: Penguin.

Hoggart, S. (1996). "Sketch: Cheer Leaders put Clapometer in Spin," *Guardian*, October 4, p. 6.

Holmes, D. (1997). *Virtual Politics: Identity and Community in Cyberspace*. London: Sage.

Jenkins, R. (1991). *A Life at the Centre*. London: Macmillan.

Jones, B., and D. Kavangh (1998). *British Politics Today*. Manchester University Press.

Jones, M. (1994). "Battle for the Middle Class Vote," *Sunday Times*, October 9, p. 13.

Jones, N. (1995). *Soundbites and Spin Doctors*. London: Cassell.

Jones, N. (1997). *Campaign 1997*. London: Indigo.

Jordan, G. (1994). "Why Bumble Bees Fly: Accounting for Public Interest Participation." *Paper presented at ECPR joint sessions*, Madrid.

Kavanagh, D. (1996a). "British Party Conferences and the Political Rhetoric of the 1990s in Government and Opposition," *British Government and Opposition* 31 (1): 27–44.

Kavanagh, D. (1996b). *British Politics*, 3rd edn. Oxford: Oxford University Press.

Kelly, R.N. (1989). *Conservative Party Conferences: The Hidden System*. Manchester: Manchester University Press.

Kelly, R.N. (1994). "The Party Conferences," in A. Seldon and S. Bell (eds), *Conservative Century*. Oxford: Oxford University Press.

Kline, S. (1997). "Image Politics: Negative Advertising Strategies and the Election Audience," in M. Nava, A. Blake, I. MacRury, and B. Richards (eds), *Buy this Book: Studies in Advertising and Consumption*. London: Routledge.

Labour Party (1997). *National Executive Committee Report*. London: Labour Party.

Lawson, N. (1992). *The View from No. 11: Memoirs of a Tory Radical*. London: Bantam.

Liberal Democrat Party (1997). *The Role and Operation of the Party Conference: Background Paper for Consultative Session*. London: LDP.

MacAskill, E. (1994). "Blair Takes Labour by Storm," *Scotsman*, October 5, p. 1.

Mack, C.S. (1997). *Business, Politics, and the Practice of Government Relations*. Westport, CT: Quorum.

McLuhan, M. (1964). *Understanding Media: The Extensions of Man*. London: Routledge.

Minkin, L. (1978). *The Labour Party Conference: A Study in Intra-party Democracy*. Manchester: Manchester University Press.

Morris, R. (1991). *Tories, From Village Hall to Westminster: A Political Sketch*. Edinburgh: Mainstream.

Packard, V. (1957). *The Hidden Persuaders*. London: Longman.

Parris, M. (1996). "Political Sketch: Houdini of Love Witnesses Chancellor's Escape," *Times*, October 11, p. 2.

Pearce, E. (1992). *Election Rides*. London: Faber.

Presthus, R. (1973). *Elite Accommodation in Canadian Politics*. London: Cambridge University Press.

Presthus, R. (1974). *Elites in the Policy Process*. London: Cambridge University Press.

Rawnsley, A. (1994). "Get Tough and Dump an Icon," *Observer*, October 9, p. 28.

Riddell, P., and P. Webster (1996). "Advice to John Major on how to beat Labour," *Times*,

Rosenbaum, M. (1997). *From Soapbox to Soundbite*. London: Macmillan.

Scammell, M. (1995). *Designer Politics: How Elections are Won*. London: Macmillan.

Schmitter, P.C., and W. Streeck (1981). "The Organisation of Business Interests: A Research Design to Study the Associative Action of Business in the Advanced Industrial Societies of Western Europe." Berlin: International Institute of Management, Labour Market Policy Discussion Paper, *Wissenschaftszentrum Berlin für Sozialforschung* as a WZB Discussion Paper, IIM/LMP 81–13.

Shipley, D., C. Egan, and K.S. Wong (1993). "Dimensions of Trade Show Exhibiting Management," *Journal of Marketing Management* 9 (1): 55–64.

Stanyer, J., and M. Scammell (1996). "On the Fringe: The Changing Nature of the Party Conference Fringe and its Coverage by the Media." *Paper presented to the Political Studies Association Conference, Glasgow University*, April 10–12.

Thatcher, C. (1983). *Diary of an Election.* London: Sidgwick and Jackson.

Thatcher, M. (1993). *The Downing Street Years.* London: Harper Collins.

*Times* (1997). "Cherie's Sister Speaks on Fringe," October 3, p. 8.

Tyler, R. (1987). *Campaign! The Selling of the Prime Minister.* London: Grafton Books.

Watkins, A. (1991). *A Conservative Coup.* London: Duckworth.

White, M. (1996). "Strip and Bang Left Faithful Startled," *Guardian*, October 5, p. 9.

White, M. (1997). "Party Animals put Conference on the Chic Social Circuit," *Guardian*, September 29, p. 9.

Whiteley, P.F., and S.J. Winyard (1987). *Pressure for the Poor.* London: Methuen.

# 16

# A UK Case: Lobbying for a new BBC Charter

LEIGHTON ANDREWS

The BBC is a unique institution in Britain, with only a few similar organizations around the world (McKinsey, 1999). The BBC is a public corporation and in the UK context provided the basic model for the development of publicly owned enterprises in the twentieth century (Mulgan, 1994: 159). It is funded by a licence fee paid by all those who own a television set. The corporation's governing constitution, its royal charter (BBC, 2003b), is renewed on a regular basis. The charter approved in 1996 is due for renewal in 2006, and the British government has already announced its initial thinking on the charter review (Jowell, 2003; Wells, 2003; Jury, 2003; DCMS, 2003a). The Secretary of State for Culture, Media and Sport has appointed a former senior civil servant as an external advisor on the review (DCMS, 2003b). There is also a general examination of public service broadcasting by Britain's new communications regulator, OFCOM (Gibson, 2003). The BBC has already put in place its internal management team to drive forward its campaign for charter renewal (BBC, 2003a; Horsman, 2003; Rouse, 2003; *Broadcast*, 2003a). The BBC has also faced challenges to the legality of the license fee (Rozenberg, 2003). Meanwhile, other broadcasters are pitching for a slice of the licence fee (Snoddy, 2003; Dowell, 2003; Brown, 2003; Milmo and Brown, 2003; Barnett, 2003).

While the present (October 2004) Culture Secretary has said that the Hutton review of relations between the BBC and the government over Gulf War coverage is entirely separate from charter renewal, she has also said the government will consider the relevant recommendations for the BBC from the Hutton inquiry (Baldwin, 2003). It is no surprise that one of those intimately involved in the battle for the charter last time round is saying the BBC needs to set the agenda (Wyatt, 2003a; *Broadcast*, 2003b). Following the publication of the Hutton report and the unprecedented resignation of both the Chairman and the Director General, the review of the BBC's charter will be more charged than normal (BBC, 2004a; Jones, 2004). The BBC now has a new Director General, Mark Thompson, and a new Chairman, Michael Grade. The BBC's new Director General appears to accept that the corporation is a year behind in its charter review planning (Burt, 2004). Paradoxically, the BBC appears to have been strengthened by the outcome of the Hutton inquiry, with public support clearly demonstrated in the opinion polls (Jones *et al.*, 2004; Watt, 2004a). Such is the impact that a review of the BBC carried out by an independent group for the Conservative Party (BPG, 2004) appears to have been shelved by the Conservative leader,

Michael Howard (Watt, 2004b). The BBC has now set out its own manifesto for its new charter, *Building Public Value* (BBC, 2004b). The corporation has also robustly defended its news journalism (BBC, 2004c). However, the Hutton fallout still endures (Dyke, 2004).

The last review of the BBC charter commenced in 1992 and was finally completed in early 1996. With the publication of memoirs by several leading BBC personalities central to the last charter renewal (Birt, 2002; Wyatt, 2003b; Hussey, 2001) this may be an appropriate time to look again at that campaign, drawing also on the present author's experience as the BBC's Head of Public Affairs between 1993 and 1996.[1]

The examination which follows will review the BBC's strategy for the review of its charter, the development of its lobbying program, and its preparations for and response to the extensive parliamentary scrutiny which took place. As a case study, while the BBC may be a unique organization, there are nevertheless examples of lobbying activity which will be recognizable and relevant to a wide range of other organizations. It is worth stating that the BBC's campaign was widely seen as highly sophisticated and successful (Jenkins, 1994; Bragg, 1994a).

Many people have commented on the powerful "baronies" within the BBC at different times during its existence. Managing communications in an organization like the BBC with a very public face and a porous culture is challenging. I noted in my diary during 1994 that it was directly parallel to managing government communications: "It is like managing the bureaucracy in government, getting each part to deliver on time and according to schedule." As a specific case study, the chapter will also contribute to the emerging research on source strategies in the media (Schlesinger, 1990). Initially focusing on sources' interaction with the media as a counter to analyses which privilege media outlets in interpreting coverage of issues and events, Schlesinger recognized that sources are organizations seeking to influence the political agenda (1990: 77), and are able to do so by engaging in "successful strategic action." He has also specifically called for further understanding of the ways in which media

organizations seek to influence the agenda of media policy (Schlesinger, 1995: 31).

Reviewing the BBC's charter follows a similar process to the development of legislation in the United Kingdom. Ordinarily, there is first a Green (or consultation) Paper, on which comments are invited from the public, Parliament, and interested parties. This is followed at a later date by the publication of a White Paper, with more definite proposals. In the case of the legislative process, this would be followed by the publication of a Bill introduced in one of the two Houses of Parliament. In the case of the BBC, the next phase would be the publication of the draft royal charter, then the adoption of the full charter, with full parliamentary debate preceding it. This was the procedure in the 1992–1996 period. The process is overseen by a government department.

## THE BBC CONSTITUTION

The BBC's governing document is the royal charter. Ostensibly, the charter is granted by the Queen. In practice, it is on the recommendation of the government of the day, following widespread consultation, including parliamentary debate and scrutiny and public consultation. The nature of this consultation means that there is considerable scope for lobbying, by the BBC and other interest groups.

Oversight of the BBC is conducted by twelve Governors who act as trustees in the public interest. They are appointed on fixed terms by the Queen on advice from the government of the day. As the BBC's Web site puts it:

> The BBC's governors safeguard its independence, set its objectives and monitor its performance. They are accountable to its license payers and Parliament, and publish an Annual Report assessing the BBC's performance against objectives.
>
> (BBC, 2003c)

The chapter will provide some evidence of the relative independence of a publicly funded public service broadcaster from the state, not least in the ability to lobby independently on issues concerning its own future. In the period under consideration the BBC was managed by a Board of Management, reporting to its Director General. The Governors were involved in the appointments of the Board of Management. The role of the Governors is defined in the royal charter (DNH, 1995a).

The BBC is funded by a license fee paid by those who have television sets. The negotiations on the BBC license fee took place during the charter campaign and gaining government support for the BBC's achievements linked both decisions.

---

### Exhibit 16.1 Chronology of Charter Renewal

The chapter describes the period of policy formation on the BBC charter, beginning with the development of the government's Green Paper on the future of the BBC, published in 1992, and ending with the adoption of the new charter from May 1, 1997. Key dates are:

1992   *November*
       Government Green Paper
       BBC *Extending Choice*

1993   *January*
       John Birt becomes Director General

1993   *April*
       BBC response to Green Paper

1993   *May*
       Select committee inquiry begins

1993   *November*
       Touche Ross report on license fee
       Government license fee announcement

1993   *December*
       Select committee report

1994   *July*
       White Paper published

1995   *February*
       Lords and Commons debates on White Paper

1995   *November*
       Draft charter and agreement published

1996   *January–February*
       Lords and Commons debates on draft charter and agreement

1996   *May*
       Charter adopted

## THE STRATEGIC CONTEXT OF THE CHARTER RENEWAL CHALLENGE

The BBC's previous charter had been renewed in 1981 for a period of fifteen years. By 1990, when Mrs Thatcher departed, the BBC had survived an unprecedented decade of government, industry, and interest-group pressure on its finances and editorial policies, and had been the subject of regular alternative proposals for its future. Mrs Thatcher made no secret of her desire to see, for example, the BBC licence fee abolished (Thatcher, 1993: 637; Birt, 2002: 225; Hussey, 2001: 336). The BBC itself had been forced to change and take on the challenges of a highly competitive broadcasting market. At the time the BBC faced its charter renewal the broadcasting environment was going through rapid change. As Patricia Hodgson, then the BBC's Head of Policy and Planning, put it in 1992:

> Satellite, cable, subscription and digital technologies are revolutionizing the industry, but it is early days yet to assess their full effect. Ten years ago, there were only four commercial television channels in the whole of Europe; now there are fifty eight.
>
> (Hodgson, 1992)

The key changes in the BBC's approach to engaging with issues of broadcasting finance and the wider market, including the development of new technologies, derive from the changes in management introduced by the new Chairman, Marmaduke Hussey, following his appointment in 1986. Hussey appointed Michael Checkland as Director General and John Birt as his deputy, with specific responsibility for News and Current Affairs. O'Malley sees these appointments as satisfying the right of the Conservative Party that the BBC was getting its act together (O'Malley, 1994: 49). Steve Barnett and Andrew Curry believe that "it is a fair conclusion that, in the years 1987–90, real damage would have been inflicted on the BBC had the Checkland-Birt reforms not been initiated in some form" (Barnett and Curry, 1994: 235).

According to Will Wyatt, from 1990 onwards everything was focused on achieving a new BBC charter (Wyatt, 2003b: 186). Director General Checkland placed John Birt in charge of this, supported by the then Director of Corporate Affairs, Howell James, and the head of the Policy and Planning Unit, Patricia Hodgson (Birt, 2002: 340). They established fifteen task forces to look at all areas of the BBC's work, staffed by up-and-coming younger executives encouraged to think "outside the box." A final report synthesizing their views was drawn up in the summer of 1992, which became the basis for *Extending Choice*, the BBC's own "manifesto" (Birt, 2002: 344).

### Threats to the BBC

During this period the BBC remained under political pressure. Private briefings on the emerging thinking of the task force process were given to then Home Secretary, Kenneth Baker. Baker was keen that the BBC should be divested of local radio, Radio 1 and Radio 2, and should take advertising on the margins of the two television channels, perhaps in the nighttime hours (Birt, 2002: 343). Barnett and Curry believe that "the prognosis at the beginning of 1991 was not optimistic" (1994: 164). Some, for example, were pushing for the licence fee to be given to a Public Service Broadcasting Council and for programs and services to be funded from that (Green, 1991; Wittstock, 1992; Veljanovski, 1989; Peacock, 1985).

Baker told the 1991 Cambridge Royal Television Convention "the BBC in the next two or three years is going to be a very different body to what it is today" (Baker, 1993). He said that the government would set out all the options on the future of the BBC that had been canvassed, so there could be a debate on all the alternatives. Baker's draft Green Paper, ready before the 1992 election, "was very serious indeed about advertising" (Barnett and Curry, 1994: 169). Birt was told it contained proposals for privatizing Radio 1 and Radio 2 (2002: 341).

### The BBC's Financial Position

The corporation was under significant financial pressure at this time. It had essentially enjoyed "three decades of inherent growth" as radio listeners had first graduated to become television viewers, paying a higher licence fee, then had converted to a higher-fee color licence (Wyatt, 2003b: 182). The 1988 broadcasting White Paper recalled that the government had determined that the BBC licence fee would rise in line with inflation only for the three years 1988–1990 (Home Office, 1988). In 1990 the BBC had suffered a below-inflation rise in the licence fee. Hussey reveals that he offered this up to the new Home Secretary, David Waddington, although the government then appointed Price Waterhouse to review the BBC's finances and scope for savings: they came up with the same proposal (Hussey, 2001: 245).

## THE BBC'S STRATEGIC OBJECTIVES: SETTING THE AGENDA

Internally, the BBC set out a number of objectives for the debate on charter renewal (Andrews, 1994). These were to:

1  Develop and communicate a confident vision of the BBC's future.
2  Demonstrate willingness to change.
3  Demonstrate increased efficiency.
4  Ensure debate is well informed.
5  Listen to a wide range of views.

In practice, this required a willingness to work with government as far as possible to create consensus; a series of initiatives to improve the BBC's efficiency; and a clear manifesto for the BBC's future. The BBC also needed to engage with a wide range of target audiences.

### Working with the Government to create Consensus

Following the 1992 election, responsibility for broadcasting passed to a new government department, the Department for National Heritage, headed by Secretary of State David Mellor, who was seen as much closer to the BBC. The department drew up a new Green Paper on the BBC's future. The first draft was supposedly so pro-BBC that even the BBC lobbied for it to be tightened up! (Barnett and Curry, 1994: 172). Mellor told Birt that if he "could define the BBC's purposes convincingly … promise to overhaul the institution … transform its efficiency, he felt for his part he could deliver the BBC whole." Mellor disagreed with Baker's views on the BBC. Early on in his period of office he made it clear publicly that he saw no funding mechanism for the BBC with "the simplicity of the licence fee" (Birt, 2002: 347).

There was extensive discussion between the BBC, Mellor, and his department during the spring and summer of 1992. At the BBC's annual joint Board of Management and Board of Governors conference, Mellor warned that it would not be easy to win support for the licence fee and the BBC must continue to demonstrate it was efficient. The corporation must also argue the case for the BBC from first principles (Birt, 2002: 348). He also told the BBC that on no account should the corporation publish *Extending Choice* before the government Green Paper was published. This would mean that the government set the terms of the debate: if the BBC went first, it could provoke a reaction on the right, which would make demands on the government to produce a different approach (Barnett and Curry, 1994: 172; Birt, 2002: 348; Wyatt, 2003b: 224).

However, the situation was not settled. Mellor himself departed the government for personal reasons. He had already warned Birt that things would not be easy: efficiency was still an issue, and so were the Governors and their role. The Treasury was arguing for the BBC to become a publisher only in the run-up to the publication of the Green Paper, but dropped its stance after a briefing on Producer Choice (Birt, 2002: 351).

Fortunately for the BBC, the new Heritage Secretary, Peter Brooke, soon declared that his views were "not a million miles" from those of Mellor (DNH, 1992a). The government's Green Paper was published on November 24, 1992 (DNH, 1992b). Introducing the Green Paper in the House of Commons, Brooke referred to the context of technological change and the growth of new television channels. He said that the BBC would need to change but also that it should continue as a major public service organization:

> The essential issues in the debate are likely to be the future objectives of public service broadcasting; the range of the BBC's programmes, services and functions; how the BBC should be financed; how it should be organised to provide its services more efficiently; and the ways of making the BBC responsive to its audiences and accountable for its services. All those issues are linked and need to be seen as part of a coherent policy for the future.
>
> (Parliamentary Debates, 1992)

This was a short summary of the key overarching questions outlined in the Green Paper. In answers to questions, Brooke confirmed his support for the licence fee. A wide range of contributions, including many from the Conservative benches, supported the BBC and opposed the idea of a Public Service Broadcasting Council. Wyatt comments (2003b: 225): "The policy and planning department, which negotiated with government, had done a good job." For Barnet and Curry, "the Checkland-Birt reform had won the political battle that would set the context for the debates to come" (1994: 174).

### A Clear Manifesto for the BBC's Future

Birt saw the Green Paper as "an elegant statement of the questions and challenges the BBC needed to address" (2002: 351). Two days later he launched *Extending Choice* (BBC, 1992), "my personal manifesto" (2002: 344), the document that would "enable us to win the argument with the main parties and with the public at large." There were four key roles for the BBC:

1  Providing comprehensive and impartial news and information.
2  Supporting the development and expression of British culture and entertainment.
3  Guaranteeing the provision of educational services.
4  Stimulating the communication of culture between Britain and overseas.

The BBC had to continue to entertain, educate, and inform, to be distinctive, and to pioneer services and programmes in areas that the market would not deliver. It should withdraw from areas where it could not make an original contribution. It also needed to demonstrate it was accountable to its audience and that it was managed efficiently (BBC, 1992).

The external reaction was clear: the BBC had won the first battle for charter renewal (Miller, 1992). Birt himself worried: "the collaboration between the government and the BBC was all too evident" (2002: 351). The BBC clearly now had "a secure and steady future," though it had "to close the end-game" (2002: 352). That battle would be fought rather more publicly, but Hussey saw the next phase as "a calm, civilized and constructive debate." Hussey believes *Extending Choice* "changed the perception of the BBC in the eyes of the mandarins" (2001: 260). But the government itself had to take pains to demonstrate that the battle was not yet over. Nearly a year later, the Secretary of State was to tell the Royal Television Society convention: "I am told there are people who believe the BBC has already won. To them I would say we are only in the early stages" (DNH, 1993a).

### Target Audiences

The BBC identified a wide range of target audiences. In the political field, these included key Ministers, civil servants and ministerial special advisors, notably in the Department of National Heritage, the Department of Trade and Industry, the Treasury and 10 Downing Street. Decision takers, influencers, and friends of the BBC were identified. One of the challenges the BBC faced in this period was the regular change of Ministers: there were four Secretaries of State for National Heritage between 1992 and 1996. Because the BBC needed cross-party support, the opposition parties were also important, and as it was a publicly funded body the corporation needed to have regard to the views of all MPs and Peers.

Media audiences included the specialist media and show-business reporters on the national papers, and the specialist broadcast industry media, as well as current affairs publications like the *Economist*. Public audiences included viewers and listeners as a whole, special interest groups like the Voice of the Listener and Viewer (VLV) and key opinion formers, particularly those with public platforms. The media industry's own top executives were also a target: not all would be pro-BBC, but few would want a commercial privatized BBC competing with their revenue base. The industry events such as the Edinburgh International Television Festival and the Royal Television Society Convention required particular focus on the BBC's communications planning (Birt, 2002: 393–396). They would also be lobbying the government intensely for their own objectives. Finally, there were the BBC's own internal audiences: its management, its staff, its talent, its advisory councils.

Addressing these target audiences required a sustained, focused, and relentless communications and lobbying campaign. This chapter deals largely with the political campaign, though this was clearly integrated with the work undertaken within the BBC's Corporate Affairs Directorate by specialists in media relations, internal communications, corporate campaigns and events, and viewer and listener relations. The BBC had begun this process in the late 1980s (Birt, 2002: 335–336) but in the context of charter renewal the campaign was stepped up.

## STRATEGIC IMPLEMENTATION

John Birt took over as Director General in January 1993. The BBC had to map out a course of action from the Green Paper to the White Paper, and from the White Paper to the final publication of the charter. There were a number of strands to this campaign. The first was to develop and refine certain of the pledges and policies in *Extending Choice*. The second was to continue to demonstrate that the BBC maintained its commitment to efficiency, since a licence fee review would commence shortly in parallel with the lead-in to the White Paper. The third strand was to maintain and build support among all audiences, from the public, BBC

employees, the media industry and consumer bodies, as well as the press and politicians.

## Refining the "manifesto"

In refining *Extending Choice*, the Director General announced a review of the BBC's programme strategy when he presented his new team to the world in January 1993. He also explained how a restructuring of the organization would underpin Producer Choice and how the BBC would redefine its commercial objectives and its international operations. The Policy and Planning Unit was to become a directorate represented at board level for the first time (Birt, 1993a). The BBC produced its own response to the Green Paper in April 1993 (BBC, 1993a). This promised the corporation would promote high-quality programmes on each channel and service; intensify the drive for efficiency; become more open and transparent; identify commercial opportunities within a public service framework; develop its international services; clarify the functions of the Governors and management; commit to an annual performance review; and listen to the public in a more proactive way (BBC, 1993a). The corporation also published a study of other public service broadcasters around the world (McKinsey, 1993).

The BBC responded to the financial pressures it faced with a series of efficiency reviews which looked at opportunities for savings in studio resources, property, and overheads in particular. From these developments eventually stemmed the new so-called "internal market," Producer Choice, which was finally launched in April 1993. Birt documents the difficulties of the implementation of the scheme (2002: 327–330), but as he notes: "Producer Choice finally persuaded Britain's politicians that the BBC had become more efficient" (2002: 330). Changes were made after a review by the BBC Producer Choice Steering Group: bulk buying was encouraged, and more importantly, the number of business units was halved (Birt, 2002: 330; McDonald, 1995; Starks, 1993; Cloot, 1994). Producer Choice produced significant savings for the BBC (Snoddy, 1994b).

The public backdrop through 1993 was difficult. Considerable management energy, not least in the Corporate Affairs directorate, was spent on firefighting. The Director General was revealed not to have been on the payroll of the BBC while he was Deputy Director General, and this had still not been regularized. This prompted weeks of speculation on his future (Birt, 2002: 360–373; Hussey, 2001: 270–275; Wyatt, 2003b: 230–233; Barnett and Curry, 1994: 202–205; Horrie and Clarke, 1994: 259–278). The introduction of Producer Choice produced floods of stories about the problems encountered in implementing the new system. Former BBC staff members were critical and older staff members such as Mark Tully occasionally made their dissatisfaction public. Changes in the popular music station Radio 1, with the departure of older disk jockeys as a new approach was developed, were never out of the tabloids (Garfield, 1998). The introduction of the new Radio Five Live service, replacing the existing Radio 5, caused tensions to rise inside the corporation. The first staff survey of the BBC provoked headlines about dissatisfaction (Snoddy, 1993a; Thynne, 1993; Culf, 1993; Frean, 1993). The BBC was accused of having leaked outtakes from the Prime Minister's interview with ITN. Within the media industry, rivals queued up to attack the BBC and its role, some arguing for the Public Service Broadcasting Council option and the break-up of the BBC (for example, Cox, 1993).

## Strategic Coordination

Driving the campaign for the BBC's charter renewal was a small Charter Renewal Steering Group. This involved the Director General, Deputy Director General, Director of Policy and Planning, Director of Corporate Affairs, Director of Personnel and Director of Finance, with other senior executives attending as appropriate. The secretariat came from the Directorate of Policy and Planning. This directorate was the BBC's "corporate brain" (Birt, 2002: 333), looking at all areas of strategy and policy, and included departments such as Corporate Strategy, Commercial Policy, Engineering Policy, Editorial Policy, and Policy

Development, as well as the coordination of the charter renewal process overall. Birt rightly described it as "the most powerful capability of its kind anywhere in European broadcasting" (2002: 333).

## THE NEW PUBLIC AFFAIRS UNIT

In February 1993 the BBC created a new Public Affairs Unit to coordinate its parliamentary lobbying in support of the charter's renewal.[2] The unit reported to the corporation's new Director of Corporate Affairs, Pamela Taylor, then her successor, appointed in 1994, from British Telecom, Colin Browne. The unit worked closely with the separate Directorate of Policy and Planning, which had responsibility for the day-to-day negotiations with government departments such as the Department of National Heritage, the DTI, and the Downing Street Policy Unit. There was some overlap between the two, and the post was appointed after interviews involving both the Director of Corporate Affairs (DCA) and the Director of Policy of Planning (DPP), Patricia Hodgson, with the Director General having a final one-to-one interview. The job description for the Head of Public Affairs included the responsibilities for monitoring government, representing and promoting the interests of the BBC to government, building relationships with government personnel, "to act as a senior BBC representative in the Corporation's dealings with governmental and other national interest groups," and "to make a major contribution to the development of policy and strategy" (BBC, 1993b).

The Directorate of Corporate Affairs was largely a communications and marketing directorate responsible for media relations, employee communications, interest-group relationships, communications with viewers and listeners, corporate events, charter renewal communications, and the marketing of the corporation (as distinct from individual programmes and services). Later, in order to provide better communications between the two directorates, as the BBC White Paper turned into a draft charter and agreement, and other issues such as European directives and a new broadcasting Bill came forward, a Public Policy Management Board was created, involving the relevant individuals in each directorate. This met every six weeks.

## The Public Affairs Strategy

The Public Affairs Unit was set explicit objectives deriving from the overall objectives set for the Directorate of Corporate Affairs, in particular to coordinate an effective communications strategy for the delivery of a new charter. These included:

1 Promoting the BBC's accountability to Parliament by establishing a strategy and framework of contact for the BBC with MPs, MEPs, and government.
2 Promoting understanding among MPs/Peers/MEPs/government about BBC policy developments.
3 Achieving a successful charter renewal by developing and orchestrating a programme of communication with key constituencies.
4 Involving BBC management and staff in this process.
5 Keeping the Board of Management and Board of Governors informed of current parliamentary/governmental issues in their area.
6 Acting as the central information gatherer on domestic and European issues.

## Proactive Monitoring and Intelligence Gathering

The unit was the first of its kind in the BBC, and the first to introduce modern public affairs techniques into the corporation. For example, it systematized the BBC's daily monitoring of parliamentary proceedings relevant to the broadcasting sector, with a regular weekly *Week at Westminster* bulletin sent round to over 100 BBC managers. This covered all developments in Parliament (questions, debates, statements, early day motions, press releases) on subjects of interest to the corporation. Astonishingly,

though this kind of document was standard practice in the corporate world, nothing like it had been published internally in the BBC before.

In order to shape the intelligence it was receiving, the unit also began to log all *corporate* (not editorial) contacts between the BBC and politicians, with a computerized database giving information on their views as expressed in meetings with BBC executives, as well as their interventions in relevant debates on broadcasting. Gradually, the unit built up profiles of all MPs.

The unit also instituted regular twice-yearly polling through MORI of MPs' views on the BBC. As well as providing evidence of their views on the license fee, the quality of BBC management and the privatization of Radio 1, the reports also enabled the unit to track the effectiveness of public affairs activity, based on MPs' recall of their contacts.

## Government Intelligence

Formally, day-to-day relations between the BBC and its "sponsor" department in government, the Department for National Heritage, were the responsibility of the BBC Secretary on the one hand and government officials on the other. In practice, the Policy and Planning Department led. The nature of the BBC meant that many individuals at a corporate level might have regular contact with Ministers and civil servants—leaving aside the editorial contacts of the corporation's political journalists. It was therefore essential that clear formal lines operated. This meant a degree of hierarchy, with the Chairman and Director General being responsible for ministerial contacts at Secretary of State level, and Policy and Planning handling the civil servants. Ministerial special advisors fell into something of a grey area.

Regular intelligence was supplied to the Charter Renewal Steering Group (CRSG) by the Public Affairs Unit on a fortnightly basis, with occasional updates when there were matters of greater urgency. Before Christmas 1993, opinions in the Cabinet clearly varied on questions such as the BBC's transmission system, the future of its radio stations, its role in making programs, and the level of the licence fee. Updates on Cabinet views and the likely timing of the White Paper were passed through to the CRSG during early 1994.

The Director General himself frequently sought additional intelligence and background, usually requested in handwritten notes known as "inky blues" (Wyatt, 2003b: 274). One that I received began "I was away in the States during Tony Blair's coronation" and asked for general background from Blair's speeches. Earlier on another had warned, "we are a leaky organization and reports like this may get passed around and leaked!"

## Managing Parliamentary Contacts

The unit had the responsibility for centrally managing the BBC's parliamentary contacts. For example, when the new Controller of Radio 1, Mathew Bannister, took up his post in the autumn of 1993, the unit coordinated a high volume of contacts for him with groups of MPs and Peers, so that he could outline the rationale for his radical changes to the schedules. He saw seventy MPs and Peers. MPs and Peers on relevant committees, and party spokespersons, were regularly courted with a programme of lunches and dinners—and briefings for those who didn't want hospitality. There was a wide range of parliamentary groups with broadcasting interests, including the All-party Media Group and the House of Lords Broadcasting Group. Some 230 MPs and Peers were seen centrally and 100 through the BBC's regions in the 1993–1994 reporting year.

The Chairman held occasional lunches for groups of MPs and there were regular briefings by the Director General and his Board of Management team, coordinated by Biddy Baxter, the former long-standing producer of the well known children's program *Blue Peter*, who worked with the Public Affairs Unit. These were highly successful set-piece events which combined briefing on BBC strategy with tours of studios.

## Briefings and Mailings

The unit also began the process of regular briefings to MPs and Peers. From April 1994 a printed parliamentary bulletin was sent out every eight weeks or so, normally timed to coincide with new BBC initiatives or policy developments. There were also targeted mailings to groups of politicians with particular interests: for example, the new Radio 3 season. Briefings were also sent out in advance of relevant debates or questions, especially to identified "friends" of the BBC, and also where needed to the Secretary of State's special advisor and the opposition front bench. Where MPs or Peers raised issues that needed answering the unit was the first port of call for a response. Popular versions of BBC documents were produced, emphasizing the theme that the BBC stood for *Broadcasting at its Best* (BBC, 1993c).

## Case Study: The National Heritage Select Committee

The first real challenge for the Public Affairs Unit was the inquiry into the Green Paper held by the National Heritage Select Committee, chaired by Gerald Kaufman, MP, a senior Labour MP. Select committees shadow government departments in the House of Commons, and their reports have to be considered by government. Kaufman had raised the prospect of his committee holding an inquiry into questions to Brooke on the day of the Green Paper publication (Parliamentary Debates, 1992).

This was an important test for the BBC. It would subject all sections of the corporation to public probing. The BBC itself was asked to provide fourteen different witnesses over nine separate hearings (Andrews, 1994). The BBC's witnesses included representatives of radio and television, the national regions, the World Service, the Finance Director, those responsible for collecting the licence fee, the Director of Policy and Planning, and ended with the Chairman and the Director General and Deputy Director General. Other hearings before the committee would include the other public service broadcasters, the satellite channels, the unions, the government, regulators, consultants, and academics.

The BBC prepared intensively for the inquiry. Background papers were drawn up assessing the weak points in the BBC's argument. Questions and draft answers were prepared. There were full-scale rehearsals, with members of the Public Affairs Unit and Policy and Planning Directorate acting as the committee. (The BBC still holds such rehearsals today: Porter, 2003.) These were video-taped so that witnesses could see their own performance. The rehearsals were a valuable opportunity to identify discrepancies between the different BBC witnesses. The Chairman, Duke Hussey, believed "I successfully oiled my way through" (2001: 277). It didn't feel like that at the time. The Chairman and Vice-chairman were rehearsed twice before their eventual appearance. Birt clearly did not enjoy the experience (Birt, 2002: 442). For us, getting fourteen people to hold the line was a significant challenge.

A full morning's technological presentation was undertaken for the committee in May 1993 at Television Centre, showing the possibilities that digital broadcasting offered for both television and radio. The presentation gave the BBC the opportunity to demonstrate practically how the corporation was at the forefront of much of the innovative thinking that was taking place in the development of new services for the Digital Age. The committee's hearings were monitored and a register of the questions it asked was kept to prepare the witnesses against the unexpected. A digest of evidence was collected. Members of the Public Affairs Unit sat in on evidence sessions by other witnesses, to take note and report back.

During the hearings we were well aware of differences in viewpoint between different members of the committee, and tried—as far as was proper—to keep close to their deliberations. On occasion, committee members would share their thinking with us. We were aware that the committee chairman, Gerald Kaufman, believed that the BBC and British broadcasting were in danger of disappearing down what he later called "an interactive plughole"

(*Television*, 1994) On the other hand, other committee members did not share his view.

The committee recommended in its report on December 9, 1993:

1   Endorsement of BBC radio channels free from advertising.
2   Continuation of the charter as the basis for BBC regulation, and an extension of the charter for a further ten years.
3   Impartiality to be written into the charter.
4   Rejection of advertising on the BBC.
5   Continued support, albeit reluctantly, for the licence fee, which was "undoubtedly good value."
6   Support for the BBC exploiting its commercial assets.
7   More autonomy for nations and regions.
8   Wider consultation on government appointments.

The committee said that the BBC was "the premier organization in the world in terms of quality" and "an international asset to the UK" (National Heritage Committee, 1993). The BBC welcomed the report as a "generous recognition of the BBC's value and achievements" (BBC, 1993d). Barnett and Curry are surprisingly negative in their assessment of the Committee's report (1994: 220). Hussey recalls:

> The Committee's report, when published, was a triumph for the BBC and another step on the road to Charter Renewal. It underwrote the position and authority of the governors, it launched the BBC in its current form, and it recommended that the licence fee continue for the last three years of the current Charter with its link to RPI.
>
> (2001: 277)

## THE 1993 LICENSE FEE SETTLEMENT

The BBC faced the challenge of a review of its funding base by Touche Ross, who were appointed by the government in June 1993 to assess the BBC's progress in achieving efficiency and revenue gains and to advise whether linking the licence fee to the retail price index was appropriate for the three remaining years of the charter. The Touche Ross inquiry was designed to build on the previous 1990 inquiry by Price Waterhouse. Birt recalls that the new Secretary of State, Peter Brooke, was "under pressure from within the government to pocket the BBC's efficiency gains by further reducing the licence fee as had happened in 1991" (Birt, 2002: 490). Leaks suggested this might happen (Hellen, 1993). Birt argued against this in public at the Cambridge RTS convention. The Director General said that without the BBC's efficiency reforms, there would have been no money for new programs: "No Producer Choice, no *Middlemarch*" (Birt, 1993c). The corporation made the case that the BBC reform programme would be "fatally" undermined if the efficiency gains could not be invested in programmes. Hussey spelt out the arguments in a letter to Brooke (Hussey, 2001: 277–279). Specifically, he warned:

> If as a result of the Touche Ross enquiry the BBC is given less than the RPI for any of the final three years of this charter it will be seen by the BBC and outsiders as a failure by the government to endorse our policies and a defeat for the forces of reform within the BBC.
>
> (2001: 278)

This argument was successful in clinching a licence fee settlement linked to the retail price index for three years. The Touche Ross review recognized the efficiency achievements that the BBC had made, and gave the corporation a solid basis for planning and a platform to deliver its program proposition for the new charter. The review confirmed that the BBC had made savings of £118 million and had reduced staff by 18 percent. The BBC itself pointed to new programs and services that had resulted from savings. The Secretary of State said in announcing his conclusion, "the good news for license fee payers is that the consultants concluded that the BBC had done well to manage its financial position during the time of considerable change" (DNH, 1993c).

## REFINING THE STRATEGY

### Accountability

The BBC's sensitivity to the political process meant that the broad strategic arguments were continually refined and reinforced with a series of new policy initiatives and strategic developments. *An Accountable BBC* was launched in December 1993. This sought to clarify responsibilities for the Board of Governors, its councils and committees. The corporation would focus more on a means of listening to license fee payers. There would be more public meetings, with a target of one per week, new seminars held by the Governors on specific themes, and a new Program Complaints Unit. Additionally there would be a handbook for licence fee payers containing basic information about the BBC, and public performance indicators for the BBC would be set down in its annual report.

### Devolution

The BBC had been under continual pressure over its programme commitments to the nations and regions of the United Kingdom. There were specific campaigns in Wales and Scotland for additional investment in the two nations, and the devolution debate in both countries was hotting up (Andrews, 1999; Marr, 1992, CSA, 1988). David Hatch, the advisor to the Director General, and a former Managing Director of Radio, developed proposals which would ensure that a third of network production was made in the nations and regions by 1997–1998, rising from about a fifth at the time. This would include an expanded amount from independent television producers. £75 million of annual production spend would be moved to the regions, and network spend in the national regions of Wales, Scotland, and Northern Ireland would increase by 67 percent (Wishart, 1994; Thynne, 1994b).

### Commercial Strategy

One of the biggest challenges was the development of the BBC's global and commercial strategy. The government was under pressure, from the commercial television companies particularly, to limit the BBC's commercial operations. The ITV companies had commissioned a study by the consultancy Booz Allen & Hamilton which indicated that Britain had a growing trade deficit with the United States. The Booz Allen & Hamilton work, presented to the select committee, forecast the deficit growing to £640 million with the rest of the world by the year 2000, with £595 million of this being with the United States (Booz Allen and Hamilton, 1993). Inside the BBC, analysts in the Policy and Planning Directorate established that, by contrast, the BBC had a trade surplus with the rest of the world of £50 million and was successful in many overseas markets (DNH, 1994: 21). The BBC was also the largest program-maker outside Hollywood and Japan, with a globally recognized brand name.

Michael Heseltine, President of the Board of Trade, wanted to know what the BBC was going to do to lead Britain's international broadcasting challenge (Birt, 2002: 464). The BBC fought this battle by spelling it out in a series of interventions on the basic principles of where the BBC would become involved in commercial activities, and a Fair Trading policy, agreed with the Treasury, which would govern the behavior of the corporation's trading arms (BBC, 1994a, b). The core principles governing the BBC's commercial activities were that the corporation would undertake only commercial activities that were compatible with its public service mission, and that no public money would be used to subsidize commercial activities (Phillis, 1994a, b, c, d, 1995; Reguly, 1996). The BBC closed down some services which were felt to be incompatible with that remit (Barnet and Curry, 1994: 223).

The BBC announced its global and commercial plans in May 1994, aiming to become the leading international player in satellite-delivered television services, through a global strategic alliance with Pearson. BBC Deputy Director General Bob Phillis also outlined a new target for the BBC's commercial revenues: these were to treble over the life of the new charter (Snoddy, 1994c; Frean, 1994a; Kane, 1994). As a result of this alliance, two new services, BBC Prime (entertainment) and BBC World (news and information), would be launched in early 1995 (BBC, 1994d, e).

## Reinforcing the Efficiency Arguments

John Birt had set the task of the BBC becoming the best-managed organization in the public sector (Snoddy, 1992). The introduction of performance-related pay and the devolution of the setting of pay to directorate and local level were two of the initiatives that illustrated this (BECTU, 1994; Frean, 1994b; Culf, 1994a, b, c; Snoddy, 1994b; Thynne, 1994a; Leapman, 1994). The introduction of these measures resulted in a strike and stoppages in mid-1994, which hit election coverage among other programmes (Pryor, 1994; Thynne, 1994b; see also BBC 1994h; Birt, 1994). The strikes provoked editorials in a number of newspapers (*Daily Telegraph*, 1994; *Times*, 1994; *Guardian*, 1994). The response of the BBC's management to the dispute was seen as a definite statement by the Conservative government of how the corporation had changed. Some Labour politicians boycotted BBC election programmes in June (Culf, 1994d). Simon Jenkins commented in the *Times* subsequently: "The BBC strike, coming just as the White Paper was being written, was a godsend" (Jenkins, 1994).

## THE WHITE PAPER: WINNING THE FIRST PHASE

It is often difficult to evaluate the success of lobbying operations. In the case of the public debate over the BBC, there is perhaps sufficient documentary evidence to attempt some quantification of this. In early 1994 the British Film Institute published a review of the responses to the government's Green Paper on the BBC. This contained a summary of the key issues where there was still controversy. These included:

1  The BBC's commercial activities.
2  The BBC's approach to the nations and regions.

3  The scope of the BBC's radio services.
4  Independent production and Producer Choice.
5  The definition of public service broadcasting.
6  The role of the Governors.
7  The BBC's accountability to the license fee payer.
8  The BBC's relationship to the overall broadcasting environment.
9  Equal Opportunities.
10 Privatization of BBC transmission.
11 The level and method of setting the licence fee.
12 The legal framework for charter renewal.

The BFI saw these as providing "the meat" in the charter debate (BFI, 1994: 7). When the government's White Paper came to be published in July 1994 it was clear that the BBC had achieved its goals in all these areas bar possibly one—that of privatization of the transmission system.

The White Paper (DNH, 1994a, b, c) *The Future of the BBC: Serving the Nation, Competing Worldwide*, published in July 1994 (and not, as Hussey (2001: 280) says, February 1995) contained a strong endorsement of the BBC's current role. As Hussey records, certain proposals such as privatization of Radio 1 and the determination of impartiality to be taken away from the Governors were only finally staved off quite late in the day (2001: 284, 302). The royal charter would be renewed for ten years. The licence fee would continue, with a review in 2001. There was strong support for the BBC's plans for commercial development and for its Fair Trading proposition. On accountability, the role of the Board of Governors would be set out in the new charter. They should take the lead in ensuring that the BBC was more responsive to public opinion, in setting objectives, and in monitoring performance. The BBC would need to consult more in advance of major change. The corporation would need to publish a statement of promises to its audiences, along the lines of the government's Citizen's Charter in public services. There was support for the expansion of digital television and radio on a terrestrial basis.

Meanwhile the issue of subscription services would simply be left open. The BBC welcomed the White Paper as a vote of confidence that would take the corporation into the next century (BBC, 1994g).

The press coverage of the White Paper demonstrated the success of the BBC, and its Director General, in achieving this outcome (Culf, 1994b; Frean and Prynne, 1994; Thynne and Jones, 1994; Snoddy, 1994c; Brown and McIntyre, 1994). Birt notes that the coverage given to him was the start of the breakdown in the relationship between him and the Chairman (Birt, 2002: 400–401). Simon Jenkins in the *Times* said that the armed forces could learn from the BBC's lobbying (Jenkins, 1994). Melvyn Bragg paid tribute to "the BBC—with its policy unit and its long-term lobbying strategy" (Bragg, 1994a).

In Parliament the reaction was broadly positive, with just one or two Conservative right-wing critics such as David Evennett and Tony Marlow raising critical notes. Other Conservatives, such as Tim Renton, were warm and supportive. Select committee chair Gerald Kaufman welcomed the White Paper as an endorsement of the select committee's report (Parliamentary Debates, 1994a).

## FROM WHITE PAPER TO NEW CHARTER

As Hussey has commented, "The White Paper did not, of course, end the debate" (Hussey, 2001: 284). A new Secretary of State was appointed soon after the White Paper, and the BBC had to spend time ensuring that he was briefed on the rationale behind the White Paper. The Chairman wrote formally to him in November 1994 with the BBC's response to the White Paper, including further detail on the BBC's commercial activities, its responsiveness to its audiences, and its plans to use new technologies.

Early in 1995 the BBC's long-awaited Program Strategy Review finally reported, two years after John Birt had set it up. *People and Programmes* said that the BBC had to connect better with the young, the less well-off, and those farthest away from London (BBC, 1995a). There was to be greater emphasis on knowledge, leisure, and regional programming. The conclusions of the review had already started to influence the development of programs (such as *The Net*) and services (such as Radio Five Live). A further £85 million was to be released for programs, including the *People's Century* series, more science, an accessible program on art, and a series on personal finance. The emphasis was that the BBC was promising "something for everyone" (Williams, 1995; Thynne, 1995), though some saw this as the BBC "appealing to the lowest common denominator" (*Times*, 1995).

The BBC also successfully launched its new services with Pearson in February 1995, taking forward its commercial plans. In the autumn of 1995 the corporation published a statement outlining its plans for the Digital Age. The BBC's plans included an extended BBC 1 and 2 in widescreen, news "when you want it," more slots for regional television and education programs and digital radio (BBC, 1995b).

## PARLIAMENTARY SCRUTINY

### Case Study  The Draft Charter and Agreement

There was extensive dialogue between the BBC's Policy and Planning Directorate and civil servants at the Department of National Heritage on the content of the charter and agreement during 1995. The charter was the constitution of the BBC, setting out the BBC's purposes and the roles of the Governors and the National Councils and Advisory Bodies. The agreement, which was between the BBC and the Secretary of State, covered the provision of the BBC's services, programme content issues, objectives for the home and overseas services, programme standards, hours of broadcasting transmission facilities, defense and emergency arrangements, funding, archives, research, and ethics (DNH, 1995a, b). The BBC was also to publish a statement of promises to licence fee payers.

The White Paper was debated in both Houses of Parliament in 1995 (Parliamentary

Debates, 1994b, 1995). The Select Committee on National Heritage also held a further session in June 1995 to review developments within the BBC since its previous inquiry in 1993. Rehearsals were again coordinated by the Public Affairs Unit in advance of the hearing. The committee's questions ranged widely over the full extent of the BBC's output, including several questions on its impartiality (NHC, 1995).

The draft charter and agreement were published on November, 27 1995—like the White Paper, reflecting a significant delay over the expected publication date. The key changes from the White Paper were:

1  The BBC's transmission services *were* to be privatized.
2  There would be an impartiality clause based on the 1990 Broadcasting Act (Evans, 1995).
3  The Governors' role would be more strictly defined in relation to impartiality and taste and decency.
4  The BBC would be required to publish a "pledges" document for the public each year.
5  The role of the National Broadcasting Councils was more strictly defined.
6  The BBC's role in the development of digital and online services was explicitly recognized.
7  The BBC was to be able to develop new commercial services funded by subscription and pay-per-view.

Not all of these issues were welcome. The BBC believed that the impartiality clause was unnecessary, for example (BBC, 1995b). The BBC had, however, seen off attempts to give this responsibility to the Broadcasting Standards Commission (Hussey, 2001: 302). However, the corporation was to be allowed to handle the sale of transmission and keep the proceeds. The BBC was broadly happy with the outcome. The journalist Maggie Brown commented in the *Guardian:* "there are whole portions of the documents which read as if they have been written by the BBC's own policy unit, which has clearly conducted some very fruitful lobbying" (Brown, 1995).

The most substantial debates on the BBC, however, concerned the draft charter and agreement themselves. The BBC went into overdrive in its lobbying on these. Between September and December 1995, 277 MPs were contacted and lobbied at BBC events. Forty Peers were briefed on the BBC's digital plans. There were meetings with the All-party Media Group, with select committee members, ministerial PPSs and others. The Public Affairs Unit worked to ensure pro-BBC speakers spoke in the debates and prepared full and detailed briefings on the charter.

The Lords presented a potentially tricky arena for both the government and the BBC at this time. The corporation's *Panorama* interview with Princess Diana had recently been aired, and friends of the BBC Chairman were aware that he had not been informed that the interview was to take place until very late in the proceedings (Birt, 2002: 408–414; Hussey, 2001: 295–297; Wyatt, 2003b: 325). The issue surfaced in early December 1995 when a group of Conservative MPs and Peers visited the corporation for one of the "Biddy Baxter" seminars. The government decided to hold an informal meeting on December 14, 1995, in advance of the full Lords debate on the drafts. This provided the government Minister in the House of Lords, Lord Inglewood, with the opportunity to address concerns and questions that were likely to be raised. There was an active, right-wing group of Tory Peers constituted in a back-bench "Broadcasting Group" convened by Lord Orr-Ewing. Their concerns were that the BBC's coverage contributed to an attack on national institutions such as the royal family, that impartiality was constantly threatened, bad language and sexual innuendo were commonplace, and the Governors seemed powerless to address these issues. One of their number, Lord Caldecote, tabled an amendment to the government's motion in the Lords to strengthen the Governors' role. This group was assiduously courted by Lord Inglewood, who was able to persuade them that significant concessions had been extracted from the BBC in the charter and agreement. Throughout this period, the BBC's Public Affairs Unit and its

Policy and Planning Directorate worked very closely with the government.

The right-wing pressure on the government was evident in the debate in contributions by Lords Caldecote, Orr-Ewing, Gibson, Chalfont, and Ackner and Viscount Cross. The broad range of Conservative Peers did, however, support the BBC, which also had support from across the House. In the end the Caldecote amendment was withdrawn, with recognition that the government had sought to listen. The impartiality clause in the new agreement, which the BBC had resisted, was a valuable weapon in the government's armoury (Parliamentary Debates, 1996a).

The Commons debate took place on February 15, 1996. There was another Secretary of State by now—Virginia Bottomley had taken over from Stephen Dorrell. In the Commons the debate was smoother, although the official opposition did complain that there should have been an informal opportunity for MPs to discuss the charter in the same way that the Lords had done. Others complained that there was no opportunity to amend the charter. But the most active critic of the BBC, by this stage, was the select committee chairman, Gerald Kaufman. Broadly, there was considerable support for the BBC, though comments focused on the role of the Governors, services for the regions and nations, and the quality of programs (Parliamentary Debates, 1996b).

## CONCLUSION

The BBC charter renewal process in the 1992–1996 period offers several lessons for the BBC's charter preparations in the period to 2006. Lobbying for the BBC's charter was a complex, multilayered and multidimensional process. The key lesson is the need for the corporation to seek to set the framework for discussions on its future. As Wyatt (2003b) has written: "The BBC's charter expires in 2006 and the campaign for its renewal looks to have started late. The trick with political campaigns is to set the agenda." Hutchinson (1999: 167) rightly comments: "The BBC won its battle to survive ... principally by making it extremely difficult for the politicians with whom it was dealing to level the kind of charges against it which they would have been most likely to bring."

Lobbying for a complex corporation, whether private or public-sector, involves a range of policy actors within and without the corporation. Success is not determined only by the organization's strategy, but is dependent on the external political context (John, 2002). It is a central dimension of corporate strategy (Andrews, 1996).

When it comes to lobbying, the media industry as a whole may be a special case:

> The media enjoy certain tactical advantages: politicians, of course, are attentive to their influence and public relations role (and perhaps grant their lobbyists more ready access than other lobbyists); the media are used to moving quickly and deploying their resources over a long campaign.
>
> (Tunstall and Palmer, 1991)

Tunstall and Machin (1999) note that media lobbies in the United States are seen as some of the most effective lobbying organizations. Croteau and Hoynes (2001) identified that the top ten US media companies spent an average of $2 million on lobbying in 1998.

The BBC, however, is a very special case (Eldridge, 1996). Because of its status, conferred by the royal charter, the BBC is intricately bound up with the media policy of the UK state. The government relies to a large degree on the BBC for information on its own services and for analysis of the media market. In the period under review, the BBC's policy and planning division carried more fire-power than the government's broadcasting policy division in the Department of National Heritage.

There has been considerable debate in media studies on the role of "primary definers" in shaping news coverage and policy outcomes (Hall et al., 1978; Schlesinger, 1990; Schlesinger and Tumber, 1994; Deacon and Golding, 1994; Manning, 2001; Davis, 2002, 2003a). "Primary

definers" are institutions which take the shape of accredited sources for the purpose of media reporting and for the definition of policy outcomes (Hall et al., 1978: 58). Government itself is the most obvious example. There is no space to go into the detail of this debate here but it is clear that the BBC, in terms of its institutional access to government, plays the role of a "primary definer" in terms of debates on the media. In Schlesinger's terms (1990: 80–82), the BBC has *institutional* status, a significant *financial base,* and *cultural capital.* In Gandy's terms (1982, 1992) the BBC in its charter debate was a significant provider of "information subsidies" to the political marketplace. As Schlesinger and Tumber have written (1994: 96):

> Just as information subsidies flow from sources to journalists, so too do they flow from pressure groups to legislators. This process may be linked to the credibility that a given group has achieved with politicians over a period of time. It is credibility and reliability that make such briefings acceptable and usable in parliamentary debate.

The BBC's 1992–1996 lobbying campaign is a good example of how the field of political communications needs to be considered as much broader than that of electoral campaign politics (Deacon and Golding, 1994). As Davis (2003b) has suggested, there is scope for a new body of research in the interaction of elite policy networks, the media, and politics—and not least in the field of media policy making.

Of course, the BBC faces substantially different challenges today than it did in the 1990s. Multichannel television is hitting hard at the BBC's audience. The BBC itself is a player in both the digital television and digital radio markets, and through its Freeview terrestrial platform is bringing digital services to millions. The unprecedented battle with the government resulting in the post-Hutton resignations brought the BBC to a nadir in its fortunes— then paradoxically provided it with a launch platform for the new charter. A new Chairman and Director General have a major opportunity to win another ten years for the BBC, with its services, system of governance, and licence fee funding intact (Burt, 2004).

## NOTES

1 The text draws on private contemporaneous notes which are cited on occasion.

2 The present author was appointed to head the unit and joined the BBC in June 1993. (*Broadcast*, 1993a, b). The unit initially consisted of the head, a deputy, a researcher, and secretary, with a further appointment of a public affairs manager recruited in November 1993. Initially based in White City, in October 1993 the unit moved into the ground floor of 4 Millbank, the building which houses most of the United Kingdom's political broadcasting journalists, in October 1993, and was to remain there for ten years. In late 1994 the deputy moved into the center of corporate affairs and a new Parliamentary Liaison Officer was appointed to the unit in early 1995. A part-time appointee worked on the BBC's behalf in Brussels, reporting to the Head of Public Affairs: during 1994 this role was made full-time and two other staff members were recruited.

## REFERENCES

Andrews, L. (1994). "The BBC White Paper: Winning Support for Change," presentation to Hawksmere Public Affairs Campaigns conference, London, December 12 (repeated June 19, 1995).

Andrews, L. (1996). "The Relationship of Political Marketing to Political Lobbying," *European Journal of Marketing* 30 (10–11).

Andrews, L. (1999). *Wales says Yes*. Bridgend: Seren Books.

Baker, K. (1991). Home Secretary's speech to the Royal Television Society Convention, Home Office.

Baker, K. (1993). *These Turbulent Years*. London: Faber.

Baldwin, T. (2003). "Gordon is so Hard to say for Blairite Survivor," *Times*, July 25, p. 12.

Barendt, E. (1994). "Legal Aspects of Charter Renewal," *Political Quarterly* 65 (1).

Barnett, S. (2003). "Caught between Alastair and the Deep Blue Tory Sea," *Observer Business*, July 13, p. 7.

Barnett, S., and A. Curry (1994). *The Battle for the BBC*. London: Aurum Press.

BBC (1992). *Extending Choice*. London: BBC.

BBC (1993a). *Responding to the Green Paper*. London: BBC.

BBC (1993b). Job description for Head of Public Affairs.

BBC (1993c). *Broadcasting at its Best*. London: BBC.

BBC (1993d). *An Accountable BBC*. London: BBC.

BBC (1994a). *The BBC's Fair Trading Commitment*. London: BBC.

BBC (1994b). *The BBC's Commercial Policy*. London: BBC.

BBC (1994c). "BBC takes Britain into Global Market with Pearson PLC," press release, May 10.

BBC (1994d). "BBC and Pearson announce European Launch Plans," press release, November 28.

BBC (1994e). "Bob Phillis calls for Industry Support for the BBC Competing Worldwide," press release, December 5.

BBC (1994f). "New Policy to boost BBC Regions," bulletin, Public Affairs Unit.

BBC (1994g). "Initial Response to White Paper," Press Office, July 6.

BBC (1994h). Bulletin for staff, May 23.

BBC (1995a). *People and Programmes*. London: BBC.

BBC (1995b). *Extending Choice in the Digital Age*. London: BBC.

BBC (2003a). "BBC Charter Renewal Project Teams and Leaders Announced," BBC Web site, accessed March 13.

BBC (2003b). Royal Charter and Agreement.

BBC (2003c). "About the BBC: How the BBC is Run," www.bbc.co.uk/info/running/, accessed December 9.

BBC (2004a). "BBC apologises as Dyke quits," January 29, http://news.bbc.co.uk/l/hi/ukpolitics/3441181.stm, accessed January 30.

BBC (2004b). *Building Public Value*. London: BBC.

BBC (2004c). "BBC Journalism: The Neil Report," www.bbc.co.uk/info/policies/neil_report.shtml, accessed February 14, 2005.

BCS (1993). *The Case for a Stronger and Less Centralist BBC*. Edinburgh: Broadcasting Campaign for Scotland.

BECTU (1994). Bulletin, January 11.

BFI (1993a). *All our Futures*, ed. Wilf Stevenson. London: British Film Institute.

BFI (1993b). BFI/BAFTA Commission of Inquiry into the Future of the BBC.

BFI (1994). *Responses to the Green Paper*, ed. Peter Goodwin and Wilf Stevenson. London: BFI.

Birt, J. (1993a). "Extending Choice: Turning Promises into Realities," mimeo, January.

Birt, J. (1993b). "The BBC." Royal Television Society Fleming Lecture, London, April.

Birt, J. (1993c). Closing remarks from final session "View from the Bridge," Royal Television Society Cambridge Convention, September 18.

Birt, J. (1994). Letter to all members of BBC staff, June 10.

Birt, J. (2002). *The Harder Path.* London: Time Warner.

Booz Allen and Hamilton (1993). Evidence to the National Heritage Select Committee, in National Heritage Committee, *The Future of the BBC*, House of Commons, December 2, London: HMSO.

BPG (2004). *Beyond the Charter.* London: Broadcasting Policy Group/Premium Publishing, also at www.beyondthecharter.com.

Bragg, M. (1994a). "Can the BBC ride Two Horses?" *Evening Standard*, July 7.

Bragg, M. (1994b). "ITV's Identity Crisis," *Guardian*, July 11.

*Broadcast* (1993a). "BBC picks Andrews as Political Arm-twister," *Broadcast*, May 14.

*Broadcast* (1993b). "The Fighter and the Fight," *Broadcast*, June 18.

*Broadcast* (2003a). "Keating takes on BBC Charter Job," *Broadcast*, February 7, p. 2.

*Broadcast* (2003b). "Wyatt: BBC must take Initiative," *Broadcast*, January 21, p. 3.

Brown, M. (1992). "BBC wins Support for Keeping Licence Fee," *Independent*, November 23.

Brown, M. (1993). "MPs urge Ten-year Extension for BBC Charter," *Independent*, December 10.

Brown, M. (1995). "The BBC: Back after the Break," *Guardian*, December 4.

Brown, M. (2003). "Countdown to 2006," *Guardian Media*, April 7.

Brown, M., and D. McIntyre (1994). "Birt's BBC is given its Reward," *Independent*, July 7.

Browne, C. (1995). "The BBC and the Renewal of the Charter," speech to Public Broadcasters' international conference "Public Broadcasting, the Cornerstone of Democracy," Prague, June 20–22.

Burt, T. (2004). "A Radically Different BBC—Apart from the Licence Fee," *Financial Times*, October 12.

Cloot, P. (1994). *BBC Producer Choice: A Case Study.* Templeton College, Oxford: Major Projects Association.

Congdon, T., *et al.* (1992). *Paying for Broadcasting.* London: Routledge.

Cox, B. (1993). "Duty and the Beast," *Guardian*, August 23.

Croteau, D. and W. Hoynes (2001). *The Business of Media.* Pine Forge, CA: Sage.

CSA (1988). "A Claim of Right for Scotland," Edinburgh: Campaign for a Scottish Assembly.

Culf, A. (1993). "BBC Survey shows Staff Fearful and Insecure," *Guardian*, July 17.

Culf, A. (1994a). "Performance Pay Plan for BBC Staff," *Guardian*, January 12.

Culf, A. (1994b). "Dispute is about future of the BBC," *Guardian*, May 25.

Culf, A. (1994c). "Labour backs Strike with BBC Boycott," *Guardian*, June 9.

Culf, A. (1994d). "Victory for Birt's BBC Revolution," *Guardian*, July 7.

*Daily Telegraph* (1994). "Disillusion at the BBC," June 10.

Davis, A. (2002). *Public Relations Democracy.* Manchester: Manchester University Press.

Davis, A. (2003a). "Whither Mass Media?" *Media, Culture and Society* 25 (5).

Davis, A. (2003b). "Public Relations and News Sources," in S. Cottle (ed.), *News, Public Relations and Power.* London: Sage.

DCMS (2003a). *Review of the BBC's Royal Charter.* London: Department of Culture, Media and Sport.

DCMS (2003b). "Tessa Jowell appoints Terry Burns to Advise on BBC Charter Review," press notice 107/03, September 18.

Deacon, D., and P. Golding (1994). *Taxation and Representation.* London: John Libbey.

DNH (1992a). "Brooke seeks Wide Debate on BBC: Speech by Peter Brooke, MP, to the Royal Television Society Autumn Symposium," press notice 74/92, October 20. London: Department of National Heritage.

DNH (1992b). *The Future of the BBC.* Green Paper, London: Department of National Heritage.

DNH (1993a). "Broadcasters need to accept Change, says Peter Brooke," press notice 126/93, London: Department of National Heritage.

DNH (1993b). *Setting the Level of the Licence Fee: A Study for the Department of National Heritage.* London: Department of National Heritage.

DNH (1993c). "Brooke announces Increases in TV Licence Fee will be in Line with Inflation," press notice 156/93, London: Department of National Heritage.

DNH (1994). *The Future of the BBC: Serving the Nation, Competing Worldwide.* London: Department of National Heritage.

DNH (1995a). Draft of the Royal Charter. London: Department of National Heritage.

DNH (1995b). Draft of the Agreement between the Secretary of State and the BBC. London: Department of National Heritage.

Dowell, B. (2003). "Government may strip BBC of £500 million in Licence Fees," *Sunday Times*, October 26.

Dyke, G. (2004). *Inside Story.* London: Harper Collins.

Eldridge, J. (1996). "A Very Special Case: The BBC from John Reith to John Birt," *Cultural Policy* 2 (2).

Evans, A. (1995). "Impartiality Duty in new BBC Constitution—Minister," Press Association, April 5.

Frean, A. (1993). "BBC Survey backs Tully's Claims," *Times*, July 17.

Frean, A. (1994a). "BBC Reforms to save Millions," *Times*, January 12.

Frean, A. (1994b). "BBC launches Satellite Deal with Media Group," *Times*, May 11.

Frean, A., and J. Prynne (1994). "Birt triumphs in Battle of the BBC," *Times*, July 7.

Gandy, O. (1982). *Beyond Agenda-setting*. Norwood, NJ: Ablex.

Gandy, O. (1992). "Public Relations and Public Policy: the Structuration of Dominance in the Information Age," in Elizabeth L. Toth and Robert L. Heath (eds), *Rhetorical and Critical Approaches to Public Relations*. Hillsdale, NJ: Erlbaum.

Garfield, S. (1998). *The Nation's Favourite*. London: Faber.

Garnham, N. (1994). "The Broadcasting Market," *Political Quarterly* 65 (1).

Gibson, O. (2003). "The Question Masters," *Media Guardian*, December 1.

Goodwin, P. (1998). *Television under the Tories*. London: British Film Institute.

Green, D. (1991). *A Better BBC*. London: Centre for Policy Studies.

*Guardian* (1994). "There goes the News," *Guardian*, June 10.

Hall, S., C. Critcher, T. Jefferson, J. Clarke, and B. Robert (1978). *Policing the Crisis*. London: Macmillan.

Hargreaves, I. (1993). *Sharper Vision*. London: Demos.

Hellen, N. (1993). "BBC faces Cut in £1.6 billion Licence Income," *Evening Standard*, August 20.

Henry, G. (1994). "Auntie's Defiant Day off Work," *Guardian*, May 25.

Hodgson, P. (1992). "Foreword," in T. Congdon *et al.*, *Paying for Broadcasting*. London: Routledge.

Home Office (1988). *Broadcasting in the 1990s: Competition, Choice and Quality*. Cm 517, London: HMSO.

Horrie, C., and S. Clarke (1994). *Fuzzy Monsters*. London: Heinemann.

Horsman, M. (2003). "Pre-emptive Strike," *Financial Times Creative Business*, February 11, p. 11.

Hussey, M. (2001). *Chance Governs All*. London: Macmillan.

Hutchinson, D. (1999). *Media Policy: An Introduction*. Oxford: Blackwell.

Jenkins, S. (1994). "Army loses OK Corral Gunfight," *Times*, July 16.

John, S. (2002). *The Persuaders*. London: Palgrave.

Jones, G. (2004). "BBC in Crisis, Blair in Clear," *Daily Telegraph*, January 29.

Jones, G., T. Leonard and M. Born (2004). "Hutton a Whitewash, say 56 percent," *Daily Telegraph*, January 30.

Jowell, T. (2003). Speech to IPPR Convention on Public Service Communications, Oxford, January 15.

Jury, L. (2003). "BBC faces Tough Review for Charter Renewal, warns Jowell," *Independent*, July 16, p. 6.

Kane, F. (1994). "City applauds BBC Alliance with Pearson," *Guardian*, May 11.

King, A. (1998). "Thatcherism and the Emergence of Sky TV," *Media, Culture and Society* 20 (2).

Leapman, M. (1994). "BBC Staff face Pay Penalties for Poor Work," *Independent*, January 12.

Manning, P. (2001). *News and News Sources*. London: Sage.

Marr, A. (1992). *The Battle for Scotland*. London: Penguin.

McDonald, O. (1995). "Producer Choice in the BBC," *Public Money and Management*, January–March.

McKinsey (1993). *Public Broadcasters around the World*. London: McKinsey & Co.

McKinsey (1999). *Public Broadcasters around the World*. London: McKinsey & Co.

Miller, J. (1992). "BBC wins the Battle, but the War is far from Over," *Sunday Times*, November 29.

Miller, N., and R. Allen (1991). *And Now for the BBC*. London: John Libbey.

Milmo, D., and M. Brown (2003). "BBC shapes Fight for new Charter," *Guardian*, April 7, p. 11.

Mulgan, G. (1994). *Politics in an Anti-political Age*. London: Polity Press.

NHC (1993). *The Future of the BBC*. National Heritage Committee, House of Commons, December 2, London: HMSO, 77–1 and 77–2.

NHC (1995). "Follow-up to Previous Inquiries." National Heritage Committee, House of Commons, June 15.

O'Malley, T. (1994). *Closedown: The BBC and Government Broadcasting Policy, 1979–1992*. London: Pluto Press.

Parliamentary Debates (1992). House of Commons, Statement on BBC, November 24.

Parliamentary Debates (1994a). House of Commons, BBC, July 6.

Parliamentary Debates (1994b). House of Lords, Debate on BBC, December 6.

Parliamentary Debates (1995). House of Commons, Debate on BBC, February 9.

Parliamentary Debates (1996a). House of Lords, BBC, January 9.

Parliamentary Debates (1996b). House of Commons, BBC, February 15.

Peacock, A. (1995). "Report of the Committee on Financing the BBC." London: HMSO.

Phillis, R. (1994a). "The BBC in the International Marketplace," speech to FT Cable and Satellite Conference, February 16.

Phillis, R. (1994b). "Serving the Nation, Competing Worldwide," speech to Royal Institute of International Affairs conference "Global Media and Multimedia Telecoms," November 7.

Phillis, R. (1994c). Speech to the Royal Television Society, December 5.

Phillis, R. (1994d). "Adapt ... and Survive," Guardian, September 26.

Phillis, R. (1995). "The BBC in the International Multimedia Marketplace," FT Cable, Satellite and New Media Conference, February 27.

PIEDA (1993). "The Economic Significance of BBC Scotland," Edinburgh: PIEDA.

Pierce, A. (1994). "News Programes taken Off Air by Twenty-four-hour BBC Strike," Times, May 25.

Porter, A. (2003). "BBC to face Commons over £300 million Loss," Sunday Times Business section, July 13, p. 9.

Pryor, N. (1994). "BBC Strikes wreck Coverage of Elections," Evening Standard, June 9.

Reguly, E. (1996). "Auntie's Guide on a Voyage to the New World," Times, October 26.

Rouse, L. (2003). "The Licence Fee Hit Squad," Television, May, p. 22.

Rozenberg, J. (2003). "Should the BBC still have a Licence to Bill?" Daily Telegraph, January 16, p. 14.

Schlesinger, P. (1990). "Rethinking the Sociology of Journalism," in M. Ferguson (ed.), Public Communication: The New Imperative. London, Sage.

Schlesinger, P. (1995). "Europeanization and the Media: National Identity and the Public Sphere," Arena, February.

Schlesinger, P., and H. Tumber (1994). Reporting Crime. Oxford: Clarendon Press.

Scottish and Westminster (1993). "Campaign launched for Scottish Broadcasting," BCS release, October 18. London: Scottish and Westminster Communications.

Simpson, C. (1993). "Campaign for More Say in Broadcasting." Glasgow Herald, October 19.

Snoddy, R. (1992). "Birt plots the Endgame," Financial Times, November 30.

Snoddy, R. (1993a). "BBC Staff Survey hits at Red Tape," Financial Times, July 17.

Snoddy, R. (1994a). "BBC's Cost-cut Drive Attacked," Financial Times, January 12.

Snoddy, R. (1994b). "Savings at BBC likely to More than Double," Financial Times, April 5.

Snoddy, R. (1994c). "BBC to Link with Pearson in World Satellite Project," Financial Times, May 10.

Snoddy, R. (2003). "Penalise BBC on Fee, says TV Chief," Times, February 7, p. 4.

Sparks, C. (1995). "The Future of Public Service Broadcasting in Britain," in Critical Studies in Mass Communication, 12, pp. 325–41.

Starks, M. (1993). "Public Services and Market Forces: The BBC Experience," Office of Public Management lecture, London: BBC.

Television (1994). G. Kaufman, "Trouble in Toytown," Television.

Thatcher, M. (1993). The Downing Street Years. London: Harper Collins.

Thynne, J. (1993). "BBC admits its Staff are Insecure and feel Swamped by Red Tape," Daily Telegraph, July 7.

Thynne, J. (1994a). "BBC to cut Perks and Pay by Results," Daily Telegraph, June 12.

Thynne, J. (1994b). "BBC diverts £75 million into Regional Programming," Daily Telegraph, April 26.

Thynne, J. (1994c). "Strike to hit BBC Election Programmes," Daily Telegraph, June 9.

Thynne, J. (1995). "BBC puts Accent on Something for Everyone," Daily Telegraph, February 16.

Thynne, J., and G. Jones (1994). "Birt celebrates Victory as BBC Escapes Intact," Daily Telegraph, July 17.

Times (1994). "Corporate Battle," Times, June 10.

Times (1995). "Enlightened View," Times, February 16.

Tunstall, J., and D. Machin (1999). The Anglo-American Media Connection. Oxford: Oxford University Press.

Tunstall, J., and M. Palmer (1991). Media Moguls. London: Routledge.

Tusa, J. (1994). "Implications of Recent Charges," Political Quarterly 65 (1).

Veljanovski, C. (ed.) (1989). Freedom in Broadcasting. London: IEA.

Watt, N. (2004a). "New Poll reveals Public Mistrust," Guardian, January 30.

Watt, N. (2004b). "Tories to Reposition Party as the Friend of the BBC," February 24.

Wells, M. (2003). "Tessa's Test for Greg," Media Guardian, January 20, p. 4.

Whittingdale, J., MP (1995). New Policies for the Media. London: CPC.

Williams, R. (1995). "BBC sets out to offer 'Something for Everyone'," Independent, February 16.

Wishart, R. (1993). "Fight for Local Control of BBC in Scotland," *Scotsman*, October 19.

Wishart, R. (1994). "BBC Scotland takes Slice of £75 million Boost," *Scotsman*, April 26.

Wittstock, M. (1992). "Bragg's Quango for Airwaves is Played Down," *Times*, November 23.

Wyatt, W. (2003a). "Time for some Different Signals from Dyke," *Broadcast*, January 31, p. 17.

Wyatt, W. (2003b). *The Fun Factory: A Life in the BBC*. London: Aurum Press.

Wyatt, W. (2003c). *The Fun Factory*. London: Aurum.

# 17

# Lobbying by US Beer Wholesalers

CONOR MCGRATH

## INTRODUCTION

The National Beer Wholesalers Association (NBWA) has become, over the 1990s, one of the most powerful lobbying groups on Capitol Hill. Birnbaum's surveys of Washington lobbyists for *Fortune* magazine (1997, 1998, 1999, 2001) provide an indicator of how much the NBWA has developed. These surveys ask Members of Congress, Congressional and White House staffers, and senior lobbyists, to rate the political influence exercised by trade associations, trade unions, and interest groups.

The National Beer Wholesalers Association has made extraordinary progress: ranked thirty-fourth in 1997, it moved to twenty-fourth in 1998, to nineteenth in 1999, and by 2001 was rated the eighth most powerful group in Washington. To put this achievement into context, NBWA has close to 2,000 members and an annual budget of $6 million; the group ranked immediately ahead of the NBWA on the most recent *Fortune* list—the US Chamber of Commerce—has over 320,000 members and spends about $100 million.

### NBWA Leadership

The consistent improvement in how the NBWA is perceived in Washington is inseparable from the influence of its current president. Dr David Rehr has been responsible for the initiation and implementation of the NBWA's government affairs strategy over the 1990s. While an undergraduate in 1980, Rehr was a volunteer in a Congressional election campaign. The Republican candidate whom he assisted won, and took Rehr to Washington with him. In December 1986, Rehr was appointed Legislative Representative (later Assistant Director for Federal Government Relations) at the National Federation of Independent Business. There, he lobbied members of the House of Representatives on issues of concern to small businesses.

Rehr joined the NBWA as Vice-President (Government Affairs) in 1992. At the time, the NBWA's lobbying efforts were largely directed at state governments, and most of its Congressional contacts were Democrats. Rehr's appointment was intended both to give the organization greater expertise in lobbying at the federal level, and to strengthen the NBWA's ties with members of the Republican Party. One political journalist notes that, by this time, "Rehr had the skills, contacts and experience to transform the previously minor DC interest group into a power to be reckoned with on Capitol Hill" (Casselman, 2001). Rehr has recalled how little political clout the NBWA had then: "On a scale of 1 to 10, the NBWA was at a 3. My job was to take it to 7.5 and eventually to 10" (cited

Table 17.1   *Top five NBWA activities identified by member companies as "very important" or "important" (percentage of member companies)*

| Activity | 1994 | 1997 | 2000 |
|---|---|---|---|
| Government lobbying | 96.6 | 96.3 | 97.5 |
| Government grassroots lobbying | 95.9 | 95.4 | 97.5 |
| Government issue dissemination | 95.3 | 93.9 | 96.1 |
| Joint Legislative Conference | 91.5 | 88.1 | 87.6 |
| NBWA Political Action Committee | 90.9 | 92.2 | 93.3 |

*Sources* NBWA Strategic Plans, 1994, 1997, 2000.

in Massing, 1998: 40). In January 2000, David Rehr was appointed President and CEO of the National Beer Wholesalers Association, responsible for all the organization's activities, staff, and budgets. In that role, he continues as the NBWA's chief Congressional lobbyist and acts as its national media spokesperson.

### Increasing Emphasis on Government Relations

Every three years, the NBWA produces a comprehensive strategic plan, based largely upon responses received to a survey in which all NBWA member companies are asked to rank in order of importance a list of over twenty NBWA activities. In 1994, 1997, and 2000, member companies ranked the various government relations programs as the association's five most important activities (as shown in Table 17.1). In each of these surveys, the only other NBWA service rated as "very important" or "important" by over 80 percent of member companies was the organization's newsletter, *Beer Perspectives,* circulated to member companies biweekly.

Thus, the NBWA's members regard government relations activities as the most important programs undertaken by the association—and they do so by a long margin. A certain circularity is evident: because members perceive that the NBWA's government relations program works, the association receives more support and interest for government relations from members, and thus it undertakes government relations programs more effectively on members' behalf.

### NBWA BACKGROUND

The role of wholesalers in the American system is not one of simply transporting beer from brewers to retailers. Rather, wholesalers actually buy beer from brewers, store it at their own warehouses, and then sell and deliver the beer to local retailers. The beer wholesaling sector in the United States contributes $8 billion annually to the US gross domestic product; directly employs 93,000 workers; has an annual direct payroll of $3.4 billion; and contributes over $4 billion in direct state and local taxes each year. A typical beer wholesaler has sales of $14 million each year, and employs 48 workers with an annual wage bill of over $1.6 million.

There are approximately 2,200 licensed beer wholesalers in America, of which nearly 2,000 are NBWA members. The proportion of beer wholesaling companies which are members of the NBWA has risen from 66 percent in 1993 to 75.3 percent in 1997, to 86 percent in 2000—a further indication of the association's development over the 1990s.

### Structure and Organization

The NBWA's staff is structured in five main groupings. Industry Affairs, headed by the vice-president, has responsibility for membership development, training, technology and industry information. The Conventions and Meetings section organizes the NBWA's annual conference and a range of smaller meetings and seminars throughout the year. The NBWA sections of most relevance to this case study are:

1  *Public Affairs:* handles media relations and publications for members.
2  *Political Affairs:* manages the association's financial contributions to politicians running for Congress.
3  *Government Affairs:* the NBWA's lobbyists (or "Washington Representatives").

Public affairs has been made the association's No. 2 priority, after government affairs. Rehr believes that public opinion and public policy have a circular relationship: opinion polls drive legislative change, which is then reflected in opinion polls. David Ruthenberg (2000–2001 NBWA chairman) has asserted that:

> In recent years, it has become necessary to add a public affairs component to supplement and complement our government affairs activities. ... It has become vitally important that we embrace talking with the media, that we talk about the great things our industry does with the general public, legislators, business and community leaders, school administrators.
>
> (Ruthenberg, 2000)

## MAXIMIZING INFLUENCE ON CAPITOL HILL

On his arrival at the National Beer Wholesalers Association in 1992, David Rehr was clear that a number of factors would dictate the extent to which any new government affairs strategy would succeed.

### Internal/Organizational Requirements

#### Redefinition of the NBWA

The most pressing need was to establish precisely how the NBWA should brand itself as an organization. Prior to Rehr's appointment, the association had no established or memorable reputation among policy makers and tended to present itself in an uncoordinated manner. He, on the other hand, firmly believed in the importance of being able to use a single logo and strap line in all of the NBWA's

communications. Rehr appreciated that if Representatives and Senators already had a mental impression of an organization before being approached by that group on any particular issue, they would be more likely to absorb the message being delivered. The slogan he devised—"Family Businesses Distributing America's Beverage"—not only defines the fundamental point about beer wholesalers in a way which is easily mentally retained, but also has the effect of protecting the NBWA's policy interests: "It's tough to be against family businesses in America, and when you say beer is America's beverage, it is a lot tougher to be against beer" (Rehr, 2001b). Rehr's general philosophy provides a sense of unity and coherence to all the NBWA's detailed statements and positions. The consistency of this simple "bottom line" self-image underpins the association's entire government affairs strategy.

### Practicality and simplicity of strategy

> I studied marketing and advertising when I was an undergraduate ... we are marketing and selling a product. ... a Bill or a regulation, or something that we want from the Government, or something that we want the Government not to do to us. So we use all the fundamental principles of advertising and marketing: Number one, we keep things very simple. Number two, we repeat [the message] constantly.
>
> (Rehr, 2001b)

Rehr views the American political system as highly competitive—Members of Congress and Senators each receive over 1,000 phone calls, faxes, e-mails and letters daily, as well as approaches by some of the 15,000 registered lobbyists on Capitol Hill. Any organization wishing to be successful at government affairs must be highly focused and utterly relentless:

> We compete against all these people every day. Sometimes they are better, frankly—we are competing against people who want to finally cure cancer ... NBWA's staff are ruthless in competing against that on behalf of our members and creating an image of who we are and what we want.
>
> (Rehr, 2001b)

## Marketing Textbooks

Rehr attributes a large part of the NBWA's effectiveness to the fact that its government affairs philosophy is based on solid and proven principles, contained in three marketing books:

1 *Marketing Warfare* (Ries and Trout, 1986) stresses the importance of developing a simple position reinforced by no more than three or four key messages which are then constantly repeated;
2 *The Twenty-two Immutable Laws of Branding* (Ries and Ries, 1998) discusses the importance of establishing a fixed identity. "To be an effective lobbyist and to be effective at public affairs you've got to have a brand: 'Coke—the real thing'. 'Beer Wholesalers— Family Businesses Distributing America's Beverage'" (Rehr, 2001b).
3 *Positioning: The Battle for your Mind* (Ries and Trout, 1981) relates how to disseminate messages which are actually absorbed and retained by their recipients.

"I believe the basis of these three books is the reason why *Fortune* magazine has said we are the eighth most influential group … $28 worth of books" (Rehr, 2001b).

## Boosting Government Affairs Internally

If a government affairs program is to be successful and effective, all members of an organization's staff must appreciate why it has such a high priority, and have some knowledge of the activities being undertaken. Rehr emphasizes the importance of concentrating on a limited number of key objectives:

> At NBWA, we try to do three things well—win legislative/executive branch issue battles; define beer wholesalers as "Family Businesses Distributing America's Beverage"; and help elect Members to the House and Senate who are "pro-beer wholesalers, pro-business" in their philosophy. In Government Affairs, we could easily involve ourselves in 100 issues—but we don't.

> (Rehr, 1997a)

This outlook ensures that the association focuses on its strengths.

The NBWA's view is that it is imperative to understand why member companies feel that they benefit from participating in the organization. So, for instance, the survey undertaken for the 2000 strategic plan revealed that members wanted to see 61 percent of all association expenditure devoted to government affairs activities. However, government affairs cannot be pursued to the exclusion of all other internal departments—the point is to achieve a synergy between government affairs and the association's other functions. Thus, a meeting held by the staff involved in government affairs, public affairs, and membership activities resulted in publication of a pamphlet entitled "Five Reasons a Membership in NBWA Protects your Bottom Line." In addition to producing a tangible rationale conveying how membership of the association makes financial sense, the exercise ensured that key groups of employees better understood what each does and why.

In addition, the products generated by government affairs programs should be used widely to increase awareness among both member companies and staff. For instance, the NBWA distributed a reprint of a major article in the *New York Times Magazine* (Massing, 1998) on its government affairs and public affairs strategy to all its member companies.

Rehr has found that the successful marketing of the government affairs program is a major factor in persuading wholesalers that NBWA membership is of value to them and their own business. Wholesalers will join and stay in the NBWA only if they perceive it to be visible and effective. Consequently, government affairs is a central focus at all NBWA meetings and in all communications to members, such as the annual report and biweekly newsletter, *Beer Perspectives*.

## Importance of Evaluation

Finally, in relation to the internal components of success, Rehr insists upon setting defined and quantifiable targets for all activities.

> What we try to do every year is just improve ourselves four to five percent … If you just do something a little bit better every year, at the

Table 17.2   *Total funds raised by the NBWA's Political Action Committee, donated to candidates for election to Congress*

| Year | Amount ($) |
| --- | --- |
| 1990 | 401,030 |
| 1993 | 637,005 |
| 1996 | 751,028 |
| 1999 | 883,803 |
| 2000 | 1,008,190 |
| 2002 | 1,170,000 |

*Source* NBWA figures.

end of ten years, guess what: everything is great. We don't try to go for a knockout, because it is not going to happen.

(Rehr, 2001b)

## Strategy for PAC Disbursements

A further element of the NBWA's efforts to influence policy makers is its strategy for financially supporting politicians running for election or re-election to Congress. Contributions are channeled through the NBWA's Political Action Committee (PAC). Table 17.2 shows that over the last decade, the total raised by the PAC (from beer wholesalers and their employees) and then donated by it to politicians has almost trebled. In the 2001–2002 election cycle, the NBWA's PAC was the twelfth largest in the United States (from a total of over 4,000). The growth of the NBWA's PAC indicates that in recent years, members' awareness of the importance of government affairs has grown. In the 2000 election, 92 percent of Congressional candidates supported by the NBWA's PAC won their seats.

Only those politicians who agree with the association's core attitudes and interests receive money from the NBWA. While this may be self-evident, in reality many organizations fund politicians simply in order to gain access to them.

We're pretty unabashed about helping our friends, and if people are against us … we try to replace them with people who are more sensitive to our needs … Most lobbying/public affairs/government affairs operations don't really think through how they give the money. They often in fact give money to people who

are their adversaries because they think they can reduce their hostility, buy them off … It doesn't really work.

(Rehr, 2001b)

PAC funds will often be made available on the recommendation of beer wholesalers around the nation who have had expressions of support from local politicians. NBWA supporters facing difficult re-election battles will be aided as much as possible by the PAC, as these politicians will obviously be particularly grateful for assistance. Equally, the NBWA will fund candidates who are standing against Members of Congress who have consistently opposed the association. Generally, the PAC provides large disbursements to fewer candidates rather than giving small amounts to many politicians, on the premise that this will maximize the association's influence with key policy makers: "With the increasing costs of campaigns, if you have a choice to give $10,000 or $500, which is the legislator going to remember?" (Rehr, 2001b).

And, because the aim of the NBWA's PAC is to ensure that Congress is pro-small businesses, a substantial majority of its contributions are made to Republicans. However, the NBWA has been careful to contribute to "those Democrats who strongly supported the beer wholesalers, including Democratic minority leader Dick Gephardt (in whose district is the headquarters of Anheuser Busch, the largest producer of beer in the US)" (Casselman, 2001).

While the PAC is important to the NBWA, it would be a mistake to overstate its role in the group's effectiveness. It certainly provides an indicator of how beer wholesalers have been persuaded by the association in recent years to become actively involved in the political and electoral processes, but equally the NBWA does not owe its success to having money available. "If we didn't have a PAC, we may not be the eighth most influential group—there's no question that helps us—but we probably would still be in the top twenty five' (Rehr, 2001b).

## Relationships with Congressional Members and Staff

The NBWA's effectiveness on Capitol Hill has been immeasurably aided by the close network Rehr developed among Republican Representatives. During 1994, Rehr received considerable support from a Republican Congressman and whip, Tom DeLay, over a campaign opposing new government regulations relating to stress injuries (which affected beer wholesalers in terms of their employees lifting cases of beer). DeLay's political philosophy perfectly matched the NBWA's goals: before entering Congress he had owned a small business, and consequently opposed bureaucratic regulation of business (indeed, he was nicknamed, "Mr DeReg").

Rehr became a key advisor to DeLay in the Republican whip's efforts to win control of the House at the 1994 election. DeLay established an informal group of industry representatives which met two synergistic purposes—it brought business lobbyists into the House Republicans' policy-making process, and it coordinated those lobbyists' PAC contributions to Republican candidates. This alliance with DeLay continued after the 1994 election, at which the Republicans did indeed win control of the House, with Newt Gingrich as Speaker and DeLay as House Majority Whip. Much of the conservative revolution which ensued was based on the advice of business lobbyists such as Rehr.

One writer relates asking Rep. Bill Paxon (then chairman of the National Republican Congressional Committee, tasked with helping to elect as many Republicans as possible to the House of Representatives) which interest groups were most significant in terms of working to ensure that Republicans would continue to control the House. Paxon mentioned Americans for Tax Reform; the National Rifle

Association (although the NBWA does not take a formal view about gun control, both organizations share an interest in electing Republican Members of Congress); the (now defunct) Christian Coalition (which advocated limited federal power); the National Federation of Independent Business (which clearly shared NBWA goals on promoting small business)—and the National Beer Wholesalers Association. Rehr described this alliance of groups as "the center-right coalition that is realigning America" (cited in Drew, 1997: 14).

However, no interest group can survive for long, much less flourish, on Capitol Hill unless it can work with legislators from both political parties. Rehr has worked deliberately to surround himself with key staff who complement his own background with House Republicans. In recent years, he has recruited lobbyists with ties to Democratic Representatives including Dick Gephardt, Martin Frost, and Harold Ford, Jr—as well as those with ties to Senate Republicans including then Assistant Minority Leader Don Nickles. Fred Hatfield, chief of staff for then Senator John Breaux (Dem., Louisiana) has said that:

> The success enjoyed by the National Beer Wholesalers Association over the last several years is due in large part because they can be trusted to provide reliable and accurate information to staffers and Members of Congress. Their relentless engagement of the legislative process and the people who work on Capitol Hill has heightened the profile and effectiveness of the NBWA.
>
> (Hatfield, 2001)

## Increasing Visibility

### Coalition Building

The NBWA has recognized that there are dozens of organizations involved in the beer industry: farmers, brewers, unions representing brewers' employees, manufacturers of beer cans and bottles, wholesalers, retailers, and consumers—a group called Beer Drinkers of America has 300,000 members. On issues which impact upon the beer industry generically, a wide-ranging alliance can be constructed to campaign with a single voice.

There are two other major trade associations in the beer industry—the Beer Institute (representing larger brewers) and the Brewers' Association of America (speaking on behalf of smaller breweries). Historically, some tension existed between the three, but they have begun to work more closely together—a process aided by the fact that the heads of all three groups are relatively young and took up their appointments at around the same time. Moreover, on "mega industry issues", the NBWA will cooperate with the vintners and distillers. Although the beer, wine, and spirits industries compete against each other for share of sales, certain issues are of common interest, such as public affairs campaigns on preventing underage drinking, or ensuring that state attorneys-general do not lodge class action lawsuits seeking to make producers responsible for alcohol abuse. However, such macro-industry cooperation remains relatively limited.

## Media Attention

Rehr believes that appropriate media coverage can help maintain an organization's visibility and profile. The publications most widely read by Washington's political and administrative elite are the *Washington Post, Washington Times, New York Times*, and *Wall Street Journal*. Therefore:

> I look for opportunities to appear in those publications when it is helpful to our mission. Every Member of Congress, every staffer, every regulator, the President of the United States, reads [them]. And if they see your organization's name there, it makes you bigger than you really are. Because again, we are competing against all these other lobbyists.
>
> (Rehr, 2001b)

## Marketing the NBWA

Aside from the daily business of lobbying legislators, the NBWA holds a number of regular events to maintain its profile on Capitol Hill. Since 1993, the NBWA has hosted an annual Oktoberfest to thank Members of Congress and

their staff for supporting the association; over 1,000 guests attended in 2002. Every Christmas, the NBWA distributes small gifts to around 2,000 Congressional staffers—a coffee cup, computer mouse pad, pencil holder, or paperclip holder—all branded with the phrase, "Family Businesses Distributing America's Beverage." "If you've got this beer wholesalers mug on your desk, every day at least once you are going to think about the beer wholesalers" (Rehr, 2001b).

Each spring since 1991, the NBWA and the two brewers' organizations have held a Joint Legislative Conference (JLC) in Washington, DC, with wholesalers and brewers from across the nation. The JLC provides a key opportunity for beer wholesalers to demonstrate the grassroots base of their government relations campaigns, and raises the association's visibility on Capitol Hill. At the JLC, beer wholesalers personally lobby their Representatives and Senators about the NBWA's three or four key legislative and policy issues. Attendance at the JLC increased from 562 in 1991 to 1,020 in 2001.

Rehr (and Beer Institute president Jeff Becker) teach beer wholesalers and brewers to regard their meetings with Representatives and Senators as "Making the Capitol Hill Sales Call" (Rehr, 2001a). He reminds wholesalers that meeting a Member of Congress to ask for support on policy issues involves a number of things:

1 "*Sales Kit.*" The NBWA and the two brewers' organizations supply this: a packet of information outlining the beer industry's position on key pieces of legislation, along with background data on the three associations and the economic contribution made by the industry. It also includes a "Capitol Hill Worksheet" on which wholesalers record the responses given by their Members of Congress to each request to support or oppose particular Bills.
2 "*Know your Product.*" Rehr runs through the main points on each legislative issue, so that wholesalers know exactly which messages to deliver during meetings.
3 "*Respond to Rebuttals.*" Wholesalers are provided with appropriate responses to a number of questions commonly asked about each issue.

4 *"Ask for the Order."* At each meeting, the beer wholesaler should ask the legislator whether he or she supports the NBWA's stance on each piece of legislation, and record the responses on their Capitol Hill Worksheet.

5 *"Follow up to Complete the Sale."* The Member of Congress should be invited to visit the wholesaler's facility in the constituency. All Capitol Hill Worksheets should be returned to NBWA staff, and finally, the wholesaler should send a note of thanks to the Member on company notepaper.

## LEGISLATIVE CAMPAIGNS

### Importance of Grassroots

NBWA members own warehouses in 99 percent of all Congressional Districts, and so can write to their local Members of Congress on particular issues from their perspectives as employers of some of the Member's constituents. The association can fax and e-mail to members alerts about legislation and urgent requests that they contact their local Members to seek their support. Wholesalers are periodically sent a questionnaire asking about the relationships they have been able to develop with their local Representatives and Senators; this information is added to the NBWA's database. The association organizes regular training sessions on government relations, and sends members frequent updates on their legislators' voting records and attitudes to key pieces of legislation. In 1994, 10–20 percent of NBWA members would respond positively if asked by the association to write or telephone their Representative or Senators to put forward the organization's position on a piece of pending legislation. By 1997 this figure had increased to 35 percent; it currently stands at around 80 percent.

### Developing a Government Relations Strategy

When designing a strategy to deal with a particular legislative issue, the NBWA follows a five-step process:

1 *Define the issue.* Reduce the purpose of the campaign to its essence, using simple language to frame the issue; and do this before your opponents define the issue to their advantage.

2 *Position the issue.* "This is the idea of thinking through in fifteen words or less why someone would want to be for it" (Rehr, 2001b). Rehr suggests that at this point, it is useful to try to explain the issue to a friend: "If the average person gets it, then I think the average Member of Congress or the average media person probably gets it too" (Rehr, 2001b).

3 *Identify tools.* Plan precisely which methods will be used to present your message.

4 *Create a quantifiable campaign.* Have a "road map" of precisely what activities you intend to undertake at each stage of the campaign, and a clear understanding of what you hope to get from each activity.

5 *Ruthless execution.* This returns to the notion that a message has to be repeated constantly: "With advertising and marketing, you have to tell someone something thirteen times before it starts to sink in" (Rehr, 2001b).

Two particular legislative campaigns will serve to highlight important aspects of the NBWA's government affairs strategy.

### Repeal of the Federal Excise Tax

A federal excise tax (FET) was first levied on beer in 1862, to help finance the Civil War. Between then and 1951, various increases brought FET on beer from $8 per barrel to $9; the rate remained constant for the next forty years. In 1990, Congress decided that, as part of the effort to reduce the national deficit, taxes should be raised on beer, jewelry, furs, expensive boats, private airplanes, and luxury cars. The increase—which came into force in 1991—doubled FET payable on a barrel of beer from $9 to $18, or 32c per six-pack of beer. This increase currently generates over $1.5 billion each year in additional government revenue. Since then, the FET payable on all these "luxury" goods has been repealed, with the exception of the beer tax.

When Rehr joined the NBWA in 1992, his legislative goals were defensive and reactive—to "make sure the tax wasn't raised again, and to be sure that anti-beer legislation didn't pass the Congress and get signed into law" (cited in Drew, 1997: 16). There was good cause to be concerned that government would regard beer as an easy target for further FET increases. In 1993, the NBWA became concerned that President Clinton intended to use a new FET increase on beer to pay for some of his health care proposals; it sent an Action Alert to all NBWA members, who lobbied the White House through letters and phone calls. When the reform package was announced, it contained no mention of tax increases on beer.

One consequence of the NBWA's strategy over recent years is that the organization now feels confident that it can undertake a proactive campaign—not merely to avoid further tax increases on beer, but to repeal the FET increase entirely. Rehr has said that "We've moved off of defense. We have to worry less about Congress raising the beer tax and can concern ourselves with trying to eliminate it" (cited in Drew, 1997: 264). Support for the campaign has demonstrably increased over the last few years. In 1997, a Bill to return to the pre-1991 tax level on beer was supported by 81 Members of Congress; a similar measure attracted 99 co-sponsors in 1998; and yet another effort to amend the law was supported in 2000 by 113 Representatives.

This ongoing campaign provides a clear example of the way in which the NBWA develops a strategy:

1  *Define the issue.* Rather than getting into a technical explanation of what is involved in a repeal of the federal excise tax increase on beer in 1991, the issue is simply framed in terms of "Roll back the beer tax."
2  *Position the issue.* Essentially, the NBWA's message is that the FET increase is unfair because it is disproportionately paid by lower-income families. "Our positioning on this is: 'Roll back the tax—it's a tax on working Americans.' The average beer drinker in America makes $28,000 a year. Everybody on Capitol Hill wants to be for cutting taxes on working people" (Rehr, 2001b).
3  *Identify tools.* The NBWA has employed various lobbying tools to promote its message: personal contact with legislators; advertisements in political magazines; grassroots lobbying by wholesalers through letters and the Joint Legislative Conferences.
4  *Create a quantifiable campaign.* Develop quantitative targets such as the number of co-sponsors supporting legislation, and the number of times the issue appears in the media.
5  *Ruthless execution.* "It is like being a broken record. For nine years, I've repeated: 'Family Businesses Distributing America's Beverage.' 'Beer: it's America's beverage.' 'Roll back the tax.'" (Rehr, 2001b).

The National Beer Wholesalers Association continues to campaign for the repeal of the 1991 FET increase on beer. On 29 March 2001, Phil English (a Republican Congressman) introduced another Bill to reduce the federal excise tax on beer to the pre-1991 level. This most recent effort attracted 226 co-sponsors. The NBWA is hopeful that it will progress through both the House and Senate in the next session of Congress.

### Repeal of the "Death Tax"

Another issue receiving much NBWA attention in recent years was repeal of the estate tax, under which property inherited upon death is taxed. This was significant for the NBWA because when a beer wholesaler died, his or her company was passed on to family members, but was subject to estate tax. Often, this meant that part or all of the business had to be sold in order to pay the estate tax. According to NBWA figures, the burden of this tax was so severe that over 70 percent of family businesses did not survive the second generation of owners. Moreover, it was argued that the time and money spent by wholesalers and their families dealing with the estate tax could be better employed in actually managing their businesses and creating new jobs. In addition, the NBWA regarded estate tax as fundamentally immoral, given that during a beer wholesaler's life, he or she had already paid taxes on the profits generated by the business.

This legislative campaign illustrates the importance attached by the NBWA to framing issues in language which makes it easier for the public and legislators to support the association's position. Originally, the NBWA (and other small business groups) referred to the issue as the "estate tax" but found that this generated little interest among the American public, so it began talking about "inheritance tax," equally unsuccessfully. More recently, the NBWA has campaigned to abolish the "death tax," as this was felt to have more resonance with the public and legislators alike. According to Rick Berman (General Counsel of the American Beverage Institute), however good an organization's lobbying capabilities are, they will not always be sufficient, because even generally supportive legislators cannot vote for a policy if to do so would be counter to public opinion.

> When the Republicans tried to repeal the estate tax, they couldn't get it going. Why? Because most people don't perceive themselves as having an estate. And they didn't perceive themselves as having an inheritance. But everyone thinks that they're going to die, and so all of a sudden, that starts to make sense ... They couldn't get traction until they changed the terms of the debate.
>
> (Berman, 2000)

In 1998, a Bill was introduced in the House of Representatives which would have gradually reduced the tax until by 2009 it would have been eliminated; that measure was supported by 133 Members of Congress, but failed to become law. During the Bill's consideration by the House Ways and Means Committee, the NBWA arranged for oral evidence to be given by two children of a beer wholesaler who had recently died:

> They told how their grandfather and then their father had worked long and hard to build the wholesalership into a stable business. Then they recounted the final few months they

and their mother spent with their father and the hardship they experienced trying to get everything in order to save the business from being taken away by the exorbitant death taxes.

> (Klopcic, 1998)

In 2000, a Financial Freedom Act—which included a provision to end the estate tax—was passed by 279 to 136 votes in the House of Representatives and by 59 to 39 votes in the Senate. However, it was then vetoed by President Clinton, and NBWA supporters were unable to muster the 67 Senate votes necessary to override a presidential veto.

In 2001, another Bill to phase out the "death tax" passed the House of Representatives on May 26 by 240 to 154 votes and moved to the Senate, where it passed on the same date by 58 to 33 votes. The Economic Growth and Tax Reconciliation Act was signed into law by President Bush on June 7, 2001, ending a long campaign by the NBWA to eliminate the "death tax".

## CONCLUSION

Trade associations such as the NBWA have long been regarded as influential interest groups. As Mack points out: "When public officials hear from an association on an issue, they know they are receiving the views of an entire industry or profession ... an association can speak with a voice of considerable power, especially if it is backed by tactics that produce voluminous mail and political communications" (1997: 167). This case study has shown how the National Beer Wholesalers Association has transformed itself into one of the most powerful groups in Washington, through the initiation and implementation of a positive, proactive, and professional government affairs strategy.

In large measure, this evolution reflects the dynamism, creative flair and leadership of its president, David Rehr. Tom DeLay, the Republican Majority Leader in the House of Representatives, has said of Rehr: "David is one of the few individuals who understands the synergy of lobbying, politics, and public relations.

His strategies have made NBWA one of the most effective groups in Washington" (DeLay, 2001).

However, the internal and external strategies pursued by the National Beer Wholesalers Association in terms of the development of its government affairs program need not be unique to that one organization. They contain valuable lessons which could usefully be adopted by the managers of other associations. While there is certainly a "chicken and egg" element to the question of whether the NBWA is increasingly focused on government relations because its members say that is their priority or whether government relations is increasingly important to members because the NBWA demonstrates its effectiveness in that area year after year, what is undoubtedly true is that a certain synergy and circularity are evident here. Moreover, such a virtuous circle can be achieved within any trade association.

Rehr has suggested that a primary factor in the NBWA's success in government affairs and public affairs is that, at all times, staff are aware that they simultaneously address three discrete audiences:

1   The key message to *NBWA members* is that the organization is proactive in terms of its government affairs and public affairs programs.
2   What the NBWA essentially wants *Members of Congress and their staff* to recall is that "NBWA = beer."
3   The fundamental point of *industry and media* liaison activity is to promote the notion that beer is good (Rehr, 1997b).

It is the synergy between these messages which has allowed the NBWA to market itself so successfully both to its own members and to Congress. Again, while the specifics are quite particular to the NBWA, in general terms all trade associations could devise a similar set of messages appropriate to their own situation.

The NBWA places a great deal of emphasis on the importance of ensuring that its member companies know exactly what the association's government affairs program is designed to achieve. Rehr has found that not only is the NBWA more effective when it has an involved and knowledgeable member base, but that the successful marketing of the government relations program is a major factor in persuading wholesalers that NBWA membership is of value to them and their own business. As a voluntary organization, wholesalers will join and stay in the NBWA only if they perceive it to be visible and effective. Consequently, government affairs is a central focus at all NBWA meetings and in all communications to members.

In learning from the success of the NBWA, leaders in any trade association working within any political system ought to keep in mind a small number of fundamental rules:

1   Ensure that government affairs is a central management function, prioritized throughout the organization.
2   Communicate the vital importance of government affairs to members, and manage their expectations of what can be achieved so that the association develops a sustainable reputation for delivering on its objectives.
3   Build excellence in government affairs through recruiting and retaining skilled and creative professionals.
4   Find the most concise and most effective means of branding the organization— and then constantly communicate that image and message.
5   Keep the strategy as straightforward and consistent as possible.
6   Make certain that every member of the organization's staff, whatever their role, understands and accepts the importance of the government affairs function.
7   Build partnerships with other organizations, and create issue-based coalitions wherever possible.
8   Know how to service the media as well as possible, and be innovative in your media relations.
9   Use your members as much as possible, and train them well in how to deliver the association's messages.
10  Having devised a simple campaign on any particular issue, be absolutely relentless in executing the plan.

# REFERENCES

Berman, R. (2000). Presentation to NBWA Annual Convention.

Birnbaum, J.H. (1997). "Washington's Power 25," *Fortune*, December 8.

Birnbaum, J.H. (1998). "The Power 25: The Influence Merchants," *Fortune*, December 7.

Birnbaum, J.H. (1999). "The Power 25: Follow the Money," *Fortune*, December 6.

Birnbaum, J.H. (2001). "The Power 25: Fat and Happy in DC," *Fortune*, May 28.

Casselman, B. (2001). Letter to the author, August 29.

DeLay, T. (2001). Letter to the author, August 29.

Drew, E. (1997). *Whatever it Takes: The Real Struggle for Political Power in America.* New York: Viking.

Hatfield, F. (2001). Letter to the author, August 27.

Klopcic, D.L. (1998). "Message from the Chairman," in NBWA Annual Report.

Mack, C.S. (1997). *Business, Politics and the Practice of Government Relations.* Westport, CT: Quorum.

Massing, M. (1998). "Why Beer Won't Go Up in Smoke," *New York Times Magazine*, March 22.

National Beer Wholesalers Association Website, www.nbwa.org.

National Beer Wholesalers Association biweekly newsletter, *Beer Perspectives.*

National Beer Wholesalers Association (1992, 1993, 1994, 1995, 1997, 1998, 1999, 2000, 2002). Annual Report.

National Beer Wholesalers Association (1994, 1997, 2000). *Strategic Plan.*

Rehr, D.K. (1997a). "Marketing your Government Relations Program." Presentation to an American Society of Association Executives seminar, January 30.

Rehr, D.K. (1997b). "Six Steps in Maximizing your Association's Voice through Government Relations and Public Relations Working Together." Presentation to an American Society of Association Executives seminar, March 27.

Rehr, D.K. (2001a). "Making the Capitol Hill Sales Call." Presentation to NBWA/BREWERS Joint Legislative Conference, April 2.

Rehr, D.K. (2001b). Interview with the author, June 13.

Ries, A., and L. Ries (1998). *The Twenty-two Immutable Laws of Branding.* New York: Harper Collins.

Ries, A., and J. Trout (1981). *Positioning: The Battle for your Mind.* New York: Warner.

Ries, A., and J. Trout (1986). *Marketing Warfare.* New York: McGraw-Hill.

Ruthenberg, D. (2000). Presentation to NBWA Annual Convention.

# 18

# Lobbying in the United States

## An Overview for Students, Scholars and Practitioners

### CLIVE S. THOMAS

There is an interesting fact about the public affairs business in the United States.[1] The United States has by far the most developed public affairs industry in the world in terms of the range and sophistication of strategies and tactics and the profession of lobbying; but, particularly in regard to the avenues and methods of lobbying, it is an aberration when compared to other democratic systems (Thomas, 1993b). The root of this lies in the unique US separation of powers governmental structure, its strong federal system, its long established individualist political culture, and the all-pervasive entrepreneurial spirit in American life.

This highly developed but aberrant US public affairs industry has important lessons for academics, students, and practitioners, both Americans and non-Americans, but particularly those acculturated in the ways of democratic parliamentary systems. This chapter is written with both groups in mind. It will alert Americans to the fact that if they study other systems or lobby in them, that significant differences exist between Washington, DC, and state capitals like Sacramento, Tallahassee, and Santa Fe from lobbying in London, Canberra or other capitals around the world. For the non-American not familiar with the US public affairs system, this chapter will

raise their awareness and help them to think like an American when studying the US system or lobbying in it.

However, those not familiar with the US system but who have some knowledge or experience with lobbying do not need to start from scratch. To understand the US system one simply needs to keep in mind the distinction between the *activity* of lobbying and the *process* and *mores* of lobbying. As this *Handbook* clearly demonstrates, the *activities* of lobbying—making contacts, building good relations with public officials to develop trust and credibility, and so on—are universal to lobbying whether in Washington, DC, Buenos Aires, Lisbon, or anywhere else. What is different are the processes—formal and informal—in regards to institutional structure, avenues of lobbying, and the local cultural rules of the lobbying game. It is these processes and mores that are essential to fully appreciate a public affairs system whether one is an academic, a student, or a practitioner. Explaining these differences in process and mores is the major purpose of this chapter.

Given the need to serve academics, students, and practitioners, this chapter provides a practical understanding of the American public affairs system by drawing on the writings of both academics and practitioners. As background to understanding the practices in the US lobbying business, the third section (pp. 284–7) examines the governmental structure and culture that produce the particular processes and mores of public affairs. The next two outline the development and present configuration of the lobbying industry in Washington, DC, and the states. In the following two (pp. 287–90 and 290–1) we explain some important aspects of strategies and tactics and examine the elusive question of group influence. Two case studies are provided at pp. 296–8 to help illustrate the points and analysis in the first seven sections and to set the scene for the ninth (p. 298), which speculates on the future direction of the US lobbying business. The chapter concludes with a review of useful sources of information for students, scholars, and practitioners. The focus of this chapter, as an overview, means that it is best to read it before the more specialist Chapter 19 about established lobbyists in the United States.

Before we move to the operation of the system, however, we first need to explain the terminology of public affairs in the United States This will be our first lesson in the cultural mores of the US lobbying business.

## A NOTE ON THE USE OF TERMS

There are some important differences between the United States and other English-speaking countries in the use of terms and language regarding interest groups and lobbying. This is the case among academics and practitioners alike. While these are not hard-and-fast differences they do generally apply. To understand both academic and popular writing on this subject, and to be taken seriously as a practitioner, it is important to know these differences and to use the American terms when in the United States or when writing about its interest-group system.

Top of the list is the term *public affairs*. As expressed in the title of this *Handbook*, in many English-speaking countries as well as in the European Union the term refers to the act of dealing with government and trying to influence its policies. But the term is rarely, if ever, used in this context in the United States. To an American the term *public affairs* has a much broader connotation than simply dealing with government: it embraces all things that have a public face, such as firms dealing with the general public or, in some cases, all matters not internal to a private organization. What is termed public affairs outside the United States is usually referred to as *lobbying*, *government relations*, or *government affairs* by Americans and their interest groups, organizations, and businesses, with lobbying being the usually preferred term.

Two common terms that might cause confusion to a non-American are *interest group* and *pressure group*. Until the early 1980s American academics used these terms interchangeably. But by the 1990s Americans scholars no longer used the term pressure group. Political practitioners, public officials and the public in general rarely use the words pressure group but most often *special interest* or simply *interest group*, *interest* or the word *lobby* used as a noun as, for example, in referring to the *environmental lobby*, the *women's lobby*, and so on. Exhibit 18.1 sets out explanations of the major terms in the lobbying industry as understood by academics and practitioners in the United States.

---

## Exhibit 18.1 The Use of Some Major Terms in US Lobbying

**Interest group** An association of individuals (e.g., a trade union) or organizations (e.g., a software manufacturer) or a public or private institution (e.g., a government department) which, on the basis of one or more shared concerns, attempts to influence government policy in its favor.

**Interest; lobby** These terms (as nouns) are used interchangeably with *interest group*; but they are more general and are used in a variety of ways. The term *lobby* always has political connotations (usually referring to a collection of interests such as business groups) but *interest* may or may not. It may simply refer to a part (a sector) of society, such as farmers or minorities, with similar concerns or a common identity, that may or may not engage in political activity. The distinction between an interest or lobby and a formal interest group is sometimes difficult to make in practice. This is because organized groups, such as women's groups, often act and are perceived as representing a broader political interest than their official membership. The term *interest* instead of *interest group* is often used when referring to government entities working to influence other governments because of the broader and less formalized nature of the constituencies represented.

**Lobbying** The interaction of a group or interest, through its lobbyist, or other representatives, with policy makers, either by *direct* means (such as using a lobbyist) or *indirect* means (such as through a public demonstration), with a view to influencing current policy or creating a relationship conducive to shaping future policy to the benefit of that group or interest.

**Lobbyist** A person designated by an interest group or interest to facilitate influencing public policy in that group or interest's favor by performing one or more of the following: (1) directly contacting public officials; (2) monitoring political and governmental activity; (3) advising on political strategies and tactics; (4) developing and orchestrating the group's lobbying effort. In Washington, DC, lobbyists are often referred to as *Washington representatives.*

**Lobbying community** A term often used by academics in the United States to refer to the individuals who lobby. Five types of lobbyists have been identified: (1) contract lobbyists, freelancers hired on a contract specifically to lobby for a client or clients; (2) in-house lobbyists, who work for a business or organization and lobby as part of their job; (3) legislative liaisons, who represent government jurisdictions or agencies; (4) volunteer or cause lobbyists, committed individuals who lobby for a cause usually for no pay; and (5) private individuals working for some personal benefit.

**Lobbying industry/Lobbying business** These are general and interchangeable terms used by practitioners and some academics; they include the lobbying community but are more all-embracing terms describing the array of interest groups, organizations (including businesses, non-profits, government jurisdictions and agencies, etc.), individuals (mainly members of the lobbying community), and lobbying and other firms and organizations (such as law, public relations, research, etc.) that are involved in lobbying either directly or by providing support services at the federal, state, and local level in the United States.

**Strategies and tactics** These terms are also often used interchangeably because they are so interrelated in practice, but they are not the same. A strategy is an overall plan for gaining access and influence and securing specific policy goals. Tactics are the specific means for achieving these goals. Ideally, a strategy will include such elements as: the goals to be achieved and what are and are not acceptable fallback positions; the identification of key policy makers to be persuaded; the ways that these policy makers will be approached and persuaded—by hired lobbyists, group personnel, group members, through phone, letter or e-mail contact, etc. The tactics of a group are the specific ways in which this strategy is implemented on a day-to-day basis. These include: which public official in which branches of government will be contacted, who will contact them, and when and how the message will be delivered. Tactics may also include a specific media or public relations campaign, even demonstrations and protests, aimed at influencing policy makers' stances.

*Source* Thomas (2004a: 3–7, 140–141, 151–154).

Two terms that are becoming increasingly common outside the United States but the use of which might puzzle many American academics and practitioners are *non-governmental organization* (NGO) and *civil society*. The term NGO is sometimes used in the United States not to refer to domestic lobbies but with reference to international organizations like Amnesty International and Greenpeace; but it is still not common even for such groups. There is no synonymous term in the United States to NGO in domestic politics. Probably the closest is *public interest group* (such as civil liberties groups) or *cause group* (such as those for the poor). The term *civil society* is rarely used in the United States to refer to the multitude of groups, organizations, and interests that make up the society *vis-à-vis* government. Again, there is no equivalent, single term in the United States. The rough American equivalent would be the word *society* or sectors of society such as the *private sector*, the *public sector*, the *non-profit sector,* and so on.

In this chapter terms are used as they are in the US lobbying business. This will help the non-American become familiar with the local lingo; and for American readers it will prevent confusion.

## THE INSTITUTIONAL AND POLITICAL CULTURAL SCENE AND ITS IMPLICATIONS FOR LOBBYING

It may be an elementary fact but it is nevertheless *the* crucial one in the lobbying business that all but the most naive lobbyist will work to affect policy by accessing the power points of a political system. In this regard the United States is quite different and in many ways unique

from the parliamentary democracies of the rest of the world. Together with these institutional arrangements the political cultural mores about lobbying determine the *processes* of lobbying as they operate in the United States.

### Institutional Structural Factors

Three structural and institutional factors combine to produce this unique environment for lobbying.

First, is the separation of the powers system that structures the relationship between the legislature, executive, and judiciary at the federal and state level. Unlike parliamentary systems, the United States gives extensive constitutional authority to the legislative branch (Congress and state legislatures) to make policy. This includes the right to veto actions of the executive. Through the principle of judicial review, the courts can declare acts of both the legislature and the executive unconstitutional. This authority has meant that in recent years the courts have become part of lobbying strategy and tactics for some interest groups.

Second, the strong federal system operating in the United States means that power is divided not only between the branches of government at the same level but also between levels (federal and state). Yet, while some policy domains are clearly the responsibility of one level, such as foreign policy being exclusively a federal—mainly presidential—responsibility, most policy areas such as education, health, and transportation have elements administered by both federal and state government (and local governments too). This means that interest groups of all types, such as teachers, universities, social issue groups (like pro- and anti-choice—abortion—groups), among a plethora of others, have to lobby at more than one level of government. That is they have to be involved in intergovernmental (IGR) lobbying activities.

Third, while political parties in the United States have become more powerful at the federal and state level since the major Republican Party victories of 1994, parties still do not have the centralizing and controlling role that they have in most other liberal democracies. This is for a variety of complex reasons. In brief: legislators in the United States often receive little funding from their party during elections and very often receive support from individuals and particularly interest groups; there is considerable local control over the choice of candidates, who must be a resident of their district and state; elected officials often build loyalties with their constituents that transcend party because ideology often plays less of a role in US politics than personality and bringing home the bacon. Furthermore, because of separately elected Houses of the Congress and state legislature (House and Senate) and because the executive (President or Governor) is separately elected, divided party control often occurs within the legislature and between the legislature and the executive branch. All this tends to undermine the controlling influence that party—particularly a majority party—has in determining avenues of access and exclusionary control over policy making.

## Political Cultural Values and Mores

It is impossible to do justice to the complexity of American political cultural values and mores in a few paragraphs. Nevertheless, there are some American traits and characteristics that are important to identify, as these influence both the processes and activities of lobbying as we distinguished between them above. The three most insightful of these are: political pragmatism and individualism; the entrepreneurial spirit applied to politics; and a moralistic streak that produces an ambivalent attitude toward interest groups.

Political pragmatism and individualism can be contrasted with the highly ideological

(mainly socialist versus conservative) and more collectivist nature of European politics. Ideology has never been as important in US politics as in Europe and socialism never took root in the United States (though the liberal wing of the Democratic Party, in effect, pursues social democratic policies). The individualistic streak undermined the establishment of trade unions that have never organized more than 30 percent of the labor force (and only 14 percent in 2004) compared to over 50 percent in most European countries and in excess of 80 percent in Sweden. This means that the conditions for neocorporatism, where government and peak associations in business and labor can set national policy, are absent because there is no one peak association representing a majority of business or labor in the United States (Salisbury, 1979; Wilson, 1982).

The all-pervasive entrepreneurial spirit in the United States has had great influence on the processes and techniques of interest-group activity. This entrepreneurial bent has been facilitated by the many avenues available to interest groups in their quest to influence public policy that are not available to the more centralized and particularly the neocorporatist systems of Western Europe. Some major developments resulting from this entrepreneurial element were: the emergence by the early twentieth century at the federal level and by the 1940s in the states of the lobbying profession, particularly the contract lobbyist; the establishment of firms in Washington, DC, and later in the states that specialize in lobbying and developing lobbying campaigns; beginning in the 1960s, the emergence of grassroots techniques to involve members in lobbying as well as the use of advertising and media campaigns to promote a lobbying effort; the rise of the political action committee (PAC) to funnel campaign money to political candidates with the hope of them aiding a group's lobbying effort once elected; and the development of an array of tactics such as coalition building, the use of the courts, and group involvement in the nomination of executive branch officials and judges. In short, the entrepreneurial and to a large extent the capitalist ethic have influenced

US interest group activity more than any other Western country.

In the late nineteenth century the unfettered application of entrepreneurial techniques to lobbying led to many abuses, especially by railroad lobbyists as America built a railroad network. This clashed with the moralistic element in American society, and the first attempts to regulate lobbying were made. Here lies a central irony in American society and particularly American politics that has accompanied the development of interest groups for over a hundred years. This is that Americans have a very ambivalent attitude toward interest groups: they join them by the tens of millions but are very skeptical of them and their actual and perceived abuses (Petracca, 1992: xix, xx; Benedict, 2004). This ambivalence has had its effect on the operation of interest-group activity. Three of the most important of these consequences are: interest groups and lobbyists often try to play down their activities such as using euphemistic titles for lobbyist (e.g. government affairs representative or legislative liaison); the United States has developed, at the federal and state levels and increasingly at the local level, the most extensive regulation of interest-group activity in the Western world; and because of the first two points, elected and appointed officials are very concerned about their dealings with lobbyists and interest groups.

## The Consequences for Interest-Group Activity and Lobbying

What, then, are the consequences—the lessons—for scholars, students, and practitioners from these institutional and political cultural differences in the US system? Six lessons are particularly important.

First, the US system is very fragmented in its policy-making process compared to all other Western democracies with their parliamentary systems, strong parties, and strong Cabinets where decision making is lodged largely with the executive branch. This means that for interest groups there are many power points in the US system—legislative, executive, and sometimes judicial—that must be covered in most lobbying efforts. For the non-American coming to study or work the US lobbying system, this may take some adjustment of thinking and strategizing. While it is certainly not a duplicate copy of the American system, lobbying in the European Union with its fragmentation of power between the member nations, the Commission, the Parliament and the European Court is a rough equivalent of the US system.

Second, the fragmented policy system gives the advantage to those groups and interests wishing to protect the *status quo* through defensive lobbying. They only have to stop a measure at one point in the system to kill it, such as a sympathetic committee chair in the House or Senate; or getting the Governor or the President to oppose it or veto it if passed. In contrast, those who want to promote something have to clear all the hurdles in the process—and these are numerous. Zeigler and van Dalen (1976: 125–127) call this situation the "advantage of the defense." This situation contrasts sharply with that in very centralized, strong party systems like Sweden, Germany, and even Britain, where support of a measure by the majority party and the Cabinet usually assures its passage.

Third, a lobbying effort often has to be mounted on several fronts, particularly by those who want to get something enacted. And this may include more than so-called *direct lobbying*; these days it increasingly includes *indirect lobbying* (see Exhibit 18.1 for definitions). Such a broad range of tactics is well known outside the United States. But they are often not appropriate or necessary in highly centralized systems, especially where some level of neocorporatist arrangements is used.

Fourth, the fragmented nature of the system plus the "advantage of the defense" means that enacting entire programs (programmatic policy making perhaps through neocorporatist arrangements) which is possible in many parliamentary systems is very difficult to achieve in the US system at any level. Instead, policy making is incremental, involving major compromise and wheeling and dealing. Even when a policy does get enacted it is usually amended, and sometimes extensively as those with power and a stake in the outcome exert their influence. However, as the number of groups in the US interest group system expands, and more and more groups get into the political fray, a situation dubbed hyperpluralism has developed where policy outcomes are less easy to predict (Salisbury, 1990).

Fifth, the first four points mean that resources—money, staff, contacts, good lobbyists, and so on—are very important in the United States. Certainly, this is true of all political systems. However, in many parliamentary systems lobbying can still be conducted by accessing a few key contacts in the bureaucracy and/or in a majority political party, involving relatively minimal resources. In contrast, as noted above, in the United States it is increasingly important to carry on a lobbying effort on many fronts and this requires substantial resources. Furthermore, evidence shows that while shoestring operations can *occasionally* be successful, those groups and interests with the most resources are usually the most successful (Thomas and Hrebenar, 2004: 117–121).

Yet resources by themselves are not sufficient. They need to be organized and oriented for lobbying purposes. Thus, one essential resource among a group's assets is political entrepreneurial skill (Salisbury, 1969). Again, while this asset is important in all interest-group systems, it is less important when there are fewer resources that need to be marshaled.

Finally, the clash between the individualistic ethos of working to get what one wants from government and the moralistic ethic that opposes unfettered power, and particularly corruption in politics, has led, as also noted earlier, to extensive regulation of lobbying in the United States. More precisely, this is *monitoring*—attempting to provide public disclosure on who is lobbying whom and on what issue—rather than *regulation*—restricting who can lobby and how and on what they can spend their money. This is because the "right to petition government" provision of the First Amendment to the US constitution protects the right to lobby. Furthermore, evidence suggests that these lobby laws do not level the political playing field in terms of power but do provide public disclosure (Thomas, 1998).

The lessons to be learned from the existence of these lobby laws for academics and students is that they are evidence of a unique lobbying environment in American politics that does not exist in other democracies. Plus, these laws constrain the actions of lobbyists and public officials alike even if they do not ultimately affect which groups are powerful and which ones are not. For the practitioner, particularly the non-American, these laws, which now exist in all fifty states and in some big cities like New York and Los Angeles as well as at the federal level in Washington, DC, mean that one needs to check their requirements and restrictions before lobbying in a particular political jurisdiction.

## THE US LOBBYING INDUSTRY: A VERY SHORT HISTORY

The origins of the lobbying business in the United States go back to at least the early nineteenth century at both the state and the federal level, and received a major boost in the Civil War (1861–1865) when merchants peddling everything from food to clothes to arms waylaid public officials as they left their lodgings in Washington, DC, to go to work (Thomas, 2004b: 151). As noted above, by the early twentieth century a small lobbying industry was established in Washington, DC, and by the 1940s in the more populated states like California, Massachusetts, and New York.

Down to the early 1960s, however, the lobbying industry in Washington, DC, and in most states was very small by today's standards. One major reason for this was that state governments and to some extent the federal government clung to a *laissez-faire* philosophy. Most lobbying involved killing proposals (defensive lobbying), the range of groups operating was narrow, consisting mainly of business, agriculture, labor, education, and governments (local governments and special districts) at both the state and the federal level, with a substantial presence by the foreign lobby in Washington, DC. Even in Washington, DC, the lobbying community was fairly small, with relatively few contract lobbyists. In some of the less populated states like Wyoming and Alaska there were less than a dozen contract lobbyists.

Several factors worked to change this situation and to expand the lobbying industry to enable its present characteristics. One theory sees the major changes as resulting from factors external to the lobbying industry, what could be termed—but rarely are by scholars— *demand-side factors*. Another explanation, the so-called *supply-side theory*, sees the expansion as being partly generated from within the lobbying business itself. The accurate explanation likely combines the two theories, though the supply-side explanation is more recent and less widely accepted. In Chapter 19 Burdett Loomis provides a good explanation of the supply-side theory. Here we outline the external factors.

These included the major increase of government activity following President Lyndon Johnson's Great Society program of the 1960s; the civil rights, women's, Native American (American Indian), and environmental movements that also got their major boost in the 1960s; and the Vietnam War. In addition, a more educated and discerning public began to see political parties as increasingly ineffective and turned to interest groups for solutions to problems. This confluence of circumstances as government came to affect the lives of more and more people and organizations and others turned to government to solve social and economic problems, produced a major expansion in interest-group activity and the lobbying industry in the 1970s, 1980s, and 1990s. Not only did the number of lobbying groups expand considerably but previously underrepresented and unrepresented groups, such as those for the poor and handicapped, and a plethora of others, gave the make-up of the so-called *group universe* a new look. The lobbying community expanded considerably and increased in professionalism at the federal and state levels and even in some large cities. The range of strategies and tactics was broadened, with increasing use of grassroots lobbying, public relations campaigns, and particularly the use of PACs, whose numbers increased from less than 100 in 1970 to nearly 4,000 in 1998, giving over $200 million to candidates in that year (Federal Election Commission, 1999; Hrebenar, 2004).

## THE LOBBYING INDUSTRY TODAY

In the early twenty-first century the lobbying industry is a major business in Washington, DC, and all fifty state capitals and has an important presence in many large cities. In Chapter 19, Loomis covers elements of the lobbying business in Washington, DC. So here we will provide an overview of the components of the business at both the federal and state levels to provide a context in which to understand the specifics of the next chapter and to make a contrast between Washington, DC, and the states.

### The Lobbying Business in Washington, DC

The developments of the last three decades have produced a thriving lobbying industry in Washington, DC, which is probably by far the largest such industry in the world. Exhibit 18.2 lists the major components of this industry. Here we make some brief comments about the three major components: interest groups and interests; lobbyists and lobbying firms; and support services.

### Interest Groups and Interests

As Loomis points out in Chapter 19, no one knows for certain how many interest groups operate in Washington, DC. Probably a good estimate of the formal organizations (those whose lobbyists are required to register) is between 15,000 and 20,000. These run the gamut from long-established interests such as businesses and business associations from Microsoft to the National Association of Manufacturers (NAM) to snack food producers, to trade unions, to many agricultural groups, and education interests (like universities). This includes a plethora of so-called *new interests* (those that have come to prominence in the past thirty years) like minority groups (women, African-Americans, and many other ethnic and racial groups). There are so-called *public interest groups* like environmentalists (such as the Sierra Club) and good government groups (such as Common Cause and the League of Women

Voters). Then there are cause groups such as pro-life and pro-choice groups, animal rights groups (such as People for the Ethical Treatment of Animals (PETA)), and the National Rifle Association (NRA), one of the most powerful groups in the nation.

Added to these formal groups are several thousand various types of governments that lobby in Washington. There are over 150 governments from around the world and many organizations such as the Organization of American States (OAS) and the United Nations (UN) that maintain offices. Over thirty states (including New York, California, and Alaska) have offices in Washington, as do many large cities. Federal agencies also work the halls of Congress and other departments to promote and protect their interests. See Nownes *et al.* (2004) for more specific details on the so-called group universe at the federal and state level.

### Lobbyists and Lobbying Firms

We explain the five types of lobbyists in Appendix 18. 2. Again, it is impossible to determine the exact number of lobbyists because many (those working for governments who lobby as part of their job) do not have to register. Many contract lobbyists form lobbying firms many of which specialize in particular policy areas such as health care, agriculture, and transportation (and even more specialized areas). As Loomis points out, many contract lobbyists (known as Washington representatives) are former Members of Congress or members of presidential staffs. What they sell to their clients is knowledge of how the system works and access to key policy makers. In-house lobbyists, on the other hand, are more likely to have come up through their profession or business (medicine, railroads, education, etc.) and next to legislative liaisons from government agencies likely constitute the largest segment of the lobbying community in Washington (Nownes, 2004a).

### Support Services

All these groups and organizations and their lobbyists need all sorts of aid to get the edge in the increasingly competitive lobbying game in Washington. As a result, what might be called a *lobbying support industry* has grown up to provide many ancillary services. These include legal advice, and many lobbying firms combine law and lobbying. There are firms to help organize lobbying campaigns (including those that will create a grassroots campaign—so-called *astroturf*, after the artificial surface developed in place of grass). Many public relations firms specialize in lobby campaign public relations and media campaigns. The last twenty years have seen a rise in the multi service lobbying firm: one that provides a one-stop-shopping option including lobbying and all the support services.

### The Lobbying Business in the States Compared with Washington, DC

For similar reasons that have produced a major expansion in the lobbying business in Washington, DC, the past thirty years have seen a major expansion in the lobbying business in all fifty states. There are, however, some major differences between the lobbying scene in the nation's capital and in the state capitals.

First, the scale of the business varies widely. At one end of the scale is California, with its 33 million people, as well as states like New York, Florida, and Texas, also with large populations, and at the other end is Wyoming, with only 500,000, and states like Alaska, Montana, and Vermont. The former have populations larger than most countries and very diversified economies so that a wide range of interests are represented in their capitals. The latter group has largely natural resource extraction economies and thus a narrower range of interests operating in their halls of government.

Second, size obviously affects the number of groups operating, the size of the lobbying community, and the support services available. California, for example, is a mini-Washington, DC, in all respects (with the exception of a large foreign lobby contingent) whereas Wyoming has a much narrower range of groups operating, only a few dozen contract lobbyists, and a few lobby support services. Major interests that need these services in states like Wyoming often go to Washington, DC, or to the larger states to get them.

Third, all this said, the actual size and extent of the lobbying community are hard to determine with accuracy across the states, and comparisons are difficult. One method used to make comparisons is to use lobby registration lists that are now available in all fifty states. However, these vary widely in their inclusiveness and generally do not require government departments and local governments (if they use in-house lobbyists) to register. For example, Florida and Arizona have much more inclusive registration laws than California or New York and the false impression that is conveyed by their lobby lists is that the former have larger lobbying industries than the latter. This is certainly not the case.

Finally, in the highly populated states, of necessity, strategies and tactics are much more developed and more fully utilized, including PAC contributions and the use of public relations and media campaigns. This is because, similar to Washington, DC, competition for the ear of policy makers is more intense. In contrast, in many less populated states a sort of "friends and neighbors" situation exists between public officials on the one hand and lobbyists and the public on the other. In this situation access to policy makers is much easier and the need to mount major million-dollar efforts using a broad range of tactics is less necessary.

## WHAT DETERMINES LOBBYING STRATEGIES AND TACTICS?

Looked at in terms of the distinction made in the introduction between the activities and processes of lobbying, in essence, strategy and tactics involve working to adapt the universal activities of lobbying to the particular processes of the system at hand. Making this adaptation is essential to the success of a lobbying effort. As noted in the introduction the lobbying strategies and tactics used in the United States are more extensive and more highly developed than in any other political system. They have been alluded to in various parts of this chapter and are also considered by Loomis in the next chapter. In addition, a comprehensive overview

of the range of strategies and tactics—both direct and indirect—used in the United States is provided in Thomas (2004a: Chapter 7). Here we explain what shapes the use of strategies and tactics in the United States for those coming to the study or practice of lobbying for the first time.

The most important point to make is that there is no *one way* to lobby on all issues at all times and across different jurisdictions (Washington and the states). The choice of a lobbying strategy and the tactics used to implement it depend on a host of factors, including the following:

1   Is it a defensive or promotional campaign or a maintenance situation (simply keeping good contacts for the time when an issue arises)? Each will dictate a different strategy and tactics.

2   Is the group or organization a well known, insider group with many contacts in government? If so, it will not need to work as much on getting access as will a new or little known organization.

3   What is the nature of the issue? Is it a highly technical issue not likely to be much in public view, such as changing a regulation (e.g. state licensing of architects) or is it an issue likely to have a high profile with the public (e.g. decriminalizing marijuana)? The former will require a narrow strategy involving the appropriate government department and perhaps the legislature. The latter will involve a much broader strategy involving direct and indirect lobbying tactics.

4   While a whole range of tactics is available to all groups (depending on their available resources) the broader the range of tactics used means that the lobbyist and group leader will have less control over the outcome. Thus, in general, the fewer individuals and elements involved in a strategy the better. For example, grassroots lobbying and media campaigns can backfire on a group if not handled properly or if circumstances change.

5   All this points to the fact that the best organized and orchestrated campaigns stand the greatest chance of success. Spontaneous

campaigns, say of a local group to get a traffic light installed where accidents occur, may work now and again, but the lack of organization of such groups often leads to their failure.

6   Increasingly, lobbying involves an IGR strategy if the federal and state governments (and even local government) have authority in an issue area such as education, including college and university education. Across the fifty states there are cultural norms that make lobbying in one state slightly different from lobbying in another. For example, a California legislator would expect a major grassroots and perhaps public relations effort on many issues whereas a North Dakota legislator would likely view this as inappropriate.

What all this means is that, even in the highly sophisticated lobbying environment of the United States with all its well tried strategies and tactics, lobbying is still an art and not a science—perhaps more so. Furthermore, the time-honored tactic of personal contacts—a lobbyist, group official, or member convincing a public official one-on-one—is still a key, and in most campaigns *the* key, tactic. This fundamental *activity* of lobbying will likely always remain as long as politics is about influence. In the United States it is simply that the competition for influence has spawned all the sophisticated, indirect *processes* of lobbying, all of which are ultimately aimed at increasing the effectiveness of one-on-one contact. Thus, the skill in lobbying is to choose among the available strategies and tactics and combine these skillfully to convince policy makers of the issue at hand. Once again, this is where the lobbyist and group leader as political entrepreneur is at a premium.

## GROUP POWER AND EFFECTIVENESS

One of the most fascinating questions about interest groups and lobbying is that relating to power or "clout" or "juice" as it's often called by practitioners. Yet this question of what constitutes power and how to acquire it and maintain it is one of the most elusive in the lobbying business. Practitioners often have a simple answer to this question: power depends on money and connections. And as we'll see below this may be in part the case. However, interest group scholars are much more cautious in their explanation of power, citing the fact that there are many variables involved. For a succinct explanation of the issues concerned and approaches to assessing interest-group power see Thomas (2004c: 192–196).

Much of the research on what constitutes group power in the United States has been conducted on the American states and not at the federal level. In this section we draw upon this research to briefly explain the three types of interest-group power as identified by political scientists, the factors seen as shaping group power, and list the most effective groups at the state level since the early 1980s.

### Single Group Power

This is the ability of a group or coalition to achieve its goals as it defines them. It is the only important assessment of the degree of success and is an internal evaluation by the group. Some groups can be very successful in achieving their goals but keep a low profile so as not to be singled out as powerful by public officials. This could be the case for several reasons. It might be because the group is only occasionally active when it has an issue, such as an association of vending machine operators working to defeat restrictions on the placing of vending machines in high schools. It could be an *ad hoc* group coming together on one issue and then disbanding when success is achieved, such as a coalition to defeat an antismoking ballot initiative in Oregon. Or it could be that the group's issue is far from public view and of minor public concern, such as working with a department to write regulations, as might be the case with hairdressers interested in the occupational licensing process. Rarely are hairdressers seen as among the most effective groups in a state; but they may be among the most successful groups in achieving their limited goals. Many groups involved in the regulatory process are very successful because they have captured their area of concern (in other words, gotten control of policy making) through dependence of bureaucrats on their expertise. The last thing most of these groups would want is public attention and to be singled out as an "effective group."

## Overall Interest Power

This is the aspect of group power that most interests the American press and the public, who are less concerned about the minutiae of government and more with high-profile issues and questions such as "Who is running the country or the state?" or "Who has real political clout?" Whereas the only important assessment of single group power is internal to a group, overall interest power is based on external assessments of informed observers. The assessment in this chapter uses the Hrebenar-Thomas study, which combined quantitative and qualitative techniques employing the first two

methods. This study has assessed overall interest power in all fifty states on five occasions (1985, 1989, 1994, 1998, and 2002). Exhibit 18.2 provides a composite of this time series assessment to present a list of the most effective interests since the early 1980s.

However, we must be clear on exactly what these assessments do and do not reveal. They reveal the interests that are viewed by policy makers and political observers as the most effective in the states over a five-year period prior to the assessment. For this reason they tend to be the most active groups or those with a high profile. The assessment should not be viewed as indicating that the groups near the top of the list always win or even win most of the time; in fact, they may win less often than some low-profile groups not listed. The place of an individual interest in the ranking, however, does indicate its level of importance as a player in state politics over the period assessed and the extent of its ability to bring political clout to bear on the issues that affect it.

---

### Exhibit 18.2 The Overall Most Effective Interests in the Fifty States Since the Early 1980s (grouped by category and more or less in rank order)

1    **Consistently the two most effective interests**
Schoolteachers' organizations (predominantly the National Education Association)
General business organizations

2    **Consistently among the ten most effective**
Utility companies and associations (telecommunications, cable television)
Lawyers (predominantly trial lawyers and state bar associations)
Hospital associations/Health care organizations
Insurance: general and medical (companies and associations)
General local government organizations (municipal leagues, county organizations, etc.)
Manufacturers (companies and associations)
General farm organizations (mainly state farm bureaus)
Physicians/state medical associations

3    **Consistently ranked among the ten to twenty most effective interests**
State and local government employees (other than teachers)
Traditional labor associations (predominantly the AFL-CIO)

Bankers' associations (includes savings and loan associations)
Contractors/builders/developers
Realtors' associations
K-12 education interests (other than teachers)
Gaming interests (race tracks/casinos/lotteries)
Individual banks and financial institutions
Environmentalists
Universities and colleges (institutions and personnel)

4 **Consistently ranked twentieth to thirtieth in effectiveness**
Truckers and private transport interests (excluding railroads)
Individual cities and towns
State agencies
Agricultural commodity organizations (stockgrowers, grain growers, etc.)
Taxpayers' interest groups
Retailers (companies and trade associations)
Individual traditional labor unions (Teamsters, UAW, etc.)
Sportsmen/hunting and fishing (includes anti-gun control groups)
Liquor, wine and beer interests
Religious interests (Churches and religious right)

5 **Usually ranked among the thirtieth to fortieth range**
Mining companies and associations
Forest product companies and associations
Tourist/hospitality interests
Oil and gas (companies and associations)
Senior citizens
Public interest/good government groups
Railroads
Tobacco interests
Pro-life/pro-choice groups
Criminal justice lobby
Women and minorities
Miscellaneous social issue groups (anti-drunk driving, anti-smoking, anti-poverty groups, etc.)

*Source* Compiled by the author from Thomas and Hrebenar (2004).

Comparing the listings over the years, what comes though most of all is the relative stability of both the types of groups that make the list and their rankings. When changes in ranking do occur, or new groups appear on the list, the changes appear to be very much influenced by the prominence of issues at the time and partisan control and the ideological persuasion of state government. Gaming, health, and insurance interests, for example, have steadily increased in perceived influence as lotteries and casinos, health care, and tort reform became issues in the states. Environmental and other liberal causes, as well as senior citizens' groups, wax and wane in strength according to who is in power in government. This is also true (though to a lesser extent) of business and development interests, which have seen a boost in their rankings since the Republican Party successes in the elections of 1994.

Today, as over the past twenty-five years, two interests far outstrip any others in terms of their perceived influence and continue to vie for the top ranking. These are general business organizations (mainly state chambers of commerce) and schoolteachers (mainly state affiliates of the National Education Association (NEA)). Utility interests have also firmly established themselves in third place on a consistent basis. The top twelve interests as listed in 2002 are essentially those that were listed as most effective in the early 1980s. Another interesting fact about these top twelve interests is that they are the only ones mentioned as effective in more than half the states. So despite the so-called "advocacy explosion" of the last thirty years it has not been paralleled by a broad range of groups being effective in most states. It is also worth noting that (again despite the advocacy explosion) there is no public interest or citizen group ranked in the top twenty interests. This top twenty (and, indeed, the entire listing) has always been dominated by economic interests, especially business and labor (including the professions). Local governments, universities, and school boards are the only interests approaching what might be considered the broad public interest. In short, the five surveys confirm what we have known since the first study of the power of state interest groups, conducted by Zeller (1954):

business and the professions remain the most effective interests in the states (as they do in Washington, DC).

This overview of group power in the states also helps us clarify a common misunderstanding among those not versed in the politics of interest groups. This is that the public visibility of a group should not be assumed to mean that it is effective or influential. Visibility is one thing, effectiveness is quite another. Many groups, such as student organizations, often have a high profile but may not be particularly effective, if at all. On the other hand, many groups with no high profile, such as many of those that worked to affect the regulatory process—like dentists and architects—may be very successful but may have a very low public profile. This, as we pointed out above, may be an important aspect of their success.

What do we know about what determines both single group and overall interest group power? Based upon Thomas and Hrebenar (2004) and other work (for example, Stone et al., 1986: 196–208), Exhibit 18.3 sets out the twelve major elements. All twelve are important but the three most important practical factors that Thomas and Hrebenar single out are the degree of necessity of the group to public officials, good lobbyist-policy maker relations, and whether the group's lobbying focus is defensive or promotional.

---

### Exhibit 18.3 Twelve Factors Determining the Influence of Individual Interest Groups and Interests

1   *The degree of necessity of group services and resources to public officials.* The more government needs the group the greater the group's leverage will be to use sanctions against government to achieve its goals, through strikes, withholding cooperation, withholding campaign contributions, etc. This is one of the bases of business power in the United States.
2   *Lobbyist-policy maker relations.* The closeness and trust between lobbyists and policy makers, as well as public officials' dependence on lobbyists and their groups for information, campaign contributions, etc. The more skillful the lobbyist the more successful the group is likely to be. It is personal contact and building of trust and credibility that are often key to lobbying success.

3    *Whether the group's lobbying focus is primarily defensive or promotional.* Because it is much easier to stop than to promote a policy, the "advantage of the defense" gives groups like business, working to prevent tax hikes and regulations, an advantage over groups such as environmentalists that are attempting to promote policies.

4    *The extent and strength of group opposition.* Obviously, the greater the opposition to a group or its cause the more difficult it will be to achieve its goals. Some groups are natural political enemies, such as environmentalists and developers, and in many cases business and labor. Other interests such as dentists and those advocating stricter laws against domestic violence and child abuse have little opposition.

5    *Legitimacy of the group and its demands: how these are perceived by the public and public officials.* A group must be viewed as legitimate, but there are degrees of legitimacy and the acceptance of groups and their demands. Most groups advocating violence are seen as illegitimate. Others, like associations of doctors and groups advocating against drunk drivers (see the case study) are given high levels of legitimacy. Still others, like labor unions, are viewed as legitimate but their demands may sometimes be viewed unfavorably.

6    *Group financial resources.* While money by itself does not translate into political power, it is the most liquid of all resources and can be used to hire staff and lobbyists, make campaign contributions, mount media and grassroots campaigns, and so on.

7    *Political, organizational, and managerial skill of group leaders.* Lobbying campaigns in any society require organization and knowledge of the political process, particularly its power points. Having group leaders with these skills–political entrepreneurial skills—is an essential element of success.

8    *Size and geographic distribution of group membership.* Generally, the larger and more geographically spread the membership of an organization, the more pressure it can bring to bear on more public officials.

9    *Potential for the group to enter into coalitions with other groups.* When a group is able to join forces with another group, or groups, it can potentially overcome its deficiencies in one or more of the previous eight factors. There is an increasing need to form coalitions as competition between groups for access to key policy makers and the ability to influence their actions intensifies due to more and more groups lobbying.

10   *Extent of group autonomy in political strategizing.* While the flexibility to join or leave a coalition can enhance a group's power, the less a group is in charge of strategy and tactics, the more its potential for achieving its goals may be compromised or not addressed at all. This is why many businesses and local governments have begun to lobby on their own in recent years while often remaining members of their broader trade or local government association.

11   *Political cohesiveness of the membership.* The more united the group the more likely it is to have its issue dealt with. Public officials are unlikely to take action if they see a group is divided.

12   *Timing and the political climate.* There are times when it is politically propitious to act on an issue and times when it is not. Making judgments on this is part of the skill— the political entrepreneurship—of lobbyists and group leaders. For example, it would not be politically wise to propose major increases in funding for a program in times of declining government revenues.

*Source* Developed by the author from Thomas and Hrebenar (2004).

## Interest-group System Power in the States

Whereas the power of single groups and the overall impact of individual interests are observed in their political mobilization and their ability to achieve their goals, group system power is much more abstract. Group system power is the array of groups and organizations, both formal and informal, and the lobbyists who represent them working to affect public policy within a state. The idea of a state interest group system is an abstraction because even though there are relations between various groups and lobbyists representing various interests, never do all the groups in a political system act in concert to achieve one goal. However, for analytical purposes, as one element of the socio-economic and political life of the state, it is the characteristics of the interest group system in a state—size, development, composition, methods of operating, and so on—in its relationship to the economy, society, and government that is particularly important in determining such things as the polilitical power structure, what public policies are pursued and which ones are not, and the extent of representation and democracy.

It is also even more difficult to assess than overall interest power because of the multiplicity of variables involved. The method most frequently used has been to garner the observations of political practitioners and political scientists regarding the importance of the players involved in the policy-making process in each state (Morehouse, 1981: 107–117; Zeller, 1954: Chapter 13 and 190–193). This was the method used over the past twenty years by Thomas and Hrebenar, though this study fine-tuned the means of categorizing and understanding changes in group system power.

## TWO CASE STUDIES

Many of the points and explanations related above can be illustrated by two contrasting case studies. The first, the failure of the Clinton health care plan, shows how even a presidential initiative can be roundly defeated given the nature of the US system. The second, Mothers Against Drunk Driving (MADD), is an example of a highly successful grassroots organization that has, of necessity, become a type of establishment group in recent years.

## Defeat of the Clinton Health Care Plan

The Clinton administration's Health Security Act of 1993 was a response to a chronic decreasing ability of Americans to afford the steadily increasing cost of health care. Its central purpose was to insure that all Americans were covered for health care that was to be underwritten by the federal government. Health insurance in America is largely dependent upon employment. In response to rising health care costs employers were either passing the costs on to employees or cutting or eliminating employee health benefits. Americans were so concerned about this trend that by 1990 public support for health care reform was at a forty-year high, and Americans overwhelmingly felt that insurance should be available to everyone. Such a reform had been a major plank in Bill Clinton's successful bid for the presidency in 1992.

The details of the course of this attempted reform and its failure are numerous and complex and much has been written on the subject (see, for example, Starr, 1995; Cigler and Loomis, 1995: 398–404). For our purposes, the gist of the story is as follows.

Although there was initially much public support this was not fully exploited and eventually was dissipated. The plan itself was very complex and not easily understood by the public, providing its opponents with ways to undermine public support. President Clinton did not do good groundwork with the major decision makers in Congress (especially the Republican Majority Leader, Bob Dole of Kansas), or with some of the major health interests that would be affected. And the President put his wife, Hilary Clinton, in charge of the effort, which did not sit well with many Washington insiders, as she was a political newcomer; plus she had a very steep learning curve on how things worked in Washington.

Major health interest groups were cool towards the plan (such as the American Medical Association (AMA)) or opposed it (such as the medical insurance and pharmaceutical industries and their trade associations). These had major allies in Congress, particularly Senator Dole. Plus, they exploited the complexities and uncertainties in the program through a masterly public relations campaign, including what has become the classic interest-group public relations ad campaign in the history of US interest-group activity. This was the "Harry and Louise" ad, where a middle-class couple, sat at their dinner table, talked about the problems they saw in the Clinton plan (Hrebenar, 1997: 123–124).

This opposition, even the concerns of Harry and Louise, would likely not have been so effective if the forces for the proposal had been united and proactive. But they were not. In this regard, Cigler and Loomis (1995: 402–403) write that while there is general agreement among most Americans and many interests that American health care, especially in its coverage and financing, requires substantial modification, this agreement is a "negative consensus" in which varying interests "have defined themselves by what they *oppose* rather than what they support." For example, the National Federation of Independent Businesses (NFIB) and the Catholic Church would like to see coverage extended to the working poor but the NFIB balked at requiring all employers to either provide health insurance or pay a tax penalty, and the Catholic Church could not reconcile itself with publicly funded abortions. Plus, as Paul Starr, former health care policy advisor to President Clinton, adds, by calling for major cuts in future Medicare spending growth, the plan lost the support of the hospital industry. For the same reason, the American Association of Retired Persons (AARP) decided not to endorse a specific plan until it was too late.

In this situation the "advantage of the defense" won the day—a massive organized effort by big-money interests to stop the plan, with little opposition from its ever fracturing alliance of supporters. So here was a campaign on the part of the Clinton administration that ignored many of the key rules of the lobby organization. The campaign failed to: consult key players beforehand; orchestrate and coalesce the forces in favor of the plan, including the public; become familiar with the intricacies of the politics of the policy area at hand (in this case health care); follow through on the lobby effort, among other things. As Paul Starr laments: "The administration had gone to the trouble of writing a bill and then left it like a foundling on the doorstep of Congress." The administration foolishly assumed that public support would insure some kind of plan. They were wrong.

## The Success of MADD

Mothers Against Drunk Driving was founded in 1980 by Candy Lightner, whose thirteen-year-old daughter had been killed by a hit-and-run driver. The driver had four previous convictions for drunk driving but had served only forty eight hours in jail, and had been arrested for a previous hit-and-run offense just two days earlier. Enraged at the laxity of the justice system and the loss of her daughter, Candy Lightner became obsessed with reforming the US drunk driving laws.

Lightner lobbied Governor Jerry Brown of California to create a state commission for studying drunk driving. After several months of daily visits to the governor's office, Brown formed the commission and made her its first member. In 1982 President Ronald Reagan asked Lightner to serve on the National Commission on Drunk Driving. By 1984 MADD had successfully lobbied Congress to raise the national legal drinking age to twenty one, a change said to save approximately 800 lives annually (Ness, 2000: 524–25).

Then MADD turned its attention to the states. It was successful in all fifty states in raising the drinking age to twenty one and lowering the legal blood alcohol limit to 0.08 or below. MADD also increased penalties for drunk driving, including: in many states, a mandatory short stay at a detention center (three to five days); and prison sentences, confiscation of vehicles and loss of a driver's license for many years for subsequent offences. In 2004 MADD had more than 600 chapters across the United States, and in 2003 reported an annual budget of $47 million (www.MADD.org).

The initial and continuing success of MADD is due to several factors rarely duplicated in American politics. First, it represented a highly emotional issue to which all Americans could relate and which it was difficult for any public official to oppose. It had a charismatic and tireless spokesperson in Candy Lightner, who illustrates the entrepreneur element related above. Probably the most important factor is that MADD cultivated strong support from key public officials. Clearly, the initial backing of Governor Jerry Brown and later of President Reagan gave the organization's goals a tremendous boost (www.MADD.org). This support helped MADD overcome the strong opposition first mounted against it by the alcohol and hospitality industries. All these factors enabled MADD to overcome the "advantage of the defense" possessed by its potential opponents.

Despite these phenomenal successes, MADD has had its internal problems and conflicts over policy as it has transformed from a grassroots organization to, in effect, an establishment interest group (including the departure of Candy Lightner). Herein lies another important lesson about group development and survival (and probably effectiveness) in US politics (and likely any country's politics). This is that often grassroots, so-called "public interest", groups cannot survive on a long-term basis as a spontaneous operation; they must develop a permanent and sophisticated organization and employ full-time and professional staff. This is simply a reality of the lobbying business in a competitive and increasingly sophisticated environment as exists in the United States.

## FUTURE DIRECTIONS OF LOBBYING IN THE UNITED STATES

What developments might be expected in the US lobbying industry in the future, say over the next twenty to thirty years? Based upon the characteristics of the system and its recent developments we can make some observations about these and their implications for both the study of interest groups and the practice of lobbying. These observations can be supplemented by the comments made by Loomis in Chapter 19. Several developments will occur in this constantly dynamic system. Seven, however, are particularly likely and worthy of note.

1  The system will continue to expand and to fragment as more and more groups and organizations (including a plethora of governments at all levels) see the need to have a presence in Washington, their state capital, city hall, and county headquarters.

2  This expansion will not be due only to new interests entering the political fray. If past trends continue, much will be a result of groups and organizations and interests beginning to lobby on their own as well as continuing to belong to a trade association or other umbrella lobbying group. This will be primarily because the specific needs of many groups and organizations cannot be entirely met by an umbrella lobbying organization.

3  The states and localities (cities, towns, counties, and special districts) will become increasingly important in policy making as they take on more responsibility, in part because the federal government will push more responsibility on to the fifty states and the tens of thousands of local government jurisdictions.

4  As there is more and more activity at the state and local level in areas in which responsibility is shared with the federal government, IGR lobbying is likely to expand considerably. There are already major examples of this with businesses like the tobacco industry and the alcohol beverage industry as well as public interest groups such as environmentalists and MADD, as we saw above.

5  Issue areas are likely to become less and less compartmentalized. That is, issues like health care will continue to affect more and more organizations and not just health groups such as doctors and hospitals. This

is also true of many other issues such as that of the environment which affect not only businesses as these impact the environment, but agricultural interests, trade unions (concerned about employment in environmentally sensitive industries), and so on. In short, many issues have a kind of political ripple affect.

6  Because of all five points noted above, the growth in coalition building between groups is likely to continue and reach new levels. A coalition is fast becoming the only way to mount a lobbying effort that stands a chance of success, given the increased competition among groups for the ear of policy makers. Most of these coalitions will be *ad hoc*, on one issue only, and will disband after the issue is won or lost. Increasingly, too, these coalitions include strange bedfellows such as trade unions and business groups, animal rights groups and pharmaceutical companies, among many others, because these coalitions suit a certain need at a certain time.

7  Finally, we can certainly expect that the entrepreneurial spirit will rise to meet the challenge of these developments by groups and lobbyists refining old techniques and developing new ones to be competitive in the lobbying game. This will include increased use of the Internet, more and more use of indirect lobbying techniques such as the media, and getting group members to help candidates get elected. Most of all, there will be an increased premium on organizing and orchestrating lobby campaigns as a means to try and outmaneuver the opposition and competition.

Given these likely developments, what are their implications? The following five points appear to be particularly significant.

1  To pick up on the last point above, organization and orchestration of a campaign will be key. An even greater premium will be placed upon organization than ever before.

2  While it always depends on the particular issue at hand, the overall trend is likely to be more and more lobbying campaigns involving multifaceted strategies—legislative, executive, the courts, grassroots, public relations, maybe also including IGR lobbying, etc.—to try and outdo the opposition and competition.

3  The major implication of the first two points is, of course, the need for increased resources. So here lies a paradox: while increased involvement of groups and interests in the US lobbying process has meant that more people and causes are represented it has made success even more dependent on resources than in the past. Consequently, as research clearly shows, those with the resources and the experience will likely continue to be successful regardless of the merits of their cause or their need.

4  The ability to build coalitions, often with former foes, will also be at a premium.

5  Mainly for the practitioner (particularly those new to the US lobbying scene), it will become more and more important to use a lobbying firm or some other entity that can help a group or organization plan and campaign and work their way through the increasingly complicated processes and interconnections that characterize lobbying in the United States.

To return to the major theme of this chapter (the interplay of the processes and activities of lobbying), even though the *activities* of lobbying will remain relatively unchanged, the *processes* of lobbying in the United States are likely to become increasingly complex. Again, ironically (though understandable in terms of the development and sophistication of political systems), as the US lobbying scene becomes more and more inclusive in the number of people represented it is becoming less and less user-friendly to the citizen lobbyist and more and more geared to the professional lobbyist and group leaders.

## USEFUL SOURCES OF INFORMATION

For the American and non-American coming to study or participate in lobbying in the United States there are many useful sources to supplement the overview provided in this chapter. Here we list some main sources in five categories: (1) academic works; (2) popular writing and "how to" books; (3) directories; (4) federal, state, and local government sources; and (5) other sources, including the Internet. Before consulting these, however, for those who need to get more of an understanding of the similarities and differences between the US and other Western political systems, a very useful source is *Only in America* (Wilson, 1998).

## Academic Sources

The academic literature on US interests groups is vast, consisting of well over a thousand books and articles and several thousand academic conference papers. Much of this literature, however, is highly academic and of little use to the beginner and to the practitioner. Useful overviews of the writing on US groups—both academic and popular—can be found in Nownes (2004) and Thomas (2004a: Chapter 6). Very readable introductory texts on federal interest-group activity are Berry (1997), Hrebenar (1997), Mahood (2000), and Nownes (2001). On interest groups at the state level, the best overview is Thomas and Hrebenar (2004) and on state lobbyists Rosenthal (2001). On lobbying in cities and towns see Christensen (1995: Chapter 10) and Schumaker (2004); and for IGR lobbying see Thomas (2004d). The subject of lobby regulation, knowledge of which is essential for practitioners but also for scholars, can be found in Thomas (1998). The most comprehensive overview of the academic literature on US interest groups is several chapters in *Research Guide to US and International Interest Groups* (Thomas, 2004, especially Chapters 2, 5, 6, 8, 9, and 14).

## Popular and "How to" Books

These fall into two categories. First are books written by journalists, lobbyists and others which attempt to convey the way that interest groups and lobbyists operate in American politics. But sometimes these are simply exposés which are entertaining but not of practical value. The second category is "how to" books

which attempt to inform on how to organize and execute a lobbying campaign.

Among the more objective books in the first category are *The Lobbyists* (Birnbaum, 1992), *The Power Game: How Washington Works* (Smith, 1988), and *Washington on $10 million a Day* (Silverstein, 1999). In the "how to" category *Lobbying Congress: How the System Works* (Wolpe and Levine, 1996) and *The Citizen's Guide to Lobbying Congress* (deKieffer, 1997) deal with lobbying at the federal level; and *Guide to State Legislative Lobbying* (Guyer and Guyer, 2000) and *In Our Own Interest* (Smith, 1979) deal with lobbying at the state level.

## Directories of Interest Groups and Lobbyists

There are numerous reference sources that list organizations, lobbyists, and lobbying firms. Most of these focus on the lobbying business in Washington, DC, but a few cover the states. It is always important to get the latest edition of these publications; though many cease publication after a few years.

The most comprehensive directories are the annual *Encyclopedia of Associations* (2004), containing information on the vast majority of membership organizations in the United States with national offices, and *Encyclopedia of Associations: Regional, State, and Local Organizations* (2001). For more specific details on over 300 major interest groups in the United States see *Encyclopedia of Interest Groups and Lobbyists in the United States* (Ness, 2000). Several other publications contain information on specific types of groups, such as the *National Trade and Professional Associations of the United States* (2001), *Public Interest Profiles 2001–2002* (2002), which is an index of citizen groups, the *2001 National Directory of Corporate Public Affairs* (Steele, 2001), and the *Annual US Union Sourcebook* (2001).

The annual editions of *Washington Representatives* (2004) contain an extensive list of lobbyists active in Washington, DC, politics. They also contain information on what groups each individual listed represents, and how he/she can be contacted. Directories of state lobbyists are sometimes produced but, given the vast numbers of lobbyists in all fifty states, they often contain only a small number of lobbyists in a state and usually only contract lobbyists (for example, *State Contract Lobbyist Directory*, 1991). But see the next section for other sources on lobbyists and their clients.

### Federal, State, and Local Government Sources

These governments are very valuable sources of information and of data for scholars and practitioners alike. The federal Restrictions of Lobbying Act of 1995 requires all lobbyists to register with the Clerk of the House of Representatives and the Secretary of the Senate, and this information is available to the public. The Federal Election Commission (FEC) keeps records on PAC contributions and other campaign information. Another important government source to consult, especially for practitioners involved with non-profit organizations, is the US Internal Revenue Code (IRC). The key section here is 501(c) which restricts expenditures on lobbying for certain non-profit organizations.

Because every state requires that lobbyists and interest groups register (though the criteria of who must register vary across states), the states are excellent sources of information on groups and their representatives. Most states publish annual—sometimes quarterly—lists of registered lobbyists and organizations. Some publish extensive data on PAC contributions, conflict of interest information, and so on. These lists are available to the public either free or for a small fee and increasingly these days on the Internet. Two other useful sources on state lobby and related laws are COGEL (Council on Governmental Ethics Laws) at www.cogel.org on the Internet; and *Lobbying, PACs, and Campaign Finance Fifty State Handbook* (2002).

### Other Sources and the Internet

There are many other useful sources of information available to the student and practitioner. We will mention just three of them here.

First, there are seminars and even certificate programs for those interested in learning the practicalities of lobbying and lobby campaign organizing. For example, George Washington University in Washington, DC, has a certificate program in this field. The University of Utah's Hinckley Institute of Politics runs seminars on lobbying. And almost every state has some public or private organization that puts on similar seminars and workshops, as do several universities and private organizations in Washington, DC.

Second, there are several magazines and other weekly, monthly, plus occasional publications that contain valuable articles on interest groups and lobbying. These include: *Campaigns and Elections, Governing, Influence,* and *Public Integrity*. The Washington, DC, publisher, Congressional Quarterly Press (www.cqpress.com), the leading publisher of government directories, books, and magazines is a very valuable source of information on lobbying and interest groups for political practitioners as well as for students and scholars.

Finally, a tremendous amount of material is available on the Internet and it is expanding daily. The federal and state interest group, lobbyist, and PAC data explained above are now almost entirely available on the Net, as is information about lobbyists, and lobbying firms, magazines and lobbying courses and seminars. One simply needs to type in key words on a search engine like Google. Most interest groups have Web sites (home pages) and dozens more create sites every day. The typical group site contains basic information on group policies, goals, and membership, as well as details on how to contact and join the group.

See Nownes (2004: 35–37) and the next chapter of this book for more details on interest-group and lobbyist directories and other useful resource information.

### NOTE

1 See the next section regarding the use (more precisely, the non-use) of the term "public affairs" to refer to interest-group activity and lobbying in the United States.

# REFERENCES

*Annual US Union Sourcebook,* 16th edn (2001). West Orange, NJ: Industrial Relations & Information Services.

Benedict, Robert C. (2004). "Public Knowledge of and Attitudes toward Interest Groups and Lobbyists in the United States." Entry 6.7. in Thomas, *Research Guide,* cited below.

Berry, Jeffrey M. (1997). *The Interest Group Society,* 3rd edn. New York: Addison Wesley Longman.

Birnbaum, Jeffrey H. (1992). *The Lobbyists: How Influence Peddlers get their Way in Washington.* New York: Times Books.

Christensen, Terry (1995). *Local Politics: Governing at the Grassroots.* Belmont, CA: Wadsworth.

Cigler, Allan J., and Burdett A. Loomis (eds) (1995). *Interest Group Politics,* 4th edn. Washington, DC: Congressional Quarterly Press.

DeKieffer, Donald E. (1997). *The Citizen's Guide to Lobbying Congress.* Chicago: Chicago Review Press.

*Encyclopedia of Associations,* 39th edn (2003). Farmington Hills, MI: Gale Group.

*Encyclopedia of Associations: Regional, State and Local Organizations,* 12th edn (2001). Detroit: Gale Research.

Federal Election Commission (1999). "FEC Issues Semi-annual Federal PAC Count," July 20.

Guyer, Robert L., and Laura K. Guyer (2000). *Guide to State Legislative Lobbying.* Gainesville, FL: Engineering the Law.

Hrebenar, Ronald J. (1997). *Interest Group Politics in America,* 3rd edn. Armonk, NY: Sharpe.

Hrebenar, Ronald J. (2004). "Political Action Committees (PAC)." Entry 7.4. in Thomas, *Research Guide,* cited below.

*Lobbying, PACs, and Campaign Finance Fifty State Handbook* (2002) compiled by the State Capital Global Law Firm Group. Minneapolis, MN: West Publishing.

Mahood, H.R. (2000). *Interest Groups in American National Politics: An Overview.* Upper Saddle River, NJ: Prentice Hall.

Morehouse, Sarah MaCally (1981). *State Politics, Parties and Policy.* New York: Holt Rinehart & Winston.

*National Trade and Professional Associations of the United States, 2001,* 36th edn. Washington, DC: Columbia Books.

Ness, Immanuel (2000). *Encyclopedia of Interest Groups and Lobbyists in the United States,* 2 vols. Armonk, NY: Sharpe.

Nownes, Anthony J. (2001). *Pressure and Power: Organized Interests in American Politics.* Boston, MA: Houghton Mifflin.

Nownes, Anthony J. (2004a). "Lobbyists in Washington, DC and the American States." Entry 7.8. in Thomas, *Research Guide,* cited below.

Nownes, Anthony J. (2004b). "Sources of Information on Interest Groups in the American Political System: An Overview." Chapter 2 in Thomas, *Research Guide,* cited below.

Nownes, Anthony J., Frank R. Baumgartner, and Beth L. Leech (2004). "The Interest Group Universe in Washington, DC and the States." Entry 6.2. in Thomas, *Research Guide,* cited below.

Petracca, Mark P. (1992). *The Politics of Interests: Interest Groups Transformed.* Boulder, CO: Westview Press.

*Public Interest Profiles, 2001–2002* (2002). Washington, DC: Foundation for Public Affairs and Congressional Quarterly Press.

Rosenthal, Alan (2001). *The Third House: Lobbyists and Lobbying in the States,* 2nd edn. Washington, DC: Congressional Quarterly Press.

Salisbury, Robert H. (1969). "An Exchange Theory of Interest Groups." *Midwest Journal of Political Science* 13: 1–32.

Salisbury, Robert H. (1979). "Why No Corporatism in America?" in P. Schmitter and G. Lehmbruch (eds), *Trends toward Corporatist Intermediation.* Beverly Hills, CA: Sage.

Salisbury, Robert H. (1990). "The Paradox of Interest Groups in Washington, DC: More Groups, Less Clout", in Anthony King (ed.), *The New American Political System.* Washington, DC: American Enterprise Institute.

Schumaker, Paul (2004). "Interest Groups in Local Politics." Entry 6.5. in Thomas, *Research Guide,* cited below.

Silverstein, Kenneth (1999). *Washington on $10 million a Day.* New York: Common Courage Press.

Smith, Dorothy (1979). *In Our Own Interest: A Handbook for the Citizen Lobbyist in State Legislatures.* Seattle: Madrona Publishers.

Smith, Hedrick (1988). *The Power Game: How Washington Works.* New York: Random House.

Starr, Paul (1995). "What Happened to Health Care Reform?" *American Prospect* 20 (winter): 20–31.

*State Contract Lobbyist Directory* (1991). Alexandria, VA: State & Federal Associates.

Steele, J. Valerie (2001). *2001 National Directory of Corporate Public Affairs,* 19th edn. Washington, DC: Columbia Books.

Stone, Clarence N., Robert K. Whelan, and William J. Murin (1986). *Urban Policy and Politics in a*

*Bureaucratic Age,* 2nd edn. Englewood Cliffs, NJ: Prentice Hall.

Thomas, Clive S., ed. (1993a). *First World Interest Groups: A Comparative Perspective.* Westport, CT: Greenwood Press.

Thomas, Clive S. (1993b). "The American Interest Group System: Typical Model or Aberration?" in Thomas, *First World Interest Groups,* cited above.

Thomas, Clive S. (1998). "Interest Group Regulation across the United States: Rationale, Development and Consequences." *Parliamentary Affairs* 51: 500–15.

Thomas, Clive S., ed. (2004a). *Research Guide to US and International Interest Groups.* Westport, CT: Praeger.

Thomas, Clive S. (2004b). "Lobbyists: Definitions, Types and Varying Designations." Entry 7.6. in Thomas, *Research Guide,* cited above.

Thomas, Clive S. (2004c). "Interest Group Power and Influence." Entry 7.17. in Thomas, *Research Guide,* cited above.

Thomas, Clive S. (2004d). "The Intergovernmental Activity of Interest Groups." Entry 6.6. in Thomas, *Research Guide,* cited above.

Thomas, Clive S., and Ronald J. Hrebenar (2004). "Interest Groups in the States," in Virginia Gray and Russell L. Hanson (eds), *Politics in the American States: A Comparative Analysis,* 8th edn. Washington, DC: Congressional Quarterly Press.

*Washington Representatives,* 27th edn (2003). Washington, DC: Columbia Books.

Wilson, Graham K. (1982). "Why is there no Corporatism in the United States?" in G. Lehmbruch and P. Schmitter (eds), *Patterns of Corporatist Policy Making.* Beverly Hills, CA: Sage.

Wilson, Graham K. (1998). *Only in America: The Politics of the United States in Comparative Perspective.* Chatham, NJ: Chatham House.

Wolpe, Bruce C., and Bertram J. Levine (1996). *Lobbying Congress: How the System Works,* 2nd edn. Washington, DC: Congressional Quarterly Press.

Zeigler, L. Harmon, and Hendrik van Dalen (1976). "Interest Groups in the States," in Herbert Jacob and Kenneth N. Vines (eds), *Politics in the American States: A Comparative Analysis,* 3rd edn. Boston, MA: Little Brown.

Zeller, Belle (1954). *American State Legislatures,* 2nd edn. New York: Crowell.

## ACKNOWLEDGMENT

The author would like to thank George Ascott, a research assistant at the University of Alaska Southeast, for his research help on the two Case Studies.

# 19

# Lobbying in the United States

*An Industry Matures*

BURDETT LOOMIS

Congress is considering legislation—developed with the help of the IT business community—that would require federal agencies to use a checklist to assess their cybersecurity risks. If this or other legislation to tighten government security is passed, what can you bring to the table?

Learn about the new business opportunities for your company at TechNews.com's third Breakfast Briefing on Homeland Security ... get an exclusive update on the current cybersecurity challenges and how government and industry can work together to address new threats.

TechNews.com announcement, for October 2, 2002 (7.00 a.m. start time for busy lobbyists)

With featured guests Senator Ron Wyden (Dem., Oregon) and Representative Sherwood Boehlert (Rep., New York), TechNews.com offered, for the bargain-basement price of $75, to bring together the diverse players in the emerging cybersecurity subfield of the fast-growing homeland security community of interests. Across Washington, DC, that same day, dozens of other such briefings were held, each with the explicit purpose of bringing the public and private sectors together to address a specialized slice of governmental policy. This is

business as usual, and it provides one small window for viewing how the lobbying industry has come to insinuate itself into every nook and cranny of US policy making. Lobbyists may not be more important in the American politics of the twenty-first century than they were in the mid-1950s or 1980s, but there are more of them, and they engage in more activities, more of the time (Cigler and Loomis, 1995).

## ORGANIZED INTERESTS AND LOBBYING: A GROWTH INDUSTRY

The literature that describes the size and scope of the interest-group/lobbying universe has roots that grow from some of the earliest behavioral studies in American politics, as with Pendleton Herring's (1929) study of group representation. Herring noted the number of trade associations (1,400) and other groups (500), and sought to assess their effectiveness. Subsequently, David Truman's *The Governmental Process* (1950) signaled the beginning of a mid-century emphasis on groups as the basic building blocks of a plural society. Truman does cite figures for numbers of groups, both in the aggregate and by category. Citing Department of Commerce figures, he reports the existence of "approximately 4,000 [national] trade, professional, civic, and other organizations" (1950: 58).

Still, few studies have attempted to pin down the overall size of the interest-group/lobbying community. The best summary of these attempts comes from Mark Petracca's valuable 1992 essay, "The Rediscovery of Interest Group Politics," in which he notes various counts of groups and lobbyists (1992, 13). These include:

1   500 organizations in contact with Congress in the 1920s.
2   300 "effective lobbies" in the late 1920s.
3   6,000 active lobbyists "more or less" and 5,000 attorneys in DC during the late 1930s, after the New Deal expansion of governmental programs.
4   400 lobbies in the 1940s and 12,000 lobbyists in DC during World War II.
5   500 continuing lobbying groups and hundreds of others representing occasional interests in 1950s Washington.
6   Between 800 and 1,200 Washington lobbyists in the late 1950s and early 1960s.
7   5,662 registered lobbyists in 1981, growing to 23,011 in 1987.
8   As of the early 1980s about 7,000 organizations maintained a presence in Washington, with about half of these representing corporations.

These figures illustrate the difficulty of assessing the number of organized interests or lobbyists (OIL) in Washington, to say nothing of groups and lobbyists in state capitals, whose growth has accelerated since the 1970s.

Moreover, traditional membership groups and trade associations have come to represent fewer and fewer of the organized interests that seek to affect policy making in Washington, state capitals, and major cities across the country. Increasingly, institutions such as corporations, non-profits, and other governmental units have reshaped the organizational mix of the organized interest universe (Salisbury, 1984). Likewise, organized interests have become more powerful players within electoral politics, first through political action committees (after the 1974 campaign finance reforms) and more

recently through soft money contributions and independent expenditures (Magleby and Monson, 2003).

The basic question here is: how large is the organized interest/lobbying establishment?[1] There are many reasonable estimates, and a host of apparently hard numbers. Petracca (1992) provides a dramatic graph that tracks the growth of "Washington interest representatives" total figures from around 4,000 in 1977 to more than 14,000 in 1991. More recently, the Senate has revised its registration of lobbyists, which offers hard data from 1996 (see below). But having accurate figures on the total number of organizations or registered lobbyists does not give us a complete picture of the group/lobby universe. Thousands of key influentials, occasional lobbyists, and support personnel fail to be included in most counts. Thus, when Kevin Phillips (1994: 43), a long-time Washington insider, sought to assess the size of the organized interest/lobbyist sector, he made a guess of around 91,000 people connected to the lobbying business in DC. And Phillips relied on the estimates and calculations of American university political scientist James Thurber, another long-time capital insider.

Despite a substantial amount of data, the disparate elements of the OIL universe defy the drawing of easy conclusions. Indeed, one thing is almost certain: no single figure will summarize the entire lobbying or organized interest sector.

## ORGANIZED INTERESTS AND LOBBYING: SIZE AND SCOPE

The first task in sorting through the size and scope of the organized interest/lobbying universe is simply to categorize the different elements. The divisions here include: lobbying and related activities; organizations and associations; overall expenditures; and measures of campaigns and other aspects of elections, such as from independent sources. No matter how accurate and clearly divided, simple numbers provide only one measure of the reach of organized interests and lobbyists.

Within all categories, a core of individuals, firms, corporations, non-profits, and other entities engage in much more activity and wield more influence that many peripheral or occasional players. Thus, the lobbying industry may be more concentrated than appears from this first cut of figures. At the same time, this smaller number of organizations and individuals may well account for the lion's share of transactions and opportunities within the sector.

### Lobbyists, Lobbying Firms, and Lawyers

Even as lobbyists are required to register with the Secretary of the Senate, and the Center for Responsive Politics tracks their numbers, definitive figures are hard to come by. Thus, Dennis Johnson (2001: 81) estimates the number of lobbyists in a range from 3,000 to 7,000. Such an estimate falls short of the 10,163 lobbyist profiles (and 3,769 for firms/organizations) in the searchable databases of the lobbying trade journal *Influence*. The Center for Responsive Politics cited 12,113 active lobbyists in 1999. The Lobby Disclosure Act's data, recorded by the Secretary of the Senate and collected since 1996, report somewhat higher figures; despite some variation, the number of lobbyists registering has averaged about 19,100 in the five years from 1998 through 2002.

Although the Senate figures will continue to offer some good baseline and trend numbers, they scarcely tell the entire story about lobbying in Washington, to say nothing of its manifestation in state capitals. Any number of high-level "rainmakers" may not register as lobbyists, in that they do not lobby in any conventional sense. They may offer strategic advice or provide a key introduction to their clients, while others do the day-to-day work of advocacy.

More systematically, some lobbyists escape the scrutiny of the Lobbying Disclosure Act (LDA), even though they often advertise their successes. In particular, grassroots lobbying remains outside the scope of the law's requirements. As the advocacy group Public Citizen (2001) observes:

Whether it's a defense contractor hiring a public relations firm to mobilize editorial boards, suppliers, and workers to lobby for government funding of an allegedly superfluous nuclear attack submarine or the National Education Association engaging a professional "Advocacy" web site to generate e-mails to Congress supporting legislation to reduce class sizes … grass-roots lobbying using state-of-the-arts communication technology is everywhere. Yet because it is not covered by the LDA, citizens are left in the dark about the special interests that are spending tens and even hundreds of millions of dollars to influence policies …

That's not to say that grassroots lobbyists and firms cannot be identified; for example, the trade journal *Campaigns and Elections* lists seventeen firms under its grassroots category heading, and the actual number is certainly higher.

Central here is that almost any single count is likely to be an undercount. A different kind of miscounting comes with lawyers/lobbyists, some of whom register, but many may not. As of 2003 more than 77,000 lawyers had registered with the Washington DC Bar (compared to 37,000 in 1983), a number that grossly overstates the number of practicing attorneys. Still, there are approximately 8,000 law firms in the capital area, and many have lobbying practices. Given that lawyers often function as, or complement, lobbyists, the count of lawyers/lobbyists will underestimate their numbers, in that even if all lawyers/lobbyists did register, there would be many more staff attorneys and paralegal assistants who would go uncounted.

In sum, the actual number of lobbyists and their support staffs is difficult to pin down. But if Thurber's 91,000 figure was even roughly accurate for the early 1990s, the number has almost certainly climbed to well over 100,000 by 2004.

### International Representation

Many lobbying firms represent foreign clients in complex international matters, as well as domestic concerns that affect both nations and the easing of relations between their clients and the United States. Patton Boggs, which sits atop the list of top earners in the lobbying field in 2001, according to *Influence*, with a lobbying revenue of over $52 million, represents various international clients, including the Abu Dhabi government, the government of Honduras, the State of Qatar, the Arab Republic of Egypt and the Sultanate of Oman.

Like many other facets of lobbying, defining the size of the international aspect of lobbying is elusive. The amounts spent by foreign entities to influence political and public opinion in the United States varies significantly (http://www.lobbying-europe.com/1.usa/indexUSA.htm). The total number of short-term registrants with the Department of Justice (DOJ) working in the United States with the intent of swaying political and public opinion was 1,956 in mid-2002. These registrants represent 589 foreign principals, which are required to disclose their activities to the DOJ in accordance with the Foreign Agents Registration Act of 1938.

## Membership Groups and Associations

The evidence is relatively clear on the overall number of membership groups and associations. Two separate reference works track these organizations. For 2003, the *Directory of Associations* lists 31,500 associations with US origins. (It also tracks some foreign groups.) The *Encyclopedia of National Associations* lists 22,000 organizations that are non-profits. Not all of these organizations have Washington, DC, offices or employ DC representatives, but they do contribute to the increasingly dense organizational world described by Olson (1982) and Rauch (1994). The *Encyclopedia* also chronicles the formation of new organizations and observes that 500 such groups are listed in 2003.

Although the non-profit interests are ordinarily regarded as severely limited in their capacity to engage in politics, especially through lobbying, Jeffery Berry (2003) details both the impact and the potential of non-profit activities. Again, the growth of non-profits provides a much expanded opportunity structure and increases the density of the overall organized interest/lobbying sector.

## Institutions

Although corporations are clearly key institutions in the mix of organized interests and lobbyists, their representation in DC is largely subsumed under the lobbying category. Our focus on institutions moves more toward the public sector. In addressing such representation Beverly Cigler (1995) differentiates between the seven major intergovernmental associations (representing, respectively, governors, state governments, state legislatures, cities, counties, mayors, and city/county managers) and various other groups and organizations. These include parts of the "intergovernmental information infrastructure," specialist associations (e.g., health, transportation, etc.), and a number of new generalist organizations, such as those representing towns/townships and regional councils. In short, the intergovernmental lobby has become exceptionally dense. Added to these groups are the five major educational associations, with their hundreds of members.

In addition to these large, umbrella organizations, individual states, cities, and universities have become increasingly active individual participants in Washington lobbying. Thus, between 1998 and 2001, the number of universities with Washington offices or lobbyists climbed from 191 to 294, with the amount being spent rising from $23 million to $42 million (Brainard, 2002). Again, these figures seriously underrepresent the amount of lobbying by higher educational institutions, in that almost all major universities have governmental affairs staffers who essentially serve as lobbyists, to say nothing of the activities by presidents and chancellors. The reason for the rise in lobbying by individual institutions is clear in that earmarked funds have grown steadily over the past decade, to the point that more than $1.8 billion was designated for specific projects in fiscal year 2002 (Brainard, 2002).

In a similar vein, more than thirty states have established Washington offices, to supplement their representation by national organizations (as well as their elected senators and representatives). The fiscal crises in the states have led some offices to close, while other states see an increased need for representation beyond that provided by national groups and their own legislators. And some cities and other governmental units have established offices or hired lobbyists to work on their behalf. For example, in 2000 the Tennessee Valley Authority—a public entity—spent more than $800,000 and used six different lobbying firms in its Washington representation. Even more noteworthy is lobbying by small cities:

> A quick look at [lobbying] firms' client lists illustrates just how diverse local lobbying in Washington, DC, has become. For every Atlanta or Philadelphia there are dozens of Sioux Citys, Akrons, and Mobiles. And for every Akron or Mobile, there are even smaller towns, many having all the name recognition of Spearfish. S.D. Registration records show that at least 306 localities with populations of less than 100,000 employed lobbyists in Washington in 2003, an increase from 120 in 1998, the earliest date from which records are available.
>
> (Metzger, 2004)

Ironically, whether state, city, or university lobbyists are truly successful—that is, bring in considerably more than their cost—is almost irrelevant. Almost all institutions will get something, and the lobbyists can claim credit, regardless of whether they influenced the outcome at all.

Whatever the metric, lobbying in the United States has become a growth industry. Whether looking at numbers of lobbyists, groups, law-lobbying firms, or expenditures, one concludes that the influence business is healthy. Growth does not occur in a vacuum, however, and the OIL sector's expansion has roots in both demand for increased activity and a burgeoning supply of lobbying personnel. Indeed, the *demand-side* aspect of the growth in number, reach, and activities of groups is relatively straightforward, and will be briefly detailed below. Less fully considered is a *supply-side* approach to these elements of growth. It may well be that the expansion of lobbying in the United States has been fueled as much by a potential supply of lobbyists as an array of well defined demands from a wide range of interests.

## THE GROWTH OF GOVERNMENT AND INCREASED DEMANDS FOR LOBBYING

The fiscal year 1930 budget for the United States stood at about $3 billion; the government did very little of any import. The fiscal year 2005 budget exceeds $2.4 trillion, and federal regulations and tax laws affect almost everyone in the society, as well as virtually every institution, from public schools to family farms to private hospitals. Changing a few lines of a tax law, as the wine-making Gallo family sought, for more than a decade, can mean tens of millions of dollars in returns.

Without going through the voluminous literature on organized interests and their demands on government, we need only return to Madison's characterization of the inherent selfishness of individuals, both by themselves and as parts of factions. Without question, organized interests make substantial, continual demands on government, even as they relate to legislators and other decision makers in complex and sophisticated ways (Ainsworth, 2002; Leech *et al.*, 2002). Although scholars and journalists have noted the requests that legislators (and executives) make of lobbyists, almost all studies view the lobbyist-legislator relationship from a demand-side perspective—even when lobbyists are providing valuable information to legislators (Hall, 1998; Wright, 1996).

The range of demands is great, as is the array of tactics and strategies designed to accomplish groups' goals. Large-scale campaigns involving broad coalitions and stealth efforts to change a line of tax law require very different lobbying efforts. Likewise, many demands simply reflect a desire to maintain a *status quo* position that is under attack. From a demand-side perspective, the growth of organized interests and lobbying derives in large part from the growth of government—both as a distributor of resources (e.g., earmarked funds for universities) and the instigator of costly regulations (e.g., keeping close track of all foreign students) (Leech *et al.*, 2002; Nivola, 1998). Without question, governmental expansion has provided increased opportunities for lobbying.

Still, the explosion in the number of lobbyists and other politically relevant professionals (consultants, pollsters, public relations personnel, lawyers, etc.) cannot be completely explained from the perspective of demands on the system. Perhaps, an increasing supply of these professionals has directly led to more demands on the Congress, the executive, and the regulatory agencies.

## A SUPPLY-SIDE APPROACH TO THE GROWTH OF LOBBYING

The basic argument is straightforward. Over the past few decades, for a host of reasons, the number of individuals who support themselves in politics generally, and lobbying specifically, has grown dramatically. There are many elements of demand in this growth, from the evolution of new industries to increases in federal funding to the expansion of regulation, all of which create incentives for influencing governmental outcomes. The stakes of governmental decisions are often high, and it makes sense for groups, corporations, candidates, and parties to purchase costly professional services to succeed at influencing public decisions.

At the same time, drawing from the well developed, if flawed, economic analogy, *the very supply of political professionals, in Washington, in state capitals, and large cities may well contribute to the growth of spending on lobbying, polling, consulting, policy-related legal work, advertising, and numerous other professions with a significant political niche (e.g., accountants).* In short, the supply of public affairs professions is large and growing. A supply-side approach to the expansion of lobbying and other political professions does not completely explain the rising costs of electoral and, especially, policy-oriented politics. But thinking through the implications of a large and growing private-sector political class offers the possibilities for new insights about the intersection of politics and policy making in national, state, and urban politics.

## Beyond Economics: Supply-Side Applications to Politics

After "supply-side economics" entered the American political lexicon during the Reagan era, its metaphorical sweep has been extended to various non-economic quarters. A survey of some recent political usages includes:

1  "Supply-side redistricting" in which politicians respond to newly drawn congressional districts mandated by voting rights legislation (Canon *et al.*, 1996).
2  The creation of competition for congressional seats by term-limited state legislators who constitute a steady supply of potential House candidates (Steen, 2002).
3  A "supply-side" perspective on Russian elections in which Richard Rose (2000) contends that the "erratic and changing supply of parties … has often worked against the possibility of holding elected leaders responsible."

On the policy front, the supply-side metaphor has appeared with energy issues, the potential growth of charter schools, and the availability of prescription drugs.

Save for energy policy, in which the supply of sources directly affects prices and demand, the use of "supply-side" terminology remains largely metaphorical. Still, it does convey an alternative approach to the general tendency to frame issues in terms of demands by groups or individuals. Indeed, policy demands are often artificial, as in so-called "astroturf lobbying," where lobbyists, sometimes acting at the behest of legislators or administration officials, create apparent demand from the public at large or within specific constituencies.

Moving more toward the politics of influence, scholars who have examined conservative think tanks and support for conservative publications develop a supply-side argument both implicitly and, on occasion, explicitly (Covington, 2003). One does not need believe in a "vast right-wing conspiracy" to acknowledge a growing supply of conservative institutions and opportunities.

In a similar vein, political scientist Michael Nelson (2002) argues that the growing number of initiatives that have been placed on state ballots are determined "not by the demands of the people but by the suppliers of initiatives." Both the conservative movement and the increase in initiatives tap into the growth of the political actions dominated by subsidized supplies of information, be it think-tank studies or arguments to sign a petition to place an issue on the ballot.

Still, rather than focusing on those who *subsidize* initiatives, the emphasis here lies with those who actually *supply* the initiatives and profit from placing them on the ballot. Nelson (2002) observes:

> Oregon's Bill Sizemore, for example, placed six initiatives before his state's voters in 2000. Political life and financial livelihood, so often in tension for elected officials, happily coincide for Sizemore. The anti-tax, anti-union organization he heads, Oregon Taxpayers United, hires the signature-gathering firm that he owns, I&R Petition Services, Inc., to qualify measures for the ballot.

All six of Sizemore's initiatives lost, but as an entrepreneur he could profit from engaging in the issue-oriented actions that served his political needs. Not only could Sizemore cause opposing groups to spend substantial funds on defeating his initiatives, he could make money while he fought for his set of conservative causes.

Various examples thus illustrate the potential for supply-side explanations for the growth of lobbying and other political endeavors. Still, politicians, journalists, and academics continue to think largely in terms of demands on the system. That is, in Harold Lasswell's (1936) famous formulation, politics emphasizes "who gets what," first, and then "when and why." But supplies of benefits and, especially, participants may be just as important, and much less obviously so.

## The Supply Side: Incentives

The story here begins with a 2003 garden-variety congressional fund raiser, held at the Capitol Hill Democratic Club. The crowd was typical—a handful of lobbyists hanging around, along with the staff and some thirsty interns. A few members of Congress strode in, mixed things up a bit, stood for photos, and walked back to the Capitol. In short, nothing extraordinary at all.

Into this setting came a number of lobbyists, ranging from a couple of the capital's biggest dogs down to a pair of neophyte advocates who had only recently begun to lobby on a full-time basis. One of the latter was Bill Nelson, namesake of his father, the Florida Senator. A brief biography on the Jefferson Government Relations site leads with this description:

> Bill Nelson brings to Jefferson significant political and campaign experience working alongside his father, US Senator Bill Nelson. Prior to his father's election to the Senate, Bill assisted him with other successful election campaigns including races for the US House of Representatives and Insurance Commissioner, Treasurer, and Fire Marshal for the state of Florida. As a personal aide to Senator Nelson, Bill traveled with his father, planned campaign events, and occasionally served as a surrogate speaker.

(www.jeffersongr.com)

The site lists no substantive accomplishments for Mr Nelson, excepting his work for his father and his knowledge of the Florida congressional delegation.

The other young lobbyist was a first-year associate in the legendary law and lobbying firm of Patton Boggs. This associate, from a state university law school in a small Midwestern state, had never worked on Capitol Hill. But over the course of his law school career he had prevailed upon Patton Boggs for summer clerkships, and had landed a job after graduation. Still a bit wet behind the ears, he was responsible for a modest set of clients and was moving into a career of Washington lobbying.

Neither of these individuals necessarily typifies those who enter the lobbying profession in contemporary American politics. Far more representative are the thousands of congressional aides who have gained valuable expertise as committee staffers before taking their knowledge and skills to the private sector. Still, the junior Nelson and the Patton Boggs lobbyist demonstrate the pull of the lobbying profession and the potential supply of Washington advocates. As the overall number of DC lobbyists grows, so too do the number of opportunities for close relatives of Senators and Representatives (Loomis and Struemph, 2003; Neubauer *et al.*, 2003). While many relatives bring substantial experience and training to their jobs, others offer little more, at least initially, than their blood ties.

At the same time, the young Patton Boggs associate similarly increases the supply of lobbyists inside the Beltway. The profession lured him to Washington, and he worked diligently to enter the influence establishment. Moreover, with no congressional or executive experience, with no state capital background, and with no blood or friendship ties to sitting legislators, the newly minted lawyer-lobbyist demonstrates how the lobbying profession can expand simply by offering the potential to work at a job that combines influence, affluence, and enjoyment.

Aside from those who grow up within the milieu of politics, few children look to the future and aspire to become lobbyists, political consultants, or election-law specialists. To be sure, an increasing number of educational programs do explicitly prepare individuals to become part of the organized interest/lobbying establishment, and these programs are both examples of a growing supply of professionalized politicians as well as producers of political pros. Still, most private-sector political occupations appear particularly alluring to those who have already taken a job—and perhaps embarked upon a career—in the lower echelons of politics or policy making.

Three incentives combine to attract individuals to this so-called "industry," in that lobbyists (including lawyer-lobbyists), consultants, and other public affairs specialists have the opportunity to (1) do well, (2) do good, and (3) have fun. One poorly kept secret about lobbying and consulting is that these professions offer real day-to-day enjoyment, as well as providing the chance to earn substantial sums and, by

and large, to pursue one's broad philosophical goals. In many ways, the incentives that draw political professionals to their occupations mirror those that entrepreneurs use to attract members to their interest groups. That is, doing well roughly equates to material incentives; doing good reflects purposive/expressive incentives; and having fun relates to the solidary/camaraderie set of incentives (Salisbury, 1969). All three incentives attract lobbyists to their jobs, and such a combination should prove a powerful draw.

### Doing Well

Lobbyists, by and large, earn a lot more than do staffers on Capitol Hill, in the executive branch, or within regulatory bodies. Indeed, the consistent flow of government personnel into lobbying and law firms reflects historic career patterns, and a trickle became a steady flow as far back as the 1930s, with F.D.R. staffers such as Tommy Corcoran establishing a private presence that enriched them and turned them into power brokers of mid-century Washington (McKean, 2003). Even though more than 900 Capitol Hill staffers earned over $100,000 in 2002, salaries peak near $150,000 (Bolton, 2002). A highly regarded tax committee staff member can command $500,000 or more from a lobbying firm, and even junior staff members can often double their income.

The career path from staffer to lobbyist is so well trodden that extended analysis is unnecessary. Rather, staffers who leave the Hill, the White House, or the bureaucracy expect to earn considerably more in the private sector than they did in the public sphere. Although some details of "doing well" will be provided below, the fact that lobbyists earn more money than staffers is not sufficient to understand the growth in the large numbers of lobbyists, lawyer-lobbyists, public affairs operatives, and other political professionals. Increasing one's income, while important for those living in the high-cost world of Washington, would not necessarily prove adequate to lure legions of staffers to corporations, associations, and lobbying firms—or, more important, to keep them there.

*Doing Good*

Although the idea of "doing well" seems unexceptional, that of "doing good" requires more thorough consideration. Most lobbyists, regardless of their background, tend to end up working for interests or groups with whom they are generally comfortable. For instance, when Kansas Governor Bill Graves, whose family once owned a large trucking business, left office in 2002, he was a natural candidate to head the American Trucking Association.

Legislators who supported business and corporate interests on Capitol Hill have little trouble in finding compatible clients. Thus, former Representative Robert Livingston's (Rep., Louisiana) fast-growing, highly lucrative lobbying firm represents more than sixty clients, ranging from drug firm Schering-Plough to several universities (www.influence.biz). As a former House Appropriations Committee chairman, Livingston is well positioned to seek earmarks and preferred treatment for a wide range of interests. At the same time, the chief executive officer of the Livingston Group is former Democratic Representative Toby Moffett, a certified liberal in his eight years as a House member (1975–1983). Though his politics have moderated to an extent, Moffett's clients remain more limited than Livingston's. And they include groups interested in health, urban affairs, geothermal energy, and student loans—an array that would scarcely cause much soul searching for most liberal Democrats.

Although partisanship has grown stronger within the K Street community in the wake of the GOP's post-1994 congressional resurgence, for many lobbyists party ties make little difference. Two mid-level trade lobbyists observed that their private sector projects, in a lobbying shop and a law firm, respectively, touched on many of the same issues as their previous government work. Their satisfaction as lobbyists came largely from their ability to continue to advocate for more free trade and economic development; in their eyes, they could continue to "do good," even as they moved to the private sector. Such a transition makes sense, in that subject-matter lobbyists will usually work within their specialty. Of course, many

personnel from regulatory agencies do end up working to modify the very regulations that they helped write. Even in such circumstances, however, the goal of making the regulations work in the real world may well give them a sense of "doing good."

The mix of motives that such individuals may face arises most often for Democratic staff and members in contract lobbying firms. In that, as of 2003, former Democratic members at sixty six outnumber their Republican counterparts at sixty two in the ranks of lobbying (and the discrepancy is greater for staff, given the extended period in which Democratic staffers far outnumbered Republican), lobbyists affiliated with the current minority party have adjusted reasonably well. Take, for example, former Representative Tom Downey (Dem., New York), currently chairman of the Downey McGrath Group, a major Washington lobbying firm. Downey formerly lobbied for Microsoft and currently lists Chevron among his group's forty six clients, which range from the oil giant and Oracle to the Union of Concerned Scientists and World Hunger Day. In the end, the necessities of commerce and the policy preferences of the partners come together to produce an overall practice that combines reasonable rewards with the chance to do good works. For Downey McGrath, the very diversity of the firm's client base allows more lucrative accounts to subsidize those interests with fewer resources, and the lobbyists can work on an overall mix of issues that provides the "expressive" sense of doing good.

By and large, association and corporate lobbyists who work for a single entity, such as the National Rifle Association or General Motors, have an easier time of equating doing good with doing well. NRA lobbyists can earn a good salary while feeling that they are on the side of the angels. To be sure, many small groups, especially those that represent disadvantaged populations in the society, must rely much more on expressive rewards for their lobbyists, and this almost certainly limits the supply of professional advocates. And the combination of doing good and doing well serves to increase the supply of lobbyists in the capital. As one prominent association head said,

"I am philosophically in tune with my organization, in tune with entrepreneurs (who are my members), and I have a lot of freedom to be entrepreneurial in my work" (personal interview).[2] Indeed, beyond serving his group and earning a good living, this lobbyist clearly enjoyed himself. As he happily concluded, his work is "not the drudgery of everyday commerce." For many lobbyists, doing good may well shade over into having fun.

### Having Fun

In his close observation of corporate lobbyists, Rogan Kersh (2002: 232–233) discovered that his sample spent about a third of their time on what he labeled "other professional" activities—beyond interacting with clients, working on legislation, addressing implementation issues, and engaging in electoral activities (largely fund raising). So, one-third of the time that a lobbyist is "at work" he or she is doing something else, which for Kersh includes "informal meetings with officials or fellow lobbyists, general research and analysis, business development, generic media commentary, and administrative office work" (2002: 232).

Much of lobbyists' activity is just not *directly* instrumental to their work. Rather, they use the freedom that Kersh describes to engage in various activities that give them pleasure. For example, many get deeply involved in presidential politics. They raise funds, advise candidates, and talk to reporters—for the most part with little sense of any future payoff, or at least no specific reward. Some might hope for a Cabinet position (as Downey did with a possible Gore presidency), but most of their activity is more avocational than vocational. Getting involved in national politics is what they do. Down the line, there may be rewards. If your candidate wins, your policy preferences may be helped, and your access may improve. But, more than anything else, national politics—especially in the presidential arena—provides the enjoyment of action; it's one way that the lobbyists can remain in the national arena.

Even at best, the rewards are not immediate. One top Republican lobbyist put it, "The benefits from a campaign are often indirect [for lobbyists and their firms]. You understand the process of decision making a little better" (interview). And some of that understanding may eventually help the client. Regardless, clients often directly subsidize the lobbyists' participation in party and electoral politics. One veteran Democratic contract lobbyist from a Washington firm has had a long history of working on party politics, largely in a previous position representing a major corporate interest. The corporation subsidized his forays into party politics with the assumption that some general benefits would accrue to it. Still, the lobbyist operated more as a free agent than as a participant in any explicit principal-agent relationship.

Though not all lobbyists enjoy the non-stop shmoozing that characterizes much of their work, lots do feed off this activity. For example, many maintain relationships with reporters and serve as media commentators, often on general politics. Overall, one lobbyist noted, the media have begun to pay a lot more attention to lobbyists and lobbying. Starting in 2000, the trade journal *Influence* was established; it has since chronicled the lobbying profession with a mix of news, editorial, and personnel items. In response, both *Roll Call* and *The Hill* have begun to pay increased attention to Washington's advocacy community. Indeed, for many top lobbyists, one key element of "having fun" is that the status of the profession has risen considerably. Journalist Tim Noah (2003) argues:

> Just a generation ago, the only two reasons even a low-ranking member might leave the House of Representatives were if he lost an election or retired. It was not a foregone conclusion that he would stay in Washington, but if he did, and he took a lobbying job, the appropriate feeling to have toward him was mild pity. Sure, he'd be paid more. But the best years of his life would be behind him. Inside his comfortable office, he'd gaze out the window and daydream about his glory days in government.

If presidential politics, socializing with elites, and heightened prestige reflect ways in which high-profile lobbyists enjoy their work, others have fun in more low-key ways. Indeed, given the large number of Washington representatives, there must be multiple ways to enjoy one's job. For many lobbyists, especially those who gain their positions more with policy expertise than with connections to major clients or with ties back to Capitol Hill, the White House, or regulatory agencies, "having fun" means continuing to work on the issues they most care about. Such a consideration links directly to "doing good," but the two incentives are complementary, not the same.

One lobbyist, who worked at a large, highly political law firm expressed great satisfaction in helping pass a modest trade Bill. "We cleaned it up, and created a good, small Bill," he said. "I discovered I'm a pretty good lobbyist," as he seeks to fight off the powerful protectionist forces that have increased the difficulty of passing trade legislation. In addition, he noted that "trade was not so partisan an issue in the early "nineties, [it was] somewhat more genteel, though less so after NAFTA" (interview). Moreover, trade alliances are fluid, and thus open up the possibility for building and renewing coalitions.

This trade lobbyist, a lawyer, felt very much at home in his law firm, in part because he was a part of a much larger lobbying unit that worked on trade policy, among other issues. Although the law firm paid well, and the lobbyist felt he could "do good," he remained motivated by his ability to have fun in addressing those issues that he thought most important.

This set of motivations closely mirrored those of a trade advocate at a pure lobbying firm, which was underwriting her international trade practice. In essence, the firm was adding to the number of trade lobbyists in DC in hopes of finding another profit center and diversifying its business (an important consideration in 2003 for a firm generally seen as leaning Democratic). With excellent executive branch and private sector credentials, this lobbyist could hope to have a positive impact on trade policy as she used her numerous contacts in the United States and Europe to ease barriers and encourage international business deals.

This trade lobbyist also noted that the relatively low levels of partisanship in the trade field made it an attractive area for someone who wanted to make things happen. This lobbyist was more of a deal maker and international coalition builder than her law-firm counterpart, and her sense of "having fun" was more attuned to bringing key players together as opposed to crafting a particular piece of legislation. In the end, though compensation and virtue provided her with strong incentives to lobby, she also expressed real satisfaction in the nature of the job itself—which allowed her to travel and to use her previous experience and contacts. In addition, given the nature of a smaller, family-like firm, she felt appreciated and part of an overall endeavor that she supported.

## Incentives and the Supply of Lobbyists

From the Bob Dole type of "rainmaker" *über*-lobbyist to the young star Bill Paxon, who surrendered a highly promising House career to become one of DC's most visible and well connected lobbyists, to former Tom DeLay chief of staff, Susan Hirschmann, who fostered a bidding war for her services, to hundreds of Hill staff members and executive branch officials and regulatory agency lawyers, those who move from government to lobbying shops, law firms, corporate offices, and trade organizations make a lot of money. And the pay scales have escalated.

The big money deals are well publicized, but overall material incentives have risen sharply. T.R. Goldman of *Influence* observes (2000):

> When John Jonas, a senior lobbyist and partner at Patton Boggs, left the Hill in 1986 as a House committee tax counsel, he was earning $53,000. He joined Patton Boggs and his salary jumped to $75,000. Now, he complains, kids leave the Hill making $53,000 expect starting salaries of $120,000. "I tell them you're not worth it for this marginal level of work," says Jonas …
>
> But he pays them anyway …

Moreover, the length of time that many staffers spend on Capitol Hill before moving to K Street has declined, from more than five years in the mid-1970s to about four years by the late 1990s. Goldman reports, "rank-and-file committee counsel—not chiefs of staff or chief counsel—from committees like Ways and Means, Finance, Judiciary, perhaps Natural Resources, can enter the private sector commanding as much as $225,000, after just three to four years on the Hill" (2000).

In short, American lobbyists often enjoy material incentives that are substantial and growing. This can certainly explain part of the increased supply of Washington representatives. Compensation levels do demonstrate the continuing demands for lobbyists' services, at least those with ties back to governmental offices. Still, money alone does not drive the lobbying industry.

If many lobbyists see financial reward as a necessary condition for employment, it is not always a sufficient one. Former Senate Judiciary Committee counsel John McMickle observes, "The biggest thing is how much better this is than the Hill in terms of hours worked, in terms of control of your life. When you work for a senator, you're at his mercy" (Goldman, 2002). Perhaps quality of life does not quite equate to "having fun," but it's in the ball park. Or a prospective lobbyist may reject the financial overtures of larger firms to work for a smaller group whose values she shares, even if the pay—while substantial—is less. In the end, it is the combination of incentives— material, expressive/purposive, and camaraderie/ lifestyle/"fun"—that both lead personnel to the lobbying profession and, perhaps more importantly, keep them there.

## Sources of Supply

Not all lobbyists come from the Hill or from the White House office of legislative affairs or regulatory or departmental staff. But lots do. In particular, those who understand processes, know the content of issues, or have strong contacts within the government—and preferably all of these—are highly valued. Beyond experience, various lobbyists—such as former legislators— have been principals within the process.

One common factoid that almost all journalists use in discussing the growth of the lobbying industry is that, of the legislators who retired in the 1970s, only 3 percent work in the lobbying field, while 22 percent of those who retired in the 1990s do so (Birnbaum, 2000: 190). Age does make a difference here, but the lure of lobbying for Members of Congress has almost certainly increased. Where else could a defeated House Member hope to double his or her salary? Of course, many legislators do not make good lobbyists, largely because they bring neither goodwill nor policy expertise with them. Their careers tend to be short.

Looking over the potential supply of lobbyists in 1960 and 2000, the growth in the number of advocates over the past forty years scarcely seems surprising, even accounting for a rise in demand. Although the number of House Members and Senators has remained constant, nothing else has. Hill staff has approximately tripled (from about 4,000 to more than 11,300) (Ornstein et al., 2002); equally important, they have become much more professional, rather than just performing the routine clerk and secretarial functions. Moreover, a staffer's average tenure on Capitol Hill has declined from 5.3 years in the 1960s to about four years in the contemporary era.

Related to the staff phenomenon has been the exploding numbers of congressional interns. A rough guess might place the number of interns on the Hill at around 2,000 (at most) in 1960 and at least 10,000 in 2000. The intern numbers are especially significant, in that over the course of a decade approaching 100,000 students, and probably considerably more, get at least a small taste of Capitol Hill (and the receptions held there, often sponsored by lobbyists). Moreover, lots more interns work in Members' district offices, which were essentially non-existent in 1960. In addition, the growth of professional staff within the executive branch, both in the White House and the departments/agencies, and the regulatory agencies provides thousands more potential lobbyists. In particular, the White House office of legislative affairs has steadily increased its numbers. The press corps has also grown substantially, and a fair number of Washington representatives come from a media background.

With a large lobbying community, and an even larger professional political community, in Washington, one additional source has begun to contribute to the growing supply of Washington representatives. More and more second-generation lobbyists are turning to the family profession, as one might expect as increasing numbers of sons and daughters grow up in the professional political environment. Although he provides no overall figures, *Influence's* Goldman (2003) describes a substantial number of second-generation advocates who have risen to significant positions within a host of DC firms—often bypassing the normal apprenticeship on Capitol Hill. Many of these younger lobbyists do know many of the key congressional players, but they are most likely to credit a simple familiarity with the process as central to their decision to become a lobbyist.

In 1960 no Washington educational institutions offered graduate degrees in lobbying, legislative affairs, or consulting; now several do, along with various state universities. Save for Brookings and a couple of other institutions, think tanks remained unexplored territory in 1960; they now house thousands of individuals who may well be lured into the lobbying profession—scarcely much of a jump for many think-tank staffers.

All in all, the sources of supply for the lobbying industry have multiplied several times over the past thirty or fourty years. Aside from more Members of Congress staying in DC to lobby, and some mid- and late-career stalwarts who leave the Hill for lucrative advocacy careers, other broad trends contribute to the increased supply. At the very bottom, internships bring tens of thousands of ambitious students to the capital from every state, while congressional offices turn out a regular stream of competent, policy-oriented, and underpaid professionals who can command higher salaries in the private sector. To a lesser extent, but at higher levels, so too do the executive branch and the regulatory agencies. The supply of would-be lobbyists shows no sign of abating, perhaps one more illustration of the profession's rising stature.

## THE LOBBYING INDUSTRY: IMPLICATIONS

At the societal level, the "influence" sector of American politics continues to grow in numbers of organized interests and lobbyists, the array of tactics used by these interests, and the amounts spent on lobbying, broadly defined, especially as it grows to incorporate much of public affairs. The demands of groups, corporations, universities, foreign entities, and myriad other organized interests, all directed at an expanding government (regardless of party and President), have fueled the growth of the lobbying industry. At the same time, supply-side incentives encourage individuals to enter the lobbying profession, as well as political consulting, public affairs, public relations, and survey research. This mix of continuing demand and increasing supply may well lead interests to embark upon more, and more expensive, lobbying initiatives, especially when the stakes for winning continue to increase.

Three broad sets of implications can be drawn from the growth of the lobbying industry in the United States. First, *few decisions are ever final*, as losers regroup and move their lobbying efforts to other venues and seek to redefine the conflict. Perhaps most noteworthy here was the continuing public lobbying efforts of the AARP, the huge senior citizens' group, *after* a major prescription drug Bill had narrowly passed through the Congress and a lengthy period of conventional lobbying. The AARP, along with the Bush administration, has fought an extended and losing battle to convince the public that the expensive Bill would be a boon to seniors.

Second, the *American lobbying industry serves as a model* for developments in many other nations. Although the United States' separation of powers/federalism system is unique in offering large numbers of venues, the basic techniques and integrated lobbying/public affairs operations have become much more common around the globe.

Third, and related, many international firms have purchased US lobbying firms, as they develop into diversified public affairs entities, with multiple profit centers across the industrialized world. Such a trend raises profound questions from a principal-agent perspective, in that a US firm that represents a particular domestic interest also functions as a profit center for a multinational corporation. To whom, exactly, does the lobbying firm owe its primary allegiance? Such a question can even be raised domestically in the United States; in 2003 a Chicago venture capital firm purchased a major lobbying firm (Dutko) with the intent of internationalizing its reach, increasing its value, and selling it off after a few years. To the extent that a lobbying firm becomes simply a piece of venture capital, its relationship to its financial principal will inevitably be at odds with some of its other principals—its clients— who expect that they have paid for the full loyalty of the firm in its role as agent.

## THE LOBBYING INDUSTRY AND "INTEREST-GROUP LIBERALISM"

> A brief working model of interest-group liberalism turns out to be a vulgarized version of the pluralist model of modern political science: (1) organized interests are homogeneous and easy to define. Any duly elected representative of any interest is taken as an accurate representative of each and every member. (2) Organized interests emerge in every sector of our lives and adequately represent most of those sectors, so that one organized group can be found effectively answering and checking some other organized group as it seeks to prosecute its claims against society. And (3) the role of government is one of insuring access to the most effectively organized, and of ratifying the agreements and adjustments worked out among competing bodies.
>
> (Theodore Lowi, *The End of Liberalism*, 1979)

If Lowi's storied characterization of "interest-group liberalism" was accurate in 1979, it is all the more so almost twenty five years later. To the extent that the notion of the OIL and the lobbying industry, and especially its consideration of organized interests, connects to a theoretical construct of American politics, it is through Lowi's (1979) formulation. Although

the study of gridlock in American politics has regularly ignored the role(s) played by organized interests (Mayhew, 1991; Binder, 2003), these groups and their highly sophisticated lobbying and public affairs efforts have become central to the difficulties that American governmental institutions face in resolving difficult issues. As Lowi observes, "the most important difference between liberal and conservative, Republicans and Democrats, is to be found in the interest groups they identify with" (1979: 51).

In the intervening quarter-century, organized interests have grown, if anything, more pervasive and more partisan; the Republican takeover of Congress, and especially the House, has increased partisanship among organized interests, as Representative Tom DeLay (Rep., Texas), first as whip, then as Majority Leader, has led a consistent (if not always successful) charge to pressure groups to employ lobbyists with GOP connections (Dunham, 2002). In addition, contribution patterns have grown increasingly partisan, as more organized interests have placed their bets (or investments) disproportionately with one party (Ferguson, 1995; Edsall, 2002).

But, beyond such moneyed partisanship, organized interests have also become more and more sophisticated in fulfilling their distinct representative roles within the American political system. Although not all corporations become actively involved in politics, most do, both on Capitol Hill and within the regulatory process (Vogel, 1989). More non-profits have joined public interest groups in providing substantial representation to sectors that have not traditionally enjoyed such protection (Berry, 1999, 2003).

The lobbying industry—in both its demand and supply-side manifestations—reacts to market forces. Lowi was describing the beginnings of a market that has matured substantially since the late 1970s. Aside from the growth of lobbying firms and their diversification in providing services, it's no wonder that there are dozens of national polling firms where there was once a handful, or that there are firms that specialize in collecting signatures for initiatives, or consultants that can provide ground-war troops for congressional campaigns. There is a burgeoning supply of professionals; there is a great deal of money; there are high stakes within policy processes that include a $2.4 trillion budget and regulatory rules that shape almost all private enterprise.

With high policy stakes, seemingly unlimited sources of funds, and a steady supply of young, well equipped professionals, the American lobbying industry, while mature, remains on the cusp of further growth. This is good for lobbyists, no doubt, but of questionable value to a political system that—absent crisis—finds ordered change extremely difficult to produce.

## NOTES

1 A note on terminology. Among American scholars the terms "interest groups" and "organized interest" are the most frequently used, although some movement toward "advocacy groups" may be gaining ground. Most studies avoid the terms "pressure groups" or "special interest groups" in that they appear pejorative.

2 Interviewees were promised anonymity.

## REFERENCES

Ainsworth, S. (2002). *Analyzing Interest Groups*. New York: Norton.

Armey, D. (1999). "The Freedom and Fairness Restoration Act," accessed at http://flattax.house.gov/proposal/flat-sum.asp.

Berry, J. (1999). *The New Liberalism*. Washington, DC: Brooking Institution.

Berry, J. (2003). *A Voice for Nonprofits*. Washington, DC: Brooking Institution.

Binder, S. (2003). *Stalemate: The Causes and Consequences of Legislative Gridlock*. Washington, DC: Brooking Institution.

Birnbaum, J. (2000). *The Money Men*. New York: Crown.

Bolton, A. (2002). "Senate Outpaces House in $100K Salaries," *The Hill*, October 7.

Brainard, J. (2002). "Some Colleges Reap Little Return Lobbying for Pork Projects," *Chronicle of Higher Education*, October 18, p. 27.

Canon, D., M. Schousen, and P.J. Sellers (1996). "The Supply Side of Congressional Redistricting: Race and Strategic Politicians," *Journal of Politics* 58 (3): 846.

Cigler, A., and B. Loomis (1995). "More than More of the Same," in *Interest Group Politics*, 4th edn. Washington, DC: CQ Press.

Cigler, B. (1995). "Not Just Another Special Interest: Intergovernmental Representation," in A. Cigler and B. Loomis, *Interest Group Politics*, 4th ed. Washington, DC: CQ Press.

Covington, S. (2003). *Covert Action Quarterly* 63, accessed at http://mediafilter.org/CAQ/caq63/caq63thinktank.html.

Dunham, R. (2002). "The GOP's Wacky War on Dem Lobbyists," *Businessweek Daily*, http://www.businessweek.com/bwdaily/dnflash/jun2002/.

Edsall, T.B. (2002). "Big Business's Funding Shift Boosts GOP," *Washington Post*, November 27, p. A1.

Ferguson, T. (1995). *The Golden Rule*. Chicago: University of Chicago Press.

Goldman, T.R. (2000). "The Rising Tide," *Influence*, August 23.

Goldman, T.R. (2002). "Kingdom of K Street Beckons Hill Staffers," *Influence*, July 10, p. 11.

Goldman, T.R. (2003). "When Lobbying is the Family Business," *Influence*, June 25.

Hall, R. (1998). "Lobbying as an Informational Subsidy." Paper presented at the Midwest Political Science Association meeting, Chicago, IL, April.

Herring, P. (1929). *Group Representation before Congress*. Washington, DC: Brooking Institution.

Steen, J. (2003). "Supply-side Competition, State Term Limits, and Congressional Elections." Paper presented at Midwest Political Science Association meeting, Chicago, April 3–6.

Johnson, D. (2001). *No Place for Amateurs: How Political Consultants are Reshaping American Democracy*. New York: Routledge.

Kersh, R. (2002). "Corporate Lobbyists as Political Actors," in A. Cigler and B. Loomis (eds), *Interest Group Politics*, 6th edn. Washington, DC: CQ Press.

Lasswell, H. (1936). *Politics: Who Gets What, When and How*. New York: McGraw-Hill/Peter Smith.

Leech, B., F. Baumgartner, T. La Pira, and N. Semanko (2002). "The Demand Side of Lobbying: Government Attention and the Mobilization of Organized Interests," Paper presented at the Midwest Political Science Association meeting, Chicago, IL, April.

Loomis, B., and M. Struemph (2003). "Organized Interests, Lobbying, and the Industry of Politics: A First-cut Overview." Paper presented at the Midwest Political Science Association meeting, Chicago, IL, April.

Lowi, T. (1969). *The End of Liberalism*. New York: Norton.

Lowi, T. (1979). *The End of Liberalism*, 2nd edn. New York: Norton.

Magleby, D., and J.Q. Monson (2003). "The Noncandidate Campaign: Soft Money and Issue Advocacy in the 2002 Congressional Elections," accessed at *PSOnline*, www.apsanet.org.

Mayhew, D. (1991). *Divided we Govern*. Cambridge, MA: Harvard University Press.

McKean, D. (2003). *Tommy the Cork*. South Royalton, VT: Steer Forth Press.

Metzger, A. (2004). "Smaller Cities Becoming Bigger K Street Clients," *Influence*, September 14.

Neubauer, C., J. Pasternak, and R. Cooper (2003). "The Senators' Sons; A Washington Bouquet: Hire a Lawmaker's Kid," *Los Angeles Times*, June 17.

Nelson, M. (2002). "Democratic Delusions: The Initiative Process in America," *American Prospect*, June 3, accessed at http://www.prospect.org.

Nivola, P. (1998). "The New Pork Barrel: What's Wrong with Regulation Today and What Reformers Need to Do to Get it Right," *Brookings Review* 16 (1): 6–9.

Noah, T. (2003). "Why Congressmen Want to be Lobbyists," http://slate.msn.com, accessed July 31.

Ornstein, N.,T. Mann and M. Malbin (2002). *Vital Statistics on Congress, 2001–2*. Washington, DC: American Enterprise Institute.

Olson, M. (1982). *The Rise and Decline of Nations*. New Haven, CT: Yale University Press.

Petracca, M. (1992). "The Rediscovery of Interest Group Politics," in *The Politics of Interests*. Boulder, CO: Westview Press.

Phillips, K. (1994). *Arrogant Capital*. Boston, MA: Little Brown.

Public Citizen (2001). "Problems with and Recommended Changes to the Federal Lobbying Disclosure System," accessed at http://www.citizen.org/congress/govt_reform.

Rauch, J. (1994). *Demosclerosis*. New York: Times Books.

Rose, R. (2000). "Putin's Russia: How Floating Parties Frustrate Democratic Accountability: A Supply Side View of Russia's Elections," *East European Constitutional Review* 9 (1–2): 5–11.

Salisbury, R. (1969). "An Exchange Theory of Interest Groups," *Midwest Journal of Political Science* 13: 1–32.

Salisbury, R. (1984). "Interest Representation: The Dominance of Institutions," *American Political Science Review* 78: 64–76.

Truman, D. (1950). *The Governmental Process*. New York: Knopf

Vogel, D. (1989). *Fluctuating Fortunes: The Political Power of Business in America*. New York: Basic Books. www.jeffersongr.com/bios/nelson.shtml, accessed June 15, 2003.

Wright, J. (1996). *Interest Groups and Congress*. Boston, MA: Allyn & Bacon. www.influence.biz, accessed July 22, 2003.

## ACKNOWLEDGMENT

Micheal Struemph has proven a most valuable research associate on this project, and his work is reflected in much of the collected data and its interpretations.

# 20

# Stakeholder Relationships in Canada

## In Partnership with the Community

JAMES SHAW AND PATRICK SHAW

Nexen Inc. is an independent, Canadian-based global energy and chemicals company listed on the Toronto and New York stock exchanges. Its Web site can be found at www.nexeninc.com. Formerly known as Canadian Occidental Petroleum Ltd, the company explores for, develops, produces, and markets crude oil and natural gas worldwide. Its core operations are located in Yemen, Western Canada, the North Sea and the Gulf of Mexico, with producing properties also being held in Nigeria.

Nexen has been producing from a sour natural gas field and operating the associated processing facility northeast of the city of Calgary, Alberta, since the early 1960s. Sour gas contains hydrogen sulphide, which can be very toxic and has a "rotten egg" odour if very small amounts are released into the air. For decades the company's presence in this region went largely unnoticed by the general public. However, as the city of Calgary rapidly grew, spurred on heavily during the 1980s by the presence of the 1988 Winter Olympic Games held in the city and surrounding region, residential development sprawled north and eastward and eventually encroached upon the company's widely distributed field facilities.

The industrial installations, such as Nexen's and other companies operating in the area,

were readily visible to any new land developers or home purchasers, and its operations had been repeatedly demonstrated to be "scientifically" safe. Despite the company's exemplary safety record, the outrage felt by the public moving into this area during the 1990s about what they perceived to be a new and risky intrusion into their lives was unexpectedly high.

Plate 20.1   *Community in close proximity to gas: once farm fields, resources are now within urban centers*

The company initially had difficulty identifying or appreciating these concerns in light of the fact that it had occupied the area in relative harmony with the agricultural community for many years. What had been a rather benign and even amicable relationship in its early days was at risk of degenerating into one of extreme frustration and a disastrous loss of respect between the company and the residents in the community where it operated. As such, the matter had serious implications for the company's public affairs professionals and its reputation.

For Nexen the drilling and production of natural gas on the city of Calgary's urban fringe was much more than a theoretical case study of conflict resolution or consultation with its neighbours in the community. In fact, the company actually needed to accelerate the rate of extraction of the potentially hazardous sour gas from the area—in part to properly deplete the resource before even more intense population densities were to encroach upon the area, and in part due to its responsibility to the government regulator overseeing the proper recovery of the energy resources in the province. In this real-life scenario, the perceptions of risk rode on the wave of an encroaching urban population where the company had successfully and safely operated for decades. For Nexen, accelerating the extraction of this resource while maintaining solid relationships in the community was fundamental to how it saw and continues to see itself aligning with, and fitting into, the communities where it operates.

## WHAT WOULD ANOTHER PUBLIC HEARING ACCOMPLISH?

As the existing provincial regulations were structured, a public hearing approach was the generally accepted vehicle for energy developers to broadly explain their resource extraction plans along with related safety and economic considerations. These hearings served as the primary opportunity for citizens to air their concerns and for companies to respond to issues and allegations related to the relevant development effort. Nexen staff recognized that strictly adhering to the letter and law of the regulatory process for assessing and managing

development around its proposed new extraction and exploration in the area would likely further deteriorate the already fragile community relationship and adversely impact its ability to operate the facilities in the focal area, even if its plans were approved by the regulator.

Nexen already developed and successfully implemented a voluntary process for public consultation and engagement that embraced the principles of "open, honest, and transparent communication." These principles are fundamental to the company's Safety, Environment, and Social Responsibility mandate and are further embodied in the "International Code of Ethics for Canadian Business" (Appendix 20.1) which Nexen played a pivotal role in developing with the Canadian federal government. Many of the successes that Nexen has enjoyed through effective stakeholder engagement and consultation found their genesis in the core ideals expressed in that particular document.[1]

Throughout its operations, the company is committed to the principles of corporate social, environmental and community responsibility. Nexen actively supports local projects and initiatives in the communities where it operates and it strives to have its performance guided by leadership in ethics, integrity, environmental protection, and safety.

Alignment between Nexen's strategy, structure and systems serves to uphold the company's core values. Nexen sees itself, and wants others to view it, as a company of conscience, where values matter. In its corporate value expressions Nexen states that it is concerned about every stakeholder, every community, and every generation. As such, the public affairs processes of community consultation and stakeholder dialogue draw upon every one of the company's management objectives.

Many industrial organizations tend to characterize the "sensitive environment" where they operate as akin to that of the biophysical domain. Often companies will describe their presence in terms of their "footprint" in the area where they somehow impact the physical environment. The tools and management practices for dealing with the biophysical domain tend to be well developed and highly advanced. In developed countries, there are

Figure 20.1    *Nexen's safety, environment, and social responsibility system*

many regulations clearly describing physical performance expectations in these areas. But in the case of sour gas exploration and development bordering a major urban centre the sensitivities faced are in large measure associated with the potential social, political, and economic interactions. The public affairs and stakeholder-oriented tools and management practices to address these are often much less definitive and far more interpretive.

Nexen's executive team strive to remain open to new approaches and have long recognized the significant responsibility within the community each member shares, including the responsibility to seek solutions where none is readily apparent. This outlook led to the development and clear articulation of guidelines for Nexen's highest-level decision making in regard to social responsibility and environmental sustainability.

Nexen's Safety, Environment and Social Responsibility (SESR) mission is to provide leadership, coordination and support to all the company's operations and administrative functions and undertake appropriate due diligence consistent with Nexen shareholders' best interests. This is evident in the company's SESR values statement, which includes specifically that the company values:

1  The experience and professionalism of our people.
2  The commitment, leadership, and accountability of all personnel for SESR performance.
3  Ongoing and open dialogue with our stakeholders.
4  The health, welfare, and safety of our people, contractors and the public.
5  The concept of sustainable development— a balance of environmental, economic and social responsibility.
6  The commitment of our people to a safe operating environment and protection of environmental quality.
7  Prompt, open, frank, and complete communication on SESR issues.

Nexen has proactively sought out opportunities over the last fifteen years to contribute to and has continuously evolved a leadership role in establishing meaningful community consultation wherever and whenever it could.

## INTEGRITY ON THE INSIDE

Throughout the company Nexen is committed to managing its performance with honesty and trust. Nexen operates under a system of "Total Governance", which means that the board, management team, and employees work together to meet corporate goals and foster a culture of integrity throughout the organization. The board takes governance seriously in all respects. The company has been known to continually exceed required disclosure standards. Mandates for all committees and the board as a whole, together with detailed disclosure of corporate governance practices, are readily available to the public in its proxy materials and can be retrieved electronically by accessing Nexen's public filings at www.sedar.com. Direction comes from the top, and all of the company's staff have responsibilities for implementing it.

## INTERNATIONAL CODE

The code (Appendix 20.1) is a statement of values/principles designed to facilitate and assist individual firms in the development of their policies and practices that are consistent with the vision, beliefs, values, and principles contained therein. Nexen played a significant role in helping define and develop this International Code for Canadian Business and subscribes to the contents throughout its global operations. When describing stakeholders, the vision is intended to include local communities, Canadian and host governments, local governments, shareholders, the media, customers and suppliers, interest groups, and international agencies. The parameters of this code directly influence how the company approaches stakeholder consultation wherever it operates.

## FOOTPRINT TO FINGERPRINT

As the regional population of northeast Calgary rapidly increased in both size and scope, a palpable shift in the public attitude toward resource development had occurred. Old and new community members alike had exhibited feelings of an escalating fear of health and safety threats which they associated with sour gas development. This fear was fueled by a lack of quality information from the company and provincial regulators about safety measures as well as real and perceived risks. Misgivings about the safety factors around sour gas development appeared to be widespread. As real estate development in the area had intensified an escalation of opposition and community tension around the existing sour gas extraction operations. The communities in northeast Calgary became progressively more frustrated. Their relationship with the company was pushed very near to the breaking point.

The community interaction was reflective of the high-risk, low-trust environment described so well by leading popular risk communication experts (Covello and Sandman, 2001). They define risk as being the combination of two very real aspects; Hazard (i.e., the scientific fact) and Outrage (i.e., the emotional catalyst). Thinking in terms of how the community stakeholders viewed the sour gas developments, rather than the way the company knew and had demonstrated it could operate, shed considerable insight on to a cooperative means for addressing the situation. Nexen was well prepared in defining the Hazard of any environment, and health, or safety threat from its operations. That meant it could feel good about addressing one half of the formula for defining Risk. It still needed an understanding of the Outrage factor evident and apparently growing in the community.

Outrage occurs when community stakeholders believe that they face personal risk that is (Sandman, 2004):

1  Involuntary/coerced.
2  Unfair.
3  Unfamiliar/exotic.

4  Memorable.
5  Unknowable/catastrophic.
6  Uncontrollable.
7  Morally relevant.
8  Untrustworthy.
9  The result of a closed process and unresponsive bureaucratic control.

Recognizing that the existing and cumbersome regulatory process for adjudicating development around new extraction and exploration would likely further deteriorate the already fragile corporate-community relationship, Nexen developed and successfully implemented a voluntary process for public consultation and engagement. Key to this initiative was that it embraced the principles of "Open, Honest and Transparent Communication". The principles fundamental to the company's SESR mandate and further embodied in the "International Code of Ethics for Canadian Business" directed Nexen's focus to be less on its footprint and more on the relationships the company wanted to be identified for—its fingerprint. Many of the successes that Nexen has enjoyed through effective stakeholder engagement and consultation have found their genesis in these core ideals.

## BRINGING VALUE TO THE SURFACE

Often there are attitudes within organizations that have to be changed in order to surface the true value of community consultation. There are additional insights about Hazard and Outrage gained from studying Covello and Sandman that bear repeating (Covello and Sandman, 2001):

1  The public responds more to outrage than to hazard.
2  Activists and the media amplify outrage, but they don't create it.
3  Outraged people don't pay much attention to hazard data.
4  Outrage isn't just a distraction from hazard. Both are legitimate and important.
5  When hazard is high, risk communications try to nurture more outrage.

6  When hazard is low, risk communicators try to reduce the outrage.
7  Organizations usually can't reduce outrage much until they change their own organization.

The human and public affairs elements, often ignored by industrial concerns in past pursuits to satisfy society's growing appetite for energy, are now very much at the forefront. The need for and the concept behind public consultation are not new. Industrial development has been aware of public opinion and used it to lever opportunities and expedience in exploration for many years. High oil and gas prices have been vigorously employed as the catalyst for increased exploration in the past. Consumers have traditionally been willing to tolerate some considerable degree of risk, disruption, and inconvenience if they thought it would support the achievement of affordable and accessible energy.

When the northeast Calgary community became aware that Nexen was to seek regulatory approval to drill additional sour gas wells into this field, the tentative relationships with the company and its local employees were pushed to breaking point. To proceed with the formal regulatory approval process, where the primary focus is on a public hearing, would have resulted in a further deterioration of relations between all members of the community and the company. Regardless of the outcome of such a potentially volatile public hearing, there could be no winner.

Nexen approached the Alberta government's energy regulator, then known as the Energy Resources Conservation Board (now known as the Alberta Energy and Utilities Board, AEUB). The company asked the board to consider an alternative to the quasi-judicial public hearing mechanism to seek resolution of possible issues involving the development application. The company and the AEUB agreed that a voluntary public consultation mechanism, outside that of the formal regulatory process, warranted an attempt. It would have been futile for the company to launch such a mechanism on its own because of the trust issues and its decreasing lack of credibility with the

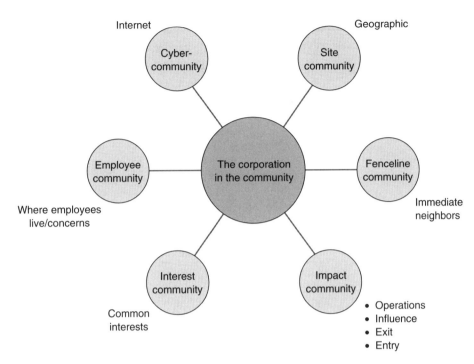

Figure 20.2   *The various communities represented at the first public consultation meeting*

community. The AEUB, as a credible and respected regulator in the province, agreed to champion the implementation of the process.

A meeting was convened by the AEUB. This initial gathering was attended by highly skeptical and even hostile representatives from the various communities in northeast Calgary and the surrounding rural area. As described by Edmund M. Burke, creator of Boston College's Center for Corporate Community Relations, in his book *Corporate Community Relations: The Principle of the Neighbor of Choice* (1999) there were many types of communities represented at that first meeting. Fence-line neighbors, community members, shopkeepers, service companies, real estate developers, city officials, provincial government agencies, and the company were all represented. The residents were asked to participate in a mediation-based, open consultation forum, which purposed to review the company's development proposal. Nexen was requested by the regulator to address the concerns raised by the community. The company was also asked to reimburse committee participants for reasonable costs

associated with individual representatives' involvement in the consultation process. An independent and neutral third-party facilitator (not a mediator) was agreed upon in advance by the community and the company, and immediately began the process of setting and organizing meetings.

The residents' expectations at the outset were best expressed by one of the key community stakeholders, who stated, "I expect we'll have a bunch of meetings, be told how safe everything is, and then they will go ahead and do whatever they intended to do in the first place." Nevertheless, over the next few months the Northeast Calgary Application Consultation Committee (NCACC) met on a regular basis. Terms of reference were agreed upon and these guided the groups' activities and actions (see Appendix 20.2).

There was an emergence of mutual respect and trust as the participants worked together, got to know one another and made progress on resolving many issues. There was the opportunity to accomplish something positive by working together. Residents and the

Table 20.1    *Stakeholder involvement mechanisms*

| Mechanism | Providing information | Understanding | Discussing the issues | Identifying common ground | Building consensus | Ensuring follow-up |
|---|---|---|---|---|---|---|
| Open house | ✠ | ✠ | ✠ | ✠ | | ✠ |
| Stakeholder meeting | ✠ | ✠ | ✠ | | | ✠ |
| Workshop | | ✠ | ✠ | ✠ | ✠ | |
| Advisor/liaison committee | | ✠ | ✠ | ✠ | ✠ | ✠ |
| Discussion paper/call for submissions | ✠ | ✠ | | | | |
| Toll-free number | ✠ | ✠ | | | | |
| Targeted briefing | ✠ | ✠ | ✠ | | | ✠ |
| Seminar | | ✠ | ✠ | | | |
| Site visit | ✠ | ✠ | ✠ | | | |
| Expert committee | | ✠ | ✠ | ✠ | | ✠ |
| Formal hearings | | ✠ | | | | |
| Informal communication | ✠ | ✠ | ✠ | ✠ | ✠ | ✠ |
| Distributing collateral materials/information | ✠ | | | | | ✠ |

company soon acknowledged the sincerity of everyone involved. According to the community "The turning point was when we started to ask probing questions and demanding answers which were dependent upon having access to normally confidential information. The Nexen people were the first to support us and agreed to full disclosure." Trustworthy behavior is the precursor to the establishment of trust.

There were many options open to the community and the company in order to reach each other, identify issues or concerns, and bring matters to the table for the committee to discuss and resolve. Examples of some of the mechanisms available in the consultation process are shown in Table 20.1.

There are four commonly recognized levels of consultation—and different levels may occur or may be needed at different times in any project cycle:

1  *Comment* when seeking input only.
2  *Dialogue* to provide a forum for identifying and discussing issues but not resolving them.
3  *Agreement* to identify common ground and agree to unresolved issues.
4  *Consensus* resolution of all issues satisfactorily to all parties.

Different approaches work best with different individuals or groups—not all are the same in terms of their interest, support, or issues. Leaders in community consultation endeavor to find ways to communicate with all stakeholders along the continuum (see Table 20.2).

Terms like "consult" and "engage" have many meanings: be clear about those issues upon which you are prepared to consult with community stakeholders and those that are non-negotiable, and define at what stages of the project you are prepared to consult and then communicate the process clearly:

1  The consultation process.
2  The business process.
3  The regulatory process.
4  The implementation planning process.
5  The follow-up and feedback plan.

In the months that followed that first meeting and the establishment of the committees, almost all of the community issues were addressed and consensus reached on their resolution. The report eventually delivered by the committee to the government regulator concluded that the residents would not object to the drilling of additional wells subject to the implementation of a number of recommendations. Important to the resolution was the need for the final government approval to include enforcement of the most stringent technological standards available, timing considerations for

Table 20.2   *Common characteristics of stakeholder populations*

| GROUP | | | | |
|---|---|---|---|---|
| Fighters | Foes | Fence sitters | Friends | Family |
| **CHARACTERISTICS** | | | | |
| Committed to making it fail | No reason to be involved in making it work | Waiting to be persuaded/convinced changes are good | See change as important, but not essential | Committed to making change really work |
| Opposed | Opposed | Let it happen | Help it happen | Make it happen |
| **BEHAVIORS** | | | | |
| Return to "good old days" Threatened antagonists Silent saboteurs, or noisy, open and confrontational | Loss of prestige, power Fear of significant increase in work load Behind the scenes | Neutral Spinning wheels Looking for signs Blank sheet | Want to succeed See general interest advantage | Believers Acceptance of need Self interest in being involved |
| Active opposition | Passive opposition | Neutral at best | Passive supporters | Active supporters |
| 20% of the population: ask them what they need; enable them to support the change | | 60% of the population: keep them informed; build their involvement | 20% of the population: engage them as change agents and champions | |

Plate 20.2   *Involving the community in the decision-making process*

continued development, emergency ignition practices, further public communication mechanisms, and residential and industrial set-back considerations.

What was originally perceived by many to be impossible only one year earlier, was ultimately achieved—a win/win benefit for all. "In the end, the success of the group was not measured by who got their own way, but rather in terms of shared pride in our conclusions and in the consensus process used in arriving at those conclusions," stated community representative Brian Holmes.

## WHAT WORKED

Key elements in the success of this consultative process were identifying a credible, strong yet neutral, facilitator, and the immediate establishment of terms of reference that governed the process. It was critical that the participants in the process represented the widest spectrum of views on the issues. In addition, it was extremely important that the participants identified the issues of concern— the company did not assume beforehand that it knew or understood the issues that were to be raised. Accordingly, a management process was clearly defined that tracked the issues and progress made in achieving resolution of those issues (see Plate 20.3).

Plate 20.3    *After the NCACC process: a paradigm shift in news headlines*

Once the issues of the sour gas operations were clearly defined, they were consolidated into four key work areas:

1   Public safety.
2   Orderly and economic development of the reserves.
3   Land use conflicts.
4   Communications.

Subcommittees of the main or plenary forum were established for these areas and each was chaired by a member of the public. At the subcommittee level, each of the issues was examined in detail, resolution sought for any outstanding areas of disagreement, and then consensus pursued before the plenary group. Government, Nexen, and outside consultants provided technical expertise when needed.

Interestingly, the residents concluded that the use of outside parties was not required.

## PUBLIC AFFAIRS LESSONS NEXEN LEARNED

Building upon these experiences and others that the company now defines within its framework of Corporate Social Responsibility, Nexen undertook to work with industry and government in the development of "The International Code of Ethics for Canadian Business." Key principles embodied in the code helped Nexen to develop a policy framework that incorporates the following in its consultation approach:

1   Local communities need to be involved in the decision making for issues that affect them.
2   Public consultation and community engagement add value and contribute towards a stable operating environment.
3   Consultation is the preferred mechanism to resolving issues with stakeholders.
4   Open, honest, and transparent relationships are critical to our success.
5   Provide meaningful and transparent consultation with all stakeholders and attempt to integrate activities with local communities.
6   It is the public that must decide what constitutes an acceptable level of risk to their lives. The company's role in this process is to help facilitate that understanding.

The Nexen experience with this process led to the development and widespread recognition of a set of prerequisites for successful public consultation:

1   There must be genuine willingness on the part of all parties to engage in the consultation process.
2   There needs be some flexibility in the positions of all parties.
3   All parties must be willing to engage in "straight talk."

4   There must be a champion to initiate and drive the process.
5   There needs to be an informed, yet neutral, third-party facilitator.

In addition, the company recognized that it is not just the scientific determination of the risk that is critical to resolving issues of concern in the community. Of equal importance is the ability to communicate that risk effectively, and to acknowledge that any "perceived" risk is as valid an issue as any scientifically proven risk. Clearly, perception is regarded as the editor of reality.

## THE PATH FORWARD

The tremendous satisfaction that emerged among the participants in the NCACC process influenced how the company currently conducts its activities with respect to public consultation and community engagement. Public consultation itself has evolved in the Alberta oil and gas industry. The industry now has clearly established guidelines to assist companies in planning their community engagement process. First developed in the 1990s, and updated in 2003 with direct input from Nexen, the "Guide for Effective Public Involvement" was developed by member companies of the Canadian Association of Petroleum Producers. An online version of this guide is available at www.capp.ca.

The five-step process is an effective tool in assisting energy exploration and development companies (or for that matter any industrial development) better understand many of the above-ground and community issues that are often not considered during the initial phases of project development (see Exhibit 20.1). These guidelines provide a very useful and directly applicable resource in fulfilling the regulatory requirements and minimum standards for consultation and notification required by the law. AEUB Guide 56 outlines these requirements and is a mandatory process for any energy development application in Alberta.

---

### Exhibit 20.1 Steps for Implementing a Public Involvement Program

1   **Establish preliminary plan**
    Identify project parameters.
    Ensure corporate commitment.
    Understand regulatory requirements.
    Factors in determining the level of public involvement.
    Gather and analyse preliminary information.
    What to look for.
    Information sources.
    Identify possible issues and stakeholders.
    Document all commitments and contracts.
    Allocate appropriate time, resources, and budget.
    Plan for public input to be incorporated into decision making.
    Wrap up Step 1.

2   **Make initial community contacts**
    Make preliminary contacts.
    Communicate with formal/informal leaders.
    Identify issues.
    Determine how stakeholders wish to be consulted.
    Wrap up Step 2.

---

3   **Prepare a detailed plan**
    Plan public involvement activities.
    Wrap up Step 3.

4   **Continue next level of public involvement and issue resolution**
    Carry out public involvement activities.
    Continue to track contracts and commitments.
    Analyse information.
    Creative problem solving and consensus building.
    Follow through with public and stakeholders.
    Wrap up Step 4.

5   **Monitor and evaluate**
    Monitor program activities.
    Monitoring approaches.
    Evaluate program.
    Wrap up Step 5.

*Source* Canadian Association of Petroleum Producers (2003), *Guide for Effective Public Involvement.* Calgary: CAPP.

---

Nexen firmly believes that community consultation is founded on building awareness, trust, accountability, and commitment in the communities in which it operates. Community consultation actively seeks to involve the public and community in the processes and decisions that may impact their lives and livelihood. The company believes that communities have the legitimate right to know about planned and ongoing activities and to participate in the decision-making process for those issues that affect them.

Nexen also believes that in identifying shared concerns, it is better able to find shared solutions and opportunities and that while it is the government that grants permits, it is the community that gives permission.

## SYNERGY GROUPS: FINGERPRINTS EVERYWHERE

Building on the success and experience of past programs, Nexen undertook a key role in the formation of a new community consultation organization that oversees an area greater than 2,700 km² with hundreds of sour gas resources and a number of operating companies. The organization, The Airdrie and Area Public and Petroleum Producers Awareness Alliance (APPA), is a community-based society that seeks to:

1   Provide a collaborative forum where community and industry can discuss and address areas of mutual concern in an open, constructive, and non-threatening environment.
2   Challenge the petroleum industry to find new ways to explore, develop, and produce hydrocarbon resources in a safe, efficient, and environmentally friendly manner.
3   Develop and encourage "best practices" for petroleum operations.
4   Demonstrate how industry and community can work together collaboratively.
5   Optimize communication with the community and affected stakeholders to recognize opportunities and reduce impacts.

Nexen saw tremendous value in working to develop a community and industry communication and awareness forum in the rural and urban fringe of Calgary given the continued development of petroleum and sour gas resources in the area. This multi-stakeholder group looks to communicate, address, and resolve public concerns about petroleum activities and energy development. The group has become a vehicle for both community and industry to communicate in a positive and responsible manner. The terms of reference are summarized by the group's mission statement and personal contract, signed by all committee members:

### APPA Mission Statement

WHEREAS: As oil and gas operators in the appa area, we recognize that our continued "public license to operate" is dependent on visible and continuous demonstration of good will and neighborly relations with nearby residents, land owners and communities, and

WHEREAS: As residents in the appa area, we have an opportunity to participate in a constructive, meaningful and open manner in a mechanism for addressing our concerns associated with being neighbors of the petroleum industry.

We, the APPA member undersigned, hereby declare that we will strive in good faith to achieve the following objectives of the Airdrie and Area Public and Petroleum Producers Awareness Alliance (APPA):

- To promote co-operation, continuing communication, distribution of information and understanding between individual oil and gas companies as well as between the oil and gas companies and the public.
- To allow for effective response to events that may impact the public, the environment or industry personnel.
- To create awareness of risks and potential impacts, to recognize opportunities to minimize these through the development of and adherence with APPA member Best Practices, and to support programs for the sustainability of renewable resources for future generations.
- To participate in discussion of concerns affecting the interests of the community, regulatory agencies and the oil and gas industry in the APPA area in an open, constructive and efficient manner.
- To assist with the development of, and to follow APPA Best Practices, which address various operational issues of concern to local residents. It is further agreed that this

commitment will extend to contractors and joint-venture partners who are under the direction of APPA member companies.
- To provide opportunities to publicly recognize positive actions by APPA members that further the aims and objectives of APPA and which contribute to positive relations between residents and the petroleum industry in the APPA area.
- In recognition of the fact that APPA is a voluntary organization, we agree to be open to various measures and encouragements as may be agreed to by the APPA membership and honor APPA Best Practices.

APPA is a community-based registered society. It works to provide a forum where the community and the petroleum industry can address areas of mutual concern, identify synergies that minimize the industry's footprint on the community, and develop "best practices" that ensure consistency in approaching areas of concern. Four committees, similar to the NCACC process established by Nexen in the early 1990s, carry out APPA's work. The committees (Communications, Safety and Health, Environment, and Operations Integration) meet every other month and are co-chaired by the community and the petroleum and energy industry. A general or plenary meeting occurs approximately every two months following the subcommittee meetings. These meetings are widely advertised so that the general public can participate (see Plate 20.4).

Plate 20.4   *APPA open house near Calgary: bringing industry and community together*

Nexen facilitated the distribution of nearly 5,000 information brochures to residents in the rural areas northeast of Calgary and organized the first multi-industry open house event for the new group. The open house and information session sought to facilitate communication of planned and ongoing activities as well as to provide a forum for education on current events and undertakings in the petroleum industry. Regulators and other key stakeholders and community interest groups were also invited to participate. Feedback mechanisms and interviews from attendees were incorporated into the performance and communications processes. APPA continues to evolve to meet the needs of the community and in 2004 a consensus was achieved through the membership to include other industrial developments. Thus the mandate will change to reflect the synergies of an expanded and renewed community consultation panel.

## THE FUTURE FOR NEXEN: RESPONSIBLE CARE®

Taking community involvement and awareness to the next step in its evolution, Nexen began a journey that few upstream oil and gas operations have embarked upon. Nexen, working with the Canadian Chemical Producers Association (CCPA), has undertaken the "Responsible Care®" initiative.[2] Responsible Care: Beyond What's Required® is a comprehensive health, safety, environment, and community issues management system established in 1985 by the CCPA to address public concerns about the manufacture, distribution, and use of chemicals.

The issues addressed by the development of Responsible Care® are much like what the oil and gas industry faces today. Nexen Chemicals and Responsible Care® have become synonymous in the company's chemical operations for more than a decade, and Nexen Chemicals has been a leader in Responsible Care® implementation since 1991. Leveraging from this experience and seeing the value added opportunities, Nexen's Oil and Gas Divisions and Canadian Nexen in Yemen have also begun the

process of implementing this highly effective management system in their operations.

Nexen Canada began the process of Responsible Care® supporting systems development at the Balzac complex sour gas processing facility near northeast Calgary in late 2000 and in October 2002 the Balzac complex became the first upstream oil and gas operation in the world to be Responsible Care® verified. "Doing the right thing, and being seen as doing the right thing" is fundamental to the Responsible Care® ethic.

The codes of practice that make up Responsible Care® have the underlying theme that addresses "the protection of people and the environment through the responsible management of … products, processes, and operations." Like the guiding principles, the codes reflect an ethic, an attitude, and even a way of thinking about the way ascribing companies conduct business and their role in society. In meeting the intent of Responsible Care® companies must be sensitive to concerns of the community and respond to them. They must develop and employ processes of regular communication and establish outreach programs to ensure that stakeholders are receiving accurate and timely information.

Nexen believes that the Responsible Care® ethic is the next step in the future of community involvement and public consultation for its industry. Meeting the community's needs for communication and involvement and addressing issues of the human environment will be the measure of the company's success as it looks to access resources in an environment of ever increasing sensitivities.

## CONCLUSION

Nexen continues to play an active and significant role in the evolution and development of public consultation in the Canadian upstream oil and gas industry. The company, and its public affairs-related professionals in particular, continue to learn from their own experiences and those of others, and contribute to the ongoing improvement of public consultation and community engagement in Canada and internationally. Nexen's efforts have been recognized for their contributions in this area by several prestigious organizations, including, among others, the Global Compact, IPIECA, the Dow Jones Sustainability Index, the International Association for Public Participation, and the Canadian Association of Petroleum Producers.

The greatest recognition though is the acknowledgement from community members when they view Nexen as a good corporate citizen and a welcome community member. These are the lasting, positive fingerprints that this company wants to leave behind.

## NOTES

1 See International Code of Ethics for Canadian Business (www.nexeninc.com).

2 Responsible Care: A Total Commitment® is a registered trademark of the Canadian Chemical Producers Association (www.ccpa.ca).

## APPENDIX 20.1 INTERNATIONAL CODE OF ETHICS FOR CANADIAN BUSINESS

### Vision

Canadian business has a global presence that is recognized by all stakeholders as economically rewarding to all parties, acknowledged as being ethically, socially and environmentally responsible, welcomed by the communities in which we operate, and that facilitates economic, human resource and community development within a stable operating environment.

We believe that:

- we can make a difference within our sphere of influence (our stakeholders);
- business should take a leadership role through establishment of ethical business principles;
- national governments have the prerogative to conduct their own government and legal affairs in accordance with their sovereign rights;
- all governments should comply with international treaties and other agreements that they have committed to, including the areas of human rights and social justice;
- while reflecting cultural diversity and differences, we should do business throughout the world consistent with the way we do business in Canada;
- the business sector should show ethical leadership;
- we can facilitate the achievement of wealth generation and a fair sharing of economic benefits;
- our principles will assist in improving relations between the Canadian and host governments;
- open, honest and transparent relationships are critical to our success;
- local communities need to be involved in decision making for issues that affect them;
- multistakeholder processes need to be initiated to seek effective solutions;
- confrontation should be tempered by diplomacy;
- wealth maximization for all stakeholders will be enhanced by resolution of outstanding human rights and social justice issues; and
- doing business with other countries is good for Canada and vice versa.

We value:

- human rights and social justice;
- wealth maximization for all stakeholders;
- operation of a free market economy;
- public accountability by governments;
- a business environment which militates against bribery and corruption;

- equality of opportunity;
- a defined code of ethics and business practice;
- protection of environmental quality and sound environmental stewardship;
- community benefits;
- good relationships with all stakeholders; and
- stability and continuous improvement within our operating environment.

## Principles

(A) Concerning Community Participation and Environmental Protection, we will:

- strive within our sphere of influence to ensure a fair share of benefits to stakeholders impacted by our activities;
- ensure meaningful and transparent consultation with all stakeholders and attempt to integrate our corporate activities with local communities as good corporate citizens;
- ensure our activities are consistent with sound environmental management and conservation practices; and
- provide meaningful opportunities for technology cooperation, training and capacity building within the host nation.

(B) Concerning Human Rights, we will:

- support and respect the protection of international human rights within our sphere of influence; and
- not be complicit in human rights abuses.

(C) Concerning Business Conduct, we will:

- not make illegal and improper payments and bribes and will refrain from participating in any corrupt business practices;
- comply with all applicable laws and conduct business activities with integrity; and
- ensure contractor's, supplier's and agent's activities are consistent with these principles.

(D) Concerning Employee Rights and Health and Safety, we will:

- ensure health and safety of workers is protected;
- strive for social justice and respect freedom of association and expression in the workplace; and
- ensure consistency with other universally accepted labour standards, related to exploitation of child labour, forced labour and non-discrimination in employment.

## APPENDIX 20.2 TERMS OF REFERENCE NORTHEAST CALGARY APPLICATION CONSULTATION COMMITTEE (NCACC)

### Purpose

The purpose of the NCACC is to provide a forum in which a wide cross-section of stakeholders can identify and coordinate a review of issues arising from Canadian Occidental Petroleum Limited's (CanadianOxy) proposal for additional sour gas development within the Crossfield Field in the immediate vicinity of the City of Calgary. The Committee will play a *consultative, advisory* and *meditative* role. Recommendations developed through the Committee are subject to the normal regulatory jurisdiction of the Energy Resources Conservation Board (ERCB) and other departments of the government of Alberta. The process is not intended to preclude full consideration of all aspects of the application at a public hearing.

## Objective

- Maximize the cooperation, communication and distribution of information between affected parties.
- Optimize the satisfaction of stakeholders wherever possible with the ultimate decisions reached.
- Minimize the time, inconvenience and cost associated with the review and decision process.

## Membership

Representatives in organizations as outlined in Attachment 1 or as modified by consensus of the Committee.

## Mandate

- To coordinate the review and assure adequate public consultation of issues in an open and honest manner.
- The role of the NCACC will be reviewed after the formal applications are filed.

## Terms of Reference

- Develop an operating procedure for NCACC.
- Identify and define significant issues of mutual interest to all key stakeholders on all aspects of drilling and operation of the proposed facilities.
- Identify and define expectations of participants.
- Advise and assist the applicant to develop a public information program for potential applications.
- Identify and coordinate any independent assessments of issues that may be required.
- Document any agreements reached, supplementary information filed, concerns raised and assurances given during the consultation and review process.
- Submit a report for consideration by the ERCB on the views of the Committee:

  i. Issues addressed.
  ii. Suitability of the project for final disposition by ERCB.
  iii. Conclusions reached and/or conditions for consideration of the ERCB should the project be approved.

## Organization

- NCACC will be chaired by a neutral third party facilitator agreed to by the Committee.
- Agenda for meetings and "invited guests" who may participate to be agreed on in advance through the chairman.
- Working meetings will be "in camera" although public meetings can be scheduled as considered appropriate.

- The Secretariat for the Committee will be provided by the ERCB.
- Stakeholders should be represented at senior levels of their organization and delegates should have a commitment to participate throughout the process.
- Each stakeholder has one formal seat at the table, but can be accompanied by advisors as appropriate.
- NCACC will make decisions on a consensus basis (no votes) with notes on the meetings taken and distributed to the stakeholders; there will be no restriction on those items which might be discussed by the Committee, but only directly relevant items will be documented.
- NCACC subcommittees may be formed to deal with specific concerns in greater detail, deliberation of the subcommittees will be brought back for consideration and disposition of the NCACC.
- NCACC may deem it advisable to hire consultants to advise it on certain technical aspects of the project. If so, it will request CanadianOxy and/or any other appropriate agency to fund the consultant study, and will not proceed to hire a consultant until proper authorization is received.
- NCACC meeting cost will be covered by CanadianOxy.
- Reasonable out of pocket expenses for NCACC members on meeting days may be covered by CanadianOxy.
- If there is a lack of agreement on any items, each party is free to play its normal role with its constituency, or at any public meeting or hearing with respect to outstanding issues.
- Regardless of the outcome of the discussions of the Committee, the final decisions on the application would have to be in conformance with the established legislation.
- Committee members will be as cooperative as possible with the other participants with respect to public release of information or communication with the media, and would seek NCACC input to the maximum extent possible regarding public releases or statements.

## Timing

NCACC will hold regular meetings as required, the location to be agreed upon by the Committee.

## NCACC Stakeholder Membership Group Representation

1   Balzac Rate Payer Association (BRPA).
2   Bow North Surface Rights Group (Bow North).
3   Federation of Calgary Communities (Federation).
4   Summer Village of Chestermere Lake (Chestermere).

5   Abbeydale Community Association (Abbeydale).
6   Applewood Park Community Association (Applewood).
7   Calgary Marlborough Community Association (Calgary Marlborough).
8   Forest Heights Hubalta Community Association (Forest Heights).
9   Marlborough Park Community Association (Marlborough Park).
10  Martindale Community Association (Martindale).
11  Monteray Park Community Association (Monteray Park).
12  Penbrooke Community Association (Penbrooke).
13  Pineridge Community Association (Pineridge).
14  Taradale Community Association (Taradale).
15  Temple Community Association (Temple).
16  Whitehorn Community Association (Whitehorn).

17  Canadian Occidental Petroleum Limited (CanadianOxy).

18  Alberta Environment (AE).

19  Alberta Public Safety Services (APSS).

20  Calgary Health Services (CHS).

21  Calgary Regional Planning Commission (CRPC).

22  City of Calgary (City).

23  Energy Resources Conservation Board (ERCB).

24  MD of Rockyview No. 44 (MD).

## REFERENCES

Burke, E.M. (1999). *Corporate Community Relations: The Principle of the Neighbor of Choice.* Westport, CT: Quorum Books.

Covello, V., and P. Sandman (2001). "Risk Communication: Evolution and Revolution," in A. Wolbarst (ed.), *Solutions to an Environment in Peril.* Baltimore, MD: Johns Hopkins University Press.

Sandman, P. (2004). "Managing Stakeholder Outrage: Corporate Citizenship on the Dark Side," comments from a keynote speech presented to the Annual International Corporate Citizenship Conference of the Center for Corporate Citizenship of Boston College, San Francisco, March 30.

# 21

# An Integrated Model: The Evolution of Public Affairs Down Under

GEOFF ALLEN

Public affairs management in Australia changed dramatically in the decade of the 1990s and continues to change as innovation in leading companies spreads through to others. The pace of change in the nature of the function has varied considerably across companies, and is more advanced in industry sectors that are more vulnerable to social and political pressures. In general, however, public affairs grew over that decade from a lower to middle level function to one increasingly accepted as more strategic and more senior.

The annual oration of the Centre for Corporate Public Affairs[1] affords an opportunity for captains of industry to reflect on its role in Australia. Introducing the first oration in 1994, Mark Rayner, then a top mining executive and later chairman of three of Australia's largest companies, said:

> In my experience Public Affairs means many different things to different Australian managers, whether it is performed in companies or in industry associations. Perhaps influenced by the team in my own company, with which I have worked very closely, I have come to accept the view of Public Affairs that seems to be the model adopted by the Centre.

This view stresses that the function should:

- contribute significantly to the way business relates to its internal and external stakeholders;
- interpret the current and future social and political environment for strategic commercial planning; and
- encourage the integration of responsibility for dealing with social and political matters with other aspects of direct line management.

More and more, the role of Public Affairs executives ought to be about driving and managing that integration.

(Rayner, 1994)

John Prescott, then CEO of Australia's largest company, BHP (now BHP Billiton), bringing the 1995 Oration to a conclusion, said:

> I spoke of the community's license to operate, and the notion of legitimacy so essential to survival. To maintain this legitimacy, and to ensure a positive environment in which to operate, requires skills and approaches which are as important as the financial, technical and marketing capabilities which we have traditionally valued.

Public affairs people play a vital role in the process, which is reflected in BHP's support for the Centre for Corporate Public Affairs, and for a more sophisticated development of public affairs specialists. They have the communication skills, the community contacts and the understanding of different audiences—internal and external—which are important to the firm's future.

In essence, they are the acknowledged authority on the social and political environments and their effect on our business. As such, they are playing an increasingly strategic role in planning, issues management and the creative use of public policy to further company goals.

The public affairs role is also evolving in other ways. It's my belief that forging closer partnerships with our communities involves changing the thinking of our managers.

(Prescott, 1995)

Dealing with social, political and industrial issues has to be part of the normal line management role, and part of the company's culture. Performance in this area is fast becoming a core function of managers. Prescott continued:

Shifting prime responsibility for external relationships to the line means that the public affairs people become the specialists. They define the need, have the primary expertise, and can still be the conscience and coach where necessary. This evolution of the role fits in with our efforts to bring community interests to the decision making table at every stage of our planning.

(Prescott, 1995)

These underlying themes of acknowledged expertise, the significance of the sociopolitical context of companies—embedding new understanding and skills in the line management task and engagement of public affairs practitioners in corporate strategic planning—reflect the role of best practice companies as perceived in Australia. However, practitioners in many companies are still struggling to have this ideal, and their potential contribution, recognized by others in their management teams.

## THE AUSTRALIAN POLITICAL SYSTEM

The Australian political system has been dubbed "Washminster," reflecting its hybrid nature and its antecedents in constitutional design. It is a federal system with six state and two small territory governments sharing power with the national government in Canberra. The federation occurred at the start of the twentieth century when six British colonies ceded some powers to a new national government. New Zealand was active in federation negotiations but declined to join the federation late in the process. Although the national government received limited, prescribed powers, with residual matters remaining with the states, subsequent forces, including a later transfer of major taxing powers, referred powers in emerging areas requiring national cohesion (such as companies and securities law) and a liberal interpretation by the High Court of the national government's foreign affairs and international trade powers, have conspired to make Canberra the main focus for corporate attention. States, however, retain most control of issues important to some industries such as environmental protection, planning and local infrastructure, some consumer law, trading hours and a large part of labor law. Accordingly companies need to manage relations at both state and national levels.

The national and most state parliaments are bicameral systems with upper Houses capable of blocking legislation. Frequently, the balance of power in state and federal upper Houses is held by independents and/or minority parties. As in Westminster, the Ministers forming the executive are drawn from the parties or coalitions with a majority in the lower House, and the executive is responsible to the Parliament.

Australian politics has been dominated by two broad groupings. The Australian Labor Party, which commenced as a product of the trade union movement, is one. Union power is still relevant but waning in the party, which can now be broadly characterized as a moderate, left-of-center and increasingly middle-class organization. On the other side is a more conservative long-standing coalition of the mainstream urban middle-class Liberal Party and a smaller agrarian-based party, the Nationals.

Since the mid-1980s both sides of politics have broadly coalesced around an elite consensus on free trade, fiscal rectitude, limited government enterprise, and a broadly similar Western Alliance foreign policy. Approaches to business regulation differ only in degree, although a major difference exists in relation to the role of unions and centralized industrial relations. Apart from industrial relations the other significant divide is between what might be called "liberal" or "socially progressive" elements and social conservatives, but this division is distributed well within both major party groupings.

Party discipline has been relatively strong and power within government is concentrated in the hands of Ministers, and particularly the Prime Minister (or Premiers in the states). Governments have been traditionally supported by powerful, professional, and independent bureaucracies. However, notwithstanding continuing great influence in some areas this power has been eroded over the 1990s by the rise of political staff in Ministers' offices, and by an increasing churn (albeit still limited and at the top echelon) of senior officials following government changes.

More important, however, has been increased contestability in policy matters from specialist consultancies providing, on the one hand, sophisticated research-based advocacy in support of various constituencies and, on the other, engaging in the new and growing field of outsourced policy work for governments. This has been accompanied also by more sophisticated and questioning media and greater general public involvement in the major debates of the day.

Another challenge to the monopoly of power in the hands of the executive has come from changes in the dynamics of politics. The minor parties, which tend to be of the left, and which have acquired the balance of power in the upper Houses, have consequently become a new necessary target for lobbying over impending legislation and are thus a target for relationship building.

## GOVERNMENT RELATIONS

In a nation of only 20 million people and seven governments the political system is relatively accessible for senior business and other interest-group representatives. For most of the twentieth century the unchallenged concentration of political power in the hands of a few top bureaucrats and senior Ministers had made public policy advocacy a relatively direct and simple matter. More recently proponents of policy have not only had to provide a good political rationale to align their objectives with the political imperatives of decision makers, they have had to provide them with a robust public policy rationale. This rationale has also to win acceptance by a wider circle in the political and policy elite, and on sensitive issues by better informed, suspicious, and more involved media and general public in vigorous open debates.

In this environment public affairs practitioners are obliged to be more sophisticated in their approach in terms of public policy and political analysis, and agenda setting. A revolution in research-based advocacy took place following the leadership of some national business organizations in the late 1970s and 1980s and has deepened consequently. However, as the political system moves more closely towards the multipoint decision making of the US system, the US experience in public advocacy, coalition building, and grassroots communication and lobbying is being explored with interest.

As in most places Australian politicians are careful not to waste their political capital. A classic illustration of policy environment in Australia was the campaign around controversial legislation to introduce a broad-based consumption tax. Prime Minister Howard had long been a champion of a shift from the relative weighting of direct and indirect taxes. Several prior attempts had been made with significant political damage to proponents and the conventional wisdom was that it was off the agenda. Business interests supporting the shift were told by the Prime Minister that if they could change the political climate to make it achievable without damaging the government, he would pursue the change. The first step for business leaders was to enter a deep dialogue with the leading NGO opponent of the change, the Australian Council of Social Services (ACOSS). After research and deep dialogue ACOSS agreed to support change under certain conditions. The business interests, led by the major CEO organization Business Council of Australia, mounted a campaign which included interest-group dialogue to reduce opposition, paid advertising, and traditional lobbying. The needle of public opinion swung sufficiently to allow the government to embrace the policy. It became the center of a national election campaign in 1998 following which the government was re-elected. After this, and the winning of some concessions in further bargaining on the detail of the new tax, sufficient support was gained within the left-leaning minor parties to achieve the necessary legislation. The coalition of major business organizations working together enabled necessary cohesion and momentum on the business side throughout this campaign.

The dynamics of advocacy are much the same on major issues for individual industries or major companies. They require a well researched and robust public policy rationale, access, and trust, involving a broadening range of political and bureaucratic decision makers. They are significantly impacted by the actions of other interested parties, particularly in the organized interest-group community, whether at the national or neighborhood levels.

It is relevant here that business, especially big business, is not held in high esteem by the general public. As in many developed countries the community considers big business to be untrustworthy and uninterested in community well-being. Many interest groups, including strident corporate critics, are more trusted, impacting the credibility of the business voice in competitive advocacy.

Not surprisingly, then, collaborative community relations and social investment programs, involving interest groups and other respected NGOs as partners, are a common tool for dialogue, building trust, and maximizing alignment of interests. The media

are a major tool for providing supportive information, framing issues, and agenda setting, and it is important for company staff to be supportive of public policy agendas, both for their own comfort and as ambassadors of the company's position.

Accordingly, at least on the big issues, all the major tools of corporate communications and community relations are employed together with government relations expertise in the task of influencing government and pursuing public policy agendas.

## AN INTEGRATED FUNCTION

The function as it is most commonly conceived in Australia integrates the two major strands of communications and government relations into a single management entity. This integration has taken place only since the mid-1980s as these roles became more strategic and as the issues environment and desired relationship with multiple stakeholders required a holistic external relations response from companies.

Key drivers of change in this issues environment were the rise of participative democracy which in turn was driven by increased public sophistication in policy debates and demand for a voice, the rise and enhanced influence in policy resolution of NGOs, and the increased power of populist minority political parties. As noted above, in the management of most significant issues there is seen to be the need for a holistic packaging of government relations, media management, other external and internal communication, and not uncommonly investor relations. The integrated function is seen to be desirable to ensure the best capacity to anticipate the behavior of those various stakeholders and opinion leaders who influence issue outcomes and a cohesive response.

A practical reason driving this integration, however, has been the limited scale of Australian businesses. Many large enterprises in Australia are divisions of multinational companies. However, the range of market capitalization of the first to the twentieth largest listed Australian company is US$48.5 billion to US$5.25 billion (at July 2004 exchange rate $A0.70 to $US1.00).

The only systematic data collection across the function in Australia is the survey undertaken every three years by the Centre for Corporate Public Affairs of its members and other leading companies. The study conducted through the second half of calendar year 2003 (Centre, 2003) throws some light on the nature and standing of public affairs practice in Australia.

The seventy seven respondents to the Centre 2003 survey consisted of some industry associations, government statutory authorities, and the public affairs departments of some other government agencies. However, the large majority were government and private sector business enterprises from Australia's top 100 companies. The Centre 2003 survey was answered in almost all cases by the organization's most senior public affairs practitioner.

On average the Centre 2003 survey found a sizable minority of listed companies had less than five professionals across these combined government relations and communications functions, more than three-quarters had fewer than twenty professionals and only 10 percent of listed companies had thirty or more. While the research data omit information from some companies at the large end of the scale and budget, the average administrative budget for the function in listed companies was only around A$6 million (US$4.2 million) (Centre, 2003). Accordingly public affairs departments are smaller than US and UK counterparts and, as noted, integrating the two clusters of function under a single executive provides critical mass and administrative advantages.

Despite these recent changes there are a number of companies in which government relations and communications are still managed in the traditional silos. In these companies, as in other companies with an integrated function but at an early stage in their evolution, the communications/public relations role is performed at a relatively low level, combining the roles of "problem dump" to deal *ad hoc* with issues necessarily late in their life cycle and "spin doctor" to put the best light possible on the corporation and its products.

In a similar vein government relations (sometimes called "regulatory affairs") practitioners simply monitor legislative and regulatory arrangements and seek where appropriate, often through technical argument, to defend interests concerning for example trade protection, taxation policy, and licensing.

As conceived within this less advanced model both the communications and government relations roles are reactive, largely involve one-way asymmetrical communication, and are seen as somewhat exotic and remote from the core management task. Accordingly practitioners are less likely to be in the information loop and in a position to contribute to strategic thinking and planning.

The name "public affairs" tends to be used in the United States and United Kingdom to connote government relations, although there appears to be a trend towards a more integrated model globally and this has been the situation in a number of major UK and US multinational companies for many years. Consistent with Australia's integrated model, however "public affairs" does not particularly connote government relations. Rather, the titles "government relations," "government and regulatory affairs," and "government relations and public policy" are commonly used—along with corporate communications—to denote a major subfunction within public affairs. Recent surveys, however, show that "corporate affairs" is even more commonly used to describe the function (see Figure 21.1). This can cause confusion because for some companies "corporate affairs" is used to describe the umbrella function covering other staff functions, including, for example, human resource management, legal, internal audit, and risk management.

The Centre 2003 survey shows the nature of subfunctions covered by the relevant department and demonstrates the degree of the integration between government relations and other aspects of corporate-community boundary spanning (see Figure 21.2). Figure 21.2 needs to be read as indicative only. Some respondent organizations may or may not, for example, undertake investor relations, have retail customers or international businesses, and there are obviously blurred lines between

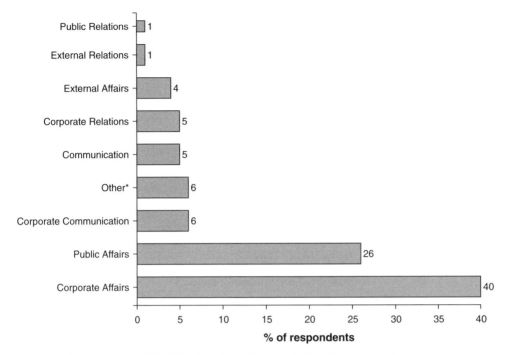

Figure 21.1    *Names for the public affairs function. Other titles include Corporate and Community Affairs and Stakeholder Comunications.* Source *Centre for Corporate Public Affairs (2003)*

brand management, corporate marketing, sponsorship, and a cluster of community relations activities. Some of these subfunctions are managed in close proximity to other lead departments and these relationships are discussed below.

Consumer affairs would frequently sit within marketing in consumer product companies. Where regulatory affairs sits outside the cluster of public affairs subfunctions this is normally in industries with a high dependence on technical regulation such as deregulated utilities, transport, and banking. Here common reporting lines are to the legal department or CFO.

In a small number of companies, for example those selling consumer non-durables with little societal or political vulnerability, low levels of government relations tasks, together with market-focused communications, would be undertaken in powerful marketing departments.

While it varies greatly across companies, the proportion of full-time professional staff working in key functional areas in Australia illustrates the level and spread of subfunctions

within an average company (see Figure 21.3). It should be noted, however, that some companies have been known recently to have more than 100 public affairs professionals and even some relatively large companies survive with only one.

Tasks, structures, and reporting relationships are continuing to change, a fact illustrated by the fact that, according to the Centre 2003 survey, a massive 48 percent of public affairs departments reported that they had been reorganized or restructured in the prior twelve months.

## STANDING AND INFLUENCE

As noted, respondents to the Centre 2003 survey were mostly the top public affairs practitioners in their companies. Of these 75 percent said they were a member of the organization's senior management team and 71 percent reported to the most senior person in the organization (chairman or CEO/managing

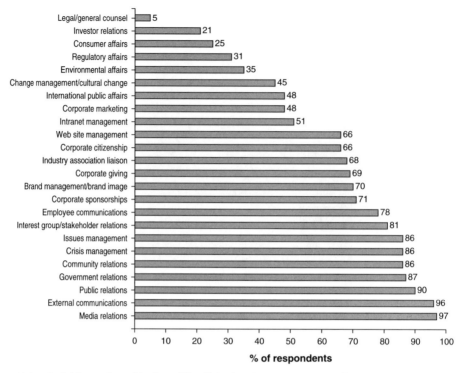

Figure 21.2   *Activities conducted in the public affairs function.* Source *Centre for Corporate Public Affairs (2003)*

director). Sixty-two percent said they were involved in routine presentations to the board on external relations issues.

In relation to the influence the function has on the strategic business planning and decision making, 75 percent of respondents said their department identifies/prioritizes issues for senior management attention, 69 percent said their department participates in the strategic planning process for the corporation, and 69 percent said the function comments on corporate strategic plans for sensitivity to emerging political/regulatory/social issues (see Figure 21.4).

An example of high-end engagement in business strategy formation is the inclusion in several companies of chapters on the medium-term future social and political context for the business in the strategic plan document, along with chapters for example on the economic and market outlook. Another example (albeit still rare) is responsibility for international

political risk assessment being placed in the hands of Public Affairs and the requirement for this department's review and report on international investment proposals before they are submitted to an executive committee and board for decision. The rationale is that the experience and skill set that go into analyzing the social, political, and regulatory issues at home are the same as those required for overseas corporate environments.

Not surprisingly the function has been mostly highly developed—in terms of scale, sophistication, internal positioning, and integration of communications and government relations—in those industries that have been most vulnerable to sociopolitical pressures. This has been clearly illustrated by the function in the oil industry since the troublesome 1970s, the mining, forestry, chemicals, and tobacco sectors in the 1980s and 1990s, and most recently pharmaceutical, alcohol, and, post-deregulation, banking and utility companies. Approaches to

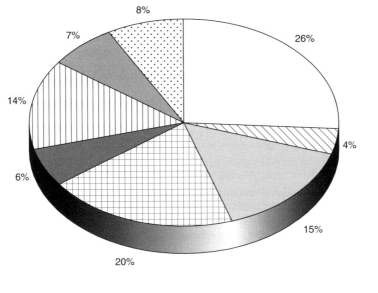

26%

4%

15%

20%

6%

14%

7%

8%

Media relations/external communications strategy

Investor relations

Stakeholder/community relations and reputation management

Government affairs/regulatory affairs/issues management

Communication strategy

Internal/employee communication

Marketing/branding

Other

Figure 21.3   *Proportion of full-time professional staff working in key functional areas.*
Source *Centre for Corporate Public Affairs (2003)*

planning for the function itself illustrate the differences in thinking in Australian companies between the old and new generation of public affairs practice.

Public affairs departments remote from strategic thinking and action tend by their nature to react to circumstances and agendas set by others. Their functional plans are less likely to be based on corporate business strategy and instead focus on subfunctional activities such as relatively disconnected government relations, media, internal communications, and community relations. Key performance indicators are more likely to assess inputs, such as their activity, rather than outcomes, measuring impact in achieving organizational objectives.

Routine public affairs products and *ad hoc* responses to unforseen events will always be important, but where plans are built around the strategic imperatives of the organization, all the tools of the integrated public affairs

function can be enlisted in function plans to achieve those objectives. Accordingly, for example, to enter a new market, or achieve sensitive regulatory change, the plans for media, government relations, stakeholder, and community relations, and these days even social investment, would coalesce around the achievement of these corporate goals. This fully articulated alignment of public affairs priorities with the most important business goals also demonstrates the value proposition of best practice public affairs.

Efforts to build function plans and subfunction plans around business's strategic imperatives have occupied Australian practitioners in recent years. In the Centre 2003 survey, respondents from around 80 percent of public affairs departments regularly prepared their own strategic plan, but of these only 45 percent stated they were formally linked to the corporate strategic plan.

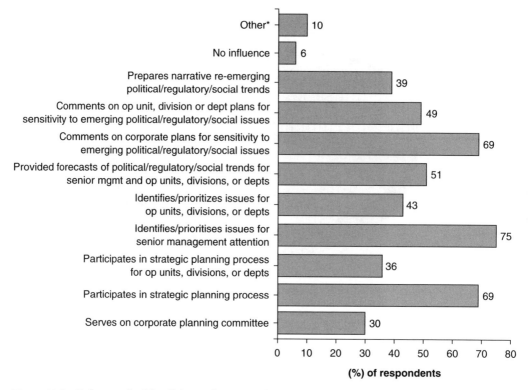

Figure 21.4   *Influence of public affairs on the strategic business planning process. Other includes: sets performance targets for operations for community and indigenous relations; injects investors' views into the process and has access to chairman and managing director on these aspects; participates in organizational risk management.* Source *Centre for Corporate Public Affairs (2003)*

## GOVERNMENT RELATIONS

As government relations management in Australia is most frequently seen as a subfunction of a broader integrated public affairs task, its specialists are most commonly in the second line of a public affairs department, sharing relative status with a communications or external relations manager. In this typical second line would be executives managing media relations, community and/or stakeholder relations, and internal communications. Invariably, however, higher-level government relations activity would also involve the head of the function, as well as the senior line manager whose issues are at stake.

Government relations managers frequently come from the ranks of Ministers' offices where,

as in Washington, they have been involved in high-level policy and political advice. A number of these political advisors will have prior experience in the civil service, which is separate from Ministers' offices, but the civil service itself has also been a direct source of a significant percentage of government relations practitioners.

The political system does not require government relations practitioners to have a legal background. The theater of lobbying is remote from the drafting of legislation, and draws more on the skills of economists, accountants, and even social policy analysts than of lawyers. Accordingly relatively few practitioners have a legal background.

Lawyers and also economists are more common in a role called "regulatory affairs," which as noted is a function common to some highly regulated industries and sometimes sits outside public affairs in technical, legal, or finance departments. This function focuses on compliance, liaison with governments on narrow technical legislation, and preparing arguments on, for example, pricing or competition policy for negotiations with business regulators. In these circumstances it is sometimes in dispute with Public Affairs, taking a technical and legalistic approach to regulators rather than the more consensual relationship-based orientation of Public Affairs.

Like Washington and Ottawa, but unlike most European countries, the political and bureaucratic capital, Canberra, is remote from most corporate headquarters. Unlike Washington, however, but with a few exceptions, public affairs practitioners are based in corporate headquarters rather than Canberra. The rationale is that the political and bureaucratic system is relatively accessible, particularly where familiarity and trust have been built over time, and it is more important for the practitioner to be close to, and understand what is happening in, the company. Government representatives are keen for market intelligence and information from the corporate world. Business is keen to understand as much as possible of the thinking and activities of government. Accordingly, such information is the currency of the constructive business-government relationship.

A majority, but by no means all, of industry associations are Canberra-based. With some rare exceptions there are no separate state-based government relations executives. State government relations are normally managed by a national government relations staff, although, where they exist, public affairs generalists in state offices of major companies would normally be involved in state government relations.

The nature of the government relations function has been relatively stable over recent years. The role and significance of industry associations have fluctuated with the competence and performance of major groups. Not unlike in the United States, associations appear to be more influential with governments that are not normally identified with business—the Australian Labor Party, and Democrats in the

United States. As elsewhere, there is a long-run trend, however, for associations to decline in active membership and influence, for short-term coalitions (sometimes with strange bedfellows) around specific issues to grow, and for larger individual companies to do their own lobbying and compete on the basis of their public policy and government relations competence.

## BRAND AND REPUTATION MANAGEMENT

There are no absolute boundaries around the integrated public affairs function in Australia. As with regulatory affairs there are a number of related specializations which may or may not be performed within public affairs departments. Where they are managed separately some companies have experienced tensions and turf wars. These subfunctions include reputation and brand management at the interface with marketing, investor relations at the interface with the finance function, and employee communications at the interface with human resource management. These will be considered in turn.

Reputation measurement and management have been among the hottest topics in public affairs in Australia in the new millennium. There are a number of reasons for this. First there is growing appreciation in business generally of reputation as an intangible asset and competitive tool. Conversely a number of corporate collapses in ignominious circumstances have reminded companies of the significance and fragility of their reputations. The relevance of reputation as a corporate competitive weapon began in the early 1990s in industries under public scrutiny, such as banks following deregulation and mining companies under attack on issues like environmental management and aboriginal land rights. Australian companies now compete on the basis of their reputations to be neighbour of choice, employer of choice, supplier of choice, business partner of choice, and to win the benefit of the doubt, where possible, with regulators. An expression of this has been the small but discernible trend for line managers to have their impact on reputation—sometimes put in terms of relations with stakeholders—as a key performance indicator and related to remuneration at risk.

A further important development has been the emergence of reputation indexes and the increasing demands of domestic and international socially responsible investment funds and their reporting and screening processes. These funds are small in Australia compared to their northern hemisphere counterparts, but are on a fast track. In any event many of Australia's largest companies seek international capital and are on, or seek to be on, the most important global indexes (Allen Consulting Group, 2000).

More controversial have been indexes designed by embryonic ratings agencies and market researchers developed for newspaper publication and linked to consultancies. In Australia, one in particular, purporting to have rankings determined on a number of criteria by around twenty organizations, a significant number of whom were NGO activists campaigning against companies they were scoring and rating (Centre, 2001a). This included the peak trade union organization adjudicating on companies challenging compulsory unionism and Greenpeace assessing the environmental reputation of chemical and uranium-producing companies. The scores and ratings were published annually with a fanfare in the national print media.

There were other serious flaws in the concept, and concern for the methodology of this high-profile ranking led to strong public criticism, not only from a large majority of senior practitioners who collectively voiced concern, but from Australia's large company CEO organization, the Business Council of Australia. This, and the lack of an appropriate current alternative, spawned a search for more acceptable methodologies for the inevitable growth of public rankings as well as the measurement of reputation as an internal management tool.

A further driver for focus on reputation has been the strong recent trend to sustainability or triple bottom-line reporting underpinned by stakeholder expectations (Allen Consulting Group, 2002). These are relatively new in their present form, but by the time of the Centre 2003 survey 74 percent of listed companies and 71 percent of independent statutory authorities said they published reports on sustainability practices. The majority published community, environment, and occupational health and safety information in a combined report produced in hard copy and online formats, reporting annually. A most recent trend has been to abandon the annual report and move to continuous disclosure online as internal data are updated.

Because of the broad social and political context of reputation management this function has been appropriated by public affairs departments and has led to an incursion into the prior ownership of brand management by marketing departments (see Figure 21.5).

Asked in the Centre 2003 survey what was the most important change in external relations over the past three years, one senior practitioner expressed a common position: "development of an integrated brand strategy that aligned the organization's entire communications/stakeholder effort." In situations like financial services and utilities, where the corporate brand and product brand are indistinguishable, there is seen to be a strong imperative to manage the corporate brand and reputation strategies in the closest possible collaboration.

Even where "brand" is seen as a product or service market issue and "reputation" is seen as an issue for customers pertaining to multiple stakeholders, alignment of these strands has been an imperative, particularly given the way in which the management of issues (public affairs), or indeed inappropriate marketing practices, can affect brand and reputation in the mind of any stakeholder. The alignment of brands, issues, and reputation can be seen as in Figure 21.6.

## COMMUNITY RELATIONS AND SPONSORSHIP

Under the emerging Australian model community relations and sponsorship activities are deeply integrated with other aspects of the

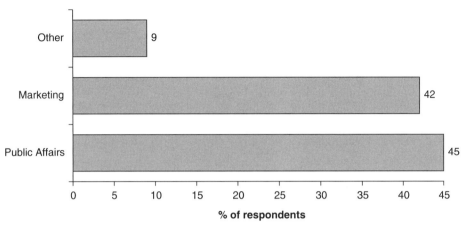

Figure 21.5   *The section of the organization that has primary responsibility for managing the corporate brand. Source Centre for Corporate Public Affairs (2003)*

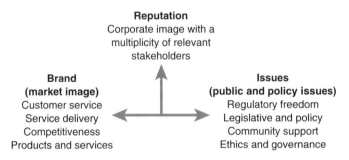

Figure 21.6   *Alignment of brand (the marketing concept of the brand) equals reputation. Source Allen Consulting Group (2002)*

public affairs task. In Australia, no doubt as elsewhere, there is a slide, with many overlaps and grey areas, from sponsorship aimed at brand awareness and sales support to community involvement or social investment aimed principally at the public good (see Exhibit 21.1).

---

**Exhibit 21.1 Sponsorship and Community Involvement: From Commercial to Philanthropic**

- *Sales support*—marketing strategies to promote uptake of products and services, which often include corporate entertainment and, when specifically targeted, should be seen as a cost of sales.
- *Cause-related marketing*, especially with retail products—"Two cents of telephone call costs on Sunday night go to handicapped children"; "Buy this cereal and help surf lifesavers."
- *Brand strategies*—brand awareness and image creation, association of company with activities that enhance desired brand or reputation characteristics.

- *Relationship building* beyond sales and marketing, using sponsorship to build useful networks and connections.
- *Political positioning* which includes both the demonstration of commitment to community values and building reputation and trust as a non-tangible asset. But also importantly to build bridges to key political/regulatory/issues advocacy opinion leaders, by association and familiarity to break down negative stereotypes and build trust. This use of community involvement or social investment has been understandably pioneered and used most actively in industries with high vulnerability to interest-group and regulatory pressures.
- *Staff engagement,* for example through matched giving or volunteer direct engagement which responds to increasing demands for employees not only to be associated with socially aware companies but to use the workplace as a channel for altruism.
- *Disinterested philanthropy* which is becoming a dated concept in public companies. The response to unsolicited requests, and particularly supporting favorite causes of powerful individuals, is passing rapidly from the public company agenda.

*Source* Allen Consulting Group (2002).

The more sponsorship is associated with a product or specific business unit market, or the more it facilitates sales relationships, the more likely it is to be run by marketing. Conversely the more it is focused on community relationship building, non-market stakeholder relations, and overall corporate reputation, the more it is likely to reside within public affairs. Where sponsorship responsibilities are split, as occurs frequently, there are dangers including positioning inconsistency, duplication of resources, cannibalization of promotional activities, and confusion with external sponsorship partners.

The subtly different orientations of marketing and public affairs departments in sponsorship and community involvement can lead to differences in language and nuance and, as indicated, there are already inconsistencies in perspective across companies or, in many cases, within them. There is a lack of clarity in many Australian companies about where marketing starts and the other goals of community involvement begin.

## COMMUNITY INVOLVEMENT

Notwithstanding the above, one of the strongest trends from the mid-1990s has been

the alignment of corporate giving with business strategy. The fullest study of corporate community involvement in Australia was undertaken in 2001 (Centre, 2001b). This project, funded by a grant from the Australian government, surveyed 115 of Australia's larger companies at both CEO and public affairs practitioner level.

About 10 percent of respondents claimed their rationale for community involvement activities was simply altruistic, "putting back to the community," and about 15 percent adopted the Friedmanite position that their social responsibilities were met exclusively by undertaking their business activities ethically and returning the surplus to shareholders.

However, for three-quarters of the companies in this study the "business case" for community involvement was claimed not only as a means of improving short-term business competitiveness but as a way to maintain trust, support, and legitimacy with the community, with governments, and with employees. They saw community involvement as a social responsibility of business but one that was also clearly aligned with the long-term commercial interest of their companies.

In addition many of those who philosophically rejected the case for community involvement are in practice actively involved in the full range of community activities, from sponsorship through staff volunteering to direct corporate giving. Since that study the trend to a hard-headed alignment with business imperatives has continued and brought new levels of sophistication in strategy and execution.

There has been a strong trend in recent years in Australia for companies to align their activities with their particular place in the market as they make choices between the smorgasbord of community involvement opportunities. Choices are often defined by the nature of an industry and its impacts (for example, resources companies with environment or indigenous affairs, banks with financial literacy) or competencies (for example, information technology companies with computer literacy). However, this alignment is sometimes overridden by other criteria such as the use of sponsorships as a tool to build stakeholder relations (the arts) or to meet neighborhood expectations (local charities and events). The strategic use of company infrastructure (physical, intellectual property, commercial expertise) has become a major feature of social investment and community relations in Australia.

There has also been a strong trend to undertake fewer, deeper engagements and to work with closer partnerships and alliances. This has been driven by several factors. One is the capacity to enhance performance and leverage impact in both program delivery and image. Another is the use of community activities to break down negative stereotypes and build relationships and mutual understanding with traditional issues adversaries, resulting in some unusual coalitions. Influenced in part by US examples, this is widely employed in industries that have had powerful NGO critics, such as the resources sector, with hostile environmental and indigenous rights organizations, and the financial services sector, responding to social welfare and consumer activists. While there are some successful exceptions, there has been a tendency to move away from collective corporate charities and other initiatives that homogenize corporate brands and diminish potential for direct corporate exposure and personal engagement.

Another recent trend in Australia has been the requirement for clear understandings between the company and its community partners around all relevant issues, including project control, branding and publicity, financial/legal obligations, key performance indicators, time frames, and arrangements for exit from and termination of supportive relationships. Mutual obligations are increasingly documented in contractual form.

In some cases acceptance by desired partners can be positioned as an implied endorsement by them, not necessarily of the company's total behavior or position on specific issues. Reputational benefits accrue from this implied endorsement. However, this is being managed with care, as relevant NGOs have critics on their own side ready to call collaboration with corporates, for example, "greenwash" or inappropriate seduction by the issues adversary.

One of the strongest business case drivers for corporate community involvement in recent years has been the rising expectation among staff, particularly younger staff, that their organization will contribute to community well-being in a manner beyond a company's core activity, and that they themselves will have an opportunity, through their place of employment, to contribute in this way. Organizations are accordingly finding ways to engage staff volunteers in their general community involvement activities, or finding opportunities specifically designed for this purpose. In some companies utilizing the special skills of staff is seen to provide the most effective form of community activity. Volunteering and matched grants to approved causes with staff involvement are among the most rapidly growing activities in Australian companies.

As a number of consultancy studies have shown, employee attitudes in major companies tend to broadly reflect the attitudes of the community at large—even on sensitive issues in which their company is involved. This high level of staff expectation of their company to be socially engaged reflects a high expectation in the Australian community. The year 2000 Millennium Poll (Environics, 1999) of twenty-three countries on corporate social responsibility shows the Australian public had the

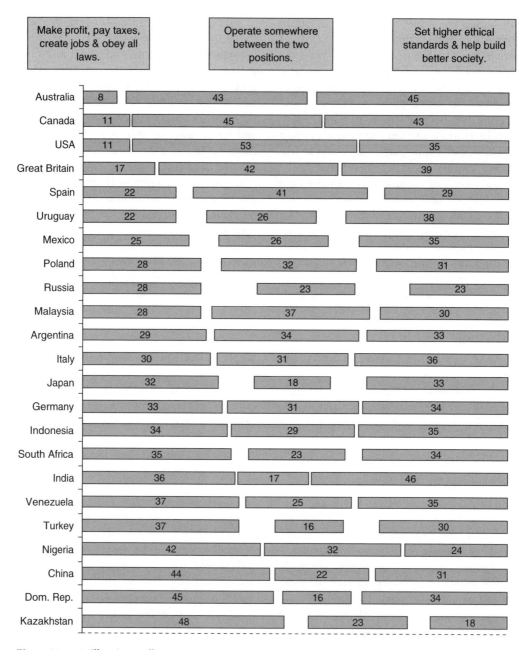

Figure 21.7   *Millennium Poll on Corporate Social Responsibility: the role of large companies in society (percentage agreeing). The Millennium Poll asked people to choose between these statements on what the role of large companies in society should be. The poll was a series of interviews with over 25,000 average citizens in twenty-three countries in mid-1999. It was conducted by Environics International in cooperation with the Prince of Wales Business Leaders Forum and the Conference Board.* Source *Millennium Poll on Corporate Social Responsibility (1999).*

highest ranking of twenty three countries on demands for large companies to help build a better society.

In the Centre 2003 survey senior public affairs practitioners were asked "What are your organization's goals for corporate social

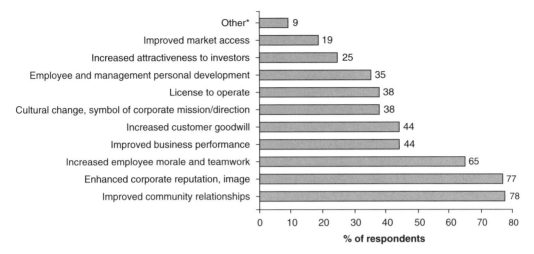

Figure 21.8    *Stated goals of corporate social responsibility.* Source *Centre for Corporate Public Affairs (2003)*

responsibility?" The responses in Figure 21.8 clearly indicate a focus on underlying business objectives.

Prior to the 1990s and for many the mid-1990s, in Australia corporate social responsibility was largely defined by "sponsorship and donations." Philanthropic and sponsorship decisions were made in an *ad hoc* manner by boards of directors. This was done without a strategic framework, and largely in response to *ad hoc*, unsolicited requests, frequently reflecting personal preferences, or as a reciprocal favor with the club or directors of other companies. This approach is now extremely rare in large public companies. Allocating the task to Public Affairs and within agreed guidelines has been for some a defensive strategy to protect directors from their mates, ahead of the development of serious business case frameworks.

Around the year 2000 there was a growth in the number of corporate "foundations" in Australia through which some or all of these activities are channeled. Unlike the United States, Australian tax law does not require an arm's-length structure and the establishment of foundations has more to do with establishing a higher profile for corporate activities than any other motive. Some of the few Australian corporate foundations have external directors, but are normally run as a branch

of, and are serviced by, the public affairs department.

## INVESTOR RELATIONS

While the misdeeds of Australian "corporate cowboys" in the 1980s were in the world league, the governance debate became intense again in the first years of the new century. Two major corporate collapses that coincided with Enron, and that had some similar characteristics, led to new regulatory pressure and in particular a focus on company audit and board practice.

The corporate response to the governance debate from around the year 2000 was led by company directors themselves and, apart from managing reputational fallout and explaining reforms, few public affairs practitioners were able to find a practical role on this issue. A key part of the process, however, was investor relations, as companies entered into dialogue with the investment community about current and future practice.

Shareholder activism, including the use of shareholder power to pursue the public interest agendas of corporate critics, is alive, well, and growing in Australia. This suggests the need for a public affairs, including issues management, skill set. As private investment and governance issues have attracted increased interest from the general media there has also been a significant shift beyond technical financial reporting in both print and electronic media so that business news is often "in the front of the paper."

Research with Australian practitioners suggests that, at least in their eyes, investor relations practitioners in the United States have been more narrowly focused on financial performance and less on broader issues of corporate assessment in Australia (although this is seen to be also a recent trend in the United States; Higgins, 2000; Unseem, 1996). As one practitioner said, "We think analysts are better in Australia. In the USA there is the tyranny of quant. and risk aversion. Good analysts here are looking for corporate body language, capability of management and things like the impact of public policy; not so much technical stuff" (Allen, 2002).

While no one questions the centrality of financial performance, balance sheet strength, and other technical financial and accounting issues, the breadth of interest by investors in Australia is attested to by the most commonly used survey of professional investor perceptions, the Corporate Confidence Index. Based on interviews with both buy and sell-side analysts, this proprietary survey ranks the relevant professional performance of fifty leading stocks. It considers issues such as anticipated earnings per share, cash flow, effective capital management, gearing, return on assets, and overall investment value. More than half the criteria explored, however, relate to issues that are the stuff of more general corporate reputation, stakeholder perceptions, and strategic positioning. These include issues such as the reputation of the board, CEO and senior management team, cohesive strategic vision, integrity and governance, competitive advantage, disclosure, transparency, quality of Web site, and so on.

Growing pressure by interest groups on the investment community, as well as companies, to report and be judged on social, environmental, and human rights criteria will further broaden the scope of required communications with the investment sector, including retail investors, as well as ethical funds.

Notwithstanding this, research by this writer for corporate clients suggests institutional investors are still strongly oriented to financial performance and see a company's reputation and competence in managing social and political pressures as a protection against regulatory and other constraints and as a proxy for sound management. Of interest is that the Australian Shareholders' Association—the major retail investor voice, led largely by retirees—has a firm policy opposing companies managing to a triple bottom line.

Studies by the Centre for Corporate Public Affairs in the mid and late 1990s showed that in around 30 percent of publicly listed companies the investor relations function was embedded in public affairs departments and around 70 percent was placed elsewhere, most commonly with the Chief Financial Officer. This was similar at that time to research conducted on US companies by the US Public Affairs Council. Scale and resources may have contributed to the integration of this function with the larger public affairs role, but there was also the view that institutional and particularly retail investors were just another stakeholder community, albeit with special interests. Because of privatization of government enterprises and demutualization, Australia has the highest number of retail investors *per capita* in the world.

Many of those Australian investor relations executives who are structurally separate in investor relations departments reporting direct to a CFO have a clear rationale for this. As one said, "It is hard to envisage anyone doing our job without a finance background, or being part of the finance team" (Allen, 2002). It should be noted, however, that a small but increasing number of investor relations executives are reporting directly to the CEO.

The Centre 2003 survey found a decline in the number of investor relations executives operating from within public affairs, a fact attributable to that function's increasing complexity, regulatory intervention, and corporate significance, leading to greater scale, seniority, and specialist professionalism. This in turn has led to the separation of investor relations as a stand-alone function. Australians perceive this

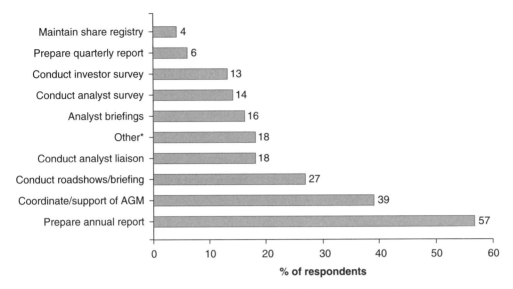

Figure 21.9   *Investor relations tasks undertaken by the public affairs department in the past twelve months. *Includes Webcast/teleconference, conduct client surveys, Web site reporting (site visits, daily inquiries). Source Centre for Corporate Public Affairs (2003)*

to be a trend in most developed Western economies. The nature of the investor relations task within public affairs departments is indicated in Figure 21.9.

This Centre 2003 survey does not reveal how the investor relations tasks divide where they are split between public affairs and a separate department. Invariably Public Affairs supports various presentations, frequently prepares the annual report, and manages the conduct of annual general meetings. Media management is often shared but, as noted, the separation of financial and general reporting on companies has become quite blurred.

Australian companies, no doubt with others, have experienced tension when poor coordination between investor and other stakeholder strategies are not harmonized. The promotion of high profitability and good prospects from one corporate function at the same time as price rises, demanding fiscal favours of governments, or plant closure from another corporate function, has been common in Australia with obvious consequences.

While tensions will arise with different stakeholders, most companies have moved to establish relationships and protocols—even colocation—to ensure consistency in strategy and execution between the public affairs and structurally separate investor relations departments.

## INTERNAL COMMUNICATIONS

The public affairs function in Australia is thought of as externally oriented. Internal activities like issues analysis and strategic advice to other managers normally focus on the external world and the company's interaction with it. The exception is internal or employee communications. Seventy-eight percent of the public affairs departments in the Centre 2003 survey had responsibility for internal communications. For most of the remainder, human resources departments would take the lead, but in almost all cases would work closely with Public Affairs.

The location of internal communications in public affairs departments has arisen from it being a subset of the media-communications silo that joined with government affairs to form the integrated model. With a heavy bias to print publications as the vehicle for talking to employees, this had naturally drawn on the journalistic skills of media and other communications staff and was therefore a natural fit.

As stakeholder concepts emerged in Australia, employees were considered as one category of stakeholder and managing communications with this was conceptually linked to stakeholder relations, a perceived function of Public Affairs. Also, through many political and reputational battles, companies in industries under challenge worked very hard to keep staff aligned with corporate positions and in a limited way to use them as purveyors of the corporate message in the task of issues management.

Internal communications became more strategic over the 1990s, moving from an emphasis on providing business information and feel-good social news to seeking to influence behavior and attitude. New technology and the philosophy of two-way face-to-face communication have driven a diversity of communications channels. Internal communications have also been a key element in cultural change programs, fashionable in the 1990s and then largely driven by human resource management.

However, post-millennium, internal communications have received new recognition and, in a number of the most progressive companies, are the centrepiece of cultural and business transformation. This is occurring where top management is deeply committed to such organizational transformation and sees culture, behavior, and staff mind set as critical to business success.

## INTERNATIONAL PUBLIC AFFAIRS

An important recent trend has been the extension of Australian public affairs offshore, and particularly to Asia. Overwhelmingly international public affairs for Australians means Asian public affairs. This is driven by the expansion of Australian companies into the region and the propensity for North American and European multinational companies to use Australian-based executives to oversee their regional practice.

It is hard to generalize in discussion of the public affairs environment in Asia because of the diversity in levels of development, cultures, political systems and structures, and philosophies in Asian business systems. However, there are some broad observations that can be usefully made.

Strategic public affairs is relatively new in Asia; European, North American, and Australian MNCs have led the way. Except with these, and a limited number of large, globally connected indigenous companies, the language and practice in Asia are still lower-order public relations.

As in parts of Europe, government relations tend to have been managed at a high level between government officials and top management of companies behind closed doors and without the need for separate specialist advice. Agreements are reached by alignment of government and business interests without fanfare or great public debate or controversy. This might be called an "insiders' game" and can be contrasted with what might be called an "outsiders' game" associated with more public adversarial-style English-speaking countries. In the latter there is a clearer separation of business and government. Vigorous debate, and open media and grassroots political leverage accompanying business advocacy, are accepted as appropriate by both sides. While they vary considerably in nature, business-government relations in all Asian countries are an insiders' game; attempting to run an outsiders' game in Asian economies would be a serious mistake.

The media generally in Asia see themselves less as ombudsmen and critics of business and government than in the West and can be more accessible to positive stories on company issues. The local-language media are less Western in style and focus, and local-language press and wire services have grown in quantity and influence. While expatriate business people tend to read, and operate through, the Western-language press, readers in government and the local markets generally are more impacted by media in their own language and consumed by their constituents and customers.

Until the early 1980s a key feature of many Asian economies was the myriad of small and medium-sized family-controlled companies; they were generally headed by their founder and had few non-family shareholders. The environment in which they flourished was homogeneous and congenial to business. For corporate external relations it was a benign environment. Consumer lobbies were not well developed. The media were generally uncritical, and journalists who behaved otherwise could be ignored at no cost to the companies and often at greater cost to themselves. Community relations and corporate giving were undertaken in the name of the family and reflected its preferences rather than the company's broader objectives.

However, success brought change to a number of family-owned companies. Many became transnational and grew too large to be owned exclusively by founders or their families. They sought public listing, needing substantial injections of funds to expand further into different industries and countries. This meant their activities and financial performance became a matter of public interest and even shareholder activism where Western institutions have acquired significant stock.

The patriarchs who founded family companies have started to retire, handing the reins to their Western-educated children. Many of these children have lived and worked overseas and have seen the public accountability required of large institutions in Western economies. As heads of public companies rather than family businesses, they understand the importance of building relationships with diverse constituencies with differing agendas and concerns. They began to recognize the need to manage public perceptions, and to place value on corporate reputations.

Regulatory environments began to change too, in response to the increasing complexity and sophistication of newly floated companies. For example, the Asian crisis in the late 1990s drew widespread attention to the inadequacies of financial regulation. Consumer lobbies have become a little stronger and quality of life issues have grown with a more prosperous educated middle class. The region's most interesting economy China, however, has been going through its own rapid change, now privatizing its vast array of state-owned enterprises, seeking the rapid growth of direct foreign investment, and building a new, sophisticated, globally connected, entrepreneurial business elite.

Finally, the expanding presence of Western multinational companies in the growing Asian markets has had a continuing impact on public affairs practice. With a rapid growth since the 1980s in direct foreign investment in the region, Western MNCs have continued to bring in their own thinking about how to operate in the field, including management approaches to government affairs and consumer relations. They have trained on the job a new generation of young and competent practitioners who are spreading out to indigenous companies, consultants, and the government sector.

## PUBLIC AFFAIRS IN THE GOVERNMENT SECTOR

One important development in Australia that received traction in the late 1990s was the emergence of public affairs management in government departments and agencies. It has been common practice to have functions entitled "public information", "communications" and "media relations", with roles that reflected these titles. More recently "public affairs" has become a common designation as the government sector has sought to replicate many aspects of the function as performed in the private sector.

Increasingly well rounded professionals are being trained or recruited from the private sector to work on the organization's relationships with external stakeholders, to deal more strategically with the media, to develop and maintain new forms of government/community sponsorships, and to apply issues management techniques to both policy and organizational issues. Specialists in the government are now turning to questions of organization brand and reputation and are adding their skills to internal communications, although the latter function is still normally within HR departments. Major government organizations like the Australian Taxation Office, Department of Environment and Heritage and Department of Defence have moved in this direction in recent years. Some departments and agencies have adopted the title "public affairs" without significantly changing their roles and practices.

As in the Westminster system, the organizational context for the practice of public affairs in the non-commercial public sector and the private sector differs significantly. Whereas in the private sector analysis of the social and political issues is used to facilitate the achievement of organizational objectives (such as production and profit) they are core activities in the government sector. A significant part of the skill set and activity of the private sector public affairs specialist is deeply embedded in, and performed by, line management in government.

While the private sector firm operates autonomously within the law and guidelines established by its board and on a relatively narrow agenda, the government agency operates within the complex framework of political (Ministerial-Cabinet) leadership, parliamentary accountability, more demanding public expectations and complex multiple agendas. In these areas where the role of the Minister, ministerial staff, and even political party ends, and where that of the public service agency starts, is movable, often contestable, and frequently controversial, particularly in the areas of public presentation and relationships with constituencies. While there are rapidly rising expectations and demands for accountability on the private sector, accountability in the public sector still exceeds that of the private sector, and levels of acceptable risk are lower.

The relatively new development of private sector-style public affairs in government is more common in service delivery agencies and has reached only a small number of policy departments. Here there is a mixed reaction from the political staff and ministers who are more protective of the government's reputation and stakeholder relations agenda. However, indications are that public affairs practice in government will continue to grow strongly and will provide the next and major wave of career opportunities for those interested in this work.

## THE AUSTRALIAN MODEL IN CONTEXT

The growth of strategic public affairs on the integrated model in Australia has been recent and rapid. As a largely derivative culture and economy, and with a significant presence of particularly US and UK multinational corporations, conceptual frameworks originating in those countries have a significant influence in Australia.

On this writer's close observation of the development of the function globally, the American companies, plus a small handful of European-minded multinationals, led developments in the function since the 1970s as they reacted to a new order of corporate criticism and regulatory activism. These developments were fed by US consultants and business school academics who invented the language for example of corporate legitimacy, sociopolitical vulnerability analysis, issues life cycles, and strategic issues management. We watched while corporate philanthropy in the United States morphed to strategic philanthropy and to the current practice of engaging critics and issues adversaries in new partnerships.

From the vantage point of Australia, innovation in public affairs concepts and practice has recently shifted somewhat to Europe, driven particularly by redefining business society relations which in turn gave rise to "the stakeholder corporation." This followed, and was linked to, community demands for environmental and social sustainability—themselves underpinned by demand for a new level of transparency and triple bottom-line reporting.

As Australian practitioners have looked north to borrow public affairs ideas and practices, they have been confronted with the cultural differences between companies based in the United States and with those in the United Kingdom and Europe. General community philosophies about the role of the corporation in society vary between (as well of course to a lesser degree within) them.

American concepts are natural products of the dominant corporate ideology, based on individualism, limited government, private property, and strong obligations of private citizenship. This no doubt emerged in part from Protestant theology, escape from government persecution, and the pioneering culture of early European settlement. European philosophies on the role of companies in the community appear to have emerged from a stronger communitarian culture where economic institutions were traditionally licensed by the state and with a different style of reciprocal obligation to the nation and community from those of American capitalism.

The European companies British American Tobacco and Shell, for example, have built stakeholder dialogue formally into their management systems; Shell's Foundation has as its mission to support "priority areas where there are meaningful NGO and/or government partnerships." In particular these companies which have each been involved in businesses in developing countries have created deep relationships with UN and other European-based organizations and involved them in their programs. An example is Unilever's partnerships with WHO, UNICEF, the Red Cross/Crescent, and UNESCO. Europeans are more inclined to sign global agreements affecting corporate social engagement or compacts. "Sustainability" and "triple bottom-line" notions are more inclined to be providing the conceptual framework for these European companies than for their American counterparts.

Whereas Europeans tend to have "sustainability reports" based on the triple bottom line and verified by externals, Americans use the language of private property, and corporations as private citizens "giving back." Motorola publishes its "Global Corporate Citizenship Report" which in 2002 stated they are "enthusiastic and proactive citizens of the greater global community." IBM claims to be pursuing a "new model of corporate citizenship" and McDonald's explains its rationale in this area by leading its statement of core values with founder Ray Croc's philosophy, "We give back to the communities in which we do business."

With the rise in Australia of powerful interest groups, diversification of power centers, and participative democracy, indigenous Australian companies—more used in the past to Westminster-style politics—are now looking to borrow American tools of grassroots lobbying and political coalition building. This is a major current focus in large Australian companies. At the same time community expectations and interest-group dynamics are driving Australians to relationships more closely akin to the stakeholder corporation, and have embraced the language and philosophy of sustainability, more akin to European than American ways of thinking. The philosophical underpinnings and language of Australian business draw on both traditions, and have selected for application elements from each which suit Australian circumstances.

Australia accordingly is a hybrid, fast adapter, but is developing its own brand of cohesive external relations and political management across a number of traditional silos. As noted, this has been historically driven by small scale and limited resources, small teams having to cover what other countries managed in silos. More recently, however, the mainstream integrated model is driven by the logic that key issues, reputation management, and strategic support for corporate business plans require the holistic application of public policy, government relations, media, internal communications, and most recently stakeholder and interest group relations, drawing on new strategic community involvement and social investment.

## NOTE

1 The Centre for Corporate Public Affairs (www.accpa.com.au) has as its members the public affairs departments of more than 100 major companies, government business enterprises, and industry associations. It provides a forum for senior practitioners to discuss issues of mutual interest, is a conduit for bringing best-practice tools and concepts to Australia, conducts research into professional practice, and provides professional development for the staff of members. The annual oration invites leading figures to comment on the relationship between business and its sociopolitical context.

## REFERENCES

Allen Consulting Group (2000). *Socially Responsible Investment in Australia.* Report commissioned by Philanthropic Trusts in Australia.

Allen Consulting Group (2002). Allen Consulting Group and Commonwealth of Australia. *Triple Bottom Line Measurement and Reporting in Australia; Making it Tangible.*

Allen, G. (2002). "Public Affairs Support for the Investor Relations Task," *Corporate Public Affairs* 12 (1).

Centre (2001a). "Behind the Age/SMH Good Reputation Index," *Corporate Public Affairs* 11 (2).

Centre (2001b). *Corporate Community Involvement; Establishing a Business Case.* Melbourne and Sydney: Centre for Corporate Public Affairs in conjunction with the Business Council of Australia. www.allenconsult.com.au/publications.

Centre (2003). *2003 Survey of Australian Public Affairs.* Melbourne and Sydney: Centre for Corporate Public Affairs.

Environics (1999). *The Millennium Poll on Corporate Social Responsibility: Global Survey on Public Opinion on the Changing Role of Companies,* with the Prince of Wales Leaders Forum and the Conference board. www.environics.net.eil.

Higgins, R.B. (2000). *Best Practice in Global Investor Relations: The Creation of Shareholder Value.* Westport, CT: Quorum Books.

Prescott, J. (1995). *1995 Annual Corporate Public Affairs Oration.* Melbourne: Centre for Corporate Public Affairs.

Rayner, M. (1994). *Introduction to 1994 Annual Corporate Public Affairs Oration.* Melbourne: Centre for Corporate Public Affairs.

Unseem, M. (1996). *Investor Capitalism: How Money Managers are changing the Face of Corporate America.* New York: Basic Books/Harper Collins.

# 22

# Emerging Markets

## Public Affairs in Germany and Austria

ANDREAS LEDERER, NIOMBO LOMBA,
AND CHRISTIAN SCHEUCHER

## PUBLIC AFFAIRS IN GERMANY

Compared to the United States, the public affairs branch in Germany is still in its infancy. In Europe public affairs has first been recognized by the European Public Relations Confederation (CERP, 1991) and defined as "the planned and predetermined endeavors of a company to exercise its rights and duties as citizens of a country, a community or an association, as well as to also encourage its staff to do it" (Schönborn, 2002). What are the bases of this branch in Germany? Which role does it play and can future developments be recognized?

### The Political System of Germany

Germany is a democratic parliamentary federation. The political system is characterized by a multiparty system and federal structures (the federation and sixteen countries). The pluralistic principle of diversity is valid in Germany (Andersen and Woyke, 2000). Political, social, and economic interest groups such as unions (e.g. Verdi) and employer associations (e.g. the Federal Association of German Industry) are

of equal sociopolitical importance. The political deliberation is interwoven and moderated by the political parties and the government. Consensus is sought and coalitions are entered into. Regarding their structure two trends can be observed in the German associations:

1 An increasing number of associations.
2 A change in the representation of companies and associations. They are not only represented by a (leading) association but take on this task themselves (Sebaldt, 1997a).

This increase of associations in Germany can already be registered since the middle of the 1970s. The first lobbying list of the German federal government contained 635 groups in 1974 (Sebaldt, 1997b). This number increased steadily; in 2003 there were already 1,781 interest groups registered (Sator, 2003).

### The Change of the Republic— from Bonn to Berlin

The young republic with Bonn as its capital was characterized by a balance of interests between unions and employer associations. This mediation of interests was a generally accepted part of the political life according to the corporate model of Bonn. The social market economy and the *Rheinische Kapitalismus* have been imprinted by the changing power of associations and built up through them. It was the task of the associations to generate the interests of their members and then to communicate them to the political system. Except for some of the very big enterprises like the Deutsche Bank or Kirch Media, single companies found it as difficult to be heard as did associations with special requests and special interests.

The work of the lobbyists was characterized by the cozy atmosphere in Bonn. Background talks and meetings in bars and restaurants were part of the daily routine in Bonn due to the size of the town and the consequent short distances (Wallrabenstein, 2003). This meant that representatives of associations were already engaged in lobbying during these times. But public affairs as currently defined had already been introduced to Germany by the large US agencies. Weber-Shandwick, Fleishman Hillard, Hill and Knowlton or Burson-Marsteller are part of this (Schönborn, 2002).

An entirely new era started with the transfer of the capital to Berlin (a change of locality and completely new government quarters). During the time in Bonn many headquarters of companies and associations were relatively close (Frankfurt, Düsseldorf, etc.) compared to the situation in Berlin (Schönborn, 2002). In the capital it was necessary to build up new representations of companies and associations. About two-thirds of the thirty DAX enterprises, for instance, have a representation in Berlin (Sator, 2003).

This change can also be registered in the political arena. Politics takes place in a larger public setting in Berlin and is becoming more transparent. The communication of the political actors is changing. Public affairs advisors focus upon the government apparatus— and to a lesser extent on the Members of Parliament. Alemann views this as "a process existing since decades, since the majority of laws, regulations, supportive measures and also of public investigative decisions is prepared and executed by the government" (Alemann, 2000). A poll taken among public affairs agencies demonstrates that the administration and the Cabinets of Ministers together are more often addressed by public affairs agencies than Members of Parliament, the media and parties (Poli-c.de, 2004).

Furthermore, the individual areas of politics are gaining ever more complexity. Members of associations and single institutions tend to increasingly represent their interests themselves. Also, the federal principle affects the economic and political action. Public affairs do not only take place on the level of the federal government but also on those of federal states and communities (Wallrabenstein, 2003) (see Figure 22.1). Not all companies and associations can be represented in Berlin. Not all of them have the required staff and know-how to lead public affairs campaigns.

## Europe is Gaining Strength

With the progression of Europe's unity more and more political decisions are made in Brussels. The number of laws and decisions concerning the member states is continuously increasing. In addition, there are developments like globalization, individualization, and information technologies which make it necessary for associations, companies, and also for (government) institutions of individual European countries to become active at the regional and even supranational levels. Therefore a campaign which may be successful in Germany can be brought to fail on the European level due to different decisions. This factor can be taken into account by having a representative in Brussels; on the other hand, a public affairs strategy should always be structured in such a way that the European standards can be considered too (Schönborn, 2002). Interestingly a poll conducted by Poli-c.de in 2004 indicates that German public affairs agencies do not take as much action on a European level as one would expect compared to the increasing importance of European policies (see Figure 22.1) (Poli-c.de, 2004).

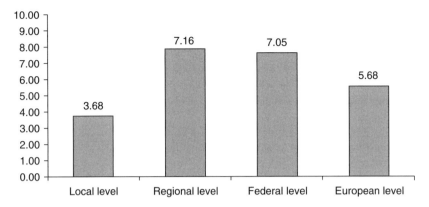

Figure 22.1   *"On what level do you lobby?"* Source *Poli-c.de (2004)*

## Berlin moves to the Center— Opportunities arising in the East

While the German capital has until now been situated on the eastern border of the European Union, it is now moving more and more into the center of Europe. The Eastern European countries are already an important strategic economic market. This will be further reinforced as a consequence of the eastward expansion of the European Union. Due to its good contacts and its location Berlin is particularly well suited for an expansion to Eastern Europe (Wallrabenstein, 2003). The special role played by Germany within the European Union will act as a support. Some public affairs agencies with a seat in Berlin have already made use of this and built up representations in the new member countries, such as Media Consulta and Publicis.

## Public Affairs of a new Kind?

The changes in the Berlin republic have led to a recognizable movement of growth in the PA branch. Political communication is used ever more deliberately by companies, associations, and other organizations. Organizations, institutions, and companies have recognized campaigns and other methods of political communication as useful strategic instruments (Schönborn, 2002). They are forced to take up a steady dialogue with politics. Repeatedly

there are political decisions taken which have consequences for entrepreneurial decisions. The economic situation and the high unemployment rate are examples of areas of concern to all companies. This work of representation and lobbying is now carried out by a large number of agencies and advisors (Schönborn, 2002). Individual consultants, public affairs departments of international agency associations, individually owned national agencies, and full-service agencies constitute the four types of agencies which make up the German political consultancy scene under a structural perspective (Lianos and Simon, 2003).

The clients of German agencies split into private enterprises and associations (more then 50 percent). In contrast the public sector is declared by 60 percent to be an infrequent client. But over 50 percent of the agencies questioned work on a regular basis for initiatives (see Figure 22.2) (Poli-c.de, 2004).

The economic data of PR agencies offering public affairs services show the growing strength of political communication in Germany which, moreover, did not decrease in 2003 in spite of the difficult economic situation. The ten top successful agencies of 2001 doubled—with a total of €18.3 million—their turnover with public affairs compared to 2000 (*PR-Report*, 2002, 2001). By comparison, the total turnover in 2003 already amounts to €17.99 million (see Table 22.1).

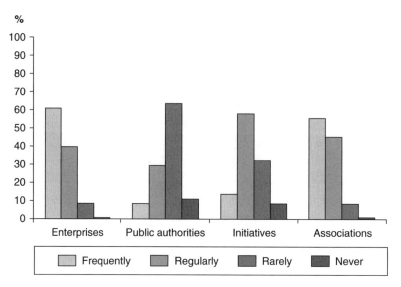

Figure 22.2    *"Who are your clients?"* Source *Poli-c.de (2004)*

Table 22.1    *Ranking of agencies with public affairs servcies, by turnover, in 2003*

| Rank | Agency | Turnover (€million) | Share of total turnover (%) |
|---|---|---|---|
| 1 | Media Consulta | 4.23 | 30 |
| 2 | fischerAppelt | 2.57 | 20 |
| 3 | Ahrens & Behrent | 1.80 | 20 |
| 4 | Hill & Knowlton | 1.76 | 20 |
| 5 | CPCompartner | 1.57 | 35 |
| 6 | RUGO Kommunikation | 1.50 | 45 |
| 7 | Topcom Communication | 1.42 | 80 |
| 8 | iserundschmidt | 1.26 | 60 |
| 9 | Trimedia | 1.23 | 10 |
| 10 | komm.passion group | 0.65 | 10 |

Source *PR-Report* (2003).

## Legal Framework

The legal conditions for public affairs and lobbying are not explicitly defined in Germany. Public appeals are regulated by the constitutional embodiment of freedom of opinion in Article 5 of the statutory law. The legal base of lobbying work is defined in Article 9, paragraph 3 on the freedom for associations and coalitions. It states that everybody has the right to form associations for the preservation and promotion of working and economic conditions. The regulation of lobbyism is laid down in the business rules of the federal government and parliament. Besides the rules of conduct applying to parliamentary representatives, which require the disclosure of any offices held in associations and unions as well as their seats on administrative boards, executive boards, and supervisory boards, the procedural rules also include the hearing rights and procedures for those associations and lobbyists who are registered on the lobbying list of the Bundestag (parliament). They are permitted to participate in official hearings and other official forms of communication (Alemann, 2000).

## Public Affairs in Society and Enterprise: Transparency Requested

How are public affairs and lobbying actually perceived in society? And how are companies designing their public affairs activities? It can

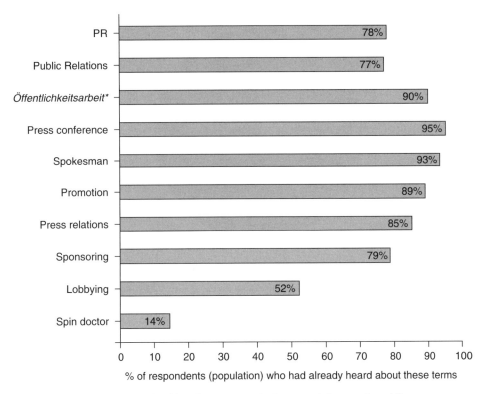

Figure 22.3    *Recognition of selected public relations terms in Germany. *German for public relations.* Source *Bentele et al. (2003)*

be stated that the concepts of "public relations" or "sponsoring" are clearly better known in the population than the concept of "lobbying." Yet, a study conducted by Bentele and Seidenglanz in 2003 disproves that terms used by public relations in Germany are not particularly well known (see Figure 22.3).

"Lobbying" is known to 52 percent of all respondents and 33 percent state they know its meaning. Within the population 66 percent view lobbying as part of public relations. Regarding the evaluation of the impact of public relations on politics—measured on a scale of 1 (very low) to 5 (very high)—the respondents gave the following ratings. The impact of public relations on politics in general ranges at 3.3, the figure applying to the design of election campaigns at 3.9. And the influence of lobbyists on politics is rated at 3.5 (Bentele and Seidenglanz, 2003).

All in all, 78 percent of the respondents accept lobbying if it takes place neither secretly nor behind locked doors excluding the public (Güttler and Klewes, 2002). Overall, the public

appears open-minded toward the influence of interest groups on politics. For instance, regarding economic politics, 82 percent of the respondents favor the participation of economic associations (Güttler and Klewes, 2002). It is requested, however, that there is transparency between economics and politics (public status), honesty (acceptance of norms), and a genuine, functioning pluralism (equality of chances) (Bentele and Seidenglanz, 2003). Yet, 44 percent are still against the political influence of companies and associations. This is explained with the acceptance of influence under the conditions already mentioned (Güttler and Klewes, 2002). But it is considered desirable and necessary that interest groups influence the political process. Groups whose sphere of interest is affected or who have competency themselves should participate in the decision-making process for certain issues. Another 26 percent of the respondents state that managers of economic enterprises are too little heard regarding

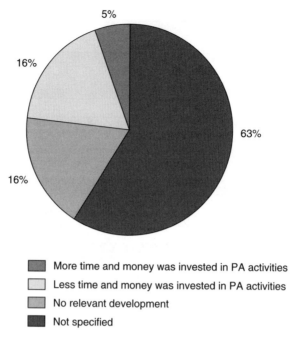

Figure 22.4   *Development of public affairs activities in German corporations in recent years.* Source *Publicis (2003)*

economic politics. This is seen in the same way by 35 percent of the population concerning associations. Young people, self-employed persons, and supporters of the established smaller parties are especially open to this type of consulting by representatives of interest groups and companies. In their view, associations can and should communicate more actively and offer solutions (Güttler and Klewes, 2002).

## Meaningful Investments

The German companies are in the meantime not only represented by associations. Two-thirds of the DAX enterprises already have representations in the capital. A survey conducted by Publicis Berlin among the public affairs representatives of German companies shows that they are increasingly looking for a stronger tie to politics. Those questioned were companies who had an office in Berlin or a representation in the capital. Of those 63 percent reported to have spent more time and money on public affairs than before. This means that the financial expenditures and the

personal resources in the area of public affairs have been raised (see Figure 22.4).

The evaluation of political representatives addressed by public affairs managers turns out to be quite differentiated from the point of view of the PA advisors. Asked about the readiness of politicians to consider the opinions of the economic sector in their own decisions, 47 percent describe it as "far-reaching." For 37 percent it is only "limited," while just 10 percent believe this readiness of politics to be "strongly present" (Publicis, 2003). An increasing role is thereby played by international activities. Internationally coordinated government relations are becoming more important. Public affairs strategies containing mutually coordinated strategies in several countries are used by 79 percent of the responding enterprises.

There was also agreement among 79 percent with the statement that worldwide operating enterprises should plan and integrate their public affairs activities on an international basis. The public affairs managers agreed by 90 percent that lobbying will gain even more importance on the supranational level

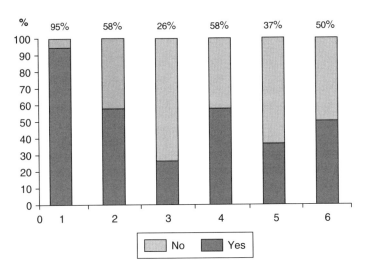

Figure 22.5 *"Where do you find the general guidelines for your actions?"*
1 *German federal law,*
2 *Code of conduct of the European Commission,*
3 *Code of Lisbon and Athens,*
4 *DeGePol behavioral index,*
5 *German Public Relations Society guidelines on public relations in politics,*
6 *own code of conduct.*
Source *poli-c.de (2004)*

(e.g. EU institutions) during the coming years. Representations in Brussels are held by 63 percent of enterprises (Publicis, 2003).

## Does a new Generation of Public Affairs Advisors Exist?

During the years 2002 and 2003 Germany experienced a broad public debate on consulting in the areas of public affairs and lobbying, which was triggered by the publication of the practices of a well known PR advisor. He supposedly paid money to active politicians and officials. These events were the reason for starting a public debate regarding the business practices of public affairs advisors and the PR branch as a whole (Wassermann, 2002).

So far the branch has not adopted a code of conduct for itself, although some PR agencies that also offer public affairs consulting accept voluntary guidelines, like the International Code of Ethics (Matrat, 1965) or the European Code of Professional Conduct in Public Relations (CERP, 1978). However, these guidelines orient themselves on public relations. This is why the European Public Relations Confederation

(CERP) accepted the European Charter for Public Affairs as a recommendation for action in 1991 (CERP, 1991).

In order to avoid concerns in approaching the branch due to scandals and resulting negative images, the establishment of a code of conduct has been considered. One example is the behavioral codex of DeGePol (2003). The Poli-c.de poll shows the understanding of general regulations for actions as a player in politics. The German agencies by 95 percent prefer the federal law as formal regulation. Fifty-eight percent commit themselves to the code of conduct of the European Commission. Compared to the informal codes of conducts (Code de Lisbonne and Code d'Athène) the codex of the German Society for Political Consulting (DeGePol) is accepted by 58 percent (see Figure 22.5) (Poli-c.de, 2004).

The German Society for Political Consulting is an association of the new generation of political public affairs advisors and campaign consultants existing since 2002. The members of DeGePol agree at the time of entry to use the behavioral codex and, among other things, to demonstrate transparency by obliging themselves to honesty toward the public and to their clients. Further items include:

1   An obligation to discretion: confidential treatment of information and no concurrent representation of opposing interests.
2   No financial stimuli: not exerting influence by using dubious or illegal means, especially of a financial nature.
3   No racist, sexist, religious, or other discrimination.
4   Respectful treatment and esteem of the professional and personal reputation of clients and colleagues.
5   A clear separation between professional activities and other political offices, mandates, and functions.
6   No activities that are likely to damage the public standing of political consultancy.

The Politikkongress (Political Congress), which first took place at the end of November 2003, as well as the journal *Politics and Communication* issued since 2002, can both be viewed as signs of professionalization and the development of a normative structure for the branch. The congress was attended by PR and PA advisors, advertising managers, representatives of communication science and political science, classical lobbyists, and press secretaries. It contained almost forty individual reports and more than seventy-five speakers (Lianos and Simon, 2003). It appears that there is a need for an exchange of thoughts, ongoing development, and professionalization within the German political communication scene.

### Will the Coming Generation have a new Educational Qualification?

Political communication and public affairs are, however, characterized by a separation between theory and practice (Klewes, 2003). Unlike the United States, political consulting in Germany is a strongly scientific system. Consequently, scientific political consulting as a rule is institutionalized, hierarchical, and not practice-oriented. Furthermore, the public as recipient is less considered compared to the United States. The development of American-style think tanks is still in its infancy. Since the influence of associations appears to be dwindling, the importance of third-party cooperations and assignments for agencies is on the rise.

In Berlin itself a new generation of political consultants, advisors for public affairs and for political communication is growing (Wallrabenstein, 2003). But a change can also be observed among the lobbyists for associations and enterprises. Those acting are younger and have a more specific education. Yet, there are presently neither any defined means of educational qualification nor are there relevant institutions for education and ongoing training in Germany.

The existing educational paths can be divided in a practical one (agency/politics) and a theoretical one (political science/communication science) with a subsequent public affairs training. The younger generation of advisors has mostly graduated from a university and then completed a traineeship in an agency. The Poli-c.de poll shows that 60 percent of the questioned German agencies describe a university degree as essential and 90 percent think of it as desirable. Whereas an ongoing training in public relations is non-relevant to more then 60 percent.

The most important qualifications for public affairs consultants according to the poll are good experience in politics and a knowledge of political science. Legal knowledge, knowledge of communication science, and experience in journalism are considered much less important. Experience in public relations and economic knowledge are considered of middle importance (see Figure 22.6) (Poli-c.de, 2004).

A university education has some deficits. Traditional political science is considered to be too theoretical. The curricula for administrative and legal studies neglect the technical requirements of political campaigns and the dynamics of political discourse, while the MBA only touches on the public life of companies and institutions. On the other hand, PR studies at German universities neglect the questions of political organization, analysis of elections, and financing (Klewes, 2003).

In order to accomplish an ongoing process of professionalization it would therefore be meaningful to create convergences of the different areas of studies and to put an interdisciplinary emphasis on studies offered for public affairs. The few already existing courses as well as the possibilities offered for ongoing training must be optimized in this sense (DeGePol, 2003).

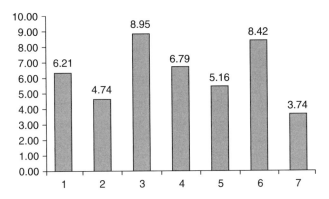

Figure 22.6   *"Which competencies qualify a lobbyist?"*
1   *Experience in public relations,*
2   *experience in journalism,*
3   *experience in politics,*
4   *grasp of economics,*
5   *legal knowledge,*
6   *expertise in political science,*
7   *expertise in communications.*
Source *poli-c.de (2004)*

Besides the studies of political science and communication science and the possibilities for study and training in the area of public relations, there are also special types of education gradually being offered in Germany. Specialized studies and additional training for public affairs and political consultancy include: the Bachelor of International Political Management degree at the Hochschule Bremen, the Master of Public Policy at the University of Erfurt, the Master of Public Affairs Management at the University for Management and Communication in Potsdam, and the seminars of the PR-Kolleg Berlin (Klewes, 2003). In fall 2005 the Hertie School of Governance in Berlin will offer a Master's in Public Policy.

The course at the Hochschule Bremen takes seven semesters. Since it is a professionally oriented course, the necessary previously acquired qualification is either the general or the specialist high school graduation, an additional proof of English-language skills, and a practicum of at least six weeks at a political institution. A course of this kind has been offered since the fall semester 2003/2004 (www.ispm.hs-bremen.de/Studium/studium.html).

The period of study in Erfurt lasts two years. The course has been offered since the fall semester of 2002 and places an emphasis not so much on political communication as

on political consulting, political field analysis, and organizational management (www.unierfurt-de/publicpolicy/). Requirements for being accepted are: graduation from a university with an above-average rating or "proof of acquisition of the required qualification on a professional or other basis" (Klewes, 2003).

Beginning in September 2004, Potsdam is offering a Master's program in Public Affairs Management. It will be a cooperation between Media Mind AG and the PR-Kolleg Berlin. It is planned to educate about 3,000 students on the bases of personal attendance and on correspondence courses up to the year 2010 (www.umk-potsdam.de/).

Regarding ongoing training, the PR-Kolleg Berlin offers three-to-five-day workshops regarding the issues "Basic Knowledge of Public Affairs," "The Public Affairs Campaign," "Public Affairs for Associations," and "Lobbying in Berlin and Brussels" (www.pr-kolleg.de).

## Good Prospects

Germany's peculiarities make up the characteristics of the development of public affairs in the country. Due to the increase in associations and the growing representation of companies and individual associations, as well as the changes following the transfer of the capital from Bonn to Berlin, a new scope for public affairs is resulting. New participants have been added to the associations and unions, PR agencies, specialized law firms, and independent professional consultants (Grunenberg, 2001). It may be assumed that there will be a partial and strategic mixture of representatives of associations and enterprises, lawyers, and public affairs advisors. The continuing development of the branch, the debates concerning codes of conduct and a special kind of education appear to be indicators for the professionalization of public affairs. But in spite of all the changes happening in the German public affairs market Germany is still far behind the situation existing in Brussels or especially in the United States. It is certain, however, that there will be an approximation to these markets soon. Particularly, an increase in the importance of public affairs for enterprises and associations can be recognized, and presumably a German variant of political communication will develop. The political scientist Ulrich von Alemann, for instance, draws the following conclusion: "To a small extent lobbyism is cogoverning. And this is not so bad at all" (Alemann, 2000).

## PUBLIC AFFAIRS IN AUSTRIA

### Lobbying as a Profession

This section evaluates the degree of professionalization of public affairs in Austria. For analysis and presentation we orient ourselves by the two meanings of the etymological root *professio*. Professional lobbying is understood as a "registered trade," as one that is exercised "as a vocation" in the sense of Max Weber's "living from politics"—making a living with lobbying somehow as a profession. The immaterial definition "living for politics" is thereby viewed as the opposite (Weber, 1992: 16). But we also understand *professio* as the "public statement, expression," meaning the public presentation of one's own profession.

This section also deals with the question to what extent there are persons in Austria who are living from lobbying in the sense of this professionalization—meaning this *professio*—and how this profession presents itself to the public.

The contribution is structured by the following topics, which will be presented and evaluated:

1 Which scope is given to full-time professional lobbyists by the consociational Austrian political system?
2 What does the public affairs agency and consulting scene in Austria look like and how has it developed?
3 How relevant and accepted is lobbying in the public debate and how has the image of lobbyists changed?
4 How far has the professionalization of public affairs advanced in Austria?
5 What does the offer of services by professional lobbyists look like?
6 What are the expectations and prospects for the branch in the future?

### Note on the Methodology

The methodology of this section is based on a series of six semi-structured interviews with renowned Austrian public affairs advisors and agency representatives. These six reputable lobbyists have been selected from a small circle of a total of about twenty persons in Austria. Furthermore, the section is based on the evaluation of the available reports in three national daily newspapers, one online news service of the communication branch, as well as a quantitative analysis of various aggregated data from established agencies (year of foundation, identification of the branch in the agency's name).[1] The contribution is also expressively based on the personal professional lobbying experiences of the authors over several years. It is to be understood as a sketch of the lobbying branch in Austria from the practitioner's point of view.

The branch—as far as it can be called such in Austria at all—is very small; this is why this survey was conducted in the form of individual interviews using a semi-structured questionnaire. It is estimated that in Austria a total of about twenty to thirty persons actually match up to the internationally adopted profile of a professional lobbyist (Bentele, 2003). We have exclusively concentrated upon persons and agencies who are acting as lobbyists on a private economic basis and who define themselves as lobbyists in publications and within the frame of this survey. All six persons questioned declared that they publicly refer to themselves as lobbyists. The period of interviewing was the time between December 9 and 22, 2003.

We did not interview persons from institutions that were not completely meeting the mentioned conditions: those active in political organizations like parties and associations, parliamentarians, government staff members, those working for non-governmental organizations (NGOs), and those employed in companies whose roles are in part touching on a political terrain (responsible for corporate affairs). The persons listed earn their living—compared to our respondents—not by the acquisition of clients on the free market und under competitive conditions, but by receiving their income from the institutions and corporations mentioned. These persons are therefore working under completely different conditions than the respondents and in many cases are even the business partners and clients of professional lobbyists.

## Political Structures

Until recently the Austrian political system was characterized by a very strong consociational structure. The most important interests were and still are institutionalized in the various chambers with compulsory memberships and membership fees. The balance of interests in the Second Republic has so far been met primarily by the institution of the *Sozialpartnerschaft* (social partnership), an informal body consisting of four institutions of employees, employers, and agriculture (Chamber of Commerce, Chamber of Labor; Austrian Federation of Unions, Presidential Conference of Chambers of Agriculture). It has mainly prepared important decisions in the area of social and economic politics on an informal basis—similar to a shadow government—since the mid-1960s, and these deci-

sions have *de facto* been frequently accepted by the government.

The chambers and the densely organized associations have been and mainly still are considerably involved in the legislative process through their representatives in Parliament as well as through the compulsory pre-parliamentary appraisal of the legal drafts issued by the Ministries (*Begutachtungsverfahren*) (Tálos, 1997: 441). The chambers and associations are in permanent consultation with the Ministries.

In the recent past, however, the importance of this Austrian tradition of balancing interests has been on the decline. One reason for this can be found in Austria's joining the European Union, which consequently led to a transfer of essential competences of the social partnership to the supranational level of the EU (Karlhofer and Tálos, 2000: 393); but it was also due to the decreasing importance of the unions, following a decline in their degree of organization, while the chambers with their compulsory memberships are suffering from a crisis of legitimacy (Karlhofer and Tálos, 2000: 390). The traditional consensus of social partners has also been challenged by the inauguration in 2000 of the first non-social democratically led government for thirty years, which views this tradition of balancing interests more distantly (Karlhofer and Tálos, 2000: 394).

However, small countries like Austria are especially exposed to the pressure of a global economy toward adaptation and restructuring in order to remain competitive. This is the background for the development of niches and spaces in which lobbyists as representatives of interests can increasingly establish themselves.

## Regulation of the Relationship between Lobbyists and Politicians

Prior to presenting a law in Parliament the government has to send the legal draft to the Chambers as part of the appraisal procedure. The Ministries usually also invite other representatives of interest groups.

There are no rules for the ways Ministries interact with professional lobbyists. The business orders of both Chambers of the Austrian

Parliament also lack regulations for the relationship between lobbyists and parliamentarians. In Austria there exists neither an official register of lobbyists nor a code of conduct for the Parliament. Yet, both chambers are permitted to have their committees seek external expertise. Experts representing certain individual interests are therefore not excluded (European Parliament, 2003: 53).

Many Members of Parliament are at the same time also functionaries of chambers and associations whose interests they represent in Parliament. In 1978 the percentage of parliamentarians who have also been full or part-time functionaries of economic associations was 55.8 percent. But this percentage dropped to 14.8 percent in 2000 (Karlhofer and Tálos, 2000: 388). In this regard no rules of incompatibility exist.

### The Lobbying Scene

As of January 2006, according to the professional association of Austrian PR agencies (PRVA) plus relevant names known in the media, there exist altogether about fifty agencies and individual advisors who are active as public affairs consultants and lobbyists in various ways.

A quantitative analysis demonstrates that for about three-quarters of the agencies no hint as to their lobbying activities can be discovered in their names, but that these agencies usually include in their names the terms "public relations," "communications," or "strategic communication" as indicators is of the branch. Only a handful of agencies call themselves agencies for "lobbying" and about ten agencies and consultants mention "public affairs" in their names.

Looking at the dates of foundation of the agencies offering public affairs consulting, it becomes obvious that they have almost exclusively been founded since the mid-1980s. For most agencies the subsequent change of direction to the business field of public affairs and lobbying is not expressed in the name. However, it can be observed that more than half of those agencies that define themselves as public affairs or lobbying agencies have been founded since 1995.

The analysis shows a clear move by existing agencies to this area of business as well as a small surge of founding agencies during recent years, who publicly declare themselves to be public affairs agencies and who are also primarily acting as such.

The growing demand for public affairs services is illustrated by the increasing turnover. In 2003, the top ten public relations agencies which offer public affairs services turned over about 8 million Euro with lobbying services (Anon., 2004). This, however, does not include the firms specializing in lobbying and public affairs. Other sources estimate a turnover of the entire PR/PA industry of about 30 million Euro (Ruzicka, 2004).

### The Public Image of Lobbyists

In Austria, representatives of interest groups have so far almost exclusively been active on an informal basis, using personal relations or memberships in political parties or associations. The professional declaration as lobbyist was unusual, and if used, it carried rather a negative connotation. Due to the dense structures and networks of associations and chambers many potential clients had doubts about the meaningfulness of financing professional lobbying for a long period of time.

Based on an analysis of reports in three national Austrian daily newspapers and one online news service of the communication branch regarding the issue of lobbying, it will be attempted to demonstrate the development of a professional image. The period of investigation lies between 1995 and the end of 2003. Primarily the frequency of the use of the word "lobbyism" has been investigated quantitatively, and secondly the image of lobbyism as a profession was looked at as presented by background reports on this topic. The following conclusions can be drawn:

1   *The public interest grows.* The distribution of the number of mentions of the word "lobbying" (see Table 22.2) allows the conclusion that the public relevance of lobbying has increased since 1995. In all media investigated there was a growing frequency of such mentions. But it must

Table 22.2  *Mentions of "lobbying" in three Austrian papers and one online news agency of the communications branch*

| Year | Der Standard | Die Presse | Wirtschaftsblatt | Horizont.at |
|------|------|------|------|------|
| 2003 | 59 | 75 | 81 | 27 |
| 2002 | 53 | 70 | 81 | 14 |
| 2001 | 55 | 56 | 68 | 12 |
| 2000 | 44 | 49 | 51 | 16 |
| 1999 | 58 | 46 | | |
| 1998 | 54 | 63 | | |
| 1997 | 46 | 42 | | |
| 1996 | | 43 | | |
| 1995 | | 25 | | |

be considered that these mentions include every use of the word "lobbying" and do not only refer to the specific use of the term as a profession. Only the increasing frequency in the online news service of the branch Horizont.at speaks clearly for a growing public relevance of the term, since it can be assumed that the mentions there refer almost exclusively to the profession.

2  *Lobbying is reaching Vienna through Brussels.* It can also be seen by the increase of various background reports that the interest has grown during the last years. The qualitative analysis of these reports regarding the image conveyed shows the development toward an emancipated, professional image of lobbyists in the public view.

Reports concerning lobbyism as a professional trade first appeared in the context of lobbying in Brussels, i.e. on the level of the European Union. The influence upon the political decision makers there is viewed as immanent to the system and as legitimate as far as the lobbying work remains transparent. Only over time do lobbyists also appear in background reports who are also offering their services on the Austrian market. The public appearance of lobbyists has been noticeably growing since the turn of the century.

Lobbying is increasingly seen as publicly relevant as Austrian lobbyists establish themselves more and more as active figures in economic life and political processes. It is therefore now possible to speak of a normalization compared to the international situation.

3  *Background of Austrian lobbyists.* The key people in agencies and among self-employed consultants have previously been politicians or civil servants, former employees of political parties or former secretaries and members of Ministers' Cabinets. But it is not only the agencies and consultants who are coming from this group; such people are also managing the public affairs departments of large companies (Anon., 2002, 2003a). The Austrian situation can be characterized as: "Essentially the community of lobbyists with their own clients (who do not represent a special interest group or only one particular client) is quite small in our country. Whoever belongs to it is usually coming from politics" (Anon, 2003a).

## Characteristics of Professionalization

Following Scammell, the listed criteria can, among other things, serve to evaluate the degree of general professionalization: control over entry, a self-regulating code of conduct, definable bodies of knowledge, full-time employment in the field, and formal organization of professionals into societies that defend professional standards and protect members' interests (Scammell, 1997: 5).

For lobbyists in Austria no control exists over entry into the branch. As Scammell points out, this criterion cannot be applied to branches like political consultants, journalists, and also lobbyists, since a control over entry would be democratically questionable in these cases. Anyway, lobbyists in Austria don't need a license like lawyers or tax consultants do.

It is difficult to say anything about the standards of general know-how in the branch in Austria. Within German-speaking countries there is only one branch journal, published in Berlin, dealing with political communication. It rarely refers to the Austrian branch or to developments in that country.

It looks different in regards to education. For some time now the area of public affairs/lobbying has been integrated in two of three postgraduate university courses in communications, for instance at the private Donau Universität Krems in the postgraduate course for Integrated Communication of the International Center of Journalism.

Among approximately ten PR studies and educational programs outside the universities one professional school offers a separate program for "Public Affairs/Lobbying". Most of the other educational programs have integrated public affairs/lobbying into their general offer in the form of reports by external visitors. Since the fall of 2002 one private university offers—in co-operation with the Public Relations Association of Austria—a PR program emphasizing the European Union. According to its director this program focuses heavily on the practice of lobbying and public affairs.

In 2004 two associations were established to represent the profession. Both have adopted voluntary codes of conduct.

As far as full-time employment is concerned, our survey shows that all interviewed agencies are employing advisors concerned exclusively with public affairs. On the other hand, the estimated turnovers with public affairs lead to the conclusion that only a very few of the self-employed consultants and agencies generate more than two-thirds of their turnover from public affairs.

## Range of Services Offered by the Profession

Regarding the *services offered* our respondents described the spectrum as follows: strategic consulting of corporations on political processes, conception and realization of the strategy, interventions, monitoring of relevant developments, as well as setting up contacts. Specific activities mentioned were also mediation in conflict situations, the confidential dissemination of information, and the personal coaching of the client regarding his relations with politics and administration.

As far as *branches* are concerned, the survey among these specialists made it clear that those branches that were formerly state-owned and run but have now been opened up to the free market now represent fields of activity for lobbyists. This target group includes primarily the media (television and radio), telecommunications, the energy sector, traffic and infrastructure. Other sectors offering good possibilities for lobbyists are the industrial kind of medicine/biotechnology and chemistry, as well as those of financing insurance and food/trade.

## The Increasing Importance of Professional Lobbying

A majority of the respondents believe that lobbying has gained importance during recent years. Reasons for this are seen in the increasing professionalization of the branch, but also the growing offer of services, and the greater complexity of issues due to the embedding of companies into the European multilevel system, which can be handled independently only by large corporations. An additional reason is seen in the difficult economic situation which forces companies to close or to reduce their own departments of public affairs at least temporarily and to buy these services externally. Under difficult economic conditions it appears that companies also have a greater interest in political processes. Another factor contributing to professionalization is the understanding that—due to the growing competitive pressure and the increasing public demands on corporations—public affairs and lobbying have become important contributors to the company's success. This is reinforced by

Table 22.3   *Rates of Austrian public affairs consultants, hourly and daily (€)*

|  | Hourly | | Daily | |
|---|---|---|---|---|
|  | Minimum | Maximum | Minimum | Maximum |
| Average | 230 | 306 | 2,000 | 2,800 |
| Extremes | 150 | 450 | 1,400 | 4,500 |

the improving public image of lobbyists. Here we can observe a process of "educating the market," which has already been achieved in most other European countries.

The liberalization of the formerly nationalized sectors of the economy like energy or telecommunications opens windows of opportunities for lobbyists of the private economic sector. Where the state formerly had a monopoly it is now possible for international competitors to enter the market. They are interested in the best possible conditions for their market entry, while the formerly state-owned Austrian corporations have an interest in holding their positions as well as possible. Chambers and associations are losing relevance in this situation, since they may only represent the interests of whole branches, not the individual, frequently competing, interests of corporations. This is confirmed by the increase in public affairs departments in the large Austrian companies. Furthermore, the public affairs activities of companies also motivate competitors to equally active lobbying activities in order to avoid disadvantaging themselves.

The added value of their work is described by those interviewed as follows: the high quality of available contacts, the special know-how of political processes, the ability to combine economic and political interests, the early recognition of problematic situations, and the ability to receive relevant information from political circles.

The question about the primary importance of knowledge of and access to persons or networks as opposed to knowledge of facts and relevant information cannot be clearly answered. The replies are balanced and many respondents stress the inseparability of both factors. The international political consultant Karl Jurka has formulated the "indispensable principle" of the branch: "No person without an issue, no issue without a person."

Regarding *fees* the survey shows (see Table 22.3) that the hourly rates are averaging between a minimum of €230 and a maximum of €300, while the figures range between €180 at the lowest and a €450 top rate. An even greater disparity can be found among the daily rates. Estimates assume for the branch a usual amount of €2,000 (Anon., 2003b). But as the survey results demonstrate, this seems to be the lower end of the scale. The average daily rate of an Austrian lobbyist lies between a €2,000 minimum and €2,800 maximum fee. Here the extremes lie at a minimum of €1,400 and a top rate of €4,500.

In order to discover the *degree of internationalization* of the branch in Austria some questions referred to the organizational structure of the agency, the background of the clients, and the area of work. The results show that public affairs consulting in Austria is cooperating internationally in different ways. There are agencies which are part of international networks as well as Austrian companies with loosely structured international partnerships. It is noticeable that large public affairs agencies operating Europe-wide or even worldwide do not have any Austrian branches so far but only loose partners. In recent years, however, there have been a few takeovers of Austrian agencies by international agency groups.

Regarding the question about the background of their clients, all respondents stated that they also worked for foreign clients. In most cases they were clients from the European Union, but occasionally also from the United States and Asia. All respondents claimed to work abroad, and also in the immediate vicinity of their clients.

*Differences from other markets* and other countries as seen by interviewees can be divided by the function of the political system and the degree of professionalization. Regarding the differences in public affairs work, which can be traced back to the particularities of the political system, they point out that the political system in Austria—due to the small size of the country—is very easy to structure, which in turn again raises the importance of personal contacts. They also stress the influential role still played for the balance of interests by the various associations in Austria.

In professional terms they mention the considerably lower rates of fees in Austria and the unclear differentiation between lobbying and public relations.

It is further noted that compared to other countries the lobbying work in Austria is more often done by corporations themselves, since the political scene is easier to overlook and contacts therefore often exist already. It is congruent with the above-mentioned greater importance of personal contact in Austria that the factors of know-how and competence are internationally regarded as of higher importance than in Austria.

## The Future

Compared to the situation ten years ago, respondents' experience of the branch of public affairs in Austria is generally more professional today in the sense of being larger, more international, and more serious. Besides, public affairs and lobbying are nowadays accepted and appear more self-assured in public, as affirmed by the analysis of the press reports.

The future of the profession is seen positively by all those questioned. Concrete expectations are tied to a further increase in acceptance of public affairs as well as increasing cooperation between institutional interests and public affairs service agents. Along with the increasing quality of the branch itself it is expected that there will be a separation of "the wheat from the chaff." Regarding business opportunities there is a general expectation of a growing market and an increase in commissions. There is rising hope of orders from the European Union, mainly from the new member states, as well as the expectation of being able to increase one's own activities in these countries.

## RÉSUMÉ

1  The political and economic framework has radically changed in Austria during the last ten years. As a consequence there are niches developing where lobbyists can establish themselves.

2  Since the 1990s some communication agencies have been able to enlarge their spectrum of services specifically in the area of public affairs and lobbying. A small "wave of foundations" of agencies that particularly devote themselves to this field and also identify themselves publicly by using the name "public affairs agency" has appeared since the late 1990s. By international comparison this scene is very small but growing.

3  The increasing frequency of public appearances by public affairs consultants referring to themselves as "lobbyists" as well as the fact that the image of lobbyism has changed to one of a professional and legitimate trade are leading to a new self-image and public image of the branch. This is affirmed by the fact that those questioned publicly refer to themselves as "lobbyists".

4  All persons foresee growth for their branch, especially within the European Union and the new member states.

5  Overall, these developments indicate a convergence towards the international standards regarding the professional understanding and image of lobbyists in Austria.

## NOTE

1 We considered relevant background reports in daily newspapers like *Die Presse* (since January 1995), *Der Standard* (since January 1997), *Wirtschaftsblatt* (since January 2000) and the Austrian online news service of the communication branch Horizont.at (since January 2000).

# REFERENCES

Alemann, Ulrich von (2000). "Vom Korporatismus zum Lobbyismus? Die Zukunft der Verbände zwischen Globalisierung, Europäisierung und Berlinisierung," *Aus Politik und Zeitgeschichte* 26–27, June 23–30.

Andersen, Uwe, and Wichard Woyke (eds) (2000). *Handwörterbuch des politischen Systems der Bundesrepublik Deutschland*, 4th edn. Bonn: Bundeszentrale für politische Bildung.

Anon. (2002). "Wenn Kontakte zu Politik und Verwaltung bares Geld wert sind," *Die Presse* (Vienna), July 24.

Anon. (2003a). "Lobbyisten. So lassen Sie die Fäden ziehen," *Wirtschaftsblatt* (Vienna), October 28.

Anon. (2003b). "Was kostet Lobbying?" *Wirtschaftsblatt* (Vienna), October 28.

Anon. (2004). "Das Bestseller–PR–Agentur Ranking 2003," *Bestseller* (Vienna), May. Source: http://www.horizont.at/news/newspdf/16953.pdf (accessed December 31, 2003).

Bender, Gunnar, and Lutz Reulecke (eds) (2003). *Handbuch des deutschen Lobbyisten. Wie ein modernes und transparentes Politikmanagement funktioniert*. Frankfurt am Main: Frankfurter Allgemeine Buch.

Bentele, Günther (2003). "Kungelei oder legitime Kommunikation? Innen- und Außenwahrnehmung des Lobbyismus." Speech delivered at the "Politikkongress," Berlin, November 24–25. Source: http://www.politikkongress.de/pdf/referent/bender.pdf (accessed December 31, 2003).

Bentele, Günther, and René Seidenglanz (2003). *PR-Images in Germany: Population Poll and Journalist Survey*. Leipzig: Institut für Kommunikations- und Medienwissenschaft, Universität Leipzig.

Bundesregierung (1949). *Grundgesetz für die Bundesrepublik Deutschland*. Bundesregierung online, www.bundesregierung.de. Source: http://www.bundesregierung.de/static/pdf/gg.pdf (accessed November 29, 2003).

CERP (1978). European Code of Professional Conduct in Public Relations (Code of Lisbon), adopted at the General Assembly of CERP in Lisbon 1978. Source: http://www.cerp.org/code/euro_code.htm (accessed December 31, 2003).

CERP (1991). European Charter for Public Affairs, 1991. Tampere: CERP Council, October 19. Source: http://www.cerp.org/code/papers_pubaffairs.htm (accessed December 31, 2003).

DeGePol (2003). *Was ist Politikberatung?* Berlin: Deutsche Gesellschaft für Politikberatung. Source:

http://www.degepol.de/downloads/degepol_online.pdf (accessed December 31, 2003).

European Parliament, Directorate General of Research (ed.) (2003). *Lobbying in the European Union: Current Rules and Practices*. Working paper. Source: www4.europarl.eu.int/estudies/internet/workingpapers/afco/pdf/104_en.pdf (accessed November 25, 2003).

Grunenberg, Nina (2001). "Politikberatung. Die Mächtigen schlau machen," *Die Zeit* (Hamburg) 28/2001.

Güttler, Alexander, and Joachim Klewes (eds) (2002). *Public Affairs Studie. Keine Angst vor der Lobby. Bürger wollen transparente Politikberatung*. Düsseldorf: Güttler + Klewes Communications Management.

Karlhofer, Ferdinand, and Emmerich Tálos (2000). "Sozialpartnerschaft unter Druck. Trends und Szenaren," in Anton Pelinka, Fritz Plasser, and Wolfgang Meixner (eds), *Die Zukunft der österreichischen Demokratie. Trends, Prognosen und Szenarien*. Vienna: Signum.

Klewes, Joachim (2003). "Kann man PA eigentlich studieren?" Speech delivered at Politikkongress, Berlin, November 24–25. Source: http://www.politikkongress.de/pdf/referent/klewes.pdf (accessed December 31, 2003).

Leif, Thomas, and Rudolf Speth (eds) (2003). *Die Stille Macht. Lobbyismus in Deutschland*. Wiesbaden: Westdeutscher Verlag.

Lianos, Manuel (2003). "Public Affairs. Das Spiel der Agenturen," *Politik und Kommunikation* 9/2003. Berlin: Politikverlag Helios.

Lianos, Manuel, and Stephanie Simon (2003). "Politikkongress und Politikaward. Ein Blick hinter die Bühnen," *Politik und Kommunikation* 12/2003. Berlin: Politikverlag Helios.

Mancini, Paola (1999). "New frontiers in Political Professionalism," *Political Communication* 16: 231–245.

Matrat, Lucien (1965). International Code of Ethics (Code of Athens). Adopted in Athens by CERP and IPRA, May. Source: http://www.cerp.org/code/international_code.htm (accessed December 31, 2003).

Poli-c.de (2004). *Agentur-Umfrage zum Thema Lobbying*, ed. Florian Busch-Janser and Mario Voigt. Source: http://www.poli-c-gev.de/poli-c/ publicaffairs/studien.html (accessed April 8, 2004).

*PR-Report* (2001). Issue 1801, October 19. Hamburg: Haymarket Media.

*PR-Report* (2002). Issue 1824, April 26. Hamburg: Haymarket Media.

*PR-Report* (2003). *Ranking Public-Affairs 2003*. Published at poli-c.de, source: http://www.poli-c-gev.

de/poli-c/publicaffairs/agenturen-ranking.html (accessed December 31, 2003).

Publicis (2003). "Public-Affairs-Umfrage 2003," Berlin: Publicis Public Relations. Source: http://www.publicis-pr.de/download/pool/paumfrage_ergebnisse.pdf (accessed December 31, 2003).

Ruzicka, Johanna (2004). "Lobbyisten lobbyieren in eigener Sache," *Der Standard* (Vienna), December 1.

Sator, Christoph (2003). "Die Lobby-Republik," Deutsche Presse-Agentur, August 1, in *Manager Magazin*. Source: http://www.manager-magazin.de/koepfe/artikel/0,2828,259242,00.html (accessed December 31, 2003).

Scammell, Margaret (1997). "The Wisdom of the War Room: US Campaigning and Americanization." Research Paper R-17, Cambridge, MA: Joan Shorenstein Center on the Press, Politics, and Public Policy, Harvard University. Source: www. ksg. harvard.edu/presspol/Research_Publications/Papers/Research_Papers/R17.pdf (accessed December 1, 2003).

Schönborn, Gregor (ed.) (2002). *Public Affairs Agenda. Politikkommunikation als Erfolgsfaktor.* Neuwied Kriftel: Luchterhand.

Sebaldt, Martin (1997a). "Verbände und Demokratie. Funktionen bundesdeutscher Interessengruppen in Theorie und Praxis," in *Aus Politik und Zeitgeschichte*, B 36–37.

Sebaldt, Martin (1997b). *Organisierter Pluralismus in Deutschland. Kräftefeld, Selbstverständnis und politische Arbeit deutscher Interessengruppen*, Opladen: Westdeutscher Verlag.

Tálos, Emmerich (1997). "Sozialpartnerschaft. Kooperation—Konzertierung—politische Regulierung," in Herbert Dachs, Peter Gerlich *et al.* (eds), *Handbuch des politischen Systems Österreichs. Die zweite Republik*, 3rd edn. Vienna: Manz.

Wagner, Joachim (2003). "Die fünfte Gewalt. Lobbyisten haben so viel Einfluss wie nie zuvor in der Geschichte der Bundesrepublik," *Die Zeit* (Hamburg) 45/2003.

Wallrabenstein, Alex (2003). "Public Affairs Boomtown Berlin," in Marco Althaus and Vito Cecere (eds) (2003). *Kampagne! Zwei neue Strategien für Wahlkampf, PR und Lobbying*, Münster, Hamburg, and London: Lit Verlag.

Wassermann, Andreas (2002). "Bisschen viel Wind," *Der Spiegel* (Hamburg) 31/2002.

Weber, Max (1992). *Politik als Beruf.* Stuttgart: Reclam.

## Other Sources

www.ispm.hs-bremen.de/Studium/studium.html
www.pr-kolleg.de
www.uni-erfurt.de/publicpolicy/
www.umk-potsdam.de/

## Sources for Empirical Analysis

### Newspapers

Online: Archive of *Die Presse*: www.diepresse.com, January 1995 to December 2003.

Online: Archive of *Der Standard*: www.derstandard.at, January 1997 to December 2003.

Online: Archive of *Wirtschaftsblatt*: www.wirtschaftsblatt.at, January 2000 to December 2003.

### Austrian online news service of the communication branch: Horizont.at

Online: Archive of Horizont.at: www.horizont.at, January 2000 to December 2003.

# 23

# Political Marketing and Public Affairs

BRUCE I. NEWMAN

This chapter will explore the link between political marketing and public affairs. In the United States, where the emphasis will be placed in this chapter, there have been efforts on the part of political parties and other political action committees and interest groups to use the influence of money to affect political outcomes at election time as well as to pass laws that benefit one group in society over another. We will investigate the role of money that comes from lobbying efforts on the part of corporations and the impact it has on campaign budgets, tactics, and the general ethical condition that exists in politics today. The chapter ends with the introduction of an innovative Strategic Framework for Lobbyists that can be used as the basis for the development of marketing strategies.

## THE ROLE OF LOBBYING IN THE UNITED STATES

In general, the role of lobbyists in the United States can be broken down into three main areas: business, union, and special interest. Business lobbyists usually hire firms such as public affairs companies to conduct their business for them. These public affairs companies are beginning to understand and use the tactics and strategies that have been well documented in the political marketing literature to date. Unions seem to be more active at the grassroots level and tend to concentrate more on influencing their own members. Special interest groups are more active with respect to issue advocacy advertising, and less sophisticated with respect to their use of political marketing methods. Although the link between political marketing and lobbying has been touched on in the literature in political marketing (Newman, 1999a, b), this chapter will be the first serious analysis of how the two can be merged into a very powerful knowledge base to be used by lobbyists to impact the decision making of political parties and politicians in their role as governing officials.

The integration of the fields of political marketing and public affairs as a hybrid model for lobbyists constitutes an important step for governments around the world that are increasingly forced to find ways of identifying business opportunities for corporations in their respective countries. It is in the interest of corporations to use political activity to secure greater sales and avoid regulation costs that make it more difficult for them to compete for business around the world. So, it should not be surprising to know that the literature finds that the most consistent explanatory factors of political activity have been firms' size, degree of government regulation, and the amount of firm or industry sales to the government (Grier et al., 1994). Among the top 500 corporations in the United States, close to 60 percent have political action committees, and the mean contribution to candidates running for public office was $80,349 (Mitchell et al., 1997).

Some have even referred to lobbyists as the fourth branch of government. Whereas both parties (Democrats and Republicans) in the United States have tried to work in a cooperative arrangement with lobbyists, the Republicans have been more proactive than the Democrats. The Republican leadership in the Senate have regular meetings with lobbyists about hiring Republicans, such as ex-chiefs of staff, or a pollster to be placed in lobbying firms. The firms then raise money for Republican candidates and help get them elected.

## WHAT IS A PAC?

A PAC is an acronym that stands for the term *political action committee* which is set up to raise and spend funds to support candidates for public office. Special interests (like the American Heart Association and trade associations like the National Roofing Contractors Association) use their political action committees to make known and further their positions on issues and policies that affect their industry. PAC money is used to support politicians who have helped these organizations in their fight on Capitol Hill.

### Who are the Top PACs?

So which corporations have given the most amount of money over the past decade in the United States? According to Opensecrets.org, a Web site devoted to the dissemination of information on lobbying, the following list of donors covers the top ten since 1989:

1   American Federation of State, County and Municipal Employees: $34,335,708.
2   National Association of Realtors: $22,840,577.
3   National Education Association: $22, 754,066.
4   Association of Trial Lawyers of America: $22,411,966.
5   International Brotherhood of Electrical Workers: $20,451,489.
6   Philip Morris: $20,106,715.
7   Carpenters and Joiners Union: $20, 100,487.
8   Teamsters Union: $19,998,665.
9   Laborers Union: $19,877,259.
10  American Medical Association: $19, 862,043.

As one looks at the figures at recent single elections, such as in the 2001–2002 cycle and 1999–2000 cycle, it becomes clear that the list of the top ten contains almost all of the same organizations listed above, with the following exceptions—the United Auto Workers, the National Auto Dealers Association, and the Machinists/Aerospace Workers Union. There is clearly a consistency in influence coming from the same lobbyists. This makes it more clear for the candidates running for election, as well as the politicians sitting in office, to know where to turn for money to finance their re-election bids as well as pet projects in Congress.

As one looks overseas to identify the political action committees that are spending the most on foreign elections, the following companies rise to the top five in the 2003–2004 cycle:

1   Brown & Williamson Tobacco: $362,550.
2   Bayer Corporation: $245,500.
3   BAE Systems North America: $243,639.
4   BASF Corporation: $219,250.
5   BP America: $204,000.

In almost all of the cases cited above, the Republicans received at least twice as much as the Democrats have.

Table 23.1    *Contributions for House candidates (%)*

| Contributor | Incumbents | Challengers |
|---|---|---|
| Individual over $200 | 15 | 18 |
| Individual $200–$1000 | 36 | 39 |
| Political action committee | 41 | 17 |
| Parties | 1 | 3 |
| Candidates | 1 | 18 |
| Miscellaneous | 6 | 4 |

*Source* Magleby (2002: 126).

## LEVEL OF SPENDING IN RECENT ELECTION CYCLES

If we go back to recent presidential cycles and track the source of money from political action committees and soft and individual donations, the amount of money coming from business, labor, and ideological organizations breaks down in the following way in 2004 (as of November, 2003):

1   Business: $66,275,578, one-third to Democrats, two-thirds to Republicans.
2   Labor: $15,841,628, seven-eighths to Democrats, one-eighth to Republicans.
3   Ideological: $7,058,590, two-fifths to Democrats, three-fifths to Republicans.

During the complete 2002 election cycle the breakdown across business, labor, and ideological organizations was:

1   Business: $200,197,589, one-third to Democrats, two-thirds to Republicans.
2   Labor: $60,271,466, nine-tenths to Democrats, one-tenth to Republicans.
3   Ideological: $44,124,760, half to Democrats, half to Republicans.

### Impact of Spending on Election Outcomes

Perhaps most important and germane to this discussion is not necessarily the amount of money spent on election campaigns, but the impact (or correlation) of the money spent on individual campaigns and the outcomes of that spending. In an authoritative edited book on the financing of the 2000 congressional election, Maglby (2002: 127) concluded that most of the candidates who raised and spent the most money won, and most of those candidates also happened to be incumbents. This of course stands to reason, as those members in Congress who have the most influence in the legislative process will be in the best position to influence laws that impact on corporations and other interested parties. A very interesting statistic is the breakdown of contributions for House of Representatives candidates (Table 23.1)

Only in the case of incumbents did the largest percentage of money come from political action committees. The political action committee's main job is to get the maximum return on their donations, seeking to win influence and goodwill with as many lawmakers as possible in Washington. There will not be a return on their investment if the recipients of their donations don't win office. Because of this political action committees are very careful where they invest their money, thereby not taking the risk on non-incumbents whom they are not familiar enough with to trust to carry out the favors they seek.

The way in which political action committees get around the limitations of the law in their support of candidates and parties is to spend their money and influence on "issue ads." Issue advertisements which raise specific concerns or even attack or support a candidate are considered to be non-political as long as they do not call for the open support or defeat of a particular candidate in an ad. This is where the influence of political marketing becomes very significant. This was part of the Supreme Court ruling in its landmark 1976 *Buckley v. Valeo* decision that set the rules for the current set of election laws. The use of

Table 23.2   *Top spending on the top ten issues*

| Industry | Total spending |
|---|---|
| 1 Miscellaneous | 41,294,326 |
| 2 Human rights | 14,286,766 |
| 3 Environment | 6,797,000 |
| 4 Gun rights | 6,680,759 |
| 5 Republican/Conservative | 6,024,761 |
| 6 Pro-Israel | 1,500,000 |
| 7 Abortion policy/Pro-choice | 799,168 |
| 8 Abortion policy/Pro-life | 715,000 |
| 9 Gun control | 420,000 |
| 10 Women's issues | 340,000 |

*Source* Opensecrets.org

issue ads became very popular during the course of elections that took place in the 1990s when religious rights groups began to make targets of selected politicians. Since then, several political action committees followed suit to express their rights as citizens of the United States by paying for such issue ads that clearly favored one candidate over another. The political parties themselves in fact have relied on issue ads to support their own cadre of candidates in recent elections. According to the Annenberg Center of the University of Pennsylvania, hundreds of millions of dollars were spent on television and radio ads alone during the recent election cycles in the United States.

According to year 2000 data, the most amount of money spent on the top ten issues based on ideological/single-issue ads broke down into the categories in Table 23.2.

As one looks at money spent by lobbyists in recent elections in the United States, the following conclusions can be drawn:

1   Contributions from political action committees to congressional candidates continue on an upward spiral.
2   Growth in soft money spending, particularly by the Democratic Party, has been essential to the party's success in recent key congressional races.
3   Parties and political action committees will continue to see redistricting changes happening in upcoming elections which will make their job even more difficult.
4   Political action committees are spending millions of dollars on issue advocacy in more targeted congressional races.

5   Political action committees are increasing their independent expenditures because they are able to directly urge voters to vote for or against a particular candidate. However, all independent expenditures must be reported to the FEC.
6   Political action committees that gave the most in recent elections were corporate political action committees in direct contributions to candidates, followed by trade associations, followed by labor political action committees, followed by ideologically oriented political action committees, with cooperatives giving the least amount of monetary support.
7   Groups like the NRA, the Christian Coalition and the AFL-CIO are semi-permanent, full-service, independent electoral organizations that work just like political parties.
8   A large proportion of PAC activity is shielded from public view, as more groups learned to take advantage of opportunities to influence electoral policies through such devices as soft money contributions to the political parties and issue advocacy advertising.

Some say the United States is in an era characterized by the "permanent campaign" where political fund raising is continual and there is a blurring of election and policy-making activity. While many have made the argument that the increase in the number and influence of political action committees implies the decline of political parties and the emergence of the influence of special interests, it is clear that the PAC system owes much of its structure to the party system. PACs are formed by groups that are sensitive to electoral shifts and partisan conflict. This sensitivity to the ebb and flow of the party system also implies that most political action committees are likely to favor one party or the other.

## THE IMPACT OF LAWS ON LOBBYISTS

Under amended FECA 1979 parties can spend money on pins, bumper stickers, voter registration, get-out-the-vote drives, and the spending does not count against the party contribution or coordinated expenditure limits for any candidate. The law also permits parties to set up a separate account for fund raising called "non-federal" or "soft" money for party activities not expressly connected to candidates.

In *Buckley v. Valeo* (1976) the Supreme Court majority ruled that there should be mandatory limits on campaign spending. Candidates spending their own money, as well as independent expenditures, are violations of a constitutional right to free speech and unconstitutional. This case applies to state and local elections as well. *Buckley v. Valeo* allows interest groups to skirt the full disclosure intention of FECA because of the right to free speech. Supreme Court footnotes to the case state that limits on spending or contributions apply only to express advocacy (i.e. "vote for," "elect," "defeat," "for Congress"). Without these words the advocacy spending is beyond the scope of FECA and the source of the funding or the amount need not be disclosed. Political action committees may engage in unlimited express advocacy for or against a candidate via "independent expenditures." Unlimited express advocacy represents internal communications with their own members, and unlimited and undisclosed issue advocacy that often supports or opposes a candidate. Political action committees may raise unlimited money for electoral purposes but face spending constraints on direct contributions.

There have been some very significant changes put into law in the United States that will have an impact on the effectiveness of lobbyists. On December 10, 2003, the Supreme Court ruled that the Congress was justified in seeking to purge national politics of the big money campaign contributions with laws that will limit large donations from corporations, unions, and individuals. At stake from the opponents of the laws were objections to the limitation of free speech (provided for by the First Amendment of the constitution of the United States) that some argued was inherent in the passing of the laws ruled justified by the Supreme Court. According to the new laws, soft money contributions (namely those contributions to political parties for use other than advocating a candidate's election or defeat) that until now gave local and state parties unlimited transfers of monies to be used for issue/ideological advertisements will now be effectively eliminated.

Hard money contributions (contributions to individual candidates to support or defeat them) will now be limited to $2,000 per election, $25,000 per year to national parties and $5,000 per year to a single political action committee. There will be a complete ban on issue ads, which are broadcast ads from independent groups, including unions and corporations, that do not advocate the election or defeat of candidates, yet refer directly to them, within sixty days of an election or thirty days of a primary. This law is the first major campaign finance legislation in thirty years, and is often referred to as McCain-Feingold (also known technically in the Congress as legislation S.1593) after its main sponsors, Senators John McCain and Russell Feingold. The law takes effect in the 2004 elections and beyond. This law will have a very big impact on funds that allowed soft money contributions to political parties to be used to get out the vote and build party strength, and not to support a particular candidate. However, many critics argued that campaigns turned to soft money donations to circumvent campaign finance rules. The national political parties have raised hundreds of millions of dollars which have in fact been used to help support specific campaigns. The central provision of McCain-Feingold prohibits parties from soliciting, receiving, or spending soft money.

## STRATEGY DEVELOPMENT BY LOBBYISTS

Firms cannot legally contribute corporate funds to political action committees, but firms can grant permission for trade associations or professional political action committees to solicit their employees for contributions. Many decisions on legislation are often made in a last-minute frenzy as legislators prepare to adjourn for the legislation session, so lobbyists need to know when to act and how to act as legislation comes up fast. It is crucial that each member of the subcommittee working on a Bill a political action committee is interested in is contacted by the committee about the Bill and gets constituents who support the Bill to contact committee members. Next, contact should be made by all members of the full committee to get their support. The Bill may be in committee for years, so there is ample time for a political action committee to get constituents to contact committee members. Political Action Committees can influence a Bill at any point in the process from committee to joint committee to either House to conference committee to the executive.

The key step in moving a political action committee's Bill to a successful vote in committee (which is the most critical step) is choosing the most influential person in the committee to join the cause of the political action committee. To get the PAC Bill through committee, a political action committee will also want to approach the strongest committee member from the minority side. Political action committees should help committees set up hearings on the Bill and be present at mark-up sessions (because the legislator or staff person may need to contact someone from the political action committee at a moment's notice, and because last-minute words with an undecided committee member are important, and because it sends the message to the legislators that the political action committee is concerned about a particular Bill).

Political action committees should try to make connections with legislators' staff members who have a lot of "behind the scenes"

power and get updates on their bill. Political action committees should recognize those staff members who have helped them. (This involves spending of some kind.) Most political action committees use ideological, access-oriented, or mixed strategies when contributing to candidates. Political action committees that use ideological strategies are similar to the two major political parties (democrats and republicans) with respect to the fact that they seek to influence the political process through the election.

Ideological political action committees give money to candidates in highly competitive races to encourage the career of up-and-coming young politicians. Ideological political action committees rarely make contributions for the purpose of gaining access to legislators because these committees seek to push pecific issues that are linked to fundamental policies and issues that politicians will rarely compromise on. Access-oriented committees make contributions mainly to gain a foothold with members of Congress who are in a position to affect regulations and appropriations on those laws that affect the specific industry in which the organization operates and that is represented by the political action committee. Access-oriented committees consider campaign contributions a tool for strengthening their relationship with important government officials. They see that contributions create goodwill to make it easier for their lobbyists to influence the legislative process. Access-oriented political action committees give more money to incumbents, and it does not have to be a competitive election for them to give money.

Mixed strategy political action committees, which include primarily trade associations and labor unions, give some money to candidates that share their views and some money to incumbents they want to keep accessible to them. It is not unusual to see committees recruiting and training candidates to run for public office, as well as serving as advisors to their campaigns in the primary and general elections. So the question that arises now is: how can a lobbyist use the knowledge base in political marketing to carry out their functions?

## THE ROLE OF POLITICAL MARKETING IN POLITICS

Politicians have relied on basic marketing skills to get elected, going back to the earliest campaigns in US history. Candidates have relied on campaign buttons, posters, political rallies, and campaign speeches to inform voters about what they stand for, who they are, and how they will help them achieve their dreams. Once in office, these same candidates turn into politicians who have to work hard to put into legislation those laws that will allow them to go back to the same voters at the next election cycle with promises fulfilled. Getting those promises fulfilled takes much more than simply relying on marketing to win office, but must depend on a whole new set of marketing methods to govern with. This is where the intersection of public affairs and marketing finds its most interesting connection, and that is the use of marketing by lobbyists to impact on the choice of laws that a politician attempts to enact (Harris *et al.*, 1999; Newman, 1994). The same principles that operate in the commercial marketplace hold true in the political marketplace: successful organizations have a market focus and are constantly engaged in doing research to better understand their customers' wants and needs. In other words, marketers must be able to anticipate their customers' wants and needs, and then develop innovative products and services on a regular basis to keep their customers brand loyal and devoted to their companies. Politicians have a similar orientation and are carrying out research on a regular basis to determine how best to represent their constituency and attempt to increase the quality of life of citizens by using the most efficient means available to them as a steward of the government (Kotler and Kotler, 1981, 1999; Newman and Sheth, 1985b).

Political marketing can be defined as:

the application of marketing principles and procedures in political campaigns by various individuals and organizations. The procedures involved include the analysis, development, execution, and management of strategic campaigns by candidates, political parties, governments, lobbyists and interest groups that seek to drive public opinion, advance their own ideologies, win elections, and pass legislation and referenda in response to the needs and wants of selected people and groups in a society.

(Newman, 1999a: xiii)

This definition can be broadened to include the use of these same methods by lobbyists who seek to influence public opinion in an attempt to influence politicians to pass laws that benefit the companies they represent.

It has literally become impossible not to incorporate a marketing orientation when running for office, or for that matter when running the country. Politics today has become more than just a campaign to get elected and re-elected, but is increasingly becoming a full-fledged marketing campaign that relies on all the same processes as a corporation would use to succeed in the marketplace. The same advanced technological methods used by corporate America to market products are being used by politicians to market themselves and their ideas. The modern-day politician at all levels of office must rely on marketing not only to win the election but to be successful as a leader after entering the White House (Wring, 1999; Butler and Collins, 1999; Perloff, 1999; Newman and Perloff, 2004). Advances in the telecommunications industry, especially interactive technology, have opened up the possibilities for corporations that are in the business of lobbying government (Johnson, 1999). To better understand the role of political marketing for lobbyists, it is critical to first understand how government is changing. Only by understanding the needs of government officials and politicians will it be possible for lobbyists to impact their decision-making process over legislation.

The amount of money being spent on the Internet represents a major opportunity for government. Some believe that the implications of this technology will be felt far more in the management and exercise of governance through the implications it has for the economy, individual liberties, and democratic processes (Harris, 2000). On the commercial side, electronic commerce has been forecast to increase from $1.2 trillion in 2003 to as high as $7.3 trillion by 2004 (Good and Schultz, 2002). Mandel and Hof (2001) believe that electronic commerce will hit $6.8 trillion in 2004, with 90 percent of that coming from business-to-business sales. Transactions on e-marketplaces are expected to reach $2.9 trillion in 2004. Business will buy $2.8 trillion in supplies over the Internet in 2004, excluding e-marketplace purchases. Lobbyists will have to make a concerted effort to account for these important trends.

## MAKING THE LEAP TO LOBBYING

The use of political marketing by lobbyists presents several different leaps in logic. Because lobbyists have to deal with many different government officials, particularly those in Congress, the job is very difficult. If lobbyists are going to successfully sell themselves to government officials, and at the same time help politicians to sell their ideas to the people and Congress, then a framework must be used that translates the value proposition that exists between government and lobbyists. A theory of political choice behavior developed by Newman (1981) and tested on several elections (Newman and Sheth, 1985a, 1987; Newman, 1999b, a) proposes a number of cognitive beliefs that may come from a wide range of sources, including the voter, word-of-mouth communication, and the mass media. In addition, the theory incorporates the influence of an individual's affiliation with groups of people in his/her social environment (Lazarsfeld et al., 1948) and the influence of party affiliation and past voting behavior (Campbell et al., 1960). The usefulness of this theory can be found in the comprehensiveness of the range of voter beliefs that are covered in so few cognitive constructs. As such, it has the potential to be used by Congress as a very powerful communication tool to develop appeals that highlight the distinctiveness of what Congress can offer interested parties over the Internet.

The fundamental axiom of the theory is that a voter/citizen is a consumer of a service offered by a politician, and, similar to consumers in the commercial marketplace, voters choose candidates based on the perceived value they offer them. The same logic can be applied to citizens seeking services from Congress. The theory proposes that there are five distinct and separate cognitive domains that drive the voter's behavior. A key proposition of the theory is that voter behavior can be driven by a combination of one or more of the domains in a given election. The generic nature of the theory makes it useful for anyone interested in understanding the relative importance of various issues, policies and other service offerings to citizens from government. The theory includes the following components:

1   *Political issues.* This dimension represents the policies a candidate advocates and promises to enact if elected to office. This dimension captures the rational considerations of a voter that normally would revolve around issues that people feel in their pocketbooks. This construct captures the same kind of appeals that are used by companies who appeal to consumers with products that promise high quality, lower prices, and other benefits that have a rational appeal.

2   *Social imagery.* This represents the stereotyping of the candidate to appeal to voters by making associations between the candidate and selected segments in society (e.g. the support that opinion leaders give to a politician. The use of imagery can be very powerful here as the candidate or political party manufactures an image in the minds of voters on the basis of his associations, with the possibility of that image being either positive or negative in the mind of the voter, depending on which group it is that the candidate is trying to associate himself with. The adaptation of this component in the commercial marketplace manifests itself through the use of prominent and well known spokespersons for companies who are used in advertisements and commercials. Similar to the same

process that is used in politics, companies create an image for their product through the sheer association of the product or company with the personality who is used.

3　*Candidate personality.* Imagery in politics is perhaps the most important avenue that can be used to sell a candidate or political party. Whereas the use of imagery was described through the use of the Social Imagery component in the model, it is also represented through the personality of the candidate in a slightly different way. Here, the candidate (or political party) is emphasizing personality traits to help reinforce and manufacture an image in the voter's mind. When we compare this to the consumer in the marketplace, marketers do play on emotions by using the right setting, appeals, and background to create a mood which affects the consumer's decision to purchase a particular brand.

4　*Situational contingency.* This dimension represents that aspect of a voter's thinking which could be swayed by "hypothetical events" described by competing parties or candidates during the course of a campaign. Winning elections is often times based on getting a small percentage of voters to switch their allegiance to another candidate or party. Marketers also rely on this dimension as the basis for appealing to consumers and getting them to switch from one brand or company to another. Common practices used to implement this value proposition come in the form of sales promotions, giveaways, and advertisements, all unexpected events from the consumer's point of view that are aimed at altering his behavior. In the government, this may be shaped by news and media reports that affect voters' and citizens' perceptions of government.

5　*Epistemic value.* This dimension appeals to a voter's sense of curiosity or novelty in choosing a candidate. Marketers rely on this tactic when appealing to consumers' desires to acquire the latest and newest products in the marketplace. Whereas the theory as it exists can be applied by lobbyists in their effort to affect the decision

making of government officials, it may be more useful to make some conceptual changes in the model so that it has a more direct application to the role of the lobbyist in government.

## LINKING PUBLIC AFFAIRS, LOBBYING, AND POLITICAL MARKETING.

The specific link between public affairs and lobbying is a much debated issue. However, this linkage was well put in an article in the *Journal of Public Affairs*, a leading source on the role of public affairs and lobbying in the world today:

> from a pragmatic point of view, the industry is engaged, one way or another, in the application of pressure and influence to produce political outcomes that are beneficial to its clients. To succeed in this enterprise requires knowledge and understanding of the prevailing political culture and dynamics of decision-making. This culture is undergoing fundamental change and the industry is falling behind in its grasp of what is happening. In any event, we are likely to see a radical transformation in the practice of public affairs in Europe, to the extent that the public affairs industry will be un-recognizable in ten years' time.
>
> (Titley, 2003: 85)

The recent elections in the United States, especially the 2004 campaign of Howard Dean, support a similar theme that is spelled out in the Titley (2003) article, which is the change that will dominate politics in the future does not rest necessarily with the elites in the formal political institutions, but with the power of public opinion. Specifically, in the case of the 2004 US presidential election, the candidacy of Howard Dean documented the fund-raising ability of a virtual unknown, and without the consent of the political elites in the Democratic Party. Through innovative use of the Internet, Dean was able to raise money from millions of small donors who allowed him to lead all other competitors going into the start of the primary season. However, after losing the Iowa caucus, it became clear that even extraordinary fund-raising ability was not enough to make him successful, and he subsequently lost the nomination to John Kerry. This is in stark contrast to the large sums of money that President Bush was able to raise in his bid to get re-elected in 2004. The President relied on the funds from lobbyists who represented corporations that the Bush administration supported during his tenure with favorable legislation. The case for less reliance on political party ideology (Newman, 2001a, b) is well made and sheds light on the need for models of citizen/voter choice behavior that can be used to understand and respond to the needs and wants of citizens in an effort to affect public opinion. As Titley (2003) makes the case for the movement from rational-based campaigns designed around few political actors to value-based arguments targeted to many political actors, it is necessary to begin to develop and adapt models that have been historically used by political marketers for use in the public affairs industry.

As we have witnessed in the United States, the Howard Dean candidacy proved that it is possible for any interested party that represents a particular ideology to have an impact on public opinion. This same technology will enable corporations to work with both the elite political actors and the citizenry to impact the development of legislation, and not be put in a position to respond to the impact of these same methods being used against corporations by single-issue interest groups. This is where public affairs, lobbying, and political marketing intersect. Instead of relying on public affairs and lobbying as tools for corporations to further their own business and political interests, political marketing will take this discussion a step further by shedding light on how political actors are using political marketing techniques to drive their policy-making and electioneering decisions. Once the decision-making process of politicians and political parties is made more clear in light of the political marketing paradigm shift that has taken place over the past few decades, only then will lobbyists be in a position to understand how to best partner with government to affect

their own business and political interests (O'Shaughnessy, 1999).

The ability of public affairs officials to rely on both rational and emotional appeals will mean a better understanding of the political marketing model. As such, it is in the interest of public affairs officials to carefully scrutinize how political marketing has shaped campaigns in recent decades around the world as they compete for more scarce resources from government. An integrated framework of public affairs and political marketing will be necessary to bridge this knowledge gap. Such a framework will fill the vacuum that exists in the public affairs industry today. This will facilitate the interplay between public affairs executives and other stakeholders in the corporation who have a direct impact on public opinion (e.g. product and brand managers, marketing research directors, marketing strategists, and other corporate players who are involved in the marketing process within a corporation).

Since we do live in an era of manufactured images (Newman, 1999c), it will become imperative that public affairs executives and lobbyists understand the tools by which organizations and individuals can shape and manufacture images in the commercial and political marketplaces.

## A STRATEGIC FRAMEWORK FOR LOBBYISTS

The basic premise behind the Strategic Framework for Lobbyists stems from the political marketing literature that emphasizes the importance of first understanding the needs and wants of the voters before establishing a campaign platform as a candidate or sitting politician (Newman, 1994, 1999a, b, 1999c; Newman and Vercic, 2003). To the lobbyist, it is imperative that there be a very clear understanding of both the politician and his/her constituency. With this in mind, the following framework puts forward four different components that allow the lobbyists the ability to draw a political profile for the party or politician before embarking on strategy development.

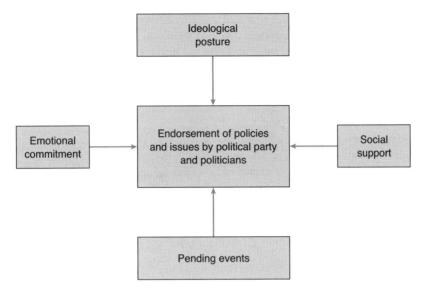

Figure 23.1 *Strategic framework for lobbyists*

If we take the Strategic Framework for Lobbyists presented in Figure 23.1, several similarities to the Theory of Political Choice Behavior emerge.

### Ideological Posture

This component reflects the issues and policies that a political party or politician supports on a philosophical level. The lobbyist will be interested in measuring the specific issues and policies that reflect the ideological orientation of the party/politician. This component is measured by a number of statements about the issues and policies that are either of interest to the party/politician or will have a direct impact on the success of that person or party in an upcoming election:

> Please indicate whether you agree or disagree that each of the following issues is important to you:
>
> *I believe my party/candidacy requires me to:*
>
> (a) Increase health care benefits.
> (b) Reduce taxes for corporations.
> (c) Etc.

The list of "hypothetical" issues is determined with qualitative research that is pertinent to the party/politician at the point in time when the lobbyist is seeking to get their support.

### Emotional Commitment

This component reflects the personal commitment that a party or politician has towards a particular segment of voters or supporters, as well as his/her own personal emotional attachment to specific issues or policies that can ostensibly help an interested organization (both profit and non-profit). This component is measured by identifying a list of feelings that reflect the party/politician's commitment to the group or issue:

> Parties and politicians support certain groups in society as well as specific issues for many personal and political reasons. Please indicate whether you experience any of the feelings I have listed below in your support of the following groups of people and issues:
>
> *I support the following issue because:*
>
> 1 I am fulfilling my promise to …
> 2 Standing up for the rights of … is important to me.
> 3 Etc.

The lobbyist will fill in the issue that is important to the organization that he/she is representing.

The list of "voter/interest groups" is determined with qualitative research that is pertinent to the party/politician at the point in time when the lobbyist is seeking to get their support.

### Social Support

This component reflects the support that a party/politician receives from a segment of voters, an interest group, a political action committee, or any other significant group of people who could influence the decision of a party or individual politician. This component takes into consideration the importance that a group of people has on the development of the image of the party/politician. However, this goes beyond the simple stereotyping of the party/politician to address the support that the group gives to a party/politician in the form of money or a volunteer network at election time. A political party or individual politician may choose to seek the support of various groups of people to manufacture an image in the minds of voters on the basis of the association of these groups to the party/politician. This component is measured by identifying a list of groups of voters/interest groups/political action committees and determining how likely it is that each group supports the party/politician in some capacity.

> In this section, I have listed a number of groups of people who are likely to be supportive of party X/politician Y. For *each* group of people, I'd like to know which you think is most or least likely to support the party/politician with money or volunteer help:
>
> 1   National Rifle Association.
> 2   Democrats.
> 3   Elderly citizens.

The lobbyist will fill in the groups that are important to the organization that he/she is representing. The list of "voter/interest groups" is determined with qualitative research that is pertinent to the party/politician at the point in time when the lobbyist is seeking to get their support.

### Pending Events

This component represents the impact of events in the world and in the specific country of the party/politician that will have a temporary impact on the voting record of the party/politician. This component is measured by listing a number of "hypothetical events" that might influence the party/politician to support a specific issue or group of people:

> Certain conditions motivate parties/politicians to behave differently than their voting record might indicate. Do you believe that the following situations would influence you to switch your support for issue X/group Y?
>
> *I would switch my support of issue X if I knew:*
>
> 1   I would lose an upcoming election.
> 2   I could attract more voters.
> 3   My party leadership would stop supporting my causes.

## Measurement of the Framework

The model is measured by first carrying out a factor analysis individually on the list of items in each of the four component areas. The factor scores from this analysis are then input into a discriminant analysis. The principal statistical technique used to provide the lobbyist with diagnostic information on how best to help the political party or individual politician to insure passage of a particular law that is pending is discriminant analysis. The objective of this method of analysis is to classify legislation into mutually exclusive and exhaustive categories. In other words, a lobbyist will be able to examine simultaneously the characteristics of two or more pending laws by performing a two or multiple-group discriminant analysis.

Technically speaking, the statistical objective behind this technique is to maximize the between-group variance of two or more segments and minimize the within-group variance of each of the segments. Therefore, discriminant analysis is used to develop a set of characteristics by which to compare two segments of people in an effort to explain the differences in their behavior.

A second major function of discriminant analysis is to enable the lobbyists to predict party/politician choice behavior. This prediction is based on a technique known as classification analysis, by which a set of probabilities is derived from the discriminant analysis. Based on these probabilities, the behavior of the politician/party is predicted to be a likely supporter of the particular organization the lobbyist is representing.

## Strategic Implications of the Framework

The Strategic Framework for Lobbyists can be used to identify the specific appeals that are laid out for the politician to use in an effort to get legislation passed in Congress (in the United States), in Parliament (in the United Kingdom) or in any other political body that decides on which laws are passed in a country. This often means that a politician will have to rely on standard marketing research methods to identify the needs and wants of citizens as well as the thinking of the politician to better position the ideas of the politician.

In politics, market segmentation has been traditionally used by political parties and politicians to target specific messages to different segments of people (Baines, 1999). For example, during the 2004 US presidential race, on the Democratic side, Howard Dean realized early on that Democrat voters were very angry about President Bush's decision to invade Iraq. With that knowledge, Dean set out to separate himself from the rest of the candidates running for the Democratic nomination by making his feelings on the war the centerpiece of his campaign. That market segmentation strategy worked quite well until the voters in the early primaries decided that they wanted not only a candidate who cared about that issue but someone who was electable. Ultimately, the segment of voters who supported Howard Dean began to slip away because of his loss in the Iowa caucus, and the increasing importance of electability in the campaign.

There were of course other voter segments casting ballots in the Democratic primaries. There were the voters who might have voted for Bush and supported his initial efforts in Iraq but became more disillusioned over time as the media began to run stories on the absence of intelligence to support the idea that

Iraq had weapons of mass destruction. These voters may have participated in the open primaries where states allow voters from either one of the two major parties to vote. Another segment could have consisted of voters who had lost their jobs since President Bush entered the White House, and were looking for a candidate who looked like he was able to restore the lost jobs in the country. We could of course list other segments, but the key point is that each of these segments represents a different group of voters who are looking for something different in a President.

Once the multiple voter segments have been identified, the candidate has to position himself in the marketplace. Positioning is a multistage process that begins with a politician making a determination of his own strengths and weaknesses as well as his opponents' strengths and weaknesses. Positioning is the process by which a politician or party conveys an image to voters in the best light possible (Nimmo, 1970). The manufacturing of an image is carried out in the media by emphasizing certain personality traits of the candidate, as well as stressing various issues (Newman, 1999c). For example, during the 2000 US presidential campaign, George W. Bush realized that as a perceived outsider to Washington, he was in a good position to criticize the system which the incumbent (Bill Clinton) had governed for the previous eight years. Similarly, Howard Dean's appeal initially was centered around the same message, namely that he was an outsider to Washington, DC, and was not contaminated by the influential people and organizations who affect the governing process. The segmentation and positioning of politicians continues on after a politician gets into office as the individual and party that he or she represents attempts to appeal to various segments of the population by passing legislation that is favorable for one group over another.

The key issue arises as to the use of the strategic lobbying framework to enable a political party or politician to more effectively segment and position the image and platform of the person or party. The framework presented in this chapter puts the party/politician in a position to make a determination with respect to the marketing strategy that should be used to influence public opinion. The lobbyist can use the strategic framework to collect information on the thinking of the politicians and voters to determine how best to position the message a politician/party sends to the multiple segments that need to be addressed. These multiple segments include: the Congress (or Parliament if it is the United Kingdom); selected segments of citizens; leaders of influential interest groups; other political leaders who will be influential in passing legislation; the media who will report on the efforts of the lobbyist and the organization he or she represents; governments in other countries who have a vested interest in the passing of legislation; and of course the sitting government which stands to either benefit or be hurt by the legislation.

## REFERENCES

Baines, P. (1999). "Voter Segmentation and Candidate Positioning," in B.I. Newman (ed.), *Handbook of Political Marketing*. Thousand Oaks, CA: Sage.

Butler, P., and N. Collins (1999). "A Conceptual Framework for Political Marketing," in B.I. Newman (ed.), *Handbook of Political Marketing*. Thousand Oaks, CA: Sage.

Campbell, A., *et al.* (1960). *The American Voter*. New York: Wiley.

Good, D.J., and R.J. Schultz (2002). "E-commerce Strategies for Business-to-business Service Firms in the Global Environment," *American Business Review* 20 (2): 111–118.

Grier, K.B., *et al.* (1994) "The determinants of Industry Political Activity, 1978–1986," *American Political Science Review* 88: 911–926.

Harris, B. (2000). "Fostering an Age of Wisdom," *Government Technology's E*, 6–7.

Harris, P., *et al.* (1999). "Limitations of Political Marketing? A Content Analysis of Press Coverage of Political Issues during the 1997 UK General Election Campaign," in B.I. Newman (ed.), *Handbook of Political Marketing*. Thousand Oaks, CA: Sage.

Johnson, D.W. (1999). "The Cyberspace Election of the Future," in B.I. Newman (ed.), *Handbook of Political Marketing*. Thousand Oaks, CA: Sage.

Kotler, P., and N. Kotler (1981). "Business Marketing for Political Candidates," *Campaigns and Elections* 2: 24–33.

Kotler, P., and N. Kotler (1999). "Political Marketing: Generating Effective Candidates, Campaigns, and Causes," in B.I. Newman (ed.), *Handbook of Political Marketing*. Thousand Oaks, CA: Sage.

Lazarsfeld, P., B. Berelson, and H. Gaudet (1948). *The People's Choice: How the Voter Makes up his Mind in a Presidential Campaign*. New York: Columbia University Press.

Magleby, D.B. (eds) (2002). *Financing the 2000 Election*. Washington, DC: Brookings Institution Press.

Mandel, M.J., and R.D. Hof (2001). "Rethinking the Internet," *Business Week*, March 26, pp. 117–22.

Mitchell, N.J., W.L. Hansen, and E.M. Jepsen (1997). "The Determinants of Domestic and Foreign Corporate Political Activity," *Journal of Politics* 59 (4): 1096–1113.

Newman, B.I. (1981). "The Prediction and Explanation of Actual Voting Behavior in a Presidential Primary Election." Unpublished doctoral dissertation, University of Illinois at Urbana–Champaign.

Newman, B.I. (1994). *The Marketing of the President: Political Marketing as Campaign Strategy*. Thousand Oaks, CA: Sage.

Newman, B.I. (1999a). "A Predictive Model of Voter Behavior," in B.I. Newman (ed.), *Handbook of Political Marketing*. Thousand Oaks, CA: Sage.

Newman, B.I. (ed.) (1999b). *Handbook of Political Marketing*. Thousand Oaks, CA: Sage.

Newman, B.I. (1999c). *The Mass Marketing of Politics: Democracy in an Age of Manufactured Images*. Thousand Oaks, CA: Sage.

Newman, B.I. (2001a). "An Assessment of the 2000 US Presidential Election: A Set of Political Marketing Guidelines," *Journal of Public Affairs* 1 (3): 210–216.

Newman, B.I. (2001b). "Image Manufacturing in the United States: Recent US Presidential Elections and Beyond," *European Journal of Marketing* 35 (9–10): 966–970.

Newman, B.I. (2002a). "The Role of Marketing in Politics," *European Journal of Political Marketing* 1 (1): 1–5.

Newman, B.I. (2002b). "Broadening the Boundaries of Marketing: Political Marketing in New Millennium," *Psychology and Marketing* 19 (12): 983–986.

Newman, B.I., and R. Perloff (2004). "Political Marketing Approaches to Political Communication," in L.L. Kaid (ed.), *Handbook of Political*

*Communication Research.* Thousand Oaks, CA: Sage Publications.

Newman, B.I., and J.N. Sheth (1985a). "A Model of Primary Voter Behavior," *Journal of Consumer Research* 12: 178–187.

Newman, B.I., and J.N. Sheth (1985b). *Political Marketing: Readings and Annotated Bibliography.* Chicago: American Marketing Association.

Newman, B.I., and J.N. Sheth (1987). *A Theory of Political Choice Behavior.* New York: Praeger.

Newman, B.I., and D.Vercic (eds) (2003). *Communication of Politics: Cross-cultural Theory Building in the Practice of Public Relations and Political Marketing.* New York: Haworth Press.

Nimmo, D. (1970). *The Political Persuaders.* Englewood Cliffs, NJ: Prentice Hall.

O'Shaughnessy, N.J. (1999). "Political Marketing and Political Propaganda," in B.I. Newman (ed.), *Handbook of Political Marketing.* Thousand Oaks, CA: Sage.

Perloff, R.M. (1999). "Elite, Popular, and Merchandised Politics: Historical Origins of Presidential Campaign Marketing," in B.I. Newman (ed.), *Handbook of Political Marketing.* Thousand Oaks, CA: Sage.

Titley, S. (2003). "How Political and Social Change will Transform the EU Public Affairs Industry," *Journal of Public Affairs* 3 (1): 83–89.

Wring, D. (1999). "The Marketing Colonizations of Political Campaigning," in B.I. Newman (ed.), *Handbook of Political Marketing.* Thousand Oaks, CA: Sage, pp. 41–54.

# PART IV

# Scholarship and Theory Building in Public Affairs

Success or failure lies in conforming to the times.

(Niccolo Machiavelli)

This final part of *The Handbook of Public Affairs* is designed to appeal more generally to the academic audiences in the readership, although several chapters, particularly the ones by Keim and Fleisher, should also appeal to practicing or potential public affairs (PA) practitioners. Each chapter offers up-to-date, leading-edge thinking about recent scholarly developments in the PA field. Part IV encompasses seven subject matter areas related to public affairs and business-government relations more generally, including:

1 Theories and theoretical roots of public affairs.
2 Advocacy management.
3 Governance and public affairs.
4 Empirical study of public affairs.
5 Issues management
6 Stakeholder management.
7 PA education.
8 Regulation and public affairs.

In Chapter 24 on the theories and theoretical roots of public affairs, Windsor notes that functional PA activities are boundary-spanning in nature, with the boundaries being established by the interface between a corporation and its external non-market environment. Similar in perception to some of the earlier chapters, he notes that this broad assignment of organizational responsibilities is a vital corporate function that remains in search of identity, conceptualization, theory, effective corporate organization, best practices, and social legitimacy (Boddewyn, 1974; Harris and Moss, 2001; Meznar and Nigh, 1993).

Windsor assesses theory and concept development with respect to the corporate PA function. Like others before him (Fleisher and Hoewing, 1992; Marcus and Irion, 1987), he observes that the function has grown in scope, importance, and professionalism. This growth becomes increasingly important in light of his view that the external environment of business is becoming more global, all levels of government more politicized, and with more stakeholders that are more effectively mobilized through applications of information and communication systems and technologies (ICSTs—see Chapter 11). Public affairs scholarship is multidisciplinary yet not a truly interdisciplinary field of study focused on understanding and improving the art of corporate PA practice. The scholarship that has accumulated to date is still largely descriptive and barely predictive. Practice remains almost wholly instrumental, but barely strategic. Windsor further suggests that both scholarship and practice inescapably occur within a neglected normative context of corporate social responsibility and the ethics of impacts on stakeholders and the public interest (Windsor, 2001; also see Carroll's Chapter 29).

This chapter distinguishes "theories" (and "models") from theoretical roots. Windsor observes that there is no "grand" theory of public affairs developed as yet—that is, no integrative or overarching framework exists. The theoretical roots of public affairs seem to be drawn from several disciplines, at the interface of which much PA research lies. These disciplines include, but are not solely limited to, communications and public relations, economics, organizational sociology, political science, and strategic management. The contributions of these various disciplines to PA scholarship and practice are identified and assessed. The normative dimension adds the disciplines of businesses in societies, business ethics, and ecological systems. In lieu of an overarching framework, the extant limited theories and models deal, in relative isolation and drawing on different theoretical roots, with piecemeal application to public affairs. This fragmented scholarship reflects the growing complexity of the business environment and the typical dispersal of PA activities within corporations.

Windsor considers the future of PA scholarship linked to improved practice in the twenty-first century. He states that corporate public affairs in the twenty-first century should focus on two central issues. One issue concerns definition of "the" public interest in a pluralistic democracy. The other issue concerns development of the competencies and resources needed to manage international public affairs in an expanding global arena for market operations and public policy making (Fleisher, 2003).

Windsor's detailed examination of the various proposed "theories" or "models" of public affairs suggests several important research questions—many of which are encompassed in various forms by chapters in this *Handbook*. What should be the objectives of corporate PA activities? Can corporations effectively integrate management of issue life cycles? Can interested parties and stakeholders influence political outcomes and public opinion? Should corporations attempt to influence political outcomes and public opinion? What PA strategies and tactics are likely to be effective? How should

firms organize internally for PA activities? What PA capabilities, competencies, and resources are important—both today and in the future? Systematically uncovering the answers to these important questions should keep PA associations, managers, practitioners, researchers, and scholars busy and interested for many years.

Chapter 25, by long-time corporate political activity researcher Gerry Keim, addresses the always interesting topic of political advocacy. In this chapter, political advocacy refers to the range of efforts exhibited by businesses that are designed to advance their public policy interests in the United States by acting individually or in concert with other businesses or politically active stakeholder groups. Political actions may be directed to state or federal policy makers in the legislative or executive branches of government as well as the judicial, although these judicially focused initiatives are not covered in this chapter due to space constraints. Because context-specific institutional settings and structures affect the opportunities and processes of public policy advocacy, the chapter's focus is limited to public policy advocacy in the United States at the state and federal levels. Keim takes an advisory perspective and considers what can be gleaned from existing research and practice to suggest how businesses can be more effective advocates for their public policy interests.

In the United States, unlike parliamentary systems, business interests are more likely to find some support in both major parties and party members are not subject to strict party discipline. Presidents, governors, and party leaders in legislatures often find some members of their party voting against their policies when the members encounter strong advocacy efforts from groups in their constituencies; consequently, advocacy efforts are more issue-focused and attempt to influence individual policy decisions made by government officials rather than trying to elect to office the candidates from particular parties.

Keim develops a rationale for business political advocacy from the perspective of an individual firm. He suggests that political advocacy is part and parcel of a competitive game; advocacy by one firm or group of firms to influence a public policy decision will often be in response to, or will generate responses by, other groups—including other businesses—with alternative or opposing interests. Keim follows by discussing lenses for examining the nature of competition among politically active stakeholders. These lenses view public policy issues by examining the evolution of the issue, the distribution of the costs and benefits of the issue, and the breadth of interest the issue attracts. These different perspectives help to inform decision makers about the likely nature of competition surrounding specific issues.

Keim proceeds to focus on the means for linking the interests of legislators and regulators with those of issue advocates. He unpacks the process of issue advocacy into three discrete and sequential phases—gaining access to policy makers, providing useful information to policy makers, and successfully influencing policy makers. He observes that effective participation in the first two phases, gaining access and supplying valuable information to decision makers, is necessary but not sufficient for a firm or other advocacy group to reach the third phase, which is influence over the decision on the policy of interest. He further expands on this point and relates it to efforts to measure the effectiveness of government relations activities in business firms.

The chapter concludes by sharing feedback gathered from focus groups of employees in several industries, discussing their experiences with advocacy efforts. Using these data, Keim identifies and examines numerous opportunities to improve business advocacy efforts. He suggests that broadening the interest in advocacy among all managers can be accomplished through interactive educational sessions; subsequently, managers can more effectively generate interest among their colleagues and subordinates (see also Chapter 8 by Showalter and Fleisher on this point). Keim finishes by offering helpful suggestions for beginning advocacy efforts in companies that have not previously participated in the public policy process.

Chapter 26 is an insightful description by John Holcomb of the multifaceted and still evolving corporate reform agenda. Since 2001

it has included most prominently the issues of investor rights and corporate governance reform. This chapter examines the changes that have taken place as a result of previous corporate scandals in the functions of corporate boards and the roles played by shareholders. The chapter goes beyond a legal analysis and instead focuses on practical changes that have occurred.

Regarding the changes in corporate boards of directors, Holcomb examines the issues of:

1 Board diligence and work load.
2 Board independence.
3 Separation of the board chair and CEO positions.
4 The pool of available board candidates.
5 Compensation of board members.
6 The growing importance of the board's compensation committee.
7 The lingering issue of multiple board memberships.

Regarding the roles played by shareholders, the chapter emphasizes the upturn in shareholder activism generally, along with providing examples of a number of key shareholder campaigns. Holcomb discusses the debate during 2004 over shareholder nomination of directors, as well as examining the evolution and growing importance of corporate governance rating services. As this chapter nicely illuminates, these issues should continue to be priorities for corporate public affairs at the highest levels of organizations for years to come.

Jennifer Griffin of George Washington University in Washington, DC, provides in Chapter 27 a review and synthesis of key contributions from empirical studies on public affairs and related corporate political activities over the past four decades. Echoing Schuler's (2002) call to pull together the research fragments in a manner that provides a comprehensive and reasonable picture of the overall phenomenon, Griffin employs a systems approach to address this task. Within a systems perspective, the focus is neither solely on the firm nor on the political institutions but simultaneously examines multiple players in the public policy process (i.e., stockholders, employees or unions, suppliers, competitors, politicians, special interest groups, etc.). This review is intentionally neither firm-centric nor institution-centric, rather it is systems-oriented and process-centric, reflecting the boundary-spanning responsibilities, challenges, and activities of public affairs.

She identifies opportunities for additional empirical research in the corporate PA and corporate political strategy field. Griffin notes that the main questions asked while systematically examining research across four decades of scholarly inquiry are:

1   Can PA and corporate political strategy be *empirically described*?
2   Can we *interpret* how corporate political strategy contributes to competitive advantage—across industries, across contexts, across geographic and political borders?
3   Can we better *understand and articulate* a common sense of meaning regarding business political strategy and how corporate public affairs adds value?

After highlighting selective research, Griffin elaborates upon three separate "waves" of research on corporate public affairs and corporate political strategy, including (1) foundational building blocks, (2) managerial challenges, and (3) blurring of boundaries. Each of these waves of research focuses on disparate literatures informing choices from disparate theoretical streams that are brought to bear by multiple players for different audiences in the art and science of public policy (Getz, 1997, 2002; Mitnick, 1993). The chapter concludes on a rather promising note that these waves continue to have strength in their own right and that the field offers plenty of opportunities for future researchers to ride a wave of their choice or even to find new waves upon which to ride.

Contributor Persey P.M.A.R. Heugens provides in Chapter 28 an insightful view of issues management (IM), viewed by many public affairs (PA) scholars to be one of the foundational pillars of the field. Heugens notes that IM has gone through a couple of unique periods of development, including an explosive growth in the late 1970s and 1980s, followed by a quieter period during the 1990s when academics had apparently moved on from the more staid IM toward corporate social responsibility and citizenship topics. Despite the apparent academic meandering away from IM research and scholarship, Heugens rightfully notes that practitioners and corporate IM applications have continued to be institutionalized and improved.

Heugens notes seven major antecedent factors that explained IM's organizational development and proliferation, including: (1) the professionalization of public affairs; (2) continuing improvements in organizations' abilities to gather environmental data and information; (3) furthering professionalization of interest groups/non-governmental organizations (NGOs); (4) the politicization of business; (5) the shifting of corporate mindsets towards social involvement and the growth of IM as an extension of social responsiveness; (6) the increased coverage of business activities by traditional as well as new media; and (7) focusing more effort on symbolic competition through the means of reputation management. These factors, most of which have now been around for at least a decade or more, show almost no likelihood of losing their importance to continue shaping the evolution of IM in the subsequent decade.

Having explained the factors that led to IM's popularity, Heugens examines key constructs and processes that are commonly found in contemporary IM systems. He presents three brief case examples drawn from IM-experienced companies Baxter International, Dow Chemical, and Heineken. In order to help readers address the often confusing intricacy evident in IM, Heugens describes a generic IM system, consisting of middle managers, top managers and issues, and IM processes, including issue identification, issue selling, issue buying, and issue response. He notes the multi-level, multi-layered complexity that pervades this generic IM system and helps the reader better understand the many avenues by which both researchers and practitioners can focus to further enhance IM system effectiveness and their organization's competitiveness. Heugens leaves readers with a renewed sense of IM's importance in the practice of public affairs as well as implicit avenues of research that are available for scholars who should find many research opportunities and intriguing research questions in this challenging area.

University of Georgia Professor Archie Carroll observes in Chapter 29 how it is becoming evident that stakeholder theory, concepts, management, measurement, and thinking are becoming staples to contemporary managers and PA executives. He suggests that there is growing support for the belief that the stakeholder model is increasingly becoming the most fitting and valuable for descriptive, normative, and instrumental purposes. The language of stakeholder theory has already swept the world of organizations as more and more managers and analysts perceive the value of diagnosing and prescribing things in stakeholder terms. He further observes that corporate PA officers were among the earliest to adopt the valuable language of stakeholders.

Theorists and practitioners alike will substantiate the stakeholder model over time as concepts are refined and applied and results are noted. Carroll shares the views of several other noted management thinkers and practitioners who strongly argue that corporate character and reputation will be a strategic item in the presently emerging business era, and that stakeholder management will be a primary means by which effective organizations fulfill this quest. From an academic and PA practitioner's point of view, and from the perspective of a leading business executive, Carroll shows the case being built for the stakeholder model of the organization.

*Handbook* co-editor Craig Fleisher addresses the education of current and prospective PA practitioners in Chapter 30. A number of important achievements in improving business-government interactions and outcomes during the past century can be traced directly to business or corporate public affairs (BCPA) initiatives. The extent to which we are able to make additional improvements in the health of business—government and corporate-stakeholder relations depends, in large part, upon the quality and preparedness of the BCPA work force, which is, in turn, dependent upon the relevance and quality of its education and training.

This chapter examines an essential component of the public affairs work force—business or corporate PA professionals—identifies roles played by BCPA practitioners, surveys the educational options available, and offers propositions for improving the state of BCPA education.

This chapter develops recommendations for how, over the next five to ten years, education, training, and research could be strengthened to meet the needs of future BCPA professionals in order to improve business-government and other stakeholder relationships. Fleisher also offers recommendations for overall improvements in BCPA professional education, training, research, and leadership. He suggests that a wide range of institutional settings, including not only post-secondary universities and colleges but also degree-granting programs in schools of business, commerce, management, marketing, public relations, public policy, other professional schools (e.g., law), consultancies, conference organizers, private and public (i.e., professional and trade) associations can play important roles in BCPA education, training, research, and leadership development. He presents ideas for many of these institutional settings that are directed toward improving the future of BCPA education around the globe.

In the *Handbook's* final chapter, Holcomb notes how the corporate scandals since the year 2001 have spawned litigation, criminal prosecutions, and new regulatory pressures on business at both the state and federal levels. He shares how some scandal-ridden firms have responded with their own internal investigations. Holcomb examines those legal and regulatory pressures, along with the impact of the most important new US law, the Sarbanes-Oxley Act (Sarbox).

The chapter also examines internal administrative reforms at the Securities and Exchange Commission, as well as the conflict between federal agencies and state regulators, as each level of government asserts its powers to grapple with the corporate scandals. Holcomb addresses the changes adopted by the self-regulatory agencies. Last but certainly not least, Holcomb also discusses two major regulatory controversies—regulation of the mutual fund industry, and the expensing of stock options.

This final part of the *Handbook* should serve as a beacon of light for readers to use in charting their own understanding of the evolving field of public affairs. It is clear that the field has made much progress both in practice and scholarship, and that much discovery and further examination continue to lie ahead. The co-editors hope that the sum total of the contributions contained within Part IV lead to further improvements in both the practice and research of public affairs, ultimately leading to improved outcomes for business, government, and society interactions and relationships.

## REFERENCES

Boddewyn, J.J. (1974). "External Affairs: A Corporate Function in Search of Conceptualization and Theory," *Organization and Administration Sciences* 5 (spring): 67–111.

Fleisher, C.S. (2003). "The Development of Competencies in International Public Affairs," *Journal of Public Affairs* 3 (1): 76–82.

Fleisher, C.S., and R. Hoewing (1992). "Strategically Managing Corporate External Relations: New Challenges and Opportunities," *Journal of Strategic Change* 1 (6): 41–51.

Getz, K.A. (1997). "Research in Corporate Political Action: Integration and Assessment," *Business and Society* 36 (1): 32–72.

Getz, K.A. (2002). "Public Affairs and Political Strategy: Theoretical Foundations," *Journal of Public Affairs* 1 (4) and 2 (1): 305–329.

Harris, P., and D. Moss (2001). "Editorial. In Search of Public Affairs: A Function in Search of an Identity," *Journal of Public Affairs* 1 (2): 102–110.

Marcus, A.A., and M.S. Irion (1987). "The Continued Growth of the Corporate Public Affairs Function," *Academy of Management Executive* 1 (3): 247–250.

Meznar, M.B., and D. Nigh (1993). "Managing Corporate Legitimacy: Public Affairs Activities, Strategies and Effectiveness," *Business and Society* 32 (1): 30–43.

Mitnick, B.M. (1993). "The Strategic Uses of Regulation—and Deregulation," in B. Mitnick (ed.), *Corporate Political Agency: The Construction of Competition in Public Affairs*. Newbury Park, CA: Sage.

Schuler, D.A. (2002). "Public Affairs, Issues Management and Political Strategy: Methodological Approaches that Count," *Journal of Public Affairs* 1 (4) and 2 (1): 336–355.

Windsor, D. (2001). "The Future of Corporate Social Responsibility," *International Journal of Organizational Analysis* 9 (3): 225–256.

# 24

# "Theories" and Theoretical Roots of Public Affairs

## DUANE WINDSOR

Public affairs activities address the interface between a corporation and its external non-market environment. This broad assignment is a vital corporate function that remains in search of identity, conceptualization, theory, effective corporate organization, best practices, and social legitimacy (Boddewyn, 1974; Harris and Moss, 2001; Meznar and Nigh, 1993). This chapter assesses theorizing and conceptualization concerning the corporate public affairs function. The function has been growing in scope, importance, and professionalism (Marcus and Irion, 1987). The external environment of business will continue to become more global and at all levels of government more politicized and with more stakeholders more effectively mobilized. Public affairs scholarship is a multidisciplinary and not yet truly interdisciplinary field of study focused on understanding and improving the art of corporate public affairs practice. The scholarship is still largely descriptive and barely predictive. Practice is almost wholly instrumental but barely strategic. Both scholarship and practice inescapably occur within a neglected normative context of corporate social responsibility and the ethics of impacts on stakeholders and the public interest (Windsor, 2001). This chapter distinguishes "theories" (and "models") from theoretical roots. There is no "grand" theory of public affairs—no integrative or overarching framework. Theoretical roots lie in several disciplines, at the interface of which public affairs research lies: communications and public relations, economics, organizational sociology, political science, and strategic management. The normative dimension adds the disciplines of businesses in societies, business ethics, and ecological systems. In lieu of an overarching framework, limited theories and models deal, in relative isolation and drawing on different theoretical roots, with piecemeal aspects of public affairs. Fragmented scholarship reflects a growing complexity of the business environment and the typical dispersal of public affairs activities within corporations. This chapter considers the future of public affairs scholarship linked to improved practice in the twenty-first century.

The public affairs function is a wide diversity of activities typically not fully coordinated or strategically planned (Richards, 2003), thus reflecting the complexity of the business environment. This chapter is a thumbnail sketch in outline of theories and theoretical roots of public affairs scholarship and practice. References are illustrative. Some afford greater depth (Getz, 2002; Griffin et al., 2001a, b; Keim, 2002; Schuler, 2002; Windsor, 2002a). This introduction addresses key terminological and taxonomic matters, and outlines the chapter's structure.

Donaldson and Preston (1995) distinguish, for stakeholder theory, among descriptive-empirical, instrumental, and normative dimensions. This tripartite distinction seems readily applicable to public affairs, heavily interlaced with stakeholder issues and the public interest. Empirical description marches with prediction: if empirical conditions C obtain, what will action A obtain in terms of outcomes O? Prescription (i.e., strategic, tactical, and organizational advice) marches with the other two dimensions. Business decision making is essentially instrumental (Jackall, 1988): what action A will work, given conditions C, toward an outcome of maximizing the firm's long-term wealth (Jensen, 2000)?

The chapter uses the terms "business" and "corporation" (or "corporate") and "firm" interchangeably for convenience. There is a small literature on small and medium firms, but most studies focus on major corporations. The firm must choose how it collaborates with its industry (Hojnacki, 1997; Mahon and McGowan, 1996).

The firm operates in a complex external environment—partly market and partly non-market. External relations are much of what a firm does (Baron, 2000). Baron identifies four elements in non-market external relations: interests (i.e., stakeholders), intelligence (competitive and political), institutions, and issues (Fleisher, 1999, 2002). Public affairs concerns all non-market dimensions of the firm's external environment. The non-market environment involves governmental institutions, the media, non-governmental organizations (NGOs) operating as active pressure groups, and stakeholder interest groups such as consumers with latent potential to be mobilized into active permanent or temporary pressure groups. Individual customers are part of the market environment. Groups of customers, or consumer advocacy pressure groups, form part of the non-market environment. The strategic goal of the corporate public affairs function is successful relationships with governments at all levels (international, national, state, and local) and other external stakeholders (NGOs, other

pressure groups, or latent interest groups) forming key elements of the non-market environment. The corporation now increasingly operates globally across multiple national boundaries and in multiple local communities. The business environment is becoming more politicized, if more privatized and deregulated in some industries; and more mobilized into more effective NGOs and other pressure groups.

The firm is also an organization of interactions among internal stakeholders (executives, directors, employees, and stockholders). It can be vitally important to influence and mobilize internal stakeholders in order to affect external stakeholders (Jensen, 2000). External image and reputation and effectiveness of the public affairs management can affect the loyalty and actions of internal stakeholders (Corley et al., 2001). An example is Halliburton's 2003 effort to mobilize employees in a "Defending Our Company" campaign concerning its no-bid contract work in Iraq. US Vice-president Dick Cheney was earlier the firm's CEO.

Public affairs is logically a subset of external relations and broader than and embedding political strategy. The public affairs function operates at the interface of community relations, corporate communications and public relations, corporate philanthropy, image and reputation management, issues management, legal affairs, media relations, political influence efforts and business-government relations, and stakeholder management activities. Accepting that modern public affairs historically grew out of community relations and political lobbying, the general tendency, in practice and scholarship, has been to regard public affairs activities as narrowly concerned with communities, issues, politics, and external stakeholders (Harris and Moss, 2001). Corporate philanthropy, legal affairs, and media relations have tended to be independent concerns. This tendency, beginning to be reversed in global practice, ignores the integrative effects of these activities in combination (Harris and Moss, 2001) in strategically responding to and shaping the firm's non-market environment and the firm's and industry's social legitimacy (Meznar and Nigh, 1993).

The remainder of the chapter is organized into three main sections. The next section addresses the rich theoretical roots of public affairs, as background for consideration of key theories and models. The subsequent section identifies and discusses those theories and models. The following section considers the less developed normative dimension and discusses the future of public affairs scholarship linked to practice in the twenty-first century. There is a brief conclusion.

## THE THEORETICAL ROOTS OF PUBLIC AFFAIRS

Public affairs permeates business but the diffused function does not march with an overarching theory of external relations or public affairs or political strategy (Getz, 2002)—and a grand theory seems unlikely (Meznar, 2002). Epstein (1969) arguably remains the best integrative effort to date. Public affairs comprises neither a unified discipline nor a profession, although more specialization and expertise may be desirable. The function lies organizationally at the interface of multiple activities and, typically, subunits of a firm (Shaffer and Hillman, 2000) and intellectually at the interface of multiple disciplines that contribute rich but not automatically compatible theoretical roots. There are partly competing theories and models rather than any integrative framework. The seven key disciplines, each outlined in a separate subsection below, are businesses in society and business ethics, communications and public relations, ecological systems, economics, organizational sociology, political science, and strategic management. (This treatment expands on Getz's (2002) pioneering taxonomic treatment.)

### Businesses in Societies and Business Ethics

The combined discipline of businesses in societies and business ethics (partly overlapping and interpenetrating) addresses the non-market environment, emphasizing business responsibilities and impacts. It is the natural (but not exclusive) home base of much public affairs scholarship. Businesses in Societies, a label capturing the global character of business (Wartick, 1997), scientifically examines descriptive empirical and instrumental dimensions. Business ethics philosophically addresses the normative dimension. A rich literature dates back at least to Bowen (1953). Three central research streams are important: prescriptive business ethics, corporate social responsibility, and global corporate citizenship constructs; the corporate social performance (CSP) framework embedding triple (or even more) bottom lines; and stakeholder management practices.

### Business Ethics, Corporate Social Responsibility, and Global Corporate Citizenship Constructs

Adam Smith (*The Wealth of Nations*, 1776) and Alfred Marshall (*Principles of Economics*, 1890) emphasized ethics and the broad social context of the marketplace.

1 Corporate social responsibility (Bowen, 1953, drawing on earlier roots) is what the firm owes legally and morally to society. The basic notion has been refined to a set of responsibilities. Carroll (1991) models this set as a pyramid with economic responsibilities (broadly goods and services, jobs, and profits) at the foundation. Legal and ethical responsibilities are the next two levels in that order. Philanthropic responsibilities form the apex. Economic and legal responsibilities are mandatory, ethical behavior is expected and tax-deductible philanthropy is desirable. Empirical studies suggest managers often think in this order.
2 Carroll is explicit that all four dimensions are infused with moral duty. A moral manager acts differently concerning each responsibility compared to an amoral or immoral manager. Jackall (1988) exposed the often morally ambiguous culture within corporations that has resulted in the recent spate of misreporting and fraud scandals.

Business ethics normatively addresses issues in legal compliance and with moral integrity (Paine, 1994). In many respects, business ethics is the application of moral philosophy (of which there are multiple schools) to analysis and prescription of corporate social responsibilities.

3    The more recent construct of global corporate citizenship reformulates corporate responsibilities to a world arena in parallel with the label Businesses in Societies. The basic notion is that firms should behave as good "citizens" defined in terms of "responsible practice" linking vision, values, and value added (Waddock, 2002). Multinational enterprises operate in many countries, in each of which the firm ought to operate as a good citizen (Logsdon and Wood, 2002). Adam Smith (*The Theory of Moral Sentiments*, 1759) defined citizenship as legal obedience and good citizenship as an effort to advance the welfare of the whole commonwealth.

### Corporate Social Performance Theory

The Businesses in Societies literature refined corporate responsibilities into a CSP approach emphasizing business social impacts in multiple dimensions. Wood (1991) reformulated this CSP perspective into an outcomes-oriented framework. This CSP template combines corporate social responsibility motives (or principles corresponding to determinants empirically), socially responsive organizational processes, and social outcomes of corporate activities. Wood's reformulation is tripartite: those three dimensions, each subdivided into three elements or subdimensions. The three motives are effectively social legitimacy, internal or organizational dynamics for "public" responsibility, and individual morality. The three elements of organizational processes are environmental assessment, issues management, and stakeholder management. The three outcomes, expressed in very general terms, are social policies, social programs, and social impacts. The CSP model becomes a predictive instrument when the elements are treated conditionally, so that "who, what, when, where, why and how" (Getz, 1997,

2002) get studied empirically with an eye to prediction of how non-market actions affect firm performance (Shaffer *et al.*, 2000). The CSP template can be cross-walked to Carroll's responsibilities construct and to the firm's stakeholder groups. The notion of performance outcomes suggests multiple bottom lines, greatly complicating strategic coordination and organizational planning. Elkington (1998) proposes three bottom lines for financial, social, and ecological performance. Jensen (2000) argues that managers can handle only one decision criterion (i.e., wealth): everything else must be a constraint on that objective and not a competing target.

### Stakeholder Management Practices

A stakeholder is any individual or group or category of individuals who can affect or be affected by the focal firm and thus could have interest in collaboration with management. Examples include ecology activists, communities, customers, employees, investors, media, governments, and suppliers. (This author excludes nature and competitors from stakeholder status.) Burmese peasants are suing Unocal over its minority investment in a pipeline project of Total (France) and the repressive Myanmar military regime. Stakeholder theory models management attempting collaboration among such various stakeholder interests (Windsor, 2002b). Freeman (1984) formalized the stakeholder approach from earlier roots. Frooman (1999) examines stakeholder influence strategies for dealing with the firm; Savage *et al.* (1991) examine the firm's influence strategies for dealing with stakeholders. One study investigates the degree to which "quality of management" is or is not synonymous with quality of stakeholder relations (Waddock and Graves, 1997). Brandenburger and Nalebuff (1996) attempt to integrate market and non-market components into a value creation network including stakeholders and competitors.

## Communications and Public Relations

Public affairs means influencing stakeholders through performance activities and outcomes and through communications efforts of various types (including propaganda). A broad conception of stakeholders includes governments and the media. There is an enormous literature in communications and public relations that cannot be referenced here. There is a substantial overlap of public affairs and public relations (Harris and Moss, 2001) in which communications strategies and tactics play a vital role. This chapter directs attention to corporate image and reputation (McLeod *et al.*, 2002). Public opinion toward business in general and toward a particular industry or firm in particular is a latent reservoir of support or opposition. Tobacco products, for example, are under increasing assault. An important issue in communications and public relations is the ambiguous distinction between political and commercial free speech. The former has constitutional guarantees in the United States; the latter does not to the same degree. Nike chose to settle out of court in a suit alleging that it manipulated commercial free speech in defending itself with respect to allegations concerning overseas contract-manufacturing labor practices.

## Ecological Systems

If not a stakeholder logically, nature must be regarded as the crucial, perhaps the overriding, aspect of corporate social performance. Nature is the fundamental requirement for human life or high material quality of life. Ecological systems thinking and evidence (Bronn and Bronn, 2002) are vital to an appreciation of corporate and stakeholder impacts on natural ecological systems. Increasingly, organized activist pressure groups advocate stronger environmental improvements. The triple bottom line approach (Elkington, 1998) includes ecological impact as a performance dimension. Informative instances are global warming and the Kyoto climate accord, the Greenpeace action against Shell's Brent Spar platform in the North Sea, the environmental lawsuit against ChevronTexaco in Ecuador and the debate over SUVs (and the associated small business tax deduction).

## Economics

Economics is the science of rational resource allocation (directed to some desired outcome) and market behavior (demand and supply activities of buyers and sellers). Operating on the supply side of the market (i.e., selling to some customer), the firm seeks to maximize its economic wealth. Four economic approaches bear on public affairs: collective action theory, public choice theory, transaction cost theory, and game theory.

### Collective Action Theory

Olson (1965) modeled (transaction) costs to individuals of grouping together, as in pressure groups and coalitions of firms, for joint action. Choices concern: deciding to lead, to follow, or to "free ride" (Lenway and Rehbein, 1991). "Free riding" is a calculation that one can obtain without costs what others pay to provide. The economics of group formation must be weighed against resulting economies of scale in information gathering and delivery (Keim, 2002). "Rational ignorance" implies that an individual adequately satisfied with outcomes should not pay to acquire costly information or to vote. (Australia requires voting in federal and state or territory elections.)

### Public Choice Theory

Public choice theory examines group decisions from a demand-and-supply perspective (Hayes, 1981). One can depict the corporation as, or as if by analogy, operating in at least three "marketplaces" (Fligstein, 1996; Mahon *et al.*, 2002): (1) for goods and services (to customers and from suppliers, including labor and investors); (2) for public policies supplied by governments; and (3) for public opinion—bearing on image, reputation, and legitimacy, as a function of ideas and perceptions held by influential stakeholders. Keim's work, noted in several references, reflects this public choice approach.

### Transaction Cost Theory

Springing from the Nobel Prize in Economics work by Ronald Coase, this perspective works from the insight that transactions between two or more parties involve some cost. Williamson (1985) has built a sophisticated set of arguments about governance arrangements for markets, organizations, and institutions. Transaction costs influence how affected parties handle all interactions and interdependencies. Multi-stakeholder collaboration is an instance.

## Game Theory

Game theory is formal mathematical or informal logical modeling of interactions among interdependent actors. An oligopolistic industry is a game-theoretic setting: competitors are interdependent and take account of each other's conduct. Multi-stakeholder collaboration is a game-theoretic setting. A "game" comprises two or more players (competing and/or cooperating), stakes or outcomes and a set of (disputable) rules for defining winner and loser. In politics or stakeholder management, the "rule of anticipated reactions" (Friedrich, 1963) instructs actors to consider the likely countermoves of other players. One can use game-theoretic reasoning about two parties (say a firm and a regulatory body, or a political action committee and a legislator) or about three or more parties (say two firms and an NGO competing for the attention of a legislator).

## Organizational Sociology

An important issue is whether public affairs functions as organizational buffer against or bridge with the environment. Meznar and Nigh (1995) suggest buffering occurs where there is environmental uncertainty but the organization is powerful; and bridging occurs where there is environmental uncertainty and top management holds an institution-oriented philosophy. Organization theory (Bacharach, 1989), grounded in sociological analysis of groups and organizations, offers two relatively abstract contributions to public affairs scholarship. These two perspectives consider the firm in terms of its resistance to, adaptation to and/or manipulation of the external environment. The two perspectives are resource dependence theory and institutional theory.

## Resource Dependence Theory

Resource dependence theory views the organization as dependent on and extracting resources from an uncertain environment (Kotter, 1979; Pfeffer and Salancik, 1978). The firm seeks to reduce dependency by reduction of uncertainty (e.g., gathering costly information) and/or manipulation of the environment (e.g., influencing public opinion).

## Institutional Theory

Institutional theory (Oliver, 1991) views the environment concretely as a system of formal or informal rules, requirements, and institutions for which the firm can develop internal political capital. There is an important question of whether such vitally important capital should be outsourced, an action that increases external dependence.

## Political Science

Political science contributes two perspectives bearing on public affairs. One perspective, addressing the demand side of public policy, concerns pressure-group politics. The other perspective, addressing the supply side of public policy, concerns legislative, regulatory, and judicial institutions and processes.

## The Interest Group Theory of Pluralism

The dominant model of US democracy is an interest group theory in which there is competition for public policy outputs (Becker, 1983; Dahl, 1961; Latham, 1952; Smith, 1995; Truman, 1951). For this chapter, an interest group is latent; a pressure group is mobilized and active. This pluralism perspective, in combination with collective action theory, generally shapes the demand side of the public affairs literature. What matters most is mobilization of interests and intensity of commitment to action.

## The Status Quo Bias Model of Public Policy Process

The supply side of public policy process examines governmental institutions (Baron, 2001b) that shape demand forces (Lowery and Gray, 1998; Schattschneider, 1960). The general view is that policy institutions exhibit, for various reasons, bias toward the *status quo*. The *status quo* is costly but not impossible to change. It is important to understand how governmental institutions operate (Arnold, 1990; Niskanen, 1975). Generally, legislators seek re-election; bureaucrats seek expansion (contrast Bertrand and Mullainathan, 2003, discussed just below).

## Strategic Management

The rich literature on business strategy is beginning to move toward a theory of strategic management integrating market and non-market components. Key aspects relevant to public affairs are agency theory, the behavioral theory of the firm, integrated strategic management theory, and population ecology theory.

### Agency Theory

Agency theory, a game-theoretic model (Eisenhardt, 1989; Jensen and Meckling, 1976), considers contracting and monitoring relationships between a principal (i.e., an investor or citizen) and an agent (i.e., an employee or legislator). The general expectation is that an agent has incentive to monopolize and conceal information and to shirk performance (Keim and Baysinger, 1988). Agency theory comes in two variants. One variant predicts empire building (Niskanen, 1975). The other predicts underperformance in favor of a "quiet life" (Bertrand and Mullainathan, 2003).

### Behavioral Theory of the Firm

Cyert and March (1963) conceptualized the behavioral theory of the firm as the internal dynamics of political coalitions (Bower and Doz, 1979). A key notion in the concept is slack or excess resources, not fully deployed. Slack resources may permit experimentation with new innovations or serve to build organizational buffers against external pressures. Slack (difficult to operationalize and measure empirically) may have complex and contradictory dynamic effects on organizational decision making (Bowen, 2002).

### Integrated Strategic Management Theory

There is no unified theory of strategic management (Campbell and Alexander, 1997). There are three broad approaches to business strategy in the literature. One emphasizes attributes of the external environment. Porter's (1980, 1985) five forces model of competitive advantage and position is a key perspective. A second approach emphasizes internal attributes of the firm, with particular attention to investing in capabilities or competencies (Fleisher, 2003). This approach stresses strategic intent (i.e., directioning). The Burgelman-Bower model (Noda and Bower, 1996) portrays organizational dynamics in terms of iterative resource allocations constituting strategic commitment (McWilliams *et al.*, 2002). A third approach emphasizes internal resources of the firm, as underlying elements of capabilities (Barney, 1991; Itami, 1987; Wernerfelt, 1984). Baron (1995a, b, 2001a) developed the case for strategically integrating market and nonmarket components.

### Population Ecology Theory

Population ecology theory views organizations as a natural population of entities competing for limited resources and space in a "territory" (Hannan and Carroll, 1992). This perspective is related to resource dependency but includes the whole population of organizations. A political ecology variant (Orssatto and Clegg, 1999) is relevant to public affairs.

## "THEORIES" OF PUBLIC AFFAIRS

This section discusses illustrative applications of "theories" and "models" of public affairs, directed to political strategy and stakeholder management—the most studied aspects. Each subsection below identifies an important question for scholars and practitioners.

Two considerations bear on identifying and understanding theories and models of public affairs. First, there is a large and disorganized literature (Meznar, 2002) on public affairs and political strategy, exceeding 1,000 items even without stakeholder items (Getz, 2002, citing Griffin *et al.*, 2001a, b). This literature includes a broad scope of disparate research issues (Getz, 2002). Meznar (2002) suggests that one obstacle facing the field is lack of coherence among existing studies. Meznar's other obstacle, discussed in the next section, concerns lack of international perspective. Hillman and Hitt (1999) comment there is no consensus on appropriate integration of multiple research issues. It is possible here only to identify what seem to be some key themes and research streams. Second, not only is there no grand theory, but such theory as exists—really piece-meal "theories" and "models" drawing on different theoretical roots—is not strong theory (Meznar, 2002). "Strong" theory means robust prediction and persuasive prescription. Scholars are not even comfortable trying to answer Getz's (1997, 2002) three proposed central questions: (1) Why do firms participate in public affairs and political strategy, and should they do so—motives and determinants? (2) What are effective and ineffective strategies and tactics for various, and likely conditional, aspects of corporate activities—prescriptive actions and inactions? (3) What are the limitations to and constraints on rational action by firms—forces bearing on choices and outcomes? Much of the literature is either atheoretical description or vague prescription—neither grounded in predictability (Getz, 2002). Atheoretical description (Stott, 2003) is, however, a vital step in science. Scholars work on pieces of a kaleidoscopic and evolving puzzle; gradual progress on explanation and prediction emerges.

Practitioners must innovate and compete for strategic advantage in this disorganized intellectual setting. There are broadly speaking three paths into (not necessarily out of) the thicket of practical questions concerning public affairs activities. One path is economic reasoning: demand-and-supply market analogy in combination with cost-benefit analysis of resource allocation. A second path is institutional reasoning: predicted functioning of governmental institutions and pressure groups and practical methods for influencing external

parties. A third path is strategic reasoning: political, stakeholder, and other external relations capabilities creating sustainable competitive advantage.

A reading of the literature suggests a loose logical schema, not amounting to any grand theory, for addressing public affairs cycles. This schema simply identifies broadly a complex set of partly overlapping questions. Generally, the schema combines insightful models proposed by Wood (1991) for CSP and Schuler (2002) for corporate political or social issue life cycles. In a life "cycle," an "issue" would move through the framework from determinants (or motives) through actions (or inaction) of various interests and institutions to outcomes. A framework suitable for prediction and action planning must include at least five components: firms, governmental institutions, media, formal and *ad hoc* pressure groups of stakeholders and latent public opinion which can be mobilized. A complex set of motives and external and internal determinants drives a firm's actions or inactions (and those of pressure groups, allies, complementors, and competitors). These actions or inactions in combination affect internal and external stakeholders. These efforts, or a lack of them, feed into the media and governmental institutions—subdivided into multiple public policy arenas. Outcomes are likely to be multidimensional. Impacts on firm performance feed back to motives and determinants. The loose framework affords scope for competition and cooperation, and models a game-theoretic setting for strategic and tactical calculations by all parties (Schuler *et al.*, 2001).

## What Should be the Objectives of Corporate Public Affairs Activities?

Determinants or motives of businesses are varied (Grier *et al.*, 1994; Lichtenberg, 1989; Mitchell *et al.*, 1997; Schuler, 1999; Vogel, 1996). Businesses have interests in predicting environmental changes and in influencing the external environment in multiple arenas and issues (Keim, 2002). The firm must decide whether to be a passive environmental adapter or an active public policy and stakeholder opinion influencer. Passive prediction without influence efforts implies advance planning of purely internal changes for responding to environmental changes. Proactive reaction influence implies trying to prevent or otherwise shape coming environmental changes. Public affairs entrepreneurship implies first-mover initiation of efforts to change the external situation (Keim, 2002). The firm must be able to scan the environment for change information and competitive intelligence (Fleisher, 1999). Executives must determine appropriate objectives: e.g., legitimacy; image and reputation; prevention of harms to the firm; acquisition of benefits to the firm; or the public interest. Different theoretical roots emphasize different objectives. Economics suggests wealth maximization. CSP literature suggests legitimacy and social impacts. Political science suggests the public interest.

## Can Corporations Effectively Integrate Management of Issue Life Cycles?

A vital question is whether firms can integrate management of issue life cycles. Integrated issue management seeks to identify risks and opportunities in advance of key audiences (Palese and Crane, 2002) within the corporate governance and strategic management framework. There is a vital need for strategic thinking (Heath, 2002) on issues management. Evidence is highly mixed, reflecting success and failure stories (Heath, 2002; Mahon and Waddock, 1992).

1   US drug companies have been struggling to prevent import of cheaper generics or re-import of their own exports through other countries (especially Canada and Mexico). The Food and Drug Administration (FDA) has taken the position that there is too large a risk of product defect. High drug prices in an aging population pressuring the federal government to incorporate drugs into social security weigh against the drug industry and shape public opinion. Generics increasingly

are being approved for developing countries beset by HIV.

2   Another example involves the 2003 business-government dispute over allowing telephone customers to register with the federal government's National Do Not Call Registry in order to block unwanted telephone solicitations. The Direct Marketing Association—a trade group with some 4,700 members and a significant number of employees (Cox News Service, 2003)—attempted to prevent the registry's operation, despite strong public opinion, and obtained two federal district court rulings that its operation would violate free speech. The association lost in the federal appeals court and the Congress raced a Bill through signed by President Bush. A National Do Not Spam Registry presently seems less likely.

3   A proposed 2003 Bill to give the FDA oversight of cigarettes, a Bill supported by Philip Morris on analysis that it might prevent more draconian measures in the future (see Friedrich, 1963), faltered over disagreements within the Senate Health Committee (O'Connell, 2003). Other cigarette firms opposed the Bill.

4   In 1987, at a Texas City refinery near Houston, a pressured storage tank was ruptured and released 6,600 gallons of hydrofluoric acid; about 1,200 persons were hospitalized and 3,000 evacuated (Drosjack, 2003). The US Public Interest Research Group (PIRG) wants a federal law requiring refinery operators to substitute less risky chemicals as a hedge against accident or terrorism. Texas has twelve refineries storing hydrofluoric acid near more than one million people; nationwide, more than 15 million live near such facilities. A Bill requiring federal agencies to identify facilities and recommend security and safety improvements has repeatedly failed due to opposition from the oil industry's National Petrochemical and Refiners Association, which contends that voluntary self-regulation and cooperation with federal agencies will suffice (Drosjack, 2003).

## Can Interested Parties Influence Political Outcomes and Public Opinion?

A central question (de Figueiredo and de Figueiredo, 2002) in public affairs scholarship and practice is the degree to which corporations or pressure groups can influence political outcomes in governmental institutions. De Figueiredo and de Figueiredo (2002) suggest that the prediction situation is complicated by interdependencies between institutions, such that stages of pressure group strategies cannot be examined in isolation. The authors looked at litigation of administrative rule making in the courts. They argue that influence strategies should reflect the ideology of the court (i.e., bias toward or against the *status quo*) and responsiveness of the court to resources.

The general view has been that business is politically a "powerful" sector (Lowi, 1964). Lindblom (1977) argued the ultimate dependence of government on private market performance. The proposition has been tested in Bauer *et al.* (1963) and Quinn and Shapiro (1991). The situation may be changing with rising mobilization of interest groups. Generally, public opinion is vaguely hostile to large business corporations and their executives—opinion rubbed raw by recent corporate scandals resulting in the Bipartisan Campaign Reform Act of 2002 and the Sarbanes-Oxley Act of 2002 (preceded by the Foreign Corrupt Practices Act of 1977). A primitive theory is that, all things being equal, business is likely to win out in competition with weaker interests—unless public opinion swings strongly in favor of an anti-business policy. But the empirical situation is generally ambiguous and reflects the contingent or conditional nature of reality in public affairs (Baumgartner and Leech, 1996; Evans, 1986; Keim and Zeithaml, 1986; Rehbein and Schuler, 1999). The empirical situation evolves with time and experience. Public policy arenas are highly and increasingly competitive (Austin-Smith and Wright, 1992).

## Should Corporations Attempt to Influence Political Outcomes and Public Opinion?

A firm must weight costs and benefits in relationship to objectives (Bhuyan, 2000; Dean *et al.*, 1998; Lenway *et al.*, 1990; Marsh, 1998). There are two competing views of the question (Richards, 2003). One view is that public affairs activities are a necessary cost of business (Schnietz and Schuler, 1999). The other view is that public affairs can be a value-added asset or competence. Richards surveys the state of valuation tools and their use for measuring the financial contribution that public affairs activities can add to the bottom line. Hillman and Keim (2001) conclude that stakeholder relations can be positive while social issues are typically negative with respect to financial performance. McWilliams and Siegel (2000) suggest that there is no clear evidence one way or the other. Stakeholder support (brand loyalty) and advocacy may be a function of the firm's image or reputation (Council on Foundations, 1996, cited by Richards, 2003). Good corporate citizenship involves support of community organizations, employee volunteers, charitable support, and direct philanthropy (Council on Foundations, 1996, cited by Richards, 2003).

## What Public Affairs Strategies and Tactics are Likely to be Effective?

Addressing this question—broadly in public affairs or narrowly in political strategy—must cope with multiple arenas, institutional complexities, varying stakeholder interests and mobilization, and so forth in an ambiguous and contingent (i.e., conditional) setting (Schuler *et al.*, 2001). The relationship between strategies and effectiveness (Meznar and Nigh, 1993) is vital but unknown except in rough outline. There are many studies—of political action committees, soft money, lobbying, stakeholder loyalty and branding, grassroots mobilization, access to legislators and regulators and legislative committees, stakeholder dialogue processes, and so on (e.g., Chin *et al.,* 2000; Gray and Lowery, 1997; Grenzke, 1989; Hall and Wayman, 1990; Hillman *et al.,* 1999; Hojnacki and Kimball, 1999). Keim (2002) draws some important inferences from the most recent membership survey of the Washington, DC-based Public Affairs Council (Hoewing, 1999). Most members naturally engage in government relations activities at federal, state, and local levels. Most members use PACs for political contributions—with wide disparities in rates of participation by employees. Just under half, in contrast, made "soft money" contributions to political party committees. Grassroots mobilization—still mostly occasional and *ad hoc* (Keim, 2002)—is vital. The Internet is increasingly important (Roper, 2002). Legislators are concerned with credibility of information and pressure, and with re-election probabilities (including campaign financing). Grassroots efforts are rated by congressional aides as most effective (Lord, 2000a, b) but not in the traditional form of mass preprinted mailings or signed petitions or modern forms such as faxes and e-mails. Personal visits by constituents (which can occur in the district) followed by personal letters and then more distantly phone calls weigh. Effectiveness rises with cost of organizing. Information from informed and interested constituents and others most likely to participate in policy-making efforts receives the most credence (Keim, 2002).

## How Should Firms Organize Internally for Public Affairs Activities?

There should be integration or at least improved coordination of activities for community relations, competitive intelligence, government relations, media relations, and stakeholder relations (Fleisher, 1999, 2001; Kaufman *et al.,* 1993; Shaffer and Hillman, 2000). Keim (2002) draws out two organizational structure findings from the Public Affairs Council survey (Hoewing, 1999). Firms are increasingly contracting out public affairs activities, including lobbying. (Outsourcing in other functions has yielded mixed results. It may dissipate essential internal capital and increase external dependence. Suppose a firm's management information systems function, outsourced, is bought by a competitor.) Decision making in public affairs—government relations departments is typically centralized, although the overall function is typically fragmented. Participative management might draw better on internal knowledge and encourage employees' political participation and support (Keim, 2002).

## What Public Affairs Competencies and Resources are Important?

Integrated strategic management of market and non-market components raises the issue of what internal competencies and resources are important, and can they be sources of sustainable competitive advantage? Skills at environmental scanning, PAC operation, lobbying, grassroots mobilization, public relations, media relations, and so forth, are important— but not necessarily unique and non-imitable. A number of procedures have been proposed: scenarios (Pedler, 2001), total quality management or TQM (Fleisher and Nickel, 1995), and analytical tools for issues management and stakeholder management (Fleisher, 2002). Multi-stakeholder dialogue is an increasingly used and important process (Svendsen, 1998). Non-market partnerships and alliances may be of continuing importance (Waddock, 1988). Sustainable competitive advantage typically involves long-term investment in unique, difficult to imitate capabilities and resources.

## PUBLIC AFFAIRS IN THE TWENTY-FIRST CENTURY

Techniques for forward planning in business are scenarios and related procedures such as Delphi expert panels (Pedler, 2001). At least so far, the twenty-first century looks difficult for corporate public affairs. The United States is at war in Afghanistan and Iraq. Diplomatic relations between the United States and the United Nations and key EU countries are strained. Various countries are targets of terrorism. Corporate fraud and misreporting scandals propelled the Bipartisan Campaign Reform Act of 2002 and the Sarbanes-Oxley Act of 2002. The Campaign Reform Act regulates political giving and corporate political speech. The Sarbanes-Oxley Act imposes stronger duties for top corporate executives and other key market actors, increases penalties for white-collar crimes, and seeks to protect whistleblowers.

## What is "The" Public Interest in a Plural Democracy?

Corporate public affairs practice is rationally directed to two targets. One target, broader in character, is securing legitimization of the firm (and by logical extension the firm's industry) from multiple societies and stakeholders. In the author's view, such legitimacy must be a resultant of contribution to the public interest (Downs, 1962). Another target, narrower in character, is securing specific benefits, or avoiding specific costs, for the firm from public policy, stakeholder action, and public opinion. The public interest is not simply an aggregation of private interests—whether politically active or inactive. Rather, the public interest is overriding and integrative—the best long-term outcomes for the commonwealth. Edmund Burke ("Speech to the Electors of Bristol", 1774) expressed the matter (to dissatisfied constituents) as the difference between a legislative representative and a trustee. The latter must sometimes disregard the immediate and local interests of the constituency represented for the greater good of the commonwealth. The public interest is not something of calculation, but something of judgment and wisdom. Ghoshal (2003) is highly critical of business schools' approach to technical education (e.g., accounting, finance, and marketing) as undergirding recent corporate scandals like Enron. Economics is geared to opinion aggregation

and market-like competition or monopolization. Strategic management is geared to the interests of the firm. The public interest, as Burke argued, may demand self-sacrifice.

## International Public Affairs: The Expanding Global Arena

Public affairs literature has focused on the United States and its neighbor Canada, and on their firms. The literature may be subject to a charge of American and subsequently Western ethnocentrism, as a barrier to progress (Meznar, 2002). There is a growing literature on public affairs in multinational corporations and various countries (e.g., Berg and Holtbrugge, 2001; Boddewyn, 1988; Boddewyn and Brewer, 1994; Hillman and Keim, 1995; Meznar, 1996); and also on political influence activities of European firms at Brussels, the seat of the European Commission and associated bureaucracy. International public affairs will likely require the development of special competencies (Fleisher, 2003). Pedler (2001) points out that, while there are increasingly global issues and authorities, regulation and control remain largely national. Businesses must deal with both national and international regimes and an increasingly mobilized civil society operating through global alliances among NGOs. Examples can be found in the public affairs activities of DaimlerChrsyler (Palese and Crane, 2002), the Trans Alliance Business Dialogue (TABD) established in 1995 with the backing of the Clinton administration and the European Commission (Hatcher, 2003), and the latter's rejection of the General Electric—Honeywell merger (Mahon et al., 2002).

## CONCLUSION

This chapter assesses "theories" and the theoretical roots of public affairs. The public affairs function addresses the interface between a corporation and its external non-market environment. Public affairs comprises a vitally important but diffused function. This broad assignment remains in search of identity, conceptualization, theory, effective corporate organization, best practices, and social legitimacy. Public affairs scholarship is multidisciplinary rather than interdisciplinary, and still largely descriptive rather than predictive. Public affairs practice is almost wholly instrumental but barely strategic. There is no "grand" theory of public affairs—no integrative or overarching framework. No such grand theory or framework seems likely. The chapter suggests some combination of corporate social performance (CSP) theory and corporate political or social issue life cycle theory. The theoretical roots of public affairs scholarship reside in several different disciplines: communications and public relations, economics, organizational sociology, political science, and strategic management. The normative context, badly neglected in practice, adds businesses in societies, business ethics, and ecological systems.

The contributions of these various disciplines to public affairs scholarship and practice are identified and assessed. Examination of the various proposed "theories" or "models" of public affairs suggests several important research questions—many of which are encompassed in various forms by chapters in this *Handbook*. What should be the objectives of corporate public affairs activities? Can corporations effectively integrate management of issue life cycles? Can interested parties influence political outcomes and public opinion? Should corporations attempt to influence political outcomes and public opinion? What public affairs strategies and tactics are likely to be effective? How should firms organize internally for public affairs activities? What public affairs competencies and resources are important? Corporate public affairs in the twenty-first century should focus on two central issues. One issue concerns definition of "the" public interest in a pluralistic democracy. The other issue concerns development of the competencies and resources needed to manage international public affairs in an expanding global arena for market operations and public policy making.

# REFERENCES

Arnold, R.D. (1990). *The Logic of Congressional Action*. New Haven, CT: Yale University Press.

Austen-Smith, D., and J.R. Wright (1992). "Competitive Lobbying for a Legislator's Vote," *Social Choice and Welfare* 9 (3): 229–257.

Bacharach, S.B. (1989). "Organizational Theories: Some Criteria for Evaluation," *Academy of Management Review* 14 (4): 496–515.

Barney, J. (1991). "Firm Resources and Sustained Competitive Advantage," *Journal of Management* 17 (1): 99–120.

Baron, D.P. (1995a). "Integrated Strategy: Market and Non-market Components," *California Management Review* 37 (2): 47–65.

Baron, D.P. (1995b). "The Nonmarket Strategy System," *Sloan Management Review* 37 (1): 73–85.

Baron, D.P. (2000). *Business and its Environment*. Upper Saddle River, NJ: Prentice Hall.

Baron, D.P. (2001a). "Private Politics, Corporate Social Responsibility, and Integrated Strategy," *Journal of Economics and Management Strategy* 10 (1): 7–45.

Baron, D.P. (2001b). "Theories of Strategic Nonmarket Participation: Majority-rule and Executive Institutions," *Journal of Economics and Management Strategy* 10 (1): 47–89.

Bauer, R.A., I. Pool, and L.A. Dexter (1963). *American Business and Public Policy: The Politics of Foreign Trade*. New York: Atherton.

Baumgartner, F.R., and B.L. Leech (1996). "The Multiple Ambiguities of 'Counteractive Lobbying'," *American Journal of Political Science* 40 (2): 521–542.

Becker, G.S. (1983). "A Theory of Competition among Pressure Groups for Political Influence," *Quarterly Journal of Economics* 98 (3): 371–400.

Berg, N., and D. Holtbrugge (2001). "Public Affairs Management Activities of German Multinational Corporations in India," *Journal of Business Ethics* 30 (1): 105–119.

Bertrand, M., and S. Mullainathan (2003). "Enjoying the Quiet Life? Corporate Governance and Managerial Preferences," *Journal of Political Economy* 111 (5): 1043–1075.

Bhuyan, S. (2000). "Corporate Political Activities and Oligopoly Welfare Loss," *Review of Industrial Organization* 17 (4): 411–426.

Boddewyn, J.J. (1974). "External Affairs: A Corporate Function in Search of Conceptualization and Theory," *Organization and Administration Sciences* 5 (spring): 67–111.

Boddewyn, J.J. (1988). "Political Aspects of MNE Theory," *Journal of International Business Studies* 19 (3): 343–363.

Boddewyn, J.J., and T.L. Brewer (1994). "International Business Political Behavior: New Theoretical Directions," *Academy of Management Review* 19 (1): 119–143.

Bowen, F.E. (2002). "Organizational Slack and Corporate Greening: Broadening the Debate," *British Journal of Management* 13 (4): 305–316.

Bowen, H.R. (1953). *Social Responsibilities of the Businessman*. New York: Harper & Row.

Bower, J.L., and Y. Doz (1979). "Strategy Formulation: A Social and Political Process," in D.E. Schendel and C.W. Hofer (eds), *Strategic Management*. Boston, MA: Little, Brown & Company.

Brandenburger, A.M., and B.J. Nalebuff (1996). *Co-opetition*. New York: Doubleday.

Bronn, P.S., and C. Bronn (2002). "Issues Management as a Basis for Strategic Orientation," *Journal of Public Affairs* 2 (4): 247–258.

Campbell, A., and M. Alexander (1997). "What's Wrong with Strategy?" *Harvard Business Review* 75 (6): 42–49.

Carroll, A.B. (1991). "The Pyramid of Corporate Social Responsibility: Toward the Moral Management of Organizational Stakeholders," *Business Horizons* 34 (4): 39–48.

Chin, M.L., J.R. Bond, and N. Geva (2000). "A Foot in the Door: An Experimental Study of PAC and Constituency Effects on Access," *Journal of Politics* 62 (2): 534–549.

Corley, K.G., P.L. Cochran, and T.G. Comstock (2001). "Image and the Impact of Public Affairs Management on Internal Stakeholders," *Journal of Public Affairs* 1 (1): 53–68.

Council on Foundations (1996). *Measuring the Value of Corporate Citizenship*. Washington, DC: Council on Foundations.

Cox News Service (2003). "Marketers Won't Give FCC No-call Data," *Houston Chronicle* 102 (October 4): 2C.

Cyert, R.M., and J.G. March (1963). *A Behavioral Theory of the Firm*. Englewood Cliffs, NJ: Prentice Hall.

Dahl, R.A. (1961). *Who Governs?* New Haven, CT: Yale University Press.

Dean, T.J., M. Vryza, and G.E. Fryxell (1998). "Do Corporate PACs Restrict Competition? An Empirical Examination of Industry PAC Contributions and Entry," *Business and Society* 37 (2): 135–156.

de Figueiredo, J.M., and R.J.P. de Figueiredo (2002). "The Allocation of Resources by Interest Groups: Lobbying, Litigation and Administrative Regulation," *Business and Politics* 4 (2): 161–181.

Donaldson, T., and L.E. Preston (1995). "The Stakeholder Theory of the Corporation: Concepts, Evidence, and Implications," *Academy of Management Review* 20 (1): 65–91.

Downs, A. (1962). "The Public Interest: Its Meaning in a Democracy," *Social Research* 29 (1): 1–36.

Drosjack, M. (2003). "Activists Push to Ban Chemical Nationwide," *Houston Chronicle* 103 (October 15): 2C.

Eisenhardt, K.M. (1989). "Agency Theory: An Assessment and Review," *Academy of Management Review* 14 (1): 57–74.

Elkington, J. (1998). *Cannibals with Forks: The Triple Bottom Line of Sustainability*. Gabriola Island, BC: New Society Publishers.

Epstein, E.M. (1969). *The Corporation in American Politics*. Englewood Cliffs, NJ: Prentice Hall.

Evans, D.M. (1986). "PAC Contributions and Roll-call Voting: Conditional Power," in A.J. Cigler and B.A. Loomis (eds), *Interest Group Politics*. Washington, DC: Congressional Quarterly Press.

Fleisher, C.S. (1999). "Public Policy Competitive Intelligence," *Competitive Intelligence Review* 10 (2): 23–36.

Fleisher, C.S. (2001). "Emerging US Public Affairs Practice: The 2000+ PA Model," *Journal of Public Affairs* 1 (1): 44–52.

Fleisher, C.S. (2002). "Analysis and Analytical Tools for Managing Corporate Public Affairs," *Journal of Public Affairs* 2 (3): 167–172.

Fleisher, C.S. (2003). "The Development of Competencies in International Public Affairs," *Journal of Public Affairs* 3 (1): 76–82.

Fleisher, C.S., and J.R. Nickel (1995). "Attempting TQM in Organizational Staff Areas: TQM as Managerial Innovation in Corporate Public Affairs," *Revenue Canadienne des Sciences de l'Administration* 12 (2): 116–127.

Fligstein, N. (1996). "Markets as Politics: A Political-Cultural Approach to Market Institutions," *American Sociological Review* 61 (4): 656–673.

Freeman, R.E. (1984). *Strategic Management: A Stakeholder Approach*. Boston, MA: Pitman.

Friedrich, C.J. (1963). "Influence and the Rule of Anticipated Reactions," in *Man and his Government: An Empirical Theory of Politics*. New York: McGraw-Hill.

Frooman, J. (1999). "Stakeholder Influence Strategies," *Academy of Management Review* 24 (2): 191–205.

Getz, K.A. (1997). "Research in Corporate Political Action: Integration and Assessment," *Business and Society* 36 (1): 32–72.

Getz, K.A. (2002). "Public Affairs and Political Strategy: Theoretical Foundations," *Journal of Public Affairs* 1 (4) and 2 (1): 305–329.

Ghoshal, S. (2003). "Business Schools Share the Blame for Enron," *Financial Times* (London), July 18, p. 19.

Gray, V., and D. Lowery (1997). "Reconceptualizing PAC Formation: It's not a Collective Action Problem, and it May be an Arms Race", *American Politics Quarterly* 25 (3): 319–346.

Grenzke, J.M. (1989). "PACs and the Congressional Supermarket: The Currency is Complex," *American Journal of Political Science* 33 (1): 1–24.

Grier, K.B., M.C. Munger, and B.E. Roberts (1994). "The Determinants of Industry Political Activity, 1978–1986," *American Political Science Review* 88 (4): 911–926.

Griffin, J.J., C.S. Fleisher, S.N. Brenner, and J.J. Boddewyn (2001a). "Corporate Public Affairs Research: Chronological Reference List 1, 1985–2000," *Journal of Public Affairs* 1 (1): 9–32.

Griffin, J.J., C.S. Fleisher, S.N. Brenner, and J.J. Boddewyn (2001b). "Corporate Public Affairs Research: Chronological Reference List 2, 1958–1984," *Journal of Public Affairs* 1 (2): 167–186.

Hall, R.L., and F.W. Wayman (1990). "Buying Time: Moneyed Interests and the Mobilization of Bias in Congressional Committees," *American Political Science Review* 84 (3): 797–820.

Hannan, M.T., and G.R. Carroll (1992). *Dynamics of Organizational Populations*. New York: Oxford University Press.

Harris, P., and D. Moss (2001). "Editorial. In Search of Public Affairs: A Function in Search of an Identity," *Journal of Public Affairs* 1 (2): 102–110.

Hatcher, M. (2003). "New Corporate Agendas," *Journal of Public Affairs* 3 (2): 32–38.

Hayes, M.T. (1981). *Lobbyists and Legislators: A Theory of Political Markets*. New Brunswick, NJ: Rutgers University Press.

Heath, R.L. (2002). "Issues Management: Its Past, Present and Future," *Journal of Public Affairs* 2 (4): 209–214.

Hillman, A.J., and M.A. Hitt (1999). "Corporate Political Strategy Formulation: A Model of Approach, Participation, and Strategy Decisions," *Academy of Management Review* 24 (4): 825–842.

Hillman, A.J., and G.D. Keim (1995). "International Variation in the Business-Government Interface: Institutional and Organizational Considerations," *Academy of Management Review* 20 (1): 193–214.

Hillman, A.J., and G.D. Keim (2001). "Shareholder Value, Stakeholder Management, and Social Issues: What's the Bottom Line?" *Strategic Management Journal* 22 (2): 125–139.

Hillman, A.J., A. Zardkoohi, and L. Bierman (1999). "Corporate Political Strategies and Firm Performance: Indications of Firm-specific Benefits from Personal Service in the US Government," *Strategic Management Journal* 20 (1): 67–81.

Hoewing, R.L. (1999). *Corporate Public Affairs: The State of Corporate Public Affairs Survey, Final Report, 1999–2000*. Washington, DC: Foundation for Public Affairs.

Hojnacki, M. (1997). "Interest Groups' Decisions to Join Alliances or Work Alone," *American Journal of Political Science* 41 (1): 61–87.

Hojnacki, M., and D.C. Kimball (1999). "The Who and How of Organizations: Lobbying Strategies in Committee," *Journal of Politics* 61 (4): 999–1024.

Itami, H. (1987). *Mobilizing Invisible Assets*. Cambridge, MA: Harvard University Press.

Jackall, R. (1988). *Moral Mazes: The World of Corporate Managers*. New York: Oxford University Press.

Jensen, M.C. (2000). "Value Maximization and the Corporate Objective Function," in M. Beer and N. Nohria (eds), *Breaking the Code of Change*. Boston, MA: Harvard Business School Press.

Jensen, M.C., and W.H. Meckling (1976). "Theory of the Firm: Managerial Behavior, Agency Costs, and Ownership Structure," *Journal of Financial Economics* 3 (2): 305–360.

Kaufman, A.M., E.J. Englander, and A.A. Marcus (1993). "Selecting an Organizational Structure for Implementing Issues Management: A Transaction Costs and Agency Theory Perspective," in B.M. Mitnick (ed.), *Corporate Political Agency*. Newbury Park, CA: Sage.

Keim, G.D. (2002). "Managing Business Political Activities in the USA: Bridging between Theory and Practice," *Journal of Public Affairs* 1 (4) and 2 (1): 362–375.

Keim, G., and B. Baysinger (1988). "The Efficacy of Business Political Activity: Competitive Considerations in the Principal-Agent Context," *Journal of Management* 14 (2): 163–180.

Keim, G., and C. Zeithaml (1986). "Corporate Political Strategy and Legislative Decision Making: A Review and Contingency Approach," *Academy of Management Review* 11 (4): 828–843.

Kotter, J.P. (1979). "Managing External Dependence," *Academy of Management Review* 4 (1): 87–92.

Latham, E. (1952). "The Group Basis of Politics: Notes for a Theory," *American Political Science Review* 46 (2): 376–397.

Lenway, S.A., and K.A. Rehbein (1991). "Leaders, Followers, and Free Riders: An Empirical Test of Variation in Corporate Political Involvement," *Academy of Management Journal* 34 (4): 893–905.

Lenway, S.A., K.A. Rehbein, and L. Starks (1990). "The Impact of Protectionism on Firm Wealth: The Experience of the Steel Industry," *Southern Economic Journal* 56 (4): 1079–1093.

Lichtenberg, F.R. (1989). "Contributions to Federal Election Campaigns by Government Contractors," *Journal of Industrial Economics* 38 (1): 31–48.

Lindblom, C.E. (1977). *Politics and Markets: The World's Political Economic Systems.* New York: Basic Books.

Logsdon, J., and D.J. Wood (2002). "Business Citizenship: From Domestic to Global Level of Analysis," *Business Ethics Quarterly* 12 (2): 155–187.

Lord, M. (2000a). "Corporate Political Strategies and Legislative Decision Making: The Impact of Corporate Legislative Influence Activities," *Business and Society* 39 (1): 76–93.

Lord, M. (2000b). "The Growth of Grassroots: Constituency Building as Political Strategy," in T. Kramer with W. Pedersen (eds), *Winning at the Grassroots: A Comprehensive Manual for Corporations and Associations.* Washington, DC: Public Affairs Council.

Lowery, D., and V. Gray (1998). "The Dominance of Institutions in Interest Representation: A Test of Seven Explanations," *American Journal of Political Science* 42 (1): 231–255.

Lowi, T.J. (1964). "American Business, Public Policy, Case Studies and Political Theory," *World Politics* 16 (4): 677–715.

Mahon, J.F., and R.A. McGowan (1996). *Industry as a Player in the Political and Social Arena.* Westport, CT: Greenwood Press.

Mahon, J.F., and S.A. Waddock (1992). "Strategic Issues Management: An Integration of Issue Life Cycle Perspectives," *Business and Society* 31 (1): 19–32.

Mahon, J.F., S.L. Wartick, and C.S. Fleisher (2002). "Editorial. Public Affairs, Issues Management, and Corporate Political Strategy: An Introduction," *Journal of Public Affairs* 4 (1): 294–304.

Marcus, A.A., and M.S. Irion (1987). "The Continued Growth of the Corporate Public Affairs Function," *Academy of Management Executive* 1 (3): 247–250.

Marsh, S. (1998). "Creating Barriers for Foreign Competitors: A Study of the Impact of Anti-dumping Actions on the Performance of US Firms," *Strategic Management Journal* 19 (1): 25–38.

McLeod, D.M., G.M. Kosicki, and J.M. McLeod (2002). "Resurveying the Boundaries of Political Communication Effects," in J. Bryant and D. Zillmann (eds), *Media Effects: Advances in Theory and Research.* Mahwah, NJ: Erlbaum.

McWilliams, A., and D. Siegel (2000). "Corporate Social Responsibility and Financial Performance: Correlation or Misspecification?" *Strategic Management Journal* 21 (5): 603–609.

McWilliams, A., D.D. Van Fleet, and K.D. Cory (2002). "Raising Rivals' Costs through Political Strategy: An Extension of Resource-based Theory," *Journal of Management Studies* 39 (5): 707–724.

Meznar, M. (1996). "Public Affairs Management in Multinational Corporations: Who Makes the Decisions?" *Journal of International Management* 2 (3): 149–175.

Meznar, M. (2002). "The Theoretical Foundations of Public Affairs and Political Strategy: Where do We Go from Here?" *Journal of Public Affairs* 1 (4) and 2 (1): 330–336.

Meznar, M.B., and D. Nigh (1993). "Managing Corporate Legitimacy: Public Affairs Activities, Strategies and Effectiveness," *Business and Society* 32 (1): 30–43.

Meznar, M.B., and D. Nigh (1995). "Buffer or Bridge? Environmental and Organizational Determinants of Public Affairs Activities in American Firms," *Academy of Management Journal* 38 (4): 975–996.

Mitchell, N.J., W.L. Hanssen, and E.M. Jepsen (1997). "The Determinants of Domestic and Foreign Corporate Political Activity," *Journal of Politics* 59 (4): 1096–1113.

Niskanen, W. (1975). "Bureaucrats and Politicians," *Journal of Law and Economics* 18 (3): 617–43.

Noda, T., and J.L. Bower (1996). "Strategy Making as Iterated Processes of Resource Allocation," *Strategic Management Journal* 17 (summer): 159–192.

O'Connell, V. (2003). "Tobacco Bill Falters as Alliances Prove to be Fragile," *Wall Street Journal,* October 3, p. B7.

Oliver, C. (1991). "Strategic Responses to Institutional Processes," *Academy of Management Review* 16 (1): 145–179.

Olson, M. (1965). *The Logic of Collective Action: Public Goods and the Theory of Groups.* Cambridge, MA: Harvard University Press.

Orssatto, R.J., and S.R. Clegg (1999). "The Political Ecology of Organizations," *Organizations and Environment* 12 (3): 263–279.

Paine, L.S. (1994). "Managing for Organizational Integrity," *Harvard Business Review* 72 (2): 106–117.

Palese, M., and T.Y. Crane (2002). "Building an Integrated Issue Management Process as a Source of Sustainable Competitive Advantage," *Journal of Public Affairs* 2 (4): 284–292.

Pedler, R.H. (2001). "Envisaging the Future: Scenarios and Public Affairs Practice," *Journal of Public Affairs* 1 (2): 113–123.

Pfeffer, J., and G.R. Salancik (1978). *The External Control of Organizations.* New York: Harper & Row.

Porter, M.E. (1980). *Competitive Strategy.* New York: Free Press.

Porter, M.E. (1985). *Competitive Advantage.* New York: Free Press.

Quinn, D.P., and R.Y. Shapiro (1991). "Business Political Power: The Case of Taxation," *American Political Science Review* 85 (3): 851–874.

Rehbein, K.A., and D.A. Schuler (1999). "Testing the Firm as a Filter of Corporate Political Action," *Business and Society* 38 (2): 144–166.

Richards, D.C. (2003). "Corporate Public Affairs: Necessary Cost or Value-added Asset?" *Journal of Public Affairs* 3 (2): 39–51.

Roper, J. (2002). "Government, Corporate or Social Power? The Internet as a Tool in the Struggle for Dominance in Public Policy," *Journal of Public Affairs* 2 (3): 113–124.

Savage, G.T., T.W. Nix, C.J. Whitehead, and J.D. Blair (1991). "Strategies for Assessing and Managing Organizational Stakeholders," *Academy of Management Executive* 5 (2): 61–75.

Schattschneider, E.E. (1960). *The Semisovereign People: A Realist's View of Democracy in America.* New York: Holt Rinehart & Winston.

Schnietz, K., and D.A. Schuler (1999). "Much Ado About Nothing? The Economic Impact of US Foreign Trade Mission Participation," *Business and Politics* 1 (2): 155–177.

Schuler, D.A. (1999). "Corporate Political Action: Rethinking the Economic and Institutional Influences," *Business and Politics* 1 (1): 83–97.

Schuler, D.A. (2002). "Public Affairs, Issues Management and Political Strategy: Methodological Approaches that Count," *Journal of Public Affairs* 1 (4) and 2 (1): 336–355.

Schuler, D.A., K.A. Rehbein, and R. Cramer (2001). "Pursuing Strategic Advantage through Political Means: A Multivariate Approach," *Academy of Management Journal* 45 (4): 659–672.

Shaffer, B., and A.J. Hillman (2000). "The Development of Business-Government Strategies by Diversified Firms," *Strategic Management Journal,* 21 (2): 175–190.

Shaffer, B., T.J. Quasney, and C.M. Grimm (2000). "Firm Level Performance Implications of Nonmarket Actions," *Business and Society* 39 (2): 126–143.

Smith, R.A. (1995). "Interest Group Influence in the US Congress," *Legislative Studies Quarterly* 20 (1): 89–139.

Stott, R. (2003). *Darwin and the Barnacle.* New York: Norton.

Svendsen, A. (1998). *The Stakeholder Strategy: Profiting from Collaborative Business Relationships.* San Francisco: Berrett Koehler.

Truman, D.B. (1951). *The Governmental Process.* New York: Knopf.

Vogel, D. (1996). *Kindred Strangers: The Uneasy Relationship between Politics and Business in America.* Princeton, NJ: Princeton University Press.

Waddock, S. (1988). "Building Successful Social Partnerships," *MIT Sloan Management Review* 29 (4): 17–23.

Waddock, S. (2002). *Leading Corporate Citizens: Vision, Values, Value Added.* Boston, MA: McGraw-Hill Irwin.

Waddock, S.A., and S.B. Graves (1997). "Quality of Management and Quality of Stakeholder Relations: Are they Synonymous?" *Business and Society* 36 (3): 250–279.

Wartick, S.L. (1997). "From 'Business and Society' to 'Businesses in Societies'," in B. Toyne and D. Nigh (eds), *International Business: An Emerging Vision.* Columbia, SC: University of South Carolina Press.

Wernerfelt, B. (1984). "A Resource-based View of the Firm," *Strategic Management Journal* 5 (2): 171–180.

Williamson, O.E. (1985). *The Economic Institutions of Capitalism.* New York: Free Press.

Windsor, D. (2001). "The Future of Corporate Social Responsibility," *International Journal of Organizational Analysis* 9 (3): 225–256.

Windsor, D. (2002a). "Public Affairs, Issues Management, and Political Strategy: Opportunities, Obstacles, and Caveats," *Journal of Public Affairs* 1 (4) and 2 (1): 382–415.

Windsor, D. (2002b). "Stakeholder Responsibilities: Lessons for Managers," *Journal of Corporate Citizenship* 6 (summer): 19–35.

Wood, D.J. (1991). "Corporate Social Performance Revisited," *Academy of Management Review* 16 (4): 691–718.

# 25

# Managing Business Political Advocacy in the United States

## Opportunities for Improved Effectiveness

GERRY KEIM

Political advocacy is a strategic move by which some businesses attempt to mitigate threats or create opportunities in their external environment. In this chapter political advocacy refers to efforts by businesses to advance their public policy interests by acting individually or in concert with other businesses or politically active groups. Political actions may be directed to state or federal policy makers in the legislative or executive branches of government. Some business advocacy efforts are also undertaken through the judicial branch, but space constraints will preclude consideration of those here. The perspective taken in this chapter will be of an advisory nature. What can be gleaned from existing research and practice to suggest how businesses can be more effective advocates for their public policy interests? Because institutional settings and structures affect the opportunities and processes of public policy advocacy, the focus of this chapter will be limited to public policy advocacy in the United States at the state and federal levels.

In the United States, unlike parliamentary systems, business interests are more likely to find some support in both major parties and

party members are not subject to strict party discipline. Presidents, governors, and party leaders in legislatures often find some members of their party voting against their policies when these members encounter strong advocacy efforts from groups in their constituencies. As a result, advocacy efforts are more issue-focused in the United States and center on trying to influence individual policy decisions made by government officials rather than trying to elect candidates from a particular party to office. While businesses engage in efforts to elect candidates who may be more sympathetic to business interests, the attention of this chapter will be limited to issue advocacy.

A rationale for business political advocacy from the perspective of an individual firm will be developed in the first section. Political advocacy is a competitive game; advocacy by one firm or a group of firms to influence a public policy decision will often be in response to, or will generate responses by, other groups—including other businesses—with different or opposing interests. In the second section three lenses for examining the nature of competition among politically active firms or groups will be discussed. These lenses will view public policy issues by examining the evolution of the issue, the distribution of the costs and benefits of the issue, and the breadth of interest the issue attracts. These different views will offer information about the likely nature of competition surrounding a specific issue.

In the third section, opportunities will be explicated for issue advocates such as firms and other groups in the process by which public policy decisions are made. This section will focus on linking the interests of legislators and regulators with those of issue advocates. The process of issue advocacy will be unpacked into three discrete and sequential phases—gaining access to policy makers, providing useful information to policy makers, and successfully influencing policy makers. Effective participation in the first two phases, gaining access and supplying valuable information to decision makers, is necessary but not sufficient for a firm or other advocacy group to reach the third phase which is influence over the decision on the policy of interest. This point will be expanded and related to efforts to measure the effectiveness of government relations activities in business firms.

In section four, feedback gathered from focus groups of employees discussing their experiences with advocacy efforts from a variety of industries will be discussed. Numerous opportunities to improve business advocacy efforts based on employee feedback will be identified and examined. Broadening the interest in advocacy among all managers can be accomplished through interactive educational sessions and managers can then more effectively generate interest among their colleagues and subordinates. The Internet will also be examined as a means to facilitate business political advocacy. The last section will offer suggestions for beginning advocacy efforts in companies that have not previously participated in the public policy process.

## RATIONALE FOR BUSINESS POLITICAL ADVOCACY

An essential part of business strategy is continuous assessment of threats and opportunities evolving in the external environment of the firm. Public policy decisions can affect current business operations as well as future opportunities. Public policy decisions may range from enforcement of environmental regulations that impact utility companies' operations, trade policies that protect domestic steel producers, new rules for health care providers, details of defense or domestic security policies that expand demand for suppliers of weapons or security systems, to rules enabling telephone customers to keep their phone numbers when switching to a service provided by rival carriers.

Businesses choose different postures regarding political advocacy (Keim, 1981; Weidenbaum, 1980). Many firms simply react when public policy decisions are made. Other firms may engage in monitoring efforts to predict what changes in existing public policies or origination of new policies are likely to occur and when this might happen. A third posture that some firms undertake is direct participation in the process by which public policy decisions are made as advocates for their particular business interests.

The first posture requires no expenditure of resources for advocacy efforts but can entail relatively large adjustment costs as firms may be forced to respond to new and unanticipated policy decisions by changing operations or revising future plans. The second posture entails some expenditure of firm resources for monitoring the public policy process at the state or federal (or both) levels but information gleaned from monitoring may enable firms to anticipate changes in public policy and make operational or planning responses over time which may be less costly than would be the case for responses to unanticipated policy decisions. The third posture requires resources to be used for monitoring and advocacy efforts to participate in public policy processes when pertinent issues are being decided. Firms doing this will gain the benefits of monitoring and sometimes may be able to shape public policy decisions in their interests, thereby directly reducing threats or gaining or enhancing opportunities that would otherwise arise from public policy decisions. Thus this third posture entails the greatest costs in terms of resources used but also may result in the greatest benefits for businesses that are successful political advocates.

## ASSESSING POLITICAL COMPETITION

Political advocacy to affect public policy decisions is a competitive endeavor (Keim and Baysinger, 1988). There are few public policy decisions that enjoy unanimous support from all constituents at any level of government. Among democracies, the United States is a particularly plural system with major political parties that are often not able to enforce discipline to ensure that all Democrats in the House of Representatives for example, or all Republicans in the Senate, support their party's position on a particular policy question. Members of the same party find it difficult to support common positions when their constituents back home have different interests from state to state or across legislative districts on the same public policy. As will be shown later, this is especially problematic for legislators when constituents active on a particular public policy issue are members of organized interest groups. Any business that engages in political advocacy is likely to encounter other groups of constituents who will be active on the same issue. Some of these groups of voters may be allies and some may be adversaries.

Most public policy issues involve multiple facets or provisions related to a central or overarching policy such as various provisions of clean air legislation. Expanding or reducing the set of allies or adversaries on most public policy issues is often a function of the willingness to compromise on specific facets or aspects of the policy in question. Making compromises on a provision to deal with pollution related to particulate matter may gain allies for a provision pertaining to carbon dioxide emissions, for example. Advocates that seek others with common positions on some aspects of the issue and who are willing to comprise on some areas of disagreement may be able to expand their coalition of allies.

The nature of competition including the number and types of competitors as well as the set of actions available to advocates will differ across issues. Several different perspectives for viewing public policy issues may help clarify differences in the nature of competition surrounding a particular issue.

Opportunities for issue advocacy change as the level of interest in a public issue by the media, organized voters, legislators, and regulators changes over time (Keim, 2001, 2002). The notion of an issue life cycle implies that different players may be interested in an issue at different times if there is an evolving interest in an issue (Baron, 1995). See Figure 25.1 for a graphical illustration of an issue life cycle.

As an example of an issue life cycle, consider a stylized review of the movement to create a single federal agency with responsibility for environmental pollution in the United States. The publication of the book *Silent Spring* written by former US Forest Service biologist and talented writer Rachel Carson in 1962, is often described as the single galvanizing event that ignited the firestorm of interest in environmental issues across the United States. The publication of this carefully detailed and clearly written warning of the dangers of using the natural environment as a dump for industrial waste was met with tremendous sales and interest among the reading public. The media took note and reporters publicized Carson's work with what today would be described as "earned media" coverage. Organized groups also took note. The Sierra Club, for example, founded in 1882 with members interested in exploring wilderness areas had grown to 16,000 members by 1960. As the Sierra Club expanded its agenda in the decade of the 1960s to include protecting air, water, and land from pollution its membership skyrocketed to 114,000 by 1970. Other conservation groups like the National Wildlife Federation also expanded their set of issues to include pollution at the same time and saw rapid increases in membership. This early part of the issue life cycle is usually characterized by existing interest groups adding the new issue to their agenda and thereby increasing their membership growth. Organized groups are usually skilled at attracting additional media attention to their issues in what is often an iterative process where

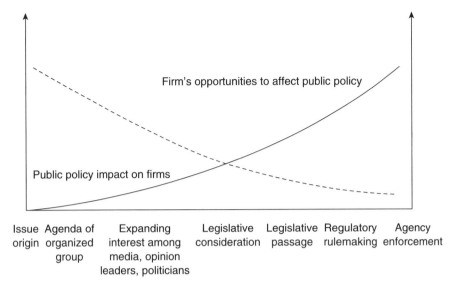

Figure 25.1   *Life cycle of an Issue.* Source *Baron (2000)*

increased media coverage leads to growing interest by more citizens and encourages groups to speak out even more on the issue. Today this is described by business and government researchers as an "information cascade" (Bonardi and Keim, forthcoming).

Intensive media coverage of an issue supported by organized groups may encourage some elected officials to add the issue to their political agenda. This is particularly likely when such groups have active members among the elected official's constituents and if there is little in the way of organized resistance among the legislator's constituents to the issue position being advocated. If significant numbers of legislators become interested in an issue, new legislative proposals are likely to be forthcoming. If new legislation is passed, new regulations may be promulgated by a regulatory agency to deal with the issue. The impact of such an issue on a firm increases as the issue moves through the issue life cycle as shown in Figure 25.1. The underlying logic is that, as the probability increases that the issue will lead to a new policy, firms will respond by incorporating the expected change of policy in their operating and planning decisions. The left-hand vertical axis in Figure 25.1 represents the increasing impact of the issue on affected firms.

Opportunities for advocacy by firms and other interested groups exist over the entire range of the issue life cycle. Many business firms, however, choose to participate only in the final stages of the life cycle by waiting until the issue attracts enough interest to result in new legislative proposals being considered before engaging in advocacy efforts to influence legislators' decisions. Advocacy efforts earlier in the issue life cycle may speed the process along if a business favors new legislation or may slow or prevent new legislation from being seriously considered if a business is against changing the *status quo*. If a business opposes a change in the *status quo*, advocacy earlier rather than later may encourage legislators not to support the issue in order to avoid antagonizing well organized constituents. Elected officials usually prefer to avoid issues that may divide their organized constituents. Members of organized groups are more likely to vote than those not part of a politically active group, and with generally declining voter participation in the United States those who *are* likely to vote become increasingly important to candidates.

Another useful way to assess the nature of competition likely to surround an issue is to examine the distribution of benefits and costs associated with the particular issue. Trade protection for a domestic industry offers a convenient example. Protecting domestic textile manufacturers from foreign competition may mean huge benefits that are concentrated on a few manufacturing firms often located in the same geographic region. The costs of such protection mean slightly higher prices for all consumers of the textile products. Millions of dollars of additional revenue concentrated among a few firms create a very strong incentive for them to be advocates for protection. Small price increases for consumers, who are not well organized and may not associate the price increases with the trade protection, create little if any incentive for the consumers to be advocates for freer trade. The lesson here is that large benefits (or costs) that are concentrated among a few well organized recipients will create strong incentives for aggressive political advocacy while widely distributed costs (or benefits) that are small in magnitude for each actor create far weaker incentives for political advocacy especially if those bearing the widely distributed costs (or benefits) are not members of an existing politically active organization.

A third perspective for assessing the nature of political competition likely to surround a particular public policy issue is to examine how widespread the appeal of the issue to the electorate is and how intense is the interest of those who care about the issue in question. Voters are able to signal their preferences for or against policy decisions at least indirectly during elections. Yet in congressional elections over the past several decades in the United States only a few issues rise to the level of interest to be considered election issues—issues that are widely salient to a significant percentage of those who actually vote. To understand the implication of this observation, consider that members of the House and Senate made in excess of 1,000 recorded votes in the 105th (1996–1998), 106th (1998–2000) and 107th Congress (2000–2002). Most of the voting decisions made by legislators did not rise to the level of salience to attract widespread voter attention. This important distinction often is not fully appreciated. Most decisions made by

legislators, and by regulators as well, are not monitored by or even observed by large segments of the electorate. Some polling data indicate that only one-third of those of voting age know the name of their member in the House of Representatives (Morin, 1996), thus it is very unlikely that many unorganized voters know much about the actual records of legislators on many of the policy votes they make. Organized interests, however, do monitor and often advocate policy positions on issues that are important to their members and they provide information to their members on the policy positions and voting records of legislators on key issues.

Successfully advocating an issue position that is contrary to the position favored by a wide segment of voters is more difficult than advocating a position on an issue that is not salient for a segment of voters (Bonardi and Keim, forthcoming; Hillman and Hitt, 1999; Keim and Zeithaml, 1986). Much of the advocacy competition in Congress and with regulatory agencies is therefore on issues where the electorate is largely ignorant and the opposition is limited to other organized groups and perhaps a small number of citizens who are unusually well informed but not likely to be organized for political action.

## ISSUE ADVOCACY AND POLITICAL EXCHANGE

The process by which public policy decisions are made can be viewed as political exchange between those who seek or demand particular policy outcomes and those who can supply them in their roles as legislators and regulators (Bonardi et al., forthcoming; Hillman and Keim, 1995). The notion of a public policy market is a useful metaphor to examine some dynamics of the give and take in the exchange process that often determines public policy outcomes. The discussion above recognizes some implications of competition on the demand side of the public policy market as various organized interest groups compete among themselves and/or with segments of the unorganized electorate in advocacy efforts to influence policy suppliers in congress, state legislatures, or government agencies. Successful advocacy also will require an understanding of the interest and constraints of relevant public policy suppliers if political exchanges are to be consummated. Knowing what other players want is an essential part of successful competition in the public policy market.

Consider the interests of elected officials. Elected officials generally seek re-election as a primary goal. This observation tends to be true for elected officials regardless of their motivation to run for office. From those who lust for the power of elected office at one extreme of the motivational spectrum to those who seek election to make the world a better place for their fellow citizens, getting re-elected is necessary in order to have the best opportunity to affect policy. Issue advocates often seek to assist re-election campaigns by providing financial support, favorable endorsements, and workers at the grassroots level to staff phone banks and distribute campaign signs and literature for candidates. At the state level, however, eighteen states have laws limiting the number of terms legislators can serve and thus re-election, at least to the same office, cannot be a goal of legislators in these states during their final term. Those seeking to influence state legislators serving in their final term in these states may find that advocacy is more difficult as it is no longer so easy to appeal to legislators' need for re-election resources and support.

In addition to re-election, legislators also bring personal values to their roles as policy makers. For example, some legislators will have strong views about protecting agricultural interests from the vagaries of market forces. Some legislators will be dedicated to fight against tax increases, while others may champion women's rights with regard to abortion, or seek to protect the natural environment from pollution. Often, but not always, these individual values will reflect the most salient values of the likely voters in the legislative district or state from which the legislator is elected. These values of individual legislators should be recognized and understood as firms think about where to direct their advocacy efforts.

A third important factor affecting legislators in their role as policy suppliers is individual legislators' concern for their party's agenda and particularly a legislator's ambitions regarding party leadership positions. For those seeking committee chairs or other leadership positions, it will be necessary to support some party policy positions that are at odds with strong advocacy efforts by firms or groups. Predicting legislators' likely policy positions is important intelligence for advocacy planning.

Re-election goals, personal values, and party considerations are all factors that may affect legislators' stand on issues. Accurately determining which legislators can be influenced and which hold steadfast positions will enable advocacy resources to be used most effectively.

When important public policies relevant to a particular business fall within the jurisdiction of "suppliers" who are regulators or other decision makers in executive branch agencies, it is important to assess their interests and constraints as well. Political appointees in government agencies serve either at the pleasure of the President, or Governor of the state, or for a fixed term of office. These individuals usually are in office for shorter time periods than are career civil servants and thus have shorter time horizons for affecting public policies. Their policy interests are related to the interests of the leader of the executive branch of government (Governor or President) who appointed them. While regulators and agency officials may not be as responsive to advocacy efforts as elected officials, they are concerned with how legislators, well organized groups and also voters view their activities. Agency prestige, budgets, and expansion or contraction of jurisdiction or mission are all subject to political influence. All agencies carry out policies that are created and modified by legislation and have their budgets approved by legislators and usually are subject to legislative oversight. These linkages provide strong if indirect connections between agency officials and politically active groups and individuals who seek to influence legislators and affect legislative policies.

The interaction of those seeking or demanding public policy decisions with those legislators or agency decision makers who are able to supply public policy can be described as "trading" or "exchange" in the public policy market. It is important to recognize that for any public policy issue there may be only a few suppliers. Suppliers are limited to those who sit on subcommittees in the legislature with jurisdiction over the issue of concern and those who make decisions in the agency with jurisdiction to implement or enforce policies and rules pertaining to the issue.

On the demand side there may be many groups and individuals with many different positions on the issue in question. As a result there is often more competition among those advocating positions on an issue than among those who can supply policy decisions on the issue (Keim and Zardkoohi, 1988). Intense competition among rival groups seeking to influence legislators often leads to a reluctance on the part of suppliers to make policy decisions if a decision will antagonize well organized constituents who may vote against them in the next election. Bank deregulation was stalled in Congress for almost two decades, for example. Issues where organized groups are able to form a coalition supporting a single position and encounter little opposition from organized opponents, as in the case of an issue with concentrated benefits and widely diffused costs such as trade protection for agricultural products, offer better opportunities for advocacy success.

Effective advocacy first requires access to relevant public policy decision makers or suppliers. Business leaders and their designated staff who invest in building personal relationships with legislators and their staff members as well as with those working in the appropriate government agencies will enjoy better access than those who do not make such investments of time and effort. Building relationships before they are needed is especially recommended. Access can be enhanced by using contract lobbyists who already have access due to previous offices held by the lobbyists or previous lobbying work with the legislators, staffers, or agency officials.

With access, businesses can provide valuable information to legislators about the economic consequences of employment and investment in the home district or state and alert legislators to important public policy issues that affect such business activity. Businesses can also provide financial and other resources that help defray election expenses and build up reserves for the next campaign. On the regulatory or agency side, businesses can provide valuable input during rule-making sessions and in other ways to inform policy making and enforcement in agencies.

The information that can be provided by businesses as advocates can be divided into two broad categories. One category is technical information about how particular public policies affect their business and the broader constituency. Businesses often have expertise in assessing costs and benefits of existing or proposed rules or policies. There are always unintended consequences of policy creation or change. By supplying information about likely effects, businesses advocates can help ensure that their concerns will be considered by policy makers. Businesses that are able to inform their employees and other constituents like suppliers, dealers, and customers about the impact of public policy decisions can also provide valuable information about the political interest in their issue or what is often called the "salience" of the issue to constituents. Legislators and their staffers and agency decision makers are usually interested in both types of information— technical information and the level of political interest in the issue. Advocates that can provide both types of information will be more effective than those that can provide only one type.

Effective advocacy, then, requires access to decision makers in the legislature and in the executive branch agencies and the ability to deliver technical and political information about the issues of most concern to the advocates. But having access and supplying both technical and political information does not ensure influence on policy decisions. Access and information provision are *necessary* but *not sufficient* capabilities.

Some of the key variables that affect decisions by public policy suppliers are beyond the control of business or other advocates. Personal values of decision makers as discussed above as well as considerations that pertain to the interests and the agenda of the political party may override the efforts of particular advocates on any issue. Likewise the efforts of opposing advocates may more than offset the efforts of a particular advocate or coalition of advocates. These factors are usually beyond the control of any advocacy group but they verify that the public policy market is often very competitive and the suppliers are affected by many factors as they make public policy decisions.

This last point bears directly on business efforts to evaluate their own advocacy endeavors (Fleisher, 1997). As described above, advocacy is a three-phase process—access, information provision, and influence. Businesses have direct control over their ability to execute the first two phases and these are necessary steps for effective advocacy. Businesses often have far less control over the third phase, as factors beyond their control come into play when policy decisions are made. Thus attempts to measure the costs and benefits of advocacy efforts by comparing the costs of resources expended with the results of targeted policy decisions may be bogus exercises.

Some management consultants beginning in the mid-1990s began recommending that businesses abandon their government relations efforts if they could not show direct impact on firm profitability. As discussed above, it is very difficult to construct valid measures directly linking advocacy efforts to the firm's bottom line because the outcome of the third phase of advocacy—the influence phase—is subject to numerous factors over which firms cannot exercise control. As a result of pressure for increased accountability of government relations activities, some firms began claiming that their advocacy efforts were the decisive factor when public policy decisions they were advocating were decided in their favor. Unless the advocates had no opposition in the public policy market, however, and public policy suppliers had no other constraints like party considerations, personal values, or other factors that may have influenced their decision, such claims of victory in the advocacy process are also likely to be bogus.

Firms can, as an alternative, utilize a second best approach to evaluating their advocacy efforts. It is possible to measure the costs associated with advocacy efforts to gain access and provide technical and political information to relevant public policy decision makers—that is, to implement the first two phases of advocacy. Efforts to improve access and supply more valuable information while lowering the costs of doing so are consistent with more efficient advocacy efforts. It is true that these measures will be input measures, not output measures, but managers sometimes must make decisions to pursue actions even when the perfect measures of costs and benefits are not available.

Choosing not to conduct government relations activities and not to participate in advocacy efforts enhances the opportunities for opponents of business to influence public policy suppliers on issues that will affect current business operations and future opportunities. Choosing not to compete in the public policy market may be even more costly than engaging in advocacy even if one loses in the competition to influence a particular policy decision. Interaction in the public policy market is ongoing and decisions by policy suppliers as well as other participants on the advocacy or demand side are likely to be influenced by moves in earlier rounds of competition. Some advocacy efforts will be more effective as a result of learning from previous experience. Some policy suppliers may be impressed by efforts made in losing advocacy efforts and therefore be more responsive in the next iteration of policy making. This makes assigning the costs and benefits of individual advocacy efforts even more difficult and less appropriate.

For businesses that decide it is too costly to engage in some advocacy efforts simply because measurement of effectiveness is difficult, there are tremendous opportunities to improve these first two phases of the advocacy process. Better access to policy makers and enhanced capabilities to supply information, particularly information about political interest among constituents in issues of concern to business firms, can be accomplished by learning from the people most affected by the success or failure of advocacy efforts—employees. Opportunities for improved advocacy will be discussed in the next section.

## MODERN MANAGEMENT AND IMPROVED BUSINESS ADVOCACY: VIEWS FROM THE FIELD

Modern management is based on a simple observation: employees have valuable information that can improve almost every business activity that requires employee support and participation. Well managed businesses gather and utilize information possessed by employees to improve their operations. Sometimes simply understanding how employees view a new initiative can vastly improve the implementation process of that initiative. Consider the example of companies implementing value-based management (VBM) like the use of Stern Stewart's Economic Value Added (EVA) as a control and reward system in the 1990s. Some firms were far more successful in terms of growth in shareholder value because they involved their employees in information exchanges and training programs to answer questions and explain how VBM systems worked and what it meant for employees (Haspeslagh *et al.*, 2001). Companies that simply hired consultants to design the VBM program and then imposed the new system of compensation on their employees were far less successful and some like AT&T even abandoned the program after several years of no results, significant costs, and widespread employee dissatisfaction.

Although corporate advocacy programs depend on employee acceptance and participation in political action committees (PACs) and efforts to provide grassroots feedback, few companies use modern management to develop these initiatives. Instead most PAC and grassroots programs are designed and implemented with little employee discussion, feedback, or education. Rather than inducing employees to participate, most companies try to direct employee participation in these efforts. There is a better way.

This author has been involved in bottom-up efforts to induce interest in business advocacy and has conducted more than fifty formal and informal focus groups and discussions with employees from a wide cross-section of industries over the past four years. The results make it clear that companies can induce interest in business advocacy efforts such as PACs and grassroots programs by listening to their employees and designing education efforts to answer questions, gather input, and build "buy in" among employees in these programs.

Employee populations usually represent the broader electorate in terms of party affiliation and self-described political ideology. Across the United States as a whole this means that in addition to many employees with Republican affiliations or leanings, many other employees will consider themselves Democrats and there will also be a sizable group of independents. Even employees from different parties and with different ideological lenses often will see common ground when discussing issues that affect job growth and business opportunities for their firm. Likewise, many employees with different party labels will see threats to their employer in a similar light. Many employees, however, may not be aware of how important public policy decisions are for existing firm operations or future opportunities. This is the first topic that must be discussed with employees and often educational efforts are needed to acquaint employees with some knowledge of how dependent their company is on existing or proposed public policy decisions.

Every employee in a pharmaceutical company or health care provider, for example, should be educated about key policies that affect opportunities for the company in the initial employee orientation. In addition to providing a conceptual base for advocacy, such educational efforts will also have positive team-building benefits as employees learn together about issues that affect *their* company. Learning how dependent a fossil fuel-based utility company is on current and future energy and environmental policies, for example, is only the first step. Employees must also learn that public policy decisions by legislators and agency officials on these issues of concern to their company are often influenced by well organized groups with interests that are very different from those of the employees. In addition to appreciating how dependent their company is on decisions made by public policy suppliers, employees must also learn how the public policy market works.

This author has extensive experience with company education efforts that inform employees about the importance of specific public policy issues to the continued success of their firm and show how other groups with opposing interests are actively seeking to influence policy suppliers on these issues. These educational sessions, when they are based on facts and logic, and not on hype and exaggeration, can have very positive effects on employees' interest in issue advocacy. Hands are raised in these sessions and employees begin to ask, "What can we do to be sure that our voices are heard when important public policy decisions are made?" When this happens employee interest is being induced. This opens the door to discussions about gaining access and supplying important information to policy makers. Advocacy initiatives based on these discussions are then at least partly owned by the employees participating.

In the course of these discussions with employees, steps to gain access to more elected officials can be examined. In the US political system, polling data consistently indicate little support for public financing of legislative elections. Similarly, most Americans do not want personal wealth to be a prerequisite for seeking elected office. After discussing these observations with employees it is easy to evolve this discussion to the role campaign contributions have in helping candidates gain the needed resources to mount serious campaigns. Providing information about the amount of money that must be raised by candidates enables employees to see why elected officials focus so much attention on fund raising. As an example, this author likes to point out that, at the federal level, candidates in races for a seat in the House of Representatives must raise $10,000 every week of the year in order to compete in the *cheapest* district races and many candidates running in House districts where media advertising is more expensive must raise several times that amount every week. The next step is to encourage employees to put themselves in the position of a legislator having to raise $10,000 or $20,000 every week and ask how many people they could afford to schedule appointments with who had not

helped them with a campaign contribution. The process of making campaign contributions in order to gain access to present information to legislators and their staffers is better understood and accepted by far greater numbers of employees when discussions like these take place.

Political education efforts with employees should also discuss the nearly even balance both political parties in the United States have in terms of appeal to voters as well as the frequent occurrence of coalitions that are formed across party lines in voting in legislatures on numerous issues. The message should be that access to members of *both* parties in legislatures is important over the long run if firms are to maximize opportunities for effective advocacy on their issues. At the federal level for example, only a few votes separate the majority and minority parties in the House and the Senate and that has been the case for the last several Congresses. Thus having access to members from both parties, which often means making campaign contributions to members of both parties, is an essential part of effective advocacy.

Employee political discussions and education efforts also must consider the competitive nature of issue advocacy. As noted earlier, highlighting the efforts of groups with opposing interests is a means to energize employee interest in issue advocacy. Extending the discussion so that employees realize that their company's access efforts will often be matched by other groups' similar efforts provides a connection to discussion of the second phase of advocacy—information provision. In the United States there is broad agreement that feedback on issues from constituents is a powerful force to which legislators in particular will pay attention (Keim, 1985; Keim and Zeithaml, 1986; Lord, 2000, 2003). Grassroots feedback provides a measure of the salience of the issue among constituent groups. Constituents who provide feedback to legislators are signaling that they are interested in and have some information about the issue. More informed constituents are, other things equal, more likely to vote (Lipset, 1981). This logic provides the link between grassroots feedback and probable impact on legislative decision making for employees. Much more needs to be done, however, to encourage employee participation in grassroots feedback efforts to "calls to action," as they are often know in the advocacy jargon.

To stimulate grassroots feedback, many businesses provide employees with information on the company position on an important issue when a policy decision is imminent and encourage employees to send their endorsement of the company position to the legislator by e-mail, letter, telegram, or phone call. Information about how to access the legislator representing the employee's district or state is included in the information describing the company's position on the issue. Information gleaned from every focus group conducted in recent years by the author reveals a serious flaw in this approach. Employees want to hear multiple positions—arguments pro and con—on the issues so they can decide which position is "correct" from their point of view. Very few companies provide multiple perspectives on issues for which they are attempting to generate employee feedback to legislators. As a result employees have at least two negative reactions to such efforts. One is that they believe their company is telling them only part of the story and this negatively affects the perceived credibility of the company in the eyes of the employees. All future grassroots efforts involve the distribution of information about relevant public policies, and source credibility is an essential factor. The second negative reaction discovered in the employee focus groups is more subtle. Employees perceive that a one-sided discussion of an issue by their company implies that employees are not expected to consider the issue but only to respond as the company directs them. In company-sponsored discussions and educational sessions many employees seem eager to think about public policy issues that affect their company but few want to be told *what* to think.

This does not mean that indicating the company position on an issue is not appropriate or desired by employees. On the contrary, most employees indicated that hearing the company's position was useful but they wanted the opportunity to compare it with the position of others—particularly adversaries. They wanted to "hear both sides and make up their own mind" as they described it in the focus groups. Links to opponents' Web sites make this very easy to do in the wired world.

This second negative reaction among employees to the common form of corporate grassroots "calls to action" is more significant than simply being an offensive action that deters support for future grassroots advocacy efforts. It represents a missed opportunity to gain valuable information that could enhance the efficiency of business advocacy efforts. Business advocacy programs, like all business activities, have limited resources and many competing uses for those resources. It is prudent to rank current and potential public policy issues along two dimensions (see Figure 25.2). Likely impact on the company is one dimension and probability to affect the outcome of the issue is the other. Employee feedback can be a very important source of information to help assess the probability of affecting the outcome of the issue. If employees, after hearing multiple points of view about an issue, do not coalesce around a common position that is supported by their company it is unlikely that the company's advocacy effort will build support among many other constituents outside the company. Thus an issue like B in Figure 25.2 may have significant impact on the company but may be an issue where the probability to influence the policy suppliers' decision is relatively low. This is an issue that may warrant close monitoring so firm plans and reaction can be altered as a decision becomes more likely but it is probably not an issue where resources should be spent on advocacy efforts—at least not grassroots advocacy efforts.

Company executives miss this important source of information when they design and operate their companies' advocacy efforts from the top down rather than from the bottom up. A related issue is the misperception by some executives that employees and executives are likely to "see issues the same way" if only the employees were as informed as their top management. Again, the focus groups provided many views to the contrary. Employees often have different mental software for processing

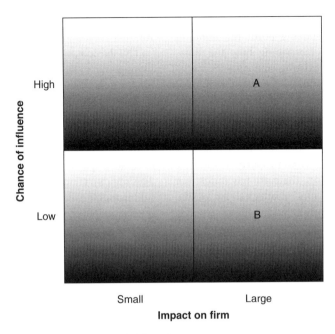

Figure 25.2    *Impact on Company versus Probability of Outcome*

information about public policy issues. Gathering information about where there may be agreement and disagreement on germane public policy issues can improve employee-based advocacy efforts significantly.

Two additional lessons can be learned from listening to employees and both are easy to incorporate in more effective advocacy programs. First, employees tend to think locally about public policy issues. It is therefore important to develop implications locally for issues that may be decided at the federal level. Having a local coordinator of advocacy efforts who can discuss local implications for the employees in Huntsville, Alabama, for example, of an issue being marked up in a committee in the US House of Representatives will be more effective than messages that suggest this Bill is bad for the company as whole. An additional implication is that, without local impact, it is more difficult to interest employees in issue advocacy.

The other lesson is to remember that employees have different ideological lenses and wear different partisan badges. Advocacy efforts that are tinged with partisan baggage, say explicit positive references to the Republican Party, will alienate many of those employees who do not

consider themselves Republicans. The common ground that can be established with employees from diverse political backgrounds is that most will be concerned about issues that threaten or enhance job growth and related opportunities for their employer.

## ACTIONS STEPS: IMPROVING OR BEGINNING EFFECTIVE ADVOCACY PROGRAMS

Employee buy-in is an essential component of effective business advocacy. Informed and concerned constituents provide the local driving force in many public policy decisions. While firms may be able to enlist the support of suppliers, customers and shareholders (Baysinger *et al.*, 1985), employees form the foundation of most effective business advocacy efforts in the United States. Employees will "buy in" to business advocacy efforts when they perceive the issue and the effort are important to them. If firms choose to compete in the public policy arena they must appeal to the best interests of their employees to join in such endeavors.

Discussions with, and education for, employees is the starting point for building employee interest. Describing how the business depends on existing and future public policy decisions should be part of employee orientation programs in all firms where public policy decisions have significant impact on current operations or future opportunities. From taxes to trade laws, product liability to privacy issues, intellectual property to Internet regulation, and so on, there are few industries that are not profoundly affected by public policy decisions. Many firms do little to acquaint their employees with the importance of public policy decisions to the success of the firm. Doing so is the first step in enlisting employee self-interest in the cause of business advocacy.

These educational discussions should address two important topics. First, they should describe how public policy decisions affect the business the employees are working in. Second, they should describe the processes by which public policy decisions are made to illustrate that many policy issues are decided with little input or attention from the general public. The US Congress provides an excellent example. When over a thousand recorded votes are made in a two-year period, many of these will never be subjected to scrutiny by the unorganized voters during elections. The logical conclusion, then, is that many decisions are made in response to the smaller numbers of voters, usually organized voters, who do scrutinize and express opinions about such issues.

Any firm can be part of this process, but if they are not, the decisions that affect firms will still be made. Policy decisions that affect their business will be made without their input but with the input of others whose interests are often quite different. This is a powerful point and employees quickly see the importance of having a seat at the table when decisions that affect their jobs are being made. There are many narrow business issues with sharply focused costs or benefits on which only a small number of constituents are active. A small number of constituents may be all that is necessary to influence a legislator's decision if many other constituents are not involved in the issue. Employees must know that they have

a chance to make a difference if their support for advocacy is to be induced.

This basic education and discussion should be ongoing so that all employees are reminded on a regular basis of the importance of public policy decisions to their business. If being informed and involved in the firm's advocacy efforts is important to senior managers, and they acknowledge this regularly, it will soon become important to most of the employees. This builds a conceptual foundation for successful business advocacy. Note that this is not built on any appeal to civic duty but on self-interest. Civic duty is a wonderful attribute but individual self-interest is in more abundant supply and is usually a more powerful motivator.

The next step is dissemination of important public policy information about issues that can affect the company. This is easy to do with Web sites that offer brief overviews—one-pagers, as they are known in politics—as well as more detailed discussions for those who want to read more. Links to opponents' Web sites or other sources of information on other points of view on the issues at hand should be included to ensure a balanced coverage of issues. These internal web sites are also very useful as sources of information for legislators, regulators, and staffers and should be available in some form to them as well. Whenever possible, discussions with employees online or in person should measure the sentiment or position of employees on emerging issues of importance to the company.

These steps will lead to the development of an employee constituency that understands the importance of business advocacy on issues pertinent to their firm and will enable employees to be informed about the details of important policy issues, including the positions of their legislators regarding these issues. This is a powerful resource that can be used to support business advocacy.

Consider a stylized scenario for utilizing an engaged and informed employee constituency to begin the advocacy process with a member of the House of Representatives. House members usually divide their districts into two or three regions with at least one staff member responsible for constituent relations in each region.

These regional staffers are like customer service representatives and are looking for problems facing constituents that the member can help solve and thereby curry favor and build name recognition with constituents. After a firm has held the discussions and educational sessions mentioned above to create an informed employee constituency, the district staff person of the House member representing the firm should be invited to the facility for a visit. After a tour and an opportunity to learn the nature of the business, lunch in a meeting room with as many employees as possible to discuss important public policy issues will provide valuable information that district staffers of legislators are seeking. The staffer will learn how many constituents are working in the company and, even more importantly, will observe how informed these constituent employees are about the issues that affect their company and how much they know about what the legislature or various government agencies are doing or not doing with regard to their issues. This information will be conveyed to the Washington office of the Member of Congress and this company and its employees are likely to be identified as politically active constituents—*read* probable voters and therefore important political customers. Future visits to the district by the legislator are likely to include plant visits to meet with these constituents and hear their concerns first-hand. The legislator and staff will correctly surmise that these constituents can be expected to vote in the next election and thus they will seek to get their votes. This is the core of the relationship between effective advocates and politicians.

Before concluding, a popular *non sequitur* should be addressed. Some observers of the US political system note the incumbents' advantage in legislative races and conclude that because incumbents are more likely to win than challengers, they will therefore be unresponsive to advocacy efforts by voters back home, especially newly organized or energized groups. Good politicians like business managers make decisions on the margin. Incumbents that ignore newly organized constituents in their district are likely to see their margin of victory shrink as those constituents vote for the challenger. Like a manager losing market share,

a successful politician in the post-election analysis will determine where the lost votes went and seek to attract those voters to his or her camp for the next election. Winning with larger percentages is not just ego-boosting, it reduces the chance for loss in the future, and increases the prestige and stature within the party. Thus even incumbents likely to be re-elected are usually responsive to the interests of well organized constituents back home. As public policy suppliers they will be responsive to the interests of good customers in their markets.

In closing, a few observations developed in another paper should be emphasized (Keim, 2002). Because the public policy market is competitive, especially on the demand side, attempting to organize business advocacy efforts in the same way that all other advocates operate is not likely to be a winning strategy. Most advocates have PACs and make contributions and most have in-house and hired lobbyists working at the state and federal levels (Schuler *et al.*, 2002). These activities are like table stakes in a poker game, they are necessary to play but not sufficient to win. What passes for "best practice" in business advocacy is seldom based on serious research, and most data are gathered from surveys of existing practitioners. The basic strategic business goal of seeking competitive advantage by creating value using practices that are difficult for competitors to copy or imitate is seldom discussed in the practice of business advocacy.

Yet, as the information gleaned from focus groups of employees makes clear, there are substantial opportunities to improve existing advocacy efforts by building from the bottom up, as many successful companies do when dealing with operating or production issues. Consider PAC support as an opportunity, for example. A few companies have a majority of their eligible employees supporting the company PAC but most companies do not. Companies with PAC support of less than a quarter of the eligible employees have little information about why employees don't support their PAC. On the grassroots side, surveys by the Public Affairs Council reveal that more and more government relations activities are being contracted out (Hoewing, 2000). This may lower costs but it eliminates opportunities for competitive advantage. Using external consultants increases the likelihood that each firm will be employing the same practices. Grassroots feedback in many firms is based on efforts to get employees and other constituents to send e-mail to legislators but this is what many other advocates are doing and the legislative offices are thus overwhelmed with e-mail, reducing the importance of any one group's efforts. On the other hand, a well informed employee constituency developed as outlined above does not need to participate in the avalanche of e-mails when issues are being decided in legislative committees. Their interests and strengths are well known to their legislators long before committee hearings are held. Lobbyists for such well organized groups need only remind legislators and staffers of the previous on-site meetings where these views were expressed and discussed. These on-site personal meetings also convey the passion and intensity of constituent feeling that e-mails can never capture or convey.

Up-side opportunities in business advocacy abound for creative managers who are willing to involve employees in the process of learning how to build interest in company advocacy efforts. Furthermore, past and existing company culture and experiences are likely to have a significant impact on the attitudes and views of employees, and cultural attributes and experiences are idiosyncratic to individual companies. What works in one company may not work in another. Each company must discover what practices and procedures will be most effective with its employees. Becoming a learning organization involves much more than copying best practices. But, it is not easy, and learning how to improve advocacy efforts by involving employees opens the door to criticism of past efforts. As long as many firms are not likely to leave the safety of following the herd, there are opportunities for competitive advantage in the practice of business advocacy for those firms willing to involve their employees in building advocacy from the bottom up. Advocacy power comes from people who are informed and involved.

## REFERENCES

Baron, D. (1995). "Integrated Strategy: Market and Nonmarket Components," *California Management Review* 37 (2): 47–65.

Baron, D. (2000). *Business and its Environment.* New York: Prentice Hall.

Baysinger, B., G. Keim, and C. Zeithaml (1985). "An Empirical Evaluation of the Potential for Including Shareholders in Corporate Constituency Programs," *Academy of Management Journal* 28: 180–200.

Bonardi, J.P., and G. Keim (forthcoming). "Corporate Political Strategies for Widely Salient Issues," *Academy of Management Review.*

Bonardi, J.P., A. Hillman, and G. Keim (forthcoming). "The Attractiveness of Political Markets: Implications for Firm Strategy," *Academy of Management Review.*

Carson, R. (1962). *Silent Spring.* London: Readers' Union.

Fleisher, C.S. (1997). *Assessing, Managing and Maximizing Public Affairs Performance.* Washington, DC: Public Affairs Council.

Haspeslagh, P., T. Noda, and F. Boulos (2001). "Managing for Value: It's Not Just about the Numbers," *Harvard Business Review* 79 (7): 65–73.

Hillman, A., and M.A. Hitt (1999). "Corporate Political Strategy Formulation: A Model of Approach, Participation and Strategy Decisions," *Academy of Management Review* 24 (4): 825–842.

Hillman, A., and G. Keim (1995). "International Variation in the Business-Government Interface: Institutional and Organizational Considerations," *Academy of Management Review* 20 (1): 193–214.

Hoewing, R. (2000). *Corporate Public Affairs: The State of Corporate Public Affairs Survey.* Washington, DC: Foundation for Public Affairs.

Keim, G. (1981). "Foundations of a Political Strategy for Business," *California Management Review* 23 (4): 41–48.

Keim, G. (1985). "Corporate Grassroots Programs in the 1980s," *California Management Review* 28 (1): 110–123.

Keim, G. (2001). "Business and Public Policy: Competing in the Political Marketplace," in M. Hitt, R. Freeman, and J. Harrison (eds), *Handbook of Strategic Management.* Malden, MA: Blackwell.

Keim, G. (2002). "Managing Business Political Activities in the USA: Bridging between Theory and Practice," *Journal of Public Affairs* 2 (1): 362–375.

Keim, G., and B. Baysinger (1988). "The Efficacy of Business Political Activity: Competitive Considerations in a Principal-Agent Context," *Journal of Management* 14 (2): 163–180.

Keim, G., and A. Zardkoohi (1988). "Looking for Leverage in the PAC Market: Corporate and Labor Contributions Considered," *Public Choice* 58: 21–34.

Keim, G., and C. Zeithaml (1986). "Corporate Political Strategies and Legislative Decision Making: A Review and Contingency Approach," *Academy of Management Review* 11: 828–843.

Lipset, S. (1981). *Political Man: The Social Bases of Politics.* Baltimore, MD: Johns Hopkins University Press.

Lord, M. (2000). "Corporate Political Strategy and Legislative Decision Making: The Impact of Corporate Legislative Influence Activities," *Business and Society* 39 (March): 76–94.

Lord, M. (2003). "Constituency Building as the Foundation for Corporate Political Strategy," *Academy of Management Executive* 17 (1): 112–124.

Morin, R. (1996). "Who's in Control? Many Don't Know or Care, Knowledge Gap Affects Attitudes and Participation," *Washington Post,* January 29, pp. A1, A6, A7.

Schuler, D., C. Rehbein, and R. Cramer (2002). "Pursuing Strategic Advantage through Political Means: A Multivariate Approach," *Academy of Management Journal* 45 (4): 659–672.

Weidenbaum, M. (1980). "Public Policy: No Longer a Spectator Sport for Business," *Journal of Business Strategy* 3 (4): 46–53.

# 26

# Public Affairs and the Governance Challenge

*Policy Actors and Corporate Reforms, 2001–2004*

JOHN M. HOLCOMB

The corporate reform agenda of the period from 2001 to 2004 has been multifaceted. It has included most prominently the issues of investor rights and corporate governance reform. This chapter will examine the changes that have taken place in the functions of corporate boards and the roles played by shareholders since the corporate scandals that have occurred since 2001. The chapter will go beyond a legal analysis and instead focus on practical changes that have occurred. Regarding the changes in corporate boards of directors, it will examine the issues of board diligence and work load, the state of independence on the board, the separation of the positions of board chair and CEO, the pool of available board candidates, compensation of board members, the growing importance of the board's compensation committee, and the lingering issue of multiple board memberships. Regarding the roles played by shareholders, the chapter will focus on the upturn in shareholder activism generally, along with examples of key shareholder campaigns. The chapter will also discuss the debate during 2004 over shareholder nomination of directors,

as well as examine the evolution and growing importance of corporate governance rating services.

As this chapter unfolds, the various policy actors are discussed in the context of each of the major issues to be examined. Those key actors fall into the following categories: political interest groups and think tanks, business and professional groups, governance rating organizations, enforcement agencies, and self-regulatory organizations. Exhibit 26.1 presents a list of the key actors in the foregoing categories that are addressed in this chapter, within the framework of the major aspects of corporate governance to be explored. Though the US Congress and the presidency have also been occasional actors on corporate reform issues, chiefly in advancing the Sarbanes-Oxley Act (Sarbox) to passage, they are really peripheral players with regards to the purview of this chapter. Characteristic of the corporate governance issue, much of the action has occurred directly between actors, bypassing the government as an intermediary. That has been especially true of interactions between shareholder groups, corporate directors, and corporate managements.

After examining the dimensions of corporate governance, including the changing roles of both directors and shareholders, the chapter will conclude with two final sections on (1) analysis of groups and actors and (2) the impact on corporate public affairs strategies. The analysis of the various groups focuses on the characteristics, strengths, and weaknesses of the actors, including both the governance reform advocates and the business sector. The final section of the chapter examines the impact of that analysis on corporate public affairs strategies and its implications for public affairs professionals in various fields, most critically those in government relations, issues management, community relations, and corporate responsibility.

---

### Exhibit 26.1 Key Actors in the US Corporate Reform Agenda, 2001–2004

POLITICAL INTEREST GROUPS AND THINK TANKS

The Corporate Library
Fund Democracy
Mutual Fund Directors Forum
Weinberg Center on Corporate Governance
National Association of Corporate Directors (NACD)
Investor Responsibility Research Center (IRRC)
Council of Institutional Investors (CII)
California Public Employee Retirement System (CalPERS)
Relational Investors
National Association of State Treasurers
American Federation of Labor–Congress of Industrial Organizations (AFL-CIO)
American Federation of State, County, and Municipal Employees (AFSCME)
Interfaith Center on Corporate Responsibility
American Enterprise Institute
Law and Economics Center
US Public Interest Research Group
Chief Executive Leadership Institute
Catalyst
Coalition for Environmentally Responsible Economies (CERES)

BUSINESS AND PROFESSIONAL GROUPS

The Business Roundtable
US Chamber of Commerce
Conference Board
Conference Board of Canada
Investment Company Institute (ICI)

GOVERNANCE RATING GROUPS

Institutional Shareholder Services (ISI)
Glass Lewis & Co.

Standard & Poor's
Moody's Investment Service
Governance Metrics International

### ENFORCEMENT AGENCIES

Securities and Exchange Commission (SEC)
Public Company Accounting Oversight Board (PACOB)
Department of Justice (DOJ)
State Attorneys General (Eliot Spitzer)
North American Securities Regulators Association

### SELF-REGULATORY ORGANIZATIONS

New York Stock Exchange (NYSE)
National Association of Securities Dealers (NASD)

## CORPORATE GOVERNANCE

> Boards are taking their jobs much more seriously, and the balance of power between executives and the board has forever been altered.
>
> (Charles Elson, Director, Weinberg Center on Corporate Governance, University of Delaware, in Michaels and Roberts, 2004)

The hopeful statement above by Charles Elson, Director of the Weinberg Center on Corporate Governance at the University of Delaware, could not have been made in the year 2000. However, due to legislative and administrative action, court decisions, and shareholder pressures, corporations have taken some positive steps to improve their governance. Elson has been a major figure in advancing that progress. He has directed the studies of his center, testified frequently before Congress on corporate reform Bills, and served on a number of corporate boards, most notably the Sunbeam board, where he was instrumental in the ousting of chief executive Al Dunlap.

Following the collapse of Enron and other corporate scandals, the spotlight focused on misbehaving management, negligent accounting firms, and passive boards of directors. Regarding corporate boards, the emphasis of reform efforts has been on board independence and board diligence. Progress has been made on both fronts, but other issues also linger, such as the separation of the positions of chief executive officer (CEO) and board chair, board compensation, multiple board memberships, shareholder activism and participation, and the effectiveness of governance rating systems.

### Diligence and Work Load

There have been some areas of positive improvement in corporate governance and board activity in the recent past. One is the area of board diligence. Boards are working harder and longer than ever before, with the help of the National Association of Corporate Directors (NACD). The NACD is a membership organization with local chapters throughout the country that meet regularly to discuss important governance issues. It also sponsors director training programs, often in partnership with leading universities, and organizes task forces and blue-ribbon commissions to examine and recommend corporate governance standards. According to Roger Raber of the NACD, directors spend an average of 250 hours per year on board business, up from

150 hours a few years ago, and audit committee members spend double that time (Dash, 2004). A study by Korn/Ferry International indicates that the average amount of time a director would spend on board business in 2001 was thirteen hours a month, an amount that is now up 50 percent to nineteen hours a month (Michaels, 2003a). Some directors report an even heavier increase in their work loads. A director of three technology companies, for instance, reports that her work load at each company has tripled, even more so in the time she spends on audit and compensation committee work (Dash, 2004). Another corroborating study from McKinsey reports that while only 10 percent of directors considered themselves actively engaged with company performance five years ago, 52 percent do so today (Michaels, 2003a).

Other improvements in board performance relate to Sarbox or New York Stock Exchange (NYSE) standards and other best practices. For instance, the Korn/Ferry International study (US Twenty-ninth Annual Board of Directors Study) found that independent directors are meeting far more frequently without the chief executive. A very high percentage (87 percent) of US directors met frequently without the chief executive present in 2003—more than double the 2002 percentage (41 percent). This experience of US directors contrasts directly with their European counterparts, where French directors met without their CEOs only 7 percent of the time and British directors did so for only 15 percent of the time (Michaels, 2003a). Further, while two-thirds of boards had a formal process to evaluate CEOs in 2002, that figure was 82 percent in 2003. Ninety percent of companies had written guidelines on corporate governance in 2003, versus 70 percent in 2002 (Michaels, 2003b). Finally, due to pressures from investors, directors are also attending annual meetings more frequently than in the past. David M. Schilling, director of global corporate accountability at the Interfaith Center for Corporate Responsibility maintains that "This should be a minimum requirement for all directors of a company," but many have failed to do so in the past (McGeehan, 2004). Evidence of board diligence and more intense focus is therefore pervasive.

## Board Independence

Recently, there has been a significant increase in the incidence of independent directors, which is seen as one of the most important best practices in corporate governance by the Sarbanes-Oxley (Sarbox) requirements, self-regulatory organizations, corporate rating systems, and shareholder activists. A study by the Investor Responsibility Research Center (IRRC) found that of 1,500 firms in widely used indexes, 83 percent now have a majority of independent directors, up from 78 percent in 2002 and 72 percent five years ago (Investor Responsibility Research Center, 2003). The average independence rating of boards has also increased, and 80 percent of recent new board members have been independent. There has also been an increase in fully independent key committees, with 80 percent of audit and compensation committees now being totally composed of independent directors (Investor Responsibility Research Center, 2003). The IRRC has studied that phenomenon, as it generates studies for its membership of institutional investors to provide guidance on how to vote on corporate reform proxy resolutions.

There is still an ongoing debate surrounding the value of independent directors, and the problems at Nortel that emerged in 2004, along with the earlier board composition issues at Enron, establish that, while board independence may well be a necessary condition for good governance, it is certainly not a sufficient condition for same. Nortel has a stellar blue-chip board on paper that nonetheless failed to properly scrutinize an overly generous bonus plan that allegedly drove accounting failures. Two of the board members had been involved in blue-ribbon corporate governance committees that issued prestigious reports. A director on several Canadian boards commented that Nortel could not have found a more distinguished board (Belson and Simon, 2004).

Various experts and authoritative bodies define "independence" in different ways, and Sarbox applies a basic definition in requiring that no audit committee member can take fees from a company for other than board service. That eliminates the possibility of either legal or consulting service, an issue that George Mitchell, the chair of Disney, faced. He stopped consulting for Disney after 2001, and his law firm did no further business with Disney after 2002. However, as a director of Staples and FedEx, he still consults to those companies, so Staples determined he did not qualify as an independent director, as he violated the "material relationship" standard of the New York Stock Exchange (NYSE), and its board removed him from the governance committee (Lublin, 2003). The activist California Public Employees Retirement System (CalPERS) opposed Mitchell's re-election to the Staples board and also opposed his elevation to become the Disney chair, since he was in a conflict situation on other boards (Lublin, 2003).

Independence is conceptually central to good corporate governance, since it alleviates conflicts of interest. As Charles Elson, Director of the Weinberg Center on Corporate Governance, states, "Go back to all those corporate scandals, and it comes down to a board that missed warning signals. The question is why, but the answer is easy. They were conflicted. And the same thing happened at the New York Stock Exchange" (Eichenwald, 2003).

The real test is that boards should not only appear independent on paper but should behave independently from the CEO and challenge management. Roderick Hills, former chair of the US Securities and Exchange Commission (SEC) comments that "if that simple thing had happened in the past, you would have eliminated all the major accounting cases." (Michaels and Roberts, 2004). Beyond having independent directors, a board culture that fosters open dissent and diligence may be even more important (Sonnenfeld, 2002).

As a response to the mutual fund crisis, the SEC has called for more independence of mutual fund boards. The SEC now requires that 75 percent of board members be independent, while the minimum for most boards currently is 51 percent, though most boards have at least two-thirds independence. Current legislative bills would ban any "interested persons" from serving on fund boards (Fried, 2004).

## Separation of Chief Executive Officer and Chair

While boards are working harder and longer, and are tending to become more independent, there has also been an increase in the number of companies that are separating the positions of CEO and chair of the board. There has been a long-standing tradition in the governance of US companies that those positions be combined, but change is even occurring in that aspect of corporate governance. Thirty percent of companies had separated the positions of chair and CEO by 2003, a quite dramatic jump from 26 percent in 2001. Almost 20 percent of companies reported having a lead director in 2003, up from only 3 percent in 2002. Overall, 23 percent of companies examined have independent board leadership of some type, an increase from 10 percent in 2002 (Investor Responsibility Research Center, 2003).

There is growing support in the United States for the so-called "European" model of separating the two positions, among corporate governance scholars (MacAvoy and Millstein, 2004) and even among former CEOs who once held both positions. There is no assurance, however, that this reform will improve governance. Witness the separation of the two positions of CEO and chair at Enron and Tyco and the establishment of the position of lead director at each company. The Conference Board, in a report issued in January, 2003, concluded that "no single board structure has yet been demonstrated to be superior in providing the oversight that leads to corporate success," and argued that a non-executive chair is appropriate in some circumstances but not in others, a view shared as well by Nell Minow of the Corporate Library and Charles Elson of the Weinberg Center on Corporate Governance (White, 2003).

The most controversial recommendation of the SEC on mutual fund reform, adopted in June of 2004, requires fund chairs to be independent, which will require that chairs at 80 percent of current funds will have to be replaced (Labaton, 2004a). Such groups as Fund Democracy, founded by former SEC lawyer Mercer Bullard, now at the University of Mississippi Law School, and the Mutual Fund

Directors Forum have supported the reform. Former SEC chair and Northwestern University law professor David Ruder chairs the Mutual Fund Directors Forum, an association primarily of independent directors of mutual funds. Ruder also organized a letter signed by all seven living former SEC chairs to current chair William Donaldson, expressing support for independent chairs for mutual funds (Coleman, 2004; Johnson, 2004). Former SEC chairs Arthur Levitt and Richard Breeden have both supported this reform publicly, writing in a *Wall Street Journal* op-ed column that "having an independent chairman without ties to the fund sponsor … is one of the best ways to improve accountability for management practices" (Levitt and Breeden, 2004). However, chief executives of such leading fund families as Vanguard, Fidelity, and T. Rowe Price have opposed the change (Fried, 2004). Fidelity's insider chair, Edward C. Johnson III, wrote an op-ed column opposing the SEC rule on independent chairs, and has backed up his case on Capitol Hill with increased lobbying and political contributions to candidates (Solomon and Hechinger, 2004a). Fidelity actually sponsored its own study demonstrating that funds with independent chairs perform worse than those funds with insider chairs, as insider-chaired funds beat 59 percent of their peers over the past ten years, while independently chaired funds beat only 48 percent of their peer funds (Coleman, 2004; Hechinger, 2004). Putnam, one of the major funds charged with violations that reached a settlement with the SEC and with the New York Attorney General, actually had an independent chair (Labaton, 2004; Solomon and Hechinger, 2004b). The Investment Company Institute, the association of mutual funds, supports more independence for mutual fund boards, but it has opposed the requirement for independent chairs and instead prefers that the independent-dominated board choose the chair (Coleman, 2004).

While the CEO of Vanguard opposed a requirement that funds have independent chairs, the founder and former CEO of Vanguard, John C. Bogle, has been a leading advocate for mutual fund reform. He argues that the previous arrangement of insiders as fund chairs presented "an unacceptable conflict of interest in the selection and compensation of fund management companies" (Bogle, 2003). In one interview before the SEC required that fund chairs be independent, Bogle complained: "Basically, the fund board is a corporate shell. You've got to change that. It must be clear that when fund chairman A negotiates with management chairman A, that they aren't the same person" (Saito-Chung, 2004). Bogle also condemns the "silence of the funds" and maintains they were partially responsible for the stock market bubble by failing to scrutinize the governance of companies in which they invested. He criticizes funds as well for failing to disclose their votes on proxy resolutions and for resisting the SEC requirement that they do so in the future (Bogle, 2003).

Scholars from conservative think tanks have meanwhile weighed in against the reform. James Glassman, a fellow at the American Enterprise Institute, believes that independent chairs and more independence on fund boards will lead to lower financial performance and to shareholder confusion, as independent board members may turn to other fund managers, e.g. Dreyfus instead of Fidelity, to run a Fidelity fund. He also maintains there is intense competition between funds, which benefits intelligent investors (Glassman, 2004). Henry Manne, founder of the Law and Economics Center at George Mason University, also criticizes mutual fund reforms and maintains that even market timing benefits shareholders and should not be regulated (Manne, 2004). Beyond the rule requiring independent fund chairs, the SEC now also requires independent directors to meet at least once a quarter without any outside directors present, and boards would be given the right to hire their own lawyers and auditors, a common practice at many funds already (Fried, 2004).

## Pool of Candidates

The pool of candidates for corporate boards must broaden, as more candidates are turning down nominations in the wake of the increase in liability exposure and the time commitment required to serve on boards. One expert at Spencer Stuart, a prominent global executive search firm, reports that "the number of people willing to serve on corporate boards is dwindling. The number of turndowns has increased dramatically over the past couple of years, from four per board slot a few years ago to maybe ten today" (Dash, 2004).

Consequently, corporations now have to look to a wider pool of candidates. Jeffrey Sonnenfeld of the Chief Executive Leadership Institute and Yale University reports that more retired leaders below the level of CEO, especially chief financial officers (CFOs), are joining corporate boards (Dash, 2004). Korn/ Ferry reports that retired audit partners are also in fashion as potential board members (Dash, 2004).

In response to Sarbox and the need to widen the pool of candidates, corporations may consider more women candidates. Women held about 13 percent of board seats at S&P 500 firms in 2002 and 10 percent of S&P 1500 firms, and they are disproportionately independent candidates, compared to their male counterparts (Hymowitz, 2003). A study by Catalyst, an organization that tracks the progress of women in the corporate world, finds some slow progress. In 2003 women held 13.6 percent of *Fortune* 500 board seats, up from 9.5 percent in 1995, and women also occupy at least 25 percent of board seats in fifty four of the 500 largest firms, up from eleven companies in 1995 (Downey, 2004). Still, fifty-four of *Fortune* 500 companies still have no female board members, and 208 firms have only one female director (Gray, 2004). A study by the Conference Board of Canada also indicates that greater gender diversity on a corporate board may improve corporate governance. Of boards of North American companies that have three or more women, 94 percent have conflict-of-interest guidelines, while only 58 percent of all-male boards do. Further, 72 percent of boards with two or more women conduct evaluations of board performance, compared to 49 percent of all-male boards (Hymowitz, 2003).

## Board Compensation

With the increase in board work load, there has been a commensurate increase in the compensation for board members. Total compensation for board members ranged from US$43,000 at small companies to US$155,000 at the 200 largest firms, with an expected rise of 15 percent in 2004, according to compensation consultants Pearl Meyer and Partners (Dash, 2004). At most companies the increase has been in cash, with much of it for extra committee work, reversing a trend of the past five years. Now, those serving on audit and compensation committees virtually receive "hazard pay."

In 2003, total compensation for board members actually decreased slightly by 4 percent to US$102,000, largely due to a decline in the value of stock option grants. With the increase in cash awards projected for 2004, awards of deferred stock, time lapsing restricted stock, and stock units are also on the rise (Investor Responsibility Research Center, 2003).

## *Governance and Financial Performance*

Many studies have examined the link between different changes in corporate governance and financial performance, and the results have been mixed. Studies show that the impact of more independent boards on financial performance has been notably weak. That was the key finding of a study based on a large sample of firms over an extended period of time (Bhagat and Black, 2002). Broadening the base from independence on corporate boards to other criteria of corporate governance, however, reveals more positive results, especially in comparing the firms with the best governance systems versus those with the worst. On that basis, increasing evidence exists for a correlation between good corporate governance and positive financial performance. Governance Metrics International, for instance, found that while the S&P 500 index increased by 2.3 percent for the year ending March, 2003, the top five firms on its governance scale rose 23.1 percent. Those five firms, with a perfect rating of 10, were Pfizer, Johnson Controls,

MBIA, Sunoco, and the SLM Corporation (Morgenson, 2003).

## Compensation Committees

While most of the recent attention has been placed on audit committees, future attention will likely be placed on compensation committees. Though both key committees must now be composed totally of independent directors, Roger Raber of the NACD refers to compensation committees as "definitely more clubby." As he states, "We have another storm to go through, and frankly, it's going to be ugly." In a survey of the 2,000 largest American corporations, more than 20 percent had compensation committees with members who had business ties to the company CEO. This is true even of General Electric, where three of the eight members of the compensation committee had business ties to GE. Additionally, the compensation committees are not required to disclose the remuneration paid to expert consultants, many of whom are often recommended by the CEO (Henriques and Fabrikant, 2002).

## Multiple Board Memberships

Given the increasing work load among board members, they are discouraged from serving on too many boards. Company bylaws today often limit CEOs to two or three outside board memberships (Dash, 2004). The standard is that senior management should be limited to three and a half boards, with a non-profit board counting as one half. For CEOs, the NACD recommends only one other corporate board position. This standard is still flagrantly violated, however. Even the new CEO of Nortel, a company that should now be even more sensitive to good governance practices, sits on a dozen other corporate boards, a practice condemned by the Council of Institutional Investors (CII) as "at the extreme end, especially at a company that is in trouble" (Michaels and Taylor, 2004). The CII is the major association of large institutional investors and public pension funds, and its former director, Sarah Teslik, has been another major voice and

pressure point for corporate governance reform. In the case of Disney's chair, George Mitchell, he relinquished five board seats but still sits on the boards of Disney, Staples, FedEx, and Starwood Hotels & Resorts (Lublin, 2003). One of the new directors for the newly constituted NYSE board is Shirley Ann Jackson, president of Rensselaer Polytechnic Institute, who also serves on eight corporate boards, as trustee to three other leading universities, and is president of the American Association for the Advancement of Science. As one experienced business columnist writes: "With all due respect to Jackson … there are not enough hours in the day to run a major research university while serving on eight corporate boards … interim chairman John Reed is perpetuating the dysfunctional system of corporate governance that he is meant to reform" (Pearlstein, 2003).

In keeping with the issue of excessive board memberships in the corporate sector, it is not uncommon for mutual fund directors to serve on the boards of 100 separate funds within a company. Marvin L. Mann, the retired CEO of Lexmark and Fidelity's lead independent director, sits on the boards of 292 Fidelity funds and earned $324,000 in 2003 (Fried, 2004). A heart surgeon sits on the board of 109 Massachusetts Financial Services (MFS) funds, and the independent trustees of Vanguard sit on 120 boards simultaneously (Anders, 2004).

## SHAREHOLDER ACTIVISM

Shareholder activism on issues across the board keeps increasing from year to year. In 2003, according to figures compiled by the Investor Responsibility Research Center, there were 1,100 shareholder resolutions submitted to major companies, up from 800 in 2002. While ninety-eight resolutions received a majority of shareholder votes in 2002, that number rose to 166 in 2003 (Petruno, 2004c). Though pension funds have been more active than mutual funds in promoting corporate governance reform, neither actually sponsors many proxy resolutions. Of almost 800 US governance proposals submitted in 2003, only thirty came from either mutual or pension funds (Brewster and Michaels, 2003). Ninety percent of all resolutions came from either individuals or union-sponsored funds. Unions ranging from the United Brotherhood of Carpenters and Joiners to the American Federation of State County and Municipal Employees (AFSCME) have sponsored resolutions, with a special concern for executive compensation (Lublin, 2004). The California Public Employee Retirement System (CalPERS), for instance, targeted only thirteen companies with resolutions in 2003 and withdrew all of them after discussions with management. CalPERS defends its record by maintaining it publishes governance policies it promotes in other ways, but its critics argue it is often conflicted from bringing genuine pressure for change in companies vital to the financial futures of its members (Brewster and Michaels, 2003). In an effort to further energize mutual and pension funds, corporate governance expert Ira Millstein is establishing a program at Baruch College. As Millstein puts it, "We want to find out why the institutions have not participated in corporate governance. Management dominance and board passivity is the result" (Michaels, 2003c).

In 2004 US labor union pension funds were the leading sponsors of shareholder resolutions, having submitted 54 percent of those in that year, versus 45 percent of the 700 resolutions in 2003 (Burr, 2004). The proxy resolution agenda for 2004 emphasized compensation and auditing and board issues, and focuses on the following issues:

1  Linking pay to performance for executive compensation packages.
2  Expensing executive options.
3  Voting on golden parachutes, or excessive severance packages.
4  Showing zero tolerance on non-audit fees.
5  Voting for ratification of the auditor.
6  Rotating auditors periodically.
7  Requiring independent boards.
8  Electing directors annually.
9  Separating the positions of CEO and chair (Burr, 2004).

An example of union activism is a campaign waged by the Communications Workers of America (CWA) and the American Federation of Labor-Congress of Industrial Organizations (AFL-CIO) against the existing corporate governance of Comcast, rated among the bottom 10 percent of companies by Institutional Shareholder Services (ISS). The CWA proposal called for elimination of the dual stock class structure at Comcast which allows CEO Brian Roberts to control the firm. The AFL-CIO proposal called for two-thirds of the Comcast board to be independent, but shareholders defeated both resolutions (Stern, 2004).

While the wave of shareholder resolutions on corporate governance issues has continued to increase over time, the new big trend of the 2004 proxy season was vigorous campaigns waged against the election of individual directors and campaigns to oust some CEOs. As Patrick McGurn, senior vice-president and special counsel at ISS, states, "This year is a good curtain raiser for the future of shareholder activism. These aren't just meaningless protest votes anymore. They are leading to meaningful change" (White, 2004) Figure 26.1 illustrates the upsurge in shareholder opposition to directors at various companies and for a variety of reasons.

Even mutual funds, long criticized by Vanguard founder John Bogel for their failure to take their fiduciary and voting responsibilities seriously, have joined the labor and pension funds in opposing certain directors. At Vanguard, for instance, the company voted for the full slate of director nominees only 29 percent of the time in 2003, a sharp contrast to the 90 percent support for management and current board members in 2002. Even though Fidelity and Vanguard have both opposed disclosure of their proxy voting records, they have more actively opposed some management positions on governance issues in 2002 and 2003. Vanguard reported that it voted against 64 percent of management stock option plans in 2002, while Fidelity voted against management's position 46 percent of the time (Hechinger and Lucchetti, 2003).

CalPERS has taken the lead among pension funds voting "no" against some board members,

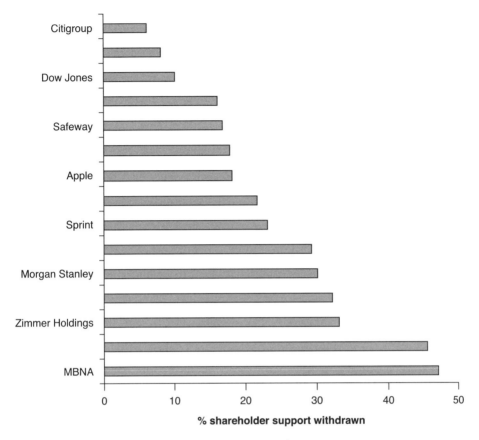

Figure 26.1    *Upsurge in Shareholder Opposition to Directors and CEOs*
Source *Adapted from: White, 2004*

and has voted against directors at such leading firms as Coca-Cola, Citigroup, Sprint, and Hewlett-Packard (Bank, 2004; Terhune and Lublin, 2004). CalPERS, along with the New York State pension fund, also opposed the re-election of Citigroup chair Sanford I. Weill, based on his role in scandals that negatively affected the company, and of CEO Charles O. Prince, due to his wife's connection to the law firm that represents the company. Perhaps not coincidentally, the Corporate Library ranked Citigroup last in corporate governance among 2,000 companies surveyed in 2003 (O'Brien, 2004).

Using their investment as leverage, pension funds also campaign for the ouster of CEOs. CalPERS was a leader in ousting Richard Grasso as CEO of the NYSE over his compensation package, just as it has attempted to pressure

Michael Eisner to step down from Disney, along with eight of the eleven directors (Verrier, 2004c). Union pension funds were also extremely active in trying to remove directors or top managers at more than 200 corporations in 2004, usually over the issue of executive compensation. The AFL-CIO targeted ten companies for such campaigns, including Apple Computer, Citigroup, and Comcast (Flanigan, 2004). Despite the increased activity by labor and such high-profile examples as Disney and Safeway, ISS actually advised its clients to withhold votes from directors in only 32 percent of companies in 2004, versus 38 percent in 2003 and 52 percent in 2002 (Taub, 2004). The key reason for the decline in advice to withhold votes is that many more small- and mid-cap companies had established key independent board committees, whereas they previously had no such panels in place (Taub, 2004).

Pension fund critics argue that CalPERS has, by contrast, been too purist on some issues and has gone overboard in opposing board members. By withholding votes from directors at 90 percent of the 2,700 corporations in its portfolio, CalPERS has generated criticism that it has both become too rigid and has gone too far in its activism (Lavelle, 2004b). Based on its strong stands for independent auditing, expensing options and other issues, CalPERS opposed former Vice President Al Gore as a director at Apple Computer and opposed nine directors at Lockheed Martin (Luchetti and Lublin, 2004). CalPERS also opposed Michael Eisner and the retention of directors at Disney, and was joined by five state pension funds in doing so, along with mutual funds like T. Rowe Price (Verrier, 2004d; Holson, 2004).

CalPERS has opposed any board member who approves of an audit firm doing any consulting for a client, a policy it has been reconsidering (Sidel, 2004). That policy goes beyond SEC rules that restrict only certain types of consulting and led CalPERS to oppose the re-election of Warren Buffet to the board of Coca-Cola. Nell Minow of The Corporate Library, which provides the leading website on corporate governance (thecorporatelibrary. com) and evaluates the governance of specific companies, roundly criticized that action by CalPERS, saying it has no business going beyond Sarbox standards in holding companies accountable (White, 2004; Petruno, 2004a). However, many companies have gone beyond the Sarbox requirements on auditor practices. In contrast to the CalPERS campaign and findings, ISS has actually found that while several hundred companies allowed audit firms to do non-audit work in 2003, that number had dwindled to fewer than 75 in 2004, including only three companies among the Standard & Poor's 500. For that and other reasons, the ISS "watch list" was half the size in 2004 than it was in 2003 (Taub, 2004).

In opposing directors at Safeway, following on the heels of a strike by Safeway workers and given the union connections of the CalPERS head, business groups and the media have criticized the pension fund for becoming too political and being mired in its own conflicts of interest (White, 2004; Petruno, 2004a). Kevin Hassett, an economic policy analyst at the American Enterprise Institute, a conservative think tank, criticized CalPERS in saying, "This is shareholder activism designed to further labor's ends" (Lavelle, 2004a). Joining the CalPERS opposition to the Safeway CEO and directors, though, were also the pension funds from Connecticut, Illinois, New York, and New York City. ISS and Glass Lewis also advised investors to oppose the Safeway CEO's re-election (Petruno, 2004b). Beyond targeting Safeway directors, CalPERS also wanted the CEO and chair Steven Burd to leave. It was not content to see him simply relinquish his position as chair, as Michael Eisner did at Disney; CalPERS wanted him out of the company (Peltz, 2004). Given that the campaign garnered only 17 percent of shareholder votes, as opposed to the 43 percent at Disney, it was not as successful in repudiating the CEO and board at Safeway.

Its campaign to oppose directors who approve of auditors that also provide any type of consulting has led it to target conscientious directors at healthy firms, though the pressure has induced some firms like Applied Materials and American Express to hire different firms to do their auditing and consulting. CalPERS has also sued the NYSE for $150 million for failing to curb specialist trading abuses (Kelly and Craig, 2003). Some also criticize CalPERS for slightly underperforming other large public pension funds over the past three years and ten years while it has been so focused on corporate governance and its own political agenda (Hoover, 2004).

The classic tool of shareholder activism, as opposed to shareholder voice, is shareholder exit from firms that are misbehaving. That is the tried and true "Wall Street Rule," which free-market advocates see as the ultimate and best check on management. Evidence of it occurring is also common, especially among the scandal-tainted mutual funds. Funds like Janus and Putnam saw huge outflows of investor dollars once New York Attorney General Eliot Spitzer and the SEC announced their charges, and overall the funds caught in the controversy each had an average of $10.7 billion in withdrawals from their stock and bond funds over the last four months of 2003 (Friedman, 2004a). In late 2003, CalPERS pulled $1.2 billion in assets from Putnam investments, after the disclosure of widespread market timing at Putnam (Atlas, 2003). Later, as improper trading allegations were levied against the Pacific Investment Management Company (PIMCO) bond-trading fund, the Illinois pension fund announced it would withdraw $250 million from PIMCO, "to send a signal to Pimco because our trustees are concerned about these allegations in the media" (Friedman, 2004b).

## Shareholder Nomination of Directors

Regarding true shareholder democracy and an increasing voice for shareholders, nothing has been more symbolically important or divisive than the SEC proposal for shareholder nominations of director candidates. As Richard Koppes, former general counsel at CalPERS reports, "I've never seen a more emotional debate between corporations and shareholders," and Nell Minow of the Corporate Library states, "If the rule as proposed goes forward, we're off to the races," (Peterson, 2004) though she earlier and accurately predicted that business would try to derail the effort as well (Day, 2003a). Sarah Teslik of the Council of Institutional Investors said, "There is nothing in the last twenty years the SEC has done that will be as important" (Day, 2003a). Barbara Roper of the Consumer Federation of America (CFA) offered somewhat less enthusiastic support when she said, "I don't know if it's the perfect approach, but I think it's a legitimate attempt to give investors more say" (Day, 2003b). John J. Sweeney, head of the AFL-CIO, also applauded the shareholder nomination initiative (Labaton, 2003). Some pension funds and labor groups continue to push for the SEC proposal, though other pension funds are willing to see it withdrawn. Among individual investors, more shareholder democracy seems to enjoy wide support. In a survey on behalf of

the AFL-CIO, Harris Interactive found that 80 percent of individuals believe they should enjoy the right to nominate directors (Michaels, 2003d). Under the original SEC proposal, the events that might trigger a shareholder-nominated director are: (1) a qualified shareholder or group of shareholders with 1 percent ownership introduces a resolution for a shareholder nominee in the following year, with the resolution supported by a majority of shareholders; (2) if 35 percent of shareholders at an annual meeting withhold votes for any director; and (3) if the board takes no action to comply with any winning proxy resolution (Lavelle, 2004c). This is a further impetus behind shareholders withholding votes from directors, since a large vote might constitute a "triggering event" leading to shareholder nominations the following year. The mere existence of the proposal has already prompted some companies to quickly implement resolutions that receive a majority of supposedly non-binding shareholder votes, as Georgia Pacific did in deciding to expense stock options. That occurred following a majority shareholder vote favoring such a resolution sponsored by the Teamsters Union. Lucent and Alcoa have also implemented popular shareholder resolutions, in an effort to avoid future shareholder nominees to their boards (Lavelle, 2004c).

Business opposition to the shareholder nominee proposal has emerged from corporate leaders such as Intel chair Andrew Grove and General Electric CEO Jeffrey Immelt, and from such groups as the Business Roundtable and the US Chamber of Commerce (Alpert, 2004). Those groups suggest the threat of special interests with narrow agendas disrupting the board is substantial and that the rule would impinge on state laws that traditionally determine how corporations operate (Day, 2004b). Henry A. McKinnell, chairman of Pfizer and co-chairman of the Business Roundtable, has said that "the proposals present the possibility of special interest groups hijacking the director election process" (Michaels and Roberts, 2004). McKinnell himself wrote an op-ed column in *The Wall Street Journal* condemning the unintended consequences of empowering "special-interest blocks of shareholders," while still endorsing the reforms of majority independent boards, totally independent key committees, disclosure of nominating committee procedures, and improved shareholder communications with the board (McKinnell, 2003). John Castellani, president of the Business Roundtable, says the proposal goes too far and may undermine the confidence of CEOs (Michaels and Roberts, 2004). The Roundtable and the Chamber of Commerce have also threatened a court fight to block implementation of the rule (Alpert, 2004; Day, 2004a; McCarty, 2004). Thomas J. Donohue, president and CEO of the US Chamber of Commerce, wrote in an op-ed column in *Investor's Business Daily* that the "replacement of experienced, involved directors with nominees beholden to a special interest will result in divisive boards that are incapable of working together as a team to oversee the performance of the company and protect the rights of shareholders" (Donohue, 2003). He even suggests a greater danger of leaks of confidential information from union and pension fund directors. Former SEC chair Harvey Pitt opposes the proposal and opts instead for candidate selections by board nominating committees. He states, "I think we will all be better off if we are spared the extension of our flawed political system to our corporate boardroom" (Michaels, 2004). Another former SEC chairman, Arthur Levitt, supports the plan and believes the fears of any major influence by shareholder nominees are overwrought, since there are so many barriers to even getting one nominee listed. He concludes, "This is a modest and well overdue step that will increase transparency and accountability in the board room … Shareholders deserve the right. The sky won't fall" (Levitt, 2004). Echoing this sentiment is the coordinator of the Shareholder Action Network, who states, "It's ridiculous that corporations feel so threatened by this when it's such a modest proposal" (Peterson, 2004). Of course, other shareholder activists argued it would be a major breakthrough for shareholder empowerment.

The Business Roundtable has countered the SEC plan with two alternatives: (1) that the triggering threshold be moved from 35 percent of shareholder votes withheld from a director to a 50 percent threshold, and (2) that the board nominating committee would have the power to nominate a new board candidate rather than the power flowing to shareholders, though one plan requires that the board must consult shareholders (Borrus, 2004; Solomon, 2004a). In analyzing the strength of the business opposition to the measure, Sarah Teslik, executive director of the Council of Institutional Investors, has stated that "The business community has accurately figured out that this rule is a significant shift in the balance of power" (Lavelle, 2004b). SEC chair William Donaldson may be willing to accept the fallback position of a 50 percent threshold and authority vested in the board nominating committee, which could alienate him from his two Democratic commissioners (Solomon, 2004a). As an indication of the political sensitivity underlying the proposal, Donaldson was backtracking from his earlier unqualified support for the proposal by mid-2004, and with the deadlock among other commissioners, it likely doomed the prospect for any new rule being passed that would affect the 2005 proxy season (Labaton, 2004b). Meanwhile, less rigid and doctrinaire pension funds (unlike CalPERS, the New York City fund, the Connecticut fund, and the North Carolina fund, for example) have expressed a willingness to see the SEC take the original plan completely off the table.

Beyond their possibly enhanced role in nominating corporate directors in the future, institutional shareholders have other nominating powers. Given the revamped board of the NYSE, CalPERS took the opportunity to nominate to its board former SEC chair Arthur Levitt and governance activist Ralph V. Whitworth, who runs Relational Investors, an investment fund that targets undervalued troubled companies for a turnaround directed by Whitworth. Whitworth is also former director of the now defunct United Shareholders of America, organized to complement T. Boone Pickens's corporate takeover campaigns (Schroeder and Kelly, 2004).

## Global Shareholder Activism

Shareholder activism is occurring on a global basis in a variety of ways. First, US institutional investors and even mutual funds are bringing pressure against companies based in other countries. Fidelity led a move to block the appointment of a British executive as chair of Carlton Communications and opposed the merger of two major Italian firms. While Fidelity prefers to work behind the scenes in the United States, Europe and the United Kingdom expect fund managers to be more active stockholders, so Fidelity International behaves more aggressively in that environment (Reilly, 2003). Not only are US institutional shareholders bringing action against firms headquartered in other countries, but investors in other countries are also organizing to lobby for corporate governance changes in their own countries. Most recently, regarding the accounting problems at Royal Dutch/Shell, two of Europe's largest pension funds based in the Netherlands are using the Shell scandal to press for more transparency, controls, and governance reforms. They favor more board independence and an independent chair, along with abolition of the company's dual share structure (Tucker and Bickerton, 2004).

## GOVERNANCE EVALUATION

While there has been improvement in director diligence and independence over the past year, and since the passage of Sarbox, the aggregate improvement in corporate governance leaves a lot of room for improvement. In its global comparisons, GovernanceMetrics International found that only fifteen firms of 1,000 US companies studied received full marks for their corporate governance. Also, in a study of 600 companies around the world, the United States finished behind the United Kingdom and Canada in corporate governance practices, with Japanese companies ranking last (Michaels, 2003e).

Among the various for-profit and non-profit corporate governance ratings systems, the most visible seems to be Institutional Shareholder Services. In 2004, for instance, it advised shareholders in Sprint to withhold their votes for the only director up for election, based on the CEO's "extravagant" compensation approved by the board (Young and Sheng, 2004). Each organization has its supporters and detractors, and ISS has been criticized often in the past for the potential conflicts of interest posed by housing client advisory services and proxy voting recommendations under the same roof. Some journalists and activist shareholders raise the specter of its client services jeopardizing the objectivity of its corporate governance ratings (Hill et al., 2003).

The once dominant position of ISS may be challenged by Glass Lewis, a relative newcomer but organized by a team that includes Lynn Turner, former chief accountant of the SEC. Among the traditional rating services, Standard & Poor's has also launched an expanding global corporate governance service directed by George Dallas in its London office. The Corporate Library and IRRC are other long-time and respected players on a rapidly expanding field where competition among quality experts may benefit investors and the market.

Given the growing number of players in the sector, there is a wide range of approaches to governance ratings, some of which conflict. ISS and Governance Metrics take a checklist approach, as do Moody's and Standard & Poor's, though the latter two traditional ratings organizations do not disclose their ratings except to their clients. IRRC does not compile ratings, though it does advise clients where companies stand on specific issues. Carol Bowie, director of the corporate governance service at IRRC questions, "How credible is this stuff if there are all these discrepancies?" ("For Investors …," 2004). Glass Lewis, which partners with IRRC on some services, also refrains from compiling governance ratings. Its chief executive Greg Taxin believes that "Issues of corporate integrity and corporate governance are fairly complex and we don't feel that one size fits all" ("For Investors …," 2004).

Institutional investors like CalPERS sometimes apply more rigid litmus tests that focus on a narrow range of factors. That may lead to conflicts with the rating organizations. As mentioned above, CalPERS will oppose any company that uses its auditor for both auditing and consulting services, whatever the type of service. That was one reason CalPERS withheld votes for Disney directors, since PricewaterhouseCoopers had been doing both auditing and consulting work for the company (Ahrens, 2004). The stricture against audit firms that provide consulting exceeds the Sarbox regulatory standard and led CalPERS to also oppose the re-election of Warren Buffet to the Coca-Cola board, a heavily criticized decision. CalPERS will also oppose any director of a company that refuses to adopt a proxy resolution that has received a majority vote of shareholders. That led CalPERS to attack Maytag, while ISS ratings put Maytag in the upper echelon of corporate governance, and Governance Metrics rates it as above average ("For Investors …," 2004).

Despite their various approaches, the rating services often converge in making the same recommendations. Glass Lewis and ISS, for example, both supported three shareholder resolutions submitted to Qwest Communications in 2004. The Association of US West Retirees submitted proposals that would have (1) barred the CEO from serving as chair, (2) required two-thirds of Qwest's directors to be free of any business relationships with the company, and (3) required a shareholder vote on extraordinary executive compensation packages. In spite of the endorsement by Glass Lewis and ISS, all three resolutions went down to defeat (McGhee, 2004). The rating services have also promoted the trend of denying votes for certain directors or even CEOs. Both ISS and Glass Lewis recommended a "no vote" on Michael Eisner at Disney and on members of the PeopleSoft board (Orwall, 2004a). Charles Elson of the Weinberg Center on Corporate Governance has said that any shareholder vote over 20 percent is significant and would force the board to further look at an issue (Holson, 2004). The resulting 43 percent vote against Eisner, according to Lynn Turner, managing director of Glass Lewis, was therefore "a two-by-four between the eyes that floored him."

In reaction, Eisner announced that he would step down as chair, but not CEO, and yield power to presiding director George Mitchell, a step some institutions found inadequate (Vise, 2004). In commenting on Eisner, Patrick McGurn of ISS stated, "He's the longest sitting CEO at a major *Fortune* 200 company and, frankly, it shows. The talent drain is well documented. Heir apparents have slipped through into the ether" (Segal, 2004). The leader of CalPERS said, "We have lost complete confidence in Mr Eisner's strategic vision and leadership in creating shareholder value" (Segal, 2004).

Since a substantial vote of 35 percent or 50 percent cast against a director may trigger a shareholder nomination at a subsequent meeting, the SEC's plan puts the proxy advisory firms like ISS and Glass Lewis in a pivotal position to drive such shareholder nominations. As Jeffrey Sonnenfeld of the Yale School of Organization and Management states, "It will put them in a kingmaker role for board nominees" (Solomon, 2004b). There is one major caveat to the efficacy of the rating systems used by any of the proxy advisory services or other rating companies, however. In the midst of a proliferation of checklists, it can leave boards uncertain what path to take. As former SEC chairman Roderick Hills maintains, "You can find legal firms that send out checklists (for compliance). That can turn boards into robots" (Michaels and Roberts, 2004).

While some rating systems with different approaches converged in their evaluation of Disney, other organizations that take seemingly similar approaches differed in their views of the Disney governance. Neither the Corporate Library nor the CII, for instance, rely on any checklist approach and tend to judge each situation on its own. Nell Minow of the Corporate Library would have given Disney a grade of F in 2003, but one year later said that Disney was a candidate for most improved governance, partially due to the advice it had received from top governance adviser Ira M. Millstein (Ahrens, 2004). Meanwhile, though, Sarah Teslik of the CII was not convinced Disney had gotten religion and said the board overhaul had been accomplished by "smoke and mirrors" (Ahrens, 2004).

Not surprisingly, rating firms that take different approaches sometimes wind up with very different evaluations of a company's governance process. ISS, with its checklist approach, for instance, gave Black and Decker a top grade of 100 percent in 2003, up from 75 percent the previous year. The Corporate Library, using a more nuanced approach, gave Black and Decker a mediocre grade, based on the CEO's pay package, the company's position on stock options, and its decision to allow auditors to do non-audit work. Furthermore, CII spotted a "potential for cronyism" at the Black & Decker board, based on board interlocks with other companies (Day, 2003c).

Beyond rating systems for corporate governance, the mutual fund scandals have prompted Morningstar to launch a fund governance rating system. It will assign grades ranging from A to F on such dimensions as board independence and pay, expenses, corporate culture, regulatory issues, and fund management compensation, as well as a total grade. There is a potential conflict of interest for Morningstar involved in its new venture, since some of the companies it rates own shares in Morningstar, and more shares will be sold through the company's initial public offering (Oster, 2004). Further, the company is launching the rating service just as it benefits from more "independent research" funds allocated through the settlement between Wall Street investment banks and the New York Attorney General. That added business opportunity will require Moningstar analysts to cover more stocks (Smith, 2004).

## ANALYSIS OF GROUPS AND ACTORS

### Shareholder Activism

This chapter now turns to an analysis of the groups promoting corporate governance reform. Professional organizations such as the NACD will continue to elevate the behavior and practices of corporate boards through its reports and director training programs. The real action, though, is likely to emanate from the shareholder side, including investors with different agendas and approaches. Institutional and other organized shareholders are exercising more pressure for changes in corporate governance, with a growing focus on the unresolved issue of executive compensation. As the shareholder movement gathers more force and momentum, it is manifesting both division within its own ranks and an expanding agenda of concern. This concluding analysis also notes the growing role of labor unions in the shareholder movement, as well as the less active role of mutual funds. While shareholder voice has grown louder, the traditional check of shareholder exit from the market remains another check on corporate misdeeds. This analysis also examines the growing importance of research and intelligence gathering by the shareholder activist movement.

### Division within the Ranks

With the growth of any social movement, internal disagreements are bound to develop along a range of issues and tactics as the groups proliferate. That has occurred within the environmental movement, as local and national groups disagree on issues and tactics, so it is not surprising that shareholder activist groups would also disagree with each other at times. In the campaign against Disney and Michael Eisner, for instance, CalPERS openly called for Eisner's removal, while the New York State Comptroller and other groups were willing to give him more time to turn Disney around. Some funds within the coalition of pension funds also argued for George Mitchell's removal from the Disney board rather than his elevation to chair, especially given his conflicts of interest, while others wanted to work with him as chair (Verrier, 2004a). In a larger sense, activists like CalPERS believe in applying outside visible pressure and being confrontational, while other pension funds not concerned about maximizing publicity prefer to work quietly behind the scenes with management.

### Expanding the Agenda

Groups often attempt to leverage their success in one area by expanding their reach into another. While the pension funds historically have not been as active as religious groups on the social agenda, some are now using their power and successes on corporate governance issues to expand their pressure tactics into other areas. This may add to the power and coalition of forces usually arrayed on less mainstream social issues. State treasurers, for instance, are using their financial leverage to combat corporate corruption in different ways. For example, they are pulling their investments from companies that move their headquarters offshore for tax reasons and are leading a campaign to run independent directors for corporate boards. The president of the National Association of State Treasurers provides the underlying rationale when he states, "Investors are used to market risk, but they're not used to integrity risk" (Wasserman, 2003).

The National Association of State Treasurers and the pension funds are also attempting to influence companies on the issues of environmental impact and climate change. Treasurers from seven states even appeared at the United Nations to demand disclosure of risks to companies and investors from climate change (Mulligan, 2003). If the government eventually caps greenhouse emissions, pension funds argue, pressuring companies on global warming now could lower long-term costs and keep them ahead of the regulatory curve. The Coalition for Environmentally Responsible Economies (CERES) has opened a dialogue with state treasurers and pension fund administrators, including CalPERS, on that issue. (Ball, 2003). CERES has coordinated its efforts with the Interfaith Center on Corporate Responsibility (ICCR), the long-time sponsor of shareholder resolutions on major social issues. As a result, four state pension funds in 2004 filed shareholder resolutions requesting that ten North American oil companies report their plans for dealing with climate change (Feder, 2004). Since 2002 such shareholder resolutions have also won a larger percentage of shareholder votes. The United States Public Interest Research Group (US PIRG) reports that the support for resolutions on climate change increased from 18 percent of the vote in 2002 to 25 percent at even more companies

in 2003, exceeding the support levels for corporate diversity resolutions in the 1970s (Seelye, 2003).

While pension funds and state treasurers have broadened their areas of concern, a major corporate governance expert believes it actually weakens their effectiveness. Charles Elson of the Weinberg Center for Corporate Governance argues, "The treasurers have made a good difference so far, but the further afield they wander, they more they risk diluting that message" (Mulligan, 2003). The corporate reform movement might also risk alienating adherents of the classical corporate model and of shareholder empowerment by emphasizing social issues and other stakeholder concerns.

### Upsurge in Union and Pension Fund Activism

This chapter has discussed the increasing roles played by labor unions and pension funds, especially as shareholder activists in submitting proxy resolutions and in withholding votes from corporate directors. As unions have lost power in workplace campaigns and in political influence, they have become more active players in corporate governance. Pension funds with a pro-labor outlook, such as CalPERS, reinforce the power of the unions but also risk politicizing investment decisions.

### Mutual Fund Silence

As discussed in the chapter, John Bogle has lamented the "silence of the funds" when it comes to exerting any pressure for corporate governance reform. Leading mutual funds like Fidelity and Vanguard have largely been active in resisting change, as when they opposed disclosure of their proxy voting records and when they opposed the rule requiring independent fund chairs. Though individual funds have basically been inactive, they are starting to scrutinize more closely the governance of companies in which they invest and are even sometimes voting against management's position on proxy resolutions and withholding votes for directors. This may become a major pressure point for corporations in the future.

## Exit from the Market

Regarding investor behavior, there is the continual choice of voice versus exit. Individuals and funds can either work for change or simply withdraw their funds from a company or mutual fund with which they disagree. Most of this chapter has discussed ways of exercising voice, by becoming more active and by promoting public policy that opens more avenues for investor participation. Sarbox, SEC rules and sanctions, state government investigations and initiatives, and NYSE standards have promoted a wide array of corporate and mutual fund reforms. Those are the most proactive ways for investors and other political interest groups to advance corporate reform. Market advocates point to the self-correcting devices within the market to harshly judge corporate and mutual fund misconduct, largely through exiting those companies and funds. Though the exit option does not do as much to prevent future misconduct as do voice options, it has played a prominent role in punishing misbehaving organizations. The chapter has addressed the moneys withdrawn after the mutual fund scandals, and investors have judged misconduct among corporations in the same way.

## Research and Corporate Monitoring

Every political movement requires a solid research foundation to promote its ideas. That has been the case with the social movements of the 1960s and 1970s, as they evolved into political interest groups and developed an array of political tactics to advance their causes. That has also been the case of the business reaction to those social movements, as the business community developed and supported its own array of think tanks at the national and local levels, many of which have had more financial support and influence than the social movements that provoked their founding.

The corporate reform movement has developed its own array of non-profit and for-profit research organizations that have focused especially on corporate governance and providing information to institutional shareholders. The two most notable non-profit organizations are the Investor Responsibility Research Center and the Corporate Library. The Weinberg Center on Corporate Governance at the University of Delaware, along with somewhat similar entities based at prominent law schools, also provide and support useful research and dialogues on corporate governance. This chapter has cited the studies and opinions of each organization on the issues of corporate governance. While there has been a search for appropriate metrics, criteria, and checklists to assess corporate governance, the non-profit centers mentioned have emphasized case-by-case judgments as they have provided expert advice and guidance to shareholders.

Meanwhile, a number of for-profit monitoring and research services have also evolved and new ones emerged to serve the needs of shareholders. These include Institutional Shareholder Services, Governance Metrics International, Standard & Poor's, and Glass Lewis & Co. ISS is the oldest of these groups, with the latter three having developed their governance services since 2001, in the wake of the corporate scandals. These groups have contributed to the search for the appropriate metrics and checklists to judge corporate governance more than have the non-profit operations. The competition among them has stimulated a healthy debate over those checklists and metrics, and this chapter has cited the conflicting opinions and evaluations of these groups. Along with the growth in these rating services have been questions regarding biases and conflicts of interest that arise when companies try to provide client services and evaluate those clients at the same time.

## IMPACT ON CORPORATE PUBLIC AFFAIRS STRATEGIES

The foregoing analysis of groups and actors suggests various corporate strategies for dealing with the corporate governance reform agenda. In some cases to be discussed, the most appropriate strategy may be collaboration and negotiation, or even outright support of the reform agenda. In cases where the reform agenda goes too far, an opposition strategy might make more sense. That strategy might also entail a research component, cultivating new allies, and developing new political coalitions. These various strategies have implications for corporate public affairs executives in various functions, including government relations, issues management, corporate responsibility, corporate contributions, and media and public relations.

Corporate governance might seem to be more internal than external to the firm and therefore to reside outside the purview of corporate public affairs executives. Even on critical high-level internal matters addressed at the board level, however, public affairs and issues management can serve a valuable role in helping senior management understand the early warning signals underlying the twists and turns of each issue and can provide an advice and intelligence function. Further, these major internal matters also have critical external components. That has been a major theme of this chapter. In many firms, various public affairs entities may have and should have developed relationships with the organizations that are playing key roles in moving the corporate governance issue forward. Where the public affairs function occupies a more central role in corporate policy making and has been less marginalized, it will play a more pivotal role in both determining and implementing the strategy on corporate governance.

In the end, all aspects of the corporate reform agenda relate to reputation management, which is a key responsibility of the CEO. The "Fifth Annual Corporate Reputation Watch Survey" sponsored in 2003 by Korn/Ferry International and Hill and Knowlton found that 65 percent of global CEOs surveyed recognized it was their personal responsibility to manage the firm's reputation, while only 14 percent placed the burden on boards of directors and only 12 percent placed it on corporate communications departments (Nosal, 2004). The CEO, however, needs to rely heavily on corporate public affairs professionals in

designing and implementing appropriate strategies to promote and improve the corporate reputation. This concluding section examines the growing importance of negotiating with shareholders, establishing structured mechanisms of interaction, and staying ahead of the curve by examining and adopting voluntary governance reforms. In so doing, public affairs executives can provide valuable advice in cultivating relationships with appropriate shareholder groups and rating services.

## Negotiate with Institutional Shareholders

Rather than confronting or hiding from institutional shareholders, many companies now invite them to meet with corporate executives to negotiate and hopefully reach an arrangement that will include withdrawal of a resolution or protest. Issues management experts and political operatives within the firm are well positioned to advise senior management on appropriate approaches to such negotiations, especially since they are experienced in dealing with the political agendas being promoted by the various pension funds.

A review of the 2004 proxy season reveals two major trends—"vigorous campaigns against individual directors and an increased willingness on the part of companies to cut deals rather than face nasty public fights" (White, 2004). Especially when proxy resolutions received a majority of shareholder votes in 2004, much more common now, corporations stopped ignoring that support and voluntarily implemented the change called for. As a result, ISS found the proxy season in 2004 quieter than in 2003, with a decline of 5 percent in shareholder resolutions making it on the ballot and a 66 percent decline in proxy fights (Taub, 2004).

Avoiding confrontation with proxy advisory services is also a good idea if a firm wants to insure the possibility of more positive evaluations. A company should not follow Disney's model of labeling Glass Lewis "an upstart company that is trying to grab publicity that diverts attention from the fact that Disney's record of building value is indisputable" (Orwall, 2004a). Disney took a more positive approach with other firms, however. Realizing institutional shareholders had major concerns over CEO succession plans at Disney, current CEO Michael Eisner and then presiding director and former US Senator George Mitchell met with leaders of the Council of Institutional Investors and of Institutional Shareholder Services to explain Disney's plans and seek feedback (Orwall, 2004b). Six of Disney's eleven directors also met with representatives of six pension funds from New York, Connecticut, North Carolina, California, and Ohio (Bayot, 2004). Related to executive succession, and given its growing importance in the eyes of shareholders, Nell Minow of the Corporate Library and others believe the board needs to assure shareholders annually that it has examined the CEO's annual medical report (Wine, 2004).

There is a danger in meeting with institutional investors, of course. The company may not receive the feedback it wants to hear. CalPERS, for instance, advised Disney to sell its theme parks to improve its return on invested capital. Richard H. Moore, the North Carolina treasurer, wrote two letters to Eisner and Mitchell following their meeting, one complaining of the lack of detail shared and the second saying the company treated the session as "a short-term public relations campaign at the expense of investors" (Orwall, 2004c). Meanwhile, dissident ex-director Roy Disney addressed the Council of Institutional Investors and compared Eisner to a "Third World dictator" (Orwall, 2004c).

If a negotiation with an institutional investor occurs over a shareholder resolution, there is of a course a chance that the negotiation will not successfully lead to a withdrawal of the resolution. If the resolution passes with a majority of the shareholder vote, the resolution is still not binding on corporate management under current rules. However, it might be prudent for the company to nevertheless implement the resolution. In the future, if shareholder nominees to the board are required, one of the trigger events might be

management's refusal to implement a resolution that has received a majority of shareholder support. Hence, the failure to adopt a popular resolution might have legal ramifications down the line, and might also create an image of resistance and injure good will with shareholders, even absent any legal consequences.

## Structured Interaction

Beyond negotiating with shareholder groups, who often represent other stakeholder interests as well, companies might consider establishing advisory panels for more structured interaction. Public affairs professionals can be extremely helpful in designing such structured interaction, since consumer affairs and community relations staff might have experience in developing advisory panels involving similar stakeholder groups. Disney claims it is considering just that, with activist institutional shareholders serving on an advisory panel as a liaison between the board and investors. George Mitchell, Disney's new chair, has said the board would even consider suggestions of independent director nominees offered by the various pension funds (Verrier, 2004b). Here again, however, if the company is going to meet with shareholder groups, it may not be prudent to minimize their clout and significance, as Mitchell did by saying they represent less than 2 percent of shares and that CEO Michael Eisner was "too busy" to meet with them (Verrier, 2004b).

## Voluntary Reforms

Perhaps the best way to deflect future pressures for corporate reforms tomorrow is to adopt voluntary reforms today. Issues management staff with their own intelligence capabilities might be helpful in discovering and promoting those best practices or reforms most suitable for a particular firm. Top management and the board would then be responsible for policy adoption and implementation. Related to the areas addressed in this chapter, voluntary reforms might include:

1  Adopting the best practices of corporate governance, based on an examination of exemplary companies and examination of the criteria used by the various rating systems, going beyond NYSE and Sarbox standards.
2  Expanding the range of board responsibilities and increasing the level of diligence and commitment by the board.
3  Expanding the avenues of voice and participation by shareholders and other stakeholders in corporate governance.
4  Being proactive in reforming executive compensation, perhaps even taking lessons from Costco and the Bridgeway Funds on limiting the amount of compensation and from IBM and General Electric on structuring stock and stock options benefits (Morgenson, 2004; Braham, 2003; Lauricella, 2004; Lohr, 2004).
5  Geting ahead of the curve by addressing issues that may be more important in the future, such as a rigorous evaluation process of board operations and corporate governance.
6  Disclosing all of the voluntary initiatives and changes to the public through the corporate Web site.

Beyond initiating proactive change, interactive mechanisms, and negotiations with investors, a corporation should also develop strategies to prevent or oppose unreasonable demands from investor groups and political interests. Those strategies and the definition of unreasonable reforms will differ from company to company and from industry to industry. The following section discusses some examples of cultivating allies, while isolating what seem to be unreasonable opponents.

## Cultivate Future Allies

To achieve its long-term goals on corporate reform measures, business might consider cultivating those investor groups more amenable to negotiation. The expertise of issues management and stakeholder engagement executives can be crucial in identifying both potential allies and implacable foes.

Among pension funds, for instance, CalPERS has been more extreme in its positions and more confrontational in its tactics, and it has been joined at various times on those issues and tactics by pension funds from Connecticut, New York, and North Carolina. Meanwhile, other state pension funds have taken more flexible positions on corporate governance and are more content to work quietly behind the scenes with corporations in which they invest. Business will likely find a friendlier welcome in dialogues and negotiations with such pension funds, though it should not foreclose the possibility of CalPERS and other groups becoming more flexible or approachable.

A comparable scene appears among the proxy advisory services and governance rating systems. Some are more rigid than others, with a checklist approach, and some weigh some criteria more heavily than others. It may make sense for corporations to carefully examine the various approaches and to align themselves with a rating system that is more compatible with their own corporate culture or governance priorities. If a company even wanted to justify its own approach versus that promoted by another rating service, it might carefully scrutinize and then highlight any ethical problems inherent to an opposing approach. For instance, if a company feels more comfortable with the approaches taken by the Corporate Library, IRRC, or Glass Lewis, it might try to accommodate one of the sets of criteria developed by those groups, while ignoring or even criticizing the criteria developed by ISS. Given the conflict-of-interest charges brought against ISS by the media, that might help strengthen a business case for dealing with other rating systems.

## REFERENCES

Ahrens, F. (2004). "Disney's New Drama: Dissension," *Washington Post*, March 1: A1.
Alpert, B. (2004). "Proxy Power: SEC May Help Dissidents Get on the Ballot," *Barron's*, March 1: 19.

Anders, G. (2004). "As Scandals Mount, Boards of Mutual Funds Feel the Heat," *Wall Street Journal*, March 17: A1.

Atlas, R.D. (2003). "Janus Tightens Trading Policies; Calpers Pulls out of Putnam," *New York Times*, November 19: C8.

Ball, J. (2003). "State Aides Mull Pension Funds and Environment," *Wall Street Journal*, November 21: A6.

Bank, D. (2004). "Calpers Won't Back Five Directors of H-P in Protest over Auditing," *Wall Street Journal*, March 11: A2.

Bayot, J. (2004). "Disney Board to Get Advice from Funds," *Los Angeles Times*, May 22: C2.

Belson, K., and B. Simon (2004). "Investors are Taking Long Hard Look at Nortel's Board," *New York Times*, May 13: W1.

Bhagat, S., and B. Black (2002). "The Non-correlation between Board Independence and Long-term Firm Performance," *Iowa Journal of Corporation Law* 27 (winter): 231–268.

Bogle, J.C. (2003). "The Emperor's New Mutual Funds," *Wall Street Journal*, July 8: A16.

Borrus, A. (2004). "Stick to your Guns, Mr Donaldson," *Business Week*, May 24: 77.

Braham, L. (2003). "Who Says Nice Guys Finish Last?" *Business Week*, June 16: 90–91.

Brewster, D., and A. Michaels (2003). "Tomorrow the SEC will Reveal plans to Make it Easier to Replace Board Members," *Financial Times*, October 7: 21.

Burr, B.B. (2004). "Corporate Governance: Activist Shareholders are "Cabbing it", to 2004 Proxy Season," *Pensions and Investments*, February 23: 3.

Coleman, M. (2004). "Funds Fight Independent Chairs, A Reform Proposed by the SEC," *Investor's Business Daily*, June 17: A1, A6.

Dash, E. (2004). "For Directors, Great Expectations (and More Pay)," *New York Times*, April 4: BU 10.

Day, K. (2003a). "SEC Chief Supports Plan to Aid Investors," *Washington Post*, July 16: A1.

Day, K. (2003b). "SEC to Back Help for Shareholders," *Washington Post*, October 7: E1.

Day, K. (2003c). "A Few Small Repairs," *Washington Post*, April 7: E1.

Day, K. (2004a). "Business Fights SEC Proposals," *Washington Post*, March 11: E1.

Day, K. (2004b). "SEC Proposes Broadening Proxy Power to Pick Boards," *Washington Post*, March 14: F6.

Donohue, T.J. (2003). "SEC Proxy Plan is a Threat to Business, Boon to Labor," *Investor's Business Daily*, December 4: A14.

Downey, K. (2004). "Survey Finds Few Female Directors," *Washington Post*, June 18: E3.

Eichenwald, K. (2003). "In String of Corporate Troubles, Critics Focus on Boards' Failings," *New York Times*, September 21: A1, A30.

Feder, B.J. (2004). "Funds Want Oil Companies to Report on Climate," *New York Times*, February 27: C3.

Flanigan, J. (2004). "Unions Gain in the Boardroom but Struggle in Contract Talks," *Los Angeles Times*, April 18: C1.

"For Investors, is Glass Half Full or Half Empty?" (2004). *Wall Street Journal*, June 17: C1, C5.

Fried, C. (2004). "Unleashing Directors and Urging them to Bark," *New York Times*, April 4: BU 27.

Friedman, J. (2004a). "Illinois Fund to Trim its Holdings at Pimco," *Los Angeles Times*, March 23: C1.

Friedman, J. (2004b). "Fund Firms in Scandal Feel Loss," *Los Angeles Times*, April 12: C1.

Fuhrmans, V. (2004). "Calpers Opposes WellPoint Deal," *Wall Street Journal*, June 15: C5.

Glassman, J.K. (2004). "Mutual Fund Folly," *Wall Street Journal*, June 24: A16.

Gray, S. (2004). "New Ideas Take Hold on Corporate Boards," *Washington Post*, January 7: E1.

Hechinger, J. (2004). "Fidelity's Johnson Seeks to Keep his Job as Insider Chairman," Wall Street Journal, March 17: C1.

Hechinger, J., and A. Lucchetti (2003). "CEOs of two Top Fund Firms Lash SEC," *Wall Street Journal*, January 15: D9.

Henriques, D.B., and G.B. Fabrikant (2002). "Deciding on Executive Pay, Lack of Independence is Seen," *New York Times* December 18: A1.

Hill, A., A. Michaels, and T. Tassell (2003). "Auditors Wary of Growing ISS Influence," *Financial Times*, May 30: A8.

Holson, L.M. (2004). "Criticism Mounting as Disney's Leader Faces Crucial Vote," *New York Times*, February 27: A1.

Hoover, K. (2004). "Calpers Activism Hits Even Healthy Firms," *Investor's Business Daily*, May 3: A1, A4.

Hymowitz, C. (2003). "In the US, What Will it Take to Create Diverse Boardrooms?" *New York Times*, July 8: B1.

Investor Responsibility Research Center (2003). "IRRC's Study Shows Corporations Overhauling Boards and Directors Pay," December 4. http://www.irrc.org/company/12052003_BoardPay.html>.

Johnson, C. (2004). "Ex-SEC Chiefs Back Mutual Funds Plan," *Washington Post*, June 16: E2.

Kelly, K., and S. Craig (2003). "Calpers Sues Big Board and Specialist Firms," *Wall Street Journal*, December 17: C1, C13.

Labaton, S. (2003). "SEC to Ease Voting for Outside Directors," *New York Times*, July 16: C1.

Labaton, S. (2004a). "SEC to Order that Funds have Outsiders as Chairmen," *New York Times*, June 22: C1.

Labaton, S. (2004b). "SEC at Odds on Plan to let Investors pick Directors," *New York Times*, July 1: C1.

Lauricella, T. (2004). "Maverick Aims at Fund Business," *Wall Street Journal*, February 2: R1, R4.

Lavelle, L. (2004a). "CalPERS: Too Fierce?" *Business Week*, June 7: 114.

Lavelle, L. (2004b). "Governance: Backlash in the Executive Suite," *Business Week*, June 14: 36–38.

Lavelle, L. (2004c). "So That's Why Boards Are Waking Up," *Business Week*, January 19: 72–73.

Levitt, A. (2004). "Let the Little Guy in the Boardroom," *New York Times*, May 24: A23.

Levitt, A., and R.C. Breeden (2004). "Our Ethical Erosion," *Wall Street Journal*, December 3, A16.

Lohr, S. (2004). "IBM to Alter how it Pays Stock Options to Officials," *New York Times*, February 25: C1.

Lublin, J.S. (2003). "Independence of Directors is Elusive Goal," *Wall Street Journal*, July 22: B1, B7.

Lublin, J.S. (2004). "Here Comes Politically Correct Pay," *Wall Street Journal*, April 12: R1, R4.

Luchetti, A., and J.S. Lublin (2004). "Calpers Targets Directors who Neglect Holders," *Wall Street Journal*, April 16: C1, C4.

MacAvoy, P.W., and I.M. Millstein (2004). *The Recurrent Crisis in Corporate Governance.* New York: Palgrave Macmillan.

Manne, H.G. (2004). "What Mutual Fund Scandal?" *Wall Street Journal*, January 8: A22.

McCarty, P. (2004). "SEC's Proxy Plan Threatened with Suit by Business Chamber," *Wall Street Journal*, March 11: A6.

McGeehan, P. (2004). "This Year, More Boards Feel Pressure to Show Up," *New York Times*, March 31: C1.

McGhee, T. (2004). "Qwest Shareholders Reject three Board Plans," *Denver Post*, May 26: 1C, 3C.

McKinnell, H. (2003). "Bad Medicine for Good Governance," *Wall Street Journal*, October 21: A18.

Michaels, A. (2003a). "Independent Directors," *Financial Times*, November 14: 8.

Michaels, A. (2003b). "CEOs under Greater Scrutiny after Big Governance Reforms," *Financial Times*, October 27: 23.

Michaels, A. (2003c). "Funds Under Fire for Lack of Initiative," *Financial Times*, October 7: 3.

Michaels, A. (2003d). "Shareholders Want Bigger Proxy Process Role," *Financial Times*, September 24: 33.

Michaels, A. (2003e). "Reforms Lose Support of Business Leaders," *Financial Times*, July 28: 24.

Michaels, A. (2004). "Pitt Hits at SEC Boardroom Plans," *Financial Times*, April 28: 27.

Michaels, A., and D. Roberts (2004). "Compliance Brings Business Benefits," *Financial Times*, April 23: 2.

Michaels, A., and P. Taylor (2004). "Nortel Chief Sits on a Dozen Boards," *Financial Times*, April 23: 30.

Morgenson, G. (2003). "Shares of Corporate Nice Guys Can Finish First," *New York Times*, April 27: BU 1.

Morgenson, G. (2004). "Two Pay Packages, Two Different Galaxies," *New York Times*, April 4: BU 1.

Mulligan, T.S. (2003). "State Treasurers Gain Critics," *Los Angeles Times*, November 28: C1.

Nosal, D. (2004). "The Impact of Public Scrutiny on CEOs and Boards," *Korn/Ferry International*, http://www.kornferry.com/Library/View Gallery. asp?CID=663&LanguageID=1&RegionID=23.

O'Brien, T.L. (2004). "New York State Fund Joins Californians in Citigroup Dissent," *New York Times*, April 14: C1.

Orwall, B. (2004a). "Disney Says it is Addressing Issue of Eisner Succession Plan," *Wall Street Journal*, February 11: B3.

Orwall, B. (2004b). "Calpers to Withhold Voting for Eisner," *Wall Street Journal*, February 26: A3, A4.

Orwall, B. (2004c). "Disney, Critics Step up courtship of Pension Funds," *Wall Street Journal*, March 29: A3, A14.

Oster, C. (2004). "A New Approach to Rating Mutual Funds," *Wall Street Journal*, May 25: D1, D2.

Pearlstein, S. (2003). "New Directors but Little Reform," *Washington Post*, November 12: E1.

Peltz, J.F. (2004). "CalPERS Blasts Safeway Decision to Retain Burd," *Los Angeles Times*, May 4: C2.

Peterson, J. (2004). "SEC Split on Aiding Investor Challenges," *Los Angeles Times*, March 8: C1.

Petruno, T. (2004a). "To Foes, CalPERS Needs to Check Itself," *Los Angeles Times*, May 23: C1.

Petruno, T. (2004b). "Backlash Confronts CalPERS," *Los Angeles Times*, May 20: C1.

Petruno, T. (2004c). "A New Era for Investor Activism?" *Los Angeles Times*, March 7: C1.

Reilly, D. (2003). "Across Atlantic, Fidelity's Voice is Loud, Public," *Wall Street Journal*, October 28: C1, C5.

Saito-Chung, D. (2004). "Saint Jack's Mission in Mutuals: Putting Shareholders in Control," *Investor's Business Daily*, April 22: A1, A6.

Schroeder, M., and Kelly, K. (2004). "Calpers Nominates NYSE Critic Levitt to Exchange Board," *Wall Street Journal*, March 26: C1.

Seelye, K.Q. (2003). "Environmental Groups Gain as Companies Vote on Issues," *New York Times*, May 29: C1.

Segal, D. (2004). "Heigh-ho or Heave-ho?" *Washington Post*, March 3: C1.

Sidel, R. (2004). "Calpers to Re-evaluate policy about Votes on Nonaudit Work," *Wall Street Journal*, June 23: C3.

Smith, R. (2004). "Quality of Morningstar's Research may Suffer," *Wall Street Journal*, May 26: C1, C5.

Solomon, D. (2004a). "SEC May Dilute Plan to Increase Holders' Power," *Wall Street Journal*, June 8: C1, C3.

Solomon, D. (2004b). "How to Pick Boards is Hotly Debated as SEC Mulls Rule," *Wall Street Journal*, March 22: A1.

Solomon, D., and J. Hechinger (2004a). "Mutual Funds', Chiefs Might Lose Strings," *Wall Street Journal*, June 22: C1, C4.

Solomon, D., and J. Hechinger (2004b). "Direct Democracy Looks for an Opening—in the Boardroom," *Wall Street Journal*, March 22: A1.

Sonnenfeld, J.A. (2002). "What Makes Great Boards Great," *Harvard Business Review* 80 (9): 106–113.

Stern, C. (2004). "Shareholders Keep Comcast Voting Structure," *Washington Post*, May 27: E2.

Taub, S. (2004). "Proxy Season Quieter in 2004, says ISS," *CFO.com*, June 18, http://www.cfo.com/printarticle/0,5317,14298|T,00.html?f=options.

Terhune, D., and J.S. Lublin (2004). "Calpers withholds Votes for Directors at Coke, Citigroup," *Wall Street Journal*, April 13: A3.

Tucker, S., and I. Bickerton (2004). "Dutch and UK Investors Link up to Lobby Shell," *Financial Times*, May 21: 1.

Verrier, R. (2004a). "Critics Won't Be Easily Brushed Off," *Los Angeles Times*, May 21: C1.

Verrier, R. (2004b). "Disney Directors Give Nod to Funds," *Los Angeles Times*, May 22: C1.

Verrier, R. (2004c). "Big Pension Funds ask Disney for a Meeting," *Los Angeles Times*, March 23: C1.

Verrier, R. (2004d). "More Pension Funds Won't Back Eisner," *Los Angeles Times*, February 27: C1.

Vise, D.A. (2004). "Some Stockholders think Disney Stopped Short," *Washington Post*, March 5: E1.

Wasserman, J. (2003). "After Scandals, State Treasurers Take Aim at Corruption," *Washington Post*, December 22: A8.

White, B. (2003). "Save the Chair for the Chief?" *Washington Post*, February 7: E1.

White, B. (2004). "Shareholders Get Firms' Attention," *Washington Post*, May 21: E1.

Wine, E. (2004). "CEO's Death Spotlights Succession," *Financial Times*, April 30: 24.

Young, S., and E. Sheng (2004). "Sprint Holders Urged to Withhold Vote for Directors," *Wall Street Journal*, April 9: B4.

# 27

# The Empirical Study of Public Affairs

## A Review and Synthesis

JENNIFER J. GRIFFIN

Corporate public affairs (PA) is often considered as both an art and a science. It resembles a field of science with PA activities being quantified, patterns identified, and responses across arenas categorized. The field remains an individualized art form with personal relationships and changing interests interacting with dynamic political systems (see also Harris and Fleisher, 2005). As a subject of science and art, tangible, intangible, visible, less visible, monetary, and non-monetary capabilities are critical at different times for different reasons for different audiences. Organizations can be in "the game" for the long term. Alternately, firms can come and go (and never return) to the political arena as they choose. Strategic choices in the political arena are made, and revisited, frequently. This chapter examines managerial choices made over the past four decades from an empirical perspective. It reviews and synthesizes empirical studies in the burgeoning field of corporate public affairs and corporate political strategy.

Recently, broad examinations of public affairs and the corporate political strategy field have been widespread. Scholarly articles have examined the field based upon: theoretical underpinnings (Getz, 1997, 2002), managerial implications (Shaffer, 1995; Mahon *et al.*, 2001), and empirical methodologies (Schuler, 2002;

Skippari *et al.*, 2003). Lists of PA-related publications originating from around the world are detailed elsewhere (Griffin *et al.*, 2001a, b). Reviews of qualitative case research on public affairs (Post and Andrews, 1990) and political strategy have been the topic of special conferences (Hillman, 2002; Schuler, 2002) and seminars (Skippari *et al.*, 2003). What has all this taught us?

Echoing Schuler's (2002) call to "reassemble the pieces (i.e., research in corporate political strategy and corporate public affairs) in a manner that gives us a complete, or even reasonable, picture of the overall phenomenon," this chapter reassembles empirical pieces, using a systems approach. The goal is to identify opportunities for additional empirical research in the corporate public affairs and corporate political strategy field. Key questions that are being asked while systematically examining research across four decades of scholarly inquiry are:

1 Can we empirically *describe* public affairs and corporate political strategy?
2 Can we *interpret* how corporate political strategy contributes to competitive advantage— across industries, across contexts, across geographic and political borders?

3 Can we better *understand and articulate* a common sense of meaning regarding business political strategy and how corporate public affairs adds value?

To reassemble the empirical research pieces, this article takes a systems perspective.[1] Within a systems perspective, the focus is neither solely on the firm nor on the political institutions but simultaneously examines multiple players in the public policy process (i.e., stockholders, employees or unions, suppliers, competitors, politicians, special interest groups, etc.). This review is intentionally neither firm-centric nor institution-centric. Rather it is systems-oriented and process-centric, reflecting the boundary spanning responsibilities, challenges, and activities of public affairs.

A systems approach is not new (e.g., Baron, 1995, 1997; Boddewyn, 2003; Boddewyn and Brewer, 1994; Brenner, 1980; Fleisher, 1993a, 1999; Getz, 2002; Mitnick, 1993; Schuler and Rehbein, 1997). The goal of this chapter is neither a grand model, a completely specified system, nor a critique of methodological approaches (Schuler, 2002). Rather it is a systematic understanding/mapping of what we have accomplished, and where the gaps in the field are in terms of empirical research.

As a boundary-spanning function, corporate public affairs is a *window in* and a *window out* of the organization, reflecting a potential for two-way exchanges of information, ideas and resources (Adams, 1976; Post, *et al.*, 1982, 1983). Public affairs systems coordinate, communicate and facilitate information into useful knowledge to be sent, filtered, refined, and transmitted in *both* directions. Firms, interdependently with the social and political systems, affect the public policy process and vice versa.

This chapter reviews and synthesizes key contributions from many diverse empirical studies on public affairs and corporate political activities over the past four decades. After highlighting selective research, the context for these studies suggests three waves of research on corporate public affairs and corporate political strategy: (1) foundational building blocks, (2) managerial challenges, (3) blurring of boundaries. Each of these waves of research focuses on

disparate literatures informing choices from disparate theoretical streams that are brought to bear by multiple players for different audiences in the art and science of public policy (Getz, 1997, 2002; Mitnick, 1993).

## SELECTIVE EMPIRICAL RESEARCH STUDIES

Selective, in-depth reviews of eighteen empirical studies—case studies, qualitative and quantitative research from top academic journals—are highlighted in Table 27.1. The list selectively identifies a few of the many empirical studies on corporate public affairs and corporate political strategy that have been published in the past twenty-five years. These frequently cited articles (Skippari *et al.*, 2003) from top scholars significantly contribute to our understanding of the art and science of the corporate public affairs and corporate political strategy field.

Aplin and Hegarty (1980) are frequently cited for a groundbreaking empirical study of corporate public affairs and corporate political strategy. Published in a top-tier management periodical, the *Academy of Management Journal*, the authors surveyed 435 legislative assistants in 1978 and conducted a within and between-subjects test on four influence strategies: political constituencies, information, public exposure/appeal, and direct pressure. Each influence strategy varied in perceived impact. Two strategies positively influenced legislators (constituency and information strategies). Two strategies were also influential, but with negative consequences on legislators (public exposure and direct pressure strategies). In 1985 Birnbaum corroborated Aplin and Hegarty's findings with a different population: for-profit and not-for-profit organizations. Firm size mattered; dependence upon the government for contracts and fear of retaliation also significantly affected the use of different political influence strategies.

In the early 1980s, a few empirical studies resulted in numerous academic publications in the management literature. In several related studies, Masters, Baysinger, Keim and Zeithaml (e.g., Masters and Baysinger, 1985; Masters and

Table 27.1 *Empirical studies of public affairs: selective sample*

| Author | Date | Journal | Population study | Research method | Dependent variable(s) | Independent variable(s) | Findings |
|---|---|---|---|---|---|---|---|
| Aplin and Hegarty | 1980 | *Academy of Management Journal* | Survey of 435 US legislative assistants in 1978 ($n = 145$, 33.3%) after both exploratory and in-depth interviews | Chi-square analysis Within subjects repeated measures design Scheffe's *post hoc* multiple comparison procedure | Four influence strategies: political constituent, information, public exposure/appeal, and direct pressure | n.a. | Business, societal interest groups and non-legislative government bodies employ different influence strategies Influence strategies varied in perceived impact Political constituent and information strategies significantly more positive impact than public exposure and direct pressure |
| Mahon | 1983 | *Journal of Corporate Social Performance and Policy* | Six chemical firms and one trade association (Chemical Manufacturers Association) | Explanatory and predictive case analysis Superfund legislative debate, 1978–1980 | Five political positions: resistance, collaborative, compromise, avoid/neglect, and accommodate | n.a. | Firm response capability affected by PA structure and conduct Patterns of corporate behavior reflect different political strategies of individual firms Patterns of strategies reflect evolution of life cycle of an issue |
| Birnbaum | 1985 | *Strategic Management Journal* | Eighteen public for-profit medical electronic firms, forty-two private and sixty-two public universities, 1980–1981 survey and archival data, ($n = 44\%$, 42% and 62%) | One-way analysis of variance *Post hoc* Scheffe test Multiple regression ($n = 69$) | Aplin and Hegarty's four influence strategies: political constituent, information, public exposure/appeal, and direct pressure | Organizational type (for-profit, not-for-profit; private and public ownership); size; dependence; fear of retaliation | Information strategies perceived more positively than pressure strategies Convergence for preferred influence strategies regardless of for-profit, not-for-profit, and ownership Firm size matters (+, direct, and increased frequency) Resource dependence significantly related to information strategies (personal visits, expert testimony) Fear of retaliation significantly related to technical reports and in contacting individual third parties |

*(Continued)*

Table 27.1  (Continued)

| Author | Date | Journal | Population study | Research method | Dependent variables(s) | Independent variable(s) | Findings |
|---|---|---|---|---|---|---|---|
| Masters and Baysinger | 1985 | *Academy of Management Journal* | *Fortune* 1000 industrial and 300 non-industrial listings, 1980; PAC receipts 1979–1980 election cycle from Federal Election Commission data | Two-stage multiple regression analysis | Firm's PAC funds | Organization size, profits, employees, and PAC history; government dependence, industry/regulatory environment; unions | Organizational and governmental environments significant variables Firm assets, employees, PAC history, industry, governmental purchases statistically related to PAC funds. Overall, $R^2 = 38\%$ |
| Masters and Keim | 1985 | *Journal of Politics* | *Fortune* 1000 industrial and 344 non-industrial listings, 1981. PAC receipts, 1981–1982 election cycle from FEC data | Logistic regression (Logit) analysis | Existence of PAC funding | No. of employees, assets, unions, profits, governmental purchases, and industry sector | Organizational variables (assets, number of employees) and regulatory environment (industry sector) are significant; Government purchasing and firm profitability not supported |
| Masters and Keim | 1986 | *Journal of Corporate Social Performance and Policy* | *Fortune* 1000 industrial and 344 non-industrial listings, 1981. PAC receipts, 1981–1982 election cycle from FEC data | Logistic regression (Logit) analysis Ordinary least squares multiple regression | Variation in corporate political action: PAC contributions and lobbying activity (DC office reps) | No. of employees, assets, unions, profits, government purchases, industry sector | Same population as 1985 article Organizational variables (assets, number of employees) and regulatory environment (industry) significant in probability of PAC and lobbying existence Profitability negatively related to lobbying and unionization positively related to PAC existence Organizational variables (assets, number of employees) and regulatory environment (industry) significantly related to amount of PAC funding and level of lobby representatives |

*(Continued)*

Table 27.1  (Continued)

| Author | Date | Journal | Population study | Research method | Dependent variable(s) | Independent variable(s) | Findings |
|---|---|---|---|---|---|---|---|
| Bhambri and Sonnenfeld | 1988 | Academy of Management Journal | Thirteen large companies from forest products and insurance industries | One-way ANOVA plus Spearman rank correlation analysis | Social performance | PA management structure: information, integration, and internal influence | • Balanced strength along each of the three structural dimensions associated with high social performance<br>• Consistent patterns of management structure at extremes of social performance ratings<br>• Institutional environments of industry create different corporate activities (e.g., task forces and steering committees) |
| Wright | 1989 | Journal of Politics | Survey over 300 outside lobbyists ($n = 143$) and PAC contributions ($n = 49$), 1983–1984 election cycle. | Group-by-group significance tests | Use of outside lobbyists and/or PAC contributions (expanding strategy); mixed strategy | n.a. | • PAC contributions used to maintain influence rather than expand influence<br>• PACs increasing in use for the House |
| Greening | 1992 | Journal of Corporate Social Performance and Policy | Survey 117 ($n = 41$, 35%) PA executives in the utility industry, 1989 | Correlation analysis and multiple regression analyses | Issues management structure (formalization, resources, committee use, integration of issues management with corporate planning, integration of issues management and line functions) | Environmental (media exposure, interest group pressure, crises) and firm variables (size, management involvement); Interaction terms | • Firms with highly developed internal structures able to avoid and/or respond to issues before they become crises<br>• Internal committees to address issues assist in avoiding negative media exposure<br>• Firms singled out by interest groups devote significant resources to manage issues, develop internal communication and coordination systems, and enact strategies |

(Continued)

Table 27.1 (Continued)

| Author | Date | Journal | Population study | Research method | Dependent variables(s) | Independent variable(s) | Findings |
|---|---|---|---|---|---|---|---|
| Greening and Gray | 1994 | *Academy of Management Journal* | Survey 451 PA executives in utility, petroleum and gas, and food processing industries (n = 103, 23%). | t-tests, analysis of variance; factor analysis; MANOVA | Issues management structure (formalization, resources, committee use, integration of issues management with corporate planning, integration of issues management and line functions) | Environmental (media exposure, interest group pressure, crises) and firm variables (size, management involvement) Interaction terms | • Extends Greening (1992)<br>• Supports integrated model combining firm-specific and environmental variables in developing appropriate issue management structures<br>• Interest-group pressures encourage internal communication and coordination systems to process information for responding to issues and developing I/M committees<br>• Media exposure did not affect I/M structure. Severe crises lead to increased resources but little structural change<br>• Large firms have formal structures, buffer core from increased visibility/scrutiny |
| Meznar and Nigh | 1995 | *Academy of Management Journal* | Survey CEO and PA exec. of 405 international firms on *Business Week* 1000 list, n = 81, 1991–1992. | Latent variable path analysis (LVPS) to explain and predict relationships within the model | Bridging (reg. and leg. compliance, speed of adapting to changing social expectations) and buffering (PAC donations, advocacy adverts, lobbying) strategies | No. of employees and assets, media mentions, luxury/necessity products, environmental uncertainty, collaborative enterprise strategy | • Firm size best predictor of buffering<br>• Visibility had no impact on buffering or bridging<br>• Increased environmental uncertainty increases both bridging and buffering strategies<br>• Firm-specific and external factors differentially affect PA strategies |
| Schuler | 1996 | *Academy of Management Journal* | Archival data, seventeen US steel firms, 1976–1989 | Multiple regression, weighted least squares due to heteroscedasticity | Political involvement: petitions and testimony | Market share; diversification; DC office; current ratio; debt to equity ratio; import penetration; domestic steel demand | • Largest firms file more petitions and provide testimony<br>• Level of domestic steel demand negatively affected filing of petitions<br>• DC office negatively related to providing testimony |

*(Continued)*

Table 27.1 (Continued)

| Author | Date | Journal | Population study | Research method | Dependent variable(s) | Independent variable(s) | Findings |
|---|---|---|---|---|---|---|---|
| Mitchell, Hansen, and Jepsen | 1997 | *Journal of Politics* | 524 firms from US *Fortune* 500 plus seventy foreign affiliates from seven largest investing countries, 1987–1988 election cycle | Multivariate analysis | PAC existence and contributions; No. of candidates | Industry concentration, government contracts, size, foreign or domestic-owned, mobilized opposing interests (unions and union PACs), media mentions, regulated (firm and industry levels) | • PAC contributions related to firm size<br>• Foreign-owned firms less likely to form PACs<br>• Media mentions and mobilized opposition positively related to PAC formation<br>• Mobilized opposition also increases likelihood of contributing PAC money to more candidates |
| Rehbein and Schuler | 1999 | *Business and Society* | 1,100 US-based, publicly traded manufacturing firms, 1990–1994 COMPUSTAT data | LISREL analysis; and goodness-of-fit tests | Corporate political action | Political environment, Economic environment, Industry structure, Firm filter | • Firm-specific characteristics significantly related to corporate political involvement<br>• Model focusing on internal firm behavior better explains corporate political activity than an economics-based model. |
| Schuler | 1999 | *Business and Politics* | 1292 US-based manufacturing companies, 1990–1994, regarding trade liberalization | Partial least squares | Corporate political action: testimony, advisory group for USTR, actions against others via USTR, PAC contributions to key committee members | Economic: unionization concentration ratio, employment rate, sales, government contracts Firm-specific: DC office and consultants, PA office, experience, free cash flow | • Firm-specific factors significantly affect firm political action in position-taking and changing public policies<br>• Economic and firm-specific factors both affect political action (51.9% variance explained)<br>• Economic factors influence organizational factors |

*(Continued)*

Table 27.1 (Continued)

| Author | Date | Journal | Population study | Research method | Dependent variable(s) | Independent variable(s) | Findings |
|---|---|---|---|---|---|---|---|
| Lord | 2000 | *Business and Society* | Survey aides in all 535 congressional offices ($n = 202$, 38%) and 500 PA executivity from Business Week 1,000 ($n = 166$, 33%) | Analysis of variance and multivariate analysis of variance of three sets (combined, congressional, corporate) | Effectiveness on legislative decision making | PAC contributions, constituency building, executive lobbying, professional lobbying, advocacy advertising | • Constituency building significantly influences legislators' choices to support or oppose legislation<br>• Emphasizes legislators' strong self-interest in serving their politically active constituencies. |
| Shaffer and Hillman | 2000 | *Strategic Management Journal* | Three anonymous diversified US-based firms | Grounded theory | n.a. | n.a. | Three types of conflict: proactive policy issues, coping with compliance costs of after-policy decisions, representation by individual business or trade/corporate groups |
| Schuler, Rehbein, and Cramer | 2002 | *Academy of Management Journal* | 1284 US-based manufacturing companies, 1990–1994, regarding trade liberalization | Multivariate regression analysis-alternating logistic regression for political activeness | Combine political tactics: PAC contributions; number of DC office staff (inside lobbyists); outside lobbyists retained, 1991–1994 | Industry: concentration, rivalry in PACs contributions, rivalry with inside lobbyists, rivalry with outside lobbyists, unions, congressional caucus.<br>Firm: sales, cash flows, government contracts. | • Industry concentration, industry political rivalry, congressional caucus, firm size and government contracts statistically related to firms using combined tactics<br>• Free cash flows and unionization not statistically significant<br>• First study to examine combined tactics |

Keim, 1985, 1986; Baysinger, 1984; Baysinger *et al.*, 1987; Zeithaml and Keim, 1985; Zeithaml *et al.*, 1988) examined large US-based firms and their political action committee (PAC) contributions from the late 1970s until the mid-1980s. This research resulted in more than a dozen empirical and theoretical articles, with different authors contributing different articles in publications such as the *Journal of Politics, Journal of Management, Academy of Management Review, Academy of Management Journal, Research in Corporate Social Performance and Policy, Strategic Management Journal*, and *California Management Review*, among others. Overall, their research suggests PAC funds were significantly affected by firm size, number of employees, PAC giving history, and the regulatory environment (industry sector) of the firm. Surprisingly, a firm's bottom-line profit was rarely, and often negatively, related to PAC funding. This PAC research led to insights into coalition building and grassroots advocacy.

A second, large-scale and groundbreaking empirical study conducted about the same time by the Boston University Research Group examined the management function challenged with managing corporate political involvement tactics and creating organizational strategies: the corporate PA function. Jim Post, Bob Dickie, Ted Murray, and John Mahon published numerous articles on corporate public affairs and related topics throughout the early and mid-1980s (e.g., Dickie, 1984; Murray, 1982; Post *et al.*, 1982, 1983; Mahon, 1983; Mahon and Murray, 1981). The initial study examined the structure, design, and conduct of PA functions in 400 large US-based firms. Often created as a firm's response to corporate crises, corporate public affairs often began with limited resources in a reactive, resistant environment and with the direct approval of the CEO. Public affairs executives worked with governmental legislators and regulators, and created strategies often reflecting a late stage, resistance/reactive, or "firefighting" mode. By the time PA executives stepped into the debate, the public policy issue was generally far along the issue life cycle (Mahon, 1989). This initial research led to

advancements in issues management and regulatory environments by examining multiple interests/stakeholders in the political negotiation process. Fifteen years later, research on corporate PA activities, resources, and processes was reinvigorated with near-simultaneous empirical studies around the world in Canada, Australia and the United States (Pedler, 1995; Centre for Corporate Public Affairs, 1996; Canadian Council for Public Affairs Advancement, 1996; Post and Griffin, 1997; see Griffin and Lenn, 1998, for a cross-national comparison).

In the early 1990s three scholars took the lead in publishing PA empirical studies. Fleisher (1992, 1993a, b, 1995, 1997), Greening (1992; Greening and Gray, 1994; Mattingly and Greening, 2001) and Meznar and Nigh (1993, 1995) separately studied benchmarking and measurement, issues management, and international PA strategies, respectively. Each author wrote numerous solo-authored and co-authored articles or books on measurement activities, structuring corporate responses, and understanding corporate PA strategies. These authors, while writing separately, began using management and organizational theories, developing models, testing hypotheses, and examining fine-grained factors differentiating PA structure and management. Fleisher studied specific indicators and measurement strategies for benchmarking PA processes, outcomes, and strategies across industries, firms, and geographic boundaries. Greening focused on issues management and how firms developed internal capabilities translating into competitive advantage. He focused on issues germane to the social, political, and legal arenas of firms, and helped spearhead broader levels of abstraction, examining interrelated aspects of firms' responses to external stimuli. Meznar, with his mentor, Nigh, extended earlier research by focusing on international business-government relations, PA structure, and buffering/bridging strategies through their examinations of multinational corporations, based primarily in the United States.

More recently, Schuler (1996, 1999) and colleagues (Rehbein and Schuler, 1999; Schuler *et al.*, 2002) compiled a database of more than

1,100 US-based manufacturing companies examining trade liberalization. This empirical research corroborates earlier findings that dual-acting pressures from internal *and* external sources simultaneously affect managerial decisions. Using fine-grained research methods, specific indicators, detailed data sources, and multiple dependent variables with viable theory-based hypotheses underscores the boundary-spanning nature of the corporate PA function. Internal, firm-specific characteristics and conditions contribute to managers' decisions of identifying priorities, deploying resources, and creating capabilities to gain competitive advantage in the political arena.

Overall, the selective review highlights disparate interests, motivations, theoretical bases, research designs, and industries involved in studying corporate public affairs and corporate political strategy. Synthesizing our collective work suggests three different waves of research utilizing differing (1) contexts, (2) conditions and (3) motivations. The field of public affairs and political strategy has converged from multiple, theoretical streams. At the same time, the field continues to diverge based on interesting research questions and improved methods. The balance of this chapter synthesizes the empirical literature by exploring the context and evolution of the fields of corporate public affairs and corporate political strategy.

## CORPORATE PUBLIC AFFAIRS: THREE WAVES OF EMPIRICAL RESEARCH

Synthesizing the empirical research suggests three waves of research: (1) foundational building blocks, (2) managerial challenges, and (3) blurring of boundaries. The first wave focuses on traditional scholarly research informing the creation of corporate public affairs and corporate political strategy. This wave includes foundational building blocks from management, political science, economics, law, and government literatures and is augmented by research from professional associations (e.g., the Conference Board, the Public

Affairs Council in Washington, DC, the Canadian Council for Corporate Public Affairs Advancement in Toronto, and the Centre for Corporate Public Affairs in Melbourne, Australia).

The second wave of research emphasizes managerial choices in deploying resources, prioritizing issues, and managing contexts in the political arena. Scholarly research on structuring the corporate PA function, political involvement activities, issues management, regulated firms/industries, as well as the growing interest in the international context of political strategy, are emphasized in this research.

The third wave of research, blurring of boundaries, is the most nascent and evolving area of empirical research. Incorporating insights from disparate literatures such as corporate strategy, international business, social actors, symbolism and marketing, this wave of research examines how firms leverage assets in gaining sustainable competitive advantage. Advantage has been defined as firm performance, political capital, incremental improvements, benchmarking, visibility, or the building of management capabilities. Multiple actors in the political and social arenas are intermixed in this research. Trade/professional associations and non-governmental organizations (NGOs) inform, enlarge, and enhance the empirical base of business-government-social interactions.

Each wave roughly follows a chronological set of empirical studies. Inevitably, the intermingling of academic ideas and the foreshadowing of significant topics of scholarly interest are apparent in each wave of research (see Table 27.2). Over the past four decades, empirical research was, at times, more internally oriented (the internal processes of the organization), and at other times more outward-oriented (role of political institutions, public policy outcomes, and corporate responses to social initiatives). More recently with a blurring of boundaries between firms and their networks of stakeholders, research focuses on how iterative stakeholder-network relations are changing the political arena.

Table 27.2   *Three waves of empirical research studies*

**1ST WAVE – FOUNDATION BUILDING**

**Political Science**
Olson, 1965; Epstein, 1969, 1980; Cobb & Elder, 1972; Vogel, 1978, 1989; Aplin & Hegarty, 1980; Steiner & Steiner, 1980; Miles, 1987; North, 1981; Mitnick, 1993 and Boddewyn, 1977, 2005; Windsor, 2005; Keim, 2002.

**Professional Associations**
Nagelschmidt, 1982; Lusterman, 1983, 1985, 1987; Mack, 1989, 1991, 1997; Pedersen, 1989; Kennerdell, 1992; Dennis, 1996; Canadian Council for Public Affairs Advancement, 1996; Foundation for Public Affairs, 1999, 2002; Pedler, 2005; Allen, 2005.

**2ND WAVE – MANAGERIAL CHALLENGES**

**Corporate Public Affairs**
Structure: Boddewyn, 1973a, 1973b, 1974; Brenner, 1980; Dickie, 1981; Mahon & Murray, 1981; Post, Dickie, Murray & Mahon, 1982, 1983; Baysinger & Woodman, 1982; Miles, 1987; Bhambri & Sonnenfeld, 1988; Fleisher, 1992; Post & the Foundation for Public Affairs, 1993; Meznar & Nigh, 1993, 1995;  Post & the Centre for Corporate Public Affairs, 1993; Pedler, 1995; Centre for Corporate Public Affairs, 1996; Griffin, 1997; Post & Griffin, 1997; Foundation for Public Affairs, 1999, 2002; Griffin & Dunn, 2004.

**Issues Management**
Chase, 1975; Ewing, 1980; Felstiner, Abel & Sarat, 1980; Mahon, 1983, 1989; Arrington & Sawaya, 1984; Heath, 1985; Ullmann, 1985; Coates, 1985; Heath & Nelson, 1986; Wartick & Rude, 1986; Wartick & Mahon, 1994; Mahon & McGowan, 1996; Heugens, 2001; Mahon, Fleisher, and Wartick, 2001; Heugens, Mahon & Wartick, 2004; Mahon, Heugens & Lamertz, 2004.

*Crises*: Greening, 1992; Greening & Gray, 1994.

**Contexts:  Regulated Firms/Industries**
Birnbaum, 1984, 1985; Ullmann, 1985; Leone, 1987; Mitnick, 1993; Mahon & McGowan, 1996; Schuler, 1996.

**Managing Political Involvement Activities**
*Political Action Committees (PACs)*: Aplin & Hegarty, 1980; Keim, 1981; Masters & Baysinger, 1985; Masters & Keim, 1985; Masters & Keim, 1986; Keim & Zeithaml, 1986; Keim & Baysinger, 1988; Dean, Vryza & Fryxell, 1998.

*Lobbying*:  MacMillan, 1981; Levitan & Cooper, 1984; Mahon, 2005.

*Grassroots*: Keim & Baysinger, 1982; Meadow, 1983; Keim, 1985; Baysinger, Keim & Zeithaml, 1987; Pedersen, 1989; Lord, 1995, 2000, 2003.

*Combinations of Tactics*: Brenner, 1980; Zeithaml & Keim, 1985; Zeithaml, Keim & Baysinger, 1988; Lenway & Rehbein, 1991; Getz, 1993; Mullery, Brenner & Perrin, 1995; Schuler, Rehbein & Cramer, 2002.

**Contexts: International, State & Local**
Dunn, Cahill & Boddewyn, 1979; Globerman & Schwindt, 1985; Ring, Lenway & Govekar, 1990; Preston & Windsor, 1992; Lenn, Brenner, Burke, Dodd-McCue, Fleisher, Lad, Palmer, Rogers, Waddock & Wokutch, 1993; Meznar & Nigh, 1993, 1995; Post and the Centre for Corporate Public Affairs, 1993; Boddewyn & Brewer, 1994; Getz, 1995; Pedler, 1995; Centre for Corporate Public Affairs, 1996; Meznar & Johnson, 1996; Griffin, Shaffer & Mahon, 1998; Doh, 1999; Oomens & van den Bosch, 1999; Young & Brewer, 1999; Blumentritt, 2003; Skippari, Eloranta, Lamberg & Parvinen 2003.

**3RD WAVE – BLURRING OF BOUNDARIES**

**Dependent Variables**
*Firm Performance*: Hillman, 2002; Hillman, Zardooki & Bierman, 1999; Shaffer, Quasney & Grimm, 2000.

*Political Capital*: Schuler, Rehbein & Cramer, 2002; Rehbein & Schuler, 2003.

*Benchmarking*: Fleisher, 1992, 1993a, 1993b, 1997.

*Insights from PA executives*: Preece, Fleisher & Toccacelli, 1995; Fleisher & Hoewing, 1992.

**Social, Political, NGO Constituencies**
Hillman & Keim, 2001; Windsor, 2002; Griffin, 2002; Epstein & Schnietz, 2002; Doh and Teegen, 2003; Griffin & Dunn, 2004.

**Corporate Strategy/Integrated Strategy**
Mahon, 1989; Mitnick, 1993; Schuler & Rehbein, 1997; Rehbein & Schuler, 1999; Greening, 1992; Baron, 1997; Shaffer & Hillman, 2000; Mattingly, 2003; Mattingly & Greening, 2001.

*Management Capabilities/Commitment*: Shaffer, 1995; Meznar & Nigh, 1995; Schuler, 1996; Schuler & Rehbein, 1997; Rehbein & Schuler, 1999; Schuler, 1999; Epstein & Schnietz, 2002; Schuler, 2002; Griffin & Dunn, 2004.

**PR/Communications/Reputation**
Grunig, 1979;Grunig & Hunt, 1984; Preece, Fleisher and Toccacelli, 1995; Fleisher, 1998, 1999; Mahon, 2002.

*Visibility*: Bonardi & Keim, 2002; Blumentritt, 2003.

## First Research Wave: Foundation Building

Early grounded research explicitly documented the need and importance to study the inter-relationships of businesses and governments (Windsor, 2002). Initially the focus was on governmental activities and actors (Epstein, 1969). Emphasizing national government with little attention to the state, local, or interregional agencies, the early management literature focused on *why* management should get involved and *how* the public policy process worked (Epstein, 1969; Lindblom, 1977; Miles, 1987; North, 1981; Olson, 1965; Vogel, 1989). The added complexity of international business-government relations underscored the importance of the CEO's commitment to government relations (Boddewyn, 1977, 2005).

For students and professionals alike, a textbook by Steiner and Steiner (1980) further solidified the field and addressed an important constituency—future managers—the students of graduate and undergraduate business school programs. Converging theoretical literatures created new opportunities to study business-government interactions from political science, management, and organizational theory/design (Windsor, 2005). Mitnick (1993) literally created the field of political agency, focusing on the unique relationship between politicians and their constituents. Electoral politics, election campaigns, and defining election issues remain important areas of inquiry today (Keim, 2002). Cobb and Elder (1972) focused on specific aspects of business-government interactions such as issues management, structure, and processes.

Professional associations, such as the Conference Board and the Public Affairs Council, were another foundational building block helping define a need and an appreciation of the importance of business-government relations. Practicing managers sought out experts in multiple academic disciplines, discussing among themselves the best practices, and organizing into professional associations. The Conference Board published a series of reports in the 1980s on business-government

relations and international public affairs (Lusterman, 1983, 1985, 1987). The US Public Affairs Council (the Council) and its non-profit research arm, the Foundation for Public Affairs (FPA), explored the multiplicity of actors, actions, and activities occurring between business and governments, special interest groups, and public interest groups. By regularly publishing the *National Directory of Corporate Public Affairs* with *Congressional Quarterly*, and surveying the "state of the art of corporate public affairs," the Council and the FPA contributed to making data on PA practices available to a wider audience (Foundation for Public Affairs, 1999, 2002; Post and the Foundation for Public Affairs, 1993).

Numerous PA executives published books on PA-related topics. Nagelschmidt (1982) edited a handbook on public affairs which was followed by Mack's books (1989, 1991, 1997). Kennerdell's book (1992) on political action committees and Lloyd Dennis's (1996) book on public affairs which in an era of change increased understanding of the role of the PA function and its activities. All in all, these pioneering PA executives help create the opportunity for ongoing interactions between PA executives and academics, as identified in the second and third waves of research.

Professional associations and corporate PA organizations with specific geographic interests later emerged around the world: the UK Centre for Public Affairs (Pedler, 2005), the Australasian Centre for Corporate Public Affairs (Allen, 2005) and the Canadian Council for Public Affairs Advancement (1996). Each professional association conducted studies, polled members, directed surveys, published manuscripts, collected anecdotal stories, created case studies to acknowledge and bring heightened awareness to the interactions between business and government around the world. Collectively, these actions increased sensitivity towards and employed different methods of inquiry to examine why, when, how, and where involvement within the political arena for public policy decision-making processes was effective.

Overall, the first wave of empirical research built upon grounded research, interviews with opinion leaders, and discussions with senior executives, governmental officials, and management experts. Aplin and Hegarty (1980), as stated earlier, were the exception. Aplin and Hegarty (1980) used fairly rigorous statistical methods to examine PAC contributions and management influence strategies. Creating a compelling logic identifying a need for, and defining research questions for, further scholarly inquiry (Epstein, 1969, 1980; Miles, 1987), this early research created a foundation for deeper empirical examinations combining quantitative and qualitative methods.

## Second Research Wave: Managerial Challenges

The second wave of research examines how organizations and managers organize their internal resources (structure, reporting relationships, budget, staffing, responsibilities, activities, etc.). It also examines how firms deploy their resources in the political arena via political involvement activities, building upon managerial capabilities, and effective issues management.

The structure, resources, and process of the corporate PA function have been academically studied for more than three decades, as discussed earlier in the selective research review. Public affairs activities, reporting relationships, senior executive titles, budgets, political involvement activities, and relationships with business-level operations have been examined since the early 1980s (Dickie, 1981; Foundation for Public Affairs, 1999, 2002; Post and Griffin, 1997; Mahon and Murray, 1981; Post et al., 1982, 1983; Fleisher, 1992; Post and the Foundation for Public Affairs, 1993; Post and Griffin, 1997). The Foundation for Public Affairs conducts biennial "state of the art corporate public affairs" studies.

At the same time, grounded research and case studies by Harvard's Miles (1987) and his former students (Bhambri and Sonnenfeld, 1988) examined PA practices in various industries, including insurance and forest products. Brenner (1980) and Baysinger and Woodman

(1982) conducted a large-scale survey on practicing PA executives and built upon Boddewyn's work in the previous decade (1973a, b, 1974). All of these studies suggest PA functions integrate different activities and different responsibilities in different firms—regardless of size, industry, and regulatory environment.

An outgrowth of the research on corporate PA structure was deeper emphasis on issues management research. Identifying, naming, and assessing blame for relevant business-government issues (Arrington and Sawaya, 1984; Chase, 1975; Coates, 1985; Ewing, 1980; Felstiner et al., 1980; Heath, 1985; Heath and Nelson, 1986; Mahon, 1989; Mahon et al., 2001). Elaborating on the issues life cycle (Mahon, 1989; Wartick and Mahon, 1994; Ullmann, 1985) and effective strategies for PA executives (Heugens, 2001; Mahon and McGowan, 1996; Wartick and Rude, 1986), the concept of a portfolio of issues (Heugens et al., 2004) and cascading arenas of resolution is emerging to capture the complex network of issues management (Mahon et al., 2004).

An outgrowth of this research focused on crisis management (Greening, 1992; Greening and Gray, 1994): how, why, and when PA executives effectively employed business-government and issues management strategies during crises.

Separately, but simultaneously, research on corporate political involvement activities also grew exponentially during this second wave of research. Building upon management literatures and the traditional political science tradition, many empirical studies of political action committees PACs were conducted (Aplin and Hegarty, 1980; Keim, 1981; Keim and Baysinger, 1988; Keim and Zeithaml, 1986; Masters and Baysinger, 1985; Masters and Keim, 1985, 1986; Dean et al., 1998). Political involvement studies examining direct lobbying (cf. MacMillan, 1981; Levitan and Cooper, 1984; Mahon, 2005) emerged. Indirect lobbying by grassroots constituencies also grew in importance. Why, when, and how to implement grassroots advocacy activities with employees, suppliers, retirees, or critical stakeholders was a natural outgrowth of political involvement activity research (Baysinger *et al.*, 1987; Keim, 1985; Lord, 1995, 2000, 2003; Meadow, 1983; Pederson, 1989).

Understanding each tactic in isolation is useful, but practicing managers often used multiple tactics in combination. Scholarly research began examining multiple tactics within the same manuscript (Brenner, 1980; Zeithaml and Keim, 1985; Zeithaml *et al.*, 1988). More recent research has combined tactics and more rigorous empirical methods to explicitly examine the trade-offs between and among political involvement tactics (cf. Getz, 1993; Lenway and Rehbein, 1991; Mullery *et al.*, 1995; Schuler *et al.*, 2002). Yet, no consensus on the best tactic for a particular issue and particular audience has emerged from these studies.

In addition to the structure and political involvement activities of PA executives, a firm's external environment was examined to see if the competitive context created unique opportunities that encouraged development of PA skills. Regulated industries, for example, are hypothesized to have different PA capabilities since regulated firms regularly interact with, have oversight and monitoring requirements of, and might even have their rate structures set by governmental agencies (Leone, 1987; Mitnick, 1993; Ullmann, 1985). Examples of scholarly research on specific regulated industries include: steel (Schuler, 1996), petrochemical (Mahon and McGowan, 1996), and high-tech (Birnbaum, 1984, 1985).

Broadening the managerial context to include international, state, and local implications became increasingly important. Studies of international public affairs and international issues management emerged (Boddewyn and Brewer, 1994; Dunn *et al.*, 1979; Ring *et al.*, 1990; Lenn *et al.*, 1993; Oomens and van den Bosch, 1999; Preston and Windsor, 1992). Some scholars focused on particular events or institutions such as the Montreal Protocol (Getz, 1995) or the World Trade Organization (WTO) (Young and Brewer, 1999). Others focused on country-specific strategies for Canadian firms (Globerman and Schwindt,

1985) or the European Union (Meznar and Johnson, 1996; Doh, 1999). Most of the international PA and political strategy empirical research, however, remains US-centric with primarily US-based researchers. Research in state and local governmental activities remains nascent (Griffin *et al.*, 1998). Yet, many opportunities await PA executives and political strategy researchers in local and international contexts (Blumentritt, 2003; Skippari *et al.*, 2003).

Underlying this wave of research were selective business and government relationships. The structure of public affairs, the process of issues management, the political involvement activities and the context of firm all contribute to shaping PA strategy. Yet, a lack of common understanding of "what is a PA function" suggesting a description of public affairs by what it does might be misleading, confounding, or erroneous. Thus, a subtle shift to focus on the purpose of PA functions and outcomes of political strategies is evident in the next wave. The blurring of boundaries between organizational studies, political science, management, and strategy is explored further in the third wave of research.

## Third Research Wave: Blurring of Boundaries

The third wave of research, "blurring of boundaries," builds upon the two previous categories: "foundation building" and "managerial challenges." Insights from political science, strategic management, and organizational theories are brought to bear to strategically examine business-government interactions and strategic public affairs. New questions were being asked. New insights, created by integrating academic literatures and closely examining managerial practices, were blurring the boundaries between firms and their institutional environments.

One key question being asked is: How effective are the outcome of the firm's PA efforts? To examine this question, academics and PA executives shifted their focus to dependent variable and management outcomes, respectively. Some argued the appropriate dependent variable was firm performance (Hillman, 2002; Hillman *et al.*, 1999; Shaffer *et al.*, 2000), others suggested creating or maintaining political capital (Rehbein and Schuler, 2003; Schuler, Rehbein and Cramer, 2002). Fleisher suggested an important outcome was improving firm practices via performance assessment and benchmarking (Fleisher, 1992, 1993a, b, 1997). Alternatively, Lord (2000) examined legislative outcomes. Insights from PA executives suggested a focus on value added, reputation, and strategically managing public affairs (Preece *et al.*, 1995; Fleisher and Hoewing, 1992). Little consensus on an appropriate dependent variable was achieved. Methodologically, quantitative studies dominate the third wave with rigorous statistical methods when examining appropriate dependent variables.

Another set of key questions is: What are the intended and unintended ripple effects of our actions? Is there a "push back" and change in the arena (from legislative to regulatory or the courts; from the courts to the court of public opinion; etc.)? This set of questions led to a strategic and purposeful integration of market and non-market strategies—integrated strategies. Empirically examining the nexus between political strategy and organizational theory (Greening, 1992; Rehbein and Schuler, 1999; Schuler and Rehbein, 1997) as well as political strategy and competitive strategy (Mahon, 1989; Mattingly, 2003; Mattingly and Greening, 2001; Mitnick, 1993; Shaffer and Hillman, 2000) ensued. Underlying this wave of research was an examination of management capabilities (Epstein and Schnietz, 2002; Rehbein and Schuler, 1999; Schuler, 1996, 2002; Schuler and Rehbein, 1997). Results of this inquiry identify no one pattern of coherent actions as being superior across contexts. Rather, a consensus is emerging that integrating political, organizational, and competitive insights (including leadership) produces superior models for understanding the field of corporate public affairs and corporate political strategy. A firm's CEO, senior PA executives, and organizational culture continue to shape how corporate PA functions are strategically managed (Pedler, 2005; Schuler, 1999, 2002;

Griffin and Dunn, 2004) and corporate political strategies are created.

Management capabilities and commitment are another promising area of research. Focusing on how firms make decisions in a variety of contexts, with a variety of resources, leveraging various relationships to achieve different ends—strategic management, resource-based view of the firm, first mover opportunity, slack resources, and institutional theory—are adding insights to business-government relations (Shaffer, 1995; Meznar and Nigh, 1995; Schuler, 1999, 2002; Epstein and Schneitz, 2002; Griffin and Dunn, 2004).

Empirical research continues to blur the boundaries among social, political (Epstein and Schnietz, 2002; Windsor, 2002) and nongovernmental (NGO) constituencies (Doh and Teegen, 2003; Griffin, 2002; Hillman and Keim, 2001). Integrating public affairs, political strategy, public relations, and communications (Grunig, 1979; Grunig and Hunt, 1984; Preece *et al.*, 1995; Fleisher, 1998, 1999) suggests new avenues of advantage, including multifaceted relationships with reputation (Mahon, 2002). This research has also led to the emergence of different organizational variables such as visibility and questions regarding the role of the media in public policy (Blumentritt, 2003; Bonardi and Keim, 2002).

A blurring of boundaries reflects the integration among various aspects of the business-government-society relationships. Simultaneously, the additional empirical research is broadening the base of inquiry within the field of corporate public affairs and corporate political strategy. The integration has brought rigor and a multilevel perspective to the examination of these complex issues while minimizing the noise and being careful of erroneous empirical conclusions.

Some fundamental questions underlie the third wave of research. *Why* do corporate PA functions exist (and continue to persist)? And, what constitutes effective political strategy? In many respects, these basic questions underscore some of the foundational principles upon which corporate PA and corporate political strategy were built. Questions of credibility, trust, reputation, legitimacy, benefit to society/public policy, and the corporate governance remain. From a management perspective, our empirical studies have only scratched the surface of understanding the notions of value added, contribution, marginal returns, performance effectiveness, and strategic direction/orientation of the PA function, specifically, and a firm's outreach philosophy more generally.

Overall, the three waves of research synthesize underlying contexts, motivations, and conditions of empirical research in the field of corporate public affairs and corporate political strategy. This chapter has selectively highlighted various management-oriented researches in corporate public affairs and political strategy. A specific detailing of the entire body of empirical political research is beyond the scope of this chapter. While there are numerous limitations to synthesizing four decades of empirical studies into three waves of research, this review encompasses more than four decades with more than 100 empirical articles from ninety different scholars. Important implications for PA executives and academic researchers are identified below.

## IMPLICATIONS AND CONCLUSIONS

The field of corporate public affairs and political strategy is multifaceted, involving complex interactions with multiple constituencies, various resources, differing interests, and serendipity. It remains as much an art as a science—even after four decades of empirical and theoretical studies from academics and professionals alike. By combining insights from a variety of different literatures, corporate political strategy gains credence from corporate strategy, stakeholder literature, issues management, international strategy, and international business. Future research into understanding the role of culture, and NGOs, will likely broaden our collective understanding and gain insights beyond the "Western" world of corporate public affairs. If properly examined, we are likely to better understand the necessary and sufficient

capabilities required for organizations to achieve effective execution of PA strategy. While anticipatory, risk-based analysis allows for reaction on some issues, an holistic strategic understanding remains undeveloped but very much in demand.

Over the past four decades, the empirical research has shifted from a focus on firm-centric tactics to strategy. Measuring what corporate PA functions are doing (e.g., balanced scorecard, benchmarking, return on investment) is being supplemented by rigorous studies to understand the longer-term issues in which an organization can viably make a difference. Some long-term issues are broader in scope than any one single company initiative. For example, trust, legitimacy, and global citizenship initiatives are being spearheaded by leading PA functions in leading companies. John Deere & Co., for example, is working closely with different contractors to develop rebuilding Iraq initiatives after the Iraqi war with the cooperation of the Department of Defense, Department of Commerce, local Iraqi businessmen, and other interested collaborators. The Gap, Westpac, and ING, for example, are early movers in publishing corporate social responsibility reports to "raise the bar" on their initiatives with their local community, philanthropic outreach, education, and corporate social activities. Organizations are strategically leveraging organizational capabilities into (as well as between and among) the social and political environments to make a difference in the lives of their employees, consumers, and local communities.

Empirically, there continues to be disagreement as to a viable and appropriate dependent variable. Is there a "best" or "only" dependent variable: firm performance, long-term firm performance, political capital, PAC contributions, access, influence, or vote counts? While it may be easy to block legislative activities or regulatory actions, are firms now more focused on effecting positive change? At the same time, new independent variables and mitigating variables are emerging, such as visibility, media citations, and intensity of stake. Whereas size was generally believed to be a driving force behind many political arena initiatives, its impact is perhaps diminishing due to strategic and selective initiatives by firms with significant stakes in policy. While size, in general, is positively related to corporate campaign contributions, the ability to gain access and affect favorable decisions is much less clear. Electoral politics (i.e., campaign contributions) is heavily favored as a research topic. More legislative and regulatory examinations in conjunction with management literatures are necessary.

This chapter, by design, is neither an exhaustive list nor indicative of what might come. A new cohort of international scholars well steeped in organizational, management, strategic, and political theories is likely to make significant contributions in the years to come (Berg, 1999; Mattingly and Greening, 2001; Skippari et al., 2003). Understanding the conditions, context, and motivations for PA strategies in multiple geographic jurisdictions from companies based around the world is particularly promising.

Overall, the field of corporate public affairss and corporate political strategy remains vibrant and engaged in a variety of important research questions. Significant contributions remain to be accomplished by executives and academic scholars regarding the art and science of public affairs. The future of the field is only limited by the imagination of the explorers.

## NOTE

1 This chapter does not take the traditional inside versus outside approach. The traditional inside/outside approach suggests that activities within the firm (the inside approach) can be examined independent of activities occurring within the firm's external context (the outside approach). An inside/outside approach is inadequate because it suggests that parallel analysis of firms and political arenas are separable (Schuler, 2002).

## REFERENCES

Adams, J.S. (1976). "The Structure and Dynamics of Behavior in Organizational Boundary Roles," pp. 1175–1199 in M.D. Dunnette (ed.), *Handbook of Industrial and Organizational Psychology*. Palo Alto, CA: Consulting Psychologists Press.

Allen, G. (2005). "An Integrated Model: The Evolution of Public Affairs Down Under," in P. Harris and Fleisher, C.S. (eds), *Handbook of Public Affairs*. London: Sage.

Aplin, J.C., and W.H. Hegarty (1980). "Political Influence: Strategies Employed by Organizations to Impact Legislation in Business and Economic Matters," *Academy of Management Journal* 23 (3): 438–450.

Arrington, C.B., and R.N. Sawaya (1984). "Managing Public Affairs: Issues Management in an Uncertain Environment," *California Management Review* 26 (4): 148–160.

Baron, D.P. (1995). "Integrated Strategy: Market and Nonmarket Components," *California Management Review* 37 (2): 47–65.

Baron, D.P. (1997). "Integrated Strategy and International Trade Disputes: The Kodak-Fujifilm Case," *Journal of Economics and Management Strategy* 6 (2): 291–346.

Baysinger, B.D. (1984). "Domain Maintenance as an Objective of Business Political Activity: An Expanded Typology," *Academy of Management Review* 9 (2): 248–258.

Baysinger, B.D., and R.W. Woodman (1982). "Dimensions of the Public Affairs/Government Relations Function in Major American Corporations," *Strategic Management Journal* 3 (1): 27–41.

Baysinger, B.D., G.D. Keim, and C.P. Zeithaml (1987). "Constituency Building as a Political Strategy in the Petroleum Industry," in A.A. Marcus, A.M. Kaufman, and D.R. Beam (eds), *Business Strategy and Public Policy: Perspectives from Industry and Academia*, New York: Quorum Books.

Berg, N. (1999). "Public Affairs Management in Multinational Corporations: Findings of an Empirical Study among German Corporations in India," in D.J. Wood and D. Windsor (eds), *Proceedings of the International Association for Business and Society*, 10: 325–330.

Bhambri, A., and J. Sonnenfeld (1988). "Organization Structure and Corporate Social Performance: A Field Study in Two Contrasting Industries," *Academy of Management Journal* 31 (3): 642–662.

Birnbaum, P. (1984). "The Choice of Strategic Alternatives under Increasing Regulation in High Technology Companies," *Academy of Management Journal* 27 (3): 489–510.

Birnbaum, P.H. (1985). "Political Strategies of Regulated Organizations as Functions of Context and Fear," *Strategic Management Journal* 6 (2): 135–150.

Blumentritt, T.P. (2003). "Foreign Subsidiaries' Government Affairs Activities: The Influence of Management and Resources," *Business and Society* 42 (2): 202–233.

Boddewyn, J.J. (1973a). "External Affairs at Four Levels in US Multinationals," *Industrial Relations* 12 (2): 239–247.

Boddewyn, J.J. (1973b). "The External Affairs Function in American Multinational Corporations," in J. Fayerweather (ed.), *International Business-Government Affairs*. New York: Ballinger.

Boddewyn, J.J. (1974). "External Affairs: A Corporate Function in Search of Conceptualization and Theory," *Organization and Administration Sciences*, spring, pp. 67–111.

Boddewyn, J.J. (main reporter) (1977). *Multinational Government Relations: An Action Guide for Corporate Management*. Washington, DC: International Business-Government Counselors.

Boddewyn, J.J. (2003). "Understanding and Advancing the Concept of 'Nonmarket,'" *Business and Society* 42 (3): 297–327.

Boddewyn, J.J., and T.L. Brewer (1994). "International Business Political Behavior: New Theoretical Directions," *Academy of Management Review* 19 (1): 119–143.

Bonardi, J-P., and G.D. Keim (2002). "Nonmarket Strategies and Election Issues: A Theoretical Framework Based on Information and Reputation Cascades." Presented at the annual Academy of Management conference, Denver, CO, August.

Brenner, S.N. (1980). "Corporate Political Activity: An Exploratory Study in a Developing Industry," in L.E. Preston (ed.), *Research in Corporate Social Performance and Policy* II. Greenwich, CT: JAI Press.

Canadian Council for Public Affairs Advancement (1996). *Corporate Public Affairs Management: The 1996 Survey of Canadian Practice*. Waterloo, ON: Canadian Council for Public Affairs Advancement.

Centre for Corporate Public Affairs (1996). *Report of Australia and New Zealand Corporate Public Affairs Survey*. Sydney: Centre for Corporate Public Affairs.

Chase, W.H. (1975). "New Standards for Measuring Public Relations: A Program for Reorganization," *Public Relations Journal* 31: 18–21.

Coates, J. (1985). *Issue Identification and Management: The State of the Art and Techniques*. Palo Alto, CA: Electric Power Research Institute.

Cobb, R.W., and C.D. Elder (1972). *Participation in American Politics: The Dynamics of Agenda Building*. Boston, MA: Allyn and Bacon.

Dean, T.J., M. Vryza, and G.E. Fryxell (1998). "Do Corporate PACs Restrict Competition? An Empirical Examination of Industry PAC Contributions and Entry," *Business and Society* 37 (2): 135–156.

Dennis, L.B. (1996). *Practical Public Affairs in an Era of Change: A Communications Guide for Business, Government, and College*. Lanham, MD: University Press of America.

Dickie, R.B. (1981). "Playing the Government Relations Game: How Companies Manage," *Journal of Contemporary Business* 10 (3): 105–118.

Dickie, R.B. (1984). "Influence of Public Affairs Offices on Corporate Planning and of Corporations on Government Policy," *Strategic Management Journal* 5 (1): 15–34.

Doh, J.P. (1999). "Regional Market Integration and Decentralization in Europe and North America: Implications for Business-Government Relations and Corporate Public Affairs," *Business and Society* 38 (4): 474–507.

Doh, J.P., and H.Teegen (2003). *Globalization and NGOs: Transforming Business, Government and Society*. New York: Praeger.

Dunn, S.W., M.F. Cahill, and J.J. Boddewyn (1979). *How Fifteen Transnational Corporations Manage Public Affairs*. Chicago: Crain Books.

Epstein, E.M. (1969). *The Corporation in American Politics*. Englewood Cliffs, NJ: Prentice Hall.

Epstein, E.M. (1980). "Business Political Activity: Research Approaches and Analytical Issues," in L.E. Preston (ed.), *Research in Corporate Social Performance and Policy* II. Greenwich, CT: JAI Press.

Epstein, M.J., and K.E. Schnietz (2002). "Measuring the Cost of Environmental and Labor Protests to Globalization: An Event Study of the Failed 1999 Seattle WTO Talks," *International Trade Journal* 15: 129–160.

Ewing, R.P. (1980). "Evaluating Issues Management," *Public Relations Journal* 36 (6): 14–16.

Felstiner, W. L.F., R.L. Abel, and A. Sarat (1980). "The Emergence and Transformation of Disputes: Naming, Blaming, Claiming …" *Law and Society Review* 15 (3–4): 631–654.

Fleisher, C.S. (1992). *"Modeling the Role of Evaluation and Measurement in the Achievement of Corporate Public Affairs Management Effectiveness."* Unpublished doctoral dissertation, University of Pittsburgh.

Fleisher, C.S. (1993a). "Assessing the Effectiveness of Corporate Public Affairs Efforts," in B.M. Mitnick (ed.), *Corporate Political Agency: The Construction of Competition in Public Affairs*. Newbury Park, CA: Sage.

Fleisher, C.S. (1993b). "Public Affairs Management Performance: An Empirical Analysis of

Evaluation and Measurement," in J.E. Post (ed.), *Research in Corporate Social Performance and Policy*. Greenwich, CT: JAI Press.

Fleisher, C.S. (ed.) (1995). *Public Affairs Benchmarking: A Comprehensive Guide*. Washington, DC: Public Affairs Council.

Fleisher, C.S. (with N. Blair and B. Hawkinson) (1997). *Assessing, Managing and Maximizing Public Affairs Performance: with Reports, Techniques, and Case Histories from Nearly Two Dozen Leading Organizations and Professionals around the Globe*. Washington, DC: Public Affairs Council.

Fleisher, C.S. (1998). "A Benchmarked Assessment of the Strategic Management of Corporate Communications," *Journal of Marketing Communications* 4 (3): 163–176.

Fleisher, C.S. (1999). "A Systems-based Synthesis of Public Affairs as a Strategic Communication Function," *Asia-Pacific Journal of Public Relations* 1 (1): 1–27.

Fleisher, C.S., and R. Hoewing (1992). "Strategically Managing Corporate External Relations: New Challenges and Opportunities," *Journal of Strategic Change* 1 (6): 41–51.

Foundation for Public Affairs (1999). *1999–2000 State of Corporate Public Affairs*. Washington, DC: Public Affairs Council.

Foundation for Public Affairs (2002). *The State of Corporate Public Affairs: Final Report*. Washington, DC: Foundation for Public Affairs.

Getz, K.A. (1993). "Selecting Corporate Political Tactics," in B. Mitnick (ed.), *Corporate Political Agency: The Construction of Competition in Public Affairs*. Newbury Park, CA: Sage.

Getz, K.A. (1995). "Implementing Multilateral Regulation: A Preliminary Theory and Illustration," *Business and Society* 34 (3): 280–316.

Getz, K.A. (1997). "Research in Corporate Political Action: Integration and Assessment," *Business and Society* 36 (1): 32–72.

Getz, K.A. (2002). "Public Affairs and Political Strategy: Theoretical Foundations," *Journal of Public Affairs* 1 (4): 305–329.

Globerman, S., and R. Schwindt (1985). "Testing Hypotheses about Business-Government Relations: A Study of the British Columbia Forest Products Industry," in L.E. Preston (ed.), *Research in Corporate Social Performance and Policy* VII. Greenwich, CT: JAI Press.

Greening, D.W. (1992). "Organizing for Public Issues: Environmental and Organizational Predictors of Structure and Process," in J.E. Post (ed.), *Research in Corporate Social Performance and Policy* XIII. Greenwich, CT: JAI Press.

Greening, D.W., and B. Gray (1994). "Testing a Model of Organizational Response to Social and Political Issues," *Academy of Management Journal* 37 (3): 467–98.

Griffin, J.J. (1997). "Corporate Public Affairs in the 1990s: Structure, Resources and Processes." Unpublished dissertation, Boston University.

Griffin, J.J. (2002). "To Brand or Not to Brand? Trade-offs in Corporate Branding Decisions," *Corporate Reputation Review* 5 (2–3): 228–240.

Griffin, J.J., and P. Dunn (2004). "Corporate Public Affairs: Commitment, Resources, and Structure," *Business and Society* 43 (2): 196–220.

Griffin, J.J., and D.J. Lenn (1998). "Corporate Public Affairs: A Cross-national Comparison," *Proceedings of the International Association for Business and Society*. Kailua-Kona, HI, June 11–14.

Griffin, J.J., B. Shaffer, and J.F. Mahon (1998). "The 'New Federalism' and the Devolution of Power from Washington: Determinants of Business Political Activity at the State Government Level." Presented at the Academy of Management annual meeting, San Diego, CA, August.

Griffin, J.J., C.S. Fleisher, S.N. Brenner, and J.J. Boddewyn. (2001a). "Corporate Public Affairs Research: Chronological Reference List, Part 1: 1985–2000," *Journal of Public Affairs* 1 (1): 9–32.

Griffin, J.J., C.S. Fleisher, S.N. Brenner, and J.J. Boddewyn (2001b). "Corporate Public Affairs Research: Chronological Reference List 2, 1958–1984," *Journal of Public Affairs* 1 (2): 169–186.

Grunig, J.E. (1979). "A New Measure of Public Opinions on Corporate Social Responsibility," *Academy of Management Journal* 22 (4): 738–764.

Grunig, J.E., and T. Hunt (1984). *Managing Public Relations*. New York: Holt Rinehart & Winston.

Harris, P. (2005). "The Management of Public Affairs in the United Kingdom," in P. Harris, and C.S. Fleisher (eds), *Handbook of Public Affairs*. London: Sage.

Harris, P., and C.S. Fleisher (eds) (2005). *The Handbook of Public Affairs*. London: Sage.

Heath, R.L. (1985). "Image and Issue Advertising: A Corporate and Public Policy Perspective," *Journal of Marketing* 49 (2): 58–68.

Heath, R.L., and R.A. Nelson (1986). *Issues Management: Corporate Public Policymaking in an Information Society*. Beverly Hills, CA: Sage.

Heugens, P.P.M.A.R. (2001). "Strategic Issues Management: Implications for Corporate Performance."

Unpublished doctoral dissertation, Rotterdam: Erasmus University.

Heugens, P.P.M.A.R., J.F. Mahon, and S. Wartick (2004). "A Portfolio Approach to Issue Adoption." Presented at the fifteenth annual International Association for Business and Society conference, March.

Hillman, A.J. (2002). "Public Affairs, Issue Management and Political Strategy: Methodological Issues that Count. A Different View," *Journal of Public Affairs* 1 (4): 356–361.

Hillman, A.J., and G.D. Keim (2001). "Shareholder Value, Stakeholder Management, and Social Issues: What's the Bottom Line? *Strategic Management Journal* 22 (2): 125–139.

Hillman, A.J., A. Zardkooki, and L. Bierman (1999). "Corporate Political Strategies and Firm Performance: Indications of Firm-specific Benefits from Personal Service in the US Government," *Strategic Management Journal* 20 (1): 67–82.

Keim, G.D. (1981). "Foundations of a Political Strategy for Business," *California Management Review* 23 (3): 41–48.

Keim, G.D. (1985). "Corporate Grassroots Programs in the 1980s," *California Management Review* 28 (1): 110–123.

Keim, G.D. (2002). "Managing Business Political Activities in the USA: Bridging between Theory and Practice," *Journal of Public Affairs* 1 (4): 362–375.

Keim, G.D., and B.D. Baysinger (1982). "Corporate Political Strategies Examined: Constituency Building may be Best of All," *Public Affairs Review* 3: 77–87.

Keim, G.D., and B.D. Baysinger (1988). "The Efficacy of Business Political Activity: Competitive Considerations in a Principal-Agent Context," *Journal of Management* 14 (2): 163–80.

Keim, G.D., and C.P. Zeithaml (1986). "Corporate Political Strategy and Legislative Decision Making: A Review and Contingency Approach," *Academy of Management Review* 11 (4): 828–843.

Kennerdell, P.B. (1992). *Managing the Business. Employee PAC: What Works, What Doesn't.* Washington, DC: Public Affairs Council.

Lenn, D.J., S.N. Brenner, L. Burke, D. Dodd-McCue, C.S. Fleisher, L.J. Lad, D.R. Palmer, K.S. Rogers, S.A. Waddock, and R.E. Wokutch (1993). "Managing Corporate Public Affairs and Government Relations: US Multinational Corporations in Europe," in J.E. Post (ed.), *Research in Corporate Social Performance and Policy* XIV. Greenwich, CT: JAI Press.

Lenway, S.A., and K. Rehbein (1991). "Leaders, Followers, and Free Riders: An Empirical Test of Variation in Corporate Political Involve-ment," *Academy of Management Journal* 34 (4): 893–905.

Leone, R. (1987). *Who Profits? How Regulation Creates Winners and Losers.* New York: Free Press.

Levitan, S., and M. Cooper (1984). *Business Lobbies: The Public Good and the Bottom Line.* Baltimore, MD: Johns Hopkins University Press.

Lindblom, C.E. (1977). *Politics and Markets: The World's Political Economic Systems.* New York: Basic Books.

Lord, M.D. (1995). "An Agency Theory Assessment of the Influence of Corporate Grassroots Political Activism," *Academy of Management Journal Best Papers Proceedings,* 55th Annual Meeting, Van, Canada, pp. 396–400.

Lord, M.D. (2000). "Corporate Political Strategy and Legislative Decision Making: The Impact of Corporate Legislative Influence Activities," *Business and Society* 39 (1): 76–93.

Lord, M.D. (2003). "Constituency Building as the Foundation for Corporate Political Strategy," *Academy of Management Executive* 17 (1): 112–24.

Lusterman, S. (1983). *Managing Business-State Government Relations.* Report 838, New York: Conference Board.

Lusterman, S. (1985). *Managing International Public Affairs.* New York: Conference Board.

Lusterman, S. (1987). *The Organization and Staffing of Corporate Public Affairs.* Report 894, New York: Conference Board.

Mack, C.S. (1989). *Lobbying and Government Relations: A Guide for Executives.* New York: Quorum Books.

Mack, C.S. (1991). *The Executive's Handbook of Trade and Business Associations: How they Work— and How to Make them Work Effectively for You.* Westport, CT: Quorum Books.

Mack, C.S. (1997). *Business, Politics, and the Practice of Government Relations.* Westport, CT: Quorum Books.

MacMillan, I. (1981). "Lobbying Strategies and Tactics," *Journal of Business Strategy* 2 (1): 73–76.

Mahon, J.F. (1983). "Corporate Political Strategies: An Empirical Study of Chemical Firm Responses to Superfund Legislation," in L.E. Preston (ed.), *Research in Corporate Social Performance and Policy* V. Greenwich, CT: JAI Press.

Mahon, J.F. (1989). "Corporate Political Strategy," *Business in the Contemporary World* 2 (1): 50–62.

Mahon, J.F. (2002). "Corporate Reputation: A Research Agenda using Strategy and Stockholder Literature," *Business and Society* 41 (4), 415–445.

Mahon, J.F., and R.A. McGowan (1996). *Industry as a Player in the Political and Social Arena: Defining the Competitive Environment.* Greenwich, CT: Quorum Books.

Mahon, J.F., and E.A. Murray (1981). "Strategic Planning for Regulated Companies," *Strategic Management Journal* 2 (3): 251–262.

Mahon, J.F., C.S. Fleisher, and S. Wartick (2001). "Public Affairs, Issues Management and Corporate Political Strategy: An Introduction," *Journal of Public Affairs* 1 (4): 294–302.

Mahon, J.F., P.M.A.R. Heugens, and K. Lamertz (2004). "Social Networks and Nonmarket Strategy," *International Journal of Public Affairs*, forthcoming.

Masters, M.F., and B.D. Baysinger (1985). "The Determinants of Funds raised by Corporate Political Action Committees: An Empirical Examination," *Academy of Management Journal* 28 (3): 654–664.

Masters, M.F., and G.D. Keim (1985). "Determinants of PAC Participation among Large Corporations," *Journal of Politics* 47: 1158–1173.

Masters, M.F., and G.D. Keim (1986). "Variation in Corporate PAC and Lobbying Activity: An Organizational and Environmental Analysis," *Research in Corporate Social Performance and Policy* 8: 249–71.

Mattingly, J.E. (2003). "Stakeholder salience, structural development, and firm performance: structural and performance correlateo of socio-political stakeholder management strategies", Unpublished doctoral dissertation. Columbia, MO: University of Missouri–Columbia.

Mattingly, J.E., and D.W. Greening (2001). "Corporate Political Strategy Formation: A Typology of Firms' Behavioral Response Patterns as Environmental Adaptations." Presented at the Academy of Management annual meetings, Washington, DC, August.

Meadow, R.G. (1983). "Political Advertising as Grassroots Lobbying: New Forms of Corporate Political Participation," *Social Science Journal* 20: 49–63.

Meznar, M.B., and J.H. Johnson (1996). "Multinational Operations and Stakeholder Management: Internationalization, Public Affairs Strategies, and Economic Performance," *Journal of International Management* 2 (4): 233–261.

Meznar, M.B., and D. Nigh (1993). "Managing Corporate Legitimacy: Public Affairs Activities, Strategies and Effectiveness," *Business and Society* 32 (1): 30–43.

Meznar, M.B., and D. Nigh (1995). "Buffer or Bridge? Environmental and Organizational Determinants of Public Affairs Activities in American firms," *Academy of Management Journal* 38 (4): 975–996.

Miles, R.H. (1987). *Managing the Corporate Social Environment: A Grounded Theory.* Englewood Cliffs, NJ: Prentice Hall.

Mitchell, N.J., W.L. Hansen, and E.M. Jepsen (1997). "The Determinants of Domestic and Foreign Corporate Political Activity," *Journal of Politics* 59: 1096–1113.

Mitnick, B.M. (1993). "The Strategic Uses of Regulation—and Deregulation," in B. Mitnick (ed.), *Corporate Political Agency: The Construction of Competition in Public Affairs.* Newbury Park, CA: Sage.

Mullery, C.B., S.N. Brenner, and N.A. Perrin (1995). "A Structural Analysis of Corporate Political Activity: An Application of MDS to the Study of Intercorporate Relations," *Business and Society* 34 (2): 147–170.

Murray, E.A., Jr (1982). "The Public Affairs Function: Report on a Large Scale Research Project," in L.E. Preston (ed.), *Research in Corporate Social Performance and Policy.* Greenwich, CT: JAI Press.

Nagelschmidt, J.S. (ed.) (1982). *The Public Affairs Handbook.* New York: American Management Association.

North, D.C. (1981). *Structure and Change in Economic History.* New York: Norton.

Olson, M., Jr (1965). *The Logic of Collective Action: Public Goods and the Theory of Groups.* New York: Harvard University Press and Schocken Books.

Oomens, M.J.H., and F.A.J. van den Bosch (1999). "Strategic Issue Management in Major European-based Companies," *Long Range Planning* 32 (1): 49–57.

Pedersen, W. (ed.) (1989). *Winning at the Grassroots: How to Succeed in the Legislative Arena by Mobilizing Employees and Other Allies.* Washington, DC: Public Affairs Council.

Pedler, R. (1995). *The Management of Public Affairs.* Occasional Papers 2. Oxford: European Center for Public Affairs.

Pedler, R. (2005). "The History and Development of Public Affairs in the European Union and the United Kingdom," in P. Harris and C.S. Fleisher (eds), *Handbook of Public Affairs.* London: Sage.

Post, J.E., and P.N. Andrews (1990). "Case Research in Corporations and Society Studies," in J.E. Post (ed.), *Research in Corporate Social*

*Performance and Policy* XII. Greenwich, CT: JAI Press.

Post, J.E., and the Centre for Public Affairs (1993). "Australian Public Affairs Practice: Results of the 1992 National Public Affairs Survey," in J.E. Post (ed.), *Research in Corporate Social Performance and Policy* XIV. Greenwich, CT: JAI Press.

Post, J.E., and the Foundation for Public Affairs. (1993). "The State of Corporate Public Affairs in the United States: Results of a National Survey," (ed.), in J.E. Post, *Research in Corporate Social Performance and Policy* XIV. Greenwich, CT: JAI Press.

Post, J.E., and J.J. Griffin (1997). *The State of Corporate Public Affairs: Final Report.* Washington, DC: Foundation for Public Affairs.

Post, J.E., R.B. Dickie, E.A. Murray, Jr, and J.F. Mahon (1982). "The Public Affairs Function in American Corporations: Development and Relations with Corporate Planning," *Long Range Planning* 15 (2): 12–21.

Post, J.E., R.B. Dickie, E.A., Murray, Jr, and J.F. Mahon (1983). "Managing Public Affairs: The Public Affairs Function," *California Management Review* 26 (1): 135–50.

Preece, S., C.S. Fleisher, and J. Toccacelli (1995). "Building a Reputation along the Value Chain," *Long Range Planning* 28 (4): 88–98.

Preston, L.E., and D. Windsor (1992). *The Rules of the Game in the Global Economy: Policy Regimes for International Business.* Boston, MA: Kluwer.

Rehbein, K., and D.A. Schuler (1999). "Testing the Firm as a Filter of Corporate Political Action," *Business and Society* 38 (2): 144–166.

Rehbein, K., and D.A. Schuler (2003). "Does a Firm's Stakeholder Orientation Affect its Political Abilities?" Presented at the annual Academy of Management meetings, Seattle, WA, August.

Ring, P.S., S.A. Lenway, and M. Govekar (1990). "Management of the Political Imperative in International Business," *Strategic Management Journal* 11 (2): 141–151.

Schuler, D.A. (1996). "Corporate Political Strategy and Foreign Competition: The Case of the Steel Industry," *Academy of Management Journal* 39 (3): 720–737.

Schuler, D.A. (1999). "Corporate Political Action: Rethinking the Economic and Organizational Influences," *Business and Politics* 1 (1): 83–97.

Schuler, D. (2002). "Public Affairs, Issues Management and Political Strategy: Methodological Approaches that Count," *Journal of Public Affairs* 1 (4): 336–355.

Schuler, D.A., and K. Rehbein (1997). "The Filtering Role of the Firm in Corporate Political Involvement," *Business and Society* 36 (2): 116–139.

Schuler, D.A., K. Rehbein, and R.D. Cramer (2002). "Pursuing Strategic Advantage through Political Means: A Multivariate Approach," *Academy of Management Journal* 45 (4): 659–672.

Shaffer, B. (1995). "Firm-level Responses to Government Regulation: Theoretical and Research Approaches," *Journal of Management* 21 (3): 495–514.

Shaffer, B., and A.J. Hillman (2000). "The Development of Business-Government Strategies by Diversified Firms," *Strategic Management Journal* 21 (2): 175–190.

Shaffer, B., T.J. Quasney, and C.M. Grimm (2000). "Firm Level Performance Implications of Nonmarket Actions," *Business and Society* 39 (2): 126–143.

Skippari, M., J. Eloranta, J-A. Lamberg, and P. Parvinen (2003). "Conceptual and Theoretical Underpinnings in the Research of Corporate Political Activity: A Bibliometric Analysis." Presented at the International Associate of Business and Society conference, Rotterdam, June.

Steiner, G.A., and J.F. Steiner (1980). *Business, Government and Society: A Managerial Perspective.* New York: Random House.

Ullmann, A.A. (1985). "The Impact of the Regulatory Life Cycle on Corporate Political Strategy," *California Management Review* 28 (1): 140–154.

Vogel, D. (1978). *Lobbying the Corporation: Citizen Challenges to Public Authority.* New York: Basic Books.

Vogel, D. (1989). *Fluctuating Fortunes: The Political Power of Business.* New York: Basic Books.

Wartick, S.L., and J.F. Mahon (1994). "Toward a Substantive Definition of the Corporate Issue Construct: A Review and Synthesis of the Literature," *Business and Society* 33 (3): 293–311.

Wartick, S.L., and R.E. Rude (1986). "Issues Management: Corporate Fad or Corporate Function?" *California Management Review* 29 (1): 124–140.

Windsor, O.D. (2002). "Public Affairs, Issues Management, and Political Strategy: Opportunities, Obstacles and Caveats," *Journal of Public Affairs* 1 (4): 382–415.

Windsor, O.D. (2005). "'Theories' and Theoretical Roots of Public Affairs," in P. Harris and

C.S. Fleisher (eds), *Handbook of Public Affairs*. London: Sage.

Wright, J.R. (1989). "PAC Contributions, Lobbying and Representation," *Journal of Politics* 51: 713–729.

Young, S., and T.L. Brewer (1999). "Global Firms, the Government Affairs Function and the WTO" Paper presented at the European International Business Academy, Manchester, UK.

Zeithaml, C.P., and G.D. Keim (1985). "How to Implement a Corporate Political Action Program," *Sloan Management Review* 26 (2): 23–31.

Zeithaml, C., G. Keim, and B.D. Baysinger (1988). "Toward an Integrated Strategic Management Process: An Empirical Review of Corporate Political Strategy," in G. Jordan (ed.), *Frontiers of Strategic Management*. Greenwich, CT: JAI Press.

## ACKNOWLEDGEMENTS

Many thanks to the editors Phil Harris and especially Craig S. Fleisher (University of Windsor) for helpful comments on this manuscript. Research assistance from Jie Jiao is warmly acknowledged. Continuing thanks to John F. Mahon (University of Maine) and Jim Post (Boston University) for compelling comments on the evolution of these ideas. Mika Skippari (Tampere University of Technology, Finland), Jim Mattingly (University of Northern Iowa) and Dan Kane (George Washington University) helped clarify ideas and grammar. All remaining errors are mine.

# 28

# Issues Management

## Core Understandings and Scholarly Development

### PURSEY P.M.A.R. HEUGENS

For many corporations, the achievement of their objectives is as dependent on the efficacy of their policies in nonmarket arenas as it is on making sound business decisions in the competitive context (Bartha, 1983). A firm's non-market environment consists of its interactions with other parties that are mediated by the public, stakeholders, government, the media, and public institutions (Baron, 1995). These political and societal forces shape a firm's market environment to a significant extent, supporting or obstructing economic exchange relationships through power (authoritative permission) and other positive or negative non-economic sanctions such as the granting or withdrawal of legitimacy (Boddewyn, 1988). Since the external environment of every firm is composed of market and non-market components, any approach to policy making must take both developments in market and in non-market environments into consideration in order to stand a chance of being successful.

Not all developments in a firm's non-market environment are equally relevant to the firm's future prosperity and room to maneuver (Bigelow *et al.*, 1991). Many firms never become directly associated with social issues like domestic violence, public drunkenness, housing crises, low trust in politicians, or the extinction of certain natural species. But there is also a class of non-market issues for which firms can be held accountable or by which they may become affected. Issues like analphabetism in the work force, the passing of constraining government regulation, the erection of trade barriers, the emergence of environmental pollution as an area of public interest, and a low availability of affordable and accessible day care centers can all critically affect an organization's ability for reaching its objectives. Once such social and political issues are durably linked to the corporation, they become a source of additional, unwanted, and unsolicited responsibilities for corporate executives that somehow must be managed (Ansoff, 1980; Moore, 1979).

Since the late 1970s, a significant body of literature has emerged from scholarly fields as diverse as sociology, psychology, business management, media studies, and public affairs that deals directly with the question of how issues—events, trends, and developments that may have a profound impact on an organization's ability to reach its objectives if they are left unattended (Ansoff, 1975; Johnson, 1983)—must be managed. The principal aim of this chapter is to review this burgeoning literature, and in doing so answer two key research questions. First, since issues management has established itself as one of the core pillars of the public affairs field in less than thirty years, an answer is sought to the question: *What explains the popularity and widespread dissemination of the issues management approach?* Second, because so many qualitatively different issues management systems are being used in the corporate world today, the following question is also addressed: *Which key constructs and processes can widely be found across the issues management systems of organizations of different size and form?* This chapter finishes with a brief conclusion section that summarizes some plausible answers to these questions.

## ANTECEDENTS OF ISSUES MANAGEMENT

Howard Chase, a veteran public affairs practitioner, coined the term "issue management" only in April of 1976. Somewhat surprisingly, perhaps, the term was almost instantaneously adopted in both the business world and in academic circles. Data from a 1982 survey of top practitioners in the public affairs field revealed that no less than 73.8 percent of the respondents believed that public issues management was either very important or extremely important to their organizations (Buchholz, 1982). Furthermore, several important books were published in the first decade after 1976 that already fully embraced the issues management logic and terminology. Examples include works like: *Management Response to Public Issues* (Buchholz *et al.*, 1985), *Social Change and Corporate Strategy* (Gollner, 1983), *Managing Public Relations* (Grunig and Hunt, 1984), *Managing External Issues* (Stanley, 1985), and *Issues Management* (Heath and Nelson, 1986).

The fame of issues management as a corporate activity continues to this day (Wartick and Heugens, 2003). The fact that many major corporations recognize issues management as an important component of their public affairs repertoire is a clear indication of this prominence. Companies like Anheuser-Busch, BASF, Coca-Cola, DaimlerChrysler, ExxonMobil, IBM, Pfizer, and Shell have all embraced the issues management function and have appointed issues managers in meaningful parts of their hierarchies. In many other corporations, top managers organize regular (usually biweekly or monthly) "issue meetings," in which previously identified issues pass in review and "ownership" of newly identified issues is attributed to non-specialized yet appropriately trained and equipped middle managers. Another important indicator for the popularity of the issues management approach is the proportion of companies that choose to attribute issues management tasks to the public affairs professionals they employ. A 1999 survey by the Foundation for Public Affairs found that 83 percent of all US companies with a public affairs department recognize issues management as a key organizational function for shaping their relations with external constituencies.

In this regard it is remarkable that issues management is losing some terrain as an object of academic study, as evidenced by a declining number of academic publications per annum on the topic (Mahon and Heugens, 2002; Wartick and Heugens, 2003). Issues management was once a very popular topic for scholarly investigation, but the academic caravan has moved on into new territory such as stakeholder management, corporate social responsibility (CSR) management, and corporate citizenship. Yet to this day, even though many corporations have adopted some form of CSR policy, individuals carrying the job title of "stakeholder manager" or "corporate citizenship manager" remain extremely rare in the corporate world, whereas almost every organization beyond a certain size has an issues manager (or even a complete issues management department) on the payroll.

In sum, issues management enjoyed almost instantaneous popularity in the business world after the term was coined in 1976. What is more, this popularity seems to continue to this day, and several respected scholars and practitioners even claim that issues management is of greater importance to the corporate sense of well-being today than it was ever before in the history of the discipline (Palese and Crane, 2002; Pratt, 2001). A key question therefore is: *What explains the popularity and widespread dissemination of the issues management approach?* Without any claims to exhaustiveness, this chapter points at seven clearly interrelated antecedent factors that have played a crucial role in the emergence and proliferation of issues management as a celebrated area of professional activity and, albeit at a more modest level, as a recognized topic of scholarly study.

## Professionalization of the Public Affairs Discipline

One of the main drivers behind the successes of the issues management field is that there has been an underlying trend towards increasing professionalization in the corporate public affairs field as a whole.[1] Business organizations have of course been forced to start managing relationships with external parties (other than consumers) ever since increases in functional specialization and in the scale of operations started decreasing the number of fully vertically integrated enterprises (Chandler, 1962), but a widespread recognition of the fact that managing the non-market environment was critical to the continued success even of organizations operating in relatively free markets did not start to dawn until after the Second World War. Nevertheless, the development of the public affairs discipline over the last sixty years has been spectacular (Griffin, 2004; Harris and Fleisher, 2004). In the United States, the first Eisenhower administration urged the establishment of the Public Affairs Council (www.pac.org) in 1956 to put an end to the polarization politics between Big Labor and Big Business. The original mission of this organization was to train and stimulate business executives to become active and effective in politics, but the organization soon became a professional organization for the advancement of the public affairs discipline in the United States. The organization now caters for the needs of more than 500 associated corporations, providing its members with unique information, training, and other resources to support their effective participation in public affairs activities at all levels. Similar organizations have since sprouted in other continents as well. In Europe, for example, the Templeton College, Oxford University-based European Centre for Public Affairs (www.publicaffairs.ac) has sought to "record, analyse and improve the conduct of public affairs" since 1986. In Australia, the Centre for Corporate Public Affairs (www.accpa.com.au) has provided professional development, training, information services and international contacts to some 100 members from the ranks of corporate Australia, industry associations, and government business enterprises since 1990. All these developments underscore the rapid professionalization, on a global level, of the public affairs discipline. This trend has greatly contributed to the success of the issues management movement, because it provides practicing issues managers with an institutional context that they can use to further their individual development and to legitimate the issues management profession as a whole.

## Developments in Organizations' Information-Gathering Capabilities

It remains doubtful as to whether the business environment in general is more complex and turbulent now than it was fifteen or fifty years ago (Krugman, 1994), regardless of numerous claims to the contrary (D'Aveni, 1994; Ilinitch *et al.*, 1996; Volberda, 1996). What *has* changed significantly, however, is the extent to which organizations are able to gather information about the economic, social, and political environments in which they have to operate. Organizations presently enjoy much greater opportunities to learn about social trends and developments in even the remotest corners of the world than their counterparts from several decades ago. Of course, as is often documented, developments in information technology and the new media have greatly enhanced organizational information-gathering capabilities

(Davenport *et al.*, 2001; Davenport and Prusak, 2000), but it would be naive to presume that the present-day abundance of information must be ascribed to technological factors alone. Other causes that have greatly increased the level of available information on many issues are: internationalization, which means that organizations have to participate in more issues in multiple countries directly, gathering information on the go (Drogendijk, 2004); information entrepreneurship, implying that companies that try to gather useful information can now choose from a greater array of dedicated consultancy firms and other information intermediaries offering corporate intelligence services than ever before (Shapiro and Varian, 1998); and new expectations concerning corporate transparency, such as those institutionalized in the US Public Company Accounting Reform and Investor Protection Act of 2002 (better known as the Sarbanes-Oxley Act), which means that organizations have to communicate more information about themselves, and by implication also that they can obtain more information about their peers. All of these factors (and many more) mean that corporate executives now face a severe form of information overload (Dutton, 1993), a literal information bombardment with which they somehow must cope. Many executives have found that setting up a well organized strategic issues management system is their best defense in this regard, because these systems allow them to identify issues early, separate the wheat from the chaff, and respond proactively only to those issues that matter most (Dutton *et al.*, 1990). In brief, the ever-increasing availability of information has contributed to the success of the issues management approach, because it represents one of the few effective tools senior executives have against the perils of information overload.

## Professionalization of Societal Interest Groups

Since 1950 more than 25,000 private, not-for-profit organizations with an international focus have debuted on the world stage (Union of International Associations, 1988). Most of these so-called non-governmental organizations (NGOs) are highly specialized, drawing members worldwide from a particular occupation, technical field, industry, or sport. Most of these organizations are relatively inconspicuous, since they are largely unknown to the larger public and since they are only moderately significant even to their members (Skjelsbaek, 1971). Others, however, are widely known and carry significant moral or political clout. Organizations like the International Red Cross (IRC), the World Wildlife Fund (WWF), Greenpeace, the International Olympic Committee (IOC), the Scout Movement, the International Air Transport Association (IATA), and the World Council of Churches (WCC) all seem to fit this bill. What characterizes these organizations is that they all embrace a number of basic world-cultural principles that are constitutive of what some have denoted as "world citizenship" (Boli and Thomas, 1997: 182): most of them embrace universalism in that they believe that humans everywhere have similar needs and share common goals; they are essentially individualistic in the sense that most NGOs accept as members only individuals or associations of individuals; and they believe in the power of voluntary association, implying that they see collective action by freely cooperating individuals as the most feasible and rational solution to social problems. It is important to recognize that the NGO landscape has been in a state of flux for several decades now. In 1971, Skjelsbaek wrote: "The NGO world is growing and changing in many ways. New organizations are added and old ones disappear … New functions are performed, new procedures adopted, and more channels of information established" (p. 423), and his words have retained their relevance to this day. In the early decades of the twenty first century, NGOs have developed themselves into the most powerful watchdog guarding the public interest against the unwarranted exercise of influence by multinational enterprises. The information-gathering capabilities, mobilization potential, and political influence of these so-called "super-NGOs" (Lador-Lederer, 1962) exceed those of many of the private sector organizations they claim to monitor. The unprecedented rise in the influence of NGOs has further cemented the popularity of issues management, as many business organizations have realized that they need to protect themselves against the sometimes arbitrary and particularistic attacks on their policies by NGOs. Proper issues management procedures allow businesses to divert such attacks by integrating the values and beliefs of a small set of highly relevant NGOs into the policy decisions they make (Heugens et al., 2002).

## Politicization of Business

It has been recognized by some that organizations, especially large and powerful ones, tend to operate as political actors (Getz, 1993; Fleisher, 1993; Schuler et al., 2002). According to Boddewyn (1988), the distinguishing characteristic in this respect is not that organizations use a variety of means—economic means such as monetary incentives, social means such as reputation, and political means such as influence—to achieve their objectives, but rather that they use these means outside the conventional market system to influence non-market stakeholders as diverse as governments, the media, communities, and opinion leaders. Bartha (1983) stresses that political behavior on behalf of the firm does not signal perversity, but is in fact a necessity. A society's economic and political subsystems are not neatly separated arenas, but are in fact interpenetrating parts of a greater whole (Preston and Post, 1975). Any large firm that tries to achieve its objectives by economic means alone will have to find out the hard way that level playing fields do not exist, and that the proficient exercise of strategic political behavior is a conditio sine qua non for organizational survival (let alone prosperity), precisely because the economic and political realms are deeply intertwined. Once we acknowledge the political roots of economic competition (and the economic roots of political competition, for that matter; Harris and Lock, 1996), it becomes possible to explain the popularity of the issues management approach. After all, a proficiently designed issues management system allows organizations to proactively monitor political trends and anticipate legislative actions, which enables them to participate more purposefully and effectively in the political process. Some have feared that issues management therefore has the potential to regress to some sort of "social gadget" (Logsdon and Palmer, 1988: 191) in the hands of corporate Molochs, a tool merely designed to promote the firm's narrow economic objectives at the expense of the interests of others. Yet, Bartha (1983) reminds us that in modern, plural societies organizations are but one of the multitude of societal groupings that strive for influence in social and political arenas. They have no special a priori status, and they can claim no precedence over others. Hence, issues management is best perceived not as an incisive weapon in the hands of a hegemonic oppressor, but rather as a relatively benign tool in the hands of one of the many players constituting the larger social arena.

## Shift in the Corporate Mind Set towards Social Involvement

Modern capitalist corporations have always been involved with extra-economic activities that evidenced a certain involvement or solidarity with society as a whole or with specific societal groups in particular (albeit often to a modest extent). But what characterizes these early forms of social involvement is that social responsibilities were integrated into the managerial creed only as voluntary activity and pertinently "not due to the recipients as a matter of right" (Sutton et al., 1956: 263). Carroll reluctantly calls this type of involvement "discretionary responsibilities" (1979: 500), because they are not enforceable and are principally left to individual judgment and choice. A fundamental shift occurred, however, due to the emergence and spread of the public corporation, which (1) separated the ownership and the control of business enterprises (such that business executives became agents who no longer owned the property they controlled; Berle and Means, 1932), and (2) provided firms with unprecedented growth opportunities, due to the diffusion of stock ownership through new and more efficient capital markets (Alchian, 1969). These developmentss mean that the discretionary nature of corporate social involvement could no longer be maintained. In the words of Preston: "it is simply inevitable that large-scale business operations will have diverse, and often unexpected, impacts on the larger society; the corporate manager can no more disclaim responsibility for these impacts than for his own reckless driving" (1975: 435). The crucial points here are twofold. First, because "stockholders in widely held corporations, for the most part, perceive themselves as passive investors rather than co-owners of a business" (Davis, 1975: 240), professional managers have to accept the social responsibilities that go hand in hand with the greater discretionary powers they enjoy because of investor non-engagement. Second, as noted by Steiner (1974: 81): "as a firm grows larger, it has an actual and potential influence on more and more people: ... it tends to become affected with a public interest." He stresses that businesses are and must remain fundamentally economic institutions, but that they do have responsibilities to help society achieve its goals, and that these responsibilities inevitably increase with organizational size. It has long been recognized that issues management is one of the main tools for shaping and enacting the social responsibilities of corporations (Wood, 1991). Since a solid issues management system allows an organization to identify its most salient stakeholder groups (Mitchell *et al.*, 1997) and to adequately assess the magnitude of consequences, probability of effect, and temporal immediacy of the issues that occupy them (Jones, 1991), issues management is perhaps the most managerially compelling tool for implementing corporate social responsibility. In the words of Wartick and Cochran (1985: 767): "social issues management is a direct extension of social responsiveness ... It provides method to an area that has been continually criticized as 'soft' and tangential to the true purpose of the corporation."

## Increase in the Media Coverage of Business

One of the telling characteristics of the present era is that there is now more recorded evidence about business conduct available in the public domain than ever before. Over the 1980s and 1990s, business reporting has been steeply on the rise. It is estimated that in the United States there were some 4,200 professional business reporters working for the top fifty newspaper markets and at national business publications like *Newsweek* and *Forbes* in 1988. Twelve years later, in 2000, there were more than 12,000 professional business journalists working at these very same media (Henriques, 2000). This steep increase in the journalistic work force is also reflected in the output they produce. A respectable newspaper like the *Washington Post*, which increased its business staff from eighteen in the early 1980s to eighty one in 2000, saw its daily page count jump from two pages (behind the sports section) to a stand-alone twelve-page daily section over the same period. For the *Los Angeles Times*, the numbers show an increase on the payroll from twenty five to ninety heads, and an expansion in the page count from six or seven pages behind sports in the 1980s to an average fourteen to eighteen-page independent section in 2000. This trend towards greater attention in the news for the conduct of businesses is of course not without consequence. The media play an important role as a *linking mechanism*, which publicly connects businesses to strategic issues (Heugens and Deephouse, 2003). The media create information on issues where it previously did not exist by ferreting for new insights; they filter the available information by focusing only on those issues that they deem newsworthy; and they translate information on these selected issues into language that much wider audiences than company experts alone can understand. The media also politicize issues by framing them in ideologically laden terms; and they disseminate their stories about businesses among a much wider audience than just those stakeholders that happen to interact with these organizations directly. These developments have greatly increased the interest in issues management, since this discipline provides organizations with a systematic procedure for keeping track of media developments (Heath and Nelson, 1986), with an analytical framework to help make the media information relevant for business decision making (Bartha, 1983), and with a set of simple rules for developing and sustaining workable relations with media organizations and other stakeholders (Heugens *et al.*, 2004).

## Shift from Substantive towards Symbolic Competition

Economic competition more and more takes the form of competition for intangible and symbolic assets, especially for reputation (Hall, 1992, 1993). Businesses no longer necessarily go head to head with one another by *substantively* offering sharper prices, better quality, and greater diversity than their rivals, but by *symbolically* manipulating the impression that they leave of these qualities in the minds of their stakeholders (Lamertz and Heugens, 2003). A burgeoning academic literature on corporate reputation now exists, and many studies have explored the positive implications good reputations have for the organizations holding them. Choi (1998) has demonstrated that multiproduct organizations with good reputations can save considerable marketing costs when they launch a new experience product under an already established brand name. Chauvin and Guthrie (1994) have asserted that a positive labor market reputation is a source of labor market information that helps reduce the firm's search costs for new personnel as well as the training costs associated with labor turnover. Kreps and Wilson (1982) and Milgrom and Roberts (1982) have shown that firms can prevent future entry into their markets (which is costly because sharing a market reduces profits) by building a reputation for "toughness," as measured by their willingness to use price-cutting tactics. Greif (1989),

finally, has pointed out that reputation can also act as a relational governance mechanism. In a fascinating study of the eleventh-century Maghribi traders, he shows how merchants controlled their overseas agents absent direct supervision or contractual safeguards. By trading exclusively with agents who were acknowledged members of a "coalition," these latter parties were forced to establish a favorable reputation for themselves to remain in the coalition, which *ex ante* linked their past conduct to their future income. Since each agent benefited more from being a coalition member than he could gain outside the coalition, his reputation as an honest trader became a self-enforcing governance mechanism cementing otherwise insecure agency relationships. Ample evidence exists that contemporary business organizations recognize the value of having an excellent reputation, and that they save no efforts when it comes to improving upon their corporate image (Fombrun, 1996). This shift toward symbolic competition is one of the main reasons why so many businesses have implemented issues management systems. Empirical research has demonstrated that issues management activities like tightening relationships with external stakeholders and building issues management capabilities by recording valuable experiences can contribute positively to better corporate reputations in the general sense and to better partial reputations on individual issues in particular (Heugens, 2002a; Wartick, 1988).

## A GENERIC ISSUES MANAGEMENT SYSTEM

Now that we have explored seven of the main factors explaining the popularity of issues management in the contemporary business world, one important question remains, notably: *Which key constructs and processes can widely be found across the issues management systems of organizations of different size and form?* In the present section of this chapter a simple issues management system will be sketched, consisting of three elementary constructs and four core processes that can be found across a wide range of businesses. The model proposed here is purposely kept as parsimonious as possible, in order to increase its generalizability across industries and organizations. It must be stressed, however, that many organizations have developed their own issues management systems, the subtleties of which cannot be captured in a model as rudimentary as the present one. In order to illustrate some of these subtleties before the more generic issues management system will be discussed, three brief case examples of contemporary issues management systems will be presented here: Dow Chemical, Heineken, and Baxter International.

Dow Chemical (www.dow.com)—whose issue priority list is legendary because of homegrown "evergreens" like Agent Orange, dioxin releases, and silicone breast implants— uses three primary working groups to integrate issue-relevant knowledge and expertise at various levels of the organization (Crane, 2001). The most senior of these groups is the Corporate Operating Board, which is composed of Dow's top managers. The Public Policy Leadership Team, chaired by the global vice-president of public affairs, is accountable for making the issue management system work "across the Dow world." Finally, the Public Policy Expertise Center, the "keeper of the toolbox," provides support services for the leadership team. An important innovation through which the Public Policy Expertise Center seeks to gain information from outside stakeholders concerning emerging public issues is the Dow EthicsLine. Concerned consumers, public interest groups, and activists can dial this toll-free help line, operated by communication specialists from an independent company, to report violations of Dow's code of business conduct or other unethical business practices. The EthicsLine initiative not only helps the Public Policy Expertise Center to monitor Dow's ethical performance, but also to identify issues while they are still in a nascent and potentially controllable stage.

Furthermore, Dutch brewing company Heineken (www.heineken.com), which has in the past been haunted by predicaments such as glass splinters in its beer bottles and presumed racism on the part of its senior executives (Klein, 2001), tends to prepare itself for challenging public issues by developing and implementing detailed crisis scenarios. These scenarios are meant to: (1) record prior experiences in the form of tangible and retrievable documents, (2) serve as instructional materials that can be used in the training of communication workers and issues managers, and (3) act as policy documents for anticipating the kinds of organizational functions and processes that instantaneously need to be activated when an issue suddenly emerges (e.g., wide-scale product recall campaigns, multilingual call centers, and support teams for the media relations staff). In order to make sure that its issues management processes remain world-class, Heineken not only benchmarks its crisis scenarios with a broad range of internal departments, but it also presents and develops them further in collaboration with dedicated consultancy firms, like public affairs and public relations consultancy firm Burson-Marsteller.

Finally, at Baxter International (www.baxter. com), a US-based health care and biotechnology company whose main issues center around bioethics in the medical field, it is common to set up multidisciplinary teams in order to avoid that policies and practices on specific issues remain diffuse across the company (Crane, 2002). The Bioethics Team, for example, represents an internal "community of knowledge" consisting of members like the Technical Council chair, six medical directors representing all of Baxter's divisions, a research and development executive, two representatives from the legal department, and the head of corporate communications. The diversity represented in this team ensures that all issue-related decisions are rooted in company-wide consensus, and that no important aspects pertaining to the issue "fall through the cracks." Baxter also tries to participate in issues that require ongoing research and an exchange of views with external audiences proactively by discussing them on its Web site. The site features a specific "issues in the news" section, which offers a short scroll-down list of the environmental, health, and safety issues with which the company is presently associated. The purpose of this page is to contribute to the discussion surrounding these issues, and hopefully steer them in a direction that is in line with the company's solution preferences (Lamertz *et al.*, 2003), by offering company-censored information expressing the Baxter perspective on these issues.

From the three corporate examples presented here, it should become obvious that issues management is an incredibly complex process, which can be organized in an almost infinite number of ways. Yet, it is still possible to uncover a number of the key constructs and processes underlying many contemporary issues management systems. In the following section (which deals with core constructs), attention will be paid to the different roles middle and upper managers play in the issues management process, as well as to the key characteristics of strategic issues. In the subsequent section (which is concerned with key issues management processes), it will be discussed how middle managers tend to identify issues, how they may go about 'selling" these issues to their superiors, how top managers can acquire more information about pertinent issues, and how they may formulate responses aimed at their management.

## Central Constructs

### Middle Management

The generic issues management system that will be proposed here consists of three central constructs, the first of which is middle management (see Figure 28.1). Middle managers are those individuals who are equipped with managerial responsibilities, who are not located at the very top of the organization, and whose primary tasks involve the supervision of lower-level managers (Fredrickson, 1984; Wooldridge and Floyd, 1990). Particularly in the context of large, bureaucratic organizations, mid-level managers have traditionally been seen as suppliers of information to the top-level managers of the organization, and reciprocally as consumers of their decisions (Thompson, 1967; Westley, 1990). Since many organizations beyond a certain size tend to be compartmentalized into many divisions, strategic business units, and departments,

Bower argued that middle managers "are the only [persons] in the organization who are in a position to judge whether [strategic] issues are being considered in the proper context" (1970: 297–298). The flip side of this compartmentalization is that middle managers tend to lack "strategic awareness" (Hambrick, 1981) in the sense that managers located at descending levels of the managerial hierarchy tend to have a declining awareness of the corporation's overall business policy and strategy.

### Top Management

The second construct that occupies a central position in the proposed issues management system is top management (see Figure 28.1). Top managers are those individuals who have overall responsibility for an organization, whose personalities and background characteristics shape organizational outcomes, and who ultimately account for what happens to the organization (Barnard, 1938; Hambrick and Mason, 1984; Selznick, 1957). Hambrick (1989: 6) has proposed four characteristics of top managers that distinguish them from individuals occupying the lower managerial echelons of the organization. First, since the major jobs of the top manager are the design of an effective organizational structure and the alignment of this internal structure with the current and expected external environment, the upper manager is principally concerned with both the internal and external spheres of the organization. Second, strategic leaders always have to ration their scarce decision-making powers, because they necessarily operate in environments characterized by ambiguity, complexity, and information overload. Third, top managers are in charge of a complex integrative task, because their jobs cut across a wide span of activities like marketing, finance, operations, and information management. Fourth, and finally, the strategic leadership task can be contrasted with leading smaller departmental units because it principally involves managing through others.

### Issues

The third and final central construct comprising the suggested issues management system is

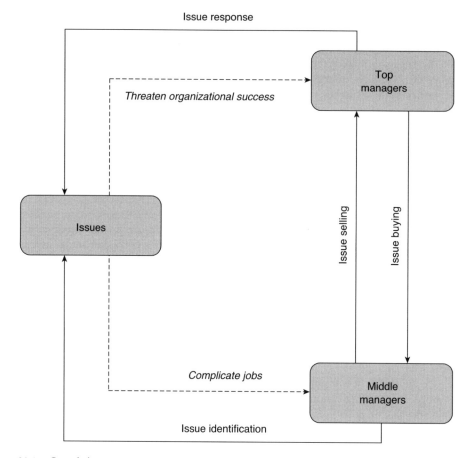

Figure 28.1   *Generic issue management system*

issues (see Figure 28.1). Issues are considered "strategic" issues (Thomas *et al.*, 1994) when they involve trends, events, or developments that have the potential to affect an organization's position and performance when left unattended (Ansoff, 1965; King, 1982). Such issues involve matters other than tactical or operational problems, and usually concern the organization and its goals in their entirety (Ginsberg, 1988). Because of the equivocality of the problems at stake, the plentitude of the stakeholder groups involved, and the entangledness of their interactions, issues tend to be ill structured (Lyles, 1981); poorly documented (Dutton *et al.*, 1983); open to multiple interpretations (Daft and Weick, 1984; Thomas and McDaniel, 1990); and characterized by a multitude of competing attributions of blame and responsibility (Heugens, 2002b). Strategic

issues therefore never surface in "prepackaged" format, but get shaped and labeled only because decision makers identify and formulate them by selectively enacting some aspects of their environment while neglecting or ignoring other aspects (Cowan, 1986; Weick, 1979).

## Core Issues Management Processes

### Issue Identification

Most (if not all) issues management systems covered in the literature argue that issues management necessarily begins with issue identification or issue diagnosis (Arrington and Sawaya, 1984; Buchholz, 1990; Wartick and Mahon, 1994). Issue identification refers to two distinct types of activities, notably: "those activities and processes by which data and stimuli are translated into focused issues (i.e. attention organizing acts) and the issues explored (i.e. acts of interpretation)" (Dutton *et al.*, 1983: 308). The first part of issue identification—the part comprised of attention organizing acts—is by far the more systematic of the two. A substantial literature exists under the heading of environmental scanning (Aguilar, 1967), which lines out numerous techniques for discovering new issues. These techniques entail, but are certainly not limited to: (1) personalized external information gathering, for example by attending professional conferences or by talking to consultants; (2) impersonalized external information gathering, for example by reading reports from trade associations or by keeping track of newspapers and magazines; (3) personalized internal information gathering, for example by talking to staff specialists or by consulting the board of directors; and (4) impersonalized internal information gathering, for example by reading management memoranda and accounting reports (Fleming, 1981).

The second part of issue identification—the part composed of acts of interpretation—is far less systematic, and is in fact not in any sense an objective process. Research suggests that, even when exposed to highly similar stimuli, top managers in different organizations will form different interpretations of the same issue (Meyer, 1982; Thomas *et al.*, 1994). Daft and Weick (1984) have noted that these differences are partially the result of socially constructed frameworks ("interpretation systems") that guide information, attention, and sense making. Dutton and Dukerich (1991) have in this respect pointed at the pivotal role of organizational identity as an interpretation system (also see Hoffman and Ocasio, 2001; Lamertz *et al.*, 2003). In their study of how the Port Authority of New York and New Jersey (a regional transportation agency) dealt with the many homeless people at its facilities, they found compelling evidence that organizational identity can both serve as an important reference point that members of the organization used for assessing the importance of the issue, and as a yardstick for determining whether the organization should or should not respond to the issue.

Caution must be taken, however, not to use organizational identity as a catchall term or as a conceptual "silver bullet" for explaining all interpretation biases in organizations. It is often possible to trace specific issue interpretations back to distinctive organizational attributes at lower levels of analysis (Thomas *et al.*, 1994). Hambrick and Finkelstein (1987), for example, argued that organization-level factors like size and type of organization create inertial forces that limit managerial discretion when it comes to creating perceptions of the environment. Furthermore, an organization's degree of specialization, operationalized as the extent to which it is vertically integrated or offers differentiated products, is likely to have a direct impact on processes of conformity and independence that contribute to how managers perceive situations and events (Gioia and Chittipeddi, 1991). Finally, Hall (1984) has contended that organizational ownership structure (public or private) provides a social setting that affects perceptions of organizational issues.

## Issue Selling

The issue management system suggested here explicitly acknowledges the different roles middle managers and top managers play in organizations. It is often middle managers rather than top executives who have their fingers on the "pulse" of the organization and are closer to customers and other stakeholder groups (Dutton *et al.*, 1997). These links often provide middle managers with intimate knowledge of what strategic issues require attention. Middle managers, as opposed to their colleagues at the top, therefore play a key role in detecting the issues that matter most to the organization and in mobilizing the resources required for their resolution (Kanter, 1982). Middle managers can mobilize these resources by affecting the resource allocation decisions of top executives, an influence they can exert by choosing when and how to bring issues to top management's attention. This process of "upward influence" (Floyd and Wooldridge, 1994) is usually referred to as "issue selling": "a voluntary, discretionary set of behaviors by which organizational members attempt to influence the organizational agenda by getting those above them to pay attention to issues of particular importance to them" (Ashford et al., 1998: 24).

Issue selling has been investigated in a variety of contexts, such as telecommunications companies in the US Midwest (Dutton et al., 1997); not-for-profit regional hospitals in the US northeast (Dutton et al., 2001); female graduates of a US Midwestern business school (Ashford et al., 1998); and a US national membership organization for women in business (Dutton et al., 2002). These studies show that middle managers can use a variety of moves to get their superiors to pay attention to the issues that matter to them (Dutton et al., 2001). For example, middle managers can try to use impression management tactics (Tedeschi, 1981) in an attempt to portray the issue they try to sell as involving bigger stakes or greater uncertainty. The logic connecting these issue characteristics to attention allocation is that top managers are motivated to pay more attention to higher payoff issues (Dutton and Ashford, 1993). Another move that is available to issue sellers is to "bundle" an issue with other issues, such that the issue is portrayed as related to and interconnected with other issues. Bundling is potentially an important move, because prior research has shown that the perceived interconnectedness of an issue with other relevant issues affects individuals' willingness to invest time and money in the issue (Dutton et al., 1990). Finally, individuals have the choice of going solo or of involving others in the selling effort (Dutton and Ashford, 1993). Prior research seems to suggest that middle managers should at least consider building a quasi-political coalition of sellers before they "go in to bat" for an issue. Dean (1987) found that successful selling of proposals for advanced manufacturing technologies was often done by proponents who sold "sideways" before securing top management involvement. Issue selling is not a risk-free undertaking, however. The process may be associated with positive career benefits for the successful seller of an important issue, but it is also not uncommon to see that selling

attempts—especially those related to issues with a negative impact—elicit a "kill the messenger" response from top managers.

## Issue Buying

Managerial work is complex and ambiguous (Katz and Kahn, 1978), and this ambiguity tends to intensify as managers move up the organizational hierarchy (Jacques, 1961). As compared with middle managers, top-level managers have to cope with a greater variety of roles that are relevant to their jobs (Mintzberg, 1973); a larger number of stakeholders that try to influence them with demands and requests (Salancik et al., 1975); and greater centrality in all kinds of causal loops that ultimately determine organizational outcomes (Weick, 1979). This increased ambiguity is problematic, because the top manager suffers from the same limits on choice as any other human being: he or she is unable to scan every aspect of the organization and its environment and selectively perceives only some of the phenomena that could impact the organization, and the bits of information he or she has chosen for processing are interpreted "through a filter woven by one's own cognitive base and values" (Hambrick and Mason, 1984: 195). Top managers are therefore extremely dependent on mid-level managers to supply them with information concerning the dormant or emerging strategic issues that threaten to affect the organization's potential for reaching desirable end states (Floyd and Wooldridge, 1996). They may therefore be expected to engage in issue-buying behavior: a voluntary, discretionary set of behaviors by which top managers attempt to identify and interpret those issues that could have an impact on the organization's ability to reach its objectives by getting their subordinates to release issue-relevant information. Issue buying by top managers comes in two generic forms, notably: (1) the facilitation of issue selling through manipulation of the organizational context, and (2) a proactive acquisition of information through feedback-seeking behavior.

First, the issue-selling literature points out that the organizational context plays a determining role in creating a general willingness among middle managers to sell issues, and that managers actively assess the organizational context before they decide to sell or keep an issue to themselves (Dutton *et al.*, 1997). An important contextual cue facilitating issue selling is top management openness (Dutton *et al.*, 2002). The literature suggests that employees are more likely to initiate change when top management appears open to suggestions and employee initiatives (Morrison and Phelps, 1999). Another factor shaping issue-selling practices is the "clubbiness" or cultural exclusivity of an organization. Dutton and her colleagues (2002) have demonstrated that the degree to which individuals believe that they are excluded from interacting with a dominant in-group is inversely related to their willingness to bring sensitive issues to the attention of the dominant coalition. A final contextual determinant of issue-selling propensities is the availability of norms favoring issue selling. When selling behaviors are seen as a legitimate and normal part of organizational life, individuals are more likely to engage in issue selling because the activity itself will less be associated with career penalties and image risk (Ashford *et al.*, 1998). Managers who want to encourage issue selling must therefore try to create an organizational context that invites employees to participate in organizational adaptation and change processes: a context in which top management is open to suggestions from all employees, regardless of tenure and rank; in which clubbiness is minimized in order to make the dominant coalition appear permeable and approachable; and in which taking initiatives is the norm rather than the exception.

Second, rather than encouraging lower-level managers to sell issues to them by manipulating the organizational context, top managers can also acquire information proactively by engaging in feedback-seeking behavior (Ashford and Tsui, 1991). Feedback seeking entails the conscious devotion of effort toward determining the correctness and adequacy of behavior for attaining valued end states (Ashford and Cummings, 1983). This proactive acquisition of information can take two separate forms. First, top managers may

monitor their subordinates for feedback by observing how they respond to various situational cues and how they adjust their behavior according to issues that threaten to complicate their jobs (see Figure 28.1). Top managers should be able to infer important information about issues that could potentially interfere with the organization's ability to reach its goals from watching how others deal with such issues in more hands-on situations (Ashford, 1986). Second, top managers may directly inquire which trends and developments mid-level managers perceive to be the greatest threats to organizational success (see Figure 28.1). Direct inquiry may yield important insights that can help top managers to at least partially overcome their selective perception of issues, precisely because middle managers can help them paint a picture of issues that is composed of direct experiences rather than armchair philosophizing and boardroom conjecturing alone. It is important to note that the value of feedback on issues is not inherent in the information itself, but derives in part from what top managers do with that information (Ashford, 1986). Feedback-seeking behavior is valuable only if the information obtained through this process is used to make adaptations to both top management conduct and corporate policy, such that the adequacy of these behaviors and policies for attaining favorable organizational outcomes and minimizing threatening issues can be enhanced (Ashford and Cummings, 1983).

## Issue Response

As was stated previously, the issues management system presented here explicitly acknowledges the different roles and responsibilities of top and middle managers in the issues management process. Whereas the identification of issues is largely the turf of (boundary-spanning) mid-level managers because of their day-to-day interactions with outside stakeholders, formulating issue responses is a top management responsibility because only senior executives enjoy the kind of discretionary power that is required to commit considerable resources to issues management activities (Hambrick, 1989). Especially in the business policy literature, organizational response is therefore described as a rational process, starting at the strategic apex of the organization and moving down through the ranks (Logsdon, 1985). Once the top management team becomes aware of an emerging social issue through issue-buying or issue-selling processes, it commits the organization to an issue response and over time institutionalizes the response into regular operating procedures (Ackerman, 1973; Ackerman and Bauer, 1976).

Through a study of the response patterns of Dutch food firms to the introduction of genetically modified food ingredients, Heugens et al. (2004) discovered four broad issue response strategies. The first, which they labeled "dialogue," entailed the development of cooperative and trust-based relationships with a broad range of external constituencies, especially those with non-economic motivations (Heugens et al., 2002; Sharma and Vredenburg, 1998). Managers using this strategy sought to avert the impact of reputational threats through an exchange of views with critical outsiders, adapting corporate policies to these outside views whenever necessary. A second strategy was named "advocacy," and was aimed at persuading external audiences that the organizational position on an otherwise controversial issue was both rationally acceptable and morally legitimate (Grunig and Grunig, 1992). Third, to avoid the organizational ownership of certain threatening issues (issue ownership may be interpreted as a strong association in the eyes of relevant publics between an organization and a societal predicament), some organizations relied on what was called a "corporate silence" strategy. This strategy is aimed at keeping the company name out of the public debate as much as possible by giving employees strict orders not to talk about the issue in public and by concentrating all external communication tasks in the hands of a relatively small number of well trained professionals (Morrison and Milliken, 2000). Fourth, and finally, organizations used a so-called "crisis communication" strategy whenever they needed to engage in a purposeful

exchange of information with interested outside constituencies under conditions of high time pressure and uncertainty. Organizations that managed crises successfully all seemed to have rules in place that allowed them to match certain crisis categories with standardized, well learnt responses (Daft and Weick, 1984; Dutton, 1993).

It must be stressed that organizations do not enjoy complete discretion when it comes to determining when to use which response. A contingency approach to issues management would suggest that the appropriateness of any response is likely to depend on the developmental stage of the issue itself. Many contributors have argued that strategic issues, much like organizations, pass through a series of sequential stages as they progress from emergence to resolution: emergence, triggering crisis, debate, and resolution (Bigelow et al., 1993; Buchholz, 1990; Fleisher and Bensoussan, 2003; Post, 1978). In the emergence stage, where we typically see an expectational gap developing between society's expectations of social conditions and the present social realities (Jacoby, 1971), organizations may rely on corporate silence strategies that allow them to lie low and avoid the additional responsibilities associated with issue ownership. During the second stage, which usually consists of a brief but intense crisis, organizations require excellent crisis communication skills to avoid that their reputations become tarnished as a consequence of their involvement with the issue. As issues evolve towards the debate or controversy stage, the gap between stakeholder expectations and firm performance becomes politicized (Post, 1978). The firms that emerge from the controversy stage as winners are usually those that have proper advocacy skills in place that allow them to state their case as compellingly as possible to third parties. Finally, in the resolution stage, the controversies between organizations and their societal stakeholders often become less bitter, and the parties involved may even assume joint responsibility for resolving the underlying problems (Gray, 1989). Organizations need strong dialogue skills at this stage, which enable them to convince the other parties with an involvement in the issue that working towards a joint solution need not necessarily be a zero-sum game. In brief, organizations cannot expect to be successful in all the stages of an issue's evolution if they only master one specific response strategy. Instead, they need to invest in a more varied response repertoire that will allow them to pursue issues throughout all consecutive phases of their life cycles.

## CONCLUSION

This chapter raised two research questions with some pertinence to the issues management field. The first research question asked: *What explains the popularity and widespread dissemination of the issues management approach?* Without any claims of exhaustiveness, this chapter has pointed in the direction of seven relevant antecedent factors. First, the ongoing professionalization of the public affairs discipline in general means that issues managers can now reflect upon themselves as members of a respectable profession, which greatly enhances the attractiveness of the discipline as a long-term career option for interested candidates (Chase, 1984). Second, rapid developments in the information-gathering capabilities of organizations have spurred the spread of the issues management function, because business executives now have a genuine need for organizational systems that help them monitor the continuous influx of new information (Davenport and Prusak, 2000). Third, the continuous professionalization and proliferation of societal interest groups has left business organizations searching for new defenses against the demands of these stakeholders, and issues management systems have established themselves as the competitive weapon of choice. Fourth, professional managers are becoming more aware that not only war but business too is a "continuation of politics by other means" (with a nod to Carl von Clausewitz), and that issues management is an excellent medium for participating in the public policy process. Fifth, as societal expectations with respect to the social involvement of

business continue to increase, executives are learning to appreciate issues management as an approach that provides substance and method to the often elusive concept of corporate social responsibility. Sixth, as the media coverage of business continues to increase, managers experience a greater need for analytical frameworks that help them make media information relevant for business decision making (Bartha, 1983). Seventh, and finally, the shift from substantive towards symbolic competition in many markets has increased the relevance of issues management as a system for building and protecting corporate reputations (Fombrun, 1996).

The second research question that was raised in the introduction of this chapter was: *Which key constructs and processes can widely be found across the issues management systems of organizations of different size and form?* It was carefully pointed out the different roles middle and upper managers play in the issues management process, because these distinctions are key to understanding the issues management systems of most organizations. Issue identification tends to be the prerogative of boundary-spanning middle managers, because they are the ones who tend to get confronted with emerging issues first by virtue of their day-to-day interactions with external stakeholders. Once an issue is identified, middle managers may autonomously take the initiative to "sell" it to top management. Alternatively, top managers may solicit for issues via so-called issue "buying" processes, by which they attempt to convince middle managers to share issue-related information with them. After top management has become cognizant of a new issue that threatens to impact the organization, it becomes their responsibility to administer an adequate response, because as senior managers they are the ones responsible for allocating resources in their organizations.

In the rugged world of practice, issues management systems can be morphed in a variety of ways to accommodate the situational needs of almost every imaginable organization. Regardless of shape or form, however, all effective issues management systems have in common that they proficiently facilitate the four core processes of issues identification, selling, buying, and response. Neglect or underdevelopment of any of these processes is likely to leave organizations in a state wherein the necessary link between analysis and action is rendered insufficient. Alternatively, organizations operating a complete and balanced issues management system—one in which each of these four core processes is well developed—are likely to reap competitive benefits from their increased ability to adjust themselves to the demands of both their market and non-market environments.

## NOTE

1 With respect to the relationship between issues management and public affairs, the latter is best regarded as the more comprehensive discipline that seeks to explore how organizations monitor and manage their business environments by influencing public policy, building strong reputations, and finding common ground with stakeholders. Issues management is then best perceived as one of the constitutive parts of the public affairs discipline, more specifically the part that focuses on the management of concrete events, trends, and developments that could have a significant impact on the ability of the organization to reach its objectives if they were left unattended.

## REFERENCES

Ackerman, R.W. (1973). "How Companies Respond to Social Demands," *Harvard Business Review* 51 (4): 88–98.

Ackerman, R.W., and R.A. Bauer (1976). *Corporate Social Responsiveness: The Modern Dilemma*. Reston, VA: Reston Publishing.

Aguilar, F.J. (1967). *Scanning the Business Environment*. New York: Macmillan.

Alchian, A. (1969). "Corporate Management and Property Rights," in *Economic Policy and the Regulation of Corporate Securities*, ed. H. Manne. Washington, DC: American Enterprise Institute.

Ansoff, H.I. (1965). *Corporate Strategy*. London: Penguin.

Ansoff, H.I. (1975). "Managing Strategic Surprise by Response to Weak Signals," *California Management Review* 18: 21–33.

Ansoff, H.I. (1980). "Strategic Issue Management," *Strategic Management Journal* 1: 131–148.

Arrington, C.B., and R.N. Sawaya (1984). "Managing Public Affairs: Issues Management in an Uncertain Environment," *California Management Review* 26: 148–160.

Ashford, S.J. (1986). "Feedback-seeking in Individual Adaptation: A Resource Perspective," *Academy of Management Journal* 29: 465–487.

Ashford, S.J., and L.L. Cummings (1983). "Feedback as an Individual Resource: Personal Strategies of Creating Information," *Organizational Behavior and Human Performance* 32: 370–398.

Ashford, S.J. and A.S. Tsui (1991). "Self-regulation for Managerial Effectiveness: The Role of Active Feedback Seeking," *Academy of Management Journal* 34: 251–280.

Ashford, S.J., N.P. Rothbard, S.K. Piderit, and J.E. Dutton (1998). "Out on a Limb: The Role of Context and Impression Management in Selling Gender-Equity Issues," *Administrative Science Quarterly* 43: 23–57.

Barnard, C.I. (1938). *The Functions of the Executive*. Cambridge, MA: Harvard University Press.

Baron, D.P. (1995). "Integrated Strategy: Market and Nonmarket Components," *California Management Review* 37: 47–65.

Bartha, P.F. (1983). "Managing Corporate External Issues: An Analytical Framework," *Business Quarterly* 47: 78–90.

Berle, A.A., and G.C. Means (1932). *The Modern Corporation and Private Property*. New York: Macmillan.

Bigelow, B., L. Fahey and J.F. Mohan (1991). "Political strategy and issues evolution: A framework for analysis and action," in K. Paul (ed.), *Contemporary Issues in Business Ethics and Politics*. Lewiston, NY: Edwin Mellen, pp. 1–26.

Bigelow, B., L. Fahey, and J.F. Mahon (1993). "A Typology of Issue Evolution," *Business and Society* 32: 18–29.

Boddewyn, J.J. (1988). "Political Aspects of MNE Theory," *Journal of International Business Studies* 19: 341–363.

Boli, J., and G.M. Thomas (1997). "World Culture in the World Polity: A Century of International Non-governmental Organization," *American Sociological Review* 62: 171–190.

Bower, J.L. (1970). *Managing the Resource Allocation Process: A Study of Corporate Planning and Investment*. Boston, MA: Division of Research, Graduate School of Business Administration, Harvard University.

Buchholz, R.A. (1982). "Education for Public Issues Management: Key Insights from a Survey of Top Practitioners," *Public Affairs Review* 3: 68.

Buchholz, R.A. (1990). *Essentials of Public Policy for Management*. Englewood Cliffs, NJ: Prentice Hall.

Buchholz, R.A., W.D. Evans, and R.A. Wagley (1985). *Management Response to Public Issues*. Upper Saddle River, NJ: Prentice Hall.

Carroll, A.B. (1979). "A Three-dimensional Conceptual Model of Corporate Performance," *Academy of Management Review* 4: 497–505.

Chandler, A.D. (1962). *Strategy and Structure: Chapters in the History of American Enterprise*. Cambridge, MA: MIT press.

Chase, W.H. (1984). *Issue Management: Origins of the Future*. Stamford, CT: Issue Action Publishers.

Chauvin, K.W., and J.P. Guthrie (1994). "Labor Market Reputation and the Value of the Firm," *Managerial and Decision Economics* 15: 534–552.

Choi, J.P. (1998). "Brand Extension as Informational Leverage," *Review of Economic Studies* 65: 655–669.

Cowan, D.A. (1986). "Developing a Process Model of Problem Recognition," *Academy of Management Review* 11: 763–776.

Crane, T.Y. (2001). "Dow Chemical Process Integrates Skills, Insights," *Corporate Public Issues and their Management* 23: 93–96.

Crane, T.Y. (2002). "Baxter Addresses Concerns through Bioethics Policy," *Corporate Public Issues and their Management* 24: 25–29.

Daft, R.L., and K.E. Weick (1984). "Toward a Model of Organizations as Interpretation Systems," *Academy of Management Review* 9: 284–295.

D'Aveni, R.A. (1994). *Hypercompetition: Managing the Dynamics of Strategic Maneuvering*. New York: Free Press.

Davenport, T.H., and L. Prusak (2000). *Working Knowledge: How Organizations Manage What They Know*. Boston, MA: Harvard Business School Press.

Davenport, T.H., J.G. Harris, D.W. De long, and A.L. Jacobson (2001). "Data to Knowledge to Results: Building an Analytic Capability," *California Management Review* 43: 117–138.

Davis, K. (1975). *Business and Society: Environment and Responsibility*. New York: McGraw-Hill.

Dean, J.W. (1987). "Building the Future: The Justification Process for New Technology," in *New Technology as Organizational Innovation*, eds J.M. Pennings and A. Buitendam. Cambridge, MA: Ballinger.

Drogendijk, R. (2004). "The Public Affairs of Internationalization: Balancing Pressures from Multiple Environments," *Journal of Public Affairs* 4 (forthcoming).

Dutton, J.E. (1993). "Interpretations on Automatic: A Different View of Strategic Issue Diagnosis," *Journal of Management Studies* 30: 339–357.

Dutton, J.E., and S.J. Ashford (1993). "Selling Issues to Top Management," *Academy of Management Review* 18: 397–428.

Dutton, J.E., and J.M. Dukerich (1991). "Keeping an Eye in the Mirror: Image and Identity in Organizational Adaptation," *Academy of Management Journal* 34: 517–554.

Dutton, J.E., L. Fathey, and V.K. Narayanan (1983). "Toward Understanding Strategic Issue Diagnosis," *Strategic Management Journal* 4: 307–323.

Dutton, J.E., S. Stumpf, and D. Wagner (1990). "Diagnosing Strategic Issues and Managerial Investment of Revenues," in *Advances in Strategic Management*, eds P. Shrivastava and R.B. Lamb. Greenwich, CT: JAI Press.

Dutton, J.E., E.J. Walton, and E. Abrahamson (1989). "Important Dimensions of Strategic Issues: Separating the Wheat from the Chaff," *Journal of Management Studies* 26: 379–396.

Dutton, J.E., S.J. Ashford, K.A. Lawrence, and K. Miner-Rubino (2002). "Red Light, Green Light: Making Sense of the Organizational Context for Issue Selling," *Organization Science* 13: 355–369.

Dutton, J.E., S.J. Ashford, R.M. O'neill, and K.A. Lawrence (2001): "Moves that Matter: Issue Selling and Organizational Change," *Academy of Management Journal* 44: 716–736.

Dutton, J.E., S.J. Ashford, R.M. O'neill, E. Hayes, and E.E. Wierba (1997). "Reading the Wind: How Middle Managers Assess the Context for Selling Issues to Top Managers," *Strategic Management Journal* 18: 407–425.

Fleisher, C.S. (1993). "Public Affairs Management Performance: An Empirical Analysis Evaluation and Measurement," in *Research in Corporate Social Performance and Policy*, ed. J.E. Post. Greenwich, CT: JAI Press.

Fleisher, C.S., and B.E. Bensoussan (2003). *Strategic and Competitive Analysis: Methods and Techniques for Analyzing Business Competition*. Upper Saddle River, NJ: Prentice Hall.

Fleming, J.E. (1981). "Public Issues Scanning," in *Research in Corporate Social Performance and Policy*, ed. L.E. Preston. Greenwich: JAI Press.

Floyd, S.W., and B.J. Wooldridge (1994). "Dinosaurs or Dynamos? Recognizing Middle Management's Strategic Role," *Academy of Management Executive* 8: 47–58.

Floyd, and B.J. Wooldrid S.W. (1996). *The Strategic Middle Manager: How to Create and Sustain Competitive Advantage*. San Francisco. Jossey Bass.

Fombrun, C.J. (1996). *Reputation: Realizing Value from the Corporate Image.* Cambridge, MA: Harvard Business School Press.

Fredrickson, J.W. (1984). "The Comprehensiveness of Strategic Decision Processes: Extension, Observations, Future Directions," *Academy of Management Journal* 27: 445–466.

Getz, K.A. (1993). "Selecting Corporate Political Tactics," in *Corporate Political Agency: The Construction of Competition in Public Affairs,* ed. B. Mitnick. Newbury Park, CA: Sage.

Ginsberg, A. (1988). "Measuring and Modeling Changes in Strategy: Theoretical Foundations and Empirical Directions," *Strategic Management Journal* 9: 559–575.

Gioia, D.A., and K. Chittipeddi (1991). "Sensemaking and Sensegiving in Strategic Change Initiation," *Strategic Management Journal* 12: 433–448.

Gollner, A.B. (1983). *Social Change and Corporate Strategy: The Expanding Role of Public Affairs.* Stamford, CT: Issue Action Publications.

Gray, B. (1989). *Collaborating: Finding Common Ground for Multiparty Problems.* San Francisco: Jossey Bass.

Greif, A. (1989). "Reputation and Coalitions in Medieval Trade: Evidence on the Maghribi Traders," *Journal of Economic History* 49: 857–882.

Griffin, J.J. (2005). "The Empirical Study of Public Affairs: A Review and Synthesis," in *Handbook of Public Affairs,* eds P. Harris and C.S. Fleisher. London: Sage. (This volume.)

Grunig, J.E., and L.A. Grunig (1992). "Models of Public Relations and Communication," in *Excellence in Public Relations and Communication Management,* ed. J.E. Grunig. Hillsdale, NJ: Erlbaum.

Grunig J.E., and T. Hunt (1984). *Managing Public Relations.* New York: Holt Rinehart and Winston.

Hall, R.I. (1984). "The Natural Logic of Management Policy Making: Its Implications for the Survival of an Organization," *Management Science* 30: 905–927.

Hall, R. (1992). "The Strategic Analysis of Intangible Resources," *Strategic Management Journal* 13: 135–144.

Hall, R. (1993). "A Framework Linking Intangible Resources and Capabilities to Sustainable Competitive Advantage," *Strategic Management Journal* 13: 607–618.

Hambrick, D.C. (1981). "Strategic Awareness within Top Management Teams," *Strategic Management Journal* 2: 263–279.

Hambrick, D.C. (1989). "Guest Editor's Introduction: Putting Top Managers Back in the Strategy Picture," *Strategic Management Journal* 10: 5–15.

Hambrick, D.C., and S. Finkelstein (1987). "Managerial Discretion: A Bridge between Polar Views of Organizational Outcomes," in *Research in Organizational Behavior,* eds L.L. Cummings and B. Staw. Greenwich, CT: JAI Press, 369–406.

Hambrick, D.C., and P.A. Mason (1984). "Upper Echelons: The Organization as a Reflection of its Top Managers," *Academy of Management Review* 9: 193–206.

Harris, P., and C.S. Fleisher (2005). "Defining Public Affairs," in *Handbook of Public Affairs,* eds P. Harris and C.S. Fleisher. London: Sage. (This volume).

Harris, P., and A. Lock (1996). "Machiavellian Marketing: The Development of Corporate Lobbying in the UK," *Journal of Marketing Management* 12: 313–328.

Heath, R.L., and R.A. Nelson (1986). *Issues Management: Corporate Public Policymaking in an Information Society.* Beverly Hills, CA: Sage.

Henriques, D.B. (2000). "Business Reporting: Behind the Curve," *Columbia Journalism Review* 39: 18–21.

Heugens, P.P.M.A.R (2002a). "Strategic Issues Management: Implications for Corporate Performance," *Business and Society* 41: 456–468.

Heugens, P.P.M.A.R. (2002b). "Managing Public Affairs through Storytelling," *Journal of Public Affairs* 2: 57–70.

Heugens, P.P.M.A.R., and D. Deephouse (2003). "The Role of the News Media as a Linking Mechanism Connecting Social Issues to Firm Impact." Working paper, Utrecht School of Economics.

Heugens, P.P.M.A.R., F.A.J. Van Den Bosch, and C.B.M. Van Riel (2002). "Stakeholder Integration: Building Mutually Enforcing Relationships," Business and Society 41: 37–61.

Heugens, P.P.M.A R., C.B.M. Van Riel, and F.A.J. Van Den Bosch (2004). "Reputation Management Capabilities as Decision Rules," *Journal of Management Studies* 41 (forthcoming).

Hoffman, A.J., and W. Ocasio (2001). "Not all Events are Attended Equally: Toward a Middle-range Theory of Industry Attention to External Events," *Organization Science* 12: 414–434.

Ilinitch, A.Y., R.A. D'Aveni, and A.Y. LEWIN (1996). "New Organizational Forms and Strategies for Managing in Hypercompetitive Environments," *Organization Science* 7: 211–220.

Jacoby, N. (1971). "What is a Social Problem?" *Center Magazine,* July/August 35–40.

Jacques, E. (1961). *Equitable Payment.* New York: Wiley.

Johnson, J. (1983). "Issues Management: What are the Issues?" *Business Quarterly* 48: 22–31.

Jones, T.M. (1991): "Ethical Decision Making by Individuals in Organizations: An Issue-contingent Model," *Academy of Management Review*, 16: 366–395.

Kanter, R.M. (1982). "The Middle Manager as Innovator," *Harvard Business Review* 60: 95–105.

Katz, D., and R.L. KAHN (1978). *The Social Psychology of Organizations.* New York: Wiley.

King, W.R. (1982). "Using Strategic Issue Analysis," *Long Range Planning* 15: 45–49.

Klein, N. (2001). *No Logo: Taking Aim at the Brand Bullies.* New York: Picador.

Kreps, D., and R. Wilson (1982). "Reputation and Imperfect Information," *Journal of Economic Theory* 27: 253–279.

Krugman, P.R. (1994). *The Age of Diminished Expectations.* Cambridge, MA: MIT Press.

Lador-Lederer, J.J. (1962). *International Non-governmental Organizations and Economic Entities: A Study in Autonomous Organization and* Ius Gentium. Leiden: Sijthoff.

Lamertz, K., and P.P.M.A.R. Heugens (2003). "The Configuration of Public Organizational Identities in the Canadian Beer Brewing Industry," Paper presented at the Annual Academy of Management Meeting August 4–6, Seattle, WA.

Lamertz, K., M.L. Martens, And P.P.M.A.R. Heugens (2003). "Issue Evolution: A Symbolic Interactionist Perspective," *Corporate Reputation Review* 6: 82–93.

Logsdon, J.M. (1985). "Organizational Responses To Environmental Issues: Oil Refining Companies And Air Pollution," In *Research in Corporate Social Performance and Policy*, ed. L.E. Preston. Greenwich, CT: JAI Press.

Logsdon, J.M., And D.R. Palmer (1988). "Issues Management and Ethics," *Journal of Business Ethics* 7: 191–198.

Lyles, M.A. (1981). "Formulating Strategic Problems: Empirical Analyses and Model Develop Ment," *Strategic Management Journal* 2: 61–75.

Mahon, J.F., and P.P.M.A.R. Heugens (2002). "Who's on First—Issues or Stakeholder Management?" In *Proceedings of the Thirteenth Annual Meeting of the International Association for Business and Society*, eds D. Windsor and S.A. Welcomer. Orono, ME: Iabs.

Meyer, A. (1982). "Adapting to Environmental Jolts," *Administrative Science Quarterly* 27: 515–537.

Milgrom, P., and J. Roberts (1982). "Predation, Reputation, and Entry Deterrence," *Journal of Economic Theory* 27: 280–312.

Mintzberg, H. (1973). *The Nature of Managerial Work.* Englewood Cliffs, NJ: Prentice Hall.

Mitchell, R.K., B.R. Agle, And D.J. Wood (1997). "Toward A Theory of Stakeholder Identification And Salience: Defining the Principle of who and What Really Counts," *Academy of Management Review* 22: 853–886.

Moore, R.H. (1979). "Planning for Emerging Issues," *Public Relations Journal* 35: 42–46.

Morrison, E.W., and F.J. Milliken (2000). "Organizational Silence: A Barrier to Change and Development in A Pluralistic World," *Academy of Management Review* 25: 706–725.

Morrison, E.W., and C.C. Phelps (1999). "Taking Charge at Work: Extrarole Efforts to Initiate Workplace Change," *Academy of Management Journal* 42: 403–419.

Palese, M., and T.Y. Crane (2002). "Building An Integrated Issues Management Process as a Source of Sustainable Competitive Advantage," Stamford, CT: Issue Action Publishers, 14.

Post, J.E. (1978). *Corporate Behavior and Social Change.* Reston, VA: Reston Publishing.

Pratt, C.B. (2001). "Issues Management: The Paradox of the Forty-Year Us Tobacco Wars," In *Handbook of Public Relations*, ed. R.L. Heath. Thousand Oaks, CA: Sage.

Preston, L.E. (1975). "Corporations and Society: The Search for a Paradigm," *Journal of Economic Literature* 13: 434–453.

Preston, L.E., and J.E. Post (1975). *Private Management And Public Policy.* Englewood Cliffs, NJ: Prentice Hall.

Salancik, G.R., B.J. Calder, K.M. Rowland, H. Leblebici, and M. Conway (1975). "Leadership as an Outcome of Social Structure and Process: A Multidimensional Analysis," In *Leadership Frontiers*, ed. J. G. Hunt and E. E. Larson. Columbus, OH: Kent University Press.

Schuler, D.A., K. Rehbein, And R.D. Kramer (2002). "Pursuing Strategic Advantage Through Political Means: A Multivariate Approach," *Academy of Management Journal* 45: 659–672.

Selznick, P. (1957). *Leadership In Administration: A Sociological Interpretation.* New York: Harper and Row.

Shapiro, C., and H.R. Varian (1998). *Information Rules: A Strategic Guide to the Network Economy.* Boston, MA: Harvard Business School Press.

Sharma, S., and H. Vredenburg (1998). "Proactive Corporate Environmental Strategy and the Development of Competitively Valuable Organizational Capabilities," *Strategic Management Journal* 19: 729–753.

Skjelsbaek, K. (1971). "The Growth of International Nongovernmental Organization in the Twentieth Century," *International Organization*, 25: 420–442.

Stanley, G.D.D. (1985). *Managing External Issues: Theory and Practice.* Greenwich, CT: JAI Press.

Steiner, G. (1974). "The Social Responsibilities of Business," in *the Changing Business Role in Modern Society*, ed. G. Steiner. Los Angeles: UCLA (Mimeo).

Sutton, F.X., S.E. Harris, C. Kaysen, and J. Tobin (1956). *The American Business Creed.* Cambridge, MA: Harvard University Press.

Tedeschi, J.T. (1981). *Impression Management Theory and Social Psychological Research.* New York: Academic Press.

Thomas, J.B., and R.R. McDaniel (1990). "Interpreting Strategic Issues: Effects of Strategy And The Information-Processing Structure of top Management Teams," *Academy of Management Journal* 33: 286–306.

Thomas, J.B., L.J. Shankster, and J.E. Mathieu (1994). "Antecedents to Organizational Issue Interpretation: The Roles of Single-Level, Cross-Level, and Content Cues," *Academy of Management Journal* 37: 1252–1284.

Thompson, J.D. (1967). *Organizations in Action: Social Science Bases of Administrative Theory.* New York: Mcgraw-Hill.

Union of International Associations (1988). *Yearbook of International Organizations.* Munich: Saur.

Volberda, H.W. (1996). "Toward the Flexible Form: How to Remain Vital In Hypercompetitive Environments," *Organization Science*, 7: 359–374.

Wartick, S.L. (1988). "How Issues Management Contributes to Corporate Performance," *Business Forum* 13: 16–22.

Wartick, S.L., And P.L. Cochran (1985). "The Evolution of the Corporate Social Performance Model," *Academy of Management Review* 10: 758–769.

Wartick, S.L., and P.P.M.A.R. Heugens (2003). "Future Directions for Issues Management," *Corporate Reputation Review* 6: 7–18.

Wartick, S.L., and J.F. Mahon (1994). "Toward A Substantive Definition of the Corporate Issue Construct: A Review and Synthesis of the Literature," *Business and Society* 33: 293–311.

Weick, K.E. (1979). *The Social Psychology of Organizing.* New York: McGraw-Hill.

Westley, F.R. (1990). "Middle Managers and Strategy: Microdynamics of Inclusion," *Strategic Management Journal* 11: 337–351.

Wood, D.J. (1991). "Corporate Social Performance Revisited," *Academy of Management Review* 16: 691–718.

Wooldridge, B., And S.W. Floyd (1990). "The Strategy Process, Middle Management Involvement, and Organizational Performance," *Strategic Management Journal* 11: 231–241.

## ACKNOWLEDGMENTS

1 I wish to thank a number of individuals who have helped me identify pockets of issues management literature that were previously unknown to me: Archie Carroll, David Deephouse, Virginia Gerde, Jennifer Griffin, Jeanne Logsdon, John Mahon, Jim Mattingly, Tim Mazur, Richard Nelson, Karen Schnietz, Robert Sexty, and Thomas Sigerstad. I also wish to acknowledge the developmental support by *Handbook of Public Affairs* editors Phil Harris and Craig Fleisher. The usual caveat applies.

# 29

# Stakeholder Management

*Background and Advances*

ARCHIE B. CARROLL

## INTRODUCTION

This chapter provides the reader with an overall perspective on the conceptual and application aspects of that body of knowledge known variously as stakeholder theory, stakeholder management, stakeholding, stakeholder analysis, or stakeholder thinking. These concepts, and this way of conceptualizing organizations, bring an inventive approach to thinking about organizations and their public affairs responsibilities, and provide a useful framework for managers who wish to improve the effectiveness of their organizations or clients.

### Background and Overview

It has long been recognized that the broad environment in which organizations find themselves has an important effect on the management, operations, and success of those organizations. Over the years, the environment of business has been conceptualized and described in a number of different ways. The environment has been thought of in terms of sub-environments such as economic, legal/political, social, and technological. The environment has also been thought of in terms of macro- and micro-divisions, in terms of strategic and operating divisions, and in other terms as well. In a major sense, the stakeholder approach introduced yet another way to think in terms of the organization's environment. And, since the public affairs function of organizations has so much to do with the organization's external environment, stakeholder management is a natural fit in terms of conceptualizing the relationship between the organization and the environment, as broadly defined.

The stakeholder concept depicts specific individuals and/or groups in the organization's environment as not only being various sub-environments, publics, or constituencies with which the organization must interact to be effective, but also as individuals or groups who have definite or clearly identifiable stakes, or investments, in the enterprise. When viewed in this way, these stakeholders, like the owners or shareholders of the firm, have some important investments in the ongoing operations and goals of the firm, and therefore, must be regarded more like they are an integral part of the organization rather than external constituencies or publics which are not part of the organization. In the context of the current discussion, we will treat stakeholder management, stakeholder thinking, or the stakeholder approach, primarily in terms of business enterprises. It should be noted, however, that the stakeholder approach is quite useful for not-for-profit, governmental, and educational organizations as well.

The stakeholder model of the firm grew out of a realization of the limitations of stockholder theory, or the stockholder model of the firm, frequently construed as built upon simplistic, short-term economic assumptions. It is not so much that the stockholder model is completely invalid, but rather that the stakeholder model more fully and accurately depicts and represents the reality managers find themselves in today. The stockholder model is deeply rooted in agency theory and fiduciary duty. In agency theory, it is held that managers (the agents) are "acting for" the owners of the enterprise and that they owe a fiduciary responsibility, or duty, to the owners. Narrowly interpreted, this economic view would hold that managers should focus on stockholders' interests, not the interests of other stakeholders.

A complicating factor here is whether one is discussing the short term or the long term. Stakeholder theorists would argue that the stockholder model is short-sighted and that tending to stakeholder interests is in the best long-term interests of the stockholders. Thus, they see no violation of agency theory or fiduciary duty. In the past several years, in particular, it has become evident from the growing body of management and marketing theory and research that concentrating on the needs and aspirations of employees and consumers, two of the major stakeholder groups, is indeed the most profitable way to attend to the stockholders' best interests.

Boatright (1997) points out that some critics of the stockholder view contend that the same conditions which create a fiduciary duty to serve the interests of stockholders also apply to other constituencies, with the result that a fiduciary duty is owed to these other constituencies

as well. In this view, officers and directors may have a fiduciary duty to other investors, such as bondholders, to protect their investments; to employees to maintain remunerative employment; to consumers to meet their needs and to protect them against harm from defective products; and so on. This notion is similar to what Goodpaster (1991) has termed a "multi-fiduciary stakeholder orientation." Such arguments tend to support the stakeholder model as an alternative to the stockholder model.

Without going too deeply into the history of the stakeholder concept, let us mark the modern era of stakeholder theory in the United States with the emergence of the popular book by R. Edward Freeman *Strategic Management: A Stakeholder Approach* (1984). Though Freeman popularized stakeholder theory within the context of strategic management, since that time it has been found useful for thinking about general management theory, strategic management, corporate governance, Business and Society relationships, marketing, and business ethics. In each of these arenas a body of literature has grown over the past twenty years.

## Values of the Stakeholder Approach

It has been argued that use of the stakeholder approach, or stakeholder management, constitutes a stakeholder model of the firm. Donaldson and Preston (1995) articulated three aspects or values of the stakeholder model which are distinct yet interrelated. Thinking of the firm using stakeholder terms, they have proposed three values—descriptive, instrumental, and normative.

First, the stakeholder model is *descriptive.* That is, it identifies and describes the relationships the corporation or organization has with groups or persons with which it interacts. The corporation is a constellation of cooperative and competitive interests possessing intrinsic value. From a public affairs perspective, the stakeholder approach helps to robustly capture the full range of relationships that firms have with external groups such as government, the media, special interest groups, and others. Understanding organizations in this way allows a fuller description or explanation of how they function.

Second, the stakeholder model is *instrumental*. It is useful in establishing the connections between the practice of stakeholder management and the resulting achievement of corporate performance goals. The fundamental premise here is that practicing effective stakeholder management should lead to the achievement of traditional organizational goals such as profitability, stability, and growth. As applied to the corporate public affairs function, it enhances the achievement of public affairs goals and aspirations.

Third, the stakeholder model is *normative*. In this perspective, stakeholders are identified by their interests in the organization whether or not the organization has any corresponding interest in them. Thus, in the normative view, the interests of all stakeholders are of intrinsic value. Stakeholders are seen as possessing value irrespective of their instrumental use to management. This is the rationalization for using stakeholder management for creating and implementing ethical organizations. In other words, the normative view of the model allows management to more completely fulfill its ethical responsibilities in the context of fulfilling its economic, legal, and philanthropic responsibilities (Carroll and Buchholtz, 2006). In summary Donaldson and Preston (1995) assert that stakeholder theory is managerial in the broadest sense of the term. It is managerial in the sense that it does not simply describe or predict but also recommends certain attitudes, structures, and practices that constitute stakeholder management, or, managing according to the stakeholder model. Such an approach, which this chapter proposes, necessitates the simultaneous attention to the legitimate interests of all appropriate stakeholders in the creation of organizational policies and practices.

## STAKEHOLDERS AND THEIR CHARACTERISTICS

Understanding the stakeholder approach to management necessitates a discussion of at least the following questions: What is a stake and a stakeholder? Who are businesses' stakeholders? How might stakeholders be perceived or categorized? What are the relevant characteristics of stakeholders which management should consider?

## What is a Stake and What is a Stakeholder?

To appreciate the concept of stakeholders, it helps to understand the idea of a stake. In traditional views of management, the exclusive or most important stakeholder seems to be the shareholders—the owners or investor group. Their stake is financial in the sense that they financed the firm. In the stakeholder view, the notion of an individual's or group's investment in the firm is perceived more broadly. A stake is an interest in or a share in an undertaking. A stake is also a claim. A claim is an assertion to a right to something. A claim is a demand for something due or believed to be due, or owed. The idea of a stake, therefore, can range from simply an interest in an undertaking at one extreme to a legal claim of ownership at the other extreme. In between these two extremes are other claims to a right to something. This "right" might be a *legal* right to certain treatment rather than a legal claim of ownership such as that held by a shareholder. Examples of legal rights include those held by employees or consumers based upon a contract or law. Employees have legal rights based upon the contract they enter into and they have certain rights which are protected by law (e.g., minimum wage, nondiscrimination in employment, safety). Consumers have legal rights based upon product/service warranties and also upon law.

The stakeholder approach recognizes *moral* rights in addition to legal rights. Moral rights might be justified claims to certain kinds of treatment which are not established by law or extend beyond that provided by law. Judgments about moral rights of employees and consumers, for example, might hinge on interpretations of what constitutes fairness, justice, or equity in relationships. An employee asserts a moral right when he or she claims "I've got a right not to be fired because I've worked here thirty years and I've given this company the best years of my life." Or, a consumer might claim, "I've got a right to a safe product after all I've paid for this" (Carroll, 1996). Groups external to the firm also assert moral rights. Underlying the motivations, claims, and activities of environmental, social, health, safety, animal rights, and other types of special interest groups, is typically a moral claim of some issue or issues which the groups think are important and should be addressed by the firm. Robert Phillips (Phillips, 2003) argues persuasively for the importance of the relationship between stakeholder theory and organizational ethics.

Given this discussion of what constitutes a stake, how might a stakeholder be defined? A stakeholder is an individual or group that claims to have one or more of the various kinds of stakes described above. Just as stakeholders *may be affected by* the actions, decisions, policies, or practices of a firm, these stakeholders also *may affect* the organization's actions, decisions, policies, or practices. With stakeholders, therefore, there is a potential two-way interaction or exchange of influence. In short, a stakeholder may be thought of as any individual or group who can affect or is affected by the actions, decisions, policies, practices, or goals of the organization (Carroll and Buchholtz, 2006).

A more narrow definition of stakeholders has been offered by Post *et al.* (2002). They define stakeholders as follows: "The stakeholders in a corporation are the individuals and constituencies that contribute, either voluntarily or involuntarily, to its wealth-creating capacity and activities, and that are therefore its potential beneficiaries and/or risk bearers." Their view of stakeholders is one that seems to emphasize individuals or groups that have more of the potential for cooperation rather than threat.

## Who are Business's Stakeholders?

In today's business environment, there are many individuals and groups who are business's stakeholders. From the business point of

view, there are certain individuals and groups that have legitimacy in the eyes of management. That is, they have a legitimate interest in, or claim on, the operations or practices of the firm. The most obvious of these groups are shareholders, employees, and customers. From the standpoint of competitive strategy, competitors might be added to the list, and from the vantage point of strategic alliances, suppliers might also be added. From the point of view of a highly plural society, which characterizes the modern business environment, stakeholders might include not only these groups but others such as the community, government, special interest groups, the media, society, or the public at large. It has also been strongly argued that the natural environment should be considered to be one of business's key stakeholders (Starik, 1993).

Years ago, scholars debated at professional meetings whether terrorists should be considered stakeholders. In the post-9/11 world, terrorists are clearly a group that business firms must anticipate and deal with because they can significantly affect the way business is conducted, especially at a global level. In short, any individual or group, and possibly the natural environment, could be thought of as a stakeholder, and therefore, it is necessary to develop a means by which managers or consultants might organize or categorize stakeholders in terms of their types and priorities (Golembiewski, 1993; Schein, 1993).

## Categorizing Stakeholders

There are a number of ways in which analysts might categorize stakeholders to facilitate effective analysis, understanding, and management. Stakeholders might be thought of as internal versus external (to the organization). Internal stakeholders might include owners, employees, and management, and various subdivisions of these groups. External stakeholders might include consumers or consumer groups, the community, special interest groups, suppliers, competitors, government, lobbyists, and the media. Another way of thinking about stakeholders is whether they should be regarded as primary or secondary. For example, primary stakeholders have been defined as those individuals or groups which have a formal, official, or contractual relationship with the firm, and all others could be seen as secondary. Alternately, their primary or secondary status could be based upon some other criteria, such as urgency to the immediate situation or decision, their power, or their legitimacy. For example, a stakeholder could move from secondary to primary status when the urgency of a claim (as in the case of a boycott, a union strike, impending government regulation, or a contaminated product) takes precedence over other considerations. In today's business environment, the media have the power to instantaneously transform a stakeholder's status with coverage on the evening news or unrelenting week-to-week coverage of a company or an issue.

At an important Toronto conference on stakeholder theory, an alternative scheme for classifying stakeholders was developed. In this scheme, stakeholders are thought of as being core, strategic, or environmental. Core stakeholders are a specific subset of strategic stakeholders, namely those that are essential for the survival of the firm. Strategic stakeholders were seen as those that are vital to the organization and the particular set of threats and opportunities it faces at a particular point in time. Environmental stakeholders were all others that formed the backdrop or general environment of the firm (Clarkson, 1995, 1998). These three categories could be perceived as a series of concentric circles with "core" at the middle, "strategic" next, and "environmental" on the outside rings.

## Stakeholder Characteristics Relevant to Decision Making

Closely related to the issue of classifying stakeholders is a consideration of pertinent stakeholder characteristics which management or public affairs executives may need to consider and which form the basis for further classifications of stakeholders. Two issues of concern in Freeman's classic book were the stakeholder's

legitimacy and their power (Freeman, 1984), perhaps building on Weber's (1947) distinction between legitimacy and power in discussing authority. Later it was determined that urgency was another vital attribute that should be factored into management's considerations. Mitchell *et al.* (1997), building upon this previous work, postulated that these were key constructs in a theory of stakeholder identification and salience: legitimacy, power, and urgency.

*Legitimacy* refers to the right of the stakeholder to hold his or her stake. It has to do with the appropriateness and relevance of the stakeholder's claims *vis-à-vis* others' claims. Legitimacy has to do with the generalized perception or assumption that the actions of an entity are desirable, proper, or appropriate within some socially constructed systems of norms, values or beliefs (Suchman, 1995). Thus, in stakeholder management, a stakeholder's legitimacy must be assessed and is always a pertinent factor in making decisions.

*Power*, as a stakeholder attribute, has to do with the stakeholder's ability to produce an effect on the company under discussion. There are many bases for power. Stakeholders that are powerful include those with extensive resources and those with high visibility. For example, a large institutional investor (trust, foundation) would be much more powerful than an individual shareholder who owns 2,000 shares of stock. As Etzioni (1964) has argued, bases for power could include coercive (force/threat), utilitarian (material incentives), or normative (symbolic influences).

*Urgency* may be defined as the "degree to which stakeholder claims call for immediate attention." Urgency could be based on the need for a timely response, or it could refer to criticality, the importance of the claim or the stakeholders' relationship to the organization (Mitchell *et al.*, 1997). Urgency may be the defining characteristic in a crisis management decision-making situation.

A stakeholder typology may be set forth based upon whether one, two, or three of the above attributes are present. A stakeholder with only power might be thought of as a "dormant" stakeholder. One with power and legitimacy might be called a "dominant" stakeholder.

A stakeholder with only urgency might be called a "demanding" stakeholder. One with urgency and power might be termed a "dangerous" stakeholder. A stakeholder with only legitimacy might be called a "discretionary" stakeholder. One with legitimacy and urgency might be termed a "dependent" stakeholder. Finally, a stakeholder with all three attributes present might be termed a "definitive" stakeholder (Mitchell *et al.*, 1997).

In summation, there are a number of different ways of thinking about stakeholders and their stakes. In considering public affairs strategy, operations or ethics, a careful analysis and thoughtful reflection upon stakeholder characteristics and the ways in which stakeholders might be categorized based upon their attributes can go a long way toward helping management teams diagnose organizational problems and improve organizational effectiveness.

## KEY QUESTIONS FOR STAKEHOLDER MANAGEMENT

Top management of a firm has the responsibilities for establishing its overall direction (goals, values, strategies, policies, operations) and seeing to it that these plans are carried out. Public affairs executives have responsibilities which devolve from these strategic considerations. Consequently, managers have both long-term and short-term responsibilities. Before the stakeholder view of the firm became necessary, the social and competitive environments were stable and management's task was relatively straightforward. Today, stakeholder management has become necessary and inevitable as many different groups demand to be recognized and satisfied.

Experts have long known of the importance of managing people and consumers as an avenue of organizational success. In one sense, then, the premise of stakeholder theory is to expand the organization's horizons and managers' thinking to be inclusive of other stakeholder groups and to see that these are groups which have a legitimate investment or stake in the enterprise's operations, as well as the power to

effect change. One could also argue that perhaps managers have been "doing stakeholder management" for decades, albeit in a piecemeal fashion, not fully perceiving the integral nature of working with stakeholders. What has been learned, however, is that today many diverse groups expect and demand to be treated as a vital part of the organization's success. While still recognizing the primacy and necessity of profits as a return on the shareholder's investments, we have also seen growing claims of other stakeholder groups—claims and expectations that they be satisfied as well.

With these perspectives in mind, it is useful to approach stakeholder management with the idea that managers can become successful stewards of stakeholders' resources by gaining knowledge about stakeholders (stakeholder analysis) and using this knowledge to predict and deal with their behaviors and actions. Our ultimate goal is to manage organizations in such a way that they are effective, efficient, and ethical. Thus, the important functions of stakeholder management are to describe, to understand, to analyze, and to manage.

Five major questions are useful for capturing the essential information that is needed to fulfill stakeholder management or to engage in stakeholder thinking (Carroll and Buchholtz, 2006). Whether one is a general manager or a public affairs officer, these questions help flesh out the essentials. These five questions include: (1) Who are the organization's stakeholders? (2) What are the stakeholders' stakes? (3) What opportunities and challenges do the stakeholders present to the firm? (4) What responsibilities (economic, legal, ethical, and philanthropic) does the firm have towards its stakeholders? (5) What strategies or actions should the firm take to best deal with stakeholder challenges and opportunities?

### Who are the Organization's Stakeholders?

A key task is to analyze the organization and its environment to determine who constitutes its stakeholders. To answer this question fully, management must not only identify generic stakeholder groups (shareholders, employees, government, consumers, etc.) as we have previously discussed, but must identify specific relevant subgroups. Within every generic stakeholder group, which are basically common to all businesses, are specific groups which may vary in terms of their legitimacy, power, and urgency. For example, a firm may need to specifically identify the subgroups of each generic group and analyze how the subgroup might place expectations or pressures on the firm.

Several examples of subgroups of generic groups would be as follows. For the generic group of *owners*, a corporation might have the following subgroups: trusts, foundations, mutual funds, board members, management owners, employee pension funds, and individual owners. For the generic group of *employees*, a corporation might find it useful to think of them in terms such as the following: young, middle-aged, older, women, men, minorities, disabled, unions, and special interests. For the general group known as *community*, subgroups might be schools, local government, chamber of commerce, local newspapers/radio, United Way, Citizens Against Taxation, residents who live close to the plant, and so on. For the generic group of *social activist groups*, relevant subgroups might include: Friends of the Earth, MADD (Mothers Against Drunk Driving), the American Civil Liberties Union, Judicial Watch, the Consumers Union, and so on. In short, companies must identify not only their generic but also their specific stakeholder groups and this may require some creative thinking.

## What are the Stakeholder's Stakes?

Once stakeholders have been identified, both generic and specific, the next challenge is to identify what are the stakes of the various groups. Even groups and individuals in the same generic category often have different specific interests, concerns, perceptions of rights, and expectations. The challenge here of management, or the public affairs office, is to identify the nature/legitimacy, power and urgency of the stakeholder's stakes. Some

judgments about legitimacy are clear. However, many are not. Within one stakeholder category, for example, it may be difficult to differentiate between legitimacy. For instance, an institutional owner of stocks (trusts, foundations, universities) may be no more legitimate than an individual owner of 500 shares. This is why it is frequently necessary to consider other criteria such as power or urgency. When power or urgency is factored in, the institutional investor, representing the holdings of millions of shares, has significantly more power and urgency. (The fund manager could quickly disinvest, thus affecting the share value of the remaining stock.)

At this stage in the process of stakeholder analysis, consideration must be given to whether the stakeholder's stake is just a casual interest, has the potential to be affected by the organization's actions, is an ownership interest, and has a legal claim or a moral claim. The stakeholders' stakes, therefore, must be carefully analyzed.

## What Opportunities or Challenges do Stakeholders Present?

Stakeholders may present an opportunity (perhaps in the form of a cooperative alliance) or a challenge (perhaps in the form of a threat) to the concerned organization. In many respects, these represent opposite sides of the coin when it comes to stakeholders. Opportunities may exist in the form of the potential for building good, productive working relationships with stakeholders. Savage *et al.* (1991) describe how Ross Laboratories, a division of Abbott Laboratories, was able to develop a cooperative relationship with some critics of its sales of infant formula in Third World countries. Ross and Abbott convinced these stakeholder groups (UNICEF and the World Health Organization) to join them in a program to promote infant health. Other firms, such as Nestlé, did not develop the potential to cooperate and suffered from consumer boycotts.

More often than not, it seems, companies see stakeholders as posing challenges or threats. Consumers complain, join activist groups, write letters to the newspapers and/or other media, file lawsuits, and quit doing business with the firm. Employees join unions, stage strikes, pickets, or walkouts, steal from employers, quit, protest to the media, file lawsuits, and so on. Special interest groups embarrass the firm with adverse publicity, boycotts, use of local and national investigative journalism opportunities, and so on.

In terms of analyzing stakeholders' potential for threat or cooperation, there are a number of factors which increase or decrease stakeholders' potential for threat or cooperation. Several illustrations are useful. Regarding *potential for threat*, the following factors may increase the potential: the stakeholder is more powerful than the organization, or the stakeholder is likely to take non-supportive action. The following factors may decrease the potential for threat: the stakeholder does not control key resources, the stakeholder is less powerful than the organization, or the stakeholder is unlikely to form any coalition. Regarding *potential for cooperation*, the following factors increase the potential: the stakeholder is likely to take action (supportive of the organization), or the stakeholder controls key resources (needed by the organization). Regarding potential for cooperation, the following factors decrease the potential: the stakeholder is unlikely to take any action, or the stakeholder is likely to take non-supportive action (Savage *et al.*, 1991). In sum, to carefully understand the potential for collaboration or possibility of threat, the stakeholders must be carefully identified, their stakes prudently assessed, and their potential for cooperation or threat cautiously assessed.

### What Responsibilities does the Firm have toward Stakeholders?

Responsibilities that firms have toward stakeholders may be assessed in terms of Carroll's four categories of economic, legal, ethical, and philanthropic responsibilities (1979, 1991) which span a range of expectations that stakeholders and the public have for business organizations. To systematically answer this question, it is possible to envision a grid with these four categories, or types, of responsibility along one axis, and a list of stakeholder groups along the other axis. If the analysis is primarily aimed at the firm's economic or strategic performance, the focus should be on the economic category (concern for financial performance). If the analysis is concerned with the firm's social responsibilities, the focus should be on the legal, ethical, and philanthropic performance (concern for society or social performance).

Of course, all these categories of performance are interrelated and do contribute to the overall performance of the enterprise; however, breaking them out into the four different types of responsibilities towards the various stakeholders provides a type of analysis that may be useful in analyzing and understanding the challenges facing the firm.

### What Strategies or Actions should Management Take?

Once responsibilities have been assessed, a business must contemplate strategies and actions for dealing with its stakeholders. In every decision situation, a number of alternative courses of action are available, and management must choose one of several that seem the best. In the previous step, a decision had to be made as to whether it was the organization's economic, legal, ethical, or philanthropic performance that was at stake. In addition, the focus could have been driven by a concern for one of the major stakeholder groups— employees, consumers, shareholders, the community, and so on. Once these basic determinations have been made, the organization faces several possible generic strategies for dealing with stakeholders that may be pursued. MacMillan and Jones (1986) pose four important questions or strategies which are still relevant. They include the following:

1  Do we deal *directly* or *indirectly* with stakeholders?
2  Do we take the *offense* or the *defense* in dealing with stakeholders?

3  Do we *accommodate, negotiate, manipulate,* or *resist* stakeholder overtures?

4  Do we employ a *combination* of the above strategies or pursue a *singular* course?

A careful analysis of the advantages and disadvantages of these strategy choices should indicate which one or several of them to employ.

If we return to the previous concept of thinking of stakeholders in terms of their potential for threat or potential for cooperation, another way of visualizing possible strategies emerges (Savage *et al.,* 1991). These researchers have proposed a two-by-two matrix depicting a typology of organizational stakeholders and resultant strategies for dealing with them. On one axis is the stakeholders' potential for threat to the organization (divided into high and low) and on the other axis is the stakeholders' potential for cooperation with the organization (divided into high and low). The resulting matrix reveals four stakeholder types and recommended strategies for dealing with each of the four types.

1  Stakeholder Type 1 is low on threat and high on potential for cooperation. This type is named *supportive* and the recommended strategy is *involve.*

2  Stakeholder Type 2 is low on threat and low on potential for cooperation and is named the *marginal* stakeholder. The recommended strategy is *monitor.*

3  Stakeholder Type 3 is high on potential threat and low on potential cooperation and is named *non-supportive.* The recommended strategy is *defend* (against).

4  Stakeholder Type 4 is high on both potential for threat and cooperation and is named a *mixed blessing.* The recommended strategy is *collaborate.*

The authors (Savage *et al.,* 1991) summarize their position regarding these four stakeholder types as follows: "managers should attempt to satisfy minimally the needs of marginal stakeholders and to satisfy maximally the needs of supportive and mixed blessing stakeholders, enhancing the latter's support for the organization".

## EFFECTIVE STAKEHOLDER THINKING AND MANAGEMENT

Both corporate executives and public affairs managers alike are concerned about solving organizational problems and improving organizational effectiveness, especially in its relationships with stakeholder groups. The above discussion has established a foundation for understanding stakeholder thinking, theory, and management. At this point, we will consider several concepts which are built upon this foundation and that are vital to appreciating the stakeholder approach.

### Stakeholder Thinking

In 1994, Juha Nasi, a Finnish professor and writer, advanced the notion of stakeholder thinking with an international conference held in Finland (Näsi, 1995; Carroll and Näsi, 1997). In addition to tracing the roots of stakeholder theory to Scandinavia in the mid-1960s, Nasi articulated a concern for stakeholder thinking that would be useful as a complement to the evolving notion of stakeholder theory. At this stage of development, Näsi (1995) asserted, "let us take theory to mean, rather loosely, a set of propositions which defines certain concepts and their interconnections." He went on to propose that "by stakeholder thinking, we mean a way to see the company and its activities through stakeholder concepts and propositions. The idea then is that 'holders' who have 'stakes' interact with the firm and thus make its operation possible" (Näsi, 1995: 21). Nasi seems to be suggesting that stakeholder thinking, that is, thinking in stakeholder terms using stakeholder concepts, is a constructive way of analyzing organizations even if we fall short of using a fully developed stakeholder theory of the firm.

The importance of stakeholder thinking was further supported by this writer, who at the Finland conference argued as follows:

> The general theme of stakeholder thinking is an appropriate and effective way of articulating a whole host of concerns which surround the

stakeholder concept or the stakeholder theory of the firm. More than anything else, it seems, the stakeholder concept envisions a way of thinking about organizations and managers' actions within and about organizations. More particularly, stakeholder thinking provides a concept for articulating, expressing, analyzing, and understanding managers in their relationships with individuals and groups "out there in the environment" known as stakeholders. At a broader level, stakeholder thinking helps us understand the business and society relationship.

(Carroll, 1995)

In summary, it could be argued that stakeholder thinking is a valuable asset in analyzing organizations and in providing a language, some concepts, and some ideas that are useful for descriptive, instrumental, and normative purposes.

## Stakeholder Management Capability

Another way of thinking about stakeholder approaches to management is through the use of what Freeman (1984) termed "stakeholder management capability" (SMC). Through this concept, Freeman suggests, managers and firms may reside at three levels of stakeholder management refinement or sophistication. Level 1—the rational level—simply entails the company identifying who its stakeholders are and what their stakes happen to be. This is the level of stakeholder identification. This actually represents a very basic level of stakeholder management. Most organizations know who their stakeholders are, but many have not carefully analyzed the nature of the stakes or their attendant power or urgency. Starik (1990) has referred to Freeman's first level of SMC as the component of "familiarization" and "comprehensiveness" because managers operating at this level are seeking to become familiar with their stakeholders and to develop a comprehensive assessment as to their identification and stakes.

Level 2 of stakeholder management capability is the process level. At this level, organizations go a step further than Level 1 and actually

develop and implement organizational processes by which the firm may scan the environment and receive relevant information about stakeholders, which is then used for decision-making purposes. Typical approaches used here include portfolio analysis processes, strategic review processes, environmental scanning, and issues management. Many public affairs activities and departments reside at this level. Starik (1990) has called Freeman's second level the level of "planning integrativeness," because management does focus on planning processes for stakeholders and integrating a consideration for stakeholders into corporate-level decision making.

Level 3, the highest and most sophisticated level of SMC, is the transactional level. This is, in a sense, the treasured bottom line for stakeholder management—the extent to which managers actually engage in transactions, or relationships, with stakeholders. At this highest level of SMC, managers take the initiative in meeting stakeholders face to face and strive to communicate with them and to be responsive to them and to anticipate their needs. Starik (1990) refers to this level as the "communication" level, which is characterized by communication, proactiveness, interactiveness, genuineness, frequency, satisfaction, and resource adequacy. Resource adequacy refers to management actually spending resources on stakeholder transactions. Level 3 defines whether the company is "walking the talk" or not.

The idea of strategic management capability is useful because it depicts on a continuum the levels through which managers and organizations might grow and mature in stakeholder management effectiveness. Firms still at Level 1 might want to re-evaluate their level of commitment to stakeholder management. Level 2 is seen as the minimal level for functioning, and Level 3 establishes the ideal level for optimizing relationships with stakeholders.

## Stakeholder Symbiosis

The topic of stakeholder symbiosis was highlighted by the Best Practices for Global Competitiveness Initiative (BPI), created and launched in 1997 by the American Productivity and Quality Center (APQC), the European Foundation for Quality Management (EFQM), Arthur Andersen, and *Fortune* magazine's Custom Projects in 1998. The group's first year's theme was "Driving Growth through Innovation, Alliances and Stakeholder Symbiosis." Stakeholder symbiosis was defined as "an emerging concept which recognizes that all stakeholders are dependent on each other for their success and financial well-being." This notion that there is interdependence among employees, suppliers, customers, shareholders, and society made some of the executives in the first year's panel somewhat uncomfortable. Many of them felt more comfortable with the idea of stakeholder management than with stakeholder symbiosis.

Nortel's David Ball (2001) cited the power of treating all stakeholders as part of the system leading to corporate success—not necessarily as equal stakeholders. Ball argued how his company had learned from benchmarking and research that best-in-class companies pay as much attention to data about employee and customer satisfaction as they do to data on current financial performance. This is based on the assumption that these measures are leading indicators of future business success. There seemed to be strong agreement among the executives that paying attention to key stakeholders paid off for their companies.

The strongest symbiotic relationships seemed to be among employee satisfaction, customer satisfaction, and profitability. Although in discussions the program participants seemed to give five key stakeholder groups equal importance, a survey by Arthur Andersen documented that the executives felt there were two tiers of stakeholders—customers, employees, and shareholders, in the first tier, and suppliers and society in the second tier. In this survey, customers dominated the importance ranking of stakeholders with a 71 percent, while shareholders and employees were virtually tied at 49 percent and 48 percent respectively (Arthur Andersen, as quoted in *Fortune* magazine, 1998). In summary, the notion of focusing on stakeholders' needs was deemed an important and vital one, but there was considerable reluctance to place all stakeholders on an equal standing.

## Stakeholder Assessment and Measurement

If stakeholders' opinions are important, it should come as no surprise that managers and consultants would desire to assess and measure stakeholders' opinions and impacts. It is useful to look at the work of one major company as an example of what is possible in this arena. Walker Information, an Indianapolis-based global firm specializing in measuring and managing stakeholders, has a firmly established reputation in the area of "customer satisfaction measurement" and has diversified its strategy to develop measurement tools, methodologies, and methods for assessing and measuring stakeholders' opinions and satisfaction. Walker Information's model focuses on the importance of corporate reputation and the roles that internal and external stakeholders play in affecting reputation. Walker Information (undated) defines corporate reputation "as the reflection of an organization as seen through the eyes of its stakeholders and expressed through their thoughts and words."

The argument presented by Walker Information substantiates the points made previously in this discussion, namely that a firm's reputation and treatment of its stakeholders are associated with the bottom line of financial success. Therefore, the assessment of stakeholders and the measurement of their attitudes and opinions are a vital component to effective management. Walker's "Reputation and Stakeholder Assessment" program employs a diagnostic model based on decades of research into customer satisfaction, value, and quality meshed with years of research into corporate character, citizenship, and reputation. The model can be applied across industries and markets, yet tailored around an in-depth understanding of one company's specific circumstances. A major deliverable of the assessment is a report showing a company's reputation relative to that of its competition and world-class leaders in other industries. The company gets an at-a-glance reference to see how it is rated across multiple stakeholder groups.

The fact that stakeholder measurements are taking their place among the other products of major research and consulting firms demonstrates that it is an idea whose time has come and we will expect to see more of it in the future.

When one considers what has happened to many corporate reputations in the early 2000s' environment of fraud and scandal, it is easy to see the relevance of stakeholder analysis and measurement to business firms. According to the *2002 Corporate Reputation Watch* (Hill and Knowlton, 2002) survey of senior executives, the potential threats of unethical behavior and media criticism represent the most serious issues now facing companies. An executive from Hill & Knowlton firmed up this view with the following statement: "Senior executives now understand that an ethical lapse can devastate a company's reputation, and that behavior is a critical component to how a company is perceived" (*Nashville Business Journal*, 2002). The issues of corporate reputation, ethical lapses, and dealing with the media are all especially pertinent to public affairs officers, and the stakeholder approach has much to offer in framing and dealing with these topics.

## Principles of Stakeholder Management

Based upon years of observation and research, a set of "principles of stakeholder management" has been developed. These principles, known as the "Clarkson Principles," were named after the late Max Clarkson, a dedicated researcher on the topic of stakeholder management. The principles are intended to provide managers with guiding precepts regarding how stakeholders should be treated. Exhibit 29.1 summarizes these principles. The key words in the principles suggest the kind of cooperative spirit that should be used in building stakeholder relationships: *acknowledge, monitor, listen, communicate, adopt, recognize, work, avoid,* and *acknowledge conflicts.*

Space does not permit commentary on these principles. However, this chapter would be remiss if they were not enumerated here for further consideration. Exhibit 29.1 presents these Principles of Stakeholder Management. Contained within these principles, or guidelines for decision making, is important wisdom regarding stakeholder management. These principles are valuable for managers at all levels and in all functions, but they are especially useful for those professionals working in the area of corporate public affairs. If followed, the organization's effectiveness will be greatly enhanced.

---

### Exhibit 29.1 Principles of Stakeholder Management, the "Clarkson Principles"

1  Managers should *acknowledge* and actively *monitor* the concerns of all legitimate stakeholders, and should take their interests appropriately into account in decision making and operations.
2  Managers should *listen* to and openly *communicate* with stakeholders about their respective concerns and contributions, and about the risks that they assume because of their involvement with the corporation.
3  Managers should *adopt* processes and modes of behavior that are sensitive to the concerns and capabilities of each stakeholder constituency.
4  Managers should *recognize the interdependence* of efforts and rewards among stakeholders, and should attempt to achieve a fair distribution of the benefits and burdens of corporate activity among them, taking into account their respective risks and vulnerabilities.

5   Managers should *work cooperatively* with other entities, both public and private, to insure that risks and harms arising from corporate activities are minimized and, where they cannot be avoided, appropriately compensated.

6   Managers should *avoid altogether* activities that might jeopardize inalienable human rights (e.g., the right to life) or give rise to risks which, if clearly understood, would be patently unacceptable to relevant stakeholders.

7   Managers should *acknowledge the potential conflicts* between (a) their own role as corporate stakeholders, and (b) their legal and moral responsibilities for the interests of stakeholders, and should address such conflicts through open communication, appropriate reporting, and incentive systems and, where necessary, third-party review.

*Source* Clarkson Centre for Business Ethics, 1999

## The Stakeholder Corporation

A useful way to wrap up this overview of stakeholder theory, thinking, and management is by reference to *The Stakeholder Corporation: A Blueprint for Maximizing Stakeholder Value*, an important book by Wheeler and Sillanpaa (1997). In many respects, one could argue that this would be the natural and logical conclusion to the evolutionary application of stakeholder management, concepts, and thinking, in practice. A brief review of Wheeler and Sillanpaa's thoughts follows. The authors assert that they have no doubt that stakeholder-inclusive companies will outperform stakeholder-exclusive companies with increasing ease in the twenty-first century.

The authors present examples of best practices from around the world which they believe demonstrate beyond reasonable doubt that stakeholder inclusion leads to better long-term business performance, including increased economic value for shareholders. The authors argue through examples from the United States and the United Kingdom that stakeholder-inclusive firms fared better than "shareholder first" companies during most of the twentieth century. They argue that the notion of stake-holding in business is not collectivist, nor is it soft in the non-competitive sense. Rather, they believe it is based on a "sophisticated view of the company as a social vehicle whose speed and steering are dependent upon careful reading of the road signs and the behavior of other road users" (Wheeler and Sillanpaa, 1997). A careful reading of this book provides practical insights into how stakeholder theory and thinking may be incorporated into organizational practice.

## USEFULNESS IN CORPORATE PUBLIC AFFAIRS

Stakeholder management, or the stakeholder approach, is strongly compatible with different conceptualizations of corporate public affairs or public affairs management. Over the years, the Public Affairs Council has defined corporate public affairs in a variety of ways. At one point it was defined as "The management function responsible for monitoring and interpreting the corporation's non-commercial environment and managing the company's response to those factors." In 2003, the Public Affairs Council stated the following to be what public affairs is all about:

> Public affairs represents an organization's efforts to monitor and manage its business environment. It combines government relations, communications, issues management and corporate citizenship strategies to influence public policy, build a strong reputation, and find common ground with stakeholders.
>
> (Public Affairs Council, 2003)

With this understanding of corporate public affairs, it is easy to see the usefulness of the stakeholder management approach. Once the notion of an organization's "environment" is invoked, it is clear that the stakeholder approach has much value. Interacting with various groups such as government and the community also yields great potential. Finally, a concern for corporate reputation is "icing on the cake" in terms of the helpfulness of these ideas.

Dealing with an organization's environment is a "bread and butter" issue for stakeholder management. Stakeholder management facilitates answering the questions: who are our stakeholders, what are their stakes and what opportunities and/or threats do they pose to the organization? These questions set the stage for assessing the organization's responsibilities to its stakeholders and deciding upon strategies for interacting with these vital stakeholders. Governmental units at all levels represent stakeholders that business must address.

The stakeholder approach is extremely valuable in issues management. As Palese and Crane (2002) have observed, issues management is "all about identifying risk and opportunity before your key audiences can." Whether one is attempting to monitor the "changing issue mix," or to design and implement an issues management process, stakeholder management serves as a useful conceptualization and tool of analysis. The identification of issues is facilitated by the stakeholder approach. It permits management to *identify* relevant stakeholders. It assists in identifying the nature of the stakeholders' stakes (casual, formal, legal, moral). It helps with the *analysis* stage in the process as an assessment of stakeholders' legitimacy, power, and urgency is considered and it helps assess their salience to the organization. These steps lead to a careful *ranking* or *prioritization* of issues, *formulation of issues responses,* and *implementation* of issue responses while monitoring stakeholders' reactions. Furthermore, once an organization rises to the transactional level of stakeholder management capability, it increases communication and enhances the chances of getting valuable feedback from the various stakeholder groups.

Finally, enhancing an organization's corporate citizenship capabilities is a natural contribution of stakeholder management. Following upon the idea that the stakeholder approach has normative value, dealing with social responsibility and business ethics issues is greatly improved using stakeholder management. Inherent in the stakeholder model is the belief that stakeholders possess intrinsic value and are to be treated accordingly.

Corporate citizenship has been described by some as a broad, encompassing term that basically embraces all that is implied in the concepts of corporate social responsibility and corporate social performance. Graves *et al.* (2001), for example, define good corporate citizenship as "serving a variety of stakeholders well." Carroll (1998) has stated that there are "four faces of corporate citizenship—economic, legal, ethical, and philanthropic." Each face, aspect, or responsibility reveals an important facet that contributes to the whole. Further, this is a stakeholder way of visualizing organizations as they are expected to fulfill these responsibilities to all stakeholders today.

Sometimes corporate citizenship is construed to be more of a narrow, focused, topic, such as "community relations." Altman visualizes corporate citizenship in this way. In this view, it embraces the functions through which business intentionally interacts with non-profit organizations, citizen, and grassroots groups, and other stakeholders at the community level. Through the concept of corporate citizenship, then, the organization is able to acquire specific, tangible goals with various stakeholder groups. In one study by Carroll *et al.* (2000), for example, it was found that both empirical and anecdotal evidence yielded the following benefits of corporate citizenship initiatives to the following stakeholder groups:

1 Improved employee relations (employee stakeholders).
2 Improved customer relationships (customer stakeholders).
3 Improved business performance (investor stakeholders).
4 Enhanced company marketing, image, and reputation (public and government stakeholders).

In summary, it is evident that the stakeholder approach may be useful to public affairs officers and managers in a variety of ways.

## CONCLUSION

It is becoming evident that stakeholder theory, concepts, management, measurement, and thinking are becoming staples to managers and public affairs executives today as we think about the new millennium. There is growing support for the belief that the stakeholder model is increasingly becoming the most fitting and valuable for descriptive, normative, and instrumental purposes. Already, the language of stakeholder theory has swept the world of organizations as more and more managers and analysts perceive the value of diagnosing and prescribing in stakeholder terms. Corporate public affairs officers were quick to adopt the language of stakeholders, and the meatier ideas of stakeholder management are turning out to be valuable as well.

Theorists and practitioners alike will substantiate the stakeholder model over time as concepts are refined and applied and results are noted. John Kay, Director of Oxford University's School of Management Studies, and founder and chairman of London Economics, a consulting firm, is one of Britain's leading management thinkers and is a strong advocate of stakeholder thinking. On the issue of why business executives still talk in shareholder value terms, Kay observes:

> The way companies in fact behave is more in accordance with a stakeholding view of the company, in which the company goal is to be a good business—and balance customer, supplier, shareholder, and other stakeholders' interests—rather than to generate shareholder wealth. Most successful managers I talk to are principally committed to running a successful business rather than to the maximization of shareholder value.

Kay goes on to say that "making commitments to stakeholders can be a source of competitive advantage" (as quoted in Davies, 1997). Frank Walker (1998), chairman of Walker Information, in an important presentation at the Conference Board's tenth annual Business Ethics conference, also strongly argued that corporate character and reputation will be strategic items in the business era we are moving to, and that stakeholder management will be a key way by which effective organizations fulfill this quest. From an academic and public affairs point of view, and from the perspective of a leading business executive, we see the case being built for the stakeholder model of the organization.

## REFERENCES

Arthur Andersen (as quoted in anony.) (1998). "Best Practices for Global Competitiveness," *Fortune* 37 (6): S1–S4.

Ball, D. (2001). *Best Practices for Global Competitiveness* (software/video learning product ZIL 123). Fairfield, NJ: ASME International.

Boatright, J.R. (1997). "Fiduciary Duty," in P.H. Werhane and R.E. Freeman (eds), *The Blackwell Encyclopedic Dictionary of Business Ethics*. Malden, MA: Blackwell.

Carroll, A.B. (1979). "A Three Dimensional Model of Corporate Performance," *Academy of Management Review* 4 (4): 497–505.

Carroll, A.B. (1991). "The Pyramid of Corporate Social Responsibility: Toward the Moral Management of Organizational Stakeholders," *Business Horizons* 34 (4): 39–48.

Carroll, A.B. (1995). "Stakeholder Thinking in Three Models of Management Morality: a Perspective with Strategic Implications," in Juha Näsi (ed.), *Understanding Stakeholder Thinking*. Helsinki: LRS Publications. pp. 47–74.

Carroll, A.B. (1996). *Business and Society: Ethics and Stakeholder Management*. Cincinnati, OH: Southwestern College Publishing..

Carroll, A.B. (1998). "The Four Faces of Corporate Citizenship," *Business and Society Review* 100–101: 1–7.

Carroll, A.B., and A.K. Bucholtz (2006). *Business and Society: Ethics and Stakeholder Management*, 6th edn. Cincinnati, OH: Southwestern College Publishing/Thompson.

Carroll, A.B. and J. Näsi (1997). "Understanding Stakeholder Thinking: Themes from a Finnish

Conference," *Business Ethics: A European Review* 6 (1): 46–51.

Carroll, A.B., K. Davenport, K.G. Lee, and D. Grisaffe (2000). "Appraising the Business Value of Corporate Citizenship." Presentation given at the International Association for Business and Society Annual meeting, March, Essex Junction, Vermont.

Clarkson, M.B.E. (1995). "A Stakeholder Framework for Analyzing and Evaluating Corporate Social Performance," *Academy of Management Review* 20 (1): 92–117.

Clarkson, M.B.E. (ed.) (1998). *The Corporation and its Stakeholders: Classic and Contemporary Readings.* Toronto, ON: University of Toronto Press.

Clarkson Centre for Business Ethics (1999). *Principles of Stakeholder Management: The Clarkson Principles.* Toronto, ON: Joseph L. Rotman School of Management, University of Toronto.

Davies, E. (1997). "Shareholders aren't Everything: John Kay," *Fortune* 135 (3): 133–134.

Donaldson, T., and L.E. Preston (1995). "The Stakeholder Theory of the Corporation: Concepts, Evidence and Implications," *Academy of Management Review* 20 (1): 65–91.

Etzioni, A. (1964). *Modern Organizations.* Englewood Cliffs, NJ: Prentice Hall.

Freeman, R.E. (1984). *Strategic Management: A Stakeholder Approach.* Boston, MA: Pitman.

Golembiewski, R.T. (1993). "Stakeholders in Consultation," in R.T. Golembiewski (ed.), *Handbook of Organizational Consultation.* New York: Marcel Dekker.

Goodpaster, K.A. (1991). "Business Ethics and Stakeholder Analysis," *Business Ethics Quarterly* 1 (1): 53–73.

Graves, S.P., S. Waddock, and M. Kelly (2001). "How Do You Measure Corporate Citizenship?" *Business Ethics* 15 (2): 17.

Hill & Knowlton (2002). *2002 Corporate Reputation Watch: Global Survey of Business Leaders' Views on Corporate Reputation Management.* London: Hill & Knowlton.

MacMillan, I.C., and P.E. Jones (1986). *Strategy Formulation: Power and Politics.* St Paul, MN: West Publishing.

Mitchell, R.K., B.R. Agle, and D.J. Wood (1997). "Toward a Theory of Stakeholder Identification and Salience: Defining the Principle of Who and What Really Counts," *Academy of Management Review* 22 (4): 853–886.

*Nashville Business Journal* (2002). "Executives See Unethical Behavior, Media Criticism as Threats," *Nashville Business Journal,* June 11, http://nashville.bizjournals.com/nashville/stories/2002/06/10/daily19.html.

Näsi, J. (ed.) (1995). *Understanding Stakeholder Thinking.* Helsinki: LSR Publications.

Palese, M., and T. Yancy Crane (2002). "Building an Integrated Issue Management Process as a Source of Sustainable Competitive Advantage," *Journal of Public Affairs* 2 (4): 284–292.

Phillips, R. (2003). *Stakeholder Theory and Organizational Ethics.* San Francisco: Berrett Koehler.

Post, J.E., L.E. Preston, and S. Sauter-Sachs (2002). *Redefining the Corporation: Stakeholder Management and Organizational Wealth.* Stanford, CA: Stanford Business Books.

Public Affairs Council (2003) www.pac.org/public/help/faq.shtml.

Savage, G.T., T.H. Nix, C.J. Whitehead, and J.D. Blair (1991). "Strategies for Assessing and Managing Organizational Stakeholders," *Administrative of Management Executive* 5 (2): 61–75.

Schein, E.H. (1993). "Models of Consultation: What do Organizations of the 1990s Need?" in R.T. Golembiewski (ed.), *Handbook of Organizational Consultation.* New York: Marcel Dekker.

Starik, M. (1990). "Stakeholder Management and Firm Performance: Reputation and Financial Relationships to US Electric Utility Consumer-related Strategies." Unpublished Ph.D. dissertation, University of Georgia.

Starik, M. (1993). "Is the Environment an Organizational Stakeholder? Naturally!" Paper presented at the fourth annual conference of the International Association for Business and Society, San Diego, CA.

Suchman, M.C. (1995). "Managing Legitimacy: Strategic and Institutional Approaches," *Academy of Management Review* 20 (3): 571–610.

Walker, F.D. (1998). "Business Ethics: Who Cares?" Speech given at the Conference Board's tenth annual Ethics Conference, New York, May 19.

Walker Information (undated). *Reputation and Stakeholder Assessment* (corporate flyer).

Weber, M. (1947). *The Theory of Social and Economic Organization.* New York: Free Press.

Wheeler, D., and M. Sillanpaa (1997). *The Stakeholder Corporation: A Blueprint for Maximizing Stakeholder Value.* London: Pitman.

# 30

# Educating Present and Future Public Affairs Practitioners

## Model Programs

CRAIG S. FLEISHER

As a maturing yet still evolving "knowledge function" within businesses or corporations, has business and corporate public affairs (BCPA) come of age? Does it have a critical need for post-secondary education, training, and developmental opportunities that are relevant and connected to practice? Can BCPA practitioners succeed in their roles and responsibilities without receiving advanced educational and continual learning opportunities? This chapter intends to provide answers to these questions and suggests specific ways to improve BCPA professionals' capabilities to address new and complex challenges at the business-government relations interface.

Business and corporate public affairs professionals have a responsibility to ensure that the relationships between their employing organizations, governmental, and societal entities are healthy. The extent to which public officials can develop appropriate policies that enhance societal benefits depends at least in part on the quality and preparedness of the business and corporate public affairs work force. If it were determined that the BCPA work force were inadequately prepared, the upgrading and improvement of the work force would be of

particular concern and need to be squarely addressed. In addition, the critical role the BCPA work force plays in responding to new sociopolitical opportunities and threats heightens the urgent need to make the changes recommended in the chapter.

Of the more than 100,000 business and corporate public affairs staffers in the United States,[1] only a small fraction receive formal public affairs training. Most BCPA professionals do not earn their degrees from post-secondary institutions in BCPA, although a fair number get them in areas like business, legal studies, management, political administration, political science, public policy, or public relations (Lindsay, 2003; Foundation for Public Affairs, 2002). Unlike members of most other professional groups, BCPA practitioners are typically not certified by either regulatory bodies or an institutionalized oversight certification body as to their competencies. The lack of any serious competency frameworks or certification bodies of BCPA professionals hampers the improvement of BCPA practice and inhibits the pursuit of professionalism (Fleisher, 1998).

Post-secondary schools and programs of BCPA can potentially play a significant role in advancing public benefit by fostering collaborations with other professional schools and degree programs, public agencies, corporations, businesses, and community organizations. These partnerships facilitate the kind of interactions required to tackle complex public and social problems that are influenced by many factors—economic, social, behavioral, environmental, and cultural. BCPA training programs should assure that education also encompasses a number of emerging content areas critical to responding to a world changing rapidly because of globalization, sociopolitical and technological advances, and rapid demographic shifts. These areas include community investment, corporate responsibility, Internet activism, communication, community-based learning and research, global competence, and sensitivity to cultural differences.

## REPRESENTATIVE ROLES FOR BCPA PRACTITIONERS

Before moving forward into an assessment of educational options for BCPA practitioners, it is worthwhile to identify the nature of roles that they could take in private sector businesses or corporations. There are a number of common roles BCPA practitioners now hold in organizations, with the following list describing the most frequently observed ones.

### Analyst

These roles involve gathering and processing information to inform efforts to solve business or corporate policy problems in the non-market environment (Fleisher, 2002a). Persons who seek careers in policy analysis enjoy working with quantitative and qualitative information to develop and assess alternatives for solving these problems. Analysts frequently have post-secondary degrees, are fluent in economics, national, or international affairs, statistics, basic understanding of law-making and legal facets, are comfortable with policy development issues, and typically have a better than average familiarity with the

business/corporate-government relationship of the sector they are assigned.

### Lobbyist/Government or Public Affairs Officer/Consultant

These roles require individuals to:

1. Use their understanding of the political system to provide non-market, political, and/or public policy advice to their organizational decision-making clients.
2. Keep abreast of non-market and political developments that might affect their decision-making clients, communicate this information to the client, and provide advice on any organizational response which might be required to address the development.
3. Identify key stakeholders in the decision-making process in public policy bodies, work to maintain relationships with these individuals and to assist clients to promote and protect their interests effectively.
4. Advocate a point of view on behalf of the organization to public policy bodies through the preparation of issue briefs and papers, communicating with officials.
5. Help bring about the passage of laws favorable to the organization they represent.

Although there is no specific background required to be a lobbyist, individuals holding these roles frequently have political science/studies and/or legal backgrounds, usually including an undergraduate degree as well as some holding a graduate degree, and are very familiar with the public policy-making process (i.e., including structures, roles, tasks, and key players) at the level they are targeting (federal, state/provincial/local, etc.). In many jurisdictions, lobbyists must be accredited, certified, licensed, or registered in order to legally operate.

### Manager/Director

These roles typically involve reporting direct to the organization's senior executive team and using scarce resources to achieve management and non-market policy/strategy objectives. Persons who hold BCPA management career positions help construct organizational solutions to problems by employing "raw materials" such as financial and human resources. Managers or directors ordinarily have undergraduate degrees as well as substantial industry experience and knowledge. Many managers or directors also hold graduate degrees in business, communication, or management and supplement their education by engaging in regular upgrading and training.

## Specialist/Project Coordinator

These roles are generally not permanent and are assigned on an as-needed basis by organizational decisions makers, typically being either the BCPA manager/director or vice-president. As such, these roles are filled by individuals who have unique knowledge, skills, or abilities specifically suited for a particular role. These positions tend to be filled by persons with lesser credentials than permanent roles, or are outsourced to external parties who specialize in the particular role area (e.g., grassroots organizations, technology applications for political action, etc.).

## Vice-President

These roles have individuals that take primary responsibility for the top-level business or corporate decisions about which public policy environmental problems their organization should address. Persons who seek vice-president positions are held accountable for these decisions in return for the authority to choose problems, establish budgets, and select alternative solutions. Vice-presidents of BCPA almost always have post-secondary degrees, typically graduate degrees, and a substantial amount (usually fifteen years or more) of business, corporate, and/or industry experience to draw upon.

## BCPA COMPETENCIES

A benchmark, "state of the field" study conducted in the United Kingdom by Cameron

(1990) suggested that one of the problems facing the field in that country was the quality of BCPA staff. Underlying this view is an understanding that some people practicing in the BCPA area may lack the necessary competencies by which to effectively perform their roles. Competencies are general descriptions of the knowledge, skills, abilities, and behaviors (KSABs) necessary for individuals to perform successfully in specified organizational areas. Competency profiles synthesize KSABs and values, and express performance requirements in behavioral terms. Competencies are mechanisms that can assist in helping organizations identify and narrow the gaps between their current stock and the ideally targeted stock of BCPA capabilities. Like other sets of organizational assets, BCPA competencies can be acquired, borrowed (i.e., in the form of outsourcing or hiring consultants/advisors), developed, diminished (i.e., through neglect, lack of use, or inappropriate utilization), enhanced, trained, or transferred, among other things.

There are a number of competencies that I believe are critical for the PA manager or practitioner to succeed in addressing international PA tasks. Specific educational achievements are classified as knowledge and skills. Knowledge outcomes identify what programs graduates need to know and understand about the field; skill outcomes entail the areas of competence necessary to be effective in the profession.

Similar with other professions, BCPA needs its practitioners to exhibit high ethical standards and a commitment for their profession. Graduates should be adaptable, responsible, thoughtful, trustworthy, and professionally oriented managers. They should be globally sensitive and have a strong appreciation for diversity and cultures besides their own. They must be equally capable of working independently or working as part of a team on their organization's strategic matters. It would be expected that a graduating Master's student in the BCPA field would demonstrate an effective ability to integrate the preceding professional attributes and demonstrate an understanding of the knowledge and skills that are summarized in Exhibit 30.1.

**Exhibit 30.1 Knowledge and Skill for Corporate Public Affairs Graduates**

**Necessary knowledge**
(what graduates should know and understand)

Communication concepts and theories
Ethical issues and trends
Institutions/structures of governance
Legal requirements and issues
Multicultural and global issues
Organizational change and development
Public affairs history
Public policy development processes
Relationships and relationship building
Societal trends
Uses of research

**Necessary skills**
(areas of competency needed to enter the profession)

Community relations and investment
Corporate reputation analysis and management
Grassroots organization and management
Issues management
Research methods and analysis
Social responsibility and responsiveness
Stakeholder management
Strategic planning and management

There remains an unanswered question as to whether undergraduate BCPA education should be pursued by universities. The issues surrounding this question likely have more to do with the demand, as opposed to the supply, side of the economic equation. Do business, corporation, and business/trade associations need, and—maybe as important—will they readily employ, bachelor's degree holders immediately upon graduating with the degree? The best way to resolve this question is to understand the current nature of the PA work force and to see whether current PA employees were able to enter the practice following the receipt of their bachelor's degrees. Fortunately, there is some survey evidence that sheds light on this question.

Studies in Canada (Canadian Council for Public Affairs Advancement, 1996) showed that practitioners rarely entered BCPA positions out of their undergraduate degrees. The majority of BCPA practitioners moved over from business line or staff positions, came to the business from the public sector, or moved into BCPA roles after having gained experience in the consulting sector. The average practitioner in the Canadian studies had spent less years in BCPA positions than they had in their businesses or corporations. Similar "state of the field" surveys in Australia (Lindsay, 2003), the United Kingdom (Cameron, 1990), and the United States (Foundation for Public Affairs, 2002) have been conducted and would tend to indicate the same relationships, although these items may not have been assessed directly. All in all, the evidence portrayed by studies conducted in several different countries appears to consistently suggest that many BCPA positions will not be filled by recent university graduates and that a university education, plus essential real-world experience and responsibilities, are what lead to the highest likelihood of BCPA employability.

The task of identifying, defining, describing the characteristics, and measuring competencies in nearly all PA activity areas, and in particular for those associated with global/international PA management (see Chapter 1 by Fleisher), is a topic ripe for academic research. Although these competency determination tasks are often conducted at the company level by human resource experts in developing or modifying job descriptions, very little research has been done looking at comparing these lists and assessing their efficacy *vis-à-vis* actual internal PA job requirements as experienced by PA managers. Another useful research project would identify proven practices in successful BCPA management in order that companies could benchmark their own practices against these standards for the purpose of improving their own performance (Fleisher, 1995).

As should be fairly clear by looking at the descriptions, most BCPA roles are held by individuals who have finished at least one university degree and have political knowledge or experience prior to entering their BCPA career paths. Pre-BCPA entry experience in the form of voluntary political work or internships, involvement with political parties, holding offices in university organizations, participating in activist/interest groups, or work placements in government or political offices (i.e., a congressional or constituency office) is nearly essential.

The majority of BCPA positions require their incumbents to exhibit comfort with various forms and medium of communication, decision making and judgment, planning, research, and people skills along with a strong interest in the public policy environment and process. Personal qualities are typically of high importance and will be, in some cases, such as for lobbyists, viewed as more influential than being able to demonstrate formal education outcomes. BCPA positions are often very demanding in terms of time and people management and require special sets of knowledge, skills and abilities to be successful.[2]

A new entrant to a BCPA position will spend a large proportion of their time on research, monitoring and responding to requests for information, but face-to-face contact with various stakeholders inside and outside the organization tends to arise quickly—initially through attending meetings, briefings, and conferences alongside more senior staff—and will increase as experience is gained. A typical career path would be from specialist/project coordinator or lobbyist to analyst, to manager/ director, to vice-president. Lobbyist is the one role where someone could spend substantial time at any point in their career and isn't necessarily associated with any particular career path or trajectory within an organization. Many business or corporate practitioners may also transition from corporate roles into consultancy roles and back again during the course of their careers (Pedler, 1995).

## PRIMARY ROUTES TO FORMAL UNIVERSITY EDUCATION IN BCPA

It is becoming increasingly evident around the globe that management qualifications have taken on increased importance among a variety of work responsibility areas the last few decades. These qualifications generally demonstrate to employers that potential or rising employees have acquired knowledge of proven practices, exemplify commitment to quality and successful outcomes, and establish benchmarks for competence and competitiveness. Whether earned by traditional face-to-face classroom methods at a post-secondary institution, via the Internet through distance learning, within a growing number of corporate universities, or through associations, the practitioner today has greater latitudes of options available by which to gain needed and/or desired credentials. Yet, as this chapter will demonstrate, not all management fields have readily established programs or credentials; correspondingly, some fields have actually made little progress toward their establishment.

Imagine a scenario in which a recent secondary school graduate has decided to pursue her wish of moving into a recognizable business and becoming a government relations officer or into a multinational corporation as an issue management practitioner. This career pursuit is *unlikely* to be on the top-twenty lists of recent or prospective secondary school graduates, but let's relax the assumption of overwhelming demand for careers in the area for a moment in order to explore the educational possibilities. What North America institutions of higher education would offer the recent secondary school graduate BCPA-oriented degree or certificate programs?[3]

There are a limited number of routes that most individuals would likely uncover in pursuing a BCPA career route: route 1 by getting a degree in public administration or affairs or route 2 by getting a degree in public relations, corporate communications, or applied communications. There may also be a very recently emerging third route in applied politics. In the paragraphs to follow, this chapter will examine each of these routes and assess their feasibility for potential BCPA professionals.

## Route 1   Degrees in Public Administration or Public Affairs

One avenue that might first appear attractive is to pursue a course of studies at an institution with an undergraduate concentration in public administration or public affairs. The Association of Public Policy Analysis and Management (APPAM, www.appam.org/services/students/) states that it:

> does not have any firm statistics on the number of undergraduate public policy degree programs in the United States. Available evidence does suggest that the number of these programs

is growing, and these programs are extremely popular among students on campuses that offer the degree. Often, the undergraduate degree focuses on specific public issues and, in comparison to a master's degree, has the luxury of devoting many courses to those issues over several semesters. Students who complete undergraduate degrees in public policy may benefit from also earning a master's degree or doctoral degree, depending on career interests and the qualifications required for employment.

The National Association of Schools of Public Affairs and Administration's (NASPAA, www.naspaa.org) Web site lists post-secondary degree programs at over 250 schools in the United States alone. Another couple of dozen programs are available in Canada. The student would have a wealth of study opportunities at well-known schools. For example, she could go to many "flagship" state universities (e.g., the Universities of Georgia, Indiana, Michigan, Washington, etc.) or prestigious universities like Princeton, Duke, and Southern California. However, are these programs designed to educate the prospective BCPA practitioner? Could an interested student study primarily for private sector career paths doing things like grassroots or issue management or lobbying? A review of the course and program offerings at these institutions would demonstrate that the answer is almost always "no." NASPAA institutions primarily prepare students for work in public service careers, not for public affairs work in the private sector.

For those individuals wanting and searching for a *graduate* degree, they would likely become aware first of schools of public administration, public affairs, or public policy. The *US News and World Report* 2002 (source: http://www.usnews.com/usnews/edu/grad/directory/dirpad/dirpadindex_brief.php) rankings placed the following institutions among its top ten: Harvard, Syracuse, Indiana, Princeton, California Berkeley, Georgia, Carnegie Mellon, Michigan, Southern California and Texas (Austin). These rankings are based on a survey of over 250 US programs from a list provided by NASPAA and the Association for Public Policy Analysis and Management (APPAM).

These schools primarily confer three degrees, consisting of the MPA (Master of Public Affairs or Master of Public Administration), MPP (Master of Public Policy), and the MPM (Master of Public Management).

The flagship MPA (Master of Public Administration) degree is the professional degree for individuals seeking public service careers in management. MPA programs develop skills and techniques used by managers to execute policies, projects, and programs addressing societal problems while paying attention to corresponding organizational, human resource, and budgetary challenges. MPA graduates work in a wide variety of public service fields and in all levels of government (federal, state, local, and regional), in non-profits organizations, in the international arena, and occasionally in the private sector. The Master of Public Policy (MPP) degree emphasizes analyzing and evaluating information to solve policy problems. As analysts, managers, and leaders, MPP graduates work with information to develop, assess, and evaluate various approaches to a myriad of societal issues. MPP degrees lead to careers in public service fields and government (federal, state, local, and regional), in non-profits, in the international arena, and occasionally in the private sector (NASPAA, 2004). Offered with lesser frequency than the MPA and MPP, the Master of Public Management (MPM) degree with primarily designed for individuals who want to take on managerial roles in public institutions and organizations.

It is also worthwhile to note that within the broader graduate public affairs category are separate rankings for specialties in city management and urban policy, criminal justice policy and management, environmental policy and management, health policy and management, information and technology management, non-profit management, public finance and budgeting, public management administration, public policy analysis, and social policy. The ten top public affairs programs previously noted are also frequently present within the top ten rankings in a good number of these specialties.

Would these public affairs degree specialties benefit the *business* or *corporate* public affairs practitioner? Nearly all of these NASPAA study areas assume the graduate is chiefly trained for government, not corporate, service. Indeed, the majority of graduates of these programs will gravitate towards and be found in public sector positions immediately after receiving their degrees. But are these degrees of equal utility to the corporate or consulting practitioner on the private sector side of the public affairs equation?

One could make an argument that several of these NASPAA-oriented Master's degrees would potentially be beneficial—in particular the MPP that emphasizes public policy analysis. The others would arguably be less beneficial on a direct basis, although each of them would add some useful knowledge and understanding to the BCPA practitioner. Among the BCPA specialties missing from these categories are stalwarts like government relations, grassroots management, issue management, lobbying, reputation management, or corporate political management.

It is the author's opinion that all of these existing, previously mentioned degree programs are likely to be of far less benefit to private sector practitioners. This is due to the very different nature of private and public sector management, particularly in terms of their unique sets of accountabilities, resources, structure, and objectives (see Baron, 1995, for further delineation of these differences). Although there likely is more cross-sector career transitioning between public and private sectors at the present time than in decades past, practitioners who have done this transition will tell you that it is relatively difficult to move from one sector to the other and that success in one sector does not necessarily translate into similar long-term success in the other. Although I do not have access to published empirical data to effectively demonstrate this phenomenon, I would propose that the vast majority of career transitions are intra-sector (e.g., public to public sector), not inter-sector. I would further propose that the relative percentage of *successful* career transitions is even higher intra-sector than inter-sector.

## Route 2    Degrees in Public Relations, Corporate Communications, or Applied Communications

Schools and departments of communication or public relations (PR) have been established for many years in post-secondary institutions. These entities usually offer either undergraduate or graduate degrees (e.g., Master of Arts, MA; Master of Science, MSc) in communications (i.e., applied, corporate, management, organizational, and/or professional) or PR. Since there is clearly some overlap between BCPA and public relations, a prospective BCPA professional might choose to seek out education in one of these programs.

Many public relations professional associations across the globe work with post-secondary institutions in accrediting their programs/courses and/or supporting their development. This would include the Public Relations Society of American (PRSA), Canadian Public Relations Society (CPRS), Institute of Public Relations (UK), Public Relations Institutes of Australia (PRIA) and New Zealand (PRINZ), among others.

There are some North American and European universities within this route that offer degree courses with a BCPA emphasis and multiple (i.e., more than three) courses. Among the best examples of these are the following:

1   Purdue University's Department of Communication offers a Master's degree in public relations/issue management and has BCPA-oriented courses available in corporate advocacy, leadership and communication, theories of public affairs, and international public relations.
2   Thames Valley University's MSc in corporate communications has more than three BCPA-oriented courses (e.g., community affairs, continuity planning, financial relations, information as intelligence, and public affairs).
3   The University of Manchester Institute of Science and Technology (UMIST) offers communication in strategic management, corporate identity and reputation management, stakeholder management,

crisis and issues management, financial communications and investor relations within its MSc in Corporate Communications degree.
4   The University of Ulster offers an MSc in political communications and public affairs that has modules in policy-making structures, research in public affairs, public affairs and lobbying, globalization and governance, public affairs applied projects, and policy analysis.
5   Charles Sturt University in Australia has a Master's degree in organization communication that offers courses in external communication issues and strategies, crisis and issue management, applied communication research, and communication technology.

Would the programs in this second route be beneficial to BCPA entry level of rising practitioners? Since many of these BCPA-emphasizing programs are new, and they are not frequently present among the so-called more "traditional" communication programs, it is still too early to tell whether they will have a significant impact on the BCPA profession. Nevertheless, these programs have a long enough track record that provides indications as to their impact in BCPA career circles. Although there clearly may be some potential benefits depending on the intensity and quality of the BCPA emphasis maintained by these programs, there are a number of criticisms commonly raised by seasoned BCPA professionals about the drawbacks of taking this route. The more prominent critiques leveled at these programs include the following:

1   Programs in this genre tend to be focused more heavily on technical/technician or otherwise tactical roles. Many of the BCPA career paths require practitioners to quickly grasp and address managerial and strategic roles in their businesses and corporations which the majority of programs in this second route insufficiently address, if they cover them at all.
2   Despite communications and public relations being described as "strategic" management functions, these programs frequently

lack or suffer from a minimalist business or management emphasis. Few of these programs offer courses in the commercial and economic functions of the BCPA professional.

3   Many lack dedicated courses in public policy institutions, structures, and processes. Government stakeholders tend to be underemphasized relative to employees, the public at large, and community groups. A few of these programs have tried to address these shortcomings by combining efforts with their university's business or management schools. This, at least, gives the students exposure to business and management education, but seldom is there a combined effort by the communications and business schools to achieve synergies and cross-functional integration of the two fields.

4   The nature of the writing taught in these programs is not that typically used for business management and corporate policy advocacy purposes. There is an emphasis on writing for specific audiences, typically more junior than the experts in governmental bodies who expect keenly crafted issue briefs or policy circulars that are often the bread and butter of BCPA practitioners.

5   These programs often emphasize methods that require gathering qualitative over, or at the relative exclusion of, quantitative data. Many programs in this route are taught by individuals trained in qualitative sciences and methods as opposed to quantitative ones. This leaves many Route 2 graduates uncomfortable with the number-crunching and quantitative emphasis often critical to advocating on behalf of business or corporate interests.

## Is there an Emerging Third Route?

If the first two routes both leave much to be desired in terms of career development and progression, where then does the *private sector* BCPA practitioner turn for higher education? In recent years, a trend has developed whereby

a number of universities have developed degree, diploma, and/or certificate programs popularly known as "practical politics," "political management," or "applied politics." These programs prepare students for careers closely akin to BCPA that, as described by John Green, Director of the Ray Bliss Institute of Applied Politics at the University of Akron, cover political activism in various forms, including campaigning, lobbying, public relations, and everything in between (Jalonick, 2002–2003). Among the best known of these programs would be (Buyer's Guide, 2003):

- The University of Akron's Master's in Applied Politics.
- American University's (Washington, DC) Master's in Applied Politics.
- George Washington University's Graduate School of Political Management (GWU GSPM) Master's in Political Management.
- New York University's MA program in Political Campaign Management.
- Regent University's MA in Political Management.
- Suffolk University's MSc in Political Science—Professional Politics.
- The University of Florida's MA program in Political Campaigning.

These universities, and the institutes attached to them, also commonly offer certificate, diploma, and/or intensive seminars/workshops in the "applied politics" field.

GWU GSPM's Dean Chris Arterton has suggested that there is increasing recognition of the role that graduate education can play in preparing students for BCPA-oriented careers among working professionals (Jalonick, 2002–2003). Arterton's school provides an outstanding example of this route's relevance to BCPA careers. The GWU GSPM confers a Master's degree in political management with academic concentrations possible in a variety of BCPA-relevant areas such as campaign management, environmental politics, issues management, lobbying, political action committees, polling and strategic research, public policy and politics, and corporate and trade association public affairs (see http://www.gwu.edu/~gspm/mapm/index.html

for further information). BCPA-relevant courses in the Master's degree in political management include:

- Advanced lobbying strategy.
- Advanced problems and strategy in political management.
- Corporate public affairs.
- Crisis management.
- Ethics and political management.
- Grassroots politics.
- Issues management.
- Leadership and politics.
- Lobbying.
- Lobbying the budget process.
- Managing government relations.
- Political action commitees.
- Political communications strategy.
- Polling.
- Public opinion dynamics.
- Quantitative analysis and political strategy.
- Statistical analysis of political data.
- Strategic management of political issues.
- Strategy and message development.

Other than these particular degrees, no other degree programs in North America actually claim to primarily focus on meeting the unique needs of private sector BCPA practitioners.[4] There have also been limited attempts outside North America to originate BCPA-related degree programs. An excellent example would be Brunel University in west London. It offers an MSc in public affairs and lobbying specifically aimed at BCPA practitioners. Courses offered in this degree program include the following:

- European Union public policy.
- Policy analysis.
- Strategic marketing.
- International business ethics.
- Structures of governance.
- Several electives on parties, politics and voters of particular EU nation states.

Nevertheless, universities are not the only providers of professionally oriented education and credentials. There have been several groups through the years that have also aimed to provide North American BCPA practitioners with advanced education opportunities. One such example is the Washington Campus (TWC), a not-for-profit educational consortium that has been around for over two decades. It describes itself as the "leading provider of executive education seminars on the US public policy process for business and not-for-profit executives" (see http://www.washcampus.edu/). For several years, the Canadian Council for Public Affairs Advancement (CCPAA) put on annually a multi-day higher educational program of courses in the BCPA field. The Washington, DC-based Public Affairs Council (PAC) puts on a set of meetings taken over three successive years called the "Public Affairs Institute," and the Issues Management Council (IMC) holds an annual conference. However, few of these efforts are directly tied to individual universities. With the notable exception of GWU GSPM, there are no other university-based North American BCPA programs of higher education.

## A Prototypical Master's Degree Program in Business or Corporate Public Affairs

The purpose of a graduate degree in business or corporate public affairs is to enable and prepare learners to acquire advanced skills and knowledge in order to effectively assume middle to senior-level leadership roles in organizations and to advance the profession as well as professionally representing their employers. It should prepare individuals for BCPA leadership, career development, and ongoing contributions to the profession and society in a global context.

Students studying for BCPA Master's degrees should learn and appreciate the role of BCPA as part of the decision-making team, and learn relevant management and public policy competencies and the skills needed to build and manage effective relationships between organizations and their stakeholders. Master's degree students should acquire advanced knowledge and understanding of the body of BCPA knowledge as well as practice, research, communication, planning, management, and advanced relationship management abilities.

I would recommend that the curriculum for a BCPA Master's degree be a program of between thirty and thirty-six credit hours (twelve semester-length courses of three semester hours a piece). Master's students should demonstrate capability and knowledge of these subject-matter areas beyond that expected of undergraduates. A sample curriculum for a graduate level degree program in BCPA is provided as Exhibit 30.2.

---

**Exhibit 30.2 Component Courses in a Model Curriculum for Master's Programs in BCPA**

BCPA-UNIQUE COURSES
(four compulsory courses + practicum component):

1   Evaluation, Measurement and Assessment of BCPA.
2   Information, Communication and Technology Systems and Processes for BCPA.
3   Research Methods for BCPA.
4   Strategic Management of BCPA.
5   + Practicum/Project in BCPA or Case Studies in BCPA or comprehensive exam.

CONTEXT COURSES
(students choose four elective courses among the following):

1   Leadership and Organizational Culture.
2   Managerial and Marketing Communications.
3   Organizational Analysis and Behavior.
4   Policy Analysis.
5   Politics of Consultation.
6   Public Policy Making: Structures and Processes.
7   Public Sector Policy.
8   Reputation and Image Management.
9   Stakeholder Management.

BUSINESS AND MANAGEMENT COURSES
(students choose four elective courses among the following):

1   Accounting.
2   Economics.
3   Finance.
4   Human Resource Management.
5   Management Information Systems.
6   Marketing (especially integrated).
7   Operations and Production.
8   Organizational Behavior and Development.

---

## Areas of Promise for Future Growth or Expansion

There is undoubtedly a shortage of post-secondary educational offerings in the North American BCPA field. Few universities or colleges have recognized or capitalized on the area as one worth pursuing in terms of curriculum and program development. In light of the consistent and often strong numbers of attendees at educational and informational meetings sponsored by profession-oriented organizations such as the Public Affairs Council (PAC), Conference Board (CB), Foundation for Public Affairs (FPA), Center for Public Affairs Management (CPAM), Issue Management Council, and Boston College Center for Community Relations (BCCCR), it would have to be assumed that there is a steady demand for these types of courses. In addition, the 2003 edition of the *National Directory of Corporate Public Affairs* lists over 14,000 contacts in the US BCPA field, and there are even more with partial BCPA responsibilities in related fields like corporate communications, investor relations, and public relations. These numbers and trends suggest that the field could benefit from institutionalized, formal, higher educational opportunities.

Several areas of opportunity exist for academic entrepreneurs to develop BCPA programs in or with higher education institutions. These include:

1  Combining or expanding existing resources and courses in areas such as corporate communications, corporate social responsibility/ethics, corporate governance, political science, policy studies, public administration, public relations, and business administration/commerce. All of these areas occasionally have a course or two in the BCPA area and could be used as sources of a curriculum that could be pulled synergistically together over a number of different faculties or departments on the typical university campus.

2  Expanding existing programs in corporate communications or public relations to recognize the communications-oriented aspects of the corporate public affairs field such as community relations, investor/shareholder relations, and integrated marketing. I explore the possibility of collaboration between public affairs and public relations further elsewhere (see Fleisher and Blair, 1999). The possible development of specializations, concentrations or minors in BCPA areas within existing corporate communications or public affairs programs is a particularly promising area for future program development that could be accomplished more easily than the greenfield development of full-service BCPA degrees.

3  Working collaboratively with membership associations such as the Public Affairs Council, Conference Board, European Council for Public Affairs, Australian Centre for Corporate Public Affairs, and Issue Management Council to develop relevant and rigorous programs from the basis of existing offerings. At some point, it would be worthwhile to get leaders of these organizations together with some of the leading academics in the field for this express task.

4  Accrediting, sponsoring, or vetting programs delivered by private companies and consultancies in areas such as grassroots management, lobbying, or issue management. This would help tackle a major problem that persists in the field whereby someone taking a course such as "Introduction to Corporate Public Affairs," or "Grassroots Management," may be taught very different things depending on which organizations and instructors are actually delivering the subject matter.

Nearly all these programs will invariably have to be focused on one of two working perspectives, the analyst or manager/administrator. BCPA analysts look at new ways of meeting top management's requests for new or modified policies or services. They perform research on social, public, economic, and environmental problems to help inform both private and public decision makers in the policy process. Analysts assemble information, organize that information for use by decision makers and propose optional courses of action. Analysis courses, although directed at different contexts, are already offered in schools of public administration, business administration, policy studies, or political science.

Corporate public affairs managers implement policies and programs, allocate resources and exist at several levels in an organization, from key executives who make decisions to the first-line supervisor. Managers are either program or staff types. The program manager, such as a grassroots program manager, is the organization's "doer." Program managers must deal with a variety of administrative issues, including establishing objectives, stimulating productivity and motivating employees. Staff managers support the work of program offices. The areas of responsibility for staff managers include budgeting and financial management, management information systems, personnel and labor relations. Schools or faculties of business management, public management, or public administration most likely have existing resources from which to launch BCPA management courses.

## Factors that Need to Come into Place for Higher Education in BCPA to Grow

The provision of higher education in BCPA will not occur by accident or through fragmented, unsystematic, and inconsistent efforts. Their probability of success will increase correspondingly with the provision of planning, resources, structures, and staff. I'd like to outline some of the primary factors that need to come into place to assist in the growth of higher educational opportunities in BCPA.

1  *The building and convergence of a common body of BCPA knowledge.* There are few "standard" academic textbooks that could be used to teach most BCPA-oriented courses, although there are a number of handbooks and popular press books that have been used for the purpose (Fleisher and Blair, 1999). The body of knowledge has certainly gotten a boost by the publication of the *Journal of Public Affairs* (UK) as a refereed outlet for academic work in BCPA. The two articles by Griffin *et al.* (2001a, b) in the *Journal of Public Affairs* provide an extensive bibliographic listing of key works in the field and could potentially be a good starting point for building consensus around a BCPA body of knowledge.

2  *Increase in the number of doctoral-trained individuals willing to supervise research and teach in the area.* There are a good number of doctoral programs in public administration or public affairs, but few if any train students in the corporate (i.e., the "BC" of the BCPA acronym) side of the equation. Some schools of business or management with doctoral programs in business environment and public policy or business, government, and society, like the University of Pittsburgh, the University of Washington, Boston, California Berkeley, or Harvard, have doctoral programs where students can choose to study BCPA. Also, PhD students and doctoral candidates in areas like strategy, organizational studies, business ethics and corporate social responsibility, public relations, communications, political science, international business, and/or marketing might consider emphasizing BCPA as the context of their doctoral research within their particular specialized fields of focus.

3  *The purposeful, regular, and systematic gathering of experience, knowledge, and wisdom from existing leaders in the field from all over the globe.* A number of individuals regularly teach, or have taught frequently, BCPA courses in North American post-secondary institutions. Exhibit 30.3 provides a list of some North American-based instructors, among others, who are recognized for their instructional activities in this field and would serve as a foundational body for creating a BCPA body of knowledge and curriculum that could be adopted by universities, supported by professional associations, and vetted by accrediting agencies.[5] The question of who or which organization will take it upon its shoulders to lead such an effort remains unanswered and keeps this body of experts from doing what needs to be done.

4  *Monetary resources in the form of program seed money, chairs, scholarships, grants, and sponsorship.* There have been some companies, foundations, and think tanks that have provided monies for the study of BCPA-related areas. Nevertheless, these have seldom led to sustained efforts to deliver new curricula or programs. This

is an educational area that some large public policy-oriented private sector organizations might find worthwhile to support if they were offered the opportunity. The opportunity to sponsor BCPA research centers may also be attractive.

5   *The effective development and management of degree programs.* Any educational program must have normative, formative, and summative assessment tools by which students can be assessed as to whether they have achieved the objectives the program intended. Techniques range from required entrance or exit examination, to supervised internship performance, to capstone courses, to major project assessment. All academic programs should practice self-assessment of their performance by means such as examining placement rates, alumni satisfaction, employer satisfaction, student evaluations, faculty-student ratios, faculty qualifications, and comparisons with other applied professional programs. External reviews by regional accreditation bodies, as well as professional associations, would also be constructive and helpful.

6   *Collaboration with existing membership organizations in the field.* Many of the existing associations, including, for example, the Conference Board, Issue Management Council, Public Affairs Council, European Centre for Public Affairs, International Association for Business and Society, Australasian Centre for Corporate Public Affairs, Washington Campus, and others, have occasionally partnered with institutions of higher education on programs. The possibility of institutionalizing these programs should be potentially attractive to both the academic and professional bodies, as each could bring a unique set of capabilities and strengths that could uniquely meet and support the other's needs.

7   *Effective marketing and promotion of BCPA to students of all ages as a viable career option.* For any of these offerings to have support over the long run, the general public must become more aware of BCPA as a legitimate career option. It is rarely discussed in secondary schools, seldom addressed in post-secondary schools, and frequently is not even well understood in the businesses and corporations in which BCPA potentially or actually serves as a crucial contributor to the accomplishment of organizational objectives.

---

**Exhibit 30.3 PhD-qualified Instructors in North America with Recognized Post-secondary BCPA Expertise**

| | |
|---|---|
| Mark Baetz | Wilfrid Laurier University |
| David P. Baron | Stanford University |
| Barry Baysinger | Kansas University |
| Tim Blumentritt | Marquette University |
| Jean Boddewyn | Baruch City University of New York |
| Jean Phillippe-Bonardi | University of Western Ontario |
| Steve Brenner | Portland State University |
| Rogene A. Buchholz | Loyola University, New Orleans |
| Archie Carroll | University of Georgia |
| Phil Cochran | University of Indiana |
| Craig S. Fleisher | University of Windsor |
| Kathleen A. Getz | American University |
| Jennifer Griffin | George Washington University |

| | |
|---|---|
| Robert Heath | University of Houston |
| Amy Hillman | Arizona State University |
| Guy Holburn | University of Western Ontario |
| John Holcomb | University of Denver |
| Julius Johnson | University of Missouri |
| Gerry Keim | Arizona State University |
| D. Jeffrey Lenn | George Washington University |
| Jeanne Logsdon | University of New Mexico |
| Michael Lord | University of North Carolina |
| Richard A. McGowan | Boston College |
| John F. Mahon | University of Maine |
| Alfred A. Marcus | University of Minnesota |
| Jim Mattingly | University of Northern Iowa |
| Martin Meznar | Arizona State University West |
| Barry Mitnick | University of Pittsburgh |
| James L. Morrison | University of North Carolina |
| Richard Alan Nelson | Louisiana State University |
| William Oberman | Penn State University |
| James Post | Boston University |
| Kathleen Rehbein | Marquette University |
| Doug Schuler | Rice University |
| Robert Sexty | Memorial University of Newfoundland |
| William Stanbury | University of British Columbia |
| John F. Steiner | California State University, Los Angeles |
| D. Wayne Taylor | McMaster University |
| David Vogle | University of California, Berkeley |
| Sandra Waddock | Boston College |
| Jim Webber | Duquesne University |
| Duane Windsor | Rice University |

In my humble opinion, I would expect to see at least a couple of new BCPA programs offered by North American institutions of higher learning in the next ten years. The higher likelihood is that we'll see these programs established more frequently outside of North America, most likely in Europe as well as in the democratic countries of Asia. The demand and the need for effective BCPA practitioners have remained stable and strong for decades and through numerous economic cycles and eras of economic and societal growth. Some universities would be wise to look at BCPA as an opportunity to grow an attractive and important field of study.

## ROLE OF OTHER INSTITUTIONS IN EDUCATING TWENTY-FIRST CENTURY PUBLIC AFFAIRS PROFESSIONALS

There has been recent growth in the number of educational programs offered by associations, consultancies, event management organizations, and within corporate bodies themselves. There have been various attempts to develop professional development programs through the years, most of which have not been sustained over longer periods of time.

Among the best examples of an ongoing effort to educate BCPA practitioners is the annual Centre for Corporate Public Affairs

(CCPA) institute sponsored by the Australian Centre for Corporate Public Affairs (ACCPA) in Melbourne. This five-day event regularly attracts rising managers in Australasia to hear from a variety of local and overseas experts, including both senior practitioners and seasoned academics. The institute's stated objectives (Australasian Center for Corporate Public Affairs, 2004) are to:

1  Provide the only comprehensive post-experience training in Australia in key practical areas of corporate public affairs and the external relations of firms and industry associations.
2  Meet particular training and professional development needs of business and government public affairs practitioners and industry association executives.
3  Expose line managers—who must interact with an increasingly complex social and political environment—to an intensive program of external relations issues, politics and management process.
4  Enhance skills and understanding, and spread state of the art techniques for monitoring external impacts and managing issues for organizational strategic advantage.

The institute is a comprehensive, residential offering. It is taught through individual and group work, lectures, case studies, various guest speakers, discussion of research and survey reports, and is associated with an annual oration. The set of subjects addressed in the institute represents a rich and varied range of topics that every BCPA practitioner needs to be familiar and comfortable with in carrying out their roles. The 2004 version of the institute included, among other things, the following subject coverage:

• Public affairs management and its evolution in Australia.
• Reputation, brand and corporate positioning.
• Issue management: tools and concepts, systems.
• Trends and developments in function management.

• Building and maintaining relationships with government.
• Corporate community involvement.
• Cultural change and strategic internal communication.
• Public affairs and organizational culture.
• Sustainability reporting.
• Community relations and risk communication.
• Crisis management and communications.
• Investor relations.
• Alliance formation and industry-level public affairs.
• Public affairs planning.
• Public policy advocacy.
• Public affairs research and practice.
• Reflections.

Despite this strong example of what can be done, there is an outstanding need for new executive forums and professional development programs designed to prepare high-potential, mid-level PA executives to manage the corporate public affairs function (Fleisher, 2002b). The major objective of these forums should be to develop, educate, and train outstanding leaders of business and corporate public affairs, and to provide networking opportunities where professionals with similar responsibilities, work experience, needs, and ambitions can learn from each other. The task of educating, training, and developing tomorrow's rising, senior, and chief BCPA executives has largely been ignored by various institutions, including both the post-secondary sector as well as the corporate. Partly as a result, some organizations have abolished or outsourced the position. Others have merged public affairs with marketing, human resources, and even legal functions. Efforts such as the CCPA institute, the Public Affairs Council's annual institute, and the European Centre for Public Affairs "Dealing with the New Brussels" series represent beneficial, serious, and sustained attempts by these concerned stakeholders to satisfy important BCPA training and development needs.

Efforts such as the CCPA institute should be replicated in other parts of the world. The

European Centre for Public Affairs and the Public Affairs Council have annual programs with similar objectives to the CCPA institute but which, in my opinion, are not as broad in scope or as rich in overall managerial context as this "benchmark" ACCPA offering.

## The Corporate Role in Educating BCPA Professionals

Corporations have an especially important role to play in seeing that BCPA practitioners of tomorrow are properly trained and able to effectively carry out their roles. The challenge is clear for corporations in ensuring their PA practitioners continue to improve their professional competences as well as improve their service in performance of both organizational and societal benefits. One way business and corporations can ensure the development of effective BCPA practitioners is to provide adequate resources for their training and development, continuous learning and up-skilling (Pinkham, 1998). Another way they can be helpful in this task is to provide support to industry associations' efforts to train BCPA skills in employees with part-time BCPA roles, as well as larger associations such as the American Chamber of Commerce Executive that has been active in helping develop BCPA practitioners.

To help make academic PA research useful beyond the walls of the university and to effectively train new BCPA practitioners to join their ranks, I'd like to call successful BCPA practitioners to action by giving consideration to their organizations and themselves doing some, if not all, of the following:

1  First of all, take a critical look at the "products" of today's BCPA and/or related education tracks. Evaluate their readiness for positions in the profession. What knowledge and skill do they lack? Establish an ongoing dialogue with BCPA educators, not just a once-a-year workshop at a conference, but regular, substantive discussion.
2  Contribute actively in BCPA education at a local university. Be a guest speaker, help with curriculum development, offer advice about assessment, and even better, instruct a course. This role can usually be facilitated by identifying a department or faculty that houses instructors teaching these courses or by contacting the public affairs officer at your local institution.
3  Volunteer your organization to serve as a host context for a case writer who can develop teaching materials for classes that accurately reflect the nature of challenges that practitioners face in the work place. There are too few case studies written in BCPA that will give future practitioners and today's students the opportunities to think through their responses to practical, real-world BCPA challenges.
4  Offer co-op positions or internships in BCPA areas for university and college students to get some practical experience in the field tackling actual issues and learning about BCPA roles in organizations. These short-term efforts can be of mutual value to both your organization in getting additional work accomplished and assessing potential future colleagues as well as to the student, who gains practical exposure and experience in the so-called "real world."
5  Participate in joint research projects with educators. Not only will this facilitate the educator-practitioner bond and expand the body of knowledge in the field, it will also yield research results that have useful practical applications.

Most university-based academics that regularly research and teach BCPA subjects will usually be more than willing to work with practitioners for the mutual benefit of both parties. More often than not, all that is needed to make these events a reality is for one party or the other to initiate contact and begin forging the relationship.

## The Practitioner's Role: Self-education and Development in BCPA

As the volume and range of BCPA educational programs are still not plentiful and readily accessible to many practitioners, upwardly aspirant BCPA practitioners must assume the critical task of pursuing their own development and education. Fortunately, this task may be the one discussed so far in this chapter where the supply of resources is most plentiful; unfortunately, many BCPA practitioners have little precious time to carry this out in their busy schedules to undergo self-development regimens. For those individuals who do make the time to do this, the following sources will be of high value:

1 Acquire and read the critical handbooks and trade books available in the field. The most critical of these are captured in the comprehensive BCPA literature review authored by Grffin *et al.* (2001a, b).
2 Regularly scan the trade publications in the field, including *Campaigns and Elections, CQ Weekly and National Journal, Roll Call, Influence: The Business of Lobbying,* and *The Hill.* In Canada, the *Hill Times* and *Inside Ottawa* are important. A regular viewing of broadcast media in the form of Canada's Public Affairs Channel (i.e., CPAC) or the USA's C-SPAN can also be educational and informational.
3 Find a seasoned mentor within your organization who will be willing to share their time and experience on a regular basis. If your organization does not have or support a mentoring program, the professional associations in the field such as the Public Affairs Council or Boston College Center for Corporate Citizenship often assist in this manner and may be able to help in identifying persons willing and able to support you in this role.
4 Obtain and keep up with the academic literature in the area by reading the *Journal of Public Affairs, Business and Society,* and the *Research in Corporate Social Performance and Policy* annual series. Also, attending an occasional conference/meeting or keeping up on the proceedings from the Academy of Management's Social Issues in Management division, the International Association of Business and Society groups can also keep

you in the loop as far as the BCPA-focused academic research goes.
5 Network and dialogue with your colleagues and peers at conferences, meetings, and workshops held by active BCPA-focused associations such as the Public Affairs Council, Issue Management Council, Conference Board Council of Public Affairs Executives, Global Public Affairs Institute, European Centre for Public Affairs, Australian Centre for Corporate Public Affairs, or Boston College Centre for Corporate Citizenship. Each of these associations also regularly publishes material that will be of interest.

## CONCLUSION

This chapter has developed recommendations for how, over the next five to ten years, education, training, and research could be strengthened to meet the needs of future BCPA professionals in order to improve business-government and other stakeholder relationships. It has also developed recommendations for overall improvements in BCPA professional education, training, research, and leadership. A wide range of institutional settings, including not only post-secondary universities and colleges but also degree-granting programs in schools of business, commerce, management, marketing, public relations, public policy, other professional schools (e.g., law), consultancies, conference organizers, and private and public (i.e., professional and trade) associations can play important roles in BCPA education, training, research, and leadership development. This chapter has presented ideas for these institutional settings that are directed toward improving the future of BCPA education around the globe.

## NOTES

1 There are no reliable numbers published of which I am aware that account for the population of PA employees in the United States or elsewhere—and certainly not a valid number of those who have full- or part-time

responsibilities in the area. The 2003 *US National Directory of Corporate Public Affairs* lists over 14,000 PA members of 1,700 large US corporations. When you consider that there are PA staffers at nearly all universities, major colleges, major agencies, and associations (trade, industry, fraternal, interest group), the number of actual practitioners is clearly much higher. Many small- to medium-sized enterprises also employ PA staffers in either a full-time or a part-time capacity.

2 Readers should consult Chapter 9 by Patrick Shaw for an elaboration of the human resource dimensions of filling BCPA positions.

3 The author is looking specifically at North America only because this area has a fifty-year history of professional associations in the field (e.g., the Washington, DC-based Public Affairs Council celebrated its fiftieth anniversary in 2004), longer than similar establishments in the European Union or in most of Asia Pacific. This focus is not to suggest that other geographic boundaries are likely to look similar; in reality, every nation-state and multi-country area is likely to have its own unique characteristics when it comes to providing education in the BCPA field.

4 I am not including programs entitled "Integrated Marketing Communications" in this grouping, because such programs tend to focus on the interface of public relations, marketing, and advertising and tend not to focus specifically on the business-government, business-public policy interfaces within which most BCPA practitioners work. Nevertheless, some IMC programs do contain a course (or sometimes even two) that would be relevant to BCPA practitioners.

5 Although I focus here upon North American resources, I should make it clear that there are some renowned experts who regularly teach BCPA courses outside of North America, including, among others, this book's co-editor as well as a number of its valuable contributors, who can and should also be involved in the systematic knowledge/wisdom gathering process I identify here.

# REFERENCES

Australasian Centre for Corporate Public Affairs (ACCPA) (2004). "The Annual Residential Training Program for Public Affairs Executives and Line Managers," brochure accessed May 30, at www.accpa.org.au.

Baron, D.P. (1995). "Integrated Strategy: Market and Nonmarket Compounds," *California Management Review* 37 (2): 47–65.

Buyer's Guide (2003). "Political Graduate Schools," *Campaigns and Elections,* October–November 1, v 23, found online at http://www.campaignline.com/.

Cameron, D. (1990). "Managing Public Affairs in British Industry," *Journal of General Management* 16 (2): 1–19.

Canadian Council for Public Affairs Advancement (CCPCA) (1996). *Corporate Public Affairs Management: The 1996 Survey of Canadian Practice.* Waterloo, ON: Canadian Council for Public Affairs Advancement.

Corbett, W.J. (1991). "EC92: Communicating in the new Europe," *Public Relations Quarterly,* winter, pp. 7–13.

Fleisher, C.S. (1995). *Public Affairs Benchmarking: a Comprehensive Guide.* Washington, DC: Public Affairs Council.

Fleisher, C.S. (1998). "Do Public Affairs Practitioners Constitute a Profession?" in *Proceedings of the Fifth Annual International Public Relations Symposium,* Bled, Slovenia.

Fleisher, C.S. (2002a). "Analysis and Analytical Tools for Managing Corporate Public Affairs, *Journal of Public Affairs* 2 (3): 167–172.

Fleisher, C.S. (2002b). "The Evolving Profile, Qualification and Roles of the Senior Public Affairs Officer," *Journal of Public Affairs* 2 (2): 90–94.

Fleisher, C.S. (2003). "The Development of Competencies in International Public Affairs," *Journal of Public Affairs* 3 (1): 76–82.

Fleisher, C.S., and N. Blair (1999). "Tracing the Parallel Evolution of Public Affairs and Public Relations: An Examination of Practice, Scholarship and Teaching," *Journal of Communication Management* 3 (3): 276–292.

Foundation for Public Affairs (2002). *The State of Public Affairs.* Biannual report. Washington, DC: Public Affairs Council.

Griffin, J.J., C.S. Fleisher, S.N. Brenner, and J.J. Boddewyn (2001a). "Corporate Public Affairs Research: Chronological Reference List 1, 1985–2000," *Journal of Public Affairs* 1 (1): 9–32.

Griffin, J.J., C.S. Fleisher, S.N. Brenner, and J.J. Boddewyn (2001b). "Corporate Public Affairs Research: Chronological Reference List 2, 1958–1984," *Journal of Public Affairs* 1 (2): 169–186.

Hall, E.T. (1976). *Beyond Culture.* Garden City, NY: Anchor Press.

Hofstede, G. (1991). *Cultures and Organizations: The Software of the Mind.* New York: McGraw-Hill.

Jalonick, M.C. (2002–2003). "Preparing for a Career in Politics, Public Affairs," *Campaigns and Elections,* December–January, pp. 79–84.

Lenn, J. (1996). "International Public Affairs: Managing within the Global Village," in L. B. Dennis (ed.), *Practical Public Affairs in an Era of Change: A Communications Guide for Business, Government and College.* Lanham, MD: University Press of America.

Lindsay, A. (2003). "Public Affairs Integrates Further into Business Strategy—and Networks Skills and Structure into Key Line Areas," *Corporate Public Affairs* (publication of the Australian Centre for Corporate Public Affairs) 13 (3–4): 1–25.

Mack, C.S. (1997). *Business, Politics, and the Practice of Government Relations.* Westport, CT: Quorum Books.

NASPAA (2004). "FAQs for Students", accessed February 12, 2005, at www.naspaa.org/students/faq/faq.asp#question_2.

National Directory of Corporate Public Affairs (NDCPA) (2003). *National Directory of Corporate Public Affairs.* Washington, DC: Columbia Books.

Pedler, R. (1995). *The Management of Public Affairs.* ECPA Occasional Papers 2. Oxford: European Centre for Public Affairs.

Pinkham, D. (1998). "Corporate Public Affairs: Running Faster, Jumping Higher," *Public Relations Quarterly,* summer, pp. 33–37.

Wartick, S., and D. Wood (1998). *International Business and Society.* New York: Blackwell.

# 31

# Public Affairs, Corporate Scandals, and Regulation

## Policy Actors and Actions

JOHN M. HOLCOMB

The corporate scandals since the year 2001 have spawned litigation, criminal prosecutions, and new regulatory pressures on business at both the state and federal levels. Some scandal-ridden firms have responded with internal investigations of their own. This chapter examines those legal and regulatory pressures, along with the impact of the most important new law, the Sarbanes-Oxley Act (Sarbox). The chapter also examines internal administrative reforms at the Securities and Exchange Commission (SEC), as well as the conflict between federal agencies and state regulators, as each level of government asserts its powers to grapple with the corporate scandals. The changes adopted by the self-regulatory agencies are also addressed. The chapter will also discuss two major regulatory controversies—regulation of the mutual fund industry, and the expensing of stock options.

Throughout the chapter, various policy actors will be discussed in the context of each of the major issues examined. Those key actors include political interest groups and think tanks, business and professional groups, internal corporate investigators, enforcement agencies, and self-regulatory organizations. Exhibit 31.1 presents a list of the key actors in the foregoing categories that are discussed in the chapter. After examining the various legal and regulatory issues, the chapter concludes with two sections, one providing a political analysis of the various groups and actors, and the other examining the impact of the regulatory challenges on corporate public affairs functions. Given the political nature of the regulatory challenges, they naturally have a major impact on the government relations and issues management functions, but they also have major implications for corporate communications, corporate contributions, and corporate responsibility functions.

## Exhibit 31.1 Key Actors in the US Corporate Reform Agenda, 2001–2004

*Political interest groups and think tanks*

The Corporate Library
Fund Democracy
Mutual Fund Directors Forum
Council of Institutional Investors (CII)
National Coalition for Corporate Reform
National Association of State Treasurers
TIAA/CREF
American Federation of Labor—Congress of
   Industrial Organizations (AFL-CIO)
International Employee Stock Options Coalition
American Enterprise Institute
Competitive Enterprise Institute
Cato Institute
Club for Growth
Brookings Institution
Center for Corporate Policy
Center for Corporate Change
Consumer Federation of America (CFA)

*Business and professional groups*

The Business Roundtable
US Chamber of Commerce
Society of Asset Allocators and Fund Timers
American Institute of Certified Public Accountants
   (AICPA)
Securities Industry Association (SIA)
Chartered Financial Analysts (CFA) Institute
Association of Corporate Counsel
Investment Company Institute (ICI)
TechNet
American Electronics Association

*Governance rating groups*

Institutional Shareholder Services (ISI)
Glass Lewis & Co.

*Internal corporate investigators*

Neil Batson
Richard Breeden
Richard Thornburg

*Enforcement agencies*

Securities and Exchange Commission (SEC)
Public Company Accounting Oversight Board
   (PACOB)

Department of Justice (DOJ)
State Attorneys General (Eliot Spitzer)
North American Securities Administrators Association

*Self-regulatory organizations*

New York Stock Exchange (NYSE)
National Association of Securities Dealers (NASD)

## REGULATION AND ENFORCEMENT ACTIONS

> Every time we turn over a rock, there are more vermin crawling beneath it.
>
> Eliot Spitzer, New York Attorney General (in Michaels and Wells, 2003)

Since 2001, there has been a gradual rise in the aggressiveness of the courts and enforcement agencies in dealing with the corporate scandals. Just as prosecutors were beginning to get some convictions and guilty pleas related to the headline scandals of Enron, WorldCom, Tyco, HealthSouth, and Adelphia after 2001, the mutual fund scandals erupted in 2003. Those led to still more investigations and prosecutions, chiefly by the Securities and Exchange Commission and by Eliot Spitzer, the Attorney General of New York. Corporations and funds in trouble have also launched internal investigations, supervised by former top SEC and law enforcement officials. These high-profile officials, especially Richard Breeden and Richard Thornburg, have become major policy actors themselves in resolving various corporate scandals. Combined with the activities of the external political interest groups and class action lawyers, they have contributed as much as or more than the formal political institutions in resolving the corporate scandals.

This section also examines the criticism by the business community of the Sarbanes-Oxley Act and the costs of compliance. That criticism has largely emanated from groups like the Business Roundtable and think tanks like the American Enterprise Institute (Borrus, 2004). Finally, this section will briefly examine some of the administrative reforms at the SEC, as well as the state-federal conflicts that have surrounded the investigations of the various corporate scandals.

### Civil Lawsuits

The number of class action lawsuits has not been rising, but has held steady at 200 over 2003–2004, according to Institutional Shareholder Services (ISS), while the amount paid to settle class action lawsuits was actually down from $2.53 billion in 2002 to $2.01 billion in 2003 (Scannell, 2004). That partially reflects the longer time cases are taking to settle, so settlement costs are likely to rise again in future years. According to Cornerstone Research, 2–3 percent of all companies were targets of such suits over the past two years (Dash, 2004). Beyond the number of suits, the settlement amounts of some suits have been quite large. Citigroup's $2.65 billion settlement of lawsuits by WorldCom investors, or $1.64 billion after taxes, is second in size only to the previous Cendant settlement for $2.85 billion. The settlement avoided potential liability of $54 billion for Citigroup. Meanwhile, class action suits against the seventeen other WorldCom underwriters continues (White, 2004; O'Brien, 2004; Morgenson, 2004a). Citigroup has also dedicated USD$6.9 billion in reserves to cover potential future litigation, which expert Jack Coffee contends may be a low estimate, subject to future increases (Michaels and Wighton, 2004). Civil litigation is still pending versus the underwriters of Enron, and two dozen class action suits have been filed against Nortel (Belson and Simon, 2004).

Beyond these shareholder lawsuits, union and state government pension funds have also been active in litigation against certain companies. The states of West Virginia and Ohio, along with the Teamsters' pension fund, have sued Freddie Mac for improper accounting that damaged the value of their holdings (Barta, 2003).

## Criminal Prosecutions

The year 2004 finally saw some progress with guilty pleas and/or convictions involving several executives at firms where little progress had earlier been evident—such as HealthSouth, WorldCom, Qwest, CSFB, Enron, and Martha Stewart, with ongoing trials of former officials at some of those firms, as well as at Adelphia and Tyco. Even prior to recent successes, former Assistant Attorney General Larry Thompson pointed out in mid-2003 that the Justice Department's task force had "obtained over 250 corporate fraud convictions or guilty pleas, including guilty pleas or convictions of at least twenty five former CEOs" (Michaels, 2003b). The SEC also filed 50 percent more fraud cases in 2003 over 2002 (Michaels, 2004a).

Beyond the rise in prosecutions, the US Sentencing Commission has also altered its guidelines in a way that might pit the interests of companies against their employers. In order to mitigate its sentence, a company gets credit for cooperating with a government investigation, and the Sentencing Commission now requires firms to waive the attorney-client privilege to receive such credit. By waiving the privilege, companies may expose their own employees to heightened liability for statements they have made to corporate counsel. One major interest group, the Association of Corporate Counsel, which represents about 16,000 corporate attorneys in 7,000 corporations, has unsuccessfully opposed the new waiver requirement (Cohen, 2004; Fields, 2004).

## Internal Investigations

From mid-2003 through mid-2004, more internal investigation reports on the corporations most tainted by scandal were released. A report on Enron's bankers, by Neil Batson, the court-appointed bankruptcy examiner, implicated Citigroup and J.P. Morgan Chase in Enron's wrongdoing. The report concluded that both banks not only knew of Enron's wrongful conduct, but facilitated it, with Citigroup receiving the brunt of the report's criticism (Chaffin and Michaels, 2003a). Batson also attacked Barclays Bank for its role in the scandal, and to a lesser extent, Deutsche Bank. It also castigated Merrill Lynch and the Canadian Imperial Bank of Commerce (CIBC) for facilitating the establishment of special purpose entities. The Batson report weakens the cases of all of the banks in their efforts to collect damages from Enron and heightens their own liability exposure to those injured by Enron (Buckley et al., 2003).

The series of reports on WorldCom by Richard Breeden, a former SEC chairman appointed as monitor, and former Attorney General Richard Thornburg, also affected the conditions from which the company could emerge from bankruptcy as MCI. It also dramatically changed the corporate governance of the firm in ways that go far beyond the terms of Sarbox or the standards of either the New York Stock Exchange (NYSE) or the SEC. Breeden forced seventy eight changes in behavior at MCI, including the separation of the CEO and chair positions, based on a 150 page governance report entitled *Restoring Trust* (Michaels, 2003f). The reforms go well beyond regulatory standards and normal best practices and include as well a board with only one insider, the CEO Michael Capellas, and ten outsiders; board meetings eight times a year; and independent directors meeting separately outside the CEO's presence for a time at each board meeting (Michaels, 2004a). Since WorldCom emerged from bankruptcy as MCI, Breeden has continued as monitor at the firm, scrutinizing decisions by Capellas and challenging decisions by the board as well (Lublin and Young, 2004). Breeden has also been investigating the problems at Hollinger, where shareholders are seeking $300 million damages for unauthorized non-compete fees negotiated by Lord Black (Kirchgaessner and Michaels, 2004).

Beyond the internal investigations supervised by Breeden and Thornburg, virtually every other firm tinged with scandal has turned to outside investigators with high-level SEC experience. There are about twenty such top-echelon individuals available for hire, and firms such as Freddie Mac, J.P. Morgan Chase, WorldCom, and Enron have done so (Michaels and Larsen, 2003).

## Sarbox Compliance Costs

Regulatory compliance costs are becoming a larger issue as steps to implement the Sarbanes-Oxley Act continue apace. Internal auditors and CFOs complain about the resources and time constraints involved. According to one recent survey, 91 percent of 200 internal auditors surveyed said their companies had identified gaps in their internal controls, and only two indicated they had completed their work in complying with Sarbox. Nearly a third of the auditors reported that Sarbox compliance efforts occupied 70–100 percent of their time, while another 23 percent reported it consumed half their time (Taub, 2004a). The largest compliance costs are due to internal controls and section 404, including related audit expenses. As of May, the audit fees for internal control work are projected to increase another 25–35 percent over the summer of 2004 (Michaels, 2004e). Due to the costs of Sarbox compliance, the costs for private firms going public have also increased by 130 percent (Taub, 2004b).

Due to the costs of compliance for public firms, many are considering going private. That figure is now 21 percent of all public firms in 2004, versus 13 percent in the previous year (Taub, 2004b). Even before 2004, the actual numbers of firms going private had steadily increased over the past three years, partially due to the tech bubble bursting as well (Reason, 2003). Even very large corporations are considering going private, according to the CEO of the Blackstone Group, and many CEOs complain that, due to Sarbox, it isn't fun being a CEO any more (Michaels and Politi, 2004). Meanwhile, some argue that many of the firms thinking of going private should

never have become public companies in the first place and were only capitalizing on the stock market boom of the 1990s (Volcker and Levitt, 2004).

Beyond private firms, there is another category of companies that are exempt by law from Sarbox regulations—so-called "controlled companies," where at least 50 percent of the voting power resides with an individual, family, or group of shareholders who vote as a bloc. Such companies are exempt from requirements on the independent composition of boards and of major committees. The Council of Institutional Investors (CII) and the Connecticut State Treasurer unsuccessfully lobbied the New York Stock Exchange and the SEC against the exemption, and several very large firms such as Coors are now exploiting the loophole (Solomon, 2004).

## Reactions to Sarbox

Despite the compliance costs, former high-level government officials have expressed support for Sarbox. Examples are former Federal Reserve chair Paul Volcker and former SEC chair Arthur Levitt, who write:

> US markets are the best in the world because they are the best regulated. We should not engage in a race to the bottom. Instead, we should lead the world to the top, and we are. Countries are emulating our reforms … and as a result, we are strengthening the world economy, not being defeated by it. While there are direct money costs involved in compliance, we believe that an investment in good corporate governance, professional integrity and transparency will pay dividends in the form of investor confidence, more efficient markets, and more market participation for the years to come.
>
> (Volcker and Levitt, 2004)

Some critics of Sarbox believe it falls far short of meaningful corporate reform, in that it does not address issues of executive compensation, evaluation of corporate boards, and shareholder participation in governance. It must be acknowledged, however, that Sarbox basically addressed corporate accounting scandals and was not meant to cure all the ills of corporate governance.

Perhaps not surprisingly, there is a backlash developing toward Sarbox within the corporate community. While some hail Sarbox as the greatest reform of corporate governance since the Securities and Exchange Acts of 1933 and 1934, many executives responsible for implementing the law are increasingly negative and skeptical of its impact. In a study by Foley and Lardner, 67 percent of business respondents in 2004 said the new reforms were too strict, compared with 55 percent who felt that way in 2003. Only 27 percent felt the reforms were "about right" (Taub, 2004b). On the other hand, a survey of 153 directors found that more than 60 percent think the law has been positive for their companies, and 70 percent believe it has been positive for their boards (Volcker and Levitt, 2004).

A survey of CFOs, sponsored by Price WaterhouseCoopers (PwC) in 2003, also showed declining support from 2002. Only 30 percent had a positive opinion of the law in 2003, down from 42 percent the previous year. Fifty percent of respondents also felt the law had had little or no impact on investor confidence (Michaels, 2003e). Some CEOs like Maurice "Hank" Greenberg of AIG have been particularly outspoken, referring to some of the regulatory requirements as "foolishness," and complaining that his firm must spend $300 million annually in compliance costs (Michaels, 2004f). Richard Scrushy, the first CEO accused of violating Sarbox provisions, has attacked the law as vague and denying him certain constitutional rights, but his standing as a critic is somewhat diminished (Michaels, 2004d).

Some scholars from conservative think tanks also decry the crisis atmosphere that produced the Sarbanes-Oxley Act. Peter J. Wallison of the American Enterprise Institute states that: "Sarbanes-Oxley was adopted hastily, and without adequate consideration by a Congress panicked about the possibility that the Enron and WorldCom cases had seriously weakened investor confidence" (Wallison, 2003). Wallison also resists the notion that independent directors will improve corporate performance. He argues that independent directors will err on

the side of caution and be risk-averse, especially in light of the recent scandals, and suggests the result may be a future of limited economic growth (Wallison, 2003).

William Donaldson, the SEC chair, acknowledged in mid-2003 that the American corporate community may have overreacted to Sarbox by becoming more risk-averse. As he stated then, "Sarbanes-Oxley unleashed batteries of lawyers across the country [with the result being] a huge preoccupation with the dangers and risks of making the slightest mistake, as opposed to a reasonable approach to legitimate business risk" (Michaels, 2003c). While lauding the impact of Sarbox in increasing investor confidence, John Thain, the CEO of the New York Stock Exchange, also sees potential pitfalls. He believes that the law, along with the reputation of the United States as a haven for anti-business litigation and class action suits, may account for the sharp decline of foreign companies listing on the New York Stock Exchange during 2002 and 2003 (Thain, 2004).

Conservative scholars and think tanks have also criticized Sarbox for concentrating too much power over corporate governance in the hands of the federal government. Corporate chartering and governance have traditionally been matters of state law in the United States, and critics now see Sarbox as leading to a federalization of corporate law, by requiring independence on the board and total independence on key committees, whilst also specifying some of the functions of key committees. The law not only injects the SEC and the national listing exchanges into the regulation of the structure, composition, and duties of the corporate board, but it also regulates some aspects of executive compensation. As one legal authority notes, "taken individually, each of Sarbanes-Oxley's provisions constitutes a significant preemption of state corporate law. Taken together, they constitute the most dramatic expansion of federal regulatory power over corporate governance since the New Deal" (Bainbridge, 2003).

Traditional federalism analysts believe that the states, as "laboratories of democracy," might generate better solutions through interstate competition, and that the one-size-fits-all approach of Sarbanes-Oxley is particularly inappropriate when trying to design governance models to fit different corporate cultures in vastly different industries. That is the conclusion of one scholar writing in a publication of the Cato Institute, a leading libertarian think tank supported by some elements of the business community (Bainbridge, 2003). Since Congress has moved so far on federalizing corporate law, it is perhaps less strange that even leading Republican legislators would now try to roll back state securities regulations and the power of state attorneys-general, as they attempted to do through the Baker Bill discussed in a later section of this chapter. Perhaps those moves appease the efficiency interests of their business supporters, but they also move counter to the trends of recent Republican administrations and to the line of federalism decisions by the Rehnquist Court.

In opposing SEC action allowing for shareholder nomination of directors, the president of the US Chamber of Commerce also raised the federalism issue. As he stated, "The SEC is proposing federalization for director responsiveness and putting itself in the role of national arbiter. This overrides the policy prerogatives historically held in this country by state legislatures and courts" (Donohue, 2003).

Some business and professional groups fight to limit the scope and impact of certain SEC rules passed to implement Sarbox, when those rules might negatively affect their activities. For instance, while investor and consumer groups wanted to totally separate auditing from consulting activities, audit firms and the American Institute of Certified Public Accountants (AICPA) battled to retain the ability to provide tax consulting to audit clients. The SEC decided not to prohibit tax services, and Lynn Turner, of Glass Lewis and former chief accountant of the SEC, reacted that "This is a big win for the auditing firms, and investors are taking it on the chin again" (Day, 2003). Meanwhile, the AICPA favored the SEC rule requiring that executives certify that their firms have internal controls in place to detect any accounting fraud or errors, known as section 404 of the law. The AICPA praised the rule as "one of the most critical components of reliable corporate reporting,"

and of course it would benefit as a profession in implementing the rule (Johnson, 2003b).

Meanwhile, there is some positive reaction to the law, especially among private firms not responsible for implementing all of it. They see some of its provisions as spurring better business practices. Almost 40 percent of nonpublic CFOs say their companies would benefit from implementing elements of the law, and that figure rises to 52 percent among CFOs of larger firms (Katz, 2003). One private firm, Cargill, has decided to follow the spirit of the law and implemented some of its auditing and disclosure provisions when revising its corporate governance standards in 2003 (Katz, 2003).

There are a number of other reasons why turning private may not allow firms to escape the Sarbox requirements. First, private firms may need to adapt their practices to prepare for the eventuality of launching an initial public offering. To secure adequate capital, firms may also have to accommodate investment banks that are starting to use Sarbox standards as the gold standard of due diligence. Finally, some states are adopting "Little Sarbanes" laws that apply to private firms as well (Katz, 2003).

## SEC Administrative Reforms

Since taking the helm at the SEC, chair William Donaldson has won praise for his vigorous, tough, and thoughtful leadership and for leading reforms to protect investors. In framing his activist agenda, particularly to reform the mutual fund industry, he has often crossed party lines to vote with the two Democratic commissioners at the SEC. As one journalist notes, "A man not known for making waves has mounted a personal campaign to overhaul the ethics of corporate America" (Peterson, 2004). In so doing, he has not won universal acclaim, as fiscally conservative and free-market groups such as the Club for Growth have criticized his regulatory proposals (Peterson, 2004). The SEC has also seen its budget more than double from 2002 to 2004, to $842 million, with an additional 710 lawyers and accountants (Borrus et al., 2003), and has also launched other internal reforms. With the sudden growth and new responsibilities of the SEC, Chairman Donaldson felt it was important to spot early any internal problems within each division. Hence, he organized a fifteen-person Office of Risk Assessment that places staff within each division to coordinate the SEC's overall policies. The office will also attempt to make internal operations more oriented to outcome than to output (Michaels, 2004b).

The SEC has also formed the Public Company Accounting Oversight Board (PCAOB), as required by Sarbox, to replace the functions once served by the American Institute of Certified Public Accountants. Barbara Roper, director of consumer protection at the Consumer Federation of America (CFA), stressed the need to have a strong accounting regulatory body at the outset and later defended its independent powers from what she called "micromanagement by the SEC" (Glater, 2002; Johnson, 2003a). Prior to the accounting body authorized by Sarbox, former SEC chair Havey Pitt had proposed a new accounting regulatory body that would supplement the activities of the AICPA. The CFA opposed that earlier proposal as creating multiple oversight bodies and potentially weak enforcement, and because the plan did not precisely specify who could serve on the board, the method of selection, and the authority to set standards (Glater, 2002; Hilzenrath and Day, 2002). The CII opposed the plan as well, saying it preferred legislation to an industry-dominated structure (Day and Hilzenrath, 2002). The Consumers Union also supported the new regulatory system authorized by Sarbox and saw it as a vast improvement over self-regulation by the AICPA and the earlier modest role by the SEC (Romero, 2002). The CFA was even skeptical of the system under Sarbox, though concerned the board would become a "captive of industry" (Hilzenrath, 2002).

The new accounting board, the PCAOB, has a standing advisory group of thirty experts and stakeholder representatives from such organizations as the CFA, the Ohio Public Employees Retirement System, the AFL-CIO, and the proxy advisory service Glass Lewis (Michaels, 2004c). Since he was appointed head of the PCAOB, William McDonough has also negotiated with

the European Union for acceptance of the extraterritorial jurisdiction of his body and has also endorsed the movement of the United States to more principles-based accounting (Michaels and Parker, 2003).

## Federal-State Relations

With the appointment of William Donaldson as chair, the SEC began to more aggressively pursue corporate and mutual fund violators. Nonetheless, both reform advocates and critics of government intervention recognize that New York Attorney General Eliot Spitzer has led the way in cleaning up the scandals. John Bogle expresses a common sentiment:

> I think the SEC deserves credit for taking the actions they've taken for trying to improve the regulations, but I think the real credit belongs to [New York] Attorney General Eliot Spitzer. He's been very aggressive. He uncovered these misdeeds, and he's been very thorough in his investigations. He's been extremely tough in resolving the issues in terms of fines and fee reductions. So it's been a very good process of federal-state teamwork. But I think everybody realizes states have taken the lead.

> (Saito-Chung, 2004)

Provoked by the aggressive law enforcement of Spitzer, and especially by his settlement with Wall Street investment banks and his attack on the sales policies of Morgan Stanley, forces within the SEC and Congress moved to curb Spitzer's influence. Representative Richard Baker (R-LA) sponsored legislation that would limit the enforcement powers of state regulators to fines and penalties, not structural reforms. Spitzer met the challenge, labeled it a "bad Bill written for the wrong reason to address a non-existent problem," and House Republicans backed away from the Bill (Michaels, 2003a, d; Smith and Solomon, 2003). The controversy surrounding Spitzer has grown, as he has stretched his resources and expanded his efforts to also challenge charities for failing to sufficiently aid 9/11 victims, grocers for their labor practices, banks for predatory lending, the federal Environmental Protection

Agency for lax enforcement, and pharmaceutical companies for drug pricing policies (Langley, 2003).

The controversy goes well beyond Spitzer, however, as other state regulators firmly oppose having their powers limited and their sails trimmed. The North American Securities Administrators Association strongly opposed the Baker Bill as harming investors, and individual state securities regulators also voiced opposition to curtailing their ability to order structural reforms in the financial services industry. The Alabama securities commissioner said that "Undermining investor protection by handcuffing local cops is a giant step backwards," and also said, "If all we can do is fine, then it becomes a cost of doing business" (Michaels, 2003a). Massachusetts Secretary of the Commonwealth William F. Galvin said the Bill "would basically neuter state protections for investors" (Masters and White, 2003). The limited number of consumer groups engaged in the issue also opposed any attack on state activism on corporate reform. Barbara Roper of the CFA called the Baker Bill "terrible." Meanwhile, industry groups like the Securities Industry Association (SIA) backed the Bill, arguing that uniform national standards are in the investors' best interests (Masters and White, 2003).

The announcement by Attorney General Edmondson of Oklahoma that he was bringing criminal charges against Bernie Ebbers of WorldCom further exacerbated the tension between the states and federal regulators on a case that Oklahoma eventually dropped (Latour et al., 2003; Gold et al., 2003). Further, at least twenty states are considering their own versions of Sarbox, with Connecticut's securities law reflecting that of Sarbox and California's going beyond the federal law in some respects (Solomon, 2003). California's Secretary of State has even proposed a Bill requiring that any company doing business in the state allow shareholders owning 2 percent of a firm's shares for at least two years to nominate candidates for the corporate board (Hiltzik, 2004). This is the first state counterpart of the SEC's divisive shareholder nomination proposal to be submitted at the state level. The general counsel of the SEC is skeptical of this trend, as he states, "the commission must ensure that state actions do not conflict with a strong, competitive, and uniform national securities market" (Solomon, 2003). Therefore, in September of 2003, the SEC and the North American Securities Administrators Association, representing state regulators, announced the formation of a working group to improve state and federal cooperation (Michaels, 2003f). Still, tensions persist and likely will as Spitzer remains more aggressive and often out in front of SEC action, regardless of his motives. Senator Paul Sarbanes (D-MD) has warned SEC chair Donaldson that a public feud with Spitzer would be counterproductive, but Donaldson has been clearly frustrated by public attacks from Spitzer's office in the media.

While state and federal cooperation/conflict was an important issue over 2004, the states also strengthened their hand by engaging in more interstate cooperation in securities regulation, among such states as New York, California, Alabama, Maine, and New Jersey (Chaffin and Michaels, 2003b). The SEC and Eliot Spitzer continue to work concurrently on several issues, whether on mutual fund abuses or on the allegedly excessive compensation and pension paid to NYSE head Richard Grasso, with Spitzer usually taking the lead. In the case of the Grasso pay package, Spitzer has used the New York Not-for-Profit Corporation Law to prosecute Grasso for misconduct, while the SEC has a higher burden to carry in prosecuting the NYSE board for fraud (Craig et al., 2004).

## Further Accounting Regulation

Beyond the increasing oversight the accounting industry is receiving from the new Public Company Accounting Oversight Board, the Federal Reserve has a rule governing banking audits, with the power to ban firms that behave improperly from auditing banks (Michaels and Silverman, 2003).

## Self-regulatory Organizations

In late 2003 under the leadership of interim chair John Reed, the New York Stock Exchange instituted a reform of its own governance. It did not go as far as some critics such as the Council of Institutional Investors desired, but it was a major step forward. The reforms included a split board, with one board supervising regulatory and compensation issues, with the other board overseeing market and trading operations. The unwieldy twenty seven person board at the time, dominated by representatives of traders and investment banks, would give way to a new eight-member board from outside the securities industry (Boland et al., 2003). The CII has also urged the NYSE to divest holdings it has in member companies, abide by the same ethical guidelines as the SEC, and disclose the charitable contributions of the NYSE Foundation, since allegedly 40 percent of those funds go to organizations which have NYSE members on their boards (Burns, 2003).

The CII, along with Nell Minow of the Corporate Library, have also advocated that the regulatory and business roles of the NYSE be divided into two separate organizations, since the organizational model of the NYSE contains inherent conflicts of interest (Boland et al., 2003). Meanwhile, the National Association of Securities Dealers (NASD) in 1995 separated itself as a non-profit regulatory group from the for-profit NASDAQ exchange. The California state treasurer, the New York state comptroller, and the California Public Employee Retirement System (CalPERS) also wanted the NYSE to separate its business from its regulatory functions and wanted increased board representation for institutional investors as well. The state treasurers and CalPERS also sued the NYSE for its specialists trading in their own accounts before placing buy and sell orders, known as "front running" (White, 2003a, Kristof, 2003). The National Coalition for Corporate Reform, which includes CalPERS and other state pension funds, takes the same position on separating business and regulatory functions and increasing investor representation (White and Day, 2003). Sarah Teslik, executive director of CII, comments, "The [NYSE] board can't work with this conflict. If the regulatory responsibilities get separated out, the governance issues go away" (Eichenwald, 2003).

She criticizes the NYSE as "both the judge and party to each dispute between broker-dealers and investors" (Thomas, 2003). Barbara Roper, director of investor protection of the Consumer Federation of America agreed the NYSE must divide its business and regulatory roles and objected to the pay package for NYSE chair Richard Grasso, as well as the appointment of Sanford Weil as public member, shortly after his firm Citigroup had agreed to pay $400 million to settle allegations its analysts had misled investors ("How to Restore …", 2003).

Regarding action by the NYSE following on the heels of the corporate scandals, it issued new rules in 2002 that listed companies would have a majority of independent directors, and that audit and compensation committees would consist entirely of independent directors, in keeping with the later provisions of Sarbox. It also required that companies would allow shareholders to vote on any stock option plan (White, 2002). The Business Roundtable offered only limited support of the rule, based on its history of favoring shareholder votes on executive stock options, but not on options for the rank and file (White, 2002).

## Mutual Fund Regulations and Penalties

SEC chair William H. Donaldson has stated:

> It is extremely troubling that so much of the conduct that led to the scandals in the mutual fund industry was, at its core, a breach of the fiduciary relationship between investment advisors and their advised funds. As fiduciaries, advisors owe their clients more than mere honesty and good faith. Recent experience suggests that all too many advisors were delivering much less.
>
> (in Johnson, 2004)

The mutual fund scandals are a new development since 2003, but are the most outrageous. They represent the worst scandal in the industry's sixty year history, and the market timing and late trading practices wound up being more common than first imagined. A Lipper survey concluded that an examination of fund flows demonstrated that one of every four global and international funds was being used by short-term arbitragers or market timers, and the SEC reported that half of all mutual funds contacted revealed they had market timing arrangements with some clients (Brewster and Michaels, 2003a). The SEC has implicated more than twenty mutual funds in the scandal (Hoover, 2004), and more than a dozen fund companies and brokerages had paid more than $2.3 billion in fines, restitution, and reduced fees in settlements by mid-2004 (Masters, 2004a), with more to come. Stephen Cutler, the SEC enforcement director, says despite the progress in combating market timing and late trading, the Commission is still "not yet through the middle innings when it comes to some of the other mutual fund issues" (Masters, 2004a).

Both William Donaldson and Eliot Spitzer have engaged in tough talk and some tough action directed toward the securities industry. Donaldson warned them at a securities conference in November, 2003, that a "backslap could easily be turned into a full nelson" (Michaels, 2003h). Meanwhile, Spitzer is trying to send strong signals that voluntary reforms are essential by issuing a "drumbeat of changes" ("Drumbeat of Change …", 2003). The SEC has also proposed other mutual fund reforms. Perhaps the most important suggestion is having a compliance officer who reports directly to the board. The SEC would also require that independent directors keep all records of deliberations over advisory fees (Fried, 2004).

The SEC and state attorneys-general have arrived at expensive settlements with fund violators since 2003. The SEC and attorneys-general of New York and Wisconsin required Richard Strong and Strong Capital Management to pay $175 million to settle fund abuses, $60 million of which will be paid personally by Richard Strong in civil penalties and restitution. Strong has also issued an apology to shareholders and accepted a lifetime ban from the securities industry. A Strong executive vice-president who approved market timing trades by Canary Capital and the fund's compliance officer, who failed to monitor such trades, also received substantial fines and were banned from the securities industry (Beltran, 2004).

In March of 2004, the SEC and the New York Attorney General's office also announced a settlement of $675 million with Bank of America and Fleet Boston Financial Corporation over fraud charges for allowing the hedge fund Canary Partners to market time its investments in Bank of America funds on a large scale (Fried, 2004; Masters, 2004b). The settlement also requires eight directors of Bank America's Nations Funds to resign. Duke University law professor James D. Cox said such "shaming will probably have an impact. Removing the directors is a really powerful message" (Masters, 2004b). In a six-month period from late 2003 to early 2004, fund violators agreed to pay $1.65 billion in fines and fee reductions to settle with various regulators (Anders, 2004; Masters, 2004b). Massachusetts Financial Services (MFS) funds agreed to a settlement of $225 million and a five-year reduction in fees, and also hired a new CEO and president as well as a new compliance director from Fidelity (Hoover, 2004). Putnam Investments agreed to pay fines of $100 million for its market timing scandal, $50 million to the SEC and the same amount to the Massachusetts Securities Division, along with $10 million more in restitution payments (Hechinger, 2004). Janus Funds paid a settlement of $236 million. The SEC, NASD, and NYSE also fined fifteen mutual funds a far less amount of $21.5 million for selectively giving "breakpoint discounts" only to certain customers (Johnson, 2004).

The SEC proposed rules in 2002 that mutual funds publish the guidelines they use to vote proxies and disclose how they cast proxy votes on behalf of their investors. That rule is now in effect, despite the ICI's persistent opposition. Fund Democracy supported disclosure, as did the CII and ISS, with the CEO of ISS, Jamie Heard, stating that "Requiring disclosure is the only way to ensure that fund managers are following their stated voting policies" (Day, 2002a). The Investment Company Institute (ICI), however, opposed disclosure, saying it thought investors didn't care how fund managers voted, and disclosure would only make funds a lightning rod for criticism by labor unions and environmental groups (Day,

2002a, b). John Bogle also supported disclosure of proxy voting records by funds, which the CEOs of Vanguard and Fidelity vehemently opposed, fearing the plan would "politicize proxy voting" (Hechinger and Lucchetti, 2003). The Competitive Enterprise Institute, a libertarian think tank in Washington, DC, also opposed the disclosure of proxy votes and argued to the SEC that forced disclosure would violate the First Amendment commercial speech rights of management investment companies. It also argued that less intrusive alternatives exist to protect the rights of investors (Cox and Kazman, 2002).

Some mutual fund reform proposals have included the abolition of 12(b)-1 fees, which is supported by the Consumer Federation of America, since funds use such fees as ways to more than compensate for the elimination of any load charges (Damato and Burns, 2004). Though regulation of mutual fund fees is opposed by even some of the critics of funds, fee reductions as part of legal settlements have been ordered. The first, with Alliance Capital, required the firm to slash its fees as much as 20 percent (Brewster and Michaels, 2003b). This is one of several areas where the SEC clashes with Spitzer's approach, since the commissioners believe fee reductions should be part only of broader rule making, not individual settlements. Mercer Bullard, head of Fund Democracy, supports Spitzer's approach of including fee reductions as part of settlements (Brewster and Michaels, 2003b). Fund Democracy has largely supported Spitzer's more aggressive measures, while criticizing the SEC for being too tepid in its regulatory and enforcement actions.

The Investment Company Institute, the association of mutual funds, supports other reforms that are basically noncontroversial. It favors restricting the use of soft dollars for investment research, believing it should be paid for from management fees rather than from shareholders' assets. Further, the ICI favors a "hard close" of 4.00 p.m. and a mandatory 2 percent redemption fee on investors who sell a fund within five days of purchasing it, in order to curtail market timing. The leading opponent of such a measure is the Society of Asset Allocators and Fund Timers, an association of financial advisers who practice market timing (Damato and Burns, 2004). The ICI also advocates regulating brokerage transactions where funds steer business to securities firms that favor the management company's funds, the type of arrangement that provoked Eliot Spitzer to prosecute Morgan Stanley (Haaga, 2003). The ICI also favors disclosure of brokerage commission as a percentage of average net assets, disclosure of the flow of assets out of and into funds, and disclosure of a fund's portfolio turnover rate (Hayashi, 2004). The Securities Industry Association, which represents brokers, parts company with the ICI on that issue, however, and has opposed mandatory disclosure of fees and commission on fund sales (Masters, 2004a).

Lest one get the impression the ICI has been a consistent advocate of reform, however, the overall picture has been quite different. The ICI, whose membership is made up of 400 mutual fund organizations, has a budget of $37 million and has blunted or co-opted most measures to reform the industry over the years (Dwyer, 2003). While publicly favoring Sarbox, it privately lobbied to insure that the law's provisions would not apply to the mutual fund industry. It also lobbied against legislation to reform the mutual fund industry, proposed by Representative Richard H. Baker (R-La). Since it is dominated by the largest fund families that have insider chairs, the ICI also consistently opposed the new requirement that fund chairs be independent of management (Dwyer, 2003). At least five of the fifteen companies represented on ICI's executive committee have been the target of investigations. Due to the resulting opposition to many reforms, Mercer Bullard of Fund Democracy stated, "There's no question the ICI's clout has been reduced as a result of this scandal" (Peterson, 2003). Fund critic John Bogle states, "They have been an incredibly powerful voice in lobbying for the mutual fund industry. Unfortunately, they have not furthered the interests of mutual fund investors" (Peterson, 2003). In a related sense, investors also indirectly fund the lobbying of the ICI, since a portion of the $31 million in dues from mutual fund members paid in 2003 was billed to shareholders rather than the fund managers. One critic observed that "they get their money from investors to lobby against the interests of investors" (Day, 2004).

Interestingly, the ICI has stronger ties to the Democratic Party and to liberal Democrats like Representative Barney Frank (D-MA), whose home state of Massachusetts is the headquarters of major funds like Fidelity, MFS, and Putnam. In fact, House Financial Services Committee chair Michael G. Oxley (R-OH) has complained that the ICI does not employ enough Republican lobbyists (Dwyer, 2003).

The ICI, Morningstar, and reform advocate John Bogle favor disclosure of fund managers' holdings in their own funds, of trading records, and of pay structures for managers, all of which would have prevented the market timing abuses (Kahn, 2004). Furthermore, Bogle has advocated an earlier closing time for fund purchases and a 2 percent redemption fee for shares held less than thirty days (Hayashi, 2003). Bogle also supported disclosure of proxy voting records by funds, which the present CEOs of Vanguard and Fidelity vehemently opposed, fearing the plan would "politicize proxy voting" (Hechinger and Lucchetti, 2003). Bogle has been the leading advocate for mutual fund reforms, has testified often before Congress, and has therefore fallen out of favor within his own industry, even within the company he founded (Bogle, 2003; Damato, 2004; Michaels, 2003g). Wall Street commentator Louis Rukeyser has said of Bogle, "Jack has been a constant gadfly pointing out to anyone who would listen important uncorrected problems in the industry. His focus on mutual fund costs and fees alone should put him in the hall of fame" (Coleman, 2003).

Former SEC chairs Arthur Levitt and Richard Breeden go along with Bogle and have recommended stringent reforms of mutual funds. They believe that all directors but one should be independent, that fund boards should have term limits and professional resources to develop independent information on fund performance, and that fund sponsors should be required to appoint investor ombudspersons to their boards in cases of extreme violations (Levitt and Breeden, 2004). Former SEC chair David Ruder also favors

the reforms passed in March 2004, requiring that fund chairs be independent and that fund boards be 75 percent independent, but he opposes regulation of fees and state regulators instituting rules for mutual funds (Henriques, 2004), a comment on Eliot Spitzer's activism and federal-state relations discussed earlier in this chapter.

Amidst all the criticism and controversy surrounding mutual funds, some funds actually exceed regulatory standards. Articles on Bridgeway Funds, based in Houston, Texas, have praised the fund family for its outstanding financial performance and for its ethics (Braham, 2003; Lauricella, 2004). It has a detailed code of ethics on its Web site (bridgewayfunds.com), prohibits market timing and late trading, requires that fund managers invest in their own funds, discloses the pay structure for fund managers and the CEO's compensation of about $350,000, and has closed most of its leading funds to new investors. That final step is a guarantee against market timing.

## Expensing Stock Options

The issue of expensing stock options continues to be a "hot button" issue for both shareholders and some corporate management. In the past few years, more than 100 of the S&P 500 firms have voluntarily begun to expense stock options, and a total of 500 firms have made the switch. Unions and other leading institutional shareholders, such as the Teachers Insurance and Annuity Association-College Retirement Equities Fund (TIAA-CREF) have been pressuring the other companies to expense options. Linda Scott, director of corporate governance for TIAA-CREF, offers two reasons for its support of expensing options—to make the financial statement more transparent and to level the field regarding other forms of equity compensation (Lahart, 2004). The Chartered Financial Analysts (CFA) Institute, which oversees the certification of those in the profession, has also endorsed expensing of options, and is establishing a Center for Financial Market Integrity to research and promote ethical conduct (Brewster, 2004). The Institute, with

70,000 members, represents fund managers and buy-side analysts. Further, the Financial Accounting Standards Board (FASB) published its proposal to require expensing of options on March 31 of 2004 (Rivlin, 2004).

Nevertheless, several prominent high-technology companies continue to resist the trend, in the face of growing pressure from their own shareholders. While 54 percent of Intel's shareholders supported a resolution calling for the expensing of options, the company's top officers continued to oppose such expensing and said they would not adopt the policy. Shareholders at Apple Computers passed a similar resolution in 2003, as did the shareholders of Hewlett-Packard and PeopleSoft in March of 2004, though management in each company would not implement the nonbinding resolutions (Bank, 2004; Rivlin, 2004). Another major tech firm, Sun Microsystems, opposes the expensing of options, despite the internal opposition on this issue from independent director Lynn Turner, former chief accountant at the SEC and now with Glass Lewis (Michaels and Waters, 2003).

In releasing its proposal, the Financial Accounting Standards Board announced it favored the binomial approach, while most US firms that expense options use the Black-Sholes equation. Opponents of the binomial approach claim it would be unworkable. While the FASB would allow individual companies to continue using the Black-Sholes method, it is adamant that large issuers of stock should switch to the binomial method (Michaels and Roberts, 2004a).

The regulatory and political aspects of the expensing issue are being driven by the FASB and by Congress, both subject to pressure from various interest groups and corporations. Though corporate leaders such as Warren Buffet and Jack Bogel are outspoken advocates in favor of expensing options, technology companies and their leaders generally are not, with the notable exceptions of GE and Microsoft. Cisco Systems has consistently opposed expensing options and said in a submission to the FASB, "Expensing of amounts that are subject to such ridiculous swings in value generated from such flawed models would be at the very least

misleading as well as irresponsible" (Michaels and Roberts, 2004b). Craig Barrett, CEO of Intel, opposed expensing options in an op-ed column in The Wall Street Journal, citing a number of economists as well as a study from the American Enterprise Institute, a conservative think tank supported by business interests (Barrett, 2004). He argued that expensing options is technically dubious and would put US high-technology companies at a disadvantage to their overseas competitors. A Bear Stearns study reveals that net income from continuing operations for S&P 500 companies would have been 8 percent less in 2003 if options had been expensed, would have been only 3 percent less in 2004, and would be even less than 3 percent in 2005. However, tech and biotech companies in the NASDAQ 100 would have seen their earnings fall by 44 percent, largely explaining the tech sector's opposition, led by the International Employee Stock Options Coalition that has lobbied for legislation to block the FASB standard (Michaels and Parker, 2004; Schroeder, 2004). TechNet, another lobby of Silicon Valley executives and venture capitalists, has also opposed expensing options and supported legislation to block the FASB decision (Weil and Cummings, 2004). Further, the American Electronics Association has organized executives from small- and mid-sized technology firms to lobby US Congress members to block the FASB proposal to expense options. Given the strength of technology firms in California, Senator Barbara Boxer (D-CA) and members of the California House delegation have sponsored bills to block the FASB (Mulligan, 2004).

Beyond GE and Microsoft, some other tech companies also broke ranks and supported the FASB's efforts to expense options. Electronic Data Systems has already done so and withdrawn its membership from the options coalition as well (Michaels and Waters, 2004). Reed Hastings, CEO of Netflix, also supported expensing options in an op-ed column for The Wall Street Journal, where he wrote that:

Amazon, Microsoft, and my company, Netflix, all voluntarily converted last year to expensing, have continued to give broad-based incentives, and innovation continues unabated. Stock options may be the symbol of the Silicon Valley culture, but it is not the essence. We innovate because it thrills us, not because of some accounting treatment.

(Hastings, 2004)

Given the large shareholder votes in favor of expensing stock options, it is that much more difficult for any political campaign by the tech sector to ultimately succeed. As Patrick McGurn, chief counsel for ISS, puts it, "Any politician who touches this is touching a real third rail now. They'd be promoting bad accounting and kowtowing to rich CEOs of tech companies dangling campaign contributions" (Morgenson, 2004b). Arguments over the methods of expensing options may be a last-ditch attempt by opposing companies to delay the inevitable.

## POLITICAL ANALYSIS OF GROUPS AND ACTORS

In analyzing the political forces both promoting and resisting regulation, this section analyzes the roles that both new and old citizen groups have played in advancing regulations. It also looks in details at the roles that various business and professional groups have played in preventing and resisting regulation, until the political forces unleashed by the corporate scandals overcame much of the resistance. In analyzing the roles played by business groups, this section both applies the capture theory of regulation to their roles and also depicts the internal division within the business community in its reaction to the corporate scandals and regulatory initiatives. This section also examines the importance of think tanks in either promoting or resisting new regulations as well.

### Citizen Group Pressure

Most of the activism to promote corporate reform has been exercised by shareholder groups, with corporations and mutual funds as the direct targets. When it comes to government regulation, there has been far less activism in a political sense by the pro-reform movement. While investor groups and research organizations have prominently advanced governance reform by targeting corporations directly, they have been far less active in lobbying for legislative or regulatory changes.

Meanwhile, the traditional consumer lobbies developed in the United States during the 1960s and 1970s have been relatively inactive on the corporate reform agenda in lobbying either Congress or the SEC. That absence of pressure is curious. Only the Consumer Federation of America has been active in lobbying and issuing public statements on legal and regulatory changes, and even that seems to represent the force of one person at the CFA. Examining the Web site of the CFA reveals no mention of corporate governance or information on the issue. While Ralph Nader continues to make statements on corporate accountability, none of the organizations in his network has actively lobbied or written on corporate governance. The Center for Corporate Policy (www.corporatepolicy.org) is linked to the Nader network and Web site and is active on executive compensation and corporate crime, but does not address the corporate governance agenda. The American Association of Retired Persons (AARP), whose membership of older citizens undoubtedly includes a large number of investors, has also been mute on corporate reform. The organization has lobbied on reform of 401-k retirement accounts but has not taken stands on Sarbox and larger issues of corporate governance. Perhaps for that reason, AEI scholar James Glassman has announced his intention to form an advocacy and research group for investors, an "AARP for investors,'" in his words (Glassman, 2004).

In speculating on the reasons for this inactivity among the traditional consumer groups, there may be several possible explanations. As older groups, they may be more fixed in their ways and have not been able to adapt to a new era of issues. Their members and/or supporters may also have placed no demands on the consumer groups to focus on corporate governance reform measures and may identify with other groups to represent them on those issues.

Finally, traditional consumer groups may also have a liberal tilt that prevents them from caring about investor issues or the "investor class," often identified with more conservative causes. Whatever the reason(s), it appears that the investor interests of most citizens have been ill served by the traditional consumer lobbies.

Filling the breach left by consumer groups on the issue has been the growing activism of US labor unions on corporate governance. They have obviously seen this as a target of opportunity, so much so that their critics have accused their pension fund activism as promoting their labor interests far more than their investor interests. One example is the campaign to remove the CEO and directors of Safeway. Labor has traditionally been active in lobbying and political influence, so it has used its lobbying clout to complement its shareholder clout on corporate governance issues, and has lobbied Congress in support of Sarbox and lobbied the SEC on regulatory initiatives. Fund Democracy, another pro-reform group led by a former SEC attorney, has lobbied the SEC on mutual fund issues.

Finally, also filling the breach left by traditional consumer groups has been a new force for change in corporate governance and accountability—former SEC chairs. All seven of them have been active in one way or the other, as public spokespersons, internal investigators, and/or corporate monitors. Most prominent among them have been Richard Breeden and Arthur Levitt. Without their leadership and courage, it is likely the movement for corporate reform would not have advanced nearly as far as it has. Complementing their efforts when it comes to mutual fund reforms has been John Bogle, founder of the Vanguard Funds, who has devoted most of his time and energy to cleaning up his own industry, criticizing it, and testifying in favor of legislative and regulatory measures.

## Business Influence

There are two aspects of business influence on the reform agenda that tend to go in opposite directions. In one sense, that influence corroborates the capture theory of regulation and indicates that business was able to wield unchecked power in creating the underlying conditions for scandals to occur. In another sense, and once the scandals had occurred, business power waned, and another feature of business influence surfaced. That feature is internal division within the ranks, corroborating the pluralist theory of politics and creating the conditions for other stakeholders to regain or assert their influence in leading to corporate reforms.

### Capture Theory

Some of the business lobbying on corporate reform measures confirms the capture theory of regulation (Stigler, 1971). According to this theory, industry often captures the economic or industry-specific regulatory agencies established to regulate them, preventing real competition from serving the public interest. Related to the corporate scandals since 2000, there have been two instances of industry capture that may have laid the foundation for the later scandals. First, the accounting industry and the American Institute for Certified Public Accountants allegedly put enough pressure on Congress and the SEC to block attempts by the agency to separate auditing and consulting (Levitt, 2002). Combining those two services under one roof helped boost the revenues of major accounting firms but contributed to the ultimate collapse of both Arthur Andersen and Enron.

Second, the Investment Company Institute, representing the major mutual funds, allegedly protected mutual fund managers more than investors and was able to block major reforms until Attorney General Eliot Spitzer of New York launched major investigations and prosecutions in 2003. In that year, the ICI failed to block the rule requiring disclosure of proxy votes, and in 2004 the ICI failed to block the rule requiring that mutual fund boards have independent chairs. In each of these cases, an iron triangle of business interests, the SEC, and Congress prevented major reform, until the corporate scandals broke the iron triangle and provided the impetus for new legislation, SEC regulations, and even voluntary changes by business. The scandals also energized the public and catalyzed the formation of new groups to challenge the business interests that previously captured the agency. Crisis events can sometimes break up political configurations that have dominated public policy in the past.

### Division within the Ranks

Just as the pro-reform groups and pension funds are divided on certain issues and tactics, the business community is also divided on issues of corporate reform. The Conference Board has been at least a moderate voice for reform, with its Commission on Public Trust and Private Enterprise advocating expensing of stock options and ways of controlling excessive executive compensation. The National Association of Corporate Directors (NACD), the primary voice for directors and sponsor of director training programs, has supported a stronger and more independent role for directors, as well as ways of controlling excessive executive compensation. The Center for Corporate Change, a group founded in Vail, Colorado, by retired CEOs and directors in 2002, has also actively promoted corporate reform through research, conferences, and awards for best governance practices. Meanwhile, the Business Roundtable and the US Chamber of Commerce have opposed reforms such as the mandatory separation of the positions of CEO and board chair and shareholder nomination of directors, even threatening to sue the SEC to block implementation of the latter rule. As mentioned in the section above, the AICPA also earlier blocked efforts by the SEC to separate the audit function from consulting.

A similar division within the business community has emerged on mutual fund reforms. While the ICI has attempted to block major reforms, the Mutual Fund Directors Form has defended a stronger and more independent role for fund directors. In some ways, it is the counterpart of the NACD in the mutual fund industry, but has assumed a lower profile. On expensing of stock options, the business community is likewise split. While most large

corporations now expense options and major business groups like the Conference Board advocate rules requiring such expensing, the technology sector continues to oppose the practice. The Employee Stock Options Coalition and TechNet, an association of Silicon Valley companies, have lobbied to block the FASB's action requiring expensing of options.

These internal divisions within the business community confirm a major premise of pluralist political theory—the business community is not monolithic and does not move as one to represent any class interest (Berry, 2000; Dahl, 1991; Polsby, 1980). The splintering within the business community also demonstrates that business is not a power elite and that some elements of the business community may win on public policy disputes while others lose. Some groups are surely more powerful than others, but occasionally less powerful elements may win by building coalitions with non-business interests to prevail. In the battle over corporate governance reform, groups representing corporate directors, institutional investors, executive reformers, former regulators, and even labor unions share viewpoints that have ultimately prevailed over groups representing entrenched top management.

### Think Tanks

The activities by think tanks on corporate reform issues partially confirm a general observation of their influence since the mid-1970s, that the original liberal think tanks have been overtaken by those sponsored and supported by business interests. While Robert Litan of the Brookings Institution, a liberal to centrist think tank, has frequently written and testified in favor of government regulation of accounting and corporate governance reform (Litan, 2002), and while Brookings itself has published books in the area, it seems to be a notable exception among liberal think tanks. The few other major liberal think tanks that have survived have generally avoided the issue.

Meanwhile, this chapter has often quoted experts and publications from conservative or libertarian think tanks, such as the American

Enterprise Institute, the Cato Institute, and the Competitive Enterprise Institute. Their work on corporate governance has simply been more pervasive than that of liberal think tanks, as it has been on a host of other economic and social issues.

This is not to say that such think tanks have been extremely influential in affecting public policy outcomes. On the contrary, they have offered criticisms and objections to proposals and rules that have ultimately passed. New corporate governance research centers, shareholder activist groups, institutional investors, governance rating services, prominent former regulators, activist attorneys-general like Eliot Spitzer, and some reform elements in the business community have outweighed the influence of both mainline business groups and the conservative/libertarian think tanks in terms of public policy outcomes.

## IMPACT ON CORPORATE PUBLIC AFFAIRS STRATEGIES

The regulation component of the corporate reform agenda logically falls in the domain of the government relations and issues management functions. In building bridges to potential allies and supporting think tanks, though, corporate contributions and corporate responsibility functions might also be involved in setting and implementing corporate strategy. Whatever the functions involved, top management and its supporting public affairs functions face some critical choices in designing corporate strategy. They must determine when to negotiate with regulators, when to engage in opposition lobbying, whether to promote state autonomy or federal preemption in regulation, which think tanks to support, and which allies to cultivate. This final section will impart thoughts on each of those choices.

### Negotiate with Regulators

There are several reasons why a company and a public affairs executive should avoid a confrontational approach with a regulator of fraud or governance issues, especially if that regulator is someone like Eliot Spitzer. Experienced government relations professionals would likely be the most important component in developing a strategy to deal with regulators. By demonizing such a regulator as a "budding demagogue," as one *Wall Street Journal* writer labeled Spitzer (Jenkins, 2004), or even questioning the regulator's political motives, a firm might destroy the possibility of a positive relationship and outcome. Even if a regulator might seem to be grandstanding, cooperation might prevent the situation from escalating. Further, a combative strategy might be seen as "obstruction of justice," converting a civil charge into a criminal charge. And also, there can be severe consequences to a firm's reputation if the regulator or the media point to the company as arrogant or out of line.

### Opposition Lobbying

In some cases, business really has no good alternative to an attempt to defeat reforms that may overreach in the eyes of that firm or its industry. Whether that strategy might entail direct or grassroots lobbying, the role of traditional government relations professionals is essential in implementing that strategy. For the tech sector, the most threatening reform has been the expensing of stock options. While most economics and business experts have favored the expensing of options, the tech sector has made at least a plausible case that the reform could injure its ability to recruit and retain top talent and might therefore injure the competitive position of the United States and domestic economic growth. While the battle appears to be a losing one for the industry, the lobbying and opinion columns by top tech executives and associations such as TechNet have made it an interesting and closer fight. Cisco Systems has opposed the FASB's expensing rule more vigorously than other companies. During the ninety-day comment period, more than two-thirds of the 2,600 comment letters came from Cisco employees, representing 7.5 percent of the company's work force. A memo by the company's CFO inspired the letter-writing campaign (Schneider, 2004). Silicon Valley workers have even staged rallies and protests against the move by the FASB to require the expensing of stock options, with signs reading "Don't Destroy the Economy; Save our Stock Options!!!" (Menn, 2004).

Some companies also see state government activism on corporate reforms as too intrusive and would prefer uniform national standards and federal pre-emption. These choices are more delicate, though, and require sensible long-term strategy development by top issues management experts. Business organizations have favored legislation such as the Baker Bill to limit the remedial powers of state regulators. There are three major caveats to consider when favoring federal over state power, however. First, many of the conservative think tanks and organizations that generally favor business concerns also promote federalism and are defenders of states' rights. By lobbying against states' rights, business undermines its own credibility and support from erstwhile conservative allies, some of whom the business community has funded over the years. Second, by opposing state activism, business implicitly also opposes very popular state officials such as Eliot Spitzer, an icon of the corporate reform movement. That in turn may provoke public skepticism and criticism of business. Third, by attacking states' rights, business also attacks the foundation of corporate law in the United States since corporations are basically chartered and regulated at the state level. It also puts business in a hypocritical position, since it has argued elsewhere against the SEC regulation on shareholder nominations to boards as unduly federalizing corporate law and undermining state authority over corporations. Business takes a politically untenable position when it argues for federalism to attack certain regulations while arguing against federalism to attack other regulations. That type of hypocrisy also alienates potential allies and undermines business credibility.

## Support Think Tanks

To fortify its opposition lobbying, business might also launch and support think tanks that support its position on what business considers overreaching corporate reforms. Here, government relations and corporate contributions professionals should jointly participate in identifying appropriate organizations to support. Of course, they have already done this to a high degree in many companies. Witness the activities and statements made by experts from such think tanks as the American Enterprise Institute, Competitive Enterprise Institute, and Cato Institute on corporate reform measures addressed in this chapter. Though few of their arguments carried the day politically, they did establish a framework within which business could pursue other political tactics as well. They also establish positions on issues that might be useful when the public sector and the media evaluate the impact of laws and regulations that did pass. Often criticisms of legal approaches are later vindicated when Congress holds oversight hearings or scholars and journalists weigh the results of those legal reforms.

## Cultivate Future Allies

To achieve its long-term political goals on corporate reform measures, business might consider cultivating those groups that have stood on the sidelines and been inactive on the agenda to this point. Here, the expertise of issues management and stakeholder engagement executives is crucial. In this sense, business might energize and mobilize latent public sentiments on corporate reform. As discussed in a previous section of this chapter, the traditional consumer lobbies have not been as active as the newer corporate governance centers and institutional shareholder groups. Business might capitalize on those opportunities by opening discussions and building more bridges to the AARP, a powerful lobby that might be approachable, given some of the moderate positions it has taken on health care reform. In this way, business might develop a coalition with groups in different sectors of concern and groups which possess different political resources and tactics than those possessed by business. Given its membership, for example, the AARP enjoys a broad base of grassroots influence by ordinary citizens, crucial to legitimizing positions in the eyes of legislators. Business might also learn to better appreciate the perspectives of investors by building bridges to organizations that better reflect investor concerns.

## REFERENCES

Anders, G. (2004). "As Scandals Mount, Boards of Mutual Funds Feel the Heat," *The Wall Street Journal*, March 17: A1.

Bainbridge, S.M. (2003). "The Creeping Federalization of Corporate Law," *Regulation* 26 (1): 26–31.

Bank, D. (2004). "Shareholders Urge that PeopleSoft Expense Options," *The Wall Street Journal*, March 26: B4.

Barrett, C.R. (2004). "More Options for Trial Lawyers," *The Wall Street Journal*, March 31: A14.

Barta, P. (2003). "Pension Funds Sue Freddie Mac over Accounting," *The Wall Street Journal*, August 11: A3, A6.

Belson, K., and B. Simon (2004). "Investors Are Taking Long Hard Look at Nortel's Board," *The New York Times*, May 13: W1.

Beltran, L. (2004). "Strong, Founder Settle for $175 Million," *CBS Marketwatch*, May 20: http://cbs.marketwatch.com/news/story.asp?guid=%7BA1E9851F%2DE320%2D420A%2DA586%2D71AAB64FB010%7D&siteid=mktw.

Berry, J.M. (2000). *The New Liberalism: The Rising Power of Citizen Groups*. Washington, DC: Brookings Institution.

Bogle, J.C. (2003). "The Emperor's New Mutual Funds," *The Wall Street Journal*, July 8: A16.

Boland, V., A. Michaels, and A. Postelnicu (2003). "NYSE Reforms to Split Regulatory and Trading Issues," *Financial Times*, November 5: 17.

Borrus, A. (2004). "Stick to your Guns, Mr Donaldson," *Business Week*, May 24: 77.

Borrus, A., M. McNamee, and P. Dwyer (2003). "The SEC Cop Means Business," *Business Week*, June 23: 110.

Braham, L. (2003). "Who Says Nice Guys Finish Last?" *Business Week*, June 16: 90–91.

Brewster, D. (2004). "Fund Managers to Speak Their Minds," *Financial Times*, May 10: 20.

Brewster, D., and A. Michaels (2003a). "Market Timers Active in One in Four Mutual Funds," *Financial Times*, October 27: 28.

Brewster, D., and A. Michaels (2003b). "Regulators' Tensions Flare over Fund Fees Deal," *Financial Times*, December 17: 32.

Buckley, N., A. Michaels, G. Silverman, and D. Wells (2003). "Barclays Slated over Enron: US Inquiry Says Bank Assisted Cover-up by Failed Energy Trader," *Financial Times*, July 29: 21.

Burns, J. (2003). "Investors Group Calls on NYSE to Make Big Governance Changes," *The Wall Street Journal*, August 7: C9.

Chaffin, J., and A. Michaels (2003a). "Newest Autopsy Implicates Wall Street in Enron Collapse," *Financial Times*, July 29: 19.

Chaffin, J., and A. Michaels (2003b). "SEC Defends Probe into Mutual Funds," *Financial Times*, November 4: 28.

Cohen, L.P. (2004). "Prosecutors' Tough New Tactics Turn Firms against Employees," *The Wall Street Journal*, June 4: A1, A8.

Coleman, M. (2003). "Mutual Fund Maven John Bogle," *Investor's Business Daily*, July 21: A3.

Cox, B., and S. Kazman (2002). "Comments of the Competititve Enterprise Institute to the Securities and Exchange Commission Concerning its Proposed Rulemaking Requiring Proxy Vote Disclosures by Management Investment Companies," September 26, File No. S7-36-02; 67 FR 60,828.

Craig, S., K. Kelly, and D. Solomon (2004). "Spitzer, SEC Open Probes into Grasso's Pay," *The Wall Street Journal*, January 9: C1, C7.

Dahl, R.A. (1991). *Democracy and its Critics*. New Haven, CT: Yale University Press.

Damato, K. (2004). "Bogle: The Man Who Told You So," *The Wall Street Journal*, January 7: C1, C12.

Damato, K., and J. Burns (2004). "Cleaning up the Fund Industry," *The Wall Street Journal*, April 5: R1.

Dash, E. (2004). "For Directors, Great Expectations (and More Pay)," *The New York Times*, April 4: BU 10.

Day, K. (2002a). "New Rules May Force Disclosure on Votes," *The Washington Post*, September 19: E1.

Day, K. (2002b). "SEC Wants Funds to Disclose Votes," *The Washington Post*, September 20: E3.

Day, K. (2003). "SEC Staff Urges Limit to Reforms," *The Washington Post*, January 22: E1.

Day, K. (2004). "Investor Fees Finance Interests of Lobbyists," *The Washington Post*, January 11: F1.

Day, K., and D.S. Hilzenrath (2002). "SEC Readies Reform Plan for Auditors," *The Washington Post*, June 20: A1.

Donohue, T.J. (2003). "SEC Proxy Plan is a Threat to Business, Boon to Labor," *Investor's Business Daily*, December 4: A14.

"Drumbeat of Change: Abuse Shows the Fund Industry Has Lost its Roots" (2003). *Financial Times*, November 11: 22.

Dwyer, P. (2003). "Breach of Trust," *Business Week*, December 15: 98–108.

Eichenwald, K. (2003). "In String of Corporate Troubles, Critics Focus on Boards' Failings," *The New York Times*, September 21: A1, A30.

Fields, G. (2004). "Sentencing Panel Adds Hurdle for Companies to Get Leniency," *The Wall Street Journal*, April 9: B3.

Fried, C. (2004). "Unleashing Directors and Urging Them to Bark," *The New York Times*, April 4: BU 27.

Glassman, J.K. (2004). "It's Morning in Asia," *The Washington Post*, July 24: F1.

Glater, J.D. (2002). "S.E.C. Proposes a New Board to Oversee Auditors," *The New York Times*, June 21: C1.

Gold, A., A. Latour, D. Berman, and Y. Dreazen (2003). "MCI and Ebbers are Charged by Oklahoma," *The Wall Street Journal*, August 28: A3, A5.

Haaga, P.G. (2003). "Mutual Integrity, Mutual Trust," *The Wall Street Journal*, December 15: A14.

Hastings, R. (2004). "Expense It!" *The Wall Street Journal*, April 5: A18.

Hayashi, Y. (2003). "Bogle Seeks Stricter Trading Rules," *The Wall Street Journal*, October 29: D9.

Hayashi, Y. (2004). "Fund Group Pushes New Disclosures," *The Wall Street Journal*, February 25: D11.

Hechinger, J. (2004). "Putnam to Pay $110 Million," *The Wall Street Journal*, April 9: C3.

Hechinger, J., and A. Lucchetti (2003). "CEOs of Two Top Fund Firms Lash SEC," *The Wall Street Journal*, January 15: D9.

Henriques, D.B. (2004). "A Sense of History, a Feeling of Betrayal," *The New York Times*, January 2: C1.

Hiltzik, M. (2004). "Is Corporate Democracy a Valid Issue in Sacramento?" *Los Angeles Times*, April 1: C1.

Hilzenrath, D.S. (2002). "Accounting Bill Advances," *The Washington Post*, June 19: E1.

Hilzenrath, D.S., and K. Day (2002). "Oversight of Auditors Tentatively Approved," *The Washington Post*, June 21: E1.

Hoover, K. (2004). "Fund Conference Digests SEC's Vote," *Investor's Business Daily*, June 24: A11.

"How to Restore Credibility at the NYSE" (2003). Wharton School of Finance and Commerce, www.knowledge.wharton.upenn.edu/index.cfm?fa=viewArticle&id=848, September 24.

Jenkins, H.W., Jr (2004). "Bored of Directors," *The Wall Street Journal*, May 26: A17.

Johnson, C. (2003a). "New Accounting Board, SEC in Dispute," *The Washington Post*, April 25: E2.

Johnson, C. (2003b). "SEC to Require Assurances of Accounting Controls," *The Washington Post*, May 27: E1.

Johnson, C. (2004). "SEC Wants Disclosures from Funds," *The Washington Post*, May 27: E1.

Kahn, V.M. (2004). "Should Managers Disclose Their Fund Stakes?" *The New York Times*, January 18: BU 5.

Katz, D.M. (2003). "Rites of Privacy," *CFO Magazine*, November 1: 9.

Kirchgaessner, S., and A. Michaels (2004). "Hollinger Sale Hit by Complications," *Financial Times*, April 19: 27.

Kristof, K.M. (2003). "CalPERS Sues NYSE, Specialist Firms," *Los Angeles Times*, December 17: C1.

Lahart, J. (2004). "Options Expensing Gets Support From Investors," *The Wall Street Journal*, May 25: C3.

Langley, M. (2003). "As his Ambitions Expand, Spitzer Draws More Controversy," *The Wall Street Journal*, December 11: A1, A8.

Latour, A., D. Berman, and S. Pulliam (2003). "Oklahoma Official Plans Charges against MCI, Former CEO Ebbers," *The Wall Street Journal*, August 27: A1, A6.

Lauricella, T. (2004). "Maverick Aims at Fund Business," *The Wall Street Journal*, February 2: R1, R4.

Levitt, A. (2002). *Take on the Street: What Wall Street and Corporate America Don't Want You to Know.* New York: Pantheon Books.

Levitt, A., and R.C. Breeden (2004). "Our Ethical Erosion," *The Wall Street Journal*, December 3, A16.

Litan, R.E. (2002). "Testimony of Robert E. Litan before the Senate Committee on Banking, Housing, and Urban Affairs," March 14.

Lublin, J.S., and S. Young (2004). "Even as MCI Makes Strides, Monitor Stays," *The Wall Street Journal*, April 20: B1, B3.

Masters, B.A. (2004a). "Beneath Market Timing, SEC Still Digging into Mutual Funds," *The Washington Post*, June 12: D12.

Masters, B.A. (2004b). "Banks Make $675 Million Deal to Settle Mutual Fund Charges," *The Washington Post*, March 16: A1.

Masters, B.A., and B. White (2003). "Donaldson Backs SEC Supremacy Bill," *The Washington Post*, July 16: E1.

Menn, J. (2004). "Silicon Valley High-tech Workers Rally in Defense of Stock Options," *Los Angeles Times*, June 25: C2.

Michaels, A. (2003a). "States Fight to Keep Regulatory Powers," *Financial Times*, July 19: 9.

Michaels, A. (2003b). "White House Praises Fraud Task Force," *Financial Times*, July 23: 26.

Michaels, A. (2003c). "After a Year of Corporate Clean-up, William Donaldson Calls for a Return to Risk-taking," *Financial Times*, July 24: 15.

Michaels, A. (2003d). "Baker Plan on State Regulators is Delayed," *Financial Times*, July 25: 13.

Michaels, A. (2003e). "Reforms Lose Support of Business Leaders," *Financial Times*, July 28: 24.

Michaels, A. (2003f). "SEC and States Try to Repair Relations," *Financial Times*, September 15: 1.

Michaels, A. (2003g). "Funds under Fire for Lack of Initiative," *Financial Times*, October 7: 3.

Michaels, A. (2003h). "Sting in the Tail of Donaldson's Message: SEC Chairman Comes out Fighting at the Security Industry's Annual Conference," *Financial Times*, November 8: 10.

Michaels, A. (2004a). "Corporate Governance," *Financial Times*, January 16: 2.

Michaels, A. (2004b). "The Patience behind the New-look SEC," *Financial Times*, February 17: 33.

Michaels, A. (2004c). "Critics to Advise on Auditing Standards," *Financial Times*, April 16: 28.

Michaels, A. (2004d). "Scrushy Defense Questions Sarbanes Legality," *Financial Times*, May 18: 26.

Michaels, A. (2004e). "Costs Leap for Public Companies," *Financial Times*, May 19: 29.

Michaels, A. (2004f). "AIG Chief Criticizes New Regulations," *Financial Times*, May 20: 26.

Michaels, A., and P.T. Larsen (2003). "Big Problems Demand the SEC Solution," *Financial Times*, December 1: 11.

Michaels, A., and A. Parker (2003). "Accountants Urged to Take Moral Stand," *Financial Times*, December 19: 31.

Michaels, A., and A. Parker (2004). "Lobbyists Stick to Their Guns over Expensing," *Financial Times*, April 1: 26.

Michaels, A., and J. Politi (2004). "Sarbanes-Oxley Driving US CEOs to Tears," *Financial Times*, May 14: 2.

Michaels, A., and D. Roberts (2004a). "FASB to Reveal Options Proposal," *Financial Times*, March 25: 31.

Michaels, A., and D. Roberts (2004b). "FASB Unveils Proposals for Options Accounting," *Financial Times*, April 1: 26.

Michaels, A., and G. Silverman (2003). "Bank Regulators Turn up Heat on Accountants," *Financial Times*, August 9: 1.

Michaels, A., and R. Waters (2003). "Sun Faces Stock Option Challenge, Board Showdown over Deducting Equity Compensation from Earnings," *Financial Times*, July 14: 19.

Michaels, A., and R. Waters (2004). "EDS Backtracks on Expensing Options," *Financial Times*, March 26: 29.

Michaels, A., and D. Wells (2003). "Spitzer Will Meet SEC in Bid to Widen Mutual Funds Probe," *Financial Times*, November 3: 23.

Michaels, A., and D. Wighton (2004). "The Scandal Bill that Keeps on Rising: Litigation Costs have Hit Citigroup hard," *Financial Times*, May 11: 30.

Morgenson, G. (2004a). "The CEO's Mad, Mad World," *The New York Times*, March 7: BU 1.

Morgenson, G. (2004b). "Litmus Test for Ethics: Options," *The New York Times*, March 21: BU 1.

Morgenson, G. (2004c). "Citigroup Agrees to a Settlement over WorldCom," *The New York Times*, May 11: A1.

Mulligan, T.S. (2004). "Options Proposal Draws Heat," *Los Angeles Times*, April 1: C1.

O'Brien, T.L. (2004). "Citigroup Assesses a Risk and Decides to Settle," *The New York Times*, May 11: C1.

Peterson, J. (2003). "Fund Lobby Loses Clout," *Los Angeles Times*, November 29: C1.

Peterson, J. (2004). "For SEC Chief, Not Business as Usual," *Los Angeles Times*, May 23: C1.

Polsby, N.B. (1980). *Community Power and Political Theory: A Further Look at Problems of Evidence and Inference*. New Haven, CT: Yale University Press.

Reason, T. (2003). "Stricter Rules and Wary Investors are Prompting More Companies to Exit the Public Markets," *CFO Magazine*, May 1: 18.

Rivlin, G. (2004). "Intel Balks at a Request to Expense Stock Options," *The New York Times*, May 20: C1.

Romero, S. (2002). "WorldCom Facing Charges of Fraud: Bush Vows Inquiry," *The New York Times*, June 27: A1.

Saito-Chung, D. (2004). "Saint Jack's Mission In Mutuals: Putting Shareholders in Control," *Investor's Business Daily*, April 22: A1, A6.

Scannell, K. (2004). "Settlement Costs for Class-action Lawsuits Fell for Firms in '03," *The Wall Street Journal*, May 10: C3.

Schneider, C. (2004). "Cisco and FASB: Options Showdown," CFO.com, May 28, http://www.cfo.com/article/1,5309,13978||T|1682,00.html?f=TodayInFinance_Inside.

Schroeder, M. (2004). "Bill Would Weaken FASB Effort to Require Expensing Options," *The Wall Street Journal*, April 21: A9.

Smith, R., and Solomon, D. (2003). "State-level Stock Cops Retain Power," *The Wall Street Journal*, July 25: C1, C5.

Solomon, D. (2003). "Zealous States Shake up Legal Status Quo," *The Wall Street Journal*, August 28: A4.

Solomon, D. (2004). "Loophole Limits Independence," *The Wall Street Journal*, April 28: C1.

Stigler, G. (1971). "The Theory of Economic Regulation," *Bell Journal of Economics* 2: 3–21.

Taub, S. (2004a). "Internal Auditors Find Control Gaps," *CFO.com*, May 26, http://www.cfo.com/article/1,5309,14039||T|1682,00.html?f=TodayInFinance_Inside.

Taub, S. (2004b). "Sarbox Costs 'Unpredictable,' Still Rising," CFO.com, May 28. http://www.cfo.com/article/1,5309,13938%7C%7CT%7C1682,00.html.

Thain, J. (2004). "Sarbanes-Oxley: Is the Price Too High?" *The Wall Street Journal*, May 27: A20.

Thomas, L. Jr (2003). "Reed Backs Reports Ideas for Changes at Big Board," *The New York Times*, October 3: C1.

Volcker, P., and A. Levitt, Jr (2004). "In Defense of Sarbanes-Oxley," *The Wall Street Journal*, June 14: A16.

Wallison, P.J. (2003). "Blame Sarbanes-Oxley," *The Wall Street Journal*, September 3: A16.

Weil, J., and J. Cummings (2004). "The Stock-option Showdown," *The Wall Street Journal*, March 9: C1.

White, B. (2002). "NYSE Proposes Board Revisions," *The Washington Post*, June 7: E3.

White, B. (2003a). "Pension Fund Officials Seek NYSE Split," *The Washington Post*, September 25: E1.

White, B. (2003b). "Pension Fund Sues NYSE, Specialist Firms," *The Washington Post*, December 17: E1.

White, B. (2004). "Citigroup to Pay WorldCom Investors $2.65 Billion," *The Washington Post*, May 11: E1.

White, B., and K. Day (2003). "NYSE to Name New Chief Executive," *The Washington Post*, December 18: E1.

# Conclusion

I think that this would be the true way to go to paradise: to learn the way to hell in order to flee it.

Machiavelli, in a letter to Guicciardini

Public affairs has grown significantly into one of the major areas of strategic management activity over the past decade. In the United States, as well as being a multibillion-dollar based business around Washington, DC, it also has its equivalent epicenters around each state government and international operations focused on the World Trade Organization and World Bank. In Europe, the bulk of the coordination of EU activity is centered on Brussels, with major activities also being focused on the prime EU capitals, London, Paris, and Berlin being particularly significant. Other public affairs centers in the European Union are growing, as with Geneva because of the WTO, and the Swiss banking system is another contact point. In Australia there is a well developed industry centered on Melbourne and Canberra, whilst other regional capitals are beginning to show steady growth and development.

What is missing in our burgeoning discipline and trade is how public affairs practice is beginning to emerge in Asia, the largest populated continent, which is predicted to dominate world trade and therefore maybe public affairs over the next few decades. Trade alliances, the development of collaborative ventures and markets, are yet to be explored and written about by the discipline. One such example is Central and Eastern Europe and their gradual incorporation into the developed-world market via core centers like Vienna, Berlin, Prague, Warsaw, and perhaps Ljubljana. The development of much of China's nascent public affairs industry is focused on key entry points such as Singapore, Shanghai, Beijing, and Hong Kong, with many specialists and international groups leading the way. How deals, legislation, and policy are developed in the People's Republic clearly is going to be a major focus of public affairs over the next decade, although one can point to the likelihood that activity will be centered on the great twenty-year plan and therefore will be very long term in nature. Similar explorations of major markets and democracies such as India and Japan and how public affairs practice is developing will also be one of the great growth areas over the period.

Predicting what will be successful strategies in public affairs is difficult. But one can be sure that the worldwide industry is professionalizing. Increasingly it is quality communicators, who understand and can connect into complex policy networks, that will be in demand in the area of public affairs. The CEO who can head up and advise on policy options will be at the forefront of public affairs and will be increasingly in demand, for shaping the business and external policy in a complex globally based stakeholder environment which will be their core business. Whether it is large corporate legal groups moving into the area to influence regulatory activity on behalf of clients or world accounting groups, international consultants will operate to amend legislation, frame better trade deals, or deal with the raft of environmental and regulatory measures that are becoming part of everyday international trade life. As energy supplies come at an ever higher premium price and demand for resources increases, so will lobbying activity and international operations to amend, champion, and modify legislation and interest group activities on behalf of clients.

As in the past decade the ability of small businesses to operate and influence world trade will remain small. Only effective transnational groupings will succeed at this, or inevitably SMEs will have limited influence. Correct strategies for them will be to form industry collaborations and then to develop transnational collaborations with interest groups and others to allow them better access into the policy and decision-making process. Sadly, there are a great many small business and interest groups at the international level who do not influence policy making, but just seem to represent interests and do little to strengthen their members' competitive position. Large multinational groups will continue to dominate public affairs and strategic policy making.

Public affairs will increasingly be seen as the strategic core business function for companies, interest groups, and government organizations that wish to compete successfully and operate internationally. Public affairs and its associated activities will increasingly be at the leading edge as an interpreter of complex governmental policies and stakeholder group demands. Corruption, illegal trade, unethical business activity, and the need for high public standards to maintain quality trade and relationships will all stimulate the growth of international public affairs. International standards of public life and comparators in ethical dealings will see significant growth.

Predicting the next ten years from 2005 is treacherous and one does feel a little like a cornered snake oil salesman at times or even a spiritualist holding a séance to find answers. Is there anybody there? What will go right? What will go wrong? From our international vantage point (both sides of the pond and now Down Under), huge growth in activity will move to Asia, and Washington, Geneva, New York and Brussels will play leading roles in developing the industry throughout that continent.

Given regulation of electoral expenditure and lobbying, increased linkages will become more evident between the funding of politicians and political campaigns. Interest group activity around this area will be increasingly more evident and easier to follow. Pressure and environmental groups may even be more open about which corporations, states and businesses they favor and disfavor (already relatively evident to many of us but not freely admitted). The broad international public may even become more aware that some interest groups have bigger budgets than many developing countries in Africa and Asia and certainly more influence on global and certain national pieces of legislation. Quality public affairs results will be carried out by the most senior staff, with a background in law, finance, business, politics or government administration. The ability to access personal networks will be core, and direct personal conversation via personal contact either face to face or by phone will still dominate. Letters and other personal communications will continue to be used by the most senior and most effective operators in the industry. At a lower level e-mail and other communications will be used, such as texting, but will be applied more at the operational, middle management level or to support general communications and campaigns. The power of personal contact and advocacy will remain to the fore.

Technology that aids high-quality interpersonal communication and which cannot be easily accessed or abused will be adopted throughout the industry. Major quality policymaking events, briefing sessions, and trade activities will still be prime events for public affairs professions to meet. But world events that attract those who want to make a noise or destroy world capitalism will not be well supported. Closed-circuit policy loops, specialist symposia, and colloquia where people can share experience and practice will still be much in demand. Political conventions and conferences will be prime places for public affairs people to meet and share practice and gain access to legislators. Pressure and interest group campaigns will increasingly utilize cellphone and equivalent communication systems to marshal campaigns and pressure legislators. Eventually a comprehensive list of mobile phone numbers worldwide will aid advocacy groups.

Finally many NGOs will almost certainly have as much influence as corporations, especially if they are honest and open in their advocacy. Trust, intelligence, and high ethical standards will remain at the heart of public affairs work.

> But one thing consoles me: when something involves a number of people, no one person in particular can be blamed.
>
> The Mandrake Root

# End Piece

The public affairs industry and associated research are rapidly evolving. We now have a good grasp of the issues in North America, Europe, Australia and New Zealand, elsewhere we have gaps. The discipline has a number of core magazines, newsletters and journals such as the *Journal of Public Affairs*, which has now published over one million words of research since 2000 and has a full international practitioner and university-based researcher editorial board. Readers of this text are invited to contribute articles to the journal courtesy of this editor at PHarris@business.otago.ac.nz. In addition, to strengthen the research fraternity of practitioners and researchers in Public Affairs and to share best practice and knowledge and aid international collaboration, we have launched a new e-mail list which we hope you will join. The list can be joined by sending an e-mail to Public-Affairs@jiscmail.ac.uk. We look forward to hearing from you.

Phil and Craig

# Index

Page numbers in *italics* refer to tables.